**Legend (example):**

| Atomic number | 24 |
|---|---|
| | **Cr** |
| Atomic mass | 52.00 |

| 1 1A | 2 2A | 3 3B | 4 4B | 5 5B | 6 6B | 7 7B | 8 8B | 9 8B | 10 | 11 1B | 12 2B | 13 3A | 14 4A | 15 5A | 16 6A | 17 7A | 18 8A |
|---|---|---|---|---|---|---|---|---|---|---|---|---|---|---|---|---|---|
| 1 **H** 1.008 | | | | | | | | | | | | | | | | | 2 **He** 4.003 |
| 3 **Li** 6.941 | 4 **Be** 9.012 | | | | | | | | | | | 5 **B** 10.81 | 6 **C** 12.01 | 7 **N** 14.01 | 8 **O** 16.00 | 9 **F** 19.00 | 10 **Ne** 20.18 |
| 11 **Na** 22.99 | 12 **Mg** 24.31 | | | | | | | | | | | 13 **Al** 26.98 | 14 **Si** 28.09 | 15 **P** 30.97 | 16 **S** 32.07 | 17 **Cl** 35.45 | 18 **Ar** 39.95 |
| 19 **K** 39.10 | 20 **Ca** 40.08 | 21 **Sc** 44.96 | 22 **Ti** 47.88 | 23 **V** 50.94 | 24 **Cr** 52.00 | 25 **Mn** 54.94 | 26 **Fe** 55.85 | 27 **Co** 58.93 | 28 **Ni** 58.69 | 29 **Cu** 63.55 | 30 **Zn** 65.41 | 31 **Ga** 69.72 | 32 **Ge** 72.64 | 33 **As** 74.92 | 34 **Se** 78.96 | 35 **Br** 79.90 | 36 **Kr** 83.80 |
| 37 **Rb** 85.47 | 38 **Sr** 87.62 | 39 **Y** 88.91 | 40 **Zr** 91.22 | 41 **Nb** 92.91 | 42 **Mo** 95.94 | 43 **Tc** (98) | 44 **Ru** 101.1 | 45 **Rh** 102.9 | 46 **Pd** 106.4 | 47 **Ag** 107.9 | 48 **Cd** 112.4 | 49 **In** 114.8 | 50 **Sn** 118.7 | 51 **Sb** 121.8 | 52 **Te** 127.6 | 53 **I** 126.9 | 54 **Xe** 131.3 |
| 55 **Cs** 132.9 | 56 **Ba** 137.3 | 57 **La** 138.9 | 72 **Hf** 178.5 | 73 **Ta** 180.9 | 74 **W** 183.9 | 75 **Re** 186.2 | 76 **Os** 190.2 | 77 **Ir** 192.2 | 78 **Pt** 195.1 | 79 **Au** 197.0 | 80 **Hg** 200.6 | 81 **Tl** 204.4 | 82 **Pb** 207.2 | 83 **Bi** 209.0 | 84 **Po** (209) | 85 **At** (210) | 86 **Rn** (222) |
| 87 **Fr** (223) | 88 **Ra** (226) | 89 **Ac** (227) | 104 **Rf** (261) | 105 **Db** (262) | 106 **Sg** (266) | 107 **Bh** (262) | 108 **Hs** (277) | 109 **Mt** (268) | 110 | 111 | 112 | (113) | 114 | (115) | 116 | (117) | 118 |

**Lanthanides / Actinides:**

| | | | | | | | | | | | | | |
|---|---|---|---|---|---|---|---|---|---|---|---|---|---|
| 58 **Ce** 140.1 | 59 **Pr** 140.9 | 60 **Nd** 144.2 | 61 **Pm** (145) | 62 **Sm** 150.4 | 63 **Eu** 152.0 | 64 **Gd** 157.3 | 65 **Tb** 158.9 | 66 **Dy** 162.5 | 67 **Ho** 164.9 | 68 **Er** 167.3 | 69 **Tm** 168.9 | 70 **Yb** 173.0 | 71 **Lu** 175.0 |
| 90 **Th** 232.0 | 91 **Pa** (231) | 92 **U** 238.0 | 93 **Np** (237) | 94 **Pu** (242) | 95 **Am** (243) | 96 **Cm** (247) | 97 **Bk** (247) | 98 **Cf** (251) | 99 **Es** (252) | 100 **Fm** (257) | 101 **Md** (258) | 102 **No** (259) | 103 **Lr** (262) |

Metals

Metalloids

Nonmetals

The 1–18 group designation has been recommended by the International Union of Pure and Applied Chemistry (IUPAC) but is not yet in wide use. No names have been assigned for elements 110–112, 114, 116, and 118. Elements 113, 115, and 117 have not yet been synthesized.

Source: Chang, R. Chemistry, 7th ed. Copyright © 2002 The McGraw-Hill Companies, Inc. New York. Reproduced wih permission.

# Principles of Environmental Engineering and Science

# The McGraw-Hill Series in Civil and Environmental Engineering

## ENGINEERING ECONOMY

**Blank and Tarquin:** *Engineering Economy*
**Humphreys:** *Jelen's Cost and Optimization Engineering*
**Riggs, Bedworth, Randhawa:** *Engineering Economics*
**Steiner:** *Engineering Economic Principles*

## ENGINEERING MATH AND STATISTICS

**Bannerjee:** *The Boundary Element Methods in Engineering*
**Barnes:** *Statistical Analysis for Engineers and Scientists: A Computer-Based Approach (IBM)*
**Ledbed:** *Formulas for Structural Dynamics*
**Milton and Arnold:** *Introduction to Probability and Statistics: Principles and Applications for Engineering and the Computing Sciences*
**Reddy:** *Introduction to the Finite Element Method*
**Rosenkrantz:** *Introduction to Probability and Statistics for Scientists and Engineers*
**Zienkiewicz and Taylor:** *The Finite Element Method: Basic Concepts and Linear Applications*

## FLUID MECHANICS

**Çengel and Turner:** *Fundamentals of Thermal-Fluid Sciences*
**Finnemore and Franzini:** *Fluid Mechanics with Engineering Applications*
**Streeter, Bedford, Wylie:** *Fluid Mechanics*
**White:** *Fluid Mechanics*

## GEOTECHNICAL ENGINEERING

**Atkinson:** *Introduction to the Mechanics of Soils and Foundations*
**Bowles:** *Foundation Analysis and Design*
**Bowles:** *Engineering Properties of Soils and Their Measurement*

## NUMERICAL METHODS

**Chapra and Canale:** *Numerical Methods for Engineers*
**Heath:** *Scientific Computing: An Introductory Survey*

## STRUCTURES

**Gaylord and Stallmeyer:** *Design of Steel Structures*
**Laursen:** *Structural Analysis*
**Leet and Bernal:** *Reinforced Concrete Design*
**Leet and Uang:** *Fundamentals of Structural Analysis*
**Leonard:** *Tension Structures: Behavior and Analysis*
**Lin and Cai:** *Probabilistic Structural Dynamics: Advanced Theory and Applications*

**Nilson:** *Design of Concrete Structures*
**Nowak and Collins:** *Reliability of Structures*
**Taly:** *Design of Modern Highway Bridges*
**Taly:** *Reinforced Masonry Structure Design*

## SURVEYING

**Anderson and Mikhail:** *Surveying: Theory and Practice*
**Wolf and DeWitt:** *Elements of Photogrammetry (with Applications in GIS)*

## STATICS, DYNAMICS, AND MECHANICS OF MATERIALS

**Barber:** *Intermediate Mechanics of Materials*
**Beer and Johnston:** *Vector Mechanics for Engineers: Statics*
**Beer and Johnston:** *Vector Mechanics for Engineers: Dynamics*
**Beer and Johnston:** *Vector Mechanics for Engineers: Statics and Dynamics*
**Beer and Johnston:** *Mechanics of Materials*
**Young:** *Roark's Formulas for Stress and Strain*

## CONSTRUCTION ENGINEERING AND PROJECT MANAGEMENT

**Raymond E. Levitt,** *Stanford University,* Consulting Editor
**Barrie and Paulson:** *Professional Construction Management*
**Bockrath:** *Contracts and the Legal Environment for Engineers and Architects*
**Callahan, Quackenbush, Rowlings:** *Construction Project Scheduling*
**Griffis and Farr:** *Construction Planning for Engineers*
**Hinze:** *Construction Contracts*
**Oberlender:** *Project Management for Engineering and Construction*
**Peurifoy, Ledbetter, Schexnayder:** *Construction Planning, Equipment, and Methods*
**Peurifoy and Oberlender:** *Estimating Construction Costs*

## TRANSPORTATION ENGINEERING

**Edward K. Morlok,** *University of Pennsylvania,* Consulting Editor
**Banks:** *Introduction to Transportation Engineering*
**Horonjeff and McKelvey:** *Planning and Design of Airports*
**Kanafani:** *Transportation Demand Analysis*
**Meyer and Miller:** *Urban Transportation Planning*
**Wells:** *Airport Planning and Management*

## WATER RESOURCES AND ENVIRONMENTAL ENGINEERING

**George Tchobanoglous,** *University of California, Davis,* Consulting Editor
**Bailey and Ollis:** *Biochemical Engineering Fundamentals*
**Benjamin:** *Water Chemistry*
**Bishop:** *Pollution Prevention: Fundamentals and Practice*
**Canter:** *Environmental Impact Assessment*
**Chanlett:** *Environmental Protection*
**Chapra:** *Surface Water Quality Modeling*
**Chow, Maidment, Mays:** *Applied Hydrology*
**Crites and Tchobanoglous:** *Small and Decentralized Wastewater Management Systems*
**Davis and Cornwell:** *Introduction to Environmental Engineering*
**Davis and Masten:** *Principles of Environmental Engineering*
**deNevers:** *Air Pollution Control Engineering*
**Eckenfelder:** *Industrial Water Pollution Control*
**Eweis, Ergas, Chang, Schroeder:** *Bioremediation Principles*
**Freeman:** *Hazardous Waste Minimization*
**LaGrega, Buckingham, Evans:** *Hazardous Waste Management*
**Linsley, Franzini, Freyberg, Tchobanoglous:** *Water Resources Engineering*
**McGhee:** *Water Supply and Sewage*
**Metcalf & Eddy, Inc.:** *Wastewater Engineering: Collection and Pumping of Wastewater*
**Metcalf & Eddy, Inc.:** *Wastewater Engineering: Treatment and Reuse*
**Peavy, Rowe, Tchobanoglous:** *Environmental Engineering*
**Rittmann and McCarty:** *Environmental Biotechnology: Principles and Applications*
**Rubin:** *Introduction to Engineering and the Environment*
**Sawyer, McCarty, Parkin:** *Chemistry for Environmental Engineering*
**Sturm:** *Open Channel Hydraulics*
**Tchobanoglous, Theisen, Vigil:** *Integrated Solid Waste Management: Engineering Principles and Management Issues*
**Wentz:** *Safety, Health, and Environmental Protection*

## OTHERS TITLES OF INTEREST

**Budynas:** *Advanced Strength and Applied Stress Analysis*
**Dally and Riley:** *Experimental Stress Analysis*
**Ugural:** *Stresses in Plates and Shells*

# Principles of Environmental Engineering and Science

**Mackenzie L. Davis**
Michigan State University—East Lansing

**Susan J. Masten**
Michigan State University—East Lansing

Boston   Burr Ridge, IL   Dubuque, IA   Madison, WI   New York   San Francisco   St. Louis
Bangkok   Bogotá   Caracas   Kuala Lumpur   Lisbon   London   Madrid   Mexico City
Milan   Montreal   New Delhi   Santiago   Seoul   Singapore   Sydney   Taipei   Toronto

# Higher Education

PRINCIPLES OF ENVIRONMENTAL ENGINEERING AND SCIENCE

Published by McGraw-Hill, a business unit of The McGraw-Hill Companies, Inc., 1221 Avenue of the Americas, New York, NY 10020. Copyright © 2004 by The McGraw-Hill Companies, Inc. All rights reserved. No part of this publication may be reproduced or distributed in any form or by any means, or stored in a database or retrieval system, without the prior written consent of The McGraw-Hill Companies, Inc., including, but not limited to, in any network or other electronic storage or transmission, or broadcast for distance learning.

Some ancillaries, including electronic and print components, may not be available to customers outside the United States.

This book is printed on acid-free paper.

International    1 2 3 4 5 6 7 8 9 0 CCW/CCW 0 9 8 7 6 5 4 3
Domestic              4 5 6 7 8 9 0 CCW/CCW 0 9 8 7 6

ISBN  0–07–235053–9
ISBN  0–07–119449–5 (ISE)

Publisher: *Elizabeth A. Jones*
Senior sponsoring editor: *Suzanne Jeans*
Developmental editor: *Lisa Kalner Williams*
Marketing manager: *Sarah Martin*
Project manager: *Jane Mohr*
Lead production supervisor: *Sandy Ludovissy*
Media project manager: *Sandra M. Schnee*
Senior media technology producer: *Phillip Meek*
Coordinator of freelance design: *Rick D. Noel*
Cover designer: *Emily Feyen*
Cover illustration: *Barbara Masten Cobb*
Lead photo research coordinator: *Carrie K. Burger*
Compositor: *Interactive Composition Corporation*
Typeface: *10/12 Times*
Printer: *Courier Westford*

**Library of Congress Cataloging-in-Publication Data**

Davis, Mackenzie Leo, 1941–
    Principles of environmental engineering and science / Mackenzie L. Davis, Susan J. Masten. — 1st ed.
      p.  cm. — (The McGraw-Hill series in civil and environmental engineering)
    Includes index.
    ISBN 0–07–235053–9 (alk. paper) — ISBN 0–07–119449–5 (alk. paper)
    1. Environmental engineering.   2. Environmental sciences.   I. Masten, Susan J.   II. Title.   III. Series.

TD145.D2623   2004
628—dc21                                                             2003046402
                                                                    CIP

www.mhhe.com

To our students, who make it worthwhile

and

To Susan Masten's grandfather, the late Jonas Nadwodny, and her father, William Masten, whose careers in water and wastewater treatment inspired her to follow in their footsteps, and for their support in encouraging her to become an engineer.

# Contents

# Preface

*Principles of Environmental Engineering and Science* is geared toward students taking an introductory, sophomore-level engineering course. The book's material is also applicable for students enrolled in upper level biology, chemistry, resource development, fisheries and wildlife, microbiology, and soil sciences courses. These students should already understand such calculus topics as differentiation, integrations, and differential equations (at an introductory level).

### Principles of *Principles*

Many of you are familiar with *Introduction to Environmental Engineering* by Mackenzie Davis and David Cornwell. Although some of the content of that text is similar to *Principles of Environmental Engineering and Science,* they are two separate books with very different objectives. *Principles* places more emphasis on scientific principles, ethics, and safety, and focuses less on engineering design. This book exposes students to a broader range of environmental topics through separate chapters on ecosystems, geological and soil resources, and agricultural effects.

True to its emphasis on an inclusive introduction to environmental topics, the first five chapters of *Principles* present the background of the discipline from which the following chapters spring. For example, Chapter 2 reviews chemistry topics essential for grasping the fundamentals of environmental engineering.

Another hallmark feature of *Principles* is its integration of mass balance. Chapter 3 introduces the concept of mass balance as a tool for problem solving and shows how it is applied in hydrology conservative systems. From this point on, mass balance explains many key environmental engineering concepts. For example, this approach illustrates conservation of soil and geological resources in Chapter 7 and develops the DO sag curve in Chapter 8 (water quality). The design equations for a completely mixed activated sludge system and a sludge mass balance are developed in Chapter 10. Mass balance accounts for the production of sulfur dioxide from the combustion of coal in Chapter 11. Finally, in Chapter 13, mass balance is used for waste auditing.

### Supplements

*Principles* offers a Website stocked with tools for both students and instructors at:

www.mhhe.com/davismasten

Students find animations that put relevant chemistry and geology topics in motion, a glossary of key terms, links to plant tours and other environmental engineering resources, and information on Chem Skill Builder, a chemistry problem-solving application with more than 1500 algorithmically generated questions.

At the *Principles* Website, instructors will find a bank of book images, lecture slides, information on Chem Skill Builder, and the *Instructor's Solutions Manual,* featuring sample course outlines and sample exams. Instructors can access these tools by contacting their local McGraw-Hill sales representative for password information.

# Acknowledgments

As with any other text, the number of individuals who have made it possible far exceeds those whose names grace the cover. At the hazard of leaving someone out, we would like to explicitly thank the following individuals for their contribution.

The following students helped to solve problems, proofread text, prepare illustrations, raise embarrassing questions, and generally make sure that other students could understand it: Shelley Agarwal, Stephanie Albert, Deb Allen, Mark Bishop, Aimee Bolen, Kristen Brandt, Jeff Brown, Amber Buhl, Nicole Chernoby, Rebecca Cline, Linda Clowater, Shauna Cohen, John Cooley, Ted Coyer, Marcia Curran, Talia Dodak, Kimberly Doherty, Bobbie Dougherty, Lisa Egleston, Karen Ellis, Craig Fricke, Elizabeth Fry, Beverly Hinds, Edith Hooten, Brad Hoos, Kathy Hulley, Lisa Huntington, Angela Ilieff, Alison Leach, Gary Lefko, Lynelle Marolf, Lisa McClanahan, Tim McNamara, Becky Mursch, Cheryl Oliver, Kyle Paulson, Marisa Patterson, Lynnette Payne, Jim Peters, Kristie Piner, Christine Pomeroy, Susan Quiring, Erica Rayner, Bob Reynolds, Laurene Rhyne, Sandra Risley, Lee Sawatzki, Stephanie Smith, Mary Stewart, Rick Wirsing, Ya-yun Wu. To them a hearty thank you!

The authors would also like to thank Pamela Augustine, David Desteiger, Cheryl Edson, John Engle, Timothy Greenleaf, Erin Henderson, Robert Little, Jeremy Mansell, Kelly Mlynarek, Brad Osinski, Shannon Simpson, Lindsay Smith, Bryan Stramecki, Brad Vernier, Marcie Wawzysko, and Adam Wosneski who also helped proofread the text, check problems and make the book more readable for students. In addition, we wish to thank Rebecca Masten-Davies for her assistance with providing a cultural experience for students by naming cities, rivers, lakes, etc. after mythological beings from the world over.

We would also like to thank the following reviewers for their many helpful comments and suggestions: David Bagley, U of Toronto; Theodore Cleveland, U of Houston; Benoit Cushman-Roisin, Dartmouth College; Brian Dempsey, Penn State U; Andrew Dzuril, Florida State U; Subhasis Ghoshal, McGill U; Mark Hernandez, U of Colorado; Howard Liljestrand, U of Texas, Austin; Taha Marhaba, NJIT; Thomas Overcamp, Clemson U; Michael Penn, U of Wisconsin, Platteville; Kelly Rusch, Louisiana State U; Richard Schuhmann, Penn State U.; Daniel Smith, U of South Florida; Helena Solo-Gabriele, U of Miami; and Scott Wells, Portland State U.

We give special thanks to Simon Davies for his contribution of Chapter 14. His efforts are sincerely appreciated. And last, but certainly not least, we wish to thank our families who have put up with us during the writing of this book, especially Rebecca and Jeffrey Masten-Davies, who gave up several Christmas vacations plus many other days during the year while their mom spent uncountable hours working on this book.

A special thanks to Macks' wife, Elaine, for putting up with the nonsense of book writing.

Mackenzie L. Davis                                                                          Susan J. Masten

# About the Authors

**Mackenzie L. Davis** is an Emeritus Professor of Environmental Engineering at Michigan State University. He received all his degrees from the University of Illinois. From 1968 to 1971 he served as a Captain in the U.S. Army Medical Services Corps. During his military service he conducted air pollution surveys at Army ammunition plants. From 1971 to 1973 he was branch chief of the Environmental Engineering Branch at the U.S. Army Construction Engineering Research Laboratory. His responsibilities included supervision of research on air, noise, and water pollution control and solid waste management for Army facilities. In 1973 he joined the faculty at Michigan State University. He has taught and conducted research in the areas of air pollution control and hazardous waste management.

In 1987 and 1989–1992, under an intergovernmental personnel assignment with the Office of Solid Waste of the U.S. Environmental Protection Agency, Dr. Davis performed technology assessments of treatment methods used to demonstrate the regulatory requirements for the land disposal restrictions ("land ban") promulgated under the Hazardous and Solid Waste Amendments.

Dr. Davis is a member of the following professional organizations: American Chemical Society; American Institute of Chemical Engineers; American Society for Engineering Education; American Meteorological Society; American Society of Civil Engineers; American Water Works Association; Air & Waste Management Association; Association of Environmental Engineering & Science Professors; and the Water Environment Federation.

His honors and awards include the State-of-the-Art award from the A.S.C.E., chapter honor member of Chi Epsilon, Sigma Xi, and election as a Diplomate in the American Academy of Environmental Engineers with certification in hazardous waste management. He has received teaching awards from the American Society of Civil Engineers Student Chapter, Michigan State University College of Engineering, North Central Section of the American Society for Engineering Education, Great Lakes Region of Chi Epsilon, and the AMOCO Corporation. He is a registered professional engineer in Illinois and Michigan.

In 2003, Dr. Davis retired from Michigan State University.

**Susan J. Masten** is a Professor in the Department of Civil and Environmental Engineering at Michigan State University. She received her Ph.D. in environmental engineering from Harvard University in 1986. She worked for several years in environmental research before joining the MSU faculty in 1989, including at the US Environmental Protection Agency Kerr Laboratory, in Ada, Oklahoma. Professor Masten's research involves the use of chemical oxidants for the remediation of soils, water, and wastewater. Her research is presently focused on the use of ozone for reducing the concentration of disinfection by-products in drinking water, controlling fouling in membranes, and reducing the toxicity of ozonation by-products formed from the ozonation of polycyclic aromatic hydrocarbons and pesticides. She also has research projects involving the use of ozone for the reduction of odor in swine manure slurry and the elimination of chlorinated hydrocarbons and semivolatile organic chemicals from soils using in-situ ozone stripping and ozone sparging.

Dr. Masten is a member of the following professional organizations: American Chemical Society, International Ozone Association, American Water Works Association and the American Society for Engineering Education. She has been on the Executive Committee of the MSU Chapter of the American Chemical Society since 1995.

Professor Masten was a Lilly Teaching Fellow during the 1994–1995 academic year. She is also the recipient of the Withrow Distinguished Scholar Award, College of Engineering, MSU, March 1995, and the Teacher-Scholar Award, Michigan State University, February 1996. Dr. Masten was also a member of the Faculty Writing Project, Michigan State University, May 1996. In 2001, she was awarded the Association of Environmental Engineering and Science Professors/Wiley Interscience Outstanding Educator Award.

Dr. Masten is a registered professional engineer in the state of Michigan.

## About the Cover Artist

**Barbara Masten Cobb,** sister of Susan Masten, attended art school before completing an associate degree in nursing in 1983. Barbara is employed as the lead floor nurse in a New Jersey nursing home but in her spare time, she is able to continue her beloved career in art.

# 1

# Introduction

1

## 1–1   WHAT IS ENVIRONMENTAL SCIENCE?

### Natural Science

In the broadest sense, science is systematized knowledge derived from and tested by recognition and formulation of a problem, collection of data through observation, and experimentation. We differentiate between social science and natural science in that the former deals with the study of people and how they live together as families, tribes, communities, races, and nations, and the latter deals with the study of nature and the physical world. Natural science includes such diverse disciplines as biology, chemistry, geology, physics, and environmental science.

### Environmental Science

Whereas the disciplines of biology, chemistry, and physics (and their subdisciplines of microbiology, organic chemistry, nuclear physics, etc.) are focused on a particular aspect of natural science, environmental science in its broadest sense encompasses all the fields of natural science. The historical focus of study for environmental scientists has been, of course, the natural environment. By this, we mean the atmosphere, the land, the water and their inhabitants as differentiated from the built environment. Modern environmental science has also found applications to the built environment or, perhaps more correctly, to the effusions from the built environment.

### Quantitative Environmental Science

Science or, perhaps more correctly, the **scientific method,** deals with data, that is, with recorded observations. The data are, of course, a sample of the universe of possibilities. They may be representative or they may be skewed. Even if they are representative they will contain some random variation that cannot be explained with current knowledge. Care and impartiality in gathering and recording data, as well as independent verification, are the cornerstones of science.

When the collection and organization of data reveal certain regularities, it may be possible to formulate a generalization or **hypothesis.** This is merely a statement that under certain circumstances certain phenomena can generally be observed. Many generalizations are statistical in that they apply accurately to large assemblages but are no more than probabilities when applied to smaller sets or individuals.

In a scientific approach, the hypothesis is tested, revised, and tested again until it is proven acceptable.

If we can use certain assumptions to tie together a set of generalizations, we formulate a theory. For example, theories that have gained acceptance over a long time are known as **laws.** Some examples are the laws of motion, which describe the behavior of moving bodies, and the gas laws, which describe the behavior of gases. The development of a **theory** is an important accomplishment because it yields a tremendous consolidation of knowledge. Furthermore, a theory gives us a powerful new tool in the acquisition of knowledge for it shows us where to look for new generalizations. "Thus, the accumulation of data becomes less of a magpie collection of facts and more of a systematized hunt for needed information. It is the existence of classification and generalization, and above all theory that makes science an organized body of knowledge."[1]

Logic is a part of all theories. The two types of logic are qualitative and quantitative logic. Qualitative logic is descriptive. For example we can qualitatively state that when the amount of wastewater entering a certain river is too high, the fish die. With qualitative logic we cannot identify what "too high" means—we need quantitative logic to do that.

When the data and generalizations are quantitative, we need mathematics to provide a theory that shows the quantitative relationships. For example, a quantitative statement about the river might state that "When the mass of organic matter entering a certain river equals $x$ kilograms per day, the amount of oxygen in the stream is $y$."

Perhaps more importantly, quantitative logic enables us to explore 'What if?' questions about relationships. For example, "If we reduce the amount of organic matter entering the stream, how much will the amount of oxygen in the stream increase?" Furthermore, theories, and in particular, mathematical theories, often enable us to bridge the gap between experimentally controlled observations and observations made in the field. For example, if we control the amount of oxygen in a fish tank in the laboratory, we can determine the minimum amount required for the fish to be healthy. We can then use this number to determine the acceptable mass of organic matter placed in the stream.

Given that environmental science is an organized body of knowledge about environmental relationships, then **quantitative environmental science** is an organized collection of mathematical theories that may be used to describe and explore environmental relationships.

In this book, we provide an introduction to some mathematical theories that may be used to describe and explore relationships in environmental science.

## 1–2 WHAT IS ENVIRONMENTAL ENGINEERING?

### Engineering

Engineering is a profession that applies science and mathematics to make the properties of matter and sources of energy useful in structures, machines, products, systems, and processes.

### Environmental Engineering

The Environmental Engineering Division of the American Society of Civil Engineers (ASCE) has published the following statement of purpose that may be used to show the relationship between environmental science and environmental engineering:

> Environmental engineering is manifest by sound engineering thought and practice in the solution of problems of environmental sanitation, notably in the provision of safe, palatable, and ample public water supplies; the proper disposal of or recycle of wastewater and solid wastes; the adequate drainage of urban and rural areas for proper sanitation; and the control of water, soil, and atmospheric pollution, and the social and environmental impact of these solutions. Furthermore it is concerned with engineering problems in the field of public health, such as control of arthropod-borne diseases, the elimination of industrial health hazards, and the provision of adequate sanitation in urban, rural, and recreational areas, and the effect of technological advances on the environment [2].

Neither environmental science nor environmental engineering should be confused with heating, ventilating, or air conditioning (HVAC), nor with landscape architecture. Neither should they be confused with the architectural and structural engineering functions associated with built environments, such as homes, offices, and other workplaces.

## 1–3 HISTORICAL PERSPECTIVE

Recognizing that environmental science has its roots in the natural sciences and that the most rudimentary forms of generalization about natural processes are as old as civilizations, then environmental science is indeed very old. Certainly, the Inca cultivation of crops and the mathematics of the Maya and Sumerians qualify as early applications of natural science. Likewise the Egyptian prediction and regulation of the annual floods of the Nile demonstrate that environmental engineering works are as old as civilization. On the other hand if you asked Archimedes or Newton or Pasteur what field of environmental engineering and science they worked in, they would have given you a puzzled look indeed! For that matter, even as late as 1687 the word *science* was not in vogue; Mr. Newton's treatise alludes only to *Philosophiae Naturalis Principa Mathematics (Natural Philosophy and Mathematical Principles)*.

Engineering and the sciences as we recognize them today began to blossom in the 18th century. The foundation of environmental engineering as a discipline may be considered to coincide with the formation of the various societies of civil engineering in the mid-1800s (e.g., the American Society of Civil Engineers in 1852). In the first instances and well into the 20th century, environmental engineering was known as sanitary engineering because of its roots in water purification. The name changed in the late 1960s and early 1970s to reflect the broadening scope that included not only efforts to purify water but also air pollution, solid waste management and the many other aspects of environmental protection that are included in the environmental engineer's current job description.

Although, we might be inclined to date the beginnings of environmental science to the 18th century, the reality is that at any time before the 1960s there was virtually no reference to environmental science in the literature.

Although the concepts of ecology had been firmly established by the 1940s and certainly more than one individual played a role, perhaps the harbinger of environmental science as we know it today was Rachel Carson and, in particular, her book *Silent Spring* [3]. By the mid-1970s environmental science was firmly established in academia, and by the 1980s recognized subdisciplines (environmental chemistry, environmental biology, etc.) that characterize the older disciplines of natural sciences had emerged.

## 1-4 HOW ENVIRONMENTAL ENGINEERS AND ENVIRONMENTAL SCIENTISTS WORK TOGETHER

There is an old saying that "Scientists discover things and engineers make them work." Like many similar old saws there is a grain of truth in the statement and part is out of date. From an educational point of view environmental engineering is founded on environmental science. Environmental science and, in particular, quantitative environmental science provides the fundamental theories used by environmental engineers to design solutions for environmental problems. In many instances the tasks and tools of environmental scientists and environmental engineers are the same.

Perhaps the best way to explain how environmental scientists and engineers work together is to give some examples:

- Early in the 20th century, a dam was built to provide water for cooling in a power plant. The impact of the dam on the oxygen in the river and its ability to support fish life was not considered. The migration of salmon in the river was not considered. To remedy the problem, environmental engineers and scientists designed a fish ladder that not only provided a means for the fish to bypass the dam but also aerated the water to increase the dissolved oxygen. The environmental scientists provided the knowledge of the depth of water and height of the steps the fish could negotiate. The environmental engineers determined the structural requirements of the bypass to allow enough water to flow around the dam to provide the required depth.

- Storm water from city streets was carrying metal and organic contaminants from the street into a river and polluting it. Although a treatment plant could have been built, a wet land mitigation system was selected to solve the problem. The slope of the channel through the wet land was designed by the environmental engineers. The provision of limestone along the channel bed to neutralize the pH and remove metals was determined by the joint work of the environmental scientists and engineers. The selection of the plant material for the wet land was the job of the environmental scientists.

- A highway rest area septic tank system was being overloaded during holiday weekend traffic. Rather than build a bigger septic system or a conventional wastewater treatment plant, an overland flow system in the median strip of the highway was selected as the solution. The engineering system to move the wastewater from the rest area to the median strip was designed by the environmental engineer. The slope of the overland flow system and its length were jointly determined by the environmental scientist and engineer. The grass cover was selected by the environmental scientist.

In each of these instances, the environmental engineer and the environmental scientist had something to contribute. Each had to be familiar with the requirements of the other to be able to come up with an acceptable solution.

## 1–5 INTRODUCTION TO PRINCIPLES OF ENVIRONMENTAL ENGINEERING AND SCIENCE

### Where Do We Start?

We have used the ASCE definition of an environmental engineer as a starting point for this book:

1. Provision of safe, palatable, and ample public water supplies
2. Proper disposal of or recycling of wastewater and solid wastes
3. Control of water, soil, and atmospheric pollution (including noise as an atmospheric pollutant)

To this list we have added those topics from environmental sciences that compliment and round out our understanding of the environment: ecosystems, risk assessment, soil and geological resources, and agricultural effects.

### A Short Outline of This Book

A short outline of this book provides an overview of the many aspects of environmental engineering and science. The first chapters present a review and introduction to the tools used in the remainder of the book. This includes a chemistry review (Chapter 2), an introduction to materials and energy balances (Chapter 3), an introduction to ecosystems (Chapter 4), and an introduction to risk assessment (Chapter 5).

The science of hydrology is introduced in Chapter 6. The principles of conservation of mass are used to describe the balance of water in nature. The physics of water behavior above and below ground will give you the quantitative tools to understand the relationships between rainfall and stream flow that you will need to understand problems of groundwater pollution.

Chapter 7 describes the fundamental relationships between geological processes, weathering, and soil formation and the quantitative means of describing soil properties, the behavior of chemicals, and microorganisms in the soil.

Water quality is a dynamic process. The interrelationships between hydraulic parameters and the chemistry and biology of lakes and streams is described in Chapter 8.

The treatment of water for human consumption is founded on fundamental principles of chemistry and physics. In Chapter 9, these are used to demonstrate methods of purifying water.

Modern treatment of municipal wastewater and some industrial wastes is based on the application of fundamentals of chemistry, microbiology, and physics. These are explained in Chapter 10.

Air pollution, though occurring naturally, is most closely related to human activities. The chemical reactions that occur and the physical processes that transport air pollutants as well as their environmental effects are discussed in Chapter 11.

Chapter 12 presents an overview of the problem of solid waste generation and its environmental effect.

Hazardous waste is the topic of Chapter 13. We examine some alternatives for pollution prevention and the treatment of these wastes as an application of quantitative environmental science to environmental engineering.

Nonpoint source pollution is the topic of Chapter 14. Agriculture is fundamental to our civilization and yet the effects of agriculture on the environment are enormous. Sound application of environmental science provides a means for sustainable development.

It has been estimated that 1.7 million workers in the United States between the ages of 50 and 59 have enough hearing loss to be awarded compensation. The environmental insult most frequently cited in connection with highways is noise. The fundamentals of physics are used in Chapter 15 to describe and mitigate noise.

The final chapter is a brief examination of ionizing radiation with an introduction to health effects of radiation.

### Le Système International d'Unités

Because this text is written using the International System of Units (SI), we thought it would be appropriate to include a brief discussion of the evolution of SI at this point. The following was extracted from the American Society for Testing Materials (ASTM) publication numbered E380:

> SI is a coherent system with seven base units for which names, symbols, and precise definitions have been established. Many derived units are defined in terms of the base units, symbols assigned to each, and, in some cases, given names, as for example, the newton (N).
>
> The decimal system of units was first conceived of in the 16th century, when there was a great confusion and jumble of units of weights and measures. It was not until 1790, however, that the French National Assembly requested the French Academy of Sciences to work out a system of units suitable for adoption by the entire world. This system, based on the meter as a unit of length and the gram as a unit of mass, was adapted as a practical measure to benefit industry and commerce.
>
> Measurement of additional quantities required for science and commerce has necessitated development of additional fundamental and derived units. Numerous other systems based on these two metric units have been used. A unit of time was added to produce the centimeter-gram-second (CGS) system adopted in 1881 by the International Congress of Electricity. By about 1900 practical measurements in metric units began to be based on the meter-kilogram-seconds (MKS) system. A fourth unit, the ampere, was added in 1950.
>
> In 1954 the 10th General Conference on Weights and Measure (CGPM) adopted a rationalized and coherent system of units based on the four MKSA units, plus the degree Kelvin as the unit of temperature and the candela as the unit of luminous intensity. In 1960 the 11th CGPM formally gave the system the full title of International System of Units, for which the abbreviation is "SI" in all languages. In 1971 the 14th CGPM added a seventh base unit, the mole, and approved the pascal (Pa) as a special name for the SI unit of pressure or stress, the newton per square meter, the siemens (S) as a special name for the unit of electrical conductance, and the reciprocal ohm (mho) or the ampere per volt [4].

The SI naming convention for factors of ten is included on the inside back cover of this book.

## 1-6 ENVIRONMENTAL SYSTEMS OVERVIEW

### Systems as Such

Before we begin in earnest, we thought it worth taking a look at the problems to be discussed in this text in a larger perspective. Engineers and scientists like to call this the **systems approach,** that is, looking at all the interrelated parts and their effects on one another. In environmental systems it is doubtful that mere mortals can ever hope to identify all the interrelated parts, to say nothing of trying to establish their effects on one another. The first thing the systems engineer or scientist does, then, is to simplify the system to a tractable size that behaves in a fashion similar

**FIGURE 1–1**

The earth as an ecosystem.

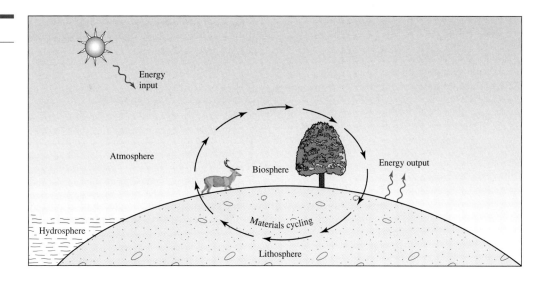

to the real system. The simplified model does not behave in detail as the system does, but it gives a fair approximation of what is going on.

In Chapter 4 we introduce the systems of natural science called ecosystems. On the large scale shown in Figure 1–1, the ecosystem sets a framework for the topics selected for this book, that is, the relationships and interactions of plants and animals with the water, air, and soil that makes up their environment. From this large scale, we present three environmental systems that serve as the focus of this book: the water resource management system (Chapters 6, 8, 9, 10 and 14), the air resource management system (Chapters 11 and 15), and the solid waste management system (Chapters 7, 12 and 13). Pollution problems that are confined to one of these systems are called **single-medium problems** if the medium is either air, water, or soil. Many important environmental problems are not confined to one of these simple systems but cross the boundaries from one to another. Such problems are referred to as **multimedia pollution problems.**

### Water Resource Management System

**Water Supply Subsystem.**  The nature of the water source commonly determines the planning, design, and operation of the collection, purification, transmission, and distribution works.* The two major sources used to supply community and industrial needs are referred to as **surface-water** and **groundwater.** Streams, lakes, and rivers are the surface water sources. Groundwater sources are those pumped from wells.

Figure 1–2 depicts an extension of the water resource system to serve a small community. The source in each case determines the type of collection works and the type of treatment works. The pipe network in the city is called the **distribution system.** The pipes themselves are often referred to as **water mains.** Water in the mains generally is kept at a pressure between 200 and 860 kilopascals (kPa). Excess water produced by the treatment plant during periods of low **demand**[†] (usually the nighttime hours) is held in a storage reservoir. The storage reservoir may be elevated (the ubiquitous water tower), or it may be at ground level. The stored water is used to meet high demand during the day. Storage compensates for changes in demand and allows a smaller treatment plant to be built. It also provides emergency backup in case of a fire.

---

*Works* is a noun used in the plural to mean "engineering structures." It is used in the same sense as art works.

[†]Demand is the use of water by consumers. This use of the word derives from the economic term meaning "the desire for a commodity." The consumers express their desire by opening the faucet or flushing the water closet (W.C.).

**FIGURE 1–2**

An extension of the water supply resource system. (*Source:* Davis, M.L., Cornwell, D.A., *Introduction to Environmental Engineering*, WCB/ McGraw-Hill: N.Y., 1998. Reprinted by permission.)

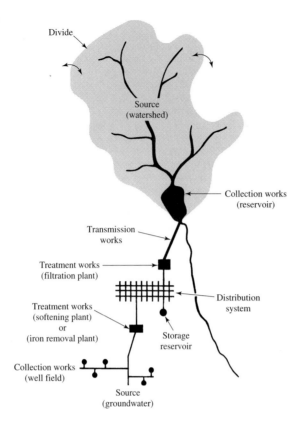

Population and water consumption patterns are the prime factors that govern the quantity of water required and hence the source and the whole composition of the water resource system. One of the first steps in the selection of a suitable water supply source is determining the demand that will be placed on it. The essential elements of water demand include average daily water consumption and peak rate of demand. Average daily water consumption must be estimated for two reasons: (1) to determine the ability of the water source to meet continuing demands over critical periods when surface flows are low or groundwater tables are at minimum elevations, and (2) for purposes of estimating quantities of stored water that would satisfy demands during these critical periods. The peak demand rates must be estimated in order to determine plumbing and pipe sizing, pressure losses, and storage requirements necessary to supply sufficient water during periods of peak water demand.

Many factors influence water use for a given system. For example, the mere fact that water under pressure is available stimulates its use, often excessively, for watering lawns and gardens, for washing automobiles, for operating air-conditioning equipment, and for performing many other activities at home and in industry. The following factors have been found to influence water consumption in a major way:

1. Industrial activity
2. Meterage
3. System management
4. Standard of living
5. Climate

The following factors also influence water consumption to a lesser degree: extent of sewer, system pressure, water price, and availability of private wells.

| TABLE 1–1 | Examples of Variation in per Capita Water Consumption | | | |
|---|---|---|---|---|
| | | **Percent of per Capita Consumption** | | |
| **Location** | **Lpcd** | **Industry** | **Commercial** | **Residential** |
| Lansing, MI | 479 | 17.33 | 40.2 | 42.5 |
| East Lansing, MI | 310 | 0 | 5 | 95 |
| Michigan State University | 307 | 0 | 1 | 99 |

*Source:* Data from local treatment plants, 1994.

The influence of industry is to increase per capita* water demand. Small rural and suburban communities will use less water per person than industrialized communities. Industry is probably the largest single factor influencing per capita water use.

The second most important factor in water use is whether individual consumers have water meters. Meterage imposes a sense of responsibility not found in unmetered residences and businesses. This sense of responsibility reduces per capita water consumption because customers repair leaks and make more conservative water use decisions almost regardless of price. Because water is so cheap, price is not much of a factor.

Following meterage closely is the aspect called system management. If the water distribution system is well managed, per capita water consumption is less than if it is not well managed. Well-managed systems are those in which the managers know when and where leaks in the water mains occur and have them repaired promptly.

Industrial activity, meterage, and system management are more significant factors controlling water consumption than are either the standard of living or the climate. The rationale for the latter two factors is straightforward. Per capita water use increases with an increased standard of living. Highly developed countries use much more water than the less developed nations. Likewise, higher socioeconomic status implies greater per capita water use than lower socioeconomic status. Higher average annual temperature implies higher per capita water use, whereas areas of high rainfall experience lower water use.

The average national value for fresh water consumption in the United States in 1990 was estimated to be 1,411 liters per capita per day (Lpcd)[5]. A similar study conducted in 1970 yielded a value of 628 Lpcd. The average single-family residence uses about 400 Lpcd. The variation in demand is normally reported as a factor of the average day. For metered dwellings the factors are as follows: maximum day = 2.2 × average day; peak hour = 5.3 × average day [6]. Some average daily figures and the contribution of various sectors to demand are shown in Table 1–1.

**Wastewater Disposal Subsystem.**   Safe disposal of all human wastes is necessary to protect the health of the individual, the family, and the community, and also to prevent the occurrence of certain nuisances. To accomplish satisfactory results, human wastes must be disposed of so that:

1. They will not contaminate any drinking water supply.
2. They will not give rise to a public health hazard by being accessible to insects, rodents, or other possible disease carriers that may come into contact with food or drinking water.
3. They will not give rise to a public health hazard by being accessible to children.
4. They will not cause violation of laws or regulations governing water pollution or sewage disposal.

---

*Per capita* is a Latin term that means "by heads." Here it means "per person." This assumes that each person has one head (on the average).

**FIGURE 1–3**

Wastewater management subsystem. (*Source:* Linsley, R.K., Fanzini, J.B. *Water Resources Engineering,* McGraw-Hill: New York, 1979. Reprinted by permission.)

5. They will not pollute or contaminate the waters of any bathing beach, shellfish-breeding ground, or stream used for public or domestic water supply purposes, or for recreational purposes.
6. They will not give rise to a nuisance due to odor or unsightly appearance.

These criteria can best be met by the discharge of domestic sewage to an adequate public or community sewer system [7]. Where no community sewer system exists, on-site disposal by an approved method is mandatory.

In its simplest form the wastewater management subsystem is composed of six parts (Figure 1–3). The source of wastewater may be either industrial wastewater or domestic sewage* or both. Industrial wastewater may be subject to some pretreatment on site if it has the potential to upset the municipal **wastewater treatment plant** (WWTP). Federal regulations refer to municipal wastewater treatment systems as **publicly owned treatment works,** or POTWs.

The quantity of sewage flowing to the WWTP varies widely throughout the day in response to water usage. A typical daily variation is shown in Figure 1–4. Most of the water used in a community will end up in the sewer. Between 5 and 10% of the water is lost in lawn watering, car washing, and other consumptive uses. Consumptive use may be thought of as the difference between the average rate that water flows into the distribution system and the average rate that wastewater flows into the WWTP (excepting the effects of leaks in the pipes).

The quantity of wastewater, with one exception, depends on the same factors that determine the quantity of water required for supply. The major exception is that underground water (groundwater) conditions may strongly affect the quantity of water in the system because of leaks. Whereas the drinking water distribution system is under pressure and is relatively tight, the sewer system is gravity-operated and is relatively open. Thus, groundwater may **infiltrate,** or leak into, the system. When manholes lie in low spots, there is the additional possibility of **inflow** through leaks in the manhole cover. Other sources of inflow include direct connections from roof gutters and downspouts, as well as sump pumps used to remove water from basement footing tiles. Infiltration and inflow (I & I) are particularly important during rainstorms. The additional water from I & I may hydraulically overload the sewer, causing sewage to back up into houses, as well as to reduce the efficiency of the WWTP. New construction techniques and materials have made it possible to reduce I & I to insignificant amounts.

Sewers are classified into three categories: sanitary, storm, and combined. Sanitary sewers are designed to carry municipal wastewater from homes and commercial establishments. With proper pretreatment, industrial wastes may also be discharged into these sewers. Storm sewers are designed to handle excess rainwater and snow melt to prevent flooding of low areas. Whereas sanitary sewers convey wastewater to treatment facilities, storm sewers generally discharge into rivers and streams. Combined sewers are expected to accommodate both municipal wastewater and stormwater. These systems are designed so that during dry periods the wastewater is carried to a treatment facility. During rain storms, the excess water is discharged directly into a river, stream, or lake without treatment. Unfortunately the stormwater is mixed with untreated sewage. Modern design practice discourages the building of combined sewers, and the continued improvement of our natural water bodies will probably require extensive replacement of combined sewers with separate systems for sanitary and storm flow.

When gravity flow is not possible or when sewer trenches become uneconomically deep, the wastewater may be pumped. When the sewage is pumped vertically to discharge into a gravity sewer at a higher elevation, the location of the sewage pump is called a lift station.

Sewage treatment is performed at the WWTP to stabilize the waste material, that is, to make it less putrescible (likely to decompose). The effluent from the WWTP may be discharged into an ocean, lake, or river (called the receiving body). Alternatively, it may be discharged onto (or into)

---

*Domestic sewage is sometimes called sanitary sewage, although it is far from being sanitary!

**FIGURE 1–4**

Typical variation in daily wastewater flow. (*Source:* Davis, M.L., Cornwell, D.A., *Introduction to Environmental Engineering*, WCB/McGraw-Hill: N.Y., 1998. Reprinted by permission.)

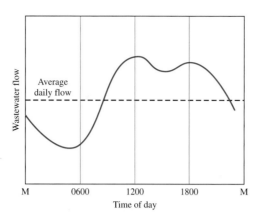

the ground or be processed for reuse. The by-product sludge from the WWTP also must be disposed of in an environmentally acceptable manner.

Whether the waste is discharged onto the ground or into a receiving body, care must be exercised not to overtax the assimilative capacity of the ground or receiving body. The fact that the wastewater effluent is cleaner than the river into which it flows does not justify the discharge if it turns out to be the proverbial "straw that breaks the camel's back."

In summary, water resource management is the process of managing both the quantity and the quality of the water used for human benefit without destroying its availability and purity.

### Air Resource Management System

Our air resource differs from our water resource in two important aspects. The first is in regard to quantity. Whereas engineering structures are required to provide an adequate water supply, air is delivered free of charge in whatever quantity we desire. The second aspect is in regard to quality. Unlike water, which can be treated before we use it, it is impractical to go about with a gas mask on to treat impure air or to use ear plugs to keep out the noise.

The balance of cost and benefit for obtaining a desired quality of air is termed **air resource management.** Cost-benefit analyses can be problematic for at least two reasons. First is the question of what is desired air quality. The basic objective is, of course, to protect the health and welfare of people. But how much air pollution can we stand? We know the tolerable limit is something greater than zero, but tolerance varies from person to person. Second is the question of cost versus benefit. We know that we don't want to spend the entire gross national product to ensure that no individual's health or welfare is impaired, but we do know that we want to spend some amount. Although the cost of control can be reasonably determined by standard engineering and economic means, the cost of pollution is still far from being quantitatively assessed.

Air resource management programs are instituted for a variety of reasons. The most defensible reasons are that (1) air quality has deteriorated and there is a need for correction, and (2) the potential for a future problem is strong.

In order to carry out an air resource management program effectively, all of the elements shown in Figure 1–5 must be employed. (Note that with the appropriate substitution of the word *water* for *air,* these elements apply to management of water resources as well.)

### Solid Waste Management

In the past, solid waste was considered a resource, and we will examine its current potential as a resource. Generally, however, solid waste is considered a problem to be solved as cheaply as possible rather than a resource to be recovered. A simplified block diagram of a solid waste management system is shown in Figure 1–6.

**FIGURE 1–5**

A simplified block diagram of an air resource management system.

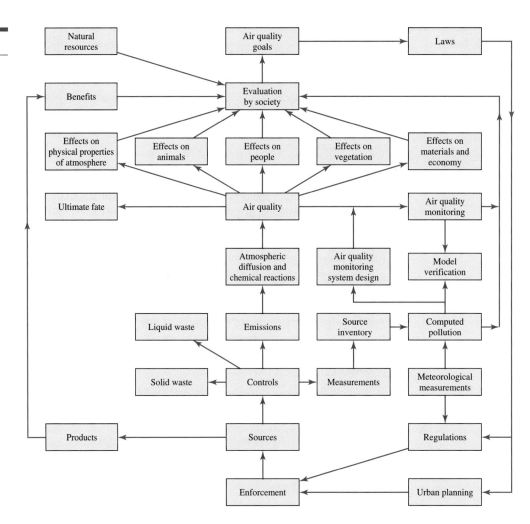

**FIGURE 1–6**

A simplified block diagram of a solid waste management system. (*Source:* Tchobanoglous, G., Theisen, H., Eliassen, R. *Solid Wastes,* McGraw-Hill: New York, 1977. Reprinted by permission.)

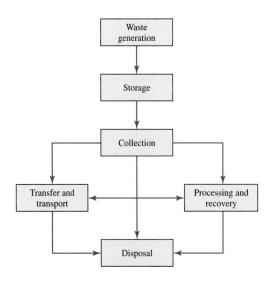

Typhoid and cholera epidemics of the mid-1800s spurred water resource management efforts, and while air pollution episodes have prompted better air resource management; nevertheless, we have yet to feel the effect of material or energy shortages severe enough to encourage modern solid waste management. The landfill "crisis" of the 1980s appears to have abated in the early 1990s due to new or expanded landfill capacity and to many initiatives to reduce the amount of solid waste generated. In 1992, 39 states and the District of Columbia had some form of recycling law. Some states have waste-reduction goals, some have recycling goals, and some have both. Some of these goals are mandatory; others are voluntary.

### Multimedia Systems

Many environmental problems cross the air–water–soil boundary. An example is acid rain that results from the emission of sulfur oxides and nitrogen oxides into the atmosphere. These pollutants are washed out of the atmosphere, thus cleansing it, but in turn polluting water and changing the soil chemistry, which ultimately results in the death of fish and trees. Thus, our historic reliance on the natural cleansing processes of the atmosphere in designing air pollution control equipment has failed to deal with the multimedia nature of the problem. Likewise, disposal of solid waste by incineration results in air pollution, which in turn is controlled by scrubbing with water, resulting in a water pollution problem.

Three lessons have come to us from our experience with multimedia problems. First, it is dangerous to develop models that are too simplistic. Second, environmental engineers and scientists must use a multimedia approach and, in particular, work with a multidisciplinary team to solve environmental problems. Third, the best solution to environmental pollution is waste minimization—if waste is not produced, it does not need to be treated or disposed of.

### Sustainability

Although pollution problems will remain with us for the foreseeable future, an overriding issue for the continuation of our modern living style and for the development of a similar living style for those in developing countries, is the question of **sustainability.** That is, how do we maintain our ecosystem in the light of major depletion of our natural resources. If, in our systems view, we look beyond the simple idea of controlling pollution to the larger idea of sustaining our environment, we see that there are better solutions for our pollution problems. For example:

- Pollution prevention by the minimization of waste production
- Life cycle analysis of our production techniques to include built-in features for extraction and reuse of materials
- Selection of materials and methods that have a long life
- Selection of manufacturing methods and equipment that minimize energy and water consumption

## 1–7   ENVIRONMENTAL LEGISLATION AND REGULATION

In the United States, our publically elected state and federal officials enact environmental laws. The laws direct the appropriate agency to develop and publish regulations to implement the requirements of the law. At the federal level, the U.S. Environmental Protection Agency (EPA) is the primary agency that develops and enforces environmental regulations. Our focus in this discussion is on federal legislation. Much of the legislation enacted at the state level is derived from federal laws.

Federal laws are termed "acts" of Congress and are given titles as well as numerical codes. For example, the Clean Water Act of 1972 (PL 92-500). Based on these acts, the EPA develops regulations. These are first published in the *Federal Register,* as proposed rules for public comment. In addition to the proposed rules, EPA publishes the data and logic they have used to establish the rules. After receiving and responding to the public comments, the final rules are published in the *Federal Register.* Once a year, in July, all the rules are published (codified) in the Code of Federal Regulations (CFR). In subsquent chapters, we touch on a few of the applicable regulations as they apply to the topic of discussion. The following discussion is focused on the legislation.

### Environmental Policy

The National Environmental Policy Act of 1969 (PL 91-190), often referred to as NEPA is an overarching environmental law that asserts that "it is the continuing responsibility of the federal government to use all practicable mensa, consistent with other essential considerations of national policy," to improve plans and programs to achieving environmental excellence. Of the many important directives of the act (which applies to all federal agencies, not just EPA) were the requirement for each agency to prepare an environmental impact statement (EIS) and the establishment of the Council on Environmental Quality (CEQ).

For any major federal action, the responsible agency must conduct an environmental impact assessment (EIA) of their proposed action before the action is implemented. The EIS must be published and public comment must be accepted before any action is taken. In a series of Supreme Court decisions, NEPA has been determined to be strictly procedural as opposed to substantive. That is, that the act is understood as controlling only how agencies go about their decisionmaking, not what they actually decide to do.

The CEQ is an information gathering and coordinating body. The act specifies that the head of the council shall aid the president by reviewing the adequacy of existing systems for monitoring and predicting environmental changes. The CEQ has chosen the role of presidential advisor as distinguished from an ombudsman or agent of the Congress.

### Wildlife and Habitat Protection

Although not alone among U.S. wildlife and habitat protection laws, the Endangered Species Act of 1966 (ESA) is the flagship enactment on wildlife protection. Like NEPA, the ESA has far-reaching components. For example, it recognizes that endangered species are dependent on ecosystems, and it is the ecosystems themselves that should be preserved. ESA directs that all federal departments and agencies shall seek to conserve endangered and threatened species and shall use their authority in furtherance of this purpose.

### Water Quality Management

**Drinking Water.**   The Safe Drinking Water Act of 1974 was the first legislation aimed at providing safe water for consumption rather than for discharge into waterways. In this legislation, Congress directed the EPA to establish drinking water standards for public water systems serving 25 or more people or having 15 or more service connections. In 1975, the EPA published the Interim Drinking Water Regulations.

In 1980, Congress added a provision to prohibit underground injection of wastes without a permit. Major modifications were added in 1986 with the passage of the Safe Drinking Water Act Amendments. The amendments converted the interim regulations to permanent status; established enforcement responsibility; prohibited the use of lead pipes, solder, and fluxes; and moved to protect sole source aquifers.

The Safe Drinking Water Act Amendments of 1996 strengthened and expanded the protection of drinking water by providing grants for compliance and enforcement, enhanced water-system capacity, operator training, and development of solutions to source pollution. In addition, it provided for public notification of violations within 24 hours (rather than 2 weeks under the old act), and annual reporting of levels of regulated contaminants to consumers. Relief from analysis of contaminants that have never been found and are unlikely to occur was given to reduce analytical costs. EPA was funded to conduct research on health effects and treatment for arsenic, radon, and *Crytosporidium.* In addition, EPA was required to develop a screening program to identify the risks posed by substances that have an effect similar to that produced by naturally occurring estrogen and to screen pesticides and other chemicals for estrogenic effects.

**Water Pollution Control.** This discussion follows that of L. Ortolano in *Environment Planning and Design* [8]. Prior to 1948, the principal responsibility for controlling water pollution was assumed by the states and by various local and regional agencies. The first institutions to deal with water pollution problems were created soon after the "sanitary awakening" of the 1850s, when waterborne diseases reached epidemic proportions.

The federal role in water pollution control began with the Public Health Service Act of 1912. This act established the Streams Investigation Station at Cincinnati to carry out water pollution research. The Oil Pollution Act was passed in 1924 to prevent oily discharges on coastal waters. During the 1930s and 1940s, there was a continuing debate over whether the federal government should take a greater role in controlling water pollution. This debate led to the limited expansion of federal powers expressed in the Water Pollution Control Act of 1948 (Table 1–2). The Federal Water Pollution Control Act (FWPCA) of 1956 was the cornerstone of early federal efforts to reduce pollution. Key elements of the act included a new program of subsidies for municipal treatment plant construction and an expanded basis for federal legal action against polluters. Increased funding for state water pollution control efforts and new support for research and training activities were also provided. Each of these programs was continued in the many amendments to the Federal Water Pollution Control Acts in the 1960s and 1970s.

The 1956 legislation mandated a program of construction grants (subsidies to help pay for municipal treatment facilities) as a response to pressures from municipalities. The cities felt that federal funds should be used to help pay for the treatment plants required by federal law. Grants made under the 1956 act could subsidize as much as one-third of the construction cost for a municipal plant, but the maximum grant for a single project was limited to $600,000. A total of $50 million per year was authorized for the program.

The Water Quality Act of 1965 carried forward many provisions of the earlier federal legislation, generally with an increase in levels of funding. The 1965 act also introduced important

**TABLE 1–2** Federal Laws Controlling Water Pollution

| Year | Title | Selected Elements of Legislation[a] |
|---|---|---|
| 1948 | Water Pollution Control Act | Funds for state water pollution control agencies<br>Technical assistance to states<br>Limited provisions for legal action against polluters |
| 1956 | Federal Water Pollution Control Act (FWPCA) | Funds for water pollution research and training<br>Construction grants to municipalities<br>Three-stage enforcement process |
| 1965 | Water Quality Act | States set water quality standards<br>States prepare implementation plans |
| 1972 | FWPCA Amendments | Zero discharge of pollutants goal<br>BPT and BAT effluent limitations<br>NPDES permits<br>Enforcement based on permit violations |
| 1977 | Clean Water Act | BAT requirements for toxic substances<br>BCT requirements for conventional pollutants |
| 1981 | Municipal Waste Treatment Construction Grants Amendments | Reduced federal share in construction grants program |

[a]The table entries include only the new policies and programs established by each of the laws. Often these provisions were carried forward in modified form as elements of subsequent legislation.

BPT = best practical treatment; BAT = best available treatment; NPDES = national pollution discharge elimination system; BCT = best conventional treatment.

new requirements for states to establish ambient water quality standards and detailed plans indicating how the standards would be met. The act also shifted responsibility for administering the federal water quality program from the U.S. Public Health Service to a separate agency, the Federal Water Pollution Control Administration, within the Department of Health, Education, and Welfare (HEW). This was not a permanent change. In 1970, a presidential reorganization order placed the water pollution control activities and several other federal environmental programs in the newly created Environmental Protection Agency (EPA).

In amending the Federal Water Pollution Control Act in 1972, Congress introduced (1) national water quality goals, (2) technology-based effluent limitations, (3) a national discharge permit system, and (4) federal court actions against sources violating permit conditions.

The 1972 amendments aimed to restore and maintain "the chemical, physical and biological integrity of the nation's waters." The amendments specified, as a national goal, that the "discharge of pollutants into navigable waters be eliminated by 1985." This also included an interim goal:

> [W]herever attainable, an interim goal of water quality which provides for the protection and propagation of fish, shellfish and wildlife and provides for recreation in and on the water [should] be achieved by July 1, 1983.

The EPA administrator was required to set effluent restrictions that met the following general requirements of the 1972 amendments: By 1977, all dischargers were to achieve "best practicable control technology currently available" (BPT); and by 1983, all dischargers were to have the "best available technology economically achievable" (BAT). After delays caused by numerous legal challenges to the EPA administrator's effluent limitations guidelines, the BPT provisions were implemented. However, the BAT requirements were so heavily disputed that Congress modified them in the Clean Water Act of 1977.

The principal criticism of the original BAT effluent limitations was that the costs of the very high required percentage reductions in residuals would be much greater than the benefits. In defining BAT, costs were considered, but only in the general context of affordability by industry. Computations of the social benefits of stringent effluent controls were not a central factor. Congress presumed the benefits of eliminating water pollutants would be substantial.

Congressional insistence on very strict effluent limitations can also be interpreted as an effort to guarantee the rights of Americans to high-quality water.

In 1977, Congress responded to critics of BAT by requiring it only for toxic substances. A different requirement was introduced for "conventional pollutants," such as biochemical oxygen demand and suspended solids. The effluent limitations guidelines for these pollutants were to be based on the best conventional pollutant control technology (BCT).

The Clean Water Act of 1977 strongly endorsed the view that waterborne toxic substances must be controlled. The text of the act included a list of 65 substances, or classes of substances, to be used as the basis for defining toxics. This list resulted from a 1976 settlement of a legal action in which several environmental organizations sued the EPA administrator for failing to issue toxic pollutant standards. This list was subsequently expanded by EPA to include 127 "priority pollutants" (Table 1–3).

Effluent limitations required by the FWPCA amendments of 1972 (and later the Clean Water Act of 1977) formed the basis for issuing "National Pollutant Discharge Elimination System" (NPDES) permits. The permit system idea stemmed from actions taken by the Department of Justice in the late 1960s. With the support of a favorable interpretation by the Supreme Court, attorneys for the United States relied on the 1899 River and Harbor Act to prosecute industrial sources of water pollution. The 1899 act, which was drafted originally to prohibit deposits of refuse in navigable waters to keep them clear for boat traffic, was interpreted in the 1960s as applying to liquid waste as well. In December 1970, the EPA administrator issued an executive order calling for a water quality management program using permits and penalties based on the River and Harbor Act of 1899. Although this program was delayed by court challenges in 1971, Congress made it a central part of the federal strategy embodied in the FWPCA amendments of 1972.

| TABLE 1–3 | EPA's Priority Pollutant List |
| --- | --- |

1. Antimony
2. Arsenic
3. Beryllium
4. Cadmium
5a. Chromium (III)
5b. Chromium (VI)
6. Copper
7. Lead
8. Mercury
9. Nickel
10. Selenium
11. Silver
12. Thallium
13. Zinc
14. Cyanide
15. Asbestos
16. 2,3,7,8-TCDD (dioxin)
17. Acrolein
18. Acrylonitrile
19. Benzene
20. Bromoform
21. Carbon tetrachloride
22. Chlorobenzene
23. Chlorodibromomethane
24. Chloroethane
25. 2-Chloroethylvinyl ether
26. Chloroform
27. Dichlorobromomethane
28. 1,1-Dichloroethane
29. 1,2-Dichloroethane
30. 1,1-Dichloroethylene
31. 1,2-Dichloropropane
32. 1,1-Dichloropropylene
33. Ethylbenzene
34. Methyl bromide
35. Methyl chloride
36. Methylene chloride
37. 1,2,2,2-Tetrachloroethane
38. Tetrachloroethylene
39. Toluene
40. 1,2-trans-Dichloroethylene
41. 1,1,1-Trichloroethane
42. 2,4 Dichlorophenol
43. Trichloroethylene
44. Vinyl chloride
45. 2-Chlorophenol
46. 2,4-Dichlorophenol
47. 2,4-Dimethylphenol
48. 2-Methyl-4-chlorophenol
49. 2,4-Dinitrophenol
50. 2-Nitrophenol
51. 4-Nitrophenol
52. 3-Methyl-4-chlorophenol
53. Pentachlorophenol
54. Phenol
55. 2,4,6-Trichlorophenol
56. Acenaphthene
57. Acenaphthylene
58. Anthracene
59. Benzidine
60. Benzo(a)anthracene
61. Benzo(a)pyrene
62. Benzo(a)fluoranthene
63. Benzo(ghi)perylene
64. Benzo(k)fluoranthene
65. Bis(2-chloroethoxy)methane
66. Bis(2-chloroethyl) Ether
67. Bis(2-chloroisopropyl) Ether
68. Bis(2-ethylhexyl) Phthalate
69. 4-Bromophenyl phenyl ether
70. Butylbenzyl phthalate
71. 2-Chloronaphthalene
72. 4-Chlorophenyl phenyl ether
73. Chrysene
74. Dibenzo(a,h)anthracene
75. 1,2-Dichlorobenzene
76. 1,3-Dichlorobenzene
77. 1,4-Dichlorobenzene
78. 3,3-Dichlorobenzidine
79. Diethyl phthalate
80. Dimethyl phthalate
81. Di-n-butyl phthalate
82. 2,4-Dinitrotoluene
83. 2,6-Dinitrotoluene
84. Di-n-octyl phthalate
85. 1,2-Diphenylhydrazine
86. Fluoranthene
87. Fluorene
88. Hexachlorobenzene
89. Hexachlorobutadiene
90. Hexachlorocyclopentadiene
91. Hexachloroethane
92. Indeno(1,2,3-cd)pyrene
93. Isophorone
94. Naphthalene
95. Nitrobenzene
96. N-Nitrosodimethylamine
97. N-Nitrosodi-n-propylamine
98. N-Nitrosodiphenylamine
99. Phenanthrene
100. Pyrene
101. 1,2,4-Trichlorobenzene
102. Aldrin
103. α-BHC
104. β-BHC
105. γ-BHC
106. δ-BHC
107. Chlordane
108. 4,4'-DDT
109. 4,4'-DDE
110. 4,4'-DDD
111. Dieldrin
112. α-Endosulfan
113. β-Endosulfan
114. Endosulfan sulfate
115. Endrin
116. Endrin aldehyde
117. Heptachlor
118. Heptachlor epoxide
119. PCB-1242
120. PCB-1254
121. PCB-1221
122. PCB-1232
123. PCB-1248
124. PCB-1260
125. PCB-1016
126. Toxaphene

*Source:* 40 CFR 131.36, July 1, 1993.

### Air Quality Management

This discussion follows that of L. Ortolano in *Environmental Planning and Design* [8]. The earliest programs to manage air quality regulated emissions from smokestacks using nuisance law municipal ordinances. The first antismoke ordinance in the United States was issued by Chicago in 1881. Little progress was made in air pollution control in the first half of the 20th century.

During the 1950s, there was a shift away from nuisance law and municipal ordinances as bases for air quality management. Two factors stimulated the development of additional air pollution control strategies. One was a tragic air pollution episode in 1948 at Donora, Pennsylvania, which caused death to 20 people and illness to several thousand. The second factor was the growing recognition of the linkage between automobile exhausts and photochemical smog.

The pattern of reliance on local agencies began to change with the passage of the Federal Air Pollution Control Act of 1955 (Table 1–4). This act established a program of federally funded research grants administered by the U.S. Public Health Service. Although the act represented an

**TABLE 1–4**     Federal Laws Controlling Air Pollution

| Year | Title | Selected Elements of Legislation[a] |
|------|-------|--------------------------------------|
| 1955 | Air Pollution Control Act | Funds for air pollution research |
| 1960 | Motor Vehicle Exhaust Act | Funds for research on vehicle emissions |
| 1963 | Clean Air Act | Three-stage enforcement process<br>Funds for state and local air pollution control agencies |
| 1965 | Motor Vehicle Air Pollution Control Act | Emission regulations for cars beginning with 1968 models |
| 1967 | Air Quality Act | Federally issued criteria documents<br>Federally issued control technique documents<br>Air quality and control regions (AQCRs) defined<br>Requirements for states to set ambient standards for AQCRs<br>Requirements for state implementation plans |
| 1970 | Clean Air Act Amendments | National ambient air quality standards<br>New source performance standards<br>Technology forcing auto emission standards<br>Transportation control plans |
| 1977 | Clean Air Act Amendments | Relaxation of previous auto emission requirements<br>Vehicle inspection and maintenance programs<br>Prevention of significant deterioration areas<br>Emission offsets for nonattainment areas<br>Study ozone depletion<br>National emission standards for hazardous air pollutants (NESHAP) |
| 1980 | Acid Precipitation Act | Development of a long-term research plan |
| 1986 | Radon Gas and Indoor Air Quality Research Act | Research program to gather data and to coordinate and assess federal action |
| 1990 | Clean Air Act Amendments | Sets attainment dates for criteria air pollutants<br>Imposes new requirements for auto emissions and establishes clean fuels program<br>Identifies 189 hazardous air pollutants to be regulated<br>Establishes 502 allowances for acid rain control<br>Establishes a national permit system<br>Sets schedule for phase out of ozone-depleting compounds |

[a]The table entries include only the new policies and programs established by each of the laws. Often these provisions were carried forward as elements of subsequent legislation.

expansion of the federal role, it was a very limited one. The legislative history of the act indicates congressional intent to restrain federal involvement and to respect the rights and responsibilities of states, counties, and cities in controlling air pollution.

The federal role was further extended by the Clean Air Act of 1963, which allowed direct federal intervention to reduce interstate pollution. The form of intervention followed the enforcement process in the Federal Water Pollution Control Act of 1956.

The first federal restrictions on auto emissions came with the Motor Vehicle Air Pollution Control Act of 1965. Based on earlier auto emission control efforts in California, the 1965 act gave the secretary of the Department of Health, Education, and Welfare authority to establish permissible emission levels for new automobiles beginning with the 1968 model year. The control of emissions from older vehicles was left to individual states.

The Air Quality Act of 1967 borrowed concepts from the Water Quality Control Act of 1965 by requiring states to develop ambient air quality standards and state implementation plans (SIPs) to achieve the standards implementation plans were to include emission requirements for controlling air pollution and a timetable for meeting the requirements. Deadlines were set for submitting ambient standards, which were to be established on a region-wide basis.

Although the Clean Air Act Amendments of 1970 continued many of the research and state aid programs established by prior legislation, several aspects of the amendments represented dramatic changes in strategy. These involved (1) the requirement that the administrator of EPA set national ambient air quality standards (NAAQS) and emission standards for selected categories of new industrial facilities, and (2) the explicit delineation (by Congress) of auto emission standards. Another manifestation of the expanded role of the federal government was the requirement of the 1970 amendments that the EPA administrator issue new source performance standards (NSPS). These standards were to control new stationary sources categorized by the administrator as contributing significantly to air pollution.

The Clean Air Act Amendments of 1977 relaxed the emission requirements somewhat and extended the compliance deadlines into the early 1980s. They also defined a concept of prevention of significant deterioration (PSD) areas and required that an area that meets the national ambient standards for a given air pollutant be declared a PSD area for that pollutant. The amendments also defined three classes of PSD areas. For each class, numerical limits indicated the maximum permissible increment of air quality degradation from all new (or modified) stationary sources of pollution in an area.

The 1977 amendments also indicated that significant new sources of pollution could locate in areas that did not meet the NAAQS, but only if certain conditions were satisfied. The amendments required that a significant new source locating in a nonattainment area (one which has not achieved the NAAQS) had to meet strict emission-reduction requirements developed by the EPA administrator. In addition, discharges from the new source had to be more than offset by reductions in emissions from other sources in the region.

In 1979, the EPA extended the concept of emission offsets, as used in nonattainment areas, to a different context: multiple sources of air pollution generated at a single site. This extension, known as the **bubble policy,** is illustrated in Figure 1-7. The figure depicts a firm that must control releases from smokestacks at two adjacent plants. Before the bubble policy, the firm had to comply with emission standards that allowed only $100 \text{ Mg} \cdot \text{d}^{-1}$ from each plant.* The total discharge was $200 \text{ Mg} \cdot \text{d}^{-1}$. The unit cost of emission controls for plant A was much higher than that for plant B, but the emission requirements were insensitive to these cost differences. Using the bubble policy, the firm is free to decide how to reduce residuals at each plant. The only restriction is that its total discharge must be no greater than $200 \text{ Mg} \cdot \text{d}^{-1}$. Imagine that a bubble surrounds the two plants. The policy allows the firm to make choices within the bubble, but the total discharge from the bubble is restricted. In the early 1980s, the original bubble policy was extended to include plants that were not at the same location (multiplant bubbles).

---

*$\text{Mg} \cdot \text{d}^{-1}$ = megagram per day. $1 \text{ Mg} = 1000 \text{ kg}$.

**FIGURE 1-7**

Illustration of bubble concept. (*Source:* Davis, M.L., Cornwell, D.A., *Introduction to Environmental Engineering,* WCB/ McGraw-Hill: N.Y., 1998. Reprinted by permission.)

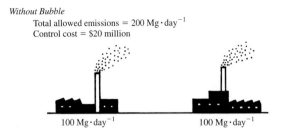

*Without Bubble*
Total allowed emissions = 200 Mg·day$^{-1}$
Control cost = $20 million

100 Mg·day$^{-1}$          100 Mg·day$^{-1}$

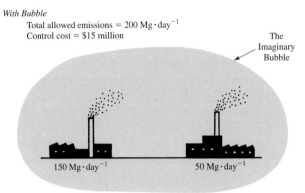

*With Bubble*
Total allowed emissions = 200 Mg·day$^{-1}$
Control cost = $15 million

The Imaginary Bubble

150 Mg·day$^{-1}$          50 Mg·day$^{-1}$

The Clean Air Act Amendments of 1990 (CAAA) mandated that the EPA promulgate more than 175 new regulations, 30 guidance documents, 35 studies, and 50 new research initiatives. The congressional mandates are categorized under 11 titles in the act. It has become common to refer to the requirements of the CAAA by title number.

In light of the fact that three previous deadlines for attainment had come and gone, Title I establishes 16 new deadlines. Although these are primarily aimed at ozone, there are also classifications for carbon monoxide and fine particulates.

Provisions relating to mobile sources are spelled out in Title II. Cars are required to have dashboard warning lights that signal whether or not pollution control equipment is working. These devices frequently have impregnated chemicals that react with the pollutants. The life expectancy of these devices, in terms of miles driven, is specified as 100,000 miles, rather than the previous requirement of 50,000 miles. Auto makers are required to produce some cars that use clean fuels such as alcohol and some that are powered by electricity. In addition, inspection and maintenance (I/M) programs for metropolitan areas have been expanded.

Because the previous legislation establishing national emission standards for hazardous pollutants (NESHAPs) based on health risk proved too cumbersome, Title III established an initial list of 189 hazardous air pollutants (HAPs) and directed EPA to establish emission standards based on technology. These standards are to be the maximum achievable control technology (MACT) for a given source category.

Under Title IV, the act outlines a new nationwide approach to the problem of acid rain. The law sets up a market-based system to lower sulfur dioxide emissions. EPA will issue emission allowances to power plants listed in the act. The allowances are set below current emission levels. Plants may meet the allowances by installing control technology or by purchasing allowances from plants that have emissions below their allowance. For example, in November of 1994, Niagara Mohawk, which serves upstate New York, and the Arizona Public Service Co. traded emission allowances for carbon monoxide and sulfur dioxide.

Unlike the Clean Water Act, no provision for permits was included in the original Clean Air Act (1963). Title V remedies this deficiency by making it unlawful to operate one of the sources listed in the act except by compliance with a permit.

Depletion of the ozone layer is addressed in Title VI of the act. A schedule for phasing out the production of ozone-destroying chemicals was promulgated in the act with provision that EPA could accelerate the schedule. In 1993, EPA established an accelerated schedule that essentially phased out the production of ozone-destroying chemicals by 2001.

### Noise Pollution Control

The following discussion on noise pollution control follows C. R. Bragdon, *Inter-noise,* and Council on Environmental Quality Reports. The city of Boston was the first to regulate noise, beginning in 1850. This ordinance was primarily concerned with noise occurring in public places that would disturb the peace. Consequently, restrictions were placed on the use of public spaces for conducting noisy activities. It was not until the beginning of the 20th century that other cities became interested in regulating noise.

In the late 1920s the health commissioner of New York City established a noise abatement commission. This commission, the first of its kind, sought to identify city noise sources, assess their effect, and recommend solutions. The commission's report, *City Noise,* published in 1930, was unique in many ways. An acoustical inventory of noise source was undertaken along with a survey of public opinion and recommendations for laws to control noise. The legislation that this widely circulated report urged was subsequently adopted by many other cities. Primary noise provisions included muffler requirements for vehicles, building construction restrictions in residential areas, the prohibition of horns and whistles, the regulation of peddlers and vendors, and the prohibition of noise from mechanical or electrical sound-making or reproducing equipment.

In 1948 the National Institute of Municipal Law Officers (NIMLO) prepared a research report to guide municipalities in controlling noise. This report, subsequently referred to as the NIMLO model ordinance, was to be widely disseminated and adopted. Until recently this ordinance has been the basis for most laws.

It was not until 1952 that specific noise emission levels appeared. These first laws contained vehicle noise level requirements expressed in decibels. Seattle, Washington, and Cincinnati, Ohio, adopted these first quantitative ordinances. Following the control of mobile noise sources were laws establishing specific fixed source limits that used the zoning ordinance as the legal basis. Chicago, Illinois, in 1955 adopted the first law that restricted land use activity that produced noise. It represented a new approach to zoning. Restrictions were not placed on the classification of industry by type (i.e., light manufacturing or heavy manufacturing) and by permitted uses, but rather on their performance in terms of noise emission. Many cities adopted provisions similar or identical to those used in Chicago.

In 1970 NIMLO modified their earlier nuisance-type ordinance, adding decibel provisions as an alternative. The League of California Cities prepared a model document that contained sound levels for zoning districts in rural, suburban, and urban areas.

In 1973 17 states had types of noise laws concerned with zoning and land use, motor vehicles, and aircraft and building codes.

Prior to 1970 the federal government's activities in noise abatement had no central focus. The emphasis was on specific activities regulated separately by individual agencies. Each noise problem was considered in isolation.

The landmark legislation in the area of occupational noise abatement was enacted in 1942 and is known as the Walsh-Healey Public Contracts Act. This act established minimum working conditions for employees of contractors who supply the federal government with materials, supplies, and equipment in excess of $10,000. However, it was not until 1969 that the secretary of labor interpreted this as applicable to noise! (*Note:* These applied only to supply contracts and not to construction contracts.)

In the 1962 amendments to the Federal Aid Highways Act, economic, social, and environmental effects were included as requirements for consideration in the development of plans for construction. The following year, the Federal Housing Administration implemented minimum standards for airborne noise and building structure noise permitted for mortgage underwriting.

The Department of Transportation Act (1966) included provisions to promote research on noise abatement with particular attention to aircraft. This was followed by the 1968 amendments to the Federal Aviation Administration Act that directed the secretary of transportation to prescribe rules for control and abatement of aircraft noise.

Environmental legislation and rule making had a banner year in 1970. The Federal Aid Highways Act was amended to direct the secretary of transportation to develop and promulgate standards for highway noise levels compatible with different land uses. The Occupational Safety and Health Act of 1970 (OSHA) enabled the secretary of labor to apply the Walsh-Healey standards with new meaning. Walsh-Healey merely excluded from bidding on federal contracts those suppliers who failed to meet minimum work condition standards. OSHA provided penalties for those suppliers, including civil and criminal law sanctions. Construction noise was brought under federal consideration in the Construction Safety Act of 1970. This act carried the Walsh-Healey provisions to the supply of construction contracts.

Also in 1970 Congress added Title IV to the Clean Air Act amendments. This act was entitled the Noise Pollution and Abatement Act of 1970, and it set up the Office of Noise Abatement and Control in the EPA. The major provision of the act was to give the EPA the discretion to identify and classify causes and sources of noise and to assess their effects. Authority for actual abatement of federal sources of noise was also included.

### Solid Waste Management

This discussion follows G. Tchobanoglous and colleagues, *Solid Wastes* [9]. Modern solid waste legislation dates from 1965 when the Solid Waste Disposal Act, Title II of Public Law 89-272, was enacted by Congress. The intent of this act was to

1. Promote the demonstration, construction, and application of solid waste management and resource recovery systems that preserve and enhance the quality of air, water, and land resources.
2. Provide technical and financial assistance to states and local governments and interstate agencies in the planning and development of resource recovery and solid waste disposal programs.
3. Promote a national research and development program for improved management techniques, more effective organizational arrangements, and new and improved methods of collection, separation, recovery, and recycling of solid wastes, and the environmentally safe disposal of nonrecoverable residues.
4. Provide for the promulgation of guidelines for solid waste collection, transport, separation, recovery, and disposal systems.
5. Provide training grants in occupations involving the design, operation, and maintenance of solid waste disposal systems.

Enforcement of this act became the responsibility of the U.S. Public Health Service (USPHS) and the Bureau of Mines. The USPHS had responsibility for most of the municipal wastes. The Bureau of Mines was charged with supervision of solid wastes from mining activities and the fossil-fuel solid wastes from power plants and industrial steam plants.

The Solid Waste Disposal Act of 1965 was amended by Public Law 95-512, the Resources Recovery Act of 1970. The act directed that the emphasis of the national solid waste management program be shifted from disposal as its primary objective to that of recycling and reuse of recoverable materials in solid wastes or to the conversion of wastes to energy.

Another feature of the 1970 act was the mandate of Congress to the secretary of health, education, and welfare to prepare a report on the treatment and disposal of hazardous wastes, including radioactive, toxic chemical, biological, and other wastes of significance to the public health and welfare. Previously, the Atomic Energy Act of 1954 had authorized the U.S. Atomic Energy Commission to manage all radioactive wastes generated by the commission and the nuclear power industry.

### Hazardous Waste Management

Part of this discussion is excerpted from J. Quarles, Federal Regulation of Hazardous Wastes [10]. For many years little attention was paid to where waste materials, including the contaminants removed from the air and the water, went. These contaminants often returned to the environment through the disposal of waste. Waste disposal practices were discovered to have caused environmental damage in many cases, especially in contamination of groundwater used as a drinking-water supply. This led Congress to enact the Resource Conservation and Recovery Act of 1976, commonly known as RCRA (and pronounced "rick-rah").

RCRA addresses the handling of hazardous waste at facilities currently operating and at those yet to be constructed. The act was designed in large part to meet disposal needs resulting from the Clean Air Act and Clean Water Act, which require industries to remove hazardous substances from their air emissions and their water discharges. Neither statute, however, ensures that the ultimate disposition of waste materials will be environmentally sound. RCRA was intended to provide that ensurance. RCRA does not, however, deal directly with abandoned sites or closed facilities where hazardous wastes have been handled or disposed of in the past. These locations are covered by the Comprehensive Environmental Response, Compensation, and Liability Act (CERCLA, pronounced "sir-klah"), commonly referred to as Superfund, enacted by Congress in 1980. Finally, RCRA also does not control the disposition of hazardous substances within the productive stream of commerce. Such substances include chemicals covered by the Toxic Substances Control Act; pesticides regulated under the Federal Insecticide, Fungicide, and Rodenticide Act; or other hazardous products subject to the Hazardous Materials Transportation Act and to other types of federal regulation.

The five major elements in the federal approach to hazardous waste management are

1. Federal classification of hazardous waste
2. Cradle-to-grave manifest (record-keeping) system
3. Federal standards for safeguards to be followed by generators, transporters, and facilities that treat, store, or dispose of hazardous waste
4. Enforcement of federal standards for facilities through a permit program
5. Authorization of state programs to operate in lieu of the federal program

The act directs the EPA to promulgate regulations necessary to put the federal program into full effect.

Unhappy with the progress in implementing RCRA, Congress in 1984 passed the Hazardous and Solid Waste Amendments (HSWA, pronounced "hiss-wah"). The scope of RCRA was significantly increased. Under the legislation,

1. Waste minimization was established as the preferred method for managing hazardous waste.
2. Untreated hazardous waste was banned from land disposal, and EPA was directed to establish treatment standards for land disposal.
3. New technology standards, such as double liners, leachate collection systems, and extensive groundwater monitoring, were established for land disposal facilities.
4. New requirements were established for small-quantity generators.
5. The EPA was directed to establish standards for underground storage tanks.
6. The EPA was directed to evaluate criteria for municipal solid waste landfills and upgrade monitoring requirements.

CERCLA provided authority for removal of hazardous substances from improperly constructed or operated active sites not in compliance with RCRA and from inactive disposal sites.

The most fundamental feature of CERCLA is that it provides basic operating authority to the federal government to take direct action to remove hazardous substances from dangerous inactive disposal sites and to assist with cleaning up emergency spills. This includes authority to carry out investigations, testing, and monitoring of disposal sites. It also includes authority to implement remedial measures to remove contaminants in the groundwater.

CERCLA earned its nickname, Superfund, from the provision of a $1.6 billion Hazardous Substance Response Trust Fund. Seven-eighths of the money is to be provided by industry through taxes on crude oil, certain petroleum products, and 42 chemical feedstocks; one-eighth is to be provided by government through appropriations from general revenues.

In cases where responsibility for the wastes that cause contamination can be traced to companies with financial resources, CERCLA places financial responsibility for the cleanup on those companies. The statute establishes a new and far-reaching set of federal laws under which liability can be imposed on such companies even when they are only indirectly involved in the ownership or operation of the facilities where the wastes were disposed. After the government has identified a site as a threat to the environment, it may call upon those liable companies to undertake the cleanup at their own cost. Alternatively, if such companies refuse to assume responsibility for the cleanup, the government can carry out the remedial program using money from the fund and then bring suit against the companies for reimbursement.

A national contingency plan (NCP) establishes the rules for how EPA will use its authority and spend its money. To qualify for expenditure of CERCLA funds, a site must appear on the national priorities list (NPL). The EPA developed the hazardous ranking system (HRS) as a method of assigning a site to the NPL. As of December 1, 2000, 1,200 sites had been placed on the NPL. In addition CERCLA contains notice requirements for all releases (spills) of reportable quantities of hazardous substances and creates a postclosure liability fund for qualified disposal facilities.

The Superfund Amendments and Reauthorization Act (SARA) of 1986 extended the provisions of CERCLA. In addition to establishing an $8.5 billion fund for cleanup, SARA establishes that EPA

1. Revise the NPL and the HRS on which it is based.
2. Revise the NCP.
3. Is authorized to subpoena documents and witnesses.
4. Can spend money to investigate sites and design remedies, and can permit private parties to conduct cleanup.
5. Has broad enforcement authority to require private parties to undertake cleanup.
6. Must impose the more stringent of federal standards or state standards.
7. May use mixed funding, that is, both federal and private money.
8. Develop an administrative record of decisions.

The Toxic Substances Control Act (TSCA) of 1976 is unique in hazardous waste legislation in that it requires disclosure of information about the toxicity of new materials before they enter into commercial manufacture. It deals with hazardous waste in only one instance: polychlorinated biphenyls (PCBs). At the federal level, rules for the disposal of PCBs are set under TSCA (pronounced "tos-ka") rather than RCRA or CERCLA.

### Atomic Energy and Radiation Management

Laws and regulations to manage radioactive materials and radiation exposure began with the Atomic Energy Act of 1946. The act established the Atomic Energy Commission (AEC) and directed it to conduct research and development on peaceful applications of fissionable and radioactive materials. The Atomic Energy Act of 1954 provided for control of uranium and thorium ("source material" for nuclear reactors), plutonium and enriched uranium (classified as special nuclear material because of their potential use in atomic weapons), and other by-products of the nuclear industry. The Energy Reorganization Act of 1974 divided the developmental and regulatory functions of the AEC between two agencies: the Energy and Research and Development Administration (ERDA) and the Nuclear Regulatory Commission (NRC). In restructuring the administration of energy-related matters after the Arab oil boycott, the Energy Organization Act of 1977 replaced ERDA with the Department of Energy (DOE). The NRC was given jurisdiction over reactor construction and operation. It regulates the possession, use, transportation, handling, and disposal of radioactive materials and wastes. The DOE is responsible for research and development and will operate defense and high-level waste repositories.

The diminishing space at low-level disposal sites led to the enactment of the Low-Level Waste Policy Act (LLWPA) in 1980. Each state is responsible for providing for the availability of capacity either within or outside the state for disposal of low-level radioactive waste generated within its borders. States were encouraged to enter into compacts with their neighbors to more efficiently manage the waste. The law allowed the compacts to exclude wastes from other regions and allowed existing disposal sites to impose surcharges for disposal of wastes from regions without sites. The surcharge was to be used for site development. Difficulties in negotiating the compacts prompted the enactment of the Low-Level Radioactive Waste Policy Act Amendments of 1985 (LLRWPAA). It stipulated that the three existing commercial sites remain open for use by all states through 1992. Annual and total limits on the volume of waste that can be sent from reactors were established. DOE is responsible for overseeing the compact arrangements with authority to allocate additional emergency capacity to reactors. The NRC can authorize emergency access to existing sites.

The Nuclear Waste Policy Act of 1982 directed DOE to develop a plan for storage of high-level radioactive waste. Following the requirements of the law, DOE began investigation of nine sites in the west and two in the east. Under the act, the EPA established standards that specified release limits for 1000 and 10,000 years after disposal.

Because of loudly voiced concern over the direction of the DOE's mission plan and the decision to abandon the search for a repository site in the east, Congress passed the Nuclear Waste Policy Act Amendments of 1987. The amendments restructured DOE's high-level waste program. The only site that would be considered would be Yucca Flats, Nevada. Furthermore, spent fuel would be required to be shipped in NRC-approved packages after notification of state and local governments. During the years 2007–2010, DOE is to study the need for a second repository.

For mixed wastes, that is, both hazardous and radioactive, RCRA and HSWA apply to the hazardous characteristic. As of 1987, disposal rules must comply with both NRC rules for radioactivity and EPA rules for hazardous constituents. Before then, only the NRC rules applied. Likewise, for leaking disposal sites, CERCLA and SARA rules apply as well as the NRC rules.

Radiation exposure from x-rays and medical diagnosis and treatment are regulated under the Radiation Control for Health and Safety Act of 1968.

## 1-8 ENVIRONMENTAL ETHICS

The birth of environmental ethics as a force is partly a result of concern for our own long-term survival, as well as our realization that humans are but one form of life, and that we share our earth with other forms of life [11].

Although it seems a bit unrealistic for us to set a framework for a discussion of environmental ethics in this short introduction, we have summarized a few salient points in Table 1–5.

| **TABLE 1–5** | An Environmental Code of Ethics |
|---|---|

1. Use knowledge and skill for the enhancement and protection of the environment.
2. Hold paramount the health, safety and welfare of the environment.
3. Perform services only in areas of personal expertise.
4. Be honest and impartial in serving the public, your employers, your clients, and the environment.
5. Issue public statements only in an objective and truthful manner.

Although these few principles seem straightforward, real-world problems offer distinct challenges. Here is an example for each of the principles listed:

- The first principle may be threatened when it comes into conflict with the need for food for a starving population and the country is overrun with locusts. Will the use of pesticides enhance and protect the environment?

- The EPA has stipulated that wastewater must be disinfected where people come into contact with the water. However, the disinfectant may also kill naturally occurring beneficial microorganisms. Is this consistent with the second principle?

- Suppose your expertise is water and wastewater chemistry. Your company has accepted a job to perform air pollution analysis and asks you to perform the work in the absence of a colleague who is the company's expert? Do you decline and risk being fired?

- The public, your employers, and your client believe that dredging a lake to remove weeds and sediment will enhance the lake. However, the dredging will destroy the habitat for muskrats. How can you be impartial to *all* these constituencies?

- You believe that a new regulation proposed by EPA is too expensive to implement, but you have no data to confirm that opinion. How do you respond to a local newspaper reporter asking for your opinion? Do you violate the fifth principle even though "your opinion" is being sought?

Below are two cases that are more complex. We have not attempted to provide pat solutions but rather have left them for you and your instructor to resolve.

### Case 1: To Add or Not to Add

A friend of yours has discovered that his firm is adding nitrites and nitrates to bacon to help preserve it. He also has read that these compounds are precursors to cancer-forming chemicals that are produced in the body. On the other hand, he realizes that certain disease organisms such as those that manufacture botulism toxin have been known to grow in bacon that has not been treated. He asks you whether he should (a) protest to his superiors knowing he might get fired; (b) leak the news to the press; (c) remain silent because the risk of dying from cancer is less than the absolute certainty of dying from botulism.

*Note:* The addition of nitrite to bacon is approved by the Food and Drug Administration. Nitrites and nitrates are, in and of themselves, not very toxic to adults. However, heating these compounds results in a reaction with the amines in proteins to form nitrosamine, which is a carcinogenic compound.

### Case 2: You Can't Do Everything At Once [12]

As an environmental scientist newly assigned to a developing country you find yourself in an isolated village with an epidemic of cholera. You have two routes of action available:

1. You can nurse and comfort the sick.
2. You can try to clean up the water supply.

Which is the ethical choice?

We think it is important to point out that many environmentally related decisions such as those described here are much more difficult than the problems presented in the remaining chapters of this book. Frequently these problems are related more to ethics or economics than to environmental engineering and environmental science. The problems arise when several courses of action are possible with no certainty as to which is best. Decisions related to safety, health, and welfare are easily resolved. Decisions as to which course of action is in the best interest of the public are much more difficult to resolve. Furthermore, decisions as to which course of action is in the best interest of the environment are at times in conflict with those which are in the best interest of the public. Whereas decisions made in the public interest are based on professional ethics, decisions made in the best interest of the environment are based on environmental ethics.

*Ethos,* the Greek word from which *ethic* is derived, means the character of a person as described by his or her actions. This character was developed during the evolutionary process and was influenced by the need for adapting to the natural environment. Our ethic is our way of doing things. Our ethic is a direct result of our natural environment. During the latter stages of the evolutionary process, *Homo sapiens* began to modify the environment rather than submit to what, millennia later, became known as Darwinian natural selection. As an example, consider the cave dweller who, in the chilly dawn of prehistory, realized the value of the saber-toothed tiger's coat and appropriated it for personal use. Inevitably a pattern of appropriation developed, and our ethic became more self-modified than environmentally adapted. Thus, we are no longer adapted to our natural environment but rather to our self-made environment. In the ecological context, over millennia such maladaptation results in one of two consequences: (1) the organism (*Homo sapiens*) dies out; or (2) the organism evolves to a form and character that is once again compatible with the natural environment [11]. Assuming that we choose the latter course, how can this change in character (ethic) be brought about? Each individual must change his or her character or ethic, and the social system must change to become compatible with the global ecology.

The acceptable system is one in which we learn to share our exhaustible resources to regain a balance. This requires that we reduce our needs and that the materials we use must be replenishable. We must treat all of the Earth as a sacred trust to be used so that its content is neither diminished nor permanently changed; we must release no substances that cannot be reincorporated without damage to the natural system. The recognition of the need for such adaptation (as a means of survival) has developed into what we now call the **environmental ethic** [11] or **environmental stewardship.**

## CHAPTER REVIEW

When you have completed studying the chapter, you should be able to do the following without the aid of your textbook or notes:

1. List the properties that distinguish science from other fields of inquiry.
2. Differentiate between natural science and social science.
3. List three disciplines of natural science.
4. Define environmental science.
5. Explain the advantage of a theory over a collection of ideas.
6. Describe the advantage of a quantitative theory over a qualitative one.
7. Identify and use the symbols of SI units.
8. Sketch and label a water resource system, including (a) source, (b) collection works, (c) transmission works, (d) treatment works, and (e) distribution works.
9. State the proper general approach to treatment of a surface water and a groundwater (see Figure 1–2).
10. Define the word *demand* as it applies to water.
11. List the five most important factors contributing to water consumption and explain why each has an effect.
12. State the rule-of-thumb water requirement for an average city on a per-person basis and calculate the average daily water requirement for a city of a stated population.
13. Define the acronyms WWTP and POTW.
14. Explain why separate storm sewers and sanitary sewers are preferred over combined sewers.
15. Explain the purpose of a lift station.
16. Identify and explain the following acronyms and concepts found in environmental legislation: BPT, BAT, BCT, NPDES, HAP, MACT, bubble policy, NIMLO, Walsh-Healey, OSHA, RCRA, and Superfund.
17. Discuss the role of environmental ethics in environmental engineering and environmental science.

## DISCUSSION QUESTIONS

**1-1**  A nonscientist has remarked that the laws of motion are *just* a theory. She implies that the laws are hypothesis that are not testable. Prepare a written response (explanation) to this remark that includes a definition of the following terms: *hypothesis, theory, law.*

**1-2**  The values for per capita water consumption in Table 1-1 are very specific to the cities noted. Determine the per capita water consumption for your college or university.

**1-3**  Using the Internet, answer the following questions regarding the Clean Air Act:

**(a)** Title II of the act addresses what kinds of pollution sources?

**(b)** What is the chemical name of the first hazardous air pollutant listed under Title III

**(c)** Section 604 of the act lists the phase-out of production of substances that deplete the ozone layer. What is the last year that carbon tetrachloride can be produced?

**1-4**  Using the Internet, determine the Website address (also known as the URL) that allows you to find information on environmental regulations published in the *Federal Register* and in the Code of Federal Regulations.

**1-5**  The Shiny Plating Company is using about 2000.0 $kg \cdot week^{-1}$ of organic solvent for vapor degreasing of metal parts before they are plated. The Air Pollution Engineering and Testing Company (APET) has measured the air in the workroom and in the stack that vents the degreaser. APET has determined that 1985.0 $kg \cdot week^{-1}$ is being vented up the stack and that the workroom environment is within occupational standards. The 1985.0 $kg \cdot week^{-1}$ is well above the allowable emission rate of 11.28 $kg \cdot week^{-1}$.

Elizabeth Fry, the plant superintendent, has asked J. R., the plant engineer, to review two alternative control approaches offered by APET and to recommend one of them.

The first method is to purchase a pollution control device to put on the stack. This control system will reduce the solvent emission to 1.0 $kg \cdot week^{-1}$. Approximately 1950.0 kg of the solvent captured each week can be recycled back to the degreaser. Approximately 34.0 kg of the solvent must be discharged to the wastewater treatment plant (WWTP). J. R. has determined that this small amount of solvent will not adversely affect the performance of the WWTP. In addition, the capital cost of the pollution control equipment will be recovered in about 2 years as a result of savings from recovering lost solvent.

The second method is to substitute a solvent that is not on the list of regulated emissions. The price of the substitute is about 10% higher than the solvent currently in use. J. R. has estimated that the substitute solvent loss will be about 100.0 $kg \cdot week^{-1}$. The substitute collects moisture and loses its effectiveness in about a month's time. The substitute solvent cannot be discharged to the WWTP because it will adversely affect the WWTP performance. Consequently, about 2000 kg must be hauled to a hazardous waste disposal site for storage each month. Because of the lack of capital funds and the high interest rate for borrowing, J. R. recommends that the substitute solvent be used. Do you agree with this recommendation? Explain your reasoning.

**1-6**  Ted Terrific is the manager of a leather-tanning company. In part of the tanning operation a solution of chromic acid is used. It is company policy that the spent chrome solution is put in 0.20-$m^3$ drums and shipped to a hazardous waste disposal facility.

On Thursday the 12th, the day shift miscalculates the amount of chrome to add to a new batch and makes it too strong. Because there is not enough room in the tank to adjust the concentration, Abe Lincoln, the shift supervisor, has the tank emptied and a new one prepared and makes a note to the manager that the bad batch needs to be reworked.

On Monday the 16th, Abe Lincoln looks for the bad batch and cannot find it. He notifies Ted Terrific that it is missing. Upon investigation, Ted finds that Rip VanWinkle, the night-shift supervisor, dumped the batch into the sanitary sewer at 3:00 A.M. on Friday the 13th. Ted makes discreet inquiries at the wastewater plant and finds that they have had no process upsets. After Ted severely disciplines Rip, he should: (Choose the correct answer and explain your reasoning.)

**(a)** Inform the city and state authorities of the illegal discharge as required by law even though no apparent harm resulted.

**(b)** Keep the incident quiet because it will cause trouble for the company without doing the public any good. No harm was done, and the shift supervisor has been punished.

**(c)** Advise the president and board of directors and let them decide whether to follow alternatives (a) or (b).

## ADDITIONAL READING

Gunn, A. S. and P. Aarne Vesilind, *Environmental Ethics for Engineers,* Chelsea, MI, Lewis Publishers, Inc., 1986.

## REFERENCES

1. Wright, R. H., *The Science of Smell,* New York: Basic Books, Inc., p. 7, 1964.
2. Environmental Engineering Division of the American Society of Civil Engineers, Statement of Purpose, *Official Register,* New York: ASCE, 1977.
3. Carson, R., *Silent Spring,* Boston: Houghton Mifflin, 1962.
4. American Society of Mechanical Engineers, *ASME Orientation and Guide for Use of SI (Metric) Units,* New York: American Society of Mechanical Engineers, 1976.
5. Gleick, P. H., ed., *Water in Crisis: A Guide to the World's Fresh Water Resources,* New York: Oxford University Press, p. 388, 1993.
6. Linaweaver, F. P., Jr., Geyer, J. C., and Wolff, J. B., "Summary Report on the Residential Water Use Research Project," *Journal of the American Water Works Association,* vol. 59, p. 267, 1967.
7. U.S. Department of Health Education and Welfare, *Manual of Septic Tank Practice* (Public Health Service Publication No. 526), Washington, DC: U.S. Government Printing Office, 1970.
8. Ortolano, L., *Environmental Planning and Design,* New York: Wiley, 1984.
9. Tchobanoglous, G., Theisen, H., and Eliassen, R., *Solid Wastes,* New York: McGraw-Hill, p. 39. 1977.
10. Quarles, J., *Federal Regulation of Hazardous Wastes.* Washington, DC: The Environmental Law Institute, 1982.
11. Vesilind, P. A., *Environmental Pollution and Control,* Ann Arbor, MI: Ann Arbor Science, pp. 214–216, 1975.
12. Adapted from Wright, R. H., *The Science of Smell,* New York: Basic Books, Inc., p. 8, 1964.

# 2

# Chemistry

## 2–1   INTRODUCTION

Environmental science is fundamentally a study of the chemistry, physics, and biology of natural systems or the environment. As such, a basic understanding of these disciplines is essential. In this chapter we will focus on a review of the fundamentals of chemistry with specific applications from environmental science.

**Chemistry** is the study of matter. **Matter** is any substance that has mass and occupies space. All objects, whether gas, liquid, or solids, are made up of elements. **Elements** cannot be broken down into simpler substances by any chemical reaction. **Compounds** are substances containing two or more elements that are combined chemically. A pure compound always contains the same elements in exactly the same proportions (**law of definite proportions** or **law of constant composition**). For example, 1.0000 g of table salt (sodium chloride, NaCl) always contains 0.3934 g of sodium and 0.6066 g of chlorine. The sodium and chlorine are chemically combined. The ratios and structural makeup of the compounds will significantly affect their properties. For example, the chemical compound glucose is made of carbon, hydrogen, and oxygen. The chemical formula is $C_6H_{12}O_6$, indicating that for every 6 atoms of carbon, there are 12 atoms of hydrogen and 6 atoms of oxygen. The compound $CH_2O$ has the same ratio of carbon : hydrogen : oxygen as glucose, but very different properties. This other compound is formaldehyde, a liquid at room temperature and toxic to humans. A **mixture** is a material, having variable composition, which can be separated by physical means. For example, table salt dissolved in water is a mixture. When you allow the water to evaporate, the table salt is left behind.

Chemical compounds made of carbon and hydrogen as the basic building block are considered **organic chemicals.** Organic chemicals can be formed either by living organisms or by synthetic chemical reactions. All other compounds are considered **inorganic chemicals.** A few simple compounds such as carbon monoxide (CO), carbon dioxide ($CO_2$), carbonates, and cyanides are considered inorganic compounds even though they contain carbon. We will discuss some of these compounds later in the chapter.

## 2–2   BASIC CHEMICAL CONCEPTS

### Atoms, Elements, and the Periodic Table

All chemical compounds are composed of atoms of the various elements as basic structural building blocks. Elements are grouped together by their basic properties, as seen in the **periodic table**. (See inside front cover for a tabular arrangement of elements.) For example, the Group IIA (alkaline earth metals) includes calcium, magnesium, and barium, all of which are found in nature as silicate rocks. These elements also occur commonly as carbonates and sulfates. All of these metals (except beryllium) react with water if present as the zero-valent pure elemental metal. Except for beryllium, all of the hydroxides of alkaline earth metals are basic. On the other side of the periodic table are the halogens (Group VIIA): fluorine, chlorine, bromine, iodine, and astatine. All of these elements are reactive nonmetals (except for astatine, whose chemistry is still not well documented). All of the halogens form stable compounds in which the element is in the $-1$ oxidation state*.

An atom is an extremely small particle of matter that retains its identity during chemical reactions. Atoms are made up of electrons, neutrons, and protons. Neutrons and protons make up the nucleus and the vast majority of the mass of atoms. The **nucleus** may also contain one or more electrons. A **proton** is a positively charged particle having a mass more than 1800 times that of an electron. A **neutron** is a particle having a mass almost equal to that of a proton, but no charge. **Electrons** move rapidly around the nucleus, forming a cloud of negative charge.

---

*The oxidation state is the charge an atom in a chemical would have if the pairs of electrons in each bond belonged to the more electronegative atom. For chemicals that are ionicly bonded the oxidation number equals the ionic charge. For covalently bonded compounds, the oxidation number represents a hypothetical charge assigned in accordance with a set of generally accepted rules.

The **atomic number (Z)** is the number of protons in the nucleus of an atom. All atoms of a particular element have the same number of protons, although the number of neutrons and electrons may vary. Therefore, an element is a substance whose atoms have the same atomic number. For example, chlorine has an atomic number of 17; it has 17 protons in the nucleus. The **mass number** of an element is the sum of the number of protons and neutrons in the nucleus of that particular element. For example, carbon-12, the most abundant form of carbon, has six protons and six neutrons. Carbon-14, used in dating ancient objects, has the same number of protons as carbon-12 (six), but eight neutrons. These different forms of carbon are known as isotopes. **Isotopes** are chemically identical forms of an element, having different numbers of neutrons. The atomic numbers of the isotopes of the same element do not vary, whereas the mass numbers do. Some elements, such as sodium, have only one naturally occurring isotope; others, such as oxygen, carbon, and nitrogen, have several naturally occurring isotopes.

The **atomic weight** of an element is the average atomic mass for the naturally occurring element, expressed in atomic mass units (amu) or daltons. The atomic weight listed on the page facing the periodic table in the front of this book is determined by taking into account the fractional abundance of an isotope, that is the fraction of each naturally occurring isotope of the particular element and the atomic weight of that particular isotope.

**EXAMPLE 2–1** In the following table, we have listed the isotopes of magnesium, the percentages at which they are found naturally, and the isotopic weights of each. Calculate the atomic weight of magnesium and compare the value you calculate to the value given in the list of elements in the front of your textbook.

| Isotope | Isotopic Mass (amu) | Fractional Abundance |
|---------|--------------------|--------------------|
| $^{24}Mg$ | 23.985 | 0.7870 |
| $^{25}Mg$ | 24.986 | 0.1013 |
| $^{26}Mg$ | 25.983 | 0.1117 |

Solution   Multiply each of the isotopic masses by its fractional abundance, then sum:

| Isotope | Isotopic Mass (amu) | Fractional Abundance | Isotopic Mass × Fractional Abundance |
|---------|--------------------|--------------------|-----------------------------------|
| $^{24}Mg$ | 23.985 | 0.787 | 18.876195 |
| $^{25}Mg$ | 24.986 | 0.1013 | 2.531082 |
| $^{26}Mg$ | 25.983 | 0.1117 | 2.902301 |
| | | Sum | 24.30958 |

Therefore, the atomic mass of magnesium is 24.3096 amu. The slight difference between this value and that in the list of atomic weights is simply due to round-off error.

### Chemical Bonds and Intermolecular Forces

All atoms that are not present in a uniatomic form are held together by chemical bonds. Molecules can be held together by intermolecular forces, which are usually weakly attractive. A **molecule** is a definite group of atoms that are chemically bonded and held together in a fixed geometric arrangement.

## FIGURE 2-1

The electronegativities of common elements (using the scale provided by Linus Pauling). (*Source:* Chang, *Chemistry*, 7th ed. Copyright © 2002, The McGraw-Hill Companies. Reproduced with permission.)

Increasing electronegativity →

Increasing electronegativity ↓

| 1A | 2A | 3B | 4B | 5B | 6B | 7B | 8B | 8B | 8B | 1B | 2B | 3A | 4A | 5A | 6A | 7A | 8A |
|---|---|---|---|---|---|---|---|---|---|---|---|---|---|---|---|---|---|
| H 2.1 | | | | | | | | | | | | | | | | | |
| Li 1.0 | Be 1.5 | | | | | | | | | | | B 2.0 | C 2.5 | N 3.0 | O 3.5 | F 4.0 | |
| Na 0.9 | Mg 1.2 | | | | | | | | | | | Al 1.5 | Si 1.8 | P 2.1 | S 2.5 | Cl 3.0 | |
| K 0.8 | Ca 1.0 | Sc 1.3 | Ti 1.5 | V 1.6 | Cr 1.6 | Mn 1.5 | Fe 1.8 | Co 1.9 | Ni 1.9 | Cu 1.9 | Zn 1.6 | Ga 1.6 | Ge 1.8 | As 2.0 | Se 2.4 | Br 2.8 | |
| Rb 0.8 | Sr 1.0 | Y 1.2 | Zr 1.4 | Nb 1.6 | Mo 1.8 | Tc 1.9 | Ru 2.2 | Rh 2.2 | Pd 2.2 | Ag 1.9 | Cd 1.7 | In 1.7 | Sn 1.8 | Sb 1.9 | Te 2.1 | I 2.5 | |
| Cs 0.7 | Ba 0.9 | La-Lu 1.0-1.2 | Hf 1.3 | Ta 1.5 | W 1.7 | Re 1.9 | Os 2.2 | Ir 2.2 | Pt 2.2 | Au 2.4 | Hg 1.9 | Tl 1.8 | Pb 1.9 | Bi 1.9 | Po 2.0 | At 2.2 | |
| Fr 0.7 | Ra 0.9 | | | | | | | | | | | | | | | | |

The two basic types of bonds are ionic and covalent. An **ionic bond** is a chemical bond formed by electrostatic attraction between positive and negative ions. With ionic bonding, one atom "gives" up or transfers at least one electron from its valence shell to the valence shell of other atom. The atom that loses electrons becomes a **cation** (positively charged ion), and the one that gains electrons becomes an **anion** (negatively charged ion). For example, the hydrogen atom in hydrofluoric acid (HF) "gives up" its electron to fluorine. In this case, the hydrogen, essentially, becomes positively charged and the fluorine, negatively charged. Compounds that tend to have a greater ability to draw an electron toward itself are known to have **high electronegativities,** * or, in this case, a greater attraction for the shared electron pair than hydrogen. In general, metals are the least electronegative elements; nonmetals are the most electronegative (Figure 2–1).

**Covalent bonding** is formed by the sharing of a pair of electrons between atoms. For example, with hydrogen gas ($H_2$) the electrons in the $1s$ orbital overlap, and each electron can occupy the space around both atoms. Thus, the electrons can be described as shared by both atoms. Other chemicals that are bonded covalently include methane ($CH_4$), ammonia ($NH_3$), and ethylene ($C_2H_4$).

In the case of hydrogen, the bonding electrons are shared equally between the atoms. However, when the two atoms are different elements, the electrons may not be shared equally. A **polar covalent bond** is a covalent bond in which the bonding electrons are not shared equally—or the probability of finding the electrons in the vicinity of one atom is greater than the probability of finding it near the other atom. For example, with HCl, the bonding electrons are more likely to be found near the chlorine atom than the hydrogen atom. Similarly, when compounds such as hydrogen and oxygen are covalently bonded together, as in water, neither the hydrogen nor the oxygen transfers an electron, so that neither atom is essentially completely charged in nature. For example, with water, one can think of the hydrogen as being partially positive in character, with oxygen being partially negative.

---

*Electronegativity is a measure of the ability of an atom in a molecule to attract bonding electrons to itself. The most widely used scale was developed by Linus Pauling. He derived electronegativity values from bond energies and assigned a value of 4.0 to fluorine. Lithium, at the left end of the same period, has a value of 1.0. In general, electronegativity decreases from right to left and from top to bottom in the periodic table.

So far we have discussed ionic and covalent bonding, which holds atoms together. However, there are other, usually weakly attractive, forces that can hold molecules together. These are **intermolecular forces.**

Three types of intermolecular forces can exist between neutral molecules: dipole–dipole forces, London (or dispersion) forces, and hydrogen bonding. **Van der Waals** forces include both dipole–dipole interactions and dispersion forces. Van der Waals forces are weak, short-range attractive forces between neutral molecules such as $Cl_2$ and $Br_2$. Dispersion forces are also weak short-range attractive forces that result from the instantaneous dipole/induced-dipole interactions that can occur because of the varying positions of the electrons as they move around the nuclei. Because molecules with greater molecular weights tend to have more electrons, dispersion forces tend to increase with molecular weight. This increase in forces is also due to the fact that larger molecules tend to be more polarizable, resulting in a greater likelihood for the formation of induced dipoles.

Hydrogen bonding occurs in substances bonded to certain very electronegative atoms. Hydrogen bonding is very important to the environmental scientist or engineer because it gives water its unique properties.

Hydrogen bonding can be investigated by studying two chemicals: fluoromethane ($CH_3F$) and methanol ($CH_3OH$). Both substances have about the same molecular weight and dipole moment. You might expect both chemicals to have similar properties, but fluoromethane is a gas at room temperature and methanol is a liquid. The boiling points of fluoromethane and methanol are $-78°C$ and $65°C$, respectively. The reason for the very different properties is the moderately strong attractive forces that exist between a hydrogen atom covalently bonded to a very electronegative atom, X, and a lone pair of electrons on another small, electronegative atom of another molecule. For example, with methanol, the partially positive hydrogen atom covalently bonded to the partially negative oxygen atom is attracted to the partially negative oxygen atom of another molecule:

These forces give methanol its properties. Similarly, hydrogen bonding occurs with water molecules, making water a liquid at room temperature, despite its low molecular weight.

### The Mole, Molar Units, and Activity Units

A **mole** is defined as **Avogadro's number** of molecules of a substance, that is, as $6.02 \times 10^{23}$ molecules of a substance. For example, a mole of benzene (a compound present in gasoline) contains $6.02 \times 10^{23}$ molecules of benzene. The molecular weight can be determined by multiplying the atomic weight of each element by the number of atoms of each element present in the substance. The **molecular formula** (a chemical formula that gives the exact number of the different atoms of an element found in the molecule) for benzene is $C_6H_6$. The **molecular weight** of a substance is the weight of a mole of that particular substance. Because the atomic weights of carbon and hydrogen are 12.01 and 1.008 amu (atomic mass units) or daltons, respectively, the molecular weight of benzene is

$$(12.01)(6) + (1.008)(6) = 78.11 \text{ g} \cdot \text{mol}^{-1} \tag{2–1}$$

Thus a mole of benzene has a mass of 78.11 g.

An **ion** is an electrically charged atom or molecule. For example, in water, calcium ions are present as cations, $Ca^{2+}$, and chlorine is present as the anion chloride ($Cl^-$).

**Molarity** is the number of moles per liter of solution. For example, a 1 molar (1 M) solution of benzene has 1 mole of benzene per liter of solution. It will be represented hereafter by the brackets [ ]. In environmental science, because the concentration of chemicals found in the environment is often quite small, we sometimes use micromoles per liter ($\mu mol \cdot L^{-1}$, or $\mu M$) as a unit.

**EXAMPLE 2–2**   A solution of calcium chloride is prepared in a 1.00-L volumetric flask. A 60.00-g sample of $CaCl_2$ is added to a small amount of water in the flask, and then additional water is added to bring the total volume of solution to 1.00 L. What is the concentration of calcium chloride in units of molarity?

Solution   The first step in solving this problem is to determine the molecular weight of calcium chloride. The atomic weights of calcium and chlorine can be obtained from the list at the front of this book. They are 40.078 amu and 35.4527 amu for calcium and chlorine, respectively. The molecular weight is

$$40.078 + 2(35.4527) = 110.98 \text{ g} \cdot \text{mol}^{-1}$$

The concentration in SI units is 60.00 g · $L^{-1}$. Converting to molar units:

$$(60.00 \text{ g} \cdot L^{-1})/(110.98 \text{ g} \cdot \text{mol}^{-1}) = 0.5406 \text{ M}$$

Alternatively, we can write the expression as

$$\frac{60 \text{ g}}{L} \times \frac{\text{mol}}{110.98 \text{ g}} = 0.5406 \text{ M}$$

in which it is easier to see how the units cancel.

Activity is defined in terms of chemical potential* and is dimensionless. It will be represented hereafter by the braces, { }. For pure phases (e.g., solid, liquid, ideal one-component gas), the activity is, by definition, one. Activity can be related to molar concentrations using the activity coefficient, essentially a factor that describes the nonideal behavior of the component in the system under study.

In dilute solutions, the total ion concentration is low (generally less than $10^{-2}$ M). The ions in such solutions can be considered to act independently of one another. As the concentration of ions in solution increases, the interaction of their electric charges affects their equilibrium relationships. This interaction is measured in terms of ionic strength. To account for high ionic strength, the equilibrium relationships are modified by incorporating activity coefficients. These are symbolized by $\gamma_{(ion)}$. Activity is then the product of the molar concentration of the species and its activity coefficient:

$$\{i\} = [i]\gamma_{(ion)} \tag{2–2}$$

Throughout this text, we will use the notation $\{i\}$ to represent the activity of a solution, whereas, $[i]$ will be used to denote molarity. For example, the activity of $Ca^{2+}$ in a 0.1 M solution of NaCl would be related to the molar concentration of calcium by the equation

$$\{Ca^{2+}\} = \gamma_{(Ca^{2+})}[Ca^{2+}] \tag{2–3}$$

One method used to calculate activity coefficients is discussed on page 46.

### Chemical Reactions and Stoichiometry

Stoichiometry is that part of chemistry concerned with measuring the proportions of elements or compounds involved in a reaction. Stoichiometric calculations are an application of the principle of conservation of mass to chemical reactions.

---

*Potential energy is the energy an object possesses because of its position in a field of force. Chemical potential is a thermodynamic quantity that is useful as a criterion for spontaneity. Chemical potential can be thought of as the tendency for a reaction to occur. For example, a reaction that has a negative potential is analogous to a pipe full of water that is flowing downhill. In the case of the pipe, water will flow by gravity. In the case of chemical potential, the reaction is thermodynamically feasible. Chemical potential, however, tells you nothing about the rate of the reaction.

A **chemical equation** is the symbolic representation of a chemical reaction in terms of chemical formulas. For example, the most widely used automobile fuel is gasoline. One of the compounds found in gasoline is octane. If octane is burned completely, only water and carbon dioxide are formed. The equation describing this reaction is

$$2C_8H_{18} + 25O_2 \longrightarrow 16CO_2 + 18H_2O \tag{2–4}$$

The chemical compounds to the left of the reaction arrow are known as **reactants;** those to the right as **products.**

In many cases it is useful to note the states or phases of the chemicals involved in the reaction. The following labels are commonly used:

$(g)$ = gas, $(\ell)$ = liquid, $(s)$ = solid, $(aq)$ = aqueous (water) solution

If we use these symbols, Equation 2–4 is written as:

$$2C_8H_{18}(\ell) + 25O_2(g) \longrightarrow 16CO_2(g) + 18H_2O(\ell) \tag{2–5}$$

**Balancing Chemical Reactions.** All chemical equations such as those presented here must be balanced, that is, there must be the same number of atoms of each element on both sides of the reaction arrow. The best way to emphasize this point is to show an example.

**EXAMPLE 2–3** Calcium can be removed from natural waters by the addition of sodium hydroxide according to the unbalanced reaction

$$Ca(HCO_3)_2 + NaOH = Ca(OH)_2 + NaHCO_3$$

Balance this reaction.

Solution    The first step is to tally all of the elements on both sides of the reaction

| Element | Reactants | Products |
|---|---|---|
| Calcium | 1 | 1 |
| Hydrogen | $(1 \times 2) + 1 = 3$ | $(1 \times 2) + 1 = 3$ |
| Carbon | $(1 \times 2) = 2$ | 1 |
| Oxygen | $(3 \times 2) + 1 = 7$ | $(1 \times 2) + 3 = 5$ |
| Sodium | 1 | 1 |

We are short one carbon atom on the product side, so multiply the number of moles of $NaHCO_3$ by 2:

$$Ca(HCO_3)_2 + NaOH = Ca(OH)_2 + 2NaHCO_3$$

Now we have two carbons, but we also have two sodium atoms, two hydrogen atoms and six oxygen atoms from the sodium bicarbonate (in addition to what we have from the calcium hydroxide).

| Element | Reactants | Products |
|---|---|---|
| Calcium | 1 | 1 |
| Hydrogen | $(1 \times 2) + 1 = 3$ | $(1 \times 2) + (1 \times 2) = 4$ |
| Carbon | $(1 \times 2) = 2$ | $\cancel{1}\ 2$ |
| Oxygen | $(3 \times 2) + 1 = 7$ | $(1 \times 2) + (3 \times 2) = 8$ |
| Sodium | 1 | $\cancel{1}\ 2$ |

Now, we need to multiply the number of moles of NaOH by 2:

$$Ca(HCO_3)_2 + 2NaOH = Ca(OH)_2 + 2NaHCO_3$$

Which results in:

| Element | Reactants | Products |
|---------|-----------|----------|
| Calcium | 1 | 1 |
| Hydrogen | $(1 \times 2) + (1 \times 2) = 4$ | $(1 \times 2) + (1 \times 2) = 4$ |
| Carbon | $(1 \times 2) = 2$ | $\cancel{1}\ 2$ |
| Oxygen | $(3 \times 2) + (1 \times 2) = 8$ | $(1 \times 2) + (3 \times 2) = 8$ |
| Sodium | $\cancel{1}\ 2$ | $\cancel{1}\ 2$ |

The equation is now balanced!

**Types of Chemical Reactions.**   Four types of reactions are of principal importance to the environmental scientist and engineer: precipitation–dissolution, acid–base, complexation or ion-association, oxidation–reduction.

**Precipitation–Dissolution Reactions.**   Some dissolved ions can react with other ions to form solid insoluble compounds, known as **precipitates.** The phase-change reaction by which dissolved chemicals form insoluble solids is called a **precipitation reaction.** A typical precipitation reaction is the formation of calcium carbonate when a solution of calcium chloride is mixed with a solution of sodium carbonate.

$$CaCl_2 + Na_2CO_3 \rightleftharpoons CaCO_3(s) + 2Na^+ + 2Cl^- \tag{2-6}$$

The $(s)$ in the preceding reaction denotes that the $CaCO_3$ is a solid. When no symbol is used to designate state, it is assumed that the chemical species is dissolved. The arrows in the reaction imply that the reaction is reversible and so could proceed to the right (i.e., the ions are combining to form a solid) or to the left (i.e., the solid is dissociating into the ions). When the reaction proceeds to the left, it is referred to as a **dissolution reaction.** Dissolution reactions are important when dealing with rocks and minerals. For example, under acidic conditions, the mineral calcite ($CaCO_3$) can dissolve to release calcium ions ($Ca^{2+}$) and $CO_3^{2-}$ (carbonate) into water. At equilibrium no additional calcium or carbonate can go into solution; the solution is said to be **saturated.** If the solution is not in equilibrium and additional calcium and carbonate can dissolve, the solution is said to be **undersaturated.** In some cases it is possible to obtain higher concentrations of the dissolved ions than what is predicted using the equilibrium constant; the solution is said to be **supersaturated.**

Some dissolution reactions can be said to proceed to completion, that is, they proceed essentially completely to the right or left. For example, if we add sodium chloride or calcium sulfate to water, these compounds will dissociate (break up) to release the associated ions.

$$NaCl(s) \longrightarrow Na^+ + Cl^- \tag{2-7}$$

$$CaSO_4(s) \longrightarrow Ca^{2+} + SO_4^{2-} \tag{2-8}$$

Although we might be inclined to state that the water contains NaCl and $CaSO_4$, these species are present in their dissolved form.

**Acid–Base (or Neutralization) Reactions.**   The general concept of acids and bases was devised by Brønsted and Lowry. A Brønsted–Lowry acid is then defined as any substance that can donate a proton to another substance and a Brønsted–Lowry base is any substance that can accept a proton. Thus proton transfer can occur only if both an acid and a base are present.

If we use A to designate an acid and B to denote a base, then the general form of an acid–base reaction is

$$HA + H_2O \rightleftharpoons H_3O^+ + A^- \tag{2-9}$$

in which HA is a stronger acid than water and water acts as the base. The reaction results in the formation of a second (conjugate) acid ($H_3O^+$) and a second (conjugate) base ($A^-$). In this reaction

$$B^- + H_3O^+ \rightleftharpoons HB + H_2O \tag{2-10}$$

$B^-$ is the base and water acts as the acid. Likewise, this reaction also results in the formation of a second acid (HB) and base ($H_2O$).

The term pH is defined as the negative log of the $H^+$ activity:

$$pH = -\log\{H^+\} \tag{2-11}$$

A solution having a pH of 7 is neutral; it is neither acidic nor basic. A solution having a pH < 7 is acidic, and a solution with a pH > 7 is basic. The pH of most natural waters lies in the range of 6 to 9, conditions necessary to support most life, although extremophilic bacteria can grow at pH values less than 4 and greater than 9. Biological activities involve acid–base reactions and, therefore, affect the pH of waters. As water moves through soils, acid–base reactions are likely to occur. Acid–base reactions occur in the atmosphere when acid rain is produced. Acids can enter the aquatic and terrestrial ecosystems due to their direct release from household, municipal, and industrial wastes. Unlike many precipitation reactions, acid–base reactions are very fast; with half-lives usually on the order of milliseconds.

Free protons cannot exist in water; they will combine with the $H_2O$ molecule to form the hydronium ion ($H_3O^+$). If we add an acid to water it will dissociate to release a proton. For example,

$$HCl \rightleftharpoons H^+ + Cl^- \tag{2-12}$$

Because hydrochloric acid (HCl) is a strong acid, this reaction will go essentially to completion. That is, one mole of HCl will produce one mole of protons. For an acid–base reaction to occur, the proton must be transferred to a base. Water is **amphoteric,** that is, it can act as either an acid or a base. In this case water would act as a base and accept the protons released by the dissociation of hydrochloric acid.

$$H_2O + H^+ \rightleftharpoons H_3O^+ \tag{2-13}$$

If we combine the preceding reactions, we obtain the overall reaction

$$HCl + H_2O \rightleftharpoons H_3O^+ + Cl^- \tag{2-14}$$

which is the actual reaction that occurs in water, although the shorthand notation shown in Equation 2–12 is often used.

If we add a base to water, it will react with hydronium ions present in the water. For example, the addition of sodium hydroxide to water results in the consumption of $H_3O^+$.

$$NaOH + H_3O^+ \rightleftharpoons 2H_2O + Na^+ \tag{2-15}$$

In this case, water acts as an acid in that it donates a proton to the base.

**Complexation Reactions.**  Complexation reactions occur in natural waters whenever the "coordination" of two (or more) atoms, molecules, or ions results in the formation of a more stable product. These reactions are important to the environmental scientist or engineer because the form of the chemical can significantly affect the toxicity, the efficiency of removal, and the biological uptake of that chemical species.

A **complex** is a compound consisting of either complex ions with other ions of opposite charge or a neutral complex species. The **complex ion** is defined as a metal ion with Lewis bases* attached to it through coordinate covalent bonding. The Lewis bases attached to the metal atom in a complex are known as **ligands.** The coordination number of a metal atom in a complex is the total number of bonds the metal atom forms with ligands. For example, with $Fe(H_2O)_6^{2+}$, $Fe^{2+}$ is the complex ion; water is the ligand; and the coordination number of the iron in this complex is 6 because six molecules of water are bonded to the iron molecule.

Oxidation–Reduction (Redox) Reactions.   Without oxidation–reduction (redox) reactions, life as we know it would be impossible. Photosynthesis and respiration are essentially a sequence of redox reactions. The cycling of nutrients in the environment is also controlled by redox reactions. Redox reactions also occur when the iron in your car rusts. In general, redox reactions are quite slow, thankfully, because no one wants to see things such as their car rapidly destroyed by rust. However, this slowness presents difficulties to the environmental scientist or engineer. With redox reactions, in the natural environment, equilibrium is rarely reached.

Redox reactions involve changes in the oxidation state of an ion and the transfer of electrons. When iron metal corrodes, it releases electrons:

$$Fe^0 \rightleftharpoons Fe^{2+} + 2e^- \qquad (2-16)$$

If one element releases electrons, then another must be available to accept the electrons. In iron pipe corrosion, hydrogen gas is often produced:

$$2H^+ + 2e^- \rightleftharpoons H_2(g) \qquad (2-17)$$

where the symbol $(g)$ indicates that the hydrogen is in the gas phase.

When balancing redox equations, you must also ensure that the number of electrons transferred is balanced. In Example 2–3, there was no change in the oxidation state of any of the elements. However in the next two examples, the oxidation state changes.

---

*A Lewis base has one (or more) pairs of electrons, which it can donate to the central metallic cation in the complex.

**EXAMPLE 2–4**   In the atmosphere, sulfur dioxide (released by coal-burning power plants) reacts relatively slowly with oxygen and water vapor to form sulfuric acid, a pollutant that has the potential to cause severe respiratory distress and acid rain.

The chemical equation is

$$SO_2 + O_2 + H_2O \longrightarrow H_2SO_4$$

Balance this reaction.

Solution   Note this reaction is not written as an equilibrium reaction. This is because the reaction proceeds essentially to completion and is not reversible. The first task is to list all of the elements present in the reaction.

| Element | Reactants | Products |
|---|---|---|
| S (sulfur) | 1 | 1 |
| O (oxygen) | 5 | 4 |
| H (hydrogen) | 2 | 2 |

Note that in this reaction the oxygen is reduced from a charge of zero (in $O_2$) to a charge of $-2$ in $H_2SO_4$. The sulfur is oxidized from a charge of $+4$ in $SO_2$ to $+6$ in $H_2SO_4$. Therefore, we must first balance the number of electrons transferred.

$$O_2 \longrightarrow 2O^{2-}$$

$$S^{4+} \longrightarrow S^{6+}$$

Four electrons must be transferred in the first reaction, whereas, two electrons are transferred in the second. Therefore, to conserve the number of electrons transferred, we must multiply the second reaction by 2.

$$O_2 + 4e^- \rightleftharpoons 2O^{2-}$$

$$2(S^{4+} \rightleftharpoons S^{6+} + 2e^-)$$

Thus, the reaction now becomes

$$2SO_2 + O_2 + H_2O \longrightarrow 2H_2SO_4$$

The next step is to add up all of the atoms of each element on both sides of the reaction. For example, on the reactant side of the reaction there are four atoms of oxygen in $2SO_2$, two atoms of oxygen in $O_2$, and one atom of oxygen in water ($H_2O$), for a total of seven atoms. Now write 7 in the table in the cell corresponding to oxygen and reactants. You should then do the same for all other elements.

| Element | Reactants | Products |
|---|---|---|
| S (sulfur) | 2 | 2 |
| O (oxygen) | 7 | 8 |
| H (hydrogen) | 2 | 4 |

Both sides of the reaction must have the same number of atoms of all elements; however, we have seven atoms of oxygen on the reactant side and eight on the product side. We are short one oxygen atom on the reactant side of the reaction. Let's first try to balance the equation by multiplying the number of water molecules by 2.

$$2SO_2 + O_2 + 2H_2O \longrightarrow 2H_2SO_4$$

The table would then become

| Element | Reactants | Products |
|---|---|---|
| S (sulfur) | 2 | 2 |
| O (oxygen) | 7̸ 8 | 8 |
| H (hydrogen) | 2̸ 4 | 4 |

The equation is now balanced!

**EXAMPLE 2–5**  The following reaction is important in lake and river sediments that are devoid of oxygen.

$$SO_4^{2-} + H^+ + CH_2O \rightleftharpoons HS^- + CO_2 + H_2O$$

Balance this reaction.

Solution  Note that this bacterially mediated reaction is reversible. First we consider the charge on the various atoms. Oxygen almost always* has a charge of $-2$. If oxygen has a charge of $-2$, then

---

*Oxygen almost always has a charge of –2; except in the diatomic state, where the charge is 0 or as a peroxide, where the charge is –1.

the charge on the sulfur in $SO_4^{2-}$ is $+6$, the charge on carbon in $CO_2$ is $+4$. Hydrogen almost always has a charge of $+1$ (except in the diatomic state, where the charge is 0). Therefore, the charge on the sulfur in $HS^-$ is $-2$, and the hypothetical charge on the carbon in $CH_2O$ is 0. If the reaction for the reduction of sulfur is

$$S(+6)O_4^{2-} \rightleftharpoons HS(-2)^-$$

we need eight electrons on the reactant side to balance the oxidation state of sulfur on the product side. The numbers in parentheses correspond to the oxidation state of sulfur.

$$S(+6)O_4^{2-} + 8e^- \rightleftharpoons HS(-2)^-$$

$([+6] + [-8] = -2)$. Now we must balance the oxidation reaction. In this reaction, carbon goes from an oxidation state of 0 to an oxidation state of $+4$. Clearly we need four electrons to balance this reaction.

$$CH_2O \rightleftharpoons CO_2 + 4e^-$$

Because we need to balance the number of electrons transferred, the next step is to multiply the previous reaction by 2:

$$2CH_2O \rightleftharpoons 2CO_2 + 8e^-$$

Our original equation becomes

$$SO_4^{2-} + H^+ + 2CH_2O \rightleftharpoons HS^- + 2CO_2 + H_2O$$

with the number of electrons transferred balanced. The next steps are similar to those presented earlier. Let's now create a table showing all atoms in the reaction.

| Element | Reactants | Products |
|---|---|---|
| S (sulfur) | 1 | 1 |
| O (oxygen) | 6 | 5 |
| C (carbon) | 2 | 2 |
| H (hydrogen) | 5 | 3 |

Because the number of carbon and sulfur atoms are already balanced, we must avoid changing the number of molecules of any species containing carbon or sulfur. We need one more atom of oxygen and two more atoms of hydrogen on the product side of the reaction. Voila! Water! Add one more molecule of water on the product side of the reaction.

$$SO_4^{2-} + H^+ + 2CH_2O \rightleftharpoons HS^- + 2CO_2 + 2H_2O$$

and the table becomes

| Element | Reactants | Products |
|---|---|---|
| S (sulfur) | 1 | 1 |
| O (oxygen) | 6 | ~~5~~ 6 |
| C (carbon) | 2 | 2 |
| H (hydrogen) | 5 | ~~3~~ 5 |

The preceding equation is now balanced!

**Reactions Involving Gases.** The transfer of gases into or from solutions is important because aquatic life could not survive if gases such as oxygen and carbon dioxide did not dissolve in water. "Pure" rainwater in equilibrium with the carbon dioxide in air would not have a pH near 5.6 were it not for the fact that carbon dioxide dissolves in water. Carbon dioxide dissolves in water by the reaction

$$CO_2(g) \rightleftharpoons CO_2(aq) \tag{2–18}$$

where the symbol (aq) indicates the aqueous phase.

Carbon dioxide can then react with water to form carbonic acid.

$$CO_2(aq) + H_2O \rightleftharpoons H_2CO_3 \tag{2–19}$$

We can also use these gas transfer reactions to our advantage. For example, ammonia can be stripped from waters by raising the pH to convert $NH_4^+$ to $NH_3$ and then providing conditions in which the ammonia will be transferred to the gas phase.

$$NH_3(aq) \rightleftharpoons NH_3(g) \tag{2–20}$$

## Chemical Equilibrium

If you add calcite to a dilute hydrochloric acid solution, the calcite will dissolve, giving off carbon dioxide bubbles, until **chemical equilibrium** has been reached. At this point the rate of the reaction proceeding to the right equals that proceeding to the left.

$$CaCO_3 + 2HCl \rightleftharpoons Ca^{2+} + CO_2(g) + H_2O + 2Cl^- \tag{2–21}$$

We define chemical equilibrium as the condition when the rate of forward reaction equals the rate of the reverse reaction.

Chemical equilibrium is always described mathematically by an equilibrium **constant.** The equilibrium constant, which is derived from chemical thermodynamic data, is numerically equivalent to the product of the concentrations of products divided by the product of the reactants, with each of the concentration terms raised to a power equivalent to the stoichiometric coefficient from the chemical reaction, where the concentrations are those at equilibrium conditions. For example, for the general reaction

$$aA + bB \rightleftharpoons cC + dD \tag{2–22}$$

the equilibrium constant, $K$, is described mathematically as

$$K = \frac{\{C\}^c\{D\}^d}{\{A\}^a\{B\}^b} \tag{2–23}$$

Note that the concentrations in Equation 2–23 must be in units of activity or in molarity (if the solution is sufficiently dilute). The **law of mass action** states that the value of the equilibrium constant expression $K$ is a constant for a particular reaction at a given temperature, and that this value is independent of the equilibrium concentrations of the chemicals substituted into the equation.

Many environmental reactions proceed rapidly, so that equilibrium calculations can be used to predict the concentrations of chemicals after some treatment process, in a body of water, or in raindrops. This is especially true with the dissolution of chemicals in a well-mixed reactor, the dissociation of acids and bases, and the dissolution of gases in raindrops or fog. Although chemical equilibrium calculations are less useful for slower reactions like the dissolution of minerals in rocks or the dissolution of gases in large bodies of water, these calculations do provide information on the concentrations of chemical species after chemical equilibrium is reached, although the time to reach these concentrations may be long.

**Solubility Calculations.** All compounds are soluble in water to a certain extent. Likewise, the concentration of all compounds is limited by how much of a chemical can be dissolved in water. Some compounds, such as NaCl, are very soluble; other compounds, such as AgCl, are very insoluble, that is, only a small amount will go into solution. If you add baking soda ($NaHCO_3$), a solid compound, to distilled water, some of the compound will go into solution. After you have added a certain mass of baking soda, no more of it will go into solution (**dissolve**). At this point, equilibrium is reached. The solubility reaction for sodium bicarbonate is written as follows.

$$NaHCO_3\ (s) \rightleftharpoons Na^+ + HCO_3^- \tag{2-24}$$

A solubility product can be written for this equation.

$$\{Na^+\}\{HCO_3^-\} = K_s \tag{2-25}$$

Solubility product constants ($K_s$) can be obtained from a variety of sources. A limited subset is presented in Table 2–1 and Appendix A–9; a more complete list is available from such sources as *The CRC Handbook of Chemistry and Physics*.

The most general form of a precipitation–dissolution reaction is

$$A_aB_b(s) \rightleftharpoons aA^{x+} + bB^{y-} \tag{2-26}$$

As stated previously, the equilibrium expression for any reaction can be written as the product of the products (taken to the appropriate stoichiometric factors) divided by the product of the reactants. You will note that in the preceding reaction the concentration of the reactant, $A_aB_b$, does not appear in the equation. This is because the solubility products were defined using activities not molar concentrations. By definition, the activity of a pure solid is 1. As such, the activity term for the reactant, assumed to be a pure solid, drops out of the equation. Thus, for any precipitation reaction we can write a solubility product

$$K_s = \{A^{x+}\}^a \{B^{y-}\}^b \tag{2-27}$$

Solubility products are often reported as $pK_s$, that is, the negative logarithm (base 10) of $K_s$.

$$pK_s = -\log_{10}(K_s) \text{ or } -\log(K_s) \tag{2-28}$$

This is done because the values of $K_s$ are often very small.

| **TABLE 2–1** | Selected Solubility Products at 25°C | | |
|---|---|---|---|
| **Substance** | **Equilibrium Reaction** | **$pK_s$** | **Application** |
| Aluminum hydroxide | $Al(OH)_3\ (s) \rightleftharpoons Al^{3+} + 3OH^-$ | 32.9 | Coagulation |
| Aluminum phosphate | $AlPO_4\ (s) \rightleftharpoons Al^{3+} + PO_4^{3-}$ | 22.0 | Phosphate removal |
| Calcium carbonate (aragonite) | $CaCO_3\ (s) \rightleftharpoons Ca^{2+} + CO_3^{2-}$ | 8.34 | Softening, corrosion control |
| Ferric hydroxide | $Fe(OH)_3\ (s) \rightleftharpoons Fe^{3+} + 3OH^-$ | 38.57 | Coagulation, iron removal |
| Ferric phosphate | $FePO_4\ (s) \rightleftharpoons Fe^{3+} + PO_4^{3-}$ | 21.9 | Phosphate removal |
| Magnesium hydroxide | $Mg(OH)_2\ (s) \rightleftharpoons Mg^{2+} + 2OH^-$ | 11.25 | Removal of calcium and magnesium |
| Dolomite $(CaMg(CO_3)_2)$ (ordered) | $CaMg(CO_3)_2 \rightleftharpoons Ca^{2+} + Mg^{2+} + 2CO_3^{2-}$ | 17.09 | Weathering of dolomitic minerals |
| Kaolinite | $Al_2Si_2O_5(OH)_4 + 6H^+ \rightleftharpoons 2Al^{3+} + 2Si(OH)_4 + H_2O$ | 7.44 | Weathering of kaolinite clays |
| Gypsum | $CaSO_4 \cdot 2H_2O \rightleftharpoons Ca^{2+} + SO_4^{2-} + 2H_2O$ | 4.58 | Weathering of gypsum minerals |

*Source:* W. Stumm, J. J. Morgan, *Aquatic Chemistry*, 3rd ed., New York: Wiley and Sons, Inc., 1996.

The solubility products are thermodynamic data and can be determined from values of Gibbs free energy* for the products and the reactants. Many solubility products have also been determined empirically, although for sparingly soluble compounds, these experimental values are often highly variable and inaccurate. Solubility products are defined for a specific temperature, usually 25°C. If the temperature is other than the reference temperature for which the solubility product was determined, a temperature correction must be used. Solubility products at temperatures other than 25°C can be calculated using the basic thermodynamic expression:

$$\frac{\partial \ln K}{\partial T} = \frac{\Delta H_r^0}{RT^2} \tag{2-29}$$

where $K$ = equilibrium constant, for example a solubility product
$T$ = absolute temperature
$\Delta H_r^0$ = change in enthalpy of reaction
$R$ = ideal gas constant
$T$ = absolute temperature (kelvins, K)

Assuming that the change in enthalpy is constant over the temperature considered, an approximate solution for Equation 2–29 is

$$\ln \frac{K_{T_2}}{K_{T_1}} = \frac{\Delta H_r^0}{R} \left( \frac{1}{T_1} - \frac{1}{T_2} \right) \tag{2-30}$$

You should also remember that thermodynamic data, such as solubility products, tell you nothing about the kinetics of the reaction (how fast it proceeds). These reactions may take seconds to reach equilibrium or hundreds of thousands of years!

---

*Gibbs free energy is a thermodynamic quantity that gives a direct criterion for the spontaneity of a reaction.

**EXAMPLE 2–6** If you add 30 g of calcite ($CaCO_3$) to a 1.00-L volumetric flask and bring the final volume to 1.00 L, what would be the concentration of calcium ($Ca^{2+}$) in solution. Assume that the calcium in solution is at equilibrium with $CaCO_3$ $(s)$ and the temperature of the solution is 25°C. The $pK_s$ for calcite is 8.48.

Solution    The pertinent reaction is

$$CaCO_3(s) = Ca^{2+} + CO_3^{2-} \qquad K_s = 10^{-pK_s} = 10^{-8.48}$$

Remember that $K_s = \{Ca^{2+}\}\{CO_3^{2-}\}$. We will assume that the solution is dilute, allowing us to approximate the activities with molar concentrations. As such, the preceding equation becomes

$$K_s = [Ca^{2+}][CO_3^{2-}]$$

For every mole of calcite that dissolves, one mole of $Ca^{2+}$ and one mole of $CO_3^{2-}$ are released into solution. At equilibrium, the molar concentration of $Ca^{2+}$ and $CO_3^{2-}$ in solution will be equal, so we may say

$$[Ca^{2+}] = [CO_3^{2-}] = s$$

Substituting $s$ for each compound in the $K_s$ expression,

$$10^{-8.48} = s^2$$

Solving for $s$ (which is equal to $Ca^{2+}$), we can determine the concentration of calcium: $Ca^{2+} = 10^{-4.24}$ or $5.75 \times 10^{-5}$ M (moles per liter) in solution. Because the concentration of calcium (and also carbonate) are so low, the assumption that the activities could be approximated by the molar concentrations was a reasonable one. Note that the amount of calcite added to the flask is irrelevant. You are asked for the equilibrium concentrations, which are independent of the "starting" conditions or the mass of calcite added, so long as the mass added exceeded the solubility.

When the background* electrolyte concentration is high (i.e., in seawater, in landfill leachates, and in activated sludge), one must take into account the effects of the ions on all equilibrium constants. Here we will investigate its effect on solubility products; however, the effects are accounted for in the same way for all types of equilibrium constants. Remember that the solubility product is defined as

$$K_s = \{A^{x+}\}^a\{B^{y-}\}^b \tag{2-31}$$

and

$$\{i\} = \gamma_i[i] \tag{2-32}$$

where $\{i\}$ is the activity of $i$, $\gamma_i$ is the activity coefficient of $i$ (in the solution having a particular composition and ionic strength) and $[i]$ is the molar concentration of $i$. Substituting $\gamma_i[i]$ into Equation 2–31, yields

$$K_s = (\gamma_A[A^{x+}])^a(\gamma_B[B^{y-}])^b \tag{2-33}$$

Activity coefficients can be determined using a number of approximations. The Davies equation is presented here because it is valid for the widest ranges of electrolyte concentrations (where ionic strength, $I$, is less than 0.5 M). The Davies equation states that

$$\log \gamma = -Az^2\left(\frac{\sqrt{I}}{1+\sqrt{I}} - 0.2I\right) \tag{2-34}$$

where $A \approx 0.5$ for water at 25°C
$z$ = charge of the ion
$I$ = ionic strength of the solution = $\frac{1}{2}\sum C_i z_i^2$
$C_i$ = molar concentration of each of the $i$th ion in solution
$z_i$ = charge on the $i$th ion

*The term *background* is used to denote those ions that also occur in solution.

**EXAMPLE 2–7**   Reexamine Example 2–6. Assume you added 30 g of calcite to water to make up 1.00 L of a solution containing 0.01 M NaCl. What would be the concentration of calcium ($Ca^{2+}$) in solution? Assume that the calcium in solution is at equilibrium with calcite ($s$) and the temperature of the solution is 25°C.

Solution   First we must calculate the concentration of the sodium chloride solution. The two ions present in this solution would be $Na^+$ and $Cl^-$. Because NaCl would completely dissociate, the concentrations of both ions would be 0.01 M. We can now calculate the ionic strength

$$I = \frac{1}{2}[(0.01)(1)^2 + (0.01)(1)^2] = 0.01 \text{ M}$$

We must now look at the two ions we are investigating: calcium and carbonate. Because the absolute value of the charge on both calcium and carbonate is the same (i.e., two), $\gamma_{Ca} = \gamma_{CO_3}$.

$$\log \gamma_{Ca} = \log \gamma_{CO_3} = -(0.5)(2)^2 \left( \frac{\sqrt{0.01}}{1 + \sqrt{0.01}} - 0.2(0.01) \right) = -0.178$$

$$\gamma_{Ca} = \gamma_{CO_3} = 10^{-0.178} = 0.664$$

Using the activity coefficient to calculate the effect of ionic strength on the solubility product, we have

$$K_s = \{Ca^{2+}\}\{CO_3^{2-}\} = \gamma_{Ca}[Ca^{2+}]\gamma_{CO_3}[CO_3^{2-}]$$

$$\frac{K_s}{\gamma_{Ca}\gamma_{CO_3}} = [Ca^{2+}][CO_3^{2-}] = \frac{10^{-8.48}}{(0.664)(0.664)} = 7.51 \times 10^{-9}$$

Solving the problem as shown in Example 2–6, we see that

$$[Ca^{2+}] = [CO_3^{2-}] = 8.7 \times 10^{-5} \text{ M}$$

**EXAMPLE 2–8**   Look at Example 2–6 one more time. Assume you added 30 g of calcite to 1 L of water having the composition given below. What would be the concentration of calcium ($Ca^{2+}$) in solution? Assume that the calcium in solution is at equilibrium with calcite (s) and the temperature of the solution is 25°C.

| Ion | Concentration (mM) | Ion | Concentration (mM) |
|-----|--------------------|-----|--------------------|
| $NO_3^-$ | 2.38 | $Mg^{2+}$ | 53.2 |
| $SO_4^{2-}$ | 28.2 | $Na^+$ | 468.0 |
| $Cl^-$ | 545.0 | $K^+$ | 10.2 |
| | | $Cu^{2+}$ | 10.2 |

$$I = \frac{1}{2}[(2.38 \times 10^{-3})(1)^2 + (2.82 \times 10^{-2})(2)^2 + (0.545)(1)^2 + (1.02 \times 10^{-2})(2)^2$$
$$+ (5.32 \times 10^{-2})(2)^2 + (0.468)(1)^2 + (1.02 \times 10^{-2})(1)^2] = 0.696 \text{ M}$$

$$\log \gamma_{Ca} = \log \gamma_{CO_3} = -(0.5)(2)^2 \left( \frac{\sqrt{0.696}}{1 + \sqrt{0.696}} - 0.2(0.696) \right) = -0.631$$

$$\gamma_{Ca} = \gamma_{CO_3} = 10^{-0.631} = 0.234$$

Using the activity coefficient to calculate the effect of ionic strength on the solubility product, we see that

$$K_s = \{Ca^{2+}\}\{CO_3^{2-}\} = \gamma_{Ca}[Ca^{2+}]\gamma_{CO_3}[CO_3^{2-}]$$

$$\frac{K_s}{\gamma_{Ca}\gamma_{CO_3}} = [Ca^{2+}][CO_3^{2-}] = \frac{10^{-8.48}}{(0.234)(0.234)} = 6.05 \times 10^{-8}$$

Solving the problem as shown in Example 2–6, we see that

$$[Ca^{2+}] = [CO_3^{2-}] = 2.5 \times 10^{-4} \text{ M}$$

You might remember from general chemistry that "like dissolves like." Calcium and carbonate ions are highly ionic. Adding sodium chloride to distilled water makes the resulting solution more ionic. As such, calcite is more soluble in the sodium chloride solution than it was in pure water. Because the ionic strength of the aqueous solution given in Example 2–8 is greater than that of the 0.01 M NaCl solution used in Example 2–7, calcite is even more soluble in this water than it is in the sodium chloride solution.

**Common Ion Effect.** In natural waters, rarely does a chemical dissolve into water that is free of the ion being dissolved. For example, as groundwater flows past calcite containing rocks, calcium will dissolve into the water by the reaction

$$CaCO_3(s) \text{ (calcite)} = Ca^{2+} + CO_3^{2-} \qquad K_s = 10^{-8.48} \tag{2-35}$$

However, rarely does this reaction occur in water that is devoid of calcium or carbonate ions at the start of the reaction. As such, the solubility of calcite decreases, and calcite will not dissolve in groundwater to the extent to which it would in a pure water.

**EXAMPLE 2–9**

What is the solubility of dolomite in water that contains $100 \text{ mg} \cdot \text{L}^{-1} CO_3^{2-}$? The solubility product of dolomite is $10^{-17.09}$. Assume that the effects of ionic strength are negligible.

**Solution**

The first step in solving this reaction is to determine the concentration of carbonate that exists in the water prior to the dissolution (solubilization) of dolomite. The molar concentration of carbonate must be calculated. The molecular weight of carbonate is $60.01 \text{ g} \cdot \text{mol}^{-1}$. Therefore, the molar concentration of carbonate is

$$(100 \text{ mg} \cdot \text{L}^{-1})(10^{-3} \text{ g} \cdot \text{mg}^{-1})(1 \text{ mol}/60.01 \text{ g}) = 0.00167 \text{ M}$$

Dolomite dissolves according to reaction

$$CaMg(CO_3)_2 = Ca^{2+} + Mg^{2+} + 2CO_3^{2-} \qquad K_s = 10^{-17.09}$$

At the start of the reaction we have $0.00167 \text{ M } CO_3^{2-}$, $0 \text{ M } Ca^{2+}$, and $0 \text{ M } Mg^{2+}$ in solution. If $s$ moles of dolomite dissolves, then we add $s$ moles of $Ca^{2+}$, $s$ moles of $Mg^{2+}$, and $2s$ moles of $CO_3^{2-}$ to the solution. At equilibrium, the concentrations of the ions of interest are the sums of the values given here. We can write this in tabular form to summarize the calculations.

| | Concentration (M) | | |
|---|---|---|---|
| | $Ca^{2+}$ | $Mg^{2+}$ | $CO_3^{2-}$ |
| Starting | 0 | 0 | 0.00167 |
| Change | $s$ | $s$ | $2s$ |
| Equilibrium | $s$ | $s$ | $0.00167 + 2s$ |

The next step is to write the equilibrium equation.

$$[Ca^{2+}][Mg^{2+}][CO_3^{2-}]^2 = K_s = 10^{-17.09}$$

Substituting from the table, we have

$$(s)(s)(0.00167 + 2s)^2 = 10^{-17.09}$$

The preceding equation can be solved numerically using a mathematical equation-solving package such as SOLVER on EXCEL or by trial and error. By trial and error, we obtained a value of $s$ of $1.704 \times 10^{-6} \text{ M}$. As such, the concentrations of $Ca^{2+}$, $Mg^{2+}$, and $CO_3^{2-}$ are $1.704 \times 10^{-6} \text{ M}$, $1.704 \times 10^{-6} \text{ M}$, and $1.673 \times 10^{-3} \text{ M}$, respectively.

In many situations, you must deal with conditions in which multiple common ions are present in the solution at the beginning of the reaction. In other cases, a solution can be supersaturated with the ions, and precipitation of a solid can occur. This next example illustrates how to solve a problem when the solution is supersaturated.

**EXAMPLE 2-10**  A solution is initially supersaturated with $CO_3^{2-}$ and $Ca^{2+}$ such that the concentrations are both $50.0 \text{ mg} \cdot L^{-1}$. When equilibrium is ultimately reached what will be the final concentration of $Ca^{2+}$?

Solution  We are starting with a solution that is supersaturated with calcium and carbonate. Over time, as equilibrium is reached, calcium carbonate will precipitate. The reaction is

$$Ca^{2+} + CO_3^{2-} = CaCO_3(s) \qquad pK_s = 8.305$$

Remember that to solve equilibrium problems, we must use molar units! The atomic weight of $Ca^{2+}$ is 40.08 amu and the molecular weight of $CO_3^{2-}$ is $60.01 \text{ g} \cdot \text{mol}^{-1}$, resulting in initial molar concentrations of $1.25 \times 10^{-3} \text{ mol} \cdot L^{-1}$ and $8.33 \times 10^{-4} \text{ mol} \cdot L^{-1}$ for $Ca^{2+}$ and $CO_3^{2-}$, respectively.

$$K_s = 10^{-pK_s} = 10^{-8.305} = [Ca^{2+}][CO_3^{2-}]$$

For every mole of $Ca^{2+}$ that precipitates from solution, one mole of $CO_3^{2-}$ also precipitates. If the amount removed is given by $s$, then

$$10^{-8.305} = 4.95 \times 10^{-9} = [1.25 \times 10^{-3} - s][8.33 \times 10^{-4} - s]$$

$$1.041 \times 10^{-6} - (2.083 \times 10^{-3})s + s^2 = 0$$

Solving for $s$, using the quadratic formula, yields

$$s = \frac{-b \pm \sqrt{b^2 - 4ac}}{2a} = \frac{2.08 \times 10^{-3} \pm \sqrt{4.34 \times 10^{-6} - 4(1.041 \times 10^{-6})}}{2}$$

$$= 8.33 \times 10^{-4} \text{ M}$$

Therefore, the final $Ca^{2+}$ concentration is

$$[Ca^{2+}] = 1.25 \times 10^{-3} \text{ M} - 8.33 \times 10^{-4} \text{ M} = 4.17 \times 10^{-4} \text{ M}$$

or

$$(4.17 \times 10^{-4} \text{ mol} \cdot L^{-1})(40 \text{ g} \cdot \text{mol}^{-1})(10^3 \text{ mg} \cdot \text{g}^{-1}) = 16.7 \text{ mg} \cdot L^{-1}$$

Note that mathematical analysis of the quadratic expression would yield two solutions, both positive, one larger than the other. The larger solution ($1.25 \times 10^{-3}$) yields a value for $s$ that is equal to the original concentrations of $Ca^{2+}$. This would yield a final concentration that is zero. Because this is physically impossible, we will discard the larger solution for $s$.

**Acid–Base Equilibria.**  Water ionizes according to the equation

$$H_2O = H^+ + OH^-$$

(2–36)

The degree of ionization of water is very small and can be measured by what is called the **dissociation** (or **ionization**) **constant** of water, $K_w$. It is defined as

$$K_w = \{OH^-\}\{H^+\} \tag{2-37}$$

and has a value of $10^{-14}$ ($pK_w = 14$) at 25°C. A solution is said to be acidic if $\{H^+\}$ is greater than $\{OH^-\}$, neutral if equal, and basic if $\{H^+\}$ is less than $\{OH^-\}$. At a temperature of 25°C and in dilute solutions (where the ionic strength effects on $K_w$ can be ignored), if $[H^+] = [OH^-] = 10^{-7}$ M, then the solution is neutral. Under the same conditions, if $[H^+]$ is greater than $10^{-7}$ M then the solution is acidic. Convenient expressions for the hydrogen and hydroxide ion concentrations are pH and pOH, respectively. The terms are defined as

$$pH = -\log\{H^+\} \tag{2-38}$$

$$pOH = -\log\{OH^-\} \tag{2-39}$$

where log = logarithm in base ten, as was used for $pK_s$ values. Therefore, a neutral (and dilute) solution at 25°C has a pH of 7 (written pH 7), an acidic solution has a pH < 7, and a basic solution has a pH > 7. Also note that by taking the logarithm of Equation 2–37, we see that

$$pH + pOH = 14 \tag{2-40}$$

at a temperature of 25°C and in dilute solutions.

Acids are classified as strong acids or weak acids. As mentioned previously, strong acids have a tendency to donate their protons to water. For example,

$$HCl = H^+ + Cl^- \tag{2-41}$$

which is actually the simplified form of

$$HCl + H_2O = H_3O^+ + Cl^- \tag{2-42}$$

showing water as a base, which accepts a proton.

Equilibrium exists between the dissociated ions and undissociated compound. With strong acids, equilibrium is such that essentially all of the acid dissociates to form the proton and the conjugate base ($Cl^-$ in the previous example). We can write the equilibrium expression as

$$K_a = \frac{[H_3O^+][Cl^-]}{[HCl]} \tag{2-43}$$

As with other equilibrium constants,

$$pK_a = -\log K_a \tag{2-44}$$

A list of important strong acids is in Table 2–2. Note the use of the single arrow to signify that, for all practical purposes, we may assume that the reaction proceeds completely to the right.

| TABLE 2–2 | Strong and Moderately Strong Acids | | | |
|---|---|---|---|---|
| | **Acid** | **Chemical Reaction** | **$pK_a$** | **Importance** |
| | Hydrochloric acid | $HCl \longrightarrow H^+ + Cl^-$ | $\approx -3$ | pH adjustment |
| | Nitric acid | $HNO_3 \longrightarrow H^+ + NO_3^-$ | $-1$ | Acid rain formation |
| | Sulfuric acid | $H_2SO_4 \longrightarrow H^+ + HSO_4^-$ | $\approx -3$ | Acid rain formation, coagulation, pH adjustment |
| | Bisulfite | $HSO_4^- \rightleftharpoons H^+ + SO_4^{2-}$ | $1.9$ | Formation in anoxic sediments |

**EXAMPLE 2–11**   If 100 mg of $H_2SO_4$ (MW $= 98$) is added to water, bringing the final volume to 1.0 L, what is the final pH?

Solution   Using the molecular weight of sulfuric acid, we find

$$\left(\frac{100\ \text{mg}}{1\ \text{L}\ H_2O}\right)\left(\frac{1\ \text{mol}}{98\ \text{g}}\right)\left(\frac{1\ \text{g}}{10^3\ \text{mg}}\right) = 1.02 \times 10^{-3}\ \text{mol} \cdot \text{L}^{-1}$$

The reaction is

$$H_2SO_4 \longrightarrow 2H^+ + SO_4^{2-}$$

and sulfuric acid is a strong acid, so we can determine the pH in the following manner. If the concentration of sulfuric acid is $1.02 \times 10^{-3}$ M, then during the dissociation of the acid $2(1.02 \times 10^{-3})$ M $H^+$ is produced. The pH is

$$\text{pH} = -\log(2.04 \times 10^{-3}) = 2.69$$

**Weak acids** are acids that do not completely dissociate in water. Equilibrium exists between the dissociated ions and undissociated compound. The reaction of a weak acid is

$$HA = H^+ + A^- \tag{2–45}$$

An equilibrium constant exists that relates the degree of dissociation to the equilibrium constant for that reaction:

$$K_a = \frac{[H^+][A^-]}{[HA]} \tag{2–46}$$

A list of weak acids important in environmental science is provided in Table 2–3. By knowing the pH of a solution (which can be easily found with a pH meter) it can be possible to get a rough idea of the degree of dissolution of the acid. For example, if the pH is equal to the $pK_a$ (i.e., $[H^+] = K_a$), then from Equation 2–46, $[HA] = [A^-]$. Because the total amount of acid species, $A_T$, equals $[HA] + [A^-]$ and $[HA] = [A^-]$, the acid is 50% dissociated. If the $[H^+]$ is two orders of

---

**TABLE 2–3**      Selected Weak Acid Dissociation Constants at 25°C

| Substance | Chemical Reaction | $pK_a$ | Significance |
|---|---|---|---|
| Acetic acid | $CH_3COOH = H^+ + CH_3COO^-$ | 4.75 | Anaerobic digestion |
| Carbonic acid | $H_2CO_3^* = H^+ + HCO_3^-$ | 6.35 | Buffering of natural |
| | $HCO_3^- = H^+ + CO_3^{2-}$ | 10.33 | waters, coagulation |
| Hydrogen sulfide | $H_2S = H^+ + HS^-$ | 7.2 | Aeration, odor control, |
| | $HS^- = H^+ + S^{2-}$ | 11.89 | anaerobic sediments |
| Hypochlorous acid | $HOCl = H^+ + OCl^-$ | 7.54 | Disinfection |
| Phosphoric acid | $H_3PO_4 = H^+ + H_2PO_4^-$ | 2.12 | Phosphate removal, |
| | $H_2PO_4^- = H^+ + HPO_4^{2-}$ | 7.20 | plant nutrient, |
| | $HPO_4^{2-} = H^+ + PO_4^{3-}$ | 12.32 | pH adjustment |

*The asterisk next to $H_2CO_3$ signifies both true carbonic acid and dissolved carbon dioxide. Because we cannot distinguish between the two, analytically, we combine the concentrations of the two compounds and refer to the sum as $H_2CO_3$-star.

magnitude (100 times) greater than the $K_a$, then

$$K_a = \frac{[H^+][A^-]}{[HA]} = \frac{100K_a[A^-]}{[HA]}$$

$$1 = \frac{100[A^-]}{[HA]}$$

$$[HA] = 100[A^-]$$

In this case pH $\ll$ p$K_a$, and the acid is found primarily in the protonated form (as HA). Conversely, if pH $\gg$ p$K_a$, then the acid is primarily in the dissociated form (A$^-$).

**EXAMPLE 2-12**   A solution of HOCl is prepared in water by adding 15 mg HOCl to a volumetric flask, and adding water to the 1.0 L mark. The final pH is measured to be 7.0. What are the concentrations of HOCl and OCl? What percent of the HOCl is dissociated? Assume the temperature is 25°C.

Solution   The dissociation reaction for HOCl is

$$HOCl = H^+ + OCl^-$$

From Table 2–3, we find the p$K_a$ is 7.54 and

$$K_a = 10^{-7.54} = 2.88 \times 10^{-8}$$

Writing the equilibrium expression in the form of Equation 2–46 and substituting the concentration of H$^+$, we find

$$K_a = \frac{[H^+][OCl^-]}{HOCl} = \frac{[1.00 \times 10^{-7}][OCl^-]}{HOCl} = 2.88 \times 10^{-8}$$

Using the previous equation, we can solve for the HOCl concentration as

$$[HOCl] = 3.47[OCl^-]$$

Because, at equilibrium, the concentration of the combination of HOCl or OCl$^-$ must equal that which was added, we can state that

$$[HOCl] + [OCl^-] = \text{molar concentration added}$$

Because we added HOCl, we need to calculate the molar concentration using the molecular weight of HOCl.

Molar concentration $= (15 \text{ mg} \cdot L^{-1})(10^{-3} \text{ g} \cdot \text{mg}^{-1})(1 \text{ mol}/52.461 \text{ g}) = 2.86 \times 10^{-4} \text{ M}$

Thus,

$$[HOCl] + [OCl^-] = 2.86 \times 10^{-4} \text{ M}$$

Substituting from the equation for HOCl concentration, we see

$$(3.47[OCl^-]) + [OCl^-] = 2.86 \times 10^{-4} \text{ M}$$

Therefore, $[OCl^-] = 6.39 \times 10^{-5}$ M. The concentration of HOCl can be calculated either by multiplying this concentration by 3.47 or subtracting this concentration from $2.86 \times 10^{-4}$ M.

$$[HOCl] = 2.86 \times 10^{-4} - 6.39 \times 10^{-5} = 2.22 \times 10^{-4} \text{ M}$$

The percentage of OCl$^-$ that is dissociated can be calculated as

$$\frac{[OCl^-]}{[HOCl] + [OCl^-]} = \frac{[6.4 \times 10^{-5}]}{[2.86 \times 10^{-4}]} = 22.4\%$$

**Equilibrium Among Gases and Liquids.** The relationship between the equilibrium concentration of gas dissolved in solution and the partial pressure of the gas is defined by Henry's law. The original formulation of Henry's law states that the partial pressure of a chemical in the gas phase ($P_{gas}$) is linearly proportional to the concentration of the chemical in the aqueous phase ($C_{aq}$).

$$P_{gas} = kC_{aq} \tag{2-47}$$

Henry's law is valid for dilute solutions and low pressures.

The confusion with Henry's law comes about because various concentration scales can be used for both the gas and aqueous phase concentrations and the proportionality constant can be written on either side of the equation, resulting in constants that are the inverse of one another. For example, one way to write Henry's law is given in Equation 2–48.

$$P_{gas} = K_H C^* \tag{2-48}$$

where $P_{gas}$ = partial pressure of the gas in equilibrium (kPa)
  $K_H$ = Henry's law constant, $kPa \cdot m^3 \cdot g^{-1}$
  $C^*$ = equilibrium concentration of gas dissolved in liquid ($g \cdot m^{-3}$)

Similarly, one can use molar and atmospheres as units. Here the equation becomes

$$C_{aq} = K_H' P_{gas} \tag{2-49}$$

where $P_{gas}$ = partial pressure of the gas in equilibrium (atm)
  $K_H'$ = Henry's law constant ($mol \cdot L^{-1} \cdot atm^{-1}$)
  $C_{aq}$ = equilibrium concentration of gas dissolved in water ($mol \cdot L^{-1}$)

Another notation to describe the equilibrium between the gas and the liquid phases uses gas-phase concentrations in units of moles per cubic meter ($mol \cdot m^{-3}$). The gas-phase concentration in moles per cubic meter can be related to the concentration in units of atmospheres by the equation,

$$(Gas) = \frac{P_{gas}}{RT} \tag{2-50}$$

where (Gas) = concentration of gas ($mol \cdot m^{-3}$)
  $P_{gas}$ = partial pressure of the gas in equilibrium (atm)
  $R$ = ideal gas constant ($atm\ m^3 \cdot mol^{-1}\ K$)
  $T$ = temperature ($K$)

Thus,

$$\frac{C_{aq}}{(Gas)} = K_H RT \left[ \frac{mol \cdot L^{-1}}{mol \cdot m^{-3}} \right] \tag{2-51}$$

For a given temperature and pressure, the equilibrium concentration of the gas in the liquid is a constant and is called the saturation concentration.

To confuse the issue even more, some scientists use mole fractions to describe the aqueous concentration of a dissolved gas. The partial pressure of a gas in air is the product of its mole fraction and the air pressure. For example, the atmosphere contains about 21% oxygen by volume, so the partial pressure would be 0.21 times the atmospheric pressure. Another useful expression of Henry's law is written as

$$X = HP_{gas} \tag{2-52}$$

where $X$ = mole fraction of the gas dissolved in the liquid at equilibrium
  $H$ = Henry's law constant ($atm^{-1}$)
  $P_{gas}$ = partial pressure of gas in equilibrium with liquid (atm)

The mole fraction of one gas in water may be calculated as

$$X_1 = \frac{[gas_1]}{[H_2O] + [gas_1] + [gas_2] + \cdots [gas_n]} \approx \frac{[gas_1]}{[H_2O]} \qquad (2\text{--}53)$$

where $[gas_1]$ = mass of dissolved gas 1.

If, in Equation 2–53, we use concentration units of moles per liter then, because the molar concentration of $H_2O = (1000 \text{ g} \cdot \text{L}^{-1})/(18 \text{ g} \cdot \text{mol}^{-1}) = 55.56 \text{ mol} \cdot \text{L}^{-1}$, Equation 2–52 can be combined to be written as

$$[gas] = 55.56 H P_g \qquad (2\text{--}54)$$

To add to the confusion over Henry's constants, the relationship between the equilibrium concentration of gas dissolved in solution can also be written, not in terms of the partial pressure of the gas but in terms of the concentration of the particular gas in air in units of milligrams per cubic meter ($mg \cdot m^{-3}$) while the aqueous concentration is also in milligrams per cubic meter. Henry's constant is essentially dimensionless. Here, the relationship is

$$C_g = K'_H C_w^* \qquad (2\text{--}55)$$

where $C_g$ = concentration of the gas in air at equilibrium ($mg \cdot m^{-3}$ air)
$K'_H$ = Henry's law constant ($mg \cdot m^{-3}$ air) $[(mg \cdot m^{-3} \text{ water})^{-1}]$
$C_w^*$ = equilibrium concentration of gas dissolved in liquid ($mg \cdot m^{-3}$ water)

The Henry's law coefficient varies both with the temperature and the concentration of other dissolved substances. Henry's law constants are given in Appendix Table A–11.

**EXAMPLE 2–13**  The concentration of carbon dioxide in water at 20°C is $1.00 \times 10^{-5}$ M. The Henry's constant for carbon dioxide dissolution in water is $3.91 \times 10^{-2}$ M atm$^{-1}$ at 20°C. What is the partial pressure of $CO_2$ in the air?

**Solution**  With Henry's law given in units of molar per atmosphere ($M \cdot atm^{-1}$), we must write the proportionality equation as

$$C_{CO_2} = K'_H P_{CO_2}$$

or

$$P_{CO_2} = \frac{C_{CO_2}}{K'_H}$$

Thus,

$$P_{CO_2} = \frac{(1.00 \times 10^{-5} \text{ M})}{3.91 \times 10^{-2} \text{ M} \cdot \text{atm}^{-1}} = 2.56 \times 10^{-4} \text{ atm}$$

**EXAMPLE 2–14**  The Henry's constant for dichloromethane (DCM) is approximately 0.5 $M \cdot atm^{-1}$ at 20°C. What is the Henry's constant in dimensionless units? If the atmospheric (gas phase) concentration of DCM was measured to be $10^{-3}$ $mg \cdot m^{-3}$, what is the concentration of DCM in the rainwater?

**Solution**  Using the relationship,

$$K'_H = \frac{H}{RT}$$

we can solve for $H$.

$$H = (0.5 \text{ M} \cdot \text{atm}^{-1})(0.082 \text{ L} \cdot \text{atm} \cdot \text{K}^{-1} \cdot \text{mol}^{-1})(273 + 20 \text{ K}) = 12.01$$

To solve for the aqueous concentration,

$$C_{\text{aq,DCM}} = HC_{\text{g,DCM}}$$

$$= (12.01)(10^{-3} \text{ mg} \cdot \text{m}^{-3}) = 1.2 \times 10^{-2} \text{ mg} \cdot \text{m}^{-3} \text{ or } 1.2 \times 10^{-5} \text{ mg} \cdot \text{L}^{-1}$$

### Reaction Kinetics

Many reactions that occur in the environment do not reach equilibrium quickly. Some examples include the disinfection of water, gas transfer into and out of bodies of water, dissolution of rocks and minerals, and radioactive decay. The study of the speed at which these reactions proceed is called reaction kinetics. The rate of reaction, $r$, is used to describe the rate of formation or disappearance of a compound. Reactions that take place in a single phase (i.e., liquid, gas, or solid) are called **homogeneous reactions**. Those that occur at surfaces between phases are called **heterogeneous reactions**. For each type of reaction, the rate may be defined as follows:

For homogeneous reactions

$$r = \frac{\text{mass of chemical species}}{(\text{unit volume})(\text{unit time})} \tag{2–56}$$

For heterogeneous reactions

$$r = \frac{\text{mass of chemical species}}{(\text{unit surface area})(\text{unit time})} \tag{2–57}$$

By convention, the production of a compound is denoted by a positive sign for the reaction rate $(+r)$, and a negative sign $(-r)$ is used to designate the disappearance of the substance of interest. Reaction rates are a function of temperature, pressure, and the concentration of reactants. For a stoichiometric reaction of the form

$$a\text{A} + b\text{B} \rightarrow c\text{C} \tag{2–58}$$

where $a$, $b$, and $c$ are the proportionality coefficients for the reactants A, B, and C, the change in concentration of compound A in a batch reactor is equal to the reaction rate equation for compound A.

$$-\frac{1}{a}\frac{d[\text{A}]}{dt} = -\frac{1}{b}\frac{d[\text{B}]}{dt} = +\frac{1}{c}\frac{d[\text{C}]}{dt} = -k[\text{A}]^{\alpha}[\text{B}]^{\beta} \tag{2–59}$$

where  [A], [B], and [C] are the concentrations of the reactants, and

$\alpha$, $\beta$, and $k$ are empirically determined constants.

The proportionality term, $k$, is called the **reaction rate constant** and is generally dependent on the temperature and pressure. Because A and B are disappearing, the sign of the reaction rate equation is negative. It is positive for C because C is being formed.

The order of reaction is defined as the sum of the exponents in the reaction rate equation. The exponents may be either integers or fractions. Some sample reaction orders are shown in Table 2–4. First-order reactions are simple; the rate constant has units of inverse time. It is common, with first-order reactions, to use the half-life $(t_{1/2})$ for the reaction; that is the time required for the concentration to reach a value one-half of its initial concentration. The half-life is defined as $\ln(0.5)/k$, or $0.693/k$.

---

**TABLE 2–4**      Example Reaction Orders

| Reaction Order | Rate Expression | Units on Rate Constant |
|---|---|---|
| Zero | $r_A = -k$ | $(\text{concentration})(\text{time})^{-1}$ |
| First | $r_A = -k[A]$ | $(\text{time})^{-1}$ |
| Second | $r_A = -k[A]^2$ | $(\text{concentration})^{-1}(\text{time})^{-1}$ |
| Second | $r_A = -k[A][B]$ | $(\text{concentration})^{-1}(\text{time})^{-1}$ |

---

**EXAMPLE 2–15**   As a result of the Aykhal Crystal detonation in 1974 (in the former Soviet Union), cesium-137 was measured (in 1993) in the soil at a concentration of $2 \times 10^4$ Bq $\cdot$ kg$^{-1}$ soil.* If the background concentration of $^{137}$Cs is 0.5 Bq $\cdot$ kg$^{-1}$ soil, how many years will it take before the concentration of $^{137}$Cs reaches background levels.

Solution   The decay of radionuclides occurs by a first-order reaction. Because $t_{1/2} = 0.693 \cdot k^{-1}$, $k = 0.693/(30 \text{ years}) = 0.0231 \text{ year}^{-1}$.

Then we can write that

$$\ln(C/C_0) = -kt$$

$$\ln(0.5/2 \times 10^4) = -(0.0231 \text{ year}^{-1})t$$

$$t = 459 \text{ years}$$

---

*The unit becquerel (Bq) describes radioactivity. It is the number of disintegrations per second.

---

For the general reaction

$$aA + bB \rightarrow cC \tag{2–58}$$

the overall reaction rate, $r$, and the individual reaction rates are related.

$$r = -\frac{r_a}{a} = -\frac{r_b}{b} = \frac{r_c}{c} \tag{2–60}$$

The reaction rate constant, $k$, must be determined experimentally by obtaining data on the concentrations of the reactants as a function of time and plotting on a suitable graph. The form of the graph is determined from the result of integration of the equations in Table 2–4. The integrated form and the appropriate graphical forms are shown in Table 2–5.

---

**TABLE 2–5**      Plotting Procedure to Determine Order of Reaction by Method of Integration

| Order | Rate Equation | Integrated Equation | Linear Plot | Slope | Intercept |
|---|---|---|---|---|---|
| 0 | $d[A]/dt = -k$ | $[A] - [A]_0 = -kt$ | $[A]$ vs. $t$ | $-k$ | $[A]_0$ |
| 1 | $d[A]/dt = -k[A]$ | $\ln[A]/[A]_0 = -kt$ | $\ln[A]$ vs. $t$ | $-k$ | $\ln[A]_0$ |
| 2 | $d[A]/dt = -k[A]^2$ | $1/[A] - 1/[A]_0 = kt$ | $1/[A]$ vs. $t$ | $k$ | $1/[A]_0$ |

Source: J. G. Henry, C. W. Heinke, *Environmental Science and Engineering*, Englewood Cliffs, NJ: Prentice Hall, 1989. p. 201. Reprinted with permission.

**EXAMPLE 2–16**   An environmental engineering student was very interested in the reaction of the chemical 2,4,6-chickenwire. She went into the lab and found that 2,4,6-chickenwire degrades in water. During her experiments she collected the data in the following table. Plot the data to determine if the reaction is zero-, first-, or second-order with respect to the concentration of 2,4,6-chickenwire.

| Time (min) | Concentration (mg · L$^{-1}$) | Time (min) | Concentration (mg · L$^{-1}$) |
|---|---|---|---|
| 0 | 10.0 | 10 | 5.46 |
| 1 | 8.56 | 20 | 4.23 |
| 2 | 8.14 | 40 | 1.26 |
| 4 | 6.96 | 80 | 0.218 |
| 8 | 6.77 | | |

**Solution**   Using the information in Table 2–5, we see that the decomposition of 2,4,6-chickenwire cannot be zero-order because for zero-order reactions, the concentration of the reactant does not vary with time. Let's graph the data on first- and second-order plots.

With the first-order plot, we graph the concentration versus time.

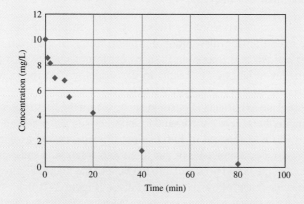

The plot is clearly nonlinear, so the degradation of 2,4,6-chickenwire is not first-order. Let's now plot the concentration of the natural log of the concentration of 2,4,6-chickenwire divided by its initial concentration versus time.

The plot is linear; a least squares regression analysis reveals a $r$-square value of 0.9921. The slope of the line (forced through zero) is 0.0486. This corresponds to a rate constant of 0.051 min$^{-1}$. Clearly, the reaction is second-order.

A special type of reaction is known as an elementary reaction. For these reactions the stoichiometric equation represents both the mass balance and the reaction process on a molecular scale, and the stoichiometric coefficients ($a$, $b$, $c$) are equivalent to the exponents in the reaction rate equation. For example, with the following elementary reaction:

$$a\text{A} + b\text{B} \rightarrow c\text{C} \tag{2-58}$$

we can a priori write the kinetic expression as

$$r_A = -k[\text{A}]^a[\text{B}]^b \tag{2-61}$$

without having to develop the kinetic expression from experimental results.

The effect of temperature on elementary reactions is described by the relationship first postulated by Arrhenius (in 1889), where

$$k = Ae^{-E_a/RT} \tag{2-62}$$

where $A$ = the Arrhenius parameter
$\quad E_a$ = the activation energy
$\quad R$ = universal gas constant
$\quad T$ = absolute temperature
$\quad e$ = exponential; $e^1 = 2.7183$

**Gas Transfer Across Air–Water Interfaces.**   An important example of time-dependent reactions is the mass transfer (dissolution or volatilization) of gas from water. The transfer of a gas between air and water is important in many environmental systems from the dissolution of oxygen from the air in lakes and streams to the stripping of carbon dioxide from chemically treated groundwater.

In 1924 Lewis and Whitman [1] postulated a two-film theory to describe the mass transfer of gases. According to their theory, the boundary between the gas phase and the liquid phase (also called the interface) is composed of two distinct films that serve as barriers between the bulk phases (Figure 2–2). For a molecule of gas to go into solution, it must pass through the bulk of the gas, the gas film, the liquid film, and into the bulk of the liquid (Figure 2–2a). To leave the liquid, the gas molecule must follow the reverse course (Figure 2–2b).

The driving force causing the gas to move, and hence the mass transfer, is the concentration gradient: $C_s - C$. $C_s$ is the saturation concentration of the gas in the liquid, and $C$ is the actual aqueous concentration. The saturation concentration is a function of temperature, pressure, and gas-phase concentration (or liquid-phase concentration, depending on which phase serves as the

**FIGURE 2–2**

Two-film model of the interface between gas and liquid: (a) absorption mode and (b) desorption mode. $C_t$ is the concentration at time, $t$. $C_s$ is the saturation concentration of the gas in the liquid.

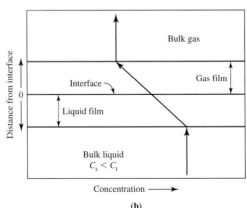

source phase). When $C_s$ is greater than $C$, the gas will go into solution. When $C$ is greater than $C_s$, the gas will volatilize from solution. $C_s$ can be determined from the relationship for Henry's constant as discussed previously.

The rate of mass transfer can be described by the following equation.

$$\frac{dC}{dt} = k_a(C_s - C) \tag{2–63}$$

where $k_a$ = rate constant or mass transfer coefficient, $(\text{time})^{-1}$. In a batch reactor, Equation 2–63 can be written as

$$r_c = k_a(C_s - C) \tag{2–64}$$

The difference between the saturation concentration and the actual concentration, $C_s - C$, is called the deficit. Because the saturation concentration is constant with temperature and pressure, this is a first-order reaction.

Integrating the above equation yields

$$\ln\left(\frac{C_s - C_t}{C_s - C_0}\right) = k_a t \tag{2–64a}$$

where $C_t$ = the aqueous concentration of the gas at any time, $t$.

---

**EXAMPLE 2–17**  A falling raindrop initially has no dissolved oxygen. The saturation concentration for oxygen in the drop of water is $9.20 \text{ mg} \cdot \text{L}^{-1}$. If, after falling for 2 s, the droplet has an oxygen concentration of $3.20 \text{ mg} \cdot \text{L}^{-1}$, how long must the droplet fall (from the start of the fall) to achieve a concentration of $8.20 \text{ mg} \cdot \text{L}^{-1}$? Assume that the rate of oxygen exchange is first-order.

Solution  We begin by calculating the deficit after 2 s, and that at a concentration of $8.20 \text{ mg} \cdot \text{L}^{-1}$:

Deficit at 2 s = $9.20 - 3.20 = 6.00 \text{ mg} \cdot \text{L}^{-1}$

Deficit at $t$ s = $9.20 - 8.20 = 1.00 \text{ mg} \cdot \text{L}^{-1}$

Now using the integrated form of the first-order rate equation from Table 2–5, noting that the rate of change is proportional to deficit and, hence, $[A] = (C_s - C)$ and that $[A]_0 = (9.20 - 0.0)$, we see that

$$\ln\left(\frac{6.00}{9.20}\right) = -k(2.00 \text{ s})$$

$$k = 0.214 \text{ s}^{-1}$$

With this value of $k$, we can calculate a value for $t$.

$$\ln\left(\frac{9.20 - 8.2}{9.20}\right) = -(0.214 \text{ s}^{-1})(t)$$

$$t = 10.4 \text{ s}$$

---

## 2–3 ORGANIC CHEMISTRY

So far much of what we have discussed in this chapter has been about inorganic chemistry. Because environmental science is very much one of the life sciences, we need to discuss organic chemistry. As mentioned previously, organic chemicals, which are those chemicals made up of carbon and hydrogen, can be produced naturally or via synthetic anthropogenic reactions. This vast and diverse group of chemicals are important because they form the basis for all life; are used in many ways, as insecticides, herbicides, hormones, antibiotics, to name a few; and can have serious deleterious effects on the environment.

Organic chemicals are divided into groups, by several different approaches. For example, we can divide up organic chemicals by the types of C—C bonding present. Alkanes are those compounds that have a single bond between adjacent carbon atoms. Alkenes have a double bond between adjacent carbon atoms, whereas the highly reactive alkynes have a triple bond between adjacent carbon atoms. With alkanes, the carbon atoms involved in the single bonds share two electrons; with alkenes the double-bonded carbons share four electrons; and with alkynes six electrons are shared by the carbons involved in the triple bonds.

### Alkanes, Alkenes, and Alkynes

Alkanes ($C_nH_{2n+2}$) are also called paraffins or aliphatic hydrocarbons. With this group of chemicals, the carbon atoms are all linked by single covalent bonds. The nomenclature used by the IUPAC (International Union of Pure and Applied Chemists) is shown in Table 2–6. The suffix -*ane* is used to distinguish alkanes from other compounds. Alkanes can be straight-chained, branched or cyclic. Some alkanes (and other organic compounds) may have the same molecular formula but different structures. These compounds are referred to as **structural isomers.** For example, *n*-hexane, 2-methylpentane, 3-methylpentane, and 2,3-dimethylbutane all have the molecular formula $C_6H_{14}$. However, the structural formulas for these chemicals all differ as shown in Figure 2–3. The chemical cyclohexane, which has six carbons, is not a structural isomer of the other hexanes listed here because its molecular formula is $C_6H_{12}$.

| TABLE 2–6 | Chemical Nomenclature for Alkanes |
|---|---|
| **Molecular Formula** | **IUPAC Name** |
| $CH_4$ | methane |
| $C_2H_6$ | ethane |
| $C_3H_8$ | propane |
| $C_4H_{10}$ | butane |
| $C_5H_{12}$ | pentane |
| $C_6H_{14}$ | hexane |
| $C_7H_{16}$ | heptane |
| $C_8H_{18}$ | octane |
| $C_9H_{20}$ | nonane |
| $C_{10}H_{22}$ | decane |

**FIGURE 2–3**

Structural isomers and IUPAC names for $C_6H_{14}$.

*n*-hexane          3-methylpentane          2-methylpentane          2,3-dimethylbutane

**FIGURE 2–4**

*Cis-* and *trans-*1,2-
dichloroethene.

*cis*-1,2-dichloroethene

*trans*-1,2-dichloroethene

**FIGURE 2–5**

Kekulé resonance
structures of benzene.

**FIGURE 2–6**

Robinson shorthand
notation for aromatic
rings.

As mentioned previously, alkenes ($C_nH_{2n}$) contain at least one double bond. Naming alkenes is similar to naming alkanes, except that the IUPAC uses *-ene* as the suffix. Common naming calls for the use of *-ylene* as the suffix. As such, $C_2H_4$ has the IUPAC name *ethene* and the common name *ethylene*. Alkenes have geometric isomers because the C=C bond is rigid (i.e., it cannot rotate), unlike in alkanes. We therefore need to remember that with alkenes there are cis and trans isomers. For example, the common industrial solvent and groundwater contaminant, dichloroethene (DCE), comes in two forms, *cis*-DCE and *trans*-DCE (Figure 2–4).

Alkynes ($C_nH_n$) are named in a similar manner to alkanes and alkenes, except IUPAC uses the suffix *-yne*. Common naming uses acetylene as the base name. For example, $H_3C—C≡C—CH_3$ is called dimethylacetylene. The alkynes are highly reactive and dangerously explosive. They are generally of lesser environmental significance because they do not last long in the environment.

### Aryl (Aromatic) Compounds

Aromatic compounds are cyclic and have alternating double bonds, in a resonance structure in which all of the carbons in the ring share the π-bond electrons, although this sharing may not always be equal, making the aromatic ring slightly polar. Benzene ($C_6H_6$) is the simplest aromatic compound and is shown in Figure 2–5 with its Kekulé resonance structure. Because of the sharing of the π-bond electrons, creating what can be thought of as a "cloud" of electrons surrounding the carbon atoms, the chemical symbol in Figure 2–6 (known as the Robinson symbol) is often used as a shorthand notation for benzene. The hydrogen atoms are assumed to be bonded to the carbon atoms.

Among the many aromatic compounds of environmental significance, three classes of compounds stand out: the benzenelike hydrocarbons (benzene, toluene, and xylene or BTX), polycyclic aromatic hydrocarbons (PAHs, also known as polynuclear aromatic hydrocarbons—PNAs), and the polychlorinated biphenyls (PCBs). The first class (BTX—shown in Figure 2–7) are found in gasoline and are common in soils contaminated by gasoline products. The next group (PAHs) is a class of fused benzene rings, which are found in many petroleum products and are by-products of the incomplete combustion of other hydrocarbons. The carcinogenic properties of some of these chemicals make them of environmental concern. Several PAHs are shown in Figure 2–8. As shown in Figure 2–9, the biphenyl compounds are composed of two benzenes covalently bonded with a single bond.

Chlorinated biphenyls (PCBs) are biphenyl compounds that have a total of one to five chlorine atoms bonded to each of the aromatic rings (in place of the hydrogen atoms). PCBs were produced in the United States until 1978 and were used extensively in transformer oils, because these compounds are essentially nonflammable. PCBs were also used in such products as carbonless copy paper, electrical insulation, and paints. Although the biphenyl itself does not appear to be toxic, chlorination of the biphenyl increases the toxicity and carcinogenicity of this class of compounds. In general, the greater the degree of chlorination, the more **recalcitrant** (less easily biodegradable) are these compounds. Although their use has been banned for more than 20 years, the presence of PCBs in the environment continues to be a problem.

**FIGURE 2–7**

BTX compounds.

benzene    toluene    xylene

**FIGURE 2–8**

Several examples of polycyclic aromatic hydrocarbons.

napthalene    anthracene    pyrene    benzo(a)pyrene

**FIGURE 2–9**

Two covalently bonded benzene rings. This is the basic unit of the biphenyl compounds.

**TABLE 2–7**         Common Functional Groups and Examples of Compounds

| Functional Group[a] | | Example Compound | |
| --- | --- | --- | --- |
| **Name** | **Chemical Structure** | **Name** | **Structure** |
| Alcohol | R—OH (on alkyl group) | ethanol | $H_3C$—$CH_2OH$ |
| Phenol | R—OH (on aryl group) | phenol | ⬡—OH |
| Aldehyde | R—CH (with =O) | acetaldehyde | $H_3CCH$ (with =O) |
| Ketone | R—C—R' (with =O) | methylethylketone | $H_3C$—C—$C_2H_5$ (with =O) |
| Ester | R—C—O—R' (with =O) | methylethylester | $H_3C$—C—O—$C_2H_5$ (with =O) |
| Ether | R—O—R' | methylethylether | $H_3C$—O—$C_2H_5$ |
| Amine | R—C—$NH_2$ | methylamine | $H_3C$—$NH_2$ |
| Amide | R—C—$NH_2$ (with =O) | methylamide | $H_3C$—C—$NH_2$ (with =O) |
| Mercaptan | R—SH | methylmercaptan | $CH_3SH$ |
| Halides | R—(Cl, Br, I, or F) | chloroform | $CHCl_3$ |
| Sulfonic acid | R—$SO_3H$ | benzenesulfonic acid | ⬡—S(=O)(=O)—OH |

[a]*Note:* R represents any functional group or hydrogen.

### Functional Groups and Classes of Compounds

The presence of other elements or groups of elements on the backbone structure of hydrocarbons changes the properties of the chemical considerably. For example, replacing a hydrogen on ethane with a hydroxyl (—OH) functional group changes the chemical from an aqueous-insoluble gas to an aqueous-soluble liquid (ethanol). Functional groups are simply groups of specific bonding arrangements of atoms in organic molecules. Common functional groups are listed in Table 2–7.

## 2–4   WATER CHEMISTRY

Because all environmental systems contain water, the properties of water play a significant role in defining environmental processes.

### Physical Properties of Water

The basic physical properties of water relevant to environmental science are density and viscosity. Density is a measure of the concentration of matter and is expressed in three ways:

1. **Mass density, ρ.** Mass density is mass per unit volume and is measured in units of kilograms per cubic meter ($kg \cdot m^{-3}$). Table A–1, in the Appendix, shows the variation of density with temperature for pure water free from air. Dissolved or suspended impurities change the density of water in direct proportion to their concentration and their own density. In most environmental science applications, it is common to ignore the density increase due to impurities in the water. However, environmental scientists and engineers cannot ignore the density of the matter when dealing with high concentrations of solutions and suspensions, such as thickened sludge or stock solutions of reagents such as lime (used in water purification), or in ocean or estuarine waters.

2. **Specific weight, γ.** Specific weight is the weight (force) per unit volume, measured in units of kilonewtons per cubic meter ($kN \cdot m^{-3}$). The specific weight of a fluid is related to its density by the acceleration of gravity, $g$, which is $9.81 \text{ m} \cdot s^{-2}$.

$$\gamma = \rho g \tag{2-65}$$

3. **Specific gravity, S.** Specific gravity is given by

$$S = \frac{\rho}{\rho_0} = \frac{\gamma}{\gamma_0} \tag{2-66}$$

where the subscript zero denotes the density of water at $3.98°C$, $1000 \text{ kg} \cdot m^{-3}$, and the specific weight of water, $9.81 \text{ kN} \cdot m^{-3}$.

For quick approximations, the density of water at commonly occuring temperatures can be taken as $1000 \text{ kg} \cdot m^{-3}$ (which is conveniently $1 \text{ kg} \cdot L^{-1}$).

4. **Viscosity.** All substances, including liquids, exhibit a resistance to movement, an internal friction. Just think of several liquids such as water, corn syrup, and molasses. The latter two are much more **viscous** than water, that is, they flow much less freely than does water. Alternatively, if you dropped a marble in each of the three fluids, you would find that the marble travels fastest in the water. The higher the viscosity of the fluid, the greater the friction, and the harder it is to pump the liquid. Viscosity is actually a measure of the friction and is presented in one of two ways:

   a. Dynamic viscosity, or absolute viscosity, $\mu$, has dimensions of mass per unit length per time, with units of kilograms per meter second ($kg \cdot m^{-1} \cdot s$) or pascal per second ($Pa \cdot s^{-1}$).

   b. Kinematic viscosity, $\nu$, is defined as the dynamic viscosity divided by the density of the fluid at that temperature.

$$\nu = \frac{\mu}{\rho} \tag{2-67}$$

It has dimensions of length squared per time with the corresponding units meters squared per second ($m^2 \cdot s^{-1}$).

### States of Solution Impurities

Substances can exist in water in one of three classifications: suspended, colloidal, or dissolved. A dissolved substance is one that is truly in solution. The substance is homogeneously dispersed in the liquid. Dissolved substances can be simple atoms or complex molecular compounds. For example, if one adds table salt to water, the dissolved sodium is present as $Na^+$, its dissociated form of NaCl. On the contrary, if one adds sugar to water, the dissolved form of sugar (glucose) is $C_6H_{12}O_6$. Dissolved substances are present in the liquid, that is, there is only one phase present. The substance cannot be removed from the liquid without accomplishing a phase change such as distillation, precipitation, adsorption, or extraction.

In **distillation** either the liquid or the substance itself is changed from a liquid phase to a gas phase in order to achieve separation. Distillation can occur in nature when salt water containing sodium chloride salt evaporates, leaving behind the sodium and chloride ions and producing a vapor that is free of sodium chloride.

In **precipitation** the substance in the liquid phase combines with another chemical to form a solid phase, thus achieving separation from the water. This occurs in a water treatment plant when lime (CaO) is added to remove hardness ions (in particular calcium and magnesium).

**Adsorption** also involves a phase change, wherein the dissolved substance attaches to the surface of solid particles. Attachment can be due to either chemical or physical attractive forces. Adsorption is important in soils, where ions such as nitrate and phosphate can attach, or sorb, to the surfaces of the soil particles.

**Liquid extraction** can separate a substance from water or a solid by extracting it into another liquid, hence a phase change from water to a different liquid. Liquid extraction is used in some environmental engineering applications, for example, petroleum-based compounds such as polycyclic aromatic hydrocarbons can be removed from soils by extracting them with such organic solvents as hexane.

Under no circumstances can physical methods such as filtration, sedimentation, or centrifugation remove dissolved substances. Activated carbon filters remove dissolved chemicals. They are not true filters, in that they do not "strain out" particles. Activated carbon works by the adsorption and absorption of dissolved substances onto the carbon itself.

Suspended solids are not truly dissolved and are large enough to settle out of solution or be removed by filtration. In this case two phases are present: the liquid water phase and the suspended-particle solid phase. Mixtures of a liquid and suspended particles are referred to as **suspensions.** The lower size range of suspended particles is 0.1–1.0 μm, about the size of bacteria. Suspended particles can range up to about 100 μm in size. Suspended solids are often defined operationally as those solids that can be filtered by a glass fiber filter and are properly called filterable solids. Suspended solids can be removed from water by physical methods such as sedimentation, filtration, and centrifugation.

Colloidal particles are usually defined on the basis of size and are generally from 0.001 to about 1 μm in size. Colloidal particles are kept in suspension by physical and chemical forces of attraction. Milk is an example of a colloidal suspension. The fat molecules are not truly dissolved but are held in suspension by attractive forces to the water. If you add acid (due to natural processes such as fermentation or the addition of vinegar), you will find that a solid precipitate forms. The acid changes the charge on the colloidal particles, allowing the colloidal particles to bind together and come out of suspension. Colloidal particles can be removed from the liquid by physical means such as ultracentrifugation or by filtration through membranes having pore sizes less than 0.45 μm. Colloidal particles cannot be removed by sedimentation unless the particles are first aggregated to form particles large enough to settle.

### Concentration Units in Aqueous Solutions or Suspensions

Concentrations of solutions can be given in a variety of units. Chemists tend to use **molarity** or **molality,** but environmental scientists and engineers use units of **milligrams per liter (mg · L$^{-1}$), parts per million (ppm),** or **percent (by weight).** In other cases, it makes more sense to use units of normality.

**Weight percent,** $P$, is sometimes employed to express approximate concentrations of commercial chemicals or of solid concentrations of sludges. The term specifies the grams of substance per 100 g of solution or suspension and is mathematically expressed as

$$P = \frac{W}{W + W_0} \times 100\% \tag{2–68}$$

where $P$ = percent of substance by weight
  $W$ = mass of substance (grams)
  $W_0$ = mass of solute (grams)

Analytical results are often given directly in mass per volume (concentration), and the units are milligrams per liter ($mg \cdot L^{-1}$). In environmental science and engineering it is often assumed that the substance does not change the density of the water. This is generally true in dilute solutes at constant temperature, but it is not valid for concentrated solutions, in air, or in cases of large temperature fluctuations. However, when this assumption is valid, we can use the density of water ($1 \, g \cdot mL^{-1}$) to develop the following conversion:

$$\left( \frac{1 \text{ mg solute}}{\text{L solution}} \right) \left( \frac{1 \text{ L}}{1000 \text{ mL}} \right) \left( \frac{1 \text{ mL}}{g} \right) \left( \frac{g}{1000 \text{ mg}} \right) = \frac{1 \text{ mg}}{10^6 \text{ mg}} = 1 \text{ ppm} \qquad (2\text{–}69)$$

or $1 \, mg \cdot L^{-1}$ equals 1 part per million (ppm). For very dilute solutions, concentrations of parts per billion (ppb) or parts per trillion (ppt) can be used. Using an analogous conversion to that given in Equation 2–69, we can see that $1 \, \mu g \cdot L^{-1} = 1$ ppb and $1 \, ng \cdot L^{-1} = 1$ ppt. Using the same assumptions, then a conversion for milligrams per liter to weight percent can be developed.

$$\frac{1 \text{ mg}}{L} \left( \frac{1 \text{ mL}}{g} \right) \left( \frac{L}{1000 \text{ mL}} \right) \left( \frac{g}{1000 \text{ mg}} \right) = \frac{1 \text{ mg}}{10^6 \text{ mg}} = \frac{1 \text{ mg}}{10^4 (100 \text{ mg})} = 10^{-4} \, P \qquad (2\text{–}70)$$

or $1 \, mg \cdot L^{-1}$ equals $1 \times 10^{-4} P$, which can be translated into $1\% = 10{,}000 \, mg \cdot L^{-1}$.

Concentrations may also be reported in units of moles per liter (molarity) or gram-equivalents per liter (normality). When working with chemical reactions it is necessary to use concentrations of molarity (see Section 2–2) or normality.

Molarity is related to milligrams per liter by

$$mg \cdot L^{-1} = \text{molarity} \times \text{molecular weight} \times 10^3$$

$$= (mol \cdot L^{-1})(g \cdot mol^{-1})(10^3 \, mg \cdot g^{-1}) \qquad (2\text{–}71)$$

A second unit, normality, is frequently used in softening and redox reactions. **Normality** is defined as the number of gram-equivalents of a substance per liter. Gram-equivalents are determined using the equivalent weight of the substance. The **equivalent weight (EW)** is the molecular weight divided by the number ($n$) of electrons transferred in redox reactions or by the number of protons transferred in acid–base reactions. The value of $n$ depends on how the molecule reacts. In an acid–base reaction, $n$ is the number of hydrogen ions that are transferred. It is easiest to conceptualize this with an example reaction. Let's consider sulfuric acid, which has a chemical formula of $H_2SO_4$. Sulfuric acid can give up two electrons to a base.

$$H_2SO_4 = 2H^+ + SO_4^{2-} \qquad (2\text{–}72)$$

The two moles of protons ($H^+$), which are released for every mole of sulfuric acid that dissociates, must be accepted by a base. For example,

$$2H^+ + 2NaOH = 2H_2O + 2Na^+ \qquad (2\text{–}73)$$

If we combine Equations 2–72 and 2–73, we can write a third equation.

$$H_2SO_4 + 2NaOH = SO_4^{2-} + 2H_2O + 2Na^+ \qquad (2\text{–}74)$$

in which two moles of protons are transferred to two moles of sodium hydroxide (the base). Thus, for sulfuric acid, the number of equivalents per mole is 2.

When working with acid–base problems, one often uses equivalent weights instead of molecular weights. The equivalent weight is simply the molecular weight divided by the number of protons transferred. Continuing with our use of sulfuric acid as an example, we see that the equivalent weight of sulfuric acid is the molecular weight ($98.08 \, g \cdot mol^{-1}$) divided by 2, or $49.04 \, g \cdot \text{g-equivalent}^{-1}$.

Determining $n$ for precipitation reactions is simply a special case of that for acid–base reactions. Here the $n$ is equal to the number of hydrogen ions that would be required to replace the cation involved in the precipitation reaction. For example, for $CaCO_3$ it would take two hydrogen ions to replace the calcium, forming $H_2CO_3$. Therefore, the number of equivalents per mole, $n$, equals 2.

In oxidation–reduction (redox) reactions, $n$ is equal to the number of electrons transferred in the reaction. For example, in the following reaction:

$$Fe^{2+} + \tfrac{1}{4}O_2 + H^+ = Fe^{3+} + \tfrac{1}{2}H_2O \tag{2-75}$$

one electron is transferred and $n$ equals 1. Here the equivalent weight of the ferrous ion is $55.85 g \cdot$ g-equivalent$^{-1}$. Obviously, it is impossible to determine the number of equivalence without knowing the reaction.

Normality (N) is the number of gram-equivalents per liter of solution and is related to molarity (M) by

$$N = nM \tag{2-76}$$

remembering that $n$ is the number of gram-equivalents per mole.

**EXAMPLE 2-18** Commercial sulfuric acid ($H_2SO_4$) is often purchased as a 93 wt% (weight percent) solution. Find the concentration of this solution of $H_2SO_4$ in units of milligram per liter, molarity, and normality. Sulfuric acid (100%) has a specific gravity of 1.839. Assume that the temperature of the solution is 15°C.

Solution We can use Equation 2–66 to find the density of a 100% sulfuric acid solution.

$$(1000.0 \text{ g} \cdot L^{-1})(1.839) = 1839 \text{ g} \cdot L^{-1}$$

From Table A–1 (Appendix), we find that at 15°C 1.000 L of water weighs 999.103 g. Following this line of reasoning, a 93% solution of $H_2SO_4$ would have a density of

$$(999.103 \text{ g} \cdot L^{-1})(0.07) + (1839 \text{ g} \cdot L^{-1})(0.93) = 1780.2 \text{ g} \cdot L^{-1} \quad \text{or} \quad 1.8 \times 10^6 \text{ mg} \cdot L^{-1}$$

The molecular weight of $H_2SO_4$ is found by looking up the atomic weights in the front of this textbook.

| Number of Atoms (n) | Element | Atomic Weight (AW) | n × AW |
|---|---|---|---|
| 2 | hydrogen, H | 1.008 | 2.016 |
| 1 | sulfur, S | 32.06 | 32.06 |
| 4 | oxygen, O | 15.9994 | 64.0 |
| | | Molecular weight | 98.08 g · mol$^{-1}$ |

The molarity is found by manipulating Equation 2–71 so as to divide the concentration (in grams per liter) by the molecular weight (in grams per mole).

$$\frac{1780.2 \text{ g} \cdot L^{-1}}{98.08 \text{ g} \cdot mol^{-1}} = 18.15 \text{ M}$$

The normality is found from Equation 2–76, realizing that $H_2SO_4$ can donate two hydrogen ions and therefore $n = 2$ g-equivalents · mol$^{-1}$.

$$N = 18.15 \text{ mol} \cdot L^{-1} (2 \text{ Eq} \cdot mol^{-1}) = 36.30 \text{ Eq} \cdot L^{-1} \quad \text{or} \quad 36.3 \text{ N}$$

**EXAMPLE 2–19**  Find the mass of sodium bicarbonate ($NaHCO_3$) that must be added a 1.00 L volumetric flask containing distilled water to make a 1.0 M solution. Find the normality of the solution.

Solution  The molecular weight of $NaHCO_3$ is 84; therefore, the mass that must be added can be determined by using Equation 2–71.

$$\text{Concentration} = (1.0 \text{ mol} \cdot \text{L}^{-1})(84 \text{ g} \cdot \text{mol}^{-1}) = 84 \text{ g} \cdot \text{L}^{-1}$$

Therefore, 84 g of sodium bicarbonate must be added to 1 L of solution to prepare a 1 M solution. Because $HCO_3^-$ is able to donate or accept only one proton, $n = 1$. Using Equation 2–76, we see that the normality is the same as the molarity.

**EXAMPLE 2–20**  Determine the equivalent weight of each of the following: $Ca^{2+}$, $CO_3^{2-}$, $CaCO_3$.

Solution  Equivalent weight was defined as EW = (Atomic or molecular weight)/$n$, where $n$ is the oxidation state, or the number of electrons or hydrogen ions transferred in the reaction of interest. The units of EW are grams per g-equivalent (g · g-Eq$^{-1}$) or milligrams per milliequivalent (mg · mEq$^{-1}$).

For calcium, $n$ is equal to its oxidation state in water, so $n = 2$. From the table in the front of the book, the atomic weight of $Ca^{2+}$ is 40.08 g · mol$^{-1}$. The equivalent weight is then

$$\text{EW} = \frac{40.08}{2} = 20.04 \text{ g} \cdot \text{g-Eq}^{-1} \qquad \text{or} \qquad 20.04 \text{ mg} \cdot \text{mEq}^{-1}$$

For the carbonate ion ($CO_3^{2-}$), $n = 2$ because carbonate can accept two protons ($H^+$). The molecular weight is calculated as shown in the following table.

| Number of Atoms (n) | Element | Atomic Weight (AW) | n × AW |
|---|---|---|---|
| 1 | carbon, C | 12.01 | 12.01 |
| 3 | oxygen, O | 15.9994 | 48.0 |
| | | Molecular weight | 60.01 g · mol$^{-1}$ |

And the equivalent weight is

$$\text{EW} = \frac{60.01 \text{ g} \cdot \text{mol}^{-1}}{2 \text{ g-Eq} \cdot \text{mol}^{-1}} = 30.01 \text{ g} \cdot \text{g-Eq}^{-1} \qquad \text{or} \qquad 30.01 \text{ mg} \cdot \text{mEq}^{-1}$$

With $CaCO_3$, $n = 2$ because two hydrogen ions are required to replace the cation ($Ca^{2+}$) to form carbonic acid ($H_2CO_3$). Its molecular weight is the sum of the atomic weight of $Ca^{2+}$ and the molecular weight of $CO_3^{2-}$ and is, therefore, equal to $40.08 + 60.01 = 100.09$. Its equivalent weight is

$$\text{EW} = \frac{100.09 \text{ g} \cdot \text{mol}^{-1}}{2 \text{ g-Eq} \cdot \text{mol}^{-1}} = 50.05 \text{ g} \cdot \text{g-Eq}^{-1} \qquad \text{or} \qquad 50.05 \text{ mg} \cdot \text{mEq}^{-1}$$

### Buffers

A solution that resists large changes in pH when an acid or base is added or when the solution is diluted is called a **buffer.** A solution containing a weak acid and its salt is an example of a buffer. Atmospheric carbon dioxide ($CO_2$) produces a natural buffer through the following reactions:

$$CO_2(g) = CO_2(aq) + H_2O = H_2CO_3^* = H^+ + HCO_3 = 2H^+ + CO_3^{2-} \qquad (2\text{--}77)$$

where $H_2CO_3^*$ = "carbonic acid" = true carbonic acid ($H_2CO_3$) and dissolved carbon dioxide

$$(CO_2\ (aq)), \text{ which cannot be distinguished analytically}$$

$$HCO_3^- = \text{bicarbonate ion}$$
$$CO_3^{2-} = \text{carbonate ion}$$

This is perhaps the most important buffer system in water. We will be referring to it several times in this and subsequent chapters as the carbonate buffer system.

Before we continue looking at the buffering of natural waters, let's review some basic carbonate chemistry. As mentioned earlier, carbonic acid dissociates to form bicarbonate.

$$H_2CO_3^* = H^+ + HCO_3^- \qquad K_{a1} = 10^{-6.35} \text{ at } 25°C \qquad (2\text{--}78)$$

Thus, we can write the equilibrium expression

$$\frac{[HCO_3^-][H^+]}{[H_2CO_3^*]} = 10^{-6.35} \qquad (2\text{--}79)$$

Similarly, bicarbonate can act as a Brønsted–Lewis acid and dissociate to form carbonate.

$$HCO_3^- = H^+ + CO_3^{2-} \qquad K_{a2} = 10^{-10.33} \text{ at } 25°C \qquad (2\text{--}80)$$

As before we can write an equilibrium expression, this time for bicarbonate.

$$\frac{[CO_3^{2-}][H^+]}{[HCO_3^-]} = 10^{-10.33} \qquad (2\text{--}81)$$

In a closed system, where the concentration of carbonate species is constant.

$$[H_2CO_3^*] + [HCO_3^-] + [CO_3^{2-}] = C_T \qquad (2\text{--}82)$$

Replacing the terms for bicarbonate and carbonate with expressions in terms of carbonate acid, we can write an expression for the concentration of carbonic acid in terms of pH.

$$[H_2CO_3^*] = C_T \left( 1 + \frac{K_{a1}}{[H^+]} + \frac{K_{a1}K_{a2}}{[H^+]^2} \right)^{-1} \qquad (2\text{--}83)$$

The following relationships are true:
   (a) $pH < pK_{a1} < pK_{a2}$; $\log[H_2CO_3^*] \approx \log C_T$
       $d(\log[H_2CO_3^*])/d(pH) = 0$ and the line for $\log[H_2CO_3^*]$ can be represented by a straight line of slope zero.
   (b) $pK_{a1} < pH < pK_{a2}$; $\log[H_2CO_3^*] \approx pK_{a1} + \log C_T - pH$
       $d(\log[H_2CO_3^*])/d(pH) = -1$ and the line for $\log[H_2CO_3^*]$ can be represented by a straight line of slope $-1$.
   (c) $pK_{a1} < pK_{a2} < pH$; $\log[H_2CO_3^*] \approx pK_{a1} + pK_{a2} + \log C_T - 2pH$
       $d(\log[H_2CO_3^*])/d(pH) = -2$ and the line for $\log[H_2CO_3^*]$ can be represented by a straight line of slope $-2$.

We can develop similar relationships for $HCO_3^-$ and $CO_3^{2-}$ such that the log of the concentrations of each of these species can be plotted. Once we have done this we can plot these relationships on a log-log graph of log concentration versus pH as shown in Figure 2–10.

**FIGURE 2–10**

Plot of pC (−log C) versus pH for the carbonate system. ($T = 25°C$, $pK_{a1} = 6.35$, $pK_{a2} = 10.33$)

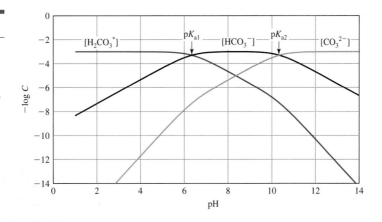

**EXAMPLE 2–21**

The pH of a water is measured to be 7.5. The concentration of bicarbonate was measured to be $1.3 \times 10^{-3}$ M. What are the concentrations of carbonate, carbonic acid, and $C_T$? Assume this system is closed to the atmosphere.

Solution

This problem can be solved using the relationships given earlier.

$$K_{a1} = \frac{[HCO_3^-][H^+]}{[H_2CO_3^*]} = 10^{-6.3}$$

and

$$\frac{[CO_3^{2-}][H^+]}{[HCO_3^-]} = 10^{-10.33}$$

Solving for $[H_2CO_3^*]$, we have

$$[H_2CO_3^*] = \frac{[HCO_3^-][H^+]}{pK_{a1}} = \frac{(1.3 \times 10^{-3})(10^{-7.5})}{10^{-6.3}} = 8.2 \times 10^{-5} \text{ M}$$

Solving for $[CO_3^{2-}]$, we have

$$[CO_3^{2-}] = \frac{pK_{a2}[HCO_3^-]}{[H^+]} = \frac{(10^{-10.33})(1.3 \times 10^{-3})}{10^{-7.5}} = 1.9 \times 10^{-6} \text{ M}$$

$$C_T = [H_2CO_3^*] + [HCO_3^-] + [CO_3^{2-}] = 8.2 \times 10^{-5} + 1.3 \times 10^{-3} + 1.9 \times 10^{-6}$$

$$= 1.384 \times 10^{-3} \text{ M} \approx 1.4 \times 10^{-3} \text{ M}$$

As depicted in Equation 2–77, the $CO_2$ in solution is in equilibrium with atmospheric $CO_2$ ($g$). Any change in the system components to the right of $CO_2(aq)$ causes the $CO_2(g)$ either to be released from solution or to dissolve. If this is true (i.e., we have an open system), the concentration of $H_2CO_3^*$ is constant with pH and $C_T$ changes as pH changes. If this is the case, the plot of log $C$ versus pH looks very different. A typical plot is shown in Figure 2–11.

**FIGURE 2–11**

pC (−log C)–pH diagram for the carbonate system ($T = 25°C$, $pK_{a1} = 6.35$, $pK_{a2} = 10.33$; $K_H = 10^{-1.5}$ M · atm$^{-1}$; $P_{CO_2} = 10^{-3.5}$ atm)

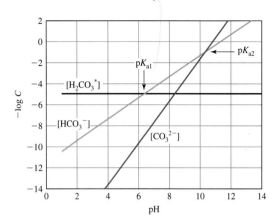

**EXAMPLE 2–22**

The pH of a water is measured to be 7.5. What are the concentrations of carbonate, bicarbonate, carbonic acid, and $C_T$? Assume this system is open to the atmosphere. The temperature is 25°C. The Henry's constant for carbon dioxide is $10^{-1.47}$ M · atm$^{-1}$ at this temperature. The partial pressure of carbon dioxide is $10^{-3.53}$ atm.

Solution

The same relationships hold true for this problem as in the previous one. Because we are given the partial pressure of carbon dioxide and the Henry's constant we can calculate the concentration of carbonic acid using the relationship

$$[H_2CO_3^*] = K_H P_{CO_2} = (10^{-1.47} \text{ M} \cdot \text{atm}^{-1})(10^{-3.53} \text{ atm}) = 10^{-5.0} \text{ M}$$

$$pK_{a1} = \frac{[HCO_3^-][H^+]}{[H_2CO_3^*]} = 10^{-6.3}$$

and

$$\frac{[CO_3^{2-}][H^+]}{[HCO_3^-]} = 10^{-10.33}$$

Solving for $[HCO_3^-]$

$$[HCO_3^-] = \frac{[H_2CO_3^*]pK_{a1}}{[H^+]} = \frac{(1.0 \times 10^{-5})(10^{-6.3})}{10^{-7.5}} = 1.6 \times 10^{-4} \text{ M}$$

Solving for $[CO_3^{2-}]$

$$[CO_3^{2-}] = \frac{pK_{a2}[HCO_3^-]}{[H^+]} = \frac{(10^{-10.33})(1.58 \times 10^{-4})}{10^{-7.5}} = 2.3 \times 10^{-7} \text{ M}$$

$$C_T = [H_2CO_3^*] + [HCO_3^-] + [CO_3^{2-}] = 1.0 \times 10^{-5} + 1.6 \times 10^{-4} + 2.3 \times 10^{-7}$$

$$= 1.70 \times 10^{-4} \text{ M} \approx 1.7 \times 10^{-4} \text{ M}$$

We can examine the character of the buffer system to resist a change in pH by considering the addition of an acid or a base and applying the **law of mass action** (Le Châtelier's principle). For example, if an acid is added to the system, the hydrogen ion concentration will increase, and the system will not be at equilibrium. To achieve equilibrium, the carbonate combines with the

**FIGURE 2-12**

Behavior of the carbonate buffer system with the addition of acids and bases or the addition and removal of $CO_2$.

*Case I: Open System*
**Acid is added to carbonate buffer system.[a]**

Reaction shifts to the left as $H_2CO_3^*$ is formed when $H^+$ and $HCO_3^-$ react.[b]
$CO_2$ is released to the atmosphere.
pH is lowered slightly because the availability of free $H^+$ (amount depends on buffering capacity).

*Case II: Open System*
**Base is added to carbonate buffer system.**

Reaction shifts to the right.
$CO_2$ from the atmosphere dissolves into solution.
pH is raised slightly because $H^+$ combines with $OH^-$ (amount depends on buffering capacity).

*Case III: Open System*
**$CO_2$ is bubbled into carbonate buffer system.**

Reaction shifts to the right because $H_2CO_3^*$ is formed when $CO_2$ and $H_2O$ react.
$CO_2$ dissolves into solution.
pH is lowered.

*Case IV: Open System*
**Carbonate buffer system is stripped of $CO_2$.**

Reaction shifts to the left to form more $H_2CO_3^*$; to replace that removed by stripping.
$CO_2$ is removed from solution.
pH is raised.

[a]Refer to Equation 2–77.
[b]The asterisk * in $H_2CO_3^*$ is used to signify the sum of $CO_2$ and $H_2CO_3$ in solution.

free protons to form bicarbonate. Bicarbonate reacts to form more carbonic acid, which in turn dissociates to $CO_2$ and water. The excess $CO_2$ can be released to the atmosphere in a thermodynamically open system. Alternatively, the addition of a base consumes hydrogen ions and the system shifts to the right, with the $CO_2$ being replenished from the atmosphere. When $CO_2$ is bubbled into the system or is removed by passing an inert gas such as nitrogen through the liquid (a process called stripping), the pH will change more dramatically because the atmosphere is no longer available as a source or sink for $CO_2$. Figure 2–12 summarizes the four general responses of the carbonate buffer system. The first two cases (I and II) are common in natural settings when the reactions proceed over a relatively long time. Cases III and IV are not common in natural settings, but may occur in engineered systems. For example in a water treatment plant, we can alter the reactions more quickly than the $CO_2$ can be replenished from the atmosphere.

**Buffering Capacity.**  We are often concerned with the ability of a water to resist changes in pH when an acid or base is added. This ability to resist change is referred to as **buffering capacity.** Water chemists use the term **alkalinity** to describe a water's ability to resist changes in pH on the addition of acid, therefore, it is also called **acid-neutralizing capacity. Acidity** describes the ability of a water to resist changes in pH due to the addition of base. Therefore, it is also called **base-neutralizing capacity.**

**Alkalinity.**  Alkalinity is defined as the sum of all titratable bases to a pH of approximately 4.5. It has units of equivalents per liter or normality (N). It is found by experimentally determining the amount of acid required to reduce the pH of the water sample to 4.5. In most freshwaters the only weak acids or bases that contribute to alkalinity are bicarbonate ($HCO_3^-$), carbonate ($CO_3^{2-}$), $H^+$, and $OH^-$. In ocean waters, the bromate species also play a significant role in determining alkalinity. The total $H^+$ that can be neutralized by water containing primarily carbonate species is

$$\text{Alkalinity} = [HCO_3^-] + 2[CO_3^{2-}] + [OH^-] - [H^+] \qquad (2\text{–}84)$$

where [ ] refers to concentrations in moles per liter. In most natural waters (pH 6–8), the OH$^-$ and H$^+$ are negligible, such that

$$\text{Alkalinity} \approx [\text{HCO}_3^-] + 2[\text{CO}_3^{2-}] \tag{2–85}$$

Note that [CO$_3^{2-}$] is multiplied by 2 because it can accept two protons. If we were to write Equation 2–85 using *normality* instead of molarity then Equation 2–84 would become

$$\text{Alkalinity} = (\text{HCO}_3^-) + (\text{CO}_3^{2-}) + (\text{OH}^-) - (\text{H}^+) \tag{2–86}$$

where ( ) refers to concentrations in units of normality.

The pertinent acid–base reactions are

$$\text{H}_2\text{CO}_3 = \text{H}^+ + \text{HCO}_3^- \qquad \text{p}K_{a1} = 6.35 \text{ at } 25°\text{C} \tag{2–78}$$

$$\text{HCO}_3^- = \text{H}^+ + \text{CO}_3^{2-} \qquad \text{p}K_{a2} = 10.33 \text{ at } 25°\text{C} \tag{2–80}$$

From the p$K$ values, some useful relationships can be found. The more important ones are as follows:

1. Below pH of 4.5, the only carbonate species present in appreciable quantity is H$_2$CO$_3$ and the concentration of OH$^-$ is negligible. Because carbonic acid does not contribute to alkalinity, in this case the alkalinity is negative (due to the H$^+$). This water would have no ability to neutralize acids, and any small addition in acid would result in a significant reduction in pH.
2. In the pH range from 7 to 8.3, HCO$_3^-$ predominates over carbonate, and the concentration of H$^+$ approximately equals the concentration of OH$^-$ (both are also small in comparison with the concentration of HCO$_3^-$). As such, the alkalinity is approximately equal to the concentration of HCO$_3^-$.
3. At a pH of greater than 12.3, the predominant carbonate species is CO$_3^{2-}$, the concentration of H$^+$ is negligible, and the concentration of OH$^-$ cannot be ignored. Here, the alkalinity equals 2[CO$_3^{2-}$] + [OH$^-$].

In environmental engineering and science, we need to differentiate between alkaline water and water having high alkalinity. Alkaline water has a pH greater than 7, and a water with high alkalinity has a high buffering capacity. An alkaline water may or may not have a high buffering capacity. Likewise, a water with a high alkalinity may or may not have a high pH.

By convention, alkalinity is not expressed in molarity units as shown in the preceding equations, but rather in **units of milligrams as CaCO$_3$ per liter** or normality (Eq $\cdot$ L$^{-1}$). In order to convert concentrations of the ions to milligrams per liter as CaCO$_3$, multiply milligrams per liter as the species by the ratio of the equivalent weight of CaCO$_3$ to the species equivalent weight.

$$\text{Milligrams per liter as CaCO}_3 = (\text{milligrams per liter as species})\left(\frac{\text{EW of CaCO}_3}{\text{EW of species}}\right) \tag{2–87}$$

The alkalinity is then determined as before, except that instead of using normality, the concentrations in units of milligrams per liter as CaCO$_3$ are added or subtracted.

**EXAMPLE 2–23**   A water contains 100.0 mg $\cdot$ L$^{-1}$ CO$_3^{2-}$ and 75.0 mg $\cdot$ L$^{-1}$ HCO$_3^-$ at a pH of 10 ($T = 25°$C). Calculate the exact alkalinity. Approximate the alkalinity by ignoring the appropriate chemical species.

Solution   First, convert CO$_3^{2-}$, HCO$_3^-$, H$^+$, and OH$^-$ to milligrams per liter as CaCO$_3$. Remember, you are given the concentrations of carbonate and bicarbonate in milligrams per liter as the species and the concentrations of H$^+$ and OH$^-$ in molar units.

The equivalent weights are

$$CO_3^{2-}: MW = 60, n = 2, EW = 30$$
$$HCO_3^-: MW = 61, n = 1, EW = 61$$
$$H^+: MW = 1, n = 1, EW = 1$$
$$OH^-: MW = 17, n = 1, EW = 17$$

and the concentrations of $H^+$ and $OH^-$ are calculated as follows: pH = 10; therefore $[H^+]$ = $10^{-10}$ M. Using Equation 2–71,

$$[H^+] = (10^{-10} \text{ mol} \cdot L^{-1})(1 \text{ g} \cdot \text{mol}^{-1})(10^3 \text{ mg} \cdot \text{g}^{-1}) = 10^{-7} \text{ mg} \cdot L^{-1}$$

Using Equation 2–37, we see that

$$[OH^-] = \frac{K_w}{[H^+]} = \frac{10^{-14}}{10^{-10}} = 10^{-4} \text{ mol} \cdot L^{-1}$$

and

$$[OH^-] = (10^{-4} \text{ mol} \cdot L^{-1})(17 \text{ g} \cdot \text{mol}^{-1})(10^3 \text{ mg} \cdot \text{g}^{-1}) = 1.7 \text{ mg} \cdot L^{-1}$$

Now, the concentrations in units of milligrams per liter as $CaCO_3$ are found by using Equation 2–87 and taking the equivalent weight of $CaCO_3$ to be 50.

$$CO_3^{2-} = 100.0 \times \left(\frac{50}{30}\right) = 167 \text{ mg} \cdot L^{-1} \text{ as } CaCO_3$$

$$HCO_3^- = 75.0 \times \left(\frac{50}{61}\right) = 61 \text{ mg} \cdot L^{-1} \text{ as } CaCO_3$$

$$H^+ = 10^{-7} \times \left(\frac{50}{1}\right) = 5 \times 10^{-6} \text{ mg} \cdot L^{-1} \text{ as } CaCO_3$$

$$OH^- = 1.7 \times \left(\frac{50}{17}\right) = 5.0 \text{ mg} \cdot L^{-1} \text{ as } CaCO_3$$

The exact alkalinity (in milligrams per liter as $CaCO_3$) is found by

$$\text{Alkalinity} = 61 + 167 + 5.0 - (5 \times 10^{-6}) = 233 \text{ mg} \cdot L^{-1} \text{ as } CaCO_3$$

## 2–5 SOIL CHEMISTRY

Although often taken for granted and, seemingly, not as valued as water and air, without soil, life on this planet would not exist. Soil is important for the production of food; the maintenance of carbon, nitrogen, and phosphorus balances; and for the construction of building materials.

Chemically, soil is a mixture of weathered rocks and minerals; decayed plant and animal material (humus and detritus); and small living organisms, including plants, animals, and bacteria. Soil also contains water and air. Typically, soil contains about 95% mineral and 5% organic matter, although the range in composition varies considerably.

The concentrations of chemicals in soil are given in mass units: parts per million, milligrams per kilogram, or micrograms per kilogram. The units vary somewhat based on the magnitude of the mass of chemical present per unit mass (usually kilograms) of soil. For example, when dealing with carbon, the concentration is usually given in percent because carbon generally accounts for about 1 to 25% of soil material. On the contrary, when working with nutrient concentrations (e.g., nitrogen, phosphorus, etc.) units of milligrams per kilogram are used. When working with many hazardous wastes, whose concentrations are usually small, we use units of parts per billion or micrograms per kilogram.

The movement of ionic nutrients such as nitrate, ammonia, and phosphate is governed by ion-exchange reactions. For example, sodium ions may be attached to the soil surface by electrostatic interactions. If water containing calcium is passed through the soil, the calcium will be preferentially exchanged for the sodium according to this reaction.

$$2(Na^+–Soil) + Ca^{2+} = Ca^{2+}–(Soil)_2 + 2Na^+ \tag{2-88}$$

By this reaction, two sodium ions are released for every ion of calcium exchanged; thus maintaining the charge balance. Thus, an important characteristic of soil is its exchange capacity. **Exchange capacity** is, essentially, the extent to which a unit mass of soil can exchange a mass of a certain ion of interest. Exchange capacity (reported in units of equivalents of ions per mass of soil) is an important characteristic of soil in terms of its ability to leach ions such as magnesium, calcium, nitrate, and phosphate.

Another important process that occurs in soils is sorption. **Sorption** is essentially the attachment of a chemical to either the mineral or organic portions of soil particles and includes both adsorption and absorption. Van der Waals forces, hydrogen bonding, or electrostatic interactions can result in the attachment of chemicals to the soil surface. In some cases, covalent bonding can actually result, and the chemical is irreversibly bound to the soil.

With low concentrations of pollutants, sorption can be described mathematically by a linear expression.

$$K_d = \frac{C_s \ (mol \cdot kg^{-1})}{C_w \ (mol \cdot L^{-1})} \tag{2-89}$$

where $C_w$ = the equilibrium concentration of the chemical in the water (mass per volume of water)

$K_d$ = a partition coefficient describing sorption equilibrium of a chemical-distribution ratio = (mass per mass of soil) (mass per volume of water)$^{-1}$

$C_s$ = the equilibrium concentration of the chemical on the soil (mass per mass of soil)

The partition coefficients of various organic pollutants can vary over at least eight orders of magnitude, depending predominately on the chemical characteristics of the pollutant, but also on the nature of the soil itself.

With most neutral organic chemicals, sorption occurs predominately on the organic fraction of the soil itself (as long as the fraction of organic material on the soil is "significant"). In these cases,

$$C_s \approx C_{om} f_{om} \tag{2-90}$$

where $C_{om}$ = concentration of organic chemical in the organic matter of the soil

$f_{om}$ = fraction of organic matter in the soil.

Combining Equations 2–88 and 2–89 yields an equation valid for neutral organic chemicals.

$$K_d = \frac{C_{om} f_{om}}{C_w} \tag{2-91}$$

## 2-6   ATMOSPHERIC CHEMISTRY

The atmosphere is a thin envelope of gases that surround the Earth's surface, held in place by gravity. As one moves higher in elevation, the Earth's gravitational forces decrease and the density of these gases also decreases. The composition of air varies with location, altitude, anthropogenic sources (e.g., factories and cars), and natural sources (e.g., dust storms, volcanoes, forest fires). The concentrations of some gases vary less than others. The essentially "nonvariable" gases make up approximately 99% (by volume) of the atmosphere. Of the variable gases, water vapor, carbon dioxide, and ozone are the most prevalent. Table 2–8 lists these gases and their volume percents.

The atmosphere is divided into several layers on the basis of temperature. The layer closest to the Earth's surface, the troposphere, extends to approximately 13 km. As shown in Figure 2–13, the temperature in this layer decreases with increasing altitude. It is estimated that

| TABLE 2–8 | Composition of the Atmosphere |
|---|---|
| **Gas** | **Percentage by Volume[a]** |
| **Nonvariable gases** | |
| Nitrogen | 78.08 |
| Oxygen | 20.95 |
| Argon | 0.93 |
| Neon | 0.002 |
| Others | 0.001 |
| **Variable gases** | |
| Water vapor | 0.1–≈5.0 |
| Carbon dioxide | 0.035 |
| Ozone | 0.000006 |
| Other gases | Trace |
| Particulate matter | Usually trace |

[a]Percentages, except for water vapor, are for dry air.

*Source:* M. L. McKinney, R. M. Schooch, *Environmental Science: Systems and Solutions,* Sudbury, MA: Jones and Bartlett Publishers, 1996. Reprinted with permission.

**FIGURE 2–13**

The Earth's atmosphere. (*Source:* U.S. Weather Bureau, *U.S. Standard Atmosphere,* U.S. Government Printing Office, Washington, D.C., 1976)

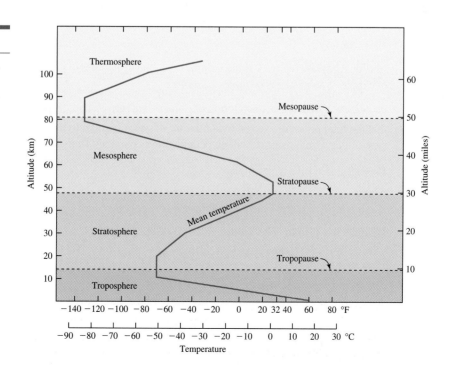

80–85% of the mass of the atmosphere is in the troposphere. The next layer is the stratosphere, which extends to an altitude of approximately 50 km. Within the stratosphere, the temperature increases with increasing altitude until it reaches approximately 0°C at the stratopause (the boundary between the stratosphere and the mesosphere). The temperature increase in the stratosphere is due to the absorption of ultraviolet radiation and the resulting heat given off by the reactions that occur. The troposphere and stratosphere contain approximately 99% of the mass of the atmosphere. In the next layer, the mesosphere, which extends to approximately 80 km, the temperature decreases with increasing altitude until it reaches a temperature of approximately −80°C. The outermost envelope around the Earth is the thermosphere, another region in which the temperature increases with increasing altitude.

One of the major differences between aqueous and atmospheric reactions is the importance of gas-phase and photochemical reactions in the latter. One of the most important gas-phase photochemical reactions that occurs in the troposphere is the formation of ozone from the reaction of ultraviolet radiation, hydrocarbons, and nitrogen oxides ($NO_x$). More details about these and other important atmospheric reactions will be presented in Chapter 11 (Air Pollution).

### Fundamentals of Gases

**Ideal Gas Law.**   The behavior of chemicals in air with respect to temperature and pressure can be assumed to be ideal (in the chemical sense) because the concentration of these pollutants are usually sufficiently low. Thus, we can assume that at the same temperature and pressure, different kinds of gases have densities proportional to their molecular masses. This may be written as

$$\rho = \frac{P \times M}{R \times T} \tag{2–92a}$$

where $\rho$ = density of gas ($g \cdot m^{-3}$)
$P$ = absolute pressure (Pa)
$M$ = molecular mass ($g \cdot mol^{-1}$)
$T$ = absolute temperature (K)
$R$ = ideal gas constant = $8.3143\ J \cdot K^{-1} \cdot mol^{-1}$ (or $Pa \cdot m^3 \cdot mol^{-1} \cdot K^{-1}$)

Because density is defined as mass per unit volume, or the number of moles per unit volume, $n/V$, the expression may be rewritten in the general form as

$$PV = nRT \tag{2–92b}$$

(the ideal gas law) where $V$ is the volume occupied by $n$ moles of gas. At 273.15 K and 101.325 kPa, one mole of an ideal gas occupies 22.414 L.

**Dalton's Law of Partial Pressures.**   In 1801, the English scientist John Dalton found that the total pressure exerted by a mixture of gases is equal to the sum of the pressures that each type of gas would exert if it alone occupied the container. In mathematical terms,

$$P_t = P_1 + P_2 + P_3 + \cdots + P_n \tag{2–93a}$$

where $P_t$ = total pressure of mixture
$P_1, P_2, P_3, P_n$ = the partial pressure of each gas*

Dalton's law also may be written in terms of the ideal gas law.

$$P_t = n_1 \frac{RT}{V} + n_2 \frac{RT}{V} + n_3 \frac{RT}{V} + \cdots \tag{2–93b}$$

$$P_t = (n_1 + n_2 + n_3 + \cdots) \frac{RT}{V} \tag{2–93c}$$

---

*That is, pressure of each gas if it were in the container alone.

Dalton's law is important in air quality assessment because stack and exhaust sampling measurements are made with instruments calibrated with air. Because combustion products have a composition entirely different from air, the readings must be adjusted ("corrected" in sampling parlance) to reflect this difference. Dalton's law forms the basis for the calculation of the correction factor.

**Concentrations of Pollutants in Air.** One must be aware that when dealing with concentrations of gases in air, the approximation of 1 ppm $= 1$ mg $\cdot$ L$^{-1}$ is no longer valid as it is with dilute aqueous solutions. This is because the density of air is not 1 g $\cdot$ mL$^{-1}$ and varies significantly with temperature. With air, concentrations are often reported in units of micrograms per cubic meter or parts per million. With air, the units of parts per million are reported on a volume–volume basis (unlike that used with aqueous concentrations, which are given on a mass–volume basis). The units of parts per million have the advantage over micrograms per cubic meter in that changes in temperature and pressure do not change the ratio of the volume of pollutant to volume of air. Thus, it is possible to compare concentrations given in parts per million, without considering effects of pressure or temperature. The concentration of particulate matter may be reported only as micrograms per cubic meter. The micrometer unit is used to report particle size.

**Converting Micrograms per Cubic Meter to Parts per Million.** The conversion between micrograms per cubic meter and parts per million is based on the fact that at standard conditions (0°C and 101.325 kPa), one mole of an ideal gas occupies 22.414 L. Thus, we may write an equation that converts the mass of the pollutant, $M_p$, in grams to its equivalent volume, $V_p$, in liters at standard temperature and pressure (STP).

$$V_p = \frac{M_p}{MW} \times 22.414 \text{ L} \cdot \text{mol}^{-1} \tag{2–94}$$

where MW is the molecular weight of the pollutant in units of grams per mole. For readings made at temperatures and pressures other than standard conditions, the standard volume, 22.414 L $\cdot$ mol$^{-1}$, must be corrected. We can use the ideal gas law to make the correction.

$$(22.414 \text{ L} \cdot \text{mol}^{-1}) \times \frac{T_2}{273 \text{ K}} \times \frac{101.325 \text{ kPa}}{P_2} \tag{2–95}$$

where $T_2$ and $P_2$ are the absolute temperature (in Kelvin) and absolute pressure (in kilopascals) at which the readings were made. Because parts per million is a volume ratio, we may write

$$\text{ppm} = \frac{V_p}{V_a + V_p} \tag{2–96}$$

where $V_a$ is the volume of air in cubic meters at the temperature and pressure at which the measurement was taken. We then combine Equations 2–94, 2–95, and 2–96 to yield Equation 2–97.

$$\text{ppm} = \frac{(M_p/MW) \times 22.414 \text{ L} \cdot \text{mol}^{-1} \times (T_2/273 \text{ K}) \times (101.325 \text{ kPa}/P_2)}{V_a \times 1000 \text{ L} \cdot \text{m}^{-3}} \tag{2–97}$$

where $M_p$ is the mass of the pollutant of interest in micrograms. The factors converting micrograms to grams and liters to millions of liters cancel one another. Unless otherwise stated, it is assumed that $V_a = 1.00$ m$^3$.

**EXAMPLE 2–24**    A 1-m$^3$ sample of air was found to contain 80 $\mu$g $\cdot$ m$^{-3}$ of SO$_2$. The temperature and pressure were 25.0°C and 103.193 kPa when the air sample was taken. What was the SO$_2$ concentration in parts per million?

Solution    First we must determine the MW of SO$_2$ from the chart inside the front cover of this book, we find

MW of SO$_2 = 32.06 + 2(15.9994) = 64.06$ g $\cdot$ mol$^{-1}$

Next we must convert the temperature from Celsius to Kelvin. Thus,

$25°C + 273\ K = 298\ K$

Now using Equation 2–97, we find

Concentration

$$= \frac{(80\ \mu g/64.06\ g \cdot mol^{-1}) \times 22.414\ L \cdot mol^{-1} \times (298\ K/273\ K) \times (101.325\ kPa/103.193\ kPa)}{m^3 \times 10^3\ L \cdot m^{-3}}$$

$= 0.030$ ppm of $SO_2$

## CHAPTER REVIEW

When you have completed studying this chapter, you should be able to do the following without the aid of your texbook or notes:

1. Define the following terms: matter, elements, compounds.
2. State the essence of the law of definite proportions (a.k.a. the law of constant composition).
3. Describe how elements are grouped in the periodic table.
4. Describe the composition of atoms.
5. Define: atomic number, mass number, and atomic weight?
6. Describe isotopes.
7. Describe the types of bonding that hold together atoms and molecules.
8. Define the following terms: molecule, molecular formula, ion, cation, and anion.
9. Describe what a chemical equation represents symbolically.
10. Be able to balance chemical equations.
11. Describe the four principal types of reactions of importance to environmental scientists and engineers.
12. Describe the law of mass action.
13. Describe how ionic strength affects equilibrium constants. Describe how we take into account the effects of ionic strength on equilibrium constants.
14. Describe the common ion effect.
15. Describe what is meant by pH and pOH.
16. Define: weak acid, strong acid, weak base, and strong base.
17. Describe Henry's law.
18. Be able to write the expressions for zero-, first-, and second-order reactions.
19. Define: alkanes, alkenes, alkynes, structural isomers, aryl (aromatic) compounds, alcohols, phenols, aldehydes, ketones, esters, ethers, amines, amides, mercaptans, halides, sulfonic acid compounds.
20. Define: mass density, specific weight, specific gravity, and viscosity.
21. Define: suspended solids and colloidal particles (in terms of the sizes of the particles).
22. Define: buffer, alkalinity, and acidity.
23. List and define three units of measure used to report air pollution data (i.e., ppm, $\mu g \cdot m^{-3}$, and $\mu m$).
24. Explain the difference between parts per million in air pollution and parts per million in water pollution.
25. Explain the effect of temperature and pressure on readings made in parts per million.
26. Calculate the concentration of a chemical species in soil in units of parts per million, milligrams per kilogram, and micrograms per kilogram.
27. What is meant by exchange capacity?

With the aid of this text, you should be able do to following:

1. Calculate the molarity or normality of a chemical given the mass added to a particular volume of solution.
2. Calculate the concentration of chemicals that precipitate given the solubility product of the precipitate.
3. Calculate the equilibrium solution concentrations given varying ionic strengths of the background electrolyte.
4. Calculate the solubility of a chemical in the presence of a common ion.
5. Perform dissociation-type calculations.
6. Use Henry's law to calculate the concentration of a gas or the concentration of the gas dissolved in a liquid (given the other).
7. Calculate the mass of chemical remaining after a first-order reaction proceeds for a given time, given the first-order rate constant.
8. Calculate the concentration of a chemical in water in units of percent by weight, molarity, normality, milligrams per liter as the chemical species, milligrams per liter as $CaCO_3$.
9. Calculate the alkalinity of a solution given the concentrations of carbonate, bicarbonate, and the pH.
10. Use the ideal gas law appropriately.
11. Use Dalton's law of partial pressures to calculate the total pressure of a mixture of gases.
12. Calculate the concentration of chemical species in a gas in units of micrograms per cubic meter, parts per million (by volume), and micrograms, as appropriate.
13. Use the distribution coefficient and the equilibrium concentration in water to calculate the equilibrium concentration on the soil.
14. Use the fraction of organic matter to calculate the concentration of the neutral organic chemical in the organic matter.

## PROBLEMS

**2-1**  For each atomic symbol, give the name of the element.
(a) Pb   (b) C   (c) Ca   (d) Zn   (e) O   (f) H   (g) Hg   (h) S   (i) N   (j) Cl
(k) Mg   (l) P

> **Answer: (a)** lead **(b)** carbon **(c)** calcium **(d)** zinc **(e)** oxygen **(f)** hydrogen **(g)** mercury
>
> **(h)** sulfur **(i)** nitrogen **(j)** chlorine **(k)** magnesium **(l)** phosphorus

**2-2**  The following table gives the number of protons and neutrons in the nucleus of various atoms. (a) Which atom is the isotope of atom A? (b) Which atom has the same mass number as atom A?

|          | **Protons** | **Neutrons** |
|----------|-------------|--------------|
| Atom A   | 13          | 15           |
| Atom B   | 12          | 15           |
| Atom C   | 13          | 16           |
| Atom D   | 15          | 17           |

**2-3**  Calculate the atomic weight of boron, B, based on the following fractional abundance data.

| **Isotope** | **Isotopic Mass (amu)** | **Fractional Abundance** |
|-------------|-------------------------|--------------------------|
| B-10        | 10.013                  | 0.1978                   |
| B-11        | 11.009                  | 0.8022                   |

> **Answer:** 10.812

**2-4**  What element has 17 protons and 18 neutrons in its nucleus?

**2-5** A solution of sodium bicarbonate is prepared by adding 45.00 g of sodium bicarbonate to a 1.00-L volumetric flask and adding distilled water until it reaches the 1.00-L mark. What is the concentration of sodium bicarbonate in units of (a) milligrams per liter, (b) molarity, (c) normality and (d) milligrams per liter as $CaCO_3$?

**Answer: (a)** $4.5 \times 10^4$ mg $\cdot$ L$^{-1}$ **(b)** 0.536 M **(c)** 0.536 N **(d)** $2.68 \times 10^4$ mg $\cdot$ L$^{-1}$ as $CaCO_3$

**2-6** Balance the following chemical equations:

(a) $CaCl_2 + Na_2CO_3 \rightleftharpoons CaCO_3 + NaCl$

(b) $C_6H_{12}O_6 + O_2 \rightleftharpoons CO_2 + H_2O$

(c) $NO_2 + H_2O \rightleftharpoons HNO_3 + NO$

(d) $C_4H_{10} + O_2 \rightleftharpoons CO_2 + H_2O$

(e) $Al(OH)_2 \rightleftharpoons Al^{2+} + OH^-$

**2-7** A magnesium hydroxide solution is prepared by adding 10.00 g of magnesium hydroxide to a volumetric flask and bringing the final volume to 1.00 L by adding water buffered at a pH of 7.0. What is the concentration of magnesium in this solution? (Assume that the temperature is 25°C and the ionic strength is negligible).

**Answer:** $5.62 \times 10^{-5}$ M

**2-8** What is the concentration of iron if the water has an ionic strength of (a) zero, (b) 0.5 M? (Assume that the temperature of the solution is 25°C.)

**2-9** A ferric phosphate solution is prepared by adding 2.4 g of ferric phosphate to a volumetric flask and bringing the final volume to 1.00 L by adding water having a phosphate concentration of 1.0 mg $\cdot$ L$^{-1}$. What is the concentration of soluble iron in this solution? (Assume that the temperature of the solution is 25°C.)

**Answer:** $1.196 \times 10^{-17}$ M

**2-10** A solution made up with calcium carbonate is initially supersaturated with $Ca^{2+}$ and $CO_3^{2-}$ ions, such that the concentrations of each are both $1.35 \times 10^{-3}$ M. When equilibrium is finally reached, what is the final concentration of calcium?

**2-11** A solution has an $H^+$ concentration of $10^{-5}$ M. (a) What is the pH of this solution? (b) What is the pOH? (Assume that the temperature of the solution is 25°C.)

**Answer: (a)** 5 **(b)** 9

**2-12** If 200 mg of HCl is added to water to achieve a final volume of 1.00 L, what is the final pH?

**2-13** A solution of acetic acid is prepared in water by adding 11.1 g of sodium acetate to a volumetric flask and bringing the volume to 1.0 L with water. The final pH is measured to be 5.25. What are the concentrations of acetate and acetic acid in solution? (Assume that the temperature of the solution is 25°C.)

**Answer:** [HA] = 0.028 M    [A$^-$] = 0.088 M

**2-14** A 0.21 m$^3$ drum contains 100 L of a mixture of several degreasing solvents in water. The concentration of trichloroethylene in the headspace (gas phase) above the water was measured to be 0.00301 atm. The Henry's constant for trichloroethylene is 0.00985 atm $\cdot$ m$^3$ $\cdot$ mol$^{-1}$ at 25°C. What is the concentration of trichloroethylene in the water in units of molarity? (Assume that the temperature of the solution is 25°C.)

**2-15** The concentration of a chemical degrades in water according to first-order kinetics. The degradation constant is 0.2 day$^{-1}$. If the initial concentration is 100.0 mg $\cdot$ L$^{-1}$, how many days are required for the concentration to reach 0.14 mg $\cdot$ L$^{-1}$?

**Answer:** 32.9 days

**2-16** The water in a pond is reaerated. Reaeration occurs according to first-order kinetics with a rate of 0.034 day$^{-1}$. If the temperature of the stream is 15°C and the initial oxygen concentration 2.5 mg $\cdot$ L$^{-1}$, how long (in days) does it take for the oxygen concentration to increase to 6.5 mg $\cdot$ L$^{-1}$? The oxygen solubility in water at 15°C is 10.15 mg $\cdot$ L$^{-1}$.

**2-17**   Hypochlorous acid decays in the presence of ultraviolet radiation. Assume that degradation occurs according to first-order kinetics and the rate of degradation was measured to be 0.12 day$^{-1}$ (at a particular sunlight intensity and temperature). Given this, how long does it take for the concentration of hypochlorous acid to reach nondetectable levels ($0.05$ mg $\cdot$ L$^{-1}$) if the initial concentration were 3.65 mg $\cdot$ L$^{-1}$?

   **Answer:** 35.8 days

**2-18**   Show that a density of 1 g $\cdot$ mL$^{-1}$ is the same as a density of 1000 kg $\cdot$ m$^{-3}$. (*Hint:* Some useful conversions are listed inside the back cover of this book.)

**2-19**   Show that a 4.50% by weight mixture contains 45.0 kg of substance in a cubic meter of water (i.e., 4.50% = 45.0 kg $\cdot$ m$^{-3}$).

   **Answer:** 45 kg $\cdot$ m$^{-3}$

**2-20**   Show that 1 mg $\cdot$ L$^{-1}$ = 1 g $\cdot$ m$^{-3}$.

**2-21**   Calculate the molarity and normality of the following:

   (a)  200.0 mg $\cdot$ L$^{-1}$ HCl
   (b)  150.0 mg $\cdot$ L$^{-1}$ H$_2$SO$_4$
   (c)  100.0 mg $\cdot$ L$^{-1}$ Ca(HCO$_3$)$_2$
   (d)  70.0 mg $\cdot$ L$^{-1}$ H$_3$PO$_4$

   **Answers:**

   | | Molarity (M) | Normality (N) |
   |---|---|---|
   | **(a)** | 0.005485 | 0.005485 |
   | **(b)** | 0.001529 | 0.003059 |
   | **(c)** | 0.0006168 | 0.001234 |
   | **(d)** | 0.000714 | 0.00214 |

**2-22**   Calculate the molarity and normality of the following:

   (a)  80 $\mu$g $\cdot$ L$^{-1}$ HNO$_3$
   (b)  135 $\mu$g $\cdot$ L$^{-1}$ CaCO$_3$
   (c)  10 $\mu$g $\cdot$ L$^{-1}$ Cr(OH)$_3$
   (d)  1000 $\mu$g $\cdot$ L$^{-1}$ Ca(OH)$_2$

**2-23**   Calculate concentration of the following in units of milligrams per liter:

   (a)  0.01000 N Ca$^{2+}$
   (b)  1.000 M HCO$_3^-$
   (c)  0.02000 N H$_2$SO$_4$
   (d)  0.02000 M SO$_4^{2-}$

   **Answers:** (a) 200.4 mg $\cdot$ L$^{-1}$ (b) 61,020 mg $\cdot$ L$^{-1}$ (c) 980.6 mg $\cdot$ L$^{-1}$ (d) 1921.2 mg $\cdot$ L$^{-1}$

**2-24**   Calculate the concentration of the following in micrograms per liter.

   (a)  0.0500 N H$_2$CO$_3$
   (b)  0.0010 M CHCl$_3$
   (c)  0.0300 N Ca(OH)$_2$
   (d)  0.0080 M CO$_2$

**2-25**   A water initially contains 40 mg $\cdot$ L$^{-1}$ of Mg$^{2+}$. The pH of the water is increased until the concentration of hydroxide ion (OH$^-$) is 0.001000 M. What is the concentration of magnesium ion in this water at this pH? Give your answer in milligrams per liter. Assume that the temperature of the solution is 25°C.

   **Answer:** 0.4423 mg $\cdot$ L$^{-1}$

**2-26**   Groundwater in Pherric, New Mexico, initially contains 1.800 mg $\cdot$ L$^{-1}$ of iron as Fe$^{3+}$. What must the pH be raised to in order to precipitate all but 0.30 mg $\cdot$ L$^{-1}$ of the iron? The temperature of the water is 25°C.

**2-27**   You made up a saturated solution of calcium sulfate (CaSO$_4$). The temperature is 25°C. You then add $5.00 \times 10^{-3}$ M sodium sulfate (Na$_2$SO$_4$). What are the concentrations of calcium and sulfate after equilibrium is reached? The pKs of CaSO$_4$ is 4.36.

   **Answer:** Ca$^{2+}$ = 0.0046 M, SO$_4^{2-}$ = 0.00956 M

**2-28** The solubility product of calcium fluoride ($CaF_2$) is $3 \times 10^{-11}$ at 25°C. Could a fluoride concentration of $1.0 \text{ mg} \cdot L^{-1}$ be obtained in water that contains $200 \text{ mg} \cdot L^{-1}$ of calcium? Show your work.

**2-29** What amount of NaOH (a strong base), in milligrams, would be required to neutralize the acid in Example 2–11?

     **Answer:** 81.568 or 81.6 mg

**2-30** The pH of a finished water from a water treatment process is 10.74. What amount of 0.02000 N sulfuric acid, in milliliters, is required to neutralize 1.000 L of the finished water, assuming that the alkalinity (buffering capacity) of the water is zero?

**2-31** How many milliliters of 0.02000 N hydrochloric acid would be required to perform the neutralization in Problem 30?

     **Answer:** 27.5 mL

**2-32** Calculate the pH of a water at 25°C that contains $0.6580 \text{ mg} \cdot L^{-1}$ of carbonic acid. Assume that $[H^+] = \left[HCO_3^-\right]$ at equilibrium and ignore the dissociation of water.

**2-33** What is the pH of a water that, at 25°C, contains $0.5000 \text{ mg} \cdot L^{-1}$ of hypochlorous acid? Assume equilibrium has been achieved. Ignore the dissociation of water. Although it may not be justified based on the data available to you, report the answer to two decimal places.

     **Answer:** pH $= 6.28$

**2-34** If the pH in Problem 33 is adjusted to 7.00, what would the $OCl^-$ concentration in milligrams per liter be at 25°C?

**2-35** Convert the following from milligrams per liter as the ion to milligrams per liter as $CaCO_3$.
  (a) $83.00 \text{ mg} \cdot L^{-1}$ $Ca^{2+}$              (d) $220.00 \text{ mg} \cdot L^{-1}$ $HCO_3^-$
  (b) $27.00 \text{ mg} \cdot L^{-1}$ $Mg^{2+}$            (e) $15.00 \text{ mg} \cdot L^{-1}$ $CO_3^{2-}$
  (c) $48.00 \text{ mg} \cdot L^{-1}$ $CO_2$ (*Hint:* $CO_2$ and $H_2CO_3$ in water are essentially the same: $CO_2 + H_2O = H_2CO_3$)

     **Answers:**
     **(a)** $Ca^{2+} = 207.25$ or $207.3 \text{ mg} \cdot L^{-1}$ as $CaCO_3$      **(d)** $HCO_3^- = 180.41$ or $180.4 \text{ mg} \cdot L^{-1}$
     **(b)** $Mg^{2+} = 111.20$ or $111.2 \text{ mg} \cdot L^{-1}$ as $CaCO_3$                 as $CaCO_3$
     **(c)** $CO_2 = 109.18$ or $109.2 \text{ mg} \cdot L^{-1}$ as $CaCO_3$      **(e)** $CO_3^{2-} = 25.02$ or $25.0 \text{ mg} \cdot L^{-1}$ $CaCO_3$

**2-36** Convert the following from milligrams per liter as the ion or compound to milligrams per liter as $CaCO_3$.
  (a) $200.00 \text{ mg} \cdot L^{-1}$ $NH_4^+$            (d) $85.05 \text{ mg} \cdot L^{-1}$ $Ca^{2+}$
  (b) $280.00 \text{ mg} \cdot L^{-1}$ $K^+$               (e) $19.90 \text{ mg} \cdot L^{-1}$ $Na^+$
  (c) $123.45 \text{ mg} \cdot L^{-1}$ $SO_4^{2-}$

**2-37** Convert the following from milligrams per liter as $CaCO_3$ to milligrams per liter as the ion or compound.
  (a) $100.00 \text{ mg} \cdot L^{-1}$ $SO_4^{2-}$           (d) $10.00 \text{ mg} \cdot L^{-1}$ $H_2CO_3$
  (b) $30.00 \text{ mg} \cdot L^{-1}$ $HCO_3^-$           (e) $150.00 \text{ mg} \cdot L^{-1}$ $Na^+$
  (c) $150.00 \text{ mg} \cdot L^{-1}$ $Ca^{2+}$

     **Answers:**
     **(a)** $SO_4^{2-} = 95.98$ or $96.0 \text{ mg} \cdot L^{-1}$      **(d)** $H_2CO_3 = 6.198$ or $6.20 \text{ mg} \cdot L^{-1}$
     **(b)** $HCO_3^- = 36.58$ or $36.6 \text{ mg} \cdot L^{-1}$      **(e)** $Na^+ = 68.91 \text{ mg} \cdot L^{-1}$
     **(c)** $Ca^{2+} = 60.07$ or $60.1 \text{ mg} \cdot L^{-1}$

**2-38**  Convert the following from milligrams per liter as $CaCO_3$ to milligrams per liter as the ion or compound.

   (a)  $10.00 \ mg \cdot L^{-1} \ CO_2$    (d)  $81.00 \ mg \cdot L^{-1} \ H_2PO_4^-$

   (b)  $13.50 \ mg \cdot L^{-1} \ Ca(OH)_2$    (e)  $40.00 \ mg \cdot L^{-1} \ Cl^-$

   (c)  $481.00 \ mg \cdot L^{-1} \ HPO_4^{2-}$

**2-39**  What is the "exact" alkalinity of a water that contains $0.6580 \ mg \cdot L^{-1}$ of bicarbonate, as the ion, at a pH of 5.66?

   **Answer:**  $0.4302 \ mg \cdot L^{-1}$ as $CaCO_3$

**2-40**  Calculate the "approximate" alkalinity (in milligrams per liter as $CaCO_3$) of a water containing $120 \ mg \cdot L^{-1}$ of bicarbonate ion and $15.00 \ mg \cdot L^{-1}$ of carbonate ion.

**2-41**  Calculate the "exact" alkalinity of the water in Problem 2–40 if the pH is 9.43.

   **Answer:**  $123.35 \ mg \cdot L^{-1}$ as $CaCO_3$

**2-42**  Calculate the "exact" alkalinity of the water in Problem 2–40 if the pH is 11.03.

**2-43**  What is the pH of a water that contains $120.00 \ mg \cdot L^{-1}$ of bicarbonate ion and $15.00 \ mg \cdot L^{-1}$ of carbonate ion?

   **Answer:**  9.43

**2-44**  What is the density of oxygen at a temperature of 273.0 K and at a pressure of 98.0 kPa?

**2-45**  Determine the density of nitrogen gas at a pressure of 122.8 kPa and a temperature of 298.0 K.

   **Answer:**  $1.39 \ kg \cdot m^{-3}$

**2-46**  Show that one mole of any ideal gas will occupy 22.414 L at STP. (STP is 273.16 K and 101.325 kPa.)

**2-47**  What volume would one mole of an ideal gas occupy at 25.0°C and 101.325 kPa?

   **Answer:**  24.46 L

**2-48**  A sample of air contains $8.583 \ mol \cdot m^{-3}$ of oxygen and $15.93 \ mol \cdot m^{-3}$ of nitrogen at STP. Determine the partial pressures of oxygen and nitrogen in $1.0 \ m^3$ of the air.

**2-49**  A $1\text{-}m^3$ volume tank contains a gas mixture of 18.32 mol of oxygen, 16.40 mol of nitrogen, and 6.15 mol of carbon dioxide. What is the partial pressure of each component in the gas mixture at 25.0°C?

   **Answer:**  $O_2$: 45.4 kPa, $N_2$: 40.6 kPa, $CO_2$: 15.2 kPa

**2-50**  Calculate the volume occupied by 5.2 kg of carbon dioxide at 152.0 kPa and 315.0 K.

**2-51**  Determine the mass of oxygen contained in a $5.0\text{-}m^3$ volume under a pressure of 568.0 kPa and at a temperature of 263.0 K.

   **Answer:**  41.56 kg

**2-52**  One liter of a gas mixture at 0°C and 108.26 kPa contains $250 \ mg \cdot L^{-1}$ of $H_2S$ gas. What is the partial pressure exerted by this gas?

**2-53**  A 28-L volume of gas at 300.0 K contains 11 g of methane, 1.5 g of nitrogen, and 16 g of carbon dioxide. Determine the partial pressure exerted by each gas.

   **Answer:**  $CH_4$: 61.2 kPa, $N_2$: 4.77 kPa, $CO_2$: 32.4 kPa

**2-54**  Given the gas mixture of Problem 2–53, how many moles of each gas are present in the 28-L volume?

**2-55**  The partial pressures of the gases in a 22,414-L volume of air at STP are: oxygen, 21.224 kPa; nitrogen, 79.119 kPa; argon, 0.946 kPa; and carbon dioxide, 0.036 kPa. Determine the gram-molecular weight of air.

   **Answer:**  28.966

**2-56**   Convert the concentration of $SO_2$ from 80 $\mu g \cdot m^{-3}$ to units of parts per million, given that the gas has a temperature of 25°C and a pressure of 101.325 kPa.

**2-57**   Convert the concentration of $NO_2$ from 0.55 ppm to units of micrograms per cubic meter, given that the gas has a temperature of 290 K and pressure of 100.0 kPa.

   **Answer:** 1048.8, or 1050 $\mu g \cdot m^{-3}$

**2-58**   A chemical is placed in a beaker containing 20 g of soil and 500 mL of water. At equilibrium, the chemical is found in the soil at a concentration of 100 mg $\cdot$ kg$^{-1}$ of soil. The equilibrium concentration of this same chemical in the water is 250 $\mu g \cdot L^{-1}$. What is the partition coefficient for this chemical on this soil?

**2-59**   A chemical, SpartanGreen, has a partition coefficient of 12,500 (mg $\cdot$ kg$^{-1}$)(mg $\cdot$ L$^{-1}$)$^{-1}$. If the concentration of this chemical in water is found to be 105 $\mu g \cdot L^{-1}$, at equilibrium, what is the concentration on the soil?

   **Answer:** 1312.5 mg $\cdot$ kg$^{-1}$

**2-60**   Derive the equation given for the half-life of a reactant.

## DISCUSSION QUESTIONS

**2-1**   Would you expect a carbonated beverage to have a pH above, below, or equal to 7.0? Explain why?

**2-2**   Explain the concentration unit of molarity to a citizen in a community with a hazardous waste site.

**2-3**   When dealing with acid rain (rainfall having a pH < 4) would a lake having a high or low alkalinity be more or less affected by this form of pollution? Explain your answer.

**2-4**   When you allow a can of carbonated beverage to sit open so that the carbon dioxide is released to the atmosphere, does the pH of the beverage remain the same, increase, or decrease? Explain your answer.

**2-5**   Would you expect the mineral kaolinite to dissolve more in a water having a high or a low pH? Explain your answer.

**2-6**   A gas sample is collected in a special gas-sampling bag that does not react with the pollutants collected but is free to expand and contract. When the sample was collected, the atmospheric pressure was 103.0 kPa. At the time the sample was analyzed the atmospheric pressure was 100.0 kPa. The bag was found to contain 0.020 ppm of $SO_2$. Would the original concentration of $SO_2$ be more, less, or the same? Explain your answer. If the concentrations were reported in units of micrograms per cubic meter, would your answer change? How?

**2-7**   What is the difference between chemical equilibrium and steady-state conditions?

## ADDITIONAL READING

**Books**

Ebbing, D. D., *General Chemistry,* Boston, MA: Houghton Mifflin Co., 1993.

Finlayson-Pitts, B. J., J. N. Pitts, Jr., *Atmospheric Chemistry,* New York: John Wiley and Sons, 1986.

Hemond, H. F., E. J. Fechner-Levy, *Chemical Fate and Transport in the Environment,* New York: Academic Press, 1999.

Larson, R. A., E. J. Weber, *Reaction Mechanisms in Environmental Organic Chemistry,* Chelsea: Lewis Publishers, 1993.

Morel, F. M., J. G. Hering, *Principles of Aquatic Chemistry,* New York: John Wiley and Sons, 1993.

Sawyer, C. N., P. L. McCarty, and G. F. Parkin, *Chemistry for Environmental Engineering,* 4th ed. New York: McGraw-Hill, 1994.

Schwarzenbach, R. P., P. M. Gschwend, and D. M. Imboden, *Environmental Organic Chemistry,* New York: John Wiley and Sons, 1993.

Snoeynick, V. L., D. Jenkins, *Water Chemistry,* New York: Wiley & Sons, 1980.

Stumm, W., J. J. Morgan, *Aquatic Chemistry,* 3rd ed. New York: John Wiley and Sons, Inc., 1996.

vanLoon, Gary W., Stephen J. Duffy, *Environmental Chemistry: A Global Perspective,* Oxford, England: Oxford University Press, 2000.

Fu Yeh, Teh, *Environmental Chemistry: Essentials of Chemistry for Engineering Practice,* vol. 4A, Upper Saddle River: Prentice Hall PTR, 1999.

**Journals**

*Acta Hydrochimica et Hydrobiologica* (Wiley-VCH)

*Advances in Environmental Research* (Elsevier)

*Applied Geochemistry* (Elsevier)

*Aquatic Geochemistry* (Kluwer)

*Archives of Environmental Contamination and Toxicology* (Springer)

*Bulletin of Environmental Contamination and Toxicology* (Springer)

*Chemosphere* (Elsevier)

*Critical Reviews in Environmental Science and Technology* (CRC)

*Environmental Science and Pollution Research* (Ecomed)

*Environmental Science and Technology* (American Chemical Society)

*Environmental Toxicology and Water Quality* (Wiley)

*International Journal of Environmental Analytical Chemistry*

*Journal of Atmospheric Chemistry* (Kluwer)

*Journal of Environmental Monitoring* (RSC)

*Journal of Environmental Quality*

*Journal of Environmental Science and Health,* Part A—Toxic/Hazardous Substances and Environmental Engineering (Marcel Dekker)

*Journal of Soil Science Society of America*

*Marine Chemistry* (Elsevier)

*Marine Environmental Research* (Elsevier)

*Marine Pollution Bulletin* (Elsevier)

*The Science of the Total Environment* (Elsevier)

*Water Environment Research*

*Water Environment and Technology*

*Water Research* (Elsevier)

*Water Science and Technology* (Elsevier)

*Water, Air, and Soil Pollution* (Kluwer)

## REFERENCE

1. Lewis, W. K., Whitman, W. G., "Principles of Gas Absorption," *Ind Eng Chem,* vol. 16, p. 1215, 1924.

# 3

# Materials and Energy Balances

## 3–1   INTRODUCTION

Materials and energy balances are key tools in achieving a quantitative understanding of the behavior of environmental systems. They serve as a method of accounting for the flow of energy and materials into and out of environmental systems. Mass balances provide us with a tool for modeling the production, transport, and fate of pollutants in the environment. Energy balances likewise provide us with a tool for modeling the production, transport, and fate of energy in the environment. Examples of mass balances include prediction of rainwater runoff (Chapter 6), determination of the solid waste production from mining operations (Chapter 7), oxygen balance in streams (Chapter 8), and audits of hazardous waste production (Chapter 13). Energy balances allow us to estimate the efficiency of thermal processes (Chapter 7), predict the temperature rise in a stream from the discharge of cooling water from a power plant (Chapter 8), and study climate change (Chapter 11).

## 3–2   UNIFYING THEORIES

### Conservation of Matter

The **law of conservation of matter** states that (without nuclear reaction) matter can neither be created nor destroyed. This is a powerful theory. It means that if we observe an environmental process carefully, we should be able to account for the "matter" at any point in time. It does not mean that the form of the matter does not change nor, for that matter, the properties of the matter. Thus, if we measure the volume a fresh glass of water on the counter on Monday and measure it again a week later and find the volume to be less, we do not presume magic has occurred but rather that matter has changed in form. The law of conservation of matter says we ought to be able to account for all the mass of the water that was originally present, that is, the mass of water remaining in the glass plus the mass of water vapor that has evaporated equals the mass of water originally present. The mathematical representation of this accounting system is called a **materials balance** or **mass balance.**

### Conservation of Energy

The **law of conservation of energy** states that energy cannot be created or destroyed. Like the law of conservation of matter, this theory means that we should be able to account for the "energy" at any point in time. It also does not mean that the form of the energy does not change. Thus, we should be able to trace the energy of food through a series of organisms from green plants through animals. The mathematical representation of the accounting system we use to trace energy is called an **energy balance.**

### Conservation of Matter and Energy

At the turn of the 20th century, Albert Einstein hypothesized that matter could be transformed to energy and vice versa. The birth of the nuclear age proved his hypothesis correct, so today we have a combined **law of conservation of matter and energy** that states that the total amount of energy and matter is constant. A nuclear change produces new materials by changing the identity of the atoms themselves. Significant amounts of matter are converted to energy in nuclear explosions. Exchange between mass and energy is not an issue in environmental applications. Thus, there are generally two separate balances for mass and energy.

## 3–3   MATERIALS BALANCES

### Fundamentals

In its simplest form a materials balance or mass balance may be viewed as an accounting procedure. You perform a form of material balance each time you balance your checkbook.

$$\text{Balance} = \text{deposit} - \text{withdrawal} \tag{3–1}$$

For an environmental process, the equation would be written

Accumulation = input − output                                              (3–2)

where accumulation, input, and output refer to the mass quantities accumulating in the system or flowing into or out of the system. The "system" may be, for example, a pond, river, or a pollution control device.

**The Control Volume.**   Using the mass balance approach, we begin solving the problem by drawing a flowchart of the process or a conceptual diagram of the environmental subsystem. All of the known inputs, outputs, and accumulation are converted to the same mass units and placed on the diagram. Unknown inputs, outputs, and accumulation are also marked on the diagram. This helps us define the problem. System boundaries (imaginary blocks around the process or part of the process) are drawn in such a way that calculations are made as simple as possible. The system within the boundaries is called the **control volume.**

We then write a materials balance equation to solve for unknown inputs, outputs, or accumulations or to demonstrate that we have accounted for all of the components by demonstrating that the materials balance "closes," that is, the accounting balances. Alternatively, when we do not have data for all inputs or outputs, we can assume that the mass balance closes and solve for the unknown quantity. The following example illustrates the technique.

**EXAMPLE 3–1**   Mr. and Mrs. Konzzumer have no children. In an average week they purchase and bring into their house approximately 50 kg of consumer goods (food, magazines, newspapers, appliances, furniture, and associated packaging). Of this amount, 50% is consumed as food. Half of the food is used for biological maintenance and ultimately released as $CO_2$; the remainder is discharged to the sewer system. The Konzzumers recycle approximately 25% of the solid waste that is generated. Approximately 1 kg accumulates in the house. Estimate the amount of solid waste they place at the curb each week.

Solution   Begin by drawing a mass balance diagram and labeling the known and unknown inputs and outputs. There are, in fact, two diagrams: one for the house and one for the people. However, the mass balance for the people is superfluous for the solution of this problem.

Write the mass balance equation for the house.

Input = accumulation in house + output as food to people + output as solid waste

Now we need to calculate the known inputs and outputs.

One half of input is food = (0.5)(50 kg) = 25 kg

This is output as food to the people. The mass balance equation is then rewritten as

50 kg = 1 kg + 25 kg + output as solid waste

Solving for the mass of solid waste:

Output as solid waste = 50 − 1 − 25 = 24 kg

The mass balance diagram with the appropriate masses may be redrawn as shown below:

We can estimate the amount of solid waste placed at the curb by performing another mass balance around the solid waste as shown in the following diagram:

The mass balance equation is

Solid waste in = output to recycle + output to curb

Because the recycled amount is 25% of the solid waste

Output to recycle = (0.25)(24 kg) = 6 kg

Substituting into the mass balance equation for solid waste and solving for output to curb;

24 kg = 6 kg + output to curb

Output to curb = 24 − 6 = 18 kg

### Time as a Factor

For many environmental problems time is an important factor in establishing the degree of severity of the problem or in designing a solution. In these instances Equation 3–2 is modified to the following form:

Rate of accumulation = rate of input − rate of output          (3–3)

where **rate** is used to mean "per unit of time." In the calculus this may be written as

$$\frac{dM}{dt} = \frac{d(\text{in})}{dt} - \frac{d(\text{out})}{dt} \qquad (3\text{–}4)$$

where $M$ refers to the mass accumulated and (in) and (out) refer to the mass flowing in or out. As part of the description of the problem, a convenient time interval that is meaningful for the system must be chosen.

**EXAMPLE 3–2** Truly Clearwater is filling her bathtub but she forgot to put the plug in. If the volume of water for a bath is 0.350 m³ and the tap is flowing at 1.32 L · min⁻¹ and the drain is running at 0.32 L · min⁻¹, how long will it take to fill the tub to bath level? Assuming Truly shuts off the water when the tub is full and does not flood the house, how much water will be wasted? Assume the density of water is 1,000 kg · m⁻³.

Solution The mass balance diagram is shown here.

Because we are working in mass units, we must convert the volumes to masses. To do this, we use the density of water.

$$\text{Mass} = (\text{volume})(\text{density}) = (\Psi)(\rho)$$

where the

$$\text{Volume} = (\text{flow rate})(\text{time}) = (Q)(t)$$

So for the mass balance equation, noting that $1.0 \text{ m}^3 = 1{,}000 \text{ L}$ so $0.350 \text{ m}^3 = 350 \text{ L}$,

$$\text{Accumulation} = \text{mass in} - \text{mass out}$$

$$(\Psi_{\text{ACC}})(\rho) = (Q_{\text{in}})(\rho)(t) - (Q_{\text{out}})(\rho)(t)$$

$$\Psi_{\text{ACC}} = (Q_{\text{in}})(t) - (Q_{\text{out}})(t)$$

$$\Psi_{\text{ACC}} = 1.32t - 0.32t$$

$$350 \text{ L} = (1.00 \text{ L} \cdot \text{min}^{-1})(t)$$

$$t = 350 \text{ min}$$

The amount of water wasted is

$$\text{Wasted water} = (0.32 \text{ L} \cdot \text{min}^{-1})(350 \text{ min}) = 112 \text{ L}$$

## More Complex Systems

A key step in the solution of mass balance problems for systems that are more complex than the previous examples is the selection of an appropriate control volume. In some instances, it may be necessary to select multiple control volumes and then solve the problem sequentially using the solution from one control volume as the input to another control volume. For some complex processes, the appropriate control volume may treat all of the steps in the process as a "black box" in which the internal process steps are not required and therefore are hidden in a black box. The following example illustrates a case of a more complex system and a method of solving the problem.

**EXAMPLE 3–3** A storm sewer network in a small residential subdivision is shown in the following sketch. The storm water flows by gravity in the direction shown by the pipes. Storm water only enters the storm sewer on east–west legs of pipe. No storm water enters on the north–south legs. The flow rate for each section of pipe is also shown by each section of pipe. The capacity of each pipe is 0.120 m³ · s⁻¹. During large rain storms River Street floods below junction number 1 because the flow of water exceeds the capacity of the storm sewer pipe. To alleviate this problem and to provide extra capacity for expansion, it is proposed to build a retention pond to hold the storm water until the storm is over and then gradually release it. Where in the pipe network should the retention pond be built to provide approximately 50% extra capacity ($0.06 \text{ m}^3 \cdot \text{s}^{-1}$) in the remaining system?

Solution    This is an example of a balanced flow problem. That is $Q_{out}$ must equal $Q_{in}$. Although this problem can almost be solved by observation, we will use a sequential mass balance approach to illustrate the technique. Starting at the upper end of the system at junction number 12, we draw the following mass balance diagram:

The mass balance equation is

$$\frac{dM}{dt} = \frac{d(in)}{dt} - \frac{d(out)}{dt}$$

Because no water accumulates at the junction

$$\frac{dM}{dt} = 0$$

and

$$\frac{d(in)}{dt} = \frac{d(out)}{dt}$$

$$(\rho)(Q_{in}) = (\rho)(Q_{out})$$

Because the density of water remains constant, we may treat the mass flow rate in and out as directly proportional to the flow rate in and out.

$$Q_{in} = Q_{out}$$

So the flow rate from junction 12 to junction 9 is $0.01 \text{ m}^3 \cdot \text{s}^{-1}$.

At junction 9, we can draw the following mass balance diagram.

0.01 m$^3 \cdot$s$^{-1}$

0.01 m$^3 \cdot$s$^{-1}$

⑨

$Q_{out} = ?$

Again using our assumption that no water accumulates at the junction and recognizing that the mass balance equation may again be written in terms of flow rates,

$$Q_{\text{from junction 9}} = Q_{\text{from junction 12}} + Q_{\text{in the pipe connected to junction 9}}$$
$$= 0.01 + 0.01 = 0.02 \text{ m}^3 \cdot \text{s}^{-1}$$

Similarly

$$Q_{\text{from junction 6}} = Q_{\text{from junction 9}} + Q_{\text{in the pipe connected to junction 6}}$$
$$= 0.02 + 0.01 = 0.03 \text{ m}^3 \cdot \text{s}^{-1}$$

and, noting that storm water enters on east–west legs of pipe

$$Q_{\text{from junction 3}} = Q_{\text{from junction 6}} + Q_{\text{in the pipe connecting junction 3 with junction 2}}$$
$$= 0.03 + 0.01 = 0.04 \text{ m}^3 \cdot \text{s}^{-1}$$

By a similar process for all the junctions, we may label the network flows as shown in the following diagram.

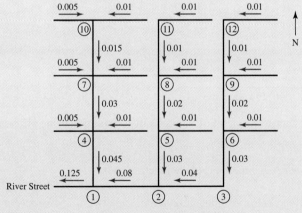

It is obvious that the pipe capacity of 0.12 m$^3 \cdot$ s$^{-1}$ is exceeded just below junction 1. By observation we can also see that the total flow into junction 2 is 0.07 m$^3 \cdot$ s$^{-1}$ and that a retention pond at this point would require that the pipe below junction 1 carry only 0.055 m$^3 \cdot$ s$^{-1}$. This meets the requirement of providing approximately 50% of the capacity for expansion.

## Efficiency

The effectiveness of an environmental process in removing a contaminant can be determined using the mass balance technique. Starting with Equation 3–4,

$$\frac{dM}{dt} = \frac{d(\text{in})}{dt} - \frac{d(\text{out})}{dt}$$

The mass of contaminant per unit of time [$d(\text{in})/dt$ and $d(\text{out})/dt$] may be calculated as

$$\frac{\text{Mass}}{\text{Time}} = (\text{concentration})(\text{flow rate})$$

For example,

$$\frac{\text{Mass}}{\text{Time}} = (\text{mg} \cdot \text{m}^{-3})(\text{m}^3 \cdot \text{s}^{-1}) = \text{mg} \cdot \text{s}^{-1}$$

This is called a **mass flow rate.** In concentration and flow rate terms, the mass balance equation is

$$\frac{dM}{dt} = C_{\text{in}} Q_{\text{in}} - C_{\text{out}} Q_{\text{out}} \tag{3--5}$$

where $dM/dt$ = rate of accumulation of contaminant in the process
$C_{\text{in}}, C_{\text{out}}$ = concentrations of contaminant into and out of the process
$Q_{\text{in}}, Q_{\text{out}}$ = flow rates into and out of the process

The ratio of the mass that is accumulated in the process to the incoming mass is a measure of how effective the process is in removing the contaminant

$$\frac{dM/dt}{C_{\text{in}} Q_{\text{in}}} = \frac{C_{\text{in}} Q_{\text{in}} - C_{\text{out}} Q_{\text{out}}}{C_{\text{in}} Q_{\text{in}}} \tag{3--6}$$

For convenience, the fraction is multiplied by 100%. The left-hand side of the equation is given the notation $\eta$. Efficiency ($\eta$) is then defined as

$$\eta = \frac{\text{mass in} - \text{mass out}}{\text{mass in}}(100\%) \tag{3--7}$$

If the flow rate in and the flow rate out are the same, this ratio may be simplified to

$$\eta = \frac{\text{concentration in} - \text{concentration out}}{\text{concentration in}}(100\%) \tag{3--8}$$

The following example illustrates a multistep solution using efficiency as part of the solution technique.

**EXAMPLE 3–4**

The air pollution control equipment on a municipal waste incinerator includes a fabric filter particle collector (known as a baghouse). The baghouse contains 424 cloth bags arranged in parallel, that is 1/424 of the flow goes through each bag. The gas flow rate into and out of the baghouse is 47 $\text{m}^3 \cdot \text{s}^{-1}$, and the concentration of particles entering the baghouse is 15 $\text{g} \cdot \text{m}^{-3}$. In normal operation the baghouse particulate discharge meets the regulatory limit of 24 $\text{mg} \cdot \text{m}^{-3}$. During preventive maintenance replacement of the bags, one bag is inadvertently not replaced, so only 423 bags are in place.

Calculate the fraction of particulate matter removed and the efficiency of particulate removal when all 424 bags are in place and the emissions comply with the regulatory requirements. Estimate the mass emission rate when one of the bags is missing and recalculate the efficiency of the baghouse. Assume the efficiency for each individual bag is the same as the overall efficiency for the baghouse.

**Solution**

The mass balance diagram for the baghouse in normal operation is shown here.

In concentration and flow rate terms, the mass balance equation is

$$\frac{dM}{dt} = C_{in}Q_{in} - C_{out}Q_{out}$$

The mass rate of accumulation in the baghouse is

$$\frac{dM}{dt} = (15{,}000 \text{ mg} \cdot \text{m}^{-3})(47 \text{ m}^3 \cdot \text{s}^{-1}) - (24 \text{ mg} \cdot \text{m}^{-3})(47 \text{ m}^3 \cdot \text{s}^{-1}) = 703{,}872 \text{ mg} \cdot \text{s}^{-1}$$

The fraction of particulates removed is

$$\frac{703{,}872 \text{ mg} \cdot \text{s}^{-1}}{(15{,}000 \text{ mg} \cdot \text{m}^{-3})(47 \text{ m}^3 \cdot \text{s}^{-1})} = \frac{703{,}872 \text{ mg} \cdot \text{s}^{-1}}{705{,}000 \text{ mg} \cdot \text{s}^{-1}} = 0.9984$$

The efficiency of the baghouse is

$$\eta = \frac{15{,}000 \text{ mg} \cdot \text{m}^{-3} - 24 \text{ mg} \cdot \text{m}^{-3}}{15{,}000 \text{ mg} \cdot \text{m}^{-3}}(100\%)$$

$$= 99.84\%$$

Note that the fraction of particulate matter removed is the decimal equivalent of the efficiency.

To determine the mass emission rate with one bag missing, we begin by drawing a mass balance diagram. Because one bag is missing, a portion of the flow ($1/424$ of $Q_{out}$) effectively bypasses the baghouse. The line around the baghouse is drawn to show this.

A judicious selection of the control volume aids in the solution of this problem. As shown in the diagram, a control volume around the overall baghouse and bypass flow yields three unknowns: the mass flow rate out of the baghouse, the rate of mass accumulation in the baghouse hopper, and the mass flow rate of the mixture. A control volume around the baghouse alone reduces the number of unknowns to two:

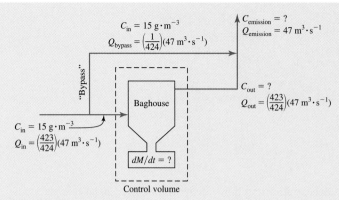

Control volume

Because we know the efficiency and the influent mass flow rate, we can solve the mass balance equation for the mass flow rate out of the filter.

$$\eta = \frac{C_{in}Q_{in} - C_{out}Q_{out}}{C_{in}Q_{in}}$$

Solving for $C_{out}Q_{out}$

$$C_{out}Q_{out} = (1 - \eta)C_{in}Q_{in}$$

$$= (1 - 0.9984)(15,000 \text{ mg} \cdot \text{m}^{-3})(47 \text{ m}^3 \cdot \text{s}^{-1})(423/424) = 1125 \text{ mg} \cdot \text{s}^{-1}$$

This value can be used as an input for a control volume around the junction of the bypass, the effluent from the baghouse and the final effluent.

A mass balance for the control volume around the junction may be written as

$$\frac{dM}{dt} = C_{in}Q_{in \text{ from bypass}} + C_{in}Q_{in \text{ from baghouse}} - C_{out}Q_{out}$$

Because there is no accumulation in the junction

$$\frac{dM}{dt} = 0$$

and the mass balance equation is

$$C_{out}Q_{out} = C_{in}Q_{in \text{ from bypass}} + C_{in}Q_{in \text{ from baghouse}}$$

$$= (15,000 \text{ mg} \cdot \text{m}^{-3})(47 \text{ m}^3 \cdot \text{s}^{-1})(1/424) + 1125 = 2788 \text{ mg} \cdot \text{s}^{-1}$$

The concentration in the effluent is

$$\frac{C_{out}Q_{out}}{Q_{out}} = \frac{2788 \text{ mg} \cdot \text{s}^{-1}}{47 \text{ m}^3 \cdot \text{s}^{-1}} = 59 \text{ mg} \cdot \text{m}^{-3}$$

The overall efficiency of the baghouse with the missing bag is

$$\eta = \frac{15,000 \text{ mg} \cdot \text{m}^{-3} - 59 \text{ mg} \cdot \text{m}^{-3}}{15,000 \text{ mg} \cdot \text{m}^{-3}}(100\%)$$

$$= 99.61\%$$

The efficiency is still very high but the control equipment does not meet the allowable emission rate of 24 mg $\cdot$ m$^{-3}$. It is not likely that a baghouse would ever operate with a missing bag because the unbalanced gas flows would be immediately apparent. However, many small holes in a number of bags could yield an effluent that did not meet the discharge standards but would otherwise appear to be functioning correctly. To prevent this situation, the bags undergo periodic inspection and maintenance and the effluent stream is monitored continuously.

### The State of Mixing

The state of mixing in the system is an important consideration in the application of Equation 3–4. Consider a coffee cup containing approximately 200 mL of black coffee (or another beverage of your choice). If we add a dollop (about 20 mL) of cream and immediately take a sample (or a sip), we would not be surprised to find that the cream was not evenly distributed throughout the coffee. If, on the other hand, we mixed the coffee and cream vigorously and then took a sample, it would not matter if we sipped from the left or right of the cup, or, for that matter, put a valve in the bottom and sampled from there, we would expect the cream to be distributed evenly. In terms of a mass balance on the coffee cup system, the cup itself would define the system boundary for the control volume. If the coffee and cream were not mixed well, then the place we take the sample from would strongly affect the value of $d(\text{out})/dt$ in Equation 3–4. On the other hand, if the coffee and cream were instantaneously well mixed, then any place we take the sample from would yield the same result. That is, any output would look exactly like the contents of the cup. This system is called a completely mixed system. A more formal definition is that **completely mixed systems** are those in which every drop of fluid is homogeneous with every other drop, that is, every drop of fluid contains the same concentration of material or physical property (e.g., temperature). If a system is completely mixed, then we may assume that the output from the system (concentration, temperature, etc.) is the same as the contents within the system boundary. Although we frequently make use of this assumption to solve mass-balance problems, it is often very difficult to achieve in real systems. This means that solutions to mass-balance problems that make this assumption must be taken as approximations to reality.

If completely mixed systems exist, or at least systems that we can approximate as completely mixed, then it stands to reason that some systems are completely unmixed or approximately so. These systems are called **plug-flow systems.** The behavior of a plug-flow system is analogous to that of a train moving along a railroad track (Figure 3–1). Each car in the train must follow the one preceding it. If, as in Figure 3–1b, a tank car is inserted in a train of box cars, it maintains its position in the train until it arrives at its destination. The tank car may be identified at any point in time as the train travels down the track. In terms of fluid flow, each drop of fluid along the direction of flow remains unique and, if no reactions take place, contains the same concentration of material or physical property that it had when it entered the plug-flow system. Mixing may or may not occur in the radial direction. As with the completely mixed systems, ideal plug-flow systems don't happen very often in the real world.

When a system has operated in such a way that the rate of input and the rate of output are constant and equal, then, of course, the rate of accumulation is zero (i.e., $dM/dt = 0$). This condition is called **steady state.** In solving mass-balance problems, it is often convenient to make an assumption that steady-state conditions have been achieved. We should note that steady state does not imply equilibrium. For example, water running into and out of a pond at the same rate is not at equilibrium, otherwise it would not be flowing. However, if there is no accumulation in the pond, then the system is at steady state.

Example 3–5 demonstrates the use of two assumptions: complete mixing and steady state.

## FIGURE 3–1

(a) Analogy of a plug-flow system and a train.
(b) Analogy when a pulse change in influent concentration occurs.

**EXAMPLE 3–5**   A storm sewer is carrying snow melt containing $1.200 \text{ g} \cdot \text{L}^{-1}$ of sodium chloride into a small stream. The stream has a naturally occurring sodium chloride concentration of $20 \text{ mg} \cdot \text{L}^{-1}$. If the storm sewer flow rate is $2000 \text{ L} \cdot \text{min}^{-1}$ and the stream flow rate is $2.0 \text{ m}^3 \cdot \text{s}^{-1}$, what is the concentration of salt in the stream after the discharge point? Assume that the sewer flow and the stream flow are completely mixed, that the salt is a conservative substance (it does not react), and that the system is at steady state.

**Solution**   The first step is to draw a mass balance diagram as shown here.

Note that the mass flow of salt may be calculated as

$$\frac{\text{Mass}}{\text{Time}} = (\text{concentration})(\text{flow rate})$$

or

$$\frac{\text{Mass}}{\text{Time}} = (\text{mg} \cdot \text{L}^{-1})(\text{L} \cdot \text{min}^{-1}) = \text{mg} \cdot \text{min}^{-1}$$

Using the notation in the diagram, where the subscript "st" refers to the stream and the subscript "se" refers to the sewer, the mass balance may be written as

Rate of accumulation of salt $= [C_{st}Q_{st} + C_{se}Q_{se}] - C_{mix}Q_{mix}$

where $Q_{mix} = Q_{st} + Q_{se}$

Because we assume steady state, the rate of accumulation equals zero and

$$C_{mix}Q_{mix} = [C_{st}Q_{st} + C_{se}Q_{se}]$$

Solving for $C_{mix}$

$$C_{mix} = \frac{[C_{st}Q_{st} + C_{se}Q_{se}]}{Q_{st} + Q_{se}}$$

Before substituting in the values, the units are converted as follows:

$$C_{se} = (1.200 \text{ g} \cdot \text{L}^{-1} \times 1000 \text{ mg} \cdot \text{g}^{-1}) = 1200 \text{ mg} \cdot \text{L}^{-1}$$

$$Q_{st} = (2.0 \text{ m}^3 \cdot \text{s}^{-1})(1000 \text{ L} \cdot \text{m}^{-3})(60 \text{ s} \cdot \text{min}^{-1}) = 120{,}000 \text{ L} \cdot \text{min}^{-1}$$

$$C_{mix} = \frac{[(20 \text{ mg} \cdot \text{L}^{-1})(120{,}000 \text{ L} \cdot \text{min}^{-1})] + [(1200 \text{ mg} \cdot \text{L}^{-1})(2000 \text{ L} \cdot \text{min}^{-1})]}{120{,}000 \text{ L} \cdot \text{min}^{-1} + 2000 \text{ L} \cdot \text{min}^{-1}}$$

$$= 39.34 \text{ or } 39 \text{ mg} \cdot \text{L}^{-1}$$

### Including Reactions

Equation 3–4 is applicable when no chemical or biological reaction takes place and no radioactive decay occurs of the substances in the mass balance. In these instances the substance is said to be **conserved.** Examples of conservative substances include salt in water and argon in air. Examples of nonconservative substances (i.e., those that react or settle out) include decomposing organic matter and particulate matter that is settling from the air.

In most systems of environmental interest, transformations occur within the system: by-products are formed (e.g., $CO_2$) or compounds are destroyed (e.g., ozone). Because many environmental reactions do not occur instantaneously, the time dependence of the reaction must be taken into account. Equation 3–3 may be written to account for time-dependent transformation as follows:

$$\text{Accumulation rate} = \text{input rate} - \text{output rate} \pm \text{transformation rate} \qquad (3\text{–}9)$$

Time-dependent reactions are called **kinetic reactions.** As discussed in Chapter 2, the rate of transformation, or reaction rate ($r$), is used to describe the rate of formation or disappearance of a substance or chemical species. With reactions, Equation 3–4 may become

$$\frac{dM}{dt} = \frac{d(\text{in})}{dt} - \frac{d(\text{out})}{dt} + r \qquad (3\text{–}10)$$

The reaction rate is often some complex function of temperature, pressure, the reacting components, and products of reaction.

$$r = -kC^n \qquad (3\text{–}11)$$

where $k$ = reaction rate constant (in $\text{s}^{-1}$ or $\text{d}^{-1}$)
  $C$ = concentration of substance
  $n$ = exponent or reaction order

The minus sign before reaction rate, $k$, indicates the disappearance of a substance or chemical species.

In many environmental problems, for example the oxidation of organic compounds by microorganisms (Chapter 8) and radioactive decay (Chapter 16), the reaction rate, $r$, may be assumed to be directly proportional to the amount of material remaining, that is the value of $n = 1$. This is known as a **first-order reaction.** In first-order reactions, the rate of loss of the substance is proportional to the amount of substance present at any given time, $t$.

$$r = -kC = \frac{dC}{dt} \qquad (3\text{–}12)$$

The differential equation may be integrated to yield either

$$\ln \frac{C}{C_0} = -kt \tag{3-13}$$

or

$$C = C_0 e^{-kt} = C_0 \exp(-kt) \tag{3-14}$$

where $C$ = concentration at any time $t$
   $C_0$ = initial concentration
   $e = \exp$ = exponential $e = 2.7183$ raised to the $-kt$ power

For simple completely mixed systems with first-order reactions, the total mass of substance ($M$) is equal to the product of the concentration and volume ($C\mathcal{V}$) and, when $\mathcal{V}$ is a constant, the mass rate of decay of the substance is

$$\frac{dM}{dt} = \frac{d(C\mathcal{V})}{dt} = \mathcal{V}\frac{d(C)}{dt} \tag{3-15}$$

Because first-order reactions can be described by Equation 3–12, we can rewrite Equation 3–10 as

$$\frac{dM}{dt} = \frac{d(\text{in})}{dt} - \frac{d(\text{out})}{dt} - kC\mathcal{V} \tag{3-16}$$

**EXAMPLE 3–6**   A well-mixed sewage lagoon (a shallow pond) is receiving $430 \text{ m}^3 \cdot \text{d}^{-1}$ of sewage out of a sewer pipe. The lagoon has a surface area of 10 ha (hectares) and a depth of 1.0 m. The pollutant concentration in the raw sewage discharging into the lagoon is $180 \text{ mg} \cdot \text{L}^{-1}$. The organic matter in the sewage degrades biologically (decays) in the lagoon according to first-order kinetics. The reaction rate constant (decay coefficient) is $0.70 \text{ d}^{-1}$. Assuming no other water losses or gains (evaporation, seepage, or rainfall) and that the lagoon is completely mixed, find the steady-state concentration of the pollutant in the lagoon effluent.

Solution   We begin by drawing the mass-balance diagram.

The mass-balance equation may be written as

Accumulation = input rate − output rate − decay rate

Assuming steady-state conditions, that is, accumulation = 0, then

Input rate = output rate + decay rate

This may be written in terms of the notation in the figure as

$$C_{\text{in}} Q_{\text{in}} = C_{\text{eff}} Q_{\text{eff}} + k C_{\text{lagoon}} \mathcal{V}$$

Solving for $C_{\text{eff}}$, we have

$$C_{\text{eff}} = \frac{C_{\text{in}} Q_{\text{in}} - k C_{\text{lagoon}} \mathcal{V}}{Q_{\text{eff}}}$$

Now calculate the values for terms in the equation. The input mass rate $(C_{in}Q_{in})$ is

$(180 \text{ mg} \cdot \text{L}^{-1})(430 \text{ m}^3 \cdot \text{d}^{-1})(1000 \text{ L} \cdot \text{m}^{-3}) = 77,400,000 \text{ mg} \cdot \text{d}^{-1}$

With a lagoon volume of

$(10 \text{ ha})(10^4 \text{ m}^2 \cdot \text{ha}^{-1})(1 \text{ m}) = 100,000 \text{ m}^3$

and the decay coefficient of $0.70 \text{ d}^{-1}$, the decay rate is

$kC\forall = (0.70 \text{ d}^{-1})(100,000 \text{ m}^3)(1000 \text{ L} \cdot \text{m}^{-3})(C_{lagoon}) = (70,000,000 \text{ L} \cdot \text{d}^{-1})(C_{lagoon})$

Now using the assumption that the lagoon is completely mixed, we assume that $C_{eff} = C_{lagoon}$. Thus,

$kC\forall = (70,000,000 \text{ L} \cdot \text{d}^{-1})(C_{eff})$

Substituting into the mass-balance equation

Output rate $= 77,400,000 \text{ mg} \cdot \text{d}^{-1} - 70,000,000 \text{ L} \cdot \text{d}^{-1} \times C_{eff}$

or

$C_{eff}(430 \text{ m}^3 \cdot \text{d}^{-1})(1000 \text{ L} \cdot \text{m}^{-3}) = 77,400,000 \text{ mg} \cdot \text{d}^{-1} - 70,000,000 \text{ L} \cdot \text{d}^{-1} \times C_{eff}$

Solving for $C_{eff}$, we have

$$C_{eff} = \frac{77,400,000 \text{ mg} \cdot \text{d}^{-1}}{70,430,000 \text{ L} \cdot \text{d}^{-1}} = 1.10 \text{ mg} \cdot \text{L}^{-1}$$

**Plug-Flow with Reaction.** As noted in Figure 3–1, in plug-flow systems, the tank car, or "plug" element of fluid, does not mix with the fluid ahead or behind it. However, a reaction can take place in the tank car element. Thus, even at steady-state, the contents within the element can change with time as the plug moves downstream. The control volume for the mass balance is the plug or differential element of fluid. The mass balance for this moving plug may be written as

$$\frac{dM}{dt} = \frac{d(\text{in})}{dt} - \frac{d(\text{out})}{dt} + \forall\frac{d(C)}{dt} \tag{3-17}$$

Because no mass exchange occurs across the plug boundaries (in our railroad car analogy, there is no mass transfer between the box cars and the tank car), $d(\text{in})$ and $d(\text{out}) = 0$. Equation 3–17 may be rewritten as

$$\frac{dM}{dt} = 0 - 0 + \forall\frac{d(C)}{dt} \tag{3-18}$$

As noted earlier, for a first-order decay reaction, the right-hand term may be expressed as

$$\forall\frac{dC}{dt} = -kC\forall \tag{3-19}$$

The total mass of substance $(M)$ is equal to the product of the concentration and volume $(C\forall)$ and, when $\forall$ is a constant, the mass rate of decay of the substance in Equation 3–18 may be expressed as

$$\forall\frac{dC}{dt} = -kC\forall \tag{3-20}$$

where the left-hand side of the equation $= dM/dt$. The steady-state solution to the mass-balance equation for the plug-flow system with first-order kinetics is

$$\ln\frac{C_{out}}{C_{in}} = -k\theta \tag{3-21}$$

or

$$C_{out} = (C_{in})e^{-k\theta} \tag{3-22}$$

where $k$ = reaction rate constant (in $s^{-1}$, $min^{-1}$, or $d^{-1}$)
  $\theta$ = residence time in plug-flow system (in s, min, or d)

In a plug-flow system of length $L$, each plug travels for a period $= L/u$, where $u$ = the speed of flow. Alternatively, for a cross-sectional area $A$, the residence time is

$$\theta = \frac{(L)(A)}{(u)(A)} = \frac{\Psi}{Q} \tag{3-23}$$

where $\Psi$ = volume of the plug-flow system (in $m^3$)
  $Q$ = flow rate (in $m^3 \cdot s^{-1}$)

Thus, for example, Equation 3–21, may be rewritten as

$$\ln\frac{C_{out}}{C_{in}} = -k\frac{L}{u} = -k\frac{\Psi}{Q} \tag{3-24}$$

where $L$ = length of the plug-flow segment (in m)
  $u$ = linear velocity (in $m \cdot s^{-1}$)

Although the concentration within a given plug changes over time as the plug moves downstream, the concentration at a fixed point in the plug-flow system remains constant with respect to time. Thus, Equation 3–24 has no time dependence.
  Example 3–7 illustrates an application of plug-flow with reaction.

**EXAMPLE 3–7**  A wastewater treatment plant must disinfect its effluent before discharging the wastewater to a near-by stream. The wastewater contains $4.5 \times 10^5$ fecal coliform colony-forming units (CFU) per liter. The maximum permissible fecal coliform concentration that may be discharged is 2000 fecal coliform $CFU \cdot L^{-1}$. It is proposed that a pipe carrying the wastewater be used for disinfection process. Determine the length of pipe required if the linear velocity of the wastewater in the pipe is $0.75 \ m \cdot s^{-1}$. Assume that the pipe behaves as a steady-state plug-flow system and that the reaction rate constant for destruction of the fecal coliforms is $0.23 \ min^{-1}$.

Solution  The mass balance diagram is sketched here. The control volume is the pipe itself.

$C_{in} = 4.5 \times 10^5 \ CFU \cdot L^{-1}$
$u = 0.75 \ m \cdot s^{-1}$
  — L = ? —
$C_{out} = 2{,}000 \ CFU \cdot L^{-1}$
$u = 0.75 \ m \cdot s^{-1}$

Using the steady-state solution to the mass-balance equation, we obtain

$$\ln\frac{C_{out}}{C_{in}} = -k\frac{L}{u}$$

$$\ln\frac{2000 \ CFU \cdot L^{-1}}{4.5 \times 10^5 \ CFU \cdot L^{-1}} = -0.23 \ min^{-1}\frac{L}{(0.75 \ m \cdot s^{-1})(60 \ s \cdot min^{-1})}$$

Solving for the length of pipe, we have

$$\ln(4.44 \times 10^{-3}) = -0.23 \text{ min}^{-1} \frac{L}{45 \text{ m} \cdot \text{min}^{-1}}$$

$$-5.42 = -0.23 \text{ min}^{-1} \frac{L}{45 \text{ m} \cdot \text{min}^{-1}}$$

$$L = 1060 \text{ m}$$

A little over 1 km of pipe is needed to meet the discharge standard. For most wastewater treatment systems this would be an exceptionally long discharge and another alternative such as a mixing reactor (discussed in the following section) would be investigated.

### Reactors

The tanks in which physical, chemical, and biochemical reactions occur, for example, in water softening (Chapter 9) and wastewater treatment (Chapter 10), are called **reactors.** These reactors are classified based on their flow characteristics and their mixing conditions. With appropriate selection of control volumes, ideal chemical reactor models may be used to model natural systems.

**Batch reactors** are of the fill-and-draw type: materials are added to the tank (Figure 3–2a), mixed for sufficient time to allow the reaction to occur (Figure 3–2b), and then drained (Figure 3–2c). Although the reactor is well mixed and the contents are uniform at any instant in time, the composition within the tank changes with time as the reaction proceeds. A batch reaction is unsteady. Because there is no flow into or out of a batch reactor

$$\frac{d(\text{in})}{dt} = \frac{d(\text{out})}{dt} = 0$$

For a batch reactor Equation 3–16 reduces to

$$\frac{dM}{dt} = -kC\mathbb{V} \tag{3–25}$$

As we noted in Equation 3–15

$$\frac{dM}{dt} = \mathbb{V}\frac{dC}{dt}$$

So that for a first-order reaction in a batch reactor, Equation 3–25 may be simplified to

$$\frac{dC}{dt} = -kC \tag{3–26}$$

Flow reactors have a continuous type of operation: material flows into, through, and out of the reactor at all times. Flow reactors may be further classified by mixing conditions. The contents of a **completely mixed flow reactor** (CMFR), also called a continuous-flow stirred tank reactor (CSTR),

**FIGURE 3–2**

Batch reactor operation. **(a)** Materials added to the reactor. **(b)** Mixing and reaction. **(c)** Reactor is drained. *Note:* There is no influent or effluent during the reaction.

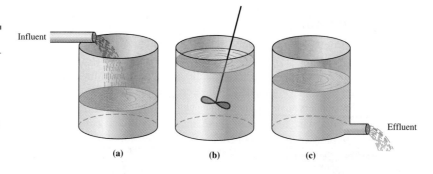

Influent

Effluent

(a)    (b)    (c)

## FIGURE 3–3

Schematic diagram of **(a)** completely mixed flow reactor (CMFR) and **(b)** the common diagram. The propeller indicates that the reactor is completely mixed.

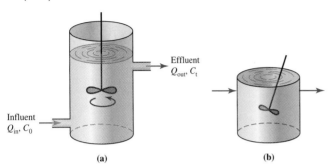

(a)         (b)

## FIGURE 3–4

Schematic diagram of a plug-flow reactor (PFR). Note: $t_3 > t_2 > t_1$.

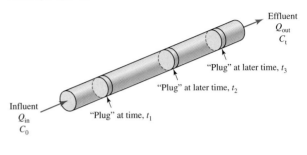

ideally are uniform throughout the tank. A schematic diagram of a CMFR and the common flow diagram notation are shown in Figure 3–3. The composition of the effluent is the same as the composition in the tank. If the mass input rate into the tank remains constant, the composition of the effluent remains constant. The mass balance for a CMFR is described by Equation 3–16.

In **plug-flow reactors** (PFR), fluid particles pass through the tank in sequence. Those that enter first leave first. In the ideal case, it is assumed that no mixing occurs in the lateral direction. Although composition varies along the length of the tank, as long as the flow conditions remain steady, the composition of the effluent remains constant. A schematic diagram of a plug-flow reactor is shown in Figure 3–4. The mass balance for a PFR is described by Equation 3–18, where the time element ($dt$) is the time spent in the PFR as described by Equation 3–23. Real continuous-flow reactors are generally something in between a CMFR and PFR.

For time-dependent reactions, the time that a fluid particle remains in the reactor obviously affects the degree to which the reaction goes to completion. In ideal reactors the average time in the reactor (**detention time** or **retention time** or, for liquid systems, **hydraulic detention time** or **hydraulic retention time**) is defined as

$$\theta = \frac{\forall}{Q} \tag{3–27}$$

where $\theta$ = theoretical detention time (in s)
     $\forall$ = volume of fluid in reactor (in m$^3$)
     $Q$ = flow rate into reactor (in m$^3 \cdot$ s$^{-1}$)

Real reactors do not behave as ideal reactors because of density differences due to temperature or other causes, short circuiting because of uneven inlet or outlet conditions, and local turbulence or dead spots in the tank corners. The detention time in real tanks is generally less than the theoretical detention time calculated from Equation 3–27.

### Reactor Analysis

The selection of a reactor either as a treatment method or as a model for a natural process depends on the behavior desired or recognized. We will examine the behavior of batch, CMFR, and PFR reactors in several situations. Situations of particular interest are the response of the reactor to a sudden increase (Figure 3–5a) or decrease (Figure 3–5b) in the steady-state influent concentration for conservative and nonconservative species (commonly called a step increase or decrease) and the response to pulse or spike change in influent concentration (Figure 3–5c). We will present the plots of the effluent concentration for each of the reactor types for a variety of conditions to show the response to these influent changes.

## FIGURE 3–5

Example influent graphs of **(a)** step increase in influent concentration, **(b)** step decrease in influent concentration, and **(c)** a pulse or spike increase in influent concentration. *Note:* The size of the change is for illustration purposes only.

(a)     (b)     (c)

## FIGURE 3–6

Batch reactor response to a step or pulse increase in concentration of a conservative substance. $C_0$ = mass of conservative substance/volume of reactor.

## FIGURE 3–7

Batch reactor response for **(a)** decay of a non-conservative substance and **(b)** for a formation reaction.

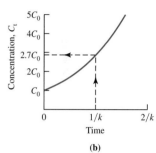

(a)     (b)

For nonconservative substances, we will present the analysis for first-order reactions. The behavior of zero-order and second-order reactions will be summarized in comparison at the conclusion of this discussion.

**Batch Reactor.** Laboratory experiments are often conducted in batch reactors because they are inexpensive and easy to build. Industries that generate small quantities of wastewater (less than $150 \text{ m}^3 \cdot \text{d}^{-1}$) use batch reactors because they are easy to operate and provide an opportunity to check the wastewater for regulatory compliance before discharging it.

Because there is no influent to or effluent from a batch reactor, the introduction of a conservative substance into the reactor either as a step increase or a pulse results in an instantaneous increase in concentration of the conservative substance in the reactor. The concentration plot is shown in Figure 3–6.

Because there is no influent or effluent, for a nonconservative substance that decays as a first-order reaction, the mass balance is described by Equation 3–26. Integration yields

$$\frac{C_t}{C_0} = e^{-kt} \tag{3–28}$$

The final concentration plot is shown in Figure 3–7a. For the formation reaction, where the sign in Equation 3–28 is positive, the concentration plot is shown in Figure 3–7b.

**EXAMPLE 3–8** A contaminated soil is to be excavated and treated in a completely mixed aerated lagoon at a Superfund site. To determine the time it will take to treat the contaminated soil, a laboratory completely mixed batch reactor is used to gather the following data. Assuming a first-order reaction, estimate the rate constant, $k$, and determine the time to achieve 99% reduction in the original concentration.

| Time (d) | Waste Concentration (mg · L⁻¹) |
|----------|-------------------------------|
| 1        | 280                           |
| 16       | 132                           |

Solution: The rate constant may be estimated by solving Equation 3–28 for $k$. Using the 1st and 16th day, the time interval $t = 16 - 1 = 15$ d

$$\frac{132 \text{ mg} \cdot \text{L}^{-1}}{280 \text{ mg} \cdot \text{L}^{-1}} = \exp[-k(15 \text{ d})]$$

$$0.4714 = \exp[-k(15)]$$

Taking the logarithm (base $e$) of both sides of the equation, we obtain

$$-0.7520 = -k(15)$$

Solving for $k$, we have

$$k = 0.0501 \text{ d}^{-1}$$

To achieve 99% reduction the concentration at time $t$ must be $1 - 0.99$ of the original concentration

$$\frac{C_t}{C_0} = 0.01$$

The estimated time is then

$$0.01 = \exp[-0.05(t)]$$

Taking the logarithm of both sides and solving for $t$, we get

$$t = 92 \text{ days}$$

**CMFR.** A batch reactor is used for small volumetric flow rates. When water flow rates are greater than 150 m³ · d⁻¹, a CMFR may be selected for chemical mixing. Examples of this application include equalization reactors to adjust the pH, precipitation reactors to remove metals, and mixing tanks (called **rapid mix** or **flash mix tanks**) for water treatment. Because municipal wastewater flow rates vary over the course of a day, a CMFR (called an **equalization basin**) may be placed at the treatment plant influent point to level out the flow and concentration changes. Some natural systems such as a lake or the mixing of two streams or the air in a room or over a city may be modeled as a CMFR as an approximation of the real mixing that is taking place.

For a step increase in a conservative substance entering a CMFR, the initial level of the conservative substance in the reactor is $C_0$ prior to $t = 0$. At $t = 0$, the influent concentration ($C_{in}$) instantaneously increases to $C_1$ and remains at this concentration (Figure 3–8a). With balanced

**FIGURE 3–8**

Response of a CMFR to **(a)** a step increase in the influent concentration of a conservative substance from concentration $C_0$ to a new concentration $C_1$. **(b)** Effluent concentration.

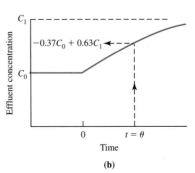

**FIGURE 3-9**

Flushing of CMFR resulting from **(a)** a step decrease in influent concentration of a conservative substance from $C_0$ to 0. **(b)** Effluent concentration.

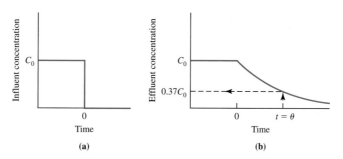

(a)

(b)

fluid flow ($Q_{in} = Q_{out}$) into the CMFR and no reaction, the mass balance equation for a step increase is

$$\frac{dM}{dt} = C_1 Q_{in} - C_{out} Q_{out} \tag{3-29}$$

where $M = C\Psi$. The solution is

$$C_t = C_0 \left[ \exp\left( -\frac{t}{\theta} \right) \right] + C_1 \left[ 1 - \exp\left( -\frac{t}{\theta} \right) \right] \tag{3-30}$$

where $C_t$ = concentration at any time $t$
$C_0$ = concentration in reactor prior to step change
$C_1$ = concentration in influent after instantaneous increase
$t$ = time after step change
$\theta$ = theoretical detention time = $\Psi/Q$
exp = exponential $e$ such that the terms in brackets immediately following are powers of $e$, that is, $e$ raised to the power of the term in the brackets, where $e = 2.7183$

Figure 3-8b shows the effluent concentration plot.

Flushing of a nonreactive contaminant from a CMFR by a contaminant-free fluid is an example of a step change in the influent concentration (Figure 3-9a). Because $C_{in} = 0$ and no reaction takes place, the mass balance equation is

$$\frac{dM}{dt} = -C_{out} Q_{out} \tag{3-31}$$

where $M = C\Psi$. The initial concentration is

$$C_0 = \frac{M}{\Psi} \tag{3-32}$$

Solving Equation 3-31 for any time $t \geq 0$, we obtain

$$C_t = C_0 \exp\left( -\frac{t}{\theta} \right) \tag{3-33}$$

where $\theta = \Psi/Q$ as noted in Equation 3-27. Figure 3-9b shows the effluent concentration plot.

**EXAMPLE 3-9**    Before entering an underground utility vault to do repairs, a work crew analyzed the gas in the vault and found that it contained 29 mg $\cdot$ m$^{-3}$ of hydrogen sulfide. Because the allowable exposure level is 14 mg $\cdot$ m$^{-3}$, the work crew began ventilating the vault with a blower. If the volume of the vault is 160 m$^3$ and the flow rate of contaminant-free air is 10 m$^3 \cdot$ min$^{-1}$, how long will it take to lower the hydrogen sulfide level to a level that will allow the work crew to enter? Assume the manhole behaves as a CMFR and that hydrogen sulfide is nonreactive in the time period considered.

**Solution** This is a case of flushing a nonreactive contaminant from a CMFR. The theoretical detention time is

$$\theta = \frac{V}{Q} = \frac{160 \text{ m}^3}{10 \text{ m}^3 \cdot \text{min}^{-1}} = 16 \text{ min}$$

The required time is found by solving Equation 3–33 for $t$

$$\frac{14 \text{ mg} \cdot \text{m}^{-3}}{29 \text{ mg} \cdot \text{m}^{-3}} = \exp\left(-\frac{t}{16 \text{ min}}\right)$$

$$0.4828 = \exp\left(-\frac{t}{16 \text{ min}}\right)$$

Taking the logarithm to the base $e$ of both sides

$$-0.7282 = -\frac{t}{16 \text{ min}}$$

$$t = 11.6 \text{ or } 12 \text{ min to lower the concentration to the allowable level}$$

Because the odor threshold for $H_2S$ is about $0.18 \text{ mg} \cdot \text{m}^{-3}$, the vault will still have quite a strong odor after 12 min.

A precautionary note is in order here. $H_2S$ is commonly found in confined spaces such as manholes. It is a very toxic poison and has the unfortunate property of deadening the olfactory senses. Thus, you may not smell it after a few moments even though the concentration has not decreased. Each year a few individuals in the United States die because they have entered a confined space without taking stringent safety precautions.

Because a CMFR is completely mixed, the response of a CMFR to a step change in the influent concentration of a reactive substance results in an immediate corresponding change in the effluent concentration. For this analysis we begin with the mass balance for a balanced flow ($Q_{in} = Q_{out}$) CMFR operating under steady state conditions with first-order decay of a reactive substance.

$$\frac{dM}{dt} = C_{in}Q_{in} - C_{out}Q_{out} - kC_{out}V \tag{3-34}$$

where $M = CV$. Because the flow rate and volume are constant, we may divide through by $Q$ and $V$ and simplify to obtain

$$\frac{dC}{dt} = \frac{1}{\theta}(C_{in} - C_{out}) - kC_{out} \tag{3-35}$$

where $\theta = V/Q$ as noted in Equation 3–27. Under steady-state conditions $dC/dt = 0$ and the solution for $C_{out}$ is

$$C_{out} = \frac{C_0}{1 + k\theta} \tag{3-36}$$

where $C_0 = C_{in}$ immediately after the step change. Note that $C_{in}$ can be nonzero before the step change. For a first-order reaction where material is produced, the sign of the reaction term is positive and the solution to the mass balance equations is

$$C_{out} = \frac{C_0}{1 - k\theta} \tag{3-37}$$

## FIGURE 3–10

Steady-state response of CMFR to **(a)** a step increase in influent concentration of a reactive substance. **(b)** Effluent concentration. *Note:* Steady-state conditions exist prior to $t = 0$.

(a)

(b)

## FIGURE 3–11

Non-steady-state response of CMFR to **(a)** step decrease from $C_0$ to 0 of influent $C_0$ reactive substance. **(b)** Effluent concentration.

(a)

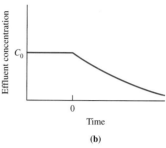

(b)

The behavior the CMFR described by Equation 3–36 is shown diagrammatically in Figure 3–10.

A step decrease in the influent concentration to zero ($C_{in} = 0$) in a balanced flow ($Q_{in} = Q_{out}$) CMFR operating under non-steady-state conditions with first-order decay of a reactive substance may be described by rewriting Equation 3–34

$$\frac{dM}{dt} = 0 - C_{out} Q_{out} - kC_{out}\Psi \tag{3–38}$$

where $M = C\Psi$. Because the volume is constant, we may divide through by $\Psi$ and simplify to obtain

$$\frac{dC}{dt} = \left(\frac{1}{\theta} + k\right)C_{out} \tag{3–39}$$

where $\theta = \Psi/Q$ as noted in Equation 3–27. The solution for $C_{out}$ is

$$C_{out} = C_0 \exp\left[-\left(\frac{1}{\theta} + k\right)t\right] \tag{3–40}$$

where $C_0$ is the effluent concentration at $t = 0$.

The concentration plots are shown in Figure 3–11.

**PFR.** Pipes and long narrow rivers approximate the ideal conditions of a PFR. Biological treatment in municipal wastewater treatment plants is often conducted in long narrow tanks that may be modeled as a PFR.

A step change in the influent concentration of a conservative substance in a plug-flow reactor results in an identical step change in the effluent concentration at a time equal to the theoretical detention time in the reactor as shown in Figure 3–12.

## FIGURE 3–12

Response of a PFR to **(a)** a step increase in the influent concentration of a conservative substance. **(b)** Effluent concentration.

(a)

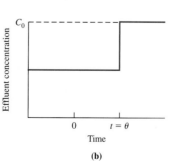

(b)

## FIGURE 3–13

Response of a PFR to **(a)** a step increase in the influent concentration of a reactive substance. **(b)** Effluent concentration.

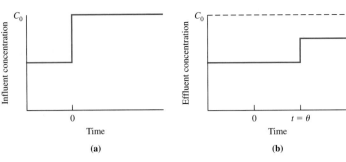

## FIGURE 3–14

Passage of a pulse change in influent concentration of a conservative substance through a PFR. $u$ is the linear velocity of the fluid through the PFR.

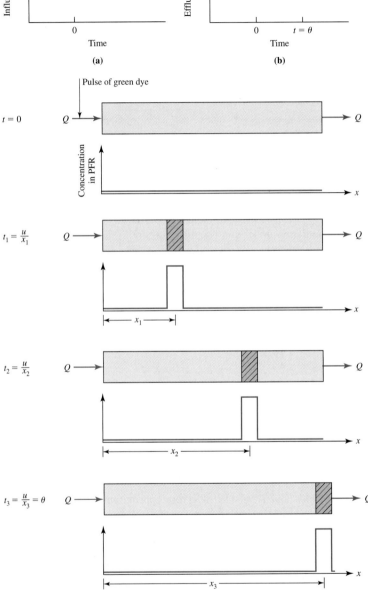

Equation 3–21 is a solution to the mass-balance equation for a steady-state first-order reaction in a PFR. The concentration plot for a step change in the influent concentration is shown in Figure 3–13.

A pulse entering a PFR travels as a discrete element as illustrated in Figure 3–14 for a pulse of green dye. The passage of the pulse through the PFR and the plots of concentration with distance along the PFR are also shown.

**Reactor Comparison.** Although first-order reactions are common in environmental systems, other reaction orders may be more appropriate. Tables 3–1 and 3–2 compare the reactor types for zero-, first-, and second-order reactions.

**TABLE 3–1** — Comparison of Steady-state Mean Retention Times for Decay Reactions of Different Order[a]

| Reaction Order | $r$ | Equations for Mean Retention Times ($\theta$) | | |
| --- | --- | --- | --- | --- |
| | | Ideal Batch | Ideal Plug Flow | Ideal CMFR |
| Zero[b] | $-k$ | $\dfrac{C_0}{k}$ | $\dfrac{(C_0 - C_t)}{k}$ | $\dfrac{(C_0 - C_t)}{k}$ |
| First | $-kC$ | $\dfrac{1}{k}$ | $\dfrac{\ln(C_0/C_t)}{k}$ | $\dfrac{(C_0/C_t) - 1}{k}$ |
| Second | $-2kC^2$ | $\dfrac{1}{2kC_0}$ | $\dfrac{(C_0/C_t) - 1}{2kC_0}$ | $\dfrac{(C_0/C_t) - 1}{2kC_t}$ |

[a]$C_0$ = initial concentration or influent concentration; $C_t$ = final condition or effluent concentration.
[b]Expressions are valid for $k\theta \le C_0$; otherwise $C_t = 0$.

**TABLE 3–2** — Comparison of Steady-state Performance for Decay Reactions of Different Order[a]

| Reaction Order | $r$ | Equations for $C_t$ | | |
| --- | --- | --- | --- | --- |
| | | Ideal Batch | Ideal Plug Flow | Ideal CMFR |
| Zero[b] $t \le C_0/k$ | $-k$ | $C_0 - kt$ | $C_0 - k\theta$ | $C_0 - k\theta$ |
| $t > C_0/k$ | | 0 | | |
| First | $-kC$ | $C_0[\exp(-kt)]$ | $C_0[\exp(-k\theta)]$ | $\dfrac{C_0}{1 + k\theta}$ |
| Second | $-2kC^2$ | $\dfrac{C_0}{1 + 2ktC_0}$ | $\dfrac{C_0}{1 + 2k\theta C_0}$ | $\dfrac{(8k\theta C_0 + 1)^{1/2} - 1}{4k\theta}$ |

[a]$C_0$ = initial concentration or influent concentration; $C_t$ = final condition or effluent concentration.
[b]Time conditions are for ideal batch reactor only.

**EXAMPLE 3–10**

A chemical degrades in a flow-balanced, steady-state CMFR according to first-order reaction kinetics. The upstream concentration of the chemical is $10 \ \text{mg} \cdot \text{L}^{-1}$ and the downstream concentration is $2 \ \text{mg} \cdot \text{L}^{-1}$. Water is being treated at a rate of $29 \ \text{m}^3 \cdot \text{min}^{-1}$. The volume of the tank is $580 \ \text{m}^3$. What is the rate of decay? What is the rate constant?

**Solution**

From Equation 3–11, we note that for a first-order reaction, the rate of decay, $r = -kC$. To find the rate of decay, we must solve Equation 3–34 for $kC$ to determine the reaction rate.

$$\frac{dM}{dt} = C_{\text{in}} Q_{\text{in}} - C_{\text{out}} Q_{\text{out}} - kC_{\text{out}} \Psi$$

For steady-state there is no mass accumulation, so $dM/dt = 0$. Because the reactor is flow-balanced, $Q_{\text{in}} = Q_{\text{out}} = 29 \ \text{m}^3 \cdot \text{min}^{-1}$. The mass balance equation may be rewritten

$$kC_{\text{out}} \Psi = C_{\text{in}} Q_{\text{in}} - C_{\text{out}} Q_{\text{out}}$$

Solving for the reaction rate, we obtain

$$r = kC = \frac{C_{\text{in}} Q_{\text{in}} - C_{\text{out}} Q_{\text{out}}}{\Psi}$$

$$= kC = \frac{(10 \ \text{mg} \cdot \text{L}^{-1})(29 \ \text{m}^3 \cdot \text{min}^{-1}) - (2 \ \text{mg} \cdot \text{L}^{-1})(29 \ \text{m}^3 \cdot \text{min}^{-1})}{580 \ \text{m}^3} = 0.4 \ \text{mg} \cdot \text{L}^{-1} \cdot \text{min}^{-1}$$

The rate constant, $k$, can be determined using the equations given in Table 3–1. For a first-order reaction in a CMFR

$$\theta = \frac{1}{k[(C_0/C_t) - 1]}$$

The mean hydraulic detention time ($\theta$) is

$$\theta = \frac{\mathbb{V}}{Q} = \frac{580 \text{ m}^3}{29 \text{ m}^3 \cdot \text{min}^{-1}} = 20 \text{ min}$$

Solving the equation from the table for the rate constant, $k$, we get

$$k = \frac{(C_0/C_t) - 1}{\theta}$$

and

$$k = \frac{(10 \text{ mg} \cdot \text{L}^{-1}/2 \text{ mg} \cdot \text{L}^{-1}) - 1}{20 \text{ min}} = 0.20 \text{ min}^{-1}$$

**Reactor Design.**  Volume is major design parameter in reactor design. In general, the influent concentration of material, the flow rate into the reactor, and the desired effluent concentration are known. As noted in Equation 3–27, the volume is directly related to the theoretical detention time and the flow rate into the reactor. Thus, the volume can be determined if the theoretical detention time can be determined. The equations in Table 3–1 may be used to determine the theoretical detention time if the decay rate constant, $k$, is available. The rate constant must be determined from the literature or laboratory experiments.

## 3–4  ENERGY BALANCES

### First Law of Thermodynamics

The **first law of thermodynamics** states that (without nuclear reaction) energy can be neither created nor destroyed. As with the law of conservation of matter, it does not mean that the form of the energy does not change. For example, the chemical energy in coal can be changed to heat and electrical power. **Energy** is defined as the capacity to do useful work. **Work** is done by a force acting on a body through a distance. One **joule** (J) is the work done by a constant force of one newton when the body on which the force is exerted moves a distance of one meter in the direction of the force. **Power** is the rate of doing work or the rate of expanding energy. The first law may be expressed as

$$Q_H = U_2 - U_1 + W \tag{3–41}$$

where $Q_H$ = heat absorbed (in kJ)
  $U_1, U_2$ = internal energy (or thermal energy) of the system in states 1 and 2 (in kJ)
  $W$ = work (in kJ)

### Fundamentals

**Thermal Units of Energy.**  Energy has many forms, among which are thermal, mechanical, kinetic, potential, electrical, and chemical. Thermal units were invented when heat was considered a substance (caloric), and the units are consistent with conservation of a quantity of substance. Subsequently, we have learned that energy is not a substance but mechanical energy of a particular form. With this in mind we will still use the common metric thermal unit of energy, the calorie.* One **calorie** (cal) is the amount of energy required to raise the temperature of one gram of water from 14.5°C to 15.5°C. In SI units 4.186 J = 1 cal.

The **specific heat** of a substance is the quantity of heat required to increase a unit mass of the substance one degree. Specific heat is expressed in metric units as $kcal \cdot kg^{-1} \cdot K$ and in SI units as $kJ \cdot kg^{-1} \cdot K$ where K is kelvins and 1 K = 1°C.

**Enthalpy** is a thermodynamic property of a material that depends on temperature, pressure, and the composition of the material. It is defined as

$$H = U + P\forall \tag{3-42}$$

where $H$ = enthalpy (in kJ)
$\quad U$ = internal energy (or thermal energy) (in kJ)
$\quad P$ = pressure (in kPa)
$\quad \forall$ = volume (in $m^3$)

Think of enthalpy as a combination of thermal energy ($U$) and flow energy ($P\forall$). Flow energy should not be confused with kinetic energy ($\frac{1}{2}Mv^2$). Historically, $H$ has been referred to as a system's "heat content." Because *heat* is correctly defined only in terms of energy transfer across a boundary, this is not considered a precise thermodynamic description and enthalpy is the preferred term.

When a non-phase-change process[†] occurs without a change in volume, a change in internal energy is defined as

$$\Delta U = Mc_v\Delta T \tag{3-43}$$

where $\Delta U$ = change in internal energy
$\quad M$ = mass
$\quad c_v$ = specific heat at constant volume
$\quad \Delta T$ = change in temperature

When a non-phase-change process occurs without a change in pressure, a change in enthalpy is defined as

$$\Delta H = Mc_p\Delta T \tag{3-44}$$

where $\Delta H$ = enthalpy change
$\quad c_p$ = specific heat at constant pressure

Equations 3–43 and 3–44 assume that the specific heat is constant over the range of temperature ($\Delta T$). Solids and liquids are nearly incompressible and therefore do virtually no work. The change in $P\forall$ is zero, making the changes in $H$ and $U$ identical. Thus, for solids and liquids, we can generally assume $c_v = c_p$ and $\Delta U = \Delta H$, so the change in energy stored in a system is

$$\Delta H = Mc_v\Delta T \tag{3-45}$$

Specific heat capacities for some common substances are listed in Table 3–3.

When a substance changes **phase** (i.e., it is transformed from solid to liquid or liquid to gas), energy is absorbed or released without a change in temperature. The energy required to cause a phase change of a unit mass from a solid to a liquid at constant pressure is called the **latent heat of fusion** or **enthalpy of fusion.** The energy required to cause a phase change of a unit mass from a liquid to a gas at constant pressure is called the **latent heat of vaporization** or **enthalpy of vaporization.** The same amounts of energy are released in condensing the vapor and freezing the liquid. For water the enthalpy of fusion at 0°C is 333 $kJ \cdot kg^{-1}$ and the enthalpy of vaporization is 2257 $kJ \cdot kg^{-1}$ at 100°C.

---

*In discussing food metabolism, physiologists also use the term *Calorie*. However, the food Calorie is equivalent to a *kilocalorie* in the metric system. We will use the units cal or kcal throughout this text.
[†]Non-phase-change means, for example, water is not converted to steam.

| **TABLE 3–3** | Specific Heat Capacities for Common Substances | |
|---|---|---|
| | **Substance** | **$c_p$ (kJ · kg$^{-1}$ · K$^{-1}$)** |
| | Air (293.15 K) | 1.00 |
| | Aluminum | 0.95 |
| | Beef | 3.22 |
| | Cement, Portland | 1.13 |
| | Concrete | 0.93 |
| | Copper | 0.39 |
| | Corn | 3.35 |
| | Dry soil | 0.84 |
| | Human being | 3.47 |
| | Ice | 2.11 |
| | Iron, cast | 0.50 |
| | Steel | 0.50 |
| | Poultry | 3.35 |
| | Steam (373.15 K) | 2.01 |
| | Water (288.15 K) | 4.186 |
| | Wood | 1.76 |

*Source:* Adapted from Hudson, R. G. *The Engineers' Manual.* John Wiley and Sons, New York (1959), p. 314; Guyton, A. C. *Textbook of Medical Physiology,* 2nd ed. W. B. Saunders, Philadelphia (1961), pp. 920–921, 950–953; Salvato, J. A., Jr. *Environmental Engineering and Sanitation,* 2nd ed. Wiley-Interscience, New York (1972), pp. 598–599; and Masters, G. M. *Introduction to Environmental Engineering and Science.* Prentice Hall, Upper Saddle River, NJ (1998), p. 30.

**EXAMPLE 3–11**

Standard physiology texts [1] report that a person weighing 70.0 kg requires approximately 2000 kcal for simple existence, such as eating and sitting in a chair. Approximately 61% of all the energy in the foods we eat becomes heat during the process of formation of the energy-carrying molecule adenosine triphosphate (ATP) [1]. Still more energy becomes heat as it is transferred to functional systems of the cells. The functioning of the cells releases still more energy so that ultimately "all the energy released by metabolic processes eventually becomes heat" [1]. Some of this heat is used to maintain the body at a normal temperature of 37°C. What fraction of the 2000 kcal is used to maintain the body temperature at 37°C if the room temperature is 20°C? Assume the specific heat of a human is 3.47 kJ · kg$^{-1}$ · K$^{-1}$.

Solution

The change in energy stored in the body is

$$\Delta H = (70 \text{ kg})(3.47 \text{ kJ} \cdot \text{kg}^{-1} \cdot \text{K}^{-1})(37°C - 20°C) = 4129.30 \text{ kJ}$$

Converting the 2000 kcal to kJ

$$(2000 \text{ kcal})(4.186 \text{ kJ} \cdot \text{kcal}^{-1}) = 8372.0 \text{ kJ}$$

So the fraction of energy used to maintain temperature is approximately

$$\frac{4129.30 \text{ kJ}}{8372.0 \text{ kJ}} = 0.49, \text{ or about } 50\%$$

The remaining energy must be removed if the body temperature is not to rise above normal. The mechanisms of removing energy by heat transfer are discussed in the following sections.

**Energy Balances.**  If we say that the first law of thermodynamics is analogous to the law of conservation of matter, then energy is analogous to matter because it too can be "balanced." The simplest form of the energy balance equation is

Loss of enthalpy of hot body = gain of enthalpy by cold body  (3–46)

**EXAMPLE 3–12**  The Rhett Butler Peach, Co. dips the peaches in boiling water (100°C) to remove the skin (a process called blanching) before canning them. The wastewater from this process is high in organic matter and it must be treated before disposal. The treatment process is a biological process that operates at 20°C. Thus, the wastewater must be cooled to 20°C before disposal. Forty cubic meters (40 m³) of wastewater is discharged to a concrete tank at a temperature of 20°C to allow it to cool. Assuming no losses to the surroundings, that the concrete tank has a mass of 42,000 kg and a specific heat capacity of 0.93 kJ · kg⁻¹ · K⁻¹, what is the equilibrium temperature of the concrete tank and the wastewater?

Solution  Assuming the density of the water is 1000 kg · m⁻³, the loss in enthalpy of the boiling water is

$$\Delta H = (1000 \text{ kg} \cdot \text{m}^{-3})(40 \text{ m}^3)(4.186 \text{ kJ} \cdot \text{kg}^{-1} \cdot \text{K}^{-1})(373.15 - T) = 62,480,236 - 167,440T$$

where the absolute temperature is 273.15 + 100 = 373.15 K.

The gain in enthalpy of the concrete tank is

$$\Delta H = (42,000 \text{ kg})(0.93 \text{ kJ} \cdot \text{kg}^{-1} \cdot \text{K}^{-1})(T - 293.15) = 39,060T - 11,450,439$$

The equilibrium temperature is found by setting the two equations equal and solving for the temperature.

$$(\Delta H)_{\text{water}} = (\Delta H)_{\text{concrete}}$$

$$62,480,236 - 167,440T = 39,060T - 11,450,439$$

$$T = 358 \text{ K or } 85°C$$

This is not very close to the desired temperature without considering other losses to the surroundings. Convective and radiative heat losses discussed later on also play a role in reducing the temperature, but a cooling tower may be required to achieve 20°C.

For an open system, a more complete energy balance equation is

Net change in energy = energy of mass entering system − energy of mass leaving system

± energy flow into or out of system  (3–47)

For many environmental systems the time dependence of the change in energy (i.e., the rate of energy change) must be taken into account. Equation 3–47 may be written to account for time dependence as follows:

$$\frac{dH}{dt} = \frac{d(H)_{\text{mass in}}}{dt} + \frac{d(H)_{\text{mass out}}}{dt} \pm \frac{d(H)_{\text{energy flow}}}{dt}$$  (3–48)

If we consider a region of space where a fluid flows in at a rate of $dM/dt$ and also flows out at a rate of $dM/dt$, then the change in enthalpy due to this flow is

$$\frac{dH}{dt} = c_{\text{p}}M\frac{dT}{dt} + c_{\text{p}}T\frac{dM}{dt}$$  (3–49)

where $dM/dt$ is the mass flow rate (e.g., in kg/s) and $\Delta T$ is the difference in temperature of the mass in the system and the mass outside of the system.

Note that Equations 3–47 and 3–48 differ from the mass-balance equation in that there is an additional term: "energy flow." This is an important difference for everything from photosynthesis (in which radiative energy from the sun is converted into plant material) to heat exchangers (in which chemical energy from fuel passes through the walls of the tubes of the heat exchanger to heat a fluid inside). The energy flow into (or out of) the system may be by conduction, convection, or radiation.

**Conduction.** Conduction is the transfer of heat through a material by molecular diffusion due to a temperature gradient. Fourier's law provides an expression for calculating energy flow by conduction.

$$\frac{dH}{dt} = -h_{tc}A\frac{dT}{dx}$$  (3–50)

where $dH/dt$ = rate of change of enthalpy (in $kJ \cdot s^{-1}$ or kW)
   $h_{tc}$ = thermal conductivity (in $kJ \cdot s^{-1} \cdot m^{-1} \cdot K^{-1}$ or $kW \cdot m^{-1} \cdot K^{-1}$)
   $A$ = surface area (in $m^2$)
   $dT/dx$ = change in temperature through a distance (in $K \cdot m^{-1}$)

Note that $1\ kJ \cdot s^{-1} = 1\ kW$. The average values for thermal conductivity for some common materials are given in Table 3–4.

**Convection.** Forced convective heat transfer is the transfer of thermal energy by means of large-scale fluid motion such as a flowing river or aquifer or the wind blowing. The convective heat transfer between a fluid at a temperature, $T_f$, and a solid surface at a temperature $T_s$, can be described by Equation 3–51.

$$\frac{dH}{dt} = h_c A(T_f - T_s)$$  (3–51)

where $h_c$ = convective heat transfer coefficient (in $kJ \cdot s^{-1} \cdot m^{-2} \cdot K^{-1}$)
   $A$ = surface area (in $m^2$)

| TABLE 3–4 | Thermal Conductivity for Some Common Materials[a] | |
|---|---|---|
| | **Material** | $h_{tc}$ (W · m$^{-1}$ · K$^{-1}$) |
| | Air | 0.023 |
| | Aluminum | 221 |
| | Brick, fired clay | 0.9 |
| | Concrete | 2 |
| | Copper | 393 |
| | Glass-wool insulation | 0.0377 |
| | Steel, mild | 45.3 |
| | Wood | 0.126 |

[a]Note that the units are equivalent to $J \cdot s^{-1} \cdot m^{-1} \cdot K^{-1}$

*Source:* Adapted from Kuehn, T. H., J. W. Ramsey, J. L. Threkeld. *Thermal Environmental Engineering.* Prentice Hall, Upper Saddle River, NJ (1998), pp. 425–427; Shortley, G., D. Williams. *Elements of Physics.* Prentice Hall, Englewood Cliffs, NJ (1955), p. 290.

## FIGURE 3–15

Sinusoidal Waves

The wavelength (λ) is the distance between two peaks or troughs.

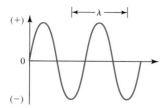

**Radiation.**  Although both conduction and convection require a medium to transport energy, radiant energy is transported by electromagnetic radiation. The radiative transfer of heat involves two processes: the absorption of radiant energy by an object and the radiation of energy by that object. The change in enthalpy due to the radiative heat transfer is the energy absorbed minus the energy emitted and can be expressed as

$$\frac{dH}{dt} = E_{abs} - E_{emitted} \tag{3-52}$$

Thermal radiation is emitted when an electron moves from a higher energy state to a lower one. Radiant energy is transmitted in the form of waves. Waves are cyclical or **sinusoidal** as shown in Figure 3–15. The waves may be characterized by their wavelength ($\lambda$) or their frequency ($\nu$). The wavelength is the distance between successive peaks or troughs. Frequency and wavelength are related by the speed of light ($c$).

$$c = \lambda \nu \tag{3-53}$$

Planck's law relates the energy emitted to the frequency of the emitted radiation.

$$E = h\nu \tag{3-54}$$

where $h$ = Planck's constant = $6.63 \times 10^{-34}$ J · s

The electromagnetic wave emitted when an electron makes a transition between two energy levels is called a **photon.** When the frequency is high (small wavelengths), the energy emitted is high. Planck's law also applies to the absorption of a photon of energy. A molecule can only absorb radiant energy if the wavelength of radiation corresponds to the difference between two of its energy levels.

Every object emits thermal radiation. The amount of energy radiated depends on the wavelength, surface area, and the absolute temperature of the object. The maximum amount of radiation that an object can emit at a given temperature is called **blackbody radiation.** An object that radiates the maximum possible intensity for every wavelength is called a **blackbody.** The term *blackbody* has no reference to the color of the body. A blackbody can also be characterized by the fact that all radiant energy reaching its surface is absorbed.

Actual objects do not emit or absorb as much radiation as a blackbody. The ratio of the amount of radiation an object emits to that a blackbody would emit is called the emissivity ($\varepsilon$). The energy spectrum of the sun resembles that of a blackbody at 6000 K. At normal atmospheric temperatures, the emissivity of dry soil and woodland is approximately 0.90. Water and snow have emissivities of about 0.95. A human body, regardless of pigmentation, has an emissivity of approximately 0.97 [1]. The ratio of the amount of energy an object absorbs to that which a blackbody would absorb is called absorptivity ($\alpha$). For most surfaces, the absorptivity is the same value as the emissivity.

Integration of Planck's equation over all wavelengths yields the radiant energy of a blackbody.

$$E_B = \sigma T^4 \tag{3-55}$$

where $E_B$ = blackbody emission rate (in W · m$^{-2}$)
  $\sigma$ = Stephan–Boltzmann constant = $5.67 \times 10^{-8}$ W · m$^{-2}$ · K$^{-4}$
  $T$ = absolute temperature (in K)

For other than blackbodies, the right-hand side of the equation is multiplied by the emissivity.

For a body with an emissivity $\varepsilon$ and an absorptivity $\alpha$ at a temperature $T_b$ receiving radiation from its environment which is a blackbody of temperature $T_{environ}$, we can express the change in enthalpy as

$$\frac{dH}{dt} = A\left(\varepsilon\sigma T_b^4 - \alpha\sigma T_{environ}^4\right) \tag{3–56}$$

where $A$ = surface area of the body (in m²)

The solution to thermal radiation problems is highly complex because of the "re-radiation" of surrounding objects. In addition the rate of radiative cooling will change with time as the difference in temperatures changes; initially the change per unit of time will be large because of the large difference in temperature. As the temperatures approach each other the rate of change will slow. In the following problem we use an arithmetic average temperature as a first approximation to the actual average temperature.

**EXAMPLE 3–13**   As mentioned in Example 3–12, heat losses due to convection and radiation were not considered. Using the following assumptions, estimate how long it will take for the wastewater and concrete tank to come to the desired temperature (20°C) if radiative cooling and convective cooling are considered. Assume that the average temperature of the water and concrete tank while cooling between 85°C (their combined temperature from Example 3–12) and 20°C is 52.5°C. Also assume that the mean radiant temperature of the surroundings is 20°C, that both the cooling tank and the surrounding environment radiate uniformly in all directions, that their emissivities are the same (0.90), that the surface area of the concrete tank including the open water surface is 56 m², and that the convective heat transfer coefficient is $13 \; J \cdot s^{-1} \cdot m^2 \cdot K^{-1}$.

Solution   The required change in enthalpy for the wastewater is

$$\Delta H = (1000 \; kg \cdot m^{-3})(40 \; m^3)(4.186 \; kJ \cdot kg^{-1} \cdot K^{-1})(325.65 - 293.15) = 5{,}441{,}800 \; kJ$$

where the absolute temperature of the wastewater is $273.15 + 52.5 = 325.65$ K.
The required change in enthalpy of the concrete tank is

$$\Delta H = (42{,}000 \; kg)(0.93 \; kJ \cdot kg^{-1} \cdot K^{-1})(325.65 - 293.15) = 1{,}269{,}450 \; kJ$$

For a total of $5{,}441{,}800 + 1{,}269{,}450 = 6{,}711{,}250$ kJ, or 6,711,250,000 J
In estimating the time to cool down by radiation alone, we note that the emissivities are the same for the tank and the environment and that the net radiation is the result of the difference in absolute temperatures.

$$E_B = \varepsilon\sigma \left(T_c^4 - T_{environ}^4\right)$$

$$= \varepsilon\sigma T^4 = (0.90)(5.67 \times 10^{-8} \; W \cdot m^{-2} \cdot K^{-4})[(273.15 + 52.5)^4 - (273.15 + 20)^4]$$

$$= 197 \; W \cdot m^{-2}$$

The rate of heat loss is

$$(197 \; W \cdot m^{-2})(56 \; m^2) = 11{,}032 \; W, \text{ or } 11{,}032 \; J \cdot s^{-1}$$

Using Equation 3–51, the convective cooling rate may be estimated.

$$\frac{dH}{dt} = h_c A(T_f - T_s)$$

$$= (13 \; J \cdot s^{-1} \cdot m^{-2} \cdot K^{-1})(56 \; m^2)[(273.15 + 52.5) - (273.15 + 20)]$$

$$= 23{,}660 \; J \cdot s^{-1}$$

The time to cool down is then

$$\frac{6,711,250,000 \text{ J}}{11,032 \text{ J} \cdot \text{s}^{-1} + 23,660 \text{ J} \cdot \text{s}^{-1}} = 193,452 \text{ s, or } 2.24 \text{ days}$$

This is quite a long time. If land is not at a premium and several tanks can be built, then the time may not be a relevant consideration. Alternatively, other options must be considered to reduce the time. One alternative is to utilize conductive heat transfer and build a heat exchanger. The heat exchanger could be used to heat the incoming water needed in the blanching process.

**Overall Heat Transfer.**  Most practical heat transfer problems involve multiple heat transfer modes. For these cases, it is convenient to use an overall heat transfer coefficient that incorporates multiple modes. The form of the heat transfer equation then becomes

$$\frac{dH}{dt} = h_0 A (\Delta T) \tag{3-57}$$

where $h_0$ = overall heat transfer coefficient (in $\text{kJ} \cdot \text{s}^{-1} \cdot \text{m}^{-2} \cdot \text{K}^{-1}$)
  $\Delta T$ = temperature difference that drives the heat transfer (in K)

Among their many responsibilities, environmental scientists (often with a job title of environmental sanitarian) are responsible for checking food safety in restaurants. This includes ensuring proper refrigeration of perishable foods. The following problem is an example of one of the items, namely the electrical rating of the refrigerator, that might be investigated in a case of food poisoning at a family gathering.

**EXAMPLE 3-14**  In evaluating a possible food "poisoning," Sam and Janet Evening evaluated the required electrical energy input to cool food purchased for a family reunion. The family purchased 12 kg of hamburger, 6 kg of chicken, 5 kg of corn, and 20 L of soda pop. They have a refrigerator in the garage in which they stored the food until the reunion. The specific heats of the food products (in $\text{kJ} \cdot \text{kg}^{-1} \cdot \text{K}^{-1}$) are hamburger: 3.22; chicken: 3.35; corn: 3.35; beverages: 4.186. The refrigerator dimensions are 0.70 m × 0.75 m × 1.00 m. The overall heat transfer coefficient for the refrigerator is $0.43 \text{ J} \cdot \text{s}^{-1} \cdot \text{m}^{-2} \cdot \text{K}^{-1}$. The temperature in the garage is 30°C. The food must be kept at 4°C to prevent spoilage. Assume that it takes 2 h for the food to reach a temperature of 4°C, that the meat has risen to 20°C in the time it takes to get it home from the store, and that the soda pop and corn have risen to 30°C. What electrical energy input (in kilowatts) is required during the first 2 h the food is in the refrigerator? What is the energy input required to maintain the temperature for the second 2 h. Assume the refrigerator interior is at 4°C when the food is placed in it and that the door is not opened during the 4-h period. Ignore the energy required to heat the air in the refrigerator, and assume that all the electrical energy is used to remove heat. If the refrigerator is rated at 875 W, is poor refrigeration a part of the food poisoning problem?

**Solution**  The energy balance equation is of the form

$$\frac{dH}{dt} = \frac{d(H)_{\text{mass in}}}{dt} + \frac{d(H)_{\text{mass out}}}{dt} \pm \frac{d(H)_{\text{energy flow}}}{dt}$$

where $dH/dt$ = the enthalpy change required to balance the input energy
  $d(H)_{\text{mass in}}$ = change in enthalpy due to the food
  $d(H)_{\text{energy flow}}$ = the change in enthalpy to maintain the temperature at 4°C

There is no $d(H)_{\text{mass out}}$.
  Begin by computing the change in enthalpy for the food products.

### Hamburger

$$\Delta H = (12 \text{ kg})(3.22 \text{ kJ} \cdot \text{kg}^{-1} \cdot \text{K}^{-1})(20°C - 4°C) = 618.24 \text{ kJ}$$

### Chicken

$$\Delta H = (6 \text{ kg})(3.35 \text{ kJ} \cdot \text{kg}^{-1} \cdot \text{K}^{-1})(20°C - 4°C) = 321.6 \text{ kJ}$$

### Corn

$$\Delta H = (5 \text{ kg})(3.35 \text{ kJ} \cdot \text{kg}^{-1} \cdot \text{K}^{-1})(30°C - 4°C) = 435.5 \text{ kJ}$$

### Beverages
Assuming that 20 L = 20 kg

$$\Delta H = (20 \text{ kg})(4.186 \text{ kJ} \cdot \text{kg}^{-1} \cdot \text{K}^{-1})(30°C - 4°C) = 2176.72 \text{ kJ}$$

The total change in enthalpy = 618.24 kJ + 321.6 kJ + 435.5 kJ + 2176.72 kJ = 3,552.06 kJ

Based on a 2-h period to cool the food, the rate of enthalpy change is

$$\frac{3,552.06 \text{ kJ}}{(2 \text{ h})(3600 \text{ s} \cdot \text{h}^{-1})} = 0.493, \text{ or } 0.50 \text{ kJ} \cdot \text{s}^{-1}$$

The surface area of the refrigerator is

0.70 m × 1.00 m × 2 = 1.40 m$^2$

0.75 m × 1.00 m × 2 = 1.50 m$^2$

0.75 m × 0.70 m × 2 = 1.05 m$^2$

for a total of 3.95 m$^2$

The heat loss through walls of the refrigerator is then

$$\frac{dH}{dt} = (4.3 \times 10^{-4} \text{ kJ} \cdot \text{s}^{-1} \cdot \text{m}^{-2} \cdot \text{K}^{-1})(3.95 \text{ m}^2)(30°C - 4°C) = 0.044 \text{ kJ} \cdot \text{s}^{-1}$$

In the first 2 h, the electrical energy required is 0.044 kJ · s$^{-1}$ + 0.50 kJ · s$^{-1}$ = 0.54 kJ · s$^{-1}$. Because 1 W = 1 J · s$^{-1}$, the electrical requirement is 0.54 kW, or 540 W. It does not appear that the refrigerator is part of the food poisoning problem.

In the second 2 h, the electrical requirement drops to 0.044 kW, or 44 W.

Note that at the beginning of this example we put "poisoning" in quotation marks because illness from food spoilage may be the result of microbial infection, which is not poisoning in the same sense as, for example, that caused by arsenic.

The result of Example 3–14 is based on an assumption of 100% efficiency in converting electrical energy to refrigeration. This is, of course, not possible and leads us to the second law of thermodynamics.

### Second Law of Thermodynamics

The second law of thermodynamics states that energy flows from a region of higher concentration to one of lesser concentration, not the reverse, and that the quality degrades as it is transformed. All natural, spontaneous processes may be studied in the light of the second law, and in all such cases a particular one-sidedness is found. Thus, heat always flows spontaneously from a hotter body to a colder one; gases seep through an opening spontaneously from a region of higher pressure to a region of lower pressure. The second law recognizes that order becomes disorder, that randomness increases, and that structure and concentrations tend to disappear. It foretells

## FIGURE 3-16

Schematic flow diagram of a Carnot heat engine. (*Source:* J. A. Richards et al. *Modern University Physics.* Addison-Wesley, Reading, MA 1960.)

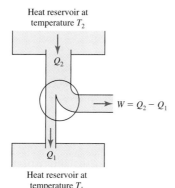

Heat reservoir at temperature $T_2$

$Q_2$

$W = Q_2 - Q_1$

$Q_1$

Heat reservoir at temperature $T_1$

elimination of gradients, equalization of electrical and chemical potential, and leveling of contrasts in heat and molecular motion unless work is done to prevent it. Thus, gases and liquids left by themselves tend to mix, not to unmix; rocks weather and crumble; iron rusts.

The degradation of energy as it is transformed means that enthalpy is wasted in the transformation. The fractional part of the heat which is wasted is termed unavailable energy. A mathematical expression called the **change in entropy** is used to express this unavailable energy.

$$\Delta s = M c_p \ln \frac{T_2}{T_1} \tag{3-58}$$

where $\Delta s$ = change in entropy
$M$ = mass
$c_p$ = specific heat at constant pressure
$T_1, T_2$ = initial and final absolute temperature
$\ln$ = natural logarithm

By the second law, entropy increases in any transformation of energy from a region of higher concentration to a lesser one. The higher the degree of disorder, the higher the entropy. Degraded energy is entropy, dissipated as waste products and heat.

Efficiency ($\eta$) or, perhaps, lack of efficiency is another expression of the second law. Sadi Carnot (1824) was the first to approach the problem of the efficiency of a heat engine (e.g., a steam engine) in a truly fundamental manner. He described a theoretical engine, now called a Carnot engine. Figure 3–16 is a simplified representation of a Carnot engine. In his engine, a material expands against a piston that is periodically brought back to its initial condition so that in any one cycle the change in internal energy of this material is zero, that is $U_2 - U_1 = 0$, and the first law of thermodynamics (Equation 3–41) reduces to

$$W = Q_2 - Q_1 \tag{3-59}$$

where $Q_1$ = heat rejected or exhaust heat
$Q_2$ = heat input

Thermal efficiency is the ratio of work output to heat input. The output is mechanical work. The exhaust heat is not considered part of the output.

$$\eta = \frac{W}{Q_2} \tag{3-60}$$

where $W$ = work output
$Q_2$ = heat input

or, using Equation 3–59

$$\eta = \frac{Q_2 - Q_1}{Q_2} \tag{3-61}$$

**FIGURE 3–17**

Schematic flow diagram of a refrigerator. (*Source:* J. A. Richards et al. *Modern University Physics.* Addison-Wesley, Reading, MA 1960).

$Q_2 = W + Q_1$

Carnot's analysis revealed that the most efficient engine will have an efficiency of

$$\eta_{max} = 1 - \frac{T_1}{T_2} \tag{3-62}$$

where the temperatures are absolute temperatures (in kelvins). This equation implies that maximum efficiency is achieved when the value of $T_2$ is as high as possible and the value for $T_1$ is as low as possible.

A refrigerator may be considered to be a heat engine operated in reverse (Figure 3–17). From an environmental point of view, the best refrigeration cycle is one that removes the greatest amount of heat ($Q_1$) from the refrigerator for the least expenditure of mechanical work. Thus, we use the **coefficient of performance** rather than efficiency.

$$\text{C.O.P.} = \frac{Q}{W} = \frac{Q_1}{Q_2 - Q_1} \tag{3-63}$$

By analogy to the Carnot efficiency,

$$\text{C.O.P.} = \frac{T_1}{T_2 - T_1} \tag{3-64}$$

**EXAMPLE 3–15** What is the coefficient of performance of the refrigerator in Example 3–14?

Solution The C.O.P. is calculated directly from the temperatures.

$$\text{C.O.P.} = \frac{273.15 + 4}{[(273.15 + 30) - (273.15 + 4)]} = 10.7$$

Note that in contrast to the heat engine, the performance increases if the temperatures are close together.

## CHAPTER REVIEW

When you have completed studying the chapter, you should be able to do the following without the aid of your textbook or notes:

1. Define the law of conservation of matter (mass).
2. Explain the circumstances under which the law of conservation of matter is violated.
3. Draw a materials-balance diagram given the inputs, outputs, and accumulation or the relationship between the variables.
4. Define the following terms: rate, conservative pollutants, reactive chemicals, steady-state conditions, equilibrium, completely mixed systems, and plug-flow systems.
5. Explain why the effluent from a completely mixed system has the same concentration as the system itself.
6. Define the first law of thermodynamics and provide one example.
7. Define the second law of thermodynamics and provide one example.
8. Define energy, work, power, specific heat, phase change, enthalpy of fusion, enthalpy of evaporation, photon, and blackbody radiation.
9. Explain how the energy-balance equation differs from the materials-balance equation.
10. List the three mechanisms of heat transfer and explain how they differ.
11. Explain the relationship between energy transformation and entropy.

With the aid of this text you should be able to do the following:

1. Write and solve mass-balance equations for systems with and without transformation.
2. Write the mathematical expression for the decay of a substance by first-order kinetics with respect to the substance.
3. Solve first-order reaction problems.
4. Compute the change in enthalpy for a substance.
5. Solve heat transfer equations for conduction, convection, and radiation individually and in combination.
6. Write and solve energy balance equations.
7. Compute the change in entropy.
8. Compute the Carnot efficiency for a heat engine.
9. Compute the coefficient of performance for a refrigerator.

## PROBLEMS

**3-1** A sanitary landfill has available space of 16.2 ha at an average depth of 10 m. Seven hundred sixty-five (765) $m^3$ of solid waste is dumped at the site 5 days a week. This waste is compacted to twice its delivered density. Draw a mass-balance diagram and estimate the expected life of the landfill in years.

   **Answer:** 16.25, or 16 years

**3-2** Each month the Speedy Dry Cleaning Company buys one barrel (0.160 $m^3$) of dry cleaning fluid. Ninety percent of the fluid is lost to the atmosphere and 10% remains as residue to be disposed of. The density of the dry cleaning fluid is 1.5940 $g \cdot mL^{-1}$. Draw a mass-balance diagram and estimate the monthly mass emission rate to the atmosphere (in kilograms per month).

**3-3** The Rappahannock River near Warrenton, VA, has a flow rate of 3.00 $m^3 \cdot s^{-1}$. Tin Pot Run (a pristine stream) discharges into the Rappahannock at a flow rate of 0.05 $m^3 \cdot s^{-1}$. To study mixing of the stream and river, a conservative tracer is to be added to Tin Pot Run. If the instruments that measure the tracer can detect a concentration of 1.0 $mg \cdot L^{-1}$, what minimum concentration must be achieved in Tin Pot Run so that 1.0 $mg \cdot L^{-1}$ of tracer can be measured after the river and stream mix? Assume that the 1.0 $mg \cdot L^{-1}$ of tracer is to be measured after complete mixing of the stream and Rappahannock has been achieved and that no tracer is in Tin Pot Run or the Rappahannock above the point where the two streams mix. What mass rate (in kilograms per day) of tracer must be added to Tin Pot Run?

   **Answer:** 263.52, or 264 $kg \cdot day^{-1}$

**3-4** In water and wastewater treatment processes a filtration device may be used to remove water from the sludge formed by a precipitation reaction. The initial concentration of sludge from a softening reaction (Chapter 9) is 2% (20,000 $mg \cdot L^{-1}$) and the volume of sludge is 100 $m^3$. After filtration the sludge solids concentration is 35%. Assume that the sludge does not change density during filtration and that liquid removed from the sludge contains no sludge. Using the mass-balance method, determine the volume of sludge after filtration.

**3-5** To remove the solution containing metal from a part after metal plating the part is commonly rinsed with water. This rinse water is contaminated with metal and must be treated before discharge. The Shinny Metal Plating Co. uses the process flow diagram shown in Figure P-3-5. The plating solution contains 85 $g \cdot L^{-1}$

Figure P-3–5

of nickel. The parts drag out $0.05 \ \text{L} \cdot \text{min}^{-1}$ of plating solution into the rinse tank. The flow of rinse water into the rinse tank is $150 \ \text{L} \cdot \text{min}^{-1}$. Write the general mass-balance equation for the rinse tank and estimate the concentration of nickel in the wastewater stream that must be treated. Assume that the rinse tank is completely mixed and that no reactions take place in the rinse tank.

**Answer:** $C_n = 28.3$, or 28 mg $\cdot$ L$^{-1}$

**3-6**   Because the rinse water flow rate for a nickel plating bath (Problem 3–5) is quite high, it is proposed that the countercurrent rinse system shown in Figure P-3–6 be used to reduce the flow rate. Assuming that the $C_n$ concentration remains the same at 28 mg $\cdot$ L$^{-1}$, estimate the new flow rate. Assume that the rinse tank is completely mixed and that no reactions take place in the rinse tank.

*Figure P-3–6*

**3-7**   If biodegradable organic matter, oxygen, and microorganisms are placed in a closed bottle, the microorganisms will use the oxygen in the process of oxidizing the organic matter. The bottle may be treated as a batch reactor, and the decay of oxygen may be treated as a first-order reaction. Write the general mass-balance equation for the bottle. Using a computer spreadsheet program you have written, calculate and then plot the concentration of oxygen each day for a period of 5 days starting with a concentration of 8 mg $\cdot$ L$^{-1}$. Use a rate constant of 0.35 d$^{-1}$.

**Answer:** Day 1 = 5.64, or 5.6 mg $\cdot$ L$^{-1}$;   Day 2 = 3.97, or 4.0 mg $\cdot$ L$^{-1}$

**3-8**   In 1908, H. Chick reported an experiment in which he disinfected anthrax spores with a 5% solution of phenol [2]. The results of his experiment are tabulated here. Assuming the experiment was conducted in a completely mixed batch reactor, determine the decay rate constant for the die-off of anthrax.

| Concentration of survivors (number $\cdot$ mL$^{-1}$) | Time (min) |
|---|---|
| 398 | 0 |
| 251 | 30 |
| 158 | 60 |

**3-9**   The concept of *half-life* is used extensively in environmental engineering and science. For example, it is used to describe the decay of radioisotopes, elimination of poisons from people, self-cleaning of lakes, and the disappearance of pesticides from soil. Starting with the mass-balance equation, develop an expression that describes the half-life ($t_{1/2}$) of a substance in terms of the reaction rate constant, $k$, assuming the decay reaction takes place in a batch reactor.

**3-10**   If the initial concentration of a reactive substance in a batch reactor is 100%, determine the amount of substance remaining after 1, 2, 3, and 4 half-lives if the reaction rate constant is 6 months$^{-1}$.

**3-11**   Liquid hazardous wastes are blended in a CMFR to maintain a minimum energy content before burning them in a hazardous waste incinerator. The energy content of the waste currently being fed is 8.0 MJ $\cdot$ kg$^{-1}$ (megajoules per kilogram). A new waste is injected in the flow line into the CMFR. It has an energy content of 10.0 MJ $\cdot$ kg$^{-1}$. If the flow rate into and out of the 0.20 m$^3$ CMFR is 4.0 L $\cdot$ s$^{-1}$, how long will it take the effluent from the CMFR to reach an energy content of 9 MJ $\cdot$ kg$^{-1}$?

**Answer:** $t = 34.5$, or 35 s

**3-12** Repeat Problem 3-11 with a new waste having an energy content of 12 MJ $\cdot$ kg$^{-1}$ instead of 10 MJ $\cdot$ kg$^{-1}$.

**3-13** A bankrupt chemical firm has been taken over by new management. On the property they found a 20,000-m$^3$ brine pond containing 25,000 mg $\cdot$ L$^{-1}$ of salt. The new owners propose to flush the pond into their discharge pipe leading to the Atlantic Ocean, which has a salt concentration above 30,000 mg $\cdot$ L$^{-1}$. What flow rate of fresh water (in m$^3$ $\cdot$ s$^{-1}$) must they use to reduce the salt concentration in the pond to 500 mg $\cdot$ L$^{-1}$ within one year?

**Answer:** $Q = 0.0025$ m$^3$ $\cdot$ s$^{-1}$

**3-14** A 1900-m$^3$ water tower has been cleaned with a chlorine solution. The vapors of chlorine in the tower exceed allowable concentrations for the work crew to enter and finish repairs. If the chlorine concentration is 15 mg $\cdot$ m$^{-3}$ and the allowable concentration is 0.0015 mg $\cdot$ L$^{-1}$, how long must the workers vent the tank with clean air flowing at 2.35 m$^3$ $\cdot$ s$^{-1}$?

**3-15** A railroad tank car derails and ruptures. It discharges 380 m$^3$ of pesticide into the Mud Lake drain. As shown in Figure P-3-15, the drain flows into Mud Lake, which has a liquid volume of 40,000 m$^3$. The water in the creek has a velocity of 0.10 m $\cdot$ s$^{-1}$, and the distance from the spill site to the pond is 20 km. Assume that the spill is short enough to treat the injection of the pesticide as a pulse, that the pond behaves as a flow-balanced CMFR, and that the pesticide is nonreactive. Estimate the time for the pulse to reach the pond and the time it will take to flush 99% of the pesticide from the pond.

**Answer:** Time to reach the pond = 2.3 days   Time to flush = 21.3, or 21 days

*Figure P-3-15*

**3-16** During a snowstorm the fluoride feeder in North Bend runs out of feed solution. As shown in Figure P-3-16, the rapid mix tank is connected to a 5-km long distribution pipe. The flow rate into the rapid mix tank is 0.44 m$^3$ $\cdot$ s$^{-1}$, and the volume of the tank is 2.50 m$^3$. The velocity in the pipe is 0.17 m $\cdot$ s$^{-1}$. If the fluoride concentration in the rapid mix tank is 1.0 mg $\cdot$ L$^{-1}$ when the feed stops, how long until the concentration of fluoride is reduced to 0.01 mg $\cdot$ L$^{-1}$ at the end of the distribution pipe. The fluoride may be considered a nonreactive chemical.

*Figure P-3-16*

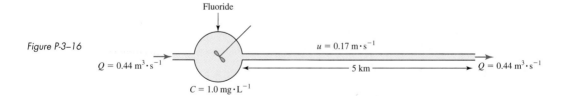

**3-17** A sewage lagoon that has a surface area of 10 ha and a depth of 1 m is receiving 8640 m$^3$ $\cdot$ d$^{-1}$ of sewage containing 100 mg $\cdot$ L$^{-1}$ of biodegradable contaminant. At steady state, the effluent from the lagoon must not exceed 20 mg $\cdot$ L$^{-1}$ of biodegradable contaminant. Assuming the lagoon is well mixed and that there are no losses or gains of water in the lagoon other than the sewage input, what biodegradation reaction rate coefficient (d$^{-1}$) must be achieved for a first-order reaction?

**Answer:** $k = 0.3478$, or 0.35 day$^{-1}$

**3-18** Repeat Problem 3-17 with two lagoons in series (see Figure P-3-18). Each lagoon has a surface area of 5 ha and a depth of 1 m.

*Figure P-3-18*

$C_{in} = 100 \text{ mg} \cdot \text{L}^{-1}$
$Q_{in} = 8640 \text{ m}^3 \cdot \text{d}^{-1}$

Lagoon 1
Area = 5 ha

Lagoon 2
Area = 5 ha

$C_{out} = 20 \text{ mg} \cdot \text{L}^{-1}$
$Q_{out} = 8640 \text{ m}^3 \cdot \text{d}^{-1}$

**3–19**  Using a spreadsheet program you have written determine the effluent concentration if the process produc-ing sewage in Problem 3–17 shuts down ($C_{in} = 0$). Calculate and plot points at 1-day intervals for 10 days. Use the graphing function of the spreadsheet to construct your plot.

**3–20**  A 90-$\text{m}^3$ basement in a residence is found to be contaminated with radon coming from the ground through the floor drains. The concentration of radon in the room is $1.5 \text{ Bq} \cdot \text{L}^{-1}$ (becquerels per liter) under steady-state conditions. The room behaves as a CMFR, and the decay of radon is a first-order reaction with a decay rate constant of $2.09 \times 10^{-6} \text{ s}^{-1}$. If the source of radon is closed off and the room is vented with radon-free air at a rate of $0.14 \text{ m}^3 \cdot \text{s}^{-1}$, how long will it take to lower the radon concentration to an acceptable level of $0.15 \text{ Bq} \cdot \text{L}^{-1}$.

**3–21**  For the following conditions determine whether a CMFR or a PFR is more efficient in removing a reactive compound from the waste stream under steady-state conditions with a first-order reaction: reactor volume = $280 \text{ m}^3$, flow rate = $14 \text{ m}^3 \cdot \text{day}^{-1}$, and reaction rate coefficient = $0.05 \text{ day}^{-1}$.

  **Answer:** CMFR $\eta = 50\%$; PFR $\eta = 63\%$

**3–22**  Compare the reactor volume required to achieve 95% efficiency for a CMFR and a PFR for the following conditions: steady-state, first-order reaction, flow rate = $14 \text{ m}^3 \cdot \text{day}^{-1}$, and reaction rate coefficient = $0.05 \text{ day}^{-1}$.

**3–23**  The water in a biological wastewater treatment system must be heated from 15°C to 40°C for the micro-organisms to function. If the flow rate of the wastewater into the process is $30 \text{ m}^3 \cdot \text{day}^{-1}$, at what rate must heat be added to the wastewater flowing into the treatment system? Assume the treatment system is com-pletely mixed and that there are no heat losses once the wastewater is heated.

  **Answer:** $3.14 \text{ GJ} \cdot \text{d}^{-1}$

**3–24**  The lowest flow in the Menominee River in July is about $40 \text{ m}^3 \cdot \text{s}^{-1}$. If the river temperature is 18°C and a power plant discharges $2 \text{ m}^3 \cdot \text{s}^{-1}$ of cooling water at 80°C, what is the final river temperature after the cool-ing water and the river have mixed? Assume the density of water is constant at $1000 \text{ kg} \cdot \text{m}^{-3}$.

**3–25**  Mr. Peepers has a 200-W electric heater in his bird bath. If the bird bath contains 2 kg of ice, how long will it take to melt the ice? Assume all the heat goes into melting the ice.

  **Answer:** 55.5 or 56 min

**3–26**  A small building that shelters a water supply pump measures 2 m × 3 m × 2.4 m high. It is constructed of 1-cm thick wood having a thermal conductivity of $0.126 \text{ W} \cdot \text{m}^{-1} \cdot \text{K}^{-1}$. The inside walls are to be main-tained at 10°C when the outside temperature is −18°C. How much heat must be supplied to maintain the desired temperature? How much heat must be supplied if the walls are lined with 10 cm of glass-wool insu-lation having a thermal conductivity of $0.0377 \text{ W} \cdot \text{m}^{-1} \cdot \text{K}^{-1}$? Assume there is no heat loss through the floor. Ignore the wood in the second calculation.

**3–27**  The radiative heat load on two surfaces of a horizontal leaf is about $1.7 \text{ kW} \cdot \text{m}^{-2}$ [3]. The leaf in turn radi-ates away a portion of this heat load. If the leaf temperature is near that of the ambient temperature, say 30°C, what fraction of the heat loss is by radiation? Assume the emissivity of the leaf is 0.95.

  **Answer:** Fraction = 0.2676 or 0.27 or 27%

**3-28**    Bituminous coal has a heat of combustion* of $31.4 \text{ MJ} \cdot \text{kg}^{-1}$. In the United States the average coal-burning utility produces an average of 2.2 kWh of electrical energy per kilogram of bituminous coal burned. What is the average overall efficiency of this production of electricity?

## DISCUSSION QUESTIONS

**3-1**    A piece of limestone rock ($CaCO_3$) at the bottom of Lake Superior is slowly dissolving. For the purpose of calculating a mass balance, you can assume

    (a)  The system is in equilibrium.          (c)  Both of the above.

    (b)  The system is at steady state.          (d)  Neither of the above.

    Explain your reasoning.

**3-2**    A can of a volatile chemical (benzene) has spilled into a small pond. List the data you would need to gather to calculate the concentration of benzene in the stream leaving the pond using the mass-balance technique.

**3-3**    In Table 3–3, specific heat capacities for common substances, the values for $c_p$ for beef, corn, human beings, and poultry are considerably higher than those for aluminum, copper, and iron. Explain why.

**3-4**    If you hold a beverage glass whose contents are at 4°C "You can feel the cold coming into your hand." Thermodynamically speaking is this statement true? Explain.

**3-5**    If you walk barefooted across a brick floor and a wood floor, the brick floor will feel cooler even though the room temperature is the same for both floors. Explain why.

## ADDITIONAL READING

Masters, G. M. *Introduction to Environmental Engineering and Science.* Prentice Hall, Upper Saddle River, NJ (1998).

Mihelcic, J. R. *Fundamentals of Environmental Engineering.* John Wiley & Sons, Inc., New York (1999).

Nazaroff, W. W., L. Alverez-Cohen. *Environmental Science Engineering.* John Wiley and Sons, New York (2001).

Reynolds, T. D., P. A. Richards. *Unit Operations and Processes in Environmental Engineering.* PWS Publishing Company, Boston, MA (1996).

Vesilind, P. A. *Introduction to Environmental Engineering.* PWS Publishing Company, Boston, MA (1997).

Wanielista, M. P., et al., *Environment and Engineering.* Brooks/Cole Engineering Division Wadsworth, Inc., Monterey, CA (1984).

## REFERENCES

1. Guyton, A. C. *Textbook of Medical Physiology,* 2nd ed. W. B. Saunders Co., Philadelphia (1961), pp. 920–921, 950–953.
2. Chick, H. "An investigation of the laws of disinfection," *Journal of Hygiene* (1908), p. 698.
3. Gates, D. M. *Energy Exchange in the Biosphere.* Harper & Row Publishers, New York (1962), p. 70.

---

*Heat of combustion is the amount of energy released per unit mass when the compound reacts completely with oxygen. The mass does not include the mass of oxygen.

# 4 Ecosystems

## 4–1 INTRODUCTION

**Ecology,** the study of the interrelationships between plants and animals that live in a particular physical environment, requires that we first define the physical environment, that is, the ecosystem that is to be studied. **Ecosystems,** short for ecological systems, are communities of organisms that interact with one another and with their physical environment, including sunlight, rainfall, and soil nutrients. Organisms within an ecosystem tend to interact with one another to a greater extent than do the organisms between ecosystems. Ecosystems can vary greatly in size. For example, a tidal pool of only about 2 m in diameter could be considered an ecosystem because the plants and animals living in this environment depend on one another and are unique to this type of system. On a larger scale, a tropical rainforest* is also an ecosystem. Even larger is our global biosphere,† which could be considered the "ultimate" Earthbound ecosystem. Within each ecosystem are **habitats**, which are defined as the place where a population‡ of organisms lives.

Ecosystems can be further defined as systems into which matter flows. Matter also leaves ecosystems; however, this flow of matter into and out of the ecosystem is small compared with the amount of matter that cycles within the ecosystem. If we think of a lake as an ecosystem, matter flows into the lake in the form of carbon dioxide that dissolves into the water, nutrients that runoff from the land, and chemicals that flow with any streams or rivers feeding the lake. Within the lake, matter flows from one organism to the next in the form of food, excreted material, or respired gases (either oxygen or carbon dioxide). This flow of matter is critical for the existence of an ecosystem.

Another characteristic of an ecosystem is that it can change with time. Later in the chapter we will discuss how lakes change (naturally or anthropogenically) over time, from a system that has very clear water, low levels of nutrients, and low numbers of a large variety of species to one that contains highly turbid water, high levels of nutrients, and large numbers of a few species. Both of these systems (the same lake at different times) are very different ecosystems. Similarly, severe flooding or droughts and extreme temperature changes or other extreme environmental conditions (e.g., volcanic activity or forest fires) can cause significant changes in an ecosystem.

Ecosystems can be natural or artificial. The lake, the tidal pool, or the forest is usually natural (although lakes can be human-made and forests can be cultivated). Constructed wetlands are increasingly being used for the treatment of storm runoff, mining wastes (acid mine drainage), or municipal sewage. Agricultural land is another example of an artificial (or human-made) ecosystem. The criteria explained earlier are met in all ecosystems, whether they are natural or artificial, large or small, long-lasting or temporary.

## 4–2 HUMAN INFLUENCES ON ECOSYSTEMS

As environmental engineers and scientists we have a responsibility to protect ecosystems and the life that resides within them. Although ecosystems change naturally, human activity can speed up natural processes by several orders of magnitude (in terms of time).

Seemingly harmless or beneficial activities can wreak havoc on the environment. For example, large-scale agricultural operations, although producing inexpensive food to feed millions, can result in the release of pesticides, fertilizers, and carbon dioxide and other greenhouse gases to the environment. Hydroelectric power is seen as a clean, renewable energy source. However, dam

---

*A tropical rainforest is an example of a biome. **Biomes** are complex communities of plants and animals in a region and a climate. These include deserts, tundra, chaparrals or scrubs, and temperate hardwood forests.

†The sum of all the regions of the earth that support ecosystems is known as the **biosphere.** The biosphere is made up of the atmosphere, the hydrosphere (the water), and the lithosphere (the soil, rocks, and minerals that make up the solid portion of earth).

‡A **population** is defined as a group of organisms of the same species living in the same place at the same time.

construction can have detrimental effects on river ecosystems, drastically reducing fish populations, as well as causing erosion of soil and vegetation during powerful water surges.

Human activity can also change ecosystems through the destruction of species. The loss of habitat can threaten the existence of individual species within an ecosystem. For example, the destruction of the rainforest in Mexico threatens the very existence of the monarch butterfly. If these forests are destroyed to the extent that the monarch loses its winter roosting grounds, **global extinction** of this butterfly could result—the complete and permanent loss of this animal species across the entire planet. However, the localized destruction of the milkweed plant deprives the butterfly of its nesting environment, resulting in **local extinction.**

The destruction of an ecosystem is not the only way humans can affect animal populations. The release of toxic chemicals can also threaten wildlife. Dichlorodiphenyltrichloroethane (DDT) is a classic example of such a chemical. The release of DDT from the 1940s to the 1960s threatened the very existence of the American bald eagle. DDT weakened the eggs laid by the female birds, so much so that they were often crushed in the nest by the mother bird. In some areas, DDT uptake from contaminated prey by the adult eagles resulted in a nearly complete failure to reproduce.

A third way species can be threatened is by the introduction of nonnative (**exotic**) species into ecosystems. The introduction of the rabbit onto Norfolk Island, the zebra mussel into the Great Lakes or the Asian fungus causing Dutch elm disease onto the U.S. east coast has had a significant impact on ecosystems. The introduction of rabbits onto Norfolk Island in 1830 resulted in the loss of 13 species of vascular plants by 1967 [1]. Scientists believe that the zebra mussel (*Dreissena polymorpha*) was introduced into the Great Lakes from the ballast water of a transatlantic freighter that previously visited a port in eastern Europe, where the mussel is common [2]. The zebra mussel can now be found in inland waters in 21 states and the Province of Ontario [3] and is thought to be responsible for the reduction of some 80% of the mass of phytoplankton in Lake Erie. Because the zebra mussel is an efficient filterer of water its presence significantly increases water clarity, allowing light to penetrate deeper into the water column, increasing the density of rooted aquatic vegetation, benthic forms of algae, and some forms of insect-like benthic organisms [2]. The mussel has also caused the near extinction of many types of native unionid clams in Lake St. Clair and the western basin of Lake Erie [2]. The zebra mussel attaches itself to the native clams, eventually killing them.

The last method by which species can become extinct is through excessive hunting, some legal, others illegal. The manatee whose habitat is the Everglades is threatened by poaching, along with harm due to boat propellers, loss of habitat and vandalism. The rhinoceros is threatened by poaching, mainly for its horns.

## 4–3   ENERGY AND MASS FLOW

Ecosystems would not be possible were it not for the flow of energy into them. The sun is the primary source of this energy because all biological life is dependent on the green plants that use sunlight as a source of energy. As such, these sunlight-using organisms are called **primary producers.** Primary producers also obtain their carbon from inorganic sources such as carbon dioxide ($CO_2$) or bicarbonate ($HCO_3^-$). As such, they are referred to as **autotrophic.** These photosynthetic organisms that obtain their carbon from inorganic sources are called **photoautotrophic.** *Trophic* is the term used to describe the level of nourishment. Trophic levels are summarized in Table 4–1.

The process by which some organisms (namely chlorophyll-containing plants) are able to convert energy from sunlight into chemical energy (in the form of sugars) is called **photosynthesis** and can be represented by the simple equation

$$6CO_2 + 6H_2O + 2800 \text{ kJ energy from sun} \xrightarrow{\text{chlorophyll}} C_6H_{12}O_6 + 6O_2 \qquad (4\text{--}1)$$

**TABLE 4–1**          Characteristic Terms for Biological Organisms Based on Energy and Carbon Sources

| Type | Energy Source | Electron Donor[a] | Carbon Source |
|---|---|---|---|
| Phototrophs | Light | | |
| Chemotrophs | Organic or inorganic compounds | | |
| Lithotrophs (subgroup of chemotrophs) | | Reduced inorganic compounds | |
| Organotrophs (subgroup of chemotrophs) | | Organic compounds | |
| Autotrophs | | | Inorganic compounds (e.g., $CO_2$) |
| Heterotrophs | | | Organic carbon |

[a]Electron donors (reducing agents) are the source of electrons that come from reduced bonds (i.e., C—H bonds). The breaking of these reduced bonds may be coupled directly or indirectly to the production of adenosine triphosphate (ATP) within the cell.

The chemical compound represented by $C_6H_{12}O_6$ is the simple sugar glucose. The rate of carbon dioxide use and, therefore, glucose production is dependent on sunlight and the number and growth rate of the photoautotrophs, along with other environmental conditions such as temperature and pH. The rate of production of biomass glucose, cells, and other organic chemicals by the primary producers is referred to as **net primary productivity** (NPP). Swamps and tropical forests, for example, have a high NPP, whereas deserts and the arctic tundra do not. The rates of production can be limited by such factors as sunlight (e.g., the growing season, insolent radiation or sunlight penetration into waters), temperature, water, or the availability of nutrients.

When plants are not photosynthesizing, for example, at night, they are respiring, that is giving off carbon dioxide in a manner similar to the way animals do. **Aerobic respiration** is simply the breakdown of organic chemicals, such as sugars and starches, by molecular oxygen to form gaseous carbon dioxide.

Some organisms are able to obtain energy through photosynthesis but are not capable of reducing carbon dioxide. Thus, they obtain carbon from reduced carbon compounds generated by other organisms. These organisms are known as **photoheterotrophs:** heterotrophic referring to the fact that carbon for cell synthesis is derived from preformed organic compounds usually produced by other organisms. This group of biota include the purple nonsulfur bacteria; the green nonsulfur bacteria; some Chrysophytes including *Chromulina, Chrysochromulina, Dinobryon,* and *Ochromonas;* some Euglenophytes including *Euglena gracilis;* some Cryptophytes; and some Pyrrhophyta (Dinoflagellates) such as *Gymnodinium* and *Gonyaulaux.*

These organisms all obtain their energy from light, and they acquire carbon from either inorganic or organic sources. Similarly, the **chemotrophs** obtain their energy from organic or inorganic carbon rather than from light. Chemotrophs can be either autotrophic, that is, they build cell mass from either inorganic forms of carbon, or heterotrophic, using organic forms of carbon to synthesize new cells and compounds. Chemotrophs can also be either lithotrophs, that is, they obtain energy by breaking inorganic chemical bonds, or organotrophs, which get energy by breaking organic chemical bonds.

Chemotrophs that are autotrophic obtain their energy from organic or inorganic compounds and use inorganic carbon compounds as a carbon source (from reduced carbon bonds). All chemoautotrophs are prokaryotic, archaea, and bacteria. These include the nitrifiers, such as *Nitrosomonas europea.* Other chemoautotrophs are bacteria that live at high temperatures and are

**FIGURE 4–1**

Trophic levels (levels of nourishment).

found in deep-sea vents. These organisms also use inorganic chemicals, including $H_2S$, $HS^-$, $S^{2-}$, $SO_3^{2-}$, iron sulfide, $Fe^{2+}$, $NH_3$, $NO_2^-$, hydrogen gas, carbon monoxide, ammonia, or nitrite, as electron acceptors. The redox state of the system considered governs the properties of the system and the predominance of species within the system. Redox chemistry was discussed in Chapter 2.

Chemoheterotrophs use inorganic or organic compounds as energy sources; however, they use only preformed reduced organic chemicals as a source of carbon for cell synthesis.

Examples of chemoheterotrophs include animals, protozoa, fungi, and bacteria. Essentially all cellular pathogens are chemoheterotrophs.

As we move up the trophic levels (Figure 4–1) from the primary producers, we find those organisms that are known as the **primary consumers.** These **chemoheterotrophic** organisms are the herbivores that eat plant material. Although chemoautotrophs may obtain energy from chemicals formed by other organisms, under most circumstances they do not consume the organism to obtain those compounds. Rather the compounds they consume were excreted by the living organism or released during the decay of the dead organisms. These organisms are often referred to as the **decomposers** (as they are a special type of consumers). The **secondary consumers,** also chemoheterotrophic organisms, are carnivores that eat the flesh of animals. In a pond ecosystem, beaver, muskrats, ducks, pond snails, and the lesser water boatman, an aquatic insect, are all primary consumers. Among the secondary consumers living in a pond are the insects (all except the lesser water boatman), leeches, otters, mink, and heron. What we have just described is the **food web,** a description of the complex relationship between organisms in an ecosystem. An example of a food web is provided in Figure 4–2.

Another term often used is the food, or biomass, pyramid, which attempts to show the quantitative relationships of energy flow by plotting the mass of biomass (all organisms) with trophic level. As we move up the food chain the amount of biomass present decreases (Figure 4–3). Consider, for instance, a meadow as an ecosytem; the vast majority of the biomass would occur as plants. The percentage of primary consumers (as the weight of biomass) would be significantly less. The mass of biomass contributed by secondary consumers would be even smaller. The reason for this decrease is that much of the food consumed by an organism higher on the trophic level is either lost as undigested waste or burned up by the organism's metabolic activity to produce heat. Very little is actually converted into body tissue that can be eaten by organisms higher up the food web.

**EXAMPLE 4–1 [4]**    A deer eats 25 kg of herbaceous material per day. The herbaceous matter is approximately 20% dry matter (DM) and has an energy content of $10\ MJ \cdot (kg\ DM)^{-1}$. Of the total energy ingested per day, 25% is excreted as undigested material. Of the 75% that is digested, 80% is lost to metabolic waste products and heat. The remaining 20% is converted to body tissue.

How many megajoules are converted to body tissue on a daily basis? Calculate the percentage of energy consumed that is converted to body tissue.

Solution    The dry matter content of the herbaceous material is calculated as

$$(25\ kg\ herbaceous\ material \cdot day^{-1}) \times (0.20\ kg\ dry\ matter \cdot (kg\ material)^{-1}) = 5.0\ kg\ DM \cdot day^{-1}$$

The energy content is calculated as

$$(10\ MJ \cdot (kg\ DM))^{-1}(5.0\ kg\ DM \cdot day^{-1}) = 50\ MJ \cdot day^{-1}$$

Now draw a schematic of the energy balance.

**FIGURE 4–2** Simplified Representation of a Food Web, Showing the Main Pathways

Food (energy) moves in the direction of the arrows. The driving force is sunlight. Depictions of the various organisms are not drawn to scale. (*Source:* http://www.epa.gov/glnpo/atlas/images/big05.gif)

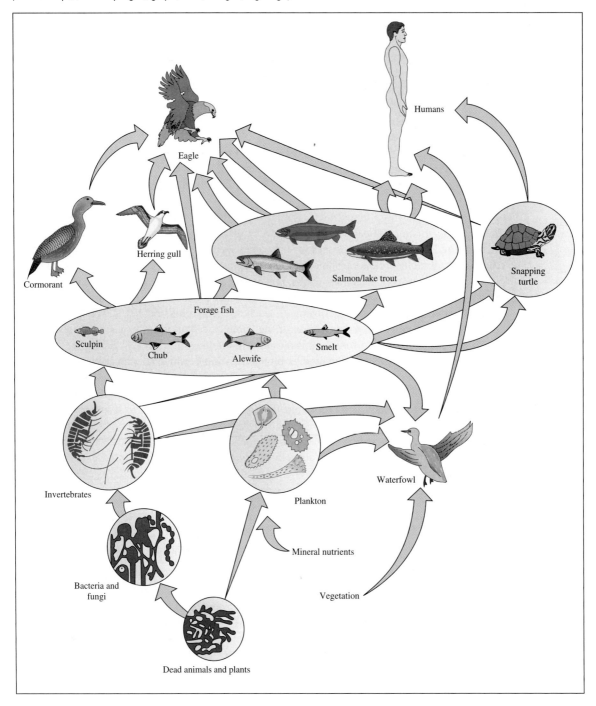

## FIGURE 4–3

A simplified illustration of the relationship between organisms in an ecosystem is the biomass, or ecological pyramid. This diagram shows both mass and energy flow.

The amount of energy digested is calculated as

$$(0.75) \times 50 \text{ MJ} \cdot \text{day}^{-1} = 37.5 \text{ MJ} \cdot \text{day}^{-1}$$

The amount of this energy that is then turned into tissue is calculated as

$$(0.2) \times 37.5 \text{ MJ} \cdot \text{day}^{-1} = 7.5 \text{ MJ} \cdot \text{day}^{-1}$$

The percentage of "consumed" energy used for body tissue is

$$\left( \frac{7.5 \text{ MJ} \cdot \text{day}^{-1}}{50 \text{ MJ} \cdot \text{day}^{-1}} \right) \times 100 = 15\%$$

This "inefficiency" of conversion of energy is further exemplified in the fact that it is often assumed that only about 10% of the energy consumed by an organism in the form of plant matter is converted into animal tissue (in Example 4–1, it was 15%). Given this, if we consider the mass balance example for lake trout (see Figure 4–2), we can determine the approximate percentage of energy used in building trout tissue.

**EXAMPLE 4–2**   For every megajoule of energy used by the phytoplankton in Lake Michigan (see Figure 4–2), how many joules of energy are used in building cell tissue in the lake trout? How many in humans? Use the following food web path:

Phytoplankton $\longrightarrow$ zooplankton $\longrightarrow$ alewife $\longrightarrow$ lake trout $\longrightarrow$ humans

**Solution**   Given the rule of thumb that only 10% of the energy consumed is converted to biomass, then

Phytoplankton $\longrightarrow$ zooplankton $\longrightarrow$ alewife $\longrightarrow$ lake trout $\longrightarrow$ humans
　　1 MJ　　　　　　0.1 MJ　　　　　0.01 MJ　　　　1000 J　　　　100 J

So far, we have focused our discussion on the trophic levels with no discussion of the type of respiration that occurs in living organisms. Basically, respiration can be aerobic, anaerobic, or anoxic. Organisms that are **aerobic** survive in oxygen-rich environments and use oxygen as the terminal electron acceptor.* Obligate aerobes can survive only in the presence of oxygen. The microorganisms *Bacillus subtilis, Pseudomonas aeruginosa,* and *Thiobacillis ferrooxidans* are examples of obligate aerobes. Humans are also obligate aerobes. The primary end products of aerobic decomposition are carbon dioxide, water and new cell tissue. **Anoxic** environments contain low concentrations (partial pressures) of oxygen. Here nitrate is usually the terminal electron acceptor. The end products of denitrification are nitrogen gas, carbon dioxide, water and new cells. **Anaerobic respiration** can occur only in the absence of oxygen or nitrate. Obligate anaerobes include *Clostridium* sp. and *Bacteroides* sp. Sulfate, carbon dioxide, and organic compounds that can be reduced serve as terminal electron acceptors. The reduction of sulfate results in the production of hydrogen sulfide, mercaptans, ammonia, and methane. Carbon dioxide and water are the major by-products. *Desulfovibrio desulfuricans* is an example of a sulfur-reducing bacterium.

Facultative anaerobes can use oxygen as the terminal electron acceptor and, under certain conditions, they can also grow in the absence of oxygen. Under anoxic conditions, a group of facultative anaerobes called denitrifiers utilizes nitrites ($NO_2^-$) and nitrates ($NO_3^-$) as the terminal electron acceptor. Nitrate nitrogen is converted to nitrogen gas in the absence of oxygen. This process is called **anoxic denitrification.**

### Bioaccumulation

So far, in this chapter we have discussed the food web and the ecological pyramid. Bioaccumulation has serious implications for the movement of chemicals in the environment. Chemicals that are hydrophobic (those that don't want to "go into" water) will tend to be lipophilic, that is, "liking lipids." As a result, these chemicals will tend to **partition** (move into) into the fat tissue of animals. This process results in bioaccumulation. **Bioaccumulation** is the total uptake of chemicals by an organism from food items (benthos, fish prey, sediment ingestion, etc.) as well as via mass transport of dissolved chemicals through the gills and epithelium [5]. When chemicals bioaccumulate, the concentration of a chemical increases over time in an organism relative to the chemical's concentration in the environment. For this to occur, these chemicals must be retained in living tissue faster than they are broken down (metabolized) or excreted. For example, if a crustacean or other "lake bottom-dwelling" organism consumes DDT or PCBs from the lake sediments, these chemicals will tend to remain in the fatty tissue of the organism. If we were to put a crustacean from a pristine environment into the contaminated lake, we would notice a corresponding increase in the concentration of the DDT in the crustacean's tissue with residence time in the lake. The problem is compounded when a small fish eats the crustacean because it eats not only the crustacean but the PCB or DDT in the tissue of the crustacean. And the process continues as a larger fish eats the smaller fish. The result of this is that these chemicals tend to biomagnify as we move up the food web.

**Biomagnification** is the process that results in the accumulation of a chemical in an organism at higher levels than are found in its own food. It occurs when a chemical becomes more and more concentrated as it moves up through a food chain. A typical food chain includes algae eaten by *Daphnia,* a water flea, eaten by an alewife eaten by a lake trout and finally consumed by a kingfisher (or human being). If each step results in bioaccumulation, then an animal at the top of the food chain, through its regular diet, will accumulate a much greater concentration of chemical than was present in organisms lower in the food chain, and biomagnification will occur.

Biomagnification is illustrated by a study of DDT, which showed that where soil levels were 10 ppm, DDT reached a concentration of 141 ppm in earthworms and 444 ppm in robins [6]. In another study (Figure 4–4), the biomagnification of PCB in the Great Lakes food web can be easily observed. Through biomagnification, the concentration of a chemical in the animal at the top of the

---

*In the oxidation of an electron donor, the electron acceptor (oxidizing agent) is reduced, that is, it accepts electrons.

**FIGURE 4–4**   Persistent Organic Chemicals such as PCBs Biomagnify

This diagram shows the degree of concentration in each level of the Great Lakes aquatic food web for PCBs (in parts per million, ppm). The highest levels are reached in the eggs of fish-eating birds such as herring gulls.
(*Source: The Great Lakes: An Environmental Atlas and Resource Book,* 3rd ed. Jointly produced by Government of Canada (Toronto, Canada) and U.S. Environmental Protection Agency, Great Lakes National Program Office, Chicago, 1995. *Note:* Better quality images are available from US EPA brail.lawrence@epa.gov)
http://www.epa.gov/glnpo/atlas/glat-ch4.html#3

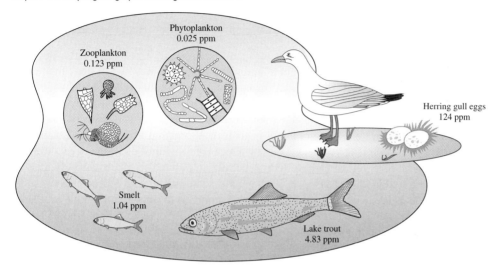

food chain may be sufficiently high to cause death or adverse effects on behavior, reproduction, or disease resistance and thus endanger that species, even though contamination levels in the air, water, or soil are low. Fortunately, bioaccumulation does not always result in biomagnification.

Another term often used (and confused) is **bioconcentration**—the uptake of chemicals from the dissolved phase [1]. Through bioconcentration, the concentration of a chemical in an organism becomes greater than its concentration in the air or water in which the organism lives. Although the process is the same for both natural and synthetically made chemicals, the term *bioconcentration* usually refers to chemicals foreign to the organism. For fish and other aquatic animals, bioconcentration after uptake through the gills (or sometimes the skin) is usually the most important bioaccumulation process.

Bioconcentration factors, the ratio of the concentration of the chemical of interest in the organism to the concentration in water, are used to measure the tendency of a chemical to accumulate in lipid tissue and to relate pollutant concentrations in the water column with that in fish using the following equation:

Concentration in fish = (concentration in water) × (bioconcentration factor)     (4–2)

These factors are important in performing risk assessment calculations for predicting the effect of a chemical on a target species.

**EXAMPLE 4–3**   The concentration of the pesticide DDT was found to be $5\ \mu g \cdot L^{-1}$ in the water of a pond. The bioconcentration factor for DDT [7] is $54{,}000\ L \cdot kg^{-1}$. What is the expected concentration of DDT in the fish living in the pond?

Solution   Concentration in fish = $(5\ \mu g \cdot L^{-1})(54{,}000\ L \cdot kg^{-1}) = 270{,}000\ \mu g \cdot kg^{-1}$,  or $270\ mg \cdot kg^{-1}$

## 4–4 NUTRIENT CYCLES

Chapter 3 focused on material and energy balances. These same balances, although very complex, hold true globally. The basic elements of which all organisms are composed are carbon, nitrogen, phosphorus, sulfur, oxygen, and hydrogen. The first four of these elements are much more limited in mass and easier to trace than are oxygen and hydrogen. Because these elements are conserved, they can be recycled indefinitely (or cycled through the environment). Because the pathways used to describe the movement of these elements in the environment are cyclic, they are referred to as the carbon, nitrogen, phosphorus, and sulfur cycles.

### Carbon Cycle

Although carbon is only the 14th by weight in abundance on earth, it is by far, one of the most important elements on earth as it is the building block of all organic substances and thus, of life, itself. Carbon is found in all living organisms, in the atmosphere (predominately as carbon dioxide and bicarbonate), in soil humus, in fossil fuels, and in rock and soils (predominately as carbonate minerals in limestone or dolomite or in shales). Although it was once thought that the largest reservoir of carbon is terrestrial (plants, geological formations, etc.), the ocean actually serves as the greatest reservoir of carbon. As can be seen in Figure 4–5, approximately 85% of world's carbon is found in the oceans.

Photosynthesis is the major driving force for the carbon cycle, shown in Figure 4–6. Plants take up carbon dioxide and convert it to organic matter. Even the organic carbon compounds in fossil fuels had their beginnings in photosynthesis. The "bound," or stored, $CO_2$ in fossil fuels is released by combustion processes. The cycling of carbon also involves the release of carbon dioxide by animal respiration, fires, diffusion from the oceans, weathering of rocks, and precipitation of carbonate minerals.

The ocean is a major sink of carbon, much of which is found in the form of dissolved carbon dioxide gas, and carbonate and bicarbonate ions. Primary productivity is responsible for the assimilation of inorganic carbon into organic forms. Productivity is limited by the concentrations of nitrogen, phosphorus, silicon, and other essential trace nutrients. The concentrations of $CO_2$ vary with depth. In shallow waters, photosynthesis is active and there is a net consumption of $CO_2$. In deeper waters, there is a net production of $CO_2$ due to respiration and decay processes. Because ocean circulation occurs over such a long time scale, the oceans take up $CO_2$ at a slower rate than the rate at which $CO_2$ from anthropogenic sources is accumulating in the atmosphere. In addition, as the amount of $CO_2$ dissolved in the ocean increases, the chemical capacity to take up more $CO_2$ decreases. The rate of uptake of $CO_2$ is driven by two main cycles: the solubility and biological pumps.

**FIGURE 4–5**

Major reservoirs of carbon (numbers in billions of metric tons) (*Source:* From Post, W. M. et al. "The global carbon cycle." *American Scientist* vol. 78, p. 315, 1990.)

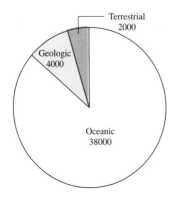

**FIGURE 4–6**

Cycling of carbon in the environment.

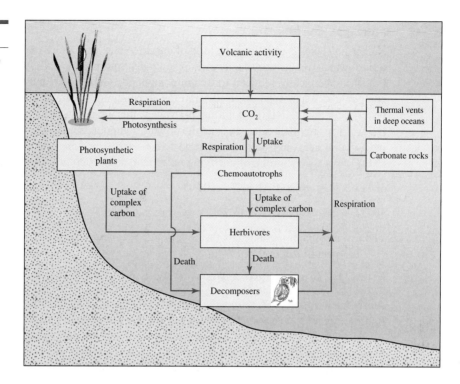

The solubility pump, as it is known, is the net driving force for dissolution of $CO_2$ into waters. Polar waters are colder at the surface than in deeper regions. As a result of the cold temperatures, $CO_2$ dissolution is enhanced in colder waters, driving dissolution of $CO_2$ from the atmosphere into the waters. Because these colder waters are denser than the warmer waters below, the colder waters tend to sink, taking with them $CO_2$. Because ocean circulation is slow, much of this $CO_2$ is "lost" to deep waters, keeping surface waters lower in $CO_2$ and driving dissolution from the atmosphere.

Phytoplankton, zooplankton and their predators, and bacteria make up the biological pump. These organisms take up carbon, resulting in a cycling of much of the carbon and nutrients found in the surface ocean waters. However, as these organisms die, they settle into deeper regions of ocean, taking with them bound $CO_2$. Additionally, as the dead organisms settle, some of this bound $CO_2$ finds its way into the ocean depths with the fecal matter of these organisms. Some is carried by currents to deeper regions. Thus, the depths of the ocean become a $CO_2$ sink, releasing carbon mainly through "upwelling" of water, diffusion across the thermocline,* and seasonal, wind-driven mixing, which brings the deep water to the surface. This mixing of the deeper waters returns nutrients and carbon to the ocean surface, continuing the cycle of photosynthesis and respiration.

Humans have affected significantly the carbon cycle through the combustion of fossil fuel, the large-scale production of livestock, and the burning of forests. Since the Industrial Revolution (the 1850s), the concentration of carbon dioxide in the atmosphere has increased from approximately 280 ppm to 360 ppm in 1999 [8]. Although there is still some debate, many scientists believe that this increase in carbon dioxide levels has resulted in an increase in global temperatures. These scientists expect that global temperatures will continue to increase, although the extent of this increase is still the subject of some contention. Global warming will be discussed in more detail in Chapter 11.

---

*As discussed in Section 4–6, the thermocline is the layer in a body of water where the temperature decreases sharply with increasing depth. Temperature changes in the thermocline exceed $1°C \cdot m^{-1}$ depth.

### Nitrogen Cycle

Nitrogen in lakes is usually in the form of nitrate ($NO_3^-$) and comes from external sources by way of inflowing streams or groundwater. When taken up by algae and other phytoplankton, the nitrogen is chemically reduced to amino compounds ($NH_2$—R) and incorporated into organic compounds. When dead algae undergo decomposition, the organic nitrogen is released to the water as ammonia ($NH_3$). At normal pH values, this ammonia occurs in the form of ammonium ($NH_4^+$). The ammonia released from the organic compounds, plus that from other sources such as industrial wastes and agricultural runoff (e.g., fertilizers and manure) is oxidized to nitrate ($NO_3^-$) by a special group of nitrifying bacteria in a two-step process called nitrification:

$$4NH_4^+ + 6O_2 = 4NO_2^- + 8H^+ + 4H_2O \tag{4-3}$$

$$4NO_2^- + 2O_2 = 4NO_3^- \tag{4-4}$$

The first reaction is mediated by the organism *Nitrosomonas* sp., the second by *Nitrobacter* sp.
The overall reaction is

$$NH_4^+ + 2O_2 = NO_3^- + 2H^+ + H_2O \tag{4-5}$$

As shown in Figure 4–7, nitrogen cycles from nitrate to organic nitrogen, to ammonia, and back to nitrate as long as the water remains aerobic. However, under anoxic conditions, for example, in anaerobic sediments, when algal decomposition has depleted the oxygen supply, nitrate is reduced by bacteria to nitrogen gas ($N_2$) and lost from the system in a process called **denitrification.** Denitrification reduces the average time nitrogen remains in the lake. Denitrification can also result in the formation of $N_2O$, (nitrous oxide). The denitrification reaction is

$$2NO_3^- + \text{organic carbon} = N_2 + CO_2 + H_2O \tag{4-6}$$

Some photosynthetic microorganisms can also fix nitrogen gas from the atmosphere by converting it to organic nitrogen and are, therefore, called nitrogen-fixing microorganisms. In lakes the most important nitrogen-fixing microorganisms are photosynthetic bacteria called cyanobacteria, also known as blue-green algae because of the pigments they contain. Because of their nitrogen-fixing ability, cyanobacteria have a competitive advantage over green algae when nitrate and ammonium concentrations are low but other nutrients are sufficiently abundant. Nitrogen fixation also occurs in the soil. The aquatic fern *Azolla* is the only fern that can fix nitrogen. It does so by virtue of a symbiotic association with a cyanobacterium (*Anabaena azollae*). *Azolla* is found worldwide and is sometimes used as a valuable source of nitrogen for agriculture. Similarly, lichens can also contribute to nitrogen fixation. For example, *Lobaria pulmonaria,* a common *N*-fixing lichen in Pacific northwest forests, fixes nitrogen by a symbiotic relationship with the cyanobacterium *Nostoc.* Lichens such as this are a major source of nitrogen in old growth forests.

Nitrogen fixation is also acomplished in the soils by almost all legumes. Nitrogen fixation occurs in the root nodules that contain bacteria (*Bradyrhizobium* for soybean, *Rhizobium* for most other legumes). The legume family (Leguminosae or Fabaceae) includes many important crop species such as pea, alfalfa, clover, common bean, peanut, and lentil. The reaction describing nitrogen fixation is

$$N_2 + 8e^- + 8H^+ + ATP \longrightarrow 2NH_3 + H_2 + ADP + P_I \tag{4-7}$$

where $P_I$ = inorganic phosphate.

Human influences on the nitrogen cycle have resulted from the manufacture and use of industrial fertilizers, fossil fuel combustion, and large-scale production of nitrogen-fixing crops. Consequently, the release of biologically usable nitrogen from soil and organic matter has increased. Nitrous oxide releases from industrial sources and the combustion of fossil fuels have also increased. The effects of nitrogen releases are significant and range from acid rain and lake

**FIGURE 4–7**

The nitrogen cycle (*Source:* O'Keefe, T. C., S. R. Elliott, R. J. Naiman, D. J. Norton. *Introduction to Watershed Ecology,* October 10, 2002. www.epa.gov/watertrain/ecology/rl.html; http://www.epa.gov/watertrain/ecology/s33.jpg)

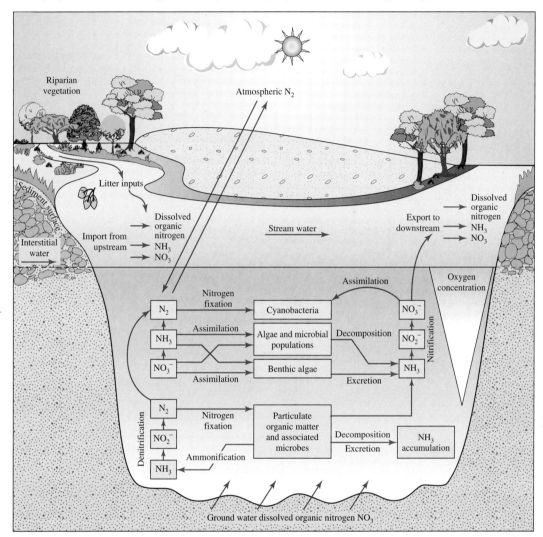

acidification to the corrosion of metals and deterioration of building materials. The effects of perturbations on the nitrogen cycle are discussed in more detail later in this book.

### Phosphorus Cycle

Phosphorus in unpolluted waters is imported through dust in precipitation or via the weathering of rock. Phosphorus is normally present in watersheds in extremely small amounts, usually existing dissolved as inorganic orthophosphate, suspended as organic colloids, adsorbed onto particulate organic and inorganic sediment, or contained in organic water. In polluted waters, the major source of phosphorus is from human activities. The only significant form of phosphorus available to plants and algae is the soluble reactive inorganic orthophosphate species ($HPO_4^{2-}$, $PO_4^{3-}$, etc.) that are incorporated into organic compounds. During algal decomposition, phosphorus is returned to the

**FIGURE 4–8**

The phosphorus cycle. (*Source: Virginia Estabrook, The Michigan Water Resource Center, Michigan Water Research Center, Central Michigan University.* http://www.cst.cmich.edu/centers/mwrc/phosphorus%20cycle.htm)

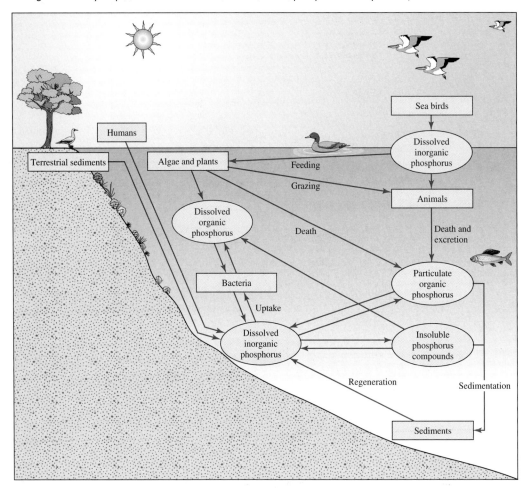

inorganic form. The release of phosphorus from dead algal cells is so rapid that only a small fraction of it leaves the upper zone of a stratified lake (the epilimnion) with the settling algal cells. However, little by little, phosphorus is transferred to the sediments; some of it in undecomposed organic matter; some of it in precipitates of iron, aluminum, and calcium; and some bound to clay particles. To a large extent, the permanent removal of phosphorus from the overlying waters to the sediments depends on the amount of iron, aluminum, calcium, and clay entering the lake along with phosphorus. The overall cycle can be seen in Figure 4–8.

**EXAMPLE 4–4**  A farmer has a 7-year rotation of corn, soybeans, and wheat and 4 years of alfalfa. Manure will be applied before corn and wheat and before seeding to alfalfa. The initial soil tests results indicate total phosphorus level of 48 kg P · hectare$^{-1}$. Manure is to be surface-applied in mid-March and disk-incorporated within 2 days of application. One-third of the organic nitrogen and 50% of the nitrogen from $NH_4$ is available to the corn crop. To obtain the desired yield of corn, the local extension agent has told the farmer to apply 100 kg of nitrogen per hectare.

The manure analysis is

- Total N = 12 g N · (kg manure)$^{-1}$
- Organic N = 6 g N · (kg manure)$^{-1}$
- $NH_4$ = 6 g N · (kg manure)$^{-1}$
- Total $P_2O_5$ = 5 g P · (kg manure)$^{-1}$
- Total $K_2O$ = 4 g K · (kg manure)$^{-1}$

Calculate the available nitrogen per kilogram of manure and the kilograms of manure per hectare that must be applied to meet the corn's nitrogen needs.

**Solution**   This is a mass balance problem. Thirty-three percent of the organic nitrogen in the manure is available to the corn, whereas, 50% of the inorganic nitrogen ($NH_4$) is available to the corn. There is 6 g organic nitrogen per kilogram of manure and 6 g inorganic nitrogen per kilogram of manure. Therefore, the available N in grams per kilogram can be calculated as

$$\text{Organic N} \times 0.33 + NH_4 \times 0.5 = 6 \text{ g N} \cdot \text{kg}^{-1} \times 0.33 + 6 \text{ g N} \cdot \text{kg}^{-1} \times 0.5$$

$$= 5 \text{ g N} \cdot (\text{kg manure})^{-1}$$

$$\text{Application rate} = \frac{\text{Crop nitrogen needs (in kg N} \cdot \text{hectare}^{-1})}{\text{Available nitrogen (in g N} \cdot (\text{kg manure})^{-1}) \times (10^{-3} \text{ g} \cdot \text{kg}^{-1})}$$

$$= \left[ \frac{100 \text{ kg N} \cdot \text{hectare}^{-1}}{(5 \times 10^{-3} \text{ kg N} \cdot (\text{kg manure})^{-1})} \right]$$

$$= 20{,}000 \text{ kg manure per hectare}$$

Human activities have led to a release of phosphorus from the disposal of municipal sewage and from concentrated livestock operations. The application of phosphorus fertilizers has also resulted in perturbations in the phosphorus cycle, although these changes are thought to be more localized than the perturbations in the other cycles. Phosphorus releases can have a significant effect on lake and stream ecosystems.

### Sulfur Cycle

Until the Industrial Revolution the effect of sulfur on environmental systems was quite small. However, with the Industrial Revolution, our use of sulfur-containing compounds as fertilizers and the release of sulfur dioxide during the combustion of fossil fuels and in metal processing has increased significantly. Mining operations have also resulted in the release of large quantities of sulfur in acid mine drainage. Like the nitrate ion, sulfate is negatively charged and is not adsorbed onto clay particles. Dissolved sulfates thus can be leached from the soil profile by excess rainfall or irrigation. In the environment, sulfur is found predominantly as sulfides ($S^{2-}$), sulfates ($SO_4^{2-}$), and in organic forms.

As with the nitrogen cycle, microorganisms play an important role in the cycling of sulfur. Bacteria are involved in the oxidation of pyrite-containing minerals, releasing large quantities of sulfate. In anaerobic environments, sulfate-reducing bacteria (*Desulfovibrio*) reduce sulfate to release hydrogen sulfide. In marine waters, the biological production of dimethylsulfide may occur. The overall cycle is shown in Figure 4–9.

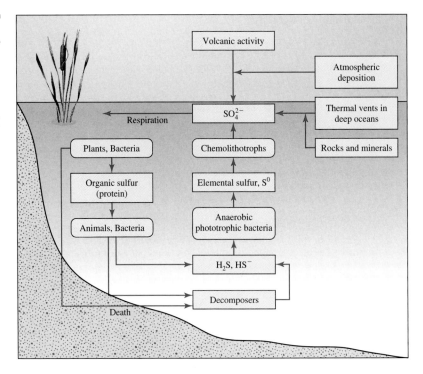

## 4–5   POPULATION DYNAMICS [9]

**Population dynamics** is the study of the changes in the numbers and composition of individuals in a population within a study unit and the factors that affect these numbers. The population can be *Escherichia coli,* moose, otters, humans, or any other unit. The study area can be a biological, geographical, political, or an engineered area. For example, if we were studying eastern timber wolves (which travel in packs of five or six), a biological unit we might investigate is the pack. A geographical area could be a mountain range, a valley, or an island. Continuing with our example, we could investigate the numbers of wolves on Isle Royale in Michigan. In this case Isle Royale would be a geographical area. A political unit might be a county, a hunting district, and so on. Lastly, an engineered area might be an aeration tank in a sewage treatment plant in which the population includes rotifers and ciliates.

As environmental scientists and engineers, evaluating population dynamics is critical to (1) understanding how environmental perturbations affect populations, (2) predicting human populations so as to determine water resource needs, (3) predicting bacterial populations in engineered systems, and (4) using populations as indicators of environmental quality. Resource development specialists and wildlife biologists also use population dynamics. They are most concerned with (1) estimating how many animals can be harvested, (2) predicting when a species or population is threatened or endangered with extinction, and (3) understanding how one population might affect another (i.e., competition or predation). Thus, an understanding of population dynamics is necessary for understanding the structure and function of communities and ecosystems.

Factors that cause populations to change may be related to or independent of the number of organisms* in the study area. These factors can be classified as either density-dependent or density-independent. Density refers to the number of organisms per unit area or volume. We usually measure plants or higher animals, in numbers of animals per hectare or per square kilometer. Bacteria, viruses and other aquatic organisms are usually measured in numbers per unit volume.

---

*We will use the term *organisms* to describe any biological species from bacteria to humans.

Density-dependent factors are, as implied, a function of density. As the density increases beyond a certain threshold, the population numbers may begin to decline. For example, as the density of bacteria in a reactor increases, they will begin to use up available resources and produce excessive amounts of waste products that may be toxic at high concentrations. The decrease in available food and other resources along with the production of waste will result in a decline in the health of the individual organisms and an increase in the death rate (**mortality**) along with a decrease in the rate of replication or reproduction. For human populations, as the density of the population increases unemployment may increase, causing people to leave the area to seek employment. Thus, the population numbers are observed to decrease as density increases. Density-independent factors are those factors that act on a population independent of the size of the population. Typical density-independent causes of mortality are weather, accidents, and environmental catastrophes (e.g., volcanos, floods, landslides, and fire).

### Bacterial Population Growth

Bacteria have been included in this section because they have a simple reproductive scheme, allowing us to more easily study the fundamentals of population dynamics and to develop the models used in this field. The dynamics of bacterial populations are also relevant to environmental scientists and engineers because of their importance in wastewater treatment and water quality.

**Bacterial Growth Requirements.**   In the discussion of the behavior of bacterial cultures that follows, we assume that all the requirements for growth are initially present. Because these requirements are fairly extensive and stringent, it is worth taking a moment to recapitulate them as follows:

1. A terminal electron acceptor
2. Macronutrients
   a. Carbon to build cells
   b. Nitrogen to build cells
   c. Phosphorus for ATP (energy carrier) and DNA
3. Micronutrients
   a. Trace metals
   b. Vitamins are required by some bacteria
4. Appropriate environment
   a. Moisture
   b. Temperature
   c. pH

**Growth in Pure Cultures.**   As an illustration, let us examine a hypothetical situation in which 1400 bacteria of a single species are introduced into a synthetic liquid medium. Initially nothing appears to happen. The bacteria must adjust to their new environment and begin to synthesize new protoplasm. On a plot of bacterial growth versus time (Figure 4–10), this phase of growth is called the **lag phase.**

At the end of the lag phase the bacteria begin to divide. Because all of the organisms do not divide at the same time, population increase is gradual. This phase is labeled the **accelerated growth phase** on the growth plot.

At the end of the accelerated growth phase, the population of organisms is large enough and the differences in generation time are small enough that the cells appear to divide at a regular rate. Because reproduction is by binary fission (each cell divides to produce two new cells), the increase in population follows in a geometric progression: $1 \rightarrow 2 \rightarrow 4 \rightarrow 8 \rightarrow 16 \rightarrow 32$, and so forth. The population of bacteria ($P$) after the $n$th generation is given by the following expression:

$$P = P_0(2)^n \tag{4–8}$$

**FIGURE 4–10**

Bacterial growth in a
pure culture: the log-
growth curve.

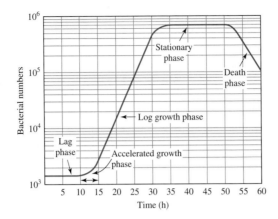

where $P_0$ is the initial population at the end of the accelerated growth phase and $n$ is the number
of generations. If we take the log of both sides of Equation 4–8, we obtain the following:

$$\log P = \log P_0 + n \log 2 \qquad (4\text{–}9)$$

This means that if we plot bacterial population on a logarithmic scale, this phase of growth would
plot as a straight line of slope $n$. The intercept $P_0$ at $t_0$ is equal to the population at the end of the accelerated growth phase. Thus, this phase of growth is called the **log growth** or **exponential growth
phase.** During this phase there are essentially no limitations to cell replication and growth.

In engineered or laboratory settings, the log growth phase tapers off as the substrate becomes
exhausted, as toxic by-products build up, as disease takes over, or as space becomes limited. Thus,
at some point the population becomes constant either as a result of cessation of fission or a balance
in death and reproduction rates. This is depicted by the **stationary phase** on the growth curve. The
stationary phase can be rather long as shown in Figure 4–10 or it can be very abrupt.

Following the stationary phase, the bacteria begin to die faster than they reproduce. This **death
phase** is due to a variety of causes that are basically an extension of those which lead to the stationary phase. The point at which this decline occurs is referred to as the **carrying capacity.**

**EXAMPLE 4–5**    If the initial density of bacteria is $10^4$ cells per liter at the end of the accelerated growth phase,
what is the number of bacteria after 25 generations?

Solution    We are told that $P_0 = 10^4$ organisms. Because we are to determine the number of bacteria after
25 generations, $n = 25$. Therefore, we can find the population after 25 generations, $P$, using
Equation 4–8.

$$P = P_0(2)^n$$
$$= 10^4(2)^{25}$$
$$= 3.36 \times 10^{11} \qquad \text{or} \qquad 3.4 \times 10^{11} \text{ cells} \cdot \text{L}^{-1}$$

**Growth in Mixed Cultures.**    In wastewater treatment, as in nature, **pure cultures*** of
microorganisms do not exist. Rather, a mixture of species compete and survive within the limits
set by the environment.

*A pure culture is one in which only a single species of microorganism is present.

**FIGURE 4–11**

Population dynamics in a closed system.

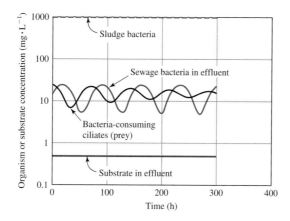

**FIGURE 4–12**

Population dynamics in an open system.

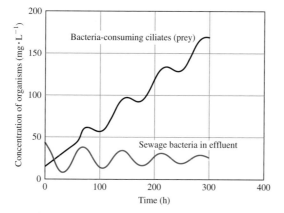

The factors governing the dynamics of the various microbial populations are food and shelter limitations, competition and predation by other organisms, and unfavorable physical conditions. The relative success of a pair of species competing for the same substrate is a function of the ability of the species to metabolize the substrate. The more successful species will be the one that metabolizes the substrate more completely. In so doing, it will obtain more energy for synthesis and consequently will achieve a greater mass.

Because of their relatively smaller size and, thus, larger surface area per unit volume, which allows a more rapid uptake of substrate, the density of bacteria will exceed that of fungi. For the same reason, the density of fungi will surpass that of protozoa and the density of filamentous bacteria will exceed that of spherical bacteria (cocci).

When the supply of soluble organic substrate becomes exhausted, the bacterial population is less successful at replicating and the predator population numbers increase. In a closed system with an initial inoculum of mixed microorganisms and substrate, the populations will cycle as the bacteria give way to higher level organisms, which in turn die for lack of food and are then decomposed by a different set of bacteria (Figure 4–11). In an open system, such as a wastewater treatment plant or a river, with a continuous inflow of new substrate, the predominant populations will change through the length of the plant or river (Figure 4–12*). This condition is known as

*Be careful interpreting this figure. Although at first glance it may appear that it indicates an inverted ecological pyramid (with more biomass in the upper trophic levels than in the lower), this is not the case because the mass of higher organisms measured in the reactor is compared with the mass of bacteria in the effluent. The actual mass of bacteria in the reactor is actually in the thousands of milligrams per liter.

**dynamic equilibrium.** It is a highly sensitive state, and changes in influent characteristics must be regulated closely to maintain the proper balance of the various populations.

### Animal Population Dynamics

The constituents that influence the rate of change in the numbers of a particular species found in the wild include such density-dependent factors as the availability of food, locations to live and build nests for their young, concentrations of toxic waste products, disease, predators, parasites, and so on. Environmental aspects such as weather, temperature, flooding, snowfall, all of which are density-independent will also affect population dynamics. As such, population dynamics involve five basic components to which all changes in population can be related: birth, death, gender ratio, age structure, and dispersal.

Clearly population dynamics are affected by the rate at which animals reproduce. A number of components affect a population's birth rate: (1) the amount and quantity of food, (2) age at first reproduction, (3) the birth interval, and (4) the average number of young born per pregnancy. A doubling in the birth (live) rate will more than double the population growth rate.

As mentioned above, several other factors affect population dynamics. **Death, or mortality, rate** is defined as the number of animals that die per unit time divided by the number of animals alive at the beginning of that time period. The gender (or sex) ratio will affect mating systems and management. **Gender ratio** is the proportion of males to females within a population. Typically, at birth, this ratio is 50:50. The mating system (monogamous vs. polygamous) will greatly affect population dynamics. In monogamous species, a decline in the population will occur if a deviation from the 50:50 gender ratio results. In polygamous species, major effects can occur if the population deviates from the 50:50 gender ratio. For example, if all females breed, a population with a ratio of 4 males for every 1 female, would result in a 40% lower birth rate than a population with a gender ratio of 50:50. If conversely, the gender ratio were 1 male:4 females and every female bred, then the birth rate would be 160% of that for a population with a gender ratio of 50:50. As expected, age structure will affect population dynamics. This is because of age-specific mortality and pregnancy rates. Dispersal is probably the poorest understood of the factors mentioned. **Dispersal** is defined as the movement of an animal from the location of its birth to a new area where it lives and reproduces. Dispersal usually does not occur until the animal is an adult, and males are usually the gender to disperse.

Population and wildlife biologists use a number of models to describe the rate of change in the numbers of individuals per unit time. The models are similar to those used for bacteria.

The simplest (exponential) model assumes that the resources necessary for population growth are unlimited. Therefore, the population grows at an exponential rate, which is the maximum rate possible for that particular species:

$$\frac{dN}{dt} = rN \tag{4-10}$$

where $dN/dt =$ the change in numbers of animals within a certain population per unit time
$r =$ the specific rate of change
$N =$ number of animals within a certain population

If $r$ is positive, the population size is increasing, if negative, the numbers are decreasing. If $r = 0$, there is no change in the population. If $N_0$ is the number of organisms at time zero, the number of organisms at any particular time, $N_t$ can be determined by integrating Equation 4–10 over that particular time period:

$$N_t = N_0 \exp(rt) \equiv N_0 e^{rt} \tag{4-11}$$

The geometric (logistic) model, like the model in Equation 4–11, assumes that resources are unlimited. It would be ridiculous to believe that there is an infinite amount of food and space to support an unlimited number of animals within a particular sized plot of land. As such, we need models that allow us to describe these limits mathematically. This model, however, assumes that growth occurs in discrete intervals described by the term λ.

$$\frac{N(t+1)}{N(t)} = \lambda = e^r \tag{4-12}$$

where  $N(t + 1)$ = population after $(t + 1)$ number in years
$N$ = population after $t$ years
$r$ = the specific growth rate (net new organisms per unit time).

The number of organisms at time, $t$, can be found from Equation 4–12.

**EXAMPLE 4–6**  Use the following data along with the exponential model to determine the population of the predicted eastern gray wolf in the state of Wisconsin in the year 2005. Compare that result with that obtained with the geometric model.

| Year | 1975 | 1980 | 1990 | 1995 | 1996 | 1997 | 1998 | 1999 |
|---|---|---|---|---|---|---|---|---|
| **Number** | 8 | 22 | 45 | 83 | 99 | 148 | 180 | 200 |

Solution  The value of $r$ in the exponential model can be determined by plotting the natural log of $N(t)/N(0)$ vs. $t$. In this case, we will use $t = 1975$ as time zero. We can then perform a linear regression to determine the slope. If we do this, we find that the slope is 0.123. Given this, we can then determine the predicted population in 2005, 30 years after the beginning of the data.

$$N(t) = N(0)e^{0.123(t)} = 8e^{0.123(30)} = 320 \text{ wolves}$$

Now using the geometric model, we can calculate the number in 2005.

Because the geometric model is applied on an interval-by-interval basis, we must develop the general formula to apply it over a time span. This is done for the first interval of 5 years.

For year 0 to year 1 we write: $8 \times \lambda = a$
For year 1 to year 2 we write: $a \times \lambda = b$
For year 2 to year 3 we write: $b \times \lambda = c$
And so on until we get year 4 to year 5: $t \times \lambda = d$.

If we work backward, substituting for the variables $a$ through $d$, we find the equation to be

$$8 \times \lambda^5 = N(5)$$

where $N(5)$ is the number of individuals 5 years later; and is equal to 22.
So

$$8 \times \lambda^5 = 22$$

Solving for $\lambda$ yields $\lambda = 1.224$.

The general equation applied to get the data in the following table is

$$\lambda = \left[\frac{N(t)}{N(0)}\right]^{1/(t-0)}$$

where $t$ is the year of calculation and 0 is the first year for which data is available.

| Year | Number | $\lambda$ |
|------|--------|-----------|
| 0 | 8 | |
| 5 | 22 | 1.224 |
| 15 | 45 | 1.122 |
| 20 | 83 | 1.124 |
| 21 | 99 | 1.127 |
| 22 | 148 | 1.142 |
| 23 | 180 | 1.145 |
| 24 | 200 | 1.144 |
| | Average | **1.147** |

Then, using the geometric growth equation, we rearrange it to solve for $N(30)$

$$N(30) = N(24) \times (1.147^6) = 455 \text{ individuals}$$

Rarely are the resources unlimited. As such, a logistic growth model, which adds a density-dependent term to describe the limitations that exist, is more useful than the simple model described earlier. This model includes a term called the carrying capacity, $K$, which is simply the numbers of individuals an area can support. As the numbers approach $K$, the mechanisms (increased mortality, decreased reproduction, increased dispersal) that result in a decrease in the rate of population growth take over. The population change can then be represented by the model:

$$\frac{dN}{dt} = rN\left[\frac{K - N}{K}\right] \tag{4-13}$$

The shape of this curve will be S-shaped or sigmoidal.

The number of individuals can be determined by integrating Equation 4–13 to obtain

$$N(t) = \frac{KN_0}{N_0 + (K - N_0)e^{-rt}} \tag{4-14}$$

**EXAMPLE 4–7**   Assume that the population of the greater roadrunner in the Guadelope Desert was 200 per hectare at the beginning of 1999. If the carrying capacity, $K$, is 600 and $r = 0.25 \cdot \text{year}^{-1}$, what is the number of roadrunners one, five and ten years later? What happens when the number of roadrunners equals $K$?

Solution   We substitute the givens into Equation 4–14 for the one year solution:

$$N(1) = \frac{600 \times 200}{200 + (600 - 200)e^{-0.25 \times 1}} = 234 \text{ roadrunners}$$

Doing the same for the five- and ten-year solutions, we get

$N(5) = 381$ roadrunners

$N(10) = 515$ roadrunners

When the number of roadrunners is 600, that is, $K$, no additional roadrunners can be sustained on this land and the population will remain at 600.

Numerous more complex models exist. These include phenomena known as monotonic damping, damped oscillations, limiting cycles, or chaotic dynamics. A number of these models can also be used to describe plant population dynamics. However, any discussion of these models is beyond the scope of this text. More information on these models can be obtained from *The Economy of Nature,* by Robert E. Ricklefs (Chapters 15 and 16, pages 326–329; 335–368).

The models discussed thus far are known as single-species models because they describe mathematically a single species of organism. Much more complex models describe the interactions between species by considering predator–prey relationships. These models show how the interactions between two species result in periodic behavior. The models use the following two differential equations to describe the numbers of predators, $K$, and prey, $P$:

$$\frac{dP}{dt} = aP - bPK \tag{4-15}$$

$$\frac{dK}{dt} = cPK - dK \tag{4-16}$$

where   $a$ = growth rate of the prey
$b$ = mortality parameter of the prey
$c$ = growth rate of the predator
$d$ = mortality parameter of the prey

These equations are often referred to as the Lotka-Volterra model. The cycling nature of these relationships can be seen in Figure 4–13.

**FIGURE 4–13**   Graphical Illustration of the Periodic Nature of Predator–Prey Relationships

The plot with the higher amplitude represents the numbers of prey, in this case, numbers of hares. The lynx is the predator. The model used here is the Lotka–Volterra predation model with initial lynx and hare populations of 1250 and 50,000, respectively. (*Source:* Wilensky, U., K. Reisman, *Thinking Like a Wolf, a Sheep or a Firefly: Learning Biology through Constructing and Testing Computational Theories—An Embodied Modeling Approach.* Center for Connected Learning and Computer-Based Modeling Northwestern University, Evanston, IL. http://www.ccl.sesp.northwestern.edu/cm/papers/bio/long/Cognition & Instruction.)

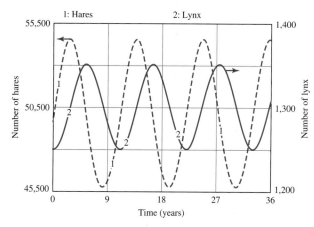

### Human Population Dynamics

Predicting the dynamics of human populations is important to environmental engineers because it is the basis for the determination of design capacity for municipal water and wastewater treatment systems and for water reservoirs. Population predictions are also important in the development of resource and pollutant management plans. Although several models are used for forecasting human populations, only the exponential model will be discussed here. Human population dynamics also depend on birth, death, gender ratio, age structure, and dispersal. In humans, cultural factors play a significant role. For example, if the average age of first pregnancy in one population is 25, and in another it is 15 and the average age of onset of menopause is 45 in both populations, the birth rates in the two populations will vary significantly. In human populations, dispersal is referred to as immigration and emigration. The effect of cultural differences can be easily illustrated using population pyramids. Population pyramids display the age by gender data of a community at one point in time. Figure 4–14 shows the population pyramids for the United States, Ghana, and Spain. Population pyramids are also useful for illustrating changes within a population over time (Figure 4–15).

Assuming an exponential growth rate, the population can be predicted using the equation

$$P(t) = P_0 e^{rt} \qquad (4\text{--}17)$$

where $P(t)$ = the population at time, $t$
$P_0$ = population at time, 0
$r$ = rate of growth
$t$ = time

The growth rate can be determined as a function of the birth rate ($b$), death rate ($d$), immigration rate ($i$), and emigration rate ($m$):

$$r = b - d + i - m \qquad (4\text{--}18)$$

where the rates are all expressed as some value per unit time.

---

**EXAMPLE 4–8**   A population of humanoids on the island of Huronth on the Planet Szacak has a net birth rate ($b$) of 1.0 individuals/(individual × year) and a net death rate ($d$) of 0.9 individuals/(individual × year). Assume that the net immigration rate is equal to the net emigration rate. How many years are required for the population to double? If in year zero, the population on the island is 85, what is the population 50 years later?

Solution   We must first calculate $r$. The net growth rate, $r$, is equal to $b - d$, or $1.0 - 0.9$ or 0.1 individuals/ individual × year. Based on this, we can calculate the projected doubling time.

$$t_{double} = \frac{\ln 2}{r} = \frac{\ln 2}{0.1} = 6.93 \text{ years}$$

The population at year 0, $N_0$, is 85.

$t = 50$ years

$$r = \frac{0.1 \text{ individuals}}{\text{individual} \times \text{year}}$$

$N_{50} = N_0 e^{rt} = 85 \times e^{(0.1)(50)} = 12{,}615$ humanoids. Hopefully the island of Huronth is quite large and able to sustain this population. Note, this model assumes that resources are unlimited. As such, the carrying capacity is not introduced into this equation.

**FIGURE 4-14**

Population pyramids for the United States, Ghana, and Spain for 2000. (*Source:* International Database, U.S. Census Bureau, International Programs Office, Washington DC, October 2002. http://www.census.gov/ipc/www/idbpyr.html)

United States: 2000

Ghana: 2000

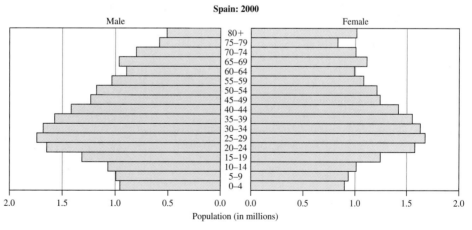

Spain: 2000

*Source*: U.S. Census Bureau, International Database.

The population of both the world and two metropolitan areas can be shown to be exponential (Figure 4–16).

One of the most difficult aspects of predicting human populations within a particular region is the accurate prediction of immigration and emigration rates. Another difficult parameter to estimate, and one that is critical for determining world population, is total fertility rate. The **total fertility rate** is the number of children a woman will have over her entire lifetime. The worldwide

**FIGURE 4–15**

Population pyramids for the United States in years 2000, 2025, and 2050 illustrating the increase in population and the "graying of America." (*Source:* U.S. Census Bureau, International Database. http://blue.census.gov/ cgi-bin/ipc/idbpyrs .pl?cty=US&out= s&ymax=250)

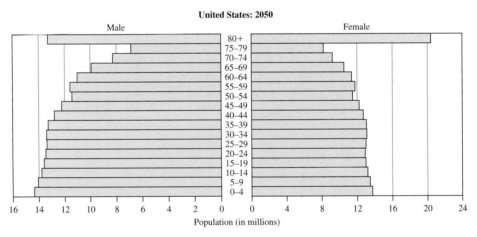

*Source*: U.S. Census Bureau, International Database.

fertility rate has been decreasing since the 1960s and is now estimated to be about 3. Although the fertility rate is decreasing there are more women in the world to give birth today than there were in the past. This results in a continued increase in population. As shown in Figure 4–17, accurately predicting the future world population depends greatly on correctly predicting the fertility rate. These differences greatly complicate policy decisions.

**FIGURE 4–16**

Population curves for the world (left) and San Diego, CA (right). (*Sources:* World population data: http://esa.un.org/unpp/ then set start date = 1950, end date = 2000, population, world http://www.census.gov/ipc/www/worldhis.html
San Diego/Tijuana data: Sweedler, A. R. Energy issues in the San Diego/Tijuana region, *Briefing Paper.* Center for Energy Studies, San Diego State University, San Diego CA, November 1999. http://www.sci.sdsu.edu/ces/CES_Res_4/Paper2.html)

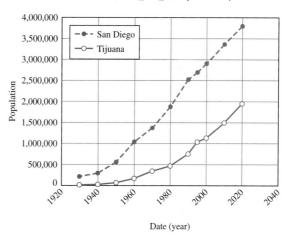

**FIGURE 4–17**

Prediction of world population using different fertility rates. Total fertility rates of 1.5, 2.1, and 2.6 children are used for low, medium, and high rates, respectively. (*Source: World Population Prospects, The 2000 Revision,* vol. III: Analytical Report. UN Population Division, Department of Economic and Social Affairs (1998) p. 61. http://www.un.org/esa/population/publications/wpp2000/chapter5.pdf (page 161))

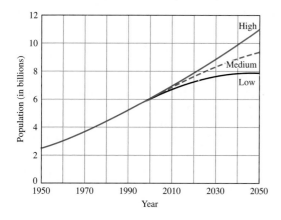

## 4–6   LAKES: AN EXAMPLE OF MASS AND ENERGY CYCLING IN AN ECOSYSTEM

Lakes provide an excellent example of the cycling of nutrients, mass, and energy within an ecosystem. In this section we will focus on the natural processes that occur in lakes and how human activities have affected these processes. You should note that any of numerous ecosystems could have been chosen as an example of these processes.

**Limnology** is the study of the ecology of inland waters. The word *limnology* comes from the Greek root *limne* meaning "pool" or "marsh." Limnologists are concerned with the relationships and productivity of freshwater biotic communities with the ever-changing physical, chemical, and biological characteristics of the waters of interest. Although we will focus on lakes, be aware that limnologists study all inland waters, including rivers, creeks, ponds, salt lakes, and even billabongs.*

### Stratification and Turnover in Deep Lakes

Nearly all deep lakes in temperate climates[†] become stratified during the summer and **overturn (turnover)** in the fall due to changes in the water temperature that result from the annual cycle of air temperature changes. In addition, lakes in cold climates undergo winter stratification and spring overturn as well. These physical processes, which are described later on, occur regardless of the water quality in the lake. Many of the lakes in the southern United States are shallow and do not tend to follow the same stratification patterns as those discussed here. Although important, the cycles exhibited by such lakes are beyond the scope of our discussion.

During the summer, the surface water of a lake is heated both indirectly by contact with warm air and directly by sunlight. Warm water, being less dense than cool water, remains near the surface until mixed downward by turbulence from wind, waves, boats, and other forces. Because this turbulence extends only a limited distance below the water's surface, the result is an upper layer of well-mixed, warm water (the **epilimnion**) floating on the lower water (the **hypolimnion**), which is poorly mixed and cool, as shown in Figure 4–18. Because of good mixing the epilimnion will be aerobic. The hypolimnion will have a lower dissolved oxygen concentration and may become anaerobic or anoxic. The intermediary layer between the epilimnion and hypolimnion is called the **metalimnion.** Within this region the temperature and density change sharply with depth. The **thermocline** may be defined as the region having a change in temperature with depth that is greater than $1°C \cdot m^{-1}$. You may have experienced the thermocline while swimming in a lake. As long as you are swimming horizontally, the water is warm, but as soon as you tread water or dive, the water turns cold. You have penetrated the thermocline. The depth of the epilimnion is related to the size of the lake. It is as shallow as 1 m in small lakes and as deep as 20 m or more in large lakes. The depth of the epilimnion is also related to storm activity in the spring when stratification is developing. A major storm at the right time will mix warmer water to a substantial depth and thus create a deeper than normal epilimnion. Once formed, lake stratification is very stable. It can be broken only by exceedingly violent storms. In fact, as the summer progresses, the stability increases because the epilimnion continues to warm, whereas the hypolimnion remains at a fairly constant temperature.

As shown in Figure 4–19, in the fall, as temperatures drop, the epilimnion cools until it is denser than the hypolimnion. The surface water then sinks, causing overturning. The water of the hypolimnion rises to the surface, where it cools and again sinks. The lake thus becomes completely mixed. If the lake is in a cold climate, this process stops when the temperature reaches 4°C because at this temperature water is the densest. Further cooling or freezing of the surface water results in winter stratification, as shown in Figure 4–19. As the water warms in the spring, it again overturns and becomes completely mixed. Thus, temperate climate lakes have at least one, if not two, cycles of stratification and turnover every year.

---

*Billabong is an aboriginal Australian word for a still body of water that collects first in the lowest areas and grows in size during a rainy season, as the rainfall becomes heavier and more frequent.

[†]Temperate climates are those without extremes of temperature and rainfall. The British Isles and the northern states of the United States have a temperate climate.

## FIGURE 4–18

Temperature and oxygen relationships in temperate eutrophic lakes.

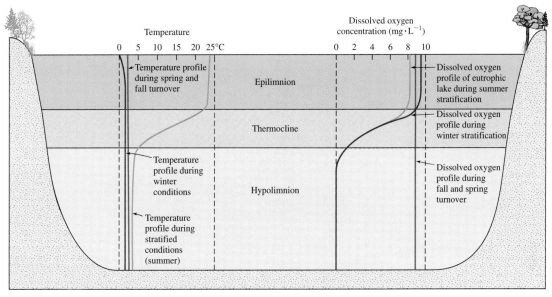

(a) Temperature profile          (b) Dissolved oxygen profile

## FIGURE 4–19

Overturn in stratified lakes. (*Source: The Great Lakes: An Environmental Atlas and Resource Book Natural Processes in the Great Lakes: Geology,* 3rd ed. Jointly produced by Government of Canada, Toronto, Ont., and the U.S. Environmental Protection Agency, Great Lakes National Program Office, Chicago, 1995. Also available at http://www.epa.gov/glnpo/atlas/glat-ch2.html#1)

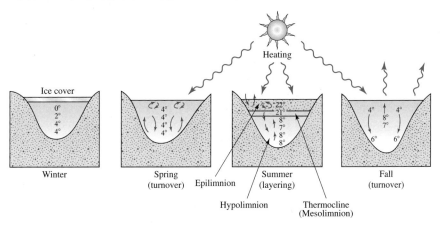

**FIGURE 4–20**

Biological zones in a temperate lake (*Source: From Water on the Web* http://wow.nrri.umn.edu/wow/under/primer/page10.html)

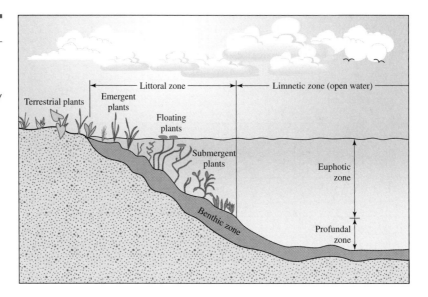

### Biological Zones

Lakes contain several distinct zones of biological activity, largely determined by the availability of light and oxygen. The most important biological zones, shown in Figure 4–20, are the euphotic, limnetic, littoral, and benthic zones.

**Limnetic Zone.**   The **limnetic zone** is layer of open water where photosynthesis can occur. Life in the limnetic zone is dominated by floating organisms (plankton) and actively swimming organisms. The producers in this zone are the planktonic algae. The primary consumers are zooplankton, such as, crustaceans and rotifers. The secondary (and higher) consumers are swimming insects and fish.

**Euphotic Zone.**   The upper layer of water through which sunlight can penetrate is called the **euphotic zone.** The depth of the euphotic zone is determined by sunlight penetration and is defined as that region of the lake where light levels are greater than 0.5–1% of that at the surface. At light intensities less than this, algae and macrophytes cannot grow. In most lakes, the euphotic zone exists within the epilimnion. However, in some very clear lakes the euphotic zone can extend well into the hypolimnion. For example, in western Lake Superior, summertime algal growth can occur at depths of up to 25 m, whereas the epilimnion only extends down about 10 m. Similarly, in Lake Tahoe, summertime algal growth has been measured at 100 m depths, whereas, the epilimnion also only extends to about 10 m depth.

In deep water, algae are the most important plants, whereas rooted plants grow in shallow water near the shore. In the euphotic zone, plants produce more oxygen by photosynthesis than they remove by respiration. Below the euphotic zone lies the **profundal zone.** The transition between the two zones is called the **light compensation point,** which corresponds roughly to the depth at which the amount of carbon dioxide being converted to sugars by photosynthesis is equal to that being released during respiration.

**Littoral Zone.**   The shallow water near the shore in which rooted (emergent) water plants (macrophytes) can grow is called the **littoral zone.** The extent of the littoral zone depends on the slope of the lake bottom and the depth of the euphotic zone. The littoral zone cannot extend deeper than the euphotic zone.

**Benthic Zone.**   The bottom sediments constitute the **benthic zone.** As organisms living in the overlying water die, they settle to the bottom where they are decomposed by organisms living

**TABLE 4–2**          Lake Classification Based on Productivity

| Lake Classification | | Chlorophyll *a* Concentration ($\mu g \cdot L^{-1}$) | Secchi Depth (m) | Total Phosphorus Concentration ($\mu g \cdot L^{-1}$) |
|---|---|---|---|---|
| Oligotrophic | Average | 1.7 | 9.9 | 8 |
| | Range | 0.3–4.5 | 5.4–28.3 | 3.0–17.7 |
| Mesotrophic | Average | 4.7 | 4.2 | 26.7 |
| | Range | 3–11 | 1.5–8.1 | 10.9–95.6 |
| Eutrophic | Average | 14.3 | 2.5 | 84.4 |
| | Range | 3–78 | 0.8–7.0 | 15–386 |
| Hypereutrophic | | > 50 | < 0.5 | Often >100 |

*Note:* Classification for oligotrophic, mesotrophic, and eutrophic lakes from Wetzel, R. G. *Limnology.* W. B. Saunders, Philadelphia, 1983, p. 767. Classification for hypereutrophic lakes from Kevern, N. R., King, D. L., Ring, R. "Lake classification systems—Part 1" *The Michigan Riparion,* February 1996, last updated December, 1999. www.mlswa.org/lkclassill.htm

in the benthic zone. Bacteria and fungi are always present. Attached algae may also be present. The presence of higher life forms, such as worms, aquatic insects, molluscs, and crustaceans, depends on the availability of oxygen.

### Lake Productivity

The productivity of a lake is a measure of its ability to support aquatic life and is often determined by measuring the amount of algal growth that can be supported by the available nutrients. Although a more productive lake will have a higher biomass concentration than a less productive one, the biomass supported is often undesirable, resulting in taste and odor problems, low dissolved oxygen levels, especially at night, excessive macrophyte growth, loss of water clarity, and proliferation of forage fish and sludge worms. Because of the important role productivity plays in determining water quality, it forms a basis for classifying lakes. Table 4–2 shows how lakes are classified based upon productivity.

Productivity is controlled by the limiting factor, which may be the concentration of nitrogen or phosphorus or the light intensity. This phenomena is known as **Liebig's law of the minimum**.* In many freshwater lakes, phosphorus is often the limiting nutrient. This is because of all the nutrients, only phosphorus is not readily available from the atmosphere or the natural water supply. Therefore, the amount of phosphorus often controls the quantity of algal growth and therefore the productivity of lakes. This can be seen from Figure 4–21 in which the concentration of chlorophyll *a* is plotted against phosphorus concentration. Chlorophyll *a*, one of the green pigments involved in photosynthesis, is found in all algae, so it is used to distinguish the mass of algae in the water from other organic material such as bacteria. It has been estimated that the phosphorus concentration should be below 0.010–0.015 mg $\cdot$ L$^{-1}$ to limit algae blooms [10].

Lakes have a natural life cycle and they change over time, although the times can be many tens of thousands of years. There are young, middle-aged, and old lakes. As lakes age, they slowly shrink as land overtakes the shores of the lake. The trees and other vegetation along the shores of the lake shed organic debris into the lake. This organic matter serves as a carbon source for the organisms in the lake. As the organic matter decays, it can become a new habitat for sedges, grasses, and rushes. This will allow rooted species to flourish where lily pads once floated on the surface. As the lake

---

*In 1840, Justin Liebig formulated the idea that the growth of a plant is dependent on the amount of foodstuff that is presented to it in minimum quantity.

**FIGURE 4–21**

Relationship between summer levels of chlorophyll *a* and measured total phosphorus concentration for 143 lakes. (*Source:* Jones, J. R., Bachmann, R. W., "Prediction of phosphorus and chlorophyll levels in lakes," *Journal of the Water Pollution Control Federation,* vol. 48, p. 2176, 1976.)

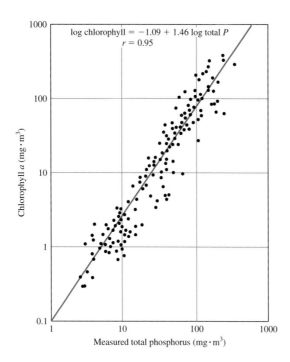

shrinks and productivity increases, the lake may become anoxic or anaerobic, resulting in a significant change in the lake ecology. This process of succession can continue until the lake becomes a marsh, then a bog, and finally a forest or grassland. This process is illustrated in Figure 4–22.

**Oligotrophic Lakes.**   **Oligotrophic** lakes have a low level of productivity due to a severely limited supply of nutrients to support algal growth. As a result, the water is clear enough that the bottom can be seen at considerable depths. In this case, the euphotic zone often extends into the hypolimnion, which is aerobic. Oligotrophic lakes, therefore, support cold-water game fish. Lake Tahoe on the California–Nevada border, Crater Lake in Oregon, and the blue waters of Lake Superior (Michigan–Wisconsin–Ontario border) are classic examples of oligotrophic lakes. However, the clarity of Lake Tahoe is decreasing due to an increase in the numbers of people residing within the watershed, and a concomitant increase in sewage discharge to the lake.

**Eutrophic Lakes.**   **Eutrophic** lakes have a high productivity because of an abundant supply of nutrients. Because the algae cause the water to be highly turbid, the euphotic zone may extend only partially into the epilimnion. As the algae die, they settle to the lake bottom where they are decomposed by benthic organisms. In a eutrophic lake, this decomposition is sufficient to deplete the hypolimnion of oxygen during summer stratification as shown in Figure 4–23. Because the hypolimnion is anaerobic during the summer, eutrophic lakes support only warm-water fish. In fact, most cold-water fish are driven out of the lake long before the hypolimnion becomes anaerobic because they generally require dissolved oxygen levels of at least 5–6 mg · $L^{-1}$. Highly eutrophic lakes may also have large mats of floating algae that typically impart unpleasant tastes and odors to the water. Halsted Bay of Lake Minnetonka (Minnesota) and the Neuse River (North Carolina) are examples of eutrophic waters.

**Mesotrophic Lakes.**   Lakes intermediate between oligotrophic and eutrophic are called **mesotrophic.** Although substantial depletion of oxygen may have occurred in the hypolimnion, it remains aerobic. Lake Ontario, Ice Lake (Minnesota), and Grindstone Lake (Minnesota) are examples of mesotrophic lakes. Lake Michigan and Lake Huron are classified as mesooligotrophic, meaning the level of productivity is higher than that of an oligotrophic lake but not quite that of a mesotrophic lake.

**FIGURE 4–22**

Succession of a lake or pond. (*Source:* Karen Heathman *Our Lakes* http://www.kidfish. bc.ca/our_lakes. htm#lifespan)

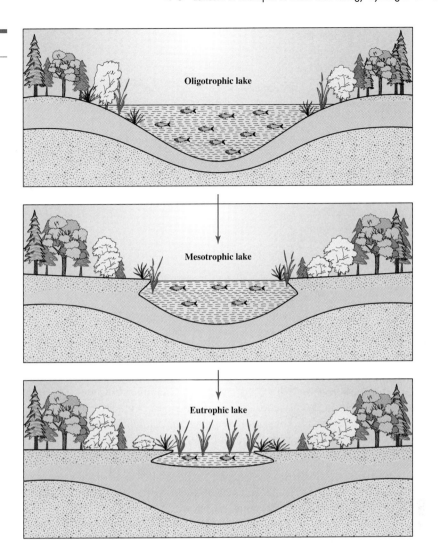

**Dystrophic Lakes.**   **Dystrophic** lakes receive a large quantity of organic material from outside the lake and have low productivity due to low nutrient concentrations. Such lakes are usually surrounded by conifer forests and are small in size. The decomposition of fallen needles results in a significant input of acid to the lake. The lake is typically yellowish brown in color, moderately clear, contains high levels of dissolved organic matter and tannin concentrations, and is acidic. These lakes also have their own characteristic algae, insects, and fish. Sphagnum moss proliferates as a thick mat on the water's surface. Organisms, such as carp, mud minnows, dragon flies and giant water bugs, which are tolerant of low oxygen levels, replace their predecessors of the eutrophic lake. There are also quantities of emergent vegetation, especially around the edges of the lake. There is zero oxygen on the deep bottom of the lake, thus no fish can survive. Aerobic life exists only in the shallow regions of a dystrophic lake during summer. Examples of dystrophic lakes are Alligator (New) Lake (North Carolina), Swan Creek Lake (North Carolina), Glen Lake, and the bog lakes of northern Michigan.

**Hypereutrophic Lakes.**   **Hypereutrophic** lakes are extremely eutrophic, with a high algal productivity level and intense algal blooms. They are often relatively shallow lakes with much accumulated organic sediment. They have extensive, dense weed beds and often accumulations of filamentous algae. They have low water clarity and high phosphate and chlorophyll concentrations. The fish and other aquatic animals in these lakes are subject to extreme shifts in oxygen

**FIGURE 4–23**

Seasonal stratification in lakes will vary with trophic levels.
T = temperature (°C);
DO = dissolved oxygen $(mg \cdot L^{-1})$

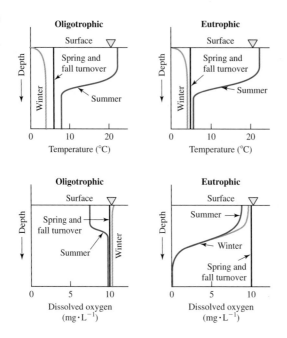

concentrations; sometimes very high and at other times very low, even depleted. These lakes are often subject to "winter kill" and even "summer kill" during which the depletion of oxygen results in an extensive kill of fish and sometimes other organisms. Recreational use of the waters in hypereutrophic lakes is often impaired. Examples of hypereutrophic lakes are Onondaga Lake (New York) and Upper Klamath Lake (Oregon).

**Senescent Lakes.**   Very old, shallow lakes in advanced stages of eutrophication are called **senescent** lakes. These lakes have thick organic sediments formed from accumulated aquatic vegetation and dead plant material. Rooted water plants exist in great abundance. These lakes are nearing extinction as a productive lake environment. They will eventually become marshes.

### Eutrophication

Eutrophication was once thought to be a natural and inevitable process in which lakes gradually become shallower and more productive through the introduction and cycling of nutrients. However, many oligotrophic lakes have remained such since the last ice age. Ultraoligotrophic lakes such as Lake Tahoe have been unproductive for millions of years. Studies in paleolimnology also suggest that lakes may undergo natural variations in productivity.

Cultural eutrophication of lakes can occur through the introduction of high levels of nutrients (usually nitrogen and phosphorus, although phosphorus is generally the more limiting of the two). This occurs due to poor management of the watershed and the input of human and animal wastes. Such changes (from oligotrophic to senescent status) can occur over a period of decades and will cease only if the input of nutrients is halted or significantly reduced. With the control of nitrogen and phosphorus inputs, the process of cultural eutrophication has greatly slowed in both Lake Erie and the Chesapeake Bay. Additional information on cultural eutrophication and its control is presented in Chapter 8.

Because of the importance of phosphorus in enhancing the rates of eutrophication, it is critical that environmental scientists and engineers be able to predict concentrations of phosphorus in lakes. A mass balance approach for a completely mixed lake at steady-state conditions can be used to determine a seasonal/annual estimate. This can be then used to determine the required control measures necessary to halt the process of eutrophication.

**FIGURE 4–24**

Simple phosphorus system.

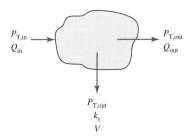

Phosphorus enters a lake in surface runoff, from wastewater discharge pipes, and from septic systems. Phosphorus is lost from the system through uptake by organisms, settling of dead biomass (containing phosphorus), and from any outfalls (streams leaving the lake). Figure 4–24 illustrates how we can develop a simple model [11] for the total phosphorus concentration, $P_T$.

$$\frac{V \, dP_T}{dt} = P_{T,in} Q_{in} - k_s P_{T,out} V - P_{T,out} Q_{out} \qquad (4\text{--}19)$$

where $V$ = volume of the hypothetical lake
$\quad P_{T,in}$ = concentration of total phosphorus in the inflow (streams entering the lake, runoff, etc.)
$\quad Q_{in}$ = inflow rate
$\quad k_s$ = phosphorus removal rate (combined settling and biological uptake)
$\quad P_{T,out}$ = concentration of total phosphorus in the lake and in the outflow (under complete mixing conditions)
$\quad Q_{out}$ = outflow rate

At steady state, $dP_T/dt = 0$, therefore

$$0 = P_{T,in} Q_{in} - k_s P_{T,out} V - Q_{out} P_{T,out} \qquad (4\text{--}20)$$

$$P_{T,out} = \frac{(P_{T,in} Q_{in})}{(k_s V + Q_{out})} \qquad (4\text{--}21)$$

If the removal rate (sometimes called the settling velocity where it does not include biological uptake) is given in units of distance per time (e.g., $m \cdot s^{-1}$), then the velocity should be multiplied by the surface area of the lake, rather than the volume.

**EXAMPLE 4–9**   Greenlawn Lake has a surface area $2.6 \times 10^6 \, m^2$. The average depth is 12 m. The lake is fed by a stream having a flow rate of $1.2 \, m^3 \cdot s^{-1}$ and a phosphorus concentration of $0.045 \, mg \cdot L^{-1}$. Runoff from the homes along the lake adds phosphorus at an average annual rate of $2.6 \, g \cdot s^{-1}$. The settling rate of the lake is $0.36 \, day^{-1}$. A river flows from the lake at a flowrate of $1.2 \, m^3 \cdot s^{-1}$. What is the steady-state concentration of phosphorus in the lake? What is the trophic state of the lake?

Solution   $0 = P_{T,stream} Q_{stream} + P_{T,runoff} - k_s P_{T,out} \, ⩝ - P_{T,out} Q_{out}$

First convert the stream phosphorus concentration to units of grams per cubic meter.

$$P_{stream} = \frac{0.045 \, mg \cdot L^{-1}(1000 \, L \cdot m^{-3})}{1000 \, mg \cdot g^{-1}} = 0.045 \, g \cdot m^{-3}$$

Therefore,

$$0 = (0.045 \, g \cdot m^{-3})(1.2 \, m^3 \cdot s^{-1}) + 2.6 \, g \cdot s^{-1}$$

$$- (0.36 \, day^{-1}) \left( \frac{1 \, day}{86,400 \, s} \right) (2.6 \times 10^6 \, m^2)(12 \, m)(P_{T,out}) - (P_{T,out})(1.2 \, m^3 \cdot s^{-1})$$

Check each product, the units should be grams per second.

$$0 = 0.054 \text{ g} \cdot \text{s}^{-1} + 2.6 \text{ g} \cdot \text{s}^{-1} - (130 \text{ m}^3 \cdot \text{s}^{-1})(P_{T,\text{out}}) - (P_{T,\text{out}})(1.2 \text{ m}^3 \cdot \text{s}^{-1})$$

$$P_{T,\text{out}} = 0.020 \text{ g} \cdot \text{m}^{-3}, \text{ or } 0.020 \text{ mg} \cdot \text{L}^{-1}$$

$$(0.020 \text{ mg} \cdot \text{L}^{-1})(1000 \text{ μg} \cdot \text{mg}^{-1}) = 20 \text{ μg} \cdot \text{L}^{-1}$$

Therefore, using Table 4-2, you can determine that the lake borders on a eutrophic state.

A discussion of how to control eutrophication is presented in Section 8–4.

## 4-7 ENVIRONMENTAL LAWS TO PROTECT ECOSYSTEMS

Since the late 1960s and early 1970s, many countries have enacted laws to protect species from extinction. Although numerous laws such as the Lacey Act of 1900 and the Migratory Bird Act of 1929 were promulgated early in the 20th century, the landmark acts protecting species were the Endangered Species Conservation Act of 1969, the Marine Mammal Protection Act of 1972, and the Endangered Species Act of 1973. The Endangered Species Act is important because it declared that endangered species "are of aesthetic, ecological, educational, historical, recreational, and scientific value to the nation and its people." It made the importation, exportation, or selling in interstate or international commence of any endangered species or any product of an endangered species illegal. It is also illegal to capture, harass, or harm any animal on the endangered species list.

In the United States another law important to the protection of ecosystems and the plants and animals within is the National Environmental Policy Act (NEPA) of 1969. NEPA is significant in that its language justifies the protection of the environment on aesthetic, cultural, and moral grounds.* The U.S. Congress recognized both the profound impact of human activity on natural environment and the critical importance of restoring and maintaining environmental quality to the overall welfare and development of humanity. Through this act, Congress sought to "foster and promote the general welfare to the overall welfare and development of man *(sic),* to create and maintain conditions under which humans and nature can exist in productive harmony, and fulfill the social, economic, and other requirements of present and future generations of Americans." One of the major aspects of the regulations promulgated under this act requires the preparation of environmental impact statements (EISs) on those major actions determined to have a significant impact on the quality of the human environment (40 CFR Part 6; Subpart A). These documents are reviewed by the U.S. EPA and must show the impact of the proposed project on the ecology of the area. Clearly, these regulations have had a profound effect on protecting the environment. If we value the environment for its own sake and for the welfare and well-being of humanity, we must work to ensure that these acts and regulations are maintained and all efforts to dilute them are halted.

## CHAPTER REVIEW

When you have completed studying this chapter, you should be able to do the following without the aid of your text or notes:

1. Define the terms *ecosystem* and *ecology*. What are the differences in these terms?
2. List the different nutrient levels of organisms. Provide the energy source, electron donor, and carbon source for each classification of organism.

---

*This act declared a national policy to encourage productive and enjoyable harmony between man (sic) and his environment; to promote efforts which will prevent or eliminate damage to the environment and biosphere and stimulate the health and welfare of man; to enrich the understanding of the ecological systems and natural resources important to the Nation; and to establish a Council on Environmental Quality.

3. Describe primary and secondary productivity. Give examples of producers, consumers, and decomposers.
4. For each type of decomposition (aerobic, anoxic, and anaerobic), list the electron acceptor and important end products.
5. Draw a typical food web for Lake Michigan.
6. Describe the difference between a food web and an ecological pyramid.
7. Describe bioaccumulation, bioconcentration, and biomagnification. How are bioconcentration factors used?
8. Describe a pure culture.
9. List the four major groups of requirements necessary for bacterial growth. List the important factors in each group.
10. Describe how the growth in a mixed culture differs from that in a pure culture.
11. Describe what is meant by dynamic equilibrium.
12. List the models used to describe animal population dynamics. List the attributes and problems associated with each model.
13. Describe what is meant by carrying capacity. Explain how it influences population growth. Do cities have a carrying capacity for humans?
14. Rank the major global pools of carbon (terrestrial vegetation and biomass, atmosphere, surface ocean, and intermediate/deep ocean) by the total mass of carbon in each. What is the predominant form of carbon in each?
15. List the major pathways in the nitrogen cycle, the chemical species that are transformed in each, and the species (give one or two examples) that accomplish each of the transformations.
16. List the major pathways in the phosphorus cycle, the chemical species that are transformed in each, and the species (give one or two examples) that accomplish each of the transformations.
17. List the major pathways in the sulfur cycle, the chemical species that are transformed in each, and the species (give one or two examples) that accomplish each of the transformations.
18. Describe the major difference between the phosphorus cycle and all other nutrient cycles.
19. Sketch and compare the epilimnion and hypolimnion with respect to the following: location in a lake, temperature, and oxygen abundance (i.e., dissolved oxygen).
20. Describe the process of stratification and overturn in lakes.
21. Define the following terms: epilimnion, hypolimnion, thermocline, and mesolimnion.
22. Define the following terms: littoral, limnetic, euphotic, profundal, and benthic zones of lakes.
22. Explain what determines the euphotic zone of a lake and what significance this has for biological growth.
23. Describe the classification of lakes as oligotrophic, mesotrophic, eutrophic, hypereutrophic, or senescent in terms of productivity, clarity, and oxygen levels.
24. Explain the process of eutrophication. Explain the difference between natural and cultural eutrophication.
25. State Leibig's law of the minimum.
26. Name the most common limiting nutrient in lakes and explain why it is most commonly limits growth.
27. List three sources of phosphorus that can be controlled to reduce cultural eutrophication.

## PROBLEMS

**4-1**   A population of purple rabbits lives on the island of Zulatop. The rabbits have a net growth rate of 0.09 year$^{-1}$. At the present time there are 176 rabbits on the island. What is the predicted number of rabbits 5, 10, and 20 years from now. Use the simple exponential growth equation to calculate the number of rabbits.

   **Answer:** $P(5) = 276$ rabbits      $P(10) = 433$      $P(20) = 1,065$

**4-2**   Recalculate the number of purple rabbits if the carrying capacity is 386 and you use the logistic equation. Assume the same number of rabbits at the present time and use the same intervals.

**4-3**   A population of spotted wolves lives on the mountain Hesperides. There were 26 wolves in the year 2054 and 54 wolves counted in 2079. Assuming exponential growth, what is the net growth rate constant?

   **Answer:** 0.029 year$^{-1}$

**4-4**   For Problem 4–3, what will the population of wolves be in 2102?

**4-5**   Using the data presented in Problem 4–3, a net growth rate of 0.04 year$^{-1}$ and a carrying capacity of 159, what will be the predicted population of wolves in the year 2102?

   **Answer:** 91 wolves

**4-6**   A population of Ladon dragons has a birth rate of 3.3 individuals/(individual × year) and a death rate of 3.2 3 individuals/(individual × year).

   (a)  What is $r$?

   (b)  Based on your answer from part a, is the population growing, declining, or remaining constant?

   (c)  Assuming exponential growth, how many years are necessary for the population to double?

   (d)  On the Wondering Rock Mountain, the population is presently 49. What will the population be in 25 years?

   (e)  If the carrying capacity were 105 on the Wondering Rock Mountain, what would the population be in 25 years (using the logistic model).

**4-7**   Suppose there is a grove of 1334 Asphodel plants on Prometheus Island located in Alcyonian Lake. The trees are growing with an $r$ of 0.21 individuals/(individual × year). The carrying capacity on the island is 3250. What is the population in 35 years, assuming a logistic growth model applies.

   **Answer:** 3247

**4-8**   Chalchihuitlicue Lake has a surface area of $4.1 \times 10^6$ m$^2$. The average depth of the lake is 15 m. The lake is fed by a stream having a flow rate of 2.02 m$^3 \cdot$ s$^{-1}$ and a phosphorus concentration of 0.023 mg $\cdot$ L$^{-1}$. A wastewater treatment plant discharges into the lake at a rate of 0.2 m$^3 \cdot$ s$^{-1}$ and a phosphorus concentration of 1.1 mg $\cdot$ L$^{-1}$. Runoff from the homes along the lake adds phosphorus at an average annual rate of 1.35 g $\cdot$ s$^{-1}$. The settling rate of phosphorus from the lake averages 0.94 year$^{-1}$. The river flows from the lake at a flow rate of 2.42 m$^3 \cdot$ s$^{-1}$. Assume evaporation and precipitation to negate each other. What is the concentration of phosphorus in the river flowing from the lake?

**4-9**   You have been conducting a water quality study of Lake Nanahuatzin, which has a surface area of $8.9 \times 10^5$ m$^2$. The average depth of the lake is 9 m. The lake is fed by a stream having a flow rate of 1.02 m$^3 \cdot$ s$^{-1}$ and a phosphorus concentration of 0.023 mg $\cdot$ L$^{-1}$. Runoff from the homes along the lake adds phosphorus at an average annual rate of 1.25 g $\cdot$ s$^{-1}$. The river flows from the lake at a flow rate of 1.02 m$^3 \cdot$ s$^{-1}$. The average phosphorus concentration in the lake is 13.2 µg $\cdot$ L$^{-1}$. Assume evaporation and precipitation negate each other. What is the calculated average settling rate of phosphorus?

   **Answer:** $1.19 \times 10^{-5}$s$^{-1}$   or   376 year$^{-1}$

**4-10**   The concentration of diazinon has been measured to be 23.3 µg $\cdot$ L$^{-1}$ in Lake Lavinia. The bioconcentration factor for diazinon is 337 L $\cdot$ kg$^{-1}$. What is the expected concentration of diazinon in fish living in Lake Lavinia?

**4-11**   The concentration of the pentachlorophenol has been measured to be 42.8 µg $\cdot$ L$^{-1}$ in Quirinus Pond. A study of the Gratiae fish revealed an average lipid concentration of 30,600 µg $\cdot$ kg$^{-1}$. What is the bioconcentration factor for this fish?

   **Answer:** 715

**4-12**   Farmer Aequitas is raising deer. She has 110 female deer age 3–15 months. The deer require 22 MJ of metabolizable energy per day during the spring months. The deer are being fed a mixture of 50% wheat and

50% silage. The wheat contains 85% dry matter (DM) and has 12.5 MJ metabolizable energy per kilogram of DM. The silage has 30% dry matter and 10.5 MJ metabolizable energy per kilogram of DM. How many kilograms of feed are required per day to feed the 110 deer?

**4-13** For Problem 4–12 calculate the energy (in megajoules) converted to body tissue on a daily basis. Assume that 19% of the feed consumed is excreted as undigested material. Of the remaining 81% that is digested, 78% is used in generating metabolic waste products and heat. The remaining 22% is incorporated into tissue.

> **Answer:** $3.92 \cdot day^{-1}$

**4-14** Using the data provided in Example 4–4, calculate the mass of phosphorus (in kilograms $P_2O_5$) and potassium (in kilograms $K_2O$) per hectare of land.

**4-15** In year 2, the farmer mentioned in Example 4–4 plans to plant soybeans. No manure is to be applied during this crop year. The soybean is a legume and can fix adequate atmospheric nitrogen to produce the desired yield of soybeans. Additional nitrogen fertilizer does not produce significant yield increases. Soybeans require 50 kg N · (hectare)$^{-1}$, 35 kg P · (hectare)$^{-1}$, and 225 kg K · (hectare)$^{-1}$ according to the local extension agent.

(a) Determine if the previous year's manure application provides enough phosphorus and potassium to meet the crop nutrient requirements of the soybeans.

(b) Estimate the remaining phosphorus and potassium after the corn is harvested. The corn crop from year 1 would have removed 52 kg of $P_2O_5$ hectare$^{-1}$ and 38 kg of $K_2O$ hectare$^{-1}$.

> **Answer:** (a) Sufficient nitrogen and phosphorus are provided. Additional potassium would be required.
> (b) 77.3 kg P · (hectare)$^{-1}$
> 48.5 kg K · (hectare)$^{-1}$

## DISCUSSION QUESTIONS

**4-1** Rank the major global pools of carbon (terrestrial vegetation and biomass, atmosphere, surface ocean, and intermediate/deep ocean) by the total mass of carbon in each. How is our consumption of fossil fuels and resultant emission of carbon dioxide changing the ratios and predominant forms of carbon in each pool?

**4-2** Why is there more standing detritus in tundra soils than in tropical rainforest soils?

**4-3** Describe how human activities are altering each of the nutrient cycles.

**4-4** Describe how phosphorus availability could control nitrogen uptake.

**4-5** How can the university you attend promote biological conservation?

**4-6** Choose an endangered species. Provide an argument, both for and against, the protection of this species.

**4-7** Is cultural eutrophication ever beneficial? Defend your position.

**4-8** Recently, several dams have been removed or breached (removal of the earthen portion while leaving the concrete intact) because they had outlived their intended purpose. Discuss the benefits and negative effects of dam removal.

**4-9** What are some environmental impacts of dams? Given the various negative effects dams have on rivers, what is the likelihood that new dams will be built? Discuss your answer.

## ADDITIONAL READING

Berner, E. K., Berner, R. A. *Global Environment: Water, Air, and Geochemical Cycles.* Prentice Hall, New York, 1996.

Claggett, H. D. *Wildlife Conservation.* Edited by The Reference Shelf, vol. 69, no. 2. H. W. Wilson, New York, 1995.

Emanoi, M. L., ed. *Encyclopedia of Endangered Species.* Gale Research, Detroit, 1994.

"Ecology"; "Endangered Species" and "Extinction (Biology)" in *McGraw-Hill Encyclopedia of Science and Technology,* 9th ed. McGraw-Hill, New York.

Horne, A., Goldman, C. *Limnology.* McGraw-Hill, New York, 1994.

Lowe, D. W., Matthews, J. R., Moseley, C. *The Official World Wildlife Fund Guide to Endangered Species of North America,* ed. by Beacham Publishing, Washington, D.C. 1990.

McCullough, D. R. *Metapopulations and Wildlife Conservation.* Island Press, Washington, D.C. 1996.

Sherry, C. J. *Endangered Species: A Reference Handbook.* ABC-CLIO, Santa Barbara, California, 1998.

Wetzel, R. G. *Limnology: Lake and River Ecosystems,* 3rd ed. Academic Press, New York, 1999.

## REFERENCES

1. Western, D., Pearl, M. C. *Conservation for the Twenty-first Century,* Oxford University Press, New York, 1989, Figure 7.2, p. 55.
2. Glassner-Schwayder, K. Zebra mussels cause economic and ecological problems in the Great Lakes. *GLSC Fact Sheet* 2000-6, August 15, 2000. U.S. Geological Survey, Great Lakes Science Center, Ann Arbor, MI. http://www.glsc.usgs.gov/information/factsheets/zebra_mussels00/zebra_mussels00.htm
3. University of Wisconsin Sea Grant Institute, Outreach Program, Nonindigenous species, zebra mussels. http://www.seagrant.wisc.edu/outreach/nis/More%20ANS/Zebra.asp http://www.seagrant.wisc.edu/communications/publications/Fish/exotics.html
4. Feeding deer by B. Mackintosh Farmnote 45/91 Department of Agriculture-Western Australia http://www.agric.wa.gov.au/agency/pubns/farmnote/1991/f04591.htm
5. Schnoor, J. L. *Environmental Modeling: Fate and Transport of Pollutants in Water, Air and Soil.* John Wiley and Sons, New York, 1996, pp. 342–343.
6. *Toxicology for the Public.* Institute for Environmental Toxicology, Michigan State University, East Lansing, MI. http://www.iet.msu.edu/Tox_for_Public/Bioaccum.htm
7. U.S. EPA, 1986, Superfund Public Health Evaluation Manual, Office of Emergency and Remedial Response, Washington, D.C.
8. Keeling, C.D., Whorf, T. P. "*Atmospheric $CO_2$ records from sites in the SIO air sampling network.*" In: *Trends: A Compendium of Data on Global Change.* Carbon Dioxide Information Analysis Center, Oak Ridge National Laboratory, Oak Ridge, TN, 1998.
9. Much of this material is taken from the following sources:
   Allison, A. *Population Control,* Penguin Books, London, 1970.
   Brewer, G. *Population Dynamics,* professor and interim chair, North Dakota State University.
   Caughley, G. *Analysis of Vertebrate Populations,* John Wiley & Sons, London, 1977.
   Edge, W. D. *Population Dynamics,* Department of Fisheries and Wildlife, Oregon State University http://www.orst.edu/instruct/fw251/notebook/population.html
   Maloney, K. *A Menagerie of Population Dynamics.* Iowa State University.
10. Vollenweider, R. A. "Input–output models with special reference to the phosphorus loading concept in limnology." *Schweizerische Zeitschrift für Hydrologie,* vol. 37, pp. 53–83, 1975.
11. Thomann, R.V., Mueller, J. A. *Principles of Surface Water Quality Modelling and Control,* New York: Harper & Row, Inc., 1987.

# 5

# Risk Perception, Assessment, and Management

## 5-1   INTRODUCTION

The concepts of risk and hazard are inextricably intertwined. **Hazard** implies a probability of adverse effects in a particular situation. **Risk** is a measure of the probability. In some instances the measure is subjective, or perceived risk. Scientists and engineers use models to calculate an estimated risk. In some instances actual data may be used to estimate the risk. We make estimates of risk for a wide range of environmental phenomena. Examples include the risk of tornadoes, hurricanes, floods, droughts, landslides, and forest fires. We have chosen to limit our discussion to the risk to human health from chemicals released to the environment.

In the last two decades an attempt has been made to bring more rigor to the risk estimation process. Today this process is called **quantitative risk assessment,** or more simply **risk assessment.** The use of the results of a risk assessment to make policy decisions is called **risk management.** Chapters 8–16 discuss alternative measures for managing risk by reducing the amount of contaminants in the environment.

## 5-2   RISK PERCEPTION [1]

The old political saying, "Perception is reality," is no less true for environmental concerns than it is for politics. People respond to the hazards they perceive. If their perceptions are faulty, risk management efforts to improve environmental protection may be misdirected.

Some risks are well quantified. For example, the frequency and severity of automobile accidents are well documented. In contrast, other hazardous activities such as those resulting from the use of alcohol and tobacco are more difficult to document. Their assessment requires complex epidemiological studies.

When lay people (and some experts for that matter) are asked to evaluate risk, they seldom have ready access to the statistics. In most cases, they rely on inferences based on their experience. People are likely to judge an event as likely or frequent if instances of it are easy to imagine or recall. Also, it is evident that acceptable risk is inversely related to the number of people participating in the activity. In addition, recent events such as a hurricane or earthquake can seriously distort risk judgments.

Table 5–1 and Figure 5–1 illustrate different perceptions of risk. Four different groups were asked to rate 30 activities and technologies according to the present risk of death from each. Three of the groups, from Eugene, Oregon, included 30 college students, 40 members of the League of Women Voters (LOWV), and 25 business and professional members of the "Active Club." The fourth group was composed of 15 people selected from across the United States because of their professional involvement in risk assessment. Table 5–1 shows how the various groups ranked the risk of the activities or technologies. The same groups were asked to estimate the mean fatality rate for the same group of activities and technologies given the fact that the annual death toll from motor vehicle accidents in the United States was 50,000. The results are plotted in Figure 5–1. The lines for "experts" and "lay groups" are lines of best fit to the results. The line at 45 degrees depicts an imaginary line of perfect fit. The steeper slope of the line for the experts' risk judgments shows that they are more closely associated with the actual annual fatality rates than those of the lay groups.

Putting risk perception in perspective, we can calculate the risk of death from some familiar causes. To begin, we recognize that we will all die at some time. So, as a trivial example, the lifetime risk of death from all causes is 100%, or 1.0. In the United States in 2001, there were about 3.9 million deaths per year. Of these, about 541,532 were cancer-related. Without considering age factors, the risk of dying from cancer in a lifetime was about

$$\frac{541,532}{3.9 \times 10^6} = 0.14$$

The annual risk (assuming a 70-year life expectancy and again ignoring age factors) is about

$$\frac{0.14}{70} = 0.002$$

| **TABLE 5–1** | Ordering of Perceived Risk for 30 Activities and Technologies[a] | | | |
|---|---|---|---|---|
| **Source of Risk** | **Group 1: LOWV** | **Group 2: College Students** | **Group 3: Active Club Members** | **Group 4: Experts** |
| Nuclear power | 1 | 1 | 8 | 20 |
| Motor vehicles | 2 | 5 | 3 | 1 |
| Handguns | 3 | 2 | 1 | 4 |
| Smoking | 4 | 3 | 4 | 2 |
| Motorcycles | 5 | 6 | 2 | 6 |
| Alcoholic beverages | 6 | 7 | 5 | 3 |
| General (private) aviation | 7 | 15 | 11 | 12 |
| Police work | 9 | 8 | 7 | 17 |
| Pesticides | 9 | 4 | 15 | 8 |
| Surgery | 10 | 11 | 9 | 5 |
| Fire fighting | 11 | 10 | 6 | 18 |
| Large construction | 12 | 14 | 13 | 13 |
| Hunting | 13 | 18 | 10 | 23 |
| Spray cans | 14 | 13 | 23 | 26 |
| Mountain climbing | 15 | 22 | 12 | 29 |
| Bicycles | 16 | 24 | 14 | 15 |
| Commercial aviation | 17 | 16 | 18 | 16 |
| Electric power | 18 | 19 | 19 | 9 |
| Swimming | 19 | 30 | 17 | 10 |
| Contraceptives | 20 | 9 | 22 | 11 |
| Skiing | 21 | 25 | 16 | 30 |
| X-rays | 22 | 17 | 24 | 7 |
| High school and college football | 23 | 26 | 21 | 27 |
| Railroads | 24 | 23 | 20 | 19 |
| Food preservatives | 25 | 12 | 28 | 14 |
| Food coloring | 26 | 20 | 30 | 21 |
| Power mowers | 27 | 28 | 25 | 28 |
| Prescription antibiotics | 28 | 21 | 26 | 24 |
| Home appliances | 29 | 27 | 27 | 22 |
| Vaccinations | 30 | 29 | 29 | 25 |

LOWV = League of Women Voters members.

[a] The ordering is based on the geometric mean risk ratings within each group. Rank I represents the most risky activity or technology.

*Source:* Adapted from: Slovic P., B. Fischoff, and S. Lichtenstein, "Rating risk," *Environment,* vol. 21, pp. 1–20, 1979.

For comparison, Table 5–2 summarizes the risk of dying from some causes of death.

In developing standards for environmental protection, the EPA often selects a lifetime incremental risk of cancer in the range of $10^{-7}$ to $10^{-4}$ as acceptable. Table 5–3 shows a comparison of other activities that, based on statistical evidence, yield a risk of $10^{-6}$.

Of course, if the risk of dying in one year is increased, the risk of dying from another cause in a later year is decreased. Because accidents often occur early in life, a typical accident

**FIGURE 5–1**

Judgments of perceived risk for experts and lay people plotted against the best technical estimates of annual fatalities for 25 technologies and activities. The lines are the straight lines that best fit the points. The experts' risk judgments are seen to be more closely associated with annual fatality rates than are the lay judgments.

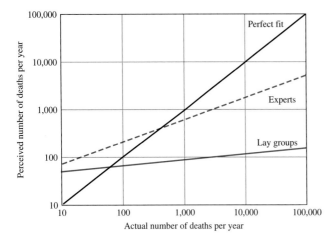

**TABLE 5–2**     Annual Risk of Death from Selected Common Human Activities

| Cause of Death | Number of Deaths in Representative Year | Individual Risk per Year |
|---|---|---|
| Black lung disease (coal mining) | 1,135 | $8 \times 10^{-3}$, or 1/125 |
| Heart attack | 724,859 | $2.7 \times 10^{-3}$, or 1/370 |
| Cancer | 541,532 | $2.0 \times 10^{-3}$, or 1/500 |
| Coal mining accident | 180 | $1.3 \times 10^{-3}$, or 1/770 |
| Fire fighting | — | $3 \times 10^{-4}$, or 1/3,333 |
| Motor vehicle | 46,000 | $2.2 \times 10^{-4}$, or 1/4,545 |
| Truck driving | 400 | $10^{-4}$, or 1/10,000 |
| Falls | 16,339 | $7.7 \times 10^{-5}$, or 1/13,000 |
| Football (averaged over participants) | | $4 \times 10^{-5}$, or 1/25,000 |
| Home accidents | 25,000 | $1.2 \times 10^{-5}$, or 1/83,333 |
| Bicycling (assuming one person per bicycle) | 1,000 | $10^{-5}$, or 1/100,000 |
| Air travel: one transcontinental trip/year | | $2 \times 10^{-6}$, or 1/500,000 |

*Sources*: National Center for Health Statistics
http://www.cdc.gov/nchs/fastats/deaths, 2001
Selected data from: Hutt, P. B., "Legal considerations in risk assessment," *Food, Drugs, Cosmetic Law Journal*, vol. 33, pp. 558–559, 1978; and Rodricks, I. and M. R. Taylor, "Application of risk assessment to good safety decision making," *Regulatory Toxicology and Pharmacology*, vol. 3, pp. 275–284, 1983.

may shorten life by 30 years. In contrast, diseases, such as cancer, cause death later in life, and life is shortened by about 15 years. Therefore, a risk of $10^{-6}$ shortens life on the average of $30 \times 10^{-6}$ years, or 15 min for an accident. The same risk for a fatal illness shortens life by about 8 min. It has been noted that smoking a cigarette takes 10 min and shortens life by 5 min [2].

| **TABLE 5–3** | Risks That Increase Chance of Death by 0.000001[a] |
|---|---|
| Smoking 1.4 cigarettes | Cancer, heart disease |
| Drinking $\frac{1}{2}$ L of wine | Cirrhosis of the liver |
| Spending 1 h in a coal mine | Black lung disease |
| Spending 3 h in a coal mine | Accident |
| Living 2 days in New York or Boston | Air pollution |
| Travelling 6 min by canoe | Accident |
| Travelling 10 miles by bicycle | Accident |
| Travelling 300 miles by car | Accident |
| Flying 1000 miles by jet | Accident |
| Flying 6000 miles by jet | Cancer caused by cosmic radiation |
| Living 2 months in Denver on vacation from New York | Cancer caused by cosmic radiation |
| Living 2 months in average stone or brick building | Cancer caused by natural radioactivity |
| One chest X-ray taken in a good hospital | Cancer caused by radiation |
| Living 2 months with a cigarette smoker | Cancer, heart disease |
| Eating 40 tablespoons of peanut butter | Liver cancer caused by aflatoxin B |
| Drinking Miami drinking water for a year | Cancer caused by chloroform |
| Living 5 years at a site boundary of a typical nuclear power plant in the open | Cancer caused by radiation |
| Drinking a thousand 24-oz. soft drinks from banned plastic bottles | Cancer from acrylonitrile monomer |
| Living 20 years near PVC plant | Cancer caused by vinyl chloride (1976 standard) |
| Living 150 years within 20 miles of a nuclear power plant | Cancer caused by radiation |
| Eating 100 charcoal broiled steaks | Cancer from benzopyrene |
| Risk of accident by living within 5 miles of a nuclear reactor for 50 years | Cancer caused by radiation |

[a]1 chance in 1 million, $10^{-6}$

*Source:* Reprinted, with permission, from: Wilson, R., "Analyzing the daily risks of life," *Technology Review,* vol. 81, pp. 41–46, 1979.

## 5–3  RISK ASSESSMENT

In 1989, the EPA adopted a formal process for conducting a baseline risk assessment [3]. This process includes data collection and evaluation, toxicity assessment, exposure assessment, and risk characterization. Risk assessment is considered to be site-specific. Each step is described briefly in the following section.

### Data Collection and Evaluation

Data collection and evaluation includes gathering and analyzing site-specific data relevant to human health concerns for the purpose of identifying substances of major interest. This step includes gathering background and site information, the preliminary identification of potential human and ecosystem exposure through sampling, and the development of a sample collection strategy.

When collecting background information, it is important to identify the following:

1. Possible contaminants
2. Concentrations of the contaminants in key sources and media (i.e., air, soil, or water) of interest, characteristics of sources, and information related to the chemical's release potential
3. Characteristics of the environmental setting that could affect the fate, transport, and persistence of the contaminants

The review of the available site information determines basic site characteristics such as air and groundwater movement or soil characteristics. With these data, it is possible to initially identify potential exposure pathways and exposure points important for assessing risk. A conceptual model of pathways and exposure points can be formed from the background data and site information. This conceptual model can then be used to help refine data needs.

## Toxicity Assessment

**Toxicity assessment** is the process of determining the relationship between the exposure to a contaminant and the increased likelihood of the occurrence or severity of adverse effects. In this discussion we will focus on adverse effects to people, but similar evaluations for plants and animals are also appropriate for evaluation of ecosystem effects. This procedure includes hazard identification and dose-response evaluation. **Hazard identification** determines whether exposure to a contaminant causes increased adverse effects for humans and to what level of severity. Dose-response evaluation uses quantitative information on the dose of the contaminant and relates it to the incidence of adverse reactions in an exposed population. Toxicity values can be determined from this quantitative relationship and used in the risk characterization step to estimate different occurrences of adverse health effects based on various exposure levels.

The single factor that determines the degree of harmfulness of a compound is the dose of that compound [4]. **Dose** is defined as the mass of chemical received by the animal or exposed individual. Dose is usually expressed in units of milligrams per kilogram of body mass ($mg \cdot kg^{-1}$). Some authors use parts per million (ppm) instead of $mg \cdot kg^{-1}$. Where the dose is administered over time, the units may be $mg \cdot kg^{-1} \cdot day^{-1}$. It should be noted that dose differs from the concentration of the compound in the medium (air, water, or soil) to which the animal or individual is exposed.

For toxicologists to establish the "degree of harmfulness" of a compound, they must be able to observe a quantitative effect. The ultimate effect manifested is death of the organism. Much more subtle effects may also be observed. Effects on body weight, blood chemistry, and enzyme inhibition or induction are examples of graded responses. Mortality and tumor formation are examples of **quantal** (all-or-nothing) responses. If a dose is sufficient to alter a biological mechanism, a harmful consequence will result. The experimental determination of the range of changes in a biologic mechanism to a range of doses is the basis of the dose-response relationship.

The statistical relationship of organism response to dose is commonly expressed as a cumulative-frequency distribution known as a **dose-response curve.** Figure 5–2 illustrates the method by which a common toxicological measure, namely the $LD_{50}$, or lethal dose for 50% of the animals, is obtained. The assumption inherent in the plot of the dose-response curve is that the test population variability follows a Gaussian distribution and, hence, that the dose-response curve has the statistical properties of a Gaussian cumulative-frequency curve.

Toxicity is a relative term. That is, there is no absolute scale for establishing toxicity; one may only specify that one chemical is more or less toxic than another. Comparison of different

## FIGURE 5–2

Hypothetical dose-response curves for two chemical agents (A and B) administered to a uniform population. NOAEL = no observed adverse effect level.

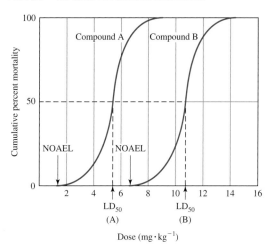

## FIGURE 5–3

Hypothetical dose-response relationships for a chemical agent administered to a uniform population.

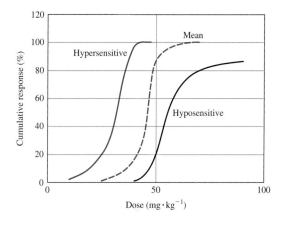

chemicals is uninformative unless the organism or biologic mechanism is the same and the quantitative effect used for comparison is the same. Figure 5–2 serves to illustrate how a toxicity scale might be developed. Of the two curves in the figure, the $LD_{50}$ for compound B is greater than that for compound A. Thus, for the test animal represented by the graph, compound A is more toxic than compound B as measured by lethality. There are many difficulties in establishing toxicity relationships. Species respond differently to toxicants so that the $LD_{50}$ for a mouse may be very different than that for a human. The shape (slope) of the dose-response curve may differ for different compounds so that a high $LD_{50}$ may be associated with a low "no observed adverse effect level" (NOAEL) and vice versa.

The nature of a statistically obtained value, such as the $LD_{50}$, tends to obscure a fundamental concept of toxicology: that there is no fixed dose that can be relied on to produce a given biologic effect in every member of a population. In Figure 5–2, the mean value for each test group is plotted. If, in addition, the extremes of the data are plotted as in Figure 5–3, it is apparent that the response of individual members of the population may vary widely from the mean. This implies not only that single-point comparisons, such as the $LD_{50}$, may be misleading, but that even knowing the slope of the average dose-response curve may not be sufficient if one wishes to protect hypersensitive individuals.

Organ toxicity is frequently classified as an acute or subacute effect. Carcinogenesis, teratogenesis, reproductive toxicity, and mutagenesis have been classified as chronic effects. A glossary of these toxicology terms is given in Table 5–4.

It is self-evident that an organ may exhibit acute, subacute, and chronic effects and that this system of classification is not well bounded.

Virtually all of the data used in hazard identification and, in particular, hazard quantification, are derived from animal studies. Aside from the difficulty of extrapolating from one species to another, the testing of animals to estimate low-dose response is difficult. Example 5–1 illustrates the problem.

| TABLE 5–4 | Glossary of Toxicological Terms | |
|---|---|---|
| | Acute toxicity | An adverse effect that has a rapid onset, short course, and pronounced symptoms. |
| | Cancer | An abnormal growth process in which cells begin a phase of uncontrolled growth and spread. |
| | Carcinogen | A cancer-producing substance. |
| | Carcinomas | Cancers of epithelial tissues. Lung cancer and skin cancer are examples of carcinomas. |
| | Chronic toxicity | An adverse effect that frequently takes a long time to run its course and initial onset of symptoms may go undetected. |
| | Genotoxic | Toxic to the genetic material (DNA). |
| | Initiator | A chemical that starts the change in a cell that irreversibly converts the cell into a cancerous or precancerous state. Needs to have a promoter to develop cancer. |
| | Leukemias | Cancers of white blood cells and the tissue from which they are derived. |
| | Lymphomas | Cancers of the lymphatic system. An example is Hodgkin's disease. |
| | Metastasis | Process of spreading or migration of cancer cells throughout the body. |
| | Mutagenesis | Mutagens cause changes in the genetic material of cells. The mutations may occur either in somatic (body) cells or germ (reproductive) cells. |
| | Neoplasm | A new growth. Usually an abnormally fast-growing tissue. |
| | Oncogenic | Causing cancers to form. |
| | Promoter | A chemical that increases the incidence to a previous carcinogen exposure. |
| | Reproductive toxicity | Decreases in fertility, increases in miscarriages, and fetal or embryonic toxicity as manifested in reduced birth weight or size. |
| | Sarcoma | Cancer of mesodermal tissue such as fat and muscle. |
| | Subacute toxicity | Subacute toxicity is measured using daily dosing during the first 10% of the organism's normal life expectancy and checking for effects throughout the normal lifetime. |
| | Teratogenesis | Production of a birth defect in the offspring after maternal or paternal exposure. |

**EXAMPLE 5–1**   An experiment was developed to ascertain whether a compound has a 5% probability of causing a tumor. The same dose of the compound was administered to 10 groups of 100 test animals. A control group of 100 animals was, with the exception of the test compound, exposed to the same environmental conditions for the same period of time. The following results were obtained:

| Group | Number of Tumors | Group | Number of Tumors |
|---|---|---|---|
| A | 6 | F | 9 |
| B | 4 | G | 5 |
| C | 10 | H | 1 |
| D | 1 | I | 4 |
| E | 2 | J | 7 |

No tumors were detected in the controls (not likely in reality).

Solution   The average number of excess tumors is 4.9%. These results tend to confirm that the probability of causing a tumor is 5%.

   If, instead of using 1000 animals (10 groups × 100 animals), only 100 animals were used, it is fairly evident from the data that, statistically speaking, some very anomalous results might be achieved. That is, we might find a risk from 1–10%.

   Note that a 5% risk (probability of 0.05) is very high in comparison with the EPA's objective of achieving an environmental contaminant risk of $10^{-7}$ to $10^{-4}$.

Animal studies are only capable of detecting risks on the order of 1%. Toxicologists employ mathematical models to extrapolate data from animals to humans.

One of the most controversial aspects of toxicological assessment is the method chosen to extrapolate the carcinogenic dose-response curve from the high doses administered to test animals to the low doses that humans actually experience in the environment. The conservative worst-case assessment is that one event capable of altering DNA will lead to tumor formation. This is called the one-hit hypothesis. From this hypothesis, it is assumed that there is no threshold dose below which the risk is zero, so that for carcinogens, there is no NOAEL and the dose-response curve passes through the origin.

Many models have been proposed for extrapolation to low doses. The selection of an appropriate model is more a policy decision than a scientific one because no data confirm or refute any model. The one-hit model is frequently used.

$$P(d) = 1 - \exp(-q_0 - q_1 d) \tag{5-1}$$

where $P(d)$ = lifetime risk (probability) of cancer
$\quad\quad d$ = dose
$\quad q_0$ and $q_1$ = parameter to fit data

This model corresponds to the simplest model of carcinogenesis, namely, that a single chemical hit will induce a tumor.

The background rate of cancer incidence, $P(O)$, may be represented by expanding the exponential as

$$\exp(x) = 1 + x + \frac{x^2}{2!} + \cdots + \frac{x^n}{n!} \tag{5-2}$$

For small values of $x$, this expansion is approximately

$$\exp(x) \approx 1 + x \tag{5-3}$$

Assuming the background rate for cancer is small, then

$$P(O) = 1 - \exp(-q_0) \approx 1 - [1 + (-q_0)] = q_0 \tag{5-4}$$

This implies that $q_0$ corresponds to the background cancer incidence. For small dose rates, the one-hit model can then be expressed as

$$P(d) \approx 1 - [1 - (q_0 + q_1 d)] = q_0 + q_1 d = P(O) + q_1 d \tag{5-5}$$

For low doses, the additional cancer risk above the background level may be estimated as

$$A(d) = P(d) - P(O) = [P(O) + q_1 d] - P(O) \tag{5-6}$$

or

$$A(d) = q_1 d \tag{5-7}$$

This model, therefore, assumes that the excess lifetime probability of cancer is linearly related to dose.

Some authors prefer a model that is based on an assumption that tumors are formed as a result of a sequence of biological events. This model is called the multistage model.

$$P(d) = 1 - \exp[-(q_0 + q_1 d + q_2 d^2 + \cdots + q_n d^n)] \tag{5-8}$$

where $q_i$ values are selected to fit the data. The one-hit model is a special case of the multistage model.

EPA has selected a modification of the multistage model for toxicological assessment, called the **linearized multistage model.** This model assumes that we can extrapolate from high doses

| **TABLE 5–5** | Slope Factors for Potential Carcinogens[a] | | |
| --- | --- | --- | --- |
| **Chemical** | **$CPS_0$** **(kg · day · mg$^{-1}$)** | **$CPS_i$** **(kg · day · mg$^{-1}$)** | |
| Arsenic | 1.5 | 15.1 | |
| Benzene | 0.029 | 0.029 | |
| Benzo(a)pyrene | 7.3 | N/A | |
| Cadmium | N/A | 6.3 | |
| Carbon tetrachloride | 0.13 | 0.0525 | |
| Chloroform | 0.0061 | 0.08 | |
| Chromium (VI) | N/A | 42.0 | |
| DDT | 0.34 | 0.34 | |
| 1,1-Dichloroethylene | 0.6 | 0.175 | |
| Dieldrin | 16.0 | 16.1 | |
| Heptachlor | 4.5 | 4.55 | |
| Hexachloroethane | 0.014 | 0.014 | |
| Methylene chloride | 0.0075 | 0.00164 | |
| Polychlorinated biphenyls | 7.7 | N/A | |
| 2,3,7,8-TCDD[b] | $1.5 \times 10^5$ | $1.16 \times 10^5$ | |
| Tetrachloroethylene[b] | 0.052 | 0.002 | |
| Trichloroethylene[c] | w | 0.006 | |
| Vinyl chloride[b] | 1.9 | N/A | |

$CPS_0$ = cancer potency slope, oral; $CPS_i$ = cancer potency slope, inhalation; w = withdrawn from IRIS.

[a] Values are frequently updated. Refer to IRIS and HEAST for current data.

[b] *Annual Health Effects Assessment Summary Tables* (HEAST) U.S. Environmental Protection Agency, 540/R-94/036, 1994.

[c] U.S. Environmental Protection Agency, National Center for Environmental Assessment
http://www.epa.gov/ncea

*Source:* With the exceptions noted this information is taken from the U.S. Environmental Protection Agency, IRIS database, October 1996.

to low doses with a straight line. At low doses, the slope of the dose-response curve is represented by a **slope factor** (SF) expressed in units of risk per unit dose, or risk (kg · day · mg$^{-1}$).

The EPA maintains a toxicological data base called IRIS (the **Integrated Risk Information System**) that provides background information on potential carcinogens. IRIS includes suggested values for the slope factor. A list of slope factors for several compounds is shown in Table 5–5.

In contrast to the carcinogens, it is assumed that for noncarcinogens there is a dose below which there is no adverse effect; that is, there is an NOAEL. The EPA has estimated the acceptable daily intake, or reference dose (RfD), that is likely to be without appreciable risk. The RfD is obtained by dividing the NOAEL by safety factors to account for the transfer from animals to humans, sensitivity, and other uncertainties in developing the data. A list of several compounds and their RfD values is given in Table 5–6.

**Limitations of Animal Studies.**   No species provides an exact duplicate of human response. Certain effects that occur in common lab animals generally occur in people. Many effects produced in people can, in retrospect, be produced in some species. Notable exceptions are toxicities dependent on immunogenic mechanisms. Most sensitization reactions are difficult

**TABLE 5–6**     RfDs for Chronic Noncarcinogenic Effects for Selected Chemicals[a]

| Chemical | Oral RfD $(mg \cdot kg^{-1} \cdot day^{-1})$ | Chemical | Oral RfD $(mg \cdot kg^{-1} \cdot day^{-1})$ |
|---|---|---|---|
| Acetone | 0.1 | Phenol | 0.6 |
| Barium | 0.05 | PCB | |
| Cadmium | 0.0005 | Aroclor 1016 | $7.0 \times 10^{-6}$ |
| Chloroform | 0.01 | Aroclor 1254 | $2.0 \times 10^{-6}$ |
| Cyanide | 0.02 | Silver | 0.003 |
| 1,1-Dichloroethylene | 0.009 | Tetrachloroethylene | 0.01 |
| Hydrogen cyanide | 0.02 | Toluene | 0.2 |
| Methylene chloride | 0.06 | 1,2,4-Trichlorobenzene | 0.02 |
| Pentachlorophenol | 0.03 | Xylenes | 2.0 |

[a] Values are frequently updated. Refer to IRIS for current data.
*Source:* U.S. Environmental Protection Agency IRIS database, 1996.

if not impossible to induce in lab animals. The procedure in transferring animal data to people is then to find the "proper" species and study it in context. Observed differences are then often quantitative rather than qualitative.

Carcinogenicity as a result of application or administration to lab animals is often assumed to be transposable to people because of the seriousness of the consequence of ignoring such evidence. However, slowly induced, subtle toxicity—because of the effects of ancillary factors (environment, age, etc.)—is difficult at best to transfer. This becomes even more difficult when the incidence of toxicity is restricted to a small hypersensitive subset of the population.

**Limitations of Epidemiological Studies.** Epidemiological studies of toxicity in human populations present four difficulties. The first is that large populations are required to detect a low frequency of occurrence of a toxicological effect. Second, a long or highly variable latency period may be needed between the exposure to the toxicant and a measurable effect. Third, competing causes of the observed toxicological response make it difficult to attribute a direct cause and effect. For example, cigarette smoking; the use of alcohol or drugs; and personal characteristics such as gender, race, age, and prior disease states tend to mask environmental exposures. Fourth, epidemiological studies are often based on data collected in specific political boundaries that do not necessarily coincide with environmental boundaries such as those defined by an aquifer or the prevailing wind patterns.

### Exposure Assessment

The objective of this step is to estimate the magnitude of exposure to chemicals of potential concern. The magnitude of exposure is based on chemical intake and pathways of exposure. The most important route (or pathway) of exposure may not always be clearly established. Arbitrarily eliminating one or more routes of exposure is not scientifically sound. The more reasonable approach is to consider an individual's potential contact with all contaminated media through all possible routes of entry. These are summarized in Table 5–7.

The evaluation of all major sources of exposure is known as **total exposure assessment** [5]. After reviewing the available data, it may be possible to decrease or increase the level of concern for a particular route of entry to the body. Elimination of a pathway of entry can be justified if

1. The exposure from a particular pathway is less than that of exposure through another pathway involving the same media at the same exposure point

| TABLE 5-7 | Potential Contaminated Media and Corresponding Routes of Exposure |
|---|---|

| Media | Routes of Potential Exposure |
|---|---|
| Groundwater | Ingestion, dermal contact, inhalation during showering |
| Surface water | Ingestion, dermal contact, inhalation during showering |
| Sediment | Ingestion, dermal contact |
| Air | Inhalation of airborne (vapor phase) chemicals (indoor and outdoor) |
|  | Inhalation of particulates (indoor and outdoor) |
| Soil/dust | Incidental ingestion, dermal contact |
| Food | Ingestion |

**2.** The magnitude of exposure from the pathway is low, or

**3.** The probability of exposure is low and incidental risk is not high

There are two methods of quantifying exposure: point estimate methods and probabilistic methods. The EPA uses the point estimate procedure by estimating the **reasonable maximum exposure** (RME). Because this method results in very conservative estimates, some scientists believe probabilistic methods are more realistic [6]. We will limit our consideration to the EPA point estimate technique.

RME is defined as the highest exposure that is reasonably expected to occur and is intended to be a conservative estimate within the range of possible exposures. Two steps are involved in estimating RME: first, exposure concentrations are predicted using a transport model such as the Gaussian plume model for atmospheric dispersion, then pathway-specific intakes are calculated using these exposure concentration estimates. The following equation is a generic intake equation.

$$CDI = C \left[ \frac{(CR)(EFD)}{BW} \right] \left( \frac{1}{AT} \right) \tag{5-9}$$

where* $CDI$ = chronic daily intake, (in mg $\cdot$ kg body weight$^{-1}$ $\cdot$ day$^{-1}$)

$C$ = chemical concentration, contacted over the exposure period (e.g., in mg $\cdot$ L$^{-1}$ water)

$CR$ = contact rate, the amount of contaminated medium contacted per unit time or event (e.g., in L $\cdot$ day$^{-1}$)

$EFD$ = exposure frequency and duration, describes how long and how often exposure occurs. Often calculated using two terms (EF and ED):

$EF$ = exposure frequency (in days $\cdot$ year$^{-1}$)

$ED$ = exposure duration (in years)

$BW$ = body weight, the average body weight over the exposure period (in kg)

$AT$ = averaging time, period over which exposure is averaged (in days)

For each different medium and corresponding route of exposure, it is important to note that additional variables are used to estimate intake. For example, when calculating intake for the inhalation of airborne chemicals, inhalation rate and exposure time are required. Specific equations for medium and routes of exposure are given in Table 5–8. Standard values for use in the intake equations are shown in Table 5–9.

---

*The notation in Equation 5–9 and subsequent expressions follows that in EPA guidance documents. The abbreviation "CDI" does **not** imply multiplication of three variables "C," "D," and "I." CDI, CR, EFD, BW, and so on are the notation for the variables. They do not refer to the product of terms.

| TABLE 5–8 | Residential Exposure Equations for Various Pathways |
|---|---|

Ingestion in drinking water

$$CDI = \frac{(CW)(IR)(EF)(ED)}{(BW)(AT)}$$ (5–10)

Ingestion while swimming

$$CDI = \frac{(CW)(CR)(ET)(EF)(ED)}{(BW)(AT)}$$ (5–11)

Dermal contact with water

$$AD = \frac{(CW)(SA)(PC)(ET)(EF)(ED)(CF)}{(BW)(AT)}$$ (5–12)

Ingestion of chemicals in soil

$$CDI = \frac{(CS)(IR)(CF)(FI)(EF)(ED)}{(BW)(AT)}$$ (5–13)

Dermal contact with soil

$$AD = \frac{(CS)(CF)(SA)(AF)(ABS)(EF)(ED)}{(BW)(AT)}$$ (5–14)

Inhalation of airborne (vapor phase) chemicals

$$CDI = \frac{(CA)(IR)(ET)(EF)(ED)}{(BW)(AT)}$$ (5–15)

Ingestion of contaminated fruits, vegetables, fish and shellfish

$$CDI = \frac{(CF)(IR)(FI)(EF)(ED)}{(BW)(AT)}$$ (5–16)

where ABS = absorption factor for soil contaminant (unitless)
AD = absorbed dose (in $mg \cdot kg^{-1} \cdot day^{-1}$)
AF = soil-to-skin adherence factor (in $mg \cdot cm^{-2}$)
AT = averaging time (in days)
BW = body weight (in kg)
CA = contaminant concentration in air (in $mg \cdot m^{-3}$)
CDI = chronic daily intake (in $mg \cdot kg^{-1} \cdot day^{-1}$)
CF = volumetric conversion factor for water = $1 L \cdot 1000 cm^{-3}$
= conversion factor for soil = $10^{-6} kg \cdot mg^{-1}$
CR = contact rate (in $L \cdot h^{-1}$)
CS = chemical concentration in soil (in $mg \cdot kg^{-1}$)
CW = chemical concentration in water (in $mg \cdot L^{-1}$)
ED = exposure duration (in years)
EF = exposure frequency (in $days \cdot year^{-1}$ or $events \cdot year^{-1}$)
ET = exposure time ($h \cdot day^{-1}$ or $h \cdot event^{-1}$)
FI = fraction ingested (unitless)
IR = ingestion rate (in $L \cdot day^{-1}$ or $mg\ soil \cdot day^{-1}$ or $kg \cdot meal^{-1}$)
= inhalation rate (in $m^3 \cdot h^{-1}$)
PC = chemical-specific dermal permeability constant (in $cm \cdot h^{-1}$)
SA = skin surface area available for contact (in $cm^2$)

*Source:* Reprinted from: *Risk Assessment Guidance for Superfund.* Volume 1, *Human Health Evaluation Manual* (part A). U.S. Environmental Protection Agency, EPA/540/1-89/002, 1989.

**TABLE 5–9**  EPA Recommended Values for Estimating Intake

| Parameter | Standard Value |
|---|---|
| Average body weight, adult | 70 kg |
| Average body weight, child[a] | |
|    0–1.5 years | 10 kg |
|    1.5–5 years | 14 kg |
|    5–12 years | 26 kg |
| Amount of water ingested daily, adult | 2 L |
| Amount of water ingested daily, child | 1 L |
| Amount of air breathed daily, adult | 20 m$^3$ |
| Amount of air breathed daily, child | 5 m$^3$ |
| Amount of fish consumed daily, adult | 6.5 g $\cdot$ day$^{-1}$ |
| Contact rate, swimming | 50 mL $\cdot$ h$^{-1}$ |
| Skin surface available, adult male | 1.94 m$^2$ |
| Skin surface available, adult female | 1.69 m$^2$ |
| Skin surface available, child | |
|    3–6 years (average for male and female) | 0.720 m$^2$ |
|    6–9 years (average for male and female) | 0.925 m$^2$ |
|    9–12 years (average for male and female) | 1.16 m$^2$ |
|    12–15 years (average for male and female) | 1.49 m$^2$ |
|    15–18 years (female) | 1.60 m$^2$ |
|    15–18 years (male) | 1.75 m$^2$ |
| Soil ingestion rate, children 1–6 years | 200 mg $\cdot$ day$^{-1}$ |
| Soil ingestion rate, persons > 6 years | 100 mg $\cdot$ day$^{-1}$ |
| Skin adherence factor, potting soil to hands | 1.45 mg $\cdot$ cm$^{-2}$ |
| Skin adherence factor, kaolin clay to hands | 2.77 mg $\cdot$ cm$^{-2}$ |
| Exposure duration | |
|    Lifetime | 70 years |
|    At one residence, 90th percentile | 30 years |
|    National median | 5 years |
| Averaging time | (ED)(365 days $\cdot$ year$^{-1}$) |
| Exposure frequency (EF) | |
|    Swimming | 7 days $\cdot$ year$^{-1}$ |
|    Eating fish and shell fish | 48 days $\cdot$ year$^{-1}$ |
| Exposure time (ET) | |
|    Shower, 90th percentile | 12 min |
|    Shower, 50th percentile | 7 min |

[a] Data in this category taken from: Copeland, T., A. M. Holbrow, J. M. Otan, et al., "Use of probabilistic methods to understand the conservatism in California's approach to assessing health risks posed by air contaminants," *Journal of the Air and Waste Management Association*, vol. 44, pp. 1399–1413, 1994.

*Source:* Data taken from: *Risk Assessment Guidance for Superfund.* Volume 1, *Human Health Evaluation Manual* (part A). U.S. Environmental Protection Agency, EPA/540/1-89/002, 1989.

**EXAMPLE 5–2** Estimate the chronic daily intake CDI of benzene from exposure to a city water supply that contains a benzene concentration equal to the drinking water standard. The allowable drinking water concentration (maximum contaminant level, MCL) is $0.005$ mg $\cdot$ L$^{-1}$. Assume the exposed individual is an adult male who consumes water at the adult rate for 70 years, that he is an avid swimmer and swims in a local pool (supplied with city water) 3 days a week for 30 min and has been doing so since he was 30 years old. He takes a long shower every day. Assume that the average air concentration of benzene during the shower is 5 $\mu$g $\cdot$ m$^{-3}$ [7]. From the literature, it is estimated that the dermal uptake from water is $0.0020$ m$^3 \cdot$ m$^{-2} \cdot$ h (This is PC in Table 5–8. PC also has units of meters per hour or centimeters per hour.) and that direct dermal absorption during showering is no more than 1% of the available benzene because most of the water does not stay in contact with skin long enough [8].

Solution From Table 5–7, we note that five routes of exposure are possible from the drinking water medium: (1) ingestion, dermal contact while (2) showering and (3) swimming, (4) inhalation of vapor while showering, and (5) ingestion while swimming.

We begin by calculating the CDI for ingestion (Equation 5–10).

$$CDI = \frac{(0.005 \text{ mg} \cdot \text{L}^{-1})(2.0 \text{ L} \cdot \text{day}^{-1})(365 \text{ days} \cdot \text{year}^{-1})(70 \text{ years})}{(70 \text{ kg})(70 \text{ years})(365 \text{ days} \cdot \text{year}^{-1})}$$

$$= 1.43 \times 10^{-4} \text{ mg} \cdot \text{kg}^{-1} \cdot \text{day}^{-1}$$

The ingestion rate (IR) and body weight (BW) were selected from Table 5–9.

Equation 5–12 may be used to estimate absorbed dose while showering.

$$AD = \frac{(0.005 \text{ mg} \cdot \text{L}^{-1})(1.94 \text{ m}^2)(0.0020 \text{ m} \cdot \text{h}^{-1})(0.20 \text{ h} \cdot \text{event}^{-1})}{(70 \text{ kg})(70 \text{ years})}$$

$$\times \frac{(1 \text{ event} \cdot \text{day}^{-1})(365 \text{ days} \cdot \text{year}^{-1})(70 \text{ years})(10^3 \text{ L} \cdot \text{m}^{-3})}{(365 \text{ days} \cdot \text{year}^{-1})}$$

$$= 5.54 \times 10^{-5} \text{mg} \cdot \text{kg}^{-1} \cdot \text{day}^{-1}$$

But only about 1% of this amount is available for adsorption in a shower because of the limited contact time, so the actual adsorbed dose by dermal contact is

$$AD = (0.01)(5.54 \times 10^{-5} \text{ mg} \cdot \text{kg}^{-1} \cdot \text{day}^{-1}) = 5.54 \times 10^{-7} \text{ mg} \cdot \text{kg}^{-1} \cdot \text{day}^{-1}$$

The surface area (SA) and exposure time were obtained from Table 5–9. The permeability constant was given in the problem statement. The exposure time is estimated by converting a long shower of 12 min to hours ($12/60 = 0.2$).

The adsorbed dose for swimming is calculated in the same fashion.

$$AD = \frac{(0.005 \text{ mg} \cdot \text{L}^{-1})(1.94 \text{ m}^2)(0.0020 \text{ m} \cdot \text{h}^{-1})(0.5 \text{ h} \cdot \text{event}^{-1})}{(70 \text{ kg})(70 \text{ years})}$$

$$\times \frac{(3 \text{ events} \cdot \text{week}^{-1})(52 \text{ weeks} \cdot \text{year}^{-1})(40 \text{ years})(10^3 \text{ L} \cdot \text{m}^{-3})}{(365 \text{ days} \cdot \text{year}^{-1})}$$

$$= 3.38 \times 10^{-5} \text{ mg} \cdot \text{kg}^{-1} \cdot \text{day}^{-1}$$

In this case, because there is virtually total body immersion for the entire contact period and because there is virtually an unlimited supply of water for contact, there is no reduction for availability. The value of ET is computed from the swimming time (30 min $= 0.5$ h $\cdot$ event$^{-1}$). The exposure frequency is computed from the number of swimming events per week and the number of weeks in a year. The exposure duration (ED) is calculated from the lifetime and beginning time of swimming $= 70 - 30$ years $= 40$ years.

The inhalation rate from showering is estimated from Equation 5–15.

$$CDI = \frac{(5\,\mu g \cdot m^{-3})(10^{-3}\,mg \cdot \mu g^{-1})(0.833\,m^3 \cdot h^{-1})(0.20\,h \cdot event^{-1})}{(70\,kg)(70\,years)}$$

$$\times \frac{(1\,event \cdot day^{-1})(365\,days \cdot year^{-1})(70\,years)}{(365\,days \cdot year^{-1})}$$

$$= 1.19 \times 10^{-5}\,mg \cdot kg^{-1} \cdot day^{-1}$$

The inhalation rate (IR) is taken from Table 5–9 and converted to an hourly basis.
For ingestion while swimming, we apply Equation 5–11.

$$CDI = \frac{(0.005\,mg \cdot L^{-1})(50\,mL \cdot h^{-1})(10^{-3}\,L \cdot mL^{-1})(0.5\,h \cdot event^{-1})}{(70\,kg)(70\,years)}$$

$$\times \frac{(3\,events \cdot week^{-1})(52\,weeks \cdot year^{-1})(40\,years)}{(365\,days \cdot year^{-1})}$$

$$= 4.36 \times 10^{-7}\,mg \cdot kg^{-1} \cdot day^{-1}$$

The contact rate (CR) was determined from Table 5–9. Other values were obtained in the same fashion as those for dermal contact while swimming.

The total exposure would be estimated as

$$CDI_T = 1.43 \times 10^{-4} + 5.54 \times 10^{-7} + 3.38 \times 10^{-5} + 1.19 \times 10^{-5} + 4.36 \times 10^{-4}$$

$$= 1.90 \times 10^{-4}\,mg \cdot kg^{-1} \cdot day^{-1}$$

From these calculations, it becomes readily apparent that, in this case, drinking the water dominates the calculation for benzene intake.

### Risk Characterization

In the risk characterization step, all data collected from exposure and toxicity assessments are reviewed to corroborate qualitative and quantitative conclusions about risk. The risk for each media source and route of entry is calculated. This includes the evaluation of compounding effects due to the presence of more than one chemical contaminant and the combination of risk across all routes of entry.

For low-dose cancer risk (risk below 0.01), the quantitative risk assessment for a single compound by a single route is calculated as

$$\text{Risk} = (\text{intake})(\text{slope factor}) \tag{5–17}$$

where intake is calculated from one of the equations in Table 5–8 or a similar relationship. The slope factor is obtained from IRIS (see, for example, Table 5–5). For high carcinogenic risk levels (risk above 0.01), the one-hit equation is used.

$$\text{Risk} = 1 - \exp[-(\text{intake})(\text{slope factor})] \tag{5–18}$$

The measure used to describe the potential for noncarcinogenic toxicity to occur in an individual is not expressed as a probability. Instead, EPA uses the noncancer hazard quotient, or hazard index (HI):

$$HI = \frac{\text{intake}}{\text{RfD}} \tag{5–19}$$

These ratios are not to be interpreted as statistical probabilities. A ratio of 0.001 does not mean that there is a one in one thousand chance of an effect occurring. If the HI exceeds unity, there may be concern for potential noncancer effects. As a rule, the greater the value above unity, the greater the level of concern.

To account for multiple substances in one pathway, EPA sums the risks for each constituent.

$$\text{Risk}_T = \sum \text{risk}_i \qquad\qquad (5\text{–}20)$$

For multiple pathways

$$\text{Total exposure risk} = \sum \text{risk}_{ij} \qquad\qquad (5\text{–}21)$$

where $i$ = the compounds and $j$ = pathways.

In a like manner, the hazard index for multiple substances and pathways is estimated as

$$\text{Hazard index}_T = \sum \text{HI}_{ij} \qquad\qquad (5\text{–}22)$$

In its guidance documents, EPA recommends segregation of the hazard index into chronic, sub-chronic, and short-term exposure. Although some research indicates that the addition of risks is reasonable [9], there is some uncertainty in taking this approach. Namely, should the risk from a carcinogen that causes liver cancer be added to the risk from a compound that causes stomach cancer? The conservative approach is to add the risks.

**EXAMPLE 5–3**   Using the results from Example 5–2, estimate the risk from exposure to drinking water containing the MCL for benzene.

Solution   Equation 5–21 in the form

$$\text{Total exposure risk} = \sum \text{risk}_j$$

may be used to estimate the risk. Because the problem is only to consider one compound, namely benzene, $i = 1$ and others do not need to be considered. Because the total exposure from Example 5–2 included each of the routes of concern for drinking water, that is, all $j$'s, the final sum may be used to compute risk. The slope factor is obtained from Table 5–5. The risk is

$$\text{Risk} = (1.90 \times 10^{-4}\ \text{mg} \cdot \text{kg}^{-1} \cdot \text{day}^{-1})(2.9 \times 10^{-2}\ \text{kg} \cdot \text{day} \cdot \text{mg}^{-1})$$

$$= 5.5 \times 10^{-6}$$

This is the total lifetime risk (70 years) for benzene in drinking water at the MCL. Another way of viewing this is to estimate the number of people that might develop cancer. For example, in a population of 2 million,

$$(2 \times 10^6)(5.5 \times 10^{-6}) = 11 \text{ people might develop cancer}$$

This risk falls within the EPA guidelines of $10^{-4}$ to $10^{-7}$ risk. It, of course, does not account for all sources of benzene by all routes. Nonetheless, the risk, compared with some other risks in daily life, appears to be quite small.

## 5–4   RISK MANAGEMENT

Though some might wish it, it is clear that establishment of zero risk cannot be achieved. All societal decisions, from driving a car to drinking water with benzene at the EPA's regulated concentration, pose a risk. Even banning the production of chemicals, as was done for PCBs, for example, does not remove those that already permeate our environment. Risk management is performed to decide the magnitude of risk that is tolerable in specific circumstances [10]. This is a policy decision that weighs the results of the risk assessment against the costs of risk reduction techniques and benefits of risk reduction as well as the public acceptance. The risk manager recognizes that if a very high certainty in avoiding risk (i.e., a very low risk, for example, $10^{-7}$) is required, the costs in achieving low concentrations of the contaminant are likely to be high.

To reduce risk, the risk manager's options fall into three categories: change the environment, modify the exposure, or compensate for the effects. Frequently, the final choice is a blend of the options. Equation 5–9 provides a glimpse of the alternatives available. These include modifying the environment by reducing the concentration of the compounds (C) through engineering measures and modifying the exposure by limiting the intake of compounds (CR) by providing warnings and dietary restrictions, or restricting access to contaminated environments and thus reducing the exposure time (EFD). Chapters 8–16 discuss alternative measures for reducing the risk of exposure to toxic compounds. The risk manager uses a benefit–cost analysis to choose the remedy.

Unfortunately, very little guidance can be provided to the risk manager. We know that people are willing to accept a higher risk for things that they expose themselves to voluntarily than for involuntary exposures and, hence, insist on lower levels of risk, regardless of cost, for involuntary exposure. We also know that people are willing to accept risk if it approaches that for disease, that is, a fatality rate of $10^{-6}$ people per person-hour of exposure [11].

## CHAPTER REVIEW

When you have finished studying this chapter, you should be able to do the following without the aid of your textbook or notes:

1. Define and differentiate between risk and hazard.
2. List the four steps in risk assessment and explain what occurs in each step.
3. Define the terms dose, $LD_{50}$, NOAEL, slope factor, RfD, CDI, IRIS.
4. Explain why it is not possible to establish an absolute scale of toxicity.
5. Explain why the average dose-response curve may not be an appropriate model for developing environmental protection standards.
6. Identify routes of exposure for the release of contaminants in multiple media.
7. Explain how risk management differs from risk assessment and the role of risk perception in risk management.

With the aid of this text, you should be able to do the following:

1. Calculate lifetime risk using the one-hit model.
2. Calculate chronic daily intake or other variables given the medium and values for the remaining variables.
3. Perform a risk characterization calculation for carcinogenic and noncarcinogenic threats by multiple contaminants and multiple pathways.

## PROBLEMS

**5-1** The recommended time weighted average air concentration for occupational exposure to water-soluble hexavalent chromium [Cr(VI)] is $0.05 \text{ mg} \cdot \text{m}^{-3}$. This concentration is based on an assumption that the individual is generally healthy and is exposed for $8 \text{ h} \cdot \text{day}^{-1}$ over a working lifetime (i.e., from age 18 to 65 years). The average work period is assumed to be $8 \text{ h} \cdot \text{day}^{-1}$, $5 \text{ days} \cdot \text{week}^{-1}$, $50 \text{ weeks} \cdot \text{year}^{-1}$. Assuming an average body weight and inhalation rate over the working life of the individual, what is the lifetime (70 years) CDI?

**Answer:** $2.2 \times 10^{-3} \text{ mg} \cdot \text{kg}^{-1} \cdot \text{day}^{-1}$

**5-2** The national ambient air quality standard for sulfur dioxide is $80 \text{ μg} \cdot \text{m}^{-3}$. Assuming a lifetime exposure ($24 \text{ h} \cdot \text{day}^{-1}$, $365 \text{ days} \cdot \text{year}^{-1}$) for an adult of average body weight, what is the estimated CDI for this concentration?

**5-3** Children are one of the major concerns of environmental exposure. Compare the CDIs for a 1-year-old child and an adult drinking a water contaminated with $10 \text{ mg} \cdot \text{L}^{-1}$ of nitrate (as N). Assume a 1-year averaging time.

**5-4**   Agricultural chemicals such as 2,4-D (2,4-dichlorophenoxyacetic acid) may be ingested by routes other than food. Compare the CDI's for ingestion of a soil contaminated with $10 \text{ mg} \cdot \text{kg}^{-1}$ of 2,4-D by a 3-year-old child and an adult. Assume both the child and adult have an equivalent exposure of 1 day per week for 20 weeks in 1 year and that the fraction of 2,4-D ingested is 0.10.

**5-5**   Estimate the chronic daily intake of toluene from exposure to a city water supply that contains a toluene concentration equal to the drinking water standard of $1 \text{ mg} \cdot \text{L}^{-1}$. Assume the exposed individual is an adult female who consumes water at the adult rate for 70 years, that she abhors swimming, and that she takes a long (20 min) bath every day. Assume that the average air concentration of toluene during the bath is $1 \text{ \mu g} \cdot \text{m}^{-3}$. Assume the dermal uptake from water (PC) is $9.0 \times 10^{-6} \text{ m} \cdot \text{h}^{-1}$ and that direct dermal absorption during bathing is no more than 80% of the available toluene because she is not completely submerged.

   **Answer:** $2.9 \times 10^{-2} \text{ mg} \cdot \text{kg}^{-1} \cdot \text{day}^{-1}$

**5-6**   Estimate the chronic daily intake of 1,1,1-trichloroethane from exposure to a city water supply that contains a 1,1,1-trichloroethane concentration equal to the drinking water standard of $0.2 \text{ mg} \cdot \text{L}^{-1}$. Assume the exposed individual is a child who consumes water at the child rate for 5 years, that she swims once a week for 30 min, and that she takes a short (10 min) bath every day. Assume her average age over the exposure period is 8. Assume that the average air concentration of 1,1,1-trichloroethane during the bath is $2 \text{ \mu g} \cdot \text{m}^{-3}$. Assume the dermal uptake from water (PC) is $0.0060 \text{ m} \cdot \text{h}^{-1}$ and that direct dermal absorption during bathing is no more than 80% of the available l,1,1-trichloroethane because she is not completely submerged.

**5-7**   Estimate the risk from occupational inhalation exposure to hexavalent chromium. (See Problem 5–1 for assumptions.)

   **Answer:** Risk $= 9.66 \times 10^{-2}$, or 0.10

**5-8**   In its rule making for burning hazardous waste in boilers and industrial furnaces [12], EPA calculated doses of various contaminants that would result in a risk of $10^{-5}$. Using the standard assumptions in Table 5–9 for an adult, estimate the concentration of hexavalent chromium that results in a lifetime inhalation risk of $10^{-5}$.

**5-9**   Characterize the risk for a chronic daily exposure by the water pathway (oral) of $0.03 \text{ mg} \cdot \text{kg}^{-1} \cdot \text{day}^{-1}$ of toluene, $0.06 \text{ mg} \cdot \text{kg}^{-1} \cdot \text{day}^{-1}$ of barium, and $0.3 \text{ mg} \cdot \text{kg}^{-1} \cdot \text{day}^{-1}$ of xylenes.

   **Answer:** HI $= 1.5$

**5-10**   Characterize the risk for a chronic daily exposure by the water pathway (oral) of $1.43 \times 10^{-4} \text{ mg} \cdot \text{kg}^{-1} \cdot \text{day}^{-1}$ of tetrachloroethylene, $1.43 \times 10^{-3} \text{ mg} \cdot \text{kg}^{-1} \cdot \text{day}^{-1}$ of arsenic, and $1.43 \times 10^{-4} \text{ mg} \cdot \text{kg}^{-1} \cdot \text{day}^{-1}$ of dichloromethane (methylene chloride).

**5-11**   Risk is a measure of probability. Probability theory tells us that the probability of a number of independent and mutually exclusive events is the sum of the probabilities of the separate events. Using this concept, estimate the lifetime (70 years) probability of death from the following: driving a motor vehicle and falling and a home accident. *Hint:* See Table 5–2.

   **Answer:** Risk $= 2.08 \times 10^{-2}$, or 0.02

**5-12**   As noted previously, risk is a measure of probability. EPA has used the 90% confidence level to select values for Table 5–9. Probability theory tells us that the probability of two independent events occurring simultaneously or in succession is the product of the individual probabilities. Using this concept, estimate the probability of ingesting 2 L of water each day and weighing 70 kg.

## DISCUSSION QUESTIONS

**5-1**   It has been stated that based on $LD_{50}$, 2,3,7,8-TCDD (tetrachlorodibenzo-*p*-dioxin) is the most toxic chemical known. Why might this statement be misleading? How would you rephrase the statement to make it more scientifically correct?

**5-2**   Which of the following individuals is at greater risk from inhalation of an airborne contaminant: a 1-year-old child; an adult female; an adult male? Explain your reasoning.

**5–3** Which of the following individuals is at greater risk from ingestion of a soil contaminant: a 1-year-old child; an adult female; an adult male? Explain your reasoning.

**5–4** A hazard index of 0.001 implies

(a) Risk $= 10^{-3}$

(b) The probability of hazard is 0.001.

(c) The RfD is small compared with the CDI.

(d) There is little concern for potential health effects.

## ADDITIONAL READING

Calabrese, E. J., E. M. Kenyon. *Air Toxics and Risk Assessment.* Lewis Publishers, Chelsea, MI (1991).

Glickman, T. S., M. Gough, editors. *Readings in Risk.* Resources for the Future, Washington, D.C. (1990).

Kamrin, M. A. *Toxicology.* Lewis Publishers, Chelsea, MI (1988).

LaGrega, D., P. L. Buckingham, and J. C. Evans. *Hazardous Waste Management.* McGraw-Hill, New York (1994).

Paustenbach, D. J., ed. *The Risk Assessment of Environmental Hazards.* John Wiley, New York (1989).

## REFERENCES

1. This discussion follows that of P. Slovic, B. Fischoff, and S. Lichtenstein, "Rating the risks," *Environment,* vol. 21, pp. 14–20 and 36–39, 1979.
2. Wilson, R. "Analyzing the daily risks of life," *Technology Review,* vol. 81, pp. 41–46, 1979.
3. *Risk Assessment Guidance for Superfund.* Volume 1, *Human Health Evaluation Manual* (part A). U.S. Environmental Protection Agency, EPA/540/1-89/002, 1989.
4. Loomis, T. A. *Essentials of Toxicology.* Lea & Febiger, Philadelphia, p. 2 (1978).
5. Butler, J. P., Greenberg, A., Lioy, P. J., et al. "Assessment of carcinogenic risk from personal exposure to benzo(*a*)pyrene in the total human environmental exposure study (THEES)," *Journal of the Air & Waste Management Association,* vol. 43, pp. 970–977, 1993.
6. Finley, B., and Paustenbach, D. "The benefits of probabilistic exposure assessment; Three case studies involving contaminated air, water, and soil." *Risk Analysis,* vol. 14, pp. 53–73, 1994.
7. McKone, T. E. "Human exposure to volatile organic compounds in household tap water: The indoor inhalation pathway," *Environmental Science & Technology,* vol. 21, pp. 1194–1201, 1987.
8. Byard, J. L. "Hazard assessment of 1,1,1-trichloroethane in groundwater." In *The Risk Assessment of Environmental Hazards,* D. J. Paustenbach, ed. John Wiley & Sons, New York, pp. 331–344 (1989).
9. Silva, E., Rajapakse, N., and Kortenkamp, A. "Something from "nothing"—Eight weak estrogenic chemicals combined at concentrations below NOECs produce significant mixture effects," *Environmental Science & Technology,* vol. 36, pp. 1751–1756, 2002.
10. *Risk Assessment in the Federal Government: Managing the Process.* National Research Council, National Academy Press, Washington, D.C., pp. 18–19 (1983).
11. Starr, C. "Social benefit versus technological risk," *Science,* vol. 165, pp. 1232–1238 (1969).
12. *Federal Register,* 56 FR 7233, 21 Feb 1991.

# 6

# Hydrology

## 6–1   FUNDAMENTALS OF HYDROLOGY

The availability of water is critical to maintaining ecosystems, as well as for communities, industry, agriculture, and commercial operations. The presence (or lack) of water at sufficient quantity and quality can significantly affect the sustainability of life. It is therefore important for the engineer and environmental scientist to have a solid understanding of our water supply and its distribution in nature.

Hydrology is a multidisciplinary subject that deals with the question of how much water can be expected at any particular time and location. The application of this subject is important to ensuring adequate water for such purposes as drinking, irrigation, and industrial uses, as well as to preventing flooding. Surface water hydrology focuses on the distribution of water on or above the earth's surface. It encompasses all water in lakes, rivers, and streams, on land and in the air. Groundwater hydrology deals with the distribution of water in the earth's subsurface geological materials, such as sand, rock, or gravel.

### The Hydrological Cycle

The **hydrological cycle** (Figure 6–1) describes the movement and conservation of water on earth. This cycle includes all of the water present on and in the earth, including salt and fresh water, surface and groundwater, water present in the clouds and that trapped in rocks far below the earth's surface.

Water is transferred to the earth's atmosphere through two distinct processes: (1) evaporation and (2) transpiration. A third process is derived from the two and is called evapotranspiration. **Evaporation** is the conversion of liquid water from lakes, streams, and other bodies of water to water vapor. **Transpiration** is the process by which water is emitted from plants through the stomata, small openings on the underside of leaves that are connected to the vascular tissue. It occurs predominantly at the leaves while the stomata are open for the passage of carbon dioxide and oxygen during photosynthesis. Because it is often difficult to distinguish between true evaporation and transpiration, hydrologists use the term **evapotranspiration** to describe the combined losses of water due to transpiration and evaporation.

---

**FIGURE 6–1**

---

The hydrological cycle. The percentages correspond to the volume in each of the different compartments. (*Source:* Montgomery, C. *Environmental Engineering,* 6th ed. McGraw-Hill, Inc., New York, 2003. Reproduced with permission.)

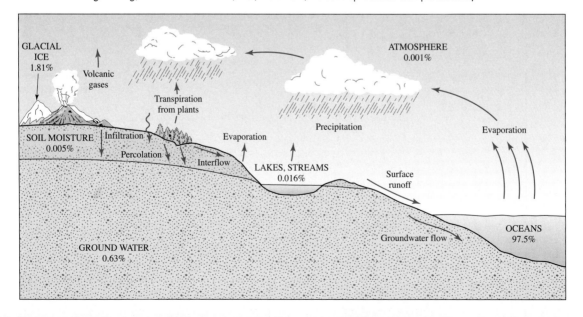

**Precipitation** is the primary mechanism by which water is released from the atmosphere. Precipitation takes several forms, the most common of which in temperate climates is rain. Additionally, water can fall as hail, snow, sleet, and freezing rain.

As water falls to the earth's surface, the droplets either run over the ground into streams and rivers (referred to as **surface runoff, overland flow,** or **direct runoff**), move laterally just below the ground surface (**interflow**), or move vertically through the soils to form groundwater (**infiltration** or **percolation**).

The movement of water through various phases of the hydrological cycle is extremely complex because it is erratic in both time and space. Here we will take a very simplistic view so as to develop a water budget. The most important terms for a water budget are evaporation (E), evapotranspiration (E$_T$), precipitation (P), infiltration (G), interflow (F), and surface runoff (R).

One of the simplest water budgets used by hydrologists is that for a lake. Let's look at how water flows into and out of a lake. Water can flow into the lake by way of any rivers or streams (natural or anthropogenic, including industrial) that flow into the lake, by surface water runoff along the banks of the lake, by precipitation that falls directly into the lake, or by seepage into the bottom sediments of the lake from groundwater. Water can flow out of the lake by way of any streams or rivers that flow from the lake; withdrawal of water for municipal, industrial, or agricultural uses; evaporation; evapotranspiration; or seepage of water through the bottom sediments of the lake. What hydrologists often wish to determine is the net amount (mass) of water that is gained or lost in the lake within a given period. Hydrologists refer to this type of problem as a **storage problem.**

To solve storage problems we must develop a mass-balance equation for the lake. In this case, the substance is water and the system is the lake. Therefore, the mass-balance equation is simply

$$\text{Mass rate of accumulation} = \text{mass rate in} - \text{mass rate out} \qquad (6\text{--}1)$$

For the lake, we can write the most general form of this equation as

$$\text{Mass rate of accumulation} = (Q_{in} + P' + R' + I'_{in} - Q_{out} - E' - E'_T - I'_{out})\rho_{water} \qquad (6\text{--}2)$$

where $Q_{in} =$ flowrate of stream(s) entering lake (in vol $\cdot$ time$^{-1}$)
$\quad\quad P' =$ rate of precipitation (in vol $\cdot$ time$^{-1}$)
$\quad\quad R' =$ rate of runoff (in vol $\cdot$ time$^{-1}$)
$\quad\quad I'_{in} =$ rate of seepage into lake (in vol $\cdot$ time$^{-1}$)
$\quad\quad Q_{out} =$ flowrate of streams exiting lake (in vol $\cdot$ time$^{-1}$)
$\quad\quad E' =$ rate of evaporation from water bodies such as lakes, rivers, and ponds
$\quad\quad\quad$ (in vol $\cdot$ time$^{-1}$)
$\quad\quad E'_T =$ rate of evapotranspiration (in vol $\cdot$ time$^{-1}$)
$\quad\quad I'_{out} =$ rate of seepage out of the lake (in vol $\cdot$ time$^{-1}$)
$\quad\quad \rho_{water} =$ density of water (in mass $\cdot$ vol$^{-1}$)

Although these problems are not inherently difficult, some confusion arises because $Q$ and $R$ are often given in units of volume per time (e.g., cubic meters per second), whereas rates of precipitation, seepage into and out of the lake, evaporation, and evapotranspiration are often given in units of length per unit time (e.g., centimeters per month or millimeters per hour). One needs to make sure that the units used are consistent (either volume per unit time or length per unit time). Because it is assumed that precipitation, seepage, evaporation, and evapotranspiration all occur over the entire surface area of the lake, we can approximate the volumetric rate by multiplying the rate (in length per unit time) by the surface area of the lake. Therefore, if we define these parameters as is typically done by hydrologists,

$\quad P =$ rate of precipitation (in mm $\cdot$ h$^{-1}$)
$\quad I_{in} =$ rate of seepage into lake (in mm $\cdot$ h$^{-1}$)
$\quad E =$ rate of evaporation (in mm $\cdot$ h$^{-1}$)
$\quad E_T =$ rate of evapotranspiration (in mm $\cdot$ h$^{-1}$)
$\quad I_{out} =$ rate of seepage out of the lake (in mm $\cdot$ h$^{-1}$)

Then Equation 6–2 becomes

$$\text{Mass rate of accumulation} = ((Q_{in} + R - Q_{out}) + (P + I_{in} - E - E_T - I_{out}) \times A_s)\rho_{water}$$

$$\times \left(\frac{1 \text{ m}}{1000 \text{ mm}^{-1}}\right)\left(\frac{1 \text{ h}}{3600 \text{ s}^{-1}}\right) \quad (6\text{–}3)$$

where $A_s$ = surface area of the lake (in m$^2$). For most systems, we can assume that the density of water is constant because the temporal changes in temperature and pressure are small. As such, we can divide both sides of Equations 6–2 or 6–3 by the density of water to yield an equation for the volumetric rate of accumulation.

**EXAMPLE 6–1**

Hvarekhshaeta Lake has a surface area of 708,000 m$^2$. Based on collected data, Drvaspa Brook flows into the lake at an average rate of 1.5 m$^3 \cdot$ s$^{-1}$ and the Vouruskasha River flows out of Hvarekhshaeta Lake at an average rate of 1.25 m$^3 \cdot$ s$^{-1}$ during the month of June. The evaporation rate was measured as 19.4 cm $\cdot$ month$^{-1}$. Evapotranspiration can be ignored because there are few water plants on the shore of the lake. A total of 9.1 cm of precipitation fell this month. Seepage is negligible. Due to the dense forest and the gentle slope of the land surrounding the lake, runoff is also negligible. The average depth in the lake on June 1 was 19 m. What was the average depth on June 30th?

**Solution**

The first step to solving this problem is to determine what we know. We know that the inputs to the lake are

$$Q_{in} = 1.5 \text{ m}^3 \cdot \text{s}^{-1}$$
$$P = 9.1 \text{ cm} \cdot \text{month}^{-1}$$
$$I_{in} = 0 \text{ (because we were told that seepage is negligible)}$$
$$R' = 0 \text{ (because we were told that runoff is negligible)}$$

We also know that the outputs from the lake are

$$Q_{out} = 1.25 \text{ m}^3 \cdot \text{s}^{-1}$$
$$E = 19.4 \text{ cm} \cdot \text{month}^{-1}$$
$$E_T = 0$$

We also know that surface area of the lake is 708,000 m$^2$ and the average depth of the lake on June 1 is 19 m.

The following is a picture of the lake as a system

Using the average values given earlier and the most general form of the mass-balance equation (6–2), the mass-balance for this lake can be reduced to

Volumetric rate of accumulation = $Q_{in} - Q_{out} + P - E$

The volumetric rate of accumulation is often referred to as the **change in storage** ($\Delta S$) and

$$\Delta S = Q_{in} - Q_{out} + P - E$$

Because the units for $Q$ and $P$ and $E$ are different, we must ensure that the proper conversions are performed, yielding the same set of units.

Therefore,

$$\Delta S = (1.5 \text{ m}^3 \cdot \text{s}^{-1})(86{,}400 \text{ s} \cdot \text{day}^{-1})(30 \text{ days} \cdot \text{month}^{-1})$$
$$- (1.25 \text{ m}^3 \cdot \text{s}^{-1})(86{,}400 \text{ s} \cdot \text{day}^{-1})(30 \text{ days} \cdot \text{month}^{-1})$$
$$+ (9.1 \text{ cm} \cdot \text{month}^{-1})(\text{m} \cdot 100 \text{ cm}^{-1})(708{,}000 \text{ m}^2)$$
$$- (19.4 \text{ cm} \cdot \text{month}^{-1})(\text{m} \cdot 100 \text{ cm}^{-1})(708{,}000 \text{ m}^2)$$
$$= 3{,}888{,}000 \text{ m}^3 \cdot \text{month}^{-1} - 3{,}240{,}000 \text{ m}^3 \cdot \text{month}^{-1}$$
$$+ 64{,}428 \text{ m}^3 \cdot \text{month}^{-1} - 137{,}352 \text{ m}^3 \cdot \text{month}^{-1}$$

Solving the preceding equation, yields

$$\Delta S = 575{,}076 \text{ m}^3 \cdot \text{month}^{-1}$$

Because $\Delta S = 575{,}076 \text{ m}^3 \cdot \text{month}^{-1}$ and the average surface area is 708,000 m², the change in depth during the month of June is

$$(575{,}076 \text{ m}^3 - \text{month})/708{,}000 \text{ m}^2 = 0.81 \text{ m} - \text{month}$$

Note that $\Delta S$ is positive. As such, the volume in the lake increased during June and, therefore, the depth increases. The new average depth on June 30 would be 19.81 m. Had a negative value for storage been calculated, then the depth of the lake would have decreased.

**More Complex Systems.**  Hydrologists often wish to look at larger systems that include lakes, rivers, the surrounding land, and even the groundwater lying in the geological materials below the land. These systems are called watersheds or basins. The **watershed,** or **basin,** is defined by the surrounding topography (Figure 6–2). The boundary of the watershed is a **divide** and is the highest elevation surrounding the watershed. All of the water that falls on the inside of the divide has the potential to flow into the streams of the basin contained within the watershed boundary (divide). Water falling outside of the divide is shed to another basin.

Before we begin to develop a water budget for a watershed, let's look at a simpler system: an impervious inclined plane, confined on all sides and having a single outlet. An example of such

---

**FIGURE 6–2**                 The Kankakee River Basin above Davis, IN

The arrows indicate that precipitation falling inside the dashed line is in the Davis watershed, whereas that falling outside is in another watershed. The dashed line then "divides" the watersheds. (*Source:* Davis M. L., D. A. Cornwell. *Introduction to Environmental Engineering,* 3rd ed. McGraw-Hill, Inc., New York, 1998.)

**FIGURE 6-3**

Schematic of a parking lot.

Inflow (*I*)

Drain    Outflow (*Q*)

**FIGURE 6-4**

Hydrograph showing constant inflow of water (e.g., rainfall) over some duration of time.

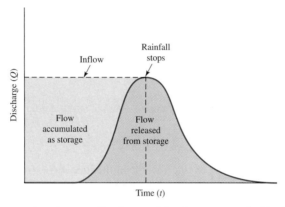

a system is a small urban parking lot, surrounded by buildings or concrete walls, and sloped in one direction (Figure 6–3). Water can flow only out of the drain.

In this system, water enters the parking lot via rainfall. The water can either remain on the parking lot in the form of puddles (**accumulated storage** or **surface detention** to the hydrologist) or flow from the parking lot (**flow released from storage**). In this case, the hydrological continuity equation (Equation 6–1) becomes

Volumetric accumulation rate = input rate − output rate          (6–4)

or

$$\frac{dS}{dt} = I - Q \tag{6–5}$$

Again, we have assumed that the density of water is constant. As such, we can express our mass balance in terms of the volumetric accumulation rate. To a hydrologist, this equation would be written as

Change in storage (in volume · time$^{-1}$)

= inflow (in volume · time$^{-1}$) − outflow (in volume · time$^{-1}$)          (6–6)

At the beginning of the rainstorm, all of the rain accumulates on the surface of the parking lot and none is released from the drain. As rain continues to fall, the amount of water stored on the parking lot surface (surface detention) increases, and eventually water begins to flow from the drain. As the rain stops, water can continue to flow from the drain, resulting in a decrease in the surface detention. Eventually, all of the water can be released from storage as it flows from the drain. In this example, we have ignored the effects of evaporation. Another example of a similar system is a bathtub that is being filled at a rate faster than it is being drained.

The flow and collection of water in the parking lot can be described by a **hydrograph,** a chart in which flow rate is plotted versus time (Figure 6–4). Note that as the water continues to flow into the system, some of that water remains in the system as accumulated storage. Once the flow of water stops (e.g., rainfall ceases), water is then released from storage as outflow. If there is no evaporation or infiltration of water, then the total mass of water flowing into the system must equal that leaving the system by way of the drain.

The same phenomenon occurs in a watershed, although the system becomes more complicated because water can infiltrate into the ground, flow over land into streams and rivers, and be

**FIGURE 6–5**

Effect of the watershed on a hydrograph. $Q_c > Q_b > Q_a$ and $t_c < t_b < t_a$.

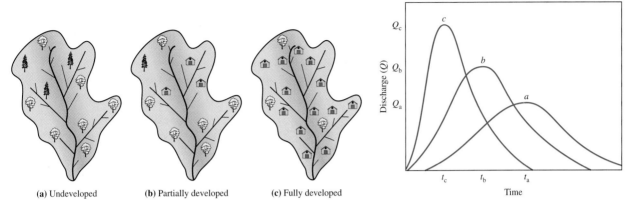

(a) Undeveloped    (b) Partially developed    (c) Fully developed

**TABLE 6–1**    Typical Runoff Coefficients

| Description of Area or Character of Surface | Runoff Coefficient | Description of Area or Character of Surface | Runoff Coefficient |
|---|---|---|---|
| Business | | Railroad yard | 0.20–0.35 |
|    Downtown | 0.70–0.95 | Natural grassy land | 0.10–0.30 |
|    Neighborhood | 0.50–0.70 | Pavement | |
| Residential | |    Asphalt, concrete | 0.70–0.95 |
|    Single-family | 0.30–0.50 |    Brick | 0.70–0.85 |
|    Multi-units, detached | 0.40–0.60 | Roofs | 0.75–0.95 |
|    Multi-units, attached | 0.60–0.75 | Lawns, sandy soil | |
| Residential, suburban | 0.25–0.40 |    Flat ($< 2\%$) | 0.05–0.10 |
| Apartment | 0.50–0.70 |    Average (2–7%) | 0.10–0.15 |
| Industrial | |    Steep ($> 7\%$) | 0.15–0.20 |
|    Light | 0.50–0.80 | Lawns, heavy soil | |
|    Heavy | 0.60–0.90 |    Flat ($< 2\%$) | 0.13–0.17 |
| Parks, cemeteries | 0.10–0.25 |    Average (2–7%) | 0.18–0.22 |
| Playgrounds | 0.20–0.35 |    Steep ($> 7\%$) | 0.25–0.35 |

*Source:* Joint Committee of the American Society of Civil Engineers and the Water Pollution Control Federation. *Design and Construction of Sanitary and Storm Sewers* (ASCE Manuals and Reports on Engineering Practice No. 37, or WPCF Manual of Practice No. 9), American Society of Civil Engineers, New York, (1969), p. 51.

caught up in puddles and depressions as surface detention. In the watersheds shown in Figure 6–5, we see that all of the water drains to a single point, a stream. The water that flows within the watershed is separated from all other watersheds by the divide. Numerous factors affect the rates at which water flows toward the stream and into the ground. For example, the steeper the slope of the land surrounding the stream, the faster the rate at which the water moves into the stream. Density and type of ground cover will also affect the rate of water transport. The denser the ground cover, the slower the rate of movement. These same factors also affect the volume of water that reaches the stream. This is represented by the runoff coefficient, some of which are given in Table 6–1. The runoff coefficient is defined as $R/P$ or the rate of water that runs off a surface divided by the rate of precipitation.

**FIGURE 6–6**

Ten-year hydrograph for Convict Creek near Mammoth Lakes, California (*Source: USGS*).

The effect of some of these factors can be observed by looking at the unit hydrographs shown in Figure 6–5. Shown here are hydrographs for three watersheds, all of which are essentially identical except for the level of development. Watershed (a) is undeveloped, that is, it is covered by dense vegetation. Watershed (b) has been partially developed, so that some vegetation remains, but numerous roads, driveways, and houses, are also present. The presence of these structures prevents infiltration, resulting in a greater fraction of the rainfall flowing over the land and into the stream. Watershed (c) is heavily developed, similar to an urban environment, where there is little open land through which the water can infiltrate. Most of the water that falls on this watershed flows rapidly into the stream. It should be noted that in watershed (c), the time to reach the maximum stream flow is the shortest. This is due to the fact that there are few trees, grasses and other plants to impede the flow in the developed watershed. As the water falls, it rushes as it falls to the nearest body of water. Also, because there is little open land through which water can infiltrate or on which it can pool, the maximum stream flow is greatest in watershed (c). These high flows can have a significant effect on humans, on stream ecosystems, and on the physical characteristics of the stream because the high flows can result in bank erosion, scouring of stream beds, and even a change in the path of the stream.

The shape of hydrographs also vary on a seasonal and annual basis. For example, the annual cycling of stream flow in Convict Creek draining the 47.2 km² watershed near Mammoth Lakes, in Mono County, California, can be seen in Figure 6–6. Each spring (March to May) snow melt contributes significantly to the streamflow. The dry season (September through April) is indicated on the hydrograph as very low flows. The unseasonably high flow (e.g., in February 1969) was perhaps due to unusually warm weather, resulting in snowmelt or rainfall.

Having developed the concept of a watershed, let's look at an example of a water budget for a watershed.

**EXAMPLE 6–2**    In 1997, the Upper Grand watershed near Lansing, Michigan, with an area of 4530 km² received 77.7 cm of precipitation. The average rate of flow measured in the Grand River, which drained the watershed, was 39.6 m³ · s⁻¹. Infiltration was estimated to occur at an average rate of $9.2 \times 10^{-7}$ m · s⁻¹. Evapotranspiration was estimated to be 45 cm · year⁻¹. What is the change in storage in the watershed?

Solution    To solve this problem, we should draw a picture, list the information we know and that which we are seeking and write the question in symbolic form.

A simple picture of the watershed is shown here.

We know the following information:

$$\text{Area} = 4530 \text{ km}^2$$

$$P = 77.7 \text{ cm} \cdot \text{year}^{-1}$$

$$\text{Infiltration} = G = 9.2 \times 10^{-7} \text{ cm} \cdot \text{s}^{-1}$$

$$E_T = 45 \text{ cm} \cdot \text{year}^{-1}$$

To solve this problem we assume that all of the flow in the river is due to runoff, so that, $R = Q_{\text{out}}$. In words, the mass-balance equation for this system can be written as

Change in storage = rate of precipitation − rate of evapotranspiration − rate of infiltration

− rate of water flowing from the stream.

Symbolically, this can be represented as

$$\Delta S = P - E_T - G - R$$

$$= 77.7 \text{ cm} \cdot \text{year}^{-1} - 45 \text{ cm} \cdot \text{year}^{-1} - (9.2 \times 10^{-7} \text{ cm} \cdot \text{s}^{-1})(60 \text{ s} \cdot \text{min}^{-1})(60 \text{ min} \cdot \text{h}^{-1})$$

$$\times (24 \text{ h} \cdot \text{day}^{-1})(365 \text{ day} \cdot \text{year}^{-1}) - R$$

We must convert $R$ from units of cubic meters per second as given to units of centimeters per year as all other terms are given. To accomplish this we must divide the flow rate by the area of the watershed it drains and perform all of the necessary unit conversions. Thus, substituting now for $R$

$$\Delta S = 77.7 \text{ cm} \cdot \text{year}^{-1} - 45 \text{ cm} \cdot \text{year}^{-1} - 29 \text{ cm} \cdot \text{year}^{-1}$$

$$- \frac{(39.6 \text{ m}^3 \cdot \text{s}^{-1})(86{,}400 \text{ s} \cdot \text{day}^{-1})(365 \text{ day} \cdot \text{year}^{-1})(100 \text{ cm} \cdot \text{m}^{-1})}{(4530 \text{ km}^2)(1000 \text{ m} \cdot \text{km}^{-1})^2}$$

Solving this equation, yields

$$\Delta S = 77.7 - 45 - 29 - 27.6 = -23.9 \text{ cm} \cdot \text{year}^{-1}$$

The negative storage means that there is a net loss of water from the watershed during this period. We can also calculate the runoff coefficient for this watershed. Remembering that the runoff coefficient equals $R/P$, then

$$\frac{R}{P} = \frac{27.6 \text{ cm}}{77.7 \text{ cm}} = 0.36$$

This value (from Table 6–1) is typical of that one would observe in a suburban area.

## 6–2    MEASUREMENT OF PRECIPITATION, EVAPORATION, INFILTRATION, AND STREAMFLOW

The development of any hydrologic continuity equation depends on the quality of the data generated. As such, it is important for the environmental scientist and engineer to have a good understanding of these parameters and how each is measured.

### Precipitation

Precipitation is the primary input quantity into the hydrologic cycle. Its accurate measurement is essential to the design of successful water resource projects, especially those pertaining to flood control.

Precipitation rates vary greatly on a regional scale. For example, as shown in Figures 6–7 and 6–8, the differences in precipitation can vary significantly, even within a few hundred kilometers.

Precipitation tends to decrease with increasing latitude because decreasing temperatures reduce atmospheric moisture. However, there are some exceptions, such as Seattle, with its rainy climate, and San Diego, which is dry. Precipitation also tends to decrease with distance from a body of water, as evidenced by the concentration of precipitation along coastlines (see Figure 6–7) and to some extent to the leeward of the Great Lakes. Mountains are also an important factor in precipitation; heavier precipitation usually occurs along the windward slope of a mountain range, whereas the leeward slope usually lies in the rain shadow. Latitude, annual temperature, and maximum possible water content all contribute to rates of precipitation. However, oceanic currents and global atmospheric patterns are also important factors.

Precipitation not only varies regionally but also temporally. These temporal changes may be more important, from an engineering perspective. Seasonal and annual variations have serious

**FIGURE 6–7**

Average annual precipitation (in inches) across the state of Washington, for the period 1961–1990. (*Source: Oregon State University—Spatial Climate Analysis Service.* www.ocs.orst.edu/pub/maps/Precipitation/Total/States/WA/wa.gif)

Oregon Climate Service
Oregon State University

| Legend (in inches) | |
|---|---|
| Under 10 | 60 to 80 |
| 10 to 20 | 80 to 100 |
| 20 to 30 | 100 to 140 |
| 30 to 40 | 140 to 180 |
| 40 to 60 | Above 180 |

Period: 1961–1990

This map is a plot of 1961–1990 annual average precipitation contours from NOAA Cooperative stations and (where appropriate) USDA-NRCS SNOTEL stations. Christopher Daly used the PRISM model to generate the gridded estimates from which this map was derived; the modeled grid was approximately 4×4 km latitude/longitude, and was resampled to 2×2 km using a Gaussian filter. Mapping was performed by Jenny Weisberg and Nathaniel DeYoung. Funding was provided by USDA-NRCS National Water and Climate Center.

## FIGURE 6–8

Annual precipitation for the southeast regional climate center state of South Carolina, for the period 1961–1990. Contour intervals = 2 in. (*Source: South Carolina Department of Natural Resources*)

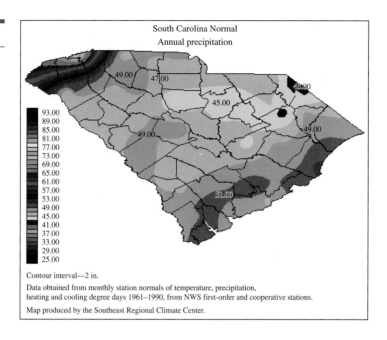

## FIGURE 6–9

Seasonal variations in precipitation in the Michigan–Huron basin (for 1994). (*Source:* Data from Yee, P. *A Report: On the 1994 Water Levels of the Great Lakes and St. Lawrence River.* Environment Canada, Cornwall, Ontario, 1995.)

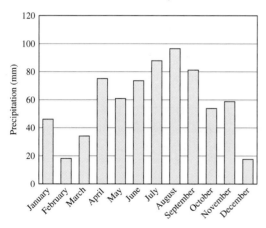

## FIGURE 6–10

Annual variations in precipitation in the Mojave Desert. (*Source:* Hereford, R., C. Longpré. *Climate History of the Mojave Desert Region, Including Data from 48 Long-term Weather Stations and an Overview of Regional Climate Variation.* Flagstaff, Arizona. http://wgsc.wr.usgs.gov/mojave/climate-history http://atmos.washington.edu/pdo)

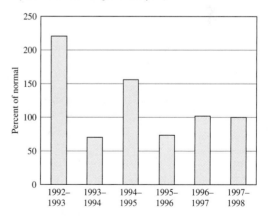

implications for water resource management. As shown in Figure 6–9, monthly precipitation rates in the Michigan–Huron basin varied by a factor of almost 5. This phenomenon is not unusual. Yearly variations can also be significant as shown in Figure 6–10. Here variations in precipitation rates vary as much as threefold. These yearly variations make it important to design reservoirs that are adequate during years of low rainfall and dams that have the capacity to ensure adequate flood control even in times of high precipitation rates.

Because floods are among the most frequent and costly natural disasters, the prediction of precipitation rates is very important. Unfortunately, predicting precipitation cycles is extremely difficult, and evidence suggests that some degree of variation may be purely random.

Hydrologists often speak of 50- or 100-year storms. This notation can be confusing because it implies a certain probability. When hydrologists speak of a 100-year storm, they are speaking of a storm with a given intensity and duration that is likely, based on records, to occur once in a 100-year period. Because storms, and therefore, floods, are stochastic* in nature, a 100-year storm can occur 2 years in a row, or even within the same year.

**Point Precipitation Analysis.**   Because accurate precipitation data are critical for the determination of flood and drought forecasting, it is important to understand how precipitation rates are determined for a given area. Precipitation can be measured using either gauges, which yield point data (i.e., data for a very limited area, often less than about 20 cm in diameter), or areal data using radar (in which the area over which the rates are averaged is much larger, generally about 2.5 km²). Each method has its advantages and disadvantages. Although rain gauges can give very accurate data for a very small region, these data must then be extrapolated over much larger regions. Data from a single nearby rain gauge are often sufficiently representative to allow their use in the design of small projects. The analysis of data from a single gauge is called **point precipitation analysis.** Radar may reasonably estimate the precipitation rate if the intensity and duration of the storm are relatively constant over the area in which measurements are taken. However, the location of mountains can interfere with the collection of critical data. Where storms can be very small in area, such as in the southwestern United States, such important data can be completely missed by the radar.

### Evaporation

Because evaporation is a significant component of the hydrologic cycle, especially in arid and semiarid climates, the determination or prediction of accurate evaporation rates is important for determining the capacity of humanmade impoundments. Variations in evaporation rates occur both on temporal (Figure 6–11) and spatial scales. Evaporation rates can be estimated using the pan evaporation method, free-water surface evaporation, and lake evaporation. **Pan evaporation** is the rate of evaporation using a standard National Weather Service (NWS) class A pan. Lake evaporation differs from pan evaporation measurements due to the heat storage capacity of the

---

*Stochastic means that the occurrence of floods can be predicted using the probability distribution of an ordered set of flood data that have been collected over time.

## FIGURE 6–11

Average monthly pan evaporation rates for Athens University of Georgia (for 1970–1971). (*Source: Data courtesy of South Carolina State Climatology Office* http://water.dnr.state.sc.us/climate/sco/pan_tables.html)

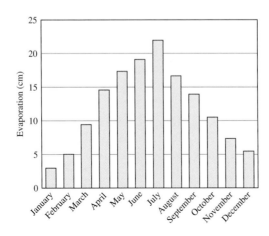

lake and wind currents. A simple method for estimating lake evaporation from class A pan evaporation measurements multiplies the pan value by 0.7.*

Another method of estimating evaporation rates is to use Dalton's equation. Dalton[†] showed that the loss of water from the surface of a lake or other body of water is a function of solar radiation, air and water temperature, wind speed, and the difference in vapor pressures at the water surface and in the overlying air. Thus, the relationship

$$E = (e_s - e_a)(a + bu) \qquad (6\text{–}7)$$

where $E$ = evaporation rate (in mm $\cdot$ day$^{-1}$)

$\quad\quad e_s$ = saturation vapor pressure (in kPa)

$\quad\quad e_a$ = vapor pressure in overlying air (in kPa)

$\quad a, b$ = empirical constants

$\quad\quad u$ = wind speed (in m $\cdot$ s$^{-1}$)

Empirical studies at Lake Hefner, Oklahoma, yielded a similar relationship.

$$E = 1.22(e_s - e_a)u \qquad (6\text{–}8)$$

From these expressions, it is apparent that high wind speeds and low humidities (vapor pressure in the overlying air) result in large evaporation rates. Note that the units for these expressions may not make much sense. This is because these are empirical expressions developed from field data. The constants have implied conversion factors in them. In applying these (and other) empirical expressions, take care to use the same units as those used by the scientists who developed the expression.

---

*Farnsworth, R. K., Thompson, E. S., Peck, E. L. 1982. *Evaporation atlas for the contiguous 48 United States.* U.S. Department of Commerce, National Oceanic and Atmospheric Administration, National Weather Service, NOAA, Technical Report NWS, Washington, D.C. (1982) 33, p. 26.

[†]Dalton, J. "Experimental essays on the constitution of mixed gases; on the force of steam or vapor from waters and other liquids, both in a Torricellian vacuum and in air; on evaporation; and on the expansion of gases by heat," *Mem Proc Manchester Lit Phil Soc* vol. 5, pp. 535–602, 1802.

**EXAMPLE 6–3**   Anjuman's Lake has a surface area of 70.8 ha. For the month of April the inflow was 1.5 m$^3 \cdot$ s$^{-1}$. The dam regulated the outflow (discharge) from Anjuman's Lake to be 1.25 m$^3 \cdot$ s$^{-1}$. If the precipitation recorded for the month was 7.62 cm and the storage volume increased by an estimated 650,000 m$^3$, what is the estimated evaporation in cubic meters and centimeters? Assume that no water infiltrates into or out of the bottom of Anjuman's Lake.

Solution   Begin by drawing the mass-balance diagram.

The mass-balance equation is.

Accumulation = input − output

The accumulation (change in storage) is 650,000 $m^3$. The input consists of the inflow and the precipitation. The product of the precipitation depth and the area on which it fell (70.8 ha) will yield a volume. The output consists of outflow plus evaporation. The change in storage can be represented by the equation

$$\Delta S = Q_{in} + P - E - Q_{out}$$

Make sure that all parameters are in the same units. The flow rates are expressed in cubic meters per second whereas $E$ and $P$ are shown in centimeters. Because we want to calculate the change in storage, we should convert all units to either units of volume per month ($m^3 \cdot month^{-1}$) or units of length per month ($cm \cdot month^{-1}$). Although hydrologists often calculate changes in storage in units of length per unit time, you should recognize that length is not conserved, rather mass (and therefore, volume, assuming a constant density) is. As such, we will solve the problem in units of volume and then calculate the change in depth. Remember also that April has 30 days.

Therefore,

$$650,000 \text{ m}^3 = (1.5 \text{ m}^3 \cdot \text{s}^{-1})(30 \text{ days})(86,400 \text{ s} \cdot \text{day}^{-1})$$

$$+ (7.62 \text{ cm})(70.8 \text{ ha})(10^4 \text{ m}^2 \cdot \text{ha}^{-1})(1 \text{ m} \cdot 100 \text{ cm}^{-1})$$

$$- (1.25 \text{ m}^2 \cdot \text{s}^{-1})(30 \text{ days})(86,400 \text{ s} \cdot \text{day}^{-1}) - E$$

Solving for $E$, we obtain

$$E = Q_{in} + P - Q_{out} - \Delta S$$
$$= 3.89 \times 10^6 \text{ m}^3 + 5.39 \times 10^4 \text{ m}^3 - 3.24 \times 10^6 \text{ m}^3 - 6.50 \times 10^5 \text{ m}^3$$
$$= 5.39 \times 10^4 \text{ m}^3$$

For an area of 70.8 ha, the evaporation rate in units of depth per month is

$$E = \frac{5.39 \times 10^4 \text{ m}^3}{(70.8 \text{ ha})(10^4 \text{ m}^2 \cdot \text{ha}^{-1})} = 0.076 \text{ m} = 7.6 \text{ cm} \cdot \text{month}^{-1}$$

**EXAMPLE 6–4**

During April, the wind speed over Anjuman's Lake was estimated to be $4.0 \text{ m} \cdot \text{s}^{-1}$. The air temperature averaged 20°C, and the relative humidity was 30%. The water temperature averaged 10°C. Estimate the evaporation rate using the Dalton's equation.

Solution

From the water temperature and Table 6–2, the saturation vapor pressure is estimated as $e_s = 1.227$ kPa. The vapor pressure in the air may be estimated as the product of the relative humidity and the saturation vapor pressure at the air temperature.

$$e_a = (2.337 \text{ kPa})(0.30) = 0.70 \text{ kPa}$$

The daily evaporation rate is then estimated to be

$$E = 1.22(1.227 - 0.70)(4.0 \text{ m} \cdot \text{s}^{-1}) = 2.57 \text{ mm} \cdot \text{day}^{-1}$$

The monthly evaporation would then be estimated to be

$$E = (2.57 \text{ mm} \cdot \text{day}^{-1})(30 \text{ days}) = 76.8 \text{ mm, or } 7.7 \text{ cm}$$

| TABLE 6–2 | Water Vapor Pressures at Various Temperatures | | | |
|---|---|---|---|---|
| | **Temperature (°C)** | **Vapor Pressure (kPa)** | **Temperature (°C)** | **Vapor Pressure (kPa)** |
| | 0 | 0.6113 | 25 | 3.1690 |
| | 5 | 0.8726 | 30 | 4.2455 |
| | 10 | 1.2281 | 35 | 5.6267 |
| | 15 | 1.7056 | 40 | 7.3814 |
| | 20 | 2.3388 | 50 | 12.344 |

*Source:* Lide, D. R. editor-in-chief, *CRC Handbook of Chemistry and Physics.* 76th ed., CRC Press, New York, (1995), pp. 6–15.

**Evapotranspiration.**  Evapotranspiration describes the total water removed from an area by transpiration (release of water vapor from plants) and by evaporation of water from soils, snow, and water surfaces. Evapotranspiration is often estimated by subtracting the total outflow for an area from the total input of water. The change in storage must be included in the calculations, unless this change is negligible.

The potential evapotranspiration rate (maximum possible loss) from a well-watered root zone (e.g., that in a golf course) can approximate the rate of evaporation that can occur over a large free-water surface. The available moisture in the root zone will limit the actual evapotranspiration rate, such that, as the root zone dries out the rate of transpiration will decrease. The rate of evapotranspiration is also a function of soil type, plant type, wind speed, and temperature. Plant types may affect evapotranspiration rates dramatically. For example, an oak tree may transpire as much as $160 \text{ L} \cdot \text{day}^{-1}$, whereas a corn plant may transpire only about $1.9 \text{ L} \cdot \text{day}^{-1}$. Although empirical models have been developed to attempt to predict rates of evapotranspiration based on the factors mentioned earlier, these models are inherently difficult to calibrate and validate due to the very complex biology and physics that govern evapotranspiration.

### Infiltration

Infiltration is the net movement of water into soil. When the rainfall rate exceeds the infiltration rate, water migrates through the surface soil at a rate that generally decreases with time until it reaches a constant value. The rate of infiltration varies with rainfall intensity, soil type, surface condition, and vegetal cover. This temporal decline in the rate is actually due to a filling of the soil pores with water and a reduction in capillary action. The change in infiltration rate with time is shown in Figure 6–12.

**FIGURE 6–12**

Effect of infiltration rate with time.

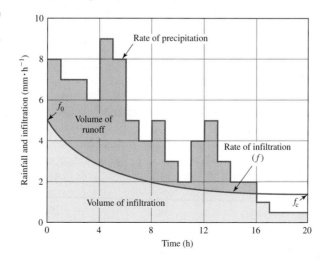

---

| **TABLE 6–3** | Parameters for Horton's Equation for Some Typical Soils | | |
|---|---|---|---|
| **Soil Type** | $f_c$ (cm · h$^{-1}$) | $f_0$ (cm · h$^{-1}$) | $k$ (h$^{-1}$) |
| Alphalpha loamy sand | 3.56 | 48.26 | 38.29 |
| Carnegie sandy loamy | 4.50 | 35.52 | 19.64 |
| Dothan loamy sand | 6.68 | 8.81 | 1.40 |
| Fuquay pebbly loamy sand | 6.15 | 15.85 | 4.70 |
| Leefield loamy sand | 4.39 | 28.80 | 7.70 |
| Troop sand | 4.57 | 58.45 | 32.71 |

*Source:* Bedient, P. B., W. C. Huber. *Hydrology and Floodplain Analysis,* 2nd ed. Addison-Wesley, Reading, MA, 1992.

Of the numerous equations developed to describe infiltration, Horton's equation* is useful for describing the rate. When the rate of rainfall exceeds the rate of infiltration, we can use Horton's equation.

$$f = f_c + (f_0 - f_c)e^{-kt} \qquad (6\text{–}9)$$

where $f$ = infiltration rate (or capacity) (in length · time$^{-1}$)
$\quad f_c$ = equilibrium, critical or final infiltration rate (in length · time$^{-1}$)
$\quad f_0$ = initial infiltration rate (in length · time$^{-1}$)
$\quad k$ = empirical constant (in time$^{-1}$)
$\quad t$ = time

Note that this equation has the same problem as many of the other mass-balance equations used by hydrologists, that is, rates are given in units of length per unit time rather than mass per unit time or volume per unit time. This occurs because obtaining a volumetric rate requires that the right hand-side of Equation 6–9 be multiplied by the surface area through which water is infiltrating, thus yielding $f$ in units of volume per unit time. However, because, by convention, hydrologists have used this notation, we have conformed to it.

As mentioned earlier soil type affects the infiltration rate of water. As one might imagine, the sandier the soil, the greater the infiltration rate. The more compacted the soil, or the greater the clay content of the soil, the slower the infiltration rate. Table 6–3 provides data for some common soil types.

Horton's infiltration can be integrated to yield an equation that represents the total volume of water that would infiltrate over a given period. The integrated form of Horton's equation is given in Equation 6–10.

$$\text{Volume} = A_s \int_0^t f \, dt = A_s \int_0^t [f_c + (f_0 - f_c)e^{-kt}] \, dt = A_s \left[ f_c t + \frac{f_0 - f_c}{k}(1 - e^{-kt}) \Big|_0^t \right] \qquad (6\text{–}10)$$

Although Horton's equation is generally applicable to most soils, several limitations apply. For sandy soils, $f_0$ exceeds most rainfall intensities. As such, all rainfall will infiltrate, and the infiltration rate will equal the precipitation rate. In these cases, Horton's equation will underpredict the infiltration rate. As mentioned previously, the infiltration capacity, $f$, decreases with cumulative infiltration volume as the pores fill up, not with time. Note that in the Horton's equation, infiltration capacity is a function of time, not cumulative infiltration volume.

---

*Horton, R. E. *Surface Runoff Phenomena: Part I, Analysis of the Hydrograph.* Horton Hydrologic Lab Pub. 101, Ann Arbor, MI, Edward Bros., 1935.

**EXAMPLE 6–5**   A soil has the following characteristics

$$f_0 = 3.81 \text{ cm} \cdot \text{h}^{-1} \qquad f_c = 0.51 \text{ cm} \cdot \text{h}^{-1} \qquad k = 0.35 \text{ h}^{-1}$$

What are the values of $f$ at $t = 12$ min, 30 min, 1 h, 2 h, and 6 h? What is the total volume of infiltration over the 6-h period in an area that is 1 m²?

Solution   Using the stated data, we can calculate the infiltration rates using Horton's equation if $i > f$ (or rate of precipitation exceeds the rate of infiltration). The volume of precipitation that infiltrated can be calculated by integrating Horton's equation over the time interval being considered.

$$\text{Volume} = A_s \int_0^t f \, dt = A_s \int_0^t [f_c + (f_0 - f_c)e^{-kt}] \, dt = A_s \left[ f_c t + \frac{(f_0 - f_c)}{-k} e^{-kt} \Big|_0^t \right]$$

Using Horton's equation, we calculate the infiltration rate for each of the desired time intervals.

| Time (h) | Infiltration Rate (cm/h) |
|---|---|
| 0.2 | 3.58 |
| 0.5 | 3.28 |
| 1 | 2.54 |
| 2 | 2.16 |
| 6 | 0.91 |

The data calculated can be plotted to show how the infiltration rate decreases with time.

The volume of water that would have infiltrated over the 6 h can be calculated.

$$\text{Volume} = A_s \left[ \left\{ (0.51)(6) + \frac{(3.81 - 0.51)}{-0.35} e^{-(0.35)(6)} \right\} \right.$$

$$\left. - \left\{ (0.51)(0) + \frac{(3.81 - 0.51)}{-0.35} e^{-(0.35)(0)} \right\} \right]$$

$$= A_s(11.3 \text{ cm}) = 1 \text{ m}^2 (11.3 \text{ cm})(1 \text{ m} \cdot 100 \text{ cm}^{-1}) = 0.113 \text{ m}^3$$

**FIGURE 6–13**

Generation of flow in a channel.

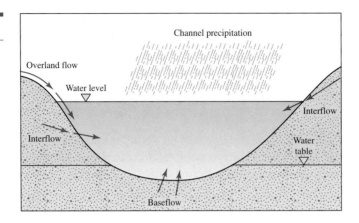

## Streamflow

As shown in Figure 6–13, flow in streams (**streamflow** to hydrologists) is generated in a number of ways. Some portion of the flow in a stream (**baseflow**) can originate from groundwater, soil, and springs. This is the portion of the streamflow that would be present even during periods of drought. **Interflow** is that portion of precipitation that infiltrates into the soil and moves horizontally through the shallow soil horizon without ever reaching the water table (**zone of saturation***). **Overland flow** is due to surface runoff and is that portion of precipitation that neither infiltrates into the soil nor evaporates nor evapotranspirates. This water flows down gradient to the nearest channel (river, stream, etc.). The final source of water in a channel is due to **channel precipitation.** This is the rainfall that actually falls into the stream or river.

The actual flow rate in a stream is determined by measuring the velocity and depth (or height of the water above a reference datum) of the water at particular cross sections in the channel. The elevation (stage) readings are calibrated in terms of streamflow. Stage measurements are commonly given in units of feet or meters. **Flow,** or discharge, the total volume of water that flows past a point on the river during some fixed time interval, is also crucial to hydrological measurements. Discharge is a measure of flowrate and can be measured in units of cubic feet per second (cfs), gallons per minute (gpm), or cubic meters per second ($m^3 \cdot s^{-1}$). Flow rate is measured at a location on the channel known as a **stream-gauging station.**

At manual recording stations, readings are made from a marked rod (staff gauge) placed in the stream (Figure 6–14). These systems require that someone visit the station to record the stage elevation.

Using automatic recording stations, the river stage can be continuously monitored and recorded. These data can be transmitted to United States Geological Service (USGS) and NWS offices using either telephone lines or satellite radios. This process allows for the remote monitoring of river elevation and prediction of flood conditions.

Automatic recording stations often use a stilling well and shelter for monitoring purposes. A stilling well and a shelter (Figure 6–15) minimize the effects of wave action and protects the piping system and valves from floating logs and other materials. For small streams, a dam with a weir plate (Figure 6–16) may be installed. This system increases the change in elevation for small changes in streamflow and makes readings more precise and accurate.

Rating curves (Figure 6–17) are required to calibrate stage measurements. These curves are constructed by USGS field personnel who periodically visit the gauging station to measure river discharge by monitoring depth and velocity of the river across a cross section of the channel.

---

*See page 209, Aquifers section.

**FIGURE 6–14**

Staff gauges for measurement of stream flow rate. (*Courtesy of Leupold & Stevens, Inc.*)

**FIGURE 6–15**

Schematic of a stilling well and shelter at a stream-gauging station.

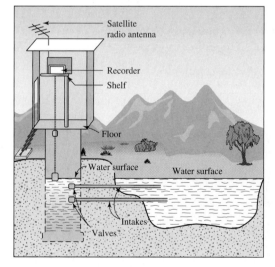

**FIGURE 6–16**

Weir for stage measurement. (*Courtesy of Leupold and Stevens, Inc.*)

FIGURE 6–17

Typical discharge curve. (*Source:* Wahl, K. L., W. O. Thomas, Jr., and R. M. Hirsch. *Stream-Gauging Program of the U.S. Geological Survey.* U.S. GEOLOGICAL SURVEY CIRCULAR 1123, Reston, Virginia, 1995.)

## 6–3 GROUNDWATER HYDROLOGY

So far, our discussion has focused on surface water. Although surface water is an important natural resource, the importance of groundwater must not be neglected. Groundwater accounts for 25.7% of the total freshwater and 98.4% of the unfrozen freshwater in the hydrosphere*. Although groundwater is renewable, the rate at which it is replenished is often much slower than the rate at which water is pumped from the water-yielding earthen layer or **aquifer.** Therefore, in locations such as Arizona, eastern Colorado, western Kansas, Texas, Oklahoma and portions of California, where groundwater is the predominant source of water, the groundwater is being "mined," that is, pumped at a rate that exceeds the rate at which it is replenished. As shown in Figure 6–18, such phenomena as saltwater intrusion and chemical and microbial contamination

*Source:* Mather, J. R. *Water Resources,* V.H. Winston and Sons, Silver Springs, MD, 1984.

FIGURE 6–18

Elements of groundwater flow. (*Source: The Nature of Water, Groundwater—A Major Link in the Hydrologic Cycle.* Environment Canada, Ottawa, Canada.
site: www.ec.gc.ca/water/en/nature/grdwtr/e-link.htm
image: http://www.ec.gc.ca/water/images/nature/grdwtr/a5f2e.htm)

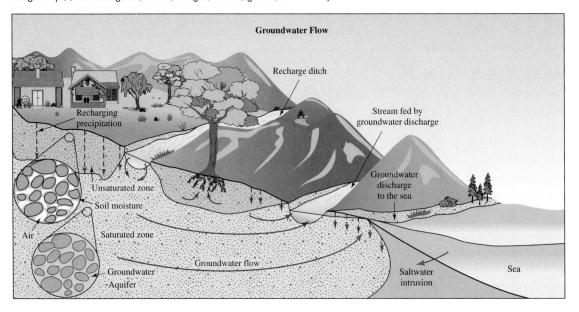

affect the quality of this important natural resource. Clearly, we must learn to better manage this resource, protecting it for future generations.

### *Aquifers*

As water drains down through the soil, it flows through the root zone and then through a zone referred to as the **unsaturated zone** (also called the **vadose zone** or the **zone of aeration**). As shown in Figure 6–18, the pores of the geologic material in the unsaturated zone are partially filled with water. The remaining portion is filled with air. The water continues to migrate vertically down through the soil until it reaches a level at which all of the openings or voids in the soils are filled with water. This zone is known as the **zone of saturation,** the **saturated zone,** or the **phreatic zone.** The water in the zone of saturation is referred to as **groundwater.** The geologic formation, through which water can flow horizontally and be pumped, is called an **aquifer.** Sand, sandstone, or other sedimentary rocks serve as good aquifers. Aquifers can also be present in other porous geologic materials, such as limestone, fractured basalt, or weathered granite.

### Unconfined Aquifers.   The upper surface of the zone of saturation in aquifers that are not confined by impermeable geologic material is called the **water table** (Figure 6–19). This type of aquifer is called a **water table aquifer,** a **phreatic aquifer,** or an **unconfined aquifer.**

The smaller void spaces in the geologic material just above the water table may contain water as a result of interactive forces between the water and the soil. The process of soil drawing water above its static level is known as **capillary action.** The zone in which this occurs is referred to as the **capillary fringe.** Although the pores in this region are saturated with water, this water cannot be thought of as a source of supply because the water held in this region will not drain freely by gravity (Figure 6–20).

In an unconfined aquifer, the water table can vary significantly with rainfall and seasons. For example, in temperate climates, in the spring when rainfall is usually high and where snow- and icemelt are significant, the water table is nearest to the ground surface. In contrast, when infiltration rates are low, such as during periods of low rainfall or when the ground surface is frozen, the water table is farthest from the surface. This process of infiltration and migration, renewing the supply of groundwater, is referred to as **recharge.**

### Perched Aquifers.   A perched aquifer is a lens of water held above the surrounding water table by an impervious geologic layer, such as bedrock or clay. It may cover an area from a few hundred square meters to several square kilometers. Drilling wells into perched aquifers can present problems because the volume of water held in these aquifers is relatively small, resulting in the well "drying out" after a short period of pumping.

## FIGURE 6–19

Schematic of groundwater aquifers.

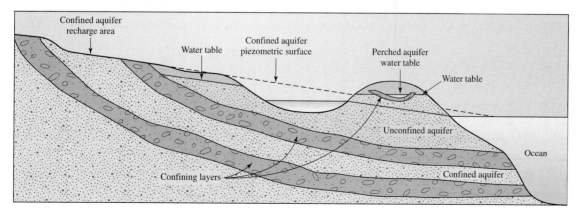

## FIGURE 6–20

Schematic drawing showing the zones of aeration and saturation and the water table. Note how the surfaces of the soil particles in the zone of aeration are partially covered by water, whereas in the zone of saturation the pores are completely filled with water. Also note that in the unpumped well, the level of water is the same as the water table. (*Source:* Montgomery, C. *Environmental Engineering,* 6th ed. McGraw-Hill, Inc., New York, 2003. Reproduced with permission.)

## FIGURE 6–21

Manometer analogy to water in an aquifer. The manometer in **(a)** is analogous to an unconfined aquifer. The manometer in **(b)** is analogous to a confined aquifer.

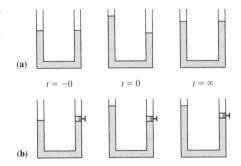

**Confined Aquifers.**   Aquifers bounded both above and below the saturated zone by impermeable layers are referred to as **confined aquifers.** The impermeable layers are called **confining layers.** Confining layers are classified either as **aquicludes** or **aquitards.** Although aquicludes are essentially impermeable to water flow and aquitards are less permeable than the aquifer, but not truly impermeable, the terms are often used interchangeably.

**Artesian Aquifer.**   The water in a confined aquifer may be under considerable pressure due to the impermeable nature of the confining layers, which restrict flow, or due to elevation differences in the aquifer. The system is analogous to a manometer. When there is no constriction in the manometer, the water level in each leg rises to the same height. This is analogous of the water properties in an unconfined aquifer and is shown in Figure 6–21a. If the water level in the left leg is raised, the increased water pressure in that leg pushes the water up in the right leg until the levels are equal again. As shown in Figure 6–21b, if the right leg is clamped shut then the water will not rise to the same level. This is analogous to the water properties in a confined aquifer. At the point where the clamp is placed, the water pressure will increase. This pressure is the result of the height of water in the left leg.

As shown in Figure 6–22, if the water in the aquifer is under pressure, it is called an **artesian aquifer.** The name *artesian* comes from the French province of Artois (Artesium in Latin) where, in the days of the Romans, water flowed to the surface of the ground from a well. When the water

**FIGURE 6–22**

Schematic showing
piezometric surface of
artesian and flowing
artesian wells. Note the
piezometric surface for
the flowing well is at
ground surface. (*Source:*
From: *Groundwater—
Nature's Hidden
Treasure, Environment*
Canada, Ottawa,
Canada, 1999.
http://www.ec.gc.ca/
water/en/info/pubs/FS/
e_FSA5.htm
image: http://www.ec
.gc.ca/water/images/
nature/grdwtr/a5f3e.jpg

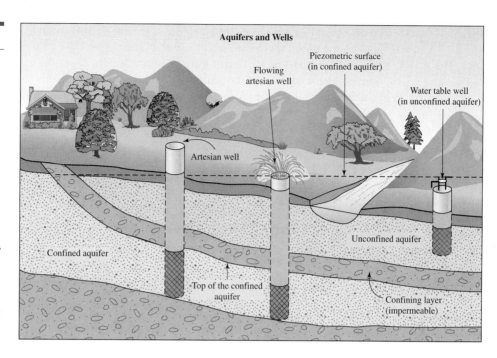

pressure in the aquifer is sufficiently high to push the water up through the geologic materials of the aquifer and overlying unsaturated zone and out onto the ground surface, the aquifer is known as a **flowing artesian aquifer.**

Water enters an artesian aquifer at some location where the confining layers intersect the ground surface. This is usually in an area of geological uplift. The exposed surface of the aquifer is called the **recharge area.** The artesian aquifer is under pressure for the same reason that the pinched manometer is under pressure, that is, because the recharge area is higher than the bottom of the top confining layer, and, thus, the height of the water above the confining layer causes pressure in the aquifer. The greater the vertical distance between the recharge area and the bottom of the top confining layer, the higher the height of the water, and the higher the pressure.

**Springs.**   Because of the irregularities in underground geologic materials and in surface topography, the water table occasionally intersects the surface of the ground or the bed of a stream, lake, or ocean. At these points of intersection, groundwater flows out of the aquifer, forming lakes, streams, or springs. The location where the water table breaks the ground surface is called a **gravity,** or **seepage spring.** Springs can result from either confined or unconfined aquifers.

**Complexities in Hydrogeology.**   The descriptions and schematics presented earlier are great simplifications of what actually occurs in nature. Aquifers are very complex and highly variable geological formations. Variations in groundwater flow occur spatially, both in the vertical and horizontal directions. Lenses of variable geologic material may be present within a formation. For example, it is not uncommon in depositional geological formations to find sand lenses within much more impermeable geologic material, such as silt and clay. Aquifer systems also have divides, analogous to that observed with surface streams. Here the groundwater flow divides into different directions, affecting the extent to which the aquifer can be tapped as a water source.

**Piezometric Surfaces and Head.**   If we place small tubes (piezometers) vertically into a confined aquifer, the water pressure will cause water to rise in the tubes just as the water in the legs of a manometer rises to a point of equilibrium. The height of the water in the tube, referred to as **piezometric head,** is a measure of the pressure in the aquifer. The piezometric head is measured using the water level in the well. An imaginary plane drawn through the points of equilibrium in several piezometers is called a **piezometric surface.** In an unconfined aquifer, the piezometric surface is the water table.

If the piezometric surface of a confined aquifer lies above the ground surface, a well penetrating into the aquifer will flow naturally without pumping. In this case the well penetrates into an artesian aquifer. If the piezometric surface is below the ground surface, the well will not flow without pumping.

The **hydraulic gradient** is the difference in the head at two locations divided by the distance between the locations and can be represented mathematically as

$$\frac{\Delta h}{L} = \frac{h_2 - h_1}{L} \tag{6-11}$$

where $\Delta h / L$ = the hydraulic gradient
$h_2$ = the head at location 2
$h_1$ = the head at location 1
$L$ = the linear distance between location 1 and location 2

**EXAMPLE 6-6**   The head in an unconfined aquifer (Figure 6–23) has been measured at four locations as shown in the following schematic.

Using this information, determine the hydraulic gradient.

**Solution**   The direction of flow is from $AC$ to $BD$. The hydraulic gradient can be calculated using Equation 6–11

$$\frac{\Delta h}{L} = \frac{h_2 - h_1}{L} = \frac{8.0 - 7.8 \text{ m}}{40 \text{ m}} = 0.005 \text{ m} \cdot \text{m}^{-1}$$

**FIGURE 6–23**

Schematic showing piezometric surface and datum in an unconfined aquifer.

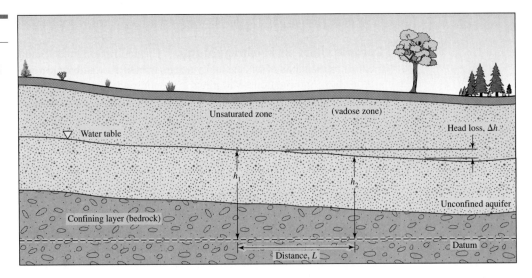

## 6–4  GROUNDWATER FLOW

Water flows along the piezometric surface from areas of higher head to lower head.

As stated earlier, in unconfined aquifers, the piezometric surface is the water table. The piezometric surface is calculated by subtracting the depth of water below the ground surface from a predefined datum. In many cases the datum is either the height of the top of the confining layer relative to sea level or the depth below ground surface (bgs).

**EXAMPLE 6–7**  You are working for a construction company and are building a school. In digging the foundation you find water at 7 m bgs. One hundred meters away, you find water at 7.5 m bgs. Choose the datum as the confining layer that is 25 m bgs. What is the piezometric surface at each point, the direction of groundwater flow, and the hydraulic gradient? *Note:* This assumes that the confining layer is parallel to the surface, which may or may not be true; however, assuming this allows us to simplify a complicated problem.

**Solution**  The first thing we should do is to draw a picture illustrating the problem. Note that at point $A$, the depth to the water table is 7.0 m, whereas at point $B$ the depth is 7.5 m. Using the datum given (at 25 m bgs), we can calculate the total head of water at each point.

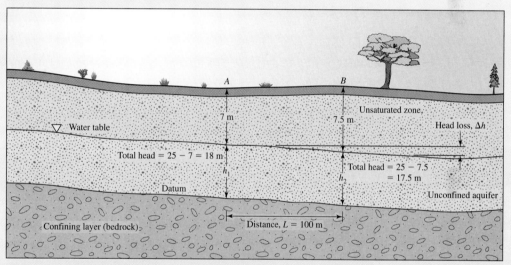

Point $A$:    Total head $= 25 - 7.0$ m $= 18$ m

Point $B$:    Total head $= 25 - 7.5$ m $= 17.5$ m

The groundwater flow is from point $A$ to $B$, from the higher piezometric surface to the lower. Using these two piezometric surfaces, the hydraulic gradient can be calculated as

$$\frac{\Delta h}{L} = \frac{h_2 - h_1}{L} = \frac{18.0 - 17.5 \text{ m}}{100 \text{ m}} = 0.005 \text{ m} \cdot \text{m}^{-1}$$

So far, we have spoken only of the direction of groundwater flow; however, in many situations, including those where we wish to predict the rate of migration of groundwater contaminants, we need to determine the rate of groundwater flow. The hydrologist, Henri Darcy, studied the flow of water through columns filled with sand and slanted on their side. He found that the rate of groundwater flow depends on the hydraulic gradient and on a property of the geological material known as the hydraulic conductivity. The **hydraulic conductivity** can be thought of as a measure of how easy it is to obtain flow of water through the porous media (i.e., the sand, gravel, etc.). For example, you might expect that water would flow much more easily through gravel than it would through very fine clay. Because water flows easily through gravel, its hydraulic conductivity would be high; however, because water does not flow readily through clay, its hydraulic conductivity would be low. Hydraulic conductivity depends on the properties of the geological material, including the grain diameter and the porosity. Hydraulic conductivities of typical geological materials are given in Table 6–4.

Hydraulic conductivity is defined as the discharge that occurs through a unit cross section of aquifer (Figure 6–24) under a hydraulic gradient of 1.00. It has units of velocity (meters per second).

| TABLE 6–4 | Typical Values of Aquifer Parameters | | |
|---|---|---|---|
| **Aquifer Material** | **Porosity (%)** | **Typical Values for Hydraulic Conductivity $(m \cdot s^{-1})$** | |
| Clay | 55 | $2.3 \times 10^{-9}$ | |
| Loam | 35 | $6.0 \times 10^{-6}$ | |
| Fine sand | 45 | $2.9 \times 10^{-5}$ | |
| Medium sand | 37 | $1.4 \times 10^{-4}$ | |
| Coarse sand | 30 | $5.2 \times 10^{-4}$ | |
| Sand and gravel | 20 | $6.0 \times 10^{-4}$ | |
| Gravel | 25 | $3.1 \times 10^{-3}$ | |
| Slate | <5 | $9.2 \times 10^{-10}$ | |
| Granite | <1 | $1.2 \times 10^{-10}$ | |
| Sandstone | 15 | $5.8 \times 10^{-7}$ | |
| Limestone | 15 | $1.1 \times 10^{-5}$ | |
| Fractured rock | 5 | $1 \times 10^{-8}$–$1 \times 10^{-4}$ | |

*Sources:* Davis, M., D. A. Cornwell. *Introduction to Environmental Engineering*, 3rd ed. McGraw-Hill, New York (1998). Todd, D. A. *Groundwater Hydrology*, 2nd ed. John Wiley and Sons, New York (1980).

**FIGURE 6–24**

Illustration of definition of hydraulic conductivity ($K$).

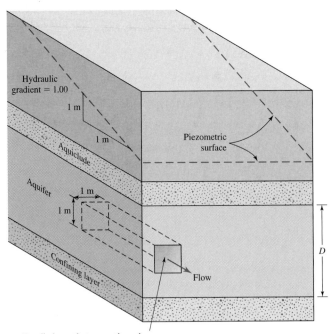

$K$ = discharge that occurs through a unit cross section 1 m square

**FIGURE 6-25**

This area is filled with solid particles. As shown in Figure 6-26, water can only flow through the pore spaces.

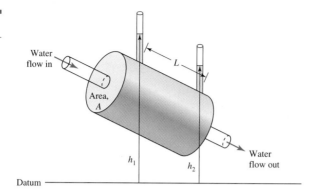

Darcy* found that when groundwater flow is laminar and the aquifer is fully saturated, the velocity of flow is proportional to both the hydraulic gradient and the hydraulic conductivity.

$$v = K\frac{\Delta h}{L} \tag{6-12}$$

where $K$ is the hydraulic conductivity (length per time) and $\Delta h/L$ is the hydraulic gradient (length per length). This equation is not valid for extremely fine materials or for fractured rock. Darcy also found that the flow rate of water, $Q$, is equal to the specific discharge (also called Darcy velocity), $v$, times the cross-sectional area through which water flows:

$$Q = vA = \left(K\frac{\Delta h}{L}\right)A \tag{6-13}$$

water flows (Figure 6-25). The actual equation used to accurately model groundwater flow is much more complicated since the hydraulic conductivity varies both in the horizontal and vertical distances and the hydraulic gradient is $\partial h/\partial L$. However, the simplified versions used here provide a basic understanding of groundwater flow.

**EXAMPLE 6-8**   Let's assume that in the previous example, the aquifer is coarse sand and that the cross-sectional area of the aquifer, through which water flows is 925 m². What is the Darcy velocity of groundwater in this aquifer? What is the specific discharge?

Solution   Using Table 6-4, we find that coarse sand has a hydraulic conductivity, $K$, of $6.9 \times 10^{-4}$ m · s⁻¹. Because the hydraulic gradient was determined to be 0.005 m · m⁻¹, the Darcy velocity of groundwater flow can be calculated as

$$v = K\left(\frac{\Delta h}{L}\right) = (6.9 \times 10^{-4}\ \text{m} \cdot \text{s}^{-1})(0.005\ \text{m} \cdot \text{m}^{-1})(86{,}400\ \text{s} \cdot \text{day}^{-1})$$

$$= 0.298\ \text{m} \cdot \text{day}^{-1}$$

The specific discharge is equal to $vA$ or

$$0.298\ \text{m} \cdot \text{day}^{-1} \times 925\ \text{m}^2 = 275.65\ \text{m}^3 \cdot \text{day}^{-1}$$

In reality, the Darcy velocity is calculated from the flowrate, $Q$, a measured parameter. As mentioned previously, the specific discharge is a flow rate, and the area used to calculate this value is the cross-sectional area of the flow shown in Figure 6-25. But water does not flow

*Henri Darcy. *Les Fontaines Publiques de la Ville de Dijon.* Victor Dalmont, Paris, pp. 570, 590–594 (1856).

**FIGURE 6–26**

Cross section of aquifer material showing voids through which water can flow.

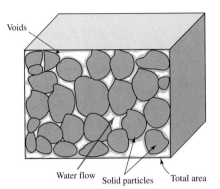

through the entire cross-sectional area since much of this area is filled with solid particles. As shown in Figure 6–26 water can only flow through the pore spaces.

As such, the average linear velocity of the water must be greater than the Darcy velocity. The average linear velocity is calculated as

$$v'_{water} = \frac{v}{\eta} \qquad (6\text{–}14)$$

where $v'_{water}$ = the average linear velocity of the water (or **seepage velocity**)

$v$ = the Darcy velocity

$\eta$ = the porosity of the geological material

**Porosity** is the ratio of the volume of voids (open spaces) in the aquifer material to the total volume. It is a measure of the maximum amount of water that can be stored in the spaces between particles of aquifer material. It does not indicate how much of this water is available to be pumped or drained from this volume of material.

**EXAMPLE 6–9**   The geological material in the column shown in Figure 6–25 is coarse sand. The piezometric surfaces, $h_1 = 10$ cm and $h_2 = 8.0$ cm. The distance between the two points where $h_1$ and $h_2$ were measured is 10.0 cm. The cross-sectional area is 10 cm$^2$. What is the linear velocity of the water flowing through the column?

Solution   The hydraulic gradient can be calculated as

$$\frac{\Delta h}{L} = \frac{h_2 - h_1}{L} = \frac{10.0 - 8.0 \text{ cm}}{10.0 \text{ cm}} = \frac{2 \text{ cm}}{10.0 \text{ cm}} = 0.2 \text{ cm} \cdot \text{cm}^{-1}$$

From Table 6–4, we see that the hydraulic conductivity, $K$, of coarse sand is equal to $6.9 \times 10^{-4}$ m $\cdot$ s$^{-1}$. The Darcy velocity can be calculated as

$$v = K \frac{\Delta h}{L} = (6.9 \times 10^{-4} \text{ m} \cdot \text{s}^{-1})(0.2 \text{ cm} \cdot \text{cm}^{-1}) = 1.38 \times 10^{-4} \text{ m} \cdot \text{s}^{-1}$$

Assuming that the porosity is 0.3 (as given in Table 6–4), then the linear velocity would be

$$v'_{water} = \frac{v}{\eta} = \frac{1.38 \times 10^{-4} \text{ m} \cdot \text{s}^{-1}}{0.3} = 4.6 \times 10^{-4} \text{ m} \cdot \text{s}^{-1}$$

From this analysis, you can see that the linear velocity of the water in the aquifer is significantly higher than the Darcy velocity.

## 6–5   SURFACE WATER AND GROUNDWATER AS A WATER SUPPLY

Groundwater and surface water provide an important natural resource. Although groundwater is hidden, it is as important as surface water. As shown in Figure 6–27a, approximately 61% of the U.S. population obtains its drinking water from surface water supplies. However, the number of public drinking-water systems that use surface water as a source is only 8% of the total (Figure 6–27b). This is because most small systems use groundwater and, as shown in Figure 6–27c, small systems vastly outnumber medium or large ones. Combined with the fact that large systems supply 80% of the population (Figure 6–27d), we see why groundwater systems account for only 39% of the per capita drinking water even though they account for 92% of the systems.

Groundwater has several characteristics that make it desirable as a water supply source over surface water. First, the groundwater system provides natural storage, which eliminates the cost of storage tanks, reservoirs, and other impoundments. Second, because the supply frequently is available at the point of demand, the cost of transmission is reduced significantly. Third, because the natural geological materials filter groundwater, groundwater is clearer and less turbid than surface water. Groundwater is less subject to seasonal fluctuations and has been more protected from pollution; however, unless we provide greater restrictions on such pollutant sources as large-scale agricultural operations, landfills, gasoline stations, and hazardous waste operations, our groundwater supplies will suffer from contamination similar to that affecting our surface water supplies.

**FIGURE 6–27**

**(a)** Percentage of the population served by drinking-water system source. **(b)** Percentage of drinking-water systems by supply source. **(c)** Number of drinking-water systems (in thousands) by size. **(d)** Population served (in millions of people) by drinking-water system size. (*Source: 1997 National Public Water Systems Compliance Report.* U.S. EPA, Office of Water. Washington, D.C. 20460. (EPA-305-R-99-002). (*Note: Small systems serve 25–3300 people; medium systems serve 3301–10,000 people; large systems serve 10,000+ people.*)

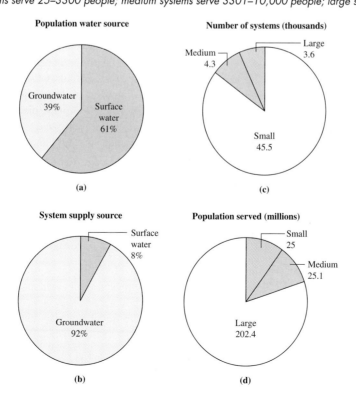

# CHAPTER REVIEW

When you have completed studying this chapter you should be able to do the following without the aid of your textbooks or notes:

1. Sketch and explain the hydrological cycle, labeling the parts as in Figure 6–1.
2. List and explain the four factors that reduce the amount of direct runoff.
3. Explain the difference between streamflow that results from direct runoff and that which results from baseflow.
4. Define evaporation, transpiration, runoff, baseflow, watershed, basin, and divide.
5. Write the basic mass-balance equation for the hydrological cycle.
6. Explain why infiltration rates decrease with time.
7. Explain why predicting water levels in streams and lakes is difficult.
8. Explain what is meant by a 100-year flood.
9. With what do precipitation rates vary and why are these variations important in water resources management?
10. Describe the different types of rainfall.
11. What are the problems associated with extrapolating rainfall gauge data to watersheds?
12. Evaporation of water from water surfaces depends on what?
13. The loss of water due to evapotranspiration depends on what?
14. What factors affect infiltration rates?
15. What method(s) can be used to estimate infiltration rates? What are the limitation(s) of this (these) method(s)?
16. Use Horton's law to estimate infiltration rates and infiltration volumes in a particular time interval.
17. Why is it important to have accurate estimates of infiltration and streamflow?
18. What is meant by streamflow and how is it determined?
19. What factors affect streamflow?
20. Explain what a unit hydrograph is.
21. Explain what factors affect the shape of a hydrograph and show how these factors change the shape.
22. Sketch the groundwater hydrological system, labeling the parts as in Figure 6–19.
23. Define the following terms: aquifer, vadose zone, unsaturated zone, zone of aeration, phreatic zone, aquitard, aquiclude, perched aquifer, confined aquifer, unconfined aquifer, hydraulic conductivity, hydraulic gradient, porosity, piezometric head (surface).
24. Explain why water in an artesian aquifer is under pressure and why water may rise above the surface in some instances and not others.
25. What factors affect the rates of water movement in the subsurface?
26. Use Horton's equation and some form of Dalton's equation to solve complex mass-balance problems.
27. Calculate the hydraulic gradient.
28. Given several hydraulic heads and the locations of the piezometers, sketch a piezometric surface.
29. Compute mass-balances for open and closed hydrological systems.
30. Estimate the volume of water loss through transpiration given the air and water temperature, wind speed, and relative humidity.
31. Determine how long is required for water to travel a certain distance in the subsurface.

## PROBLEMS

**6-1**   Lake Kickapoo, TX, is approximately 12 km in length by 2.5 km in width. The inflow for the month of April is 3.26 $m^3 \cdot s^{-1}$ and the outflow is 2.93 $m^3 \cdot s^{-1}$. The total monthly precipitation is 15.2 cm and the evaporation is 10.2 cm. The seepage is estimated to be 2.5 cm. Estimate the change in storage during the month of April.

   **Answer:** $1.61 \times 10^6 \, m^3$

**6-2**   A 4000-$km^2$ watershed receives 102 cm of precipitation in a year. The average flow of the river draining the watershed is 34.2 $m^3 \cdot s^{-1}$. Infiltration is estimated to be $5.5 \times 10^{-7}$ cm $\cdot s^{-1}$ and evapotranspiration is estimated to be 40 cm $\cdot$ year$^{-1}$. Determine the change in storage in the watershed over a year. Compute the runoff coefficient for this watershed.

**6-3**   Using the values of $f_0$, $f_c$, and $k$ for a Dothan loamy sand, find the infiltration rate at times of 12, 30, 60, and 120 min. Compute the total volume of infiltration over 120 min in an area 1 $m^2$. Assume that the rate of precipitation exceeds the rate of infiltration throughout the storm event.

   **Answer:** Rates are 83, 77, 72, and 68 mm $\cdot$ h$^{-1}$ for times of 12, 30, 60, and 120 min, respectively. The volume = 144 $m^3$ (for an area of 1 $m^2$).

**6-4**   Infiltration data from an experiment yield an initial infiltration rate of 4.70 cm $\cdot$ h$^{-1}$ and a final equilibrium infiltration rate of 0.70 cm $\cdot$ h$^{-1}$ after 60 min of steady precipitation. The value of $k$ was estimated to be 0.1085 h$^{-1}$. Determine the total volume of infiltration (in an area 1 $m^2$) for the following storm sequence: 30 mm $\cdot$ h$^{-1}$ for 30 min, 53 mm $\cdot$ h$^{-1}$ for 30 min, 23 mm $\cdot$ h$^{-1}$ for 30 min.

**6-5**   Using the empirical equation developed for Lake Hefner (Equation 6–8), estimate the evaporation from a lake on a day that the air temperature is 30°C, the water temperature is 15°C, the wind speed is 9 m $\cdot$ s$^{-1}$, and the relative humidity is 30%.

   **Answer:** 4.7 mm $\cdot$ day$^{-1}$

**6-6**   The Dalton-type evaporation equation implies that there is a limiting relative humidity above which evaporation will be negligible regardless of the wind speed. Using the Lake Hefner empirical equation, estimate the relative humidity at which evaporation will be zero if the water temperature is 10°C and the air temperature is 25°C.

**6-7**   Four monitoring wells have been placed around a leaking underground storage tank. The wells are located at the corners of a 1-ha square. The total piezometric head in each of the wells is as follows: NE corner, 30.0 m; SE corner, 30.0 m; SW corner, 30.6 m: NW corner 30.6 m. Determine the magnitude and direction of the hydraulic gradient.

   **Answer:** Hydraulic gradient = $6 \times 10^{-3}$ m $\cdot$ m$^{-1}$; direction is from west to east.

**6-8**   After a long wet spell, the water levels in the wells described in Problem 6–7 were measured and found to be the following distances from the ground surface: NE corner, 3.0 m; SE corner, 3.0 m; SW corner, 3.6 m; NW corner, 3.6 m. A confining layer of bedrock exists at a depth of 25 m bgs. Assume that the ground surface is at the same elevation for each of the wells. Determine the magnitude and direction of the hydraulic gradient.

**6-9**   A gravelly sand has hydraulic conductivity of $6.1 \times 10^{-4}$ m $\cdot$ s$^{-1}$, a hydraulic gradient of 0.00141 m $\cdot$ m$^{-1}$, and a porosity of 20%. Determine the Darcy velocity and the average linear velocity.

   **Answer:** Darcy velocity = $8.6 \times 10^{-7}$ m $\cdot$ s$^{-1}$; average linear velocity = $4.3 \times 10^{-6}$ m $\cdot$ s$^{-1}$.

**6-10**   Two piezometers have been placed along the direction of flow in a confined aquifer that is 30.0 m thick. The piezometers are 280 m apart. The difference in piezometric head between the two is 1.4 m. The aquifer hydraulic conductivity is 50 m $\cdot$ day$^{-1}$, and the porosity is 20%. Estimate the travel time for water to flow between the two piezometers.

## DISCUSSION QUESTIONS

**6-1**  An artesian aquifer is under pressure because of the weight of the overlying geological strata. Is this sentence true or false? If it is false, rewrite the sentence to make it true.

**6-2**  As a field engineer you have been asked to estimate how long you would have to measure the discharge from a mall parking lot before the maximum discharge would be achieved. What data would you have to gather to make the estimate?

**6-3**  When a flood has a recurrence interval (return period) of 5 years, it means that the chance of another flood of the same or less severity occurring next year is 5%. Is this sentence true or false? If it is false, rewrite the sentence to make it true.

## ADDITIONAL READING

### Books

Bouwer, H. *Groundwater Hydrology,* McGraw-Hill, New York (1978).

Chow, V. T., D. R. Maidment, L. W. Mays. *Applied Hydrology.* McGraw-Hill, New York (1988).

Davis, M., D. Cornwell. *Introduction to Environmental Engineering*, 3rd cd. McGraw-Hill, New York (1998).

Freeze, A. R., J. A. Cherry. *Groundwater.* Prentice-Hall, Englewood Cliffs, NJ (1979).

Linsley, Jr., R. K., J. B. Franzini, D. L. Freyburg, and G. Tchobanoglous. *Water Resources Engineering,* 4th ed. McGraw-Hill, New York (1992).

Linsley, Jr., R. K., M. A. Kohler, J. L. E. Paulhus. *Hydrology for Engineers,* 3rd ed. McGraw-Hill, New York (1982).

McCuen, R. H. *Hydrologic Analysis and Design,* 2nd ed. Prentice-Hall, Englewood Cliffs, NJ (1998).

Ponce, V. M. *Engineering Hydrology Principles and Practices.* Prentice-Hall, Englewood Cliffs, NJ (1989).

Viessman, W., G. L. Lewis, J. W. Knapp. *Introduction to Hydrology,* 3rd ed. Harper & Row, New York (1989).

### Journals

*Water Resources Bulletin*

*Water Resources Research*

*Groundwater Monitoring and Remediation*

# 7

# Geological and Soil Resources

## 7–1 INTRODUCTION

We live on the third rock from the sun. That rock provides not only a place to stand but also mineral resources and soils that form a component of the earth's ecosystem that we need to survive. Although we separate geological and soil resources for the purpose of discussion, they are intimately linked with other environmental components such as air, water, and life. From an environmental perspective, we are concerned with the depletion of our natural resources, the effects on the environment of our use of these resources, and the effects of disposal of our wastes on these resources.

## 7–2 THE ROCK CYCLE

The cycle of rock formation (Figure 7–1) begins at earth's molten core—the **magma. Igneous rocks,** the ancestors of all other rocks are "fire-formed," that is, they were once a hot, molten mass of magma. Lava flowing from a volcano forms **extrusive** igneous rock. **Intrusive** igneous rock cools many kilometers below the land surface and is only exposed after extensive erosion.

**FIGURE 7–1**         The Rock Cycle, Shown Diagrammatically

Uninterrupted, the cycle will continue completely around the outer margin of the diagram from magma through igneous rocks, sediments, sedimentary rocks, metamorphic rocks, and back again to magma. The cycle may be interrupted, however, at various points along its course and follow the path of one of the arrows crossing through the interior of the diagram.

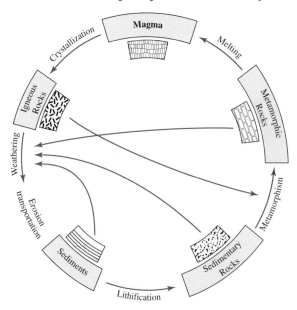

**Sedimentary** rocks are made up of redeposited broken debris from other rocks. This broken debris may be mechanically formed by deposition of the fragments from water, wind, or ice. Some examples are shale and sandstone. Alternatively, sedimentary rocks may be formed by chemical precipitation. Limestone and rock salt are examples of chemical precipitation. The process of **lithification** transforms sediments into hard rock by compaction and cementation. Sedimentary rocks are characterized by layering or **stratification.**

The third type of rock is called **metamorphic** because it has changed form. Pressure, heat, and chemically active fluids may play a role in transformation of the rock. If the metamorphic rock is subjected to sufficient heat and pressure to lose its identity and return to a molten state, the cycle is completed.

The rock cycle may be interrupted at any number of points as shown in Figure 7–1.

## 7–3  MINERAL CONCENTRATION

The numerous geological materials in use today may be classified into two broad categories: metals (e.g., aluminum, copper, iron) and nonmetals (e.g., diamonds, limestone, and phosphate rock). Although these materials may be found in some quantity almost anywhere, they are considered mineral deposits only when their concentration can be worked at a profit.

A convenient way of discussing mineral deposits is to classify them on the basis of the geologic processes that have concentrated them. These include igneous activity, weathering, sedimentation, and precipitation. Of course, many rocks are valuable in their original condition. Building stone and sand fall in this category.

### Igneous Activity

Some mineral deposits result because of the size of their ions. They do not combine readily with the common rock-forming minerals. These elements may crystallize early in the cooling of the magma and settle out of the magma solution or they may crystallize late and be injected into surrounding rocks. Diamonds are, for example, formed where carbon has been trapped by magma under extremely high pressure. Deposits of chromium, nickel, and platinum became concentrated in cooling magma, and because they were more dense than the rock-forming minerals, they settled out during crystallization.

### Weathering

The action of water, air, and living matter to break the rock down is called **weathering.** One action of weathering is to chemically alter the geologic compounds to a form that allows the desired elements to be extracted economically. Aluminum, for example, is one of the most common elements in the earth's crust, but it occurs in forms (aluminosilicates) that cannot be extracted cheaply. Weathering breaks down the aluminosilicates, that in turn, become hydrous oxides of aluminum (bauxite) that can more readily be extracted.

Iron has been concentrated by the removal of undesired components. Percolating ground water, removes the silica from the parent rock and concentrates iron in the form of $Fe_2O_3$.

A third form of weathering is the solution and redeposition of the desired elements. Here, groundwater dissolves the mineral, for example, copper, and carries it from a place of lower concentration to another location where it is deposited.

### Sedimentary Processes

Flowing water moves great quantities of mineral matter along stream and creek, accumulating heavier minerals in the channel bottoms. Gold, tin, and, iron, in particular, are concentrated this way.

### Precipitation

The concentration of compounds in solution above their solubility results in precipitation. Limestone, which is predominantly calcium carbonate, and phosphate rock (calcium fluorophosphate) are initially formed by precipitation.

| | U.S. and World Reserves of Some Common Metals | | |
|---|---|---|---|
| **TABLE 7-1** | | | |
| **Metal** | **U.S. (Tg[a])** | **World (Tg)** | |
| Aluminum | 38 | 21,000 | |
| Copper | 57 | 340 | |
| Iron | 3360 | 65,400 | |

[a]Tg = teragrams = $10^{12}$ g

*Source:* U.S. Bureau of Mines, *Mineral Facts and Problems.* U.S. Department of the Interior, 1985.

## 7-4   ROCK AND MINERAL RESOURCES

### Reserves

Resources that are replaceable over short time periods (years, decades, or centuries at the most) such as food crops, forests, grasslands, are called **renewable. Nonrenewable** resources, such as copper and iron deposits, are those formed over geologic periods. In terms of human needs, once the deposit is exhausted, the depletion is permanent.

The question is not whether the world is running out of minerals but rather what are we willing to pay and what environmental effects will be incurred. Let us first look at the question of "running out." That portion of the identified mineral resource that can be economically mined at the time of the calculation is called the mineral **reserve.** Because of changes in technology and the change in consumer willingness to pay, the reserve may change even though the mass of mineral does not. The estimated U.S. and world reserves of three metals are shown in Table 7–1. How long will the reserves last? Several types of estimates are possible. For example, we can estimate the length of time, assuming current consumption rates (demand) with no new discoveries or changes in extraction technology. Alternatively, we can assume some growth in demand with no new discoveries or changes in extraction technology. The length of time that current reserves will last with a constant demand is expressed as

$$T_s = \frac{F}{A} \tag{7-1}$$

where $T_s$ = time until exhaustion (in years)
  $F$ = mass of mineral reserve (in Tg)
  $A$ = annual demand (in $Tg \cdot year^{-1}$)

The length of time that current reserves will last with a growth in demand is expressed as

$$F = A\left[\frac{(1+i)^n - 1}{i}\right] \tag{7-2}$$

where $i$ = annual increase in demand as a fraction
  $n$ = the number of years to consume the reserve

Example 7–1 shows how to make these two kinds of estimates.

**EXAMPLE 7-1**   In 2001, the international production of iron was 1060 Tg [1]. Assuming the 2001 demand remains constant, how long will world reserves last? World production increased 1.2% from 1996 to 1997. If that rate of increase remains constant, how long will world reserves last?

Solution   If the demand remains constant (Equation 7–1), the world reserve will last

$$\frac{65,400 \text{ Tg}}{1060 \text{ Tg} \cdot year^{-1}} = 61.70, \text{ or } 62 \text{ years}$$

If the demand rises at a rate of 1.2%, then we can use the following growth expression:

$$65,400 \text{ Tg} = 1060 \text{ Tg} \cdot \text{year}^{-1} \left[ \frac{(1 + 0.012)^n - 1}{0.012} \right]$$

Solving for $n$

$$(61.70)(0.012) = (1.012)^n - 1$$

$$1.74 = (1.012)^n$$

Taking the log of both sides

$$\log(1.74) = \log[(1.012)^n] = n \log[1.012]$$

$$0.2406 = n(0.0052)$$

$$n = 46.45 \text{ or } 46 \text{ years}$$

This example illustrates the finite nature of our mineral resources. However, both estimates incorporate a number of assumptions that are not realistic. They both assume no changes in technology, no further discoveries of new ores, and, perhaps most importantly, that the grade of the ore must remain the same as it is today to be economically feasible to mine. In general, we have been able to extract lower grade ores with increases in technology as shown in Figure 7–2. It has been estimated that even with marginal grade ores, at current rates of growth, the maximum reserve capacity for aluminum, copper and iron will be exhausted in 160, 33, and 78 years, respectively [2]. In addition, the cost of extracting these ores may be prohibitive.

### Environmental Impacts

**Energy.**   Although we tend to think of cost in terms of dollars, a more realistic measure of cost for extraction of minerals is the energy required to mine and process them. Table 7–2 gives some examples of the energy expenditures in mining and concentrating some common metallic ores. These expenditures do not include the energy to fabricate a metallic product such as a beverage can or bumper.

It is estimated that approximately 1% of the world's energy resource is used for aluminum production each year and over 5% of the world's energy is used in steel production [3].

**Waste.**   Because the rock from which minerals are mined contains only a fraction of the mineral, a substantial amount of rock waste is generated by mining. In the United States, the annual

**FIGURE 7–2**

Since 1905, the quality of copper ore mined in the United States has declined from 2.5% to about 0.5%. (*Source: U.S. Bureau of Mines 1990.*)

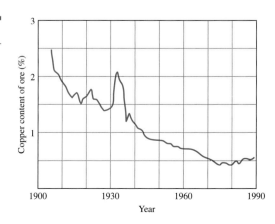

| **TABLE 7–2** | Energy Expenditures in Mining and Concentrating Some Common Metallic Ores | | |
|---|---|---|---|
| **Ore** | **Grade (%)** | **Energy (MJ · kg$^{-1}$ of metal)** | |
| Aluminum | 25 | 235 | |
| Copper | 0.7 | 74 | |
| Iron | 30 | 3.0 | |

*Sources:* Data reprinted from: Atkins, P. R., H. J. Hitter, and D. Wiloughby, "Some energy and environmental impacts of aluminum usage." In: *Energy and Environment in the 21st Century,* J. W. Testor, ed. MIT Press, Cambridge, MA (1991); and from Hayes, E. T., "Energy implications of materials recovery." In: *Materials: Renewable and Nonrenewable Resources,* P. H. Abelson and A. L. Hammond, eds. American Association for the Advancement of Science, Washington, D.C. (1976).

production of nonfuel mineral mining waste is estimated to be 1.0–1.3 petagrams (Pg) [3]. This is about seven times the amount of municipal solid waste generated in U.S. cities. In the following example, a simple mass balance of ore excavation and concentration illustrates why there is so much waste rock.

**EXAMPLE 7–2**  Estimate the amount of waste rock generated in producing 100 kg of copper from an ore containing 0.5% copper.

Solution  The mass-balance diagram is shown here.

The mass-balance equation is

$$\text{Accumulation} = M_{\text{Cu in rock}} - M_{\text{Cu out}}$$

At steady state the accumulation = 0.

At 0.5% concentration, the amount of copper in the ore is

$$M_{\text{Cu in rock}} = (0.005)(M_{\text{rock}})$$

This is also the amount of copper produced ($M_{\text{Cu out}}$). So

$$M_{\text{Cu out}} = (0.005)(M_{\text{rock}})$$

Because the $M_{\text{Cu out}}$ is 100 kg,

$$(M_{\text{rock}}) = \frac{100 \text{ kg}}{0.005} = 200{,}000 \text{ kg}$$

This waste rock does not include the soil cover (**overburden**) that is removed to expose the ore.

The waste generated in producing the mineral is not limited to waste rock. Additional waste includes wastewater and air pollutants from the smelting operations. If the ore contained sulfides, then rainwater leaching through the waste rock piles (**tailings**) will become acidified. Erosion of the waste rock piles results in increased loads of suspended solids in nearby streams and rivers. The suspended solids settle and smother hatcheries and clog gills of fish. An estimated 16,000 km of streams have been damaged by leaching from mine tailings.

Smelting operations frequently release sulfur dioxide and volatile heavy metals (e.g., lead and arsenic) to the atmosphere. Smelting operations are estimated to produce 8% of the worldwide sulfur emissions [3].

**Terrain Effects.**   Although the land directly involved in mining may seem small, it is far from insignificant. In the United States over 1.3 million ha (an area approximately the size of Connecticut) have been disturbed by surface mining [4]. In addition to being unsightly, without reclamation, this disturbed land is no longer viable as a support system for renewable resources. In some cases the mined land poses hazards from cave-ins and subsidence of the land surface beneath the roads and cities built above the mines. At some surface mines, landslides are an imminent danger.

### Resource Conservation

All methods of resource conservation are not equal. Some yield more or longer term benefits than others. There is a hierarchy of resource conservation. The preferred order is reduced consumption, material substitution, and finally, recycling.

**Reduced Consumption.**   Since the 1970s, the use of raw materials in the United States and Europe has leveled off or even declined a bit. Part of this trend is explained by the fact that the western industrialized nations have a firmly built infrastructure and major construction of public works is less common than in the past. In addition, the economies of the industrialized nations are reorienting to high-technology goods and consumer services that demand less raw materials. This trend, of course, does not include the developing countries, where the demand for minerals will remain high.

Other, more proactive, means of reducing consumption include product design, process management, and dematerialization. Products that do not wear out as quickly and that are easy to disassemble to recover materials at the end of their usefulness all contribute to reduced consumption. Germany has imposed requirements on their automobile manufacturers that require them to take back and recycle old automobiles. Companies like BMW and Volkswagen have redesigned their cars to be disassembled to recover parts.

Better process management improves efficiency and reduces the amount of waste material generated. This has benefit for production economics as well as reduced consumption of raw materials.

Another strategy, called **dematerialization,** is to reduce the size of the product while performing the intended function. For example, a smaller, lighter car still provides the transportation function but uses a smaller amount of mineral resources. Miniaturization in the electronics industry is a classic example of the savings in materials.

Dematerialization must be considered carefully. In some cases a smaller, lighter product may result in a less durable product that will, over time, use more material than a heavier, more durable product.

**Material Substitution.**   A simple way to reduce the demand for mineral resources is to produce more durable goods. Frequently, this means substituting a more durable material for a less durable one. A classic example is the substitution of plastic parts for steel on automobiles. The plastic does not corrode, and, thus extends the life of the body.

Alternatively, a material may be substituted because it performs the same function more efficiently. Fiber optic cables in place of copper telephone wire not only reduce the use of a vanishing mineral resource but also provide better communication service.

**Recycling.**   The law of conservation of mass tells us that the minerals we have mined do not disappear. Although they have served their useful life as a product, the mineral content is still there. One of the more obvious solutions to the resource limit problem is recycling. In 1993, 15.6 Tg of metals was disposed of in municipal solid waste systems. Iron accounted for 76% of the mass, and aluminum accounted for 17%. Since the early 1970s the effort to recycle has increased substantially. For example, in 1997, the U.S. Geologic Survey [1] reported that recycled aluminum accounted for 41% of the production of finished metal and that recycled copper accounted for 17% of the production. The fact that only 35% of the discarded aluminum was recovered implies there is room to grow in this effort.

The advantage of recycling is also reflected in a reduction in energy consumption. For example, the energy to produce aluminum stock from recycled metal is 5.1 MJ $\cdot$ kg$^{-1}$ compared with 235 MJ $\cdot$ kg$^{-1}$ required to produce it from ore.

On the down side, recycling has practical limits. The second law of thermodynamics cannot be violated. Each use results in some deterioration or loss through transformation. Normal wear and tear will result in the loss of some metal. Some loss will be in the form of corrosion, some will be in the form of microscopic abrasive loss, and some will be dissipative loss (e.g., in dyes, paints, inks, cosmetics, and pesticides). In the process of recovery, the crushing, grinding, and remelting will cause some additional loss.

The amount of metal available at the end of each cycle of reclamation may be approximated as a first-order decay.

$$\frac{dM}{dn} = -kM \tag{7-3}$$

where $dM/dn$ = change in mass of metal per cycle of reclamation (in kg $\cdot$ cycle$^{-1}$)
$\qquad k$ = decay constant (cycle$^{-1}$)
$\qquad M$ = mass recovered in previous cycle (in kg)

The solution to this equation yields

$$M = M_0 e^{-kn} \tag{7-4}$$

where $M$ = mass recovered (in kg)
$\qquad M_0$ = original mass (in kg)
$\qquad k$ = decay constant (cycle$^{-1}$)
$\qquad n$ = number of cycles

**EXAMPLE 7-3**    Assume that you could track a single aluminum beverage can (with a mass of 16 g) through several cycles of reclamation and that a 10% "loss" occurred in each recovery cycle. How much new aluminum must be supplied to replace the loss at the end of the third reclamation?

Solution    The decay constant is not known but may calculated from the assumptions. For the first cycle, the amount of mass recovered is 90% of the original mass (100 − 10% loss). So

$$\frac{M}{M_0} = 0.90 = e^{-kn}$$

where $n = 1$

Taking the natural logarithm of both sides and solving for $k$, we obtain

$$\ln(0.90) = \ln[e^{-k(1)}]$$

$$-0.1054 = -k(1)$$

$$k = 0.1054 \text{ cycle}^{-1}$$

The approximate mass remaining at the end of the third cycle is

$$M = M_0 e^{-kn} = (16 \text{ g}) \exp[(-0.1054)(3)]$$

$$= (16 \text{ g})(0.7290) = 11.664 \text{ g}$$

The approximate mass of new aluminum that must be supplied to replace the loss at the end of the third reclamation is then

$$16 \text{ g} - 11.664 = 4.336, \text{ or } 4.3 \text{ g}$$

Another way of expressing the limits of recycling is to estimate the equivalent mass of metal if it is recycled an infinite number of times. Or, perhaps, the equivalent mass if it is recycled a given number of times. In the first instance, this may be determined by the sum of a series.

$$\sum_{k=0}^{\infty} M_k = M_0 + M_0 f + M_0 f^2 + \cdots + M_0 f^n = \frac{M_0}{1 - f} \tag{7-5}$$

where $M_0$ = original mass (in kg)
$\quad\quad f$ = fraction recovered
$\quad\quad n$ = number of cycles

and $0 < f > 1$ and $n = \infty$
In the second instance, this may be determined by the sum of the series:

$$\sum_{k=0}^{n} M_k = M_0 + M_0 f + M_0 f^2 + \cdots + M_0 f^{n-1} = \frac{M_0(f^n - 1)}{f - 1} \tag{7-6}$$

where $f$ is not = 1 and $n < \infty$.

**EXAMPLE 7–4**  What is the equivalent mass of aluminum saved if the beverage can in Example 7–3 is recycled an infinite number of times?

Solution  Using the data from Example 7–3 and Equation 7–5, we obtain

$$\sum M_k = \frac{16 \text{ g}}{1 - 0.90} = 160 \text{ g}$$

## 7–5  ENERGY RESOURCES

Until about 300 years ago, the majority of human energy needs were supplied by human and animal labor; water power; wind; and wood and other burnable organic matter such as agricultural waste, dung, and peat (now lumped together as **biomass**). With the advent of the Industrial Revolution in the late 18th and early 19th centuries, water power remained important, but fossil fuels (primarily coal) began to be used on a large scale. Over the course of the 20th century petroleum products assumed a major role in supplying our energy needs.

The United States is both a major producer and major consumer of primary energy in the world. In 1999, the United States produced 19% of the world's primary energy and consumed 25% of its primary energy [5]. Approximately 85% of our energy consumption is in the form of fossil fuels. Thirty-seven percent of our energy use is for transportation. Although our per capita

**FIGURE 7–3**

Per capita energy consumption in the United States (MJ/capita = megajoules per person). (*Source: U.S. Energy Information Administration.*)

**FIGURE 7–4**

U.S. energy consumption (PJ = petajoules). (*Source: U.S. Energy Information Administration.*)

energy consumption has stabilized in the last three decades, our total energy consumption has grown enormously in the last 40 years (Figures 7–3 and 7–4).

### Coal Formation

About 2% of the radiant energy of the sun that reaches the earth is absorbed by plants. By photosynthetic processes, they use this energy to synthesize biomass. The solar energy stored in this organic matter is normally dissipated by oxidation and decay shortly after the plant dies; however, if the dead plant material falls in a swamp-like environment and is buried by sediments, the oxidative processes are inhibited. A thick accumulation of partially decayed plant material buried under other decaying plant material or sediment is known as **peat.** Peat is used as a fuel but is not a coal.

As the peat becomes buried under an increasingly thicker layer of dead plant matter and sediment, it is compressed and its temperature rises. The water and some hydrogen and oxygen are driven out. The peat becomes drier and richer in carbon. Over time the peat becomes **lignite,** the first-formed, poorest quality coal.

With increased pressure and heat exerted over a long period the lignite evolves into **bituminous** (soft coal) and then **anthracite** (hard coal). Typical anthracite coal is about 95% carbon. It is the highest quality coal.

It is estimated that it takes about 30,000 years of continuous plant growth to form a 1 m thick lens of coal. Although coal has formed over long periods, the most massive quantities were formed during the Carboniferous period from about 360 to 285 million years ago.

### Petroleum Formation

**Petroleum**\* is an inclusive term used to describe a wide range of gaseous, liquid, and solid hydrocarbon compounds occurring naturally in the earth. The formation of petroleum follows a natural process similar to that for coal, with the exception that the source is mostly aquatic organisms that settled to the bottom of shallow nutrient-rich seas on continental platforms. Five requirements must be fulfilled for a petroleum deposit of economic significance to occur [4].

- An original environmental setting that favors the rapid accumulation of organic-rich deposits, typically, a marine lagoon that gradually subsides.

---

\*From the Latin *petra,* meaning "rock," and *oleum,* meaning "oil"; hence "rock oil."

## FIGURE 7–5

Typical geologic and structural traps for oil and gas. Porous rocks such as sandstone can act as reservoirs for fluids if adjacent rocks act as impermeable seals. **(a)** Salt dome. **(b)** Anticline. **(c)** Fault. **(d)** Stratigraphic trap. (*Source:* Reprinted, with permission from: Coates, D. R., *Environmental Geology,* John Wiley & Sons, New York, pp. 152, 156, 215, 1981.)

**(a)** Salt dome

**(b)** Anticline

**(c)** Fault

**(d)** Stratigraphic

- An appropriate source bed that retains the oil during the sedimentation cycle. These are generally fine-grained sediments that protect the oil from dissipation or migration.
- A proper rock reservoir. This strata is contiguous with the source rock and sufficiently permeable that the petroleum is easily released when pumped. Most often, the rock reservoir is a sandstone or limestone.
- A geologic structure that serves as a trap to prevent the complete disappearance of the petroleum from the reservoir rock. Common traps are shown in Figure 7–5. They include salt domes (U.S. Gulf Coast), anticlines (Middle East), faults (California), and stratigraphic traps (Pennsylvania and New York).
- Crustal stability after formation of the petroleum and collection in the trap. Additional earth deformation after formation of the petroleum; the folding and faulting may release it to formations where it is too disseminated to recover profitably.

Petroleum may occur in forms that are not fluid. **Tar sands,** as the name implies, are sands laden with petroleum that is too viscous to flow. They have sufficient petroleum content that, if they occur at shallow depths, they can mined with surface mining techniques. The Athabasca Field in Alberta, Canada, contains a 60 m thick deposit of tar sand that covers an area over 77,000 km$^2$ [4]. **Oil shale,** or sometimes "shale-oil," may contain sufficient hydrocarbon to yield a liquid oil when heated. Scotland and Estonia have produced oil from shale since the mid-19th century.

### Fossil Fuel Reserves

How do you compare a kilogram of coal with a liter of oil? Or, for that matter, a liter of oil with a liter of natural gas? To make any useful comparison of fossil fuel reserves we must use an energy basis. For fossil fuels, the **net heating value** (NHV) serves as a common denominator for comparison. Typical values for NHV of some common fuels are shown in Table 7–3.

That portion of the identified fossil fuels that can be economically recovered at the time of the calculation is called the **proven commercial energy reserve.** Because of changes in technology and the change in consumer willingness to pay, the reserve may change even though the mass of fuel does not. The estimated U.S. and world reserves are shown in Table 7–4.

We can perform the same computations as we did with the mineral reserves to estimate the length of time these resources will last. At 1991 consumption rates, world coal reserves will last over 200 years, whereas oil and gas will last about 45–50 years [3].

| TABLE 7–3 | Typical Values of Net Heating Value | |
|---|---|---|

| Material | Net Heating Value (MJ · kg$^{-1}$) |
|---|---|
| Charcoal | 26.3 |
| Coal, anthracite | 25.8 |
| Coal, bituminous | 28.5 |
| Fuel oil, no. 2 (home heating) | 45.5 |
| Fuel oil, no. 6 (bunker C) | 42.5 |
| Gasoline (regular, 84 octane) | 48.1 |
| Natural gas[a] | 53.0 |
| Peat | 10.4 |
| Wood, oak | 13.3–19.3 |
| Wood, pine | 14.9–22.3 |

[a]Density take as 0.756 kg · m$^{-3}$

| TABLE 7–4 | U.S. and World Proven Commercial Energy Reserves of Fossil Fuels[a] | |
|---|---|---|

| Fuel | North America (EJ[b]) | World (EJ) |
|---|---|---|
| Coal | 6500 | 25,700 |
| Oil | 137 | 6100 |
| Natural gas | 199 | 6100 |
| Total Reserves | 6836 | 37,900 |

[a]Coal data are for 1998, oil and gas for 1997. (*Source:* Data from: Energy Information Agency, U.S. Department of Energy, 1999)

www.era.doe.gov

[b]Exajoules $= 10^{18}$ J $= 10^{12}$ MJ

### Nuclear Energy

Fission and fusion are the two potential reactions that may be used to generate nuclear energy. During nuclear fission, a neutron penetrates the nucleus of a fissionable atom (a radioactive isotope of uranium or plutonium) and splits it into daughter products while releasing energy. To generate energy by fusion, isotopes of a light element such as hydrogen are fused together to form a heavier element such as helium. In this process energy is released. All commercially operating nuclear reactors are based on fission reactions.

The two main isotopes of uranium are $^{235}$U and $^{238}$U. Of these, about 99.3% of the naturally occurring uranium is nonfissionable $^{238}$U. To induce a sustained fission reaction, the probability that excess neutrons from one fission reaction will cause other fissionable atoms to be split is increased by increasing the concentration of fissionable material or by slowing down the neutrons so they are more likely to be captured by $^{235}$U than $^{238}$U.

Although $^{238}$U is not fissionable, a $^{238}$U atom that captures a neutron will be transformed to fissionable plutonium ($^{239}$Pu). This is the basis of "breeder reactors." The National Academy of Science estimated that the transformation of abundant $^{238}$U to $^{239}$Pu could satisfy the U.S. electricity requirements for over a hundred thousand years [3]. Yet, there are no breeder reactors operating in the United States. Both environmental concerns and the potential for nuclear weapons proliferation have restricted the U.S. development of this energy source.

### *Environmental Impacts*

**Waste from Resource Recovery.**   Roughly 52% of the coal mined in the United States comes from surface mining. The remainder is from underground mines. Underground coal mining generates relatively small amounts of rock waste. **Strip mining,** in contrast generates large quantities of waste in the form of overburden. Up to 30 m of overburden may be removed to gain access to the coal.

The **spoil banks** from removed overburden or **tailings** from deep mines are sources of dust, excess erosion, and air pollution from fires and water pollution from acid mine drainage. Excess erosion from high-relief terrain can change relatively low sediment yields of 10 Mg · km$^{-2}$ from forested sites to over 11,000 Mg · km$^{-2}$ from excavated sites. The residual, low-grade coal in abandoned deep mines and spoil piles catch fire from spontaneous combustion, lighting or human activities. These fires are difficult, if not impossible, to control. The poor combustion conditions yield large quantities of particulates and sulfur oxides. Both ground water and surface water pollution, called **acid mine drainage** (AMD), result from rain water leaching through abandoned mines, spoil, and tailings. Although not exclusively associated with coal, sulfide minerals such as iron pyrite (FeS$_2$) frequently occur in coal beds. Once exposed to the atmosphere and bacterial action, the pyrite is oxidized to form sulfuric acid.

$$4FeS_2 + 15O_2 + 2H_2O \longrightarrow 2Fe_2(SO_4)_3 + 2H_2SO_4 \qquad\qquad (7\text{–}7)$$

This solution leaches into streams and lends them a red or yellow color from the iron precipitates. The acidic water is extremely lethal to aquatic life.

Coal mining, especially in water-poor areas of the west can have adverse effects on the groundwater supply. The water table around Decker, Montana, was lowered 15 m because of strip mining operations [4]. Mining operations may also "behead" the recharge areas of aquifers.

Compared with other forms of resource extraction, drilling for oil and natural gas has produced minimal environmental deterioration. Unfortunately, as oil and natural gas exploration intensifies to replace depleting supplies, more environmentally sensitive areas are being explored. The damage from road building and other exploration activities frequently surpasses the actual well-drilling operation.

Oil spills and leaking pipelines are notorious sources of water pollution. Large quantities of gasoline and other petroleum products evaporate into the atmosphere and contribute to the formation of ozone.

As with mineral mining, uranium mining produces rock waste. A major difference, however, is that the uranium tailings are frequently radioactive.

**Waste in Energy Production.**   Perhaps more insidious than the recovery of fossil and nuclear fuels, is the generation of wastes in the production of energy. The burning of fossil fuels releases air pollutants, such as sulfur oxides, nitrogen oxides, and particulates. The sulfur content of the fuel directly affects the mass of sulfur dioxide released. Coal, with the highest concentration of sulfur, contributes the most SO$_2$. Fuel oil has less sulfur and is frequently chosen as a substitute for coal to reduce SO$_2$ emissions. Natural gas has virtually no sulfur and, thus, no SO$_2$ emissions. Because the **ash** content (the unburnable mineral matter) of coal is high, it is also a major source of particulate pollutants. Fuel oil has less ash and less emissions. Natural gas has no ash and no emissions. All three release nitrogen oxides because the reaction chemistry does not depend on the nitrogen content of the fuel. Other pollutants from fossil fuels include toxic metals such as mercury, which occur in trace amounts in coal.

Although, nuclear energy production does not release air pollutants, the spent fuel is highly radioactive and poses an as yet unresolved solid waste disposal problem. The sheer volume of coal ash is a major solid waste disposal problem. About 30% of the ash settles out as **bottom ash** in the firing chamber of the power plant. The remaining **fly ash** must be captured by the air pollution control equipment. The following example illustrates how large a volume this ash might occupy for a large coal-fired power plant.

**EXAMPLE 7-5**  A coal-fired power plant converts about 33% of the coal's energy into electrical energy. For a large 800-MW electrical output, estimate the volume of ash that is produced in a year if the anthracite coal has a NHV of 31.5 MJ · kg$^{-1}$, an ash content of 6.9%, and the bulk density of the ash is about 700 kg · m$^{-3}$. Assume that 99.5% of the ash is captured by a combination of the air pollution control equipment and settling in the combustion chamber.

Solution  The solution to this problem begins with an energy balance. The energy-balance diagram is shown here. Because the output is in terms of power (work per unit time), the energy-balance equation is written in the form of power. At steady state, the energy-balance equation is

Input power = output power$_1$ + output power$_2$

where output power$_1$ is the power delivered to the electric distribution system and output power$_2$ is waste heat. From the definition of efficiency (see Chapter 3)

$$\eta = \frac{\text{output power}}{\text{input power}}$$

the input energy for the power plant is

$$\text{Input power} = \frac{\text{output power}}{\eta} = \frac{800 \text{ MW}_e}{0.33} = 2424 \text{ MW}_t$$

where MW$_e$ refers to megawatts electrical power and MW$_t$ refers to megawatts thermal power. Converting to units of joules per second, we obtain

$$(2424 \text{ MW}_t) \left( \frac{1 \text{ MJ} \cdot \text{s}^{-1}}{\text{MW}} \right) = 2424 \text{ MJ} \cdot \text{s}^{-1}$$

The amount of ash is determined from a mass balance for the coal. The mass-balance diagram is shown here. At steady state, the mass-balance equation is

Coal ash in = coal ash in stack gas + coal ash in bottom of boiler

The coal ash entering the boiler is found from the burning rate and the ash content of the coal. Using the NHV of 31.5 MJ · kg$^{-1}$ for anthracite, the amount of coal required is

$$\frac{2424 \text{ MJ} \cdot \text{s}^{-1}}{31.5 \text{ MJ} \cdot \text{kg}^{-1}} = 76.95 \text{ kg} \cdot \text{s}^{-1} \text{ of coal}$$

The ash input is then

$(76.95 \text{ kg} \cdot \text{s}^{-1} \text{ of coal})(0.069) = 5.31 \text{ kg} \cdot \text{s}^{-1}$

With a 99.5% capture efficiency in collecting the ash, the mass of ash to be disposed of is

$(0.995)(5.31 \text{ kg} \cdot \text{s}^{-1}) = 5.28 \text{ kg} \cdot \text{s}^{-1}$

In a year this would amount to

$(5.28 \text{ kg} \cdot \text{s}^{-1})(86,400 \text{ s} \cdot \text{day}^{-1})(365 \text{ days} \cdot \text{year}^{-1}) = 1.67 \times 10^8 \text{ kg} \cdot \text{year}^{-1}$

The volume will be

$$\frac{1.67 \times 10^8 \text{ kg} \cdot \text{year}^{-1}}{700 \text{ kg} \cdot \text{m}^{-3}} = 2.4 \times 10^5 \text{ m}^3 \cdot \text{year}^{-1}$$

This is a very large volume.

The inefficiency of the conversion of fuels into work results in the generation of waste heat. For automobiles and other dispersed energy consumers (light bulbs, refrigerators, and electric motors, for example), the environmental effect is sufficiently dispersed to be of little consequence. However, the generation of power also generates such a large amount of waste heat that the environmental effects may be serious. Thermal pollution of rivers is not limited to fossil fuel power plants but also includes nuclear plants. Example 7–6 illustrates how waste heat affects a stream.

**EXAMPLE 7–6**    Using the power plant from Example 7–5, and assuming that 15% of the waste heat goes up the stack and that 85% must be removed by cooling water, estimate the flow rate of cooling water required if the change in temperature of the cooling water is limited to 10°C. If the stream has a flow rate of 63 m$^3$ · s$^{-1}$ and a temperature of 18°C above the intake to the power plant, what is the temperature after the cooling water and the stream water have mixed?

Solution    The energy balance diagram for the power plant is shown here.

At steady state, the energy balance equation is

Input power = output power$_1$ + output power$_2$

From Example 7–5, input power = 2424 MW$_t$ and output power$_1$ = 800 MW$_e$, so

Output power$_2$ = 2424 MW − 800 MW = 1624 MW$_t$

Of this the stack losses are

$(0.15)(1624 \text{ MW}_t) = 243.6 \text{ MW}_t$

and the river water must store

$(0.85)(1624 \text{ MW}_t) = 1380.4 \text{ MW}_t$

Using Equation 3–44, we obtain

$$\frac{dH}{dt} = c_p \Delta T \frac{dM}{dt}$$

where $dH/dt = 1380.4$ MW$_t$, $c_p =$ specific heat of water from Table 3–3 is 4.186, and $\Delta T =$ the allowable temperature rise of 10°C. First converting units, we see

$$(1380.4 \text{ MW}_t) \left( \frac{1 \text{ MJ} \cdot \text{s}^{-1}}{\text{MW}} \right) = 1380.4 \text{ MJ} \cdot \text{s}^{-1}$$

then, noting that $\Delta T = 10°C = 10$ K, solve Equation 3–44 for $dM/dt$

$$\frac{dM}{dt} = \frac{1380.4 \text{ MJ} \cdot \text{s}^{-1}}{(4.186 \text{ MJ} \cdot \text{Mg}^{-1} \cdot \text{K}^{-1})(10 \text{ K})} = 32.98 \text{ Mg} \cdot \text{s}^{-1}$$

Using a density of water of 1000 kg · m$^{-3}$ (or 1 Mg · m$^{-3}$), the required volumetric flow rate is

$$\frac{32.98 \text{ Mg} \cdot \text{s}^{-1}}{1 \text{ Mg} \cdot \text{m}^{-3}} = 32.98, \text{ or } 33 \text{ m}^3 \cdot \text{s}^{-1}$$

To find the increase in stream temperature, we solve Equation 3–44 for $\Delta T$.

$$\Delta T = \frac{1380.4 \text{ MJ} \cdot \text{s}^{-1}}{(4.186 \text{ MJ} \cdot \text{Mg}^{-1} \cdot \text{K}^{-1})(63 \text{ m}^3 \cdot \text{s}^{-1})(1 \text{ Mg} \cdot \text{m}^{-3})} = 5.23 \text{ K, or } 5.23°C$$

Because the upstream temperature was 18°C, the downstream temperature will be

18°C + 5.23°C = 23.23, or 23°C.

This will have a dramatically adverse effect on aquatic life in the stream.

### Terrain Effects

Coal mining has the most serious effect on terrain. About 26,000 ha of strip mining is done each year in the United States. In 1998, it was estimated that over 400,000 ha had been strip mined in the United States [3]. Underground mines are notorious for land subsidence, including sudden collapses of the shafts that destroy homes, roads, and utilities. More than 800,000 ha of land in the United States has already subsided due to underground mining [4].

### Alternative Energy Sources

**Hydropower.** Hydropower exploits the most fundamental of physics principles by converting the potential energy of stored water to kinetic energy of falling water. The falling water passes through a turbine that drives an electrical generator. Unlike fossil fuels, hydropower is a renewable resource because the water is renewed through the hydrologic cycle. Although naturally occurring water falls have been used to generate hydropower, dams have been the major method of storing the water and raising the elevation to gain potential energy. From the definition of potential energy, the amount of energy available is a function of both the mass of water available and the elevation difference that can be created by damming up the water.

$$E_p = mg(\Delta Z) \tag{7–8}$$

where $E_p =$ potential energy (in J)

$m =$ mass (in kg)

$g =$ acceleration due to gravity

$\quad = 9.81$ m · s$^{-2}$

$\Delta Z =$ head, the difference in elevation between the water surface at the top of the dam and the turbine (in m)

Ignoring the losses in energy from friction, the kinetic energy of the falling water is equal to the potential energy. This provides us with a method for estimating the velocity of the falling water. The definition of kinetic energy ($E_k$) is

$$E_k = \frac{1}{2}mv^2 \tag{7-9}$$

where $v =$ velocity of water (in m · s$^{-1}$)

If we set the two equations equal to each other, we can solve for the velocity

$$v = [(2g)(\Delta Z)]^{0.5} \tag{7-10}$$

The power available may be estimated from the time rate at which work is done by the falling water. This is the mass flow rate of water traveling through a distance equal to the head.

$$\text{Power} = g(\Delta Z)\frac{dM}{dt} \tag{7-11}$$

where $dM/dt =$ mass flow rate of water (in kg · s$^{-1}$)
$\qquad\qquad = \rho Q$
$\qquad \rho =$ density of water (in kg · m$^{-3}$)
$\qquad Q =$ flow rate of water (in m$^3$ · s$^{-1}$)

Example 7-7 illustrates how the potential energy and power may be estimated.

**EXAMPLE 7-7**   The Hoover Dam on the Colorado River at the Arizona–Nevada border is the highest dam in the United States. It has a maximum height of 223 m and a storage capacity of about $3.7 \times 10^{10}$ m$^3$. What is the potential energy of the Hoover Dam and reservoir? If the maximum discharge is 950 m$^3$ · s$^{-1}$, what is the electrical capacity of the generating plant?

Solution   Assuming the density of water is 1000 kg · m$^{-3}$ and applying the potential energy equation:

$$E_p = (3.7 \times 10^{10} \text{ m}^3)(1000 \text{ kg} \cdot \text{m}^{-3})(9.81 \text{ m} \cdot \text{s}^{-2})(111.5 \text{ m})$$

$$= 4.05 \times 10^{16} \text{ J, or 40.5 PJ}$$

Note that the final units are

$$\left(\frac{\text{kg} \cdot \text{m}}{\text{s}^2}\right)(\text{m}) = \text{N} \cdot \text{m} = \text{J}$$

and that the average head (223 m/2 = 111.5 m) is used for the calculation.

Of course, all of this energy cannot be recovered. The estimate assumes all of the water is at the average head, that the reservoir is filled to maximum capacity, and that the maximum height is equal to the maximum head when, in fact, the maximum head is the distance between the maximum elevation of the reservoir pool and the turbines. In addition, the efficiency of converting the flowing water to mechanical energy to turn the turbine and generator is less than 100%.

At a flow rate of 950 m$^3$ · s$^{-1}$, the electrical capacity is

$$\text{Power} = (9.81 \text{ m} \cdot \text{s}^{-2})(223 \text{ m})(1000 \text{ kg} \cdot \text{m}^{-3})(950 \text{ m}^3 \cdot \text{s}^{-1}) = 2.08 \times 10^9 \text{ J} \cdot \text{s}^{-1}$$

$$= 2.08 \times 10^9 \text{ W} = 2080 \text{ MW}$$

The actual rating of the Hoover dam is 2000 MW. The average electrical power delivered may be considerably less than this because the average flow rate of water is less.

In 1997, the United States had a hydropower capacity of about 134 GW (gigawatts). This accounted for about 10% of the nation's electrical capacity [5]. Most of this is developed at large dams such Hoover and Glen Canyon in Arizona. It is unlikely, however, that any more large-scale plants will be built in the United States.

The combination of feasible topography for such dams and their negative environmental effects prohibit further expansion of large-scale projects. Dams and the reservoirs they create, flood large tracts of land. For example, Lake Mead, the reservoir behind Hoover Dam, covers an area of 640 km$^2$. Natural habitats of a wide variety of biota are destroyed to accommodate such projects. Villages, homes, farms, and other natural resources are also lost. Frequently, the reservoir traps sediments and nutrients normally supplied to downstream ecosystems while altering the dissolved oxygen, temperature, and mineral composition of the water.

An alternative source of hydropower is the 70,000 small dams already in existence in the United States. These provide an opportunity to develop so called "low-head" hydropower. Because the flow rates are low and the elevation differences are small, these projects are marginal economically.

**Biomass.**   Second only to hydropower in terms of renewable energy used in the United States, biomass burning provides about 1% of our nation's electrical capacity [5]. In developing countries, up to 90% of the energy may be supplied by biomass. Biomass energy includes wastes, standing forests, and energy crops. In the United States, the "wastes" include wood scraps, pulp and paper scraps, and municipal solid wastes. In developing countries it may also include animal wastes. In the United States, surplus corn is the principal energy crop used to produce ethanol for use as a fuel.

The environmental effects are both positive and negative. Certainly, recovering the fuel value from wastes that would otherwise be buried is a positive aspect of burning biomass. The use of standing forests, especially those harvested in an unsustainable manner, results in the creation of a wasteland. Soil erosion and deprivation of the replenishing nutrients have long-term irreparable consequences. Energy crops, in particular the conversion of corn to ethanol, are of benefit but are not very efficient because of the low energy content and the difficulty in converting it to ethanol. For all of the biomass, burning results in air pollution emissions.

**Geothermal.**   The principal employed in geothermal power is to tap the natural heat from earth's magma. The energy may be used directly to heat buildings or to produce electricity from vented steam or by heating water to produce steam. Unfortunately, geothermal power is not practical everywhere. The most likely places lie along the plate margins where the magma comes close to the surface (e.g., in Iceland). In the United States, geothermal power supplies about half of the electrical energy provided by biomass.

Because the magma is not likely to cool down for a long time, geothermal power is considered a renewable energy source. For the most part, it is environmentally benign. Excess heat may cause thermal pollution problems, and potential pollution from $H_2S$ in the vented gas, as well as heavy metals in the water are of concern and may require substantial investments to control.

**Wind.**   Even casual observation of hurricanes and tornadoes reveals that the wind has power. Sails and windmills have been used to harness the energy from lesser winds for centuries.

The force of the wind on a flat plate held normal to it is expressed as

$$F = \frac{1}{2} A \rho v^2 \qquad\qquad (7\text{--}12)$$

where $F$ = force (in N)
$\quad A$ = area of plate (in m$^2$)
$\quad \rho$ = density of air (in kg $\cdot$ m$^{-3}$)
$\quad v$ = wind speed (in m $\cdot$ s$^{-1}$)

If the force moves the plate through a distance, then work is done. The product of (distance)$(A)(\rho)$ = mass, which is the definition of kinetic energy (Equation 7–9).

Two characteristics of Equation 7–12 are important in developing wind power. The first, well noted by sailors in "putting on more sail," is that the larger the area, the greater the force captured. The second is less obvious. That is, that the force is proportional to the square of the velocity, and power (kilowatts) is proportional to the cube of velocity (force × velocity). It is a characteristic of the wind that the velocity increases with distance above ground. Thus, a wind mill will be more effective if it is placed at a higher elevation above the ground than a lower one.

Modern wind turbines for generation of electrical power are placed on towers ranging from 30 to 90 m in height in "wind farms." Each wind turbine generates 50–500 kW.

Although wind power is environmentally benign, it is not very dependable. Furthermore, the sound of 50 or more whirring propellers is not something most people want in their backyard. None-the-less, it has been forecast that up to 12% of the world demand for electricity could be provided by wind in the next two decades. Some of the U.S. leaders in wind power are the states of Oregon and Washington. They have installed 460 turbines that will supply enough electricity for 70,000 homes and businesses.

**Solar.**  In 20 days time, the earth receives energy from the sun equal to all of the energy stored as fossil fuels. This resource may be captured directly, as is done with greenhouses; passively, for example with thermal masses to absorb solar radiation; or, actively, through water heaters, photovoltaic cells, or parabolic mirrors.

To be economically realistic solar energy collection is limited to places with a lot of sunshine; Michigan is not an ideal setting. Furthermore, direct and passive systems are difficult to implement as a retrofit to existing structures. The system needs to be designed together. The active solar collection systems require large areas of land and are very expensive to install.

Although photovoltaic systems are 300% cheaper now than they were in 1982, currently, less than 0.03% of energy demand is supplied by solar devices. In the long term, 20–50 years, this fraction will need to increase to off-set the diminishing supply of oil and natural gas. Solar energy is the only truly renewable energy source that can sustain human requirements in the coming millennia.

### Energy Conservation

Numerous examples illustrate methods for energy conservation. Not all of these are practical, and some have limited value because of the small segment of the energy demand that they affect. The several examples selected for discussion here were chosen because they are a large portion of the demand.

In the United States approximately one-third of the energy consumption is used in residential heating, cooling, and lighting systems [3]. Improved insulation has a dramatic effect on reduction of energy consumption. From Equation 3–50, we may note that the effectiveness of insulation is a function of both its thermal conductivity and thickness. In the heating and air conditioning market it is more common to refer to the **resistance** (R) of the insulation than its thermal conductivity. The resistance is the reciprocal of the thermal conductivity.

$$R = \frac{1}{h_{tc}} \tag{7–13}$$

where $h_{tc}$ = thermal conductivity

Larger values of $R$ imply better insulating properties. When multiple layers of different materials are used, the combined resistance may be estimated as

$$R_T = R_1 + R_2 + \cdots + R_i \tag{7–14}$$

The resistance form of Equation 3–50 is

$$\frac{dH}{dt} = \frac{1}{R_T}(A)(\Delta T) \qquad (7\text{–}15)$$

where $A$ = surface area (in $m^2$)

$\Delta T$ = difference in temperature (in K)

$R_T$ = resistance (in $m^2 \cdot K \cdot W^{-1}$)

Example 7–8 illustrates the value of additional roofing insulation.

**EXAMPLE 7–8**

A typical residential construction from the 1950s consisted of the layers shown in the drawing. Estimate the heat loss with the existing insulation scheme and with an additional 20 cm of organic bonded-glass fiber insulation, if the indoor temperature is to be maintained at 20°C and the outdoor temperature is 0°C.

Asphalt shingle
Felt
Plywood, 9.5 mm

Attic air, 1 m

Insulation, blanket & batt, 90 mm

Gypsum, 9.5 mm

**Solution**

The resistance values are obtained from Table 7–5. Assuming a 1-$m^2$ surface area, the total resistance for the original construction in units of $m^2 \cdot K \cdot W^{-1}$ is calculated as

$R$ = asphalt + felt + plywood + air + insulation + gypsum

$$= 0.077 + 0.21 + 0.10 + \frac{1000 \text{ mm}}{90 \text{ mm}}(0.4) + 2.29 + 0.056 = 7.18 \text{ m}^2 \cdot K \cdot W^{-1}$$

where the ratio 1000/90 is the number of 90 mm air spaces in 1 m of air in the attic.

From Equation 7–15, we get

$$\frac{dH}{dt} = \frac{1}{7.18 \text{ m}^2 \cdot K \cdot W^{-1}}(1 \text{ m}^2)(20 - 0)$$

$$= 2.79 \text{ W}$$

The additional insulation will add resistance. To be in consistent units, we must multiply by the thickness of the insulation.

$$R = (27.7 \text{ m} \cdot K \cdot W^{-1})(0.20 \text{ m}) = 5.54 \text{ m}^2 \cdot K \cdot W^{-1}$$

The new resistance is then

$$R_T = 7.18 + 5.54 = 12.72$$

and the heat loss is

$$\frac{dH}{dt} = \frac{1}{12.72 \text{ m}^2 \cdot K \cdot W^{-1}}(1 \text{ m}^2)(20 - 0)$$

$$= 1.57 \text{ W}$$

This is about 56% of the original heat loss.

**TABLE 7–5**                Typical Values of Resistance for Common Building Materials

| Building Material | $R$ $(m \cdot K \cdot W^{-1})$ | R for thickness shown $(m^2 \cdot K \cdot W^{-1})$ |
|---|---|---|
| Building board | | |
|   Gypsum, 9.5 mm | | 0.056 |
|   Particle board | 7.35 | |
| Building membrane (felt) | | |
|   Two layers, 0.73 kg $\cdot$ m$^{-2}$ felt | | 0.21 |
| Glass | | |
|   Single glazing, 3 mm | | 0.16 |
|   Double glazing, 6 mm air space | | 0.32 |
|   Triple glazing, 6 mm air space | | 0.47 |
| Insulating material | | |
|   Blanket and batt | | |
|   Mineral fiber from glass, | | |
|     $\approx$ 90 mm | | 2.29 |
|     $\approx$ 150 mm | | 3.32 |
|     $\approx$ 230 mm | | 5.34 |
|     $\approx$ 275 mm | | 6.77 |
|   Glass fiber, organic bonded | 27.7 | |
|   Loose fill milled paper | 23 | |
|   Spray applied polyurethane foam | 40 | |
| Roofing | | |
|   Asphalt shingles | | 0.077 |
|   Built-up, 10 mm | | 0.058 |
| Masonry | | |
|   Brick | 1.15 | |
|   Concrete | 0.6 | |
| Siding materials | | |
|   Hardboard, 11 mm | | 0.12 |
|   Plywood, 9.5 mm | | 0.10 |
|   Aluminum or steel, over sheathing, | | |
|     Hollow-backed | | 0.11 |
|     Insulating board backed, 9.5 mm | | 0.32 |
|     Insulating board backed, 9.5 mm, foil | | 0.52 |
| Soils | 0.44 | |
| Still air, 90 mm | | 0.4 |

*Source:* Data used from: ASHRAE, *Handbook of Fundamentals,* American Society of Heating and Air Conditioning Engineers (1993).

Electric motors account for about half of the electricity used in the United States [6]. Oversized motors and constant-speed motors both contribute to inefficient use of electricity. Pumps driven by electric motors are often regulated by adjusting valves instead of the speed of the motor itself. The excess electrical energy is wasted as heat.

Old power plants rarely achieve efficiencies above 35%. In part this occurs because the waste heat is sent to a nearby river or other water body rather than being used elsewhere. **Cogeneration** power plants use the waste heat to heat buildings, thus making much more efficient use of the fuel.

Transportation accounts for 42% of all the primary energy use in the United States [5]. Automobiles and other light-duty vehicles use about 80% of the energy consumed in transportation. Increased efficiency has raised the milage of automobiles from $7.7 \text{ km} \cdot \text{L}^{-1}$ in the mid-1970s to $11.8 \text{ km} \cdot \text{L}^{-1}$ in 1992. Yet, this increase in efficiency was far outstripped by the growth in the number of vehicle-miles traveled. Worldwide, more than 700 million vehicles are on the road, and the growth rate is about 35 million per year.

Some energy conservation techniques are to increase the number of passengers by offering commuter lanes and parking incentives. It has been estimated that if every commuter car carried an average of one more person, 700,000 barrels of oil (about 4.3 PJ of energy) would be saved each day. Mass transit would improve this even more. On a global scale, these techniques are only marginal in reducing the oil depletion. Only a major revolution in transportation modes, for example switching to bicycles, will provide any benefit, and that may come too late.

The tragedy of the ultimate depletion of our oil resource is not that we will need to find other modes of travel or even that we will not have enough energy but rather that we will have expended a valuable resource that could better be used in making durable goods that can only be made from petroleum.

## 7–6   SOIL FORMATION AND PROPERTIES

### Weathering

**Weathering** is the process by which rock is broken down into fragments by the combined action of water, gases, and living matter. In a classic exhibition of the second law of thermodynamics, the decomposition proceeds inexorably toward a decrease in free energy and increased entropy. The decay of **parent material,** whether igneous, sedimentary, or metamorphic rock, is insufficient to form soil. **Soil** is distinguished from loose, weathered material or **regolith,** by the presence of plant and animal life. The presence of life is critical to the formation of soil. Through death and decay, plants and animals provide organic matter that forms the **humus.** Soil animals also perform an important function in mixing soil particles and aerating the soil. Soil microorganisms also decompose the organic matter and release nutrients necessary for plant life.

### Soil Components

The relative proportions of a representative agricultural soil are shown in Figure 7–6. Mineral matter from weathered rocks and organic matter from plants and animals constitute about 50% of the volume. Air and water occupy the **pore space** (openings or voids between the soil particles) to constitute the other half of the soil volume. The proportions of air and water vary depending on climatic conditions. As precipitation infiltrates into the pore spaces, the air volume decreases. When the soil dries by evaporation and drainage, the amount of air in the pore spaces increases.

**Soil Mineral Matter.**   Soil minerals are derived from the parent material by weathering. **Primary minerals** are those remaining unaltered from the original material. These include

**FIGURE 7–6**

Volume composition of a
silt loam surface soil
when in good condition
for plant growth. The air
and water in a soil are
extremely variable, and
their proportions
determine in large
degree the soil's
suitability for plant
growth.

**TABLE 7–6**   Annual Rate of Organic Carbon Returned by Litter

| Land Use or Vegetation Type | Organic Carbon $(Mg \cdot ha^{-1})$ |
|---|---|
| Alpine and arctic forest | 0.1 |
| Arable farming (cereals) | 1–2 |
| Temperate grassland | 2–4 |
| Coniferous forest | 1.5–3 |
| Deciduous forest | 1.5–4 |
| Tropical rainforest (Columbia) | 4–5 |
| Tropical rainforest (west Africa) | 10 |

*Source:* Data used from: White, R. E., *Introduction to the Principles and Practice of Soil Science,* John Wiley &
Sons, New York, pp. 24, 34, 152, 156 (1979).

minerals such as quartz that are very resistant to weathering. **Secondary minerals** are those that
are produced by weathering reactions with air and water to form oxides and hydroxides of the
primary minerals. One of the important hydrolysis reactions is that of silicate minerals to
form clays. **Clays,** which are minute particles composed of silicon, aluminum, oxygen, and
hydrogen, fall into four classifications: **kaolinite, montmorillonite, illite,** and **amorphous clays.**
The first three have a recognizable crystal structure. The basic clay structure is a **micelle** composed of layers of silicon and aluminum arranged alternately with oxygen atoms in a sandwich-
like structure.

**Soil Organic Matter.**   The debris of plants, animal residues, and excreta contribute to the
organic fraction of the soil. Some average values for the annual litter fall in terms of organic carbon
are given in Table 7–6. These values do not include contributions from root death and decay that may
amount to one-third to one-half of the litter fall. Timber fall may equal the litter fall in carbon but it
is not as readily decomposable. These values may be compared with the carbon contribution from
dairy manure that contributes $3.5–4.5\,Mg \cdot ha^{-1} \cdot year^{-1}$ in highly productive pastures [7].

**FIGURE 7-7**

Mass balance of carbon in soil.

The dead organic matter is colonized by a variety of microorganisms that derive energy from the oxidation of the complex molecules of plant and animal matter. In this process they **mineralize** essential elements by converting them from their organic forms to inorganic forms, such as ammonium, phosphate, and sulfate. This process makes them available for the succeeding generations of plants. Some of the organic carbon is released as carbon dioxide.

Gains of organic matter through litter decomposition are offset by losses through leaching and decomposition, a process called **turnover.** The rate of change in organic matter may be expressed as a mass-balance problem as illustrated in Figure 7–7. The input of carbon is equal to the addition of carbon through litter minus the transformation of carbon to $CO_2$, biomass, and pools of chemically and physically stabilized organic matter. Note that there is no "output" of carbon. If we assume the addition of litter is a constant and that the transformation may be expressed as a first-order reaction, then the mass-balance expression is

$$\frac{dC}{dt} = L - kC \qquad (7\text{–}16)$$

where $dC/dt$ = rate of change of organic carbon content of soil (in $Mg \cdot ha^{-1}$)
  $L$ = the annual addition of litter (in $Mg \cdot ha^{-1} \cdot year^{-1}$)
  $k$ = rate constant, assuming decomposition is a simple first-order reaction (in $years^{-1}$)
  $C$ = the carbon content of the soil (in $Mg \cdot ha^{-1}$)

If we assume steady-state conditions, then $dC/dt = 0$, and Equation 7–16 may be written as

$$L = kC \qquad (7\text{–}17)$$

and the turnover time is defined as

$$\frac{C}{L} = \frac{1}{k}$$

Theoretically, this is the time for all the organic carbon in the soil to be replaced. An estimate of turnover is presented in Example 7–9.

**EXAMPLE 7-9**   The annual contribution of carbon to the soil ($L$) at Rothamsted, England, has been estimated as 5–6% of the soil organic, $C$. Estimate the turnover time for this soil.

Solution   Using the 5% value, then

$$\frac{L}{C} = 0.05 \ year^{-1}$$

and the turnover time is

$$\frac{1}{0.05 \ year^{-1}} = 20 \ years$$

Using radioactive carbon dating, the half-life of carbon in the soil has been estimated to be between 1450 and 3700 years, depending on the depth of the soil [7]. Obviously, carbon compounds in the soil have a great range of decomposability, and a single rate constant does not account for the transformation.

**FIGURE 7–8**  Soil Water Potential

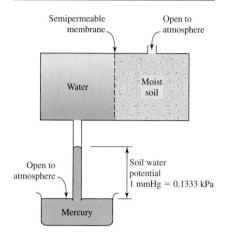

**FIGURE 7–9**

Soil moisture tension curves for three representative mineral soils. The curves show the relationship obtained by slowly drying completely saturated soils.

Decomposition of plant materials results in the release of complex organic molecules of high molecular weight that are phenolic in character. Because of their similarity to humus in soil they are often referred to as humic substances, or humic acid. They are important in the treatment of drinking water because their presence in surface water results in the formation of carcinogenic disinfection by-products (see Chapter 9). They are also important in soils because of their ability to complex metals and, hence, reduce their transport. This is an important mechanism in containing the movement of metals in contaminated aquifers (see Chapter 13).

**Soil Water.**   The amount of water in the soil is, of course, not constant. The retention and movement of soil water, its uptake and translation in plants, and its loss to the atmosphere are all energy-related phenomena. We use **free energy** to characterize the energy status of water. Following the second law of thermodynamics, water will move from zones of high free energy to zones of lower free energy. A soil saturated with water has a high free energy. The water will tend to migrate from the saturated soil to a dry soil that has a lower free energy. The difference in free energy from one contiguous site to another is termed the **total soil water potential.** The soil water potential is illustrated in Figure 7–8. Because the soil reduces the free energy of the soil water, it is a negative potential and is often referred to as suction or **tension.** A common means of expressing soil water tension is in terms of the height of a unit water column whose mass just equals the tension under consideration. Although this may be directly measured, for example in centimeters of water, it is convenient to use kilopascals (kPa) as the unit of measure.

Figure 7–9 illustrates soil moisture–energy curves for three typical soils. The soil moisture–energy curve has a practical significance in describing the movement of water and the uptake of water by plants.

The dynamic behavior of soil moisture may be illustrated by describing the processes that follow a heavy rain or irrigation that raises the soil moisture to saturation. At this point the tension is essentially zero and water moves downward by gravity forces (**drainage**).

Following the rain or irrigation, there will be a continued downward movement of some of the water in response to the hydraulic gradient. After a few days, this rapid downward movement will become negligible. The soil is then said to be at **field capacity.** At that time the water has moved out of the larger pores and its place has been taken by air. The capillaries are still filled with water and will supply plants with moisture. The soil tension will be about 0.1–0.3 kPa.

**FIGURE 7–10**

Moisture relationships in soil. (*Source:* Pfeffer, J. T., *Solid Waste Management Engineering*, Prentice Hall, Upper Saddle River, NJ, 1992. Reprinted by permission.)

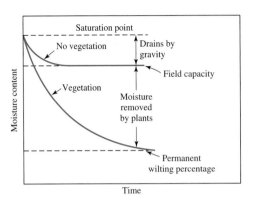

Plants take up the water and lose it through evapotranspiration and evaporation directly from the soil. As the soil dries, plants begin to wilt during the daytime. At first the plants regain their vigor during the night as the rate of demand from the plants slows to the rate of supply. Without replenishment of the water, the rate of supply will diminish to a point that the plants will remain permanently wilted. They are not dead but will die if water is not added. The soil moisture content at this stage is called the **permanent wilting percentage.** The soil tension will be about 15 kPa for most crop plants. These relationships are illustrated in Figure 7–10.

**Soil Air.**   When the soil pores are not occupied by water, they will be occupied by air. The soil air has a different composition than atmospheric air.

The biota in the soil produce $CO_2$ by their respiration. Thus, $CO_2$ builds up in the soil air and is present in concentrations that may be 300 times that found in the ambient atmosphere. The transfer of oxygen into the soil pores and the movement of carbon dioxide out of the pores is carried out by gaseous diffusion, that is the random movement of molecules from zones of higher concentration to zones of lower concentration. In open, porous soils the transfer readily occurs. These soils are called well aerated. In contrast, soils with dense structures and small pore spaces will be poorly aerated.

Soils with excess moisture, for example a saturated soil, may suffer a complete lack of oxygen because of microbial activity. This will be disastrous for plants acclimated to good aeration.

**Soil Organisms.**   Higher plants transform energy from the sun and convert it into stored energy in the form of plant biomass. Plants are the primary producers of organic matter in the soil. Their roots grow and die, and in so doing they supply other soil organisms with food and energy. At the same time, the roots modify the soil physically by pushing through cracks and making new openings of their own. The amount of root residue of crops remaining after a harvest may be as large as 15–40% of the mass of aboveground crop [8]. Good crops of oats, corn, and sugar will leave about 2500, 4500, and 8500 kg $\cdot$ ha$^{-1}$ of root residues, respectively.

Earthworms are generally more important in the consumption of leaf litter than all the other invertebrates together. They feed exclusively on dead organic matter. They migrate between the litter layer and the mineral soil and in the course of feeding ingest prodigious quantities of soil. As much as 34 Mg $\cdot$ ha$^{-1}$ of soil mass passes through their bodies [8]. The mineral as well as the organic soil passing through their bodies is subject to digestive enzymes and a grinding action within the animals. Earthworms also serve to increase aeration and drainage by their burrows. They mix and granulate soil by dragging undecomposed matter into their burrows.

The soil microorganisms consist primarily of bacteria, fungi, actinomycetes, algae, and protozoa. Although the earthworms are important in transforming litter to humus, these microorganisms are the main decomposers. Most species of bacteria found in soil are **heterotrophs,** that require complex organic molecules for growth. They secrete enzymes that break down macromolecules into relatively simple substances such as glucose and amino acids that can be absorbed by the organisms. Fungi are the chief cause of decay of hard, woody tissue. The actinomycetes, though less tolerant of acid soil, are better able to decompose lignin and complex soil organic compounds than either fungi or bacteria. The algae are photosynthetic and are therefore confined to the soil surface. The blue-green algae are important because they can reduce atmospheric nitrogen and incorporate it into amino acids, thus making a substantial contribution to the nitrogen status of the soil. Nearly all of the protozoa prey on other smaller organisms such as bacteria and algae. They may be important in regulating bacterial numbers but are not sufficiently abundant to be a major factor in organic matter decay and nutrient release.

### Soil Properties

**Particle Size Distribution.**   Soils have a continuous spectrum of particle sizes demonstrated by the frequency distribution shown in Figure 7–11. Two methods are used to find the particle size distribution. For particles greater than 0.075 mm in diameter, the soil is placed on top of a series of screens (**sieves**) with progressively smaller openings (Table 7–7) and separated by shaking. The mass retained on each sieve is determined.

**FIGURE 7–11**

Particle-size distribution curves. (*Source:* From: Das, B. M., *Principles of Geotechnical Engineering*, PWS Publishing Company, Boston, p. 44, 1994. Reprinted with permission.)

**TABLE 7–7**        U.S. Standard Sieve Sizes

| Sieve No. | Opening (mm) | Sieve No. | Opening (mm) | Sieve No. | Opening (mm) |
|---|---|---|---|---|---|
| 4 | 4.750 | 20 | 0.850 | 100 | 0.150 |
| 6 | 3.350 | 30 | 0.600 | 140 | 0.106 |
| 8 | 2.360 | 40 | 0.425 | 170 | 0.088 |
| 10 | 2.000 | 50 | 0.300 | 200 | 0.075 |
| 12 | 1.68 | 60 | 0.250 | 270 | 0.053 |
| 16 | 1.180 | 70 | 0.210 | | |
| 18 | 1.00 | 80 | 0.180 | | |

For particles smaller than 0.075 mm, hydrometer analysis is used to determine the particle size. This procedure is based on an assumption that all particles are spheres and that the velocity of soil particles can be expressed by Stokes' law.

$$v_s = \frac{g(\rho_s - \rho)d^2}{18\mu} \tag{7-18}$$

where $v_s$ = settling velocity (in $m \cdot s^{-1}$)
$\quad g$ = acceleration due to gravity (in $m \cdot s^{-2}$)
$\quad \rho_s$ = density of particle (in $kg \cdot m^{-3}$)
$\quad \rho$ = density of fluid (in $kg \cdot m^{-3}$)
$\quad d$ = diameter of particle (in m)
$\quad \mu$ = dynamic viscosity (in $Pa \cdot s$)

Noting that the velocity may be written as $h/t$, where $h$ is the depth from the liquid surface and $t$ is the time that all particles of diameter $d$ will have fallen below $h$, another expression may given

$$d = K\left(\frac{h}{t}\right) \tag{7-19}$$

where $K$ is the collection of the constants. Thus, by sampling the mass per unit volume at a given depth, after a given time, the diameter may be calculated. A hydrometer measures the specific gravity of the fluid. Because the specific gravity is a function of the amount of soil particles per unit volume, the hydrometer may be calibrated to give the amount of soil that is still in suspension. By knowing the amount of soil in suspension, $h$, and $t$, we can calculate the percentage of soil by mass finer than a given diameter.

**Texture.** In practice it is convenient to divide this continuous distribution into several class intervals based on the size of the particles. Examples of four systems are shown in Figure 7–12. Because real soils are a combination of particle sizes, it is useful to have descriptive terms to describe these mixtures or **textures.** The U.S. Department of Agriculture's soil texture classification scheme is shown in Figure 7–13. Example 7–10 illustrates how to use the chart.

**FIGURE 7-12**

Classification of soil particles according to size by four systems. The U.S. Department of Agriculture system is used in this text. (*Source:* Coates, D. R., *Environmental Geology,* John Wiley & Sons, New York, 1981. Reprinted by permission.)

**FIGURE 7–13**

U.S. Department of Agriculture textural classification. (*Source: Soil Survey Staff, Soil Taxonomy,* U.S. Dept of Agriculture Handbook 436, 1975.)

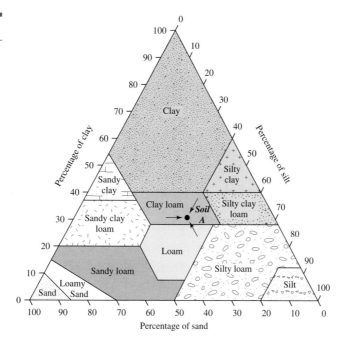

**EXAMPLE 7–10**

The results of a particle size distribution show that a sample is 30% sand, 40% silt and 30% clay. Determine the soil textural class for this soil.

Solution

Enter the chart on the clay side at the 30% line and draw a horizontal line. Enter the chart on the silt side at 40% and draw a line toward the 60% sand line until it intersects the horizontal line from clay. The intersection point will coincide with a line drawn from the sand side starting at 30% and drawn toward 70% clay. The arrows in Figure 7–13 exhibit this construction.

The soil texture is identified as a "clay loam."

**Mass-Volume Relationships.** To quantitatively describe a soil we begin with the definition of the components of the volume and mass. The total volume of a soil sample can be expressed as

$$\mathbf{V}_T = \mathbf{V}_s + \mathbf{V}_v = \mathbf{V}_s + \mathbf{V}_w + \mathbf{V}_a \qquad (7\text{–}20)$$

where $\mathbf{V}_T$ = total volume of soil
$\quad \mathbf{V}_s$ = volume of soil solids
$\quad \mathbf{V}_v$ = volume of voids
$\quad \mathbf{V}_w$ = volume of water in voids
$\quad \mathbf{V}_a$ = volume of air in voids

Assuming the mass of air is negligible, the total mass can be expressed as

$$M_T = M_s + M_w \qquad (7\text{–}21)$$

where $M_T$ = total mass of soil
$\quad M_s$ = mass of soil solids
$\quad M_w$ = mass of water

With these definitions we can express the three common volume relationships: void ratio, porosity, and degree of saturation. The **void ratio** is

$$\epsilon = \frac{V_v}{V_s} \tag{7-22}$$

The **porosity** is

$$n = \frac{V_v}{V_T} \tag{7-23}$$

The **degree of saturation** ($S$) is

$$S = \frac{V_w}{V_v} \tag{7-24}$$

It is usually expressed as a percentage. It differs from the **moisture content** (also called water content), which is expressed on a mass basis.

$$W = \frac{M_w}{M_s} \tag{7-25}$$

The density is expressed as

$$\rho_s = \frac{M_T}{V_T} \tag{7-26}$$

The density of the particles differs from the **bulk density** in that the bulk density includes both the solids and the pore spaces, whereas the particle density refers only to the soil solids. Because the moisture content varies with climatic conditions, a common reference is the dry density, in which the sample is oven-dried to exclude the water fraction.

Typical values of the mass-volume relationships for a variety of different textures of soil are shown in Table 7-8.

**TABLE 7-8**  Typical Soil Porosities, Void Ratios and Bulk Densities in Natural State

| Type of Soil | Porosity (n) | Void Ratio (ε) | Moisture Content (W%[a]) | Bulk Density (Mg · m⁻³) |
|---|---|---|---|---|
| Clay, soft glacial | 0.55 | 0.9–1.4 | 30–50 | 1.17–1.48 |
| Clay, stiff glacial | 0.37 | 0.6 | 20 | 1.73 |
| Glacial till | 0.20 | 0.25 | 10 | 2.12 |
| Loam | 0.6 | | | 1.0 |
| Loess | | 0.9 | 25 | 1.38 |
| Sand, uniform loose | 0.45 | 0.85 | 30 | 1.45 |
| Sand, uniform dense | 0.35 | 0.5 | 15–20 | 1.75–1.83 |
| Silty sand, angular loose | 0.40 | 0.65 | 25 | 1.59 |
| Silty sand, angular dense | 0.30 | 0.4 | 15 | 1.86 |

[a]Natural moisture content in saturated state.

*Sources:* Adapted from: Brady, N.C., *The Nature and Properties of Soils*, 9th ed., Macmillan, New York, pp. 264, 431–432, 549 (1990); Das, B. M., *Principles of Geotechnical Engineering*, PWS Publishing Company, Boston, p. 44 (1994); Peck, R. B., W. E. Hanson, and T. H. Thornburn, *Foundation Engineering*, John Wiley & Sons, New York, p. 21 (1953).

| **TABLE 7–9** | Typical Cation-Exchange Capacities | |
|---|---|---|
| **Soil** | | **CEC** $(mEq \cdot g^{-1})$ |
| Clay | | 0.30 |
| Silt loam | | 0.20 |
| Sand | | 0.05 |
| Humus | | 2.00 |

*Source:* From: Aswathanarayana, U., *Geoenvironment, An Introduction,* A. A. Balkema, Rotterdam, The Netherlands, p. 51, 1995.

**Cation-Exchange Capacity.**   The inorganic and organic soil solids possess a residual electrical charge. The clay particles are charged because of internal substitution of elements of the same coordination number but different valence. In addition, the broken edges of the crystal structure of the clay mineral have unneutralized valences where bonds have been broken. The organic humus possess a charge because of the dissociation of carboxyl and phenolic groups. Both the clay and humus have a net negative charge. The net charge on the clay is permanent for typical soil pH values. The net charge on the humus is a function of pH because it influences the dissociation of the carboxyl and phenolic groups.

In neutral to alkaline soils, the negative charge is balanced by exchangeable cations such as $Ca^{2+}$, $Mg^{2+}$, $Na^+$, and $K^+$ that are held around the soil particle by electrostatic attraction. In acid soils $H^+$ and $Al^{3+}$ predominate. These cations are subject to replacement by other cations through a process called **cation exchange.** A conceptual reaction may be written as

$$\text{Ca-soil particle} + 2H^+ \rightleftharpoons 2H\text{-soil particle} + Ca^{2+} \tag{7–27}$$

This reaction is reversible and follows the law of mass action; that is, high concentrations of $H^+$ will displace the reaction to the right and high concentrations of $Ca^{2+}$ will displace the reaction to the left. The ability of one ion to displace another is also a function of the charge of the ion. The greater the charge, the greater the sorption to the clay particle, so that $M^{3+}$ will displace $M^{2+}$ at a lower concentration than another $M^{2+}$ ion.

The ability of a soil to exchange cations is called the **cation-exchange capacity** (CEC). The common unit of expression for CEC is milliequivalents per 100 g of soil. Typical values for CEC are given in Table 7–9.

Exchangeable cations become available to higher plants and microorganisms as hydrogen ions from the root hairs or microorganisms exoenzymes replace nutrient cations from the soil particles. The cations floating in the soil solution are adsorbed onto the surfaces of the roots and soil organisms, where they may be assimilated.

## 7–7  SOIL RESOURCES

### Energy Storage

The soil is a storage place for energy. The primary source of energy is the sun. Plant photosynthesis captures this energy. It is brought to the soil by litter fall, by plant roots, by animals, and by oxidation of some minerals by microorganisms. The energy input to the soil is used to drive reactions involved in the food chain and in the transformations soil organisms perform on the soil components.

### Plant Production

Because of the diversity of soils and the uses we make of them, no single measure comparable to those we used for mineral or energy reserves can be used for soils. However, the intimate relationship between plants and soil as well as our dependence on those plants leads us to use forest land and agricultural production potential as a measure of the soil resource. In doing this, we obviously slight forest potential, ecosystem habitat, and a wide variety of other basis for evaluating the soil resource.

The estimated area of the world land mass covered by forests is about $40 \times 10^6$ km$^2$. Of this area, North America, South America, and Russia each have about $8 \times 10^6$ km$^2$. In 1996, this amounted to about 0.7 ha of forest per person [9]. In the United States, the area of forested land has stabilized at 1920 levels; each year more trees are grown than are harvested [10]. In contrast, it is estimated that the world forest resource will be reduced to 0.46 ha per person by 2025 [9]. Unfortunately, the major losses of forest land will be in areas that have the least amount of forest land.

**Arable** land is land that is or that can be cultivated. Agriculturally productive land consists of arable land and that which is not arable but is suitable for grazing. The total world land area is about $13 \times 10^9$ ha (Table 7–10). About half of this land is nonarable. It is desert, swampland, or mountainous. About 25% of the land supports enough vegetation to provide grazing for animals but otherwise is unsuitable for cultivation [8].

How can we evaluate the reserve capacity of the soil resource? In terms of cultivated land per person (see Table 7–10), the total potentially arable land is more than double that being cultivated. In terms of "consumption," the amount of grain area harvested per person declined from 0.23 ha in 1950 to 0.13 ha in 1998 in spite of a doubling of the world's population. This is a result of the introduction of modern agricultural practices, including mineral fertilization, specially bred varieties, and the application of pesticides and herbicides. In a worst case scenario, if we assume that no further advances are made in improving **yields** (mass of crop $\cdot$ ha$^{-1}$) and that population growth continues at its current rate, then all of the arable land will have to be put into production by 2050 [11].

Compounding the difficulty in assessing the reserve capacity of the soil resource, is the question of sustainability. Can we continue modern agricultural practices without destroying the resource?

---

**TABLE 7-10**  Population and Cultivated Land on Each Continent

| Continent | Population in 2001[a] (millions) | Area ($10^6$ ha) Total[b] | Area ($10^6$ ha) Potentially arable[b] | Cropland[c] | Cropland (ha per capita) |
|---|---|---|---|---|---|
| Africa | 823 | 2966 | 733 | 183 | 0.22 |
| Asia | 3277[d] | 2679 | 627 | 455 | 0.14 |
| Australia, New Zealand and Oceania | 31 | 843 | 154 | 48 | 1.55 |
| Europe | 729 | 473 | 174 | 140 | 0.19 |
| North America | 486 | 2139 | 465 | 274 | 0.56 |
| South America | 351 | 1753 | 680 | 139 | 0.40 |
| Russia and Baltic | 460 | 2234 | 356 | 232 | 0.50 |
| Total | 6157 | 13,087 | 3189 | 1471 | 0.24 |

[a]From Bureau of Census, U.S. Dept. of Commerce, estimated 2002.
[b]From The President's Science Advisory Committee Panel on World Food Supply, 1967.
[c]From *World Resources*, A report of the International Institute for Environment and Development and World Resources Institute, Washington, D.C., 1987.
[d]Asia does not include Russia and the Baltic states.

## 7–8   **PARAMETERS OF SUSTAINABILITY**

The chief soil factors influencing plant growth are nutrient supply, soil acidity, soil salinity (with special reference to arid and semiarid land), texture and structure, and depth available for rooting. These are discussed in the next sections in the context of sustainability.

### Nutrient Cycling

There are 16 elements without which green plants cannot grow: C, H, O, N, P, S, Ca, Mg, K, Cl, Fe, Mn, Zn, Ci, B, and Mo. The first ten are called **macronutrients,** and the last six are called **micronutrients.** Carbon, hydrogen, and oxygen are abundant in the atmosphere and hydrosphere and are not of concern in sustainability. The main limiting factors on plant growth are nitrogen, phosphorous, potassium, and sulfur. Of these, nitrogen is often the most important.

The flow of nutrients is continuous among the soil (inorganic store), the living organisms in the soil (biomass store), and the residues and excreta of living organisms (organic store). Nitrogen is fixed from the atmosphere by soil and root nodule bacteria. It may also be dissolved in rainwater in the form of ammonium. These are the only two external sources of nitrogen. The remainder is supplied in recycled form from the breakdown of dead plant material and animal excreta. This cyclic process is diagrammed in Figure 7–14. If a crop is grown and the plant products such as leaves, stems, roots, and fruit are removed, the nitrogen must be replaced by fertilizer to remain sustainable for plant growth. Crops planted on cleared ground rapidly decrease in productivity after 2–3 years [12]. In the absence of an efficient root network, the rapid leaching of nitrogen makes the addition of nitrogenous fertilizer ineffective as well as being very expensive. The classic example of this problem is that of the tropical rain forests of South America, central Africa, and South East Asia, where subsistence farmers cut and burn the trees to clear land for growing crops. The ash provides some of the nutrients to sustain crops for a few years but the thin layers of soil, the low cation-exchange capacities, and heavy rainfall result in not only the removal of macronutrients but also micronutrients. The subsistence nature of the activity precludes expenditures for mineral fertilizers to replenish the soil.

**FIGURE 7–14**

The nitrogen cycle in the soil ecosystem.

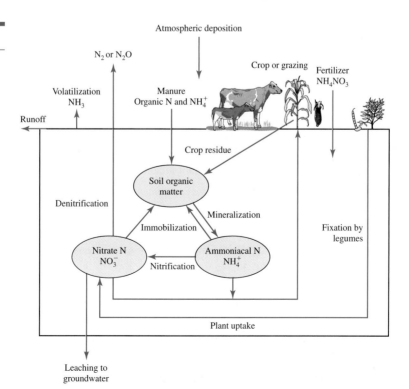

**FIGURE 7–15**

The phosphorus cycle in
the soil ecosystem.

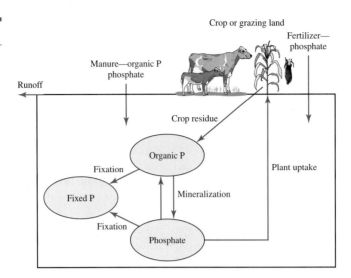

Cycling processes are also evident for phosphorus (Figure 7–15). Phosphorus is derived
from both the decay of organic matter and from the soil minerals. In highly leached soils, cycling
may be the only source of phosphorus. The form of phosphorus is as calcium phosphate in alkaline soils and as aluminum or iron phosphates in acid soils. The availability of phosphorus compounds is pH-dependent. They are most available at neutral pH values.

Potassium is also available from mineral weathering. In leached soils, the available potassium is bound up in organic cycles.

Some similarities between the sulfur and nitrogen cycles is evident (Figure 7–16). Each is
largely held in the organic fraction of the soil and each is dependent on microbial action for transformation.

### Soil Acidity

Efficient cycling, among other things, depends on a soil pH that favors the soil faunal activity and
the breakdown of organic matter by bacteria and fungi. At unfavorable pH values, organic matter
will accumulate without releasing its nutrient store. The acidity of leaf litter may have a substantial effect on the soil pH.

Crops vary in their pH tolerance. For example, alfalfa, sugar beets, some clover, lettuce,
peas, and carrots grow best in alkaline soils (pH 7–8); barley, wheat, maize, rye, and oats flourish in circumneutral soils (pH 6.5–7.5); potatoes thrive in acid soil (pH 5) [12]. For many plants,
the ability to adapt to varying soil acidity is not well understood. However, tolerance to aluminum toxicity appears to be important in acid soils and the ability to take up iron appears to be
important in alkaline soils.

### Soil Salinity

**Osmosis** is defined as the spontaneous transport of a solvent from a dilute solution to a concentrated solution across an ideal semipermeable membrane such as a plant cell wall that impedes
passage of the solute but allows the solvent to flow. In most soils this assists the flow of water
from the less concentrated soil solution to the more concentrated cell contents.

In saline soils, the soil solution concentration is high and the gradient is reversed; plants wilt
because their uptake of water is inhibited. **Saline** soils, sometimes called **white alkali** because of
a light-colored surface incrustation that is one of their characteristics, have excess soluble salts
that are mostly chlorides and sulfates of sodium, calcium, and magnesium. These can be readily
leached out with water that has lower concentrations of these salts. **Saline-sodic** soils contain
large quantities of soluble salts and enough adsorbed sodium to seriously affect most plants.

**FIGURE 7–16**

The sulfur cycle
(*Source:* Reprinted, with
permission, from: Sawyer
C. N., P. L. McCarty, and
G. F. Parkin, *Chemistry
for Environmental
Engineering and Science,*
5th ed., McGraw-Hill,
New York, p. 671.)

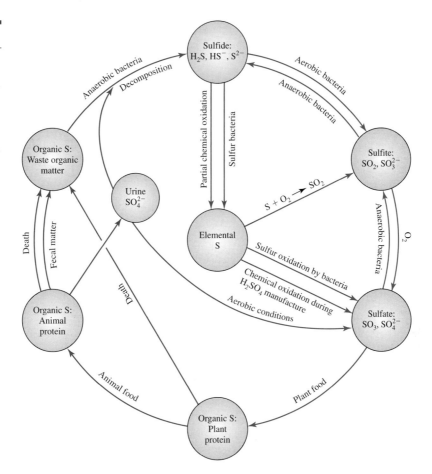

Unlike saline soils, leaching will raise the soil pH and the release of sodium will disperse the mineral colloids, which, in turn, results in a tight impervious soil. Leaching of saline-sodic soils leads to sodic soils. **Sodic** soils do not contain large amount of salts. The detrimental effects result from release of sodium, causing both plant toxicity and structural changes to the soil.

The effects of salt on plants varies depending on the plant. Barley, sugar beets, cotton, and sugar cane have good tolerance to saline soils. Rye, wheat, oats, and rice have a moderate tolerance. Orange, grapefruit, beans, and some clovers have poor tolerance [12].

In arid and semiarid areas, in which evapotranspiration exceeds precipitation, soil moisture supplies are often insufficient to sustain plant growth. Irrigation is an obvious technique to overcome this deficiency. With high evaporation, the salts in the water will tend to be left behind as the water evaporates. Thus, irrigation in areas of high evaporation can lead to high salinity in the soil. Repeated use of water for irrigation, which happens as irrigation from a river percolates through the soil back into the river and is used again and again downstream, leads to increased salt levels in the water and salinization of the soil by downstream users.

Worldwide, crop production is limited by the effects of salinity on about 50% of irrigated lands. In the United States, the problem affects about 30% of irrigated lands [13]. The sustainability of crop production on these lands is of concern.

### Texture and Structure

Groups of clay, silt, and sand particles aggregate together to form soil structures (often called **peds**). Without soil structures the soil would have few pores for air, water, and plant roots to penetrate.

A crucial process in the formation of structures is clay flocculation. Dispersed clay particles are separated from one another in individual layers of cations–usually sodium. Flocculated clay particles are linked together by other cations, especially calcium. Dispersed clay soils are very dense because the particles are packed closely together. This is why cultivation of soils rich in sodium is difficult.

## 7–9 SOIL CONSERVATION

### Soil Management

The capacity of a soil to consistently produce a crop depends on management of the soil. This goes beyond the mere application of fertilizer. Other soil attributes such as structure, drainage, and organic matter content must also be managed.

**Soil Fertility.** **Liebig's law of the minimum** states that the growth of a plant depends on the amount of foodstuff presented to it in minimum quantity. For example, a soil with abundant amounts of nitrogen will not be productive if the water available is insufficient. As noted previously, plants must have both macronutrients and micronutrients in sufficient quantity. There is an optimum level for each of these nutrients. Deficiencies will stunt growth. Excesses will be toxic. In natural systems, nutrients extracted from the soil are returned as leaf litter. When the crop is removed, there is no replenishment and the soil's nutrient store will be depleted. To maintain soil fertility nutrients must be replaced by other means.

For centuries, the use of animal manures as fertilizer has been synonymous with successful and stable agriculture. Not only do manures return organic matter and plant nutrients to the soil but they also return a high proportion of the solar energy captured by plants (Figure 7–17). Although mineral fertilizers containing nitrogen, phosphorus, and potassium provide the major macronutrients, they alone may not be sufficient. The return of organic matter also aids the maintenance of soil structure.

Crop rotation and laying the land fallow are also recognized techniques for sustained agricultural production. The rotation of legume plants that live symbiotically with the microorganisms that fix nitrogen replenishes the nitrogen supply. Fallow land that produces a grass cover provides a natural replenishment of organic matter that may be plowed back into the soil.

Liming of the soil may also be required to maintain fertility. Repeated application of nitrate fertilizers results in increased acidity of the soil. Some decay processes also will result in acidification. In addition to pH adjustment, liming reduces the toxicity of acid-soluble trace elements, improves soil structure, and increases the availability of calcium as a nutrient for soil organisms and plants.

**Structural Form and Stability.** Form determines the packing and pore space in the soil that provides aeration and water retention. Stability determines how the structures will behave when they are plowed.

Organic matter, calcium carbonate, aluminum and iron hydroxides, and silica all act to cement soil grains together and make their structures more durable. If the soil is wet the, "cement" dissolves and the structure becomes unstable. Silt soils are particularly susceptible to structural deterioration because the particles are not cohesive enough nor are they coarse enough to prevent packing.

The addition of manures and lime can help to form more stable structures. In some cases, for example, silty clays, drainage may improve their stability. The most significant factor is the timeliness of cultivation—when the surplus water has drained off for the consistency and structure of the soil to withstand the manipulation without breaking down. Limiting tillage is also of value in reducing the compaction by farm equipment. The structure of sandy soils and loam soils with a high organic content are of less concern because they can withstand the manipulation better.

### Soil Erosion

**Erosion** is the transport of soil by water and wind. Although geologic erosion is the mechanism by which sedimentary deposits are formed, short-term erosion due to anthropogenic activities is

## FIGURE 7–17

Diagram of the approximate energy flow for the United States food chain (in billions of joules) showing the high proportion of the energy ultimately found in animal manures.

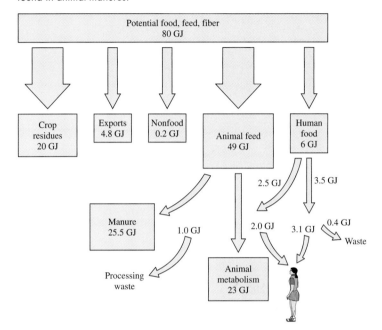

## FIGURE 7–18

Kinetic energy millimeter of rain in relation to rainfall intensity.

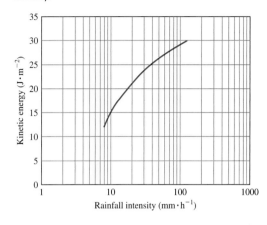

detrimental to the soil resource. Erosion is damaging to the soil fertility because mainly the nutrient-rich surface soil is removed. "No other soil phenomenon is more destructive worldwide than is soil erosion."[8]

In the United States, sediment in streams from soil erosion is estimated to be $3.6 \text{ Pg} \cdot \text{year}^{-1}$. Losses from agricultural lands ranged from 1 to $90 \text{ Mg} \cdot \text{ha}^{-1}$. The average annual loss from croplands is $16.4 \text{ Mg} \cdot \text{ha}^{-1}$. The maximum level that can be tolerated if soil productivity is to be maintained is about $11 \text{ Mg} \cdot \text{ha}^{-1}$ [8].

**Erosion by Water.**   To erode soil, work must done to disrupt the soil aggregation and to move the soil particles. Energy is supplied by the kinetic energy of the falling raindrops and running water. The energy of falling raindrops is at least 200 times that of running water [7]. Raindrop energy increases with the mass of the drop and the square of its terminal velocity. Both characteristics are a function of rainfall intensity (Figure 7–18).

The major factors affecting accelerated erosion are included in the **universal soil loss equation** (USLE):

$$A = (R)(K)(LS)(C)(P) \tag{7–28}$$

where $A$ = predicted soil loss (in $\text{Mg} \cdot \text{ha}^{-1}$)
  $R$ = rainfall erosion index
  $K$ = soil erodibility factor
  $LS$ = topographic factor, a function of
    $L$ = length (in m)
    $S$ = slope (%)
  $C$ = crop management factor
  $P$ = conservation practice factor

**FIGURE 7-19**

Average annual values of the rainfall erosion index in the United States. Note the high values in parts of the east and the generally low values in the west. (*Source:* Reprinted from: Wischmeier, W. J., and D. D. Smith, *Predicting Rainfall Erosion Loss—A Guide to Conservation Planning.* Agriculture Handbook No. 537, U.S. Department of Agriculture, Washington, D.C., 1978.)

**TABLE 7-11**     Computed *K* Values for Soils on Erosion Research Stations

| Soil | Source of Data | Computed K | Soil | Source of Data | Computed K |
|------|----------------|------------|------|----------------|------------|
| Dunkirk silt loam | Geneva, NY | 0.69[a] | Mexico silt loam | McCredie, MO | 0.28 |
| Keene silt loam | Zanesville, OH | 0.48 | Cecil sandy loam | Clemson, SC | 0.28[a] |
| Lodi loam | Blacksburg, VA | 0.39 | Cecil sandy loam | Watkinsville, GA | 0.23 |
| Cecil sandy clay loam | Watkinsville, GA | 0.36 | Tifton loamy sand | Tifton, GA | 0.10 |
| Marshall silt loam | Clarinda, IA | 0.33 | Bath flaggy silt loam with surface stones > 5 cm removed | Arnot, NY | 0.05[a] |
| Hagerstown silty clay loam | State College, PA | 0.31[a] | | | |
| Austin silt | Temple, TX | 0.29 | | | |

[a]Evaluated from continuous fallow. All others were computed from rowcrop data.

*Source:* Reprinted from: Wischmeier, W. J., and D. D. Smith, *Predicting Rainfall Erosion Loss—A Guide to Conservation Planning.* Agricultural Handbook No. 537, U.S. Department of Agriculture, Washington, D.C., 1978.

The rainfall erosion index is a function of intensity and total rainfall. Average annual values for the United States are shown in Figure 7–19.

The soil erodibility factor is low for soils in which the water infiltrates readily. Selected values of *K* are shown in Table 7–11.

The topographic factor includes the effects of both the slope and the length on the velocity of the water flow. Theoretically, a doubling of the velocity enables the water to move particles 64 times larger, to carry 32 times more mass in suspension, and makes the erosive power 4 times greater. The topographic factor for selected combinations of length and slope are shown in Table 7–12.

The *C* value indicates the influence of cropping systems on soil loss. The *C* value depends on the crop being grown, crop stage, tillage, and other management factors. Table 7–13 gives example values for *C*.

The conservation practice factor reflects the benefits of contouring, strip cropping, and other similar conservation practices (see discussion in following sections). Example *P* factors are listed in Table 7–14.

**TABLE 7–12**  The Topographic Factor (*LS*)[a] for Selected Combinations of Slope Length and Steepness

| Slope (%) | Slope Length (m) | | | | |
|---|---|---|---|---|---|
| | **15.35** | **30.5** | **45.75** | **61.0** | **91.5** |
| 2 | 0.163 | 0.201 | 0.227 | 0.248 | 0.280 |
| 4 | 0.303 | 0.400 | 0.471 | 0.528 | 0.621 |
| 6 | 0.476 | 0.673 | 0.824 | 0.952 | 1.17 |
| 8 | 0.701 | 0.992 | 1.21 | 1.41 | 1.72 |
| 10 | 0.968 | 1.37 | 1.68 | 1.94 | 2.37 |
| 12 | 1.280 | 1.80 | 2.21 | 2.55 | 3.13 |

[a]Note that the factor increases with both percent slope and length of slope.

*Source:* Reprinted from: Wischmeier, W. J., and D. D. Smith, *Predicting Rainfall Erosion Loss—A Guide to Conservation Planning.* Agricultural Handbook No. 537, U.S. Department of Agriculture, Washington, D.C., 1978.

**TABLE 7–13**  Crop Management or *C* Values for Different Crop Sequences in Northern Illinois[a]

| Crop Sequence[b] | Conventional Tillage[c] | | Minimum Tillage | | No Tillage | |
|---|---|---|---|---|---|---|
| | Residue Left | Residue Removed | Residue Level (kg) | | Residue Level (kg) | |
| | | | 458–907 | 908–1816 | 458–907 | 908–1816 |
| Continuous soybeans (Sb) | 0.49 | — | 0.33 | — | 0.29 | — |
| Continuous corn (C) | 0.37 | 0.47 | 0.31 | 0.07 | 0.29 | 0.06 |
| C–Sb | 0.43 | 0.49 | 0.32 | 0.12 | 0.29 | 0.06 |
| C–C–Sb | 0.40 | 0.47 | 0.31 | 0.12 | 0.29 | 0.06 |
| C–C–Sb–G–M | 0.20 | 0.24 | 0.18 | 0.09 | 0.14 | 0.05 |
| C–Sb–G–M | 0.16 | 0.18 | 0.15 | 0.09 | 0.11 | 0.05 |
| C–C–G–M | 0.12 | 0.16 | 0.13 | 0.08 | 0.09 | 0.04 |

[a]Note the dominating effect of tillage systems and of the maintenance of soil cover. Values would differ slightly in other areas but the principles illustrated would pertain.

[b]Crop abbreviations: C = corn; Sb = soybeans; G = small grain (wheat or oats); M = meadow.

[c]Spring plowed; assumes high crop yields.

*Source:* Selected data taken from: Walker, R. D., "USLE, A quick way to estimate your erosion losses," *Crops and Soil,* vol. 33, pp. 10–13, (1980).

**TABLE 7–14**  *P* Values for Contour-Farmed Terraced Fields in Relation to Slope Gradient

| Slope | Contour Factor | Stripcrop Factor |
|---|---|---|
| 1–2 | 0.60 | 0.30 |
| 3–8 | 0.50 | 0.25 |
| 9–12 | 0.60 | 0.30 |
| 13–16 | 0.70 | 0.35 |
| 17–20 | 0.80 | 0.40 |
| 21–25 | 0.90 | 0.45 |

*Source:* Reprinted from: Wischmeier, W. J., and D. D. Smith, *Predicting Rainfall Erosion Loss—A Guide to Conservation Planning.* Agricultural Handbook, No. 537, U.S. Department of Agriculture, Washington, D.C., 1978.

**EXAMPLE 7-11** Using the USLE estimate, determine the annual soil loss for a farm in central Indiana that has a Marshall silt loam with a slope of 2% and an average slope length of 91.5 m. The land is in continuous corn cultivation, and the farmer uses conventional tillage up and down the slope and leaves the residue.

Solution From Figure 7–19 select a rainfall erosion index of 175. The value for $K$ is 0.33 from Table 7–11. The value of $LS$ is 0.280 from Table 7–12, and the value of $C$ is 0.37 from Table 7–13. Because the farmer tills up and down hill, the value for $P$ is 1.0.

The annual soil loss is then

$$A = (R)(K)(LS)(C)(P)$$
$$= (175)(0.33)(0.280)(0.37)(1.0) = 5.98 \text{ or } 6 \text{ Mg} \cdot \text{ha}^{-1}$$

**Erosion by Wind.** Turbulent eddies of the wind lift up on the edges of soil particles. If the effective diameter of the soil particle is less than 0.06 mm in diameter, the particle becomes airborne and remains suspended for a long time. Particles between 0.06 and 0.2 mm in diameter are lifted in a "jump" that is followed by a long flat trajectory back to the ground level, where it either bounces or comes to rest after transmitting its kinetic energy to other particles that may be knocked upward. This process is called **saltation.** Particles between 0.2 and 1 mm frequently creep or roll along. Movement by saltation accounts for more than 50% of wind erosion [7]. Particles larger than 1 mm on the surface protect the smaller particles under them from erosion. Thus, over long periods, as small particles are blown from the surface to expose larger ones below the amount of erosion by "normal" winds is reduced. This is particularly important in desert environments that lack vegetative cover. It is also a reason why offroad vehicles are particularly harmful to desert soils. They destroy the natural balance by removing the protective layer of large particles.

**Conservation Measures.** We can identify several methods for limiting soil erosion by water from the USLE: by reducing the steepness of the slopes cultivated and the length of water runoff by contour plowing (along lines of equal elevation) rather than up and down hill or strip cropping by alternating tilled crops such as corn with untilled crops such as hay and grain; by crop management practices to reduce $C$ through minimum tillage or no tillage.

Wind erosion is more difficult to control. Wind breaks help slow the velocity and shorten the fetch* of the wind, but the most effective method is a healthy vegetative cover on a moist soil.

## CHAPTER REVIEW

When you have completed studying this chapter; you should be able to do the following without the aid of your textbook or notes:

1. Identify the three forms of rock in the rock cycle and explain how they are formed.
2. List the four processes that concentrate minerals.
3. Explain the difference between renewable and nonrenewable resources.
4. List the three methods of mineral resource conservation and give an example of each.
5. Describe three environmental effects of mining operations.
6. Define the following terms: weathering, mineral reserve, strip mining, overburden, tailings, spoil banks, dematerialization.
7. Describe the process of coal formation and identify the forms of combustible material formed in each stage, that is peat, lignite, bituminous, and anthracite.

---

*Distance the wind travels without being inhibited by orographic or vegetation effects.

8. Describe the process of petroleum formation and explain how it differs from the formation of coal.
9. Describe three environmental effects of coal mining.
10. Describe five nonfossil fuel alternative energy sources.
11. Define the following terms: acid mine drainage, bottom ash, fly ash, thermal resistance, cogeneration.
12. Sketch a pie chart of the soil components and identify the fractions.
13. Sketch a graph of soil moisture content versus time after a precipitation event and identify the saturation point, field capacity, and permanent wilting percentage.
14. Explain the role of soil microorganisms in the formation of soil.
15. Give two examples of soil as a resource.
16. Describe the role of each of the following in determining the sustainability of soil: nutrient cycling, soil acidity, soil salinity, texture and structure.
17. Explain Liebig's law of the minimum as it pertains to crop production.
18. List three techniques that may be employed to maintain soil fertility.
19. List two techniques for maintaining soil structure and form.
20. Describe two measures for reducing soil erosion by water.
21. Define the following terms: clay, turnover, bulk density, CEC, arable land, macronutrients, micronutrients, osmosis, saline soils, sodic soils, contour plowing, strip cropping, saltation.

With the aid of this text you should be able to do the following:

1. Determine one of the following, given the required data: the time until exhaustion of a mineral or energy reserve with a constant demand, the time until exhaustion of a mineral or energy reserve with a growth in demand, mass of mineral reserve, annual demand.
2. Perform mass-balance calculations on mining operations.
3. Estimate the mass recovered at the end of each cycle of reclamation of a material.
4. Estimate the equivalent mass for a material recycled an infinite number of times or a given number of times.
5. Estimate the amount of sulfuric acid produced from an ore with a given pyrite concentration.
6. Perform an energy balance on a thermal power plant or other fossil fuel-burning facility.
7. Perform an energy balance on a hydropower facility.
8. Perform an energy balance on a heated or cooled structure.
9. Perform carbon, nitrogen, and phosphorus balances for soil.
10. Calculate soil turnover.
11. Plot soil grain size distributions from sieve analysis.
12. Determine soil texture from grain size analysis.
13. Perform soil mass-volume calculations.
14. Estimate the soil loss from water erosion using the USLE.

## PROBLEMS

**7–1**  One author has estimated that the time until exhaustion for aluminum is 224 years if the world production remains constant. What is the annual demand based on this estimate?

   **Answer:** $94 \, \text{Tg} \cdot \text{year}^{-1}$

**7–2**  The world production of aluminum increased 3% from 1996 to 1997. Rework Problem 7–1 using this rate of increase in demand to estimate the annual demand in 1996.

**7–3**  In 1997, the United States produced 63 Tg of iron from ore with an iron content of 63.2%. Estimate the amount of waste rock generated in mining this ore if the production remains constant until the U.S. reserve is depleted.

   **Answer:** 5316.45 or 5300 Tg, or 5.3 Pg

**7–4**   As the supply of high-grade ores are used up, lower grade ores are used to produce minerals. One author has claimed that the amount of waste rock increases exponentially as the grade of ore decreases.

(a)   Assuming that you are producing 100 kg of metal product, calculate the kilograms of waste rock per kilogram of metal for ore containing 50%, 25%, 10%, 5%, and 2.5% metal.

(b)   Write a general expression for the calculation in part (a). Is it exponential?

**7–5**   If the decay constant for recovery of a metal is 0.0202 cycle$^{-1}$, what is the percent recovery for each cycle?

**Answer:** 98%

**7–6**   In the United States approximately 1.6 Mg · year$^{-1}$ of aluminum is used in beverage cans. If 63% of this is recovered and recycled each year, what is the equivalent mass if it is recycled an infinite number of times?

**7–7**   Equation 7–4 may be used to estimate the mass recovered at the end of a given cycle. Equation 7–6 may be used to estimate the equivalent mass after a given number of cycles. Calculate the mass recovered after each of the first three cycles for an aluminum beverage can (Example 7–3) using Equation 7–4 and compare the answer with that from Equation 7–6.

**Answer:** For 3rd cycle $M_{TOTAL} = 39.0$ g, $M_K = 43.4$ g

**7–8**   In 1997, the U.S. Geologic Survey estimated that 17% of the demand for copper in the United States was supplied by recycled copper. If the demand for copper remains constant at the 2001 rate of 2.6 Tg · year$^{-1}$, how many years will be added to the time until exhaustion of the U.S. reserve?

**7–9**   What percent recovery in recycling will be required to double the time to exhaustion for U.S. reserves of copper if the demand remains constant at the 2001 rate of 2.6 Tg · year$^{-1}$.

**Answer:** 58.48, or 58%

**7–10**   What percent recovery in recycling will be required to double the time to exhaustion for U.S. reserves of copper if the demand increases at a rate 1.0% · year$^{-1}$ from the 2001 rate of 2.6 Tg · year$^{-1}$.

**7–11**   What is the time until exhaustion for world reserves for copper if the remaining copper is recycled 50%? Assume the world demand remains constant at the 2001 rate of 13.7 Tg · year$^{-1}$.

**Answer:** 49.6, or 50 years

**7–12**   It has been estimated that at 1991 consumption rates, the world's coal reserve will last 200 years. Estimate the world consumption rate in 1991.

**7–13**   A conventional coal-fired power plant has an efficiency of about 33%. Assuming that all the coal in Problem 7–12 was used to generate electricity (it was not), estimate the time until exhaustion if the efficiency was raised to 40%.

**Answer:** 242 years

**7–14**   Using the Internet, determine the pH of the Tiogar River near Mansfield, PA. Is this river suffering from acid mine drainage? (*Hint:* http://waterdata.usgs.gov/nwis. Search under "Real Time" data)

**7–15**   It has been proposed that coal from the western United States be substituted for the coal in Example 7–5 to reduce the ash disposal volume. The western coal has an ash content of 4.0% and an NHV of 23.6 MJ · kg$^{-1}$. Is this a good idea? Estimate the volume of ash produced for the power plant specified in Example 7–5.

**Answer:** $1.84 \times 10^5$ m$^3$ · year$^{-1}$

**7–16**   It has been proposed that an evaporative cooling tower be used to replace the once-through cooling water in Example 7–6. At what rate must the water be provided from the river to offset the water lost in the cooling tower?

**7–17**   A house built in the 1950s has 14.86 m$^2$ of single-glazed windows. Estimate the heat loss with the existing single-glazed window and the loss if the windows are replaced with (a) double-glazed, (b) triple-glazed windows. Assume the indoor temperature is 30°C and the outdoor temperature is 0°C.

**Answer:** Single-glazed $= 1.86 \times 10^3$ W; double-glazed $= 9.29 \times 10^2$ W

**7-18**  A 25-W compact fluorescent light bulb (CFL) produces the light equivalent of a 100-W incandescent bulb. The population of North America is estimated to be about 305 million. Estimate the amount of coal to light one 100-W incandescent light bulb for each person for one year and the amount of coal that would be saved if each incandescent bulb was replaced with a CFL. Assume the coal has a NHV of 28.5 MJ $\cdot$ kg$^{-1}$ and the power plants are 33% efficient.

**7-19**  A university computer lab has 32 machines. Each machine draws 400 W of power, most of which is given off as heat. Assuming that 100% of the electrical demand is given off as heat, estimate the amount of energy that is wasted each year if the computers are left running during the 8 h at night that the lab is closed. (*Note:* The computers draw virtually as much power when they are in the "sleep mode" as they do when they are active.)

> **Answer:**  135 GJ

**7-20**  As noted in the discussion following Example 7–9, the estimated turnover time from carbon dating far exceeds that estimated from the litter contribution of carbon to the soil. One explanation for this discrepancy is that the $K$ values come in a range, depending on the transformation that is occurring.

Based on the half-lives of 1450 and 3700 years, the value of $K$ ranges from $4.78 \times 10^{-4}$ year$^{-1}$ (for 1450 years) to $1.87 \times 10^{-4}$ year$^{-1}$ (for 3700). The organic carbon content of arable soils is about 50 Mg $\cdot$ ha$^{-1}$ (to a depth of 25 cm). Using the larger $K$ value, estimate the fraction of the 1 Mg $\cdot$ ha$^{-1}$ $\cdot$ year$^{-1}$ of litter that falls that is incorporated into the soil. Assume steady-state conditions.

**7-21**  Using the U.S. Department of Agriculture textural classification, determine the texture of the following soil: 16% sand; 37% silt, 47% clay.

> **Answer:**  Clay

**7-22**  The U.S. Department of Agriculture textural classification is based on that fraction of soil that passes the No. 10 sieve. If a large fraction of the soil has a particle size greater than the No. 10 sieve, a correction is required to use the chart. For example, a soil containing 20% gravel (greater than No. 10 sieve), 10% sand, 30% silt, and 40% clay will have a corrected composition of 12.5% sand, 37.5% silt and 50.0% clay. Write an expression that shows how the correction is calculated.

**7-23**  Equations 7–20, 7–22, and 7–23 can be used to find an expression that relates porosity ($n$) and void ratio ($\epsilon$). Develop an expression that will allow you to calculate the void ratio from the porosity and use it to calculate the void ratio for loam in Table 7–8.

> **Answer:**  $\epsilon = 1.50$

**7-24**  Equations 7–20, 7–22, and 7–23 can be used to find an expression that relates porosity ($n$) and void ratio ($\epsilon$). Develop an expression that will allow you to calculate the porosity from the void ratio and use it to calculate the porosity for loess in Table 7–8.

**7-25**  In Example 7–11, the farmer had the land in continuous corn cultivation and used no conservation protection. Estimate the soil loss if a conventional tillage corn-corn-wheat-meadow rotation was employed with residue left and the field was contour-plowed.

> **Answer:**  1.16 or 1 Mg $\cdot$ ha$^{-1}$

## DISCUSSION QUESTIONS

**7-1**  If you are given a choice of bagging your groceries in a paper or a plastic bag, which do you select because it is manufactured from a renewable resource? Explain your choice.

**7-2**  A bicycle manufacturer is considering changing from steel wheel rims to rims made from either aluminum or titanium alloy. From a resource conservation point of view, which alternative would you recommend? Using the hierarchy of resource conservation, explain your choice.

**7-3**  A forest area growing on a sandy soil has been harvested to permit agricultural production. Municipal wastewater is available to provide irrigation. Corn is planted but does not yield well despite the abundant application of nitrogen, phosphorus, and potassium. What component of the soil is missing?

**7–4** Why is irrigation of farmland in the southwest potentially damaging to long-term production, but irrigation in the Great Lakes area is not likely to be damaging to the soil?

**7–5** As a new home owner you decide that you would like to have a vegetable garden. The soil is a silty-clay. What can you add to the soil to improve its structure?

## ADDITIONAL READING

Masters, G. M. *Introduction to Environmental Engineering and Science,* Prentice Hall, Upper Saddle River, NJ (1998).

## REFERENCES

1. U.S. Geological Survey, *Mineral Year Book* (2001). http://minerals.usgs.gov/minerals/pubs/commodity/myb
2. Ophuls, W., and A. S. Boyan. *Ecology and the Politics of Scarcity Revisited,* W. H. Freeman, New York, p. 76 (1992).
3. McKinney, M. L., and R. M. Schoch. *Environmental Science: Systems and Solutions,* Jones and Bartlett Publishers, Boston, pp. 191, 202, 268 (1998).
4. Coates, D. R. *Environmental Geology,* John Wiley & Sons, New York, pp. 99, 152, 156, 215 (1981).
5. Energy Information Agency, U.S. Department of Energy (1999). www.eia.doe.gov
6. Masters, G. M. *Introduction to Environmental Engineering and Science,* 2nd ed., Prentice Hall, Upper Saddle River, NJ, p. 569 (1998).
7. White, R. E. *Introduction to the Principles and Practice of Soil Science,* John Wiley & Sons, New York, pp. 24, 34, 152, 156 (1979).
8. Brady, N. C. *The Nature and Properties of Soils,* 9th ed, Macmillan, New York, pp. 264, 431, 432, 549 (1990).
9. World Conservation Monitoring Centre, Cambridge, UK (1998). http://www.wcmc.org.uk/forest/data
10. U.S. Forest Service (1999). http://www.fs.fed.us/agenda
11. Meadows, D. H., D. L. Meadows, and J. Randers. *Beyond the Limits: Confronting Global Collapse, Envisioning a Sustainable Future,* Chelsea Green Publishing Co., Post Mills, VT, p. 51 (1992).
12. Courtney F. M., and S. T. Trudgill. *The Soil, An Introduction to Soil Study,* Edward Arnold Publishers, London, pp. 60–61 (1984).
13. Jacoby, M. "Botanists design plants with a taste for salt," *Chemical & Engineering News,* p. 9, August 23, 1999.

# 8

# Water Quality Management

## 8–1   INTRODUCTION

How we use the water in lakes, rivers, ponds, and streams is greatly influenced by the quality of the water found in them. Activities such as fishing, swimming, boating, shipping, and waste disposal have very different requirements for water quality. Water of a particularly high quality is needed for drinking water supplies. In many parts of the world, the introduction of pollutants from human activity has seriously degraded water quality, even to the extent of turning pristine trout streams into foul open sewers with few life forms and fewer beneficial uses.

Water quality managers are concerned with controlling pollution from human activity so as to ensure that the water is suitable for its intended uses. Water quality management is also the science of knowing how much waste is too much for a particular water body. To know how much waste can be tolerated (the technical term is **assimilated**) by a water body, water quality managers must know the type of pollutants discharged and the manner in which they affect water quality. They must also know how water quality is affected by natural factors such as the mineral heritage of the watershed, the geometry of the terrain, and the climate of the region. A small, tumbling mountain brook will have a very different assimilative capacity from a sluggish, meandering lowland river, and lakes are different from moving waters.

Originally, the intent of water quality management was to protect the intended uses of a water body while using water as an economic means of waste disposal within the constraints of its assimilative capacity. In 1972, the Congress of the United States enacted the Federal Water Pollution Control Act Amendments of 1972, which established that it was in the national interest to "restore and maintain the chemical, physical, and biological integrity of the nation's waters." In addition to making the water safe to drink, the Congress also established a goal of ensuring "water quality which provides for the protection and propagation of fish, shellfish, and wildlife, and provides for recreation in and on the water." By understanding how pollutants affect water quality, an environmental engineer can properly design the treatment facilities to remove these pollutants to acceptable levels or can help to choose chemicals to be used in a specific process that will not have a deleterious effect on the environment. Traditionally, environmental engineers have focused their efforts on the former, that is, on end-of-pipe treatment, but current thinking demands that the environmental engineer become involved in looking at the entire process to minimize the formation of the pollution in the first place, by choosing chemicals that do not harm the environment, recycling chemicals on site and other means appropriate for the specific process or industry under consideration.

This chapter deals first with the major types of water pollutants and their sources. In the remainder of the chapter, water quality management in rivers and lakes is discussed, placing the emphasis on the categories of pollutants found in domestic wastewaters. For both rivers and lakes, the natural factors affecting water quality will be discussed as the basis for understanding how human activities affect water quality.

## 8–2   WATER POLLUTANTS AND THEIR SOURCES

The wide range of pollutants discharged to surface waters can be grouped into broad classes.

### Point Sources

Domestic sewage and industrial wastes are called **point sources** because they are generally collected by a network of pipes or channels and conveyed to a single point of discharge into the receiving water. Domestic sewage consists of wastes from homes, schools, office buildings, and stores. The term **municipal sewage** includes domestic sewage along with any industrial wastes that are permitted to be discharged into the sanitary sewers. In general, point source pollution can be reduced or eliminated through waste minimization and proper wastewater treatment prior to discharge to a natural water body.

### Nonpoint Sources

Urban and agricultural runoff are characterized by multiple discharge points and are called **nonpoint sources.** Often the polluted water flows over the surface of the land or along natural drainage channels to the nearest water body. Even when urban or agricultural runoff waters are collected in pipes or channels, they are generally transported the shortest possible distance for discharge, so that treatment at each outlet is not economically feasible. Much of nonpoint source pollution occurs during rainstorms or spring snowmelt, resulting in large flow rates that make treatment even more difficult. Reduction of agricultural nonpoint source pollution generally requires changes in land use practices and improved education. Urban storm water runoff (including that from streets, parking lots, golf courses, and lawns) can transport pollutants such as nitrogen and phosphorus from fertilizers, herbicides applied to lawns and golf courses, oil, greases, ethylene glycol (used in antifreeze), and cut grass and other organic debris.

Nonpoint pollution from urban storm water and, in particular, storm water collected in **combined sewers** that carry both storm water and municipal sewage may require major engineering work to correct. The original design of combined sewers provided a flow structure that diverted excess storm water mixed with raw sewage (above the design capacity of the wastewater treatment plant) directly to the nearest river or stream. The elimination of **combined sewer overflow** (CSO) may involve not only the construction of separate storm and sanitary sewers but also the creation of storm water retention basins and expanded treatment facilities to treat the storm water. This is particularly complex and expensive because the combined sewers frequently occur in the oldest, most developed portions of the community, thus disrupting paved streets, utilities, and commercial activities during construction activities. The installation of combined sewers is now prohibited in the United States.

### Oxygen-Demanding Material

Anything that can be oxidized in the receiving water resulting in the consumption of dissolved molecular oxygen is termed **oxygen-demanding material.** This material is usually biodegradable organic matter but also includes certain inorganic compounds. The consumption of **dissolved oxygen,** DO (pronounced "dee oh"), poses a threat to fish and other higher forms of aquatic life that must have oxygen to live. The critical level of DO varies greatly among species. For example, brook trout may require about 7.5 mg $\cdot$ L$^{-1}$ of DO, whereas carp can survive at 3 mg $\cdot$ L$^{-1}$. As a rule, the most desirable commercial and game fish require high levels of dissolved oxygen. Oxygen-demanding materials in domestic sewage come primarily from human waste and food residue. Particularly noteworthy among the many industries that release oxygen-demanding wastes are the food-processing and paper industries. Almost any naturally occurring organic matter, such as animal droppings, crop residues, or leaves, which is released into the water from nonpoint sources, will contribute to the depletion of DO.

### Nutrients

Nitrogen and phosphorus, two nutrients of primary concern, are considered pollutants when they become too much of a good thing. All living things require these nutrients for growth. Thus, they must be present in rivers and lakes to support the natural food web.* Problems arise when nutrient levels become excessive and the food web is grossly disturbed, causing some organisms to proliferate at the expense of others. As will be discussed in a later section, excessive nutrients often lead to large growths of algae, which in turn become oxygen-demanding material when they die and settle to the bottom. Some major sources of nutrients are phosphorus-based detergents, fertilizers, food-processing wastes, as well as animal and human excrement.

---

*In simplistic terms, a food web is the collection of interrelated organisms in which the lower levels are the "prey" and the upper levels are the "predators." See Chapter 4 for a more detailed discussion of the food web.

### Pathogenic Organisms

Pathogenic microorganisms found in wastewater include bacteria, viruses, and protozoa excreted by diseased persons or animals. When discharged into surface waters, they make the water unfit for drinking (i.e., nonpotable). If the concentration of pathogens is sufficiently high, the water may also be unsafe for swimming and fishing. Certain shellfish can be toxic because they concentrate pathogenic organisms in their tissues, making the toxicity levels in the shellfish much greater than the levels in the surrounding water. Issues involving the occurrence of the protozoan pathogens *Cryptosporidium* and *Giardia* and resulting outbreaks of gastrointestinal infections will be discussed in more detail in Chapter 9.

Bacteria that have developed immunity to antibiotics are of major concern to environmental professionals. Although the occurrence of these organisms in hospitals is well documented, the presence of antibiotic-resistant bacteria in surface waters was not demonstrated until the late 1990s. Ash and colleagues [1] sampled 15 U.S. rivers for bacteria resistant to ampicillin, a synthetic penicillin. Antibiotic-resistant bacteria were found in both rural and urban environments with no observable pattern. The Rio Grande was also sampled for antibiotic-resistant bacteria, this time using the antibiotic vancomycin [2]. Antibiotic-resistant bacteria were most commonly found downstream of El Paso; resistance was detected in up to 30% of the bacteria isolated from there. Equally disturbing was the discovery that 30–40% of the bacteria in the streams in rural Dubuque, Iowa, were resistant to tetracycline, and 1% of the bacteria appeared to be immune to this antibiotic [3]. Clearly the resistance of the bacteria detected reflects our heavy dependence on antibiotics and may significantly alter the future effectiveness of antibiotics [4].

### Suspended Solids

Organic and inorganic particles that are carried by wastewater into a receiving water are termed **suspended solids** (SS). When the speed of the water is reduced by flow into a pool or a lake, many of these particles settle to the bottom as sediment. In common usage, the word *sediment* also includes eroded soil particles that are being carried by water even if they have not yet settled. Colloidal particles, which do not settle readily, cause the turbidity found in many surface waters. Organic suspended solids may also exert an oxygen demand. Inorganic suspended solids are discharged by some industries but result mostly from soil erosion, which is particularly bad in areas of logging, strip mining, and construction. As excessive sediment loads are deposited into lakes and reservoirs, the turbidity increases, light penetration decreases, the bacterial population often increases, and the solids deposit on the bottom of the water body, destroying the habitat for many benthic organisms. Even in rapidly moving mountain streams, sediment from mining and logging operations has destroyed many habitats for aquatic organisms. For example, salmon eggs can only develop and hatch in stream beds of loose gravel. As the pores between the pebbles are filled with sediment, the eggs suffocate and the salmon population is reduced.

### Salts

Although most people associate salty water with oceans and salt lakes, all water contains some salt. These salts are often measured by evaporation of a filtered water sample. The salts and other matter that don't evaporate are called **total dissolved solids** (TDS). A problem arises when the salt concentration in fresh water increases to the point where the natural population of plants and animals is threatened or the water is no longer useful for public water supplies or irrigation. High concentrations of salts are discharged by many industries, and the use of salt to melt ice on roads during the winter causes high salt levels in urban runoff, especially during the spring snowmelt. Of particular concern in arid regions, where water is used extensively for irrigation, is that the water picks up salts every time it passes through the soil on its way back to the river. In addition, evapotranspiration causes the salts to be further concentrated. Thus, the salt concentration continuously increases as the water moves downstream. If the concentration gets too high, crop damage or soil poisoning can result.

## Toxic Metals and Toxic Organic Compounds

Agricultural runoff often contains pesticides and herbicides that have been used on crops. Urban runoff is a major source of zinc (originating from tire wear) in many water bodies. Many industrial wastewaters contain either toxic metals or toxic organic substances. If discharged in large quantities, many of these materials can render a body of water nearly useless for a long time. The lower James River in Virginia can now only be used as a shipping channel because of large industrial discharges of highly toxic and persistent organic compounds. Many toxic compounds are concentrated in the food web, making fish and shellfish unsafe for human consumption. Thus, even small quantities of toxic compounds in the water can be incompatible with the natural ecosystem and many human uses.

Another more recent concern is the presence of pharmaceutical chemicals in water and wastewater. Scientists in Germany and Switzerland have detected these chemicals and their metabolites in municipal wastewaters and surface waters [5] although no detrimental effects on humans have been shown. Nevertheless, because of the effects of some of these chemicals (namely fluvoxamine) on male mussels, many scientists are concerned that the presence of these chemicals in waters may have subtle effects on humans and wildlife [6]. Clearly, the discussion on antibiotic-resistant bacteria should raise alarms because the presence of antibiotics in natural environments has the potential to result in antibiotic-resistant bacterial strains.

## Endocrine-Disrupting Chemicals

The class of chemicals known as endocrine disrupters, or EDCs, has received significant interest from the scientific community, regulatory agencies, and the general public. EDCs include the polychlorinated biphenyls, commonly used pesticides such atrazine and other triazine chemicals, and the phthalates (as shown in Table 8–1). EDCs can mimic estrogens, androgens, or thyroid hormones, or their antagonists. They can also interfere with the regulation of reproductive and developmental processes in mammals, birds, reptiles, and fish [7]. The chemicals can also alter the normal physiological function of the endocrine system and can affect the synthesis of hormones in the body. EDCs can also target tissues where the hormones exert their effects. Although laboratory studies have indicated the potential effects of these chemicals on humans and wildlife,

| **TABLE 8–1** | Endocrine-Disrupting Chemicals | | | |
|---|---|---|---|---|
| **Group 1 Chlorinated Organics** | **Group 2 Industrial Chemicals** | **Group 3 Polymers with Molecular Weights ≤ 1000** | **Group 4 Substances Controlled under the Toxic Substances Control Act** | **Group 5 Pesticides** |
| 2,4,5-Trichlorophenol (S) | Hydrazine (P) | Fluoropolyol | PAHs (K) | Malathion (S) |
| PCB (K) | Bisphenol A (P) | Methoxypolysiloxane (P) | Triazines (K) | 1,2-Dibromo-3-chloropropane |
| 2,3,7,8–TCDD (K) | Transplatin (S) | Polyethylene oxide (S) | Lead (K) | Pyrethroids (S) |
| Pentachlorophenol (K) | Benzoflumethiazide | Poly(isobutylene) | Mercury (K) | Dicamba (S) |
| | Propanthelinebromide (S) | Polyurethane (S) | Endosulfans | Aldicarb (P) |
| | p-Nitrotoluene | | Kepone (S) | Aldicarb nitrofen (S) |
| | Obidoxime chloride (S) | | | |

P = probable EDC; S = suspected EDC; K = known EDC; PCB = polychlorinated biphenyl; TCDD = tetrachlordibenzo-p-dioxin; PAH = polycyclic aromatic hydrocarbons.

Source: O. A. Sadik, and D. M. Witt. Monitoring endocrine-disrupting chemicals. Environ. Sci. Technol. 33: 368A-374A, 1999.

much research still needs to be conducted before the environmental effects of these chemicals can be ascertained at low concentrations and low exposure rates. Most of the studies conducted have done so *in vitro,* and few *in vivo* studies have confirmed these results. Also, at present, there is no suitable characterization method to evaluate most EDCs in biota or biological media. Moreover, monitoring and surveillance studies of EDCs and their metabolites are expensive, laborious, and difficult.

### Arsenic

Arsenic is a naturally occurring element in the environment. Its occurrence in groundwater is largely the result of minerals dissolving naturally from weathered rocks and soils, mainly from iron oxides or sulfide minerals. High arsenic concentrations in groundwater have been documented in parts of Maine, Michigan, Minnesota, South Dakota, Oklahoma, and Wisconsin. Groundwater in many regions of these states have been shown to have arsenic concentrations [8] exceeding 10 mg $\cdot$ L$^{-1}$. Figure 8–1 shows those areas of the United States where arsenic in groundwater is problematic. Arsenic in groundwater is also challenging environmental scientists and engineers in other areas of the world including India, Taiwan, and Bangladesh, where a World Health Organization study has revealed that between 33 and 77 million of Bangladesh's 125 million people are at risk of arsenic poisoning from groundwater.

Arsenic poisoning from groundwater can have numerous health effects, ranging from circulatory disorders, gastrointestinal upsets, diabetes, peripheral neuropathies, and skin lesions [9]. Epidemiologic studies conducted in several countries (including Taiwan, Japan, England, Hungary, Mexico, Chile, and Argentina) have linked arsenic-contaminated drinking water to skin cancer. Increased mortality from internal cancers of liver, bladder, kidney, and lungs has also been reported [9].

On October 31, 2001, the U.S. EPA lowered the drinking water maximum contaminant level (MCL) from 50 to 10 $\mu$g $\cdot$ L$^{-1}$. At the previous level of 50 $\mu$g $\cdot$ L$^{-1}$, the lifetime risk for all cancers was calculated to be on the order of 1 in 100. Following the National Research Councils report *Arsenic in Drinking Water* [10] EPA proposed an arsenic MCL of 5 $\mu$g $\cdot$ L$^{-1}$. A maximum contaminant level goal (MCLG) of zero was proposed. Despite EPA policy, which has been to set the MCL as close as feasible to the MCLG, taking into account technological

**FIGURE 8–1**

Counties with arsenic concentrations exceeding possible new maximum contaminant levels in 10% or more of groundwater samples. (*Source:* Welch, A. H., S. A. Watkins, D. R. Helsel, and M. F. Focazio. Arsenic in ground-water resources of the United States. *U.S. Geological Survey Fact Sheet* 063-00, 2000.)

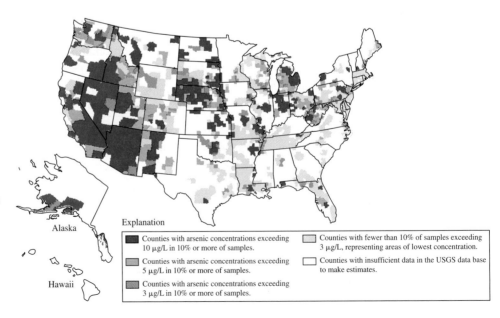

Explanation

- Counties with arsenic concentrations exceeding 10 μg/L in 10% or more of samples.
- Counties with arsenic concentrations exceeding 5 μg/L in 10% or more of samples.
- Counties with arsenic concentrations exceeding 3 μg/L in 10% or more of samples.
- Counties with fewer than 10% of samples exceeding 3 μg/L, representing areas of lowest concentration.
- Counties with insufficient data in the USGS data base to make estimates.

Alaska

Hawaii

feasibility and cost-effectiveness, the MCL was not set at 5, but at $10 \, \mu g \cdot L^{-1}$. At a level of $10 \, \mu g \cdot L^{-1}$ the lifetime excess risks for combined lung and bladder cancers were calculated to be 30 per 10,000 people for women and 30 per 10,000 for men [11]. These risks can be compared with the MCLs set for many other carcinogenic compounds, which are set based on risks of 1:100,000 to 1:1,000,000.

### Heat

Although heat is not often recognized as a pollutant, those in the electric power industry are well aware of the problems of disposing of waste heat. Also, waters released by many industrial processes are much warmer than the receiving waters. In some environments an increase in water temperature can be beneficial. For example, production of clams and oysters can be increased in some areas by warming the water. On the other hand, increases in water temperature can have negative effects. Many important commercial and game fish, such as salmon and trout, live only in cool water. In some instances the discharge of heated water from a power plant can completely block salmon migration. Heat is being theorized as one of the potential causes of the feminization of genetically male Chinook salmon in the Columbia River near Hanford, Washington. Apparently, excessively high water temperatures or abnormal temperature fluctuations during egg development can cause a genetically male embryo to develop functioning female sex organs [12]. Higher temperatures also increase the rate of oxygen depletion in areas where oxygen-demanding wastes are present. Because temperature increases result in a decrease in oxygen solubility, this increased extent of oxygen depletion along with higher temperatures causes a very pronounced deterioration in the water quality.

## 8–3 WATER QUALITY MANAGEMENT IN RIVERS

The objective of water quality management is to control the discharge of pollutants so that water quality is not degraded to an unacceptable extent below the natural background level. Controlling waste discharges, however, must be a quantitative endeavor. We must be able to measure the pollutants, predict their effect on water quality, determine the background water quality that would be present without human intervention, and decide the levels acceptable for intended uses of the water.

To most people, the tumbling mountain brook, crystal clear and icy cold, fed by melting snow is safe to drink and the epitome of high water quality.* Certainly a stream in that condition is a treasure, but we cannot expect the Mississippi River to have the same water quality. It never did and never will. Yet both need proper management if the water is to remain usable. The mountain brook may serve as the spawning ground for desirable fish and must be protected from heat and sediment as well as chemical pollution. The Mississippi, however, is already warmed from hundreds of kilometers of exposure to the sun and carries the sediment from thousands of square kilometers of land. But even the Mississippi can be damaged by organic matter and toxic chemicals. Fish do live there and the river is used as a water supply for millions of people.

The effect of pollution on a river depends both on the nature of the pollutant and the unique characteristics of the individual river.† Some of the most important characteristics include the volume and speed of water flowing in the river, the river's depth, the type of bottom, and the surrounding vegetation. Other factors include the climate of the region, the mineral heritage of the watershed, land use patterns, and the types of aquatic life in the river. Water quality management for a particular river must consider all these factors. Thus, some rivers are highly susceptible to

---

*Water from this stream may or may not be safe to drink, however appealing it may appear. Runoff containing pathogenic organisms, such as *Cryptosporidum parvum* and *Giardia lambia,* excreted in the feces of wildlife can cause disease in humans. This is a good reason to disinfect all surface waters intended for human consumption.

†Here we will use the word *river* to include streams, brooks, creeks, and any other channel of flowing, freshwater.

pollutants such as sediment, salt, and heat, whereas others can tolerate large inputs of these pollutants without much damage.

Some pollutants, particularly oxygen-demanding wastes and nutrients, are so common and have such a profound effect on almost all types of rivers that they deserve special emphasis. This is not to say that they are always the most significant pollutants in any one river, but rather that no other pollutant category has as much overall effect on our nation's rivers. For these reasons, the next sections of this chapter will be devoted to a more detailed look at how oxygen-demanding material and nutrients affect water quality in rivers.

### Effect of Oxygen-Demanding Wastes on Rivers

The introduction of oxygen-demanding material, either organic or inorganic, into a river depletes the dissolved oxygen in the water. This poses a threat to fish and other higher forms of aquatic life if the concentration of oxygen falls below a critical point. To predict the extent of oxygen depletion, it is necessary to know how much waste is being discharged and how much oxygen will be required to degrade the waste. However, because oxygen is continuously being replenished from the atmosphere and from photosynthesis by algae and aquatic plants, as well as being consumed by organisms, the concentration of oxygen in the river is determined by the relative rates of these competing processes. Organic oxygen-demanding materials are commonly measured by determining the amount of oxygen consumed during degradation in a manner approximating degradation in natural waters. This section begins by considering the factors affecting oxygen consumption during the degradation of organic matter, then moves on to inorganic nitrogen oxidation. Finally, the equations for predicting dissolved oxygen concentrations in rivers from degradation of organic matter are developed and discussed.

### Biochemical Oxygen Demand

The amount of oxygen required to oxidize a substance to carbon dioxide and water may be calculated by stoichiometry if the chemical composition of the substance is known. This amount of oxygen is known as the **theoretical oxygen demand** (ThOD).

**EXAMPLE 8–1** Compute the ThOD of $108.75 \text{ mg} \cdot \text{L}^{-1}$ of glucose ($C_6H_{12}O_6$).

**Solution** We begin by writing a balanced equation for the reaction.

$$C_6H_{12}O_6 + 6O_2 \longrightarrow 6CO_2 + 6H_2O$$

Next, compute the gram molecular weights of the reactants using the table on the inside front cover of the book.

| Glucose | Oxygen |
|---|---|
| $6C = 72$ | $(6)(2)O = 192 \text{ g} \cdot \text{mol}^{-1}$ |
| $12H = 12$ | |
| $6O = 96$ | |
| $\overline{180 \text{ g} \cdot \text{mol}^{-1}}$ | |

Thus, it takes 192 g of oxygen to oxidize 180 g of glucose to $CO_2$ and $H_2O$.

The ThOD of $108.75 \text{ mg} \cdot \text{L}^{-1}$ of glucose is

$$(108.75 \text{ mg} \cdot \text{L}^{-1} \text{ of glucose})\left( \frac{192 \text{ g} \cdot \text{mol}^{-1} O_2}{180 \text{ g} \cdot \text{mol}^{-1} \text{ glucose}} \right) = 116 \text{ mg} \cdot \text{L}^{-1} O_2$$

In contrast to the ThOD, the **chemical oxygen demand,** COD (pronounced "see oh dee"), is a measured quantity that does not depend on one's knowledge of the chemical composition of the substances in the water. In the COD test, a strong chemical oxidizing agent (chromic acid) is mixed with a water sample and then refluxed. The difference between the amount of oxidizing agent at the beginning of the test and that remaining at the end is used to calculate the COD.

If the oxidation of an organic compound is carried out by microorganisms using the organic matter as a food source, the oxygen consumed is known as **biochemical oxygen demand,** or BOD (pronounced "bee oh dee"). The test is a bioassay that uses microorganisms in conditions similar to those in natural water to measure indirectly the amount of biodegradable organic matter present. **Bioassay** means to measure by biological means. The actual BOD is almost always less than the ThOD due to the incorporation of some of the carbon into new bacterial cells. Thus, a portion of soluble carbon is removed but will not be measured in the BOD test.

To measure the BOD of a water, a water sample is inoculated with bacteria that consume the biodegradable organic matter to obtain energy for their life processes. Because the organisms also use oxygen in the process of consuming the waste, the process is called **aerobic decomposition.** This oxygen consumption is easily measured. The greater the amount of organic matter present, the greater the amount of oxygen used. The BOD test is an indirect measurement of organic matter because we actually measure only the change in dissolved oxygen concentration caused by the microorganisms as they degrade the organic matter. Although not all organic matter is biodegradable and the actual test procedures lack precision, the BOD test is still the most widely used method of measuring organic matter because of the direct conceptual relationship between BOD and oxygen depletion in receiving waters.

Only under rare circumstances will the ThOD and the COD be equal. If the chemical composition of all of the substances in the water is known and they are capable of being completely oxidized chemically, then the two measures of oxygen demand will be the same. A waste containing only simple sugars would fall into this category. The BOD is never equal to the ThOD or COD because some carbon is always converted to biomass or waste organic compounds and this soluble organic matter, which is removed during the test, is not measured, as discussed earlier.

When a water sample containing degradable organic matter is placed in a closed container and inoculated with bacteria, the oxygen consumption typically follows the pattern shown in Figure 8–2. During the first few days the rate of oxygen depletion is rapid because of the high concentration of organic matter present. As the concentration of organic matter decreases, so does the rate of oxygen consumption. During the last part of the BOD curve, oxygen consumption is mostly associated with the decay of the bacteria that grew during the early part of the test. It is generally assumed that the rate at which oxygen is consumed is directly proportional to the concentration of degradable organic matter remaining at any time. As a result, the BOD curve in

**FIGURE 8–2**

BOD and oxygen-equivalent relationships.

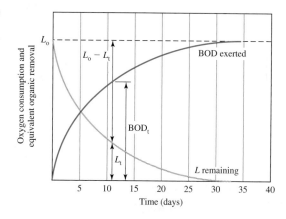

Figure 8–2 can be described mathematically as a first-order reaction. Using our definition of reaction rate and reaction order from Chapter 3, this may be expressed as

$$\frac{dL}{dt} = -r_A \tag{8-1}$$

where $L$ = oxygen equivalent of the organic chemicals remaining (in $mg \cdot L^{-1}$)

$-r_A = -kL$

$k$ = reaction rate constant (in $days^{-1}$)

Rearranging Equation 8–1 and integrating yields

$$\frac{dL}{L} = -k\,dt \tag{8-2}$$

$$\int_{L_0}^{L_t} \frac{dL}{L} = -k \int_0^t dt \tag{8-3}$$

$$\ln \frac{L_t}{L_0} = -kt \tag{8-4}$$

or

$$L_t = L_0 e^{-kt} \tag{8-5}$$

where $L_0$ = oxygen equivalent of organics at time = 0.

$L_t$ = oxygen equivalent of the organic chemicals remaining at time, $t$ ($mg \cdot L^{-1}$)

Rather than $L_t$, our interest is in the amount of oxygen used in the consumption of the organics ($BOD_t$). From Figure 8–2, it is obvious that $BOD_t$ is the difference between the initial value of $L_0$ and $L_t$, so

$$BOD_t = L_0 - L_t$$
$$= L_0 - L_0 e^{-kt}$$
$$= L_0(1 - e^{-kt}) \tag{8-6}$$

$L_0$ is often referred to as the **ultimate** BOD, that is, the maximum oxygen consumption possible when the waste has been completely degraded. Equation 8–6 is called the BOD rate equation. Note that lowercase $k$ is used for the reaction rate constant in base $e$.

---

**EXAMPLE 8–2**  If the 3-day BOD ($BOD_3$) of a waste is 75 $mg \cdot L^{-1}$ and the BOD decay constant, $k$, is 0.345 $day^{-1}$, what is the ultimate BOD?

Solution  Substitute the given values into Equation 8–6 and solve for the ultimate BOD, $L_0$.

$$75 = L_0(1 - e^{-(0.345\ days^{-1})(3\ days)}) = 0.645 L_0$$

or

$$L_0 = \frac{75}{0.645} = 116\ mg \cdot L^{-1}$$

---

You should note that the ultimate BOD ($L_0$) is defined as the maximum BOD exerted by the waste. It is denoted by the horizontal dotted line in Figure 8–2. Because $BOD_t$ approaches $L_0$ asymptotically, it is difficult to assign an exact time to achieve the ultimate BOD. Indeed, based on Equation 8–1, it is achieved only in the limit as $t$ approaches infinity. However, from a practical point of view, we can observe that when the BOD curve is approximately horizontal, the ultimate

| TABLE 8–2 | Typical Values for the BOD Rate Constant | |
| --- | --- | --- |
| | **Sample** | $k(20°C)$ $(day^{-1})$ |
| | Raw sewage | 0.35–0.70 |
| | Well-treated sewage | 0.12–0.23 |
| | Polluted river water | 0.12–0.23 |

BOD has been achieved. In Figure 8–2, we would take this to be at about 35 days. In computations, we use a rule of thumb that if $BOD_t$ and $L_0$ agree when rounded to three significant figures, then the time to reach ultimate BOD has been achieved. Given the uncertainties of the BOD test, there are occasions when rounding to two significant figures would be realistic.

Although the ultimate BOD best expresses the concentration of degradable organic matter, it does not, by itself, indicate how rapidly oxygen will be depleted in a receiving water. Oxygen depletion is related to both the ultimate BOD and the BOD rate constant ($k$). Although the ultimate BOD increases in direct proportion to the concentration of degradable organic matter, the numerical value of the rate constant is dependent on the following:

1. The nature of the waste
2. The ability of the organisms in the system to use the waste
3. The temperature

**Nature of the Waste.** There are thousands of naturally occurring organic compounds, and not all of them can be degraded with equal ease. Simple sugars and starches are rapidly degraded and will therefore have a very large BOD rate constant. Cellulose (for example, toilet paper) degrades much more slowly, and compounds such as the higher molecular weight polycyclic aromatic hydrocarbons, highly chlorinated compounds such as DDT, chlorpyriphos, PCBs, caffeine, or many of the estrogenic compounds used in birth control pills are almost undegradable in the BOD test or in conventional wastewater treatment. In some cases, as with many of the phenolic compounds, the compound is actually toxic to the microorganisms, killing them so that little or no degradation of the waste can occur. Other compounds are intermediate between these extremes. The BOD rate constant for a complex waste depends very much on the relative proportions of the various components. Table 8–2 is a summary of typical BOD rate constants. The lower rate constants for treated sewage compared with raw sewage result from the fact that easily degradable organics are more completely removed than less readily degradable organics during wastewater treatment.

**Ability of Organisms to Use Waste.** Any given microorganism is limited in its ability to use organic compounds. As a consequence, many organic compounds can be degraded by only a small group of microorganisms. In a natural environment receiving a continuous discharge of organic waste, that population of organisms that can most efficiently use this waste will predominate. However, the culture used to inoculate the sample used in the BOD test may contain only a very small number of organisms that can degrade the particular organic compounds in the waste. This problem is especially common when analyzing industrial wastes. The result is that the BOD rate constant would be lower in the laboratory test than in the natural water. To avoid this undesirable outcome the BOD test should be conducted with organisms that have been acclimated* to the waste so that the rate constant determined in the laboratory is comparable to that in the river.

---

*The word *acclimated* means that the organisms have had time to adapt their metabolisms to the waste or that organisms that can use the waste have been given the chance to predominate in the culture.

**Temperature.** Most biological processes speed up as the temperature increases and slow down as the temperature drops. Because oxygen use is caused by the metabolism of microorganisms, the rate of its use is similarly affected by temperature. Ideally, the BOD rate constant should be experimentally determined for the temperature of the receiving water. There are two difficulties with this ideal. Often the temperature of the receiving water changes throughout the year, so a large number of tests would be required to define $k$. An additional difficulty is the task of comparing data from various locations having different temperatures. Laboratory testing is therefore done at a standard temperature of 20°C, and the BOD rate constant is adjusted to the temperature of the receiving water using the following expression.

$$k_T = k_{20}(\theta)^{T-20} \qquad\qquad\qquad (8\text{--}7)$$

where $T$ = temperature of interest (in °C)

$\qquad k_T$ = BOD rate constant at the temperature of interest (in days$^{-1}$)

$\qquad k_{20}$ = BOD rate constant determined at 20°C (in days$^{-1}$)

$\qquad \theta$ = temperature coefficient [13]. For typical domestic wastewater, this has a value of 1.135 for temperatures between 4 and 20°C and 1.056 for temperatures between 20 and 30°C.

---

**EXAMPLE 8-3**    A waste is being discharged into a river that has a temperature of 10°C. What fraction of the maximum oxygen consumption has occurred in 4 days if the BOD rate constant, $k$, determined in the laboratory under standard conditions is 0.115 day$^{-1}$ (*Note:* All rate constants are base $e$.)?

**Solution**    Determine the BOD rate constant, $k$, for the waste at the river temperature using Equation 8–7.

$$k_{10°C} = 0.115(1.135)^{10-20}$$

$$= 0.032 \text{ day}^{-1}$$

Use this value of $k$ in Equation 8–6 to find the fraction of maximum oxygen consumption occurring in 4 days.

$$\frac{BOD_4}{L_0} = [1 - e^{-(0.032 \text{ days}^{-1})(4 \text{ days})}]$$

$$= 0.12$$

---

### Laboratory Measurement of Biochemical Oxygen Demand

To be as consistent as possible, it is important to standardize testing procedures when measuring BOD. In the paragraphs that follow, the standard BOD test is outlined with emphasis placed on the reason for each step rather than the details. The detailed procedures can be found in *Standard Methods for the Examination of Water and Wastewater* [14], which is the authoritative reference of testing procedures in the water pollution control field.

**Step 1.** A special 300-mL BOD bottle (Figure 8–3) is completely filled with a sample of water that has been appropriately diluted and inoculated with microorganisms. The bottle is then stoppered to exclude air bubbles. Samples require dilution because the only oxygen available to the organisms is dissolved in the water. The most oxygen that can dissolve is about 9 mg $\cdot$ L$^{-1}$, so the BOD of the diluted sample should be between 2 and 6 mg $\cdot$ L$^{-1}$. Samples are diluted with a special dilution water that contains all of the trace elements required for bacterial metabolism so that degradation of the organic matter is not limited by lack of bacterial growth. The dilution water also contains an inoculum of microorganisms so that all samples tested on a given day contain approximately the same type and number of microorganisms.

## FIGURE 8-3

### BOD Bottles

The point on the end of the stopper is to ensure that no air is trapped in the bottle. The bottle in the center is shown with the stopper in place. Water is placed in the small cup formed by the lip. This acts as a seal to further exclude air. The bottle on the right is shown with plastic wrap over the stopper. This is to prevent evaporation of the water seal. (*Photo courtesy of Harley Seeley of the Instructional Media Center, Michigan State University.*)

The ratio of undiluted to diluted sample is called the **sample size,** usually expressed as a percentage, while the inverse relationship is called the **dilution factor.** Mathematically, these are

$$\text{Sample size } (\%) = \frac{\text{volume of undiluted sample}}{\text{volume of diluted sample}} \times 100 \tag{8-8}$$

$$\text{Dilution factor} = P = \frac{\text{volume of wastewater sample}}{\text{volume of wastewater plus dilution water}} \tag{8-9}$$

The appropriate sample size to use can be determined by dividing $4 \text{ mg} \cdot \text{L}^{-1}$ (the midpoint of the desired range of diluted BOD) by the estimated BOD concentration in the sample being tested. A convenient volume of undiluted sample is then chosen to approximate this sample size. The dilution factors given earlier are not to be used when the sample size is small compared with the total volume because under such conditions the seed/dilution water will contribute significantly to the BOD. For low dilutions, the more complex equation given in Equation 8-10a should be used.

**EXAMPLE 8-4**

The BOD of a wastewater sample is estimated to be $180 \text{ mg} \cdot \text{L}^{-1}$. What volume of undiluted sample should be added to a 300-mL bottle? Also, what are the sample size and dilution factor using this volume? Assume that $4 \text{ mg} \cdot \text{L}^{-1}$ BOD can be consumed in the BOD bottle.

**Solution 1**

Estimate the sample size needed.

$$\text{Sample size} = \frac{4 \text{ mg} \cdot \text{L}^{-1}}{180 \text{ mg} \cdot \text{L}^{-1}} \times 100 = 2.22\%$$

Estimate the volume of undiluted sample needed because the volume of diluted sample is 300 mL.

Volume of undiluted sample $= 0.0222 \times 300 \text{ mL} = 6.66 \text{ mL}$

Therefore a convenient sample volume would be 7.00 mL.

Compute the actual sample size and dilution factor.

$$\text{Sample size} = \frac{7.00 \text{ mL}}{300 \text{ mL}} \times 100 = 2.33\%$$

$$\text{Dilution factor} = P = \frac{7 \text{ mL}}{300 \text{ mL}} = 0.0233$$

**Solution 2** Although environmental engineers have traditionally used this approach for determining dilution factors for BOD analysis, we could use a more fundamental approach: that of the mass-balance equation (which is inherently what was done in Solution 1). Let's, think about what we are attempting to do. We have a BOD bottle to which we add wastewater and dilution water. The wastewater has an estimated BOD of 180 mg $\cdot$ L$^{-1}$, and the dilution water has a BOD of zero.

The total volume in the BOD bottle is $\Psi_{ww} + \Psi_{dw}$ or the volume of the wastewater plus the volume of the dilution water. The total mass of BOD in the BOD bottle can be calculated from

$$\text{BOD}_{ww} \times \Psi_{ww} + \text{BOD}_{dw} \times \Psi_{ww} = (180 \text{ mg} \cdot \text{L}^{-1})(\Psi_{ww}) + (0 \text{ mg} \cdot \text{L}^{-1})(\Psi_{dw})$$

We also know that the size of a BOD bottle is 300 mL, so that

$$\Psi_{dw} + \Psi_{ww} = 300 \text{ mL} = 0.300 \text{ L}$$

The problem statement indicates that we want a final concentration of BOD of 4 mg $\cdot$ L$^{-1}$. Thus, the final mass of BOD in the bottle is

$$(4 \text{ mg} \cdot \text{L}^{-1})(0.300 \text{ L}) = 1.2 \text{ mg}$$

If we equate this to the total BOD we calculated earlier, then

$$\text{BOD}_{ww} \times \Psi_{ww} + \text{BOD}_{dw} \times \Psi_{ww} = (180 \text{ mg} \cdot \text{L}^{-1})(\Psi_{ww}) + (0 \text{ mg} \cdot \text{L}^{-1})(\Psi_{dw}) = 1.2 \text{ mg}$$

We can solve for $\Psi_{ww} = 1.2$ mg/180 mg $\cdot$ L$^{-1} = 0.00667$ L. Let's multiply this value by 1000 to obtain the answer in milliliters because that is the more appropriate answer: 6.67 mL. This is the same answer we obtained earlier. Again, as stated there, when actually performing a BOD analysis, you would choose a volume that is easier to dispense, such as 7.00 mL.

**Step 2.** Blank samples containing only the inoculated dilution water are also placed in BOD bottles and stoppered. Blanks are required to estimate the amount of oxygen consumed by the added inoculum in the absence of the sample.

**Step 3.** The stoppered BOD bottles containing diluted samples and blanks are incubated in the dark at 20°C for the desired number of days. For most purposes, a standard time of 5 days is used. To determine the ultimate BOD and the BOD rate constant, additional times are used. The samples are incubated in the dark to prevent photosynthesis from adding oxygen to the water and invalidating the oxygen consumption results. As mentioned earlier, the BOD test is conducted at a standard temperature of 20°C so that the effect of temperature on the BOD rate constant is eliminated and results from different laboratories can be compared.

**Step 4.** After the desired number of days has elapsed, the samples and blanks are removed from the incubator and the dissolved oxygen concentration in each bottle is measured. The BOD of the undiluted sample is then calculated using the following equation:

$$BOD_t = \frac{(DO_{b,t} - DO_{s,t})}{P}$$ (8-10)

where $DO_{b,t}$ = dissolved oxygen concentration in blank (blank) after $t$ days of incubation
   (in $mg \cdot L^{-1}$)
   $DO_{s,t}$ = dissolved oxygen concentration in sample after $t$ days of incubation
   (in $mg \cdot L^{-1}$)
   $P$ = dilution factor

The preceding equation is valid only when the BOD of the seed water or the dilution water is negligible. If the BOD of the dilution or seed water is significant, then the following equation must be used.

$$BOD_t = \frac{(DO_{s,i} - DO_{s,t}) - (DO_{b,i} - DO_{b,t})f}{P}$$ (8-10a)

where $DO_{b,t}$ and $DO_{s,t}$ are defined earlier and
   $DO_{s,i}$ = the initial DO of the sample
   $DO_{b,i}$ = the initial DO of the blank (seed) control
   $f$ = ratio of seed in diluted sample to seed in seed control
   = (% seed in diluted sample)/(% seed in seed control)
   = (volume of seed in diluted sample)/(volume of seed in seed control)

**EXAMPLE 8-5** What is the $BOD_5$ of the wastewater sample of Example 8-4 if the DO values for the blank and diluted sample after 5 days are 8.7 and 4.2 $mg \cdot L^{-1}$, respectively?

Solution  Substitute the appropriate values into Equation 8-10.

$$BOD_5 = \frac{8.7 - 4.2}{0.0233} = 204.5, \text{ or } 205 \ mg \cdot L^{-1}.$$

Note that because the sample was not seeded $f = 1$.

### Additional Notes on Biochemical Oxygen Demand

Although the 5-day BOD has been chosen as the standard value for most wastewater analysis and for regulatory purposes, ultimate BOD is actually a better indicator of total waste strength. For any one type of waste having a defined BOD rate constant, the ratio between ultimate BOD and $BOD_5$ is constant so that $BOD_5$ indicates relative waste strength. For different types of wastes having the same $BOD_5$, the ultimate BOD is the same only if, by chance, the BOD rate constants are the same. This is illustrated in Figure 8-4 for a municipal wastewater having a $k = 0.345 \ day^{-1}$ and an industrial wastewater having a $k = 0.115 \ day^{-1}$. Although both wastewaters have a $BOD_5$ of 200 $mg \cdot L^{-1}$, the industrial wastewater has a much higher ultimate BOD and can be expected to have a greater effect on dissolved oxygen in a river. For the industrial wastewater, a smaller fraction of the BOD was exerted in the first 5 days due to the lower rate constant.

**FIGURE 8–4**

The effect of $k$ on ultimate BOD for two wastewaters having the same BOD$_5$.

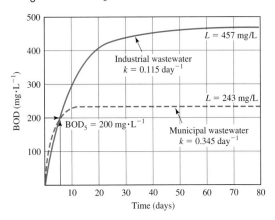

**FIGURE 8–5**

The effect of $k$ on BOD$_5$ when the ultimate BOD is constant.

Proper interpretation of BOD$_5$ values can also be illustrated in another way. Consider a sample of polluted river water for which the following values were determined using standard laboratory techniques: BOD$_5$ = 50 mg · L$^{-1}$, and $k$ = 0.2615 day$^{-1}$. The ultimate BOD calculated from Equation 8–6 is, therefore, 68 mg · L$^{-1}$. However, because the river temperature is 10°C, the $k$ value in the river is calculated to be 0.0737 day$^{-1}$ (using Equation 8–7). As shown graphically in Figure 8–5, the laboratory value of BOD$_5$ seriously overestimates the actual oxygen consumption in the river. Again, a smaller fraction of the BOD is exerted in 5 days when the BOD rate constant is lower.

The 5-day BOD was chosen as the standard value for most purposes because the test was devised by sanitary engineers in England, where the River Thames has a travel time to the sea of less than 5 days, so there was no need to consider oxygen demand at longer times. Because no other time is any more rational than 5 days, this value has become firmly entrenched in the profession.

### Nitrogen Oxidation

Until now our unstated assumption has been that only the carbon in organic matter is oxidized. Actually many organic compounds, such as proteins, also contain nitrogen that can be oxidized with the consumption of molecular oxygen. Because the mechanisms and rates of nitrogen oxidation are distinctly different from those of carbon oxidation, the two processes must be considered separately. Logically, oxygen consumption due to oxidation of carbon is called **carbonaceous BOD** (CBOD), and that due to nitrogen oxidation is called **nitrogenous BOD** (NBOD).

The organisms that oxidize the carbon in organic compounds to obtain energy cannot oxidize the nitrogen in these compounds. Instead, the nitrogen is released into the surrounding water as ammonia (NH$_3$). At normal pH values, this ammonia is actually in the form of the ammonium cation (NH$_4^+$). The ammonia released from organic compounds, plus that from other sources such as industrial wastes and agricultural runoff (i.e., fertilizers), is oxidized to nitrate (NO$_3^-$) by a special group of nitrifying bacteria as their source of energy in a process called **nitrification.** The overall reaction for ammonia oxidation is

(*nitrification*)

$$NH_4^+ + 2O_2 \xrightarrow{\text{microorganisms}} NO_3^- + H_2O + 2H^+ \qquad (8\text{–}11)$$

From this reaction the theoretical NBOD can be calculated as follows:

$$NBOD = \frac{\text{grams of oxygen used}}{\text{grams of nitrogen oxidized}} = \frac{(2 \text{ moles})(32 \text{ g O}_2 \cdot \text{mol}^{-1})}{(1 \text{ mole})(14 \text{ g N} \cdot \text{mol}^{-1})}$$

$$= 4.57 \text{ g O}_2 \cdot \text{g}^{-1} \text{ N} \qquad (8\text{–}12)$$

The actual nitrogenous BOD is slightly less than the theoretical value due to the incorporation of some of the nitrogen into new bacterial cells, but the difference is only a few percent.

Because nitrogen can be present in numerous forms ($NH_3$, $NH_4^+$, $NO_3^-$, $NO_2^-$ and various organic compounds), it is often convenient to report concentrations of nitrogenous compounds in units of milligrams per liter as N. For example, it is often convenient for environmental engineers to report ammonia concentrations as "ammonia nitrogen," that is as $NH_3$–N.

**EXAMPLE 8–6**   (a) Compute the theoretical NBOD of a wastewater containing $30 \text{ mg} \cdot L^{-1}$ of ammonia as nitrogen.
(b) If the wastewater analysis was reported as $30 \text{ mg} \cdot L^{-1}$ of ammonia ($NH_3$), what would the theoretical NBOD be?

**Solution**   In the first part of the problem, the amount of ammonia was reported as $NH_3$–N. Therefore, we can use the theoretical relationship developed from Equation 8–11.

$$\text{Theoretical NBOD} = (30 \text{ mg NH}_3\text{–N} \cdot L^{-1})(4.57 \text{ mg O}_2 \cdot \text{mg}^{-1} \text{ N}) = 137 \text{ mg O}_2 \cdot L^{-1}$$

To answer part (b), we must convert milligrams per liter of ammonia to milligrams per liter as $NH_3$–N by multiplying by the ratio of gram molecular weights of N to $NH_3$.

$$(30 \text{ mg NH}_3 \cdot L^{-1})\left(\frac{14 \text{ g N} \cdot \text{mol}^{-1}}{17 \text{ g NH}_3 \cdot \text{mol}^{-1}}\right) = 24.7 \text{ mg N} \cdot L^{-1}$$

Now we may use the relationship developed from Equation 8–11.

$$\text{Theoretical NBOD} = (24.7 \text{ mg N} \cdot L^{-1})\left(\frac{4.57 \text{ mg O}_2}{\text{mg N}}\right) = 113 \text{ mg O}_2 \cdot L^{-1}$$

The rate at which the NBOD is exerted depends heavily on the number of nitrifying organisms present. Few of these organisms occur in untreated sewage, but the concentration is high in a well-treated effluent. When samples of untreated and treated sewage are subjected to the BOD test, oxygen consumption follows the pattern shown in Figure 8–6. In the case of untreated sewage, the NBOD is exerted after much of the CBOD has been exerted. The lag is due to the time it takes for the nitrifying bacteria to reach a sufficient population for the amount of NBOD exertion to be significant compared with that of the CBOD. In the case of the treated sewage, a higher population of nitrifying organisms in the sample reduces the lag time. Once nitrification begins, however, the NBOD can be described by Equation 8–6 with a BOD rate constant comparable to that for the CBOD of a well-treated effluent ($k = 0.08$ to $0.2 \text{ day}^{-1}$). Because the lag before the nitrogenous BOD is highly variable, $BOD_5$ values are often difficult to interpret. When

**FIGURE 8–6**

BOD curves showing both carbonaceous (CBOD) and nitrogenous (NBOD) BOD.

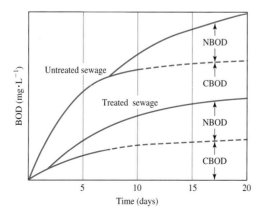

measurement of only carbonaceous BOD is desired, chemical inhibitors are added to stop the nitrification process. The rate constant for nitrification is also affected by temperature and can be adjusted using Equation 8–7.

### DO Sag Curve

The concentration of dissolved oxygen in a river is an indicator of the general health of the river. All rivers have some capacity for self-purification. As long as the discharge of oxygen-demanding wastes is well within the self-purification capacity, the DO level will remain high, and a diverse population of plants and animals, including game fish, can be found. As the amount of waste increases, the self-purification capacity can be exceeded, causing detrimental changes in plant and animal life. The stream loses its ability to cleanse itself, and the DO level decreases. When the DO drops below about 4 to 5 mg · L$^{-1}$, most game fish will have been driven out. If the DO is completely removed, fish and other higher animals are killed or driven out, and extremely noxious conditions result. The water becomes blackish and foul-smelling as the sewage and dead animal life decompose under anaerobic conditions (i.e., without oxygen).

One of the major tools of water quality management in rivers is assessing the capability of a stream to absorb a waste load. This is done by determining the profile of DO concentration downstream from a waste discharge. This profile is called the DO sag curve (Figure 8–7) because the DO concentration dips as oxygen-demanding materials are oxidized and then rises again further downstream as the oxygen is replenished from the atmosphere and photosynthesis. As depicted in Figure 8–8, the biota of the stream are often a reflection of the dissolved oxygen conditions in the stream.

To develop a mathematical expression for the DO sag curve, the sources of oxygen and the factors affecting oxygen depletion must be identified and quantified. The only significant sources of oxygen are reaeration from the atmosphere and photosynthesis of aquatic plants. Oxygen depletion is caused by a larger range of factors, the most important being the BOD, both carbonaceous and nitrogenous, of the waste discharge, and the BOD already in the river upstream of the waste discharge. The second most important factor is that the DO in the waste discharge is usually less than that in the river. Thus, the DO at the river is often reduced as soon as the waste is added, even before any BOD is exerted. Other factors affecting dissolved oxygen depletion include nonpoint source pollution, the respiration of organisms living in the sediments (**benthic demand**), and the respiration of aquatic plants. Following the classical approach, the DO sag equation will be developed by considering only initial DO reduction, ultimate BOD, and reaeration from the atmosphere.

**Mass-Balance Approach.** Simplified mass balances help us understand and solve the DO sag curve problem. Three conservative (those without chemical reaction) mass balances may be used to account for initial mixing of the waste stream and the river. DO, ultimate BOD, and

**FIGURE 8–7**

Typical DO sag curve.

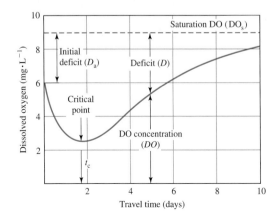

## FIGURE 8-8

Oxygen sag downstream of an organic source. (*Source: U.S. EPA.*)

## FIGURE 8-9

Schematic diagram of the mixing of the waste stream.

## FIGURE 8-10

Mass-balance diagram for BOD and DO mixing.

temperature all change as the result of mixing of the waste stream and the river. Once these are accounted for, the DO sag curve may be viewed as a nonconservative mass balance, that is, one with reactions. We can illustrate the mixing of the waste stream and the transport of the waste using the schematic diagram in Figure 8–9.

Through the discharge pipe, the waste stream flows into the river. The rectangle across the river at the location of the discharge pipe becomes the control volume around which we will develop our mass-balance expression. We will assume that the pollutant discharged from the pipe remains in this control volume and the entire volume moves downstream as a single entity. At time zero the volume is located at the pipe. The diagram illustrates the location of the volume at two subsequent times. For this case, we have two inputs and one output. The conservative mass-balance diagram for oxygen (mixing only) is shown in Figure 8–10. The product of the water flow and the DO concentration yields a mass of oxygen per unit of time.

$$\text{Mass of DO in wastewater} = Q_w \text{DO}_w \tag{8–13}$$

$$\text{Mass of DO in river} = Q_r \text{DO}_r \tag{8–14}$$

where $Q_w$ = volumetric flow rate of wastewater (in $\text{m}^3 \cdot \text{s}^{-1}$)
$Q_r$ = volumetric flow rate of the river (in $\text{m}^3 \cdot \text{s}^{-1}$)
$\text{DO}_w$ = dissolved oxygen concentration in the wastewater (in $\text{g} \cdot \text{m}^{-3}$)
$\text{DO}_r$ = dissolved oxygen concentration in the river (in $\text{g} \cdot \text{m}^{-3}$)

The mass of DO in the river after mixing equals the sum of the mass fluxs.

$$\text{Mass of DO after mixing} = Q_w DO_w + Q_r DO_r \qquad (8\text{--}15)$$

In a similar fashion for ultimate BOD,

$$\text{Mass of BOD after mixing} = Q_w L_w + Q_r L_r \qquad (8\text{--}16)$$

where $L_w$ = ultimate BOD of the wastewater (in mg $\cdot$ L$^{-1}$)
$\quad\quad\quad L_r$ = ultimate BOD of the river (in mg $\cdot$ L$^{-1}$)

The concentrations of DO and BOD after mixing are the respective masses per unit time divided by the total flow rate (i.e., the sum of the wastewater and river flows).

$$DO = \frac{Q_w DO_w + Q_r DO_r}{Q_w + Q_r} \qquad (8\text{--}17)$$

$$L_a = \frac{Q_w L_w + Q_r L_r}{Q_w + Q_r} \qquad (8\text{--}18)$$

where $L_a$ = initial ultimate BOD after mixing.

**EXAMPLE 8–7**  The town of Viracocha discharges 17,360 m$^3$ $\cdot$ day$^{-1}$ of treated wastewater into the Pachacamac Creek. The treated wastewater has a BOD$_5$ of 12 mg $\cdot$ L$^{-1}$ and a BOD decay constant, $k$, of 0.12 day$^{-1}$ at 20°C. Pachacamac Creek has a flow rate of 0.43 m$^3$ $\cdot$ s$^{-1}$ and an ultimate BOD, $L_0$, of 5.0 mg $\cdot$ L$^{-1}$. The DO of the river is 6.5 mg $\cdot$ L$^{-1}$ and the DO of the wastewater is 1.0 mg $\cdot$ L$^{-1}$. Compute the DO and initial ultimate BOD, $L_0$, after mixing.

Solution  The DO after mixing is given by Equation 8–17. To use this equation we must convert the wastewater flow to compatible units, that is, to cubic meters per second.

$$Q_w = \frac{(17,360 \text{ m}^3 \cdot \text{day}^{-1})}{(86,400 \text{ s} \cdot \text{day}^{-1})} = 0.20 \text{ m}^3 \cdot \text{s}^{-1}$$

The DO after mixing is then

$$DO = \frac{(0.20 \text{ m}^3 \cdot \text{s}^{-1})(1.0 \text{ mg} \cdot \text{L}^{-1}) + (0.43 \text{ m}^3 \cdot \text{s}^{-1})(6.5 \text{ mg} \cdot \text{L}^{-1})}{0.20 \text{ m}^3 \cdot \text{s}^{-1} + 0.43 \text{ m}^3 \cdot \text{s}^{-1}} = 4.75 \text{ mg} \cdot \text{L}^{-1}$$

Before we can determine the initial ultimate BOD after mixing, we must first determine the ultimate BOD of the wastewater. Solving Equation 8–6 for the ultimate BOD, $L_0$:

$$L_0 = \frac{BOD_5}{(1 - e^{-kt})} = \frac{12 \text{ mg} \cdot \text{L}^{-1}}{(1 - e^{-(0.12 \text{ day}^{-1})(5 \text{ days})})} = \frac{12 \text{ mg} \cdot \text{L}^{-1}}{(1 - 0.55)} = 26.6 \text{ mg} \cdot \text{L}^{-1}$$

Note that we used the subscript of 5 days in BOD$_5$ to determine the value of $t$ in the equation. Now setting $L_w = L_0$, we can determine the initial ultimate BOD after mixing, $L_a$, using Equation 8–18.

$$L_a = \frac{(0.20 \text{ m}^3 \cdot \text{s}^{-1})(26.6 \text{ mg} \cdot \text{L}^{-1}) + (0.43 \text{ m}^3 \cdot \text{s}^{-1})(5.0 \text{ mg} \cdot \text{L}^{-1})}{0.20 \text{ m}^3 \cdot \text{s}^{-1} + 0.43 \text{ m}^3 \cdot \text{s}^{-1}} = 11.86, \text{ or } 12 \text{ mg} \cdot \text{L}^{-1}$$

For temperature, we must consider a heat balance rather than a mass balance. This is an application of a fundamental principle of physics:

$$\text{Loss of heat by hot bodies} = \text{gain of heat by cold bodies} \qquad (8\text{–}19)$$

The **change in enthalpy** or "heat content" of a mass of a substance may be defined by the following equation:

$$H = mC_p\Delta T \qquad (8\text{–}20)$$

where $H$ = change in enthalpy (in J)
$m$ = mass of substance (in g)
$C_p$ = specific heat at constant pressure (in $J \cdot g^{-1} \cdot K^{-1}$)
$\Delta T$ = change in temperature (in K)

The specific heat of water varies slightly with temperature. For natural waters, a value of 4.19 will be a satisfactory approximation. Using our fundamental heat loss = heat gain equation, we may write

$$(m_w)(4.19)\Delta T_w = (m_r)(4.19)\Delta T_r \qquad (8\text{–}21)$$

The temperature after mixing is found by solving this equation for the final temperature by recognizing that $\Delta T$ on each side of the equation is the difference between the final river temperature ($T_f$) and the starting temperature of the wastewater and the river water, respectively.

$$T_f = \frac{Q_w T_w + Q_r T_r}{Q_w + Q_r} \qquad (8\text{–}22)$$

**Oxygen Deficit.**   The DO sag equation has been developed using oxygen deficit rather than dissolved oxygen concentration, to make it easier to solve the integral equation that results from the mathematical description of the mass balance. The oxygen deficit is the difference between the saturation value (at the particular temperature of the water) and the actual dissolved oxygen concentration

$$D = DO_s - DO \qquad (8\text{–}23)$$

where $D$ = oxygen deficit (in $mg \cdot L^{-1}$)
$DO_s$ = saturation concentration of dissolved oxygen (in $mg \cdot L^{-1}$)
$DO$ = actual concentration of dissolved oxygen (in $mg \cdot L^{-1}$)

The saturation value of dissolved oxygen is heavily dependent on water temperature; it decreases as the temperature increases. Values of $DO_s$ for freshwater are given in Table A–2 of Appendix A.

**Initial Deficit.**   The beginning of the DO sag curve occurs at the point where a waste discharge mixes with the river. The initial deficit is calculated as the difference between saturated DO and the concentration of the DO after mixing (Equation 8–17).

$$D_a = DO_s - \frac{Q_w DO_w + Q_r DO_r}{Q_{mix}} \qquad (8\text{–}24)$$

where $D_a$ = initial deficit after river and waste have mixed (in $mg \cdot L^{-1}$)
$DO_s$ = saturation concentration of dissolved oxygen at the temperature of the river after mixing (in $mg \cdot L^{-1}$)

**EXAMPLE 8–8**   Calculate the initial deficit of the Pachacamac Creek after mixing with the wastewater from the town of Viracocha (see Example 8–7 for data). The stream temperature is 10°C, and the wastewater temperature is 10°C.

Solution   With the stream temperature, the saturation value of dissolved oxygen ($DO_s$) can be determined from the table in Appendix A. At 10°C, $DO_s = 11.33$ mg $\cdot$ L$^{-1}$. Because we calculated the concentration of DO after mixing as 4.75 mg $\cdot$ L$^{-1}$ in Example 8–7, the initial deficit after mixing is

$$D_a = DO_s - DO_{mix} = 11.33 \text{ mg} \cdot \text{L}^{-1} - 4.75 \text{ mg} \cdot \text{L}^{-1} = 6.58 \text{ mg} \cdot \text{L}^{-1}$$

Because wastewater commonly has a higher temperature than river water, especially during the winter, the river temperature downstream of the discharge is usually higher than that upstream. Because we are interested in downstream conditions, it is important to use the downstream temperature when determining the saturation concentration of dissolved oxygen.

**DO Sag Equation.**   Numerous models have been developed to describe the change in BOD in a river or stream with distance (or time) from a wastewater outfall. The level of complexity of these models varies greatly. The simplest model and the basis for all other models is the classical Streeter–Phelps model [15]. This model assumes that

1. The river is completely and uniformly mixed in the horizontal direction across the river, and in the vertical direction with depth.
2. There is no dispersion of the pollutant as it moves downstream as shown in Figure 8–11.

This means that in the three-dimensional section shown in Figure 8–11 as box A, the chemical (e.g., DO and BOD) is completely mixed and that the concentration of the chemical is the same in all locations in the box. The assumption that no dispersion takes place means that each rectangular cross-section moves down the stream as a packet. The shape of this packet does not change with distance downstream.

The Streeter–Phelps model has essentially two reaction terms: reaeration and deoxygenation. Reaeration describes the rate at which oxygen is replenished and is a function of the stream properties. As you might expect, the greater the turbulence, the more rapids, the greater the rate of reaeration. Reaeration will also depend on the oxygen deficit. The greater the oxygen deficit, the greater the reaeration rate. Thus, the rate at which oxygen is transferred from the air into the stream or river (reaeration) is linearly proportional to the dissolved oxygen deficit (the difference between the concentration of dissolved oxygen in the water and the solubility of oxygen in water at that temperature). The kinetics and modeling of oxygen dissolution are discussed in Chapter 2, Reaction Kinetics. Thus,

Rate of reaeration $= k_r(DO_s - DO) = k_r D$ (8–25)

where $k_r =$ the reaeration coefficient (in time$^{-1}$)
   $DO_s =$ the dissolved oxygen concentration at saturation (in mass $\cdot$ volume$^{-1}$)
   $D =$ DO deficit $= (DO_s - DO)$

**FIGURE 8–11**

Cross section of stream flow. Each rhomboid represents the location of a control volume as it moves downstream in the river.

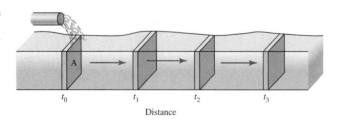

The reaeration coefficient is very much dependent on the physical characteristics of the river. The greater the velocity in the stream, the greater the reaeration coefficient will be. O'Connor and Dobbins [16] found that the reaeration coefficient is related to the stream velocity and depth using the following equation.

$$k_r = \frac{3.9u^{1/2}}{h^{3/2}} \tag{8–26}$$

where $k_r$ = the reaeration coefficient at 20°C (day$^{-1}$)
$u$ = the average stream velocity (in m · s$^{-1}$)
$h$ = the average stream depth (in m)

Note the factor of 3.9 is necessary to make the equation dimensionally correct. The units of velocity must be in meters per second, whereas depth must be in meters. Reaeration coefficients, typically, vary from 0.1 for small ponds to > 1.15 for rapids and waterfalls. The reaeration coefficient can be adjusted for temperature changes using the relationship.

$$k_r = k_{r,20}\theta^{(T-20)} \tag{8–27}$$

where $k_{r,20}$ = the reaeration coefficient for a temperature of 20°C
$\theta$ = temperature coefficient (1.024)
$T$ = temperature (in °C)

**EXAMPLE 8–9**    A stream containing no biochemical oxygen demand (this is a hypothetical situation and rarely occurs) has a DO of 5.00 mg · L$^{-1}$ and a flow rate, $Q$, of 8.70 m$^3$ · s$^{-1}$. The temperature of the stream is 18°C. The average velocity in the stream is 0.174 m · s$^{-1}$. The average depth, $H$, of the stream is 5 m. Determine the reaeration coefficient, $k_r$, and the rate of reaeration.

Solution    To solve this problem we must first determine the reaeration coefficient at 20°C, using Equation 8–26.

$$k_r = \frac{3.9u^{1/2}}{h^{3/2}} = \frac{3.9(0.174 \text{ m} \cdot \text{s}^{-1})^{1/2}}{(5.00 \text{ m})^{1.5}}$$

$$= \frac{3.9(0.417)}{11.18} = 0.146 \text{ day}^{-1}$$

We must also take into account the fact that the stream is not at 20°C but at 18°C. Thus we must use the equation

$$k_r = k_{r,20}\theta^{(T-20)} = (0.146)(1.024)^{(18-20)} = 0.139 \text{ day}^{-1}$$

The oxygen deficit is calculated by taking the difference between the saturation value (9.54 mg · L$^{-1}$—from Appendix A–2) and the dissolved oxygen concentration:

$$D = 9.54 - 5.0 = 4.54 \text{ mg} \cdot \text{L}^{-1}$$

Thus, according to Equation 8–25, the rate of reaeration equals

$$(0.139 \text{ day}^{-1})(4.54 \text{ mg} \cdot \text{L}^{-1}) = 0.632 \text{ mg} \cdot \text{L}^{-1} \cdot \text{day}^{-1}$$

Now, let's consider the rate at which DO disappears from the stream as a result of microbial action (M) or what is commonly referred to as the **rate of deoxygenation.** The rate of deoxygenation at any point in the river is assumed to be proportional to the BOD remaining at that point, so that

$$\text{Rate of deoxygenation} = k_d L_t \tag{8-28}$$

where $k_d$ = the deoxygenation rate (time$^{-1}$)

$\quad\quad L_t$ = BOD remaining at some time after the wastes enter the stream (mass · time$^{-1}$)

Most models make the assumption that $k_d$ is equal to the constant, $k$, that is, the rate constant obtained using the BOD test. Thus, using Equation 8–5, we can write Equation 8–28 in terms of the ultimate BOD.

$$\text{Rate of deoxygenation} = k_d L_0 e^{-k_d t} \tag{8-29}$$

(Because the rate of deoxygenation is temperature-dependent, $k_d$ must be corrected for temperature by correcting $k$ for temperature.) Although the assumption that $k = k_d$ is reasonable for deep, slow-moving streams, it is a poor assumption for turbulent, shallow, rapidly moving streams. For such streams:

$$k_d = k + \frac{u}{h}\eta \tag{8-30}$$

where $k$ = BOD rate constant (at 20°C)

$\quad\quad u$ = average velocity of stream flow (in length · time$^{-1}$)

$\quad\quad h$ = average depth of stream (in length)

$\quad\quad \eta$ = bed activity coefficient (ranges from 0.1 for stagnant or deep water to 0.6 for rapidly flowing water)

The deoxygenation coefficient can be corrected for temperature using Equation 8–7 and coefficients used to correct BOD rate constants for temperature.

**EXAMPLE 8-10**   Determine the deoxygenation rate constant for the reach of Pachacamac Creek (Examples 8–7 and 8–8) below the wastewater outfall (discharge pipe). The average speed, $u$, of the stream flow in the creek is 0.03 m · s$^{-1}$. The depth, $h$, is 5.0 m and the bed-activity coefficient, $\eta$, is 0.35. What is the rate of deoxygenation, in units of mg · L$^{-1}$ · day$^{-1}$?

Solution   From Example 8–7, the value of the BOD decay constant, $k$, is 0.12 day$^{-1}$. Using Equation 8–30, the deoxygenation rate constant, $k_d$, at 20°C is

$$k_d = 0.12 \text{ day}^{-1} + \frac{0.03 \text{ m} \cdot \text{s}^{-1}}{5.0 \text{ m}}(0.35) = 0.1221, \text{ or } 0.12 \text{ day}^{-1}$$

Note that the units are not consistent. As we have noted before, empirical expressions, such as that in Equations 8–26 and 8–30, may have implicit conversion factors. Thus, you must be careful to use the same units as those used by the author of the equation.

We also note that the deoxygenation rate constant of 0.1221 day$^{-1}$ is at 20°C. In Example 8–8, we noted that the stream temperature was 10°C. Thus, we must correct the estimated $k_d$ value using Equation 8–7.

$$k_d \text{ at } 10°C = (0.1221 \text{ day}^{-1})(1.135)^{10-20} = (0.1221)(0.2819)$$

$$= 0.03442, \text{ or } 0.034 \text{ day}^{-1}$$

From Example 8–7, we know that the ultimate BOD immediately after mixing, $L_t$, is 12 mg $\cdot$ L$^{-1}$. Then using Equation 8–28, we obtain

Rate of deoxygenation $= k_d L_t$

$$= 0.034 \text{ day}^{-1} \times 12 \text{ mg} \cdot \text{L}^{-1}$$

$$= 0.408 \text{ mg} \cdot \text{L}^{-1} \cdot \text{day}^{-1}$$

The DO sag curve (Streeter–Phelps model) is simply a mass-balance approach to calculating or predicting the DO level downstream in a river. Using the mass-balance approach introduced in Chapter 3, we can develop the sag curve using a one-dimensional general continuity equation for a constituent in water. Here, the constituent is oxygen and the equation is

$$\frac{\partial C}{\partial t} = \bar{D}_x \frac{\partial^2 C}{\partial x^2} - \bar{v}_x \frac{\partial C}{\partial x} + \sum (\text{reactions}) \qquad (8\text{–}31\text{a})$$

where $\bar{v}_x$ = downstream velocity in the $x$ direction
   $\bar{D}_x$ = dispersion coefficient in the $x$ direction

Here we will ignore the dispersion term and impose steady-state conditions. As such, the first two terms of Equation 8–31a drop out, and the equation is reduced to an ordinary differential equation.

$$\bar{v}_x \frac{dC}{dx} = \sum (\text{reactions}) \qquad (8\text{–}31\text{b})$$

We can obtain the reaction terms by combining Equations 8–25 and 8–28 because the oxygen deficit is a function of the competition between oxygen use and reaeration from the atmosphere. Also if we use the notation used previously, that is, $D$ for deficit, we obtain the equation

$$\bar{v}_x \frac{dD}{dx} = k_d L - k_r D \qquad (8\text{–}31\text{c})$$

where $\dfrac{dD}{dx}$ = the change in oxygen deficit ($D$) with respect to unit of distance
(in mg $\cdot$ L$^{-1}$ $\cdot$ day)

   $k_d$ = deoxygenation rate constant (in day$^{-1}$)
   $L$ = ultimate BOD of river water (in mg $\cdot$ L$^{-1}$)
   $k_r$ = reaeration rate constant (in day$^{-1}$)
   $D$ = oxygen deficit in river water (in mg $\cdot$ L$^{-1}$)

Often, environmental engineers and scientists want to represent the previous equation in terms of travel time downstream. This can be easily accomplished if we recognize that

$$\text{Time} = \frac{x}{\bar{v}_x} \qquad (8\text{–}32)$$

Therefore, we can write Equation 8–31c as

$$\frac{dD}{dt} = k_d L - k_r D \qquad (8\text{–}31\text{d})$$

By integrating Equation 8–31d, and using the boundary conditions (at $t = 0$; $D = D_a$ and $L = L_a$; and at $t = t$, $D = D_t$, and $L = L_t$), the DO sag equation is obtained:

$$D_t = \frac{k_d L_a}{k_r - k_d}(e^{-k_d t} - e^{-k_r t}) + D_a(e^{-k_r t}) \tag{8-33}$$

where $D_t$ = oxygen deficit in river water after exertion of BOD for time, $t$ (in mg $\cdot$ L$^{-1}$)
$\quad L_a$ = initial ultimate BOD after river and wastewater have mixed (Equation 8–28)
$\qquad$ (in mg $\cdot$ L$^{-1}$)
$\quad k_d$ = deoxygenation rate constant (in day$^{-1}$)
$\quad k_r$ = reaeration rate constant (in day$^{-1}$)
$\quad t$ = time of travel of wastewater discharge downstream (in days)
$\quad D_a$ = initial deficit after river and wastewater have mixed (Equation 8–24) (in mg $\cdot$ L$^{-1}$)

When $k_r = k_d$, Equation 8–33 reduces to

$$D_t = (k_d t L_a + D_a)(e^{-k_d t}) \tag{8-34}$$

where the terms are as previously defined.

---

**EXAMPLE 8-11**

A city of 200,000 people disposes of 1.05 m$^3 \cdot$ s$^{-1}$ of treated sewage that still has a BOD$_u$ of 28.0 mg $\cdot$ L$^{-1}$ and 1.8 mg $\cdot$ L$^{-1}$ of DO into a river. Upstream from the outfall, the river has a flowrate of 7.08 m$^3 \cdot$ s$^{-1}$ and a velocity of 0.37 m $\cdot$ s$^{-1}$. At this point, the BOD$_u$ and DO in the river are 3.6 and 7.6 mg $\cdot$ L$^{-1}$, respectively. The saturation value of DO (at the temperature of the river) is 8.5 mg $\cdot$ L$^{-1}$. The deoxygenation coefficient, $k_d$, is 0.61 day$^{-1}$, and the reaeration coefficient, $k_r$, is 0.76 day$^{-1}$. Assume complete mixing and that the velocity in the river is the same upstream and downstream of the outfall.

1. What is the oxygen deficit and the BOD$_u$ just downstream from the outfall (just after mixing, before any reaction can occur)?
2. What is the DO 16 km downstream?

**Solution**

1. Using Equation 8–17, we can calculate the concentration of dissolved oxygen in the river after mixing.

$$DO_{mix} = \frac{(1.8 \text{ mg} \cdot \text{L}^{-1})(1.05 \text{ m}^3 \cdot \text{s}^{-1}) + (7.08 \text{ m}^3 \cdot \text{s}^{-1})(7.6 \text{ mg} \cdot \text{L}^{-1})}{1.05 \text{ m}^3 \cdot \text{s}^{-1} + 7.08 \text{ m}^3 \cdot \text{s}^{-1}} = 6.85 \text{ mg} \cdot \text{L}^{-1}$$

Initial deficit = $D_a = 8.5 - 6.85 = 1.6$ mg $\cdot$ L$^{-1}$.

$\qquad$ Similarly, using Equation 8–18, we can calculate the concentration of ultimate BOD in the river after mixing.

$$L_{a,mix} = \frac{(28 \text{ mg} \cdot \text{L}^{-1})(1.05 \text{ m}^3 \cdot \text{s}^{-1}) + (3.6 \text{ mg} \cdot \text{L}^{-1})(7.08 \text{ m}^3 \cdot \text{s}^{-1})}{8.13 \text{ m}^3 \cdot \text{s}^{-1}} = 6.75 \text{ mg} \cdot \text{L}^{-1}$$

2. DO 16 km downstream

$$t = \frac{(16 \text{ km})(1000 \text{ m} \cdot \text{km}^{-1})}{(0.37 \text{ m} \cdot \text{s}^{-1})(3600 \text{ s} \cdot \text{h}^{-1})(24 \text{ h} \cdot \text{day}^{-1})} = 0.50 \text{ days}$$

Using Equation 8–33,

$$D_t = \frac{(0.61)(6.75)}{(0.76 - 0.61)}[\exp(-(0.61)(0.50)) - \exp(-(0.76)(0.50))]$$

$$+ 1.6 \exp(-(0.76)(0.50))$$

$$= 2.56 \text{ mg} \cdot \text{L}^{-1}$$

therefore DO = 8.5 mg $\cdot$ L$^{-1}$ − 2.56 mg $\cdot$ L$^{-1}$ = 5.9 mg $\cdot$ L$^{-1}$

To relate travel time to a physical distance downstream, we must also know the average stream velocity. Once $D$ has been found at any point downstream, the DO can be found from Equation 8–33. Note that it is physically impossible for the DO to be less than zero. If the deficit calculated from Equation 8–33 is greater than the saturation DO, then all the oxygen was depleted at some earlier time and the DO is zero. If the result of your calculation yields a negative DO, report it as zero because concentration values cannot be less than zero.

The lowest point on the DO sag curve with respect to dissolved oxygen, which is called the **critical point,** is of major interest because it indicates the worst conditions in the river with respect to dissolved oxygen. The time to the critical point ($t_c$) can be found by differentiating Equation 8–33, setting it equal to zero, and solving for $t$ using base it $e$ values for $k_r$ and $k_d$.

$$t_c = \frac{1}{k_r - k_d} \ln\left[\frac{k_r}{k_d}\left(1 - D_a\frac{k_r - k_d}{k_d L_a}\right)\right] \tag{8–35}$$

or when $k_r = k_d$,

$$t_c = \frac{1}{k_d}\left(1 - \frac{D_a}{L_a}\right) \tag{8–36}$$

and the critical deficit ($D_c$) is then found by using this critical time in Equation 8–33.

$$D_c = \frac{k_d L_a}{k_r - k_a}(e^{-k_d t_c} - e^{-k_r t_c}) + D_a(e^{-k_r t_c}) \tag{8–37}$$

In some instances there may not be a sag in the DO downstream. The lowest DO may occur in the mixing zone. In these instances Equation 8–35 will not give a useful value.

---

**EXAMPLE 8–12**   Using the data presented in Example 8–11,

1. Calculate the critical time and distance.
2. What is the minimum DO?

Solution   1. Using Equation 8–35, we can calculate the critical time, $t_c$.

$$t_c = \frac{1}{0.76 - 0.61}\ln\left\{\frac{0.76}{0.61}\left[1 - \frac{1.6(0.76 - 0.61)}{(0.61)(6.75)}\right]\right\}$$

$$= 1.07 \text{ days}$$

$$\text{Flow} = 1.2 \text{ ft} \cdot \text{s}^{-1}$$

$$x = (1.07 \text{ days})(1.2 \text{ ft} \cdot \text{s}^{-1})(3600 \text{ s} \cdot \text{h}^{-1})(24 \text{ h} \cdot \text{day}^{-1})$$

$$= 1.1 \times 10^5 \text{ ft} = 20.9 \text{ miles}$$

2. Using the critical time, $t_c$, for $t$, we can use Equation 8–33 to calculate the "critical deficit":

$$D = \frac{(0.61)(6.75)}{(0.76 - 0.61)}\{\exp[-(0.61)(1.07)] - \exp[-(0.76)(1.07)]\}$$

$$+ 1.6 \exp[-(0.76)(1.07)]$$

$$= 2.8 \text{ mg} \cdot \text{L}^{-1}$$

therefore, the minimum DO $= 8.5 \text{ mg} \cdot \text{L}^{-1} - 2.8 \text{ mg} \cdot \text{L}^{-1} = 5.7 \text{ mg} \cdot \text{L}^{-1}$

**EXAMPLE 8–13**   Determine the DO concentration at a point 5 km downstream from the Viracocha discharge into the Pachacamac Creek (Examples 8–7, 8–8, 8–10). Also determine the critical DO and the distance downstream at which it occurs.

Solution   All of the appropriate data are provided in the three previous examples. With the exceptions of the travel time, $t$, and the reaeration rate, the values needed for Equations 8–33 and 8–35 have been computed in Examples 8–7, 8–8, and 8–10. The first step then is to calculate $k$.

$$k_r \text{ at } 20°C = \frac{(3.9)(0.03 \text{ m} \cdot \text{s}^{-1})^{0.5}}{(5.0 \text{ m})^{1.5}} = 0.0604 \text{ day}^{-1}$$

Because $k_r$ is given for 20°C and the stream temperature is at 10°C, Equation 8–7 must be used to correct for the temperature difference.

$$k_r \text{ at } 10°C = (0.0604 \text{ day}^{-1})(1.024)^{10-20} = (0.0604)(0.7889) = 0.04766 \text{ day}^{-1}$$

Note that the temperature coefficient is the one associated with Equation 8–27.

The travel time $t$ is computed from the distance downstream and the speed of the stream.

$$t = \frac{(5 \text{ km})(1{,}000 \text{ m} \cdot \text{km}^{-1})}{(0.03 \text{ m} \cdot \text{s}^{-1})(86{,}400 \text{ s} \cdot \text{day}^{-1})} = 1.929 \text{ day}$$

Although it is not warranted by the significant figures in the computation, we have elected to keep four significant figures because of the computational effects of truncating the extra digits.

The deficit is estimated using Equation 8–33.

$$D_t = \frac{(0.03442)(11.86)}{0.04766 - 0.03442}[e^{-(0.03442)(1.929)} - e^{-(0.04766)(1.929)}] + 6.58[e^{-(0.04766)(1.929)}]$$

$$= (30.83)(0.9358 - 0.9122) + 6.58(0.9122)$$

$$= 6.7299 \text{ or } 6.73 \text{ mg} \cdot \text{L}^{-1}$$

and the dissolved oxygen is

$$DO = 11.33 - 6.73 = 4.60 \text{ mg} \cdot \text{L}^{-1}$$

The critical time is computed using Equation 8–35.

$$t_c = \frac{1}{0.04766 - 0.03442} \ln\left\{ \left(\frac{0.04766}{0.03442}\right) \left[1 - 6.58 \times \frac{(0.04766 - 0.03442)}{(0.03442)(11.86)}\right] \right\}$$

$$= 6.45 \text{ days}$$

Using $t_c$ for the time in Equation 8–33, we can calculate the critical deficit as

$$D_c = \frac{(0.03442)(11.86)}{0.04766 - 0.03442}[e^{-(0.03442)(6.45)} - e^{-(0.04766)(6.45)}] + 6.58[e^{-(0.04766)(6.45)}]$$

$$= 6.85 \text{ mg} \cdot \text{L}^{-1}$$

and the critical DO is

$$DO_c = 11.33 - 6.85 = 4.48 \text{ mg} \cdot \text{L}^{-1}$$

The critical DO occurs downstream at a distance of

$$(6.45 \text{ days})(86{,}400 \text{ s} \cdot \text{day}^{-1})(0.03 \text{ m} \cdot \text{s}^{-1})\left(\frac{1 \text{ km}}{1000 \text{ m}}\right) = 16.7 \text{ km}$$

from the wastewater discharge point. (Remember that 0.03 m · s⁻¹ is the speed of the stream.)

**Management Strategy.**   The beginning point for water quality management in rivers using the DO sag curve is to determine the minimum DO concentration that will protect the aquatic life in the stream. This value, called the **DO standard,** is generally set to protect the most sensitive species that exist or could exist in the particular river. For a known waste discharge and a known set of river characteristics, the DO sag equation can be solved to find the DO at the critical point. If this value is greater than the standard, the stream can adequately assimilate the waste. If the DO at the critical point is less than the standard, then additional waste treatment is needed. Usually, the environmental engineer has control over just two parameters: $L_a$ and $D_a$. By increasing the efficiency of the existing treatment processes or by adding additional treatment steps, the ultimate BOD of the waste discharge can be reduced, thereby reducing $L_a$. Often a relatively inexpensive method for improving stream quality is to reduce $D_a$ by adding oxygen to the wastewater to bring it close to saturation prior to discharge. To determine whether a proposed improvement will be adequate, the new values for $L_a$ and $D_a$ are used to determine whether the DO standard will be violated at the critical point. As a last resort, mechanical reaeration of rivers can be accomplished to artificially increase $k_r$ and therefore decrease $D_a$. However, this measure is both costly to install and operate.

When using the DO sag curve to determine the adequacy of wastewater treatment, it is important to use the river conditions that will result in the least DO concentration. Usually these conditions occur in the late summer when river flows are low and temperatures are high. A frequently used criterion is the 10-year, 7-day low flow, which is the recurrence interval of the average low flow for a 7-day period. Low river flows reduce the dilution of the waste entering the river, causing higher values for $L_a$ and $D_a$. The value of $k_r$ is usually reduced by low river flows because of reduced velocities. In addition, higher temperatures increase $k_d$ more than $k_r$ and also decrease DO saturation, thus making the critical point more severe.

---

**EXAMPLE 8–14**   The Tlaloc Company is considering opening one of two possible plants on either the Tezcatlipoca River or on its twin, the Quetzalcoatl River. Among the decisions to be made are what effect the plant discharge will have on each river and which river would be affected less. Effluent data from the Tlaloc canning plants A and B are considered to be representative of the potential discharge characteristics. In addition, measurements from each river at summer low-flow conditions are available.

| Effluent Parameter | Plant A | Plant B |
|---|---|---|
| Flow (in $m^3 \cdot s^{-1}$) | 0.0500 | 0.0500 |
| Ultimate BOD at 25°C (in $kg \cdot day^{-1}$) | 129.60 | 129.60 |
| DO (in $mg \cdot L^{-1}$) | 0.900 | 0.900 |
| Temperature (in °C) | 25.0 | 25.0 |
| $k$ at 20°C (in $day^{-1}$) | 0.110 | 0.0693 |

| River Parameter | Tezcatlipoca River | Quetzalcoatl River |
|---|---|---|
| Flow (in $m^3 \cdot s^{-1}$) | 0.500 | 0.500 |
| Ultimate BOD at 25°C (in $mg \cdot L^{-1}$) | 19.00 | 19.00 |
| DO (in $mg \cdot L^{-1}$) | 5.85 | 5.85 |
| Temperature (in °C) | 25.0 | 25.0 |
| Speed (in $m \cdot s^{-1}$) | 0.100 | 0.200 |
| Average depth (in m) | 4.00 | 4.00 |
| Bed-activity coefficient | 0.200 | 0.200 |

Four combinations must be evaluated:

Plant A on the Tezcatlipoca River     Plant B on the Tezcatlipoca River
Plant A on the Quetzalcoatl River     Plant B on the Quetzalcoatl River

**Solution**   Note that for the purpose of explaining the calculations, the number of significant figures given for the data is greater than can probably be measured. The only difference in the combinations is the change in deoxygenation and reaeration coefficients. Thus, we need calculate only one value of $L_a$ and one value of $D_a$.

We begin by converting the mass flux of ultimate BOD (in $kg \cdot day^{-1}$) to a concentration (in $mg \cdot L^{-1}$). Following our general approach for calculating concentration from mass flow, we divide the mass flux (in $kg \cdot day^{-1}$) by the flow of the water carrying the waste ($Q_w$, $Q_r$, or the sum $Q_w + Q_r$):

$$\frac{\text{Mass flux of ultimate BOD discharged (in } kg \cdot day^{-1})}{\text{Flow of water-carrying waste (in } m^3 \cdot s^{-1})}$$

The mass flux units are then converted to milligrams per day and the water flow to liters per day so that the days cancel.

$$\frac{(\text{Mass flux in units of } kg \cdot day^{-1}) \times (1 \times 10^6 \, mg \cdot kg^{-1})}{(\text{Flow rate } Q \text{ in units of } m^3 \cdot s^{-1}) \times (86,400 \, s \cdot day^{-1})(1 \times 10^3 \, L \cdot m^{-3})}$$

For either plant A or B,

$$L_w = \frac{(129.60 \, kg \cdot day^{-1})(1 \times 10^6 \, mg \cdot kg^{-1})}{(0.0500 \, m^3 \cdot s^{-1})(86,400 \, s \cdot day^{-1})(1 \times 10^3 \, L \cdot m^{-3})}$$

$$= \frac{129.60 \times 10^6 \, mg}{4.320 \times 10^6 \, L}$$

$$= 30.00 \, mg \cdot L^{-1}$$

Now we can compute the mixed BOD using Equation 8–18.

$$L_a = \frac{(0.0500)(30.00) + (0.500)(19.00)}{0.0500 + 0.500}$$

$$= 20.0 \, mg \cdot L^{-1}$$

From Table A–2 of Appendix A, we find that the DO saturation at 25°C is $8.38 \, mg \cdot L^{-1}$. Then using Equation 8–24, we determine the initial deficit:

$$D_a = 8.38 - \frac{(0.0500)(0.900) + (0.500)(5.85)}{0.0500 + 0.500}$$

$$= 8.38 - 5.4$$

$$= 2.98 \, mg \cdot L^{-1}$$

For the combination of plant A discharging to the Tezcatlipoca River, the reaeration and deoxygenation coefficients are calculated using Equation 8–26 and Equation 8–30, respectively

$$k_d = 0.110 + \frac{0.100 \times 0.200}{4.00}$$

$$= 0.115 \, day^{-1} \text{ at } 20°C$$

and

$$k_r = \frac{3.9(0.100)^{0.5}}{(4.00)^{1.5}}$$

$$= 0.154 \, day^{-1} \text{ at } 20°C$$

Because the temperature of the river is 25°C and the wastewater effluent temperature is also 25°C, we do not have to calculate a temperature after mixing. However, we will have to adjust $k_d$ and $k_r$ to 25°C. For $k_d$, we use Equation 8–7 with a value of $\theta$ of 1.056.

$$k_d = 0.115(1.056)^{25-20}$$

$$= 0.151 \text{ day}^{-1}$$

From the discussion that follows Equation 8–27, we note that $\theta = 1.024$ for reaeration, and thus

$$k_r = 0.154(1.024)^{25-20}$$

$$= 0.173 \text{ day}^{-1}$$

Although perhaps not justified by the coefficients, we round to three significant figures because we will want to calculate travel time to two decimal places.

Now we have all the information we need to calculate the time to the critical point. Using Equation 8–35, we obtain

$$t_c = \frac{1}{0.173 - 0.151} \ln \left\{ \frac{0.173}{0.151} \left[ 1 - 2.98 \left( \frac{0.173 - 0.151}{0.151 \times 20.0} \right) \right] \right\}$$

$$= 45.45 \ln\{1.146[1 - 2.98(0.02185)]\}$$

$$= 5.18 \text{ days}$$

Using this value for $t$ in Equation 8–33, we can calculate the deficit at the critical point.

$$D_c = \frac{(0.151)(20.0)}{0.173 - 0.151} [e^{-(0.151)(5.18)} - e^{-(0.173)(5.18)}] + 2.98[e^{-(0.173)(5.18)}]$$

$$= 137.3[(0.0493)] + 2.98[1.224]$$

$$= 6.763 + 1.242$$

$$= 7.99 \text{ mg} \cdot \text{L}^{-1}$$

Using $D_c$ and the appropriate value for the DO saturation that we obtained earlier from Table A–2, we can calculate the DO at the critical point.

$$\text{DO} = \text{DO}_s - D$$

$$= 8.38 - 7.99 = 0.39 \text{ mg} \cdot \text{L}^{-1}$$

Thus, the lowest DO for the plant A–Tezcatlipoca River combination is 0.39 mg $\cdot$ L$^{-1}$, and it occurs at a travel time of 5.18 days downstream from the plant A outfall. Because the Tezcatlipoca River travels at a speed of 0.100 m $\cdot$ s$^{-1}$, this would be

$$\frac{(0.100 \text{ m} \cdot \text{s}^{-1})(5.18 \text{ days})(86{,}400 \text{ s} \cdot \text{day}^{-1})}{1000 \text{ m} \cdot \text{km}^{-1}} = 44.8 \text{ km}$$

downstream.

The results of the other combinations are summarized in the following table.

| | **Plant A** | | **Plant B** | |
|---|---|---|---|---|
| | **Tezcatlipoca River** | **Quetzalcoatl River** | **Tezcatlipoca River** | **Quetzalcoatl River** |
| $k_d$ | 0.151 | 0.151 | 0.104 | 0.104 |
| $k_r$ | 0.173 | 0.245 | 0.173 | 0.245 |
| $t_c$ | 5.18 | 4.11 | 5.86 | 4.47 |
| $D$ | 7.98 | 6.62 | 6.51 | 5.32 |
| DO | 0.40 | 1.76 | 1.87 | 3.06 |

The best combination is the plant B on the Quetzalcoatl River. This is because of the four options, the deficit is the lowest and the minimum DO the greatest for plant B on the Quetzalcoatl River.

**FIGURE 8–12**

Effect of $k_d$ and $k_r$ on DO sag curve. Note that the velocity in the Quetzalcoatl River is twice that in the Tezcatlipoca River.

Using a spreadsheet program, we have generated the DO values for a series of times for each of the combinations and plotted the results in Figure 8–12. From this figure we can make the following general observations:

1. Increasing the reaeration rate, while holding everything else as it is, reduces the deficit and decreases the critical time.
2. Decreasing the reaeration rate, while holding everything else as it is, increases the deficit and increases the critical time.
3. Increasing the deoxygenation rate, while holding everything else as it is, increases the deficit and decreases the critical time.
4. Decreasing the deoxygenation rate, while holding everything else as it is, decreases the deficit and increases the critical time.

**Nitrogenous BOD.**   Up to this point, only carbonaceous BOD has been considered in the DO sag curve. However, in many cases nitrogenous BOD has at least as much influence on dissolved oxygen levels. Modern wastewater treatment plants can routinely produce effluents with $CBOD_5$ of less than 30 mg · $L^{-1}$. A typical effluent also contains approximately 30 mg · $L^{-1}$ of nitrogen, which would mean an NBOD of about 137 mg · $L^{-1}$ if it were discharged as ammonia (see Example 8–6). Nitrogenous BOD can be incorporated into the DO sag curve by adding an additional term to Equation 8–33.

$$D = \frac{k_d L_a}{k_r - k_d}(e^{-k_d t} - e^{-k_r t}) + D_a(e^{-k_r t}) + \frac{k_n L_n}{k_r - k_n}(e^{-k_n t} - e^{-k_r t}) \qquad (8\text{–}38)$$

where $k_n$ = the nitrogenous deoxygenation coefficient (in day$^{-1}$)

$L_n$ = ultimate nitrogenous BOD after waste and river have mixed (in mg · $L^{-1}$)

and the other terms are as previously defined.

It is important to note that with the additional term for NBOD, it is not possible to find the critical time using Equation 8–35. Instead, it must be found by a trial and error solution of Equation 8–38.

### Other Factors Affecting DO Levels in Rivers.

The classical DO sag curve assumes that there is only one point-source discharge of waste into the river. In reality, this is rarely the case. Multiple point sources can be handled by dividing the river up into reaches with a point source at the head of each reach. A **reach** is a length of river specified by the engineer on the basis of its homogeneity, that is, channel shape, bottom composition, slope, and so on. The oxygen deficit and residual BOD can be calculated at the end of each reach. These values are then used to determine new values of $D_a$ and $L_a$ at the beginning of the following reach. Nonpoint source pollution can also be handled this way if the reaches are made small enough. Nonpoint source pollution can also be incorporated directly into the DO sag equation for a more sophisticated analysis. Dividing the river into reaches is also necessary whenever the flow regime changes because the reaeration coefficient would also change. In small rivers, rapids play a major role in maintaining high DO levels. Eliminating rapids by dredging or damming a river can have a severe effect on DO, although DO levels immediately downstream of dams are usually high because of the turbulence of the falling water.

Some rivers contain large deposits of organic matter in the sediments. These can be natural deposits of leaves and dead aquatic plants or can be sludge deposits from wastewaters receiving little or no treatment. In either case, decomposition of this organic matter places an additional burden on the stream's oxygen resources because the oxygen demand must be supplied from the overlying water. When this benthic demand is significant, compared with the oxygen demand in the water column, it must be included quantitatively in the sag equation.

Aquatic plants can also have a substantial effect on DO levels. During the day, their photosynthetic activities produce oxygen that supplements the reaeration and can even cause oxygen supersaturation. However, plants also consume oxygen for respiration processes. Although there is a net overall production of oxygen, plant respiration can severely lower DO levels during the night. Plant growth is usually highest in the summer when flows are low and temperatures are high, so that large nighttime respiration requirements coincide with the worst cases of oxygen depletion from BOD exertion. In addition, when aquatic plants die and settle to the bottom, they increase the benthic demand. As a general rule, large growths of aquatic plants are detrimental to the maintenance of a consistently high DO level.

### Effect of Nutrients on Water Quality in Rivers

Although oxygen-demanding wastes are definitely the most important river pollutants on an overall basis, nutrients can also contribute to deteriorating water quality in rivers by causing excessive plant growth. Nutrients are those elements required by plants for their growth. They include, in order of abundance in plant tissue: carbon, nitrogen, phosphorus, and a variety of trace elements. When sufficient quantities of all nutrients are available, plant growth is possible. By limiting the availability of any one nutrient, further plant growth is prevented.

Some plant growth is desirable because plants form the base of the food chain and thus support the animal community. However, excessive plant growth can create a number of undesirable conditions, such as thick slime layers on rocks and dense growths of aquatic weeds.

The availability of nutrients is not the only requirement for plant growth. In many rivers, the turbidity caused by eroded soil particles, bacteria, and other factors prevents light from penetrating far into the water, thereby limiting total plant growth in deep water. It is for this reason that slime growths on rocks usually occur only in shallow water. Strong water currents also prevent rooted plants from taking hold, and thus limit their growth to quiet backwaters where the currents are weak and the water is shallow enough for light to penetrate.

**Effects of Nitrogen.**   Nitrogen is detrimental to a receiving body for four reasons:

1. In high concentrations, ammonia in its unionized form is toxic to fish.
2. Ammonia, $NH_3$, in low concentrations, and nitrate, $NO_3^-$, serve as nutrients for excessive growth of algae.
3. The conversion of $NH_4^+$ to $NO_3^-$ consumes large quantities of dissolved oxygen.
4. During the common practice of disinfecting wastewater effluent using chlorination, the chlorine ($Cl_2$) and hypochlorous acid/hypochlorite ($HOCl/OCl^-$) can react with any ammonia present in the water, forming chloramines. The chloramines, which are not removed during dechlorination prior to discharge, are more toxic than either chlorine and hyporchlorous acid/hypochlorite.

**Effects of Phosphorus.**   The major harmful effect of phosphorus is that it serves as a vital nutrient for the growth of algae. If the phosphorus availability meets the growth demands of the algae, algae are produced in excess. When the algae die, they become an oxygen-demanding organic material as bacteria seek to degrade them. This oxygen demand frequently overtaxes the DO supply of the water body and, as a consequence, causes fish to die.

**Management Strategy.**   The strategy for managing water quality problems associated with excessive nutrients is based on the sources for each nutrient. Except under rare circumstances, there is plenty of carbon available for plant growth. Plants use carbon dioxide, which is available from the bicarbonate alkalinity of the water and from the bacterial decomposition of organic matter. As carbon dioxide is removed from the water, it is replenished from the atmosphere. Generally, the major source of trace elements is the natural weathering of rock minerals, a process over which the environmental scientist and engineer has little control. However, because acid rain caused by air pollution accelerates the weathering process, air pollution control can help reduce the supply of trace elements. The removal of trace elements from wastewater is difficult. In addition, such small amounts of trace elements are needed for plant growth that nitrogen or phosphorus is more likely to be the limiting nutrient. Therefore, the practical control of nutrient-caused water quality problems in streams is based on removal of nitrogen or phosphorus from wastewaters before they are discharged.

## 8–4   WATER QUALITY MANAGEMENT IN LAKES

### Control of Phosphorus in Lakes

In Chapter 4 the problem of eutrophication and its effect on ecosystems was discussed. Because phosphorus is usually the limiting nutrient, control of cultural eutrophication must be accomplished by reducing the input of phosphorus to the lake. Once the input is reduced, the phosphorus concentration will gradually fall as phosphorus is buried in the sediment or flushed from the lake. Other strategies for reversing or slowing the eutrophication process, such as precipitating phosphorus with additions of aluminum (alum) or removing phosphorus-rich sediments by dredging, have been proposed. However, if the input of phosphorus is not also curtailed, the eutrophication process will continue. Thus, dredging or precipitation alone can result only in temporary improvement in water quality. In conjunction with reduced phosphorus inputs, these measures can help speed up the removal of phosphorus already in the lake system. Of course, the need to speed the recovery process must be weighed against the potential damage from inundating shoreline areas with sludge and stirring up chemicals buried in the sediment.

To be able to reduce phosphorus inputs, it is necessary to know the sources of phosphorus and the potential for their reduction. The natural source of phosphorus is the weathering of rock. Phosphorus released from the rock can enter the water directly, but more commonly it is taken up by plants and enters the water in the form of dead plant matter. It is exceedingly difficult to reduce the natural inputs of phosphorus. If these sources are large, the lake is generally naturally eutrophic. For many lakes the principal sources of phosphorus are the result of human activity. The most important sources are municipal and industrial wastewaters, seepage from septic tanks, and agricultural runoff that carries phosphorus fertilizers into the water. The relative contributions of various sources of phosphorus are illustrated in the following example.

**EXAMPLE 8–15**   The ficticious Vadatajs Lake in Cerlalicing has a surface area of $9.34 \times 10^7 \text{ m}^2$ and depth of 10 m. The lake receives a yearly average of 107 cm of precipitation. The lake receives phosphorus from the following sources:

1. The wastewater treatment plant for the city of Astrid discharges into the lake. The average water usage for the residents of the city is $350 \text{ L} \cdot \text{capita}^{-1} \cdot \text{day}^{-1}$. There are 54,000 residents of this city. The total phosphate level in the sewage influent is $10 \text{ mg} \cdot \text{L}^{-1}$ (yearly average). The wastewater treatment plant removes 90% of the phosphorus.
2. The city has recently renovated its sewage collection system, separating the storm water from the sewage, installing a combined sewer system. The storm water is discharged into the lake after treatment through a sand filter that removes 50% of the phosphorus. The storm sewers serve an area that is $9.5 \text{ km}^2$, having a runoff coefficient of 0.40. The phosphorus concentration in the untreated storm water is $0.75 \text{ mg} \cdot \text{L}^{-1}$.
3. The lake is fed by a pristine stream, having an average yearly flow rate of $0.65 \text{ m}^3 \cdot \text{s}^{-1}$. The stream has an average total phosphorus concentration of $0.05 \text{ mg} \cdot \text{L}^{-1}$.
4. Farmland lies to the east of the lake. It has a drainage area of $150 \text{ km}^2$. Manure is applied in early spring before the crops are sown. The phosphorus loading to the land is $0.42 \text{ kg} \cdot \text{km}^{-2} \cdot \text{year}^{-1}$. The crops remove 60% of the phosphorus applied. The runoff coefficient on this land is 0.30. (This loading to the lake can be averaged throughout the year).
5. The phosphorus settling rate from the lake is $2.8 \times 10^{-8} \text{ s}^{-1}$.

Calculate the total phosphorus concentration in the lake. What is the trophic state of the lake? You may assume that the rate of evaporation is equal to the rate of precipitation.

**Solution**   Let's draw a picture of this lake.

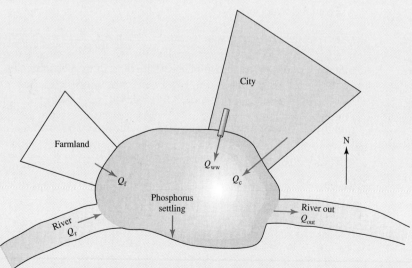

We must first calculate all of our **flow rates:**
The flowrate in the pristine stream, $Q_r$, is given as $0.65 \text{ m}^3 \cdot \text{s}^{-1}$.

The flowrate from the wastewater treatment plant is

$$Q_{ww} = (350 \text{ L} \cdot \text{capita}^{-1} \cdot \text{day}^{-1})(54{,}000 \text{ people})\left(\frac{1 \text{ m}^3}{1000 \text{ L}}\right)\left(\frac{1 \text{ day}}{86{,}400 \text{ s}}\right) = 0.219 \text{ m}^3 \cdot \text{s}^{-1}$$

The runoff for the city must be calculated from the precipitation rate and the drainage area. The precipitation rate is 107 cm $\cdot$ year$^{-1}$. The drainage area is 9.5 km$^2$. The runoff rate is 0.40.

$$Q_c = (107 \text{ cm} \cdot \text{year}^{-1})\left(\frac{1 \text{ m}}{100 \text{ cm}}\right)\left(\frac{1 \text{ year}}{(365 \text{ days} \cdot \text{year}^{-1})(86{,}400 \text{ s} \cdot \text{day}^{-1})}\right)$$

$$\times \ (9.5 \text{ km}^2)\left(\frac{1000 \text{ m}}{1 \text{ km}}\right)(0.40)$$

$$= 0.129 \text{ m}^3 \cdot \text{s}^{-1}$$

The runoff for the farmland is calculated in a similar fashion to that from the city. Here the drainage area is 15 km$^2$. The runoff rate is 0.30.

$$Q_f = \left(107 \text{ cm} \cdot \text{year}^{-1}\right)\left(\frac{1 \text{ m}}{100 \text{ cm}}\right)\left(\frac{1 \text{ year}}{(365 \text{ days} \cdot \text{year}^{-1})(86{,}400 \text{ s} \cdot \text{day}^{-1})}\right)$$

$$\times \ (150 \text{ km}^2)\left(\frac{1000 \text{ m}}{1 \text{ km}}\right)^2(0.3)$$

$$= 1.53 \text{ m}^3 \cdot \text{s}^{-1}$$

Remembering that the rate of evaporation equals the rate of precipitation, the total flow into the lake equals

$$Q_r + Q_{ww} + Q_c + Q_f = (0.65 + 0.219 + 0.129 + 1.53) \text{ m}^3 \cdot \text{s}^{-1} = 2.53 \text{ m}^3 \cdot \text{s}^{-1}.$$

To maintain a mass balance for water, the flowrate out of the lake must equal the flow rate in (this assumes that the volume lost to seepage and evaporation equals the volume in from precipitation). Thus,

$$Q_{out} = 2.53 \text{ m}^3 \cdot \text{s}^{-1}$$

Next we wish to calculate the phosphorus loading.

When the flow rate and concentration are given, then the rate of mass in equals $Q \times C$. This will be the case for all of the flows except that from the farmland.

From the river (inflow)

$$M_r = (0.65 \text{ m}^3 \cdot \text{s}^{-1})(0.05 \text{ mg} \cdot \text{L}^{-1})\left(\frac{1000 \text{ L}}{1 \text{ m}^3}\right)\left(\frac{1 \text{ g}}{1000 \text{ mg}}\right) = 0.033 \text{ g} \cdot \text{s}^{-1}$$

From the wastewater treatment plant, where 90% of the phosphorus is removed

$$M_{ww} = (0.219 \text{ m}^3 \cdot \text{s}^{-1})(10 \text{ mg} \cdot \text{L}^{-1})(1 - 0.90)\left(\frac{1000 \text{ L}}{1 \text{ m}^3}\right)\left(\frac{1 \text{ g}}{1000 \text{ mg}}\right) = 0.219 \text{ g} \cdot \text{s}^{-1}$$

From the city (storm sewer), where 50% is removed by treatment

$$M_c = (0.129 \text{ m}^3 \cdot \text{s}^{-1})(0.75 \text{ mg} \cdot \text{L}^{-1})(1 - 0.50)\left(\frac{1000 \text{ L}}{1 \text{ m}^3}\right)\left(\frac{1 \text{ g}}{1000 \text{ mg}}\right) = 0.048 \text{ g} \cdot \text{s}^{-1}$$

From the farmland, we must use the application rate. The crops use 60% of the phosphorus, so only 40% is available for release.

$$M_f = (0.42 \text{ kg} \cdot \text{km}^{-2} \cdot \text{year}^{-1})(150 \text{ km}^2)(0.40)\left(\frac{1000 \text{ g}}{1 \text{ kg}}\right)\left(\frac{1 \text{ year}}{365 \text{ days}}\right)\left(\frac{1 \text{ day}}{86{,}400 \text{ s}}\right)$$

$$= 7.99 \times 10^{-4} \text{ g} \cdot \text{s}^{-1}$$

Therefore, the total mass of phosphorus into the lake is

$$M_{in} = M_r + M_{ww} + M_c + M_f = (0.033 + 0.219 + 0.048 + 7.99 \times 10^{-4}) \text{ g} \cdot \text{s}^{-1} = 0.301 \text{ g} \cdot \text{s}^{-1}$$

We must now calculate the **mass of phosphorus out.** We will assume steady-state conditions and complete mixing. Phosphorus can leave through settling or from the river leaving the lake. Remember from Chapter 2, that we can write the degradation terms as $dC/dt = -kC_{lake}\Psi$, where $k$ is the rate constant, $C_{lake}$ is the concentration in the lake, and $\Psi$ is the volume. The term for the loss of chemical from the outflow of the lake is $C_{lake}Q_{out}$.

We can now write our **complete mass-balance equation:**

$$\frac{d(\text{Mass})}{dt} = \text{Phosphate in} - \text{phosphate out}$$

or, more specifically,

$$\frac{d(\text{Mass})}{dt} = \text{Phosphate from wastewater} + \text{phosphate from river} + \text{phosphate from farmland}$$
$$+ \text{phosphate from the city storm sewers} - \text{phosphate lost to settling}$$
$$- \text{phosphate lost in outflow from lake}$$

We can write this mathematically as we did in Chapter 2.

$$\frac{d(\text{Mass})}{dt} = C_r Q_r + C_{ww} Q_{ww} + C_c Q_c + C_f Q_f - k_s C_{lake}\Psi - C_{lake} Q_{out}$$

where $k_s$ = settling constant for phosphorus
$V$ = volume of the lake

We have already calculated the total mass of phosphorus that flows into the river.

$$M_{in} = C_r Q_r + C_{ww} Q_{ww} + C_c Q_c + C_f Q_f = 0.301 \text{ g} \cdot \text{s}^{-1}$$

Therefore,

$$\frac{d(\text{Mass})}{dt} = M_{in} - k_s C_{lake} V - C_{lake} Q_{out}$$
$$= 0.301 \text{ g} \cdot \text{s}^{-1} - (2.8 \times 10^{-8} \text{ s}^{-1})C_{lake}(9.34 \times 10^7 \text{ m}^2)(10 \text{ m}) - C_{lake}(2.53 \text{ m}^3 \cdot \text{s}^{-1})$$

Setting $d(\text{Mass})/dt = 0$ for steady-state conditions, allows us to solve the above equation for $C_{lake}$.

$$0.301 \text{ g} \cdot \text{s}^{-1} - (26.15 \text{ m}^3 \cdot \text{s}^{-1})C_{lake} - (2.53 \text{ m}^3 \cdot \text{s}^{-1})C_{lake}$$
$$= \frac{0.301 \text{ g} \cdot \text{s}^{-1}}{28.68 \text{ m}^3 \cdot \text{s}^{-1}} = C_{lake}$$

$$C_{lake} = 0.0105 \text{ g} \cdot \text{m}^{-3}$$

Because we need to compare this to values in units of milligrams per liter, we must convert our answer.

$$C_{lake} = (0.0105 \text{ g} \cdot \text{m}^{-3})\left(\frac{1000 \text{ mg}}{\text{g}}\right)\left(\frac{1000 \text{ μg}}{\text{mg}}\right)\left(\frac{\text{m}^3}{1000 \text{ L}}\right) = 10.5 \text{ μg} \cdot \text{L}^{-1}$$

Therefore, as shown in Table 4–2, the trophic state of the lake is mesotrophic. Even with all of the measures taken, more must be taken to ensure the quality of the lake.

### Municipal and Industrial Wastewaters.

All municipal sewage contains phosphorus from human excrement. Many industrial wastes are also high in this nutrient. In these cases, the only effective way of reducing phosphorus is through advanced waste treatment processes, which are discussed in Chapter 10. Prior to the late 1980s, municipal wastewater also contained large quantities of phosphorus from detergents containing polyphosphate, which is a chain of phosphate ions (usually three) linked together. The polyphosphate binds with minerals in water to make the detergent a more effective cleaning agent. By the 1970s, phosphorus loading from detergents was approximately twice that from human excrement. Phosphorus from detergents can be removed by advanced waste treatment, but phosphorus can also be removed from detergents so that it never enters the wastewater to begin with. Today's detergents do not contain phosphate because the manufacturers have replaced it with other chemicals. As a direct application of the waste minimization philosophy, by the late 1980s all states that surround the Chesapeake Bay have passed laws banning phosphate detergents as a rapid method of reducing phosphorus inputs to lakes.

**Septic Tank Seepage.**    The shores of many lakes are dotted with homes and summer cottages, each with its own septic tank and tile field for waste disposal. As treated wastewater moves through the soil toward the lake, phosphorus is adsorbed by soil particles, especially clay. Thus, during the early life of the tile field, very little phosphorus gets to the lake. However, over time, the capacity of the soil to adsorb phosphorus is exceeded and any additional phosphorus will pass on into the lake, contributing to eutrophication. The time it takes for phosphorus to break through to the lake depends on the type of soil, the distance to the lake, the amount of wastewater generated, and the concentration of phosphorus in that wastewater. To prevent phosphorus from reaching the lake, it is necessary to put the tile field far enough from the lake that the adsorption capacity of the soil is not exceeded. If this is not possible, it may be necessary to replace the septic tanks and tile fields with a sewer to collect the wastewater and transport it to a treatment facility.

**Agricultural Runoff.**    Because phosphorus is a plant nutrient, it is an important ingredient in fertilizers. As rainwater washes off fertilized fields, some of the phosphorus is carried into streams and then into lakes. Most of the phosphorus not taken up by growing plants is bound to soil particles. Bound phosphorus is carried into streams and lakes through soil erosion. Waste minimization can be applied to control phosphorus loading to lakes from agricultural fertilization by encouraging farmers to fertilize more often with smaller amounts and to take effective action to stop soil erosion.

### Acidification of Lakes

As shown in Chapter 2, pure rainwater is slightly acidic. As we discussed there, $CO_2$ dissolves in water to form carbonic acid ($H_2CO_3$). The equilibrium concentration of $H_2CO_3$ results in a rainwater pH of approximately 5.6. Thus, acid rain is usually defined to be precipitation with a pH less than 5.6. The phenomena now known as acid rain was first described by Svante Oden (Sweden) in 1968 when he demonstrated that precipitation over the Scandinavian countries was becoming more acidic (Figure 8–13). Thus, began a major effort throughout the world to discover exactly what was

---

**FIGURE 8–13**

The earliest studies identifying the change in the pH of precipitation were conducted by Svante Oden. The data here shows the pH of rainfall in Oslo, Norway, where most of Oden's studies were conducted. (*Source:* Figure 22.15m, Botkin, D. B., E. A. Keller, *Environmental Science: Earth as a Living Planet,* 2nd ed. John Wiley and Sons, New York,1998.)

**FIGURE 8–14**

Hydrogen ion concentration as pH from measurements of rainwater. (*Source: National Atmospheric Deposition Program (NRSP-3)/National Trends Network (2003). NADP Program Office, Illinois State Water Survey, 2204 Griffith Dr. Champaign, IL 61820.* http://nadp.sws.uiuc.edu/isopleths/maps1997/phfield.gif.)

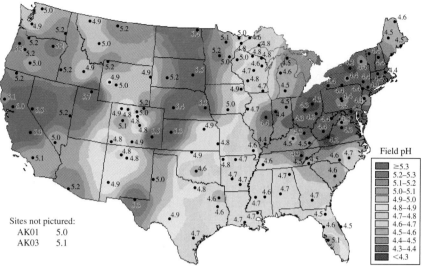

Sites not pictured:
AK01    5.0
AK03    5.1

Field pH

| | |
|---|---|
| | ≥5.3 |
| | 5.2–5.3 |
| | 5.1–5.2 |
| | 5.0–5.1 |
| | 4.9–5.0 |
| | 4.8–4.9 |
| | 4.7–4.8 |
| | 4.6–4.7 |
| | 4.5–4.6 |
| | 4.4–4.5 |
| | 4.3–4.4 |
| | <4.3 |

National Atmospheric Deposition Program/National Trends Network
http://nadp.sws.uiuc.edu

**FIGURE 8–15**

Acid rain formation. (*Source: U.S. EPA* http://www.epa.gov/acidrain/effects/diagram.html.)

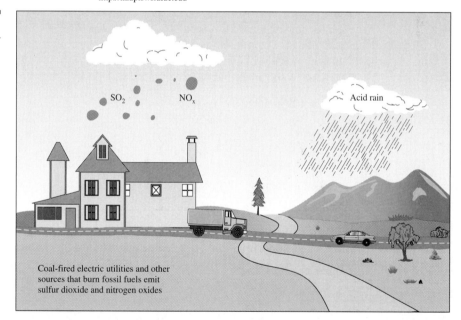

$SO_2$    $NO_x$    Acid rain

Coal-fired electric utilities and other sources that burn fossil fuels emit sulfur dioxide and nitrogen oxides

causing this decrease in pH and how extensive it was. It was discovered that the northeastern United States and Canada frequently record rainwater pH values between 4 and 5 (Figure 8–14). Since its discovery, we have also found that acid rain has caused, among other phenomena

- A complete eradication of some fish species, such as the brook trout, in hundreds of lakes in the Adirondacks.
- The acidification of >1350 of mid-Atlantic Highland streams
- The acidification of approximately 580 streams in the mid-Atlantic Coastal Plain
- The acidification of >90% of streams in the New Jersey Pine Barrens

After much research, it was found that these low pH values have been attributed to emissions of sulfur and nitrogen oxides from the combustion of fossil fuels. As shown in Figure 8–15, the release of sulfur and nitrogen oxides into the air results in the formation of nitric and sulfuric acids, which can then deposit as rain, fog droplets, or snow onto plants, structures, lakes, and so on. Because the deposition can occur in both the wet and dry form, acid rain is better termed **acid deposition.**

**EXAMPLE 8–16**   A chemical analysis has revealed the following composition for the rain falling on the city of Bakermono.

$$1.38 \text{ mg} \cdot \text{L}^{-1} \text{ HNO}_3$$
$$3.21 \text{ mg} \cdot \text{L}^{-1} \text{ H}_2\text{SO}_4$$
$$0.354 \text{ mg} \cdot \text{L}^{-1} \text{ HCl}$$
$$0.361 \text{ mg} \cdot \text{L}^{-1} \text{ NH}_3$$

What is the pH of the rainwater?

Solution   Nitric, sulfuric, and hydrochloric acids are all strong acids, which would be completely dissociated in water. Ammonia is a weak base.

All waters must be electroneutral, that is, have no excess of either cations or anions. The electroneutrality expression for this water is

$$[\text{H}^+] + [\text{NH}_4^+] = [\text{NO}_3^-] + 2[\text{SO}_4^{2-}] + [\text{Cl}^-] + [\text{OH}^-]$$

where the concentrations are given in moles per liter.

Note: Although hydroxide is not given in the chemical composition, it is present, as it is in *all* water.

We must convert all of the preceding concentrations to units of moles per liter, which can be done by dividing the concentration given by the molecular weight and then converting that number to units of moles per liter.

For example, the molecular weight of nitric acid is

$$(1.008) + (14.01) + 3(16.0) = 63.02 \text{ g} \cdot \text{mol}^{-1}$$

Therefore,

$$\frac{(1.38 \text{ mg HNO}_3 \cdot \text{L}^{-1})\left(\frac{1 \text{ g}}{1000 \text{ mg}}\right)}{63.02 \text{ g} \cdot \text{mol}^{-1}} = 2.19 \times 10^{-5} \text{ M}$$

The remaining calculations are given in the following table:

| Chemical Species | Concentration (mg · L$^{-1}$) | Molecular Weight (g · mol$^{-1}$) | Concentration (M) |
|---|---|---|---|
| HNO$_3$ | 1.38 | 63.018 | $2.18985 \times 10^{-5}$ |
| H$_2$SO$_4$ | 3.21 | 98.076 | $3.27297 \times 10^{-5}$ |
| HCl | 0.354 | 36.458 | $9.7098 \times 10^{-6}$ |
| NH$_3$ | 0.361 | 17.034 | $2.11929 \times 10^{-5}$ |

$$\sum(\text{anions}) = [\text{NO}_3^-] + 2[\text{SO}_4^{2-}] + [\text{Cl}^-] + [\text{OH}^-]$$

We need to make the following approximation to solve this problem.

$$[\text{NO}_3^-] + 2[\text{SO}_4^{2-}] + [\text{Cl}^-] \gg [\text{OH}^-]$$

so we can ignore [OH$^-$]. Therefore,

$$\sum(\text{anions}) = 2.19 \times 10^{-5} + (2)(3.28 \times 10^{-5}) + 9.71 \times 10^{-6} \text{ M} = 9.70 \times 10^{-5} \text{ M}$$

Ammonium dissociates to form ammonia. The equilibrium constant is $10^{-9.3}$. Therefore, at acidic pH all of the ammonia would be in the form of the ammonium ion, NH$_4^+$.

Therefore,

$$[H^+] + [NH_4^+] = \sum(\text{anions}) = 9.70 \times 10^{-5}$$

$$[H^+] = \sum(\text{anions}) - [NH_4^+]$$

$$= 9.70 \times 10^{-5} - 2.12 \times 10^{-5} = 7.58 \times 10^{-5} \text{ M}$$

$$pH = -\log(7.58 \times 10^{-5}) = 4.12$$

The assumptions are reasonable because the pH is acidic.

$$[OH^-] = 10^{-(14-4.12)} \text{ M} = 10^{-9.88} \text{ M} = 1.32 \times 10^{-10} \text{ M}$$

This concentration, is in fact, much less than the concentration of the other anions.

Fish, and in particular trout and Atlantic salmon, are very sensitive to low pH levels. Most are severely stressed if the pH drops below 5.5, and few are able to survive if the pH falls below 5.0. If the pH falls below 4.0, cricket frogs and spring peepers experience mortalities in excess of 85%. This is shown in the work of Ryan and Harvey [17], who found that in Patten Lake, Ontario, Canada, which had become severely acidified, the number of fish ages 2–5 years old was essentially nonexistant (Figure 8–16).

High aluminum concentrations are often the trigger that kills fish. Aluminum is abundant in soil but it is normally bound up in the soil minerals. At conventional pH values aluminum rarely occurs in solution. Acidification of the water releases highly toxic $Al^{3+}$ to the water. This is seen in Figure 8–17, showing the relationship between pH and aluminum concentrations in Swedish clearwater lakes [18]. The lower the pH, the higher the aluminum concentration. Thus, the organisms are stressed not only by the low pH but also by the high aluminum concentrations.

Acid deposition can have numerous other stress effects on aquatic organisms, including

- failure to reproduce
- gill damage resulting in respiratory problems
- failure of eggs to hatch
- interference with Ca uptake (with molluscs)

**FIGURE 8–16**

Age distribution of fish in Patten Lake. (*Source:* Dickson, W. "Properties of acidified waters." In: *Ecological Impact of Acid Precipitation.* D. Drablosand, A. Tollan, eds. SNSF, Sandefjord, Norway, pp. 75–83, 1980.)

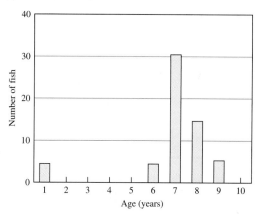

**FIGURE 8–17**

The relationship between pH and aluminum concentrations in Swedish clearwater lakes.

Most lakes are buffered by the carbonate buffer system (see Chapter 2). To the extent that the buffer capacity of the lake is not exceeded, the pH of the lake will not be appreciably affected by acid rain. If there is a source of bicarbonate to replace that consumed by the acid rain, the buffering capacity can be quite large. Calcareous soils are those containing large quantities of calcium carbonate ($CaCO_3$). The dissolution of calcium carbonate will release carbonate into solution, which can be protonated to form bicarbonate. As such, lakes formed in calcareous soils tend to be resistant to acidification.

**EXAMPLE 8-17**   Acidic rainfall infiltrates into a geological formation that is predominantly dolomite, a commonly occurring rock-forming mineral. In 1940, the average pH of the groundwater was 6.6. By 1995, the average yearly groundwater pH was 5.6. Assuming that as the groundwater percolates through the dolomite it is at equilibrium, calculate the calcium and magnesium at the two pHs. Assume that the temperature is 25°C and that the concentration of calcium, magnesium, and carbonate in the rainwater is negligible.

Solution   Dolomite has the chemical structure $CaMg(CO_3)_2$ and a $pK_s$ of 17.09. We will assume that the rainfall contains no calcium or magnesium. If the rainfall is at equilibrium with carbon dioxide, then the concentration of carbonic acid is $10^{-5}$ M (see Chapter 2, we have also assumed that the partial pressure of carbon dioxide in the atmosphere is $10^{-3.5}$ atm).

The equilibrium expression for the dissolution of dolomite is

$$CaMg(CO_3)_2 = Ca^{2+} + Mg^{2+} + 2CO_3^{2-}$$

The solubility expression is

$$[Ca^{2+}][Mg^{2+}][CO_3^{2-}]^2 = 10^{-17.09}$$

We will assume this because the concentration of calcium and magnesium are zero in the rainfall. Because equimolar amounts of both ions will dissolve into the percolating water, we can assume that the concentration of each cation equals $s$. For every one mole of calcium that dissolves, two moles of carbonate will also dissolve. Recognizing that the carbonate that dissolves can react to form carbonic acid and bicarbonate, we can write that:

$$C_T = [H_2CO_3^*] + [HCO_3^-] + [CO_3^{2-}] = 2s$$

We should also remember from Chapter 2, that the equilibrium expression for the dissociation of carbonic acid into carbonate is

$$H_2CO_3^* = 2H^+ + CO_3^{2-} \quad K = 10^{-6.3} \times 10^{-10.3} = 10^{-16.6}$$

We should also remember that the equilibrium expression for the dissociation of bicarbonate is

$$HCO_3^- = H^+ + CO_3^{2-} \quad pK = 10.3$$

At a pH of 6.6,

$$\frac{[CO_3^{2-}][H^+]^2}{[H_2CO_3^*]} = 10^{-16.6} = \frac{[CO_3^{2-}]10^{-13.2}}{[H_2CO_3^*]}$$

Thus, $[H_2CO_3^*] = 10^{3.4}[CO_3^{2-}]$

$$\frac{[CO_3^{2-}][H^+]}{[HCO_3^-]} = 10^{-10.3} = \frac{[CO_3^{2-}]10^{-6.6}}{[HCO_3^-]}$$

Thus, $[HCO_3^-] = 10^{3.7}[CO_3^{2-}]$

$$C_T = [H_2CO_3^*] + [HCO_3^-] + [CO_3^{2-}] = 10^{3.4}[CO_3^{2-}] + 10^{3.7}[CO_3^{2-}] + [CO_3^{2-}]$$

$$= 7.52 \times 10^3[CO_3^{2-}] = 2s$$

Therefore,

$$[CO_3^{2-}] = \frac{2s}{7.52 \times 10^3}$$

From the solubility expression

$$(s)(s)\left(\frac{2s}{7.52 \times 10^3}\right)^2 = 10^{-17.09}$$

Solving for $s$,

$s = 0.00327 \text{ M} = [Ca^{2+}] = [Mg^{2+}]$ at a pH of 6.6.

At pH 5.6, $s = 0.0207 \text{ M} = [Ca^{2+}] = [Mg^{2+}]$

As you can see, as we decreased the pH from 6.6 to 5.6, the concentration of calcium and magnesium that dissolved in the water increased by approximately sixfold.

Other factors that affect the susceptibility of a lake to acidification are the permeability and depth of the soil, the make up of the bedrock, the slope and size of the watershed, and the type of vegetation. Thin, impermeable soils provide little time for contact between the soil and the precipitation. This reduces the potential for the soil to buffer the acid precipitation. Likewise, small watersheds with steep slopes reduce the time for buffering to occur. Deciduous foliage tends to decrease acidity. Coniferous foliage tends to yield runoff that is more acidic, than the precipitation itself. Granite bedrock offers little potential to buffer acid rain. Galloway and Cowling [19] used bedrock geology to predict areas where lakes are potentially most sensitive to acid rain (Figure 8–18). You should note that the predicted areas of sensitivity are also those subjected to very acid precipitation.

The control of lake acidification is related to the control of atmospheric emissions of sulfur and nitrogen oxides. The role of air pollution in acid deposition is discussed in more detail in Chapter 11.

## 8–5  WATER QUALITY IN ESTUARIES [20]

An **estuary** is formed along the coastline where freshwater from rivers and streams flows into the ocean. It is a place of transition, where the freshwater mixes with the salty seawater. These partially enclosed bodies of water are influenced by tides but are protected from the full force of

**FIGURE 8–18**

Regions in North America Containing Lakes Sensitive to Acidification by Acid Precipitation

The shaded areas have igneous or metamorphic bedrock geology; the unshaded areas have calcereous or sedimentary bedrock geology. Regions having low alkalinity lakes are concurrent with regions of igneous and metamorphic bedrock geology.

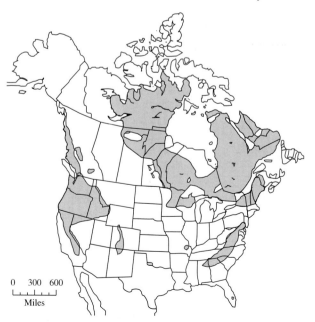

0   300  600
Miles

ocean waves, winds, and storms by the reefs, barrier islands, peninsulas, or the surrounding mainland that define an estuary's seaward boundary.

Estuaries vary greatly in size and shape. They are more commonly known by such names as bays, lagoons, harbors, inlets, or sounds, although not all water bodies by those names are estuaries. The defining feature of an estuary is the mixing of fresh and salt water. San Francisco Bay, Puget Sound, Chesapeake Bay, Boston Harbor, and Tampa Bay are examples of estuaries.

Estuaries are complex and specialized ecosystems formed out of a cycle of wetting and drying, and the submersion and reappearance of aquatic organisms. It is the movement of water that has created the distribution and specialization of organisms in estuaries. The rivers and oceans provide estuaries with an abundance of life-giving nutrients, resulting in an ecosystem that contains more life than a comparably sized plot of agricultural, forested, or grassy land. Within an estuary, many different types of habitats, including shallow open waters, freshwater and salt marshes, sandy beaches, mud and sand flats, rocky shores, oyster reefs, mangrove forests, river deltas, tidal pools, sea grass and kelp beds, and wooded swamps are found. Shore birds, fish, crabs and lobsters, marine mammals, clams and other shellfish, marine worms, sea birds, and reptiles are just some of the animals that make their homes in and around estuaries.

Estuaries could be called the "cradle" of many birds, fish, and other life because the estuary often provides sanctuary to nesting and spawning animals. It is also the ideal spot for tired, resting birds on their long migrations.

In addition to serving as a nursery and sanctuary for much wildlife, the estuary performs many other functions. As the sediment and pollutant-laden water flows from the uplands through fresh and salt marshes, much of the sediments and pollutants are filtered out, creating cleaner and clearer water. Wetland plants and soils buffer the forces of the ocean, absorbing floodwaters and dissipating storm surges. This protects upland organisms as well as valuable real estate from storm and flood damage. Salt marsh grasses and other estuarine plants also help prevent erosion and stabilize the shoreline.

Under siege from excessive nutrients, pathogen contamination, toxic chemicals, alteration of freshwater inflow, loss of habitat, and the introduction of invasive species, our estuaries are in serious danger. In the last 30 or so years, estuaries have experienced declines in fish and wildlife, the introduction of invasive species, deterioration in water quality, and a reduction in overall ecosystem health.

In Chapter 4, we discussed how nutrients such as nitrogen and phosphorus are necessary for the growth of plants and animals and sustaining a healthy aquatic ecosystem. In excess, however, nutrients can contribute to fish disease, "red and brown tides," algae blooms, and low dissolved oxygen. Proliferation of algae can prevent sunlight from penetrating the water, depriving underwater seagrasses of light. Animals that depend on seagrasses for food or shelter leave the area or die. Decreased oxygen levels result in the death of fish and shellfish. In addition, excessive algal growth, resulting in brown and red tides, has been linked to fish kills, manatee deaths, and negative effects on scallops. Increased numbers of algae may also cause foul smells and decreased aesthetic value. Sources of nutrients include point and nonpoint sources, such as sewage treatment plant discharges, stormwater runoff from lawns and agricultural lands, faulty or leaking septic systems, sediment in runoff, animal wastes, atmospheric deposition originating from power plants or vehicles, and groundwater discharges.

Pathogens pose a health threat to swimmers, surfers, divers, and seafood consumers. Fish and filter feeding organisms, such as molluscs and crabs, concentrate pathogens in their tissues and may cause illness to those consuming them. Pathogen contamination can result in the closure of shellfishing areas and bathing beaches. Sources of pathogens include urban and agricultural runoff, boat and marina waste, faulty or leaky septic systems, sewage treatment plant discharges, combined sewer overflows, illegal sewer connections, and waste from pets or wildlife.

Toxic chemicals, such as metals, polycyclic aromatic hydrocarbons (PAHs), polychlorinated biphenyls (PCBs), heavy metals, and pesticides, enter waterways through stormdrains; industrial discharges and runoff from lawns, streets and farmlands; sewage treatment plants; and from atmospheric deposition. Many toxic contaminants are also found in sediments and are resuspended into the environment by dredging and boating activities. Benthic organisms are exposed to these chemicals and may pose a risk to human health if consumed. As a result fishery and shellfish beds may need to be closed, and consumption advisories may be issued.

One effect of the global nature of our transportation system has been the introduction of nonnative or exotic species. These species are offered free rides in ballast water, on the hulls of ships and can thereby circumvent strict regulations governing the conveyance of nonnative species across international or state boundaries. Some introduced (nonnative) species have contributed to the eradication of some native flora and fauna populations and drastically reduced others, fundamentally altering the food web. As some herbivorous species overpopulate wetlands, the overgrazing of vegetation and the resultant degradation and loss of marsh has resulted. Other effects include (1) modification of nutrient cycles or soil fertility; (2) increased erosion; and (3) interference with navigation, agricultural irrigation, sport and commercial fishing, recreational boating, and beach use.

In an attempt to protect ecosystems, the Chesapeake Bay Agreement and the National Estuary Program (NEP) was created. The Chesapeake Bay, protected under its own federally mandated program, was the first estuary in the United States to be targeted for restoration and protection. In 1983, the governors of Maryland, Virginia, and Pennsylvania, the mayor of the District of Columbia, and the EPA administrator signed the Chesapeake Bay Agreement. This agreement set forth the plans to protect and improve the water quality in the Chesapeake Bay. In 1987, amendments to the Clean Water Act gave rise to the National Estuary Program. The goal of this program is to identify, restore, and protect nationally significant estuaries of the United States, focusing not just on improving water quality but on maintaining the integrity of the whole ecosystem, as well as its economic, recreational, and aesthetic values.

## 8-6   WATER QUALITY IN OCEANS

Oceans cover about 71% of the earth's surface. They play an important role in global cycling of carbon dioxide. They also help regulate the cycling of nitrogen and phosphorus. The oceans are also a critical resource, providing food, biochemical compounds, minerals, and recreation.

Coral reefs are fragile, unique, and vibrant ecosystems. Each coral reef supports a different collection of organisms, algae, plants, and animals. These coral reefs support thousands of jobs and billions of dollars in annual revenues from tourism, recreation, and fishing. They are valuable sources of new medicines and biochemical compounds, help prevent shoreline erosion, and provide life-saving protection from storms [21].

Despite their unique and priceless value, the world's coral reefs are at significant danger from marine pollution, warming temperatures in seas, deposition of sediments, and unsustainable fishing practices. Fertilizers can kill the algae that live within the coral. High nutrient levels from off-shore sewage and agricultural discharges and open ocean dumping can result in algae blooms. The algae consume oxygen, choking the coral reefs and attracting predators, such as sea urchins and crown-of-thorn seastars, which destroy living coral. Warmer oceans are thought to result in coral bleaching in which the entire reef turns white as a result of the death of the algae within the coral that give it its brilliant color. Oil pollution can destroy the coral by coating the surfaces and preventing oxygen uptake. The chemicals in the oil can poison the water in which the coral live.

Another specialized ocean ecosystem is the kelp forest. Kelp forests are found along rocky coastlines at depths of 6–30 m. Within these forests of kelp, a type of brown algae, thrive many varieties of fish and other sea creatures, including sea urchins, sea cucumbers, and seastars. Sponges and bryozoans also live along the bottom, as do many varieties of fish and eels. This fragile ecosystem can be disrupted by human activities, such as ocean disposal of municipal sewage and manure from livestock production operations. This can cause an increase in the number of urchins, which will cause widespread destruction of the forests as the urchins dislodge the kelp from its stronghold on the ocean floor.

**FIGURE 8-19**

Sources of oil pollution in
marine environments.
(*Source: Ocean Planet:
Smithsonian, Marine
Pollution 1: Oil Pollution*
http://seawifs
.gsfc.nasa.gov/
OCEAN_PLANET/HTML/
peril_oil_pollution.html.)

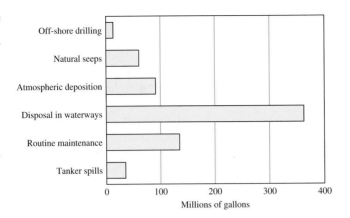

We have seen how pollution can have devastating effects on ocean ecosystems. Let's step back and look at the sources of these pollution and how as a society we can protect the oceans.

Although large oil spills make headlines, it is apparent from Figure 8–19 that the problem of oil pollution is much larger than just that of tanker spills. Used engine oil spilled on roads and other surfaces can end up in waterways, eventually flowing into the ocean. Bilge cleaning and other ship operations release millions of gallons of oil into navigable waters, in thousands of discharges of just a few gallons each. Hydrocarbons released by automobiles, power plants, and industry are deposited as rainfall or as dry deposition into waterways that flow into the ocean or directly into the ocean. Seepage from the ocean bottom and eroding sedimentary rocks releases oil. Only about 5% of oil pollution in oceans results from major tanker accidents; however, a spill can disrupt sea and shore life for great distances. Finally, spills and operational discharges from offshore oil production can result in ocean pollution.

Until fairly recently, the disposal of chemicals, sewage, and solid waste in the ocean was a common practice. In the United States, the Marine Protection, Research, and Sanctuaries Act Title I (MPRSA) limited ocean dumping. Until 1988, when the Ocean Dumping Ban Act (P.L. 100–688) amended MPRSA, it was permissible to dump sewage sludge and industrial waste in the open ocean. Although ocean dumping is predominantly banned by international law, the United States continues to allow the disposal of sediments and other materials dredged from harbors, marinas, estuaries, and bays. Much of this material contains toxic chemicals. The ocean dumping of mine waste, known as "submarine tailings disposal" is widely practiced in Southeast Asia and the Pacific.

As a result of ocean dumping along with the transport of chemicals from waterways and from the air into the ocean, toxic chemicals can be found in all the earth's oceans. Although more critical in coastal regions, these chemicals can also have a deleterious effect on ocean ecosystems. We have discussed some of the effects of chemicals on coral reefs. Bottom-dwelling fish exposed to toxic compounds released during oil spills are also susceptible. The exposed fish may develop liver disease and reproductive and growth problems. Recent news reports from the FDA warn pregnant women or women desiring to become pregnant to avoid consumption of shark, swordfish, king mackerel, and tilefish. These and other types of fish, such as tuna, can accumulate mercury. When ingested during pregnancy, mercury can damage the central nervous system of the fetus, resulting in slower cognitive development of children [22]. Toxins released during algae blooms (resulting from excessive nutrients) have resulted in the death of sea lions and are now thought to harm the already endangered humpback and blue whales. The toxin, demoic acid, has been found in anchovies, sardines, and krill, organisms in the food chain of the whales [23].

Improper disposal of solid waste materials can have devastating effects on oceanic wildlife. Animals can drown or be strangled after becoming tangled in discarded or lost fishing gear, or

**TABLE 8–3**  An Inventory of the Litter Found on Ducie Atoll

| Item | Number Found | Item | Number Found |
|---|---|---|---|
| Buoys, intact or shards | 179 | Pieces of plastic pipe | 29 |
| Crates (bread, bottle) | 14 | Pieces of rope | 44 |
| Plastic bottles (drinks, toiletries) | 71 | Fluorescent tubes and light bulbs | 12 |
| Glass bottles (from 15 countries) | 171 | Aerosol cans | 7 |
| Jars | 18 | Food/drink cans | 7 |
| Broken plastic pieces | 268 | Other | 34 |
| Bottle tops | 74 | | |

suffer and even die from eating plastics and other garbage. Ducie Atoll, in the Pitcairn Islands, located in the South Pacific almost 300 miles from the nearest inhabited island and over 3000 miles from the nearest continent, is one of the most remote islands in the world. An important breeding area for seabirds, the atoll is, unfortunately, littered with as much trash as some European beaches. Yet when a scientist visited in 1991, he found over 950 pieces of trash in a 1.5-mile (2.4-km) stretch of beach [24]. An inventory of the litter found is given in Table 8–3.

The Clean Water Act of 1972 is the principal U.S. federal statute protecting navigable waters and adjoining shorelines from pollution. It forms the foundation for other regulations detailing specific requirements for pollution prevention and response measures. Section 311 of the CWA addresses pollution from oil and hazardous substance releases, providing EPA and the U.S. Coast Guard with the authority to establish a program for preventing, preparing for, and responding to oil spills that occur in navigable waters of the United States. EPA implements provisions of the Clean Water Act through a variety of regulations, including the National Contingency Plan and the Oil Pollution Prevention regulations.

In 1969, a devastating oil spill off the coast of Santa Barbara, California, left beaches covered in an oily coating and killed large numbers of marine animals. In 1972, to protect our oceans and coastlines, Congress passed the Coastal Zone Management Act (CZMA) and the Marine Protection, Research, and Sanctuaries Act (commonly known as the Ocean Dumping Act). Through these acts three programs were created to protect and maintain our nation's marine and coastal environments. These programs are the Coastal Zone Management Program, the National Estuarine Research Reserve System, and the National Marine Sanctuaries Program. The CZMA created a national system to protect and manage coastal and ocean resources, to conserve designated areas, to balance economic, environmental and cultural activities, and to promote science-based resource management decisions. The Marine Protection, Research, and Sanctuaries Act regulates the disposal of all materials into marine waters that are within U.S. jurisdiction.

The National Estuarine Research Reserve System and the National Marine Sanctuaries Program are complementary, one focusing on estuaries and the other on the open ocean. Both programs were developed from the CZMA. The mission of these programs is to study marine ecosystems and develop methods for species and habitat protection, habitat restoration, and pollution control. Through the National Marine Sanctuaries Program, over 46,500 $km^2$ of ocean and coastal waters from the North Atlantic to the South Pacific are protected. In 2000, the Estuaries and Clean Waters Act was passed by Congress to promote and develop programs for the restoration of estuarine habitats using sound scientific and technical principals. Also in 2000, former President Clinton signed an executive order directing the U.S. EPA to better protect beaches, coasts, and ocean waters from pollution by developing Clean Water Act regulations that strengthen water quality protection for coastal and ocean waters. In developing these regulations, EPA was to set higher levels of protection in especially valued or vulnerable areas.

On January 14, 2002, the George W. Bush administration overturned stricter environmental standards for the nation's wetlands and streams. The new permitting system is likely to result in an increase in the loss of wetlands and in the destruction of stream quality. On September 19, 2002, the Coastal and Estuarine Land Protection Act was passed by the Senate Committee on Commerce, Science, and Transportation, S.2608. This act amends the CZMA to allow States' National Estuarine Research Reserve units to acquire sensitive or threatened coastal lands through a federal grant program. This act would help protect coastal lands from further development. At present, this act has not been promulgated into law. It is hoped through stricter regulations we can protect our marine environments from the devastation resulting from uncontrolled disposal of our waste materials.

## 8–7   GROUNDWATER QUALITY

### Contaminant Migration in Groundwaters

The contamination of aquifers (see Chapter 6 for a detailed description of groundwater flow and aquifers) with chemicals or microbes can (and has) resulted in the significant deterioration of the quality of groundwater. Contamination can result from a variety of sources, including

- discharge from improperly operated or located septic systems
- leaking underground storage tanks
- improper disposal of hazardous and other chemical wastes
- spills from pipelines or transportation accidents
- recharge of groundwater with contaminated surface water
- leaking dumps and landfills
- leaking retention ponds or lagoons

The types of contaminants that can pollute an aquifer are highly varied. Some of the more common contaminants include

- benzene, toluene, xylene, and ethylbenzene (BTEX) from gasoline spills
- tetrachloroethylene, trichloroethylene, trichloroethane from dry cleaning and degreasing operations
- radionuclides from weapons manufacturing, research facilities, and hospitals
- polycyclic aromatic hydrocarbons from diesel fuel, crude oil, and other petroleum product spills
- salts from various chemical processes
- fertilizers and pesticides from agricultural operations and the manufacture of these chemicals
- nitrates from agricultural operations
- pathogens from septic systems

The migration of contaminants in soils and aquifers is very much dependent on the properties of the chemical and the geologic material. The more water-soluble a chemical, the more likely it will move vertically down through the soil to the aquifer and migrate with the water, as shown in Figure 8–20. For example, chemicals such as nitrate, methyl tertiary butyl ketone (an additive to gasoline), and methamidophos (a pesticide), which are soluble in water, are less likely to sorb (attach) to the soil or aquifer solids. These chemicals are likely to move through the soil to an underlying aquifer.

Many chemicals are only sparingly soluble in water and when they migrate in groundwater often do so as a separate nonaqueous phase. As such, these chemicals are known as nonaqueous

**FIGURE 8–20**

Dissolved contamination plume.

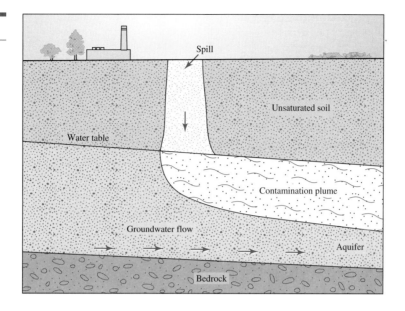

**FIGURE 8–21**

Immiscible plume of chemicals that are less dense (LNAPLs) than and insoluble in water.

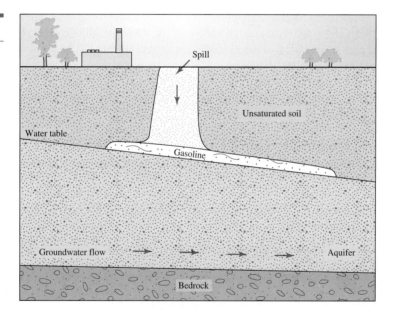

phase liquids (NAPLs). The NAPLs are subdivided into two categories, based on their relative density with water. The light NAPLs (or LNAPLs) are less dense than water and will tend to "float" on the water table as shown in Figure 8–21. Some of the chemical will dissolve into the groundwater, whereas, if the compound is volatile, some volatilize into the pore spaces of the unsaturated zone and move in the gas phase. Examples of LNAPLs include gasoline, and aviation fuel; and some of the chemicals these mixtures contain such as benzene, toluene, xylene (BTX). The dense NAPLs (DNAPLs), on the contrary, have a greater density than that of water and will tend to "sink" in the aquifer until they reach an impervious barrier like bedrock. DNAPLs will tend to "pool" on top of the bedrock, slowly releasing chemicals into the groundwater. Chemicals such as trichloroethylene, tetrachloroethylene and PCB–laden oils are examples of DNAPLs. The migration of DNAPLs is shown in Figure 8–22.

**FIGURE 8-22**

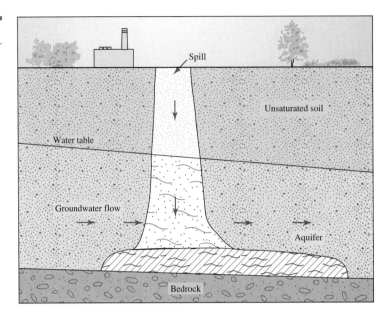

Immiscible plume of chemicals that are more dense (DNAPLs) than and insoluble in water.

Chemicals such as chrysene (present in diesel fuel) and PCBs are very insoluble in water and are not likely to move great distances in soils, and therefore, not likely to contaminate aquifers. To predict contaminant migration, we must revisit Darcy's equation.

Although a few contaminants can move at rates faster than water, most contaminants will move either at the same rate or slower than water. The relative velocities of the water and contaminant are a function of the contaminant and water characteristics. For example, organic chemicals that are more soluble in water will be **retarded** by the geologic material to a lesser degree than those organic chemicals that are relatively insoluble in water. The pH of the water will also affect retardation. For example, at low pH (and in the absence of oxygen) iron will be present predominately as Fe(II). This form of iron is quite soluble and will move with the water. On the contrary, if the pH is high ($>6$) and oxygen is present, iron will be present as Fe(III), which is much less soluble in water. The Fe(III) will precipitate and therefore, not move with the groundwater. The extent to which chemicals are retarded in water is defined by the **retardation coefficient, $R$.** $R$ is defined as

$$R = \frac{v'_{water}}{v'_{cont}} \tag{8-39}$$

where $v'_{water}$ = the linear velocity of the groundwater
$v'_{cont}$ = the linear velocity of the contaminant

The retardation coefficient is a function of the hydrophobicity of the contaminant and on the soil properties. For neutral hydrophobic organic chemicals,

$$R = 1 + \left(\frac{\rho_b}{\eta}\right) K_{oc} f_{oc} \tag{8-40}$$

where $\rho_b$ = bulk density of the soil
$\eta$ = the porosity of the soil (as a fraction)
$K_{oc}$ = partition coefficient into the organic carbon fraction of the soil
$f_{oc}$ = fraction of organic carbon in the soil.

A table of retardation coefficients of some typical groundwater contaminants is given in Table 8-4.

**TABLE 8–4**      Retardation Coefficients of Typical Groundwater Contaminants[a,b]

| Compound | Soil Type I $\rho_b = 1.4$ $n = 40\%$ $f_{oc} = 0.002$ | Soil Type II $\rho_b = 1.6$ $n = 30\%$ $f_{oc} = 0.005$ | Soil Type III $\rho_b = 1.75$ $n = 55\%$ $f_{oc} = 0.05$ |
|---|---|---|---|
| Benzene | 1.2 | 1.7 | 5.3 |
| Toluene | 1.7 | 3.6 | 17.0 |
| Aniline | 1.1 | 1.2 | 2.2 |
| Di-n-propyl phthalate | 5.6 | 19.0 | 110.0 |
| Fluorene | 23.0 | 86.0 | 500.0 |
| n-Pentane | 7.0 | 24.0 | 140.0 |

[a]Formulas used for computation of $K_{oc}$ values are from Schwarzenbach, R. P., P. M. Gschwend, and D. M. Imboden. *Environmental Organic Chemistry.* John Wiley and Sons, New York (1993), p. 274.

[b]Data used in computations are from Schwarzenbach, R. P., P. M. Gschwend, and D. M. Imboden. *Environmental Organic Chemistry,* John Wiley and Sons, New York (1993).

Note: $\rho_b$ = bulk density, $g/cm^3$; $n$ = porosity, %; $f_{oc}$ = fraction of soil that is organic carbon.

**EXAMPLE 8–18**      Two houses are located adjacent to each other. House A has a septic system located 60 m upgradient from the drinking water well for house B. The owner of house A disposed of a pesticide down the drain, causing the septic field to become contaminated with this pesticide. The linear velocity of the water in the unconfined aquifer used for drinking water is $4.7 \times 10^{-6}$ m · s$^{-1}$.

Assuming that the pesticide does not degrade in the soil and that it has a retardation coefficient of 2.4, how many days will it take for the pesticide to reach the well of house B?

Solution      Given that the retardation coefficient is defined as

$$R = \frac{v'_{water}}{v'_{cont}}$$

$$v'_{cont} = \frac{v'_{water}}{R} = \frac{4.7 \times 10^{-6} \text{ m} \cdot \text{s}^{-1}}{2.4} = 1.96 \times 10^{-6} \text{ m} \cdot \text{s}^{-1}$$

Because the distance between the septic field and the well is 60 m, the travel time is

$$\frac{\text{Distance}}{v'} = \left( \frac{60 \text{ m}}{1.96 \times 10^{-6} \text{ m} \cdot \text{s}^{-1}} \right) \left( \frac{\text{days}}{86,400 \text{ s}} \right) = 354 \text{ days}$$

Therefore, it will take 354 days for the pesticide to reach the drinking well. One should note that no mention is made here of the concentration of the chemical. The concentration depends on the mass of contaminant released and on the quantity of water flowing, effectively diluting the chemical.

Note that this is a much simplified solution of a complex problem that involves the use of extensive groundwater models.

As with other aqueous environments, the United States has promulgated numerous laws to protect groundwater resources. For example, the Safe Drinking Act protects sole-source aquifers, that is, those aquifers that are the sole supply of drinking water for a particular region. The Resource Conservation and Recovery Act (RCRA) protects groundwater by regulating the disposal of hazardous chemicals. The Comprehensive Environmental Response, Compensation and Liability Act (CERCLA) helps to protect groundwater resources by mandating and providing funding for the cleanup of abandoned hazardous waste sites. Clearly, groundwater is much too valuable a natural resource to allow it to become damaged by human activities. It is our hope that the financial and technical resources are provided by governments and industries to protect our groundwater for generations to come.

## CHAPTER REVIEW

When you have completed studying this chapter, you should be able to do the following without the aid of your text or notes:

1. List the major pollutant categories (there are four) that are produced by each of the four principal sources of wastewater.
2. List the two nutrients of primary concern with respect to a receiving body of water.
3. Define biochemical oxygen demand (BOD).
4. Explain the procedure for determining BOD and specify the nominal values of temperature and time used in the test.
5. List three reasons why the BOD rate constant may vary.
6. Sketch a graph showing the effect of varying rate constant on 5-day BOD if the ultimate BOD is the same, and the effect on ultimate BOD if the 5-day BOD is the same.
7. Using Equation 8–11 in your answer, explain what causes nitrogenous BOD.
8. Sketch a series of curves that show the deoxygenation, reaeration, and DO sag in a river. Show the effect of a change in the deoxygenation or reaeration rate on the location of the critical point and the magnitude of the DO deficit.
9. List three reasons why ammonia nitrogen is detrimental to a receiving body of water and its inhabitants.
10. List three sources of phosphorus that must be controlled to reduce cultural eutrophication of lakes.
11. Define acid rain.
12. Explain why acid rain is of concern.
13. Explain the role of calcareous soils in protecting lakes from acidification.
14. Other than rainwater pH, list six variables that determine the extent of lake acidification and explain how increasing or decreasing the value of each might be expected to change the extent of acidification.

With the aid of this text or a list of equations you should be able to do the following:

1. Calculate the $BOD_5$, given the sample size and oxygen consumption, or calculate the sample size, given the allowable oxygen consumption and estimated $BOD_5$.
2. Calculate the ultimate BOD ($L_0$), given the BOD exerted ($BOD_t$) in time, $t$, and rate constant, or calculate the rate constant, $k$, given $L_0$ and $BOD_t$.
3. Calculate a new $k$ for a temperature other than 20°C, given a value at $T$°C.
4. Calculate the BOD rate constant ($k$) and ultimate BOD ($L_0$) from experimental data of BOD versus time.
5. Calculate the oxygen deficit, $D$, in a length of stream (reach), given the required input data.
6. Calculate the critical oxygen deficit, $D_c$, at the critical point.
7. Calculate the rate of pollutant transport using retardation coefficients.

## PROBLEMS

**8-1**  Glutamic acid ($C_5H_9O_4N$) is used as one of the reagents for a standard to check the BOD test. Determine the theoretical oxygen demand of 150 mg $\cdot$ L$^{-1}$ of glutamic acid. Assume the following reactions apply.

$$C_5H_9O_4N + 4.5O_2 \longrightarrow 5CO_2 + 3H_2O + NH_3$$

$$NH_3 + 2O_2 \longrightarrow NO_3^- + H^+ + H_2O$$

**Answer:** 212 mg $\cdot$ L$^{-1}$

**8-2**  Bacterial cells have been represented by the chemical formula $C_5H_7NO_2$. Compute the theoretical oxygen demand (in grams $O_2 \cdot$ mol$^{-1}$ of cells), assuming the following reactions apply.

$$C_5H_7NO_2 + 5O_2 \longrightarrow 5CO_2 + 2H_2O + NH_3$$

$$NH_3 + 2O_2 \longrightarrow NO_3^- + H^+ + H_2O$$

**8-3**  If the $BOD_5$ of a waste is 220.0 mg $\cdot$ L$^{-1}$ and the ultimate BOD is 320.0 mg $\cdot$ L$^{-1}$, what is the rate constant?

**Answer:** $k = 0.233$ day$^{-1}$

**8-4**  If the BOD of a municipal wastewater at the end of 7 days is 60.0 mg $\cdot$ L$^{-1}$ and the ultimate BOD is 85.0 mg $\cdot$ L$^{-1}$, what is the rate constant?

**8-5**  The BOD rate constant is 0.233 day$^{-1}$ for a municipal wastewater. The $BOD_5$ was measured to be 250 mg $\cdot$ L$^{-1}$. What is the ultimate BOD?

**Answer:** 363 mg $\cdot$ L$^{-1}$

**8-6**  The BOD rate constant is 0.433 day$^{-1}$ for a municipal wastewater. The $BOD_5$ was measured to be 272 mg $\cdot$ L$^{-1}$. What is the ultimate BOD?

**8-7**  Assuming that the data in Problem 8–3 were taken at 20°C, compute the rate constant at a temperature of 15°C.

**Answer:** $k = 0.124$ day$^{-1}$

**8-8**  Assuming that the data in Problem 8–4 were taken at 25°C, compute the rate constant at 16°C.

**8-9**  A sample of municipal sewage is diluted to 1% by volume prior to running a $BOD_5$ analysis. After 5 days the oxygen consumption is determined to be 2.00 mg $\cdot$ L$^{-1}$. What is the $BOD_5$ of the sewage?

**Answer:** $BOD_5 = 200$ mg $\cdot$ L$^{-1}$

**8-10**  What sample size (in percent) is required for a $BOD_5$ of 350.0 mg $\cdot$ L$^{-1}$ if the oxygen consumed is to be limited to 6.00 mg $\cdot$ L$^{-1}$?

**8-11** If the ultimate BOD values of two wastes having $k$ values of 0.3800 day$^{-1}$ and 0.220 day$^{-1}$ are 280.0 mg · L$^{-1}$, what would be the 5-day BOD for each?

**Answer:** For $k = 0.38$ day$^{-1}$, BOD$_5$ = 238 mg · L$^{-1}$; for $k = 0.22$ day$^{-1}$, BOD$_5$ = 187 mg · L$^{-1}$

**8-12** If the BOD$_5$ values for two livestock wastes having $k$ values of 0.3800 day$^{-1}$ and 0.240 day$^{-1}$ are 16230.0 mg · L$^{-1}$, what would be the ultimate BOD for each?

**8-13** Using the data from Problem 8–1, calculate the NBOD of glutamic acid. Assume the concentration of glutamic acid is 0.1 mM.

**Answer:** CBOD = 14.4 mg O$_2$ · L$^{-1}$ and NBOD = 6.4 g mO$_2$ · L$^{-1}$

**8-14** Using the data from Problem 8–2, calculate the NBOD of bacterial cells.

**8-15** The Waramurungundi tannery with a wastewater flow of 0.011 m$^3$ · s$^{-1}$ and a BOD$_5$ of 590 mg · L$^{-1}$ discharges into the Djanggawul Creek. The creek has a 10-year, 7-day low flow of 1.7 m$^3$ · s$^{-1}$. Upstream of the Waramurungundi tannery, the BOD$_5$ of the creek is 0.6 mg · L$^{-1}$. The BOD rate constants ($k$) are 0.115 day$^{-1}$ for the Waramurungundi tannery and 3.7 day$^{-1}$ for the creek. Calculate the initial ultimate BOD after mixing.

**Answer:** 9.27 mg · L$^{-1}$

**8-16** A short distance downstream from the Waramurungundi tannery in Problem 8–15, a glue factory and a municipal wastewater treatment plant also discharge into Djanggawul Creek. The wastewater flows and ultimate BOD$_5$ for these discharges are listed in the following table. Determine the initial ultimate BOD after mixing of the creek and the three wastewater discharges.

| Source | Flow (m$^3$ · s$^{-1}$) | Ultimate BOD (mg · L$^{-1}$) |
|---|---|---|
| Glue factory | 0.13 | 255 |
| Municipal WWTP | 0.02 | 75 |

**8-17** Compute the deoxygenation rate constant and reaeration rate constant (base $e$) for the following wastewater and stream conditions.

| Source | $k$ (day$^{-1}$) | Temperature (°C) | $H$ (m) | Velocity (m · s$^{-1}$) | $\eta$ |
|---|---|---|---|---|---|
| Wastewater | 0.20 | 20 | | | |
| Amaunet Stream | | 20 | 3.0 | 0.5 | 0.4 |

**Answer:** $k_d = 0.40$ day$^{-1}$; $k_r = 0.53$ day$^{-1}$

**8-18** During flood stage, the stream conditions in Problem 8–17 change as shown in the following table. Determine the values of $k_d$ and $k_r$ for flood conditions.

| Source | $k$ (day$^{-1}$) | Temperature (°C) | $H$ (m) | Velocity (m · s$^{-1}$) | $\eta$ |
|---|---|---|---|---|---|
| Wastewater | 0.20 | 20 | | | |
| Amaunet Stream | | 20 | 4.0 | 2.5 | 0.5 |

**8-19** The initial ultimate BOD after mixing of the Bergelmir River is 12.0 mg · L$^{-1}$. The DO in the Bergelmir River after the wastewater and river have mixed is at saturation. The river temperature is 10°C. At 10°C, the deoxygenation rate constant ($k_d$) is 0.30 $day^{-1}$, and the reaeration rate constant ($k_r$) is 0.40 $day^{-1}$. Determine the critical point ($t_c$) and the critical DO.

> **Answer:** $t_c = 2.88$ days. Critical DO $= 7.53$ mg $\cdot$ $L^{-1}$

**8-20** Repeat Problem 8–19, assuming the river temperature rises to 15°C so that $k_d$ and $k_r$ change.

**8-21** The discharge from the Renenutet sugar beet plant causes the DO at the critical point to fall to 4.0 mg $\cdot$ $L^{-1}$. The Meskhenet Stream has a negligible BOD and the initial deficit after the river and wastewater have mixed is zero. What DO will result if the concentration of the waste ($L_w$) is reduced by 50%? Assume that the flows remain the same and that the saturation value of DO is 10.83 mg $\cdot$ $L^{-1}$ in both cases.

> **Answer:** DO $= 7.4$ mg $\cdot$ $L^{-1}$

**8-22** The Audhumla town council has asked that you determine whether the discharge of the town's wastewater into the Einherjar River will reduce the DO below the state standard of 5.00 mg $\cdot$ $L^{-1}$ at Gotterdämmerung, 5.79 km downstream, or at any other point downstream. The pertinent data are as follows:

| Parameter | Wastewater | Einherjar River |
|---|---|---|
| Flow (in $m^3 \cdot s^{-1}$) | 0.280 | 0.877 |
| Ult-BOD at 15°C | 6.44 | 7.00 |
| DO (in mg $\cdot$ $L^{-1}$) | 1.00 | 6.00 |
| $k_d$ at 28°C (in $day^{-1}$) | N/A | 0.199 |
| $k_r$ at 28°C (in $day^{-1}$) | N/A | 0.370 |
| Speed (in m $\cdot$ $s^{-1}$) | N/A | 0.650 |
| Temperature (in °C) | 28 | 28 |

> **Answers:** DO at Gotterdämmerung $= 4.75$ mg $\cdot$ $L^{-1}$
> Critical DO $= 4.72$ mg $\cdot$ $L^{-1}$ at $t_c = 0.3149$ day

**8-23** The town of Edinkira has filed a complaint with the state department of natural resources (DNR) that the city of Quamta is restricting its use of the Umvelinqangi River because of the discharge of raw sewage. The DNR water quality criterion for the Umvelinqangi River is 5.00 mg $\cdot$ $L^{-1}$ of DO. Edinkira is 15.55 km downstream from Quamta. What is the DO at Edinkira? What is the critical DO and where (at what distance) downstream does it occur? Is the assimilative capacity of the river restricted? The following data pertain to the 7-year, 10-day low flow at Quamta.

| Parameter | Wastewater | Umvelinqangi River |
|---|---|---|
| Flow (in $m^3 \cdot s^{-1}$) | 0.1507 | 1.08 |
| $BOD_5$ at 16°C (in mg $\cdot$ $L^{-1}$) | 128.00 | N/A |
| $BOD_u$ at 16°C (in mg $\cdot$ $L^{-1}$) | N/A | 11.40 |
| DO (in mg $\cdot$ $L^{-1}$) | 1.00 | 7.95 |
| $k$ at 20°C (in $day^{-1}$) | 0.4375 | N/A |
| Speed (in m $\cdot$ $s^{-1}$) | N/A | 0.390 |
| Depth (in m) | N/A | 2.80 |
| Temperature (in °C) | 28 | 28 |
| Bed-activity coeff. | N/A | 0.200 |

**8-24** Under the provisions of the Clean Water Act, the U.S. Environmental Protection Agency established a requirement that municipalities had to provide secondary treatment of their waste. This was defined to be treatment that resulted in an effluent $BOD_5$ that did not exceed 30 mg $\cdot$ $L^{-1}$. The discharge from Quamta (Problem 8–23) is clearly in violation of this standard. Given the data in Problem 23, rework the problem, assuming that Quamta provides treatment to lower the $BOD_5$ to 30.00 mg $\cdot$ $L^{-1}$.

**8-25** If the population and water use of Quamta (Problems 8–23 and 8–24) are growing at 5% per year with a corresponding increase in wastewater flow, how many years' growth may be sustained before secondary treatment becomes inadequate? Assume that the treatment plant continues to maintain an effluent $BOD_5$ of $30.00 \ mg \cdot L^{-1}$.

**Answer:** $n = 1.73$ year's growth if we impose the constraint that the critical DO cannot be less than $5.0 \ mg \cdot L^{-1}$.

**8-26** When ice covers a river, it severely limits the reaeration. There is some compensation for the reduced aeration because of the reduced water temperature. The lower temperature reduces the biological activity and, thus, the deaeration rate and, at the same time, the DO saturation level increases. Assuming a winter condition, rework Problem 8–23 with the reaeration reduced to 0 and the river water temperature at 2°C.

**8-27** What combination of BOD reduction and wastewater DO increase is required so the Audhumla wastewater in Problem 8–22 does not reduce the DO below $5.00 \ mg \cdot L^{-1}$ anywhere along the Einherjar River? Assume that the cost of BOD reduction is three to five times that of increasing the effluent DO. Because the cost of adding extra DO is high, limit the excess above the minimum amount such that the critical DO falls between $5.00$ and $5.25 \ mg \cdot L^{-1}$.

**Answer:** Raising the wastewater DO to $2.7 \ mg \cdot L^{-1}$ is the most cost-effective remedy.

**8-28** What amount of ultimate BOD (in $kg \cdot day^{-1}$) may Quamta (Problem 8–23) discharge and still allow Edinkira $1.50 \ mg \cdot L^{-1}$ of DO above the DNR water quality criteria for assimilation of its waste?

**8-29** Assuming that the mixed oxygen deficit ($D_a$) is zero and that the ultimate BOD ($L_r$) of the Manco Capac River above the wastewater outfall from Urcaguary is zero, calculate the amount of ultimate BOD (in $kg \cdot day^{-1}$) that can be discharged if the DO must be kept at $4.00 \ mg \cdot L^{-1}$ at a point 8.05 km downstream. The stream deoxygenation rate ($k_d$) is $1.80 \ day^{-1}$ at 12°C, and the reaeration rate ($k_r$) is $2.20 \ day^{-1}$ at 12°C. The river temperature is 12°C. The river flow is $5.95 \ m^3 \cdot s^{-1}$ with a speed of $0.300 \ m \cdot s^{-1}$. The Urcaguary wastewater flow is $0.0130 \ m^3 \cdot s^{-1}$.

**Answer:** Mass flux $= 1.14 \times 10^4 \ kg \cdot day^{-1}$ of ultimate BOD

**8-30** Calculate the DO at a point 1.609 km downstream from a waste discharge point for the following conditions. Report answers to two decimal places. Rate constants are already temperature adjusted.

| Parameters | Stream |
| --- | --- |
| $k_d$ | $1.911 \ day^{-1}$ |
| $k_r$ | $4.49 \ day^{-1}$ |
| Flow | $2.4 \ m^3 \cdot s^{-1}$ |
| Speed | $0.100 \ m \cdot s^{-1}$ |
| $D_a$ (after mixing) | $0.00$ |
| Temperature (in °C) | $17.00$ |
| ult-BOD (after mixing) | $1100.00 \ kg \cdot day^{-1}$ |

**8-31** Assume that the Urcaguary wastewater (Problem 8–29) also contains $3.0 \ mg \cdot L^{-1}$ of ammonia nitrogen with a stream deoxygenation rate of $0.900 \ day^{-1}$ at 12°C. What is the amount of ultimate carbonaceous BOD (in $kg \cdot day^{-1}$), that Urcaguary can discharge and still meet the DO level of $4.00 \ mg \cdot L^{-1}$ at a point 8.05 km downstream? Assume also that the theoretical amount of oxygen will ultimately be consumed in the nitrification process.

**Answer:** Mass flux $= 6.2 \times 10^3 \ kg \cdot day^{-1}$

**8-32** An aquifer has a hydraulic gradient of 0.00086, a hydraulic conductivity of $200 \ m \cdot day^{-1}$ and a porosity of 0.23. A chemical with a retardation factor of 2.3 contaminates the aquifer. What is the linear velocity of the contaminant? How long will it take for the contaminant to travel 100 m in the aquifer?

## DISCUSSION QUESTIONS

**8-1** Students in a graduate-level environmental engineering laboratory took samples of the influent (raw sewage) and effluent (treated sewage) of a municipal wastewater treatment plant. They used these samples to determine the BOD rate constant ($k$). Would you expect the rate constants to be the same or different? If different, which would be higher and why?

**8-2** If it were your job to set standards for a water body and you had a choice of either $BOD_5$ or ultimate BOD, which would you choose and why?

**8-3** A summer intern has turned in his log book for temperature measurements for a limnology survey. He was told to take the measurements in the air 1 m above the lake, 1 m deep in the lake, and at a depth of 10 m. He turned in the following results but did not record which temperatures were taken where. If the measurements were made at noon in July in Missouri, what is your best guess as to the location of the measurements (i.e., air, 1-m deep, 10-m deep)? The recorded values were: 33°C, 18°C, and 21°C.

**8-4** If the critical point in a DO sag curve is found to be 18 km downstream from the discharge point of untreated wastewater, would you expect the critical point to move upstream (toward the discharge point), downstream, or remain in the same place, if the wastewater is treated?

**8-5** You have been assigned to conduct an environmental study of a remote lake in Canada. Aerial photos and a ground-level survey reveal no anthropogenic waste sources are contributing to the lake. When you investigate the lake, you find a highly turbid lake with abundant mats of floating algae and a hypolimnion DO of $1.0 \text{ mg} \cdot \text{L}^{-1}$. What productivity class would you assign to this lake? Explain your reasoning.

**8-6** The lakes in Illinois, Indiana, western Kentucky, the lower peninsula of Michigan, and Ohio do not appear to be subject to acidification even though the rainwater pH is 4.4. Based on your knowledge (or what you can discover by research) of the topography, vegetation, and bedrock, explain why the lakes in these areas are not acidic.

## ADDITIONAL READING

Davis, M., and D. Cornwell. *Introduction to Environmental Engineering,* 3rd ed. McGraw-Hill, New York (1998).

Morton, S. D. *Water Pollution Causes and Cures.* Mimir Publications, Madison, Wisconsin (1976).

Nemerow, N. L. *Scientific Stream Pollution Analysis.* McGraw-Hill, New York (1974).

Tchobanoglous, G., E. D. Schroeder. *Water Quality.* Addison Wesley, Reading, Massachusetts (1985).

## REFERENCES

1. Ash, R. J., B. Mauck, M. Morgan, et al. "Antibiotic resistant bacteria in U.S. rivers" (Abstract Q-383). In: *Abstracts of the 99th General Meeting of the American Society for Microbiology.* Chicago, May 30–June 3, 1999, p. 607.

2. Sternes, K. L. "Presence of high-level vancomycin resistant enterococci in the Upper Rio Grande" (Abstract Q-63). In: *Abstracts of the 99th General Meeting of the American Society for Microbiology.* Chicago, May 30–June 3, 1999, p. 545.

3. Bennett, J., and G. Kramer. "Multidrug resistant strains of bacteria in the streams of Dubuque County, Iowa" (Abstract Q-86). In: *Abstracts of the 99th General Meeting of the American Society for Microbiology.* Chicago, May 30–June 3, 1999, p. 464.

4. Raloff, J. "Waterways carry antibiotic resistance," *Science News Online* 6/5/99. http://www.sciencenews.org/sn_arc99/6_5_99/fobl.htm

5. Buser, H. R., T. Poiger, and M. D. Muller. "Occurrence and environmental behavior of the chiral pharmaceutical drug iboprofen in surface waters and waste water," *Environmental Science Technology,* vol. 33(15): pp. 2529–2535 (1999).

   Buser, H. R., T. Poiger, and M. D. Muller. "Occurrence and fate of the pharmaceutical drug diclofenac in surface waters: Rapid photodegradation in a lake," *Environmental Science Technology,* vol. 32(22): pp. 3449–3456 (1998).

   Buser, H. R., M. D. Muller, and N. Theobald. "Occurrence of the pharmaceutical drug clofibric acid and the herbicide mecoprop in various Swiss lakes and in the North Sea," *Environmental Science Technology,* vol. 32(1): pp. 188–192 (1998).

6. Sedlak, D. L., J. L. Gray, and K. E. Pinkston. "Understanding microcontaminants in recycled water," *Environmental Science Technology,* vol. 34: pp. 508A–515A (2000).

7. Sadik, O. A., and D. M. Witt. "Monitoring endocrine-disrupting chemicals," *Environmental Science Technology,* vol. 33: pp. 368A–374A (1999).

   Harries, J. E., T. Runnalls, E. Hill, et al. *Development of a Reproductive Performance Test for Endocrine Disrupting Chemicals Using Pair-Breeding Fathead Minnows (Pimephales promelas),* vol. 34(14), pp. 3003–3011 and references cited within these two articles.

8. Welch, A. H., Helsel, D. R., Focazio, M. J., et al. "Arsenic in ground water supplies of the United States." In: *Arsenic Exposure and Health Effects,* W. R. Chappell, C. O. Abernathy, and R. L. Calderon, eds. Elsevier Science, New York, pp. 9–17 (1999).

9. Chen, C. J., C. W. Chen, M. M. Wu , and T. L. Kuo, "Cancer potential in liver, lung, bladder and kidney due to inorganic arsenic in drinking water," *British Journal of Cancer,* vol. 66, pp. 888–892 (1992).

10. National Research Council. *Arsenic in Drinking Water.* National Academy Press, Washington, D.C. (1999).

11. National Research Council. *Update: Arsenic in Drinking Water.* National Academy Press, Washington D.C. (2001).

12. Nagler, J. J., J. Bouma, G. H. Thorgaard, et al. "High incidence of a male-specific genetic marker in phenotypic female chinook salmon from the Columbia River," *Environmental Health Perspectives,* vol. 109(1): pp. 67–69 (2001).

13. Schroepfer, G. J., M. L. Robins, and R. H. Susag, "Research program on the Mississippi River in the vicinity of Minneapolis and St. Paul," *Advances in Water Pollution Research,* vol. 1, Part 1, p. 145 (1964).

14. American Public Health Association. *Standard Methods for the Examination of Water and Wastewater,* 19th ed., Washington, DC, 1995.

15. Streeter, H. W., and E. B. Phelps. *A Study of the Pollution and Natural Purification of the Ohio River,* U.S. Public Health Service Bulletin No. 146 (1925).

16. O'Connor, D. J., and W. E. Dobbins. "Mechanism of reaeration in natural streams," *American Society of Civil Engineers Transactions,* vol. 153, p. 641 (1958).

17. Ryan, P. M., and H. H. Harvey. "Growth responses of yellow perch, Perca flavescens (Mitchill), to lake acidification in La Cloche Mountains of Ontario," *Environmental Biology of Fish,* vol. 5: pp. 97–108 (1980).

18. Dickson, W. "Properties of acidified waters," In: *Ecological Impact of Acid Precipitation,* D. Drablosand A. Tollan, eds. SNSF, Sandefjord, Norway, pp. 75–83 (1980).

19. Galloway, J. N., and E. B. Cowling. "The effects of precipitation on aquatic and terrestrial ecosystems: A proposed precipitation chemistry network," *Journal of the Air Pollution Control Association,* vol. 28, pp. 229–235 (1978).

20. Much of this section is taken from the following sources: US EPA National Estuary Program: About Estuaries.
    http://www.epa.gov/owow/estuaries/about1.htm
    National Estuarine Research Reserve System: An introduction to estuaries. Belle W. Baruch Institute for Marine Biology and Coastal Research
    http://inlet.geol.sc.edu/nerrsintro.html

21. U.S. EPA Coral Reefs
    http://www.epa.gov/owow/oceans/yoto/oceanrpt/coral.html

22. Neergaard, L. "FDA: While Pregnant, Limit Fish," Associated Press, *Lansing State Journal,* January 13, 2001.

23. "Toxin Might Hurt Endangered Whales," Associated Press, January 13, 2001.

24. Benton, T. "Oceans of Garbage," *Nature,* vol. 352: p. 113 (1991).

# 9

# Water Treatment

## 9–1   INTRODUCTION

Public drinking-water systems provide drinking water to 90% of U.S. residents. In the United States 170,000 water systems are classified as public. Of these, approximately 55,000 community water systems serve 252.5 million people. **Public systems** are defined as serving at least 25 persons per day for 60 days or more out of the year. **Community water systems** supply water to the same population year-round and include, for example, cities, townships, subdivisions, and trailer parks. **Nontransient noncommunity systems** are those that regularly supply water to at least 25 of the same people at least 6 months per year but not year-round. These include schools, factories, office buildings and hospitals that have their own water supply. **Transient noncommunity systems** provide water in locations, such as restaurants, motels, campgrounds, and service stations, where people do not remain for long periods. Some 20,255 non-transient noncommunity water systems serve 6.2 million people, while 16.8 million people are served by 95,754 transient noncommunity water systems [1].

In the United States and in most developed countries, residents can be confident that their health will not be jeopardized because of poor quality water. In the period 1971 through 1996, fewer than 55 waterborne disease outbreaks occurred each year [2]. On the contrary, in many developing nations, clean water is the exception rather than the rule. As former EPA Administrator Russel F. Train remarked,

> Something like 40 percent of the human race does not have adequate access to safe water. Waterborne diseases are estimated to kill more than 25,000 people daily. Schistosomiasis and filariasis, the world's largest causes of blindness, affect—according to one estimate— some 450 million people in more than 70 nations. There are, economist Barbara Ward has said, cities in the developing world where 60 percent of the children born die of infantile gastritis before the age of five . . . [3]

It is no accident that the United States, the United Kingdom, and other developed countries have an outstanding water supply record. Since the early 1900s, engineers have been working to reduce waterborne disease. Figure 9–1 shows the incidence of typhoid fever in Philadelphia from 1890 to 1935. This decrease in waterborne diseases is typical as public water supply treatment has increased. Philadelphia received its water from rivers and distributed the water untreated until about 1906, when slow sand filters were put into use. An immediate reduction in the incidences of typhoid fever was realized.

Disinfection of the water by the addition of chlorine further decreased the number of typhoid cases. A still greater decrease was accomplished after 1920 by careful control over infected persons who had become carriers. Since 1952 the death rate from typhoid fever in the United States has been less than 1 per 1,000,000. Many developed countries and organizations have committed their technological and financial resources to creating reasonable access to safe and adequate drinking water for still developing nations in recognition of the principle that safe water is a fundamental right of all people.

**FIGURE 9–1**

Typhoid fever cases per 100,000 population from 1890 to 1935, Philadelphia.

Water that can be consumed in any desired amount without concern for adverse health effects is termed **potable water.** Just because water is potable (pronounced POH-tah-ble) does not necessarily mean that it tastes good. However, **palatable water,** which is pleasing to drink, is not necessarily safe. Over time we have learned that water must be both potable and palatable, because if it is not palatable people will turn to untreated water that may not be safe. The widespread availability of potable water in the United States does not mean that water systems have no operational or control deficiencies. As populations increase, so must water production. Often increased production requires the use of new water sources that contain higher contaminant levels. As production increases while plant capacity remains the same, the task of producing potable water becomes increasingly difficult. The scientific community is continually making advances in identifying contaminants and discovering potential long-term health effects of constituents that had not been previously identified. At the same time that some scientists are assessing existing pollutants, others are producing new chemicals at a tremendous rate.

### Water Quality

All naturally occurring water supplies are recharged by precipitation. Although generally considered pure, rainwater may, and often does, contain impurities. These impurities, however, are much lower in concentration than that found in water once it reaches the earth's surface. Surface water presents many opportunities for the introduction of mineral and organic substances, microorganisms, and other forms of pollution (contamination).* When water runs over or through the ground surface, it may pick up particles of soil. This is noticeable in the water as cloudiness, or turbidity.† It also picks up particles of organic matter and bacteria. As surface water seeps downward into the soil and through the underlying material to the water table, most of the suspended particles are filtered out. This natural filtration may be partially effective in removing bacteria and other particulate materials. However, the chemical characteristics of the water may change and vary widely when it comes in contact with mineral deposits. As surface water seeps down to the water table, it dissolves some of the minerals contained in the soil and rocks. Groundwater, therefore, often contains more dissolved minerals than surface water.

The following four categories are used to describe drinking-water quality:

1. Physical: Physical characteristics relate to the quality of water for domestic use and are usually associated with the appearance of water, its color or turbidity, temperature, and, in particular, taste and odor.

---

*Pollution as used in this text means the presence in water of any foreign substances (organic, inorganic, radiological, or biological) that tend to lower its quality to such a point that it constitutes a health hazard or impairs the usefulness of the water.

†Turbidity, a measure of the decrease in light penetration, is a relative standard. A sample is compared against various standards. The different standards employed are similar, although not exactly the same. For our purposes we will simply refer to the measure of turbidity as a turbidity unit (TU). For a given particle size, the higher the turbidity, the higher the concentration of colloidal particles.

2. Chemical: The chemical characterization of drinking water includes the identification of its components and their concentrations.
3. Microbiological: Microbiological agents are important to public health and may also be significant in modifying the physical and chemical characteristics of water.
4. Radiological: Radiological factors must be considered in areas where the water may have come in contact with radioactive substances. The radioactivity of the water is of public health concern.

Consequently, in the development of a water supply system, it is necessary to examine carefully all the factors that might adversely affect the intended use of a water supply source.

## Physical Characteristics

As mentioned earlier, water suppliers monitor such physical characteristics as turbidity, color, taste and odor, and temperature. Turbidity is caused by the presence of suspended material such as clay, silt, finely divided organic material, plankton, and other particulate material in water. Although turbidity may not adversely affect health, these particles may harbor microbiological contaminants that are harmful to human health or that decrease the effectiveness of disinfectants.

Dissolved organic material from decaying vegetation and certain inorganic matter may cause color in water. Excessive blooms of algae or the growth of aquatic microorganisms may also impart color. Color can also be caused by inorganic metals such as iron or manganese, or by humic substances, which are formed from the degradation of leaves and other organic debris. Although color itself is not usually objectionable from the standpoint of health, its presence is aesthetically displeasing and suggests that the water needs appropriate treatment.

Foreign matter such as organic compounds, inorganic salts, or dissolved gases can cause taste and odor in water. Certain types of algae, especially the blue-green algae, can also impart foul tastes and odors.

The most desirable drinking waters are consistently cool and do not have temperature fluctuations of more than a few degrees. Groundwater and surface water from mountainous areas generally meet these criteria. Most individuals find that water having a temperature between 10–15°C is most palatable.

## Chemical Characteristics

Water treatment plants monitor for a variety of inorganic and organic constituents, including chloride, fluorides, sodium, sulfate, nitrates, and more than 120 organic chemicals. Some of these chemicals are monitored for health reasons; others for more esthetic purposes. For example, iron and manganese rarely pose a health threat, whereas, the presence of nitrate can cause methemoglobinemia (blue baby syndrome) in infants. Nitrates most often originate from the application of agricultural fertilizers, whereas iron and manganese are naturally occurring. However, all three chemical species are viewed as contaminants because of their effects on water quality.

## Microbiological Characteristics

Water for drinking and cooking purposes must be made free from disease-producing organisms (pathogens), such as viruses, bacteria, protozoa, and helminths (worms). Within the United States, the most common causal agent of waterborne diseases is the protozoal parasite *Giardia lamblia* [4]. Some organisms that cause disease in humans originate with the fecal discharges of infected individuals. Others are contained in the fecal discharge of animals.

Unfortunately, the specific disease-producing organisms present in water are not easily identified. The techniques for comprehensive bacteriological examination are complex and time-consuming. As such, it has been necessary to develop tests that indicate the relative degree of contamination in terms of an easily defined quantity.

The most widely used bacteriological assay estimates the number of microorganisms of the coliform group. This grouping includes two genera: *Escherichia coli* and *Aerobacter aerogenes*.

The name of the group is derived from the word *colon.* Although *E. coli* are common inhabitants of the intestinal tract, *Aerobacter* are common in the soil, on leaves, and on grain; on occasion they cause urinary tract infections. The test for these microorganisms, called the **total coliform test,** was selected for the following reasons:

1. The coliform group of organisms usually inhabits the intestinal tracts of humans and other mammals. Thus, the presence of coliforms is an indication of fecal contamination of the water.
2. Even in acutely ill individuals, the number of coliform organisms excreted in the feces outnumbers the disease-producing organisms by several orders of magnitude. The large numbers of coliforms make them easier to culture than disease-producing organisms.
3. The coliform group of organisms survives in natural waters for relatively long periods, but does not reproduce effectively in this environment. Thus, the presence of coliforms in water implies fecal contamination rather than growth of the organism because of favorable environmental conditions. These organisms also survive better in water than most of the bacterial pathogens. This means that the absence of coliforms is a reasonably safe indication that pathogens are not present.
4. The coliform group of organisms is relatively easy to culture. Thus, laboratory technicians can perform the test without expensive equipment.

Current research indicates that testing for *E. coli* specifically may be warranted. Some agencies consider testing for *E. coli* rather than total coliforms as a better indicator of biological contamination. One strain of *E. coli* (0157) produces a potent toxin (vero toxin) that causes cell damage, leading to the development of bloody diarrhea. The potentially fatal toxin can also cause liver and kidney damage. As such, the development of rapid screening techniques specific for this strain of *E. coli* is the focus of much research.

Although molecular tests for pathogens are not commercially available for use in the drinking-water industry at present, much research is being conducted to allow for their use in the future. These techniques use DNA sequencing of genes to identify specific species of organisms. With this method, hundreds of thousands of complementary DNA (cDNA*) strands of known sequence are arrayed on a standard glass microscope slide.

RNA is extracted from bacteria that have been isolated from the sample water and then are labeled with a fluorescent dye and bonded to the DNA on the slide. The fluorescent signal of the "spot" on the array is used to help identify the organism.

### Radiological Characteristics

The development and use of atomic energy as a power source and the mining and processing of radioactive materials, as well as naturally occurring radioactive materials, have made it necessary to establish limiting concentrations for the intake of radioactive substances into the body, including that in drinking water.

### Water Quality Standards

Prior to 1974, there was no consistent set of drinking-water regulations throughout the United States. In that year Congress enacted the Safe Drinking Water Act (SWDA), requiring the U.S. EPA to set uniform nationwide drinking-water standards. State public health departments are responsible for ensuring that U.S. regulations or more stringent state regulations (if they exist) are met.

With the promulgation of the act, EPA has issued drinking-water standards, or **maximum contaminant levels (MCLs).** These standards limit the amount of each substance that can be

---

*Synthetic DNA reverse transcribed from a specific RNA through the action of the enzyme reverse transcriptase.

present in a treated water. Presently there are more than 80 MCLs.* All MCLs are set at levels to protect human health. For most contaminants, the limits are determined by assessing the cancer and noncancer risks from exposure to a chemical in drinking water. In setting MCLs for carcinogenic compounds, EPA sets the level so as to limit an individual's added risk of cancer from exposure to that contaminant between 1:10,000 and 1,000,000 over a lifetime. For microbiological contaminants such as *Giardia lamblia* and chemical contaminants that pose an immediate threat, the standards are set so as to protect human health.

With the act, EPA has promulgated two types of drinking-water standards. The first, described earlier, are the primary standards, which are designed to protect human health and for which MCLs exist. The second type, or secondary drinking-water standards, is based on providing esthetically pleasing water. The secondary MCLs (SMCLs) are recommendations and, as such, are not mandatory.

In 1996, President Clinton signed the Safe Drinking Water Amendments into law. These amendments require that water utilities provide more complete information pertaining to water quality to their customers. Consumer confidence reports documenting the source of each person's drinking water, monitoring results, and providing information concerning health concerns associated with SDWA violations are required. The amendments also encourage more public involvement and emphasize source water protection by focusing more on identifying potential causes of contamination of drinking water source waters before they occur. Federal law also now requires certification of plant operators.

For some contaminants, EPA has not defined an MCL but instead specifies a specific treatment technique. For those contaminants, the notation TT (treatment technique) is used in place of an MCL. The treatment techniques are specific processes used to treat the water. Some examples include coagulation and filtration, lime softening, and ion exchange. These processes will be discussed in the following sections. EPA now recommends that water be essentially free of some contaminants, such as lead. Other contaminants falling into this category include benzene, carbon tetrachloride, dioxin, trichloroethylene, and vinyl chloride. Standards pertaining to disinfection are discussed in detail in Section 9–6.

**Other Standards.** Although, EPA has set maximum levels of possible contaminants in drinking waters, individual states may require compliance with more stringent regulations. In addition, other agencies such as the American Water Works Association or the World Health Organization have their own set of recommendations or goals [5]. In Europe, the European Union sets standards [6].

### Water Classification and Treatment Systems

**Water Classification by Source.** Although salt water is used as a drinking-water supply (e.g., in the desert regions along the Persian Gulf), freshwater is the preferred source. As such, the remaining discussion will focus only on freshwater supplies. Potable water is most conveniently classified as to its source, that is, groundwater or surface water. Groundwater is pumped from wells drilled into aquifers. As mentioned in Chapters 6 and 8, the quantity and quality of water available depends on the type of geological formation forming the aquifer and the properties of the contaminant, itself. Drinking-water wells can be shallow (less than 50 ft) or deep (greater than 50 ft). Although, in general, the deeper the well, the greater the level of protection from contamination, deep wells only provide protection when the wells are properly designed and operated so that surface contamination is prevented. The severity of the consequences for overlooking this fact were, unfortunately, exemplified by an incident in Walkerton, Ontario. In May 2000, one of the wells supplying drinking water to the city of Walkerton (about 180 km north of Toronto) became

---

*A full list of the primary and secondary drinking-water contaminants and their associated MCLs or SMCLs can be found on the US EPA website.
http:/www.epa.gov/OGWDW/wot/howsafe.html

**TABLE 9–1**                     General Characteristics of Groundwater and Surface Water

| Ground | Surface |
|---|---|
| Constant composition | Varying composition |
| High mineral content | Low mineral content |
| Low turbidity | High turbidity |
| Low or no color | Color |
| May be bacteriologically safe | Microorganisms present |
| No dissolved oxygen | Dissolved oxygen |
| High hardness | Low hardness |
| $H_2S$, Fe, Mn | Tastes and odors |
| Possible chemical toxicity | Possible chemical toxicity |

**FIGURE 9–2**

Flow diagram of a
conventional surface-
water treatment plant
(coagulation plant).

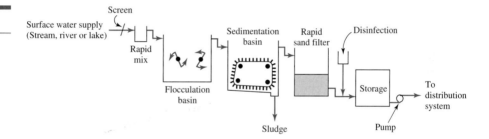

contaminated with animal waste during a heavy rainstorm. Failure of the chlorination system
along with contamination of wells with *E. coli* 0157, a highly toxic strain of the bacteria, resulted
in seven confirmed deaths and more than 1000 cases of illness.

Surface water includes rivers, lakes, and reservoirs. In general, surface and groundwater can
be characterized as shown in Table 9–1.

**Treatment Systems.**   Water treatment facilities come in one of three generally acceptable
variations: (1) limited treatment plants, (2) coagulation plants, and (3) softening plants. **Limited
treatment plants** generally have a high-quality water source and employ very specific treatment
techniques that address specific water quality issues. Some of these techniques include disinfection, corrosion control, fluoridation, iron/manganese removal, and softening. Under most regulations, limited treatment plants are used only for the treatment of groundwater as a raw water
source. **Coagulation plants** are typically used to treat surface water and **softening plants** to treat
waters having a high hardness level, typically groundwater. In a coagulation plant, rapid mixing,
flocculation, sedimentation, filtration, and disinfection are employed to remove color, turbidity,
taste and odors, and bacteria. Additional operations usually include bar racks or coarse screens.
The more contaminated a water source, the more extensive and expensive is the requisite treatment. Because many chemicals are difficult and costly to remove and because routine analysis
for many others is neither cost-effective nor practical, it is better to prevent contamination in the
first place, minimizing the need for treatment.

Figure 9–2 shows a typical flow diagram of a coagulation plant. The raw (untreated) surface
water enters the plant via low-lift pumps. Usually screening has taken place prior to pumping.
During mixing, chemicals called **coagulants** are added and rapidly dispersed through the water.
The chemical reacts with the colloidal particles to form larger particles.

Once the particles are a sufficient size to precipitate, they are usually removed by gravity
(sedimentation). This minimizes the amount of solids applied to the filters. For treatment works
with high-quality raw water, it may be possible to omit sedimentation and perhaps flocculation

**FIGURE 9–3**

Flow diagram of a water-softening plant.

basins. This modification is called **direct filtration.** With direct filtration, coagulants may be added directly to the piping network just prior to filtration. An in-line mixer provides mixing, and flow in the pipe allows for flocculation. **Filtration** is the final polishing (removal) of particles. During filtration the water is passed through sand or similar media to screen out the fine particles that did not settle.

**Disinfection** is the addition of chemicals (usually chlorine or ozone) that reduce the number of pathogenic organisms to levels that will not cause disease. Storage is provided to meet peak demands and to allow the plant to operate on a uniform schedule. The high-lift pumps provide sufficient pressure to convey the water to its ultimate destination.

The precipitated chemicals, original turbidity, and suspended material are removed from the sedimentation basins and from the filters. This sludge must be disposed of properly.

Although softening plants are similar to coagulation plants, the two use different chemicals. Additionally, although both employ settling, the solids contact chamber in a softening plant is different from a sedimentation tank used in a coagulation plant. The primary function of a softening plant is to remove hardness (predominantly calcium and magnesium). The design considerations in a softening plant (a typical flow diagram for which is shown in Figure 9–3), are different from those in filtration facilities. Also the chemical doses are much higher in softening, and the corresponding sludge production is greater.

During rapid mixing, chemicals are added to react with and precipitate the minerals that produce hardness. Precipitation occurs in the reaction basin. The other unit operations are the same as in a filtration plant except for the additional recarbonation step employed in softening to adjust the final pH.

In the next two sections of this chapter, we discuss the chemistry of coagulation and softening, respectively. The subsequent sections describe the physical processes themselves. These are applicable to both filtration and softening plants.

## 9–2  RAPID MIXING, FLOCCULATION, AND COAGULATION

Coagulation is used to remove turbidity, color, and bacteria from drinking waters. The goal of coagulation is to change the surface charge on the particles so they can stick together to form larger particles that will settle by gravity. Although chemists tend to use the term *coagulation* to describe this change in surface charge and subsequent adhesion process, environmental engineers often use the term to describe the entire process by which larger particles and dissolved ions are removed by gravity settling or precipitation. In this chapter we will use the term *coagulation* to describe the removal of particulate matter and the term *softening* for the removal of dissolved hardness ions (predominantly calcium and magnesium).

### Colloid Stability and Destabilization

In natural waters, colloids are stable because the surface of these particles are like-charged, and they, therefore, repel one another. Additionally, colloidal particles are too small to effectively settle by gravity. For an extended definition of colloids  (or colloidal particles) see page 64 of this text.

**FIGURE 9–4**

Schematic coagulation curves for several different coagulants.

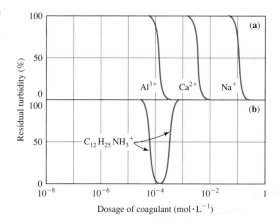

Coagulation results in a change in the surface charge on the particles. This is necessary in surface water because most of the colloidal particles are derived from clays, which have a net negative surface charge. The particles act like magnets: when the same poles (e.g., north) are pointed at each other, the magnets repel. The negatively charged particles also repel. The goal of the coagulant is to neutralize the charge on the surface so that when the particles contact one another in the flocculation basin they "stick together" to form settlable particles called **floc.** The energy imparted during a collision will (for some percentage of the particles) be sufficient to cause the particles to flocculate. If enough particles adhere to one another, they will "grow" to a settleable size. It is also important that the mixing speed in the flocculator not be so fast as to shear or break apart the floc particles.

As one might expect, the higher the concentration of the positive ion added, the greater the extent to which the surface charge is neutralized (Figure 9–4a). The greater the concentration of sodium ions added, the lower the residual turbidity. The same phenomenon can be observed with $Ca^{2+}$ and $Al^{3+}$, except that the greater the charge on the dissolved cation, the lower the concentration necessary. Although colloid destabilization may seem like a simple phenomenon from the discussion given here, it is actually more complex. As seen in Figure 9–4b, the addition of dodecyl ammonium ions, which also have a charge of 1, has a much greater effect than does the addition of sodium ions. This occurs because the long chain of the $C_{12}$ group when attached to a particle essentially pushes the particle out of the water so that it is more likely to interact with other particles. Additionally, if too much dodecyl ammonium is added, restabilization of the colloids occurs, and the turbidity increases. This is because the excess ions adsorbed to the surface results in a net positive surface charge, causing the colloids to again repel. This process is called **restabilization.**

### Coagulants

As previously mentioned, a coagulant is a chemical that is added to the water to cause the particles to coagulate. A coagulant has three key properties:

1. **Trivalent cation.** As discussed previously, naturally occurring colloids are most commonly negatively charged, hence cations are required to achieve charge neutralization. As shown in Figure 9–4a, trivalent cations are much more effective than monovalent or divalent simple cations, such as sodium and calcium.
2. **Nontoxic.** Obviously, for the production of potable water, the coagulant must be nontoxic.
3. **Insoluble in the neutral pH range.** High concentrations of the coagulant in treated water are undesirable. Therefore, a coagulant is usually relatively insoluble at the pH values desired.

The two most commonly used metallic coagulants are aluminum ($Al^{3+}$) and ferric iron ($Fe^{3+}$). Both meet the preceding three requirements, and their reactions are outlined here.

**Aluminum Sulfate.** Aluminum sulfate can be purchased as either dry or liquid alum $(Al_2(SO_4)_3 \cdot 14H_2O)$. Commercial alum has an average molecular weight of 594, with approximately 14 waters of hydration.

Alum reacts with alkalinity according to the following reaction:

$$Al_2(SO_4)_3 \cdot 14H_2O + 6HCO_3^- \rightleftharpoons 2Al(OH)_3(s) + 6CO_2 + 14H_2O + 3SO_4^{2-} \tag{9-1}$$

such that each mole of alum added uses six moles of alkalinity and produces six moles of carbon dioxide. The preceding reaction shifts the carbonate equilibrium and decreases the pH. However, as long as sufficient alkalinity is present and $CO_2(g)$ is allowed to evolve, the pH will not be drastically reduced. When sufficient alkalinity is not present to neutralize the sulfuric acid production, the pH may be lowered significantly due to the formation of sulfuric acid.

$$Al_2(SO_4)_3 \cdot 14H_2O \rightleftharpoons 2Al(OH)_3(s) + 3H_2SO_4 + 8H_2O \tag{9-2}$$

If pH control is a problem, lime or sodium carbonate may be added to neutralize the acid, thereby stabilizing the pH.

Two important factors in coagulant addition are pH and dose. The optimum dose and pH must be determined from laboratory jar tests. The optimal pH range for alum is approximately 5.5–6.5, with adequate coagulation possible at pH between 5 and 8 under some conditions.

**EXAMPLE 9–1**  A water treatment plant with an average flow of $Q = 0.044$ m³ · s⁻¹ treats its water with alum $(Al_2(SO_4)_3 \cdot 14H_2O)$ at a dose of 25 mg · L⁻¹. Alum coagulation is used to remove particulate matter, reduce the concentration of organic matter, and reduce the alkalinity of the water according to Equation 9–1. If the organic matter concentration is reduced from 8 mg · L⁻¹ to 3 mg · L⁻¹, determine the total mass of alkalinity consumed and the total mass of dry solids removed per day.

**Solution**  First determine the total amount of alkalinity consumed. We do this by noting that, according to Equation 9–1, for each mole of alum added, six moles of alkalinity (bicarbonate form) are removed. Now convert the alum dose into molar units using its molecular weight of 594.35 g · mol⁻¹

$$\frac{(25 \text{ mg} \cdot \text{L}^{-1})(10^{-3} \text{ g} \cdot \text{mg}^{-1})}{594.35 \text{ g} \cdot \text{mol}^{-1}} = 4.206 \times 10^{-5} \text{ mol} \cdot \text{L}^{-1} \text{ of alum}$$

Thus, with $4.206 \times 10^{-5}$ mol · L⁻¹ of alum added, the amount of $HCO_3^-$ removed is simply six times that, or

$$(6)(4.206 \times 10^{-5}) = 0.000252 \text{ mol} \cdot \text{L}^{-1} \text{ of } HCO_3^- \text{ or } 2.52 \times 10^{-4} \text{ eq} \cdot \text{L}^{-1} \text{ of alkalinity}$$

To find the total alkalinity removed per day, simply multiply the preceding number by the average flow of the plant

$$(0.000252 \text{ eq} \cdot \text{L}^{-1})(0.044 \text{ m}^3 \cdot \text{s}^{-1})(1000 \text{ L} \cdot \text{m}^{-3})(86{,}400 \text{ s} \cdot \text{day}^{-1}) = 959.4 \text{ eq} \cdot \text{day}^{-1}$$

Converting to a mass basis, using the equivalent weight of bicarbonate to be 61 g · mol⁻¹, yields

$$959.4 \text{ eq} \cdot \text{day}^{-1} \times 61 \text{ g} \cdot \text{eq}^{-1} = 58{,}526 \text{ g} \cdot \text{day}^{-1}, \text{ or } 58.5 \text{ kg} \cdot \text{day}^{-1}$$

For the second part of the problem we note that for every mole of alum added, two moles of solid precipitate. So, the amount of solid is

$$\left(\frac{2 \text{ mol Al(OH)}_3}{\text{mol alum}}\right)(4.206 \times 10^{-5} \text{ mol} \cdot \text{L}^{-1} \text{ of alum}) = 8.41 \times 10^{-5} \text{ mol} \cdot \text{L}^{-1} \text{ of Al(OH)}_3$$

Again putting this number on a per day basis yields,

$$(8.41 \times 10^{-5} \text{ mol} \cdot \text{L}^{-1})(0.044 \text{ m}^3 \cdot \text{s}^{-1})(1000 \text{ L} \cdot \text{m}^{-3})(86,400 \text{ s} \cdot \text{day}^{-1}) = 319.8 \text{ mol} \cdot \text{day}^{-1}$$

converting to mass basis, using the molecular weight of aluminum hydroxide ($78 \text{ g} \cdot \text{mol}^{-1}$), we obtain

$$319.8 \text{ mol} \cdot \text{day}^{-1} \times 78 \text{ g} \cdot \text{mol}^{-1} = 24944 \text{ g} \cdot \text{day}^{-1}, \text{ or } 24.9 \text{ kg} \cdot \text{day}^{-1}$$

The total solids removed also include the settled organic material. We know, based on the influent and effluent levels or $8 \text{ mg} \cdot \text{L}^{-1}$ and $3 \text{ mg} \cdot \text{L}^{-1}$, respectively, that the total organic material removed is simply $5 \text{ mg} \cdot \text{L}^{-1}$. (Note that milligrams per liter of organic material is a very simple approximation and that the normal measurement of such difficult-to-measure substances is normally given as turbidity.) Simply multiply this number by the plant flow to determine the total organic matter settled per day.

$$5 \text{ mg} \cdot \text{L}^{-1} \times 0.044 \text{ m}^3 \cdot \text{s}^{-1} \times 1000 \text{ L} \cdot \text{m}^{-3} \times 86,400 \text{ s} \cdot \text{day}^{-1} = 19,008,000 \text{ mg} \cdot \text{day}^{-1}$$

or

$$19.0 \text{ kg} \cdot \text{day}^{-1}$$

So, by adding the mass fluxes of aluminum hydroxide and settled organic matter sludges, the total amount of dry solids removed per day is calculated.

$$24.9 \text{ kg} \cdot \text{day}^{-1} + 19.0 \text{ kg} \cdot \text{day}^{-1} = 43.9 \text{ kg} \cdot \text{day}^{-1}$$

**Iron.**   Ferric cations can be supplied by adding either ferric sulfate ($Fe_2(SO_4)_3 \cdot 7H_2O$) or ferric chloride ($FeCl_3 \cdot 7H_2O$). The properties of iron with respect to coagulation efficiency, dose, and pH curves are similar to those of alum. An example of the reaction of $FeCl_3$ in the presence of alkalinity is

$$FeCl_3 \cdot 7H_2O + 3HCO_3^- \rightleftharpoons Fe(OH)_3(s) + 3CO_2 + 3Cl^- + 7H_2O \tag{9–3}$$

and without alkalinity

$$FeCl_3 + 3H_2O \rightleftharpoons Fe(OH)_3(s) + 3H^+ + Cl^- \tag{9–4}$$

If the alkalinity is insufficient, the addition of ferric chloride results in the release of three moles of protons ($H^+$) for every mole of ferric chloride added. The release of protons lowers the pH. Ferric salts generally have a wider pH range for effective coagulation than aluminum, that is, pH ranges from 4 to 9.

**Coagulant Aids.**   The three basic types of coagulant aids are activated silica, clay, and polymers.

Activated silica is sodium silicate that has been activated with sulfuric acid, alum, carbon dioxide, or chlorine. When activated silica is added to water; it produces a stable sol (i.e., solid colloidal particles dispersed in a liquid) that has a negative surface charge. The activated silica can react with the positively charged metal hydroxide floc, resulting in a larger, denser floc that settles faster and enhances enmeshment. The addition of activated silica is especially useful for treating highly colored, low-turbidity waters because it increases the density of the floc. However, because activation of silica requires proper equipment and close operational control, many plants are hesitant to use it.

Clays can act much like activated silica in that they have a slight negative charge and can increase the density of the flocs, thus increasing the settling of the floc. Clays are also most useful for treating colored, low-turbidity waters.

The most effective polymers used in water treatment as coagulant aids are the anionic and nonionic polymers. Polymers are long-chain carbon compounds of high molecular weight that have many active sites. Dodecyl ammonium (see Figure 9–4b) is a cationic polymer. The active

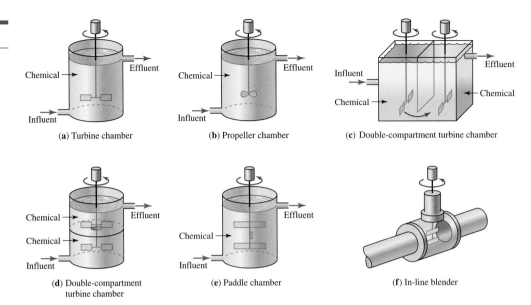

(a) Turbine chamber   (b) Propeller chamber   (c) Double-compartment turbine chamber

(d) Double-compartment turbine chamber   (e) Paddle chamber   (f) In-line blender

sites adhere to flocs, joining them together and producing a larger, tougher floc that settles better. The type of polymer, dose, and point of addition must be determined for each water and requirements may change within a plant on a seasonal, or even daily, basis.

### Mixing and Flocculation

Clearly, if the chemical reactions in coagulating and softening a water are going to take place, the chemical must be mixed with the water. In this section we will begin to look at the physical methods needed to produce chemical coagulation and softening.

**Mixing,** or **rapid mixing** as it is called, is the process whereby the chemicals are quickly and uniformly dispersed in the water. Ideally, the chemicals would be instantaneously dispersed throughout the water. During coagulation and softening, the chemical reactions that take place in rapid mixing form precipitates. Either aluminum hydroxide or iron hydroxide forms during coagulation, whereas calcium carbonate and magnesium hydroxide forms during softening. The precipitates created in these processes must be brought into contact with one another so they can form flocs. This contacting process is called **flocculation** and is accomplished by slow, gentle mixing.

Axial flow

**Rapid Mix.** Rapid mixing is probably the most important physical operation affecting coagulant dose efficiency. The chemical reaction in coagulation is completed in less than 0.1 s; therefore, it is imperative that mixing be as instantaneous and complete as possible. Rapid mixing can be accomplished within a tank with a vertical shaft mixer or within a pipe using specialized mixing systems. Other methods, such as Parshall flumes, hydraulic jumps, baffled channels, or air mixing, may also be used. Typical tank or inline mixing configurations are shown in Figure 9–5.

Propeller

For dissolution of $CaO/Ca(OH)_2$ mixtures for softening, detention times on the order of 5 to 10 min may be required. Inline mixers are not used to blend softening reagents.

The volume of a rapid mix tank is calculated using the equation

$$\forall = Qt_d \qquad (9\text{–}5)$$

Turbine

The volume seldom exceeds 8 $m^3$ because of mixing equipment and geometry constraints. The mixing equipment consists of an electric motor, gear-type speed reducer, and either a turbine or axial-flow impeller as shown in Figure 9–6. The turbine impeller provides more turbulence and is preferred for rapid mixing.

Often rules-of-thumb [7] are used to design rapid mix tanks. It has been found that the design liquid depth should be 0.5–1.1 times the basin diameter or width. The impeller diameter should

## FIGURE 9–7

Paddle flocculator.

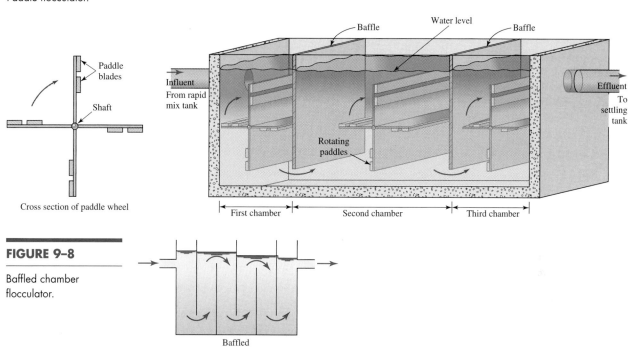

## FIGURE 9–8

Baffled chamber flocculator.

be between 0.30 and 0.50 times the tank diameter or width, and the vertical baffles should extend into the tank about 10% of the tank width or diameter.*

**Flocculation.**   Whereas rapid mix achieves successful mixing of the water and the coagulant, flocculation provides the conditions necessary for optimal particle growth so that sedimentation can occur successfully. The objective of flocculation is to allow the particles to collide, adhere to one another, and grow to a size that will settle readily. Mixing must be sufficient so that when collisions occur they have enough energy for the particles to stick together. On the other hand, too much mixing can shear particles (they break apart), and the resulting particles will be too small for sedimentation to occur effectively. The major design parameter used in flocculation is the velocity gradient, $G$. This parameter describes the degree of mixing; the higher the $G$ value, the more vigorous the mixing. A detailed discussion of the application of the $G$ value in the design of water and wastewater plants is beyond the scope of this text.

Flocculation is usually accomplished with an axial-flow impeller (see Figure 9–6), a paddle flocculator (Figure 9–7), or a baffled chamber (Figure 9–8). Axial-flow impellers have been recommended over the other types of flocculators [8] shown in Figure 9–6.

**Upflow Solids Contact.**   Mixing, flocculation, and clarification may be conducted in a single tank such as that shown in Figure 9–9. The influent raw water and chemicals are mixed in the center cone-like structure. The solids flow down under the cone (sometimes called a "skirt"). As the water flows upward, the solids settle to form a sludge blanket. This design is called an upflow solids-contact basin. The main advantage of this unit is its reduced size. The units are best suited to treating feed water that has a relatively constant quality. It is often favored for softening because the characteristics of groundwater are relatively constant, and the sludge blanket provides further opportunity to drive the precipitation reactions to completion.

*Personal communication, J3I, Inc., Holland. MI, May 1990.

**FIGURE 9–9**

Typical upflow solids contact unit (*Source:* Adapted, with permission, from American Water Works Association. *Water Treatment Plant Design*, 2nd ed., McGraw-Hill, New York, 1990.)

Zone A — rapid mix
Zone B — flocculation and solids contact
Zone C — upflow and sludge-blanket zone

**EXAMPLE 9–2**

The abandoned Catequil Street Water Treatment Plant is to be turned into a research facility treating $0.044 \text{ m}^3 \cdot \text{s}^{-1}$. A low-turbidity iron coagulation plant has been proposed with the following design parameters:

Rapid mix $t_0 = 10 \text{ s}$     Water temperature $= 18°C$

Size the rapid-mix basin.

Solution

The volume of the rapid-mix tank by Equation 9–5 is

$$∀ = (Q)(t_0) = (0.044 \text{ m}^3 \cdot \text{s}^{-1})(10 \text{ s}) = 0.44 \text{ m}^3$$

Because this volume is less than our guideline of 8 m³ as the maximum volume for a rapid-mix tank, we can use a tank of 0.44 m³. To ensure water production even in the event of a major equipment failure, it is necessary to build some redundancy into the water treatment system; therefore, we need two tanks. Because the volume of this tank is quite small, use two 0.44 m³ tanks and alternate their usage.

Using a depth-to-diameter (or width) ratio of 0.75, we obtain

Depth $= 0.75 ×$ diameter

and remembering that the volume of a cylinder equals

$$\text{Volume} = \frac{\pi d^2}{4} × \text{depth}$$

where $d =$ diameter

we get,

$$\text{Volume} = \left(\frac{\pi d^2}{4}\right)(0.75d) = 0.44 \text{ m}^3$$

Solving for $d = 0.907$ m.

Therefore, the surface area of the tank (to keep the volume near 0.44 m³) would be

$$\text{Surface area} = \frac{\pi d^2}{4} = 0.646 \text{ m, or } 0.65 \text{ m}$$

and the depth would be

$$\text{Depth} = \frac{\text{volume}}{\text{surface area}} = \frac{0.44 \text{ m}^3}{0.65 \text{ m}^2} = 0.68 \text{ m}$$

This set of calculations presents a practical problem; we are unlikely to find a tank with these dimensions. Let's pick a tank that is 1 m in diameter and 0.75 m in depth. Now, we must check that this choice does not adversely affect the quality of the design, that is, we must ensure that the tank is large enough to hold the specified volume of 0.44 m³. The designed tank volume is

$$\text{Volume} = \frac{\pi d^2}{4} \times \text{depth} = \frac{\pi (1)^2}{4} \times 0.75 = 0.59 \text{ m}^3$$

This volume is fine. The detention time is

$$\frac{0.59 \text{ m}^3}{0.044 \text{ m}^3 \cdot \text{s}^{-1}} = 13.4 \text{ min}$$

Thus, the detention time is within suggested guidelines.

## 9-3 SOFTENING

### Hardness

The term *hardness* is used to characterize a water that does not lather well; causes a scum in the bathtub; and leaves hard, white, crusty deposits (scale) on coffee pots, tea kettles, and hot water heaters. The failure to lather well and the formation of scum on bathtubs is the result of the reactions of calcium and magnesium with the soap. For example, the scum on bathtub forms according to the following reaction:

$$Ca^{2+} + 2(Soap)^- \rightleftharpoons Ca(Soap)_2(s) \tag{9-6}$$

As a result of this complexation reaction, soap cannot interact with the dirt on clothing, and the calcium–soap complex itself forms undesirable precipitates. Additionally, hardness minerals result in valves sticking due to the formation of calcium carbonate crystals in the valve and scaling on pipes.

**Hardness** is defined as the sum of all polyvalent cations (in consistent units). The common units of expression are milligrams per liter ($mg \cdot L^{-1}$) as $CaCO_3$ or milliequivalents per liter ($mEq \cdot L^{-1}$). Qualitative terms used to describe hardness are listed in Table 9–2. Because many people object to water containing hardness greater than 150 $mg \cdot L^{-1}$ as $CaCO_3$, suppliers of public water have considered it a benefit to soften the water, that is, to remove some of the hardness. A common water treatment goal is to provide water with a hardness in the range of 60 to 120 $mg \cdot L^{-1}$ as $CaCO_3$.

Although all polyvalent cations contribute to hardness, the predominant contributors are calcium and magnesium. Thus, our focus for the remainder of this discussion will be on those two minerals.

| TABLE 9–2 | Hard Water Classification According to the Water Quality Association | |
|---|---|---|
| | **Term** | **Concentration Range ($mg \cdot L^{-1}$ as $CaCO_3$)** |
| | Soft | < 17.1 |
| | Slightly hard | 17.1–60 |
| | Moderately hard | 60–120 |
| | Hard | 120–180 |
| | Very hard | > 180 |

**FIGURE 9–10**

Natural process by which water is made hard.

The natural process by which water becomes hard is shown schematically in Figure 9–10. As rainwater enters the topsoil, the respiration of microorganisms increases the $CO_2$ content of the water. As shown in Equation 2–19, $CO_2$ reacts with water to form $H_2CO_3$. Limestone, which is made up of solid $CaCO_3$ and $MgCO_3$, reacts with the carbonic acid to form calcium bicarbonate [$Ca(HCO_3)_2$] and magnesium bicarbonate [$Mg(HCO_3)_2$]. Although $CaCO_3$ and $MgCO_3$ are both insoluble in water, the bicarbonates are quite soluble. Gypsum ($CaSO_4$) and $MgSO_4$ may also go into solution to contribute to the hardness.

Because calcium and magnesium usually predominate, it is often convenient in performing softening calculations on these types of waters to *approximate* the total hardness (TH) of a water as the sum of those elements

$$TH = Ca^{2+} + Mg^{2+} \qquad (9\text{--}7)$$

where the concentrations of each element are in consistent units ($mg \cdot L^{-1}$ as $CaCO_3$ or $mEq \cdot L^{-1}$). Total hardness is often broken down into two components: (1) that associated with the $HCO_3^-$ anion (called carbonate hardness and abbreviated CH), and (2) that associated with other anions (called noncarbonate hardness and abbreviated NCH).* Total hardness, then, may also be defined as

$$TH = CH + NCH \qquad (9\text{--}8)$$

**Carbonate hardness** is defined as the amount of hardness equal to the total hardness or the total alkalinity, whichever is less. Carbonate hardness can be removed by heating the water, because the solubility of calcium and magnesium bicarbonates and carbonates [$CaCO_3$, $MgCO_3$, $Ca(HCO_3)_2$, $Mg(HCO_3)_2$] decreases with increasing temperature. As such, carbonate hardness is often called **temporary hardness** because heating the water removes it.

**Noncarbonate hardness** is defined as the total hardness in excess of the alkalinity.[†] If the alkalinity is equal to or greater than the total hardness, then there is no noncarbonate hardness. Noncarbonate hardness accounts for that portion of the calcium and magnesium (and other polyvalent ions) that is associated with ions other than bicarbonate and carbonate, including sulfate, nitrate, and chloride. Noncarbonate hardness is called **permanent hardness** because it is not removed when water is heated.

The relationships between total hardness, carbonate hardness, and noncarbonate hardness are illustrated in Figure 9–11. In Figure 9–11a, the total hardness is 250 $mg \cdot L^{-1}$ as $CaCO_3$, the carbonate hardness is equal to the alkalinity ($HCO_3^- = 200$ $mg \cdot L^{-1}$ as $CaCO_3$), and the noncarbonate hardness is equal to the difference between the total hardness and the carbonate hardness

---

*Note that this does not imply that the compounds exist as compounds in solution. They are dissociated.

[†]When the pH is between 6.5 and 8.3, $HCO_3^-$ is the dominant form of alkalinity, and total alkalinity can be approximated as the concentration of $HCO_3^-$.

**FIGURE 9–11**

Relationships between total hardness, carbonate hardness, and noncarbonate hardness. The pH of the water is between 6.5 and 8.3.

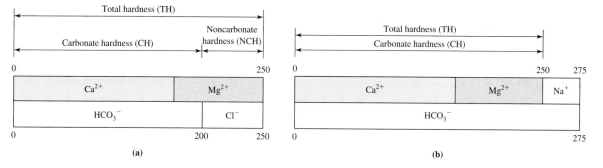

(a)
(b)

($NCH = TH - CH = 250 - 200 = 50 \, \text{mg} \cdot \text{L}^{-1}$ as $CaCO_3$). In Figure 9–11b, the total hardness is again 250 mg · L$^{-1}$ as $CaCO_3$. However, because the alkalinity ($HCO_3^-$) is greater than the total hardness, and because the carbonate hardness cannot be greater than the total hardness (see Equation 9–8), the carbonate hardness is equal to the total hardness, that is, 250 mg · L$^{-1}$ as $CaCO_3$. With the carbonate hardness equal to the total hardness, then all of the hardness is carbonate hardness and there is no noncarbonate hardness. Note that in both cases we have assumed that the pH is between 6.5 and 8.3 because $HCO_3^-$ is the only form of alkalinity present.

**EXAMPLE 9–3** A sample of water having a pH of 7.2 has the following concentration of ions.
Calculate the total hardness, the carbonate hardness, the alkalinity and the total dissolved solids for the following ions.

| Ion | Concentration (as the ion) | Ion | Concentration (as the ion) |
|---|---|---|---|
| $Ca^{2+}$ | 40 mg · L$^{-1}$ | $HCO_3^-$ | 110 mg · L$^{-1}$ |
| $Mg^{2+}$ | 10 mg · L$^{-1}$ | $SO_4^{2-}$ | 67.2 mg · L$^{-1}$ |
| $Na^+$ | 11.8 mg · L$^{-1}$ | $Cl^-$ | 11 mg · L$^{-1}$ |
| $K^+$ | 7.0 mg · L$^{-1}$ | | |

| Ion | Concentration (mg · L$^{-1}$) | M.W. (mg · mmol$^{-1}$) | \|n\| | Eq. Wt. (mg · mEq$^{-1}$) | Concentration (mEq · L$^{-1}$) | Concentration (mg · L$^{-1}$ as CaCO$_3$) |
|---|---|---|---|---|---|---|
| $Ca^{2+}$ | 40.0 | 40.1 | | | | |
| $Mg^{2+}$ | 10.0 | 24.3 | | | | |
| $Na^+$ | 11.8 | 23.0 | | | | |
| $K^+$ | 7.0 | 39.1 | | | | |
| $HCO_3^-$ | 110.0 | 61.0 | | | | |
| $SO_4^{2-}$ | 67.2 | 96.1 | | | | |
| $Cl^-$ | 11.0 | 35.5 | | | | |

**Solution**   First prepare a table like the following.

Next, determine the value of $n$ for each of the ions. In most cases, it will be the oxidation state as given.* Now divide the molecular weight by the number of equivalents per mole, $n$, to determine the equivalent weight of each of the ions. For example, the molecular weight of calcium can be expressed as $40.1 \ \mathrm{mg \cdot mmol^{-1}}$ and the number of equivalents is $2 \ \mathrm{mEq \cdot mmol^{-1}}$.

| Ion | Concentration $(\mathrm{mg \cdot L^{-1}})$ | M.W. $(\mathrm{mg \cdot mmol^{-1}})$ | $\lvert n \rvert$ | Eq. Wt. $(\mathrm{mg \cdot mEq^{-1}})$ | Concentration $(\mathrm{mEq \cdot L^{-1}})$ | Concentration $(\mathrm{mg \cdot L^{-1}}$ as $CaCO_3)$ |
|---|---|---|---|---|---|---|
| $Ca^{2+}$ | 40.0 | 40.1 | 2 | 20.05 | | |
| $Mg^{2+}$ | 10.0 | 24.3 | 2 | 12.15 | | |
| $Na^+$ | 11.8 | 23.0 | 1 | 23.0 | | |
| $K^+$ | 7.0 | 39.1 | 1 | 39.1 | | |
| $HCO_3^-$ | 110.0 | 61.0 | 1 | 61.0 | | |
| $SO_4^{2-}$ | 67.2 | 96.1 | 2 | 48.05 | | |
| $Cl^-$ | 11.0 | 35.5 | 1 | 35.5 | | |

The concentration of each of the ions given in milliequivalents per liter can be determined by dividing the concentration given in milligrams per liter by the equivalent weight. For example, for calcium:

$$[Ca^{2+}] = \frac{40.0 \ \mathrm{mg \cdot L^{-1}}}{20.05 \ \mathrm{mg \cdot mEq^{-1}}} = 1.995 \ \mathrm{mEq \cdot L^{-1}}$$

The table now becomes

| Ion | Concentration $(\mathrm{mg \cdot L^{-1}})$ | M.W. $(\mathrm{mg \cdot mmol^{-1}})$ | $\lvert n \rvert$ | Eq. Wt. $(\mathrm{mg \cdot mEq^{-1}})$ | Concentration $(\mathrm{mEq \cdot L^{-1}})$ | Concentration $(\mathrm{mg \cdot L^{-1}}$ as $CaCO_3)$ |
|---|---|---|---|---|---|---|
| $Ca^{2+}$ | 40.0 | 40.1 | 2 | 20.05 | 1.995 | |
| $Mg^{2+}$ | 10.0 | 24.3 | 2 | 12.15 | 0.823 | |
| $Na^+$ | 11.8 | 23.0 | 1 | 23.0 | 0.513 | |
| $K^+$ | 7.0 | 39.1 | 1 | 39.1 | 0.179 | |
| $HCO_3^-$ | 110.0 | 61.0 | 1 | 61.0 | 1.80 | |
| $SO_4^{2-}$ | 67.2 | 96.1 | 2 | 48.05 | 1.40 | |
| $Cl^-$ | 11.0 | 35.5 | 1 | 35.5 | 0.31 | |

Finally, the concentration of each of the ions can be determined in units of milligrams per liter as $CaCO_3$ by multiplying the concentration in milliequivalents per liter by the equivalent weight of $CaCO_3$ (which is $50.0 \ \mathrm{mg \cdot mEq^{-1}}$). Therefore, the concentration of calcium in units of milligrams per liter as $CaCO_3$ is

$$(1.995 \ \mathrm{mEq \cdot L^{-1}}) \times (50 \ \mathrm{mg \cdot mEq^{-1}}) = 99.8 \ \mathrm{mg \cdot L^{-1}} \text{ as } CaCO_3$$

---

*A review of determining the number of equivalents can be found on Section 2–4 in Chapter 2: Chemistry.

| Ion | Concentration (mg · L⁻¹) | M.W. (mg · mmol⁻¹) | \|n\| | Eq. Wt. (mg · mEq⁻¹) | Concentration (mEq · L⁻¹) | Concentration (mg · L⁻¹ as $CaCO_3$) |
|---|---|---|---|---|---|---|
| $Ca^{2+}$ | 40.0 | 40.1 | 2 | 20.05 | 1.995 | 99.8 |
| $Mg^{2+}$ | 10.0 | 24.3 | 2 | 12.15 | 0.823 | 41.2 |
| $Na^+$ | 11.8 | 23.0 | 1 | 23.0 | 0.513 | 25.7 |
| $K^+$ | 7.0 | 39.1 | 1 | 39.1 | 0.179 | 8.95 |
| $HCO_3^-$ | 110.0 | 61.0 | 1 | 61.0 | 1.80 | 90.0 |
| $SO_4^{2-}$ | 67.2 | 96.1 | 2 | 48.05 | 1.40 | 70.0 |
| $Cl^-$ | 11.0 | 35.5 | 1 | 35.5 | 0.31 | 15.5 |

The table can be completed.

In completing this problem, you should check your math and make sure if sampling and analysis is complete and accurate, the sum of the concentrations of cations and ions should be equal to within ± 10%. In this case,

$$\sum (\text{cations}) = \sum (\text{anions})$$

$$175.6 \text{ mg} \cdot L^{-1} \text{ as } CaCO_3 = 175.6 \text{ mg} \cdot L^{-1} \text{ as } CaCO_3$$

The exact total hardness is the sum of the multivalent cations

$$[Ca^{2+}] + [Mg^{2+}] = 99.8 + 41.2 = 141 \text{ mg} \cdot L^{-1} \text{ as } CaCO_3$$

The carbonate hardness (CH) is equal to that portion of the hardness associated with carbonate and bicarbonate species, that is, the alkalinity,

$$(HCO_3^-) + (CO_3^{2-}) + (OH^-) - (H^+)$$

Because the pH is between 6.5 and 8.3, the concentration of carbonate is negligible and the concentrations of hydroxide ($OH^-$) and the hydrogen ions ($H^+$) essentially cancel each other. Therefore,

$$\text{Alkalinity} = (HCO_3^-) + (\cancel{CO_3^{2-}}) + (\cancel{OH^-}) - (\cancel{H^+}) \approx (HCO_3^-)$$

$$= 90.0 \text{ mg} \cdot L^{-1} \text{ as } CaCO_3$$

Because the total hardness is 141 mg · L⁻¹ as $CaCO_3$ and the carbonate hardness is defined as that portion of hardness associated with carbonate and bicarbonate, the concentration of carbonate hardness is equal to the alkalinity, or

$$CH = 90.0 \text{ mg} \cdot L^{-1} \text{ as } CaCO_3$$

The noncarbonate hardness (NCH) is equal to the

$$\text{Total hardness} - CH = 141 - 90.0 = 51.0 \text{ mg} \cdot L^{-1} \text{ as } CaCO_3$$

Finally, the total dissolved solids (TDS) is equal to the sum of all the cations and anions using the concentrations in milligrams per liter as the ion. The reason you can use concentrations as milligrams per liter as the ions is because the TDS is determined by evaporating all of the water and determining the mass of the remaining ions.

$$TDS = 40.0 + 10.0 + 11.8 + 7.0 + 110.0 + 67.2 + 11.0 = 257 \text{ mg} \cdot L^{-1}$$

Bar charts of water composition are often useful in understanding the process of softening. By convention, the bar chart is constructed with cations in the upper bar and anions in the lower bar. In the upper bar, calcium is placed first and magnesium second because calcium concentrations usually exceed that of magnesium. Other cations follow without any specified order. The lower bar is constructed with bicarbonate placed first because in most waters it is the predominant anion. Other anions follow without any specified order. Construction of a bar chart is illustrated in Example 9–4.

**EXAMPLE 9–4**   Given the following analysis of a groundwater (pH = 7.6), construct a bar chart of the constituents, with concentrations given as milligrams per liter as $CaCO_3$.

| Ion | $mg \cdot L^{-1}$ as ion | Molecular Weight $(g \cdot mol^{-1})$ | Number of Equivalents $(Eq \cdot mol^{-1})$ | Concentration $(Eq \cdot L^{-1})$ | Concentration $(mg \cdot L^{-1}$ as $CaCO_3)$ |
|---|---|---|---|---|---|
| $Ca^{2+}$ | 150.3 | 40.08 | 2 | 7.5 | 375 |
| $Fe^{3+}$ | 1.19 | 55.85 | 3 | 0.064 | 3.2 |
| $Mg^{2+}$ | 14.6 | 24.31 | 2 | 1.20 | 60 |
| $Na^+$ | 100 | 22.99 | 1 | 4.35 | 217.5 |
| $Cl^-$ | 201.4 | 35.45 | 1 | 5.68 | 284.0 |
| $HCO_3^-$ | 450.3 | 61.02 | 1 | 7.38 | 369.0 |

**Solution**   The concentrations of the ions have been converted to $CaCO_3$ equivalents. The results are plotted in Figure 9–12.

The sum of the cation concentrations is 655.7 mg $\cdot$ L$^{-1}$ as $CaCO_3$. The (exact) total hardness is 438.2 mg $\cdot$ L$^{-1}$ as $CaCO_3$. The anions total 653.0 mg $\cdot$ L$^{-1}$ as $CaCO_3$. The carbonate hardness is 369.0 mg $\cdot$ L$^{-1}$ as $CaCO_3$ and the noncarbonate hardness is 69.2 mg $\cdot$ L$^{-1}$ as $CaCO_3$. The discrepancy between the concentrations of cations and anions is the result of other ions that were not measured. If a complete analysis were conducted, and no analytical error occurred, the number of equivalents of cations would equal exactly the number of equivalents of anions. Typically, a complete analysis will vary within ± 10% because of analytical errors.

**FIGURE 9–12**

Bar graph of groundwater constituents.

Softening can be accomplished by either the lime–soda process or by ion exchange. Both methods are discussed in the following sections.

## Lime–Soda Softening

In lime–soda softening it is possible to calculate the chemical doses necessary to remove hardness. Hardness precipitation is based on the following two solubility reactions:

$$Ca^{2+} + CO_3^{2-} \rightleftharpoons CaCO_3(s) \tag{9–9}$$

and

$$Mg^{2+} + 2OH^- \rightleftharpoons Mg(OH)_2(s) \tag{9–10}$$

The objective is to precipitate the calcium as $CaCO_3$ and the magnesium as $Mg(OH)_2$. To precipitate calcium, the pH of the water must be raised to about 10.3. To precipitate magnesium, the pH must be raised to about 11. If the naturally occurring bicarbonate alkalinity ($HCO_3^-$) is insufficient for the $CaCO_3(s)$ precipitate to form (i.e., there is noncarbonate hardness), we must add $CO_3^{2-}$ (in the form of $Na_2CO_3$). Because magnesium is more expensive to remove than is calcium, we leave as much $Mg^{2+}$ in the water as possible. Additionally, it is more expensive to remove noncarbonate hardness than carbonate hardness because we must add another chemical to provide the $CO_3^{2-}$. Therefore, utilities leave as much noncarbonate hardness in the water as possible.

**Softening Chemistry.** The chemical processes used to soften water are a direct application of the law of mass action. We increase the concentration of $CO_3^{2-}$ or $OH^-$ (or both) by the addition of chemicals and drive the reactions given in Equations 9–9 and 9–10 to the right. Insofar as possible, we convert the naturally occurring bicarbonate alkalinity ($HCO_3^-$) to carbonate ($CO_3^{2-}$) by the addition of hydroxyl ions ($OH^-$). Hydroxyl ions cause the carbonate buffer system (Equation 2–77) to shift to the right and, thus, provide the carbonate for the precipitation reaction (Equation 9–9).

The common source of hydroxyl ions is calcium hydroxide ($Ca(OH)_2$). Many water treatment plants find it more economical to buy **quicklime** ($CaO$), commonly called lime, than hydrated lime ($Ca(OH)_2$). The quicklime is converted to hydrated lime at the water treatment plant by mixing $CaO$ and water to produce a slurry of $Ca(OH)_2$, which is fed to the water for softening. This process is called **slaking.** When carbonate ions must be supplied, the most common chemical chosen is sodium carbonate ($Na_2CO_3$). Sodium carbonate is commonly referred to as **soda ash** or soda.

**Softening Reactions.** The softening reactions are regulated by controlling the pH. First, any free acids are neutralized. Then pH is raised to precipitate the $CaCO_3$; if necessary, the pH is raised further to remove $Mg(OH)_2$. Finally, if necessary, $CO_3^{2-}$ is added to precipitate the noncarbonate hardness.

Six important softening reactions are discussed here. In each case, the chemical that has been added to the water is printed in bold type. Remember that ($s$) designates the solid form, and hence indicates that the substance has been removed from the water as a solid precipitate. The following reactions are presented sequentially, although in reality they occur simultaneously.

1. **Neutralization of carbonic acid ($H_2CO_3$).** To raise the pH, we must first neutralize any free acids present in the water. Carbonic acid is the principal naturally occurring acid present in unpolluted water.* You should note that no hardness is removed in this step.

$$H_2CO_3 + \textbf{Ca(OH)}_2 \rightleftharpoons CaCO_3(s) + 2H_2O \tag{9–11}$$

2. **Precipitation of carbonate hardness due to calcium.** As mentioned previously, we must raise the pH to about 10.3 to precipitate calcium carbonate. To achieve this pH we must convert all of the bicarbonate to carbonate. The carbonate then serves as the common ion for the precipitation reaction.

$$Ca^{2+} + 2HCO_3^- + \textbf{Ca(OH)}_2 \rightleftharpoons 2CaCO_3(s) + 2H_2O \tag{9–12}$$

3. **Precipitation of carbonate hardness due to magnesium.** If we need to remove carbonate hardness that results from the presence of magnesium, we must add more lime to achieve a

---

*$CO_2$ and $H_2CO_3$ in water are essentially the same: $CO_2 + H_2O = H_2CO_3$. Thus, the equivalents per mole ($n$) for $CO_2$ is 2.

pH of about 11. The reaction may be considered to occur in two stages. The first stage occurs when we convert all of the bicarbonate to carbonate as accomplished in step 2.

$$Mg^{2+} + 2HCO_3^- + \textbf{Ca(OH)}_2 \rightleftharpoons MgCO_3 + CaCO_3(s) + 2H_2O \qquad (9\text{–}13)$$

Note that the hardness of the water did not change because $MgCO_3$ is soluble. The addition of more lime is necessary to remove the hardness due to magnesium.

$$Mg^{2+} + CO_3^{2-} + \textbf{Ca(OH)}_2 \rightleftharpoons Mg(OH)_2(s) + CaCO_3(s) \qquad (9\text{–}14)$$

4. **Removal of noncarbonate hardness due to calcium.** If we need to remove noncarbonate hardness due to calcium, no further increase in pH is required. Instead we must provide additional carbonate in the form of soda ash.

$$Ca^{2+} + \textbf{Na}_2\textbf{CO}_3 \rightleftharpoons CaCO_3(s) + 2Na^+ \qquad (9\text{–}15)$$

5. **Removal of noncarbonate hardness due to magnesium.** If we need to remove noncarbonate hardness due to magnesium, we must add both lime and soda. The lime provides the hydroxyl ion for precipitation of the magnesium.

$$Mg^{2+} + \textbf{Ca(OH)}_2 \rightleftharpoons Mg(OH)_2(s) + Ca^{2+} \qquad (9\text{–}16)$$

Note that although the magnesium is removed, no change in the hardness occurs because the calcium is still in solution. To remove the calcium we must add soda ash.

$$Ca^{2+} + \textbf{Na}_2\textbf{CO}_3 \rightleftharpoons CaCO_3(s) + 2Na^+ \qquad (9\text{–}17)$$

Note that this is the same reaction as the one to remove noncarbonate hardness due to calcium.

**EXAMPLE 9–5**   The groundwater from the ficticious Yuhwa Aquifer contains $2.3 \times 10^{-5}$ M $CO_2$. It is being pumped at a rate of $200 \text{ L} \cdot \text{s}^{-1}$ to serve the residents of the town of Haemosu. Determine the mass (in kilograms) of hydrated lime that must be added each day to neutralize the carbon dioxide present in this water. Calculate the mass (in kilograms) of calcium carbonate produced on a daily basis.

Solution   Equation 9–11 shows that we need one mole of hydrated lime for every mole of $CO_2$ present in the water. Therefore, we need $2.3 \times 10^{-5}$ M of hydrated lime. To calculate the mass needed,

$$(2.3 \times 10^{-5} \text{ M})(200 \text{ L} \cdot \text{s}^{-1})(86{,}400 \text{ s} \cdot \text{day}^{-1})(74.096 \text{ g Ca(OH)}_2 \cdot \text{mol}^{-1})(10^{-3} \text{ kg} \cdot \text{g}^{-1})$$

$$= 29.4 \text{ kg} \cdot \text{day}^{-1}$$

As shown in Equation 9–11, we also produce one mole of calcium carbonate for every one mole of carbon dioxide we neutralize. Therefore, we produce

$$(2.3 \times 10^{-5} \text{ M})(200 \text{ L} \cdot \text{s}^{-1})(86{,}400 \text{ s} \cdot \text{day}^{-1})(100.09 \text{ g CaCO}_3 \cdot \text{mol}^{-1})(10^{-3} \text{ kg} \cdot \text{g}^{-1})$$

$$= 39.8 \text{ kg CaCO}_3 \text{ day}^{-1}$$

**Process Limitations and Empirical Considerations.**   Lime–soda softening cannot produce a water completely free of hardness because of the solubility of $CaCO_3$ and $Mg(OH)_2$, the physical limitations of mixing and contact, and the lack of sufficient time for the reactions to go to completion. Thus, the minimum calcium hardness that can be achieved is about $30 \text{ mg} \cdot \text{L}^{-1}$ as $CaCO_3$, and the minimum magnesium hardness is about $10 \text{ mg} \cdot \text{L}^{-1}$ as $CaCO_3$. Because of the slimy condition that results when soap is used with water that is too soft, we normally strive for a final total hardness on the order of $75$–$120 \text{ mg} \cdot \text{L}^{-1}$ as $CaCO_3$.

To achieve reasonable removal of hardness in a practical time period, an excess of $Ca(OH)_2$ greater than the stoichiometric amount is usually provided. Based on our empirical experience, a minimum excess of 20 mg $\cdot$ L$^{-1}$ of $Ca(OH)_2$ expressed as $CaCO_3$ must be provided.

Magnesium in excess of about 40 mg $\cdot$ L$^{-1}$ as $CaCO_3$ forms scales on heat exchange elements in hot water heaters. Because of the expense of removing magnesium, we normally remove only that magnesium that is in excess of 40 mg $\cdot$ L$^{-1}$ as $CaCO_3$. For magnesium removals less than 20 mg $\cdot$ L$^{-1}$ as $CaCO_3$, the basic excess of lime mentioned earlier is sufficient to ensure good results. For magnesium removals between 20 and 40 mg $\cdot$ L$^{-1}$ as $CaCO_3$, we must add an excess of lime equal to the magnesium to be removed. For magnesium removals greater than 40 mg $\cdot$ L$^{-1}$ as $CaCO_3$, the excess lime we need to add is 40 mg $\cdot$ L$^{-1}$ as $CaCO_3$. Addition of excess lime in amounts greater than 40 mg $\cdot$ L$^{-1}$ as $CaCO_3$ does not appreciably improve the reaction kinetics.

**EXAMPLE 9–6**

The groundwater mentioned in Example 9–5 contains $2.3 \times 10^{-5}$ M $CO_2$. It also contains 300 mg $\cdot$ L$^{-1}$ as $CaCO_3$ of carbonate hardness due to calcium and 50 mg $\cdot$ L$^{-1}$ as $CaCO_3$ of carbonate hardness due to magnesium. It is treated at the same rates mentioned in Example 9–5. You are to remove all of the carbonate hardness due to calcium but do not need to remove the magnesium ions. Assume that you remove all but 20 mg $\cdot$ L$^{-1}$ (as $CaCO_3$) of the calcium ions. What mass of calcium carbonate sludge is produced on a daily basis?

**Solution**

Using Equation 9–12 we see that for every mole of calcium removed we need one mole of hydrated lime and we produce two moles of calcium carbonate sludge. Because we remove all but 20 mg $\cdot$ L$^{-1}$ as $CaCO_3$ of the calcium ions, we must remove 280 mg $\cdot$ L$^{-1}$ as $CaCO_3$. We must convert this to a molar basis.

$$\frac{(280 \text{ mg} \cdot \text{L}^{-1} \text{ as } CaCO_3)}{(100.09 \text{ mg} \cdot \text{mmol}^{-1} CaCO_3)} = 2.80 \text{ mmol} \cdot \text{L}^{-1} \text{ as } Ca^{2+}, \text{ or } 2.80 \times 10^{-3} \text{ mol} \cdot \text{L}^{-1}$$

Therefore according to the stoichiometry given in Equation 9–12, we produce $5.60 \times 10^{-3}$ mol $\cdot$ L$^{-1}$ $CaCO_3$ sludge. In units of kilograms per day, the mass of sludge equals

$$(5.6 \times 10^{-3} \text{ M})(200 \text{ L} \cdot \text{s}^{-1})(86{,}400 \text{ s} \cdot \text{day}^{-1})(100.09 \text{ g } CaCO_3 \cdot \text{mol}^{-1})(10^{-3} \text{ kg} \cdot \text{g}^{-1})$$

$$= 9690 \text{ kg} \cdot \text{day}^{-1} \text{ of } CaCO_3$$

We also produced 39.8 kg $\cdot$ day$^{-1}$ of $CaCO_3$ sludge in neutralizing the carbon dioxide according to Equation 9–11. Therefore, the total mass of sludge produced each day is 9730 kg.

### Ion-Exchange Softening

**Ion exchange** can be defined as the reversible exchange of an ion on a solid phase with an ion of like charge in an aqueous phase. The most general form of an ion-exchange reaction is

$$n\text{R}-\text{X}^+ + \text{Y}^{n+} \rightleftharpoons \text{R}_n-\text{Y}^{n+} + n\text{X}^+ \tag{9–18}$$

Note that an equivalent number of ions are exchanged in this reaction. In water treatment, ion exchange is most often used for metal removal. Because of its simplicity, ion exchange is most commonly used for in-home water-softening systems. Here the reaction can be represented as

$$Ca^{2+} + 2\text{NaR} \rightleftharpoons \text{R}_2Ca + 2Na^+ \tag{9–19}$$

where R represents the solid ion-exchange material. By this reaction, calcium has been removed from the water and replaced by an equivalent amount of sodium, that is, two sodium ions for each calcium ion. In this reaction, the alkalinity would remain unchanged because there is no reaction or exchange of anions. The exchange results in essentially 100% removal of the hardness from the water until the exchange capacity of the ion-exchange material is reached, as shown in Figure 9–13. When the ion-exchange material becomes saturated, no hardness will be

**FIGURE 9–13**

Idealized breakthrough curve of a fixed bed adsorber. (*Source:* Treybal, R. E., *Mass Transfer Operations,* McGraw-Hill, New York, 1968. Reprinted by permission.)

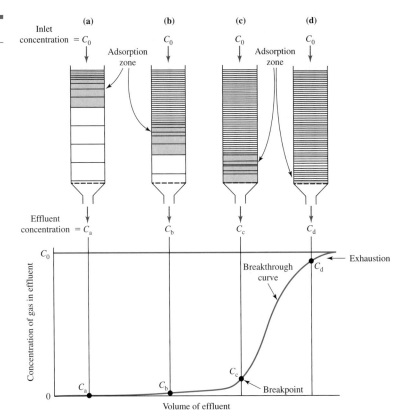

removed. At this point breakthrough is said to have occurred because the hardness ions pass through the ion-exchange adsorber. When the effluent hardness concentration exceeds a predetermined level, breakthrough is said to have occurred. At this point, the ion exchanger is taken out of service, and the ion-exchange material is regenerated. That is, the hardness is removed from the material by passing water containing highly concentrated solution of $Na^+$ through the ion exchanger. The mass action of having so much $Na^+$ in the water causes the sodium ions to be preferentially exchanged for the hardness ions.

$$R_2Ca + 2Na^+ + 2Cl^- \rightleftharpoons 2NaR + Ca^{2+} + 2Cl^- \tag{9–20}$$

The ion-exchange material can now be used to remove more hardness. The $CaCl_2$ is a waste stream that must be disposed of.

Some large water treatment facilities use ion-exchange softening, but the most common application is for residential water softeners. The ion-exchange material can either be naturally occurring clays, called zeolites, or synthetically made resins. Several manufacturers produce synthetic resins. The resins or zeolites are characterized by the amount of hardness that they remove per volume of resin material and by the amount of salt required to regenerate the resin. The synthetically produced resins have a much higher exchange capacity and require less salt for regeneration.

**Hardness Removal with Ion-Exchange Resins.**   Because the resin removes virtually 100% of the hardness, it is necessary to bypass a portion of the water and then blend to obtain the desired final hardness.

**EXAMPLE 9–7**   A home water softener has 0.1 m³ of ion-exchange resin with an exchange capacity of $62 \text{ kg} \cdot \text{m}^{-3}$. The four home residents each use water at a rate of $400 \text{ L} \cdot \text{day}^{-1}$. The well water they are using contains $340.0 \text{ mg} \cdot \text{L}^{-1}$ of hardness as $CaCO_3$. It is desirable to soften it to achieve a total hardness of $100 \text{ mg} \cdot \text{L}^{-1}$ as $CaCO_3$. What should the bypass flow rate be?

Solution
As always, you first need to draw a picture. The system used is shown in the box with the dotted line.

$$Q_{total} = Q_{bypass} + Q_{IX}$$

For the designated system,

$$Q_{IX}C_{IX} + Q_{bypass}C_{bypass} = Q_{total}C_{desired}$$

The hardness concentration after ion exchange treatment can be assumed to be zero. The concentration in the bypass is the same as $C_0$, or 340 mg · L$^{-1}$ as CaCO$_3$. The total flow rate is $(400 \text{ L} \cdot \text{capita}^{-1} \cdot \text{day}^{-1}) \times 4 = 1600 \text{ L} \cdot \text{day}^{-1}$.

$$(Q_{IX})(0) + Q_{bypass}(340 \text{ mg} \cdot \text{L}^{-1}) = (1600 \text{ L} \cdot \text{day}^{-1})(100 \text{ mg} \cdot \text{L}^{-1})$$

$$Q_{bypass} = \frac{(1600 \text{ L} \cdot \text{day}^{-1})(100 \text{ mg} \cdot \text{L}^{-1})}{340 \text{ mg} \cdot \text{L}^{-1}} = 470.6, \text{ or } 471 \text{ L} \cdot \text{day}^{-1}$$

## 9–4 SEDIMENTATION

### *Overview*

Surface water containing high turbidity may require sedimentation prior to subsequent treatment. Because the detention time of sedimentation basins (also called clarifiers or settling tanks) is usually 2–4 h, only those particles that can settle in this time will be removed. Sedimentation basins (Figure 9–14) are usually rectangular or circular with either a radial or upward water flow pattern. Sludge that is withdrawn from the bottom of sedimentation basins may in some cases be discharged back to the river.

The clarifier is designed so as to remove the settled water from the basin without carrying away any of the floc particles. In ideal reactors, the average velocity of the fluid is equal to its

**FIGURE 9–14**

A sedimentation basin: **(a)** empty **(b)** full. (*Photos courtesy of Central Coastal Water Authority.*)

(a)

(b)

flow rate divided by the area through which it flows, that is,

$$v = \frac{Q}{A_c} \qquad (9\text{--}21)$$

where $v$ = water velocity (in $m \cdot s^{-1}$) $\equiv$ overflow rate
$\qquad Q$ = water flow (in $m^3 \cdot s^{-1}$)
$\qquad A_c$ = cross-sectional surface area (in $m^2$)

To reduce the turbulence caused by the rushing water as it leaves the tank, a series of troughs, called weirs, are put in place to provide a large area for the water to flow through and minimize the velocity in the sedimentation tank near the outlet zone. The weirs then feed into a central channel or pipe for transport of the settled water. Figure 9–15 shows various weir arrangements. The length of weir required is a function of the type of solids. The heavier the solids, the harder it is to scour them, and the higher the allowable outlet velocity. Therefore, heavier particles require a shorter length of weir than do lighter particles. The units for weir overflow rates are $m^3 \cdot day^{-1} \cdot m^{-1}$, which is water flow ($m^3 \cdot day^{-1}$) per unit length of weir (m).

**EXAMPLE 9–8**   The research plant in fictitious Anextiomarus uses low-turbidity raw water and is designing its overflow weir at a loading rate of $175 \ m^3 \cdot day^{-1} \ m^{-1}$. If its plant flow rate is $0.044 \ m^3 \cdot s^{-1}$, how many linear meters of weir is required?

Solution

$$\frac{(0.044 \ m^3 \cdot s^{-1} \times 86{,}400 \ s \cdot d^{-1})}{175 \ m^3 \cdot day^{-1} \cdot m^{-1}} = 21.7, \text{ or } 22 \ m$$

### Determination of Settling Velocity (v_s)

When designing an ideal sedimentation tank, the settling velocity ($v_s$) of the particle to be removed must first be determined and then the overflow rate ($v_0$) (determined using Equation 9–21) must be set at some value less than or equal to $v_s$.

Determination of the particle-settling velocity is different for different types of particles. Settling properties of particles are often categorized into one of three classes:

**Type I Sedimentation.**   Type I sedimentation is characterized by particles that settle discretely at a constant velocity. They settle as individual particles and do not flocculate or stick to other particles during settling. Examples of these particles are sand and grit material. Generally speaking, the only applications of type I settling are during presedimentation for sand removal, prior to coagulation in a potable water plant, in settling of sand particles during cleaning of rapid sand filters, and in grit chambers (see Section 10–5).

**Type II Sedimentation.**   Type II sedimentation is characterized by particles that flocculate during sedimentation. Because they flocculate, their size is constantly changing; therefore, the settling velocity is changing. Generally the settling velocity increases with depth and extent of flocculation. These types of particles occur with alum or iron coagulation, in primary sedimentation basins (see Section 10–6), and in settling tanks in trickling filtration (see Section 10–7, pages 396 ff).

**Type III, or Zone, Sedimentation.**   In zone sedimentation the particles are at a high concentration (greater than $1000 \ mg \cdot L^{-1}$) such that the particles tend to settle as a mass, and a distinct clear zone and sludge zone are present. Zone settling occurs in lime-softening sedimentation, activated-sludge sedimentation (see Section 10–7, pages 398 ff), and in sludge thickeners (see Section 10–11, pages 421 ff).

**FIGURE 9–15**

Weir arrangements: **(a)** rectangular; **(b)** circular. (*Source: Walker Process Equipment, Inc., Division of Chicago Bridge and Iron Company (Bulletin Numbers 9-W-65, 1973, and 1600-S-107, 1972) Aurora, IL.*)

(a)

(b)

**FIGURE 9–16**

Forces acting on a free-falling particle in a fluid ($F_D$ = drag force; $F_G$ = gravitational force; $F_B$ = buoyancy force).

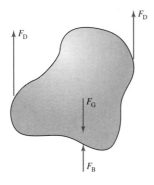

### Determination of Overflow Rate ($v_0$)

Although there are several ways of determining effective particle-settling velocities and consequently of determining overflow rates, the only method we will discuss here is the calculation used for type I sedimentation.

In the case of type I sedimentation, the particle-settling velocity can be calculated and the basin designed to remove a specific size particle. In 1687, Sir Isaac Newton showed that a particle falling in a quiescent fluid accelerates until the frictional resistance, or drag, on the particle is equal to the gravitational force of the particle (Figure 9–16). Some 200 years later, Sir George Gabriel Stokes [9] found that the terminal settling velocity of a sphere falling under quiescent conditions could be described by the following equation.

$$v_s = \frac{g(\rho_s - \rho)d^2}{18\mu} \tag{9–22}$$

where $\rho_s$ = density of particle (in $kg \cdot m^{-3}$)
  $\rho$ = density of fluid (in $kg \cdot m^{-3}$)
  $g$ = acceleration due to gravity (in $m \cdot s^{-2}$)
  $d$ = diameter of spherical particle (in m)
  $\mu$ = dynamic viscosity (in Pa-s)
  18 = a constant

Equation 9–22 is called Stokes' law. It is valid only at laminar flow conditions; that is, where the Reynolds number, $R$, < 1. **Dynamic viscosity** (also called absolute viscosity) is a function of the water temperature. A table of dynamic viscosities (Table A–1) is given in Appendix A.

**EXAMPLE 9–9**  Determine the surface area of a settling tank for the city of Ziusudra. The design flow is $0.044 \ m^3 \cdot s^{-1}$. Use a design overflow rate of $20 \ m \cdot day^{-1}$. Find the depth of the clarifier for the given overflow rate and detention time.

Solution  **1.** Find the surface area.
First change the flow rate to compatible units.

$$(0.044 \ m^3 \cdot s^{-1})(86,400 \ s \cdot day^{-1}) = 3801.6 \ m^3 \cdot day^{-1}$$

Using Equation 9–21 and an overflow rate of $20 \ m^3 \cdot day^{-1}$, the surface area is

$$A_s = \frac{3801.6 \ m^3 \cdot day^{-1}}{20 \ m \cdot day^{-1}} = 190.08 \ m^2, \text{ or } 190 \ m^2$$

Common length-to-width ratios for settling are between 2:1 and 5:1, and lengths seldom exceed 100 m. A minimum of two tanks is always provided.

Let's continue with our design, assuming that we can use two tanks, each with a width of 12 m, a total surface area of 190 $m^2$ would imply a tank length of

Length = 190 $m^2$ / (2 tanks)(12 m wide) = 7.9 m, or 8 m

This does not meet our length-to-width ratio of 2:1 through 5:1. The next step would be to choose a smaller width. Let's try 6 m.

Length = 190 m²/(2 tanks)(6 m wide) = 15.8, or 16 m

This does meet the length-to-width ratio requirement.

2. Find the tank depth.

First find the total tank volume from Equation 9–5, using a detention time of 120 min (assumed) based on the rule of thumb that the detention time should be 2–4 h.

$$\Psi = (0.044 \text{ m}^3 \cdot \text{s}^{-1})(120 \text{ min})(60 \text{ s} \cdot \text{min}^{-1}) = 316.8 \text{ m}^3, \text{ or } 320 \text{ m}^3$$

This would be divided into two tanks as noted earlier. The depth is found as the total tank volume divided by the total surface area.

$$\text{Depth} = \frac{320 \text{ m}^3}{190 \text{ m}^2} = 1.684 \text{ m, or } 1.7 \text{ m}$$

This depth would not include the sludge storage zone.

The final design would then be two tanks, each having the following dimensions: 6 m wide × 16 m long × 1.7 m deep plus sludge storage depth.

## 9–5 FILTRATION

As the water flows over the weirs and exits the sedimentation tank, it still contains particles that were too small to settle or somehow escaped removal due to fluid patterns. As such, the turbidity of the settling tank effluent ranges from 1 to 10 TU, with a typical value being 3 TU. To reduce this turbidity to 0.3 TU, a filtration process is normally used. In addition, to comply with the Surface Water Treatment Rule (SWTR) under the Safe Drinking Water Act (SDWA), all surface waters and ground waters that are under the influence of surface water must be treated using filtration.

Filtration is the process by which water flows slowly through a bed of granular media, usually sand, anthracite coal, or garnet. As the water passes through the medium, particles become trapped due to several mechanisms: interception, flocculation, straining, and sedimentation. The densest particles are "strained" like spaghetti is strained through a colander. These particles are simply too large to pass through the pore spaces of the medium and become trapped in the upper depths of the filter. Particles flowing at a sufficiently low velocity are "intercepted" and attach by weak electrostatic forces to the filter medium. If the water is chemically treated prior to filtration, additional flocculation can occur, allowing particle size to grow so that these larger particles can be removed by the other mechanisms. Heavy particles settle out on the filter medium.

As the pore spaces within the filter medium fill up with particles, the velocity of the water increases, causing some of the particles to be sheared off the medium. These particles then flow only to be trapped deeper in the filter. Once the pore spaces are filled to some "capacity," the turbidity level exceeds a critical value and the filter bed needs to be backwashed. Also as the extent to which the pores fill with particles increases, the head loss through the filter continues to increase and it becomes increasingly more difficult to pass water through the filter.

Filters can operate as either slow or rapid sand filters. The first slow sand filter was installed in London, England, in 1829 [10]. Although the first slow sand filter was installed in the United States in 1872, slow sand filtration never became widely accepted there. Rapid sand or mechanical filtration became the process of choice instead.

Slow sand filters conventionally use only sand (with a gravel support layer), but rapid sand filters use a variety of media. Single-medium beds use only sand, but dual-media filters use sand and anthracite coal. Mixed-media beds use coal, sand, and garnet.

With the promulgation of more stringent regulations for the removal of *Giardia* cysts and *Cryptosporidium* oocysts, filtration is becoming even more widely used in the United States.

Slow sand filters are more effective at removing biological particles than are rapid sand filters. This is because the *schmutzdecke* layer, which forms on the surface of sand filters, has smaller pore spaces than do the media used in rapid sand filters, hence achieving more effective filtration. Additionally, the *schmutzdecke* is biologically active, allowing for the biodegradation of a portion of the naturally occurring organic matter that causes problems in distribution systems.

The most important design parameter in sizing filters is the loading rate. The loading rate is the flow rate of water applied per unit area of the filter. It is the velocity of the water approaching the face of the filter.

$$v_a = \frac{Q}{A_s} \qquad (9\text{-}23)$$

where $v_a$ = face velocity (in $m \cdot day^{-1}$) = loading rate (in $m^3 \cdot day^{-1} \cdot m^{-2}$)
 $Q$ = flow rate onto filter surface (in $m^3 \cdot day^{-1}$)
 $A_s$ = surface area of filter (in $m^2$)

With slow sand filters, water is applied to the sand at a loading rate of 2.9 to 7.6 $m^3 \cdot day^{-1} \cdot m^{-2}$. As mentioned earlier, filters naturally clog as the pore spaces begin to fill with the particles being removed. Once this happens the filter must be cleaned. With slow sand filters this is accomplished by removing floating material, draining the water until the water level is 4–5 cm below the surface of the sand and then scraping off the top 6–12 mm of sand. Cleaning cycles may be from one to several months. Slow sand filters are well-suited for small communities. Although they require large areas of land, slow sand filters are reliable, require less operator time than rapid sand filters, and have low technical operational demands [10].

Rapid sand filters have graded (layered) sand within the bed. The sand grain size distribution is selected to optimize the passage of water while minimizing the passage of particulate matter. Rapid sand filters can also be operated as dual-media filters with sand and anthracite coal. The coal, being lighter and having larger pore spaces than the sand, effectively traps the larger particles in the upper depths of the filter bed.

Rapid sand filters are cleaned in place by forcing water upward through the sand. This operation is called **backwashing.** The washwater flow rate is such that the sand is expanded and the filtered particles are removed from the bed. After backwashing, the sand settles back into place. The largest particles settle first, resulting in a fine sand layer on top and a coarse sand layer on the bottom. The backwash water is either pumped directly to the sanitary sewer for disposal or is treated using sedimentation. The supernatent from the settling ponds is either discharged to the source water or the sanitary sewer and the sludge are landfilled.

Traditionally, rapid sand filters have been designed to operate at a loading rate of 120 $m^3 \cdot day^{-1} \cdot m^{-2}$. Experiments conducted at the Chicago water treatment plant [11] have demonstrated that satisfactory water quality can be obtained with rates as high as 235 $m^3 \cdot day^{-1} \cdot m^{-2}$. Dual-media filters are operated up to loading rates of 300 $m^3 \cdot day^{-1} \cdot m^{-2}$. Usually, a minimum of two filters are constructed to ensure redundancy. For larger plants ($> 0.5\ m^3 \cdot s^{-1}$), a minimum of four filters is suggested [12]. The surface area of the filter tank (often called a filter box) is generally restricted in size to about 100 $m^2$.

In the mid-1980s, deep-bed monomedia filters came into use. These filters are designed to achieve higher loading rates while producing lower finished water turbidities. The filters typically consist of 1.0–1.5-mm diameter anthracite about 1.5–2.5 m deep. They operate at loading rates up to 800 $m^3 \cdot day^{-1} \cdot m^2$.

**EXAMPLE 9–10** As part of their proposed new research treatment plant, Anextiomarus is planning to use five banks of rapid sand filters after their sedimentation tanks. Each bank of sand filters has six filters, operated in parallel. Each filter bed has a surface area of 3 m × 2 m. The design flow rate is 0.044 $m^3 \cdot s^{-1}$. If the design loading rate to the filter is 150 $m^3 \cdot day^{-1} \cdot m^{-2}$, what total filter surface area should be provided and how many banks of filters need to be operational? What is the loading rate when one filter is out of service?

Single bank of filters
(all banks operated in parallel)

Solution    The surface area required is the flow rate divided by the loading rate.

$$A = \frac{Q}{V_a} = \frac{(0.044 \ \text{m}^3 \cdot \text{s}^{-1})(86{,}400 \ \text{s} \cdot \text{day}^{-1})}{150 \ \text{m}^3 \cdot \text{day}^{-1} \cdot \text{m}^{-2}} = 25.34 \ \text{m}^2$$

If the maximum surface area of any one tank is 6 m², then the number of filters required is

$$\text{Number} = \frac{25.34}{6} = 4.22$$

Because we cannot build 0.22 filter, we need to round to an integer. Normally, we build an even number of filters to make construction easier and to reduce costs. In this case we would propose to build four filters and check to see that the design loading does not exceed our guideline values. With four filters the loading would be

$$v_a = \frac{Q}{A_s} = \frac{(0.044 \ \text{m}^3 \cdot \text{s}^{-1})(86{,}400 \ \text{s} \cdot \text{day}^{-1})}{(4 \ \text{filters})(6 \ \text{m}^2 \cdot \text{filter}^{-1})} = 158.4 \ \text{m} \cdot \text{day}^{-1}$$

This is less than the 235 m · day$^{-1}$ recommended maximum loading rate and would be acceptable except that many states require that the filter capacity be sufficient to handle the design flow rate with one filter out of service. Therefore, we must check the loading with three filters in service.

$$v_a = \frac{Q}{A_s} = \frac{(0.044 \ \text{m}^3 \cdot \text{s}^{-1})(86{,}400 \ \text{s} \cdot \text{day}^{-1})}{(3 \ \text{filters})(6 \ \text{m}^2 \cdot \text{filter}^{-1})} = 211.4 \ \text{m} \cdot \text{day}^{-1}$$

This is less than the 235 m · day$^{-1}$ recommended maximum loading rate and is acceptable. Thus, we would build one bank of four filters.

Figure 9–17 shows a cutaway of a rapid sand filter. The bottom of the filter consists of a support medium and collection system. The support medium is designed to keep the sand in the filter and prevent it from leaving with the filtered water. Layers of graded gravel (large on bottom, small on top) traditionally have been used for the support. A perforated pipe is one method of

**FIGURE 9–17**

Typical cross section of a rapid sand filter. (*Source: American Water Works Association, Water Treatment Plant Design, 1969. Reprinted by permission.*)

collecting the filtered water. On top of the support medium is a layer of graded sand. The wash-water troughs collect the backwash water used to clean the filter. The troughs are placed high enough above the sand layer so that sand will not be carried out with the backwash water.

## 9–6   DISINFECTION

Disinfection is used in water treatment to kill pathogens (disease-producing microorganisms) present in water that would cause mild to fatal illness if ingested. Disinfection is not the same as sterilization. Sterilization implies the destruction of all living organisms. Drinking water need not be sterile but simply devoid of pathogens at levels that would cause disease.

Four categories of human enteric pathogens are normally of concern: bacteria, viruses, protozoa, and amebic cysts. Effective disinfection must be capable of destroying all four. During the last decade, it has become clear that specific microbial pathogens, such as *Cryptosporidium,* are highly resistant to traditional disinfectants. In 1993, the presence of *Cryptosporidium parvum* oocysts in treated water caused 400,000 people in Milwaukee to experience intestinal illness. More than 4000 were hospitalized, and at least 50 deaths have been attributed to the disease. Cryptosporidiosis outbreaks have also occurred in several other states over the past several years. To protect the general public from waterborne diseases, the U.S. EPA has established maximum contaminant level goals (MCLGs) for viruses, bacteria and protozoa (i.e., *Giardia lamblia* and *Cryptosporidium parvum*). These regulations also include treatment technique requirements for filtered and unfiltered systems that are designed to disinfect against or remove these microbial pathogens. Under the Interim Enhanced Surface Water Treatment Rule, water supplies (surface water or groundwater supplies under the influence of surface water serving more than 10,000 people) are required to attain a MCLG of zero for *Cryptosporidium* and systems that filter need to achieve a 2-log removal of *Cryptosporidium* oocysts.

To be of practical service, such water disinfectants must possess the following properties:

1. They must destroy the kinds and numbers of pathogens that may be present in water within a practical period of time over an expected range of water temperatures.
2. They must be effective at the variable compositions, concentrations, and conditions of the waters to be treated.
3. They must be neither toxic to humans and domestic animals nor unpalatable or otherwise objectionable in required concentrations.
4. They must be dispensable at reasonable cost and safe and easy to store, transport, handle, and apply.
5. Their strength or concentration in the treated water must be determined easily, quickly, and (preferably) automatically.
6. They must persist within disinfected water in a sufficient concentration to provide reasonable residual protection against its possible recontamination before use.
7. They must not form toxic by-products due to their reactions with any naturally occurring material in the water.

### Disinfection Kinetics

Under ideal conditions, the rate of kill of a type of microorganism can be described by Chick's law [13], which states that the number of organisms destroyed with respect to time is proportional to the number of organisms.

$$\frac{dN}{dt} = -kN \tag{9–24}$$

where $N$ = the number of organisms
$k$ = a first-order rate constant

Under actual conditions, the rate of kill may depart significantly from Chick's law. Increasing rates of kill (with time) may occur because of the time necessary for the disinfectant to damage and inactivate the organism. Decreased rates of kill may occur because of declining concentrations of disinfectant in solution or poor distribution of organisms and disinfectant. To account for these deviations, numerous modifications of Chick's law have been proposed.

In the United States the concept of CT (C = concentration of disinfectant; T = detention time in disinfectant basin) is used to determine the required dose of a disinfectant. The concept is based on Chick's law and data that indicate the required chemical dose necessary to achieve a particular level of treatment for a particular pH and temperature. The time used in this approach is referred to as the T-10 value, or the time that it takes for 10% of a dye slug to flow from the tank. Tables of CT values have been prepared by the U.S. EPA and are used in designing and operating disinfection systems.

### Disinfectants and Disinfection By-Products

**Disinfection by-products (DPBs)** are formed when disinfectants used in water treatment plants react with bromide or naturally occurring organic matter present in the source water. Different disinfectants produce different types or amounts of disinfection by-products. Disinfection by-products for which U.S. EPA drinking-water regulations have been set include trihalomethanes (THMs), haloacetic acids (HAA), bromate, and chlorite. These chemicals are regulated under the Stage 1 Disinfection/Disinfection By-Product (D/DBP) Rule, published in December 1998 and requiring water systems to use treatment methods to reduce the formation of disinfection by-products (Table 9–3).

**Trihalomethanes (THMs)** are a group of four chemicals that form when chlorine-based disinfectants react with naturally occurring organic matter in water. The THMs are chloroform, bromodichloromethane, dibromochloromethane, and bromoform.

**Haloacetic acids (HAAs)** are a group of chemicals that form when certain disinfectants react with naturally occurring organic and inorganic matter in water. The regulated haloacetic acids, known as HAA5, are: monochloroacetic acid, dichloroacetic acid, trichloroacetic acid, monobromoacetic acid, and dibromoacetic acid. Bromate is formed when ozone reacts with naturally occurring bromide found in source water. Chlorite can be formed during the generation of chlorine dioxide.

Since the discovery of chlorination by-products in drinking water in 1974, numerous toxicological and epidemiological studies have been conducted. These studies have shown several disinfection by-products to be carcinogenic or to cause reproductive or developmental disorders in laboratory animals. Some considerable uncertainty surrounds the laboratory and epidemiological studies that have been conducted, and extensive debate is ongoing in the scientific community about the significance of these contradictory findings. Taking a conservative approach, EPA

| TABLE 9–3 | Regulations under the Stage 1 D/DBP Rule | | |
|---|---|---|---|
| **Disinfection By-Product** | **Current Regulatory Limit** | **Stage 1 D/DBP Rule Limit** | **Date Effective** |
| THMs | 100 ppb, annual average | 80 ppb, annual locational running average | December 2001, for large surface water public utilities December 2003 for small surface water and all groundwater systems |
| HAAs | | 60 ppb, annual locational running average | Same as above |
| Bromate | | 10 ppb, annual average | Same as above |
| Chlorite | | 1 ppm, monthly average | Same as above |

believes the weight of evidence presented by the available epidemiological studies on chlorinated drinking water and toxicological studies on individual disinfection by-products supports a potential hazard concern and warrants regulatory action, such as that taken in the Stage 1 D/DBP Rule. Extensive research is currently underway to better understand the potential risks attending exposure to disinfection by-products.

### Chlorine Reactions in Water

In the United States, chlorine has been the most commonly used disinfectant. When used properly, chlorine is effective, and practical. It has several advantages over other disinfectants. It is long-lasting and, therefore, provides a residual in the distribution system. Chlorine acts to kill pathogens by first penetrating through the cell wall then destroying enzymes within the cytoplasm. It has been used not only as a disinfectant but also to control slime and algae; to destroy unpleasant taste and odor-causing compounds; and to oxidize iron, manganese, and hydrogen sulfide. The major disadvantages of chlorine are the formation of chlorinated by-products due to the reaction of chlorine with naturally occurring organic matter and the lack of effectiveness of chlorine in inactivating *Cryptosporidium* oocysts.

The effectiveness of chlorine depends on several factors, including

- **Dosage** (i.e., concentration). For chlorine to be effective it must be present at a sufficiently high concentration to inactivate the pathogens.
- **Contact time.** Chlorine must be in physical contact with the pathogens for a sufficient time to achieve inactivation. Chlorine is ineffective at inactivating *Cryptosporidium* oocysts.
- **Turbidity.** The presence of particles (turbidity) essentially hides the pathogen from the disinfectant.
- **Other reactive species.** The presence of other reactive species, such as ammonia, can consume the disinfectant, thereby, reducing the concentration available for inactivation, along with producing toxic chemicals as discussed previously.
- **pH.** Chlorine is most effective at pH values less than 7.5.
- **Water temperature.** As the temperature increases the rate of disinfection increases; however, chlorine becomes less stable.

Chlorine may be added as the gas ($Cl_2$), as sodium hypochlorite (NaOCl), or as calcium hypochlorite [$Ca(OCl)_2$]. In water, chlorine gas very rapidly hydrolyzes to form HOCl and hydrochloric acid (HCl).

$$Cl_2(g) + H_2O \rightleftharpoons HOCl + H^+ + Cl^- \tag{9–25}$$

This reaction is pH-dependent. At the conditions found in most water treatment systems, this reaction is essentially complete, and no dissolved chlorine gas is present. Because hypochlorous acid is a weak acid, it dissociates to form $OCl^-$ according to the reaction

$$HOCl \rightleftharpoons H^+ + OCl^- \tag{9–26}$$

Because the $pK_a$ for this reaction is 7.54 at 25°C, at pH values above this, essentially all of the chlorine is present as $OCl^-$, whereas below a pH 7.54, hypochlorous acid predominates. This is significant because hypochlorous acid is a much more effective disinfectant than hypochlorite.

### Chlorine Dioxide

Another very strong oxidant is chlorine dioxide. Chlorine dioxide ($ClO_2$) must be generated on-site by combining chlorine and sodium chlorite. Chlorine dioxide is often used as a primary disinfectant, inactivating the bacteria and cysts. Chloramine is then used as a secondary disinfectant to provide a residual in the distribution system because chlorine dioxide does not maintain a residual long enough to be useful as a distribution system disinfectant. The advantage of chlorine dioxide over chlorine is that chlorine dioxide does not react with naturally occurring organic matter to

| TABLE 9–4 | CT Values (mg-min-L$^{-1}$) for 99.9% *Giardia* Cyst Inactivation at a pH 6.0–9.0 | | | | | |
|---|---|---|---|---|---|---|
| **Temperature** | **1°C** | **5°C** | **10°C** | **15°C** | **20°C** | **25°C** |
| Chlorine dioxide | 81 | 54 | 40 | 27 | 21 | 14 |
| Chlorine | 273 | 192 | 144 | 96 | 72 | 48 |
| Ozone | 2.9 | 1.9 | 1.43 | 0.95 | 0.72 | 0.48 |
| Chloramines | 3800 | 2200 | 1850 | 1500 | 1100 | 750 |

*Source:* United States Environmental Protection Agency. *Disinfection Profiling and Benchmarking Guidance Manual* EPA-815-R-99-013, August 1999.

*Note:* Chlorine 1°C actually at 0.5°C; dose for chlorine 1.6 mg · L$^{-1}$. Other doses unspecified; pH for chlorine 7.5, other oxidants are given as range 6–9.

form THMs. The major disadvantage of chlorine dioxide is the potential formation of chlorite and chlorate, which are potential human carcinogens.

### Ozonation

Ozone is a sweet-smelling, unstable gas. It is a form of oxygen in which three atoms of oxygen are combined to form the molecule $O_3$. Because of its instability, it is generated at the point of use. Ozone is produced from air or oxygen, and the air exiting the generation equipment can contain up to 13% ozone in oxygen.

Ozone is widely used in drinking-water treatment in Europe and is continuing to gain popularity in the United States. It is a powerful oxidant, more powerful even than hypochlorous acid. Table 9–4 shows the CT values for ozone, chlorine dioxide, and chloramine for 3-log inactivation (99.9% removal) of *Giardia* cysts, indicating the effectiveness of ozone as a disinfectant.

In addition to being a strong oxidant, ozone has the advantage of not forming THMs or any of the chlorinated DBPs. A disadvantage of ozone is that it does form some low-molecular-weight compounds that can react with chlorine-based disinfectants to produce chlorinated aldehydes and ketones. Another disadvantage is that, unless the low-molecular-weight compounds formed from the reaction of ozone with naturally occurring organic matter are removed, the regrowth of bacteria in the distribution system can be problematic. As with chlorine dioxide, ozone does not persist in the water, decaying back to oxygen in minutes. Therefore, a typical flow schematic adds ozone either to the raw water or between the sedimentation basins and filter for primary disinfection, then adds chloramine after the filters as the distribution system disinfectant.

### Ultraviolet Radiation

Ultraviolet (UV) radiation has the potential to inactivate pathogens. It is employed by submerging UV lamps into the water to be treated. Multiple lamps are used to provide greater coverage. The major factor in achieving good microorganism kill is the ability of the UV light to pass through the water to get to the target organism. Thus, the lamps must be kept free of slime and precipitates, and the water must be free of turbidity.

UV performs very well against both bacteria and viruses. Its major disadvantages are that it leaves no residual protection for the distribution system and is very expensive.

## 9–7   OTHER TREATMENT PROCESSES FOR DRINKING WATER

### Membrane Processes

Membrane processes are being used more commonly in water treatment because of their ability to remove small particles, including *Cryptosporidium* oocysts and *Giardia* cysts. These processes are classified into reverse osmosis (RO), nanofiltration (NF), microfiltration (MF), and ultrafiltration (UF). RO is capable of removing ionic substances as small as 1–15 Å in diameter. The process accomplishes this by essentially applying a pressure that exceeds the osmotic pressure of the solution, thereby forcing the water across a membrane, leaving a brine solution behind. NF membranes are capable of rejecting high percentages of multivalent ions and divalent cations while allowing monovalent ions to pass. UF and MF membranes reject molecules on the basis of size, retaining particles larger than about 15–200 and 200–1000 Å, respectively.

### Advanced Oxidation Processes (AOPs)

AOPs are processes designed to produce hydroxyl radicals (˙OH). Hydroxyl radicals are highly reactive, nonselective oxidants able to decompose many organic compounds. Two AOPs are the combinations of ozone and hydrogen peroxide and ozone and UV radiation. AOPs are most commonly used for the oxidation of chemicals that cannot be removed by other means.

### Carbon Adsorption

Carbon adsorption is essentially the same as that described in Chapter 8, with the attachment of chemical compounds onto soil particles. Here, in water treatment, the adsorbent (solid) is activated carbon, either granular (GAC) or powdered (PAC). Activated carbon is most commonly used for the removal of taste- and odor-causing compounds, as well some synthetic organic compounds. The major disadvantage of activated carbon is that the problematic compounds are not destroyed but simply transferred from one matrix, water, to another, carbon surfaces. Additionally, when used for the removal of nonpolar compounds, a GAC filter typically lasts 90–120 days before it loses its adsorptive capacity. Because of its short life, the GAC needs to be regenerated. Regeneration can be accomplished by heating the activated carbon to about 900°C to drive off the adsorbed organic chemicals. Air pollution control devices are necessary to prevent the release of any unburned organic chemicals. This is clearly an expensive proposition. Although a GAC can be used for the removal of THMs, its capacity is very low and the carbon may only last up to 30 days.

### Aeration

Aeration is used in drinking-water treatment primarily for the oxidation of iron and for the removal of volatile organic chemicals. Soluble iron can be removed by the following reaction:

$$4Fe(HCO_3)_2 + O_2 + 2H_2O \rightleftharpoons 4Fe(OH)_3 + 8CO_2 \tag{9-27}$$

The rate of oxidation of Fe(II) can be expressed by the rate law [14].

$$\frac{-d[Fe(II)]}{dt} = \frac{k[O_2(aq)]}{[H^+]^2}[Fe(II)] \tag{9-28}$$

where $k = 3 \times 10^{-12}$ min$^{-1}$ · mol$^{-1}$ at 20°C. At pH values greater than 7 the rate of iron oxidation is rapid (> 90% removal in less than 10 min).

Manganese oxidation is much slower than that of ferrous iron. At conventional temperatures oxidation of Mn(II) is not extensive at pH values below 9 unless catalytic oxidation is used.

Aeration can also be used for the removal of volatile organic chemicals, such as trichloroethylene and tetrachloroethane. When aeration is used for such means, treatment of the off-gas is necessary to avoid the release of these chemicals into the atmosphere. Countercurrent operation, whereby the stripping gas and the water flow in opposite directions, is often used for maximum removal of the chemicals.

A typical air-stripping unit is shown in Figure 9–18.

**FIGURE 9–18**

A typical air-stripping unit. (*Source: Remco Engineering* http://www.remtech-eng.com/towers.html; Tri-Pak Packing Material: http://www.jaeger.com)

## 9–8   WATER PLANT RESIDUALS MANAGEMENT

Water treatment plants produce a number of waste streams (residuals), which can be divided into five general categories.

1. Settling sludge formed during the removal of turbidity using alum or iron salts.
2. Filter backwash water and associated solids
3. Softening sludges
4. Waste streams from ion-exchange regeneration, reverse osmosis reject streams, or spent activated carbon
5. Contaminated air streams generated during aeration processes

The precipitated chemicals and other materials removed from water to make it potable and palatable are termed **sludge.** Satisfactory treatment and disposal of water treatment plant sludge can be the single most complex and costly operation in the plant.

The sludges withdrawn from coagulation and softening plants are composed largely of water (as much as 98%). Thus, for example, 20 kg of solid chemical precipitate is accompanied by 980 kg of water. Assuming equal densities for the precipitate and water (a bad assumption at best), approximately 1 $m^3$ of sludge is produced for each 20 kg of chemicals added to the water. For even a small plant (say 0.05 $m^3 \cdot s^{-1}$), this might mean up to 800 $m^3 \cdot year^{-1}$ of sludge—a substantial volume to say the least!

The most logical sludge management program attempts to use the following approach in disposing of the sludge:

1. Minimization of sludge generation
2. Chemical recovery of precipitates

**3.** Sludge treatment to reduce volume

**4.** Ultimate disposal in an environmentally safe manner

### Mass-Balance Analysis

Clarifier sludge production can be estimated by a mass-balance analysis of the sedimentation basin. Because no reaction is taking place, the mass-balance Equation (3–2) reduces to the form

$$\text{Accumulation rate} = \text{input rate} - \text{output rate} \tag{9–29}$$

**EXAMPLE 9–11**   A coagulation treatment plant with a flow of $0.044 \text{ m}^3 \cdot \text{s}^{-1}$ is dosing alum at $33.0 \text{ mg} \cdot \text{L}^{-1}$. No other chemicals are being added. The raw water/suspended solids concentration is $47.0 \text{ mg} \cdot \text{L}^{-1}$. The effluent/suspended solids concentration is measured at $10.0 \text{ mg} \cdot \text{L}^{-1}$. The sludge solids content is 1.05%, and the specific gravity of the sludge solids is 2.61. What volume of sludge must be disposed of each day?

**Solution**   The mass-balance diagram for the sedimentation basin is shown here.

Let's first perform a mass balance on the suspended solids,

$$C_{\text{in}} = 47.0 \text{ mg} \cdot \text{L}^{-1}$$

$$C_{\text{out}} = 10.0 \text{ mg} \cdot \text{L}^{-1}$$

Therefore, for every liter of water treated (47.0 − 10.0) or $37.0 \text{ mg} \cdot \text{L}^{-1}$ suspended solids is removed in the sludge each day. The mass of suspended solids sludge can be calculated as

$$Q_{\text{in}}C_{\text{removed}} = (0.044 \text{ m}^3 \cdot \text{s}^{-1})(37.0 \text{ mg} \cdot \text{L}^{-1})(1000 \text{ L} \cdot \text{m}^{-3})(86{,}400 \text{ s} \cdot \text{day}^{-1})$$

$$\times (10^{-6} \text{ kg} \cdot \text{mg}^{-1})$$

$$= 140.66 \text{ kg} \cdot \text{day}^{-1}$$

Now let's look at the amount of sludge produced by the addition of alum. Using Equation 9–1, we see that there are two moles of aluminum hydroxide $(Al(OH)_3)$ produced for every mole of alum added. The molecular weight of alum is $594.35 \text{ g} \cdot \text{mol}^{-1}$. The molecular weight of aluminum hydroxide is $78.00 \text{ g} \cdot \text{mol}^{-1}$. Therefore, using basic stoichiometric relationships, we obtain the alum dose in moles per liter

$$\frac{33.0 \text{ mg} \cdot \text{L}^{-1}}{594.35 \text{ g} \cdot \text{mol}^{-1}} \left( \frac{\text{g}}{1000 \text{ mg}} \right) = 5.55 \times 10^{-5} \text{ mol} \cdot \text{L}^{-1}$$

And the concentration of aluminum hydroxide precipitated

$$= \left( \frac{2 \text{ mol Al(OH)}_3}{\text{mole alum}} \right) (5.55 \times 10^{-5} \text{ mol} \cdot \text{L}^{-1}) = 1.11 \times 10^{-4} \text{ mol} \cdot \text{L}^{-1}$$

Converting the concentration of aluminum hydroxide to units of $\text{mg} \cdot \text{L}^{-1}$, we obtain

$$(1.11 \times 10^{-4} \text{ mol} \cdot \text{L}^{-1})(78.00 \text{ g} \cdot \text{mol}^{-1})(1000 \text{ mg} \cdot \text{g}^{-1}) = 8.66 \text{ mg} \cdot \text{L}^{-1}$$

Thus, the mass of dry aluminum hydroxide sludge produced each day is

$$(0.044 \text{ m}^3 \cdot \text{s}^{-1})(8.66 \text{ mg} \cdot \text{L}^{-1})(1000 \text{ L} \cdot \text{m}^{-3})(86{,}400 \text{ s} \cdot \text{day}^{-1})(10^{-6} \text{ kg} \cdot \text{mg}^{-1})$$

$$= 32.9 \text{ kg} \cdot \text{day}^{-1}$$

Thus the total sludge production is

$$140.66 + 32.9 = 173.6 \, \text{kg} \cdot \text{day}^{-1}$$

Because this is a dry mass and the sludge has only 1.05% solids, we must account for the volume of water in estimating the volume to be removed each day. The solids content is defined as the

$$\text{Solids content as percent} = \frac{\text{mass}_{(\text{solids})}}{\text{mass}_{(\text{solids})} + \text{mass}_{(\text{water})}} \times 100$$

$$1.05 = \frac{173.6}{173.6 + \text{mass}_{(\text{water})}} \times 100$$

$$\text{Mass}_{(\text{water})} = 16,360 \, \text{kg} \cdot \text{day}^{-1}$$

Now we use the definition of density (mass per unit volume) to find the volume of sludge and water. The specific gravity of the solids is 2.65, and the density of water is $1000 \, \text{kg} \cdot \text{m}^{-3}$.

$$\text{Volume} = \frac{\text{mass}}{\text{density}}$$

$$V_{\text{T}} = \text{volume of solids} + \text{volume of water}$$

$$= \frac{173.6 \, \text{kg} \cdot \text{day}^{-1}}{2.65 \times 1000 \, \text{kg} \cdot \text{m}^{-3}} + \frac{16,360 \, \text{kg} \cdot \text{day}^{-1}}{1000 \, \text{kg} \cdot \text{m}^{-3}}$$

$$= 0.066 + 16.36$$

$$= 16.43 \, \text{m}^3 \cdot \text{day}^{-1}$$

Obviously, the solids account for only a small fraction of the total volume. This is why sludge dewatering is an important part of the water treatment process.

### Sludge Treatment

The treatment of solid/liquid wastes produced in water treatment processes involves the separation of the water from the solid constituents to the degree necessary for the selected disposal method. The required degree of treatment is therefore a direct function of the ultimate disposal method.

Several sludge treatment methodologies have been practiced in the water industry. Figure 9–19 shows the most common sludge-handling options available, listed by general categories of thickening, dewatering, and disposal. In choosing a combination of the possible treatment process trains, it is probably best to first identify the available disposal options and their requirements for a final cake solids concentration. Most landfill applications will require a "handleable" sludge and this may limit the type of acceptable dewatering devices. Methods and costs of transportation may affect the decision of "how dry is dry enough." The criterion should not be to simply reach a given solids concentration but rather to reach a solids concentration of desired properties for the handling, transport, and disposal options available.

Table 9–5 shows a generalized range of results that have been obtained for final solids concentrations from different dewatering devices for coagulant and lime sludges.

**FIGURE 9–19**

Common sludge-handling options.

| TABLE 9-5 | Range of Cake Solid Concentrations Obtainable | |
|---|---|---|
| | **Lime Sludge**<br>(%) | **Coagulation Sludge**<br>(%) |
| Gravity thickening | 15–30 | 3–4 |
| Basket centrifuge | 10–15 | |
| Scroll centrifuge | 55–65 | 10–20 |
| Belt filter press | 10–15 | |
| Vacuum filter | 45–65 | n/a |
| Pressure filter | 55–70 | 30–45 |
| Sand drying beds | 50 | 20–25 |
| Storage lagoons | 50–60 | 7–15 |

**FIGURE 9-20**

Continuous-flow gravity thickener. (*Source: Metcalf & Eddy, Wastewater Engineering, Treatment & Reuse, 4th edition, McGraw-Hill, New York, 2003. Reprinted by permission.*)

To give you an understanding of these solids concentrations, a sludge cake with 35% solids would have the consistency of butter, whereas a 15% sludge would have a consistency much like rubber cement.

After removal of the sludge from the clarifier or sedimentation basin, the first treatment step is usually thickening. Thickening assists the performance of any subsequent treatment, gets rid of much water quickly, and helps to equalize flows to the subsequent treatment device. An approximation for determining sludge volume reduction via thickening is given by

$$\frac{V_2}{V_1} = \frac{P_1}{P_2} \tag{9-30}$$

where $V_1$ = volume of sludge before thickening (in m³)
$\quad V_2$ = volume of sludge after thickening (in m³)
$\quad P_1$ = percent of solids concentration of sludge before thickening
$\quad P_2$ = percent of solids concentration after thickening

Thickening is usually accomplished by using circular settling basins similar to a clarifier (Figure 9–20). Thickeners can be designed based on pilot evaluations or using data obtained from similar plants. Lime sludges are typically loaded at $100–200 \, \text{kg} \cdot \text{day}^{-1} \cdot \text{m}^{-2}$, and coagulant sludge loading rates are about $15–25 \, \text{kg} \cdot \text{day}^{-1} \cdot \text{m}^{-2}$.

Following thickening of the sludge, dewatering can take place by either mechanical or non-mechanical means. In nonmechanical devices, sludge is spread out, allowing the free water to drain away and the remaining water to evaporate. Sometimes the amount of free water available to drain is enhanced by natural freeze–thaw cycles. In mechanical dewatering, some type of device is used to force the water out of the sludge.

We begin our discussion with the nonmechanical methods and follow with the mechanical methods.

**Lagoons.**   A **lagoon** is essentially a large pond dug out for containment of the sludge. Lagoons can be constructed as either storage lagoons or dewatering lagoons. **Storage lagoons** are designed to store and collect the solids for some predetermined length of time. They generally have decant capabilities but no underdrain system. Storage lagoons should be equipped with sealed bottoms to protect the groundwater. Once the storage lagoon is full or the decant can no longer meet discharge limitations, it must be abandoned or cleaned. To facilitate drying, the standing water may be removed by pumping, leaving a wet sludge. Coagulant sludges can only be expected to reach a 7–10% solids concentration in storage lagoons. The remaining solids must be either cleaned out wet or allowed to evaporate. Depending on the depth of the wet solids, evaporation can take years. The top layers will often form a crust, preventing evaporation of the bottom layers of sludge.

The primary difference between a dewatering lagoon and a storage lagoon is that a **dewatering lagoon** has a sand and underdrain bottom, similar to a drying bed. Dewatering lagoons can be designed to achieve a dewatered sludge cake. The advantage of a dewatering lagoon over a drying bed is that storage is built into the system to assist in meeting peak solids production or to help in handling sludge during wet weather. Compared with conventional drying beds, bottom sand layers have the disadvantage of plugging up with multiple loadings, thereby increasing the required surface area. Polymer treatment can be useful to prevent clogging.

**Sand-Drying Beds.**   Sand-drying beds operate on the simple principle of spreading the sludge out and letting it dry. As much water as possible is removed by drainage or decanting, and the rest of the water must evaporate until the desired final solids concentration is reached. Sand-drying beds have been built simply by cleaning an area of land, dumping the sludge, and hoping something happens. At the other end of the spectrum sophisticated automated drying systems have been built.

The dewatering of sludge on sand beds is accomplished by two major methods: drainage and evaporation. The removal of water from sludge by drainage is a two-step process. First, the water is drained from the sludge, into the sand, and out the underdrains. This process may last a few days until the sand is clogged with fine particles or until all the free water has drained away. Further drainage by decanting can occur once a supernatant layer has formed (if beds are provided with a means of removing surface water). Decanting for removal of rain water can also be particularly important with sludges that do not crack.

The water that does not drain or is not decanted must evaporate. Obviously, annual rainfall rates play a role here. Phoenix would be a more efficient area for a sand bed than Seattle!

The filtrate from the sand-drying beds can be recycled, treated, or discharged to a watercourse depending on its quality. Laboratory testing of the filtrate should be performed in conjunction with sand-drying bed pilot testing before a decision is made about what is to be done with it.

**Freeze Treatment.**   Dewatering sludge by either of the nonmechanical methods may be enhanced by physical conditioning of the sludge through alternate freezing and thawing cycles. The freeze–thaw process dehydrates the sludge particles by freezing the water that is closely associated with the particles. The dewatering process takes place in two stages. The first reduces sludge volume by selectively freezing the water molecules. Next, the solids are dehydrated when they become frozen. When thawed, the solid mass forms granular-shaped particles. This coarse material readily settles and retains its new size and shape. This residue sludge dewaters rapidly and makes suitable landfill material.

The supernatant liquid from this process can be decanted, leaving the solids to dewater by natural drainage and evaporation. Pilot-scale systems can be used to evaluate this method's effectiveness and to establish design parameters. Elimination of rain and snow from the dewatering system by the provision of a roof enhances the process considerably.

**FIGURE 9-21**

Solid bowl centrifuge.

**FIGURE 9-22**

Vacuum filter. (*Courtesy of Komline-Sanderson Engineering Corporation.*)

**Centrifuging.**   A centrifuge uses centrifugal force to speed up the separation of sludge particles from the liquid. In a typical unit (Figure 9–21), sludge is pumped into a horizontal, cylindrical bowl, rotating at 800–2000 rpm. Polymers used for sludge conditioning are also injected into the centrifuge. The solids are spun to the outside of the bowl, where they are scraped out by a screw conveyor. The liquid, or centrate, is returned to the treatment plant. Centrifuges are very sensitive to changes in the concentration or composition of the sludge, as well as to the amount of polymer applied.

**Vacuum Filtration.**   A vacuum filter consists of a cylindrical drum, covered with a filtering material or fabric, which rotates partially submerged in a vat of conditioned sludge (Figure 9–22). A vacuum is applied inside the drum to extract water, leaving the solids, or filter cake, on the filter medium. As the drum completes its rotational cycles, a blade scrapes the filter cake from the filter and the cycle begins again.

**Continuous Belt Filter Press (CBFP).**   The belt filter press operates on the principle that bending a sludge cake contained between two filter belts around a roll introduces shear and compressive forces in the cake, allowing water to work its way to the surface and out of the cake, thereby reducing the cake's moisture content. The device employs double moving belts to continuously dewater sludges through one or more stages of dewatering (Figure 9–23).

**FIGURE 9–23**

Continuous belt filter press. (*Source:* U.S. Environmental Protection Agency, *Process Design Manual, Sludge Treatment and Disposal,* 1979.)

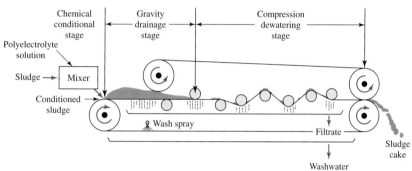

**FIGURE 9–24**

Schematic cross section of a fixed volume recessed plate filter assembly. (*Source:* U.S. Environmental Protection Agency, *Process Design Manual, Sludge Treatment and Disposal,* 1979.)

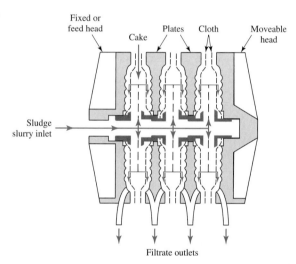

### Plate Pressure Filters.

The basic component of a plate filter is a series of recessed vertical plates. Each plate is covered with cloth to support and contain the sludge cake. The plates are mounted in a frame consisting of two bead supports connected by two horizontal parallel bars. A schematic cross section is illustrated in Figure 9–24. Conditioned sludge is pumped into the pressure filter and passes through feed holes in the filter plates along the length of the filter and into the recessed chambers. As the sludge cake forms and builds up in the chamber, the pressure gradually increases to a point where further sludge injection would be counterproductive. At this time the injection ceases.

### Ultimate Disposal

After all possible sludge treatment has been accomplished, a residual sludge remains, which must be sent for ultimate disposal. Of the many theoretical alternatives for ultimate disposal, only two are of practical interest:

1. Landfilling
2. Land spreading

As discussed in Chapter 12, municipal solid wastes can be disposed of in landfills. Landfills are well-engineered facilities that are located, designed, operated, monitored during operation and after closure, closed, cleaned up when necessary, and financed according to federal regulations. These regulations were promulgated to protect human health and the environment. New landfills are designed to collect and treat potentially harmful landfill gases so that they are not released to the environment. Landfill gases may also be used for energy production. Organic sludges may be incinerated and then applied over land.

Sludges may also be land applied as soil conditioners or amendments. The major environmental concerns regarding such disposal methods are the release of pathogenic organisms and the presence of toxic chemicals. Unlike wastewater sludges, water treatment sludges rarely have sufficiently high organic matter contents to render their putrescible organic compounds problematic.

In the past, ocean disposal of sludges was common; however, concern over the degradation of ocean environments has rendered this method unacceptable. Ocean dumping was banned under the U.S. Ocean Dumping Ban Act of 1988, as described in Chapter 8.

## CHAPTER REVIEW

When you have completed studying this chapter you should be able to do the following without the aid of your textbook or notes:

1. Define: pathogen, SDWA, MCL, MCLG, VOC, SOC, DBP, THM, and SWTR.
2. Define potable and palatable and explain why we must provide drinking water that is both potable and palatable.
3. Distinguish among dissolved substances, suspended solids, and colloidal substances based on their size and the mechanism by which they can be removed from water.
4. List the four categories of water quality for drinking water.
5. Identify the microorganism group used as an indicator of fecal contamination of water and explain why it was selected. What are its limitations?
6. Sketch a water-softening plant and a filtration plant, labeling all of the parts and explaining their functions. Show where chemicals are added and residuals produced.
7. Describe the process of coagulation.
8. Differentiate between coagulation and flocculation.
9. Explain the effect of pH on alum and ferric chloride solubility.
10. List the basic types of coagulant aids; explain how each aid works and when it should be employed.
11. Define hardness in terms of the chemical constituents that cause it and the results as seen by the users of hard water.
12. Using diagrams and chemical reactions, explain how water becomes hard.
13. Given the total hardness and alkalinity, calculate the carbonate hardness and noncarbonate hardness.
14. Calculate the theoretical detention time or volume of a tank if you are given the flow rate and the volume or detention time.
15. Define overflow rate in terms of liquid flow and settling-basin geometry, and state its units.
16. Explain the difference among type I, type II, and type III sedimentation.
17. Compare slow sand filters, rapid sand filters, and dual-media filters with respect to operating procedures and relative loading rates.
18. Explain how a rapid sand filter is cleaned.
19. Explain why a disinfectant that has a residual is preferable to one that does not.
20. Write the equations for the dissolution of chlorine gas in water and the subsequent dissociation of hypochlorous acid.
21. Define the terms thickening, conditioning, and dewatering.

22. List and describe three methods of nonmechanical dewatering of sludge.
23. List and describe four mechanical methods of dewatering of sludge.

With the aid of the text or a list of equations you should be able to do the following:

1. Calculate the gram equivalent weight of a chemical or compound.
2. Calculate consumption of alkalinity for a given dose of alum or ferric chloride (given the equations).
3. Calculate the production of $CO_2$, $SO_4^{2-}$, or acid for a given dose of alum or ferric chloride and the chemical equations.
4. Calculate the amount of lime (as $CaCO_3$) that must be added if insufficient alkalinity is present in order to neutralize the acid produced by the addition of alum or ferric chloride to a given water (given the equations).
5. Calculate the fraction of the "split" for a lime–soda softening system or an ion-exchange softening system.
6. Size rapid-mix and flocculation basins.
7. Size a sedimentation basin and estimate the required weir length.
8. Size a rapid sand filter. Determine how many filters of particular size are needed along with the flow rate through the filters.

## PROBLEMS

**9-1** The following mineral analysis was reported for a water sample taken from well No. 1 at the Eastwood Manor Subdivision near McHenry, Illinois. [15]

Well No. 1, Lab No. 02694, November 9, 1971    Bicarbonate = 611

(*Note:* All reported as mg · L$^{-1}$ as the ion unless stated otherwise.)

| Mineral | Concentration | MW | Mineral | Concentration | Equt. |
|---|---|---|---|---|---|
| Iron (2+) | 0.2 | | Silica ($SiO_2$) | 20.0 | |
| Manganese (2+) | 0.0 | | Fluoride | 0.35 | |
| Ammonium | 0.5 | | Boron | 0.1 | |
| Sodium | 4.7 | 23 | Nitrate | 0.0 | |
| Potassium | 0.9 | | Chloride | 4.5 | 35.5 |
| Calcium | 67.2 | 40.1 mg/mm | Sulfate | 29.0 | |
| Magnesium | 40.0 | 24.3 | Alkalinity | 284.0 as $CaCO_3$ | |
| Barium | 0.5 | | pH (as recorded) | 7.6 units | |

Determine the total, carbonate, and noncarbonate hardness (in mg · L$^{-1}$ as $CaCO_3$) using the predominant polyvalent cation definition in Section 9–3.

**Answers:**

$$TH = 332.8 \text{ mg} \cdot L^{-1} \text{ as } CaCO_3$$
$$CR = 284.0 \text{ mg} \cdot L^{-1} \text{ as } CaCO_3$$
$$NCR = 48.8 \text{ mg} \cdot L^{-1} \text{ as } CaCO_3$$

**9-2** Calculate the total, carbonate, and noncarbonate hardness in Problem 9–1 using all of the polyvalent cations. What is the percent error in using only the predominant cations?

**9-3** The following mineral analysis was reported for a water sample taken from well No. 1 at Magnolia, Illinois [16]. Determine the total, carbonate, and noncarbonate hardness (in mg · L$^{-1}$ as $CaCO_3$), using the predominant polyvalent cation definition of hardness.

Well No. 1, Lab No. B109535, April 23, 1973

(*Note:* All reported as mg · L$^{-1}$ as the ion unless stated otherwise.)

| Mineral | Concentration | Mineral | Concentration |
|---------|---------------|---------|---------------|
| Iron | 0.42 | Zinc | 0.01 |
| Manganese | 0.04 | Silica ($SiO_2$) | 20.0 |
| Ammonium | 11.0 | Fluoride | 0.3 |
| Sodium | 78.0 | Boron | 0.3 |
| Potassium | 2.6 | Nitrate | 0.0 |
| Calcium | 78.0 | Chloride | 9.0 |
| Magnesium | 32.0 | Sulfate | 0.0 |
| Barium | 0.5 | Alkalinity | 494.035 $CaCO_3$ |
| Copper | 0.01 | pH (as recorded) | 7.7 units |

**Answer:** TH $= 327.19$ mg $\cdot$ L$^{-1}$ as $CaCO_3$, CH $= 327.19$ mg $\cdot$ L$^{-1}$ as $CaCO_3$, NCH $= 0$

**9-4** The following mineral analysis was reported for Michigan State University well water [17]. Determine the total, carbonate, and noncarbonate hardness (in mg $\cdot$ L$^{-1}$ as $CaCO_3$).

(*Note:* All units are mg $\cdot$ L$^{-1}$ as the ion unless otherwise stated.)

| Mineral | Concentration | Mineral | Concentration |
|---------|---------------|---------|---------------|
| Fluoride | 1.1 | Silica ($SiO_2$) | 13.4 |
| Chloride | 4.0 | Bicarbonate | 318.0 |
| Nitrate | 0.0 | Sulfate | 52.0 |
| Sodium | 14.0 | Iron | 0.5 |
| Potassium | 1.6 | Manganese | 0.07 |
| Calcium | 96.8 | Zinc | 0.27 |
| Magnesium | 30.4 | Barium | 0.2 |

**9-5** What is the volume required for a rapid-mix basin that is to be used to treat 0.05 m$^3 \cdot$ s$^{-1}$ of water if the detention time is 60 s?     $V = Q(t_0)$

**Answer:** 3 m$^3$

**9-6** Two parallel flocculation basins are to be used to treat a water flow of 0.150 m$^3 \cdot$ s$^{-1}$. If the design detention time is 20 min, what is the volume of each tank?

**9-7** If a 1.0 m$^3 \cdot$ s$^{-1}$ flow water treatment plant uses ten sedimentation basins with an overflow rate of 15 m$^3 \cdot$ day$^{-1} \cdot$ m$^2$, what should be the surface area (m$^2$) of each tank?

**Answer:** 576.0 m$^2$

**9-8** Assuming a conservative value for an overflow rate, determine the surface area (m$^2$) of each of two sedimentation tanks that together must handle a flow of 0.05162 m$^3 \cdot$ s$^{-1}$ of lime softening floc. Use an overflow rate of 57 m$^3 \cdot$ day$^{-1} \cdot$ m$^{-2}$.

**9-9** Repeat Problem 9–7 for an alum or iron floc with an overflow rate of 20 m$^3 \cdot$ day$^{-1} \cdot$ m$^{-2}$.

**Answer:** 111 m$^2$

**9-10** For a flow of 0.8 m$^3 \cdot$ s$^{-1}$, how many rapid sand filter boxes of dimensions 10 m $\times$ 10 m are needed for a loading rate of 110 m$^3 \cdot$ day$^{-1} \cdot$ m$^{-2}$?

**9-11** If a dual-media filter with a loading rate of 300 m$^3 \cdot$ day$^{-1} \cdot$ m$^{-2}$ were built instead of the standard filter in Problem 9–10, how many filter boxes would be required?

**Answer:** Four filters (rounding to next largest even number)

**9-12** The water flow meter at the Westwood water plant is malfunctioning. The plant superintendent tells you the four dual-media filters (each 5.00 m $\times$ 10.0 m) are loaded at a velocity of 280 m $\cdot$ day$^{-1}$. What is the flow rate through the filters (in m$^3 \cdot$ s$^{-1}$)?

## DISCUSSION QUESTIONS

**9-1**  Explain the word turbidity in terms that the mayor of a community could understand.

**9-2**  Which of the chemicals added to treat a surface water aids in making the water palatable?

**9-3**  Microorganisms play a role in the formation of hardness in groundwater. True or false? Explain.

**9-4**  If no bicarbonate is present in a well water that is to be softened to remove magnesium, which chemicals must you add?

**9-5**  In the United States, chlorine is preferred as a disinfectant over ozone because it has a residual. Why is the presence of a residual important? In recent years ozone has been replacing chlorine as the primary disinfectant in the United States. What are the advantages and disadvantages of this?

**9-6**  A new water-softening plant is being designed for Lubbock, Texas. The climate is dry and land is readily available at a reasonable cost. What methods of sludge dewatering would be most appropriate? Explain your reasoning.

**9-7**  Since the attacks on the World Trade Center and the Pentagon on September 11, 2001, it has become apparent that we must provide sufficient security to protect our drinking-water supplies. What measures can be taken to ensure such protection?

**9-8**  In May 2000, in Walkerton, Ontario, an outbreak of enteric illness occurred due to contamination of the public water supply with *E. coli*. The outbreak killed five people and sickened hundreds. What led to the contamination and what could have prevented it? How could the water treatment plant be redesigned to prevent such an occurrence in the future?

**9-9**  In Haiti, less than half the population has access to safe water. The poverty level approaches that in sub-Saharan Africa, with an average income in 2002 around $1.40 per day. What measures could be taken to better provide safe drinking water for this population?

## ADDITIONAL READING

**Books**

American Water Works Association. *Water Quality and Treatment,* 3rd ed. McGraw-Hill, New York (2000).

American Water Works Association. *Water Treatment Plant Design,* 2nd ed. McGraw-Hill, New York (1990).

Benefield, L. D., J. F. Judkins, Jr., and B. L. Weand. *Process Chemistry for Water and Wastewater Treatment.* Prentice Hall, Englewood Cliffs, NJ (1982).

Clark, J. W., W. Viessman, and M. J. Hammer. *Water Supply and Pollution Control.* Harper & Row, New York (1977).

Davis, M., and D. Cornwell. *Introduction to Environmental Engineering,* 3rd ed. McGraw-Hill, New York (1998).

Droste, R. L. *Theory and Practice of Water and Wastewater Treatment.* Wiley, New York (1997).

Henry J. G., and G. W. Heinke. *Environmental Science and Engineering.* Prentice Hall, Englewood Cliffs, NJ (1989).

Kiely, G. *Environmental Engineering.* McGraw-Hill, London (1997).

Masters, G. M. *Introduction to Environmental Engineering and Science.* Prentice Hall, Englewood Cliffs, NJ (1991).

Montgomery, J. M. Consulting Engineers, Inc., *Water Treatment Principles and Design.* Wiley, New York (1985).

Peavy, H. S., D. R. Rowe, and G. Tchobanoglous. *Environmental Engineering.* McGraw-Hill, New York (1979).

Ray, B. T. *Environmental Engineering.* PWS, Boston, MA (1995).

Reynolds T. D., and P. A. Richards. *Unit Operations and Processes in Environmental Engineering,* 2nd ed., PWS, Boston, MA (1996).

Sincero A. P., and G. A. Sincero. *Environmental Engineering, A Design Approach.* Prentice Hall, Upper Saddle River, NJ (1996).

Steel E. W., and T. J. McGhee. *Water Supply and Sewerage.* McGraw-Hill, New York (1979).

Tchobanoglous G., and F. D. Schroeder. *Water Quality.* Addison Wesley, Reading, MA (1985).

Vesilind, P. A. *Introduction to Environmental Engineering.* PWS, Boston, MA (1997).

**Journals**

*Journal of the American Water Works Association*

*Water Research*

## REFERENCES

1. *Public Drinking Water Systems Facts and Figures.* U.S. Environmental Protection Agency, Office of Ground Water and Drinking Water, 1998 data
   http://www.epa.gov/safewater/pws/factoids.html

2. Levy, D. A., Bens, M. S., Craun, G. F., et al., "Surveillance for waterborne-disease outbreaks—United States, 1995–1996." *Mortality and Morbidity Weekly Reports,* Surveillance Summaries, December 11, 1998, 47(SS-5); 1–34.
   http://www.cdc.gov/epo/mmwr/preview/mmwrhtml/00055820.htm

3. Excerpted from remarks by former EPA Administrator Russel F. Train delivered before the Los Angeles World Affairs Forum, December 16, 1976.

4. *Morbidity and Mortality Weekly Reports,* March 1, 1990/39(SS-1); 1–9
   http://www.cdc.gov/epo/mmwr/preview/mmwrhtml/00001596.htm

5. WHO guidelines can be obtained at
   http://www.who.int/water_sanitation_health/GDWQ/Summary_tables/Sumtab.htm

6. AWWA Standards: AWWA Standards Set, AWWA, 1999.

7. Reynolds, T. D., *Unit Operations and Processes in Environmental Engineering,* PWS-Kent Publishing, Boston, MA, pp. 33–54 (1982).

8. Hudson, H. E. *Water Clarification Processes Practical Design and Evaluation.* Van Nostrand Reinhold, New York, pp. 115–117 (1981).

9. Stokes, G. G. "On the theories of the internal friction of fluids in motion, and of the equilibrium and motion of elastic solids," *Transactions of the Cambridge Philosophical Society,* vol. 8, pp. 287–319 (1845).

10. Spitzer, E. F. *Back to Basics Guide to Slow Sand Filtration.* American Water Works Association, Denver, CO (1993).

11. American Water Works Association. *Water Quality and Treatment.* McGraw-Hill, New York, p. 259 (1971).

12. Montgomery, J. M. *Water Treatment Principles and Design.* Wiley, New York, p. 535 (1985).

13. Chick, H. "Investigation of the law of disinfection," *Journal of Hygiene.* vol. 8, p. 92 (1908).

14. Stumm, W., and J. J. Morgan. *Aquatic Chemistry: Chemical Equilibria and Rates in Natural Waters,* 3rd. ed. John Wiley and Sons, New York (1996).

15. Woller, D. M., and E. W. Sanderson. *Public Water Supplies in McHenry County* (Illinois State Water Survey, publication No. 6019), Urbana, Illinois (1976).

16. Woller, D. M., and F. W. Sanderson. *Public Groundwater Supplies in Putnam County* (Illinois State Water Survey, Publication No. 60-15), Urbana, Illinois (1976).

17. Michigan Department of Public Health. *Annual Dora Summary* (1979).

# 10

# Wastewater Treatment

## 10-1   INTRODUCTION

Wastewater has historically been considered a nuisance to be discarded in the cheapest, least offensive manner possible. This meant the use of on-site disposal systems such as the pit privy and direct discharge into our lakes and streams. Over the last century it has been recognized that this approach has an undesirable effect on the environment. This led to the variety of treatment techniques that characterize today's municipal treatment systems, which are the focal point of this chapter. As we look forward it becomes obvious that in the interest of sustainability as well as fundamental economic efficiency, we must view wastewater as a raw material to be conserved. Clean water is a scarce commodity and should be treated, so it must be conserved and reused. The contents of wastewater are often viewed as a pollutants. The abundance of nutrients such as phosphorus and nitrogen are in some treatment schemes (as discussed in Section 10–10) recovered for crop growth. This approach must become more prevalent to achieve a sustainable future. The organic compounds in wastewater are a source of energy. Currently we use the processes described in Section 10–12 to recover some of this energy. Future efforts will focus on improving the efficiency of energy use in the wastewater.

## 10-2   CHARACTERISTICS OF DOMESTIC WASTEWATER

### Physical Characteristics

Fresh, aerobic, domestic wastewater has been said to have the odor of kerosene or freshly turned earth. Aged, septic sewage is considerably more offensive to the olfactory sense. Fresh sewage is typically gray in color. Septic sewage is black. This color results from the precipitation of iron sulfide.

Wastewater temperatures normally range between 10 and 20°C. In general, the temperature of the wastewater will be higher than that of the water supply because of the addition of warm water from households and heating within the plumbing system of the structure.

One cubic meter of wastewater weighs approximately 1,000,000 g and will contain about 500 g of solids. One-half of the solids will be dissolved solids such as calcium, sodium, and soluble organic compounds. The remaining 250 g will be insoluble. The insoluble fraction consists of about 125 g of material that will settle out of the liquid fraction in 30 min under quiescent conditions (these are called **settleable solids**). The remaining 125 g will remain in suspension for a very long time (these are called **suspended solids**). The result is that wastewater is highly turbid.

### Chemical Characteristics

Because the number of chemical compounds found in wastewater is almost limitless, we normally restrict our consideration to a few general classes. These classes often are better known by the name of the test used to measure them than by what is included in the class. The biochemical oxygen demand ($BOD_5$) test, which we discussed in Chapter 8, is a case in point. Another closely related test is the chemical oxygen demand (COD) test.

The COD test is used to determine the oxygen equivalent of the organic matter that can be oxidized by a strong chemical oxidizing agent (potassium dichromate) in an acid medium. The COD of a waste, in general, will be greater than the $BOD_5$ because more compounds can be oxidized chemically than can be oxidized biologically. $BOD_5$ is typically less than ultimate BOD, which is less than COD, except for totally biodegradable waste.

The COD test can be conducted in about an hour. If it can be correlated with $BOD_5$, it can be used to aid in the operation and control of the wastewater treatment plant (WWTP).

Total Kjeldahl* nitrogen (TKN) is a measure of the total organic and ammonia nitrogen in the wastewater. TKN gives a measure of the availability of nitrogen for building cells, as well as the potential nitrogenous oxygen demand that will have to be satisfied.

Phosphorus may appear in many forms in wastewater, among which are the orthophosphates, polyphosphates, and organic phosphate. For our purpose, we will lump all of these together under the heading "total phosphorus (as P)."

Three typical compositions of untreated domestic wastewater are summarized in Table 10–1. The pH for all of these wastes will be in the range of 6.5 to 8.5, with a majority being slightly on the alkaline side of 7.0.

### Characteristics of Industrial Wastewater

Industrial processes generate a wide variety of wastewater pollutants. The characteristics and levels of pollutants vary significantly from industry to industry. The Environmental Protection Agency has grouped the pollutants into three categories: conventional, nonconventional, and priority pollutants. The conventional and nonconventional pollutants are listed in Table 10–2. The priority pollutants are listed in Chapter 1 in Table 1–3.

Because of the wide variety of industries and levels of pollutants, we can only present a snapshot view of the characteristics. A sampling of a few industries for two conventional pollutants is shown in Table 10–3.

A similar sampling for nonconventional pollutants is shown in Table 10–4.

---

*Pronounced "kell dall" after J. Kjeldahl, who developed the test in 1883.

**TABLE 10-1**  Typical Composition of Untreated Domestic Wastewater

| Constituent | Weak | Medium | Strong |
|---|---|---|---|
| | (all mg · L⁻¹ except settleable solids) | | |
| Alkalinity (as $CaCO_2$)[a] | 50 | 100 | 200 |
| BOD$_5$ (as $O_2$) | 100 | 200 | 300 |
| Chloride | 30 | 50 | 100 |
| COD (as $O_2$) | 250 | 500 | 1000 |
| Suspended solids (SS) | 100 | 200 | 350 |
| Settleable solids (in mL · L⁻¹) | 5 | 10 | 20 |
| Total dissolved solids (TDS) | 200 | 500 | 1000 |
| Total Kjeldahl nitrogen (TKN) (as N) | 20 | 40 | 80 |
| Total organic carbon (TOC) (as C) | 75 | 50 | 300 |
| Total phosphorus (as P) | 5 | 10 | 20 |

[a]This amount of alkalinity is the contribution from the waste. It is to be added to the naturally occuring alkalinity in the water supply. Chloride is exclusive of contribution from water-softener backwash.

**TABLE 10-2**  EPA's Conventional and Nonconventional Pollutant Categories

| Conventional | Nonconventional |
|---|---|
| Biochemical oxygen demand (BOD$_5$) | Ammonia (as N) |
| Total suspended solids (TSS) | Chromium (VI) (hexavalent) |
| Oil and grease | Chemical oxygen demand (COD) |
| Oil (animal, vegetable) | COD/BOD$_7$ |
| Oil (mineral) | Fluoride |
| pH | Manganese |
| | Nitrate (as N) |
| | Organic nitrogen (as N) |
| | Pesticide active ingredients (PAI) |
| | Phenols, total |
| | Phosphorus, total (as P) |
| | Total organic carbon (TOC) |

*Sources:* Code of Federal Regulations, 40 CFR parts 413.02, 464.02, 467.02, and 469.12.

**TABLE 10-3**  Examples of Industrial Wastewater Concentrations for BOD$_5$ and Suspended Solids

| Industry | BOD$_5$ (mg · L⁻¹) | Suspended Solids (mg · L⁻¹) |
|---|---|---|
| Ammunition | 50–300 | 70–1700 |
| Fermentation | 4500 | 10,000 |
| Slaughterhouse (cattle) | 400–2500 | 400–1000 |
| Pulp and paper (kraft) | 100–350 | 75–300 |
| Tannery | 700–7000 | 4000–20,000 |

| TABLE 10–4 | Examples of Industrial Wastewater Concentrations for Nonconventional Pollutants | |
|---|---|---|
| **Industry** | **Pollutant** | **Concentration (mg · L$^{-1}$)** |
| Coke by-product (steel mill) | Ammonia (as N) | 200 |
| | Organic nitrogen (as N) | 100 |
| | Phenol | 2000 |
| Metal plating | Chromium (VI) | 3–550 |
| Nylon polymer | COD | 23,000 |
| | TOC | 8800 |
| Plywood-plant glue waste | COD | 2000 |
| | Phenol | 200–2000 |
| | Phosphorus (as PO$_4$) | 9–15 |

## 10–3 ON-SITE DISPOSAL SYSTEMS

In less densely populated areas where lot sizes are large and houses are spaced widely apart it is often more economical to treat human waste on-site, rather than use a sewer system to collect the waste and treat it at a centralized location. On-site systems are generally small and may serve individual homes, small housing developments (clusters), or isolated commercial establishments, such as small hotels or restaurants. In the United States about 25% of the population is serviced by on-site wastewater treatment systems. In some states as much as 50% of the population uses on-site systems within rural and suburban communities [1]. As many people chose to move to rural and outer suburban areas the number of decentralized systems is increasing. It is estimated that as much as 40% of new housing construction is taking place in areas that are not connected to municipal sewers.

### Alternative On-Site Treatment and Disposal Systems with Water

**Septic Tanks and Absorption Fields.** About 85–90% of the on-site wastewater disposal systems are conventional septic systems. A conventional septic system consists of three parts: the **septic tank,** a distribution box, and an absorption field (also called a leach or drain or tile field) (Figure 10–1). The septic tank and tile field are a unit. Neither part will function as intended without the other.

The main function of the septic tank (Figure 10–2) is to remove large particles and grease, which would otherwise clog the tile field. Heavy solids settle to the bottom where they undergo biological decomposition. Grease floats to the surface and is trapped. It is only slightly decomposed.

The size of the tank depends on the expected wastewater flow. The tank should be large enough to accommodate a holding time for water in a septic tank of at least 24 h. For individual homes the following guidelines can be used: 3 m$^3$ tank minimum; 4 m$^3$ for a three-bedroom house; 5 m$^3$ for a four-bedroom house, and 6 m$^3$ for a five-bedroom house.

Bacterial action in the tank helps to degrade the organic matter in the wastewater. The BOD$_5$ of the wastewater is also reduced by the separation of the solids from the liquid. For domestic systems, the BOD$_5$ of the influent is typically 210 mg · L$^{-1}$. The septic tank effluent has a BOD$_5$ of about 180 mg · L$^{-1}$ without an effluent filter and about 130 mg · L$^{-1}$ if an effluent filter is used in the system. Usually the BOD$_5$ limit to allow wastewater to be discharged to surface waters is 20 mg · L$^{-1}$ or less, so the BOD$_5$ of a septic effluent is too high to allow for surface water discharge. However, as further treatment occurs in the soil, absorption fields can be used to safely dispose of the partially treated septic tank effluent. A distribution box is used to distribute the septic tank effluent throughout the absorption field. The absorption field usually consists of a series

**FIGURE 10–1**

Schematic of a conventional septic system. (*Source:* R. Crites and G. Tchobanoglous, *Small Decentralized Wastewater Management Systems,* WCB/McGraw-Hill, Boston, MA, 1998. Reprinted by permission.)

Risers to ground surface for easy access

Distribution box

Perforated absorption drainline or pressure distribution pipe with orifices

Wastewater from residence

Tightline

Single or two compartment septic tank with an effluent filter and gravity discharge or an effluent filter and pump for pressure dosing

Observation port

**FIGURE 10–2**

Definition sketch for the sludge, clear water, and scum zones that form in a septic tank. (*Source:* R. Crites and G. Tchobanoglous, *Small Decentralized Wastewater Management Systems,* WCB/McGraw-Hill, Boston, MA, 1998. Reprinted by permission.)

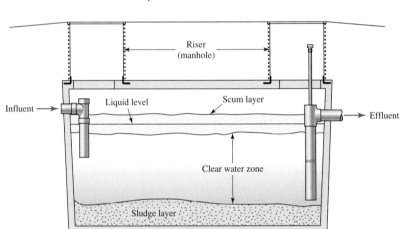

Riser (manhole)

Influent

Liquid level

Scum layer

Effluent

Clear water zone

Sludge layer

**FIGURE 10–3**

Typical cross section through conventional absorption trench. (*Source:* R. Crites and G. Tchobanoglous, *Small Decentralized Wastewater Management Systems,* WCB/McGraw-Hill, Boston, MA, 1998. Reprinted by permission.)

Native soil backfill

Fabric or building paper

15-cm minimum

5-cm minimum rock over pipe

90-cm max

10-cm distribution pipe

15-cm minimum of rock under pipe

30-cm minimum

Side wall absorption area (both sides)

2–6-cm diameter washed drainrock

45–60-cm minimum

of trenches that contain perforated PVC pipes that are about 10 cm in diameter. The pipes are placed over a 15-cm deep layer of drainrock and then buried with an additional layer of drainrock. The drainrock is covered with building fabric or building paper (which helps to prevent the migration of fines into the drainrock), and finally the trench is filled in using native soil (Figure 10–3). The trenches should be separated by a distance of at least 2 m.

When the system is operational, bacteria produce a slime layer at the bottom of the trench. This layer, commonly called the **clogging mat,** creates a barrier that slows the movement of water into the surrounding soil, which allows the flow in the surrounding soil to remain unsaturated, permitting air to move through the soil. This maintains aerobic conditions, which are essential to proper treatment of the effluent.

The size of the absorption area depends on the wastewater flow and the permeability of the surrounding soil. The permeability of the soil is determined by a percolation (or perc) test. The perc test is conducted by digging a hole of a prescribed size, filling it with water, and measuring the rate at which the water disappears into the soil. A preferred method for determining the suitability of the site is to dig one or more trenches in the area proposed for the absorption field and visually inspect them. An inspector looks for unsuitable soils such as clays and the presence of **mottled soils,** that is, those having blotches of different color. Mottled soils are an indication that the groundwater table has, at some time, risen to a level where it may interfere with the absorption field.

Most septic systems will fail eventually. The normal lifetime of an absorption field is 20–30 years. After that time the soil around the field becomes clogged with organic matter and the system will not operate properly. Many factors can cause the system to fail prematurely. Roots can block pipes, or the pipes may be crushed if a vehicle is driven over the field. The system may also fail if the absorption field is hydraulically overloaded or if substances that are toxic to soil bacteria, such as solvents, paints, pesticides, or softener salt are disposed of down the drain. However, the most common reason for premature failure is improper maintenance. Because the rate of biodegradation in septic tanks is slow, the solids that settle in the tank tend to accumulate over time. If these solids are not removed, the clear water zone between the sludge layer and the scum layer becomes too small, leading to an increased carry over of solids to the absorption field. If too many solids reach the absorption field then it can become clogged, resulting in premature failure of the field. To prevent the accumulation of too much sludge and scum in a septic tank they should be periodically removed. The rate of accumulation of sludge depends on the use of the system. It is suggested that the level of sludge in the tank be checked annually, though usually a domestic system will only need to be pumped out once every 2–3 years.

**Septic Tank and Absorption Field Modifications.**  As mentioned earlier, often the reason for the failure of absorption fields in poorly draining soils is excessive growth of the clogging mat. Reduction of the BOD of the wastewater can reduce the rate of growth of the mat. Two types of treatment systems commonly used to reduce the wastewater BOD are aerobic treatment systems and sand filters.

**Aerobic Systems.**  A wide range of aerobic treatment systems are available. The common feature of these units is the use of some mechanism to inject or circulate air inside the treatment tank. If sufficient air is introduced, then aerobic conditions can be achieved in the wastewater. Because aerobic degradation is rapid, good removal of BOD can be achieved under these conditions, which reduces the rate of growth of the clogging mat and extends the life of the absorption field.

**Sand Filter Systems.**  The sand filter is also an aerobic treatment system. The components of a typical sand filter are illustrated in Figure 10–4. The filter consists of a bed of granular material (usually sand, but other materials such as anthracite can be used). The surface of the bed is intermittently dosed with wastewater that percolates through the sand to the bottom of the filter. The sand bed is dosed anywhere from 12 to 72 times a day. The size of the dose should be such that the sand bed does not become saturated. This allows the wastewater to flow as a thin film around the sand particles, so good contact between the wastewater and the air can be achieved. Sand filters may be single-pass or multipass. Single-pass sand filters are commonly called **intermittent sand filters** (ISFs). In a single-pass system the wastewater is collected in the underdrain and passed onto an absorption field or other disposal system. In a multipass system a

**FIGURE 10–4**

Schematic of modern intermittent sand filter: **(a)** plan view and **(b)** typical cross section. (*Courtesy Orenco Systems, Inc.*)

(a) Plan view

(b) Typical cross section

portion of the treated wastewater is recycled back through the sand bed. Recirculation dilutes the wastewater coming from the septic tank. By diluting the strength of the effluent, higher application rates can be used. Recirculating sand filters require three to five times less area than single-pass sand filters. Also, better nitrogen removal is achieved in recirculating sand filters due to nitrification–denitrification (see Chapter 4).

**Dosing Systems.** Another solution to the clogging problem can be to replace the conventional absorption trenches with a disposal system that is less prone to failure. In a conventional absorption field the effluent flows by gravity into the trenches. The gravity system may be replaced by a dosing system, similar to that used in a sand filter. This helps to maintain unsaturated conditions in the soil surrounding the trench.

**Shallow Absorption Fields.** In these systems the distribution piping is often covered with large half pipe rather than gravel. The trenches are only about 0.25 m deep. Better treatment can be achieved, as the upper soil layers have a higher concentration of microbes.

### On-Site Treatment and Disposal Systems for Unfavorable Site Conditions

Where site conditions are unfavorable for conventional septic systems, alternative treatment–disposal systems may be required. Among the limitations that might preclude the installation of a conventional system are high groundwater tables, shallow limiting layers of bedrock, very slowly or rapidly permeable soils, close proximity to surface water, and small lot size.

**FIGURE 10–5**

Typical cross section through mound effluent disposal system. (*Source:* R. Crites and G. Tchobanoglous, *Small Decentralized Wastewater Management Systems,* WCB/McGraw-Hill, Boston, MA, 1998. Reprinted by permission.)

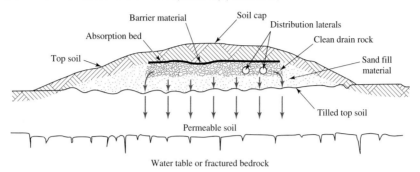

**Mound Systems.**   Mounds were first developed at the North Dakota Agricultural College in the 1940s and were known as NODAK systems. The components of a typical mound system are illustrated in Figure 10–5. Mounds are both treatment and disposal systems because the effluent from the mound percolates directly into the native soil. The design overcomes certain site restrictions such as slowly permeable soils, shallow permeable soils over porous bedrock, and permeable soils with high water tables. A mound system is a pressure-dosed absorption system that is elevated above the natural soil surface. Effluent from the septic tank is pumped or siphoned to the elevated absorption area and distributed through a piping network located in the coarse aggregate at the top of the mound. The effluent then passes through the aggregate and infiltrates the sand fill. Treatment occurs in the sand and in the fill below the sand bed. As the water percolates downward it spreads out over a large area. The size of the mound must be such that the area of native soil under the mound, called the **basal area,** is large enough that wastewater does not seep out of the base or sides of the mound. During construction of mound systems, special attention should be given to ensure that the basal area of the system is properly scarified, and that compaction of the basal area by earthmoving equipment is minimal. Compaction of the top layer of the soil can greatly reduce the rate of infiltration into the soil.

**Barriered Landscape Water-Renovation System (BLWRS).**   In the summer of 1969, Dr. A. Earl Erickson demonstrated the efficacy of using a BLWRS (pronounced "blowers," like "flowers") to denitrify water containing 100 mg $\cdot$ L$^{-1}$ of nitrate. Subsequently, he and his associates demonstrated that the BLWRS could be used to renovate both dairy cow and swine feedlot wastewater (Table 10–5) [2]. The system is, of course, equally applicable to domestic wastewater.

The BLWRS differs from the NODAK mound system in that the mound of soil is underlain by an impervious water barrier (Figures 10–6a and 10–6b). As the renovated water passes beyond the edge of the barrier, it may be collected in drains or be allowed to recharge the aquifer. The mound is constructed of a fine sand. The dimensions of the BLWRS depend on the soil texture and expected wastewater application rates. A 0.15-m layer of topsoil is used to cover the sand. A water-hardy grass (quack grass or volunteer weed cover) must be established on the surface and banks to maintain the soil's permeability and stability.

The wastewater is spread on the top of the mound by a sprinkler. As the wastewater percolates down, the organic particles are filtered out and remain on the surface. The particles are oxidized by soil microorganisms. The soluble organic compounds and other ions move into the aerobic soil zone. Most of the soluble organic matter is oxidized by bacteria in the highly active aerobic soil. The phosphate ions are held on the clay fraction of the soil and sand bed. [Iron slag or limestone (or both) can be used to enhance the phosphorus adsorption capacity.] The ammonium ions are

**TABLE 10–5** BLWRS Wastewater Renovation Efficiencies

| | Average Influent Concentration (mg · L⁻¹) | Average Effluent Concentration (mg · L⁻¹) | Efficiency (%) |
|---|---|---|---|
| Swine waste[a] | | | |
| $BOD_5$ | 1131 | 8.9 | 98.3 |
| P | 18 | 0.02 | 99.9 |
| Suspended solids | 3000 | NIL | ≈100.0 |
| TKN | 937 | 187.4 | 80.0 |
| Dairy waste[b] | | | |
| $BOD_5$ | 1637.0 | 18.9 | 98.8 |
| P | 38.5 | 0.22 | 99.4 |
| Suspended solids | 4400.0 | NIL | ≈100 |
| TKN | 917.0 | 27.5 | 97.0 |

[a]Average application rate of 15 mm · day⁻¹ for 503 days.

[b]Average application rate of 8.8 mm · day⁻¹ for 450 days.

*Source:* Data taken from: Erickson, A. E., B. G. Ellis, J. M. Tiedge, et al., *Soil Modification for Denitrification and Phosphate Reduction of Feedlot Waste.* Environmental Protection Agency Report No. EPA-66012-74-057. U.S. Government Printing Office, Washington, D.C. (1974).

**FIGURE 10–6**

**(a)** Common dimensions of barriered landscape water-renovation system (BLWRS); **(b)** water chemistry change in a BLWRS. (*Source:* Reprinted, with permission, from: Davis, M. L., and D. A. Cornwell, *Introduction to Environmental Engineering,* 3rd ed. McGraw-Hill, New York, NY, p. 360, 1998.)

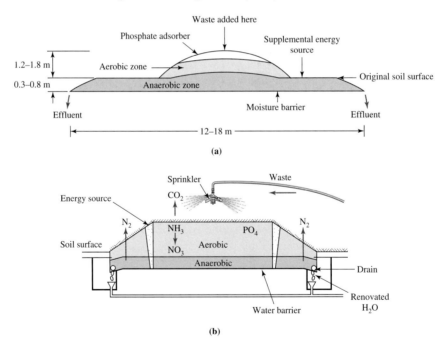

held on the soil until they are nitrified to nitrate. The downward movement of the nitrified water is stopped by the barrier. The water then is forced to move laterally through the anoxic layer. Denitrification occurs as the waste passes out of the carbon source.

The BLWRS must be operated in a cyclic fashion to allow the soil microorganisms time to degrade the waste and to maintain aerobic conditions in the soil. Application rates between 9 and 18 mm of wastewater per day may be used provided that the BLWRS is "rested" for one-third of the time. The physical conditions of the soil govern the application rates. Ponding on the surface indicates excessive application rates.

### Other On-Site Treatment and Disposal Options

Constructed wetlands can be used for on-site wastewater treatment and disposal. The use of these systems is more common in warmer climates. In arid areas, evapotranspiration beds are an alternative to conventional absorption beds. In an evapotranspiration system, water-tolerant vegetation is planted in a shallow sand bed. The plant roots draw the water up through the sand and it is evaporated or transpired to the atmosphere.

Treated domestic wastewater can be reused. However, because of the risks posed by pathogens in the water the reuse of domestic wastewater in on-site systems is not common. Some alternatives for reuse are drip irrigation and toilet flushing.

### Alternative On-Site Treatment–Disposal Systems Without Water

In areas away from population centers, such as national or state parks, remote roadside rest areas, or vacation homes, there may be no reliable water supply. The absence of a water supply or water scarcity may preclude the use of flush toilets. In this case, other systems for the disposal of human waste need to be considered. Commonly used systems are the pit privy and vault, chemical, and composting toilets. Vault, chemical, and composting toilets are closed systems, so there is "zero" discharge from these systems on-site. The waste produced is collected and disposed of elsewhere. For this reason, these systems may also be used in environmentally sensitive areas where the discharge of wastewater may be environmentally unacceptable.

**The Pit Privy.**   Although most modern environmental engineering and science texts would skip this subject, the mere existence of 10,000 of these or their modern equivalent in the United States is just too much for us to ignore. Furthermore, junior engineers and environmental scientists are the most likely candidates for designing, erecting, operating, dismantling, and closing the beasts.

Figure 10–7 provides most of the information you will ever need about the construction of an outhouse. The slab is usually poured over flat ground on top of roofing paper. The riser hole is formed using 12-gauge galvanized iron. Once the slab has set, it is lifted into place over the pit. The concrete is a 1:2:3 mix, that is, one part Portland cement, two parts sand, and three parts gravel less than 25 mm in diameter.

The principle of operation of the pit privy is that the liquid materials percolate into the soil through the cribbing (an open lattice box) and the solids "dry out." A pit of the dimensions shown in Figure 10–7 should last a family of four about 10 years. Rainwater is to be prevented from entering the pit. A cup of kerosene at weekly intervals discourages mosquito breeding, and odors can be reduced by the use of a cup of hydrated lime. Unfortunately, the lime also slows the decomposition of paper, so its use is not encouraged. Disinfectants should never be used.

**The Vault Toilet.**   This is the modern version of the pit privy. Its construction is the same as that of the pit privy with the exception that the pit is formed as a watertight vault. A special truck (fondly called a "honey wagon") is used to pump out the vault at regular intervals. Because of the liquefying action of the bacteria and biological decomposition in the liquid (rather than in the soil as occurs with the pit privy), vault toilets are much more odiferous than the old pit privies. Many masking agents (perfumes) and disinfectants are available to mitigate the stench. Unfortunately, most of them have unpleasant odors themselves. If electricity is at hand, an ozone generator, set to vent into the gas space above the waste, are very effective in odor reduction.

**The Chemical Toilet.**   The airplane toilet, the coach-bus toilet, and the self-contained toilets of recreation vehicles are all versions of the chemical toilet. The essence of the system is a strong disinfectant chemical used to carry the waste to a holding tank and render it inoffensive until it can be pumped. Although these vehicular systems are quite effective, the chemical must be selected taking into account its effect on the treatment system that ultimately must receive it. The

## FIGURE 10–7

Construction details of the pit privy: **(a)** cross section; **(b)** plan of concrete slab; and **(c)** details of riser form. (*Source:* Reprinted, with permission, from: Ehlers, V. M., and E. W. Steel, *Municipal and Rural Sanitation*, McGraw-Hill, New York, 1943.)

chemical toilet has not found wide acceptance in permanent installations due to the cost of the chemical and to the impracticality of maintenance.

**The Composting Toilet.** A composting toilet consists of a large tank located directly below the toilet room. Wastes enter the tank through a large-diameter chute that connects to the toilet. No water is used for the toilet, but a bulking agent (such as wood shavings) is added to improve liquid drainage and aeration. A small fan draws air through the tank and up the vent pipe to ensure adequate oxygen for decomposition and odorless operation. The liquid in the waste is evaporated leaving a compost. The finished compost can be removed from the lower end of the tank about once each year. It can be used as a fertilizer. Power requirements for the system are very low, so if power from an electrical grid is not available, the electrical requirements can be met from an independent generating system, such as a photovoltaic system.

## 10–4 MUNICIPAL WASTEWATER TREATMENT SYSTEMS

**FIGURE 10–8**

Degrees of treatment. (*Source:* Reprinted, with permission, from: Davis, M. L., and D. A. Cornwell, *Introduction to Environmental Engineering*, 3rd ed., McGraw-Hill, New York, NY, p. 362, 1998.)

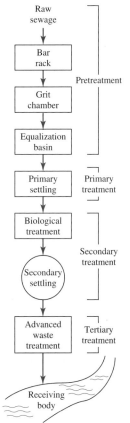

The alternatives for municipal wastewater treatment fall into three major categories (Figure 10–8): (1) primary, (2) secondary, and (3) advanced treatment. It is commonly assumed that each of the degrees of treatment noted in Figure 10–8 includes the previous steps. For example, primary treatment is assumed to include the pretreatment processes: bar rack, grit chamber, and equalization basin. Likewise, secondary treatment is assumed to include all the processes of primary treatment: bar rack, grit chamber, equalization basin, and primary settling tank.

The purpose of pretreatment is to provide protection to the wastewater treatment plant (WWTP) equipment that follows. In some older municipal plants the equalization step may not be included.

The major goal of primary treatment is to remove from wastewater those pollutants that will either settle or float. Primary treatment will typically remove about 60% of the suspended solids in raw sewage and 35% of the $BOD_5$. Soluble pollutants are not removed. At one time, this was the only treatment used by many cities. Now federal law requires that municipalities provide secondary treatment. Although primary treatment alone is no longer acceptable, it is still frequently used as the first treatment step in a secondary treatment system. The major goal of secondary treatment is to remove the soluble $BOD_5$ that escapes the primary process and to provide added removal of suspended solids. Secondary treatment is typically achieved by using biological processes. These provide the same biological reactions that would occur in the receiving water if it had adequate capacity to assimilate the wastewater. The secondary treatment processes are designed to speed up these natural processes so that the breakdown of the degradable organic pollutants can be achieved in a relatively short time. Although secondary treatment may remove more than 85% of the $BOD_5$ and suspended solids, it does not remove significant amounts of nitrogen, phosphorus, or heavy metals, nor does it completely remove pathogenic bacteria and viruses.

In cases where secondary levels of treatment are inadequate, additional treatment processes are applied to the secondary effluent to provide advanced wastewater treatment (AWT). These processes may involve chemical treatment and filtration of the wastewater—much like adding a typical water treatment plant to the tail end of a secondary plant—they may involve applying the secondary effluent to the land in carefully designed irrigation systems where the pollutants are removed by a soil–crop system. Some of these processes can remove as much as 99% of the $BOD_5$, phosphorus, suspended solids and bacteria, and 95% of the nitrogen. They can produce a sparkling clean, colorless, odorless effluent indistinguishable in appearance from a high-quality drinking water. Although these processes and land treatment systems are often applied to secondary effluent for advanced treatment, they have also been used in place of conventional secondary treatment processes.

Most of the impurities removed from the wastewater do not simply vanish. Some organic compounds are broken down into harmless carbon dioxide and water. Most of the impurities are removed from the wastewater as a solid, that is, sludge. Because most of the impurities removed from the wastewater are present in the sludge, sludge handling and disposal must be carried out carefully to achieve satisfactory pollution control.

### Pretreatment of Industrial Wastes

In municipalities, industrial wastewaters can pose serious hazards because wastewater collection and treatment systems have not been designed to treat them. The wastes can damage sewers and interfere with the operation of treatment plants. They may pass through the WWTP untreated or they may concentrate in the sludge, rendering it a hazardous waste.

The Clean Water Act gives the EPA the authority to establish and enforce pretreatment standards for discharge of industrial wastewaters into municipal treatment systems. Specific objectives of the pretreatment program are [3]

- To prevent the introduction to the WWTPs of pollutants that will interfere with the operation of a WWTP, including interference with its use or disposal of municipal sludge

- To prevent the introduction into WWTPs of pollutants that will pass through the treatment works or otherwise be incompatible with such works

- To improve opportunities to recycle and reclaim municipal and industrial wastewaters and sludge

EPA has established "prohibited discharge standards" that apply to all nondomestic discharges to the WWTP and "categorical pretreatment standards" that are applicable to specific industries [4, 5]. Congress assigned the primary responsibility for enforcing these standards to local WWTPs. In the general pretreatment regulations, industrial users are prohibited from introducing the following into a WWTP [3]:

1. Pollutants that create a fire or explosion hazard in the municipal WWTP
2. Pollutants that will cause corrosive structural damage to the municipal WWTP
3. Solid or viscous pollutants in amounts that will cause obstruction to the flow in the WWTP resulting in interference
4. Any pollutant, including oxygen-demanding pollutants (such as BOD), released in a discharge at a flow rate or concentration that will cause interference with the WWTP
5. Heat in amounts that will inhibit biological activity in the WWTP
6. Petroleum oil, nonbiodegradable cutting oil, or products of mineral oil origin in amounts that will cause interference or will pass through
7. Pollutants that result in the presence of toxic gases, vapors, or fumes within the POTW in a quantity that may cause acute worker health and safety problems
8. Any trucked or hauled pollutants, except at discharge points designated by the POTW

## 10–5 UNIT OPERATIONS OF PRETREATMENT

Several devices and structures are placed upstream of the primary treatment operation to provide protection to the WWTP equipment. These devices and structures are classified as pretreatment because they have little effect in reducing $BOD_5$. In industrial WWTPs, where only soluble compounds are present, bar racks and grit chambers may be absent. Equalization is frequently required in industrial WWTPs.

### Bar Racks

Typically, the first device encountered by the wastewater entering the plant is a **bar rack,** the primary purpose of which is to remove large objects that would damage or foul pumps, valves, and other mechanical equipment. Rags, logs, and other objects that find their way into the sewer are removed from the wastewater on the racks. In modern WWTPs, the racks are cleaned mechanically. The solid material is stored in a hopper and removed to a sanitary landfill at regular intervals.

Bar racks (or bar screens) may be categorized as trash racks, manually cleaned racks, and mechanically cleaned racks. Trash racks have large openings, 40–150 mm, and are designed to prevent very large objects such as logs from entering the plant. These are normally followed by racks with smaller openings. Manually cleaned racks have openings that range from 25 to 50 mm. As mentioned earlier, manually cleaned racks are not frequently employed. They do find application in bypass channels that are infrequently used. Mechanically cleaned racks have openings ranging from 5 to 40 mm. Maximum channel approach velocities range from 0.6 to 1.2 m $\cdot$ s$^{-1}$. Regardless of the type of rack, two channels with racks are provided to allow one to be taken out of service for cleaning and repair.

### Grit Chambers

Inert dense material, such as sand, broken glass, silt, and pebbles, is called **grit.** If these materials are not removed from the wastewater, they abrade pumps and other mechanical devices, causing undue wear. In addition, they have a tendency to settle in corners and bends, reducing flow capacity and, ultimately, clogging pipes and channels.

Three basic types of grit-removal devices are available: velocity-controlled (also known as a horizontal-flow grit chamber), aerated, and constant-level short-term sedimentation basins. We will discuss only the first because it can be analyzed by means of the classical laws of sedimentation for discrete, nonflocculating particles (Type I sedimentation). Stokes' law (See Chapter 9) may be used for the analysis and design of horizontal-flow grit chambers if the horizontal liquid velocity is maintained at about 0.3 m · s$^{-1}$. Liquid velocity control is achieved by placing a specially designed weir at the end of the channel. A minimum of two channels must be employed so that one can be out of service without shutting down the treatment plant. Cleaning may be either by mechanical devices or by hand. Mechanical cleaning is favored for plants having average flows over 0.04 m$^3$ · s$^{-1}$. Theoretical detention times are set at about 1 min for average flows. Washing facilities are normally provided to remove organic material from the grit.

**EXAMPLE 10–1**   Will a grit particle with a radius of 0.10 mm and a specific gravity of 2.65 be collected in a horizontal grit chamber that is 13.5 m in length if the average grit-chamber flow is 0.15 m$^3$ · s$^{-1}$, the width of the chamber is 0.56 m, and the horizontal velocity is 0.25 m · s$^{-1}$? The wastewater temperature is 22°C.

Solution   Before we can calculate the terminal settling velocity of the particle, we must gather some information from Table A–1 in Appendix A. At a wastewater temperature of 22°C, we find the water density to be 997.774 kg · m$^{-3}$. We will use 1000 kg · m$^{-3}$ as a sufficiently close approximation. Because the particle radius is given to only two significant figures, this approximation is reasonable. From the same table, we find the viscosity to be 0.995 mPa · s. As noted in the footnote to Table A–1, we must multiply this by 10$^{-3}$ to obtain the viscosity in units of pascal seconds (Pa · s). Using a particle diameter of 0.20 × 10$^{-3}$ m, we can calculate the terminal settling velocity using Stokes law (Equation 9–22)

$$v_s = \frac{9.80(2650 - 1000)(0.20 \times 10^{-3})^2 (\text{m} \cdot \text{s}^{-2})(\text{kg} \cdot \text{m}^{-3})(\text{m}^2)}{18(0.000995)(\text{kg} \cdot \text{m} \cdot \text{m}^{-2} \cdot \text{s}^{-2})(\text{s})}$$

$$= 3.61 \times 10^{-2} \text{ m} \cdot \text{s}^{-1}, \text{ or} \approx 36 \text{ mm} \cdot \text{s}^{-1}$$

Note that the product of the specific gravity of the particle (2.65) and the density of water is the density of the particle ($\rho$).

With a flow of 0.15 m$^3$ · s$^{-1}$ and a horizontal velocity of 0.25 m · s$^{-1}$, the cross-sectional area of flow may be estimated to be

$$A_c = \frac{0.15 \text{ m}^3 \cdot \text{s}^{-1}}{0.25 \text{ m} \cdot \text{s}^{-1}} = 0.60 \text{ m}^2$$

The depth of flow is then estimated by dividing the cross-sectional area by the width of the channel.

$$h = \frac{0.60 \text{ m}^2}{0.56 \text{ m}} = 1.07 \text{ m}$$

If the grit particle in question enters the grit chamber at the liquid surface, it will take $h/v$ seconds to reach the bottom.

$$t = \frac{1.07 \text{ m}}{0.0361 \text{ m} \cdot \text{s}^{-1}} = 29.6 \text{ s}$$

Because the chamber is 13.5 m in length and the horizontal velocity is 0.25 m · s$^{-1}$ the liquid remains in the chamber.

$$t = \frac{13.5 \text{ m}}{0.25 \text{ m} \cdot \text{s}^{-1}} = 54 \text{ s}$$

Thus, the particle will be captured in the grit chamber.

### Comminutors

Devices that chop up wastewater solids (rags, paper, plastic, and other materials) by revolving cutting bars are called **comminutors.** These devices are placed downstream of the grit chambers to protect the cutting bars from abrasion. They are used as a replacement for the downstream bar rack but must be installed with a hand-cleaned rack in parallel in case they fail.

### Equalization

**Flow equalization** is not a treatment process per se but a technique that can be used to improve the effectiveness of both secondary and advanced wastewater treatment processes. Wastewater does not flow into a municipal wastewater treatment plant at a constant rate; the flow rate varies from hour to hour, reflecting the living habits of the area served. In most towns, the pattern of daily activities sets the pattern of sewage flow and strength. Above-average sewage flows and strength occur in midmorning. The constantly changing amount and strength of wastewater to be treated makes efficient process operation difficult. Also, many treatment units must be designed for the maximum flow conditions encountered, which actually results in their being oversized for average conditions. The purpose of flow equalization is to dampen these variations so that the wastewater can be treated at a nearly constant flow rate. Flow equalization can significantly improve the performance of an existing plant and increase its useful capacity. In new plants, flow equalization can reduce the size and cost of the treatment units.

Flow equalization is usually achieved by constructing large basins that collect and store the wastewater flow and from which the wastewater is pumped to the treatment plant at a constant rate. These basins are normally located near the head end of the treatment works, preferably downstream of pretreatment facilities such as bar screens, comminutors, and grit chambers. Adequate aeration and mixing must be provided to prevent odors and deposition of solids. The required volume of an equalization basin is estimated from a mass balance of the flow into the treatment plant with the average flow the plant is designed to treat. From Chapter 3, starting with Equation 3–4

$$\frac{dM}{dt} = \frac{d(\text{in})}{dt} - \frac{d(\text{out})}{dt}$$

and writing in terms of the mass of water

$$\frac{d(\rho \forall)}{dt} = \frac{d(\rho \forall)_{\text{in}}}{dt} - \frac{d(\rho \forall)_{\text{out}}}{dt} \qquad (10\text{--}1)$$

where $\rho$ = density of water

Assuming that the density of water is constant and factoring it out, the equation yields

$$\frac{d(\forall)}{dt} = \frac{d(\forall)_{\text{in}}}{dt} - \frac{d(\forall)_{\text{out}}}{dt} \qquad (10\text{--}2)$$

The term on the left is the change in storage of water in the equalization basin. The term $d(\forall)_{\text{in}}/dt$ = the flow into the basin, which we normally designate as $Q_{\text{in}}$. Similarly, $d(\forall)_{\text{out}}/dt$ = the flow out the basin, which we normally designate as $Q_{\text{out}}$.

Thus, in conventional terms we write

$$\frac{d(\forall)}{dt} = Q_{in} - Q_{out} \tag{10-3}$$

To determine the storage required in a time interval, we rewrite Equation 10–3 as

$$d(\forall) = Q_{in}(dt) - Q_{out}(dt) \tag{10-4}$$

For finite time intervals this is

$$\Delta\forall = Q_{in}(\Delta t) - Q_{out}(\Delta t) \tag{10-5}$$

This may also be written in terms of volume of wastewater entering and leaving the equalization basin because the product $Q(\Delta t)$ is a volume

$$\Delta\forall = \forall_{in} - \forall_{out} \tag{10-6}$$

To determine the maximum volume required, the sum of $\Delta\forall$ is determined over a cycle that fills and empties the equalization basin. The variable $Q_{out}$ is set to be the average flow over the cycle. The maximum value of $\Delta\forall$ is the required storage.

**EXAMPLE 10–2**   Design an equalization basin for the following cyclic flow pattern. Provide a 25% excess capacity for equipment, unexpected flow variations, and solids accumulation. Evaluate the effect of equalization on the mass loading of $BOD_5$.

| Time (h) | Flow $(m^3 \cdot s^{-1})$ | $BOD_5$ $(mg \cdot L^{-1})$ | Time (h) | Flow $(m^3 \cdot s^{-1})$ | $BOD_5$ $(mg \cdot L^{-1})$ |
|---|---|---|---|---|---|
| 0000 | 0.0481 | 110 | 1200 | 0.0718 | 160 |
| 0100 | 0.0359 | 81 | 1300 | 0.0744 | 150 |
| 0200 | 0.0226 | 53 | 1400 | 0.0750 | 140 |
| 0300 | 0.0187 | 35 | 1500 | 0.0781 | 135 |
| 0400 | 0.0187 | 32 | 1600 | 0.0806 | 130 |
| 0500 | 0.0198 | 40 | 1700 | 0.0843 | 120 |
| 0600 | 0.0226 | 66 | 1800 | 0.0854 | 125 |
| 0700 | 0.0359 | 92 | 1900 | 0.0806 | 150 |
| 0800 | 0.0509 | 125 | 2000 | 0.0781 | 200 |
| 0900 | 0.0631 | 140 | 2100 | 0.0670 | 215 |
| 1000 | 0.0670 | 150 | 2200 | 0.0583 | 170 |
| 1100 | 0.0682 | 155 | 2300 | 0.0526 | 130 |

**Solution**   Because of the repetitive and tabular nature of the calculations, a computer spreadsheet is ideal for this problem. The spreadsheet solution is easy to verify if the calculations are set up with judicious selection of the initial value. If the initial value is the first flow rate greater than the average after the sequence of nighttime low flows, then the last row of the computation should result in a storage value of zero.

The first step is to calculate the average flow. In this case it is $0.05657 \text{ m}^3 \cdot s^{-1}$. Next, the flows are arranged in order beginning with the time and flow that first exceeds the average. In this case it is at 0900 h with a flow of 0.0631 $m^3 \cdot s^{-1}$. The tabular arrangement is shown in the following table. An explanation of the calculations for each column follows.

| Time | Flow $(m^3 \cdot s^{-1})$ | $V_{in}$ $(m^3)$ | $V_{out}$ $(m^3)$ | $dS$ $(m^3)$ | $\sum dS$ $(m^3)$ | $BOD_5$ $(mg \cdot L^{-1})$ | $M_{BOD-in}$ $(kg)$ | $S$ $(mg \cdot L^{-1})$ | $M_{BOD-out}$ $(kg)$ |
|------|------|------|------|------|------|------|------|------|------|
| 0900 | 0.0631 | 227.16 | 203.65 | 23.51 | 23.51 | 140 | 31.80 | 140.00 | 28.51 |
| 1000 | 0.067 | 241.2 | 203.65 | 37.55 | 61.06 | 150 | 36.18 | 149.11 | 30.37 |
| 1100 | 0.0682 | 245.52 | 203.65 | 41.87 | 102.93 | 155 | 38.06 | 153.83 | 31.33 |
| 1200 | 0.0718 | 258.48 | 203.65 | 54.83 | 157.76 | 160 | 41.36 | 158.24 | 32.23 |
| 1300 | 0.0744 | 267.84 | 203.65 | 64.19 | 221.95 | 150 | 40.18 | 153.06 | 31.17 |
| 1400 | 0.075 | 270 | 203.65 | 66.35 | 288.3 | 140 | 37.80 | 145.89 | 29.71 |
| 1500 | 0.0781 | 281.16 | 203.65 | 77.51 | 365.81 | 135 | 37.96 | 140.51 | 28.62 |
| 1600 | 0.0806 | 290.16 | 203.65 | 86.51 | 452.32 | 130 | 37.72 | 135.86 | 27.67 |
| 1700 | 0.0843 | 303.48 | 203.65 | 99.83 | 552.15 | 120 | 36.42 | 129.49 | 26.37 |
| 1800 | 0.0854 | 307.44 | 203.65 | 103.79 | 655.94 | 125 | 38.43 | 127.89 | 26.04 |
| 1900 | 0.0806 | 290.16 | 203.65 | 86.51 | 742.45 | 150 | 43.52 | 134.67 | 27.43 |
| 2000 | 0.0781 | 281.16 | 203.65 | 77.51 | 819.96 | 200 | 56.23 | 152.61 | 31.08 |
| 2100 | 0.067 | 241.2 | 203.65 | 37.55 | 857.51 | 215 | 51.86 | 166.79 | 33.97 |
| 2200 | 0.0583 | 209.88 | 203.65 | 6.23 | 863.74 | 170 | 35.68 | 167.42 | 34.10 |
| 2300 | 0.0526 | 189.36 | 203.65 | −14.29 | 849.45 | 130 | 24.62 | 160.69 | 32.73 |
| 0000 | 0.0481 | 173.16 | 203.65 | −30.49 | 818.96 | 110 | 19.05 | 152.11 | 30.98 |
| 0100 | 0.0359 | 129.24 | 203.65 | −74.41 | 744.55 | 81 | 10.47 | 142.42 | 29.00 |
| 0200 | 0.0226 | 81.36 | 203.65 | −122.29 | 622.26 | 53 | 4.31 | 133.61 | 27.21 |
| 0300 | 0.0187 | 67.32 | 203.65 | −136.33 | 485.93 | 35 | 2.36 | 123.98 | 25.25 |
| 0400 | 0.0187 | 67.32 | 203.65 | −136.33 | 349.6 | 32 | 2.15 | 112.79 | 22.97 |
| 0500 | 0.0198 | 71.28 | 203.65 | −132.37 | 217.23 | 40 | 2.85 | 100.46 | 20.46 |
| 0600 | 0.0226 | 81.36 | 203.65 | −122.29 | 94.94 | 66 | 5.37 | 91.07 | 18.55 |
| 0700 | 0.0359 | 129.24 | 203.65 | −74.41 | 20.53 | 92 | 11.89 | 91.61 | 18.66 |
| 0800 | 0.0509 | 183.24 | 203.65 | −20.41 | 0.12 | 125 | 22.91 | 121.64 | 24.77 |

The third column converts the flows to volumes using the time interval (1 h) between flow measurements.

$$V = (0.0631 \text{ m}^3 \cdot \text{s}^{-1})(1 \text{ h})(3600 \text{ s} \cdot \text{h}^{-1}) = 227.16 \text{ m}^3$$

The fourth column is the average volume that leaves the equalization basin.

$$V = (0.05657 \text{ m}^3 \cdot \text{s}^{-1})(1 \text{ h})(3600 \text{ s} \cdot \text{h}^{-1}) = 203.65 \text{ m}^3$$

The fifth column is the difference between the inflow volume and the outflow volume.

$$\Delta V = V_{in} - V_{out} = 227.16 \text{ m}^3 - 203.65 \text{ m}^3 = 23.51 \text{ m}^3$$

The sixth column is the cumulative sum of the difference between the inflow and outflow. For the second time interval, it is

$$\text{Storage} = dS = 37.55 \text{ m}^3 + 23.51 \text{ m}^3 = 61.06 \text{ m}^3$$

Note that the last value for the cumulative storage is 0.12 $m^3$. It is not zero because of round-off truncation in the computations. At this point the equalization basin is empty and ready to begin the next day's cycle.

The required volume for the equalization basin is the maximum cumulative storage. With the requirement for 25% excess, the volume would then be

Storage volume = $(863.74 \text{ m}^3)(1.25) = 1079.68$, or $1080 \text{ m}^3$

The mass of $BOD_5$ flowing into the equalization basin is the product of the inflow ($Q$) the concentration of $BOD_5$ ($S_0$), and the integration time ($\Delta t$).

$$M_{\text{BOD-in}} = (Q)(S_0)(\Delta t)$$

The mass of $BOD_5$ flowing out of the equalization basin is the product of the average outflow ($Q_{\text{avg}}$), the average concentration ($S_{\text{avg}}$) in the basin, and the integration time ($\Delta t$):

$$M_{\text{BOD-out}} = (Q_{\text{avg}})(S_{\text{avg}})(\Delta t)$$

The average concentration is determined as

$$S_{\text{avg}} = \frac{(\forall_i)(S_0) + (\forall_s)(S_{\text{prev}})}{\forall_i + \forall_s}$$

where $\forall_i$ = volume of inflow during the time interval $\Delta t$ (in $\text{m}^3$)
$S_0$ = average $BOD_5$ concentration during time interval $\Delta t$ (in $\text{g} \cdot \text{m}^{-3}$)
$\forall_s$ = volume of wastewater in the basin at the end of the previous time interval (in $\text{m}^3$)
$S_{\text{prev}}$ = concentration of $BOD_5$ in the basin at the end of the previous time interval previous $S_{\text{avg}}$ (in $\text{g} \cdot \text{m}^{-3}$)

Noting that $1 \text{ mg} \cdot \text{L}^{-1} = 1 \text{ g} \cdot \text{m}^{-3}$, the first row (the 0900 h time) computations are

$$M_{\text{BOD-in}} = (0.0631 \text{ m}^3 \cdot \text{s}^{-1})(140 \text{ g} \cdot \text{m}^{-3})(1 \text{ h})(3600 \text{ s} \cdot \text{h}^{-1})(10^{-3} \text{ kg} \cdot \text{g}^{-1}) = 31.8 \text{ kg}$$

$$S_{\text{avg}} = \frac{(227.16 \text{ m}^3)(140 \text{ g} \cdot \text{m}^{-3}) + 0}{227.16 \text{ m}^3 + 0} = 140 \text{ mg} \cdot \text{L}^{-1}$$

$$M_{\text{BOD-out}} = (0.05657 \text{ m}^3 \cdot \text{s}^{-1})(140 \text{ g} \cdot \text{m}^{-3})(1 \text{ h})(3600 \text{ s} \cdot \text{h}^{-1})(10^{-3} \text{ kg} \cdot \text{g}^{-1}) = 28.5 \text{ kg}$$

Note that the zero values in the computation of $S_{\text{avg}}$ are valid only at startup of an empty basin. Also note that in this case $M_{\text{BOD-in}}$ and $M_{\text{BOD-out}}$ differ only because of the difference in flow rates. For the second row (1000 h), the computations are

$$M_{\text{BOD-in}} = (0.0670 \text{ m}^3 \cdot \text{s}^{-1})(150 \text{ g} \cdot \text{m}^{-3})(1 \text{ h})(3600 \text{ s} \cdot \text{h}^{-1})(10^{-3} \text{ kg} \cdot \text{g}^{-1}) = 36.2 \text{ kg}$$

$$S_{\text{avg}} = \frac{(241.20 \text{ m}^3)(150 \text{ g} \cdot \text{m}^{-3}) + (23.51 \text{ m}^3)(140 \text{ g} \cdot \text{m}^{-3})}{241.20 \text{ m}^3 + 23.51 \text{ m}^3} = 149.11 \text{ mg} \cdot \text{L}^{-1}$$

$$M_{\text{BOD-out}} = (0.05657 \text{ m}^3 \cdot \text{s}^{-1})(149.11 \text{ g} \cdot \text{m}^{-3})(1 \text{ h})(3600 \text{ s} \cdot \text{h}^{-1})(10^{-3} \text{ kg} \cdot \text{g}^{-1})$$

$$= 30.37 \text{ mg} \cdot \text{L}^{-1}$$

Note that $\forall_s$ is the volume of wastewater in the basin at the end of the previous time interval; therefore, it equals the accumulated $dS$. The concentration of $BOD_5$ ($S_{\text{prev}}$) is the average concentration at the end of previous interval ($S_{\text{avg}}$) and *not* the influent concentration for the previous interval ($S_0$).

For the third row (1100 h), the concentration of $BOD_5$ is

$$S_{\text{avg}} = \frac{(245.52 \text{ m}^3)(155 \text{ g} \cdot \text{m}^{-3}) + (61.06 \text{ m}^3)(149.11 \text{ g} \cdot \text{m}^{-3})}{245.52 \text{ m}^3 + 61.06 \text{ m}^3} = 153.83 \text{ mg} \cdot \text{L}^{-1}$$

## 10–6 **PRIMARY TREATMENT**

With the screening completed and the grit removed, the wastewater still contains light organic suspended solids, some of which can be removed from the sewage by gravity in a sedimentation tank. These tanks can be round or rectangular. The mass of settled solids is called **raw sludge.** The sludge is removed from the sedimentation tank by mechanical scrapers and pumps (Figure 10–9). Floating materials, such as grease and oil, rise to the surface of the sedimentation tank, where they are collected by a surface-skimming system and removed from the tank for further processing.

Primary sedimentation basins (primary tanks) are characterized by type II flocculant settling. The Stoke's equation cannot be used because the flocculating particles are continually changing in size, shape, and, when water is entrapped in the floc, specific gravity. No mathematical relationship is adequate to describe type II settling. Laboratory tests with settling columns are used to develop design data.

Rectangular tanks with common-wall construction are frequently chosen because they are advantageous for sites with space constraints. Typically, these tanks range from 15 to 100 m in length and 3 to 24 m in width. Circular tanks have diameters from 3 to 90 m.

As in water treatment clarifier design discussed in Chapter 9, overflow rate is the controlling parameter for the design of primary settling tanks. At average flow, overflow rates typically range from 25 to 60 $m^3 \cdot m^{-2} \cdot day^{-1}$ (or 25–60 $m \cdot day^{-1}$). When waste-activated sludge is returned to the primary tank, a lower range of overflow rates is chosen (25–35 $m \cdot day^{-1}$). Under peak flow conditions, overflow rates may be in the range of 80 to 120 $m \cdot day^{-1}$.

Hydraulic detention time (see discussion in Section 3–3 for definition) in the sedimentation basin ranges from 1.5 to 2.5 h under average flow conditions. A 2.0-h detention time is typical.

The Great Lakes-Upper Mississippi River Board of State Sanitary Engineers (GLUMRB) recommends that weir loading (hydraulic flow over the effluent weir) rates not exceed 120 $m^3 \cdot day^{-1}$ of flow per meter of weir length ($m^3 \cdot day^{-1} \cdot m^{-1}$) for plants with average flows less than 0.04 $m^3 \cdot s^{-1}$. For larger flows, the recommended rate is 190 $m^3 \cdot day^{-1} \cdot m^{-1}$ [6]. If the side water depths exceed 3.5 m, the weir loading rates have little effect on performance.

As mentioned previously, approximately 50–60% of the raw sewage suspended solids and as much as 30–35% of the raw sewage $BOD_5$ may be removed in the primary tank.

**FIGURE 10–9**

Primary settling tank. (*Source:* Reprinted, with permission, from: Davis, M. L., and D. A. Cornwell, *Introduction to Environmental Engineering*, 3rd ed., McGraw-Hill, New York, NY, p. 373, 1998.)

**EXAMPLE 10-3**   Evaluate the following primary tank design with respect to detention time, overflow rate, and weir loading.

*Design Data*

Flow $= 0.150 \text{ m}^3 \cdot \text{s}^{-1}$           Length $= 40.0$ m (effective)
Influent suspended solids $= 280 \text{ mg} \cdot \text{L}^{-1}$     Width $= 10.0$ m
Sludge concentration $= 6.0\%$           Liquid depth $= 2.0$ m
Efficiency $= 60\%$                Weir length $= 75.0$ m

Solution   The detention time is simply the volume of the tank divided by the flow.

$$\theta = \frac{\forall}{Q} = \frac{40.0 \text{ m} \times 10.0 \text{ m} \times 2.0 \text{ m}}{0.150 \text{ m}^3 \cdot \text{s}^{-1}} = 5333.33 \text{ s, or } 1.5 \text{ h}$$

This is a reasonable detention time.

The overflow rate is the flow divided by the surface area.

$$v_0 = \frac{0.150 \text{ m}^3 \cdot \text{s}^{-1}}{40.0 \text{ m} \times 10.0 \text{ m}} \times 86{,}400 \text{ s} \cdot \text{day}^{-1} = 32 \text{ m} \cdot \text{day}^{-1}$$

This is an acceptable overflow rate.

The weir loading (WL) is calculated in the same fashion.

$$\text{WL} = \frac{0.150 \text{ m}^3 \cdot \text{s}^{-1}}{75.0 \text{ m}} \times 86{,}400 \text{ s} \cdot \text{day}^{-1} = 172.8, \text{ or } 173 \text{ m}^3 \cdot \text{day}^{-1} \cdot \text{m}^{-1}$$

This is an acceptable weir loading.

## 10–7   UNIT PROCESSES OF SECONDARY TREATMENT

### Overview

The basic ingredients needed for conventional aerobic secondary biologic treatment are the availability of many microorganisms, good contact between these organisms and the organic material, the availability of oxygen, and the maintenance of other favorable environmental conditions (e.g., favorable temperature and sufficient time for the organisms to work). A variety of approaches have been used in the past to meet these basic needs. The most common approaches for municipalities are the trickling filter process and the activated sludge process. Lagoons are employed when wastewater flows are not large and land space is available.

### Role of Microorganisms

The stabilization of organic matter is accomplished biologically using a variety of microorganisms, which convert the colloidal and dissolved carbonaceous organic matter into various gases and into protoplasm. Because protoplasm has a specific gravity slightly greater than that of water, it can be removed from the treated liquid by gravity settling.

It is important to note that unless the protoplasm produced from the organic matter is removed from the solution, complete treatment will not be accomplished because the protoplasm, which itself is organic, will be measured as BOD in the effluent. If the protoplasm is not removed, the only treatment that will be achieved is that associated with the bacterial conversion of a portion of the organic matter originally present to various gaseous end products [7].

### Classification of Microorganisms

As discussed in Chapter 4, microorganisms may be classified by their trophic levels, that is, by their energy and carbon source and their relationship to oxygen. They also may be classified by their preferred temperature regime.

Each species of bacteria reproduces best within a limited range of temperatures. Four temperature ranges are used to classify them. Those that grow best at temperatures below 20°C are called **psychrophiles. Mesophiles** grow best at temperatures between 25 and 40°C. Between 45 and 60°C, the **thermophiles** grow best. Above 60°C, **stenothermophiles** grow best. The growth range of facultative thermophiles extends from the thermophilic into the mesophilic range. These ranges are qualitative and somewhat subjective. You will note the gaps between 20 and 25°C and between 40 and 45°C. Don't make the mistake of saying that an organism that grows well at 20.5°C is a mesophile. The rules just aren't that hard and fast. Bacteria will grow over a range of temperatures and will survive at a very large range of temperatures. For example, *Escherichia coli,* classified as mesophiles, will grow at temperatures between 20 and 50°C and will reproduce, albeit very slowly, at temperatures down to 0°C. If frozen rapidly, they and many other microorganisms can be stored for years with no significant death rate.

### Some Organisms of Interest in Wastewater Treatment

**Bacteria.**   The highest population of microorganisms in a wastewater treatment plant will belong to the bacteria. They are single-celled organisms that use soluble food. Conditions in the treatment plant are adjusted so that chemoheterotrophs predominate. No particular species is selected as "the best."

**Fungi.**   Fungi are multicellular, nonphotosynthetic, heterotrophic organisms. Fungi are obligate aerobes that reproduce by a variety of methods, including fission, budding, and spore formation. Their cells require only half as much nitrogen as bacteria, so that in a nitrogen-deficient wastewater, they predominate over the bacteria [8].

**Algae.**   This group of microorganisms are photoautotrophs and may be either unicellular or multicellular. Because of the chlorophyll contained in most species, they produce oxygen through photosynthesis. In the presence of sunlight, the photosynthetic production of oxygen is greater than the amount used in respiration. At night they use up oxygen in respiration. If the daylight hours exceed the night hours by a reasonable amount, there is a net production of oxygen.

**Protozoa.**   Protozoa are single-celled organisms that can reproduce by **binary fission** (dividing in two). Most are aerobic chemoheterotrophs, and they often consume bacteria. They are desirable in wastewater effluents because they act as polishers in consuming the bacteria.

**Rotifers and Crustaceans.**   Both rotifers and crustaceans are animals—aerobic, multicellular chemoheterotrophs. The rotifer derives its name from the apparent rotating motion of two sets of cilia on its head. The cilia provide mobility and a mechanism for catching food. Rotifers consume bacteria and small particles of organic matter.

Crustaceans, a group that includes shrimp, lobsters, and barnacles, are characterized by their shell structure. They are a source of food for fish and are not found in wastewater treatment systems to any extent except in underloaded lagoons. Their presence is indicative of a high level of dissolved oxygen and a very low level of organic matter.

### Bacterial Biochemistry

**Metabolism.**   The general term that describes all of the chemical activities performed by a cell is **metabolism.** This in turn is divided into two parts: catabolism and anabolism. **Catabolism** includes all the biochemical processes by which a substrate is degraded to end products with the release of energy. Substrate is food. For our application, "food" is the organic material from the human digestive tract and other biodegradable wastes. In wastewater treatment, the substrate is oxidized. The oxidation process releases energy that is transferred to an energy carrier that stores it for future use by the bacterium (Figure 10–10). Some chemical compounds released by catabolism are used by the bacterial cell for its life functions.

**FIGURE 10–10**

General scheme of bacterial metabolism. (*Source:* Reprinted, with permission, from: Davis, M. L., and D. A. Cornwell, *Introduction to Environmental Engineering,* 3rd ed., McGraw-Hill, New York, NY, p. 343, 1998.)

**TABLE 10–6**    Waste Decomposition End Products

| Substrates | Representative End Products | |
|---|---|---|
| | **Aerobic and Anoxic Decomposition** | **Anaerobic Decomposition** |
| Proteins and other organic nitrogen compounds | Amino acids<br>Ammonia $\longrightarrow$ nitrites<br>$\longrightarrow$ nitrates*<br>Alcohols $\longrightarrow CO_2 + H_2O$<br>Organic acids | Amino acids<br>Ammonia<br>Hydrogen sulfide<br>Methane Carbon dioxide<br>Alcohols<br>Organic acids |
| Carbohydrates | Alcohols $\longrightarrow CO_2 + H_2O$<br>Fatty acids | Carbon dioxide<br>Fatty acids<br>Methane |
| Fats and related substances | Fatty acids + glycerol<br>Alcohols $\longrightarrow CO_2 + H_2O$<br>Lower fatty acids | Fatty acids + glycerol<br>Carbon dioxide<br>Alcohols<br>Lower fatty acids<br>Methane |

*Under anoxic conditions the nitrates are converted to nitrogen gas.
*Source:* After Pelczar, M. J., and R. D. Reid, *Microbiology,* McGraw-Hill, New York (1958).

**Anabolism** includes all the biochemical processes by which the bacterium synthesizes new chemical compounds needed by the cells to live and reproduce. The synthesis process is driven by the energy that was stored in the energy carrier.

### Decomposition of Waste

The type of electron acceptor available for catabolism determines the type of decomposition (i.e., aerobic, anoxic, or anaerobic) used by a mixed culture of microorganisms. Each type of decomposition has peculiar characteristics that affect its use in waste treatment.

**Aerobic Decomposition.**    From our discussion of bacterial metabolism you will recall that molecular oxygen ($O_2$) must be present as the terminal electron acceptor for decomposition to proceed by aerobic oxidation. As in natural water bodies, the oxygen is measured as DO. When oxygen is present, it is the only terminal electron acceptor used. Hence, the chemical end products of decomposition are primarily carbon dioxide, water, and new cell material (Table 10–6). Odiferous gaseous end products are kept to a minimum. In healthy natural water systems, aerobic decomposition is the principal means of self-purification.

A wider spectrum of organic material can be oxidized aerobically than by any other type of decomposition. This fact, coupled with the fact that the final end products are oxidized to a very low energy level, results in a more stable end product (i.e., one that can be disposed of without damage to the environment and without creating a nuisance condition) than can be achieved by the other decomposition systems.

Because of the large amount of energy released in aerobic oxidation, most aerobic organisms are capable of high growth rates. Consequently, there is a relatively large production of new cells in comparison with the other oxidation systems. This means that more biological sludge is generated in aerobic oxidation than in the other oxidation systems.

Aerobic decomposition is the method of choice for large quantities of dilute wastewater ($BOD_5$ less than 500 mg $\cdot$ L$^{-1}$) because decomposition is rapid, efficient, and has a low odor potential. For high-strength wastewater ($BOD_5$ is greater than 1000 mg $\cdot$ L$^{-1}$), aerobic decomposition is not suitable because of the difficulty in supplying enough oxygen and because of the large amount of biological sludge produced. In small communities and in special industrial applications where aerated lagoons are used, wastewaters with $BOD_5$ up to 3000 mg $\cdot$ L$^{-1}$ may be treated satisfactorily by aerobic decomposition.

**Anoxic Decomposition.**  Some microorganisms can use nitrate ($NO_3$) as the terminal electron acceptor in the absence of molecular oxygen. Oxidation by this route is called **denitrification.**

The end products from denitrification are nitrogen gas, carbon dioxide, water, and new cell material. The amount of energy made available to the cell during denitrification is about the same as that made available during aerobic decomposition. As a consequence, the rate of production of new cells, although not as high as in aerobic decomposition, is relatively high.

Denitrification is of importance in wastewater treatment where nitrogen must be removed to protect the receiving body. In this case, a special treatment step is added to the conventional process for removal of carbonaceous material. Denitrification will be discussed in detail later.

One other important aspect of denitrification is the final clarification of the treated wastewater. If the environment of the final clarifier becomes anoxic, the formation of nitrogen gas will cause large globs of sludge to float to the surface and escape from the treatment plant into the receiving water. Thus, it is necessary to ensure that anoxic conditions do not develop in the final clarifier.

**Anaerobic Decomposition.**  To achieve anaerobic decomposition, molecular oxygen and nitrate must not be present as terminal electron acceptors. Sulfate ($SO_4$), carbon dioxide, and organic compounds that can be reduced serve as terminal electron acceptors. The reduction of sulfate results in the production of hydrogen sulfide ($H_2S$) and a group of equally odiferous organic sulfur compounds called **mercaptans.**

The anaerobic decomposition (**fermentation**) of organic matter generally is considered to be a two-step process. In the first step, complex organic compounds are fermented to low-molecular-weight fatty acids (**volatile acids**). In the second step, the organic acids are convened to methane. Carbon dioxide serves as the electron acceptor. Anaerobic decomposition yields carbon dioxide, methane, and water as the major end products. Additional end products include ammonia, hydrogen sulfide, and mercaptans. As a consequence of these last three compounds, anaerobic decomposition is characterized by an unbelievably horrid stench.

Because only small amounts of energy are released during anaerobic oxidation, the amount of cell production is low. Thus, sludge production is low. We make use of this fact in wastewater treatment by using anaerobic decomposition to stabilize sludges produced during aerobic and anoxic decomposition.

Direct anaerobic decomposition of wastewater generally is not feasible for dilute waste although some researchers are exploring the use of anaerobic systems for treatment of dilute wastes such as groundwater contaminated with hazardous waste. The optimum growth temperature for the anaerobic bacteria is at the upper end of the mesophilic range. Thus, to get reasonable biodegradation, we must elevate the temperature of the culture. For dilute wastewater, this is not practical. For concentrated wastes ($BOD_5$ greater than 1000 mg $\cdot$ L$^{-1}$), anaerobic digestion is quite appropriate but it is almost always polished by aerobic treatment to meet discharge standards in the United States.

### Population Dynamics

**The Microbial Ecosystem.** In the discussion of the behavior of bacterial cultures that follows, the inherent assumption is that all the requirements for growth are initially present. The requirements for growth and the dynamic behavior of the microbial ecosystem were discussed extensively in Chapter 4. In wastewater treatment, as in nature, pure cultures of microorganisms do not exist. Rather, a mixture of species compete and survive within the limits set by the environment. **Population dynamics** is the term used to describe the time-varying success of the various species in competition. It is expressed quantitatively in terms of relative mass of microorganisms.

The prime factor governing the dynamics of the various microbial populations is the competition for food. The second most important factor is the predator–prey relationship.

The relative success of a pair of species competing for the same substrate is a function of the ability of the species to metabolize the substrate. The more successful species will be the one that metabolizes the substrate more completely. In so doing, it will obtain more energy for synthesis and consequently will achieve a greater mass.

**The Monod Equation.** For the large numbers and mixed cultures of microorganisms found in waste treatment systems, it is convenient to measure biomass rather than numbers of organisms. Frequently, this is done by measuring suspended solids or volatile suspended solids (those that burn at $550 \pm 50°C$). When the wastewater contains only soluble organic matter, the volatile suspended solids test is reasonably representative. The presence of organic particles (which is often the case in municipal wastewater) confuses the issue completely. In the log-growth phase (discussed in Section 4–5), the rate of growth of bacterial cells can be defined as

$$r_g = \mu X \tag{10-7}$$

where $r_g$ = growth rate of the biomass (in mg $\cdot$ L$^{-1}$ $\cdot$ $t^{-1}$)
$\mu$ = specific growth rate constant (in $t^{-1}$)
$X$ = concentration of biomass (in mg $\cdot$ L$^{-1}$)

Because $dX/dt = r_g$ for a batch reactor (see Equation 3–26) we may write the following rate expression for biomass increase in a batch reactor

$$\frac{dX}{dt} = \mu X \tag{10-8}$$

Because of the difficulty of direct measurement of $\mu$ in mixed cultures, Monod developed a model equation that assumes that the rate of food use, and therefore the rate of biomass production, is limited by the rate of enzyme reactions involving the food compound that is in shortest supply relative to its need [9]. The Monod equation is

$$\mu = \frac{\mu_m S}{K_s + S} \tag{10-9}$$

where $\mu_m$ = maximum specific growth rate constant (in $t^{-1}$)
$S$ = concentration of limiting food in solution (in mg $\cdot$ L$^{-1}$)
$K_s$ = half saturation constant (in mg $\cdot$ L$^{-1}$)
= concentration of limiting food when $\mu = 0.5\mu_m$

The relationship between the growth rate constant and limiting food concentration ($S$) follows a hyperbolic function as shown in Figure 10–11.

**FIGURE 10–11**

Monod growth rate constant as a function of limiting food concentration. (*Source:* Reprinted, with permission, from: Davis, M. L., and D. A. Cornwell, *Introduction to Environmental Engineering*, 3rd ed., McGraw-Hill, New York, NY, p. 351, 1998.)

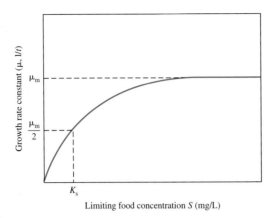

Two limiting cases are of interest in the application of Equation 10–9 to wastewater treatment systems. In those cases where there is an excess of the limiting food, then $S \gg K$ and the growth rate constant, $\mu$ is approximately equal to $\mu_m$. Equation 10–7 then becomes zero-order in substrate, $S$, that is, it is independent of the substrate. At the other extreme, when $S \ll K_s$, the system is food-limited and the growth rate becomes first-order with respect to substrate.

Equation 10–9 assumes only growth of microorganisms and does not take into account natural die-off. It is generally assumed that the death or decay of the microbial mass is a first-order expression in biomass and hence Equations 10–7 and 10–9 are expanded to

$$r_g = \frac{\mu_m S X}{K_s + S} - k_d X \qquad (10\text{–}10)$$

where $k_d$ = endogenous decay rate constant (in $t^{-1}$).

If all of the food in the system were converted to biomass, the rate of food use, $r_{su}$, would equal the rate of biomass production. Because of the inefficiency of the conversion process, the rate of food use will be greater than the rate of biomass use, so

$$r_{su} = \frac{1}{Y}(r_g) \qquad (10\text{–}11)$$

where $Y$ = decimal fraction of food mass convened to biomass

= yield coefficient, in milligrams per liter of food used, $\frac{mg \cdot L^{-1} \text{ biomass}}{mg \cdot L^{-1} \text{ food used}}$

Combining Equations 10–7, 10–9, and 10–11, we obtain

$$r_{su} = \frac{1}{Y} \frac{\mu_m S X}{(K_s + S)} \qquad (10\text{–}12)$$

Equations 10–10 and 10–12 are a fundamental part of the development of the design equations for wastewater treatment processes.

### Trickling Filters

A trickling filter consists of a bed of coarse material (called **media**), such as stones, slats, or plastic materials, over which wastewater is applied. Trickling filters have been a popular biologic treatment process. The most widely used design for many years was simply a bed of stones from 1 to 3 m deep through which the wastewater passed. The wastewater is typically distributed over the surface of the media by a rotating arm (Figure 10–12).

As the wastewater trickles through the bed, a microbial growth establishes itself on the surface of the media in a fixed film. The wastewater passes over the stationary microbial population, providing contact between the microorganisms and the organic compounds in the wastewater.

**FIGURE 10–12**

Trickling-filter plant with enlargement of trickling filter. (*Source:* Reprinted, with permission, from: Davis, M. L., and D. A. Cornwell, *Introduction to Environmental Engineering,* 3rd ed., McGraw-Hill, New York, NY, p. 375, 1998.)

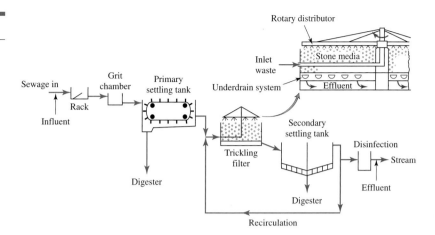

Trickling filters are not primarily a filtering or straining process as the name implies. The rocks in a rock filter are 25–100 mm in diameter and, hence, have openings too large to strain out solids. They are a means of providing large amounts of surface area where the microorganisms cling and grow in a slime on the rocks as they feed on the organic matter.

Excess growths of microorganisms wash from the rock media and would cause undesirably high levels of suspended solids in the plant effluent if not removed. Thus, the flow from the filter is passed through a sedimentation basin to allow these solids to settle out. This sedimentation basin is referred to as a **secondary clarifier;** or **final clarifier,** to differentiate it from the sedimentation basin used for primary settling.

Although rock trickling filters have performed well for years, they have certain limitations. Under high organic loadings, the slime growths can be so prolific that they plug the void spaces between the rocks, causing flooding and failure of the system. Also, the volume of void spaces is limited in a rock filter that restricts the circulation of air and the amount of oxygen available for the microbes. This limitation, in turn, restricts the amount of wastewater that can be processed.

To overcome these limitations, other materials have become popular for filling the trickling filter. These materials include modules of corrugated plastic sheets and plastic rings. These media offer larger surface areas for slime growths (typically 90 $m^2$ of surface area per cubic meter of bulk volume, as compared with 40–60 $m^2 \cdot m^{-3}$ for 75-mm rocks) and greatly increase void ratios for increased air flow. The materials are also much lighter than rock, so that the trickling filters can be much taller without facing structural problems. Although rock in filters is usually not more than 3 m deep, synthetic media depths may reach 12 m, thus reducing the overall space requirements for the trickling-filter portion of the treatment plant.

Trickling filters are classified according to the applied hydraulic and organic load. The hydraulic load may be expressed as cubic meters of wastewater applied per day per square meter of bulk filter surface area ($m^3 \cdot day^{-1} \cdot m^{-2}$) or, preferably, as the depth of water applied per unit of time ($mm \cdot s^{-1}$ or $m \cdot day^{-1}$). Organic loading is expressed as kilograms of $BOD_5$ per day per cubic meter of bulk filter volume ($kg \cdot day^{-1} \cdot m^{-3}$). Common hydraulic loadings range from 1 to 170 $m \cdot day^{-1}$ and organic loadings range from 0.07 to 1.8 kg $BOD_5 \cdot day^{-1} \cdot m^{-2}$ [10].

An important element in trickling filter design is the provision for return of a portion of the effluent to flow through the filter. This practice is called **recirculation.** The ratio of the returned flow to the incoming flow is called the **recirculation ratio.** Recirculation is practiced in stone filters for the following reasons:

1. To increase contact efficiency by bringing the waste into contact more than once with active biological material
2. To dampen variations in loadings over a 24-h period. The strength of the recirculated flow lags behind that of the incoming wastewater. Thus, recirculation dilutes strong influent and supplements weak influent

**FIGURE 10-13**

Two-stage trickling-filter plant. (*Courtesy of Dow Chemical Company.*)

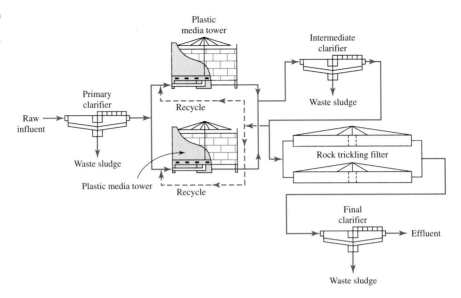

3. To raise the DO of the influent
4. To improve distribution over the surface, thus reducing the tendency to clog and also reduce filter flies
5. To prevent the biological slimes from drying out and dying during nighttime periods when flows may be too low to keep the filter wet continuously

Recirculation may or may not improve treatment efficiency. The more dilute the incoming wastewater, the less likely it is that recirculation will improve efficiency.

Recirculation is practiced for plastic media to provide the desired wetting rate to keep the microorganisms alive. Generally, increasing the hydraulic loading above the minimum wetting rate does not increase $BOD_5$ removal. The minimum wetting rate normally falls in the range of 25 to 60 m · day$^{-1}$.

Two-stage trickling filters (Figure 10–13) provide a means of improving the performance of filters. The second stage acts as a polishing step for the effluent from the primary stage by providing additional contact time between the waste and the microorganisms. Both stages may use the same media or each stage may have different media as shown in Figure 10–13. The designer will select the types of media and their arrangement based on the desired treatment efficiencies and an economic analysis of the alternatives.

### Activated Sludge

The activated sludge process is a biological wastewater treatment technique in which a mixture of wastewater and biological sludge (microorganisms) is agitated and aerated. The biological solids are subsequently separated from the treated wastewater and returned to the aeration process as needed.

The activated sludge process derives its name from the biological mass formed when air is continuously injected into the wastewater. In this process, microorganisms are mixed thoroughly with the organic matter in the wastewater under conditions that stimulate their growth through use of the organic matter as food. As the microorganisms grow and are mixed by the agitation of the air, the individual organisms clump together (flocculate) to form an active mass of microbes (biologic floc) called **activated sludge.**

In practice, wastewater flows continuously into an aeration tank (Figure 10–14) where air is injected to mix the activated sludge with the wastewater and to supply the oxygen needed for the organisms to break down the organic matter. The mixture of activated sludge and wastewater in the aeration tank is called **mixed liquor.** The mixed liquor flows from the aeration tank to a secondary clarifier where the activated sludge is settled out. Most of the settled sludge is returned to the

## FIGURE 10–14

Conventional activated sludge plant. (*Source:* Reprinted, with permission, from: Davis, M. L., and D. A. Cornwell, *Introduction to Environmental Engineering*, 3rd ed., McGraw-Hill, New York, NY, p. 382, 1998.)

## FIGURE 10–15

Activated sludge aeration tank under air, East Lansing, MI, Wastewater Treatment Plant. (*Photo by Harley Seeley, Michigan State University.*)

aeration tank (and hence is called **return sludge**) to maintain the high population of microbes that permits rapid breakdown of the organic matter. Because more activated sludge is produced than is desirable in the process, some of the return sludge is diverted to the sludge handling system for treatment and disposal. In conventional activated sludge systems, the wastewater is typically aerated for 6–8 h in long, rectangular aeration basins. About 8 $m^3$ of air is provided for each cubic meter of wastewater treated. Sufficient air is provided to keep the sludge in suspension (Figure 10–15). The air is injected near the bottom of the aeration tank through a system of perforated pipes or porous stones called **diffusers.** The volume of sludge returned to the aeration basin is typically 20–30% of the wastewater flow.

The activated sludge process is controlled by wasting a portion of the microorganisms each day in order to maintain the proper amount of microorganisms to efficiently degrade the $BOD_5$. **Wasting** means that a portion of the microorganisms is discarded from the process. The discarded microorganisms are called **waste activated sludge** (WAS). A balance is then achieved between growth of new organisms and their removal by wasting. If too much sludge is wasted, the concentration of microorganisms in the mixed liquor will become too low for effective treatment. If too little sludge is wasted, a large concentration of microorganisms will accumulate and, ultimately, overflow the secondary tank and flow into the receiving stream.

**FIGURE 10–16**

Completely mixed
biological reactor with
solids recycle.

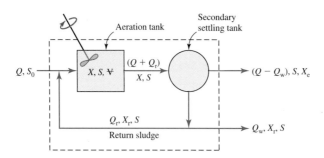

The **mean cell residence time** $\theta_c$ also called **solids retention time** (SRT) or **sludge age,** is defined as the average amount of time that microorganisms are kept in the system. This differs from the **hydraulic detention time** ($\theta$), which is the average time the wastewater is in the tank.

Many modifications of the conventional activated sludge process have been developed to address specific treatment problems. We have selected the completely mixed flow process for further discussion.

### Completely Mixed Activated Sludge Process.

The design formulas for the completely mixed activated sludge process are a mass-balance application of the equations used to describe the kinetics of microbial growth. A mass-balance diagram for the completely mixed system (CMFR) is shown in Figure 10–16. The mass-balance equations are written for the system boundary shown by the dashed line. Two mass balances are required to define the design of the reactor: one for biomass and one for food (soluble $BOD_5$).

Under steady-state conditions, the mass balance for biomass may be written as

Biomass in influent + biomass accumulated = biomass in effluent + biomass wasted     (10–13)

The biomass in the influent is the product of the concentration of microorganisms in the influent ($X_0$) and the flow rate of wastewater ($Q$). The concentration of microorganisms in the influent is measured as suspended solids ($mg \cdot L^{-1}$). The biomass that accumulates in the aeration tank is the product of the volume of the tank ($\forall$) and the Monod expression for growth of microbial mass (Equation 10–10)

$$(\forall)\left(\frac{\mu_m SX}{K_s + S} - k_d X\right) \tag{10–14}$$

The biomass in the effluent is the product of flow rate of treated wastewater leaving the plant ($Q - Q_w$) and the concentration of microorganisms that does not settle in the secondary clarifier ($X_e$). The flow rate of wastewater leaving the plant does not equal the flow rate into the plant because some of the microorganisms must be wasted. The flow rate of wasting ($Q_w$) is deducted from the flow exiting the plant.

The biomass that is wasted is the product of concentration of microorganisms in the WAS flow ($X_r$) and the WAS flow rate ($Q_r$). The mass-balance equation may be rewritten as

$$(Q)(X_0) + (\forall)\left(\frac{\mu_m SX}{K_s + S} - k_d X\right) = (Q - Q_w)(X_e) + (Q_w)(X_r) \tag{10–15}$$

where $Q$ = wastewater flow rate into the aeration tank (in $m^3 \cdot day^{-1}$)

$X_0$ = microorganism concentration (volatile suspended solids or VSS* entering aeration tank (in $mg \cdot L^{-1}$)

$\forall$ = volume of aeration tank (in $m^3$)

---

*Suspended solids means that the material will be retained on a filter, unlike dissolved solids such as NaCl. The amount of the suspended solids that volatilizes at $500 \pm 50°C$ is taken to be a measure of active biomass concentration. The presence of nonliving organic particles in the influent wastewater will cause some error (usually small) in the use of volatile suspended solids as a measure of biomass.

$\mu_m$ = maximum growth rate constant (in days$^{-1}$)

$S$ = soluble BOD$_5$ in aeration tank and effluent (in mg $\cdot$ L$^{-1}$)

$X$ = microorganism concentration (mixed-liquor volatile suspended solids or MLVSS*) in the aeration tank (in mg $\cdot$ L$^{-1}$)

$K_s$ = half velocity constant
   = soluble BOD$_5$ concentration at one-half the maximum growth rate (in mg $\cdot$ L$^{-1}$)

$k_d$ = decay rate of microorganisms (in days$^{-1}$)

$Q_w$ = flow rate of liquid containing microorganisms to be wasted (in m$^3$ $\cdot$ day$^{-1}$)

$X_e$ = microorganism concentration (VSS) in effluent from secondary settling tank (in mg $\cdot$ L$^{-1}$)

$X_r$ = microorganism concentration (VSS) in sludge being wasted (in mg $\cdot$ L$^{-1}$)

At steady-state, the mass-balance equation for food (soluble BOD$_5$) may be written as

Food in influent + food consumed = food in effluent + food in WAS     (10–16)

The food in the influent is the product of the concentration of soluble BOD$_5$ in the influent ($S_0$) and the flow rate of wastewater ($Q$). The food that is consumed in the aeration tank is the product of the volume of the tank ($\Psi$) and the expression for rate of food use (Equation 10–12)

$$(\Psi)\left(\frac{\mu_m SX}{Y(K_s + S)}\right) \tag{10-17}$$

The food in the effluent is the product of flow rate of treated wastewater leaving the plant ($Q - Q_w$) and the concentration of soluble BOD$_5$ in the effluent ($S$). The concentration of soluble BOD$_5$ in the effluent ($S$) is the same as that in the aeration tank because we have assumed that the aeration tank is completely mixed. Because the BOD$_5$ is soluble, the secondary settling tank will not change the concentration. Thus, the effluent concentration from the secondary settling tank is the same as the influent concentration.

The food in the waste activated sludge flow is the product of the concentration of soluble BOD$_5$ in the influent ($S$) and the WAS flow rate ($Q_r$). The mass-balance equation for steady-state conditions may be rewritten as

$$(Q)(S_0) - (\Psi)\left(\frac{\mu_m SX}{Y(K_s + S)}\right) = (Q - Q_w)S + (Q_w)(S) \tag{10-18}$$

where $Y$ = yield coefficient (see Equation 10–11).

To develop working design equations we make the following assumptions:

1. The influent and effluent biomass concentrations are negligible compared with that in the reactor.
2. The influent food ($S_0$) is immediately diluted to the reactor concentration in accordance with the definition of a CMFR.
3. All reactions occur in the CMFR.

From the first assumption we may eliminate the following terms from Equation 10–15: $QX_0$, and $(Q - Q_w)X_e$ because, $X_0$ and $X_e$ are negligible compared with $X$. Equation 10–15 may be simplified to

$$(\Psi)\left(\frac{\mu_m SX}{K_s + S} - k_d X\right) = (Q_w)(X_r) \tag{10-19}$$

For convenience, we may rearrange Equation 10–19 in terms of the Monod equation

$$\left(\frac{\mu_m S}{K_s + S}\right) = \frac{(Q_w)(X_r)}{(\Psi)(X)} + k_d \tag{10-20}$$

---

*Mixed-liquor volatile suspended solids is a measure of the active biological mass in the aeration tank. The term *mixed liquor* implies a mixture of activated sludge and wastewater.

Equation 10–18 may also be rearranged in terms of the Monod equation

$$\left(\frac{\mu_m S}{K_s + S}\right) = \frac{Q}{\Psi}\frac{Y}{X}(S_0 - S) \tag{10–21}$$

Noting that the left side of Equations 10–20 and 10–21 are the same, we set the right-hand side of these equations equal and rearrange to give

$$\frac{(Q_w)(X_r)}{(\Psi)(X)} = \frac{Q}{\Psi}\frac{Y}{X}(S_0 - S) - k_d \tag{10–22}$$

Two parts of this equation have physical significance in the design of a completely mixed activated sludge system. The inverse of $Q/\Psi$ is the hydraulic detention time ($\theta$) of the reactor.

$$\theta = \frac{\Psi}{Q} \tag{10–23}$$

The inverse of the left side of Equation 10–22 defines the mean cell-residence time ($\theta_c$).

$$\theta_c = \frac{\Psi X}{Q_w X_r} \tag{10–24}$$

The mean cell-residence time expressed in Equation 10–24 must be modified if the effluent biomass concentration is not negligible. Equation 10–25 accounts for effluent losses of biomass in calculating $\theta_c$.

$$\theta_c = \frac{\Psi X}{Q_w X_r + (Q - Q_w)(X_e)} \tag{10–25}$$

From Equation 10–20, it can be seen that once $\theta_c$ is selected, the concentration of soluble $BOD_5$ in the effluent ($S$) is fixed

$$S = \frac{K_s(1 + k_d\theta_c)}{\theta_c(\mu_m - k_d) - 1} \tag{10–26}$$

Typical values of the microbial growth constants are given in Table 10–7. Note that the concentration of soluble $BOD_5$ leaving the system ($S$) is affected only by the mean cell-residence time and not by the amount of $BOD_5$ entering the aeration tank or by the hydraulic detention time. It is also important to reemphasize that $S$ is the soluble $BOD_5$ and not the total $BOD_5$. Some fraction of the suspended solids that do not settle in the secondary settling tank also contributes to the $BOD_5$ load to the receiving body. To achieve a desired effluent quality both the soluble and insoluble fractions of $BOD_5$ must be considered. Thus, using Equation 10–26 to achieve a desired effluent quality ($S$) by solving for $\theta_c$ requires that some estimate of the $BOD_5$ of the suspended solids be made first. This value is then subtracted from the total allowable $BOD_5$ in the effluent to find the allowable $S$.

$$S = \text{total } BOD_5 \text{ allowed} - BOD_5 \text{ in suspended solids} \tag{10–27}$$

| TABLE 10–7 | Values of Growth Constants for Domestic Wastewater | | | |
|---|---|---|---|---|
| | | | **Value[a]** | |
| **Parameter** | **Basis** | | **Range** | **Typical** |
| $K_s$ | $mg \cdot L^{-1}\ BOD_5$ | | 25–100 | 60 |
| $k_d$ | $days^{-1}$ | | 0.025–0.075 | 0.06 |
| $\mu_m$ | $days^{-1}$ | | 2–10 | 5 |
| $Y$ | $mg\ VSS \cdot mg^{-1}\ BOD_5$ | | 0.4–0.8 | 0.6 |

[a]Values at 20°C.

Source: Metcalf & Eddy, Inc., *Wastewater Engineering: Treatment, Disposal, and Reuse*, 3rd ed., McGraw-Hill, New York, p. 394 (1991).

From Equation 10–22 it is also evident that the concentration of microorganisms in the aeration tank is a function of the mean cell-residence time, hydraulic detention time, and difference between the influent and effluent concentrations.

$$X = \frac{\theta_c(Y)(S_0 - S)}{\theta(1 + k_d\theta_c)}$$

(10–28)

**EXAMPLE 10–4**   The town of Gatesville has been directed to upgrade its primary WWTP to a secondary plant that can meet an effluent standard of 30.0 mg · L$^{-1}$ BOD$_5$ and 30.0 mg · L$^{-1}$ suspended solids. They have selected a completely mixed activated sludge system.

Assuming that the BOD$_5$ of the suspended solids may be estimated as equal to 63% of the suspended solids concentration, estimate the required volume of the aeration tank. The following data are available from the existing primary plant.

Existing plant effluent characteristics
Flow = 0.150 m$^3$ · s$^{-1}$
BOD$_5$ = 84.0 mg · L$^{-1}$

Assume the following values for the growth constants: $K_s$ = 100 mg · L$^{-1}$ BOD$_5$; $\mu_m$ = 2.5 day$^{-1}$; $k_d$ = 0.050 day$^{-1}$; $Y$ = 0.50 mg VSS · mg$^{-1}$ BOD$_5$ removed.

**Solution**   Assuming that the secondary clarifier can produce an effluent with only 30.0 mg · L$^{-1}$ suspended solids, we can estimate the allowable soluble BOD$_5$ in the effluent using the 63% assumption and Equation 10–27.

$S$ = BOD$_5$ allowed − BOD$_5$ in suspended solids
  = 30.0 − (0.630)(30.0) = 11.1 mg · L$^{-1}$

The mean cell-residence time can be estimated with Equation 10–26 and the assumed values for the growth constants,

$$11.1 = \frac{(100.0)[1 + (0.050)(\theta_c)]}{\theta_c(2.5 - 0.050) - 1}$$

Solving for $\theta_c$

$(11.1)(2.45\theta_c - 1) = 100.0 + 5.00\theta_c$

$27.20\theta_c - 11.1 = 100.0 + 5.00\theta_c$

$\theta_c = \dfrac{111.1}{22.2} = 5.00$, or 5.0 days

If we assume a value of 2000 mg · L$^{-1}$ for the MLVSS, we can solve Equation 10–28 for the hydraulic detention time.

$$2000 = \frac{5.00(0.50)(84.0 - 11.1)}{\theta[1 + (0.050)(5.00)]}$$

$$\theta = \frac{2.50(72.9)}{2000(1.25)} = 0.073 \text{ day, or } 1.8 \text{ h}$$

The volume of the aeration tank is then estimated using Equation 10–23.

$$1.8 = \frac{V}{(0.150 \text{ m}^3 \cdot \text{s}^{-1})(3600 \text{ s} \cdot \text{h}^{-1})}$$

$V$ = 972 m$^3$, or 970 m$^3$

A commonly used parameter in regulating the performance of the activated sludge process is the food to microorganism ratio ($F/M$), which is defined as

$$\frac{F}{M} = \frac{Q S_0}{V X} \tag{10-29}$$

The units of the $F/M$ ratio are

$$\frac{\text{mg BOD}_5 \cdot \text{day}^{-1}}{\text{mg MLVSS}} = \frac{\text{mg}}{\text{mg} \cdot \text{day}}$$

The $F/M$ ratio is controlled by wasting part of the microbial mass, thereby reducing the MLVSS. A high rate of wasting causes a high $F/M$ ratio. A high $F/M$ yields organisms that are saturated with food. The result is that efficiency of treatment is poor. A low rate of wasting causes a low $F/M$ ratio, which yields organisms that are starved. This results in more complete degradation of the waste.

A long $\theta_c$ (low $F/M$) is not always used, however, because of certain tradeoffs that must be considered. A long $\theta_c$ means a higher requirement for oxygen and, thus, higher power costs. Problems with poor sludge "settleability" in the final clarifier may be encountered if $\theta_c$ is too long. However, because the waste is more completely degraded to final end products and less of the waste is converted into microbial cells when the microorganisms are starved at a low $F/M$, there is less sludge to handle.

Because both the $F/M$ ratio and the cell detention time are controlled by wasting of organisms, they are interrelated. A high $F/M$ corresponds to a short $\theta_c$, and a low $F/M$ corresponds to a long $\theta_c$. $F/M$ values typically range from 0.1 to 1.0 mg $\cdot$ mg$^{-1}$ $\cdot$ day$^{-1}$ for the various modifications of the activated sludge process.

**EXAMPLE 10–5**   Two "fill and draw," batch-operated sludge tanks are operated as follows:

Tank A is settled once each day, and half the liquid is removed with care not to disturb the sludge that settles to the bottom. This liquid is replaced with fresh settled sewage. A plot of MLVSS concentration versus time takes the shape shown in the following figure.

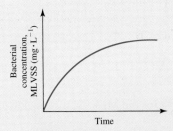

Tank B is not settled; rather, once each day, half the mixed liquor is removed while the tank is being violently agitated. The liquid is replaced with fresh settled sewage. A plot of MLVSS concentration versus time is shown in the following figure.

A comparison of the operating characteristics of the two systems is shown in the following table.

| Parameter | Tank A | Tank B |
|---|---|---|
| F/M | Low | High |
| $\theta_c$ | Long | Short |
| Sludge produced | None | Much |
| Oxygen required | High | Low |
| Power | High | Low |

The optimum choice is somewhere between these extremes. A balance must be struck between the cost of sludge disposal and the cost of power to provide oxygen (air).

**EXAMPLE 10–6**  Compute the $F/M$ ratio for the new activated sludge plant at Gatesville (Example 10–4).

**Solution**  Using the data from Example 10–4 and Equation 10–29, we obtain

$$\frac{F}{M} = \frac{(0.150 \ m^3 \cdot s^{-1})(84.0 \ mg \cdot L^{-1})(86{,}400 \ s \cdot day^{-1})}{(970 \ m^3)(2000 \ mg \cdot L^{-1})}$$

$$= 0.56 \ mg \cdot mg^{-1} \cdot day^{-1}$$

This is well within the typical range of $F/M$ ratios.

**Sludge Return.**  The purpose of sludge return is to maintain a sufficient concentration of activated sludge in the reactor basin. The return sludge pumping rate may be determined from a mass balance around the settling tank in Figure 10–16. Assuming that the amount of sludge in the secondary settling tank remains constant (steady-state conditions) and that the effluent suspended solids ($X_e$) are negligible, the mass balance is

$$\text{Accumulation} = \text{inflow} - \text{outflow} \tag{10–30}$$

$$0 = (Q + Q_r)(X') - (Q_r X'_r + Q_w X'_r) \tag{10–31}$$

where  $Q$ = wastewater flow rate (in $m^3 \cdot day^{-1}$)
  $Q_r$ = return sludge flow rate (in $m^3 \cdot day^{-1}$)
  $X'$ = mixed liquor suspended solids (MLSS) (in $g \cdot m^{-3}$)
  $X'_r$ = maximum return sludge concentration (in $g \cdot m^{-3}$)
  $Q_w$ = sludge wasting flow rate (in $m^3 \cdot day^{-1}$)

Solving for the return sludge flow rate, we get

$$Q_r = \frac{QX' - Q_w X'_r}{X'_r - X'} \tag{10–32}$$

Frequently, the assumption that the effluent suspended solids are negligible is not valid. If the effluent suspended solids are significant, the mass balance may then be expressed as

$$0 = (Q + Q_r)(X') - (Q_r X'_r + Q_w X'_r + (Q - Q_w)X_e) \tag{10–33}$$

Solving for the return sludge flow rate, we see that

$$Q_r = \frac{QX' - Q_w X_r' - (Q - Q_w)X_e}{X_r' - X'} \tag{10-34}$$

Note that $X_r'$ and $X'$ include both the volatile and inert fractions. Thus, they differ from $X_r$ and $X$ by a constant factor. With the volume of the tank and the mean cell-residence time, the sludge wasting flow rate can be determined with Equation 10–24 if the maximum return sludge concentration ($X_r'$) can be determined.

**EXAMPLE 10-7**    In the continuing saga of the Gatesville plant expansion, we now wish to estimate the return sludge pumping rate. Based on the aeration tank design (Example 10–4) and an informed, reliable source, we have the following data:

*Design data*
   Flow $= 0.150 \, \text{m}^3 \cdot \text{s}^{-1}$
   MLVSS $(X) = 2000 \, \text{mg} \cdot \text{L}^{-1}$
   MLSS $(X') = 1.43 \, (\text{MLVSS})$
   Return sludge concentration $(X_r') = 10{,}000 \, \text{mg} \cdot \text{L}^{-1}$
   Effluent suspended solids $(X_e)$ may be assumed to be negligible

Solution    The return sludge flow rate may be computed from Equation 10–32. To use this equation we must first estimate the sludge wasting flow rate ($Q_w$). Solving Equation 10–24 for $Q_w$, we obtain

$$Q_w = \frac{\forall X}{\theta_c X_r}$$

Note that $X_r$ is the microorganism concentration (MLVSS) in the sludge being wasted. As noted earlier $X_r$ differs from $X_r'$ by a constant factor. In this case the ratio of MLSS/MLVSS is given so we can estimate $X_r$ as

$$X_r = \frac{X_r'}{1.43} = \frac{10{,}000 \, \text{mg} \cdot \text{L}^{-1}}{1.43} = 6993 \, \text{mg} \cdot \text{L}^{-1}$$

Now using the data from Example 10–4, we can compute $Q_w$.

$$Q_w = \frac{(970 \, \text{m}^3)(2000 \, \text{mg} \cdot \text{L}^{-1})}{(5 \, \text{days})(6993 \, \text{mg} \cdot \text{L}^{-1})} = 55.48 \, \text{m}^3 \cdot \text{day}^{-1}$$

To compute the return sludge flow rate, we convert the wastewater flow rate to units of cubic meters per day and determine the anticipated concentration of the MLSS using the ratio of MLSS/MLVSS.

$$Q = (0.150 \, \text{m}^3 \cdot \text{s}^{-1})(86{,}400 \, \text{s} \cdot \text{day}^{-1}) = 12{,}960 \, \text{m}^3 \cdot \text{day}^{-1}$$

and

$$\text{MLSS} = 1.43(2000 \, \text{mg} \cdot \text{L}^{-1}) = 2860 \, \text{mg} \cdot \text{L}^{-1}$$

Noting that $1 \, \text{mg} \cdot \text{L}^{-1} = 1 \, \text{g} \cdot \text{m}^{-3}$, the return sludge concentration is $10{,}000 \, \text{mg} \cdot \text{L}^{-1}$ and ignoring the effluent suspended solids, the return sludge flow rate is then

$$Q_r = \frac{(12{,}960 \, \text{m}^3 \cdot \text{day}^{-1})(2860 \, \text{g} \cdot \text{m}^{-3}) - (55.48 \, \text{m}^3 \cdot \text{day}^{-1})(10{,}000 \, \text{g} \cdot \text{m}^{-3})}{10{,}000 \, \text{g} \cdot \text{m}^{-3} - 2860 \, \text{g} \cdot \text{m}^{-3}}$$

$$= 5113, \text{ or } 5000 \, \text{m}^3 \cdot \text{day}^{-1}$$

**Sludge Production.**   The activated sludge process removes substrate, which exerts an oxygen demand by converting the food into new cell material and degrading this substrate while generating energy. This cell material ultimately becomes sludge, which must be disposed of. Despite the problems in doing so, researchers have attempted to develop enough basic information on sludge production to permit a reliable design basis. Heukelekian and Sawyer both reported that a net yield of 0.5 kg MLVSS $\cdot$ kg$^{-1}$ BOD$_5$ removed could be expected for a completely soluble organic substrate [11]. Most researchers agree that, depending on the inert solids in the system and the SRT, 0.40–0.60 kg MLVSS $\cdot$ kg$^{-1}$ BOD$_5$ removed will normally be observed.

The amount of sludge that must be wasted each day is the difference between the amount of increase in sludge mass and the suspended solids (SS) lost in the effluent.

$$\text{Mass to be wasted} = \text{increase in MLSS} - \text{SS lost in effluent} \tag{10–35}$$

The net activated sludge produced each day is determined by

$$Y_{obs} = \frac{Y}{1 + k_d\theta_c} \tag{10–36}$$

and

$$P_x = Y_{obs}Q(S_0 - S)(10^{-3} \text{ kg} \cdot \text{g}^{-1}) \tag{10–37}$$

where $P_x$ = net waste activated sludge produced each day in terms of VSS (in kg $\cdot$ day$^{-1}$)
     $Y_{obs}$ = observed yield (in kg MLVSS $\cdot$ kg$^{-1}$ BOD$_5$ removed)

Other terms are as defined previously.

The increase in MLSS may be estimated by assuming that VSS is some fraction of MLSS. It is generally assumed that VSS is 60–80% of MLVSS. Thus, the increase in MLSS in Equation 10–37 may be estimated by dividing $P_x$ by a factor of 0.6–0.8 (or multiplying by 1.25–1.667). The mass of suspended solids lost in the effluent is the product of the flow rate ($Q - Q_w$) and the suspended solids concentration ($X_e$).

**EXAMPLE 10–8**   Estimate the mass of sludge to be wasted each day from the new activated sludge plant at Gatesville (Examples 10–4 and 10–7).

Solution   Using the data from Example 10–4, calculate $Y_{obs}$.

$$Y_{obs} = \frac{0.50 \text{ kg VSS} \cdot \text{kg}^{-1} \text{ BOD}_5 \text{ removed}}{1 + [(0.050 \text{ day}^{-1})(5 \text{ days})]} = 0.40 \text{ kg VSS} \cdot \text{kg}^{-1} \text{ BOD}_5 \text{ removed}$$

The net waste activated sludge produced each day is

$$P_x = (0.40)(0.150 \text{ m}^3 \cdot \text{s}^{-1})(84.0 \text{ g} \cdot \text{m}^{-3} - 11.1 \text{ g} \cdot \text{m}^{-3})(86,400 \text{ s} \cdot \text{day}^{-1})(10^{-3} \text{ kg} \cdot \text{g}^{-1})$$

$$= 377.9 \text{ kg} \cdot \text{day}^{-1} \text{ of VSS}$$

The total mass produced includes inert materials. Using the relationship between MLSS and MLVSS in Example 10–7, we obtain

$$\text{Increase in MLSS} = (1.43)(377.9 \text{ kg} \cdot \text{day}^{-1}) = 540.4 \text{ kg} \cdot \text{day}^{-1}$$

The mass of solids (both volatile and inert) lost in the effluent is

$$(Q - Q_w)(X_e) = (0.150 \text{ m}^3 \cdot \text{s}^{-1} - 0.000642 \text{ m}^3 \cdot \text{s}^{-1})(30 \text{ g} \cdot \text{m}^{-3})(86,400 \text{ s} \cdot \text{day}^{-1})$$

$$\times (10^{-3} \text{ kg} \cdot \text{g}^{-1})$$

$$= 387.13, \text{ or } 390 \text{ kg} \cdot \text{day}^{-1}$$

The mass to be wasted is then

Mass to be wasted $= 540.4 - 387.13 = 153.27$, or $150$ kg $\cdot$ day$^{-1}$

Note that this mass is calculated as dry solids. Because the sludge is mostly water, the actual mass will be considerably larger.

**Oxygen Demand.** Oxygen is used in those reactions required to degrade the substrate to produce the energy required for cell synthesis and for respiration. For long SRT systems, the oxygen needed for cell maintenance can be of the same order of magnitude as substrate metabolism. A minimum residual of 0.5 to 2 mg $\cdot$ L$^{-1}$ DO is usually maintained in the reactor basin to prevent oxygen deficiencies from limiting the rate of substrate removal.

An estimate of the oxygen requirements may be made from the BOD$_5$ of the waste and amount of activated sludge wasted each day. If we assume all of the BOD$_5$ is converted to end products, the total oxygen demand can be computed by converting BOD$_5$ to BOD$_L$. Because a portion of waste is converted to new cells that are wasted, the BOD$_L$ of the wasted cells must be subtracted from the total oxygen demand. An approximation of the oxygen demand of the wasted cells may be made by assuming cell oxidation can be described by the following reaction:

$$C_5H_7NO_2 + 5O_2 \rightleftharpoons 5CO_2 + 2H_2O + NH_3 + \text{energy cells} \tag{10-38}$$

The ratio of gram molecular weights is

$$\frac{\text{Oxygen}}{\text{Cells}} = \frac{5(32)}{113} = 1.42 \tag{10-39}$$

Thus the oxygen demand of the waste activated sludge may be estimated as $1.42(P_x)$

The mass of oxygen required may be estimated as

$$M_{O_2} = \frac{Q(S_0 - S)(10^{-3} \text{ kg} \cdot \text{g}^{-1})}{f} - 1.42(P_x) \tag{10-40}$$

where $Q =$ wastewater flow rate into the aeration tank (in m$^3 \cdot$ day$^{-1}$)
$S_0 =$ influent soluble BOD$_5$ (in mg $\cdot$ L$^{-1}$)
$S =$ effluent soluble BOD$_5$ (in mg $\cdot$ L$^{-1}$)
$f =$ conversion factor for converting BOD$_5$ to ultimate BOD$_L$
$P_x =$ waste activated sludge produced (see Equation 10–37)

The volume of air to be supplied must take into account the percent of air that is oxygen and the transfer efficiency of the dissolution of oxygen into the wastewater.

**EXAMPLE 10–9**  Estimate the volume of air to be supplied (m$^3 \cdot$ day$^{-1}$) for the new activated sludge plant at Gatesville (Examples 10–4 and 10–8). Assume that BOD$_5$ is 68% of the ultimate BOD and that the oxygen transfer efficiency is 8%.

**Solution**  Using the data from Examples 10–4 and 10–8, we see that

$$M_{O_2} = \frac{(0.150 \text{ m}^3 \cdot \text{s}^{-1})(84.0 \text{ g} \cdot \text{m}^{-3} - 11.1 \text{ g} \cdot \text{m}^{-3})(86{,}400 \text{ s} \cdot \text{day}^{-1})(10^{-3} \text{ kg} \cdot \text{g}^{-1})}{0.68}$$

$$- 1.42(377.9 \text{ kg} \cdot \text{day}^{-1} \text{ of VSS})$$

$$= 1389.4 - 536.6 = 852.8 \text{ kg} \cdot \text{day}^{-1} \text{ of oxygen}$$

From Table A–5 in Appendix A, air has a density of $1.185 \text{ kg} \cdot \text{m}^{-3}$ at standard conditions. By mass, air contains about 23.2% oxygen. At 100% transfer efficiency, the volume of air required is

$$\frac{852.8 \text{ kg} \cdot \text{day}^{-1}}{(1.185 \text{ kg} \cdot \text{m}^{-3})(0.232)} = 3101.99, \text{ or } 3100 \text{ m}^3 \cdot \text{day}^{-1}$$

At 8% transfer efficiency, we get

$$\frac{3101.99 \text{ m}^3 \cdot \text{day}^{-1}}{0.08} = 38,774.9, \text{ or } 38,000 \text{ m}^3 \cdot \text{day}^{-1}$$

**Process Design Considerations.**   The SRT selected for design is a function of the degree of treatment required. A high SRT (or older sludge age) results in a higher quantity of solids being carried in the system and creates a higher degree of treatment. A long SRT also results in the production of less waste sludge.

If industrial wastes are discharged to the municipal system, several additional concerns must be addressed. Municipal wastewater generally contains sufficient nitrogen and phosphorus to support biological growth. The presence of large volumes of industrial wastewater that is deficient in either of these nutrients will result in poor removal efficiencies. Addition of supplemental nitrogen and phosphorus may be required. The ratio of nitrogen to $BOD_5$ should be 1:32. The ratio of phosphorus to $BOD_5$ should be 1:150.

Although toxic metals and organic constituents may be at low enough levels that they do not interfere with the operation of the plant, two other untoward effects may result if they are not excluded in a pretreatment program. Volatile organic compounds may be stripped from solution into the atmosphere in the aeration tank. Thus, the WWTP may become a source of air pollution. The toxic metals may precipitate into the waste sludges. Thus, otherwise nonhazardous sludges may be rendered hazardous.

Oil and grease that pass through the primary treatment system will form grease balls on the surface of the aeration tank. The microorganisms cannot degrade this material because it is not in the water where they can physically come in contact with it. Special consideration should be given to the surface-skimming equipment in the secondary clarifier to handle the grease balls.

**Secondary Clarifier Design Considerations.**   Although the secondary settling tank is an integral part of both the trickling filter and the activated sludge process, environmental engineers have focused particular attention on the secondary clarifier used after the activated sludge process. A secondary clarifier is important because of the high solids loading and fluffy nature of the activated sludge biological floc. Also, it is highly desirable that sludge recycle be well thickened. Secondary settling tanks for activated sludge are generally characterized as having type III settling. Some authors would argue that types I and II also occur.

One of the continuing difficulties with the design of secondary settling tanks is accurately predicting effluent suspended solids concentrations as a function of common design and operating parameters. Little theoretical work has been conducted, and empirical correlations have been less than satisfactory.

### Oxidation Ponds

Treatment ponds have been used to treat wastewater for many years, particularly as wastewater treatment systems for small communities [12]. Many terms have been used to describe the different types of systems employed in wastewater treatment. For example, in recent years, *oxidation pond* has been widely used as a collective term for all types of ponds. Originally, an **oxidation pond** was a pond that received partially treated wastewater, whereas a pond that received raw wastewater was known as a sewage lagoon. **Waste stabilization pond** has been used as an all-inclusive term that refers to a pond or lagoon used to treat organic waste by biological and physical processes. These processes would commonly be referred to as self-purification if they took place in a stream. To avoid confusion, we will use the following classification [13].

1. **Aerobic ponds:** Shallow ponds, less than 1 m in depth, where dissolved oxygen is maintained throughout the entire depth, mainly by the action of photosynthesis
2. **Facultative ponds:** Ponds 1–2.5 m deep, which have an anaerobic lower zone, a facultative middle zone, and an aerobic upper zone maintained by photosynthesis and surface reaeration
3. **Anaerobic ponds:** Deep ponds that receive high organic loadings such that anaerobic conditions prevail throughout the entire pond depth
4. **Maturation, or tertiary, ponds:** Ponds used for polishing effluents from other biological processes. Dissolved oxygen is furnished through photosynthesis and surface reaeration. This type of pond is also known as a **polishing pond**
5. **Aerated lagoons:** Ponds oxygenated through the action of surface or diffused air aeration

**Aerobic Ponds.** The aerobic pond is a shallow pond in which light penetrates to the bottom, thereby maintaining active algal photosynthesis throughout the entire system. During the daylight hours, large amounts of oxygen are supplied by the photosynthesis process; during the hours of darkness, wind mixing of the shallow water mass generally provides a high degree of surface reaeration. Stabilization of the organic material entering an aerobic pond is accomplished mainly through the action of aerobic bacteria.

**Anaerobic Ponds.** The magnitude of the organic loading and the availability of dissolved oxygen determine whether the biological activity in a treatment pond will occur under aerobic or anaerobic conditions. A pond may be maintained in an anaerobic condition by applying a $BOD_5$ load that exceeds oxygen production from photosynthesis. Photosynthesis can be reduced by decreasing the surface area and increasing the depth. Anaerobic ponds become turbid from the presence of reduced metal sulfides. This restricts light penetration to the point that algal growth becomes negligible. Anaerobic treatment of complex wastes involves two distinct stages. In the first stage (known as **acid fermentation**), complex organic materials are broken down mainly to short-chain acids and alcohols. In the second stage (known as **methane fermentation**), these materials are convened to gases, primarily methane and carbon dioxide. The proper design of anaerobic ponds must result in environmental conditions favorable to methane fermentation. Anaerobic ponds are used primarily as a pretreatment process and are particularly suited for the treatment of high-temperature, high-strength wastewaters. However, they have been used successfully to treat municipal wastewaters as well.

**Facultative Ponds.** Of the five general classes of lagoons and ponds, facultative ponds are by far the most common type selected as wastewater treatment systems for small communities. Approximately 25% of the municipal wastewater treatment plants in this country are ponds, and about 90% of these ponds are located in communities of 5000 people or fewer. Facultative ponds are popular for such treatment situations because long retention times facilitate the management of large fluctuations in wastewater flow and strength with no significant effect on effluent quality. Also capital, operating, and maintenance costs are less than those of other biological systems that provide equivalent treatment.

A schematic representation of a facultative pond operation is given in Figure 10–17. Raw wastewater enters at the center of the pond. Suspended solids contained in the wastewater settle to the pond bottom, where an anaerobic layer develops. Microorganisms occupying this region do not require molecular oxygen as an electron acceptor in energy metabolism but rather use some other chemical species. Both acid fermentation and methane fermentation occur in the bottom sludge deposits.

**FIGURE 10–17**

Schematic diagram of facultative pond relationships.

The facultative zone exists just above the anaerobic zone. This means that molecular oxygen will not be available in the region at all times. Generally, the zone is aerobic during the daylight hours and anaerobic during the hours of darkness.

Above the facultative zone, an aerobic zone exists that has molecular oxygen present at all times. The oxygen is supplied from two sources. A limited amount is supplied from diffusion across the pond surface; however, the majority is supplied through the action of algal photosynthesis.

Two rules of thumb commonly used in Michigan in evaluating the design of facultative lagoons are as follows:

1. The $BOD_5$ loading rate should not exceed $22 \; kg \cdot ha^{-1} \cdot day^{-1}$ on the smallest lagoon cell.
2. The detention time in the lagoon (considering the total volume of all cells but excluding the bottom 0.6 m in the volume calculation) should be 6 months.

The first criterion is to prevent the pond from becoming anaerobic. The second criterion is to provide enough storage to hold the wastewater during winter months when the receiving stream may be frozen or during the summer when the flow in the stream might be too low to absorb even a small amount of BOD.

### Rotating Biological Contactors

The **rotating biological contactor** (RBC) process consists of a series of closely spaced discs (3–3.5 m in diameter) mounted on a horizontal shaft and rotated while about one-half of their surface area is immersed in wastewater (Figure 10–18). The discs are typically constructed of light-weight plastic. The speed of rotation of the discs is adjustable.

When the process is placed in operation, the microbes in the wastewater begin to adhere to the rotating surfaces and grow there until the entire surface area of the discs is covered with a 1–3-mm layer of biological slime. As the discs rotate, they carry a film of wastewater into the air; this wastewater trickles down the surface of the discs, absorbing oxygen. As the discs complete their rotation, the film of water mixes with the reservoir of wastewater, adding to the oxygen in the reservoir and mixing the treated and partially treated wastewater. As the attached microbes pass through the reservoir, they absorb other organic compounds for breakdown. The excess growth of microbes is sheared from the discs as they move through the reservoir. These dislodged organisms are kept in suspension by the moving discs. Thus, the discs serve several purposes:

1. They provide media for the buildup of attached microbial growth.
2. They bring the growth into contact with the wastewater.
3. They aerate the wastewater and the suspended microbial growth in the reservoir.

**FIGURE 10–18**

Photo of RBC and
diagram of RBC treatment
system. (*Courtesy of
Waker Process
Equipment, Division of
McNish Corporation.*)

The attached growths are similar in concept to a trickling filter, except the microbes are
passed through the wastewater rather than the wastewater passing over the microbes. Some of the
advantages of both the trickling filter and activated sludge processes are realized.

As the treated wastewater flows from the reservoir below the discs, it carries the suspended
growths out to a downstream settling basin for removal. The process can achieve secondary effluent quality or better. By placing several sets of discs in series, it is possible to achieve even
higher degrees of treatment, including biological conversion of ammonia to nitrates.

## 10–8   DISINFECTION

The last treatment step in a secondary plant is the addition of a disinfectant to the treated wastewater. The addition of chlorine gas or some other form of chlorine is the process most commonly
used for wastewater disinfection in the United States. The chemistry of chlorine reactions and
by-products discussed in Chapter 9 also apply to wastewater disinfection. Chlorine is injected
into the wastewater by automated feeding systems. Wastewater then flows into a basin, where it
is held for about 15 min to allow the chlorine to react with the pathogens.

There is concern that wastewater disinfection may do more harm than good. Early U.S. EPA
rules calling for disinfection to achieve 200 fecal coliforms per 100 mL of wastewater have been
modified to a requirement for disinfection only during the summer season when people may
come into contact with contaminated water. There were three reasons for this change. The first
was that the use of chlorine and, perhaps, ozone causes the formation of organic compounds that

are carcinogenic. The second was the finding that the disinfection process was more effective in killing the predators to cysts and viruses than it was in killing the pathogens themselves. The net result was that the pathogens survived longer in the natural environment because there were fewer predators. The third reason was that chlorine and, in particular, the chloramines formed in reactions with ammonia, are very toxic to fish.

Dechlorination reduces the effects of using chlorine as a disinfectant. Other processes such as ultraviolet light may be used in place of chlorine.

## 10–9   ADVANCED WASTEWATER TREATMENT

Although secondary treatment processes, when coupled with disinfection, may remove over 85% of the BOD and suspended solids and nearly all pathogens, only minor removal of some pollutants, such as nitrogen, phosphorus, soluble COD, and heavy metals, is achieved. In some circumstances, these pollutants may be of major concern. In these cases, processes capable of removing pollutants not adequately removed by secondary treatment are used in what is called tertiary wastewater treatment, or advanced wastewater treatment (AWT). The following sections describe available AWT processes. In addition to solving tough pollution problems, these processes improve the effluent quality to the point that it is adequate for many reuse purposes, and may convert what was originally a wastewater into a valuable resource too good to throw away.

### Filtration

Secondary treatment processes, such as the activated sludge process, are highly efficient for removal of biodegradable colloidal and soluble organics. However, the typical effluent contains a much higher $BOD_5$ than would be expected from theory. The typical BOD is approximately $20$–$50$ mg $\cdot$ L$^{-1}$. This is principally because the secondary clarifiers are not perfectly efficient at settling out the microorganisms from the biological treatment processes. These organisms contribute both to the suspended solids and to the $BOD_5$ because the process of biological decay of dead cells exerts an oxygen demand.

By using a filtration process similar to that used in water treatment plants, it is possible to remove the residual suspended solids, including the unsettled microorganisms. Removing the microorganisms also reduces the residual $BOD_5$. Conventional sand filters identical to those used in water treatment can be used, but they often clog quickly, thus requiring frequent backwashing. To lengthen filter runs and reduce backwashing, it is desirable to have the larger filter grain sizes at the top of the filter. This arrangement allows some of the larger particles of biological floc to be trapped at the surface without plugging the filter. Multimedia filters accomplish this by using low-density coal for the large grain sizes, medium-density sand for intermediate sizes, and high-density garnet for the smallest size filter grains. Thus, during backwashing, the greater density offsets the smaller diameter so that the coal remains on top, the sand remains in the middle, and the garnet remains on the bottom.

Typically, plain filtration can reduce activated sludge effluent suspended solids from 25 to 10 mg $\cdot$ L$^{-1}$. Plain filtration is not as effective on trickling filter effluents because these effluents contain more dispersed growth. However, the use of coagulation and sedimentation followed by filtration can yield suspended solids concentrations that are virtually zero. Typically, filtration can achieve 80% suspended solids reduction for activated sludge effluent and 70% reduction for trickling filter effluent.

### Carbon Adsorption

Even after secondary treatment, coagulation, sedimentation, and filtration, soluble organic materials that are resistant to biological breakdown may persist in the effluent. The persistent materials are often referred to as **refractory organic compounds.** Refractory organic compounds can be detected in the effluent as soluble COD. Secondary effluent COD values are often $30\text{–}60 \text{ mg} \cdot \text{L}^{-1}$.

The most practical available method for removing refractory organic compounds is by adsorbing them on activated carbon [14]. Adsorption is the accumulation of materials at an interface. The interface, in the case of wastewater and activated carbon, is the liquid–solid boundary layer. Organic materials accumulate at the interface because of physical binding of the molecules to the solid surface. Carbon is activated by heating in the absence of oxygen. The activation process results in the formation of many pores within each carbon particle. Because adsorption is a surface phenomenon, the greater the surface area of the carbon, the greater its capacity to hold organic material. The vast areas of the walls within these pores account for most of the total surface area of the carbon, which makes it so effective in removing organic compounds.

After the adsorption capacity of the carbon has been exhausted, it can be restored by heating it in a furnace at a temperature sufficiently high to drive off the adsorbed organic material. Keeping oxygen at very low levels in the furnace prevents carbon from burning. The organic compounds are passed through an afterburner to prevent air pollution. In small plants where the cost of an on-site regeneration furnace cannot be justified, the spent carbon is shipped to a central regeneration facility for processing.

### Phosphorus Removal

All the polyphosphates (molecularly dehydrated phosphates) gradually hydrolyze in aqueous solution and revert to the ortho form ($PO_4^{3-}$) from which they were derived. For example, tetrasodium pyrophosphate ($Na_4P_2O_7$) hydrolyzes in aqueous solution to form monohydrogen phosphate ($HPO_4^{2-}$) typically found in wastewater.

$$Na_4P_2O_7 + H_2O \rightleftharpoons 2Na_2HPO_4 \qquad (10\text{–}41)$$

The removal of phosphorus to prevent or reduce eutrophication is typically accomplished by chemical precipitation using one of three compounds. The precipitation reactions for each are shown here.

Using ferric chloride:

$$FeCl_3 + HPO_4^{2-} \rightleftharpoons FePO_4 \downarrow + H^+ + 3Cl^- \qquad (10\text{–}42)$$

Using alum:

$$Al_2(SO_4)_3 + 2HPO_4^{2-} \rightleftharpoons 2AlPO_4 \downarrow + 2H^+ + 3SO_4^{2-} \qquad (10\text{–}43)$$

Using lime:

$$5Ca(OH)_2 + 3HPO_4^{2-} \rightleftharpoons Ca_5(PO_4)_3OH \downarrow + 3H_2O + 6OH^- \qquad (10\text{–}44)$$

You should note that ferric chloride and alum reduce the pH, whereas lime increases it. The effective range of pH for alum and ferric chloride is between 5.5 and 7.0. If there is not enough naturally occurring alkalinity to buffer the system to this range, then lime must be added to counteract the formation of $H^+$.

The precipitation of phosphorus requires a reaction basin and a settling tank to remove the precipitate. When ferric chloride and alum are used, the chemicals may be added directly to the aeration tank in the activated sludge system. Thus, the aeration tank serves as a reaction basin. The precipitate is then removed in the secondary clarifier. This is not possible with lime because the high pH required to form the precipitate is detrimental to the activated sludge organisms. In some wastewater treatment plants, the $FeCl_3$ (or alum) is added before the wastewater enters the primary sedimentation tank. This improves the efficiency of the primary tank but may deprive the biological processes of needed nutrients.

**EXAMPLE 10–10**   If a wastewater has a soluble orthophosphate concentration of 4.00 mg · L$^{-1}$ as P, what theoretical amount of ferric chloride will be required to remove it completely?

Solution   From Equation 10–42, we see that one mole of ferric chloride is required for each mole of phosphorus to be removed. The pertinent gram molecular weights are as follows:

$FeCl_3 = 162.21$ g

$P = 30.97$ g

With a PO$_4$–P of 4.00 mg · L$^{-1}$, the theoretical amount of ferric chloride would be

$$4.00 \times \frac{162.21}{30.97} = 20.95, \text{ or } 21.0 \text{ mg} \cdot L^{-1}$$

Because of side reactions, solubility product limitations, and day-to-day variations, the actual amount of chemical to be added must be determined by jar tests on the wastewater. You can expect that the actual ferric chloride dose will be 1.5–3 times the theoretically calculated amount. Likewise, the actual alum dose will be 1.25–2.5 times the theoretical amount.

### Nitrogen Control

Nitrogen in any soluble form (NH$_3$, NH$_4^+$, NO$^-$ and NO$_3^-$, but not N$_2$ gas) is a nutrient and may need to be removed from wastewater to help control algal growth in the receiving body. In addition, nitrogen in the form of ammonia exerts an oxygen demand and can be toxic to fish. Removal of nitrogen can be accomplished either biologically or chemically. The biological process is called **nitrification–denitrification.** The chemical process is called **ammonia stripping.**

**Nitrification–Denitrification.**   The natural nitrification process can be forced to occur in the activated sludge system by maintaining a cell detention time ($\theta_c$) of 15 days in moderate climates and over 20 days in cold climates. The nitrification step is expressed in chemical terms as follows:

$$NH_4^+ + 2O_2 \rightleftharpoons NO_3^- + H_2O + 2H^+ \tag{10–45}$$

Of course, bacteria must be present to cause the reaction to occur. This step satisfies the oxygen demand of the ammonium ion. If the nitrogen level is not of concern for the receiving body, the wastewater can be discharged after settling. If nitrogen is of concern, the nitrification step must be followed by anoxic denitrification by bacteria:

$$2NO_3^- + \text{organic matter} \rightleftharpoons N_2 + CO_2 + H_2O \tag{10–46}$$

As indicated by the chemical reaction, organic matter is required for denitrification. Organic matter serves as an energy source for the bacteria. The organic matter may be obtained from within or outside the cell. In multistage nitrogen-removal systems, because the concentration of BOD$_5$ in the flow to the denitrification process is usually quite low, a supplemental organic carbon source is required for rapid denitrification. (BOD$_5$ concentration is low because the wastewater previously has undergone carbonaceous BOD removal and the nitrification process.) The organic matter may be either raw, settled sewage or a synthetic material such as methanol (CH$_3$OH). Raw, settled sewage may adversely affect the effluent quality by increasing the BOD$_5$ and ammonia content.

**Ammonia Stripping.**   Nitrogen in the form of ammonia can be removed chemically from water by raising the pH to convert the ammonium ion into ammonia, which can then be stripped from the water by passing large quantities of air through the water. The process has no effect on nitrate, so the activated sludge process must be operated at a short cell detention time to prevent nitrification. The ammonia stripping reaction is

$$NH_4^+ + OH^- \rightleftharpoons NH_3 + H_2O \tag{10-47}$$

The hydroxide is usually supplied by adding lime. The lime also reacts with $CO_2$ in the air and water to form a calcium carbonate scale, which must be removed periodically. Low temperatures cause problems with icing and reduced stripping ability. The reduced stripping ability is caused by the increased solubility of ammonia in cold water.

## 10-10  LAND TREATMENT

An alternative to the previously discussed AWT processes for producing an extremely high-quality effluent is offered by an approach called land treatment. Land treatment is the application of effluents, usually following secondary treatment, on the land by one of the several available conventional irrigation methods. This approach uses wastewater, and often the nutrients it contains, as a resource rather than considering it as a disposal problem. Treatment is provided by natural processes as the effluent moves through the natural filter provided by soil and plants. Part of the wastewater is lost by evapotranspiration, and the remainder returns to the hydrologic cycle through overland flow or the groundwater system. Most of the groundwater eventually returns, directly or indirectly, to the surface water system.

Land treatment of wastewaters can provide moisture and nutrients necessary for crop growth. In semiarid areas, insufficient moisture for peak crop growth and limited water supplies make this water especially valuable. The primary nutrients (nitrogen, phosphorus, and potassium) are reduced only slightly in conventional secondary treatment processes, so that most of these elements are still present in secondary effluent. Soil nutrients that are consumed each year by crop removal and by losses through soil erosion may be replaced by the application of wastewater. Land application is the oldest method used for treatment and disposal of wastes. Cities have used this method for more than 400 years. Several major cities, including Berlin, Melbourne, and Paris, have used "sewage farms" for at least 60 years for waste treatment and disposal. Approximately 600 communities in the United States reuse municipal wastewater treatment plant effluent in surface irrigation.

Land treatment systems use one of the three basic approaches [15]:

1. Slow rate
2. Overland flow
3. Rapid infiltration

Each method, shown schematically in Figure 10–19, can produce renovated water of different quality, can be adapted to different site conditions, and can satisfy different overall objectives.

### Slow Rate

Irrigation, the predominant land application method in use today, involves the application of effluent to the land for treatment and for meeting the growth needs of plants. The applied effluent is treated by physical, chemical, and biological means as it seeps into the soil. Effluent can be applied to crops or vegetation (including forest land) either by sprinkling or by surface techniques, for purposes such as

1. Avoidance of surface discharge of nutrients
2. Economic return from use of water and nutrients to produce marketable crops
3. Water conservation by exchange when lawns, parks, or golf courses are irrigated
4. Preservation and enlargement of greenbelts and open space

Where water for irrigation is valuable, crops can be irrigated at consumptive use rates ($3.5$–$10 \ \text{mm} \cdot \text{day}^{-1}$, depending on the crop), and the economic return from the sale of the crop can

**FIGURE 10–19**

Methods of land application. (*Source:* U.S. Environmental Protection Agency, *Land Treatment of Municipal Wastewater, Design Factors I,* U.S. Government Printing Office, Washington, DC, Jan., 1976.)

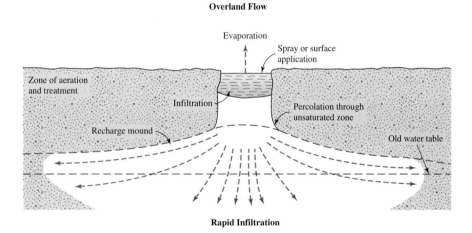

be balanced against the increased cost of the land and distribution system. On the other hand, where water for irrigation is of little value, hydraulic loadings can be maximized (provided that renovated water quality criteria are met), thereby minimizing system costs. Under high-rate irrigation ($10\text{–}15 \text{ mm} \cdot \text{day}^{-1}$), water-tolerant grasses with high nutrient uptake become the crop of choice.

### Overland Flow

Overland flow is a biological treatment process in which wastewater is applied over the upper reaches of sloped terraces and allowed to flow across the vegetated surface to runoff collection ditches. Renovation is accomplished by physical, chemical, and biological means as the wastewater flows in a thin sheet down the relatively impervious slope.

Overland flow can be used as a secondary treatment process where discharge of a nitrified effluent low in BOD is acceptable or as an advanced wastewater treatment process. The latter objective will allow higher rates of application ($18 \text{ mm} \cdot \text{day}^{-1}$ or more), depending on the degree of advanced wastewater treatment required. Where a surface discharge is prohibited, runoff can be recycled or applied to the land in irrigation or infiltration–percolation systems.

### Rapid Infiltration

In infiltration–percolation systems, effluent is applied to the soil at higher rates by spreading in basins or by sprinkling. Treatment occurs as the water passes through the soil matrix. System objectives can include

1. Groundwater recharge
2. Natural treatment followed by pumped withdrawal or the use of underdrains for recovery
3. Natural treatment where renovated water moves vertically and laterally in the soil and recharges a surface watercourse

Where groundwater quality is being degraded by salinity intrusion, groundwater recharge can reverse the hydraulic gradient and protect the existing groundwater. Where existing groundwater quality is not compatible with expected renovated quality, or where existing water rights control the discharge location, a return of renovated water to surface water can be designed, using pumped withdrawal, underdrains, or natural drainage. In Phoenix, Arizona, for example, the native groundwater quality is poor, and the renovated water is to be withdrawn by pumping, with discharge into an irrigation canal.

## 10–11  SLUDGE TREATMENT

In the process of purifying wastewater, another problem is created—sludge. The higher the degree of wastewater treatment, the larger the residue of sludge that must be handled. The exceptions to this rule are where land applications or polishing lagoons are used. Satisfactory treatment and disposal of the sludge can be the single most complex and costly operation in a municipal wastewater treatment system [14]. The sludge is made of materials settled from the raw wastewater and of solids generated in the wastewater treatment processes.

The quantities of sludge involved are significant. For primary treatment, they may be 0.25–0.35% by volume of wastewater treated. When treatment is upgraded to activated sludge, the quantities increase to 1.5 to 2.0% of this volume of water treated. Use of chemicals for phosphorus removal can add another 1.0%. The sludges withdrawn from the treatment processes are still largely water; as much as 97%. Sludge treatment processes, then, are concerned with separating the large amounts of water from the solid residues. The separated water is returned to the wastewater plant for processing.

### Sources and Characteristics of Various Sludges

Before we begin the discussion of the various treatment processes, it is worthwhile to recapitulate the sources and nature of the sludges that must be treated.

**Grit.**  The sand, broken glass, nuts, bolts, and other dense material that is collected in the grit chamber is not true sludge in the sense that it is not fluid. However, it still requires disposal. Because grit can be drained of water easily and is relatively stable in terms of biological activity (it is not biodegradable), it is generally trucked directly to a landfill without further treatment.

**Primary or Raw Sludge.**  Sludge from the bottom of the primary clarifiers contains 3–8% solids (1% solids = 1 g solids $\cdot$ 100 mL$^{-1}$ sludge volume), which is approximately 70% organic. This sludge rapidly becomes anaerobic and is highly odiferous.

**Secondary Sludge.**  This sludge consists of microorganisms and inert materials that have been wasted from the secondary treatment processes. Thus, the solids are about 90% organic. When the supply of air is removed, this sludge also becomes anaerobic, creating noxious conditions if not treated before disposal. The solids content depends on the source. Wasted activated sludge is typically 0.5–2% solids, whereas trickling filter sludge contains 2–5% solids. In some cases, secondary sludges contain large quantities of chemical precipitates because the aeration tank is used as the reaction basin for the addition of chemicals to remove phosphorus.

**Tertiary Sludges.** The characteristics of sludges from the tertiary treatment processes depend on the nature of the process. For example, phosphorus removal results in a chemical sludge that is difficult to handle and treat. When phosphorus removal occurs in the activated sludge process, the chemical sludge is combined with the biological sludge, making the latter more difficult to treat. Nitrogen removal by denitrification results in a biological sludge with properties very similar to those of waste activated sludge.

### Solids Computations

Because most WWTP sludges are primarily water, the volume of the sludge is primarily a function of the water content. Thus, if we know the percent solids and the specific gravity of the solids, we can estimate the volume of the sludge. The solid matter in wastewater sludge is composed of fixed (mineral) solids and volatile (organic) solids. The volume of the total mass of solids may be expressed as

$$\Psi_{solids} = \frac{M_s}{S_s \rho} \qquad (10\text{-}48)$$

where $M_s$ = mass of solids (in kg)
$S_s$ = specific gravity of solids
$\rho$ = density of water = $1000 \text{ kg} \cdot \text{m}^{-3}$

Because the total mass is composed of fixed and volatile fractions, Equation 10–48 may be rewritten as

$$\frac{M_s}{S_s \rho} = \frac{M_f}{S_f \rho} + \frac{M_v}{S_v \rho} \qquad (10\text{-}49)$$

where $M_f$ = mass of fixed solids (in kg)
$M_v$ = mass of volatile solids (in kg)
$S_f$ = specific gravity of fixed solids
$S_v$ = specific gravity of volatile solids

The specific gravity of the solids may be expressed in terms of the specific gravities of the fixed and solid fractions by solving Equation 10–49 for $S_s$.

$$S_s = M_s \left( \frac{S_f S_v}{M_f S_v + M_v S_f} \right) \qquad (10\text{-}50)$$

The specific gravity of sludge ($S_{sl}$) may be estimated by recognizing that, in a similar fashion to the fractions of solids, the sludge is composed of solids and water so that

$$\frac{M_{sl}}{S_{sl} \rho} = \frac{M_s}{S_s \rho} + \frac{M_w}{S_w \rho} \qquad (10\text{-}51)$$

where $M_{sl}$ = mass of sludge (in kg)
$M_w$ = mass of water (in kg)
$S_{sl}$ = specific gravity of sludge
$S_w$ = specific gravity of water

It is customary to report solids concentrations as percent solids, where the fraction of solids ($P_s$) is computed as

$$P_s = \frac{M_s}{M_s + M_w} \qquad (10\text{-}52)$$

and the fraction of water $(P_w)$ is computed as

$$P_w = \frac{M_w}{M_s + M_w} \qquad (10\text{--}53)$$

Thus, it is more convenient to solve Equation 10–48 in terms of percent solids. If we divide each term in Equation 10–51 by $(M_s + M_w)$ and recognize that $M_{sl} = M_s + M_w$, then Equation 10–51 may be expressed as

$$\frac{1}{S_{sl}\rho} = \frac{P_s}{S_s\rho} + \frac{P_w}{S_w\rho} \qquad (10\text{--}54)$$

If the specific gravity of water is taken as 1.0000, as it can be without appreciable error; then solving for $S_{sl}$ yields

$$S_{sl} = \frac{S_s}{P_s + (S_s)(P_w)} \qquad (10\text{--}55)$$

With these expressions you can calculate the volume of sludge $(\forall_{sl})$ with the following equation.

$$\forall_{sl} = \frac{M_s}{(\rho)(S_{sl})(P_s)} \qquad (10\text{--}56)$$

**EXAMPLE 10-11**   Using the following primary settling tank data, determine the daily sludge production.

*Operating Data*
Flow $= 0.150 \text{ m}^3 \cdot \text{s}^{-1}$
Influent suspended solids $= 280.0 \text{ mg} \cdot \text{L}^{-1} = 280.0 \text{ g} \cdot \text{m}^{-3}$
Removal efficiency $= 59.0\%$
Sludge concentration $= 5.00\%$
Volatile solids $= 60.0\%$
Specific gravity of volatile solids $= 0.990$
Fixed solids $= 40.0\%$
Specific gravity of fixed solids $= 2.65$

Solution   We begin by calculating $S_s$. We can do this without calculating $M_s$, $M_f$, and $M_v$ directly by recognizing that they are proportional to the percent composition.
  With

$$M_s = M_f + M_v$$

$$= 0.400 + 0.600 = 1.00$$

Then Equation 10–50 gives the following:

$$S_s = \frac{(2.65)(0.990)}{[(0.990)(0.400)] + [(2.65)(0.600)]}$$

$$= 1.321, \text{ or } 1.32$$

The specific gravity of the sludge is calculated with Equation 10–55.

$$S_{sl} = \frac{1.321}{0.05 + [(1.321)(0.950)]}$$

$$= 1.012, \text{ or } 1.01$$

The mass of the sludge is estimated from the incoming suspended solids concentration and the removal efficiency of the primary tank.

$$M_s = 0.59 \times 280.0 \text{ mg} \cdot \text{L}^{-1} \times 0.15 \text{ m}^3 \cdot \text{s}^{-1} \times 86{,}400 \text{ s} \cdot \text{day}^{-1} \times 10^{-3} \text{ kg} \cdot \text{g}^{-1}$$

$$= 2.14 \times 10^3 \text{ kg} \cdot \text{day}^{-1}$$

The sludge volume is then calculated with Equation 10–56.

$$\forall_{sl} = \frac{2.14 \times 10^3 \text{ kg} \cdot \text{day}^{-1}}{1000 \text{ kg} \cdot \text{m}^{-3} \times 1.012 \times 0.05}$$

$$= 42.29, \text{ or } 42.3 \text{ m}^3 \cdot \text{day}^{-1}$$

### Sludge Treatment Processes

The basic processes for sludge treatment are

1. *Thickening:* Separating as much water as possible by gravity or flotation.
2. *Stabilization:* Converting the organic solids to more refractory (inert) forms so that they can be handled or used as soil conditioners without causing a nuisance or health hazard through processes referred to as "digestion." (These are biochemical oxidation processes.)
3. *Conditioning:* Treating the sludge with chemicals or heat so that the water can be readily separated.
4. *Dewatering:* Separating water by subjecting the sludge to vacuum, pressure, or drying.
5. *Reduction:* Convening the solids to a stable form by wet oxidation or incineration. (These are chemical oxidation processes; they decrease the volume of sludge, hence the term reduction.)

Although a large number of alternative combinations of equipment and processes are used for treating sludges, the basic alternatives are fairly limited. The ultimate depository of the materials contained in the sludge must either be land, air, or water. Current policies discourage practices such as ocean dumping of sludge. Air pollution considerations necessitate air pollution control facilities as part of the sludge incineration process.

**Thickening.** Thickening is usually accomplished in one of two ways: the solids are floated to the top of the liquid (**flotation**) or are allowed to settle to the bottom (**gravity thickening**). The goal is to remove as much water as possible before final dewatering or digestion of the sludge. The processes involved offer a low-cost means of reducing sludge volumes by a factor of 2 or more. The costs of thickening are usually more than offset by the resulting savings in the size and cost of downstream sludge-processing equipment.

In the flotation thickening process (Figure 10–20) air is injected into the sludge under pressure (275–550 kPa). Under this pressure, a large amount of air can be dissolved in the sludge. The

**FIGURE 10–20**

Air flotation thickener. (*Source:* Reprinted with permission, from: Davis, M.C. and D. A. Cornwell, *Introduction to Environmental Engineering*, 3rd Ed., McGraw-Hill, New York, 1998.)

sludge then flows into an open tank where, at atmospheric pressure, much of the air comes out of solution as minute bubbles. The bubbles attach themselves to particles of sludge solids and float them to the surface. The sludge forms a layer at the top of the tank; this layer is removed by a skimming mechanism for further processing. The process typically increases the solids content of activated sludge from 0.5–1% to 3–6%. Flotation is especially effective on activated sludge, which is difficult to thicken by gravity.

Gravity thickening is a simple and inexpensive process that has been used widely on primary sludges for many years. It is a sedimentation process similar to that which occurs in all settling tanks. Sludge flows into a tank that is very similar in appearance to the circular clarifiers used in primary and secondary sedimentation; the solids are allowed to settle to the bottom where a heavy-duty mechanism scrapes them to a hopper from which they are withdrawn for further processing. The type of sludge being thickened has a major effect on performance. The best results are obtained with purely primary sludges. As the proportion of activated sludge increases, the thickness of settled sludge solids decreases. Purely primary sludges can be thickened from 1–3% to 10% solids. The current trend is toward using gravity thickening for primary sludges and flotation thickening for activated sludges, and then blending the thickened sludges for further processing.

**EXAMPLE 10–12**

One hundred cubic meters (100.0 m$^3$) of mixed sludge at 4.0% solids is to be thickened to 8.0% solids. Assuming that the specific gravity is not appreciably different from that of water and that it does not change during thickening, what is the approximate volume of the sludge after thickening?

Solution

A 4.0% sludge contains 4.0% by mass of solids and 96.0% water by mass. We can approximate the relationship between volume and percent solids based on a mass balance around the thickener. The mass-balance diagram appears as follows:

The mass-balance equation is then

$$C_1 V_1 - C_2 V_2 - C_3 V_3 = 0$$

If we assume the supernatant concentration ($C_3$) is much less than the influent and effluent concentrations ($C_1$ and $C_2$), then we can make the assumption that $C_3 = 0$. Then

$$C_1 V_1 = C_2 V_2$$

and

$$V_2 = \frac{C_1 V_1}{C_2}$$

In this case then, the volume of sludge after thickening would be

$$V_2 = \frac{(0.040)(100.0 \text{ m}^3)}{0.080} = 50.0 \text{ m}^3$$

Thus, we can see a substantial reduction in the volume that must be handled by thickening the sludge from 4 to 8% solids.

**Stabilization.**   The principal purposes of sludge stabilization are to break down the organic solids biochemically so that they are more stable (less odorous and less putrescible) and more dewaterable, and to reduce the mass of sludge [16]. If the sludge is to be dewatered and burned, stabilization is not used. Two basic stabilization processes are in use. One is carried out in closed tanks devoid of oxygen and is called **anaerobic digestion.** The other approach injects air into the sludge to accomplish **aerobic digestion.**

The aerobic digestion of biological sludges is nothing more than a continuation of the activated sludge process. When a culture of aerobic heterotrophs is placed in an environment containing a source of organic material, the microorganisms remove and use most of this material. A fraction of the organic material removed will be used for the synthesis of new biomass. The remaining material will be channeled into energy metabolism and oxidized to carbon dioxide, water, and soluble inert material to provide energy for both synthesis and maintenance (life-support) functions. Once the external source of organic material is exhausted, however, the microorganisms enter into **endogenous respiration,** where cellular material is oxidized to satisfy the energy of maintenance (i.e., energy for life-support requirements). If this condition is continued over an extended period, the total quantity of biomass will be considerably reduced. Furthermore, that portion remaining will exist at such a low energy state that it can be considered biologically stable and suitable for disposal in the environment. This forms the basic principle of aerobic digestion.

Aerobic digestion is accomplished by aerating the organic sludges in an open tank resembling an activated sludge aeration tank. Like the activated sludge aeration tank, the aerobic digester must be followed by a settling tank unless the sludge is to be disposed of on land in liquid form. Unlike the activated sludge process, the effluent (supernatant) from the clarifier is recycled back to the head end of the plant. This is because the supernatant is high in suspended solids ($100–300 \ mg \cdot L^{-1}$), $BOD_5$ (to $500 \ mg \cdot L^{-1}$), TKN (to $200 \ mg \cdot L^{-1}$), and total P (to $100 \ mg \cdot L^{-1}$).

Because the fraction of volatile matter is reduced, the specific gravity of the digested sludge solids will be higher than it was before digestion. Thus, the sludge settles to a more compact mass, and the clarifier underflow concentration can be expected to reach 3%.

The anaerobic treatment of complex wastes is thought to occur in three stages as shown in Figures 10–21 and 10–22 [17, 18]. In the first stage, complex waste components, including fats, proteins, and polysaccharides, are hydrolyzed to their component subunits. This is accomplished by a heterogeneous group of facultative and anaerobic bacteria. These bacteria then subject the products of hydrolysis (triglycerides, fatty acids, amino acids, and sugars) to fermentation and

**FIGURE 10–21**

Schematic diagram of the patterns of carbon flow in anaerobic digestion.

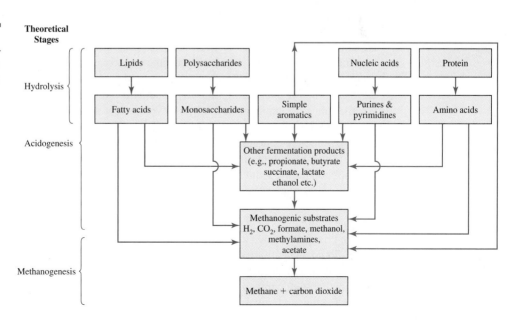

**FIGURE 10–22**

Steps in anaerobic digestion process with energy flow.

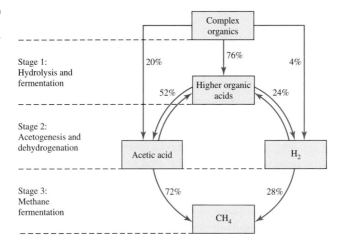

other metabolic processes, leading to the formation of simple organic compounds and hydrogen in a process called **acidogenesis** or **acetogenesis.** The organic compounds are mainly short-chain (volatile) acids and alcohols. In the first two stages little stabilization of BOD or COD is realized. In the third stage, the end products of the second stage are converted to gases (mainly methane and carbon dioxide) by several different species of strictly anaerobic bacteria. Thus, it is here that stabilization of the organic material occurs, a stage generally referred to as **methane fermentation.** Even though the anaerobic process is presented as being sequential in nature, all stages take place simultaneously and synergistically.

The bacteria responsible for acid fermentation are relatively tolerant to changes in pH and temperature and have a much higher rate of growth than the bacteria responsible for methane fermentation. As a result, methane fermentation is generally assumed to be the rate-controlling step in anaerobic waste treatment processes.

Considering 35°C as the optimum temperature for anaerobic waste treatment, Lawrence and Mimes propose that, in the range of 20 to 35°C, the kinetics of methane fermentation of long- and short-chain fatty acids will adequately describe the overall kinetics of anaerobic treatment [19]. Thus, the kinetic equations we presented to describe the completely mixed activated sludge process are equally applicable to the anaerobic process.

Two types of anaerobic digestion processes are used today: the standard-rate process and the high-rate process.

The standard-rate process does not employ sludge mixing, but rather the digester contents are allowed to stratify into zones. Sludge feeding and withdrawal are intermittent rather than continuous. The digester is generally heated to increase the rate of fermentation and therefore decrease the required retention time. Retention time ranges between 30 and 60 days for heated digesters. The organic loading rate for a standard-rate digester is between 0.48 and 1.6 kg total volatile solids per cubic meter of digester volume per day.

The major disadvantage of the standard-rate process is the large tank volume required because of long retention times, low loading rates, and thick scum-layer formation. Only about a third of the tank volume is used in the digestion process. The remaining two-thirds of the tank volume contains the scum layer, stabilized solids, and the supernatant. Because of this limitation, systems of this type are generally used only at treatment plants having a capacity of 0.04 $m^3 \cdot s^{-1}$ or less.

The high-rate system evolved as a result of continuing efforts to improve the standard-rate unit. In this process, two digesters operating in series separate the functions of fermentation and solids–liquid separation (see Figure 10–23). The contents of the first-stage, high-rate unit are thoroughly mixed, and the sludge is heated to increase the rate of fermentation. Because the contents are thoroughly mixed, temperature distribution is more uniform throughout the tank volume. Sludge feeding and withdrawal are continuous or nearly so. The retention time required for the

**FIGURE 10–23**

Schematic of a high-rate anaerobic digester.

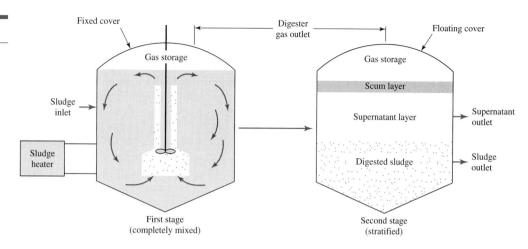

first-stage unit is normally between 10 and 15 days. Organic loading rates vary between 1.6 and 8.0 kg total volatile solids per cubic meter of digester per day.

The primary functions of the second-stage digester are solids–liquid separation and residual gas extraction. First-stage digesters may be equipped with fixed or floating covers. Second-stage digester covers are often of the floating type, and second-stage units are generally unheated.

The first-stage digester of a high-rate system approximates a completely mixed reactor without solids recycle. Hence, the biological SRT and the hydraulic retention time are equal for this system. As with the aerobic digesters, the most important operating parameters affecting VSS reduction are solids retention time and digestion temperature.

The BOD remaining at the end of digestion is still quite high. Likewise, the suspended solids may be as high as 12,000 mg · L$^{-1}$, whereas the TKN may be on the order of 1000 mg · L$^{-1}$. Thus, the supernatant from the secondary digester (in the high-rate process) is returned to the head end of the WWTP. The settled sludge is conditioned and dewatered for disposal.

**Sludge Conditioning.** Several methods are available for conditioning sludge to facilitate the separation of the liquid and solids. One of the most commonly used is the addition of coagulants such as ferric chloride, lime, or organic polymers. Ash from incinerated sludge has also found use as a conditioning agent. As happens when coagulants are added to turbid water, chemical coagulants act to clump the solids together so that they are more easily separated from the water. In recent years, organic polymers have become increasingly popular for sludge conditioning. Polymers are easy to handle, require little storage space, and are very effective. The conditioning chemicals are injected into the sludge just before the dewatering process and are mixed with the sludge.

Another conditioning approach is to heat the sludge at high temperatures (175–230°C) and pressures (1000–2000 kPa). Under these conditions, much like those of a pressure cooker, water that is bound up in the solids is released, improving the dewatering characteristics of the sludge. Heat treatment has the advantage of producing a sludge that dewaters better than chemically conditioned sludge. The process has the disadvantages of relatively complex operation and maintenance and the creation of highly polluted cooking liquors that, when recycled to the treatment plant, impose a significant added treatment burden.

**Sludge Dewatering.** The most popular method of sludge dewatering in the past has been the use of sludge drying beds. These beds are especially popular in small plants because of their simplicity of operation and maintenance. In 1977, two-thirds of all U.S. wastewater treatment plants used drying beds; one-half of all the municipal sludge produced in the United States was dewatered by this method. Although the use of drying beds might be expected in the warmer, sunny regions, they are also used in several large facilities in northern climates.

Operational procedures common to all types of drying beds involve the following steps:

1. Pump 0.20–0.30 m of stabilized liquid sludge onto the drying bed surface.
2. Add chemical conditioners continuously, if conditioners are used, by injection into the sludge as it is pumped onto the bed.
3. When the bed is filled to the desired level, allow the sludge to dry to the desired final solids concentration. (This concentration can vary from 18 to 60%, depending on several factors, including type of sludge, processing rate needed, and degree of dryness required for lifting. Nominal drying times vary from 10 to 15 days under favorable conditions, to 30–60 days under barely acceptable conditions.)
4. Remove the dewatered sludge either mechanically or manually.
5. Repeat the cycle.

Sand drying beds are the oldest, most commonly used type of drying bed. Many design variations are possible, including the layout of drainage piping, thickness and type of gravel and sand layers, and construction materials. Sand drying beds for wastewater sludge are constructed in the same manner as water treatment plant sludge-drying beds. Sand drying beds can be built with or without provision for mechanical sludge removal and with or without a roof. When the cost of labor is high, newly constructed beds are designed for mechanical sludge removal.

When space is limited or climatic conditions make sand drying beds prohibitively expensive, vacuum filters may be used. A vacuum filter consists of a cylindrical drum covered with a filtering material or fabric, which rotates partially submerged in a vat of conditioned sludge. A vacuum is applied inside the drum to extract water, leaving the solids, or **filter cake,** on the filter medium. As the drum completes its rotational cycle, a blade scrapes the filter cake from the filter and the cycle begins again. In some systems, the filter fabric passes off the drum over small rollers to dislodge the cake. There is a wide variety of filter fabrics, ranging from Dacron to stainless steel coils, each with its own advantages. The vacuum filter can be applied to digested sludge to produce a sludge cake dry enough (15–30% solids) to handle and dispose of by burial in a landfill or by application to the land as a relatively dry fertilizer. If the sludge is to be incinerated, it is not stabilized. In this case, the vacuum filter is applied to the raw sludge to dewater it. The sludge cake is then fed to the furnace to be incinerated.

The continuous belt filter presses (CBFP) equipment (Figure 10–24) used in treating waste water sludges is the same as that used for water treatment plant sludges. The CBFP is successful with many normal mixed sludges. Typical dewatering results for digested mixed sludges with initial feed solids of 5% give a dewatered cake of 19% solids at a rate of $32.8 \text{ kg} \cdot \text{h}^{-1} \cdot \text{m}^{-2}$. In general, most of the results with these units closely parallel those achieved with rotary vacuum filters. An advantage of CBFPs is that they do not have the sludge pickup problem that sometimes occurs with rotary vacuum filters. Additionally, they have a lower energy consumption.

## FIGURE 10–24

Continuous belt filter press. (*Courtesy of Komline-Sanderson Engineering Corporation.*)

**Reduction.** If sludge use as a soil conditioner is not practical, or if a site is not available for landfill using dewatered sludge, cities may turn to the alternative of sludge reduction, that is incineration. Incineration completely evaporates the moisture in the sludge and combusts the organic solids to a sterile ash. To minimize the amount of fuel used, the sludge must be dewatered as completely as possible before incineration. The exhaust gas from an incinerator must be treated carefully to avoid air pollution.

## 10–12  SLUDGE DISPOSAL

### Ultimate Disposal

The WWTP process residuals (leftover sludges, either treated or untreated) are the bane of design and operating personnel. Of the five possible disposal sites for residuals, two are feasible and only one is practical. Conceivably, one could ultimately dispose of residues in the following places: in the air, in the ocean, in "outer space," on the land, or in the marketplace. Disposal in the air by burning is in reality not ultimate disposal but only temporary storage until the residue falls to the ground. Although incineration is widely practiced as a sludge treatment device, the ash and residues from air pollution control devices must be disposed of. Disposal of sewage sludge at sea by barging is now prohibited in the United States. "Outer space" is not a suitable disposal site. Thus, we are left with land disposal and use of the sludge to produce a product.

For ease of discussion, we have divided land disposal into three categories: land spreading, landfilling, and dedicated land disposal. We have grouped all of the utilization ideas under one category.

### Land Spreading

The practice of applying WWTP residuals for the purposes of recovering nutrients, water, or reclaiming despoiled land such as strip mine spoils is called **land spreading.** In contrast to the other land disposal techniques, land spreading is land-use intensive. Application rates are governed by the character of the soil and the ability of the crops or forests on which the sludge is spread to accommodate it. Land application may be limited by heavy metals (e.g., chromium, lead, and mercury) that poison the soil (See Sludge Disposal Regulations, p. 428).

### Landfilling

Sludge landfill can be defined as the planned burial of wastewater solids, including processed sludge, screenings, grit, and ash, at a designated site. The solids are placed into a prepared site or excavated trench and covered with a layer of soil. The soil cover must be deeper than the depth of the plow zone (about 0.20–0.25 m). For the most part, landfilling of screenings, grit, and ash is accomplished with methods similar to those used for sludge landfilling.

### Dedicated Land Disposal (DLD)

**Dedicated land disposal** is the application of heavy sludge loadings to some finite land area that has limited public access and has been set aside or dedicated for all time to the disposal of wastewater sludge. Dedicated land disposal does not mean in-place use. No crops may be grown. Dedicated sites typically receive liquid sludges. Although application of dewatered sludges is possible, it is uncommon. In addition, disposal of dewatered sludge in landfills is generally more cost-effective.

### Utilization

Wastewater solids may sometimes be used beneficially in ways other than as a soil nutrient. Of the several methods worthy of note, composting and cofiring with municipal solid waste are two that have received increasing amounts of interest in the last few years. The recovery of lime and the use of the sludge to form activated carbon have also been in practice to a lesser extent.

### Sludge Disposal Regulations

The regulations that govern the use or disposal of sewage sludge are codified as 40 CFR Part 503 and have become known as the "503 regulations." The regulations apply to sewage sludge generated from the treatment of domestic sewage that is land-applied, placed on a surface disposal site, or incinerated in an incinerator that accepts only sewage sludge. The regulations do not apply to sludge generated from treatment of industrial process wastes at an industrial facility, hazardous sewage sludge, sewage sludge with PCB, concentrations of 50 mg $\cdot$ L$^{-1}$ or greater, or drinking water sludge.

## CHAPTER REVIEW

When you have completed studying this chapter, you should be able to do the following without the aid of your textbook or notes:

1. For each type of decomposition (aerobic, anoxic, and anaerobic), list the electron acceptor, important end products, and relative advantages and disadvantages as a waste treatment process.
2. List a BOD value for strong, medium, and weak municipal waste.
3. Explain the differences among pretreatment, primary treatment, secondary treatment, and tertiary treatment, and show how they are related.
4. Sketch a graph showing the average variation of daily flow at a municipal WWTP.
5. Define and explain the purpose of equalization.
6. Sketch, label, and explain the function of the parts of an activated sludge plant and a trickling filter plant.
7. Define $\theta_c$, SRT, and sludge age, and explain their use in regulating the activated sludge process.
8. Explain the purpose of the $F/M$ ratio and define $F$ and $M$ in terms of BOD$_5$ and mixed liquor volatile suspended solids.
9. Explain the relationship between $F/M$ and $\theta_c$.
10. Explain how cell production is regulated using $F/M$ or $\theta_c$.
11. Compare two systems operating at two different $F/M$ ratios.
12. Compare the positive and negative effects of disinfection of wastewater effluents.
13. List the four common AWT processes and the pollutants they remove.
14. Explain why removal of residual suspended solids effectively removes residual BOD$_5$.
15. Describe refractory organics and the method used to remove them.
16. List three chemicals used to remove phosphorus from wastewaters.
17. Explain biological nitrification and denitrification either in words or with an equation.
18. Explain ammonia stripping either in words or with an equation.
19. Describe the three basic approaches to land treatment of wastewater.
20. State the two major purposes of sludge stabilization.
21. Explain the purpose of each of the sludge treatment steps and describe the major processes used.
22. Describe the locations for ultimate disposal of sludges and the treatment steps needed prior to ultimate disposal.

With the aid of this text, you should be able to do the following:

1. Determine whether a grit particle of given diameter and density will be captured in a given velocity-controlled grit chamber, or determine the minimum diameter that will be captured under a given set of conditions.
2. Determine the required volume of an equalization basin to dampen a given periodic flow.

3. Determine the effect of equalization on mass loading of a pollutant.

4. Evaluate or size primary and secondary sedimentation tanks with respect to detention time, overflow rate, solids loading, and weir loading.

5. Estimate the soluble $BOD_5$ in the effluent from a completely mixed activated sludge plant, determine the mean cell residence time or the hydraulic detention time to achieve a desired degree of treatment, and determine the wasting flow rate to achieve a desired mean cell residence time or $F/M$ ratio.

6. Calculate the $F/M$ ratio given an influent $BOD_5$, flow, and detention time, or calculate the volume of the aeration basin given $F/M$, $BOD_5$, and flow.

7. Determine return sludge concentration or flow rate.

8. Calculate the required mass of sludge to be wasted from an activated sludge process given the appropriate data.

9. Calculate the theoretical mass of oxygen required and the amount of air required to supply it given the appropriate data.

10. Perform a sludge mass balance, given the separation efficiencies and appropriate mass flow rate.

## PROBLEMS

**10-1**  If a particle having a 0.0170-cm radius and density of $1.95 \text{ g} \cdot \text{cm}^{-3}$ is allowed to fall into quiescent water having a temperature of 4°C, what will be the terminal settling velocity? Assume the density of water $= 1000 \text{ kg} \cdot \text{m}^{-3}$.

   **Answer:** $3.82 \times 10^{-2} \text{ m} \cdot \text{s}^{-1}$

**10-2**  If the terminal settling velocity of a particle falling in quiescent water having a temperature of 15°C is $0.0950 \text{ cm} \cdot \text{s}^{-1}$, what is its diameter? Assume a particle density of $2.05 \text{ g} \cdot \text{cm}^{-3}$ and density of water equal to $1000 \text{ kg} \cdot \text{m}^{-3}$.

**10-3**  A treatment plant being designed for Cynusoidal City requires an equalization basin to even out flow and BOD variations. The average daily flow is $0.400 \text{ m}^3 \cdot \text{s}^{-1}$. The following flows and $BOD_5$ have been found to be typical of the average variation over a day. What size equalization basin, in cubic meters, is required to provide for a uniform outflow equal to the average daily flow? Assume the flows are hourly averages.

| Time | Flow $(\text{m}^3 \cdot \text{s}^{-1})$ | $BOD_5$ $(\text{mg} \cdot \text{L}^{-1})$ | Time | Flow $(\text{m}^3 \cdot \text{s}^{-1})$ | $BOD_5$ $(\text{mg} \cdot \text{L}^{-1})$ |
|---|---|---|---|---|---|
| 0000 | 0.340 | 123 | 1200 | 0.508 | 268 |
| 0100 | 0.254 | 118 | 1300 | 0.526 | 282 |
| 0200 | 0.160 | 95 | 1400 | 0.530 | 280 |
| 0300 | 0.132 | 80 | 1500 | 0.552 | 268 |
| 0400 | 0.132 | 85 | 1600 | 0.570 | 250 |
| 0500 | 0.140 | 95 | 1700 | 0.596 | 205 |
| 0600 | 0.160 | 100 | 1800 | 0.604 | 168 |
| 0700 | 0.254 | 118 | 1900 | 0.570 | 140 |
| 0800 | 0.360 | 136 | 2000 | 0.552 | 130 |
| 0900 | 0.446 | 170 | 2100 | 0.474 | 146 |
| 1000 | 0.474 | 220 | 2200 | 0.412 | 158 |
| 1100 | 0.482 | 250 | 2300 | 0.372 | 154 |

   **Answer:** $\forall = 6110 \text{ m}^3$

**10–4**  What volume equalization basin is required to even outflow and BOD variations shown in the following data? Assume the flows are hourly averages.

| Time | Flow $(m^3 \cdot s^{-1})$ | $BOD_5$ $(mg \cdot L^{-1})$ | Time | Flow $(m^3 \cdot s^{-1})$ | $BOD_5$ $(mg \cdot L^{-1})$ |
|---|---|---|---|---|---|
| 0000 | 0.0875 | 110 | 1200 | 0.135 | 160 |
| 0100 | 0.0700 | 81 | 1300 | 0.129 | 150 |
| 0200 | 0.0525 | 53 | 1400 | 0.123 | 140 |
| 0300 | 0.0414 | 35 | 1500 | 0.111 | 135 |
| 0400 | 0.0334 | 32 | 1600 | 0.103 | 130 |
| 0500 | 0.0318 | 42 | 1700 | 0.104 | 120 |
| 0600 | 0.0382 | 66 | 1800 | 0.105 | 125 |
| 0700 | 0.0653 | 92 | 1900 | 0.116 | 150 |
| 0800 | 0.113 | 125 | 2000 | 0.127 | 200 |
| 0900 | 0.131 | 140 | 2100 | 0.128 | 215 |
| 1000 | 0.135 | 150 | 2200 | 0.121 | 170 |
| 1100 | 0.137 | 155 | 2300 | 0.110 | 130 |

**10–5**  Compute and plot the unequalized and the equalized hourly BOD mass loadings to the Cynusoidal City WWTP (Problem 10–3). Using the plot and computations, determine the following ratios for BOD mass loading: peak to average; minimum to average; peak to minimum.

    **Answers:**

| | Unequalized | Equalized |
|---|---|---|
| P/A | 1.97 | 1.47 |
| M/A | 0.14 | 0.63 |
| P/M | 14.05 | 2.34 |

**10–6**  Repeat Problem 10–5 using the data from Problem 10–4.

**10–7**  Using an overflow rate of $26.0 \text{ m} \cdot day^{-1}$ and a detention time of 2.0 h, size a primary sedimentation tank for the average flow at Cynusoidal City (Problem 10–3). What would the overflow rate be for the unequalized maximum flow? Assume 15 sedimentation tanks with length to width ratio of 4.7.

    **Answers:**
    Tank dimensions = 15 tanks @ 2.17 m deep × 4.34 m × 20.4 m.
                      Maximum overflow rate $39.3 \text{ m} \cdot day^{-1}$

**10–8**  Determine the surface area of a primary settling tank sized to handle a maximum hourly flow of $0.570 \text{ m}^3 \cdot s^{-1}$ at an overflow rate of $60.0 \text{ m} \cdot day^{-1}$. If the effective tank depth is 3.0 m, what is the effective theoretical detention time?

    **Answers:**  Surface area = 820.80, or 821 $m^2$; $t_0 = 1.2$ h

**10–9**  If an equalization basin is installed ahead of the primary tank in Problem 10–8, the average flow to the tank is reduced to $0.400 \text{ m}^3 \cdot s^{-1}$. What is the new overflow rate and detention time?

**10–10**  Using the assumptions given in Example 10–4, the rule of thumb values for growth constants, and the further assumption that the influent $BOD_5$ was reduced by 32.0% in the primary tank, estimate the liquid volume of an aeration tank required to treat the wastewater in Problem 10–3. Assume an MLVSS of $2000 \text{ mg} \cdot L^{-1}$.

    **Answer:**  $V$ = 4032, or 4000 $m^3$

**10–11**  Repeat Problem 10–10 using the wastewater in Problem 10–4.

**10–12** Using a spreadsheet program you have written, rework Example 10–4 using the following MLVSS concentrations instead of the 2000 mg $\cdot$ L$^{-1}$ used in the example: 1000 mg $\cdot$ L$^{-1}$; 1500 mg $\cdot$ L$^{-1}$; 2500 mg $\cdot$ L$^{-1}$; and 3000 mg $\cdot$ L$^{-1}$.

**10–13** Using a spreadsheet program you have written, determine the effect of MLVSS concentration on the effluent soluble BOD$_5$ ($S$) using the data in Example 10–4. Assume the volume of the aeration tank remains constant at 970 m$^3$. Use the same MLVSS values used in Problem 10–12.

**10–14** If the $F/M$ of a 0.4380 m$^3$ $\cdot$ s$^{-1}$ activated sludge plant is 0.200 day$^{-1}$, the influent BOD$_5$ after primary settling is 150 mg $\cdot$ L$^{-1}$, and the MLVSS is 2200 mg $\cdot$ L$^{-1}$, what is the volume of the aeration tank?

> **Answer:** Volume $= 1.29 \times 10^4$ m$^3$

**10–15** Two activated sludge aeration tanks at Turkey Run, Indiana, are operated in series. Each tank has the following dimensions: 7.0 m wide $\times$ 30.0 m long $\times$ 4.3 m effective liquid depth. The plant operating parameters are as follows:

Flow = 0.0796 m$^3$ $\cdot$ s$^{-1}$　　　　　　　　　　　　MLVSS = 1500 mg $\cdot$ L$^{-1}$
Soluble BOD$_5$ after primary settling = 130 mg $\cdot$ L$^{-1}$　　MLSS = 1.40 (MLVSS)

Determine the following: aeration period, $F/M$ ratio.

> **Answers:** Aeration period = 6.3 h; $F/M$ = 0.33 mg $\cdot$ mg$^{-1}$ $\cdot$ d$^{-1}$

**10–16** The 500-bed Lotta Hart Hospital has a small activated sludge plant to treat its wastewater. The average daily hospital discharge is 1200 L $\cdot$ day$^{-1}$ per bed, and the average soluble BOD$_5$ after primary settling is 500 mg $\cdot$ L$^{-1}$. The aeration tank has effective liquid dimensions of 10.0 m wide $\times$ 10.0 m long $\times$ 4.5 m deep. The plant operating parameters are as follows:

MLVSS = 2000 mg $\cdot$ L$^{-1}$
MLSS = 1.20 (MLVSS)
Return sludge concentration = 12,000 mg $\cdot$ L$^{-1}$

Determine the following: Aeration period and $F/M$ ratio.

**10–17** Using the following assumptions, determine the sludge age, cell wastage flow rate, and return sludge flow rate for the Turkey Run WWTP (Problem 10–15).

Assume:

Suspended solids in the effluent are negligible　　Bacterial decay rate = 0.040 day$^{-1}$
Wastage is from the aeration tank　　　　　　　　Effluent BOD$_5$ = 5.0 mg $\cdot$ L$^{-1}$ (soluble)
Yield coefficient = 0.40　　　　　　　　　　　　Return sludge concentration = 9130 mg $\cdot$ L$^{-1}$

> **Answers:** $\theta_c$ = 11.50 days; $Q_w$ = 0.00182 m$^3$ $\cdot$ s$^{-1}$; $Q_r$ = 0.0214 m$^3$ $\cdot$ s$^{-1}$

**10–18** Using the following assumptions, determine the solids retention time and the cell wastage flow rate for the Lotta Hart Hospital WWTP (Problem 10–16).

Assume:

Suspended solids in effluent = 30.0 mg $\cdot$ L$^{-1}$　　Bacterial decay rate = 0.060 day$^{-1}$
Wastage is from the return sludge line　　　　　Inert fraction of suspended solids = 66.67%
Yield coefficient = 0.60　　　　　　　　　　　Allowable BOD in effluent = 30.0 mg $\cdot$ L$^{-1}$

**10–19** Determine the daily and annual primary sludge production for a WWTP having the following operating characteristics:

Operating data:

Flow = 0.0500 m$^3$ $\cdot$ s$^{-1}$　　　　　　　　　Specific gravity of volatile solids = 0.970
Influent suspended solids = 155.0 mg $\cdot$ L$^{-1}$　　Fixed solids = 30.0%
Removal efficiency = 53.0%　　　　　　　　　Specific gravity of fixed solids = 2.50
Volatile solids = 70.0%　　　　　　　　　　　Sludge concentration = 4.50%

> **Answer:** $V_{sl}$ = 7.83 m$^3$ $\cdot$ day$^{-1}$

**10–20**  Repeat Problem 10–19 using the following data:

Operating data:

| | |
|---|---|
| Flow $= 2.00 \text{ m}^3 \cdot \text{s}^{-1}$ | Volatile solids $= 68.0\%$ |
| Influent suspended solids $= 179.0 \text{ mg} \cdot \text{L}^{-1}$ | Specific gravity of volatile solids $= 0.999$ |
| Removal efficiency $= 47.0\%$ | Fixed solids $= 32.0\%$ |
| Sludge concentration $= 5.20\%$ | Specific gravity of fixed solids $= 2.50$ |

**10–21**  The Pomdeterra wastewater treatment plant produces thickened sludge that has a suspended solids concentration of 3.8%. They are investigating a filter press that will yield a solids concentration of 24%. If they now produce 33 $\text{m}^3 \cdot \text{day}^{-1}$ of sludge, what annual volume savings will they achieve if they install the press?

**Answer:** 10,138 or 10,000 $\text{m}^3 \cdot \text{year}^{-1}$

**10–22**  Ottawa's anaerobic digester produces 13 $\text{m}^3 \cdot \text{day}^{-1}$ of sludge with a suspended solids concentration of 7.8%. What volume of sludge must they dispose of each year if their sand drying beds yield a solids concentration of 35%?

## DISCUSSION QUESTIONS

**10–1**  You are touring the research labs of the environmental engineers at your university. Two biological reactors are in a controlled temperature room that has a temperature of 35°C. Reactor A has a strong odor but reactor B has virtually no odor. What electron acceptors are being used in each reactor?

**10–2**  If the state regulatory agency requires tertiary treatment of a municipal wastewater, what, if any, processes would you expect to find preceding the tertiary process?

**10–3**  What is the purpose of recirculation and how does it differ from return sludge?

**10–4**  In which of the following cases is the cost of sludge disposal higher?

(a)  $\theta_c = 3$ days      (b)  $\theta_c = 10$ days

**10–5**  Would an industrial wastewater containing only $NH_4$ at a pH of 7.00 be denitrified if pure oxygen was bubbled into it? Explain your reasoning.

## ADDITIONAL READING

### Books

Benefield, L. D., and C. W. Randall, *Biological Process Design for Wastewater Treatment,* Prentice Hall, Upper Saddle River, NJ (1980).

Davis, M., and D. Cornwell. *Introduction to Environmental Engineering,* 3rd ed. McGraw-Hill, New York (1998).

Droste, R. L., *Theory and Practice of Water and Wastewater Treatment,* Wiley, New York (1997).

Grady, C. P. L., and H. C. Lim, *Biological Wastewater Treatment Theory and Applications.* Marcel Dekker, New York (1980).

Henry, J. G., and G. W. Heinke, *Environmental Science and Engineering,* Prentice Hall, Upper Saddle River, NJ (1989).

Kiely, G., *Environmental Engineering,* McGraw-Hill, London (1997).

Masters, G. M., *Introduction to Environmental Engineering and Science,* Prentice Hall, Upper Saddle River, NJ (1998).

Metcalf & Eddy, Inc., and G. Tchobanoglous, *Wastewater Engineering: Treatment, Disposal, Reuse,* McGraw-Hill, New York (1991).

Peavy, H. S., D. R. Rowe, and G. Tchobanoglous, *Environmental Engineering,* McGraw-Hill, New York (1985).

Ray, H. T., *Environmental Engineering,* PWS Publishing, New York (1995).

Reynolds, T. D., and P. A. Richards, *Unit Operations and Processes in Environmental Engineering,* 2nd ed., PWS Publishing, Boston, MA (1996).

Sincero, A. P., and G. A. Sincero, *Environmental Engineering: A Design Approach,* Prentice Hall, Upper Saddle River, NJ (1996).

Tchobanoglous, G., and E. D. Schroeder, *Water Quality,* Addison Wesley, Reading, MA (1983).

Vesilind, P. A., *Introduction to Environmental Engineering,* PWS Publishing, Boston, MA (1997).

Vesilind, P. A., G. C. Hartman, and E. T. Skene, *Sludge Management & Disposal,* Lewis Publishers, Inc., Chelsea, MI (1986).

**Journals**

*Water Environment and Technology* (Water Environment Federation)

*Water Environment Research* (formerly *Journal of the Water Pollution Control Federation*)

*Water Environment and Technology*

*Water Research*

## REFERENCES

1. U.S. Environmental Protection Agency, *Response to Congress on the Use of Decentralized Wastewater Treatment Systems,* EPA Report No. 832-R-97-001b. Washington, D.C. (1997).
2. Erickson, A. E., B. G. Ellis, J. M. Tiedje, et al., *Soil Modification for Denitrification and Phosphate Reduction of Feedlot Waste* (Environmental Protection Agency Report No. EPA-66012-74-057), U.S. Government Printing Office, Washington, D.C. (1974).
3. Task Force on Pretreatment of Industrial Wastes of the Water Environment Federation, *Pretreatment of Industrial Wastes, Manual of Practice No. FD-3,* Water Environment Federation, Alexandria, VA, pp. 15, 20 (1994).
4. Code of Federal Regulations, 40 CFR 403.5.
5. Code of Federal Regulations, 40 CFR 405-71.
6. Great Lakes-Upper Mississippi River Board of State Sanitary Engineers, *Recommended Standards for Sewage Works,* 1978 ed., Health Education Service, Inc., Albany, NY, pp. 60–63 (1976).
7. Metcalf & Eddy, Inc., and G. Tchobanoglous, *Wastewater Engineering: Treatment, Disposal, Reuse,* McGraw-Hill, New York, p. 360 (1991).
8. McKinney, R. E., *Microbiology for Sanitary Engineers,* McGraw-Hill, New York, p. 40 (1962).
9. Monod, J., "The growth of bacterial cultures," *Annual Review of Microbiology,* vol. 3, pp. 371–394 (1949).
10. Joint Task Force of the American Society of Civil Engineers and the Water Pollution Control Federation, *Design of Municipal Wastewater Treatment Plants,* Book Press, Inc., Brattleboro, VT, p. 680 (1992).
11. Heukelekian, H., H. Orford, and R. Manganelli, "Factors affecting the quantity of sludge production in the activated sludge process," *Sewage & Industrial Wastes,* vol. 23, p. 8, 1951; and Sawyer, C. N., "Bacterial nutrition and synthesis," *Biological Treatment of Sewage and Industrial Wastes,* vol. 1, p. 3 (1956).
12. Benefield, L. D., and C. W. Randall, *Biological Process Design for Wastewater Treatment,* Prentice Hall, Upper Saddle River, NJ, pp. 322–324, 338–340, 353–354 (1980).
13. Caldwell, D. H., D. S. Parker, and W. R. Uhte, *Upgrading Lagoons* (Environmental Protection Agency Technology Transfer Seminar Publication. U.S. Government Printing Office, Washington, D.C. (1973).
14. U.S. Environmental Protection Agency, *Environmental Pollution Control Alternatives: Municipal Wastewater,* Environmental Protection Agency Technology Transfer Publication No. EPA 625/5-76-012, U.S. Government Printing Office, Washington, D.C., pp. 33–35, 54–55 (1976).
15. Pound, C. E., R. W. Crites, and D. A. Griffes, *Land Treatment of Municipal Wastewater Effluents, Design Factors I* (Environmental Protection Agency Technology Transfer Seminar Publication), U.S. Government Printing Office, Washington, D.C. (1976).
16. The discussion on stabilization follows L. D. Benefield and C. W. Randall, *Biological Process Design for Wastewater Treatment,* pp. 256–264, 461–464, 479; and U.S. Environmental Protection Agency, *Environmental Pollution Control Alternatives: Municipal Wastewater,* pp. 60–61.
17. Speece, R. E. "Anaerobic biotechnology for industrial wastewater," *Environmental Science and Technology,* vol. 17, pp. 416A–427A (1983).
18. Holland, K. T., J. S. Knapp, and J. G. Shoesmith, *Anaerobic Bacteria,* Chapman and Hall, New York (1987).
19. Lawrence, A. W., and T. R. Mimes, "Discussion paper," *Journal of the Sanitary Engineering Division, American Society of Civil Engineers,* vol. 97, p. 121 (1971).

# 11

# Air Pollution

## 11-1   AIR POLLUTION PERSPECTIVE

Air pollution is of public health concern on the micro, meso, and macro scales. Indoor air pollution results from products used in construction materials, the inadequacy of general ventilation, and geophysical factors that may result in exposure to naturally occurring radioactive materials. Industrial and mobile sources contribute to mesoscale air pollution that contaminates the ambient air that surrounds us outdoors. Macroscale (or global) effects include transport of ambient air pollutants over large distances. Examples of macroscale effects include acid rain and ozone pollution. Global effects of air pollution result from sources that may potentially change the upper atmosphere, examples of which include depletion of the ozone layer and global warming. Although micro- and macroscale effects are of concern, our focus will predominately be on mesoscale air pollution.

## 11-2   FUNDAMENTALS

### Pressure Relationships and Units of Measure

The fundamental relationships of pressure and the units of measure used in discussing air pollution were presented in Chapter 2: they are **micrograms per cubic meter** ($\mu g \cdot m^{-3}$), **parts per million** (ppm), and the **micrometer** ($\mu m$). Micrograms per cubic meter and parts per million are measures of concentration and are both used to indicate the concentration of a gaseous pollutant. Conversion from one of these units to the other was discussed in Chapter 2. The concentration of particulate matter may be reported only as micrograms per cubic meter. The micrometer is used to report particle size.

The advantage to the unit ppm that frequently makes it the unit of choice is that it is a volume-to-volume ratio. (Note that the usage of ppm is different from that in water and wastewater, which is a mass-to-mass ratio.) Changes in temperature and pressure do not change the ratio of the volume of pollutant gas to the volume of air that contains it. Thus, it is possible to compare parts per million readings from Denver and Washington, DC, as well as day and night readings in regions with large variations in temperature without further conversion.

### Relativity

Before we launch into the esoterics of air pollution, let's take a moment to consider the application of the units ppm and $\mu m$ in daily life. Four crystals of common table salt in one cup of granulated sugar is approximately equal to 1 ppm on a volume-to-volume basis. Figure 11–1 should help you visualize the size of a micrometer. Note that a hair has an average diameter of approximately 80 $\mu m$.

**FIGURE 11–1**

Relative sizes of small particles.

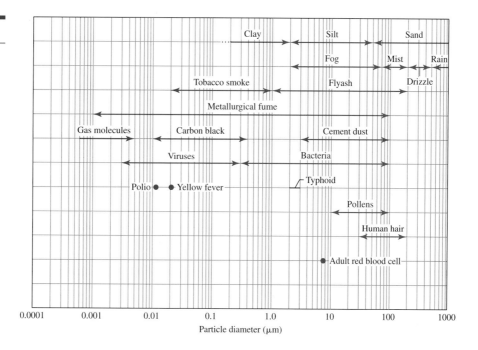

**FIGURE 11–2**

Work done on gas.

### Adiabatic Expansion and Compression

Air pollution meteorology is, in part, a consequence of the thermodynamic processes of the atmosphere. One such process is adiabatic expansion and contraction. An **adiabatic process** is one that takes place with no addition or removal of heat and with sufficient slowness so the gas can be considered to be in equilibrium at all times.

As an example, let us consider the piston and cylinder in Figure 11–2. The cylinder and piston face are assumed to be perfectly insulated. The gas is at pressure, $P$, a force, $F$, equal to the product of the pressure and area of the face of the piston, $A$, must be applied to the piston to maintain equilibrium. If the force is increased and the volume is compressed, the pressure will increase, and work will be done on the gas by the piston. Because no heat enters or leaves the gas, the work will contribute increasing the thermal energy of the gas in accordance with the first law of thermodynamics (Equation 3–41), that is,

(Heat added to gas) = (increase in thermal energy) + (external work done by or on the gas)

Because the left side of the equation is zero (because it is an adiabatic process), the increase in thermal energy is equal to the work done. The increase in thermal energy is reflected by an increase in the temperature of the gas. If the gas is expanded adiabatically, its temperature will decrease.

## 11–3  AIR POLLUTION STANDARDS

The 1970 Clean Air Act (CAA) required the U.S. EPA to investigate and describe the environmental effects of any air pollutant emitted by stationary or mobile sources that may adversely affect human health or the environment. The EPA used these studies to establish the National Ambient Air Quality Standards (NAAQS). These standards are for the ambient air, that is, the outdoor air that normally surrounds us. EPA calls the pollutants listed in Table 11–1 **criteria**

**TABLE 11-1**        National Ambient Air Quality Standards (NAAQS)

| Criteria Pollutant | Standard Type | Concentration ($\mu g \cdot m^{-3}$) | Concentration (ppm) | Averaging Period or Method | Allowable Exceedances[a] |
|---|---|---|---|---|---|
| CO | Primary | 10,000 | 9 | 8-hour average | Once per year |
| | Primary | 40,000 | 35 | 1-hour average | Once per year |
| Lead | Primary and secondary | 1.5 | | Maximum arithmetic mean measured over a calendar quarter | |
| $NO_2$ | Primary and secondary | 100 | 0.053 | Annual arithmetic mean | |
| Ozone | Primary and secondary | 235 | 0.12 | Maximum hourly average | Once per year |
| Ozone[b] | Primary and secondary | 157 | 0.08 | 8-h average | [c] |
| Particulate matter ($PM_{10}$)[d] | Primary and secondary | 150 | | 24-h average | One day per year |
| | Primary and secondary | 50 | | Annual arithmetic mean | |
| ($PM_{2.5}$)[b] | Primary and secondary | 65 | | 24-h average | One day per year |
| | | 15 | | Annual arithmetic mean | |
| $SO_2$ | Primary | 80 | 0.03 | Annual arithmetic mean | |
| | Primary | 365 | 0.14 | Maximum 24-h concentration | Once per year |
| $SO_2$ | Secondary | 1300 | 0.5 | Maximum 3-h concentration | Once per year |

[a]Allowable exceedances may actually be an average value over a multiyear period.
[b]Proposed by EPA July 1997.
[c]Average fourth highest concentration over 3-year period.
[d]Particulate matter standard applies to particles with an aerodynamic diameter $\leq 10\ \mu m$.
*Source:* Code of Federal Regulations, 40 CFR 50.4–50.12, 2002.

**pollutants** because they were developed on health-based criteria. The **primary standard** was established to protect human health with an "adequate margin of safety." The **secondary standards** are intended to prevent environmental and property damage. In 1987, the EPA revised the NAAQS. The standard for hydrocarbons was dropped and the standard for total suspended particulates (TSP) was replaced with a particulate standard based on the mass of particulate matter with an aerodynamic diameter less than or equal to 10 $\mu m$. This standard is referred to as the $PM_{10}$ standard. In 1997 a new $PM_{2.5}$ standard was added.

States are divided into air quality control regions (AQRs). An AQR that has air quality equal to or better than the primary standard is called an **attainment area.** Those areas that do not meet the primary standard are called **nonattainment areas.**

Under the 1970 CAA, the EPA was directed to establish regulations for **hazardous air pollutants** (HAPs) using a risk-based approach. These were called NESHAPs—national emission standards for hazardous air pollutants. Because EPA had difficulty defining "an ample margin of safety" as required by the law, only seven HAPs were regulated between 1970 and 1990: asbestos, arsenic, benzene, beryllium, mercury, vinyl chloride, and radionuclides. The Clean Air Act Amendments of 1990 directed EPA to establish a HAP emissions control program based on technology for 189 chemicals (Table 11–2). EPA will establish emission allowances based on **maximum achievable control technology** (MACT) for 174 categories of industrial sources that potentially emit 9.08 Mg per year of a single HAP or 22.7 Mg per year of a combination of HAPs. A MACT can include process changes, material substitutions, or air pollution control equipment.

| **TABLE 11–2** | Hazardous Air Pollutants (HAPs) | |
|---|---|---|
| Acetaldehyde | Chloroprene | Ethyl chloride (Chloroethane) |
| Acetamide | Cresols/Cresylic acid | Ethylene dibromide (Dibromoethane) |
| Acetonitrile |   (isomers and mixture) | Ethylene dichloride (1,2-Dichloroethane) |
| Acetophenone | o-Cresol | Ethylene glycol |
| 2-Acetylaminofluorene | m-Cresol | Ethylene imine (Aziridine) |
| Acrolein | p-Cresol | Ethylene oxide |
| Acrylamide | Cumene | Ethylene thiourea |
| Acrylic acid | 2,4-D, salts and esters | Ethylidene dichloride (1,1-Dichloroethane) |
| Acrylonitrile | DDE | Formaldehyde |
| Allyl chloride | Diazomethane | Heptachlor |
| 4-Aminobiphenyl | Dibenzofurans | Hexachlorobenzene |
| Aniline | 1,2-Dibromo-3-chloropropane | Hexachlorobutadiene |
| o-Anisidine | Dibutylphthalate | Hexachlorocyclopentadiene |
| Asbestos | 1,4-Dichlorobenzene(p) | Hexachloroethane |
| Benzene (including benzene | 3,3-Dichlorobenzidene | Hexamethylene-1,6-diisocyanate |
|   from gasoline) | Dichloroethyl ether | Hexamethylphosphoramide |
| Benzidine |   [Bis(2-chloroethyl)ether] | Hexane |
| Benzotrichloride | 1,3-Dichloropropene | Hydrazine |
| Benzyl chloride | Dichlorvos | Hydrochloric acid |
| Biphenyl | Diethanolamine | Hydrogen fluoride (Hydrofluoric acid) |
| Bis(2-ethylhexyl)phthalate (DEHP) | N,N-Diethyl aniline (N,N-Dimethylaniline) | Hydrogen sulfide |
| Bis(chloromethyl)ether | Diethyl sulfate | Hydroquinone |
| Bromoform | 3,3-Dimethoxybenzidine | Isophorone |
| 1,3-Butadiene | Dimethyl aminoazobenzene | Lindane (all isomers) |
| Calcium cyanamide | 3,3'-Dimethyl benzidine | Maleic anhydride |
| Caprolactam | Dimethyl carbamoyl chloride | Methanol |
| Captan | Dimethyl formamide | Methoxychlor |
| Carbaryl | 1,1-Dimethyl hydrazine | Methyl bromide (Bromomethane) |
| Carbon disulfide | Dimethyl phthalate | Methyl chloride (Chloromethane) |
| Carbon tetrachloride | Dimethyl sulfate | Methyl chloroform |
| Carbonyl sulfide | 4,6-Dinitro-o-cresol, and salts |   (1,1,1-Trichloroethane) |
| Catechol | 2,4-Dinitrophenol | Methyl ethyl ketone (2-Butanone) |
| Chloramben | 2,4-Dinitrotoluene | Methyl hydrazine |
| Chlordane | 1,4-Dioxane (1,4-Diethyleneoxide) | Methyl iodide (Iodomethane) |
| Chlorine | 1,2-Diphenylhydrazine | Methyl isobutyl ketone (Hexone) |
| Chloroacetic acid | Epichlorohydrin | Methyl isocyanate |
| 2-Chloroacetophenone |   (1-chloro-2,3-epoxypropane) | Methyl methacrylate |
| Chlorobenzene | 1,2-Epoxybutane | Methyl tert butyl ether |
| Chlorobenzilate | Ethyl acrylate | 4,4-Methylene bis(2-chloroaniline) |
| Chloroform | Ethyl benzene | Methylene chloride (Dichloromethane) |
| Chloromethyl methyl ether | Ethyl carbamate (Urethane) | Methylene diphenyl diisocyanate (MDI) |
| | | (continued) |

---

**TABLE 11–2**   Hazardous Air Pollutants (HAPs) (*continued*)

| | | |
|---|---|---|
| 4,4'-Methylenedianiline | Propylene oxide | Vinyl bromide |
| Naphthalene | 1,2-Propylenimine (2-Methyl aziridine) | Vinyl chloride |
| Nitrobenzene | Quinoline | Vinylidene chloride (1,1-Dichloroethylene) |
| 4-Nitrobiphenyl | Quinone | Xylenes (isomers and mixture) |
| 4-Nitrophenol | Styrene | o-Xylenes |
| 2-Nitropropane | Styrene oxide | m-Xylenes |
| N-Nitroso-N-methylurea | 2,3,7,8-Tetrachlorodibenzo-p-dioxin | p-Xylenes |
| N-Nitrosodimethylamine | 1,1,2,2-Tetrachloroethane | Antimony compounds |
| N-Nitrosomorpholine | Tetrachloroethylene | Arsenic compounds |
| Parathion | (Perchloroethylene) | (inorganic, including arsine) |
| Pentachloronitrobenzene (Quintobenzene) | Titanium tetrachloride | Beryllium compounds |
| Pentachlorophenol | Toluene | Cadmium compounds |
| Phenol | 2,4-Toluene diamine | Chromium compounds |
| p-Phenylenediamine | 2,4-Toluene diisocyanate | Cobalt compounds |
| Phosgene | o-Toluidine | Coke oven emissions |
| Phosphine | Toxaphene (chlorinated camphene) | Cyanide compounds[a] |
| Phosphorus | 1,2,4-Trichlorobenzene | Glycol ethers[b] |
| Phthalic anhydride | 1,1,2-Trichloroethane | Lead compounds |
| Polychlorinated biphenyls (Aroclors) | Trichloroethylene | Manganese compounds |
| 1,3-Propane sultone | 2,4,5-Trichlorophenol | Mercury compounds |
| beta-Propiolactone | 2,4,6-Trichlorophenol | Fine mineral fibers[c] |
| Propionaldehyde | Triethylamine | Nickel compounds |
| Propoxur (Baygon) | Trifluralin | Polycyclic organic matter[d] |
| Propylene dichloride | 2,2,4-Trimethylpentane | Radionuclides (including radon)[e] |
| (1,2-Dichloropropane) | Vinyl acetate | Selenium compounds |

[a]X'CN where X = H' or any other group where a formal dissociation may occur. For example KCN or Ca(CN)$_2$.

[b]Includes mono- and di-ethers of ethylene glycol, diethylene glycol, and triethylene glycol R-(OCH$_2$CH$_2$)$_n$-OR' where

n = 1, 2, or 3

R = alkyl or aryl groups

R' = R, H, or groups which, when removed, yield glycol ethers with the structure: R-(OCH$_2$CH)$_n$-OH. Polymers are excluded from the glycol category.

[c]Includes mineral fiber emissions from facilities manufacturing or processing glass, rock, or slag fibers (or other mineral derived fibers) of average diameter 1 micrometer or less.

[d]Includes organic compounds with more than one benzene ring, and which have a boiling point greater than or equal to 100°C.

[e]A type of atom which spontaneously undergoes radioactive decay.

*Note:* For all listings that contain the word *compounds* and for glycol ethers, the following applies: Unless otherwise specified, these listings are defined as including any unique chemical substance that contains the named chemical (i.e., antimony, arsenic, etc.) as part of that chemical's infrastructure.

*Source:* Public Law 101-549, Nov. 15, 1990.

## 11–4   EFFECTS OF AIR POLLUTANTS

### *Effects on Materials*

**Mechanisms of Deterioration.**   Five mechanisms of deterioration have been attributed to air pollution: abrasion, deposition and removal, direct chemical attack, indirect chemical attack, and electrochemical corrosion [1].

Solid particles of large enough size and traveling at high enough speed can cause deterioration by abrasion. With the exception of soil particles in dust storms, most air pollutant particles either are too small or travel at too slow a speed to be abrasive.

Small liquid and solid particles that settle on exposed surfaces do not cause more than aesthetic deterioration. For certain monuments and buildings, such as the White House, this form of deterioration is in itself quite unacceptable. For most surfaces, the cleaning process itself causes the damage. Sandblasting of buildings is an obvious case in point. Frequent washing of clothes weakens their fiber, and frequent washing of painted surfaces dulls their finish.

Solubilization and oxidation–reduction reactions typify direct chemical attack. Frequently, water must be present as a medium for these reactions to take place. Sulfur dioxide and $SO_3$ in the presence of water react with limestone ($CaCO_3$) to form calcium sulfate ($CaSO_4$) and gypsum ($CaSO_4 \cdot 2H_2O$). Both $CaSO_4$ and $CaSO_4 \cdot 2H_2O$ are more soluble in water than $CaCO_3$, and both are leached away when it rains. The tarnishing of silver by $H_2S$ is a classic example of an oxidation–reduction reaction.

Indirect chemical attack occurs when pollutants are absorbed and then react with some component of the absorbent to form a destructive compound. The compound may be destructive because it forms an oxidant, reductant, or solvent. Furthermore, a compound can be destructive by removing an active bond in some lattice structure. Leather becomes brittle after it absorbs $SO_2$, which reacts to form sulfuric acid because of the presence of minute quantities of iron in the leather. The iron acts as a catalyst for the formation of the acid. A similar result has been noted for paper.

Oxidation–reduction reactions cause local chemical and physical differences on metal surfaces. These differences, in turn, result in the formation of microscopic anodes and cathodes. Electrochemical corrosion results from the potential that develops in these microscopic batteries.

**Factors That Influence Deterioration.**   Moisture, temperature, sunlight, and position of the exposed material are among the more important factors that influence the rate of deterioration.

Moisture, in the form of humidity, is essential for most of the mechanisms of deterioration to occur. Metal corrosion does not appear to occur even at relatively high $SO_2$ pollution levels until the relative humidity exceeds 60%. On the other hand, humidities above 70–90% will promote corrosion without air pollutants. Rain reduces the effects of pollutant-induced corrosion by dilution and washing away of the pollutant.

Higher air temperatures generally result in higher reaction rates. However, when low air temperatures are accompanied by cooling of surfaces to the point where moisture condenses, then the rates may be accelerated.

In addition to the oxidation effect of its ultraviolet wave lengths, sunlight stimulates air pollution damage by providing the energy for pollutant formation and cyclic reformation. The cracking of rubber and the fading of dyes have been attributed to ozone produced by these photochemical reactions.

The position of the exposed surface influences the rate of deterioration in two ways. First, whether the surface is vertical or horizontal or at some angle affects deposition and wash-off rates. Second, whether the surface is an upper or lower one may alter the rate of damage. When the humidity is sufficiently high, the lower side usually deteriorates faster because rain does not remove the pollutants as efficiently.

### Effects on Vegetation
**Cell and Leaf Anatomy.**   Because the leaf is the primary indicator of the effects of air pollution on plants, we shall define some terms and explain how the leaf functions. A typical plant cell has three main components: the cell wall, the protoplast, and the inclusions. Much like human skin, the cell wall is thin in young plants and gradually thickens with age. Protoplast is the term used to describe the protoplasm of one cell. It consists primarily of water, but it also includes protein, fat, and carbohydrates. The nucleus contains the hereditary material (DNA), which controls the operation of the cell. The protoplasm located outside the nucleus is called cytoplasm. Within the cytoplasm are tiny bodies or plastids. Examples include chloroplasts, leucoplasts, chromoplasts, and mitochondria. Chloroplasts contain the chlorophyll that manufactures the plant's food

**FIGURE 11–3**

Cross section of intact leaf. (*Source:* I. Hindawi, *Air Pollution Injury to Vegetation,* National Air Pollution Control Administration, U.S. Department of Health, Education and Welfare, Raleigh, N.C., 1970.)

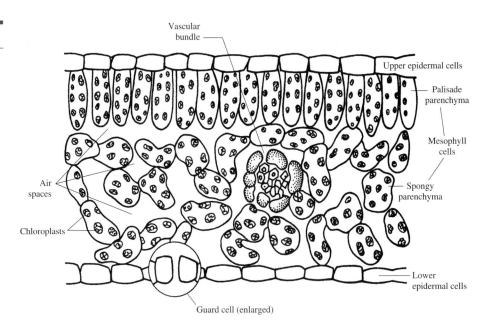

through photosynthesis. Leucoplasts convert starch into starch grains. Chromoplasts are responsible for the red, yellow, and orange colors of the fruit and flowers.

A cross section through a typical mature leaf (Figure 11–3) reveals three primary tissue systems: the epidermis, the mesophyll, and the vascular bundle (veins). Chloroplasts are usually not present in epidermal cells. The opening in the underside of the leaf is called a stoma. (The plural of stoma is stomata.) The mesophyll, which includes both the palisade parenchyma and the spongy parenchyma, contains chloroplasts and is the food production center. The vascular bundles carry water, minerals, and food throughout the leaf and to and from the main stem of the plant.

The guard cells regulate the passage of gases and water vapor in and out of the leaf. When it is hot, sunny, and windy, the processes of photosynthesis and respiration increase. The guard cells open, which allows increased removal of water vapor that otherwise would accumulate because of the increased transport of water and minerals from the roots.

**Pollutant Damage.**   Ozone injures the palisade cells [2]. The chloroplasts condense and ultimately the cell walls collapse. This results in the formation of red-brown spots that turn white after a few days. The white spots are called **fleck.** Ozone injury appears to be the greatest during midday on sunny days. The guard cells are more likely to be open under these conditions and thus allow pollutants to enter the leaf.

Plant growth may be inhibited by continuous exposure to 0.5 ppm of $NO_2$. Levels of $NO_2$ in excess of 2.5 ppm for periods of 4 h or more are required to produce **necrosis** (surface spotting due to plasmolysis or loss of protoplasm).

Sulfur dioxide injury is also typified by necrosis, but at much lower levels. A concentration of 0.3 ppm for 8 h is sufficient [3]. Lower levels for longer periods of exposure will produce a diffuse chlorosis (bleaching).

The net result of air pollutant damage goes beyond the apparent superficial damage to the leaves. A reduction in surface area results in less growth and small fruit. For commercial crops this results in a direct reduction in income for the farmer. For other plants the net result is likely to be an early death.

Fluoride deposition on plants not only causes them damage but may result in a second untoward effect. Grazing animals may accumulate an excess of fluoride that mottles their teeth and ultimately causes them to fall out.

**Problems of Diagnosis.**    Various factors make it difficult to diagnose actual damage from air pollution. Droughts, insects, diseases, herbicide overdoses, and nutrient deficiencies all can cause injury that resembles air pollution damage. Also, combinations of pollutants that alone cause no damage are known to produce acute effects when combined [2]. This effect is known as **synergism.**

### Effects on Health

**Susceptible Population.**    Under the best circumstances it is difficult to assess the effects of air pollution on human health. Personal pollution from smoking results in exposure to air pollutant concentrations far higher than the low levels found in the ambient atmosphere. Occupational exposure may also result in pollution doses far above those found outdoors. Tests on rodents and other mammals are difficult to interpret and apply to human anatomy. Tests on human subjects are usually restricted to those who would be expected to survive. This leads us to a question of environmental ethics. If the allowable concentration levels (standards) are based on results from tests on rodents, they would be rather high. If the allowable concentration levels must also protect those with existing cardiorespiratory ailments, they should be lower than those resulting from the observed effects on rodents.

We noted earlier that the air quality standards were established to protect public health with an "adequate margin of safety." In the opinion of the administrator of the EPA, the standards must protect the most sensitive responders. Thus, as you will note in the following paragraphs, the standards have been set at the lowest level of observed effect. This decision has been attacked by some theorists. They say it would make better economic sense to build more hospitals [4]. However, one also might apply this kind of logic in establishing speed limits for highways, that is, raise the speed limit and build more hospitals, junk yards, and cemeteries!

**Anatomy of the Respiratory System.**    The respiratory system is the primary indicator of air pollution effects in humans. The major organs of the respiratory system are the nose, pharynx, larynx, trachea, bronchi, and lungs (Figure 11–4). The nose, pharynx, larynx, and trachea together are called the upper respiratory tract (URT). The primary effects of air pollution on the URT are aggravation of the sense of smell and inactivation of the sweeping motion of cilia, which remove mucus and entrapped particles. The lower respiratory tract (LRT) consists of the branching structures known as bronchi and the lung itself, which is composed of grape-like clusters of sacs called alveoli. The alveoli are approximately 300 μm in diameter. The walls of alveoli are lined with capillaries. Carbon dioxide diffuses through the capillary wall into the alveolus, and oxygen diffuses out of the alveolus into the blood cell. The difference in partial pressure of each of the gases causes it to move from the higher to lower partial pressure.

**Inhalation and Retention of Particles.**    The degree of penetration of particles into the LRT is primarily a function of the size of the particles and the rate of breathing. Particles greater than 5–10 μm are screened out by the hairs in the nose. Sneezing also helps the screening process. Particles in the 1–2-μm size range penetrate to the alveoli. These particles are small enough to bypass screening and deposition in the URT; however, they are big enough that their terminal settling velocity allows them to deposit where they can do the most damage. Particles that are less than 0.5 μm in diameter may diffuse to the alveolus cell wall but do not have a large enough terminal settling velocity to be removed efficiently. Smaller particles diffuse to the alveolar walls. Refer to Figure 11–1 and note the air pollutants that fall in the critical particle size range.

**Chronic Respiratory Disease.**    Several long-term diseases of the respiratory system are seriously aggravated by and perhaps may be caused by air pollution. Airway resistance is the narrowing of air passages because of the presence of irritating substances. The result is that breathing becomes difficult. **Bronchial asthma** is a form of airway resistance that results from an allergy. An asthma "attack" is the result of the narrowing of the bronchioles because of a swelling of the mucous membrane and a thickening of the secretions. The bronchioles return to normal after the

**FIGURE 11–4**

The respiratory system. (*Source:* A. Vander, J. Sherman, D. Luciano, *Human Physiology*, 8th Edition, McGraw-Hill, NY, 2001, Reprinted by permission.)

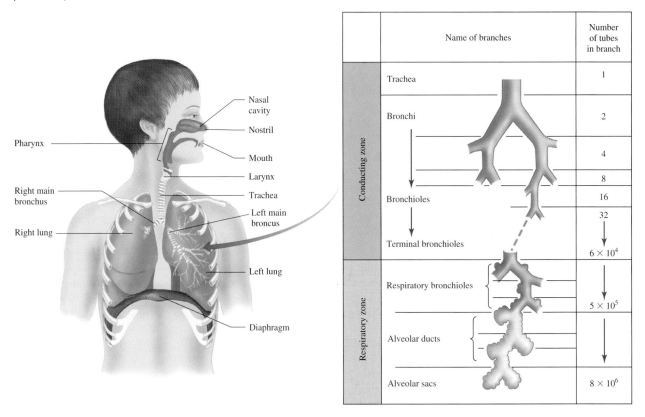

attack. **Chronic bronchitis** is currently defined to be present in a person when excess mucus in the bronchioles results in a cough for 3 months a year for two consecutive years. Lung infections, tumors, and heart disease must be absent. **Pulmonary emphysema** is characterized by a breakdown of the alveoli. The small grape-like clusters become a large nonresilient balloon-like structure. The amount of surface area for gas exchange is reduced drastically. **Cancer of the bronchus** (lung cancer) is characterized by abnormal, disorderly new cell growth originating in the bronchial mucous membrane. The growth closes off the bronchioles. It is usually fatal.

**Carbon Monoxide (CO).**   This colorless, odorless gas is lethal to humans within a few minutes at concentrations exceeding 5000 ppm. CO reacts with hemoglobin in the blood to form carboxyhemoglobin (COHb). Hemoglobin has a greater affinity for CO than it does for oxygen. Thus, the formation of COHb effectively deprives the body of oxygen. At COHb levels of 5 to 10%, visual perception, manual dexterity, and ability to learn are impaired. A concentration of 50 ppm of CO for 8 h will result in a COHb level of about 7.5%. At COHb levels of 2.5 to 3%, people with heart disease are not able to perform certain exercises as well as they might in the absence of COHb. A concentration of 20 ppm of CO for 8 h will result in a COHb level of about 2.8% [5]. (We should note here that the average concentration of CO inhaled in cigarette smoke is 200–400 ppm!) The sensitive populations are those with heart and circulatory ailments, chronic pulmonary disease, developing fetuses, and those with conditions that cause increased oxygen demand, such as fever from an infectious disease.

**Hazardous Air Pollutants (HAPs).**   Most of the information on the direct effects of hazardous air pollutants (also known as air toxics) on human health comes from studies of industrial workers. Exposure to air toxics in the workplace is generally much higher than in the ambient air. We know relatively little about the specific effects of the HAPs at the low levels normally found in ambient air.

The HAPs regulated under the NESHAP program were identified as causal agents for a variety of diseases. For example, asbestos, arsenic, benzene, coke oven emissions, and radionuclides may cause cancer. Beryllium primarily causes lung disease but also affects the liver, spleen, kidneys, and lymph glands. Mercury attacks the brain, kidneys, and bowels. Other potential effects from the HAPs are birth defects and damage to the immune and nervous systems [6].

**Lead (Pb).**    In contrast to the other major air pollutants, lead is a cumulative poison. A further difference is that it is ingested in food and water, as well as being inhaled. Of that portion taken by ingestion, approximately 5–10% is absorbed in the body. Between 20 and 50% of the inspired portion is absorbed. Those portions that are not absorbed are excreted in the feces and urine. Lead is measured in the urine and blood for diagnostic evidence of lead poisoning.

An early manifestation of acute lead poisoning is a mild anemia (deficiency of red blood cells). Fatigue, irritability, mild headache, and pallor indistinguishable from other causes of anemia occur when the blood level of lead increases to $60–120 \ \mu g \cdot 100 \ g^{-1}$ of whole blood. Blood levels in excess of $80 \ \mu g \cdot 100 \ g^{-1}$ result in constipation and abdominal cramps. When an acute exposure results in blood levels of lead greater than $120 \ \mu g \cdot 100 \ g^{-1}$, acute brain damage (encephalopathy) may result [7]. Such acute exposure results in convulsions, coma, cardiorespiratory arrest, and death. Acute exposures may occur over a period of one to three weeks.

Chronic exposure to lead may result in brain damage characterized by seizures, mental incompetence, and highly active aggressive behavior. Weakness of extensor muscles of the hands and feet and eventual paralysis may also result.

Atmospheric lead occurs as a particulate. The particle size range is between 0.16 and 0.43 $\mu$m. Before the ban on lead in automobile fuels, nonsmoking residents of suburban Philadelphia exposed to approximately $1 \ \mu g \cdot m^{-3}$ of lead in air had blood levels averaging $1.1 \ \mu g \cdot 100 \ g^{-1}$. At the same time, nonsmoking residents of downtown Philadelphia exposed to approximately $2.5 \ \mu g \cdot m^{-3}$ of lead had blood levels averaging $20 \ \mu g \cdot 100 \ g^{-1}$ [8].

**Nitrogen Dioxide ($NO_2$).**    The oxides of nitrogen are referred to collectively as $NO_x$. Exposure to $NO_2$ concentrations above 5 ppm for 15 min results in cough and irritation of the respiratory tract. Continued exposure may produce an abnormal accumulation of fluid in the lung (pulmonary edema). The gas is reddish brown in concentrated form and gives a brownish yellow tint at lower concentrations. At 5 ppm it has a pungent sweetish odor. The average $NO_2$ concentration in tobacco smoke is approximately 5 ppm. Slight increases in respiratory illness and decrease in pulmonary function have been associated with concentrations of about 0.10 ppm [9]. You should note that all of these concentrations are very high with respect to the NAAQS value in Table 11–1.

**Photochemical Oxidants.**    Although the photochemical oxidants include peroxyacetyl nitrate (PAN), acrolein, peroxybenzoyl nitrates (PBzN), aldehydes, and nitrogen oxides, the major oxidant is ozone ($O_3$). Ozone is commonly used as an indicator of the total amount of oxidant present. Oxidant concentrations above 0.1 ppm result in eye irritation. At a concentration of 0.3 ppm, cough and chest discomfort are increased. Those people who suffer from chronic respiratory disease are particularly susceptible.

**PM$_{10}$.**    As noted earlier, large particles are not inhaled deeply into the lungs. This is why EPA switched from an air quality standard based on total suspended matter (TSP) to one based on particles with an aerodynamic diameter less than 10 $\mu$m (PM$_{10}$). Studies in the United States, Brazil, and Germany have related higher levels of particulates to increased risk of respiratory, cardiovascular, and cancer-related deaths, as well as pneumonia, lung function loss, hospital admissions, and asthma [10].

Some investigations have pointed toward particle sizes smaller than 2.5 $\mu$m as a major contributor to elevated death rates in polluted cities [11]. These epidemiological investigations are based on statistical correlations. At that time they did not find wide acceptance in the scientific community. This was primarily because of the lack of a suitable biological mechanism to explain what causes the deaths. Nonetheless, in order to provide an "adequate margin of safety" the EPA administrator proposed a new standard based on $PM_{2.5}$ in July 1997. A 5-year scientific review was completed in 2002. The EPA must complete the designation of nonattainment areas by 2005. The states will have until 2017 to meet this new standard.

**Sulfur Oxides ($SO_x$) and Total Suspended Particulates (TSP).** The sulfur oxides include sulfur dioxide ($SO_2$), sulfur trioxide ($SO_3$), their acids, and the salts of their acids. Rather than try to separate the effects of $SO_2$ and $SO_3$, they are usually treated together. There is speculation that a definite synergism exists whereby fine particulates carry absorbed $SO_2$ to the LRT. The $SO_2$ in the absence of particulates would be absorbed in the mucous membranes of the URT.

Patients suffering from chronic bronchitis have shown an increase in respiratory symptoms when the TSP levels exceeded 350 $\mu$g $\cdot$ m$^{-3}$ and the $SO_2$ level was above 0.095 ppm. Studies made in Holland at an interval of 3 years showed that pulmonary function improved as $SO_2$ and TSP levels dropped from 0.10 ppm and 230 $\mu$g $\cdot$ m$^{-3}$ to 0.03 ppm and 80 $\mu$g $\cdot$ m$^{-3}$, respectively.

**Air Pollution Episodes.** The word *episode* is used euphemistically to describe air pollution disasters. Indeed, it was the shock of these disasters that stimulated the first modern legislative action to require control of air pollutants. The characteristics of the three major episodes are summarized in Table 11–3. Careful study of the table will reveal that all of the episodes had some things in common. Comparison of these situations and others where no episode occurred (i.e., where the number of dead and ill was considerably less) has revealed that four ingredients are essential for an episode. If one ingredient is omitted, fewer people will get sick and only a few people can be expected to die. The crucial ingredients are: (1) a large number of pollution sources, (2) a restricted air volume, (3) failure of officials to recognize that anything is wrong, and (4) the presence of water droplets of the "right" size [12].

| **TABLE 11–3** | Three Major Air Pollution Episodes | | |
|---|---|---|---|
| | **Meuse Valley, Belgium, 1930 (Oct. 1–5)** | **Donora, Pennsylvania, 1948 (Oct. 2–31)** | **London, 1952 (Dec. 5–9)** |
| Population | No data | 12,300 | 8,000,000 |
| Weather | Anticyclone, inversion, and fog | Anticyclone, invasion, and fog | Anticyclone, inversion, and fog |
| Topography | River valley | River valley | River plain |
| Most probable source of pollutants | Industry (including steel and zinc plants) | Industry (including steel and zinc plants) | Household coal-burning |
| Nature of the illnesses | Chemical irritation of exposed membranous surfaces | Chemical irritation of exposed membranous surfaces | Chemical irritation of exposed membranous surfaces |
| Number of deaths | 63 | 17 | 4000 |
| Time of deaths | Began after second day of episode | Began after second day of episode | Began on first day of episode |
| Suspected proximate cause of irritation | Sulfur oxides with particulates | Sulfur oxides with particulates | Sulfur oxides with particulates |

*Source:* World Health Organization, *Air Pollution*, 1961, p. 180.

Although a sufficient quantity of any pollutant is lethal by itself, it is generally agreed that some mix is required to achieve the results seen in these episodes. Atmospheric levels of individual pollutants seldom rise to lethal levels without an explosion or transportation accident. However, the proper combination of two or more pollutants will yield untoward symptoms at much lower levels. The sulfur oxides and particulates were the most suspect in the three major episodes.

The meteorology must be such that little air movement occurs, thus preventing the dilution of the pollutants. Although a valley is most conducive to a stagnation effect, the London episode proved that it isn't necessary. The stagnant conditions must persist for several days. Three days appears to be the minimum.

Tragically, each of these hazardous air pollution conditions became lethal because of the failure of city officials to notice anything strange. If they have no measurements of pollution levels or reports from hospitals and morgues, city authorities have no reason to alert the public, shut down factories, or restrict traffic.

The last and, perhaps, most crucial element is fog.* The fog droplets must be of the "right" size, namely, in the 1–2-$\mu$m diameter range or, perhaps, in the range below 0.5 $\mu$m. As mentioned earlier, these particle sizes are most likely to penetrate into the LRT. Pollutants that dissolve into the fog droplet are thus carried deep into the lung and deposited there.

## 11–5  ORIGIN AND FATE OF AIR POLLUTANTS

### Carbon Monoxide

Incomplete oxidation of carbon results in the production of carbon monoxide. The natural anaerobic decomposition of carbonaceous material by soil microorganisms releases approximately 160 Tg[†] of methane ($CH_4$) to the atmosphere each year worldwide [13]. The natural formation of CO results from an intermediate step in the oxidation of the methane. The hydroxyl radical ($OH\cdot$) serves as the initial oxidizing agent. It combines with $CH_4$ to form an alkyl radical [14]:

$$CH_4 + OH\cdot \rightleftharpoons CH_3\cdot + H_2O \tag{11–1}$$

This reaction is followed by a complex series of 39 reactions, which we have oversimplified to the following:

$$CH_3\cdot + O_2 + 2(h\nu) \rightleftharpoons CO + H_2 + OH\cdot \tag{11–2}$$

This says that $CH_3\cdot$ and $O_2$ are each zapped by a photon of light energy ($h\nu$). The symbol $\nu$ stands for the frequency of the light. The $h$ is Planck's constant = $6.626 \times 10^{-34}$ J $\cdot$ Hz$^{-1}$.

**Anthropogenic sources** (those associated with the activities of human beings) include motor vehicles, fossil fuel burning for electricity and heat, industrial processes, solid waste disposal, and miscellaneous burning of such things as leaves and brush. Approximately 600–1250 Tg of CO is released by incomplete combustion of organic carbon in these sources. Motor vehicles account for more than 60% of the emission.

No significant change in the global atmospheric CO level has been observed over the past 20 years. Yet the worldwide anthropogenic contribution of combustion sources has doubled over the same period. Because no apparent change has occurred in the atmospheric concentration, a number of mechanisms (**sinks**) have been proposed to account for the missing CO. The major sink is reaction with hydroxyl radicals to form carbon dioxide. Removal by soil microorganisms and diffusion into the stratosphere are minor routes of removal. It has been estimated that these sinks annually consume an amount of CO that equals or exceeds the production [15].

*The word *smog* is a term coined by Londoners before World War I to describe the combination of smoke and fog that accounted for much of their weather. Los Angeles smog is a misnomer because little smoke and no fog is present. In fact, as we shall see later, Los Angeles smog cannot occur without a lot of sunshine. "Photochemical smog" is the correct term to describe the Los Angeles haze.

[†]One teragram = $1 \times 10^{12}$ g

### Hazardous Air Pollutants (HAPs)

The EPA has identified 166 categories of major sources and 8 categories of area sources for the HAPs listed in Table 11–2 [16]. The source categories represent a wide range of industrial groups: fuel combustion, metal processing, petroleum and natural gas production and refining, surface-coating processes, waste treatment and disposal processes, agricultural chemicals production, and polymers and resins production. There are also a number of miscellaneous source categories, such as dry cleaning and electroplating.

In addition to these direct emissions, air toxics can result from chemical formation reactions in the atmosphere. These reactions involve chemicals emitted to the atmosphere that are not listed HAPs and may not be toxic themselves, but can undergo atmospheric transformations to generate HAPs. For organic compounds present in the gas phase, the most important transformation processes involve photolysis and chemical reactions with ozone, hydroxyl radicals (OH·), and nitrate radicals [6]. **Photolysis** is the chemical fragmentation or rearrangement of a chemical upon the adsorption of radiation of the appropriate wavelength. Photolysis is only important during the daytime for those chemicals that absorb strongly within the solar radiation spectrum. Otherwise, reaction with OH· or $O_3$ is likely to predominate. The HAPs most often formed are formaldehyde and acetaldehyde.

The major removal mechanisms appear to be OH abstraction or addition. The reaction products lead to the formation of CO and $CO_2$. Eighty-nine of the 189 HAPs have atmospheric lifetimes of less than a day.

### Lead

Volcanic activity and airborne soil are the primary natural sources of atmospheric lead. Smelters and refining processes, as well as incineration of lead-containing wastes, are major point sources of lead. Approximately 70–80% of the lead that used to be added to gasoline was discharged to the atmosphere.

Submicrometer-sized lead particles, which are formed by volatilization and subsequent condensation, attach to larger particles or they form nuclei before they are removed from the atmosphere. Once they have attained a size of several microns, they either settle out or are washed out by rain.

### Nitrogen Dioxide

Bacterial action in the soil releases nitrous oxide ($N_2O$) to the atmosphere. In the upper troposphere and stratosphere, atomic oxygen reacts with the nitrous oxide to form nitric oxide (NO).

$$N_2O + O \rightleftharpoons 2NO \tag{11-3}$$

The atomic oxygen results from the dissociation of ozone. The nitric oxide further reacts with ozone to form nitrogen dioxide ($NO_2$).

$$NO + O_3 \rightleftharpoons NO_2 + O_2 \tag{11-4}$$

The global formation of $NO_2$ by this process is estimated to be 12 Tg (as N) annually [15].

Combustion processes account for 74% of the anthropogenic sources of nitrogen oxides. Although nitrogen and oxygen coexist in our atmosphere without reaction, their relationship is much less indifferent at high temperatures and pressures. At temperatures in excess of 1600 K, they react.

$$N_2 + O_2 \overset{\Delta}{\rightleftharpoons} 2NO \tag{11-5}$$

If the combustion gas is rapidly cooled after the reaction by exhausting it to the atmosphere, the reaction is quenched and NO is the by-product. The NO in turn reacts with ozone or oxygen to form $NO_2$. The anthropogenic contribution to global emissions of $NO_2$ by this route amounted to 24 Tg (as N) in 1992 [13].

**FIGURE 11–5**

Interaction of hydrocarbons with atmospheric nitrogen oxide photolytic cycle. (*Source:* U.S. Department of Health, Education and Welfare, *Air Quality Criteria for Photochemical Oxidants,* National Air Pollution Control Administration Publication No. AP-63, U.S. Government Printing Office, Washington, DC, 1970.)

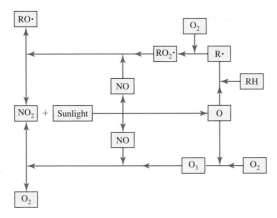

Ultimately, the $NO_2$ is converted to either $NO_2^-$ or $NO^-$ in particulate form. The particulates are then washed out by precipitation. The dissolution of nitrate in a water droplet allows for the formation of nitric acid ($HNO_3$). This, in part, accounts for "acid" rain found downwind of industrialized areas.

### Photochemical Oxidants

Unlike the other pollutants, the photochemical oxidants result entirely from atmospheric reactions and are not direct emissions from either people or nature; thus, they are called **secondary pollutants.** They are formed through a series of reactions that are initiated by the absorption of a photon by an atom, molecule, free radical, or ion. Ozone is the principal photochemical oxidant. Its formation is usually attributed to the nitrogen dioxide photolytic cycle. Hydrocarbons modify this cycle by reacting with atomic oxygen to form free radicals (highly reactive organic species). The hydrocarbons, nitrogen oxides, and ozone react and interact to produce more nitrogen dioxide and ozone. This cycle is represented in summary form in Figure 11–5. The whole reaction sequence depends on an abundance of sunshine. A result of these reactions is the photochemical "smog" for which Los Angeles is famous.

### Sulfur Oxides

Sulfur oxides may be both primary and secondary pollutants. Power plants, industry, volcanoes, and the oceans emit $SO_2$, $SO_3$, and $SO_4^{2-}$ directly as primary pollutants. In addition, biological decay processes and some industrial sources emit $H_2S$, which is oxidized to form the secondary pollutant $SO_2$. In terms of sulfur, approximately 10 Tg is emitted annually by natural sources. Approximately 75 Tg of sulfur may be attributed to anthropogenic sources each year [15].

The most important oxidizing reaction for $H_2S$ appears to be one involving ozone:

$$H_2S + O_3 \rightleftharpoons H_2O + SO_2 \qquad (11–6)$$

The combustion of fossil fuels containing sulfur yields sulfur dioxide in direct proportion to the sulfur content of the fuel.

$$S + O_2 \rightleftharpoons SO_2 \qquad (11–7)$$

This reaction implies that for every gram of sulfur in the fuel, two grams of $SO_2$ is emitted to the atmosphere. Because the combustion process is not 100% efficient, we generally assume that 5% of the sulfur in the fuel ends up in the ash, that is, 1.90 g $SO_2$ per gram of sulfur in the fuel is emitted.

**EXAMPLE 11–1**   An Illinois coal is burned at a rate of 1.00 kg · s$^{-1}$. If the analysis of the coal reveals a sulfur content of 3.00%, what is the annual rate of emission of $SO_2$?

Solution   Using the mass-balance approach, we begin by drawing the following mass-balance diagram.

The steady-state mass balance equation may be written as

$$S_{in} = S_{ash} + S_{SO_2}$$

From the problem data, the mass of "sulfur in" is

$$S_{in} = 1.00 \text{ kg} \cdot s^{-1} \times 0.030 = 0.030 \text{ kg} \cdot s^{-1}$$

In one year,

$$S_{in} = 0.030 \text{ kg} \cdot s^{-1} \times 86,400 \text{ s} \cdot day^{-1} \times 365 \text{ day} \cdot year^{-1} = 9.46 \times 10^5 \text{ kg} \cdot year^{-1}$$

The sulfur in the ash is 5% of the input sulfur.

$$S_{ash} = (0.05)(9.46 \times 10^5 \text{ kg} \cdot year^{-1}) = 4.73 \times 10^4 \text{ kg} \cdot year^{-1}$$

The amount of sulfur available for conversion to $SO_2$ is

$$S_{SO_2} = S_{in} - S_{ash} = 9.46 \times 10^5 - 4.73 \times 10^4 = 8.99 \times 10^5 \text{ kg} \cdot year^{-1}$$

The amount of sulfur formed is determined from the proportional weights of the oxidation reaction (Equation 11–7).

$$S + O_2 \rightleftharpoons SO_2$$

$$MW = 32 + 32 = 64$$

The amount of sulfur dioxide formed is then 64/32 of the sulfur available for conversion.

$$S_{SO_2} = \frac{64}{32} \times 8.99 \times 10^5 \text{ kg} \cdot year^{-1} = 1.80 \times 10^6 \text{ kg} \cdot year^{-1}$$

The ultimate fate of most of the $SO_2$ in the atmosphere is conversion to sulfate salts, which are removed by sedimentation or by washout with precipitation. The conversion to sulfate is by either of two routes: catalytic oxidation or photochemical oxidation. The first process is most effective if water droplets containing $Fe^{3+}$, $Mn^{2+}$, or $NH_3$ are present.

$$2SO_2 + 2H_2O + O_2 \rightleftharpoons 2H_2SO_4 \tag{11-8}$$

At low relative humidities, the primary conversion process is photochemical oxidation. The first step is photoexcitation* of the $SO_2$.

$$SO_2 + h\nu \rightleftharpoons \overset{*}{S}O_2 \tag{11-9}$$

---

*Photoexcitation is the displacement of an electron from one shell to another, thereby storing energy in the molecule. Photoexcitation is represented in reactions by a star ( ★ ).

The excited molecule then readily reacts with $O_2$ to form $SO_3$.

$$\overset{*}{S}O_2 + O_2 \rightleftharpoons SO_3 + O \tag{11–10}$$

The trioxide is very hygroscopic (readily retains moisture) and consequently is rapidly converted to sulfuric acid:

$$SO_3 + H_2O \rightleftharpoons H_2SO_4 \tag{11–11}$$

This reaction in large part accounts for acid rain (i.e., precipitation with a pH value less than 5.6) found in industrialized areas. Normal precipitation has a pH of 5.6 due to the carbonate buffer system.

### Particulates

Sea salt, soil dust, volcanic particles, and smoke from forest fires account for about 2.9 Pg (petagrams) of particulate emissions each year. Anthropogenic emissions from fossil fuel burning and industrial processes account for emissions of 110 Tg per year [17]. Secondary sources of particulates include the conversion of $H_2S$, $SO_2$, $NO_x$, $NH_3$, and hydrocarbons. $H_2S$ and $SO_2$ are converted to sulfates. $NO_x$, and $NH_3$ are converted to nitrates. The hydrocarbons react to form products that condense to form particles at atmospheric temperatures. Natural sources of secondary pollutants yield about 240 Tg annually. Anthropogenic sources yield about 340 Tg annually [17].

Dust particles that are **entrained** (picked up) by the wind and carried over long distances tend to sort themselves out to the sizes between 0.5 and 50 $\mu$m in diameter. Sea salt nuclei have sizes between 0.05 and 0.5 $\mu$m. Particles formed as a result of photochemical reactions tend to have very small diameters ($< 0.4$ $\mu$m). Smoke and fly ash particles cover a wide range of sizes from 0.05 to 200 $\mu$m or more. Particle mass distributions in urban atmospheres generally exhibit two maxima: one is between 0.1 and 1 $\mu$m in diameter; the other is between 1 and 30 $\mu$m. The smaller fraction is the result of condensation. The coarse fraction consists of fly ash and dust generated by mechanical abrasion.

Small particles are removed from the atmosphere by accretion to water droplets, which grow in size until they are large enough to precipitate. Larger particles are removed by direct washout by falling raindrops.

## 11–6  MICRO AND MACRO AIR POLLUTION

Air pollution problems may occur on three scales: micro, meso, and macro. Microscale problems range from those covering less than a centimeter to those the size of a house or slightly larger. Mesoscale air pollution problems are those of a few hectares up to the size of a city or county. Macroscale problems extend from counties to states, nations, and in the broadest sense, the globe. Much of the remaining discussion in this chapter is focused on the mesoscale problem. In this section we will address the general microscale and macroscale problems recognized today.

### Indoor Air Pollution

People who live in cold climates may spend from 70 to 90% of their time indoors. In the last two decades, researchers have become interested in identifying sources, concentrations, and effects of air pollutants that arise in conventional domestic residences. The startling results indicate that, in certain instances, indoor air may be substantially more polluted than the outdoor air.

Carbon monoxide from improperly operating furnaces has long been a serious concern. In numerous instances, people have died from furnace malfunction. More recently, chronic low levels of CO pollution have been recognized. Gas ranges, ovens, pilot lights, gas and kerosene space heaters, and cigarette smoke all contribute (Table 11–4). Although little or no effort has been

**TABLE 11–4**    Tested Combustion Sources and Their Emission Rates

| Source | Range of Emission Rates[a] (mg · MJ$^{-1}$) | | | | |
| | NO | NO$_2$ | NO$_x$ (as NO$_2$) | CO | SO$_2$ |
|---|---|---|---|---|---|
| Range-top burner[b] | 15–17 | 9–12 | 32–37 | 40–244 | c |
| Range oven[d] | 14–29 | 7–13 | 34–53 | 12–19 | c |
| Pilot light[e] | 4–17 | 8–12 | f | 40–67 | c |
| Gas space heaters[g] | 0–15 | 1–15 | 1–37 | 14–64 | c |
| Gas dryer[h] | 8 | 8 | 20 | 69 | c |
| Kerosene space heater[i] | 1–13 | 3–10 | 5–31 | 35–64 | 11–12 |
| Cigarette smoke[j] | 2.78 | 0.73 | f | 88.43 | c |

[a]The lowest and highest mean values of emission rates for combustion sources tested in milligrams per megajoule (mg · MJ$^{-1}$).

[b]Three ranges were evaluated. Reported values are for blue flame conditions.

[c]Combustion source is not emitting pollutant.

[d]Three ranges were evaluated. Ovens were operated for several different settings (bake, broil, self-clean cycle, etc.)

[e]One range was evaluated with all three pilot lights, two top pilot lights and a bottom pilot.

[f]Emission rates not reported.

[g]Three space heaters including one conductive, radiant, and catalytic were tested.

[h]One gas dryer was evaluated.

[i]Two kerosene heaters, including a convective and radiant type, were tested.

[j]One type of cigarette. Reported emission rates are in milligrams per cigarette (800 mg tobacco per cigarette)

*Source:* Moschandreas, D. J., J. D. Zabpansky, and D. S. Peltas, *Characteristics of Emissions from Indoor Combustion Sources,* Gas Research Institute Report No. 85/0075, Chicago, IL, May, 1985.

**TABLE 11–5**    Mean Respirable Particulates (RSP), CO, and CO$_2$ Levels Measured on the Test Floor

| | RSP ($\mu$g · m$^{-3}$) | CO (ppm) | CO$_2$ (ppm) |
|---|---|---|---|
| **Period 1** | | | |
| Floor | 26 | 1.67 | 624 |
| Lounge | 51 | 1.98 | 642 |
| **Period 2** | | | |
| Floor | 18 | 1.09 | 569 |
| Lounge | 189 | 2.40 | 650 |

*Source:* Lee, H. K., T. K. McKenna, L. N. Renton, et al., "Impact of a new smoking policy on office air quality," *Indoor Air Quality in Cold Climates, Transactions of the Air Pollution Control Association,* Pittsburgh, PA, April, 1985.

exerted to reduce or eliminate the danger from ranges, ovens, and so forth, the public has come to expect that the recreational habits of smokers should not interfere with the quality of the air others breathe. The results of a general ban on cigarette smoking in one office are shown in Table 11–5. Smokers were allowed to smoke only in the designated lounge area. Period 1 was prior to the implementation of the new policy. It is obvious that the new policy had a positive effect outside of the lounge.

**FIGURE 11–6**

Respirable suspended particulate levels as a function of smoking. (*Source:* Hosein, R., F. Silverman, P. Corey, et al., "The relationship between pollutant levels in homes and potential sources," *Transactions, Indoor Air Quality in Cold Climates, Hazards and Abatement Measures,* Air Pollution Control Association, Pittsburgh, pp. 250–260, April, 1985.)

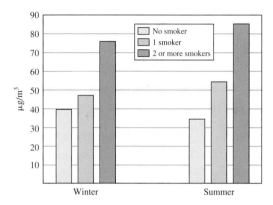

Nitrogen oxide sources are also shown in Table 11–4. $NO_2$ levels have been found to range from 70 $\mu g \cdot m^{-3}$ in air-conditioned houses with electric ranges to 182 $\mu g \cdot m^{-3}$ in non-air-conditioned houses with gas stoves [18]. The latter value is quite high in comparison with the national ambient air quality limits. $SO_2$ levels were found to be very low in all houses investigated. On the other hand, respirable particulate matter (RSP) was found to increase with one smoker and to rise dramatically with two (Figure 11–6).

Bacteria, viruses, fungi, mites, and pollen are collectively refered to as **bioaerosols.** They require a reservoir (for storage), an amplifier (for reproduction), and a means of dispersal. Most bacteria and viruses in indoor air come from humans and pets. Other microorganisms and pollen are introduced from the ambient air through either natural ventilation or through the intakes of building air-handling systems. Humidifiers, air-conditioning systems, and other places where water accumulates are potential reservoirs for bioaerosols.

Radon is not regulated as an ambient air pollutant but has been found in dwellings at alarmingly high concentrations. We will address the radon issue in depth in Chapter 16. Radon is a radioactive gas that emanates from natural geologic formations and, in some cases, from construction materials. It is not generated from the activities of the householder as is true for the pollutants discussed earlier.

Over 300 volatile organic compounds (VOCs) have been identified in indoor air. Aldehydes, alkanes, alkenes, ethers, ketones, and polynuclear aromatic hydrocarbons (PAHs) are among them. Although they are not all present all the time, frequently several are present at the same time.

Formaldehyde ($CH_2O$) has been singled out as one of the more prevalent, as well as one of the more toxic, compounds [19]. Formaldehyde may not be generated directly by the activity of the homeowner. It is emitted by a variety of consumer products and construction materials including pressed wood products, insulation materials (urea-formaldehyde foam insulation in trailers has been particularly suspect), textiles, and combustion sources. In one study, $CH_2O$ concentrations ranged from 0.0455 ppm to 0.19 ppm [20]. Some mobile homes in Wisconsin had concentrations as high as 0.65 ppm. (For comparison, the American Society of Heating, Refrigeration and Air Conditioning Engineers (ASHRAE) set a guideline concentration of 0.1 ppm.)

Unlike the other air pollution sources that continue to emit as long as there is anthropogenic activity (or in the case of radon, for geologic time), $CH_2O$ is not regenerated unless new materials are brought into the residence. If the house is ventilated over time, the concentration will drop.

The primary source of heavy metals indoors is from infiltration of outdoor air and soil and dust that is tracked into the building. Arsenic, cadmium, chromium, mercury, lead, and nickel have been measured in indoor air. Lead and mercury may be generated from indoor sources such as paint. Old lead paint is a source of particulate lead as it is abraded or during removal. Mercury vapor is emitted from latex-based paints that contain diphenyl mercury dodecenyl succinate to prevent fungus growth.

It is doubtful any regulatory effort will be made to reduce the emissions of these pollutants in the near future. Thus, the house or apartment dweller has little recourse other than to replace gas appliances, remove or cover formaldehyde sources, and put out the smokers.

### Acid Rain

Unpolluted rain is naturally acidic because $CO_2$ from the atmosphere dissolves to a sufficient extent to form carbonic acid (see Chapter 2). The equilibrium pH for pure rainwater is about 5.6. Measurements taken over North America and Europe have revealed lower pH values. In some cases individual readings as low as 3.0 have been recorded. The average pH in rain over the United States in 1997 is shown in Figure 8–14.

Chemical reactions in the atmosphere convert $SO_2$, $NO_x$, and VOCs to acidic compounds and associated oxidants (Figure 11–7). The primary conversion of $SO_2$ in the eastern United States is through the aqueous phase reaction with hydrogen peroxide ($H_2O_2$) in clouds. Nitric acid is formed by the reaction of $NO_2$ with OH radicals formed photochemically. Ozone is formed and then protected by a series of reactions involving both $NO_x$ and VOCs.

As discussed in Section 8–4, the concern about acid rain relates to potential effects of acidity on aquatic life, damage to crops and forests, and damage to building materials. Lower pH values may affect fish directly by interfering with reproductive cycles or by releasing otherwise insoluble aluminum, which is toxic. Dramatic die back of trees in central Europe has stimulated concern that similar results could occur in North America. It is hypothesized that the acid rain leaches calcium and magnesium from the soil (see Figure 9–10). This lowers the molar ratio of calcium to aluminum, which, in turn, favors the uptake of aluminum by the fine roots, ultimately leading to their deterioration.

In 1980, Congress authorized a 10-year study to assess the causes and effects of acidic deposition. This study was titled the National Acid Precipitation Assessment Program (NAPAP). In September 1987, the NAPAP released an interim report that indicated that acidic precipitation appeared to have no measurable and consistent effect on crops, tree seedlings, or human health, and that a small percentage of lakes across the United States were experiencing pH values lower than 5.0 [21]. On the other hand, oxidant damage was measurable. The NAPAP reported to Congress in 1992 that there remains no evidence of widespread decline of forest tree species caused by acidic deposition [22]. Eighty-one selected sites in the Northeast and upper Midwest have been monitored for acidity since the early 1980s. Most of the lakes and streams experienced no measurable

### FIGURE 11–7

Acid rain precursors and products.

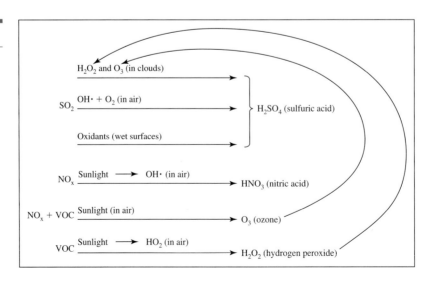

changes in acidity. Sulfate levels decreased while nitrate levels increased. The widespread decrease in sulfate concentration parallels the general decrease in national emissions of sulfur dioxide since 1980. However, acidic deposition has been firmly implicated as a causal factor in northeastern the decline of the red spruce at high elevations. The effect is to reduce midwinter cold tolerance by 4–10°C. A major new finding was that some watersheds in regions receiving high nitrogen deposition are becoming nitrogen-saturated, but there is no direct evidence of the source of the nitrate leaching from these watersheds.

Although these conclusions appear to be reassuring, many uncertainties remain. These include questions about the distribution and type of natural and anthropogenic VOCs; relative importance of air pollutants versus natural stresses in causing the decline of forests above the cloud base; probability and percentage of lakes likely to become more acidic at present levels of air pollution emissions over the next few decades; importance of acidic episodes on fish populations; and possible long-term health effects of acidic aerosols.

Approximately 70% of the $SO_2$ emissions in the United States are attributable to electric utilities. To decrease the $SO_2$ emissions, the Congress developed a two-phase control program under Title IV of the 1990 Clean Air Act Amendments. Phase I sets emission allowances for 110 of the largest emitters in the eastern half of the United States Phase II will include smaller utilities. The utilities may buy or sell allowances. Each allowance is equal to about 1 Mg of $SO_2$ emissions. If a company does not expend its maximum allowance, it may sell it to another company. As a result of this **market-based system** utility emissions have decreased by 9 million Mg. In May 1993 NAPAP reported a 10% decrease in $SO_2$, a 6% decrease in $NO_x$, and a 17% decrease in VOC emissions.

### Ozone Depletion

Without ozone, every living thing on the earth's surface would be incinerated. (On the other hand, as we have already noted, ozone can be lethal.) The presence of ozone in the upper atmosphere (20–40 km and up) provides a barrier to ultraviolet (UV) radiation. The small amounts of UV rays that do seep through provide you with your summer tan. Too much UV, however, will cause skin cancer. Although oxygen also serves as a barrier to UV radiation, it absorbs only over a narrow band centered at a wavelength of 0.2 μm. The photochemistry of these reactions is shown in Figure 11–8. The M refers to any third chemical (usually $N_2$).

In 1974, Molina and Rowland revealed a potential air pollution threat to this protective ozone shield [23]. It is noteworthy that they, along with Paul Crutzen, jointly received the Nobel Prize in chemistry for their research. They hypothesized that chlorofluorocarbons ($CF_2Cl_2$ and $CFCl_3$-often abbreviated as CFC), which are used as aerosol propellants and refrigerants, react with ozone (Figure 11–9). The frightening aspects of this series of reactions are that the chlorine atom removes ozone from the system, and that the chlorine atom is continually recycled to

**FIGURE 11–8**

Photoreactions of ozone.

**FIGURE 11–9**

Ozone destruction by chlorofluoromethane.

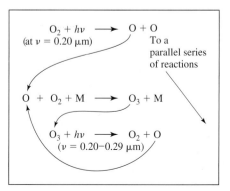

convert more ozone to oxygen. It has been estimated that a 5% reduction in ozone could result in nearly a 10% increase in skin cancer [24]. Thus, CFCs that are rather inert compounds in the lower atmosphere become a serious air pollution problem at higher elevations.

By 1987, the evidence that CFCs destroy ozone in the stratosphere above Antarctica every spring had become irrefutable. In 1987, the ozone hole was larger than ever. More than half of the total ozone column was wiped out and essentially all ozone disappeared from some regions of the stratosphere.

Research confirmed that the ozone layer, on a worldwide basis, shrunk approximately 2.5% in the period from 1976–1986 [25]. Initially, it was believed that this phenomenon was peculiar to the geography and climatology of Antarctica and that the warmer northern hemisphere was strongly protected from the processes that lead to massive ozone losses. Studies of the North Pole stratosphere in the winter of 1989 revealed that this is not the case [26].

In September 1987, the Montreal Protocol on Substances That Deplete the Ozone Layer was developed. The protocol, which has been ratified by 36 countries and became effective in January 1989, proposed that CFC production first be frozen and then reduced 50% by 1998. Yet, under the terms of the protocol, the chlorine content of the atmosphere would continue to grow because the fully halogenated CFCs have such long lifetimes in the atmosphere. $CF_2Cl_2$, for example, has a lifetime of 110 years [27]. Eighty countries met at Helsinki, Finland, in the spring of 1989 to assess new information. The delegates gave their unanimous assent to the five-point Helsinki Declaration:

1. All join the 1985 Vienna Convention for the Protection of the Ozone Layer and the follow-up Montreal Protocol
2. Phase out production and consumption of ozone-depleting CFCs no later than 2000
3. Phase out production and consumption as soon as feasible of halons and such chemicals as carbon tetrachloride and methyl chloroform that also contribute to ozone depletion
4. Commit themselves to accelerated development of environmentally acceptable alternative chemicals and technologies
5. Make relevant scientific information, research results, and training available to developing countries [28]

The Montreal Protocol was strengthened in 1990 and 1992. The current terms of the treaty banned production of CFCs, carbon tetrachloride, and methyl chloroform as of January 1996. A ban on halon production took effect in January 1995 [29].

A number of alternatives to the fully chlorinated and, hence, more destructive CFCs have been developed. The two groups of compounds that emerged as significant replacements for the CFCs are hydrofluorocarbons (HFCs) and hydrochlorofluorocarbons (HCFCs). In contrast to the CFCs, HFCs and HCFCs contain one or more C—H bonds. This makes them susceptible to attack by OH radicals in the lower atmosphere. Because HFCs do not contain chlorine, they do not have the ozone-depleting potential associated with the chlorine cycle shown in Figure 11–9. Although HCFCs contain chlorine, this chlorine is not transported to the stratosphere because OH scavenging in the troposphere is relatively efficient.

The implementation of the Montreal Protocol appears to be working. Worldwide CFC production has dropped by more than 50% since 1986. In 1993 alone, it dropped 15%. Buildup of CFCs and halons has slowed, and the levels of methyl chloroform have been declining since 1991 [30, 31]. Because the HCFCs contribute to ozone depletion, albeit at a lower level than CFCs, it is anticipated that the peak chlorine levels will continue to rise until the year 2006 if chemical firms make use of their full allocation of HCFCs [32].

The picture of the future development or retreat of the ozone hole is blurred by both the weather and volcanic eruptions. A very cold spring and strong winds forming a polar vortex that prevents replenishment of ozone-rich air will result in development of a large ozone hole in the Northern Hemisphere. The eruption of Mount Pinatubo (Phillippines) in 1991 contributed sulfuric acid aerosols that cause ozone depletion that adds to the effect of anthropogenic contributions.

**FIGURE 11-10**

Average global temperature for 1000 years. (*Source:* Mann, M. E., R. S. Bradley, M. K. Hughes, "Northern Hemisphere temperatures during the past millennium: inferences, uncertainties, and limitations," *Geophysical Research Letters,* vol. 26, 1999. Reprinted by permission.)

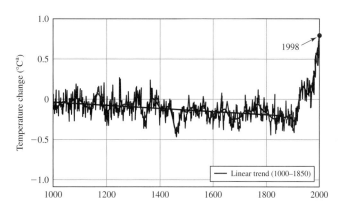

## Global Warming

Unlike ozone, carbon dioxide is relatively transparent to shortwave UV light from the sun. It does, however, absorb and emit longwave radiation at wavelengths typical of the earth and atmosphere. Hence, $CO_2$ acts much like the glass on a greenhouse. It lets in shortwave radiation from the sun that heats the ground surface, but it restricts the loss of heat by radiation from the ground surface. The more $CO_2$ in the atmosphere, the more effective it is in restricting the outflow of radiative energy.

The hypothesis is that increasing levels of $CO_2$ leads to global warming. As shown in Figure 11–10, almost every year since 1990 has been hotter than the preceding year. The average global surface temperature was higher in 1998 than in any time in the past 1000 years.

Since the first systematic measurements were made at Mauna Loa in Hawaii in 1958, $CO_2$ levels have risen from 315 to 360 ppm [33]. From analysis of air trapped in ice cores in Greenland and Antarctica, we know that preindustrial levels of $CO_2$ were about 280 ppm. The ice core records indicate that, over the last 160,000 years, no fluctuations of $CO_2$ have been larger than 70 ppm [34]. Other gases have now been recognized as contributing to the greenhouse effect. Methane ($CH_4$), nitrous oxide ($N_2O$), and CFCs are similar to $CO_2$ in their radiative behavior. Even though their concentrations are much lower than $CO_2$, these gases are now estimated to trap about 60% as much longwave radiation as $CO_2$. In recent studies, a drop-off in the rate of methane accumulation has occurred. In 1989–1990, atmospheric methane was increasing at a rate of about 10 or 11 ppb per year. An abrupt decrease to about 2 ppb per year occurred in 1992. This decrease has been attributed to a reduction in natural gas leaks such as those from pipelines [34].

The bulk of the carbon dioxide that has been added to the atmosphere has been attributed to the combustion of fossil fuel. In the 1980s, massive deforestation was identified as a possible contribution. Both the burning of timber and the release of carbon from bacterial degradation contribute. Perhaps more important, deforestation removes a mechanism for removing $CO_2$ from the atmosphere (commonly referred to as a **sink**). In normal respiration, green plants use $CO_2$ as a carbon source. This $CO_2$ is fixed in the biomass by photosynthetic processes. A rapidly growing rain forest can fix between 1 and 2 kg per year of carbon per square meter of ground surface. Cultivated fields, in contrast, fix only about 0.2–0.4 $kg \cdot m^{-2}$, and this amount is recycled by bioconsumption and conversion to $CO_2$.

Attempts to understand the consequences of global warming are based on mathematical models of the global circulation of the atmosphere and oceans. To date these models have a "good news–bad news" conclusion. Based on a 1–3.5°C rise in global temperature, the following good news is predicted for North America [24, 35]:

1. A decrease in heating costs (partly offset by increased air-conditioning cost)
2. A longer growing season for crops
3. Much easier navigation in the Arctic seas

The bad news:

1. Drier crop conditions in the Midwest and Great Plains, requiring more irrigation
2. Widespread melting of permanently frozen ground with adverse effects on building technology in Alaska and northern Canada
3. A rise in sea level up to 0.5 m that would result in an increase in the severity of flooding, damage to coastal structures, destruction of wetlands, and saltwater intrusion into drinking-water supplies in coastal areas such as Florida

On a global scale, the affects on human health may be catastrophic. Aside from heat stress, which in itself is no small thing, malaria and dengue fever—transmitted by mosquitoes—will increase in areas of increased precipitation as well as increased temperature [36]. The Intergovernmental Panel on Climate Change (IPCC) estimates between 50 and 80 million additional cases of malaria alone will result from the forecast temperature change [37].

There is still much speculation about the cause-and-effect relationship of changes in greenhouse gas concentrations and the possible outcomes. "At present it is not possible to make a very confident statement about the relative contributions of specific natural and anthropogenic forcings to observed climate change. One of the main reasons is that fully realistic simulations of climate change due to the combined effects of all anthropogenic and natural forcings mechanisms have yet to be computed." [38]

Obviously, there is still considerable disagreement about the potential for global warming. On the other hand, the consequences of ignoring these trends are sufficiently dramatic that intensive research will continue in the next decade. Even without the risks of climate change, improvements in energy efficiency to reduce greenhouse gas emissions and to eliminate CFCs are justified. The expectation of damages from climate change provides a rationale for pursuing these programs vigorously.

## 11-7 AIR POLLUTION METEOROLOGY

### The Atmospheric Engine

The atmosphere is somewhat like an engine. It is continually expanding and compressing gases, exchanging heat, and generally creating chaos. The driving energy for this unwieldy machine comes from the sun. The difference in heat input between the equator and the poles provides the initial overall circulation of the earth's atmosphere. The rotation of the earth coupled with the different heat conductivities of the oceans and land produce weather.

**Highs and Lows.**   Because air has mass, it also exerts pressure on things under it. Like water, which we intuitively understand to exert greater pressures at greater depths, the atmosphere exerts more pressure at the surface than it does at higher elevations. The highs and lows depicted on weather maps are simply areas of greater and lesser pressure. The elliptical lines shown on more detailed weather maps are lines of constant pressure, or **isobars.** A two-dimensional plot of pressure and distance through a high- or low-pressure system would appear as shown in Figure 11–11. Figure 11–11a shows a plan view of a high-pressure system in $x/y$ coordinates with the highest pressure (102.8 kPa) in the center. The lower portion of Figure 11–11a shows a plot of pressure versus distance $(x)$ for a cross section through the plan view along the line $AA$. This cross section has the appearance of a hill with the highest pressure corresponding to the H in the plan view of the high. A similar plot for a low-pressure system is shown in Figure 11–11b. Here a cross section through the line $BB$ shows a valley with the lowest pressure corresponding to the L in the plan view of the low.

The wind flows from the higher pressure areas to the lower pressure areas. On a nonrotating planet, the wind direction would be perpendicular to the isobars (Figure 11–12a). However, because the earth rotates, an angular thrust called the Coriolis effect is added to this motion. The resultant

**FIGURE 11–11**

High- and low-pressure systems.

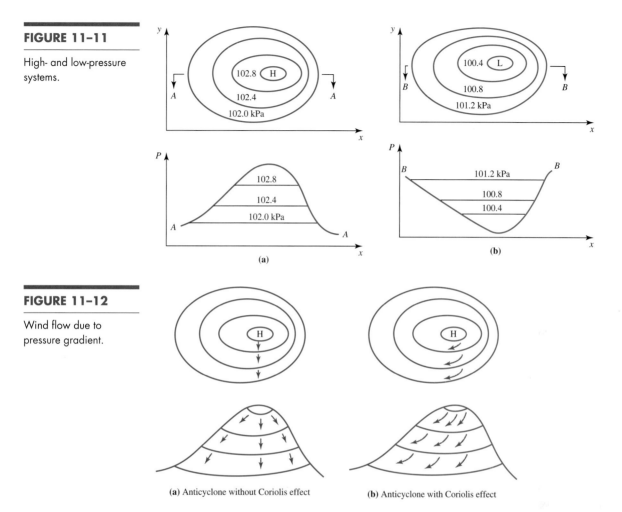

(a)

(b)

**FIGURE 11–12**

Wind flow due to pressure gradient.

(a) Anticyclone without Coriolis effect

(b) Anticyclone with Coriolis effect

wind direction in the Northern Hemisphere is as shown in Figure 11–12b. The technical names given to these systems are **anticyclones** for highs and **cyclones** for lows. Anticyclones are associated with good weather. Cyclones are associated with foul weather. Tornadoes and hurricanes are the foulest of the cyclones.

Wind speed is in part a function of the steepness of the pressure surface. When the isobars are close together, the pressure **gradient** (slope) is said to be steep and the wind speed relatively high. If the isobars are well spread out, the winds are light or nonexistent.

### Turbulence

**Mechanical Turbulence.** In its simplest terms, we may consider turbulence to be the addition of random fluctuations of wind velocity (i.e., speed and direction) to the overall average wind velocity. These fluctuations are caused, in part, by the fact that the atmosphere is being sheared. The shearing results from the fact that the wind speed is zero at the ground surface and rises with elevation to near the speed imposed by the pressure gradient. The shearing results in a tumbling, tearing motion as the mass just above the surface falls over the slower moving air at the surface. The swirls thus formed are called **eddies.** These small eddies feed larger ones. As you might expect, the greater the mean wind speed, the greater the mechanical turbulence. The more mechanical turbulence, the easier it is to disperse and spread atmospheric pollutants.

**Thermal Turbulence.** Like all other things in nature, the rather complex interaction that produces mechanical turbulence is confounded and further complicated by a third party. Heating of the ground surface causes turbulence in the same fashion that heating the bottom of a beaker full of water causes turbulence. At some point below boiling, you can see density currents rising off the bottom. Likewise, if the earth's surface is heated strongly and in turn heats the air above it, thermal turbulence will be generated. Indeed, the "thermals" sought by glider pilots and hot air balloonists are these thermal currents rising on what otherwise would be a calm day.

The converse situation can arise during clear nights when the ground radiates its heat away to the cold night sky. The cold ground, in turn, cools the air above it, causing a sinking density current.

### Stability

The tendency of the atmosphere to resist or enhance vertical motion is termed **stability.** It is related to both wind speed and the change of air temperature with height (**lapse rate**). For our purpose, we may use the lapse rate alone as an indicator of the stability condition of the atmosphere.

There are three stability categories. When the atmosphere is classified as **unstable,** mechanical turbulence is enhanced by the thermal structure. A **neutral** atmosphere is one in which the thermal structure neither enhances nor resists mechanical turbulence. When the thermal structure inhibits mechanical turbulence, the atmosphere is said to be **stable.** Cyclones are associated with unstable air. Anticyclones are associated with stable air.

**Neutral Stability.**    The lapse rate for a neutral atmosphere is defined by the rate of temperature increase (or decrease) experienced by a parcel of air that expands (or contracts) **adiabatically** (without the addition or loss of heat) as it is raised through the atmosphere. This rate of temperature decrease $(-dT/dz)$ is called the **dry adiabatic lapse rate,** designated by the Greek letter gamma ($\Gamma$). It has a value of approximately $-1.00°C \cdot 100 \text{ m}^{-1}$. (*Note:* This is not a slope in the normal sense, i.e., it is not $dy/dx$.) In Figure 11–13a, the dry adiabatic lapse rate of a parcel of air is shown as a dashed line and the temperature of the atmosphere (ambient lapse rate) is shown as a solid line. Because the ambient lapse rate is the same as $\Gamma$, the atmosphere is said to have a neutral stability.

**Unstable Atmosphere.**    If the temperature of the atmosphere falls at a rate greater than $\Gamma$ the lapse rate is said to be **superadiabatic** and the atmosphere is unstable. Using Figure 11–13b, we can see that this is so. The actual lapse rate is shown by the solid line. If we capture a balloon full of polluted air at elevation A and adiabatically displace it 100 m vertically to elevation B, the temperature of the air inside the balloon will decrease from 21.15 to 20.15°C. At a lapse rate of $-1.25°C \cdot 100 \text{ m}^{-1}$, the temperature of the air outside the balloon will decrease from 21.15 to 19.90°C. The air inside the balloon will be warmer than the air outside; this temperature difference gives the balloon buoyancy. It will behave as a hot gas and continue to rise without any further mechanical effort. Thus, mechanical turbulence is enhanced and the atmosphere is unstable. If we adiabatically displace the balloon downward to elevation C, the temperature inside the balloon would rise at the rate of the dry adiabat. Thus, in moving 100 m, the temperature will increase from 21.15 to 22.15°C. The temperature outside the balloon will increase at the superadiabatic lapse rate to 22.40°C. The air in the balloon will be cooler than the ambient air and the balloon will have a tendency to sink. Again, mechanical turbulence (displacement) is enhanced.

**Stable Atmosphere.**    If the temperature of the atmosphere falls at a rate less than $\Gamma$ it is called **subadiabatic,** and the atmosphere is stable. If we again capture a balloon of polluted air at elevation A (Figure 11–13c) and adiabatically displace it vertically to elevation B, the temperature of the polluted air will decrease at a rate equal to the dry adiabatic rate. Thus, in moving 100 m, the temperature will decrease from 21.15 to 20.15°C as before. However, because the ambient lapse rate is $-0.5°C \cdot 100 \text{ m}^{-1}$, the temperature of the air outside the balloon will have dropped to only

**FIGURE 11–13**

Lapse rate and displaced air volume. (*Source: Atomic Energy Commission, Meteorology and Atomic Energy, U.S. Government Printing Office, Washington, D.C., 1955.)*

20.65°C. Because the air inside the balloon is cooler than the air outside the balloon, the balloon will have a tendency to sink. Thus, the mechanical displacement (turbulence) is inhibited.

In contrast, if we displace the balloon adiabatically to elevation C, the temperature inside the balloon would increase to 22.15°C, and the ambient temperature would increase to 21.65°C. In this case, the air inside the balloon would be warmer than the ambient air and the balloon would tend to rise. Again, the mechanical displacement would be inhibited.

There are two special cases of subadiabatic lapse rate. When there is no change of temperature with elevation, the lapse rate is called **isothermal.** When the temperature increases with elevation, the lapse rate is called an **inversion.** The inversion is the most severe form of a stable temperature profile. It is often associated with restricted air volumes that cause air pollution episodes.

**EXAMPLE 11–2**   Given the following temperature and elevation data, determine the stability of the atmosphere.

| Elevation (m) | Temperature (°C) |
|---|---|
| 2.00 | 14.35 |
| 324.00 | 11.13 |

Solution   Begin by determining the existing lapse rate.

$$\frac{\Delta T}{\Delta Z} = \frac{T_2 - T_1}{Z_2 - Z_1}$$

$$= \frac{11.13 - 14.35}{324.00 - 2.00} = \frac{-3.22}{322.00} = -0.0100°C \cdot m^{-1} = -1.00°C \cdot 100\ m^{-1}$$

Now we compare this with $\Gamma$ and find that they are equal. Thus, the atmospheric stability is neutral.

### Terrain Effects

**Heat Islands.**   A heat island results from a mass of material, either natural or anthropogenic, that absorbs and reradiates heat at a greater rate than the surrounding area. This causes moderate to strong vertical convection currents above the heat island. The effect is superimposed on the prevailing meteorological conditions and is nullified by strong winds. Large industrial complexes and small to large cities are examples of places that would have a heat island.

Because of the heat island effect, atmospheric stability will be less over a city than it is over the surrounding countryside. Depending upon the location of the pollutant sources, this can be either good news or bad news. First, the good news: For ground level sources such as automobiles, the bowl of unstable air that forms will allow a greater air volume for dilution of the pollutants. Now the bad news: Under stable conditions, plumes from tall stacks would be carried out over the countryside without increasing ground level pollutant concentrations. Unfortunately, the instability caused by the heat island mixes these plumes to the ground level.

**Land–Sea Breezes.**   Under a stagnating anticyclone, a strong local circulation pattern may develop across the shoreline of large water bodies. During the night, the land cools more rapidly than the water. The relatively cooler air over the land flows toward the water (a land breeze, Figure 11–14). During the morning the land heats faster than water. The air over the land becomes relatively warm and begins to rise. The rising air is replaced by air from over the water body (a sea or lake breeze, Figure 11–15).

The effect of the lake breeze on stability is to impose a surface-based inversion on the temperature profile. As the air moves from the water over the warm ground, it is heated from below. Thus, for stack plumes originating near the shoreline, the stable lapse rate causes a fanning plume that does not disperse close to the stack (Figure 11–16). The lapse condition grows to the height

**FIGURE 11–14**

Land breeze during the night.

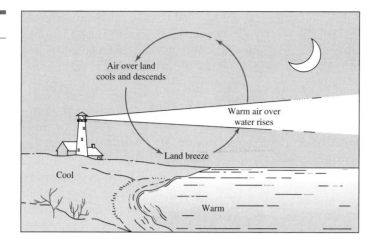

**FIGURE 11–15**

Lake breeze during the day.

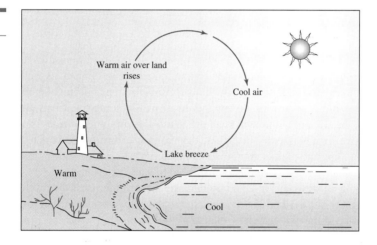

**FIGURE 11–16**

Effect of lake breeze on plume dispersion.

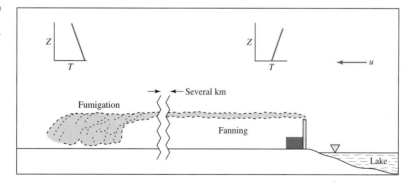

of the stack as the air moves inland. At some point inland, unstable conditions develop and the plume rapidly descends to the ground causing a "fumigation" at the ground surface.

**Valleys.** When the general circulation imposes moderate to strong winds, valleys that are oriented at an acute angle to the wind direction channel the wind. The valley effectively peels off part of the wind and forces it to follow the direction of the valley floor.

Under a stagnating anticyclone, the valley will set up its own circulation. Warming of the valley walls will cause the valley air to be warmed. It will become more buoyant and flow up the valley. At night the cooling process will cause the wind to flow down the valley.

Valleys oriented in the north–south direction are more susceptible to inversions than level terrain. The valley walls protect the floor from radiative heating by the sun. Yet the walls and floor are free to radiate heat away to the cold night sky. Thus, under weak winds, the ground cannot heat the air rapidly enough during the day to dissipate the inversion that formed during the night.

## 11–8 ATMOSPHERIC DISPERSION

### Factors Affecting Dispersion of Air Pollutants

The factors that affect the transport, dilution, and dispersion of air pollutants can generally be categorized in terms of the emission point characteristics, the nature of the pollutant material, meteorological conditions, and the effects of terrain and anthropogenic structures. We have discussed all of these except the source conditions. Now we wish to integrate the first and third factors to describe the qualitative aspects of calculating pollutant concentrations. We shall follow this with a simple quantitative model for a point source. More complex models for point sources (in rough terrain, in industrial settings, or for long time periods), area sources, and mobile sources are left for more advanced texts.

**Source Characteristics.** Most industrial effluents are discharged vertically into the open air through a stack or duct. As the contaminated gas stream leaves the discharge point, the plume tends to expand and mix with the ambient air. Horizontal air movement will tend to bend the discharge plume toward the downwind direction. At some point between 300 and 3000 m downwind, the effluent plume will level off. While the effluent plume is rising, bending, and beginning to move in a horizontal direction, the gaseous effluents are being diluted by the ambient air surrounding the plume. As the contaminated gases are diluted by larger and larger volumes of ambient air, they are eventually dispersed toward the ground.

The plume rise is affected by both the upward inertia of the discharge gas stream and by its buoyancy. The vertical inertia is related to the exit gas velocity and mass. The plume's buoyancy is related to the exit gas mass relative to the surrounding air mass. Increasing the exit velocity or the exit gas temperature will generally increase the plume rise. The plume rise, together with the physical stack height, is called the **effective stack height.**

The additional rise of the plume above the discharge point as the plume bends and levels off is a factor in the resultant downwind ground level concentrations. The higher the plume rises initially, the greater distance there is for diluting the contaminated gases as they expand and mix downward.

For a specific discharge height and set of plume dilution conditions, the ground level concentration is proportional to the amount of contaminant materials discharged from the stack outlet for a specific period. Thus, when all other conditions are constant, an increase in the pollutant discharge rate will cause a proportional increase in the downwind ground level concentrations.

**Downwind Distance.** The greater the distance between the point of discharge and a ground level receptor downwind, the greater will be the volume of air available for diluting the contaminant discharge before it reaches the receptor.

**Wind Speed and Direction.** The wind direction determines the direction in which the contaminated gas stream will move across local terrain. Wind speed affects the plume rise and the rate of mixing or dilution of the contaminated gases as they leave the discharge point. An increase in wind speed will decrease the plume rise by bending the plume over more rapidly. The decrease in plume rise tends to increase the pollutant's ground level concentration. On the other hand, an increase in wind speed will increase the rate of dilution of the effluent plume, tending to lower the downwind concentrations. Under different conditions, one or the other of the two wind speed effects becomes the predominant effect. These effects, in turn, affect the distance downwind of the source at which the maximum ground level concentration will occur.

**Stability.**   The turbulence of the atmosphere follows no other factor in power of dilution. The more unstable the atmosphere, the greater the diluting power. Inversions that are not ground-based, but begin at some height above the stack exit, act as a lid to restrict vertical dilution.

### Dispersion Modeling

**General Considerations and Use of Models.**   A dispersion model is a mathematical description of the meteorological transport and dispersion process that is quantified in terms of source and meteorologic parameters during a particular time. The resultant numerical calculations yield estimates of concentrations of the particular pollutant for specific locations and times.

To verify the numerical results of such a model, actual measured concentrations of the particular atmospheric pollutant must be obtained and compared with the calculated values by means of statistical techniques. The meteorological parameters required for use of the models include wind direction, wind speed, and atmospheric stability. In some models, provisions may be made for including lapse rate and vertical mixing height. Most models will require data about the physical stack height, the diameter of the stack at the emission discharge point, the exit gas temperature and velocity, and the mass rate of emission of pollutants.

Models are usually classified as either short-term or climatological models. Short-term models are generally used under the following circumstances: (1) to estimate ambient concentrations where it is impractical to sample, such as over rivers or lakes, or at great distances above the ground; (2) to estimate the required emergency source reductions associated with periods of air stagnation under air pollution episode alert conditions; and (3) to estimate the most probable locations of high, short-term, ground-level concentrations as part of a site selection evaluation for the location of air monitoring equipment.

Climatological models are used to estimate mean concentrations over a long period or to estimate mean concentrations that exist at particular times of the day for each season over a long period. Long-term models are used as an aid in understanding atmospheric transport over long distances. We will be concerned only with short-term models in their most simple application.

**Basic Point Source Gaussian Dispersion Model.**   The basic Gaussian diffusion equation assumes that atmospheric stability is uniform throughout the layer into which the contaminated gas stream is discharged. The model assumes that turbulent diffusion is a random activity and hence the dilution of the contaminated gas stream in both the horizontal and vertical direction can be described by the Gaussian or normal equation. The model further assumes that the contaminated gas stream is released into the atmosphere at a distance above ground level that is equal to the physical stack height plus the plume rise ($\Delta H$). The model assumes that the degree of dilution of the effluent plume is inversely proportional to the wind speed ($u$). The model also assumes that pollutant material that reaches ground level is totally reflected back into the atmosphere like a beam of light striking a mirror at an angle. Mathematically, this ground reflection is accounted for by assuming a virtual or imaginary source located at a distance of $-H$ with respect to ground level, and emitting an imaginary plume with the same source strength as the real source being modeled. The same general idea can be used to establish other boundary layer conditions for the equations, such as limiting horizontal or vertical mixing.

**The Model.**   We have selected the model equation in the form presented by D. B. Turner [39]. It gives the ground level concentration ($\chi$) of pollutant at a point (coordinates $x$ and $y$) downwind from a stack with an effective height ($H$) (Figure 11–17). The standard deviation of the plume in the horizontal and vertical directions is designated by $s_y$ and $s_z$, respectively. The standard deviations are functions of the downward distance from the source and the stability of the

**FIGURE 11-17**

Plume dispersion
coordinate system.
(*Source:* Turner, D. B.,
*Workbook of Atmospheric
Dispersion Estimates,* U.S.
Department of Health,
Education and Welfare,
Public Health Service,
National Center for Air
Pollution Control,
Publication No. 999-AP-
26, U.S. Government
Printing Office,
Washington, D.C.,
1967.)

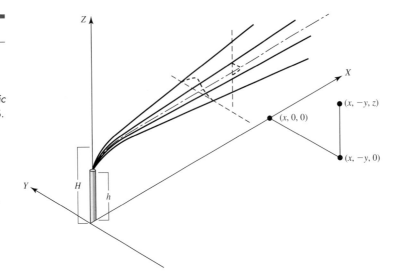

atmosphere. The equation is as follows:

$$\chi(x, y, 0, H) = \left[\frac{E}{\pi s_y s_z u}\right]\left[\exp\left[-\frac{1}{2}\left(\frac{y}{s_y}\right)^2\right]\right]\left[\exp\left[-\frac{1}{2}\left(\frac{H}{s_z}\right)^2\right]\right] \tag{11-12}$$

where $\chi(x, y, 0, H)$ = downwind concentration at ground level (in $g \cdot m^{-3}$)
$\quad\quad E$ = emission rate of pollutant (in $g \cdot s^{-1}$)
$\quad\quad s_y, s_z$ = plume dispersion (in m)
$\quad\quad u$ = wind speed (in $m \cdot s^{-1}$)
$\quad\quad x, y, z,$ and $H$ = distances (in m)
$\quad\quad$ exp = exponential $e$ such that terms in brackets immediately following are
$\quad\quad\quad\quad$ powers of $e$, that is, $e[\quad]$, where $e = 2.7182$

The value for the effective stack height is the sum of the physical stack height ($h$) and the plume rise $\Delta H$.

$$H = h + \Delta H \tag{11-13}$$

$\Delta H$ may be computed from Holland's formula as follows [40]:

$$\Delta H = \frac{v_s d}{u}\left[1.5 + \left(2.68 \times 10^{-2}(P)\left(\frac{T_s - T_a}{T_s}\right)d\right)\right] \tag{11-14}$$

where $v_s$ = stack velocity (in $m \cdot s^{-1}$)
$\quad\quad d$ = stack diameter (in m/s)
$\quad\quad u$ = wind speed (in m)
$\quad\quad P$ = pressure (in kPa)
$\quad\quad T_s$ = stack temperature (K)
$\quad\quad T_a$ = air temperature (K)

The values of $s_y$ and $s_z$ depend on the turbulent structure or stability of the atmosphere. Figures 11–18 and 11–19 provide graphical relationships between the down wind distance $x$ in kilometers and values of $s_y$ and $s_z$ in meters. The curves on the two figures are labeled A through F. The label A refers to very unstable atmospheric conditions, B to unstable atmospheric conditions, C to slightly unstable conditions, D to neutral conditions, E to stable conditions, and F to very stable atmospheric conditions. Each of these stability parameters represents an averaging time of approximately 3–15 min.

Other averaging times may be approximated by multiplying by empirical constants, for example, 0.36 for 24 h. Turner presented a table (Table 11–6) and discussion that allows an estimate of stability based on wind speed and the conditions of solar radiation.

**FIGURE 11–18**

Horizontal dispersion coefficient. (*Source:* Turner, D. B., *Workbook of Atmospheric Dispersion Estimates*, U.S. Department of Health, Education and Welfare, Public Health Service, National Center for Air Pollution Control, Publication No. 999-AP-28, U.S. Government Printing Office, Washington, D.C., 1967.)

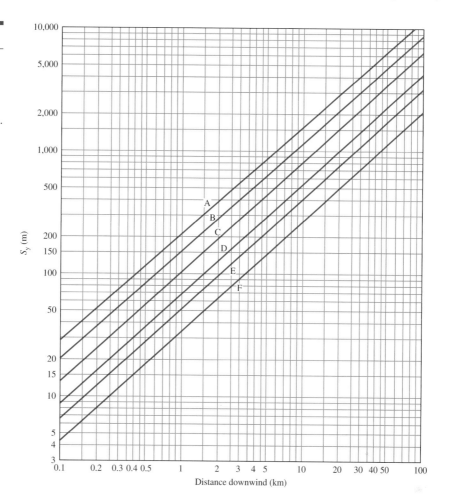

| | **Day**[a] | | | **Night**[a] | |
|---|---|---|---|---|---|
| **Surface Wind Speed (at 10 m) (m · s⁻¹)** | **Incoming Solar Radiation** | | | **Thinly Overcast or ≥ $\frac{4}{8}$ Low Cloud** | **≤ $\frac{3}{8}$ Cloud** |
| | **Strong** | **Moderate** | **Slight** | | |

**TABLE 11–6**   Key to Stability Categories

| **Surface Wind Speed (at 10 m) (m · s⁻¹)** | **Strong** | **Moderate** | **Slight** | **≥ $\frac{4}{8}$ Low Cloud** | **≤ $\frac{3}{8}$ Cloud** |
|---|---|---|---|---|---|
| <2 | A | A–B | B | | |
| 2–3 | A–B | B | C | E | F |
| 3–5 | B | B–C | C | D | E |
| 5–6 | C | C–D | D | D | D |
| >6 | C | D | D | D | D |

[a]The neutral class, D, should be assumed for overcast conditions during day or night. Note that "thinly overcast" is not equivalent to "overcast."

*Notes:* Class A is the most unstable and class F is the most stable class considered here. Night refers to the period from one hour before sunset to one hour after sunrise. Note that the neutral class, D, can be assumed for overcast conditions during day or night, regardless of wind speed.

"Strong" incoming solar radiation corresponds to a solar altitude greater than 60 degrees with clear skies; "slight" insolation corresponds to a solar altitude from 15 to 35 degrees with clear skies. Table 170, Solar Altitude and Azimuth, in the Smithsonian Meteorological Tables, can be used in determining solar radiation. Incoming radiation that would be strong with clear skies can be expected to be reduced to moderate with broken ($\frac{5}{8}$ to $\frac{7}{8}$ cloud cover) middle clouds and to slight with broken low clouds.

*Source:* Turner, D. B., *Workbook of Atmospheric Dispersion Estimates,* U.S. Department of Health, Education and Welfare, Public Health Service, National Center for Air Pollution Control, Publication No. 999-AP-28, Government Printing Office, Washington, D.C., 1967.

**FIGURE 11–19**

Vertical dispersion coefficient. (*Source:* Turner, D. B., *Workbook of Atmospheric Dispersion Estimates,* U.S. Department of Health Education and Welfare, Public Health Service, National Center for Air Pollution Control, Publication No. 999-AP-28, U.S. Government Printing Office, Washington, D.C., 1967.)

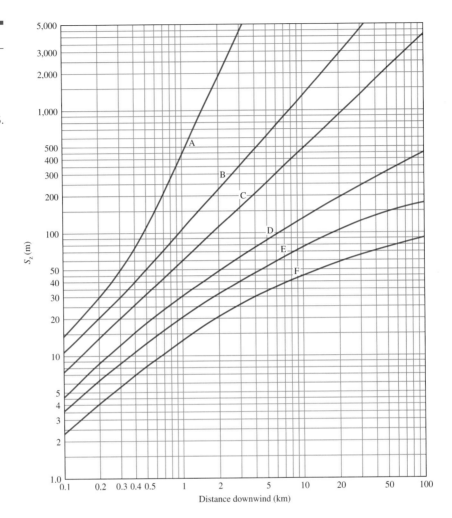

For computer solutions of the dispersion model, it is convenient to have an algorithm to express the stability class lines in Figures 11–17 and 11–18, D. O. Martin has developed the following equations that provide an approximate fit [41].

$$s_y = ax^{0.894} \tag{11-15}$$

$$s_z = cx^d + f \tag{11-16}$$

where the constants $a$, $c$, $d$, and $f$ are defined in Table 11–7. These equations were developed to yield $s_y$ and $s_z$ in meters for downwind distance $x$ in kilometers.

As noted earlier, the wind speed varies with height. Unless the wind speed at the effective height of the plume ($H$) is known, the wind speed must be corrected to account for the change in speed with elevation. For elevations up to a few hundred meters a power law expression of the following form may be used to estimate the wind speed at heights other than that of the measurement.

$$u_2 = u_1 \left( \frac{z_2}{z_1} \right)^p \tag{11-17}$$

where $u_2$ = windspeed at elevation $z_2$
$u_1$ = windspeed at elevation $z_1$
$p$ = function of the terrain roughness and the stability

EPA's recommended values for $p$ are shown in Table 11–8.

**TABLE 11–7**  Values of $a$, $c$, $d$, and $f$ for Calculating $s_y$ and $s_z$

| Stability Class | x < 1 km | | | | x ≥ 1 km | | |
|---|---|---|---|---|---|---|---|
| | a | c | d | f | c | d | f |
| A | 213 | 440.8 | 1.941 | 9.27 | 459.7 | 2.094 | −9.6 |
| B | 156 | 100.6 | 1.149 | 3.3 | 108.2 | 1.098 | 2 |
| C | 104 | 61 | 0.911 | 0 | 61 | 0.911 | 0 |
| D | 68 | 33.2 | 0.725 | −1.7 | 44.5 | 0.516 | −13 |
| E | 50.5 | 22.8 | 0.678 | 1.3 | 55.4 | 0.305 | −34 |
| F | 34 | 14.35 | 0.74 | −0.35 | 62.6 | 0.18 | −48.6 |

Source: Martin, D. O., "Comment on the change of concentration standard deviations with distance," *Journal of the Air Pollution Control Association*, vol. 26, pp. 145–146, 1976.

**TABLE 11–8**  Exponent $p$ Values for Rural and Urban Regimes

| Stability Class | Rural | Urban | Stability Class | Rural | Urban |
|---|---|---|---|---|---|
| A | 0.07 | 0.15 | D | 0.15 | 0.25 |
| B | 0.07 | 0.15 | E | 0.35 | 0.30 |
| C | 0.10 | 0.20 | F | 0.55 | 0.30 |

Source: *User's Guide for ISC3 Dispersion Models*, Vol. II, EPA-454/B-95-003b, U.S. Environmental Protection Agency, September, 1995.

**EXAMPLE 11–3**  It has been estimated that the emission of $SO_2$ from a coal-fired power plant is 1656.2 g · s⁻¹. At 3 km downwind on an overcast summer afternoon, what is the centerline concentration of $SO_2$ if the wind speed at the top of the stack (120.0 m) is 4.50 m · s⁻¹? (*Note:* "centerline" implies $y = 0$.)

**Stack parameters:**
Height = 120.0 m
Diameter = 1.20 m
Exit velocity = $10.0 \text{ m} \cdot \text{s}^{-1}$
Temperature = 315°C

**Atmospheric conditions:**
Pressure = 95.0 kPa
Temperature = 25.0°C

**Solution**  We begin by determining the effective stack height ($H$).

$$\Delta H = \frac{(10.0 \text{ m} \cdot \text{s}^{-1})(1.20 \text{ m})}{4.50 \text{ m} \cdot \text{s}^{-1}} \left\{ 1.5 + \left[ 2.68 \times 10^{-2}(95.0) \left( \frac{588 \text{ K} - 298 \text{ K}}{588 \text{ K}} \right) (1.20 \text{ m}) \right] \right\}$$

$$= 8.0 \text{ m}$$

$$H = 120.0 + 8.0 = 128.0 \text{ m}$$

Next, we must determine the atmospheric stability class. The footnote to Table 11–6 indicates that the D class should be used for overcast conditions.

Because the wind speed measurement was taken at the top of the stack and the effective stack height ($H$) is not significantly different from the stack height, we will ignore the power law correction for wind speed.

From Equations 11–15 and 11–16 we can determine that at 3 km downwind with a D stability the plume standard deviations are

$$s_y = 68(3)^{0.894} = 181.6 \text{ m}$$

$$s_z = 44.5(3)^{0.516} - 13 = 65.4 \text{ m}$$

Thus,

$$\chi = \left[ \frac{1656.2}{\pi (181.6)(65.4)(4.50)} \right] \left\{ \exp \left[ -\frac{1}{2} \left( \frac{0}{181.6} \right)^2 \right] \right\} \left\{ \exp \left[ -\frac{1}{2} \left( \frac{128.0}{65.4} \right)^2 \right] \right\}$$

$$= 1.45 \times 10^{-3} \ g \cdot m^{-3}, \ or \ 1.5 \times 10^{-3} \ g \cdot m^{-3} \ of \ SO_2$$

**FIGURE 11–20**

Effect of elevated inversion on dispersion.

**Inversion Aloft.** When an inversion is present, the basic diffusion equation must be modified to take into account the fact that the plume cannot disperse vertically once it reaches the inversion layer. The plume will begin to mix downward when it reaches the base of the inversion layer (Figure 11–20). The downward mixing will begin at a distance $X_L$ downwind from the stack. The $X_L$ distance is a function of the stability in the layer below the inversion. It has been determined empirically that the vertical standard deviation of the plume can be calculated with the following formula at the distance $X_L$.

$$s_z = 0.47(L - H) \tag{11–18}$$

where $L$ = height to bottom of inversion layer (in m)
$\quad\quad H$ = effective stack height (in m)

When the plume reaches twice the distance to initial contact with the inversion base, the plume is said to be completely mixed throughout the layer below the inversion. Beyond a distance equal to $2X_L$ the centerline concentration of pollutants may be estimated by using the following equation.

$$\chi = \frac{E}{(2\pi)^{1/2} s_y u L} \tag{11–19}$$

Note that $s_y$ is determined by the stability of the layer below the inversion and the distance to the receptor using either Figure 11–18 or Equation 11–15. We call this the "inversion" or "short form" of the dispersion equation.

**EXAMPLE 11–4**  Determine the distance downwind from a stack at which we must switch to the inversion form of the dispersion model given the following meteorologic situation:

| | |
|---|---|
| Effective stack height: 50 m | Cloud cover: none |
| Inversion base: 350 m | Time: 1130 h |
| Wind speed: 7.3 m · s⁻¹ at the effective stack height | Season: summer |

**Solution**  Determine the stability class using Table 11–6. At > 6 m · s⁻¹ with strong radiation, the stability class is C.
   Calculate the value of $s_z$.

$$s_z = 0.47(350 - 50 \ m) = 141 \ m$$

Using Figure 11–19, find $X_L$. With $s_z = 141$, draw a horizontal line to stability class C. Drop a vertical line to the "distance downwind." Find $X_L = 2.5$ km.

Therefore, at any distance equal to or greater than 5 km downwind ($2X_L$), use the inversion form of the equation (Equation 11–19).

For distances less than 5 km, we use Equation 11–12 with $s_z$ determined from the distance to the point of interest and the stability. Thus, in no case do we use $s_z$ computed from Equation 11–18 to calculate $\chi$.

## 11–9 INDOOR AIR QUALITY MODEL

If we envision a house or room in a house or other enclosed space as a simple box (Figure 11–21), then we can construct a simple mass-balance model to explore the behavior of the indoor air quality as a function of infiltration of outdoor air, indoor sources and sinks, and leakage to the outdoor air. If we assume the contents of the box are well mixed, then

Rate of pollutant increase in box = rate of pollutant entering box from outdoors

+ rate of pollutant entering box from indoor emissions

− rate of pollutant leaving box by leakage to outdoors

− rate of pollutant leaving box by decay          (11–20)

or

$$\Psi\frac{dC}{dt} = QC_a + E - QC - kC\Psi \tag{11–21}$$

where $\Psi$ = volume of box (in $m^3$)

$\quad C$ = concentration of pollutant ($g \cdot m^{-3}$)

$\quad Q$ = rate of infiltration of air into and out of box (in $m^3 \cdot s^{-1}$)

$\quad C_a$ = concentration of pollutant in outdoor air (in $g \cdot m^{-3}$)

$\quad E$ = emission rate of pollutant into box from indoor source (in $g \cdot s^{-1}$)

$\quad k$ = pollutant reaction rate coefficient (in $s^{-1}$)

Reaction rate coefficients for a selected list of pollutants are given in Table 11–9. The general solution for Equation 11–21 is

$$C_t = \frac{(E/\Psi) + C_a(Q/\Psi)}{(Q/\Psi) + k}\left\{1 - \exp\left[-\left(\frac{Q}{\Psi} + k\right)t\right]\right\} + C_0 \exp\left[-\left(\frac{Q}{\Psi} + k\right)t\right] \tag{11–22}$$

The steady-state solution for Equation 11–22 may be found by setting $dC/dt = 0$ and solving for $C$.

$$C_\infty = \frac{QC_a + E}{Q + k\Psi} \tag{11–23}$$

**FIGURE 11–21**

Mass-balance model for indoor air pollution.

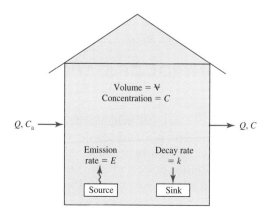

Volume = $\Psi$
Concentration = $C$

$Q, C_a \longrightarrow$          $\longrightarrow Q, C$

Emission rate = $E$          Decay rate = $k$

Source          Sink

**TABLE 11-9**      Reaction Rate Coefficients for Selected Pollutants

| Pollutant | $k$ (s$^{-1}$) | Pollutant | $k$ (s$^{-1}$) |
|---|---|---|---|
| CO | 0.0 | Particulates ($< 0.5$ μm) | $1.33 \times 10^{-4}$ |
| HCHO | $1.11 \times 10^{-4}$ | Radon | $2.11 \times 10^{-6}$ |
| NO | 0.0 | SO$_2$ | $6.39 \times 10^{-5}$ |
| NO$_x$ (as N) | $4.17 \times 10^{-5}$ | | |

*Source:* Traynor, G. W., J. R. Allen, M. G. Apte, *Indoor Air Pollution from Portable Kerosene-Fired Space Heaters, Woodburning Stoves, and Wood Burning Furnaces,* Lawrence Berkeley Laboratory, Report No. LBL-14027, March, 1982.

When the pollutant is conservative and does not decay with time or have a significant reactivity, $k = 0$. In the special case when the pollutant is conservative and the ambient concentration is negligible and the initial indoor concentration is zero, Equation 11–21 reduces to

$$C_t = \frac{E}{Q} \left\{ 1 - \exp\left[ -\left(\frac{Q}{V}\right) t \right] \right\} \tag{11-24}$$

**EXAMPLE 11-5**

An unvented kerosene heater is operated for 1 h in an apartment having a volume of 200 m³. The heater emits SO$_2$ at a rate of 50 μg · s$^{-1}$. The ambient air concentration ($C_a$) and the initial indoor air concentration ($C_0$) of SO$_2$ are 100 μg · m$^{-3}$. If the rate of ventilation is 50 L · s$^{-1}$, and the apartment is assumed to be well mixed, what is the indoor air concentration of SO$_2$ at the end of 1 h?

**Solution**

The concentration may be determined using the general solution form of the indoor air quality model (Equation 11–22). The decay rate for SO$_2$ from Table 11–9 is $6.39 \times 10^{-5}$ s$^{-1}$ and 50 L · s$^{-1}$ is equivalent to 0.050 m³ · s$^{-1}$.

$$C_t = \frac{(50 \text{ μg} \cdot \text{s}^{-1}/200 \text{ m}^3) + 100 \text{ μg} \cdot \text{m}^{-3}(0.050 \text{ m}^3 \cdot \text{s}^{-1}/200 \text{ m}^3)}{(0.050 \text{ m}^3 \cdot \text{s}^{-1}/200 \text{ m}^3) + 6.39 \times 10^{-5} \text{ s}^{-1}}$$

$$\times \left\{ 1 - \exp\left[ \left( \frac{0.050 \text{ m}^3 \cdot \text{s}^{-1}}{200 \text{ m}^3} + 6.39 \times 10^{-5} \text{ s}^{-1} \right) (3600 \text{ s}) \right] \right\}$$

$$+ (100 \text{ μg} \cdot \text{m}^{-3}) \exp\left[ -\left( \frac{0.050 \text{ m}^3 \cdot \text{s}^{-1}}{200 \text{ m}^3} + 6.39 \times 10^{-5} \text{ s}^{-1} \right) (3600 \text{ s}^{-1}) \right]$$

$$= 876.08[1 - \exp(-1.13)] + 100 \exp(-1.13)$$

$$= 876.08(1 - 0.323) + 100(0.323)$$

$$= 593.09 + 32.3 = 625.39, \text{ or } 630 \text{ μg} \cdot \text{m}^{-3}$$

## 11-10   AIR POLLUTION CONTROL OF STATIONARY SOURCES

### Gaseous Pollutants

**Absorption.** Control devices based on the principle of absorption attempt to transfer the pollutant from a gas to a liquid phase. This is a mass-transfer process in which the gas dissolves in the liquid. The dissolution may or may not be accompanied by a reaction with an ingredient of the liquid. **Mass transfer** is a diffusion process wherein the pollutant gas moves from points of higher concentration to points of lower concentration. The removal of the pollutant gas takes place in three steps:

**FIGURE 11–22**

Spray chamber.

**FIGURE 11–23**

Absorption systems.

**Plate tower**          **Packed tower**

1. Diffusion of the pollutant gas to the surface of the liquid
2. Transfer across the gas–liquid interface (dissolution)
3. Diffusion of the dissolved gas away from the interface into the liquid

Structures such as spray chambers (Figure 11–22) and towers or columns (Figure 11–23) are two classes of devices employed to absorb pollutant gases. In scrubbers, which are a type of spray chamber, liquid droplets are used to absorb the gas. In towers, a thin film of liquid is used as the absorption medium. Regardless of the type of device, the solubility of the pollutant in the liquid must be relatively high. If water is the solute, this generally limits the application to a few inorganic gases such as $NH_3$, $Cl_2$, and $SO_2$. Scrubbers are relatively inefficient absorbers but have the advantage of being able to simultaneously remove particulates. Towers are much more efficient absorbers but they become plugged by particulate matter.

The amount of absorption that can take place for a nonreactive solution is governed by the partial pressure of the pollutant. For dilute solutions, as we have in pollution control systems, the relationship between partial pressure and the concentration of the gas in solution is given by Henry's law.

$$P_g = K_H C_{equil} \tag{11–25}$$

where $P_g$ = partial pressure of gas in equilibrium with liquid (in kPa)

$\qquad K_H$ = Henry's law constant (in kPa $\cdot$ m$^3$ $\cdot$ g$^{-1}$)

$\qquad C_{equil}$ = concentration of pollutant gas in the liquid phase (in g $\cdot$ m$^{-3}$)

Equation 11–25 implies that the partial pressure of the gas must increase as the liquid accumulates more pollutant or else it will come out of solution. Because the liquid is removing pollutant from the gas phase, the partial pressure is decreasing as the gas is cleaned. This is just the reverse of what we want to happen. The easiest way to get around this problem is to run the gas and liquid in opposite directions, called **countercurrent flow.** In this manner, the high concentration gas is absorbed into a liquid with a high pollutant concentration. The lower concentration gas is absorbed by liquid with no pollutants in it.

**Adsorption.**    Adsorption is a mass-transfer process in which the gas is bonded to a solid. It is a surface phenomenon. The gas (the adsorbate) penetrates into the pores of the solid (the adsorbent)

**FIGURE 11–24**

Adsorption system.

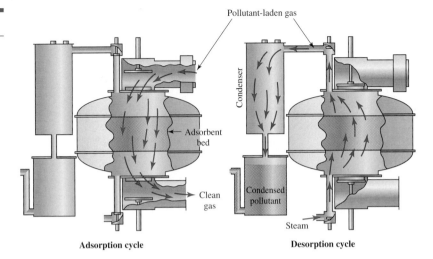

Pollutant-laden gas

Condenser

Adsorbent bed

Clean gas

Condensed pollutant

Steam

**Adsorption cycle**          **Desorption cycle**

but not into the lattice itself. The bond may be physical or chemical. Electrostatic forces hold the pollutant gas when physical bonding is significant. Chemical bonding is by reaction with the surface. Pressure vessels having a fixed bed are used to hold the adsorbent (Figure 11–24). Active carbon (activated charcoal), molecular sieves, silica gel, and activated alumina are the most common adsorbents. Active carbon is manufactured from nut shells (coconuts are great) or coal subjected to heat treatment in a reducing atmosphere. Molecular sieves are dehydrated zeolites (alkali-metal silicates). Sodium silicate is reacted with sulfuric acid to make silica gel. Activated alumina is a porous hydrated aluminum oxide. The common property of these adsorbents is a large "active" surface area per unit volume after treatment. They are very effective for treating hydrocarbon pollutants. In addition, they can capture $H_2S$ and $SO_2$. One special form of molecular sieve can also capture $NO_2$. With the exception of the active carbons, adsorbents have the drawback that they preferentially select water before any of the pollutants. Thus, water must be removed from the gas before it is treated. All of the adsorbents are subject to destruction at moderately high temperatures ($150°C$ for active carbon, $600°C$ for molecular sieves, $400°C$ for silica gel, and $500°C$ for activated alumina). They are very inefficient at these high temperatures. In fact, their activity is regenerated at these temperatures!

The relation between the amount of pollutant adsorbed and the equilibrium pressure at constant temperature is called an **adsorption isotherm.** The equation that best describes this relation for gases is the one derived by Langmuir [42].

$$W = \frac{aC_g^*}{1 + bC_g^*}$$
(11–26)

where $W$ = amount of gas per unit mass of adsorbent (in kg $\cdot$ kg$^{-1}$)
   $a, b$ = constants determined by experiment
   $C_g^*$ = equilibrium concentration of gaseous pollutant, (in g $\cdot$ m$^{-3}$)

In the analysis of experimental data, Equation 11–26 is rewritten as follows:

$$\frac{C_g^*}{W} = \frac{1}{a} + \frac{b}{a}C_g^*$$
(11–27)

In this arrangement, a plot of ($C_g^*/W$) versus $C_g^*$ should yield a straight line with a slope of ($b/a$) and an intercept equal to ($1/a$).

In contrast to absorption towers where the collected pollutant is continuously removed by flowing liquid, the collected pollutant remains in the adsorption bed. Thus, while the bed has sufficient capacity, no pollutants are emitted. At some point in time, the bed will become saturated with pollutant. As saturation is approached, pollutant will begin to leak out of the bed, a process

## FIGURE 11–25

Adsorption wave and breakthrough curve. (*Source:* Treybal, R. E., *Mass Transfer Operations,* McGraw-Hill, New York, 1968. Reprinted by permission.)

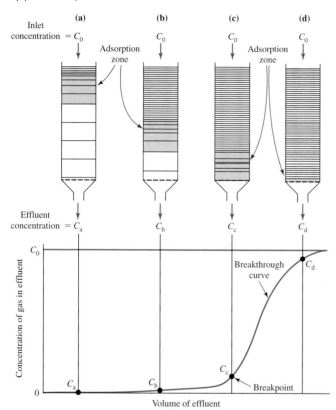

## FIGURE 11–26

Direct flame incineration.

called **breakthrough.** When the bed capacity is exhausted, the influent and effluent concentration will be equal. A typical breakthrough curve is shown in Figure 11–25. To allow for continuous operation, two beds are provided; while one is collecting pollutant, the other is being regenerated. The concentrated gas released during regeneration is usually returned to the process as recovered product.

**Combustion.**   When the contaminant in the gas stream is oxidizable to an inert gas, combustion is a possible alternative method of control. Typically, CO and hydrocarbons fall into this category. Both direct flame combustion by afterburners (Figure 11–26) and catalytic combustion have been used in commercial applications.

Direct flame incineration is the method of choice if two criteria are satisfied. First, the gas stream must have an energy concentration greater than $3.7 \ \text{MJ} \cdot \text{m}^{-3}$. At this energy concentration, the gas flame will be self-supporting after ignition. Below this point, supplementary fuel is required. The second requirement is that none of the by-products of combustion be toxic. In some cases the combustion by-product may be more toxic than the original pollutant gas. Direct flame incineration has been successfully applied to varnish-cooking, meat-smokehouse, and paint bake-oven emissions.

Some catalytic materials enable oxidation to be carried out in gases that have an energy content of less than $3.7 \ \text{MJ} \cdot \text{m}^{-3}$. Conventionally, the catalyst is placed in beds similar to adsorption beds. Frequently, the active catalyst is a platinum or palladium compound. The supporting lattice is usually a ceramic. Aside from expense, a major drawback of catalysts use is their susceptibility to poisoning by sulfur and lead compounds in trace amounts. Catalytic combustion has successfully been applied to printing-press, varnish-cooking, and asphalt-oxidation emissions.

### Flue Gas Desulfurization

Flue gas desulfurization (FGD) systems fall into two broad categories: nonregenerative and regenerative. In **nonregenerative** systems the reagent used to remove the sulfur oxides from the gas stream is used and discarded. In **regenerative** systems the reagent is recovered and reused. In terms of the number and size of systems installed, nonregenerative systems dominate.

**Nonregenerative Systems.**   There are nine commercial nonregenerative systems [43]. All have reaction chemistries based on lime ($CaO$), caustic soda ($NaOH$), soda ash ($Na_2CO_3$), or ammonia ($NH_3$).

The $SO_2$ removed in a lime/limestone-based FGD system is converted to sulfite. The overall reactions are generally represented by [44]

$$SO_2 + CaCO_3 \rightleftharpoons CaSO_3 + CO_2 \tag{11-28}$$

$$SO_2 + Ca(OH)_2 \rightleftharpoons CaSO_3 + H_2O \tag{11-29}$$

when using limestone and lime, respectively. Part of the sulfite is oxidized with the oxygen content in the flue gas to form sulfate.

$$CaSO_3 + \tfrac{1}{2}O_2 \rightleftharpoons CaSO_4 \tag{11-30}$$

Although the overall reactions are simple, the chemistry is quite complex and not well defined. The choice between lime and limestone, the type of limestone, and method of calcining and slaking can influence the gas–liquid–solid reactions taking place in the absorber.

The principal types of absorbers used in the wet scrubbing systems include Venturi scrubber–absorbers, static packed scrubbers, moving-bed absorbers, tray towers, and spray towers [45].

Spray dryer-based FGD systems consist of one or more spray dryers and a particulate collector*. The reagent material is typically a slaked lime slurry or a slurry of lime and recycled material. Although lime is the most common reagent, soda ash has also been used. The reagent is injected in droplet form into the flue gas in the spray dryer. The reagent droplets absorb $SO_2$ while being dried. Ideally, the slurry or solution droplets are completely dried before they hit the wall of the dryer vessel. The flue gas stream becomes more humidified in the process of evaporation of the reagent droplets, but it does not become saturated with water vapor. This is the single most significant difference between spray dryer FGD and wet scrubber FGD. The humidified gas stream and a significant portion of the particulate matter (fly ash, FGD reaction products, and unreacted reagent) are carried by the flue gas to the particulate collector located downstream of the spray dryer vessel [46].

### Control Technologies for Nitrogen Oxides

Almost all nitrogen oxide ($NO_x$) air pollution results from combustion processes. They are produced from the oxidation of nitrogen bound in the fuel, from the reaction of molecular oxygen and nitrogen in the combustion air at temperatures above 1600 K (see Equation 11–5), and from the reaction of nitrogen in the combustion air with hydrocarbon radicals. Control technologies for

---

*Historically, from a mass-transfer point of view, spray drying refers to the evaporation of a solvent from an atomized spray. Simultaneous diffusion of a gaseous species into the evaporating droplet is not true spray drying. Nonetheless, many authors have adopted the term "*spray drying*" as synonymous with dry scrubbing.

NO$_x$ are grouped into two categories: those that prevent the formation of NO$_x$ during the combustion process and those that convert the NO, formed during combustion into nitrogen and oxygen [47].

**Prevention.**   The processes in this category employ the fact that reduction of the peak flame temperature in the combustion zone reduces NO$_x$ formation. Nine alternatives have been developed to reduce flame temperature.

1. Minimizing operating temperatures
2. Fuel switching
3. Low excess air
4. Flue gas recirculation
5. Lean combustion
6. Staged combustion
7. Low NO$_x$, burners
8. Secondary combustion
9. Water–steam injection

Routine burner tune-ups and operation with combustion zone temperatures at minimum values reduce the fuel consumption and NO$_x$ formation. Converting to a fuel with a lower nitrogen content or one that burns at a lower temperature will reduce NO$_x$ formation. For example, petroleum coke has a lower nitrogen content and burns with a lower flame temperature than coal. On the other hand, natural gas has no nitrogen content but burns at a relatively high flame temperature and, thus, produces more NO$_x$ than coal.

Low excess air and flue gas recirculation work on the principle that reduced oxygen concentrations lower the peak flame temperatures. In contrast, in lean combustion, additional air is introduced to cool the flame.

In staged combustion and low NO$_x$ burners, initial combustion takes place in a fuel-rich zone that is followed by the injection of air downstream of the primary combustion zone. The downstream combustion is completed under fuel-lean conditions at a lower temperature.

Staged combustion consists of injecting part of the fuel and all of the combustion air into the primary combustion zone. Thermal NO$_x$ production is limited by the low flame temperatures that result from high excess air levels.

Water–steam injection reduces thermal NO$_x$ emissions by lowering the flame temperature.

**Postcombustion.**   Three processes may be used to convert NO$_x$ to nitrogen gas: selective catalytic reduction (SCR), selective noncatalytic reduction (SNCR), and nonselective catalytic reduction (NSCR).

The SCR process uses a catalyst bed (usually vanadium-titanium, or platinum-based and zeolite) and anhydrous ammonia (NH$_3$). After the combustion process, ammonia is injected upstream of the catalyst bed. The NO$_x$ reacts with the ammonia in the catalyst bed to form N$_2$ and water.

In the SNCR process ammonia or urea is injected into the flue gas at an appropriate temperature (870–1090°C). The urea is converted to ammonia, which reacts to reduce the NO$_x$ to N$_2$ and water.

NSCR uses a three-way catalyst similar to that used in automotive applications. In addition to NO$_x$ control, hydrocarbons and carbon monoxide are convened to CO$_2$ and water. These systems require a reducing agent similar to CO and hydrocarbons upstream of the catalyst.

### Particulate Pollutants

**Cyclones.**   For particle sizes greater than about 10 μm in diameter, the collector of choice is the cyclone (Figure 11–27). This is an inertial collector with no moving parts. The particulate-laden gas is accelerated through a spiral motion, which imparts a centrifugal force to the particles.

**FIGURE 11–27**

Reverse flow cyclone. (*Source:* Crawford, M., *Air Pollution Control Theory*, McGraw-Hill, New York, 1976. Reprinted by permission.)

**FIGURE 11–28**

Baghouse.

The particles are hurled out of the spinning gas and impact on the cylinder wall of the cyclone. They then slide to the bottom of the cone. Here they are removed through an airtight valving system.

As the diameter of the cyclone is reduced, the efficiency of collection is increased; however, the pressure drop also increases. This increases the power requirements for moving the gas through the collector. Because an efficiency increase will result, even if the tangential velocity remains constant, the efficiency may be increased without increasing the power consumption by using multiple cyclones in parallel (**multiclones**).

Cyclones are quite efficient for particles larger than 10 μm. Conversely, they are not very efficient for particles 1 μm or less in diameter. Thus, they are employed only for coarse dusts. Some applications include controlling emissions of wood dust, paper fibers, and buffing fibers.

**Filters.** When high efficiency control of particles smaller than 5 μm is desired, a filter may be selected as the control method. Two types are in use: (1) the deep bed filter, and (2) the baghouse (Figure 11–28). The deep bed filter resembles a furnace filter. A packing of fibers is used to intercept particles in the gas stream. For relatively clean gases and low volumes, such as air conditioning systems, these are quite effective. For dirty industrial gas with high volumes, the baghouse is preferable.

The fundamental mechanisms of collection by filters include screening or sieving because the particles are larger than the openings between the fibers, interception by the fibers themselves, and electrostatic attraction because of the difference in static charge on the particle and fiber. Once a dust cake begins to form on the fabric, sieving is probably the dominant mechanism.

The bags are made of either natural or synthetic fibers. Synthetic fibers are widely used as filtration fabrics because of their low cost, better temperature- and chemical-resistance characteristics, and small fiber diameter. Bag life varies between 1 and 5 years. Two years is considered normal. Bag diameters range from 0.1 to 0.35 m. Their lengths vary between 2 and 10 m. The bags are suspended from the toe and fastened by a collar at the open end. They are arranged in groups in separate compartments.

Reverse-air baghouses operate by directing the dirty gas into the inside of the bag. The particulate matter is collected on the inside of the bag in much the same manner as a vacuum cleaner bag. The bags are cleaned by isolating a compartment and reversing the gas flow. The reverse flow combined with the inward collapse of the bag causes the collected dust cake to fall into the hopper below.

Pulse-jet baghouses are designed with frame structures, called cages, that support the bags. The particulate matter is collected on the outside of the bag. The dust cake is removed by directing a pulsed jet of compressed air into the bag. This causes a sudden expansion of the bag. Dust is removed primarily by inertial forces as the bag reaches maximum expansion.

Baghouses have found a wide variety of applications. Examples include the carbon black industry, cement crushing, feed and grain handling, gypsum, limestone crushing, and sanding machines. Baghouse application to boiler flue gas is finding wide acceptance currently, in contrast to past practice. This is because of the better thermal properties of the bag material. Cotton and wool fiber bags, for example, cannot be used for sustained temperatures above 90–100°C. Glass fiber bags, however, can be used at temperatures up to 260°C. Of all of the particulate control devices, only the filtration method has potential to include the addition of adsorption media to facilitate concurrent removal of gas phase contaminants. Baghouse sizing is based on the ratio of filter area to gas flow rate ($m^3 \cdot s^{-1} \cdot m^{-2}$ of cloth area). Note that this air-to-cloth ratio is a velocity ($m \cdot s^{-1}$). An average value would be about 0.01 $m^3 \cdot s^{-1} \cdot m^{-2}$ for a woven fabric in a conventional baghouse.

**Liquid Scrubbing.**   When the particulate matter to be collected is wet, corrosive, or very hot, the fabric filter may not work. Liquid scrubbing might. Typical scrubbing applications include control of emission of talc dust, phosphoric acid mist, foundry cupola dust, and open hearth steel furnace fumes.

Liquid scrubbers vary in complexity. Simple spray chambers are used for relatively coarse particle sizes. For high-efficiency removal of fine particles, the combination of a Venturi scrubber followed by a cyclone would be selected (Figure 11–29). The underlying principle of operation of the liquid scrubbers is that a differential velocity between the droplets of collecting liquid and the particulate pollutant allows the particle to impinge onto the droplet. Because the droplet–particle combination is still suspended in the gas stream, an inertial collection device is placed downstream to remove it. Because the droplet enhances the size of the particle, the collection efficiency of the inertial device is higher than it would be for the original particle without the liquid drop.

**Electrostatic Precipitation (ESP).**   High-efficiency, dry collection of particles from hot gas streams can be obtained by electrostatic precipitation of the particles. The ESP is usually constructed of alternating plates and wires (Figure 11–30). A large direct current potential (30–75 kV) is established between the plates and wires, which results in the creation of an ion field between the wire and plate (Figure 11–31a). As the particle-laden gas stream passes between the wire and the

**FIGURE 11–29**

Venturi scrubber.

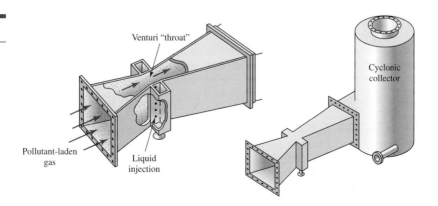

Venturi "throat"

Cyclonic collector

Pollutant-laden gas

Liquid injection

**FIGURE 11–30**

Electrostatic precipitator with **(a)** wire in tube, **(b)** wire and plate. (*Source: Training Course Manual in Air Pollution, Control of Particulate Emissions*, National Center for Air Pollution Control, U.S. Department of Health, Education and Welfare, Cincinnati, OH, 1967.)

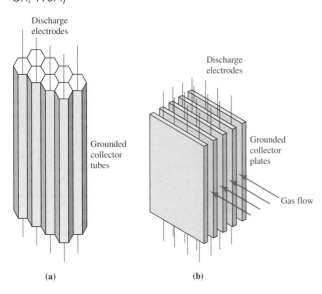

(a)                              (b)

**FIGURE 11–31**

Particle charging and collection in ESP. (*Source: Training Course Manual in Air Pollution, Control of Particulate Emissions*, National Center for Air Pollution Control, U.S. Department of Health, Education and Welfare, Cincinnati, OH, 1967.)

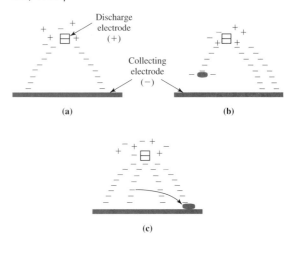

plate, ions attach to the particles, giving them a net negative charge (Figure 11–31b). The particles then migrate toward the positively charged plate, where they stick (Figure 11–31c). The plates are rapped at frequent intervals and the agglomerated sheet of particles falls to a hopper.

Unlike the baghouse, the gas flow between the plates is not stopped during cleaning. The gas velocity through the ESP is kept low (less than $1.5 \text{ m} \cdot \text{s}^{-1}$) to allow particle migration. Thus, the terminal settling velocity of the sheet is sufficient to carry it to the hopper before it exits the precipitator.

One operational problem of ESPs is of particular note. **Fly ash** is a generic term used to describe the particulate matter carried in the effluent gases from furnaces burning fossil fuels. ESPs often are used to collect fly ash. The strongest force holding fly ash to the collection plate is electrostatic and is caused by the flow of current through the fly ash. The fly ash acts like a resistor and, hence, resists the flow of current. This resistance to current flow is called the **resistivity of the fly ash.** It is measured in units of ohms per centimeter ($\Omega \cdot \text{cm}^{-1}$). If the resistivity is too low (less than $10^4 \ \Omega \cdot \text{cm}^{-1}$), not enough charge will be retained to produce a strong force and the particles will not "stick" to the plate. Conversely, and often more importantly, if the resistivity is too high (greater than $10^{10} \ \Omega \cdot \text{cm}^{-1}$), there is an insulating effect. The layer of fly ash breaks down locally and a local discharge of current (**back corona**) from the normally passive collection electrode occurs. This discharge lowers the sparkover voltage and produces positive ions that decrease particle charging and, hence, collection efficiency.

The presence of $SO_2$ in the gas stream reduces the resistivity of the fly ash. This makes particle collection relatively easy. However, the mandate to eliminate $SO_2$ emissions has frequently been satisfied by switching to low-sulfur coal. The result has been increased particulate emissions. This problem can be resolved by adding conditioners such as $SO_3$ or $NH_3$ to reduce the resistivity or by building larger precipitators.

Electrostatic precipitators have been used to control air pollution from electric power plants, Portland cement kilns, blast furnace gas, kilns and roasters for metallurgical processes, and mist from acid production facilities.

## 11–11  AIR POLLUTION CONTROL OF MOBILE SOURCES

### *Engine Fundamentals*

Before we examine some cures for the pollution from the common gasoline automobile engine, it may be useful to compare the three familiar types of engines: gasoline, diesel, and jet.

**The Gasoline Engine.**  In the typical automobile engine with no air pollution controls, a mixture of fuel and air is fed into a cylinder and is compressed and ignited by a spark from the spark plug. The explosive energy of the burning mixture moves the pistons. The pistons' motion is transmitted to the crankshaft that drives the car. The burnt, spent mixture passes out of the engine and out through the tail pipe.

One kilogram of gasoline can burn completely when mixed with about 15 kg of air. For maximum power, however, the proportion of air to fuel must be less. Most driving takes place at less than the 15-to-1 air-to-fuel ratio. Combustion is incomplete, and substantial amounts of material other than carbon dioxide and water are discharged through the tail pipe. One result of having an inadequate supply of air is the emission of carbon monoxide instead of carbon dioxide. Other by-products are unburned gasoline and hydrocarbons.

Because of the high temperatures and pressures that exist in the cylinder, copious amounts of $NO_x$ are formed (see Equation 11–5).

**The Diesel Engine.**  The diesel engine differs from the four-stroke gasoline engine in two respects. First, the air supply is unthrottled; that is, its flow into the engine is unrestricted. Thus, a diesel normally operates at a higher air-to-fuel ratio than does a gasoline engine. Second, there is no spark ignition system. The air is heated by compression. That is, the air in the engine cylinder is squeezed until it exerts a pressure high enough to raise the air temperature to about 540°C, which is enough to ignite the fuel oil as it is injected into the cylinder.

A well-designed, well-maintained, and properly adjusted diesel engine will emit less CO and hydrocarbons than the four-stroke engine because of the diesel's high air-to-fuel ratio. The higher operating temperatures, however, lead to substantially higher $NO_x$ emissions.

**The Jet Engine.**  Large commercial aircraft that use the thrust of compressed gases for propulsion may contribute significant amounts of particulates and $NO_x$ to urban atmospheres.

Propulsion is obtained when air drawn into the front of the engine is compressed and then heated by burning fuel. The expanding gas passes through turbine blades, which drive the compressor. The gas then exits the engine through an exhaust nozzle.

**Effect of Design and Operating Variables on Emissions.**  The list of variables that affect internal combustion (automobile) emissions includes the following [48]:

1. Air-to-fuel ratio
2. Load or power level
3. Speed
4. Spark timing
5. Exhaust back pressure
6. Valve overlap
7. Intake manifold pressure
8. Combustion chamber deposit buildup
9. Surface temperature
10. Surface-to-volume ratio
11. Combustion chamber design
12. Stroke-to-bore ratio
13. Displacement per cylinder
14. Compression ratio

A discussion of all of these items is beyond the scope of an introductory text such as this. Therefore, we shall restrict ourselves to a few of the variables that serve to illustrate the kinds of problems encountered in trying to design pollution out of an internal combustion engine.

The air-to-fuel ratio (A/F) is fairly easy to regulate. As we noted previously, it has a direct effect on all three emissions. As shown in Figure 11–32a, the A/F of 14.6 is the **stoichiometric**

## FIGURE 11–32

Effect of air-to-fuel ratio **(a)** on emissions, and **(b)** on power and economy. (*Source:* Seinfeld, J. H., *Air Pollution,* John Wiley & Sons, New York, 1986. Reprinted by permission.)

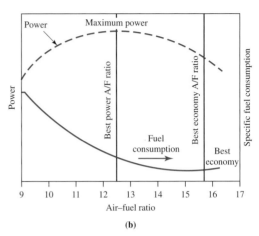

(a)

(b)

mixture for complete combustion.* At lower ratios, both CO and HC emissions increase. At higher ratios, to about 15.5, $NO_x$ emissions increase. At very lean mixtures (high A/F ratios), the $NO_x$ emission begins to decrease. Thus, one of the approaches taken to control emissions is to set the A/F ratio at a very lean setting. This is why a cold engine is hard to start. At an A/F greater than 17, the gas mixture will not ignite properly. We would be remiss if we did not show the relationship between A/F and fuel economy and "power" (Figure 11–32b).

Increasing the engine speed (not the speed of the vehicle) decreases the emission of hydrocarbons. This occurs because of decreases in the unburned fuel in the cylinder crevices and decreases in the quench gas (the gas above the piston) not reacted in the chamber. $NO_x$ emissions increase until a peak value is reached in A/F. Retarding the ignition timing decreases the HC emissions as a result of decreasing the unburned fuel from the crevices. $NO_x$ emissions also decrease with increased retarding. Little or no change occurs in CO emissions until the retard becomes excessive, at which point CO emissions go up. Lowering the compression ratio decreases both the HC and $NO_x$ emissions. It has almost no effect on CO emissions. Of course, lower compression ratios mean a slower response.

### Control of Automobile Emissions

**Blowby.**   The flow of air past the moving vehicle is directed through the crankcase to rid it of any gas–air mixture that has blown past the pistons, any evaporated lubricating oil, and any escaped exhaust products. The air is drawn in through a vent and emitted through a tube extending from the crankcase at a rate that depends on the speed of the car. About 20–40% of the car's total hydrocarbon emissions are sent into the atmosphere from the crankcase. These emissions are called crankcase blowby. All vehicles manufactured after 1963 are required to have a positive crankcase ventilation (PCV) valve to eliminate blowby emissions.

**Fuel Tank Evaporation Losses.**   Evaporation of volatile hydrocarbons (VOCs) from the fuel tank is controlled by one of two systems. The simplest system is to place an activated charcoal adsorber in the tank vent line. Thus, as the gasoline expands during warm weather and forces vapor out of the vent, the VOCs are trapped on the activated carbon.

---

*Note that *stoichiometric* (stoi-chio-met-ric) means "combined in exactly the proper proportions according to their molecular weight."

An alternative method is to vent the tank to the crankcase, but with this method, it is more difficult to achieve 100% control than with the activated charcoal system.

**Carburetor Evaporation Losses.**  During engine operation, the hydrocarbon vapors generated in the carburetor are vented internally to the engine intake system. After the engine is shut off, the gasoline in the float bowl continues to evaporate because of the high temperature in the engine compartment. This phenomenon is called **hot soak.** These losses may be controlled by the use of an activated carbon adsorption system (called a **canister**) or by venting the vapors to the crankcase. The canister system is preferred. Modern fuel injection systems do not have carburetors and thus avoid evaporation losses.

**Engine Exhaust.**  The number of techniques for reducing engine exhaust emissions far exceeds the list of engine variables that contribute to the production of emissions. In general, the control strategies can be grouped into three categories: engine modifications, fuel system modifications, and exhaust treatment devices. To some extent all three techniques have been employed. The stringent requirements of the Clean Air Act have led to the general adoption of catalytic converter exhaust treatment systems.

A three-way catalyst is currently employed as the most effective means of reducing emissions. It provides for the simultaneous oxidation of hydrocarbons and CO and the reduction of $NO_x$. The catalyst materials are either noble metals or base metals deposited on an inert support material.

The major problems with the catalysts are their susceptibility to "poisoning" by lead, phosphorus, and sulfur, and their poor wear characteristics under thermal cycling. The poisoning problem is solved by removing the lead, phosphorus, and sulfur from the fuel.

Another approach being implemented is fuel modification. The use of lead in fuels was completely phased out by January 1996. In addition, diesel fuel refining is being changed so that it will contain less sulfur and emit 20% less VOCs. Lowering the gasoline vapor pressure (called the **Reid vapor pressure**) reduces hydrocarbon emissions. Oxyfuel is yet another alternative. Oxyfuel is one with more oxygen to allow the fuel to burn more efficiently. Other alternatives include alcohols, liquified petroleum gas, and natural gas.

**Inspection–Maintenance (I/M) Programs.**  The devices installed by automobile manufacturers are extremely successful in minimizing the pollution from the exhaust and from evaporating fuel. However, as with other aspects of running an automobile, these devices wear out and fail. Because their failure does not inhibit the operation of the automobile, they are not likely to be repaired by the owner. In those areas that have exceeded the NAAQS (nonattainment areas), inspection–maintenance programs have been implemented to ensure that the control devices are in good working order. These programs require periodic checks of the exhaust and, in some instances, the evaporative controls. If the vehicle fails the inspection, the owner is required to provide the required maintenance and have the vehicle reinspected. Failure to pass the inspection may be cause to deny the issuance of license plates or tags.

## 11–12  WASTE MINIMIZATION

The best and first step in any air pollution control strategy should be to minimize the production of pollutants in the first place. Because a large proportion of air pollutants results from the combustion of fossil fuels, an obvious approach to waste minimization is to conserve energy. Modern technology has yielded more efficient furnaces that improve fuel use, but simple measures such as turning off the lights in unoccupied rooms, turning down the heat at night and, in factories, during weekends and holidays, can have a dramatic effect. Because of the interrelationship between energy consumption and water supply, water conservation also reduces air pollution. In a similar manner, building smaller, lighter automobiles reduces air pollution because less fuel is burned to propel them, but alternatives such as mass transit, walking, and bicycles can contribute significantly to reduced fuel consumption. Alternative sources of energy such as solar, wind, and nuclear also reduce air pollution emissions. (Nuclear power, of course, has a series of pollution problems that may outweigh the benefits of reduced air pollution.)

The chlorofluorocarbon destruction of the ozone layer can only be resolved by waste minimization. Preventing the escape of CFCs from refrigeration systems, the use of alternative propellants for spray cans, and similar measures are the only ones that will be successful because control devices make no sense. Waste minimization is, in fact, the method of control specified by the Montreal Protocol. In a similar fashion, the production of ozone in the lower atmosphere can only be reduced by minimizing the release of precursor hydrocarbons and the production of $NO_x$. Reduced use of solvents and the substitution of water-based paints for solvent-based paints are examples of methods to reduce hydrocarbon release.

## CHAPTER REVIEW

When you have completed studying this chapter; you should be able to do the following without the aid of your textbook or notes:

1. List the six criteria air pollutants for which the U.S. EPA has designated NAAQS.
2. List and define three units of measure used to report air pollution data (i.e., ppm, $\mu g \cdot m^{-3}$, and $\mu m$).
3. Explain the difference between ppm in air pollution and ppm in water pollution.
4. Explain the effect of temperature and pressure on readings made in ppm.
5. Explain the influence of moisture, temperature, and sunlight on the severity of air pollution effects on materials.
6. Differentiate between acute and chronic health effects from air pollution.
7. State which particle sizes are more important with respect to alveolar deposition and explain why.
8. Explain why it is difficult to define a causal relationship between air pollution and health effects.
9. List three potential chronic health effects of air pollution.
10. List four common features of air pollution episodes and identify the locations of three "killer" episodes.
11. Discuss the natural and anthropogenic origin of the six criteria air pollutants and identify the likely mechanisms for their removal from the atmosphere.
12. Identify one indoor air pollution source for each of the following pollutants: $CH_2O$, CO, $NO_x$, Rn, respirable particulates, and $SO_x$.
13. Define the term *acid rain* and explain how it occurs.
14. Discuss the photochemistry of ozone in the upper atmosphere using the pertinent chemical reactions. Discuss the hypothesized effect of chlorofluorocarbons on these reactions.
15. Explain the term *greenhouse effect,* its hypothesized cause, and why it is being debated, pro and con.
16. Determine the stability (ability to dissipate pollutants) of the atmosphere from vertical temperature readings.
17. Explain why valleys are more susceptible to inversions than is flat terrain.
18. Explain why lake breezes and land breezes occur.
19. Explain how a lake breeze adversely affects the dispersion of pollutants.
20. State the theoretical principle on which each of the following air pollution control devices operates. (a) absorption column (either a packed tower or plate tower), (b) adsorption column, (c) either afterburner or catalytic combustor, (d) cyclone, (e) baghouse, (f) Venturi scrubber, and (g) electrostatic precipitator.
21. Select the correct air pollution control device for a given pollutant and source.
22. Discuss the pros and cons of FGD and the problem of fly ash resistivity.

**23.** Explain the difference between prevention and postcombustion techniques for reduction of nitrogen oxide emissions and give one example of each.

**24.** Sketch the relationship between air-to-fuel ratio and emission of CO, HC, and $NO_x$ from automobiles.

With the aid of this text, you should be able to do the following:

**1.** Solve gas law problems.
**2.** Convert parts per million (ppm) to micrograms per cubic meter ($\mu g \cdot m^{-3}$) and vice versa.
**3.** Calculate the amount of $SO_2$ that will be released from burning coal or fuel oil with a given sulfur content in percent.
**4.** Calculate the ground level concentration of air pollutants released from a stationary elevated source or the emission rate ($E$) for a given ground level concentration.

## PROBLEMS

**11-1** Given the following temperature profiles, determine whether the atmosphere is unstable, neutral, or stable. Show all work and explain choices.

| (a) $Z$ (m) | $T$ (°C) | (b) $Z$ (m) | $T$ (°C) | (c) $Z$ (m) | $T$ (°C) |
|---|---|---|---|---|---|
| 2 | −3.05 | 10 | 5.11 | 18 | 14.03 |
| 318 | −6.21 | 202 | 3.09 | 286 | 16.71 |

   **Answers: (a)** Neutral; **(b)** Unstable; **(c)** Stable (inversion)

**11-2** Determine the atmospheric stability for each of the following temperature profiles. Show all work and explain choices.

| (a) $Z$ (m) | $T$ (°C) | (b) $Z$ (m) | $T$ (°C) | (c) $Z$ (m) | $T$ (°C) |
|---|---|---|---|---|---|
| 1.5 | −4.49 | 12 | 28.05 | 8 | 18.55 |
| 349 | 0.10 | 279 | 19.67 | 339 | 17.93 |

**11-3** Given the following observations, use the Key to Stability Categories (Table 11–6) to determine the stability.

(a) Clear winter morning at 9:00 A.M.; wind speed of 5.5 $m \cdot s^{-1}$

(b) Overcast summer afternoon at 1:30 P.M.; wind speed of 2.8 $m \cdot s^{-1}$

(c) Clear winter night at 2:00 A.M.; wind speed of 2.8 $m \cdot s^{-1}$

(d) Summer morning at 11:30 A.M.; wind speed of 4.1 $m \cdot s^{-1}$

   **Answers: (a)** D; **(b)** D; **(c)** F; **(d)** B

**11-4** Determine the atmospheric stability category of the following observations.

(a) Clear summer afternoon at 1:00 P.M.; wind speed of 1.6 $m \cdot s^{-1}$

(b) Overcast summer night at 1:30 A.M.; wind speed of 2.1 $m \cdot s^{-1}$

(c) Overcast winter morning at 9:30 A.M.; wind speed of 6.6 $m \cdot s^{-1}$

(d) Thinly overcast winter night at 8:00 P.M.; wind speed of 2.4 $m \cdot s^{-1}$

**11-5** A power plant in a college town is burning coal on a cold, clear winter morning at 8:00 A.M. with a wind speed of 2.6 $m \cdot s^{-1}$ measured at 30 m elevation and an inversion layer with its base at a height of 697 m. The effective stack height is 30 m. Calculate the distance downwind $X_L$ at which the plume released will reach the inversion layer and begin to mix downward.

   **Answer:** 5.8 km

**11-6** A factory releases a plume into the atmosphere on an overcast summer afternoon. At what distance downwind will the plume begin mixing downward if an inversion layer exists at a base height of 414 m and the windspeed is 1.8 $m \cdot s^{-1}$ measured at the effective stack height is 45 m?

**11-7**   Given the same power plant and conditions as were found in Example 11–3, determine the concentration of $SO_2$ at a point 4 km downwind and 0.2 km perpendicular to the plume centerline ($y = 0.2$ km) if there is an inversion with a base height of 328 m.

   **Answer:** $1.16 \times 10^{-3}$ g $\cdot$ m$^{-3}$

**11-8**   On a clear summer afternoon with a wind speed of 3.20 m $\cdot$ s$^{-1}$ measured at 100 m elevation, the TSP concentration was found to be 1520 $\mu$g $\cdot$ m$^{-3}$ at a point 2 km downwind and 0.5 km perpendicular to the plume centerline from a coal-fired power plant. Given the following parameters and conditions, determine the TSP emission rate of the power plant:

**Stack parameters:**          **Atmospheric conditions:**

   Height = 75.0 m                   Pressure = 100.0 kPa
   Diameter = 1.50 m              Temperature = 28.0°C
   Exit velocity = 12.0 m $\cdot$ s$^{-1}$
   Temperature = 322°C

## DISCUSSION QUESTIONS

**11-1**   A gas sample is collected in a special gas sampling bag that does not react with the pollutants collected but is free to expand and contract. When the sample was collected, the atmospheric pressure was 103.0 kPa. At the time the sample was analyzed the atmospheric pressure was 100.0 kPa. The bag was found to contain 0.020 ppm of $SO_2$. Would the original concentration of $SO_2$ be more, less, or the same? Explain.

**11-2**   Under which of the following conditions would you expect the strongest inversion (largest positive lapse rate) to form?

(a)  Foggy day in the fall after the leaves have fallen    (b)  Clear winter night with fresh snow on the ground

(c)  Clear summer morning just before sunrise

Explain why.

**11-3**   Cement dust is characterized by very fine particulates. The exhaust gas temperatures from a cement kiln are very hot. Which of the following air pollution control devices would appear to be appropriate? Explain the reasoning for your selection.

(a)  Venturi scrubber   (b)  Baghouse   (c)  Electrostatic precipitation

**11-4**   Photochemical oxidants are not directly attributable to either people or natural sources. Why, then, are automobiles singled out as the major cause of the formation of ozone?

**11-5**   Explain why the $PM_{2.5}$ standard is more appropriate than a TSP for protection of human health.

## ADDITIONAL READING

Calabrese, E. J., *Air Toxics and Risk Assessment,* Lewis Publishers, Chelsea, MI (1991).

Cooper, C. D., and F. C. Alley, *Air Pollution Control: A Design Approach,* Waveland Press, Prospect Heights, IL (1994).

Davis, W. T., *Air Pollution Engineering Manual,* Air & Waste Management Association, John Wiley & Sons, Inc., New York (2000).

Davis, M., and D. Cornwell. *Introduction to Environmental Engineering,* 3rd ed. McGraw-Hill, New York (1998).

Flagan, R. C., *Fundamentals of Air Pollution Engineering,* Prentice Hall, Upper Saddle River, NJ (1988).

Hines, A. L., T. K. Ghosh, S. K. Loyalka, et al., *Indoor Air Quality & Control,* Prentice Hall, Upper Saddle River, NJ (1993).

Intergovernmental Panel on Climate Change, *IPCC Second Assessment: Climate Change, 1995,* Joint publication of the World Meteorological Organization and the United Nations Environmental Programme (1995).

Turner, D. B., *Workbook of Atmospheric Dispersion Estimates,* 2nd ed., Lewis Publishing, Ann Arbor, MI (1994).

Wark, K., C. F. Warner, and W. T. Davis, *Air Pollution, Its Origin and Control,* 3rd ed., Addison-Wesley, Menlo Park, CA (1998).

## REFERENCES

1. The discussions on mechanisms of deterioration and factors that influence deterioration follow J. B. Yocom and R. O. McCaldin, "Effects on materials and the economy," *Air Pollution,* VI, 2nd ed., A. C. Stern, ed., Academic Press, New York, 1968.

2. Hindawi, I., *Air Pollution Injury to Vegetation,* U.S. Department of Health, Education and Welfare, National Air Pollution Control Administration (Publication No. AP-7 1), U.S. Government Printing Office, Washington DC, p. 13, 1971.

3. O'Gara, P. J., "Sulfur dioxide and fume problems and their solutions," *Industrial Engineering Chemistry,* vol. 14, p. 744, 1922.

4. Connolly, C. H., *Air Pollution and Public Health,* Holt, Rinehart & Winston, New York, p. 7, 1972.

5. Ferris, B. G., "Health effects of exposure to low levels of regulated air pollutants," *Journal of the Air Pollution Control Association,* vol. 28, pp. 482–497, 1978.

6. Kao, A. S., "Formation and removal reactions of hazardous air pollutants," *Journal of the Air and Waste Management Association,* vol. 44, pp. 683–696, 1994.

7. Goyer, R. A. and J. J. Chilsolm, "Lead," In: *Metallic Contaminants and Human Health,* Douglas H. K. Lee, ed., Academic Press, New York, pp. 57–95, 1972.

8. U.S. Department of Health, Education and Welfare, *Survey of Lead in the Atmosphere of Three Urban Communities* (U.S. Public Health Service Publication No. 999-AP-12), U.S. Government Printing Office, Washington, DC, 1965.

9. The discussion on nitrogen dioxide, photochemical oxidants, sulfur oxides, and total suspended particulates follows B. G. Ferris, "Health effects of exposure to low levels of regulated air pollutants," *Journal of the Air Pollution Control Association,* vol. 28, pp. 485–491, 1978.

10. Reichhardt, T., "Weighing the health risks of airborne patrticulates," *Environmental Science and Technology,* vol. 29, pp. 360A–364A, 1995.

11. Pope, C. A., M. J. Thun, M. M. Namboodri, et al., "Particulate air pollution as a predictor of mortality in a prospective study of U.S. adults," *American Journal of Respiratory and Critical Care Medicine,* vol. 151, pp. 669–674, 1995.

12. Goldsmith, J. R., "Effects of air pollution human health," *Air Pollution,* A. C. Stern, ed., Academic Press, New York, pp. 554–557, 1968.

13. Intergovernmental Panel on Climate Change, *Climate Change 1994: Radiative Forcing of Climate Change and an Evaluation of the IPCC IS92 Emission Scenarios,* Cambridge University Press, Cambridge, UK, 1995.

14. Wofsy, C., J. C. McConnell, and M. H. McElroy, "Atmospheric $CH_4$, CO, and $CO_2$," *Journal of Geophysical Research,* vol. 67. pp. 4477–4493, 1972.

15. Seinfeld, J. H. and S. N. Pandis, *Atmospheric Chemistry and Physics,* John Wiley & Sons, Inc., New York, pp. 59, 70, 85, 1998.

16. Federal Register, "Initial list of categories of sources under section 1 12(c)(1) of the Clean Air Act Amendments of 1990," *Federal Register,* 57, p. 31576, 1992.

17. Kiehl, J. T., and H. Rodhe, "Modeling geographic and seasonal forcing due to aerosols," In: *Aerosol Forcing of Climate,* R. J. Charlson and J. Heintzenberg, eds., John Wiley & Sons, New York, pp. 281–296, 1995.

18. Hosein, R., F. Silverman, P. Coreg, et al., "The relationship between pollutant levels in homes and potential sources," *Transactions, Indoor Air Quality in Cold Climates, Hazards and Abatement Measures,* Air Pollution Control Association, Pittsburgh, pp. 250–260, April 1985.

19. Hines, A. L., T. K. Ghosh, S. K. Loyalka, et al., *Indoor Air Quality & Control,* Prentice Hall, Upper Saddle River, NJ, p. 21, 1993.

20. Dumont, R. S., "The effect of mechanical ventilation on Rn, $NO_2$, and $CH_2O$ concentrations in low leakage houses and a simple remedial measure for reducing Rn concentration," *Transactions, Indoor Air Quality in Cold Climates, Hazards and Abatement Measures,* Air Pollution Control Association, Pittsburgh, pp. 90–104, April 1985.

21. Lefohn, A. S., and S. V. Krupa, "Conference overview," *Acidic Precipitation, A Technical Amplification of NAPAP's Findings,* Proceedings of an APCA International Conference, Pittsburgh. PA, p. 1, January 1988.

22. National Acid Precipitation Assessment Program, 1992 Report to Congress, pp. 5–6.
23. Molina, M. J., and F. S. Rowland, "Stratospheric sink for chlorofluoromethanes: Chlorine atom catalysed destruction of ozone," *Nature,* vol. 248, pp. 810–812, 1974.
24. Interdepartmental Committee for Atmospheric Sciences, *The Possible Impact of Fluorocarbons and Hydrocarbons on Ozone* (Federal Council for Science and Technology, National Science Foundation Publication No. ICAS 18aFY 75), U.S. Government Printing Office, Washington, DC, p. 3, May 1975.
25. Zurer, P. S., "Studies on ozone destruction expand beyond antarctic," *C&E News,* pp. 18–25, May 30, 1988.
26. Zurer, P. S., "Scientists find arctic may face ozone hole," *C&E News,* p. 5, February 27, 1989.
27. Reisch, M., and P. S. Zurer, "CFC production: DuPont seeks total phaseout," *C&E News,* p. 4, April 4, 1988.
28. Sullivan, D. A., "International gathering plans ways to safeguard atmospheric ozone," *C&E News,* pp. 33–36, June 26, 1989.
29. Zurer, P., "Scientists expect ozone loss to peak about 1998," *C&E News,* p. 5, September 12, 1994.
30. Newman, A., "CFC phase-out moving quickly," *Environmental Science & Technology,* 28, p. SSA, 1994.
31. Zurer, P., "Global monitoring shows ozone treaty is working," *C&E News,* pp. 7–8, July 17, 1995.
32. Rose, J., "HCFCs may slow ozone layer recovery," *Environmental Science & Technology,* vol. 28, p. 111A, 1994.
33. Hileman, B., "Global warming," *C&E News,* pp. 25–44, March 13, 1989.
34. Hileman, B., "Global warming update," *C&E News,* p. 31, February 28, 1994.
35. Hare, F. K., and T. C. Hutchinson, "Human environmental disturbances," In: *Environmental Science and Engineering,* J. G. Henry and G. W. Heinke, eds., Prentice Hall, Upper Saddle River, NJ, pp. 117–119, 1996.
36. Martens, P., "How will climate change affect human health," *American Scientist,* vol. 87, 534–541, 1999.
37. Intergovernmental Panel on Climate Change APR 2000. http://www.gcrio.org/edu.html
38. Barnett, T. P., K. Harselman, M. Chelliah, et al., "Detection and attribution of recent climate change: A status report," *Bulletin of the American Meteorological Society,* vol. 80, p. 2631, 1999.
39. Turner, D. B., *Workbook of Atmospheric Dispersion Estimates* (U.S. Department of Health, Education and Welfare, Public Health Service, National Center for Air Pollution Control, Publication No. 999-AP-28), U.S. Government Printing Office. Washington, DC, p. 6, 1967. (*Note:* Turner provides guidelines on the accuracy of this model. It is an estimating tool and not a definitive model to be used indiscriminately.)
40. Holland, J. Z., *A Meteorological Survey of the Oak Ridge Area* (U.S. Atomic Energy Commission Report No. ORO-99), U.S. Government Printing Office, Washington, DC, p. 540, 1953.
41. Martin, D. O., "Comment on the change of concentration standard deviations with distance," *Journal of the Air Pollution Control Association,* vol. 26, pp. 145–146, 1976.
42. Langmuir, I., "The adsorption of gases on plane surfaces of glass, mica, and platinum," *Journal of the American Chemical Society,* vol. 40, p. 1361, 1918.
43. Hance, S. B., and J. L. Kelly, *Status of Flue Gas Desulfurization Systems,* Paper No. 91-157.3, 84th Annual Meeting of the Air and Waste Management Association, 1991.
44. Karlsson, H. T., and H. S. Rosenberg, "Technical aspects of lime/limestone scrubbers for coal fired power plants, Part I Process chemistry and scrubber systems," *Journal of the Air Pollution Control Association,* vol. 30(6), pp. 710–714, 1980.
45. Black & Veatch Consulting Engineers, *Lime FGD Systems Data Book,* 2nd ed., EPRI Publication No. CS-2781, 1983.
46. Cannell, A. L., and M. L. Meadows, "Effects of recent operating experience on the design of spray dryer FGD systems," *Journal of the Air Pollution Control Association,* vol. 35(7), pp. 782–789, 1985.
47. Prasad, A., "Air pollution control technologies for nitrogen oxides," *The National Environmental Journal,* May/June, pp. 46–50, 1995.
48. Patterson, D. J., and N. A. Henein, *Emissions from Combustion Engines and Their Control,* Ann Arbor Science, Ann Arbor, MI, p. 143, 1972.

# 12

# Solid Waste Engineering

## 12–1   **PERSPECTIVE**

**Solid waste** is a generic term used to describe the things we throw away. It includes objects the lay audience commonly calls garbage, refuse, and trash. The U.S. EPA regulatory definition is broader in scope. It includes any discarded item; things destined for reuse, recycle, or reclamation; sludges; and hazardous wastes. The regulatory definition specifically excludes radioactive wastes and in situ mining wastes.

We have limited the discussion in this chapter to solid wastes generated from residential and commercial sources. Sludges were discussed in Chapters 9 and 10. Hazardous waste will be discussed in Chapter 13 and radioactive waste in Chapter 16.

### *Magnitude of the Problem*

Solid waste disposal creates a problem primarily in highly populated areas. In general, the more concentrated the population, the greater the problem becomes, although some very populated areas have developed creative solutions to minimize the problems. Various estimates have been made of the quantity of solid waste generated and collected per person per day. In 1998, the U.S. EPA estimated that the national average rate of solid waste generated was $2.02 \text{ kg} \cdot (\text{capita})^{-1} \text{ day}^{-1}$, up from $1.2 \text{ kg} \cdot (\text{capita})^{-1} \text{ day}^{-1}$ in 1960 [1]. On this basis, in 1998, the United States produced 200 Tg of solid waste. It is estimated that by 2005, the United States will produce annually 217 Tg of solid waste, at $2.13 \text{ kg} \cdot (\text{capita})^{-1} \text{ day}^{-1}$. EPA's goals for the nation are to recycle 35% of the municipal solid waste (MSW) generated by 2005, thereby reducing waste generation to $1.95 \text{ kg} \cdot (\text{capita})^{-1} \text{ day}^{-1}$.

Social customs result in significant variations in the mass of waste generated. For example, more frequent collections tend to result in an increase in the total amount of material collected. Increasing use of in-home garbage disposal units tends to decrease the mass of food waste disposed as MSW. As the extent of usage of packaged and prepared food increases, so does the mass of packaging waste, whereas the amount of raw food waste disposed decreases. The total mass of waste is lower in lower income areas, whereas the percentage of food waste increases.

Residential locations (including multifamily dwellings) generate approximately 55–65% of all MSW. Averages are subject to adjustment depending on many local factors. Studies show wide differences in amounts collected by municipalities because of differences in climate, living standards, time of year, education, location, and collection and disposal practices.

As observed in Figure 12–1, on both a total mass and a mass per capita basis, the United States generates more solid waste per year than any other industrialized nation. This difference would be significantly greater if the United States were not also a leader in the recycling of municipal waste, as shown in Figure 12–2. This data can be used to begin to size MSW landfills and determine numbers of trucks necessary to collect MSW as is accomplished in Example 12–1.

**FIGURE 12–1**

Variability of the masses of MSW generated by major country. (*Source: Characterization of Municipal Solid Waste in the United States: 1999 Update, Executive Summary.* EPA 530-July 1999.)

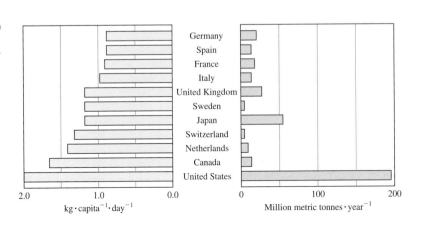

**FIGURE 12–2**

Variability of recycling patterns of MSW by major countries. (*Source: Characterization of Municipal Solid Waste in the United States: 1999 Update, Executive Summary.* EPA 530-July 1999.)

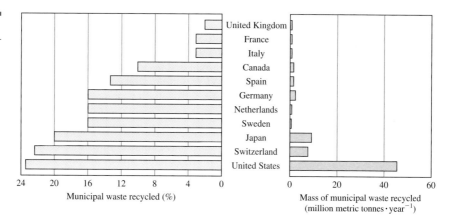

## 12–2 CHARACTERISTICS OF SOLID WASTE

The terms *refuse* and *solid waste* are used more or less synonymously, although the latter term is preferred. Solid waste can be classified in several different ways. The point of origin is important in some cases, so classification, as shown in Table 12–1, as domestic, institutional, commercial, industrial, street, demolition, or construction may be useful. The nature of the material may

| TABLE 12–1 | Sources of Solid Wastes Within a Community | |
|---|---|---|
| **Source** | **Typical Facilities, Activities, or Locations Where Wastes Are Generated** | **Types of Solid Wastes** |
| Residential | Single family and multifamily detached dwellings, low-, medium-, and high-rise apartments, etc. | Food wastes, paper, cardboard, plastics, textiles, leather, yard wastes, wood, glass, tin cans, aluminum, other metals, ashes, street leaves, special wastes (including bulky items, consumer electronics, white goods, yard wastes collected separately, batteries, oil, and tires), household hazardous wastes |
| Commercial | Stores, restaurants, markets, office buildings, hotels, motels, print shops, service stations, auto repair shops, etc. | Paper, cardboard, plastics, wood, food waste, glass, metals, special wastes (see above), hazardous wastes, etc. |
| Institutional | Schools, hospitals, prisons, governmental centers | As above in commercial |
| Construction and demolition | New construction sites, road repair/renovation sites, razing of buildings, broken pavement | Wood, steel, concrete, dirt, etc. |
| Municipal services (excluding treatment facilities) | Street cleaning, landscaping, catch basin cleaning, parks and beaches, other recreational areas | Special wastes, rubbish, street sweepings, landscape and tree trimmings, catch basin debris, general wastes from parks, beaches, and recreational areas |
| Treatment plant sites; municipal incinerators | Water, wastewater, and industrial treatment processes, etc. | Treatment plant wastes, principally composed of residual sludges |
| Municipal solid waste[a] | All of the above | All of the above |
| Industrial | Construction, fabrication, light and heavy manufacturing, refineries, chemical plants, power plants, demolition, etc. | Industrial process wastes, scrap materials, etc. Nonindustrial wastes including food wastes, rubbish, ashes, demolition and construction wastes, special wastes, hazardous wastes |
| Agricultural | Field and row crops, orchards, vineyards, dairies, feedlots, farms, etc. | Spoiled food wastes, agricultural wastes, rubbish, hazardous wastes. |

[a]The term *municipal solid waste* (MSW) normally is assumed to include all of the wastes generated in a community with the exception of industrial process wastes and agricultural solid wastes.

*Source:* G. Tschobanoglous, H. Theisen, and S. Vigil, *Integrated Solid Waste Management*, McGraw-Hill, New York, 1993, p. 41.

be important, so classification can be made on the basis of organic, inorganic, combustible, non-combustible, putrescible, and nonputrescible fractions. The classification of solid waste is usually used for choosing the treatment, collection, recycling, and disposal options.

**Putrescible waste** is the animal and vegetable waste resulting from the handling, preparation, cooking, and serving of food. It is composed largely of degradable organic matter and moisture. It also includes small amounts of free liquids. Putrescible wastes originate primarily in home kitchens, stores, markets, restaurants, and other places where food is stored, prepared, or served. This type of waste decomposes rapidly, particularly in warm weather, and may quickly produce undesirable odors. Putrescible wastes have some commercial value as animal food and as a base for commercial feeds; however, this use may be precluded by health considerations.

**Municipal solid waste,** commonly known to the lay audience as garbage, is a subset of solid waste and is defined as durable goods (e.g., appliances, tires, batteries), nondurable goods, containers and packaging, food wastes, yard trimmings and miscellaneous organic wastes from residential, commercial, and industrial nonprocess sources.

The average municipal solid waste composition in the United States in 1996 is shown in Figure 12–3.

As shown in Figure 12–4, the composition of MSW varies across the globe. Composition of MSW depends on numerous factors, including climate, frequency of collection, usage patterns of in-home garbage disposal units, social customs, per capita income, use and density of food and other material packaging, recycling patterns (e.g., implementation of curbside recycling).

The density of solid waste is the mass of solids waste per unit volume. The density of loose combustible refuse is approximately $115 \text{ kg} \cdot \text{m}^{-3}$, and the density of collected solid waste is 180 to $450 \text{ kg} \cdot \text{m}^{-3}$. In the landfill, compacted solid waste can have a density ranging from 350 to $500 \text{ kg} \cdot \text{m}^{-3}$, and the density of well compacted solid waste can range from 600 to $750 \text{ kg} \cdot \text{m}^{-3}$. Within a landfill, the density will depend on compaction and depth of the waste, the age of the waste, the composition of the waste and its moisture content. Unfortunately, where density is reported, rarely do these reports provide information to properly interpret the meaning of the density value given.

**FIGURE 12–3**

Typical composition of MSW. Other includes miscellaneous inorganic wastes and electrolytes from urine and feces in disposable diapers. (*Source: Characterization of Municipal Solid Waste in the United States: 1999 Update, Executive Summary.* EPA 530- July 1999.)

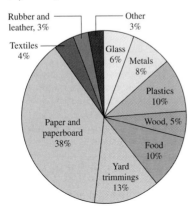

**FIGURE 12–4**

Variable composition of MSW across the globe. (*Source: Characterization of Municipal Solid Waste in the United States: 1999 Update, Executive Summary.* EPA 530- July 1999.)

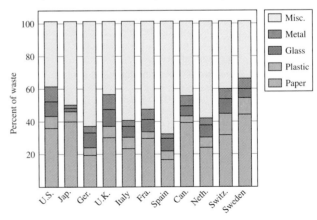

**EXAMPLE 12–1**   A town of 20,000 in Germany generates 0.95 kg · (capita)$^{-1}$ day$^{-1}$ of MSW. A town of the same size in the United States generates 1.9 kg · (capita)$^{-1}$ day$^{-1}$ of MSW.

1. How much MSW is generated in each town?
2. How many trucks would be needed to collect the waste twice weekly? The trucks each have a capacity of 4.5 t (metric tons) and operate 5 days per week. Assume that the trucks average two loads per day at 75% capacity.
3. If each of the towns recycles waste in percentages given in Figure 12–4, determine the mass of MSW that is enters the landfill. If, the density of the waste is 280 kg · m$^{-3}$, what is the volume of MSW?

Solution    1. The amount of MSW generated is simply the number of people multiplied by the per capita MSW generation rate.
   For the German town:

$$20{,}000 \text{ people} \times 0.95 \text{ kg} \cdot (\text{person})^{-1} \text{ day}^{-1} = 19{,}000 \text{ kg} \cdot \text{day}^{-1}$$

   For the U.S. town:

$$20{,}000 \text{ people} \times 1.9 \text{ kg} \cdot (\text{person})^{-1} \text{ day}^{-1} = 38{,}000 \text{ kg} \cdot \text{day}^{-1}$$

2. To determine the number of collection trucks needed by each town, first calculate the total amount generated by each town on a weekly basis:
   For the German town:

$$19{,}000 \text{ kg} \cdot \text{day}^{-1} \times 7 \text{ days} = 133{,}000 \text{ kg} \cdot \text{week}^{-1}$$

   For the U.S. town:

$$38{,}000 \text{ kg} \cdot \text{day}^{-1} \times 7 \text{ days} = 266{,}000 \text{ kg} \cdot \text{week}^{-1}$$

Next, determine the capacity of each truck.

$$2 \text{ loads} \cdot \text{day}^{-1} (0.75 \times 4.5 \text{ t per truck load})(1000 \text{ kg/t}) = 6750 \text{ kg} \cdot \text{day}^{-1} \cdot \text{truck}^{-1}$$

Next, determine the total collection demand that must be met by an unknown number of trucks. Two collections occur (effectively splitting the demand in half) for each residence during the 5-day workweek.
   For the German town:

Using the MSW generation rates calculated earlier, each week the German town generates 133,000 kg of MSW. Because the waste is collected twice a week, each truck collects

66,500 kg every 2.5 days (during a 5-day work week)

   Similarly, for the U.S. town, each truck collects,

133,000 kg every 2.5 days (during a 5-day work week)

Finally, calculate how many trucks are needed to fill this demand by dividing the total collection demand by the capacity for a single truck.
   For the German town:

$$\frac{(66{,}500 \text{ kg})}{(2.5 \text{ days})(6750 \text{ kg} \cdot \text{day}^{-1} \cdot \text{truck}^{-1})} = 3.94, \text{ or 4 trucks}$$

   For the U.S. town:

$$\frac{(133{,}000 \text{ kg})}{(2.5 \text{ days})(6750 \text{ kg} \cdot \text{day}^{-1} \cdot \text{truck}^{-1})} = 7.88, \text{ or 8 trucks}$$

3. The mass of waste that enters the landfill is simply the total amount of MSW produced minus the amount recycled. The volume is then calculated by dividing the mass by the density.

For the German town:

$$19{,}000 \text{ kg} \cdot \text{day}^{-1} - (0.16 \times 19{,}000 \text{ kg} \cdot \text{day}^{-1}) = 15960 \text{ kg} \cdot \text{day}^{-1}$$

$$\frac{(15960 \text{ kg} \cdot \text{day}^{-1})}{(280 \text{ kg} \cdot \text{m}^{-3})} = 57 \text{ m}^3 \cdot \text{day}^{-1}$$

For the U.S. town:

$$38{,}000 \text{ kg} \cdot \text{day}^{-1} - (0.23 \times 38{,}000 \text{ kg} \cdot \text{day}^{-1}) = 29{,}260 \text{ kg} \cdot \text{day}^{-1}$$

$$\frac{(29{,}260 \text{ kg} \cdot \text{day}^{-1})}{(280 \text{ kg} \cdot \text{m}^{-3})} = 104.5 \text{ m}^3 \cdot \text{day}^{-1}$$

## 12–3 SOLID WASTE MANAGEMENT

**FIGURE 12–5**

Elements of a solid waste management system.

In discussing solid waste management, we must consider the waste from the point of generation to the point of final disposal. As shown in Figure 12–5, solid waste management is a complex process, involving multiple steps.

As indicated in Figure 12–5, the first step in solid waste management is the generation of the waste. Once a material no longer has value to its owner, it is considered waste. As discussed earlier in this chapter, the generation of waste varies by country, socioeconomic status, and as a result of many other practices.

Once the waste is generated on site, it must be processed in some way. This processing may include washing, separation, and storage so as to recycle some portion of the waste. Public law and education significantly affect this step. For example, in some communities it is illegal to discard lawn clippings and other similar biomass in the regular trash collection. This material must be disposed of during separate trash collections. Educating the public as to the importance of recycling will affect this step also.

Waste collection is the next step in the management process. Collection includes picking up solid wastes and emptying containers into suitable vehicles for transport. This step also includes the collection of recyclable material. As will be discussed in the next section, collection and transport of waste represents a significant fraction of the total cost of waste management.

The collected waste can be transferred to a central storage facility or to a processing facility. If processing occurs, it usually includes mass and volume reduction, along with separation into the various components that can be reused. The separated waste may at this point become a valuable commodity. In effect, it is no longer a waste. The organic portion of the waste can be transformed into heat by chemical means (usually incineration) or into fuel gas or compost (by biologically mediated reactions).

The final steps include transport and disposal. The most common means of final disposal is landfilling.

## 12–4 SOLID WASTE COLLECTION

The solid waste collection policies of a city begin with decisions made by elected representatives about whether collection is to be made by (1) city employees (municipal collection), (2) private firms that contract with city government (contract collection), or (3) private firms that contract with private residents (private collection).

Elected officials may also determine what type of solid wastes are to be collected and from whom. In some municipalities broad classes of solid wastes (e.g., yard waste) are not accepted for general collection. In others, certain materials (e.g., tires, furniture, or dead animals) may be excluded. Hazardous wastes are excluded from regular collections. The nature of the service may be governed by limitations of disposal facilities or by the opinion of the legislative body as to what service should be performed. Almost all municipal systems collect residential waste, but only about one-third collect industrial waste.

The final decision concerning collection, which is made by the elected officials, is the frequency of collection. The proper frequency for the most satisfactory and economical service is governed by the amount of solid waste that must be collected and by climate, cost, and public requests. For the collection of solid waste that contains putresible waste, the maximum period should not be greater than

1. The normal time for the accumulation of the amount that can be placed in containers of reasonable size
2. The time it takes for fresh putresible waste to decay and emit foul odors under average storage conditions
3. The length of the fly-breeding cycle, which, during the hot summer months, is less than 7 days.

In the last three decades the prevailing frequency of collection has changed from twice a week pickup to once a week. The increased use of once per week service is due to two factors. First, unit costs are reduced when frequency is cut from twice to once per week. Second, the increased percentage of paper and decreased volume of putresible wastes permit longer periods of acceptable storage.

Once policy has been set, the actual method of collection is determined by engineers or managers. Major considerations include how the solid waste will be collected, how the crews will be managed, and how the trucks will be routed. A more complete discussion of collection methods, estimation, and routing is beyond the scope of this text.

## 12–5  WASTE AS RESOURCE

### Background and Perspective

The earth's prime mineral deposits are limited. As high-quality ores are depleted, lower grade ores must be used. Lower grade ores require proportionately greater amounts of energy and capital investment to extract. In a broad economic context, the long-term reasonableness of a market-accounting system that applies only current development costs to our use of depletable, nonrenewable natural resources such as aluminum, copper, iron, and petroleum should be viewed with concern. High rates of virgin raw material extraction result in high rates of solid waste production. In the United States, blatant mispricing—including the "depletion allowance" on minerals and unreasonably low rail rate fares on ores in contrast to scrap—is in no small way responsible for the exploitation of mineral deposits and the large amounts of solid waste generated. Furthermore, our high-waste, low-recycle lifestyle is inherently wasteful of a bountiful endowment of natural resources.

Our renewable resources, primarily timber, are also under siege. Our preference for overpackaged items, in combination with a wanton lack of care in our forests, has strained nature's capacity for growth and replenishment. Europe, India, and Japan have long been faced with a want of timber. We in the United States should learn from their predicaments.

The prevention of waste generation (resource conservation) and the productive use of waste material (resource recovery) represent means of alleviating some of the problems of solid waste management. At one time in our history, resource recovery played an important role in our industrial production. Until the mid-20th century, salvage (reprocessing of wastes to recover an original raw material, now called *recycling*) from household wastes was an increasingly important source of materials. In the 5 years preceding 1939, recycled copper, lead, aluminum, and paper supplied 44, 39, 28, and 30%, respectively, of the total raw materials shipments to fabricators in the United States [2]. Ultimately, it became more economical to process virgin materials than to use recovered ones.

In principle, processable MSW could provide 95 and 73% of our nation's needs in glass and paper, respectively. However, in the categories of metals, plastics, and wood, only a fraction of the annual needs of the country is recoverable from MSW. Much of the paper and glass that is recoverable in principle could, in practice, never be reclaimed. The EPA, in 1974, estimated the actual potential recovery, expressed as a percentage of U.S. consumption, to be iron, 6.7%; aluminum, 8.4%; copper, 4.7%; lead, 2.8%; tin, 18.9%; and paper, 14.0%. Comparing these values with those available in 1998 indicates the success of recycling programs. In terms of energy production, if all the MSW collected in the United States were converted to energy, it would supply 3–5% of the nation's need. This would be enough to supply all of our residential and commercial lighting requirements [3]. Although some communities might be able to generate 7–10% or more of their need, nationally the actual potential is probably on the order of 0.5%.

In light of these facts, it is not difficult to see why "recovery for recovery's sake" or "energy recovery for energy conservation" receive scant attention except in times of national emergency or failure of the local sanitary landfill to accommodate the waste being generated. The fact that, under our current market-accounting system, resource conservation and resource recovery, except in locally favorable situations, costs more than landfilling is a further disincentive to the conservation of our natural resources. Why, then, should any governing body even consider resource conservation and resource recovery? The answer, simply stated, is "to protect our environment." In the same context that we have attempted to control air and water pollution, we have an obligation to leave our descendants something better than the accumulated litter of our squandering habits. Although there will be some expected cost, that cost should be minimized. EPA has set as a national goal that 32% of all solid waste should be recycled by 2005. Many states are moving to enact this goal as a requirement.

Individual states have enacted over 500 laws on recycling, ranging from purchasing preferences to comprehensive recycling goals [4]. More than 6000 reuse centers around the country recycle materials ranging from specialized programs for building materials or unneeded materials in schools to local programs such as Goodwill and the Salvation Army, according to the Reuse Development Organization. Eleven states have bottle deposit regulations. Twenty-two states have yard waste bans [5]. In the 50 states and the District of Columbia, there are over 3780 yard waste compositing programs and over 9500 curbside recycling programs [5]. The EPA has estimated the increases in recovery for recyclables as shown in Table 12–2. It estimates that overall recovery increased from 6.4% in 1960 to 16.2% in 1990 to 28% in 1997 [5].

| TABLE 12–2 | Recycling Rates for Some MSW Components | | |
|---|---|---|---|
| **Material** | **1990 Recycling Rate (%)[a]** | **1997 Recycling Rate (%)[b]** | **2000 Projected Recycling Rate (%)[b]** |
| Paper and paperboard | 28.6 | 41.7 | 44–46 |
| Glass | 19.9 | 24.3 | 29–33 |
| Steel | 23.0[c] | 38.4 | 41–46 |
| Aluminum | NA | 31.2 | 37–39 |
| Plastics | 2.2 | 5.2 | 6–7 |
| Yard trimmings | 12.0 | 41.4 | 52–54 |
| Rubber and leather | NA | 11.7 | 14.5–15.9 |
| Wood | NA | 5.1 | 8.6–10 |
| Clothing and other textiles | NA | 12.9 | 13–14.7 |

NA = Data not available
[a] U.S. EPA *Reusable News,* Fall 1992.
[b] Characterization of MSW in the U.S.: 1998 Update, US EPA, Washington, DC.
[c] Combined data for all metals.

### Green Chemistry and Green Engineering

"Green chemistry" and "green engineering" are changing the way engineers design and fabricate. As we begin to look at the big picture of how engineering decisions affect the environment and our planet's life, we are finally beginning to try to solve environmental problems before they happen. Rather than using "end-of-the-pipe" treatment techniques, engineers are attempting to select materials, design manufacturing processes, and enhance energy conservation to minimize their effects on the environment. Where appropriate the effect of these decisions on MSW management are considered in the following sections.

### Recycling

Recycling can also be described as closed-loop or open-loop. **Closed-loop, or primary, recycling** is the use of recycled products to make the same or similar products. Examples of primary recycling include the use of glass bottles to make other types of glass bottles or aluminum cans to make new aluminum cans. **Secondary recycling** is the use of recycled materials to make new products with different characteristics than the originals. For example, milk jugs made of high-density polyethylene (HDPE) can be recycled into toys or drainage pipes. **Tertiary recycling** is the recovery of chemicals or energy from postconsumer waste materials. Many electronic companies, for instance, recover the solvents used in their manufacturing processes and distill them for reuse.

At the lowest and most appropriate technological level, recycled materials are separated at the source by the consumer (**source separation**). This is the most appropriate level because it requires the minimum expenditure of energy. With stringent goals for recycling, municipalities are looking at detailed recycling options.

#### Methods of Collecting Recyclable Materials.

Generally, the collection options available to a municipality for residential use include curbside collection and drop-off centers. Recycled materials can be collected by a community and then taken to a material-processing facility or to material transfer stations, where the material is sorted and separated via mechanical means.

The primary method of collecting dry recyclables in the United States today is curbside collection. This has the advantage of being easier on the resident than having to drive to a recycling center. There are two basic types of curbside collection for recycling. In the first, the homeowner is given a number of bins or bags. The homeowner separates the refuse as it is used, placing it in the appropriate bin. On collection day the container is placed on the curb. The primary disadvantage of supplying home storage containers is the cost, which can represent a significant investment. A second method of curbside recycling is to provide the homeowner with only one bin, into which is placed all the recyclable materials. Curbside personnel then separate material as it is being picked up, placing each type of material into a separate compartment in the vehicle.

A second collection alternative is a drop-off center. Because recycling is a community-specific operation, a drop-off system must be designed around and in consideration of conditions particular to the area of involvement. To evaluate and select the most appropriate drop-off system, we must consider critical factors such as location, materials handled, population, number of centers, operation, and public information. When drop-offs are used to supplement curbside programs, fewer and smaller drop-off sites may be required than that necessary when curbside programs are not implemented. When drop-off sites are the only, or primary, recycling system in a community, the system must provide for increased capacity. Careful planning to accommodate traffic flow, as well as storage and collection of materials, must be part of the siting activity.

The convenience of a drop-off center will directly affect the amount of citizen participation. Strategically locating a drop-off center in an area of high traffic flow, where the center is highly visible, will encourage a greater level of participation. Even rural areas with widely scattered populations can provide good locations for drop-offs. Rural homeowners have certain common travel patterns that bring them to a few locations at regular intervals—to a grocery store, church, or post office, to name a few.

**Recycling of Materials.**   Several types of materials are commonly recycled, including glass, metals (Al, Fe, Cu, steel), paper, and plastics. Paper (especially newspaper and cardboard) is easily recycled. Recycling paper involves the removal of inks, glue, and coatings. The paper is then reconverted to pulp that can be pressed into new paper. Because this process results in the breakdown of some of the paper fibers and a reduction in strength of the paper, new pulp material must be added to the recycled paper. By 1995, 40% of the paper produced in the United States was being recycled. Old corrugated cardboard boxes account for more than 50% of the paper that is recycled. More than a third of all paper and paperboard recycled in the world is recycled in the United States.

In 1990, some 54 billion pounds of plastic materials were produced in the United States. Of the various forms of plastics that are produced and can be recycled, high-density polyethylene is the most common. Known by the Society of Plastics Industry code, #2-HDPE, this type is used to produce milk bottles, detergent bottles, and film products such as produce bags. Recycled HDPE is also used for the production of protective wrap, grocery bags, and molded products such as toys and pails. Polyethylene terephthlate (#1-PETE) is most commonly used originally in the production of carbonated soft drink bottles. Some states have ensured the recycling of a large percentage of this material through "bottle bills," requiring deposits on soft drink bottles. Although this has been successful in the recycling of soft drink containers, as the consumption of bottled water has increased, so has the disposal of water bottles as MSW because they are not always covered by bottle bill regulations.

Glass is one of the easiest materials to recycle. Almost all of the glass that is recycled is made into new glass containers and bottles. A small amount is used to make other products, such as glass wool, fiberglass insulation, paving material, and building products. Nevertheless, in the United States, in 1996, only 36% of the glass produced was recycled. From Figure 12–6, it is clear that much work still must be done to encourage more recycling of glass products in the United States.

The most commonly recycled metals are iron and steel. MSW contains about 8% metal waste (before recycling). "Tin" cans are made almost entirely of steel. In fact, one ton of "tin" cans contains only 3.8 lb of tin. Approximately 97% of all metal food containers are made of steel. Because of its relative ease of collection and processing, 58.2% of all steel cans produced in 1996 were recycled. The major impediment to recycling of cans is the high cost of transportation. For recycling of this material to be economical, the cost of collection, transportation, and processing must be less than the cost of producing new steel.

Other metals that can be recycled include aluminum, copper, lead, nickel, tin, and zinc. Virtually all nonferrous metals can be recycled if they are sorted and free of foreign products. Although this is not a problem with aluminum cans, this restriction discourages the recycling of many nonferrous metals. Today, 100% of all soda and beer cans are made of aluminum and the average aluminum beverage cans contain about 51% postconsumer recycled aluminum. As can be

**FIGURE 12–6**

Glass products in MSW. (*Source: USEPA, Characterization of Municipal Solid Waste in the U.S. 1996 Update. Government Printing Office, Washington, D.C.*)

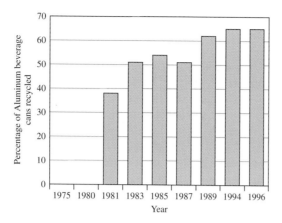

**FIGURE 12–7**

Percentage of recycled aluminum beverage cans sold and recycled. (*Data from: The Aluminum Association, 1997, and the Can Manufacturers Institute, 1997.*)

seen from Figure 12–7, the percentage of aluminum cans recycled each year rose steadily until 1994. Unfortunately, the percentage of cans recycled has leveled off at 65%. More needs to be done to ensure the continued increase in the percentage of this important resource that is recycled.

**Improving the Market for Recyclables.**    Over the last decade the market and prices for recycled materials have fluctuated widely. Among the factors that affect the market and prices are

- Economic conditions
- Overall demand
- Demand for products specifically made partially or entirely from recovered materials
- Quality of recovered materials (contamination problems)
- Capacity to use recovered material in a process
- Excess capacity to produce virgin material
- Transportation costs
- Export markets
- Differences between supply and demand
- Legislation

The market for recycled paper products varies greatly and is highly sensitive to economic conditions. During a recession, the demand for newspapers, books, and other paper products decreases significantly, reducing the demand for all paper; thus the supply of recovered paper will exceed demand. Export markets also vary greatly; for example, as paper recovery in Europe and Asia increases, their demand for U.S. recycled paper decreases. If export demand decreases, the price of recovered material also decreases, and the supply will exceed the demand. On the contrary, if the export demand increases, the price of recovered material also increases, and the demand will exceed the supply. The quality of the recovered material is an important factor in determining desirability of the material to the paper industry. The quality can be enhanced by better separation of the particular types of paper from each other and from other materials such as plastics or glass. The cost of virgin paper will also directly affect paper recovery. Strong legislature governing recycling will enhance the recovery of paper, weakening regulations will have the opposite effect. Thus, the market for recovered paper is enhanced by

- A strong economy
- Export demand
- Separation of paper from other materials
- High cost for virgin material
- Strong regulations

Most recovered glass is used by glass container manufacturers. Some recovered glass is used by fiberglass manufacturers and in making glass aggregates and abrasives. As with paper, the recovery of glass can be enhanced by the separation of glass from other materials to decrease the level of contamination. The market for recovered glass depends on the tolerance for colored glass contamination in the production process. For example, green glass fabrication can accept up to 50% different colors, whereas contamination must be less than 5% in flint (colorless) glass production. The distance to market, and therefore, transportation costs, will play a significant role in recycling. These costs can be decreased by attempting to increase the density of material when transported to market.

Aluminum containers have been the most sought-after recovered material because the conversion of scrap aluminum into new material offers considerable cost savings over production from newly mined and processed bauxite. Because the aluminum market can absorb more recovered material, an increase in the extent of aluminum recovery is feasible. Recovery could be enhanced by

- The reduction in contamination by separating aluminum from other metals
- Strong "bottle laws"
- The availability of a high street price for used beverage containers

The recovery of steel from residential use in MSW depends greatly on the willingness of the steel industry to use recycled material. In 1997, about 50% of the steel processed in the United States was recovered material; about 6% was from MSW. As the steel industry has been actively promoting recovery and recycling steel, the market appears positive.

HDPE and PETE materials account for about 80% (by mass) of the recovered plastic in MSW. The market for recovered plastic varies greatly with plastic type. As long as the supply of virgin HDPE remains low, the price for recovered HDPE will be favorable. An oversupply of virgin PETE material has kept the price of and demand for recovered PETE low. The regulations governing the recycling of plastic materials have also been weakened. Consequently, the market for recovered plastics can be enhanced by

- Strengthening recycling regulations
- Reducing production of virgin PETE.

Compost, described in detail in the next subsection, can be produced from components of MSW such as yard trimmings, food wastes, and soiled paper. These products can be mixed with non-MSW feed stocks, including livestock manure, industrial food waste, and wastewater sludges. The market for compost material can be enhanced through

- The production of high-quality and consistent material that has general customer acceptability
- The production of products with specific nutrient content depending on individual customer needs and demands
- The education of consumers as to the benefits of using compost
- Strong regulations governing the disposal of yard trimmings

### Composting

**Composting** is the controlled decomposition of organic materials, such as leaves, grass, and food scraps, by microorganisms [6]. The result of this decomposition process is compost, a crumbly, earthy-smelling, soil-like material. Because MSW in the United States contains up to about 25% yard trimmings and food scraps, composting of this material can greatly reduce the amount of waste that ends up in landfills or incinerators.

The material to be composted contains both carbon and nitrogen sources. Leaves, straw, and woody materials serve as a major carbon source. Grass and food scraps provide significant nitrogen. A ratio of 30 parts carbon to 1 part nitrogen is necessary to achieve optimal microorganism growth and energy production. Odor and other problems can occur if the carbon to nitrogen ratio is not 30:1.

The decomposition of organic materials in composting involves both physical and chemical processes. During decomposition, organic materials are broken down through the metabolic activities of various invertebrates present in composting material, including mites, millipedes, beetles, sowbugs, earwigs, earthworms, slugs, and snails. These organisms need adequate moisture and oxygen to degrade the organic materials in the most efficient manner.

Microbes in the pile create considerable heat and essentially "cook" the compost. Temperatures between 25 and 55°C are common in properly maintained large-scale compost piles. Backyard compost piles may not reach these levels. These high temperatures are necessary for rapid composting as well as for destroying weed seeds, insect larvae, and potentially harmful bacteria. When the compost is finished, it has a crumbly texture throughout the pile.

More than 67% of the MSW generated in the United States can be composted. When MSW is to be composted, recyclables, such as glass and aluminum, and noncompostable material must be removed prior to composting. The remaining material, which is predominately organic in nature, can then be composted. Aerated windrows, are the most common method. In-vessel composting, in which the material is left to decompose while enclosed in a temperature- and moisture-controlled chamber, can also be used. Composting of MSW using aerobic digestors is used in some European countries. Prior to digestion, the MSW can be combined with livestock manure or food-processing wastes. The finished compost can be sold, given away, or used by the company or municipality in local landscaping or agricultural projects.

### Source Reduction

If our standard of living is to be sustainable, we must find ways to better reuse the materials we create. We simply cannot continue to dispose of 2 kg of refuse per day per person. Thus, it is necessary that we focus our efforts on "source reduction" or preventing the formation of waste in the first place. We need to design, manufacture, purchase, and use materials in ways that minimize the amount and toxicity of the waste we generate. By practicing source reduction we also reduce the costs of and problems associated with recycling, composting, landfilling, or incinerating waste. We also conserve precious natural resources and reduce pollution. Source reduction can be accomplished in numerous ways.

**Waste Reduction and Process Modification.**    Source reduction can be accomplished by reducing the quantity of materials generated before they are ever ready for recycling or reuse. This includes the redesign of products or packages to reduce the quantity of material used. For example, in 1977 the mass of a 2-L soft drink bottle was 68 g. Today, the same size bottle has a mass of only 51 g. Although the amount of plastic in each bottle may seem inconsequential, this reduction has kept 115 million kg of plastic per year out of the waste stream. Companies can also use packaging that reduces the amount of damage or spoilage, thereby reducing the mass of material that must be discarded.

Nontoxic materials can be substituted for toxic ones. For example, soy-based or water-based inks can be used. Lead foil on wine bottles can be replaced with aluminum, which can be easily recycled. Freon can be replaced with non-ozone-consuming chemicals. High-temperature hydrocarbons and silicone oil have replaced PCBs in transformers and other electrical equipment. Transformers have also been redesigned and retrofitted to allow for the use of lubricants and insulators other than PCBs.

The mass of waste material can be reduced if manufacturers design products that have longer lives and are easily repaired. Assuming that more durable goods will cost more, consumers must also be willing to have damaged equipment repaired.

Businesses and individuals can modify their practices to reduce waste. For example, e-mail can be used to distribute messages instead of letters. Reports can be copied on both sides of a page. Additionally, mailing lists can be routinely updated to ensure that mail is not being sent astray. Individuals can request to be removed from mailing lists to reduce the amount of un-wanted and waste mail. Products can be purchased in bulk quantities to reduce waste.

**Reuse of Products.**   Other ways of source reduction are the reuse of durable goods (e.g., appliances, furniture, computers) by repairing them when they are broken or refurbishing them when they are out-dated, donating them to charity and community groups, or selling them to others that have a direct use for them. Ideally, products should be used more than once, either for the same purpose or for a different one. Reusing, when possible, is preferable to recycling because the item does not need to be reprocessed before it can be used again. Some ways that items can be reused are

- Using durable coffee mugs rather than disposable cups
- Using cloth napkins or towels rather than paper napkins or towels
- Refilling water bottles from the tap rather than buying disposable water bottles
- Donating old magazines or surplus equipment to charity
- Reusing boxes for other purposes
- Using plastic containers for storage rather than using disposable plastic bags
- Turning empty jars into containers for leftover food or other items
- Purchasing refillable pens and pencils
- Participating in a paint collection and reuse program

**Education and Legislation.**   Source reduction may be implemented by educating people about the benefits of such actions or by enforcement, for example through the use of fees or deposits. Legislation requiring mandatory refunds or deposits on both returnable and non-returnable beverage containers has been and will continue to be hotly contested by the beverage and beverage container industries. In those states that have enacted mandatory refund or deposit legislation (e.g., California, Connecticut, Delaware, Iowa, Maine, Massachusetts, Michigan, New York, Oregon, Rhode Island, and Vermont), there is strong evidence to show that the claims of lost jobs and lost business are either unfounded or are offset by increases in jobs and business in other sectors.

These programs have been a great success. Between 90 and 95% of the bottles are returned and 80–85% of the cans are returned. In Oregon, a reduction in total roadside litter of 39% by item count and 47% by volume was reported after the second year of implementation of its law. Furthermore, for glass containers there is a significant energy savings in that a glass bottle reused ten times consumes less than a third of the energy of a single-use container. Average reuse cycles vary from 10 to 20 times per container.

Other materials such as residual ash and solids from incineration can be used as source material. For example, industrial waste consisting of fly ash from power plants has been used as a raw material for manufacturing building materials. Concrete-like blocks have been produced from oil shale and coal fly ash [7]. Fly ash has also been used in the construction of roads. Chicken manure has been incinerated to produce a source material for phosphorus production, as an additive/basic material for fertilizer production, and as a basic road-building material [8].

## 12–6   SOLID WASTE REDUCTION

### Combustion Processes
**Fundamentals of Combustion.**   Combustion is a chemical reaction in which the elements in the fuel are oxidized in the presence of excess oxygen. The major oxidizable elements in the fuel, in this case, the solid waste, are carbon and hydrogen. To a lesser extent sulfur and nitrogen are also present. With complete oxidation, carbon is oxidized to carbon dioxide, hydrogen to water, and sulfur to sulfur dioxide. Some fraction of the nitrogen may be oxidized to nitrogen oxides.

## FIGURE 12–8

Combustion chambers in a mass-fired incinerator. **(a)** Martin grate (*Courtesy of Ogden Martin Systems, Inc.*) and **(b)** Dusseldorf grate (*Courtesy of American Ref-Fuel, Inc.*)

(a)                    (b)

The combustion reactions are a function of oxygen, time, temperature, and turbulence. Sufficient excess of oxygen must be available to drive the reaction to completion in a short time. As shown in Figure 12–8, the oxygen is most frequently supplied by forcing air into the combustion chamber. Over 100% excess air may be provided to ensure sufficient excess. Sufficient time must be provided for the combustion reactions to proceed to completion. The amount of time is a function of the combustion temperature and the turbulence in the combustion chamber. Some minimum temperature must be exceeded to initiate the combustion reaction (i.e., to ignite the waste). Higher temperatures also yield higher quantities of nitrogen oxide emissions, so there is a trade-off in destroying the solid waste and forming air pollutants. Mixing of the combustion air and the combustion gases is essential for the completion of the reaction.

As the solid waste enters the combustion chamber and its temperature increases, volatile materials are driven off as gases. Rising temperatures cause the organic components to thermally "crack" and form gases. When the volatile compounds are driven off, fixed carbon remains. When the temperature reaches 700°C, the carbon is ignited. To achieve destruction of all the combustible material (**burn out**), it is necessary to achieve 700°C throughout the bed of waste and ash [9].

In the **flame zone** the hot volatilized gases mix with oxygen. This reaction is very rapid, going to completion within 1–2 s if the air and turbulence are sufficient.

The evolution of solid waste combustion has led to higher temperatures both for destroying toxic compounds and increasing the opportunity to use the waste as an energy source by producing steam.

**Heating Value of Waste.** The heating value of waste is measured in kilojoules per kilogram ($kJ \cdot kg^{-1}$) and is determined experimentally using a bomb calorimeter. A dry sample is placed in a chamber and burned. The heat released at a constant temperature of 25°C is calculated from a heat balance. Because the combustion chamber is maintained at 25°C, combustion water produced in the oxidation reaction remains in the liquid state. This condition produces the maximum heat release and is defined as the **higher heating value** (HHV).

In actual combustion processes, the temperature of the combustion gas remains above 100°C until the gas is discharged into the atmosphere. Consequently, the water from combustion processes is always in the vapor state. The heating value for combustion is termed the **lower heating value** (LHV). The following equation gives the relationship between HHV and LHV:

$$LHV = HHV - [(\Delta H_v)(9H)] \tag{12-1}$$

where $\Delta H_v$ = heat of vaporization of water = $2420 \ kJ \cdot kg^{-1}$

$H$ = hydrogen content of combusted material

**FIGURE 12–9**

Cross-sectional drawing of a conventional mass-fired incinerator. (*Courtesy of Ogden Martin Systems, Inc.*)

The factor of 9 results because 1 gram mole of hydrogen will produce 9 gram moles of water (i.e., 18/2). Note that this water is only that resulting from the combustion reaction. If the waste is wet, the free water must also be evaporated. The energy required to evaporate this water may be substantial, resulting in a very inefficient combustion process from the point of view of energy recovery. The ash content also reduces the energy yield because it reduces the proportion of dry organic matter per kilogram of fuel and because it retains some heat when it is removed from the furnace.

### Types of Incinerators

**Conventional (Mass-Fired) Incineration.**  Mass-fired incinerators are the most common form of MSW incineration. The basic arrangement of the conventional incinerator is shown in Figure 12–9. These systems can accept refuse that has received little pretreatment other than the removal of oversized items, such as kitchen stoves and mattresses. Local programs for the removal of potentially hazardous chemicals such as pesticides and other hazardous household chemicals are necessary to prevent environmental damage. Because the refuse is generally not pretreated, although it may have some heat value, it is normally quite wet and is not **autogenous** (self-sustaining in combustion) until it is dried. Conventionally, auxiliary fuel is provided for the initial drying stages. Because of the large amount of particulate matter generated in the combustion process, some form of air pollution control device is required. Normally, electrostatic precipitators (discussed in Chapter 11) are chosen. Bulk volume reduction in incinerators is about 90%. Thus, about 10% of the material still must be carried to a landfill.

**Refuse-Derived Fuel Facilities.**  **Refuse-derived fuel** (RDF) is the combustible portion of solid waste that has been separated from the noncombustible portion through processes such as shredding, screening, and air classifying [10]. By processing municipal solid waste (MSW), refuse-derived fuel containing 12–16 MJ · kg$^{-1}$ can be produced from 55–85% of the refuse received. This system is also called a **supplemental fuel system** because the combustible fraction is typically marketed as a fuel to outside users (utilities or industries) as a supplement to coal or other solid fuels in their existing boilers.

In a typical system, MSW is fed into a trommel, or rotating screen, to remove glass and dirt, and the remaining fraction is conveyed to a shredder for size reduction. Shredded wastes may

**FIGURE 12–10**

Southeastern Virginia Public Service Authority's RDF plant.

then pass through an air classifier to separate the light fraction (plastics, paper, wood, textiles, food wastes, and smaller amounts of light metals) from the heavy fraction (metals, aluminum, and small amounts of glass and ceramics).

The light fraction, after being routed through a magnetic system to remove ferrous metals, is ready for fuel use. The heavy fraction is conveyed to another magnetic removal system for recovery of ferrous metals. Aluminum may also be recovered. The remaining glass, ceramics, and other nonmagnetic materials from the heavy fraction are then sent to the landfill.

The first full-scale plant to prepare RDF has been in operation in Ames, Iowa, since 1975. Subsequently, other plants using similar technology have been designed and constructed. Figure 12–10 shows the process flow diagram for the Southeastern Virginia Public Service Authority's RDF plant.

**Modular Incinerators.**   **Modular incinerators** are usually prefabricated units with capacities of 5–120 tons of solid waste per day. Most produce steam as the sole energy product. Most modular incinerators use a system involving two combustion chambers. The gases produced in the first chamber flow to the second chamber where they are burned more completely. The second chamber often serves as the only air pollution control device. Other modular units employ additional air pollution control equipment and are, thus, able to control emissions as effectively as mass-burn facilities. Although many modular units plan to retrofit existing controls to meet more stringent standards, others will close due to the expense associated with upgrading units to meet these stringent air emission standards. As a result, interest in modular incinerators is decreasing.

**Fluidized-Bed Incinerators.** Fluidized bed incinerators have been used extensively in Japan and are becoming more common elsewhere in the world. In a **fluidized bed incinerator,** sand is heated to about 1500°F by oil or gas. The sand is blown around, or "fluidized," in the incinerator by a blower that sends air from the bottom upward. As the sludge enters the bottom of the incinerator, the heated fluidized sand hits the sludge, both breaking it apart and burning it.

This type of incinerator requires front-end preprocessing of waste. Glass and metals must be removed from the refuse to be incinerated. Fluidized bed incinerators can, however, successfully burn wastes of widely variable moisture and heat content, such as paper and wood. Combustion and heat recovery in fluidized-bed incinerators are very efficient and the level of pollutant emissions is low.

Fluidized bed systems appear to be more consistent in their operation than mass-burn incinerators and may be more effectively operated to control emissions, reduce residual ash production, and achieve high energy conversion efficiencies. Fluidized bed incinerators are able to co-combust fuels, meaning that for example, they can burn municipal waste with coal or propane. These type of incinerators appear to be more effective than small sized mass-burn incinerators.

### Public Health and Environmental Issues

The combustion of MSW can result in the emission of particulate matter, acid gases ($SO_x$, HCl, HF), $NO_x$ (primarily NO and $NO_2$), carbon monoxide, organics, and heavy metals. Carbon dioxide emissions are not significant; if all MSW were incinerated, then $CO_2$ emissions would contribute < 2% of that produced during each year in the United States.

The heavy metals are distributed in the bottom ash, in fly ash, and in particulate matter released in gases. Lead and cadmium will be distributed between the bottom* and fly ashes. Many of the other metals will be found in the fly ash[†]. Until 1998, this ash could be disposed of in a Subtitle C landfill because the EPA deemed the ash exempt from hazardous waste regulations. However, in 1998, the U.S. Supreme Court ruled that if the ash generated by MSW incinerators fails federal toxicity tests it must be treated as a hazardous waste.

$NO_x$, which is produced by the reaction of air during combustion at high temperatures, is often present in the off-gases from MSW incinerators. $NO_x$ is known to have adverse effects on respiratory function and contribute to acid rain. HCl and $SO_2$ will also be produced in the off-gas. Particulate matter is known to have adverse public health and environmental effects as described in Chapter 11 (Air Pollution). Any mercury in the waste feed will be volatilized into the off-gases. MSW incinerators are the largest single source of dioxins, furans, and dioxin-like PCBs[‡] [11]. The EPA has estimated that 1100 g TEq · year$^{-1}$ of these chemicals were released in 1995. Emissions standards and guidelines have been promulgated for new and existing large (>250 tons · day$^{-1}$) municipal waste combustion (MWC) facilities, and proposed for small MWC facilities (35–250 tons · day$^{-1}$). EPA estimates that when full compliance with the MWC rules is attained, the annual emissions resulting from MSW incinerators will decline significantly

---

*Bottom ash** is the solid residue that falls through the grate of the incinerator. It is considerably larger in size than fly ash.

[†]**Fly ash** is the fine particulate in the smoke stream. It is collected in precipitators, filters, scrubbers.

[‡]Dioxin then is a collective name for 75 different polychlorinated dibenzo-*p*-dioxins. There are 135 different polychlorinated-dibenzo furans. These compounds can be extremely toxic substances to some animal species. The most toxic is 2,3,7,8-tetrachlorodibenzo-*p*-dioxin (2,3,7,8-TCDD), in which chlorine atoms are present at positions 2, 3, 7, and 8 in the dioxin molecule. This dioxin is the most commonly studied because it's extremely toxic for some laboratory animals, but its human health effects at very low concentrations and exposures have been debated considerably. 2,3,7,8-TCDD was the dioxin present in Agent Orange used as a defoliant in Vietnam and was also the major toxic chemical in the Seveso (Italy) disaster in 1976. On July 10, 1976, a plant producing a disinfectant (2,4,5-trichlorophenol) released an estimated 2 kg of TCDD-equivalent dioxins over 20 min on approximately 20 km$^2$ of land. A few days later wild and domestic animals (chickens, birds, rabbits, and some dogs) died. Children who were playing outdoors at the time suffered skin burns known as chloracne. Over 700 people were evacuated from the most highly contaminated areas. A 1993 study published in the *Journal of Epidemiology* suggests that residents of Seveso were beginning to exhibit excess cancers, at the time of the study.

to about 24 g TEq · year$^{-1}$ [12]. The 2000 NRC report [13] suggests that maximal achievable control technology (MACT) standards will still not adequately address the release of dioxins along with mercury and lead. The dioxin and dioxin-like compounds are persistent in the environment. When these chemicals enter the aquatic environment, they pass through the food web and accumulate in fish, wildlife, and, ultimately, in people.

Other organic chemicals emitted during the incineration of plastics include the polycyclic aromatic hydrocarbons (PAHs). Polystyrenes appear to yield the highest concentrations of PAHs. PAHs are of concern because many are known or potential carcinogens. Because the PAHs are hydrophobic, they are known to bioaccumulate and move up the food web.

**Human Health Effects.**   Few epidemiological studies of the effects of MSW incinerators on human health have been conducted. A French study [14] found that the purchase of respiratory medications decreased with distance away from a refuse incinerator; however, no causal relationships were discovered. A 3-year study of acute respiratory effects on humans as a result of MSW landfills found no difference in the prevalence of respiratory symptoms among residents in communities near a MSW incinerator and those in a comparison community [15]. Several studies have indicated that residents living in the vicinity of incinerators have higher incidences of respiratory disease than those living in areas at a distance from the incinerator. A comprehensive study of the incidence of cancer in 14 million people living in Great Britain near MSW incinerators found no causal relationship [16]. Although the incidence rates increased with proximity to MSW incinerators, the excess cancers could be attributed to higher unemployment, overcrowding, and lower socioeconomic class.

Studies of MSW incinerator workers show a greater risk of adverse health effects due to greater exposure to pollutants than is true for residents living near the MSW incinerator. Lead, cadmium, and mercury appear to pose the greatest risk to workers [17]. The NRC report, *Waste Incineration and Public Health,* suggests that proposed and recently promulgated regulations governing the use of MACTs will have little effect on the health of incinerator workers [13].

### Other Thermal Treatment Processes

In addition to incineration, MSW can be processed by pyrolysis or gasification. **Pyrolysis** is the thermal processing of a material in the absence of oxygen. **Gasification** is the partial combustion in which a fuel is burned with less than a stoichiometric amount of oxygen. It is an energy-efficient technique for the reduction in waste volume and for recovering energy. Both processes convert the solid waste into gaseous, liquid, and solid fuels. The main difference in the two systems is that pyrolysis uses an external heat source to drive the endothermic reactions, whereby gasification reactions are self-sustaining.

## 12-7  DISPOSAL BY SANITARY LANDFILL

Although source reduction, reuse, recycling, and composting can divert large portions of MSW from landfill disposal, some waste still must be placed on land. Before 1979, MSW could be disposed of in what was known as a "dump" or, in many cases, an open and large pile. Dumping garbage in large open piles created several problems. As the garbage decomposed, it was unsightly and foul-smelling and attracted insects, gulls, rats, and other rodents. These animal "vectors" were problematic to human health because of the diseases they can carry. Uncontrolled fires, either set or spontaneously combusting, beleaguered open dumps. As rain seeped through the garbage, it carried with it harmful bacteria and hazardous chemicals into the groundwater and nearby lakes or streams. As a result of these problems, open dumps were banned by the EPA in 1979 and have been replaced by sanitary landfills.

Today, about 55% of the MSW generated is disposed of at sanitary landfills. A **sanitary landfill** is a land disposal site employing an engineered method of disposing of solid wastes on land in a manner that minimizes environmental hazards by spreading the solid wastes to the smallest

**FIGURE 12–11**

Years of remaining U.S. landfill capacity, by state. (*Source: BioCycle Magazine, April, 1999.* http://www.epa.gov/epaoswer/non-hw/muncpl/mswdata .htm#item1)

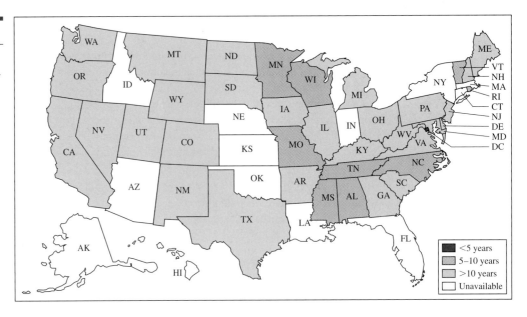

practical volume, and applying and compacting cover material at the end of each day. According to the EPA, modern landfills are well-engineered facilities that are located, designed, operated, monitored, closed, cared for after closure, cleaned up when necessary, and financed to ensure compliance with federal regulations. Others, however, believe that these views provide a false sense of security. Some believe that groundwater contamination by landfills is inevitable, that the landfills will require periodic maintenance in perpetuity, and that we are simply transferring the economical and public health burdens associated with disposal of MSW to future generations [18].

Federal regulations governing MSW disposal, namely the Subtitle D of the Resource Conservation and Recovery Act of 1991 [19], were established to protect human health and the environment. In addition, Subtitle D landfills*, built under these regulations, can collect potentially harmful landfill gas emissions and convert the gas into energy.

Since 1988, the number of landfills has decreased from about 8000 to 2314 in 1998. However, the average size of the landfill has increased. Although, some years ago, the major concern was that we would have already exceeded the capacity of existing landfills, this does not appear to be the case today. The number of years remaining for disposal of MSW varies greatly by region. As shown in Figure 12–11 most of the states are estimated to have more than 10 years of landfill capacity remaining. This is contradictory to what has been estimated elsewhere, that is, the landfills in the Northeast have essentially no time remaining, whereas those in the intermountain West have some 50 years. The landfills in the rest of the country have somewhere between 7 and 11 years [20].

### Site Selection

Site location is perhaps the most difficult obstacle to overcome in the development of a sanitary landfill. Opposition by local citizens eliminates many potential sites. In choosing a location for a landfill, consideration should be given to the following variables:

- Restricted locations such as wetlands, flood plains, and seismic impact areas
- Public opposition
- Proximity to major roadways

---

*Because municipal landfills are regulated under Subtitle D of RCRA, they are often referred to as "Subtitle D landfills."

- Load limits on roadways and bridges
- Underpass limitations
- Traffic patterns and congestion
- Location of the groundwater table and sole-source aquifers
- Soil conditions and topography
- Availability of cover material
- Climate (e.g., floods, mud slides, snow)
- Zoning requirements
- Buffer areas around the site (e.g., high trees on the site perimeter)
- Location of historic buildings, endangered species, and similar environmental factors

In October of 1991, under Subtitle D of RCRA, the EPA promulgated new federal regulations for landfills. These included siting criteria that include restrictions on distances from airports, flood plains, and fault areas, as well as limitations on construction in wetlands, seismic impact areas, and other areas of unstable geology such as landslide areas and those susceptible to sink holes. Other restrictions may apply. For example, a landfill that is less than a mile from a drinking-water intake must comply with the specific groundwater-monitoring regulations under 40 CFR 258.51–258.55 (October 9, 1994). Landfills should also be greater than 10,000 ft from airport runway used by turbojet equipment.

In siting landfills the concerns of nearby neighbors must be addressed. Due to the nature of MSW landfills and the concomitant truck traffic, MSW landfills are often considered to be poor neighbors and, result in a significant decrease in property values for distances of several kilometers surrounding the facility. The use of adequate land buffers between the landfilling operation and adjacent properties can significantly reduce the landfill's effect on the value of adjacent properties. Nevertheless, these buffers do not avoid other effects of MSW landfills, such as truck traffic, air pollution, and impaired views. In many cases it is necessary to provide more than the fair market value for the property. Payment can be made by those generating the waste (who often don't want the waste in their own backyards) along with those operating the landfill and profiting from the waste. On the positive site, landfills do bring some economic benefits, mainly in the way of jobs and a tax base.

One of the major sociological issues associated with landfills is that of environmental justice. A growing number of persons believe that landfill and other solid waste-processing operations, such as recycling plants, are disproportionately located in lower socioeconomic areas and predominately in communities populated by people of color. Consider the case of Chicago's 10th ward, where the Metropolitan Sanitary District of Greater Chicago proposed to enlarge a 650-acre landfill by converting 290 acres of wetlands into landfill. Through organizational efforts including large public meetings, demonstrations, and political meetings with the then candidate for Mayor Harold Washington, a local action group succeeded in blocking the landfill [21].

### *Operation*

The most commonly used method of operation at sanitary landfills is called the **area method** (Figure 12–12). The area method uses a three-step process: spreading the waste, compacting it, and covering it with soil.

In the area method, the solid waste is deposited on the surface, compacted, then covered with a layer of compacted soil, called the **daily cover,** at the end of the working day. Use of the area method is seldom restricted by topography; flat or rolling terrain, canyons, and other types of depressions are all acceptable.

A profile view of a typical landfill is shown in Figure 12–13. The waste and daily cover placed in a landfill during one operational period form a **cell.** The operational period is usually 1 day. The waste is dumped by the collection and transfer vehicles onto the working **face.** It is spread in 0.4–0.6-m layers and compacted. At the end of each day **cover** material is placed over the cell. The cover material may be native soil or other approved materials. Recommended

**FIGURE 12–12**

The area method.

**FIGURE 12–13**

Sectional view through a sanitary landfill. (*Source:* G. Tchobanoglous, H. Theisen, and S. Vigil, *Integrated Solid Waste Management,* McGraw-Hill, New York, 1993. Reprinted by permission.)

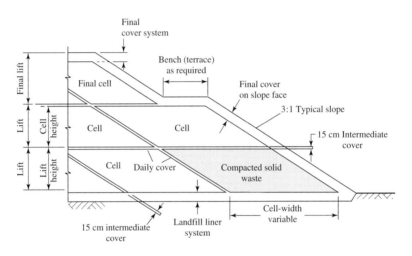

**TABLE 12–3**        Recommended Depths of Cover

| Type of Cover | Minimum Depth (m) | Exposure Time (days) |
|---|---|---|
| Daily | 0.15 | < 7 |
| Intermediate | 0.30 | 7–365 |
| Final | 0.60 | > 365 |

depths of cover for various exposure periods are given in Table 12–3. The dimensions of a cell are determined by the amount of waste and the operational period. A **lift** may refer to the placement of a layer of waste or the completion of the horizontal active area of the landfill. In Figure 12–13 a lift is shown as the completion of the active area of the landfill. The first lift is called a **fluffy lift** because the waste is not compacted until 2 m of waste is deposited. This is done to prevent damage to the liner as a result of the heavy compaction equipment. An extra layer of intermediate cover may be provided if the lift is exposed for long periods. The active area may be up to 300 m in length and width. Trenches vary in length from 30 to 300 m with widths of 5 to 15 m. The trench depth may be 3 to 9 m [22].

**Benches** are used where the height of the landfill exceeds 15–20 m. They are used to maintain the slope stability of the landfill, for the placement of surface water drainage channels, and for the location of landfill gas collection piping.

**Final cover** is applied to the entire landfill site after all landfilling operations are complete. A modern final cover will contain several different layers of material to perform very specific functions.

Additional considerations in the operation of the landfill are those required by the 1991 Subtitle D regulations promulgated by EPA. These require exclusion of hazardous waste, use of cover materials, disease vector control, explosive gas control, air quality measurements, access control, runoff and run-on controls, surface water and liquids restrictions, and groundwater monitoring, as well as record keeping [19].

**EXAMPLE 12–2**  Determine the area required for a new landfill site with a projected life of 30 years for a population of 250,000 generating $2.02 \text{ kg} \cdot (\text{capita})^{-1} \text{ day}^{-1}$. The density of the compacted waste is $470 \text{ kg} \cdot \text{m}^{-3}$. The height of the landfill cannot exceed 15 m.

Solution  This is really just a mass-balance problem. Assuming that what goes into the landfill compacted remains in the landfill for perpetuity (which is not too bad an assumption, given that food has been found virtually intact some 25–30 years after it was placed in landfills), the volume of landfill necessary can be calculated as

$$\frac{(250{,}000 \text{ people})[2.02 \text{ kg} \cdot (\text{capita}^{-1}) \text{ day}^{-1}]}{(470 \text{ kg} \cdot \text{m}^{-3})} = 1074 \text{ m}^3 \cdot \text{day}^{-1}$$

Therefore, over 30 years, the volume required is

$$(1074 \text{ m}^3 \cdot \text{day}^{-1})(365 \text{ days} \cdot \text{year}^{-1})(30 \text{ years}) = 11{,}760{,}300 \text{ m}^3$$

If we have a 15-m height constraint, then we need an area of

$$\frac{11{,}760{,}300 \text{ m}^3}{15 \text{ m}} = 784{,}020 \text{ m}^2, \text{ or } 78.4 \text{ ha}$$

Note that for simplicity, the solution did not include the volume of the daily cover that would have been used. The solution also does not take into consideration settlement of the waste due to decomposition and consolidation. Dealing with these issues is a task for subsequent upper-division courses in solid waste management.

### Environmental Considerations

Disease vectors (carriers of disease) and water and air pollution should not be a problem in a properly operated and maintained landfill. Good compaction of the waste, daily covering with good compaction of the cover, and good housekeeping are musts to control flies, rodents, and fires.

Burning, which may cause air pollution, is never permitted at a sanitary landfill. If accidental fires should occur, they must be extinguished immediately using soil, water, or chemicals.

Odors, dust, and wind-blown litter can be controlled by covering the wastes quickly and carefully, and by sealing any cracks that may develop in the cover. Dust can also be controlled by using typical dust mitigation techniques such as the application of water or biodegradable oils to the soils being excavated.

### Leachate

**Leachate,** liquid that passes through the landfill, extracts dissolved and suspended matter from the waste material. The liquid enters the landfill from external sources such as rainfall, surface drainage, groundwater, and the liquid in and produced from the decomposition of the waste.

Solid wastes placed in a sanitary landfill may undergo a number of biological, chemical, and physical changes. Aerobic and anaerobic decomposition of the organic matter results in both

| **TABLE 12–4** | Typical Data of the Composition of Leachate from New and Mature Landfills | | |
|---|---|---|---|
| | **Value (mg · L$^{-1}$)** | | |
| | **New Landfill (< 2 years)** | | **Mature Landfill (>10 years)** |
| **Constituent** | **Range** | **Typical** | |
| BOD$_5$ (5-day biochemical oxygen demand) | 2000–30,000 | 10,000 | 100–200 |
| TOC (total organic carbon) | 1500–20,000 | 6000 | 80–160 |
| COD (chemical oxygen demand) | 3000–60,000 | 18,000 | 100–500 |
| Total suspended solids | 200–2000 | 500 | 100–400 |
| Organic nitrogen | 10–800 | 200 | 80–120 |
| Ammonia nitrogen | 10–800 | 200 | 20–40 |
| Nitrate | 5–40 | 25 | 5–10 |
| Total phosphorus | 5–100 | 30 | 5–10 |
| Ortho phosphorus | 4–80 | 20 | 4–8 |
| Alkalinity as CaCO$_3$ | 1000–10,000 | 3000 | 200–1000 |
| pH (no units) | 4.5–7.5 | 6 | 6.6–7.5 |
| Total hardness as CaCO$_3$ | 300–10,000 | 3500 | 200–500 |
| Calcium | 200–3000 | 1000 | 100–400 |
| Magnesium | 50–1500 | 250 | 50–200 |
| Potassium | 200–1000 | 300 | 50–400 |
| Sodium | 200–2500 | 500 | 100–200 |
| Chloride | 200–3000 | 500 | 100–400 |
| Sulfate | 50–1000 | 300 | 20–50 |
| Total iron | 50–1200 | 60 | 20–200 |

*Source:* G. Tchobanoglous, H. Theisen, and S. Vigil, *Integrated Solid Waste Management,* McGraw-Hill, New York, 1993. Reprinted by permission.

gaseous and liquid end products. Some materials are chemically oxidized. Some solids are dissolved in water percolating through the fill. A range of leachate compositions is listed in Table 12–4. The volatile organic chemicals produced by this decomposition in the landfill gas often contribute to contamination of groundwater because they dissolve in the leachate as it passes through the landfill.

**Quantity.** The amount of leachate generated from a landfill site may be estimated using a hydrologic mass balance for the landfill. Those portions of the global hydrologic cycle (see Chapter 6) that typically apply to a landfill site include precipitation, surface runoff, evaporation, transpiration (when the landfill cover is completed), infiltration, and storage. Similar to the mass balance equations developed in Chapter 6, we can write that

$$\Delta S = P - E - R + G' - F \tag{12–2}$$

where $\Delta S$ = change in storage
$\quad\quad P$ = precipitation
$\quad\quad E$ = evaporation
$\quad\quad R$ = surface water runoff
$\quad\quad G'$ = infiltration from groundwater
$\quad\quad F$ = percolation from landfill as leachate

Precipitation may be estimated in the conventional fashion from climatological records. Surface runoff or run-on may be estimated using the various engineering techniques that are beyond the scope of this book. Evaporation and transpiration are often lumped together as *evapotranspiration (E)*. Evaporation rates may be estimated from regional data such as that provided by the U.S. Geologic Service [23]. Transpiration data may be obtained from plant science textbooks and other sources [24, 25], from direct measurements [26, 27] and from modeling efforts [28]. Infiltration (and exfiltration) may be estimated using Darcy's law (Equation 6–8). Until the landfill becomes saturated, some of the water that infiltrates will be stored in both the cover material and the waste. The quantity of water that can be held against the pull of gravity is referred to as **field capacity** (Figure 7–8). Theoretically, when the landfill reaches its field capacity, leachate will begin to flow. Then, the potential quantity of leachate is the amount of moisture within the landfill in excess of the field capacity. In reality, the field capacity does not have to be exceeded and leachate will begin to flow almost immediately because of channeling in the waste through the waste material.

Although field capacity is often used, it does have limitations. For example, the criteria for deciding when leachate just begins to flow is difficult and depends on the frequency of sampling and the accuracy with which moisture content can be measured.

As mentioned previously, the amount of leachate to leave (exfiltrate from) the landfill can be determined using Darcy's law. Leachate systems are designed to have hydraulic conductivities on the order of $10^{-9}$ m · s$^{-1}$. When using compacted clay liners, the thickness should be approximately 1 m.

---

**EXAMPLE 12–3**    Calculate the volumetric flow rate of leachate through a compacted clay liner if the area of the landfill is 15 ha and the liner thickness is 1 m. The hydraulic conductivity is $7.5 \times 10^{-10}$ m · s$^{-1}$. Assume that the head of water is 0.6 m.

Solution    First determine the Darcy velocity for the leachate through the clay layer using Equation 6–8.

$$v = K\left(\frac{\Delta h}{\Delta L}\right) = (7.5 \times 10^{-10} \text{ m} \cdot \text{s}^{-1})(0.6 \text{ m}/1 \text{ m}) = 4.5 \times 10^{-10} \text{ m} \cdot \text{s}^{-1}$$

To determine the flow, simply apply the continuity equation ($Q = vA$)

$$Q = (4.5 \times 10^{-10} \text{ m} \cdot \text{s}^{-1})(15 \text{ ha})(10^4 \text{ m}^2 \cdot \text{ha}^{-1}) = 6.75 \times 10^{-5} \text{ m}^3 \cdot \text{s}^{-1}$$

This solution assumes that there is no collection system. However, because we add a collection system in landfills, thus decreasing the hydraulic head, the infiltration of leachate out of the liner and to groundwater is minimized.

---

The EPA and the Army Engineer Research and Development Center (formerly Waterways Experiment Station) developed a computer model of the hydrologic balance called the Hydrologic Evaluation of Landfill Performance (HELP) [29]. The program contains extensive data on the characteristics of various soil types, precipitation patterns, and evapotranspiration–temperature relationships as well as the algorithms to perform a routing of the moisture flow through the landfill. Although simple to use, the HELP model overestimates leachate production, often by a factor of 2–3. This can be a costly mistake because it could result in a significant overdesign of the leachate collection and treatment system.

**Control of Leachate.**    To prevent the seepage of leachate from the landfill and thus, to avoid groundwater contamination, strict leachate control measures are required. Under the 1991 Subtitle D rules (40 CFR 258) promulgated by EPA, new landfills must be lined in a specific

**FIGURE 12–14**

A composite liner and leachate collection system.

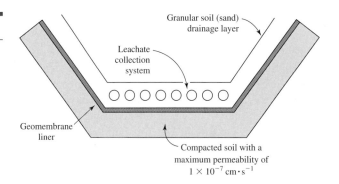

manner or meet maximum contaminant levels for the groundwater at the landfill boundary. The specified liner system includes a synthetic membrane (**geomembrane**) at least 30 mils (0.76 mm) thick supported by a compacted soil liner at least 0.6 m thick. The soil liner must have a hydraulic conductivity of no more than $1 \times 10^{-7}$ cm $\cdot$ s$^{-1}$. Flexible membrane liners consisting of HDPE must be at least 60 mils thick [19]. A schematic of the EPA specified liner system is shown in Figure 12–14.

Several geomembrane materials are available, examples of which include PVC, HDPE, chlorinated polyethylene (CPE), and ethylene propylene diene monomer (EPDM). Designers show a strong preference for PVC and especially for HDPE. Recently, geosynthetic clay liners have been used as bottom liners and final covers. These are not as thick as liners that use compacted clay yet are fast and easily installed and have low hydraulic conductivities. The use of bentonite clays allows the liner to be self-sealing in the event of damage.

Although the geomembranes are highly impermeable (hydraulic conductivities are often less than $1 \times 10^{-12}$ cm $\cdot$ s$^{-1}$), they can be easily damaged or improperly installed. Damage may occur during construction by construction equipment, by failure due to tensile stress generated by the overburden, tearing as a result of differential settling of the supporting soil, puncture from sharp objects in the overburden, puncture from coarse aggregate in the supporting soil, and tearing by landfill equipment during operation. Installation errors primarily occur during seaming when two pieces of geomembrane must be attached or when piping must pass through the liner. A liner placed with adequate quality control should have fewer than three to five defects per hectare.

The soil layer under the geomembrane acts as a foundation for the geomembrane and as a backup for control of leachate flow to the groundwater. Compacted clay generally meets the requirement for a hydraulic conductivity of less than $1 \times 10^{-7}$ cm $\cdot$ s$^{-1}$. In addition to having a low permeability, it should be free of sharp objects greater than 1 cm in diameter, graded evenly without pockets or hillocks, compacted to prevent differential settlement, and free of cracks.

**Leachate Collection.**   Under the 1991 Subtitle D rules [19], the leachate collection system must be designed so that the depth of leachate above the liner does not exceed 0.3 m. The leachate collection system is designed by sloping the floor of the landfill to a grid of underdrain pipes* that are placed above the geomembrane. A 0.3-m-deep layer of granular material (e.g., sand) with a high hydraulic conductivity (EPA recommends greater than $1 \times 10^{-2}$ cm $\cdot$ s$^{-1}$) is placed over the geomembrane to conduct the leachate to the underdrains. In addition to carrying the leachate, this layer also protects the geomembrane from mechanical damage from equipment and solid waste. In some instances a **geonet** (a synthetic matrix that resembles a miniature chain link fence), with a **geofabric** (an open-weave cloth) protective layer to keep out the sand, is placed under the sand and above the geomembrane to increase the flow of leachate to the pipe system.

---

*__Underdrain pipes__ are perforated pipes designed to collect the leachate.

**Leachate Treatment.** The composition of landfill leachate varies greatly, but is generally highly contaminated with ammonia, organic contaminants measured as chemical oxygen demand (COD) and biological oxygen demand (BOD), halogenated hydrocarbons, and heavy metals. In addition, leachate usually contains high concentrations of inorganic salts—mainly sodium chloride, carbonate, and sulfate. Thus, it must be collected and treated before discharge. Leachate from young landfills with large deposits of municipal waste, for example, will often contain very high concentrations of ammonia and organic chemicals. In contrast, leachate from old landfills will have high salt concentrations with distinctly lower ammonia, heavy metals, and organic chemical concentrations. Therefore, state-of-the-art leachate treatment plants should be designed as multistage units that can cope with the changing leachate characteristics over time.

Landfill leachate treatment varies greatly. In some cases, the collected leachate is sent without any pretreatment to municipal wastewater treatment plants, where it is treated along with municipal wastewater. In other cases, the collected leachate is pretreated by chemical flocculation followed by sedimentation and filtration before it is sent to the municipal wastewater system. In other cases, it is necessary to treat the leachate separately on site before discharge. One such possibility of a treatment system is to use a two-stage activated sludge process—nitrification–denitrification—for ammonia, COD, and BOD removal. This may not yield sufficient treatment, and further processing may be required to remove residual COD. Several options include activated carbon and ozone. However, none of these treatment processes will remove the high salt content. In cases where salts must be removed, reverse osmosis (RO) can be employed for desalination. A common treatment process combination is biological pretreatment of the leachate followed by an RO stage. On site treatment of the leachate can be achieved by recycling the flow through the landfill, allowing the microorganisms additional opportunity to degrade the biodegradable material in the leachate.

### Methane and Other Gas Production

The principal gaseous products emitted from a landfill (methane and carbon dioxide) are the result of microbial decomposition. Typical concentrations of landfill gases and their characteristics are summarized in Table 12–5. During the early life of the landfill, the predominant gas is carbon dioxide, which is produced from aerobic decomposition of the waste. During this time the nitrogen ($N_2$) gas concentration is also high. As the landfill matures, the gas is composed almost equally of carbon dioxide and methane. In the methanogenic phase, the concentration of nitrogen will decrease. Once methanogenesis is complete, methane generation will cease.

**TABLE 12–5** Typical Constituents Found in MSW Landfill Gas

| Component | Percent (dry volume basis) | Characteristic | Value |
|---|---|---|---|
| Methane | 45–60 | Temperature (°C) | 35–50 |
| Carbon dioxide | 40–60 | Specific gravity | 1.02–1.05 |
| Nitrogen | 2–5 | Moisture content | Saturated |
| Oxygen | 0.1–1.0 | High heating value (in $kJ \cdot m^{-3}$) | 16,000–20,000 |
| Sulfides, disulfides, mercaptans, etc. | 0–1.0 | | |
| Ammonia | 0.1–1.0 | | |
| Hydrogen | 0–0.2 | | |
| Carbon monoxide | 0–0.2 | | |
| Trace constituents | 0.01–0.06 | | |

*Source:* G. Tchobanoglous, H. Theisen, and S. Vigil, *Integrated Solid Waste Management*, McGraw-Hill, New York, 1993. Reprinted by permission.

Methane is explosive in the presence of oxygen when it is present at concentrations greater than 40%. Methane release is also a concern because it is a greenhouse gas and can damage crops planted in the vicinity of the landfill. As such, its movement must be controlled. The heat content of this landfill gas mixture ranges from 16,000–20,000 kJ $\cdot$ m$^{-3}$. Although not as substantial as methane alone (37,750 kJ $\cdot$ m$^{-3}$), landfill gas has sufficient economic value that many landfills have been tapped with wells to collect and use methane for energy production.

Typically, landfill gas contains numerous other compounds besides carbon dioxide, methane, and ammonia. Because of the toxicity of the trace gases emitted from landfills, these gases are of concern. More than 150 compounds have been measured at various landfills. Many of these nonmethane organic chemicals (NMOC) may be classified as hazardous air pollutants (HAPs) or volatile organic chemicals (VOCs). The occurrence of significant VOC concentrations is often associated with older landfills that previously accepted industrial and commercial wastes containing these compounds. The concentrations of ten compounds measured in landfill gases from several California sites are shown in Table 12–6. Other emissions may include nitrogen oxides (NO$_x$), sulfur dioxide, hydrogen chloride (HCl), and particulate matter.

The rate of emissions is governed by the rates of gas production and transport. Gas production is controlled by biological and chemical decomposition along with volatilization. The transport of the gases is controlled by the rates of gas diffusion, advection, and convection.

**Landfill gas** (LFG) collection systems can be active or passive. **Active systems** provide a pressure gradient to force the gas from the cells. Mechanical blowers or compressors are used. **Passive systems** allow a natural pressure gradient to build up, which causes the gas to move from the cells into the collection devices.

**TABLE 12–6**  Concentrations of Specified Air Contaminants Measured in Landfill Gasses (in ppb)

| | Landfill Site | | | | | | |
|---|---|---|---|---|---|---|---|
| Compound | Yolo Co. | City of Sacramento | Yuba Co. | El Dorado Co. | L.A.-Pacific (Ukiah) | City of Clovis | City of Willits |
| Vinyl chloride | 6900 | 1850 | 4690 | 2200 | <2 | 66,000 | 75 |
| Benzene | 1860 | 289 | 963 | 328 | <2 | 895 | <18 |
| Ethylene dibromide | 1270 | <10 | <50 | <1 | <1 | <1 | <0.5 |
| Ethylene dichloride | nr | nr | nr | <20 | 0.2 | <20 | 4 |
| Methylene chloride | 1400 | 54 | 4500 | 12,900 | <1 | 41,000 | <1 |
| Perchloroethylene | 5150 | 92 | 140 | 233 | <0.2 | 2850 | 8.1 |
| Carbon tetrachloride | 13 | <5 | <7 | <5 | <0.2 | <5 | <0.2 |
| 1,1,1-TCA[a] | 1180 | 6.8 | <60 | 3270 | 0.52 | 113 | 0.8 |
| TCE[b] | 1200 | 470 | 65 | 900 | <0.6 | 895 | 8 |
| Chloroform | 350 | <10 | <5 | 120 | <0.8 | 1200 | <0.8 |
| Methane | nr | nr | nr | nr | 0.11% | 17% | 0.14% |
| Carbon dioxide | nr | nr | nr | nr | 0.12% | 24% | <0.1% |
| Oxygen | nr | nr | nr | nr | nr | 10% | 21% |

nr: Not reported by operator.

[a]1,1,1-TCA: 1,1,1-trichloroethane, methyl chloroform.

[b]TCE: Trichloroethane, trichloroethylene.

*Source: The Landfill Gas Testing Program: A Report to the Legislature,* State of California Air Resources Board, Stationary Source Division, June, 1988.

LFG can be purified to produce a gas that can be recovered for energy generation. Alternatively, open combustion using flares can be employed to burn off LFG. Thermal incinerators operate at a sufficiently high temperature to oxidize the VOCs in the LFG to carbon dioxide and water. Purification techniques can use adsorption, absorption, or membranes. Because gas collection systems are not 100% efficient, emissions of methane and other LFGs will nevertheless occur.

**EXAMPLE 12-5**  A landfill with a gas collection system is in operation and serves a population of 200,000. MSW is generated at a rate of $1.95 \text{ kg} \cdot (\text{capita})^{-1} \text{day}^{-1}$. Gas is produced at an annual rate of $6.2 \text{ L} \cdot \text{kg}^{-1}$ of MSW delivered to the landfill. The gas contains 55% methane. Gas recovery is 15% of that generated. The heat content of the landfill gas is approximately $17,000 \text{ kJ} \cdot \text{m}^{-3}$ (a value lower than the theoretical value because of dilution of the methane with air during recovery). The landfill company and a developer have proposed to build a subdivision in the vicinity of the landfill and pipe the methane generated to the homes to be used for heating. The homes are estimated to use an average of $110 \times 10^6 \text{ kJ}$ of heat energy each year. Peak usage during winter is 1.5 times the average usage. How many homes can be built in the subdivision?

Solution  This is essentially a mass and energy-balance problem, in which solid waste is being disposed of in a landfill. Methane is generated during the decomposition of the waste. The methane is used by the homes for heating. The energy generated in the landfill must equal the energy consumed by the homeowners.

The amount of methane generated is equal to
(Amount of waste disposed in landfill per person on yearly basis)
× (Number of people served by landfill)
× (Rate of gas production per mass of solid waste)
× (Fraction of methane in gas)

$$= [1.95 \text{ kg} \cdot (\text{capita})^{-1} \text{ day}^{-1}](365 \text{ days} \cdot \text{year}^{-1})(200,000 \text{ persons})(6.2 \text{ L gas} \cdot \text{kg}^{-1})(0.55)$$

$$= 4.85 \times 10^8 \text{ L methane} \cdot \text{year}^{-1}$$

But only 15% is recovered.

$$(4.85 \times 10^8 \text{ L methane} \cdot \text{year}^{-1})(0.15) = 7.28 \times 10^7 \text{ L methane} \cdot \text{year}^{-1}$$

The heat content of the methane recovered is

$$(17,000 \text{ kJ} \cdot \text{m}^{-3})(7.28 \times 10^7 \text{ L} \cdot \text{year}^{-1})(10^{-3} \text{ m}^3 \cdot \text{L}^{-1}) = 1.24 \times 10^9 \text{ kJ} \cdot \text{year}^{-1}$$

Energy to heat the homes during times of peak demand (i.e., winter) must be supplied:

Peak demand = Averaged usage × 1.5

$$= (110 \times 10^6 \text{ kJ} \cdot \text{year}^1)(1.5) = 1.65 \times 10^8 \text{ kJ} \cdot \text{home}^{-1} \cdot \text{year}^{-1}$$

$$\text{Number of homes that can be heated} = \frac{\text{energy generated}}{\text{energy required per home}}$$

$$= \frac{1.24 \times 10^9 \text{ kJ} \cdot \text{year}^{-1}}{1.65 \times 10^8 \text{ kJ} \cdot \text{home}^{-1} \cdot \text{year}^{-1}} = 7.5 \text{ homes}$$

Because we can't heat a fraction of a home, then we can build seven homes.

**Leachate Monitoring.**  Under EPA regulations, all landfill operators must monitor for both gaseous and liquid contaminants that have the potential to be released from the landfill. The goal of any groundwater monitoring plan is to have reliable and representative information on aquifer characteristics, groundwater flow directions, and chemical and physical characteristics of groundwater being monitored. The goals of surface water monitoring are to assess the characteristics of surface waters that have the potential to be affected by leachate releases, contaminated groundwater seepage, or contaminated surface water run-off. The monitoring of surface and groundwater allows the landfill operators to demonstrate that the landfill is performing as designed, to provide data that the leachate is not infiltrating into the groundwater, to identify risks associated with improved operation of the landfill and to identify when the landfill no longer poses a risk to human or environmental health.

### Landfill Design

The design of the landfill has many components, including site preparation, buildings, monitoring wells, size, liners, leachate collection system, final cover, and gas collection system. In the following discussion we will limit ourselves to introductory consideration of the design of the size of the landfill, the selection of a liner system, the design of a leachate collection system, and a discussion of the final cover system.

To estimate the volume required for a landfill, it is necessary to know the amount of refuse being produced and the density of the in-place, compacted refuse. The volume of refuse differs markedly from one city to another because of local conditions.

Salvato recommends a formula of the following form for estimating the annual volume required [30].

$$\Psi_{LF} = \frac{PEC}{D_c} \tag{12-3}$$

where $\Psi_{LF}$ = volume of landfill (in $m^3$)
$P$ = population
$E$ = ratio of cover (soil) to compacted fill = $(\Psi_{sw} + \Psi_c)/\Psi_{sw}$
$\Psi_{sw}$ = volume of solid waste (in $m^3$)
$\Psi_c$ = volume of cover (in $m^3$)
$C$ = average mass of solid waste collected per capita per year (in kg · person$^{-1}$)
$D_c$ = density of compacted fill (in kg · m$^{-3}$)

The density of the compacted fill depends somewhat on the equipment used at the landfill site and the moisture content of the waste. Compacted solid waste densities vary from 300 to 700 kg · m$^{-3}$. Nominal values are generally in the range of 475 to 600 kg · m$^{-3}$.

---

**EXAMPLE 12-6**  How much landfill space does Apocatequil County require for 20 years of operation? You may assume that 142,000 persons are being served by this landfill and that each person generates 2.0 kg · day$^{-1}$ of waste. The density of the uncompacted waste is 106 kg · m$^{-3}$ and a compaction ratio of 4.2 can be used. The ratio of cover to compacted fill is 1.9.

Solution  Apply Equation 12–3.

$$\Psi_{LF} = \frac{PEC}{D_c} = \frac{(142,000\,\text{persons})(2.0\,\text{kg} \cdot \text{day}^{-1})(365\,\text{days} \cdot \text{year}^{-1})(1.9)}{(106\,\text{kg} \cdot \text{m}^{-3})(4.2)} = 442,400\,\text{m}^3$$

Multiply by 20 years.

$$442,400 \times 20 = 8,848,000 = 8,900,000\,\text{m}^3$$

Had we not considered the volume of cover material we would have determined the volume to be $4.66 \times 10^6\,\text{m}^3$.

### *Landfill Closure*

The major function of the final cover is to prevent moisture from entering the finished landfill. If no moisture enters, then at some time the leachate production will reach minimal proportions and the chance of groundwater contamination will be minimized.

Modern final cover design consists of a surface layer, biotic barrier, drainage layer, hydraulic barrier, foundation layer, and gas control. The surface layer is to provide suitable soil for plants to grow. This minimizes erosion. A soil depth of about 0.3 m is appropriate for grass. The biotic barrier is to prevent the roots of the plants from penetrating the hydraulic barrier. At this time, there does not seem to be an optimal material for this barrier. The drainage layer serves the same function here as in the leachate collection system—that is, it provides an easy flow path to a grid of perforated pipes. This collection piping system is subject to differential settling and may fail because of it. Some designers do not recommend installing it because they prefer to use the funds to develop a thicker hydraulic barrier. The hydraulic barrier serves the same function as the liner by preventing movement of water into the landfill. The EPA recommends a composite liner consisting of a geomembrane and a low hydraulic conductivity soil that also serves as the foundation for the geomembrane. This soil also protects the geomembrane from the rough aggregate in the gas control layer. The gas control layer is constructed of coarse gravel that acts as a vent to carry the gases to the surface. If the gas is to be collected for its energy value, a series of gas recovery wells is installed. A negative pressure is placed on these wells to draw the gas into the system.

Completed landfills generally require maintenance because of uneven settling. Maintenance consists primarily of regrading the surface to maintain good drainage and filling in small depressions to prevent ponding and possible subsequent groundwater pollution. The final soil cover should be about 0.6 m deep.

Completed landfills have been used for recreational purposes, such as parks, playgrounds, or golf courses. Parking lots and storage areas are other final uses. Because of the characteristic uneven settling and gas evolution from landfills, construction of buildings on completed landfills should be avoided.

On occasion, one-story buildings and runways for light aircraft might be constructed. In such cases, it is important to avoid concentrated foundation loading, which can result in uneven settling and cracking of the structure. The designer must provide the means for the gas to dissipate into the atmosphere and not into the structure.

## CHAPTER REVIEW

When you have completed studying this chapter you should be able to do the following without the aid of your textbook or notes:

1. State the average mass of solid waste produced per capita per day in the United States in 1998.
2. Define the following terms: refuse, solid waste, putrescible waste.
3. List the elements of a solid waste management system.
4. Explain how policy makers decide how and how often solid waste is to be collected.
5. Define the following terms: resource conservation, resource recovery, closed-loop recycling, open-loop recycling, composting.
6. List the methods of collecting recyclable materials.
7. List the common materials that can be recycled. Be able to discuss the specific issues pertaining to each material.
8. Discuss how the market for recyclable materials can be improved.
9. Define what is meant by reuse of durable goods. Describe several methods of reuse.
10. Discuss how education and legislation affect source reduction.
11. Define the following terms: combustion, pyrolysis, gasification. What is the difference among these processes?

12. List the different types of incinerators. Explain how an incinerator operates.
13. List the major public health and environmental issues dealing with incinerators.
14. List and discuss the factors pertinent to the selection of a landfill site.
15. Describe the methods of constructing a sanitary landfill.
16. Explain the purpose of daily cover in a sanitary landfill and state the minimum desirable depth of daily cover.
17. Define leachate and explain why it occurs.
18. Sketch a sanitary landfill that includes proper cover and a leachate collection system.
19. Define or explain the following terms: HHV, LHV, RDF, source separation.
20. Explain the effect of source separation on the heating value of solid waste and on the potential for hazardous air pollution emissions.

With the aid of this text or a list of equations you should be able to do the following:

1. Determine the volume and mass of solid waste from various establishments.
2. Estimate the volume and area requirements for a landfill.
3. Compute the LHV given the HHV and the chemical formula for a compound to be burned.
4. Estimate the volumetric flow rate of leachate.
5. Estimate methane generation and energy production rates.

## PROBLEMS

**12-1**  The Bailey Stone Works employs six people. Assuming that the density of uncompacted waste is $480 \, \text{kg} \cdot \text{m}^{-3}$, determine the annual volume of solid waste produced by the stone works assuming a waste generation rate of $1 \, \text{kg} \cdot \text{capita}^{-1} \cdot \text{day}$.

**Answer:** $4.6 \, \text{m}^3 \cdot \text{year}^{-1}$

**12-2**  The student population of a high school is 881. The school has 30 standard classrooms. Assuming a 5-day school week with solid waste pickups on Wednesday and Friday before school starts in the morning, determine the size of storage container required. Assume waste is generated at a rate of $0.11 \, \text{kg} \cdot (\text{capita})^{-1} \, \text{day}$ plus 3.6 kg per room and that the density of uncompacted solid waste is $120.0 \, \text{kg} \cdot \text{m}^{-3}$. Standard container sizes are as follows (all in $\text{m}^3$): 1.5, 2.3, 3.0, and 4.6.

**12-3**  The Nairyosangha landfill located in Peshdadians serves a population of 562,400 people generating MSW at a rate of $1.89 \, \text{kg} \cdot \text{capita}^{-1} \cdot \text{day}$. The volume of the landfill is $11,240,000 \, \text{m}^3$. At the present time, 63% of the landfill is used. The ratio of cover to compacted fill is 1.9. Determine projected life remaining for the landfill. Assume the density of the compacted waste to be $490 \, \text{kg} \cdot \text{m}^{-3}$.

**Answer:** 2.76 years

**12-4**  The Sibzianna landfill serves a population of 253,000. Each week 325 trucks bring a total of 2180 t of MSW to the landfill. Each truck averages two loads per day. The trucks each have a capacity of 4.5 t, and operate 5 days per week.

(a) How much MSW is generated per person? Give your answer in $\text{kg} \cdot \text{capita}^{-1} \cdot \text{day}$

(b) What is the average load (in metric tonnes) in each truck when they arrive at the landfill? At what capacity are the trucks operating?

(c) If, the density of the waste is $265 \, \text{kg} \cdot \text{m}^{-3}$, what is the volume of MSW disposed of at the landfill each week?

**12-5**  Professor Dexter has made measurements of her household solid waste, shown in the following table. If the container volume is $0.0757 \, \text{m}^3$, what is the average density of the solid waste produced in her household during the period of time from March 18th through April 8th? Assume that the mass of each empty container is 3.63 kg.

| Date | Can Number | Gross Mass[a] (kg) | Date | Can Number | Gross Mass[a] (kg) |
|---|---|---|---|---|---|
| March 18 | 1 | 7.26 | April 8 | 1 | 6.35 |
| | 2 | 7.72 | | 2 | 8.17 |
| March 25 | 1 | 10.89 | | 3 | 8.62 |
| | 2 | 8.17 | | | |
| | 3 | 7.26 | | | |

[a]Container plus solid waste.

**Answer:** Average density $= 58.4 \text{ kg} \cdot \text{m}^{-3}$

**12–6** A sanitary landfill is being designed to handle solid waste generated by Binford, Vermont, at a rate of $50 \text{ Mg} \cdot \text{day}^{-1}$. It is expected that the waste will be delivered by compactor truck on a $5 \text{ days} \cdot \text{week}^{-1}$ basis. The density as spread is $122 \text{ kg} \cdot \text{m}^{-3}$. It will be spread in 0.50-m layers and compacted to 0.25 m. Assuming three such lifts per day and a daily cover of 0.15 m, determine the following: (a) annual volume of landfill consumed in cubic meters, and (b) daily horizontal area covered by the solid waste. Ignore the soil volume between stacks.

**12–7** Calculate the volumetric flow rate of leachate through a compacted clay liner if the area of the landfill is 21 ha and the liner thickness is 1.3 m. The hydraulic conductivity is $2.5 \times 10^{-10} \text{ m} \cdot \text{s}^{-1}$. Assume that the head of water is 0.8 m.

**Answer:** $2.8 \text{ m}^3 \cdot \text{day}^{-1}$

**12–8** A developer plans to build a completely self-contained city on the Planet Zaqar. The city will have a population of 555,000. The homes in the city are to be heated with methane gas generated at the landfill. The landfill will have a gas collection system. Through education and conservation, MSW generation will be reduced to a rate of $0.45 \text{ kg} \cdot \text{capita}^{-1} \cdot \text{day}$. It is anticipated that gas can be produced at an annual rate of $25 \text{ L gas kg}^{-1}$ of MSW delivered to the landfill and that the gas will contain 58% methane. Gas recovery is 25% of that which is generated. The heat content of the methane gas is approximately $18,000 \text{ kJ} \cdot \text{m}^{-3}$ (a value lower than the theoretical value because of dilution of the methane with air during recovery). The homes are estimated to use an average $40 \times 10^6 \text{ kJ}$ of heat energy each year. Peak usage during winter is 1.5 times the average usage. Is this proposal feasible from the standpoint of generating sufficient heat for domestic use? What are alternative sources of "waste" materials that could be used as a resource to generate heat?

**12–9** A landfill that is 12 ha in area has a liner of thickness 0.9 m. Each year $1700 \text{ m}^3$ of leachate is collected. The hydraulic conductivity of the liner is $3.9 \times 10^{-10} \text{ m} \cdot \text{s}^{-1}$. What is the head of water above the liner?

**Answer:** 1.04 m

## DISCUSSION QUESTIONS

**12–1** Which of the following soil types would be suitable for (a) liner, (b) drainage layer, (c) gas venting?
(1) Gravel (>2.5 cm diameter)
(2) Glacial till ($K = 10^{-7} \text{ cm} \cdot \text{s}^{-1}$)
(3) Clay ($K = 1 \times 10^{-9} \text{ cm} \cdot \text{s}^{-1}$)
(4) Silt ($K = 1 \times 10^{-6} \text{ cm} \cdot \text{s}^{-1}$)
(5) Coarse sand ($K = 0.1 \text{ cm} \cdot \text{s}^{-1}$)
(6) Fine sand ($K = 0.001 \text{ cm} \cdot \text{s}^{-1}$)

**12–2** Although the market value of compost is negligible, many communities have implemented yard waste composting systems. Explain why.

**12–3** Discuss the characteristics of waste that are favorable for biological treatment, thermal processing, recycling, and landfilling.

**12–4** Discuss at least two aspects of concern of a municipal waste landfill.

**12–5** Discuss why biological treatment of solid waste is used extensively in Western Europe and Palestine but not in the United States.

**12–6** What is the effect of biowaste composting on gas production from a landfill?

## ADDITIONAL READING

**Books**

Bishop, P. L., *Pollution Prevention,* McGraw Hill, New York (2000).

Davis, M., and D. Cornwell. *Introduction to Environmental Engineering,* 3rd ed. McGraw-Hill, New York (1998).

Landreth, R. E., P. A. Rebers, *Municipal Solid Wastes: Problems and Solutions,* CRC Lewis Publishers, Boca Raton, FL (1996).

McBean, E. A., F. A. Rovers, G. J. Farquhar, *Solid Waste Landfill Engineering and Design,* Prentice Hall, Englewood Cliffs, NJ (1995).

Ostler, N. K., *Environmental Technology Series, Volume V: Waste Management Concepts,* Prentice Hall, Englewood Cliffs, NJ (1998).

Pfeffer, J. T., *Solid Waste Management Engineering,* Prentice Hall, Englewood Cliffs, NJ (1992).

Rhyner, C. R., *Waste Management and Resource Recovery,* CRC Lewis Publishers, Boca Raton, FL (1995).

Shah, K. L., *Basics of Solid and Hazardous Waste Management Technology,* Prentice Hall, Englewood Cliffs, NJ (2000).

Tchobanoglous, G., H. Theisen, and R. Eliassen, *Solid Wastes, Engineering Principles and Management Issues,* McGraw-Hill, New York (1993).

Tchobanoglous, G., H. Theisen, and S. Vigil, *Integrated Solid Waste Management,* McGraw-Hill, New York (1993).

**Journals**

*Journal Air and Waste Management Association*

*Waste Age*

*World Wastes*

## REFERENCES

1. U.S. Environmental Protection Agency, *Municipal Solid Waste Generation, Recycling, and Disposal in the United States: Facts and Figures for 1998,* EPA 530-F-00-024, April 2000.
2. National Center for Resource Recovery, Inc., *Resource Recovery from Municipal Solid Waste,* Lexington Books, Lexington, MA (1974).
3. Vence, T. D., and D. L. Powers, "Resource recovery systems, Part l: Technological comparison," *Solid Wastes Management/Resource Recovery Journal,* p. 26, May 1980.
4. *State Recycling Laws Update, 2000.* Raymond Communications College Park, MD, 20740. http://www.raymond.com/state/
5. U.S. Environmental Protection Agency, *Characterization of Municipal Solid Waste in the United States: 1998 Update,* Government Printing Office, Washington, D.C., 1998.
6. U.S. EPA, Municipal Solid Waste, Composting http://www.epa.gov/epaoswer/non-hw/muncpl/compost.htm
7. The Center for Desert Architecture and Urban Planning, Jacob Blaustein Institute for Desert Research-Ben-Gurion University of the Negev, Midreshet Ben-Gurion, Israel http://www.bgu.ac.il/CDAUP/building.htm#2
8. Phosphate Recovery, The Natural History Museum, London, England, 2003 http://www.nhm.ac.uk/mineralogy/phos/manure.htm
9. Pfeffer, J. T., *Solid Waste Management Engineering,* Prentice Hall, Upper Saddle River, NJ, p. 172, 1992.
10. The discussions on refuse-derived fuel, modular incinerators, and water wall combustion follows T. D. Vence and D. L. Powers, "Resource recovery systems, Part l, Technological comparison," *Solid Waste Management/Resource Recovery Journal,* pp. 26–28, 32, 34, 72, 92, 93, May, 1980.
11. U.S. EPA and Environment Canada, 2000. *Draft Report on PCDD* (Dioxins) *and PCDF* (Furans) *Sources and Regulations* (May 26, 2000) and Addendum (August, 2000). http://www.epa.gov/glnpo/bns/dioxin/PCDD_DF.regs.pdf

12. U.S. EPA. 1998. *The Inventory of Sources of Dioxin in the United States* (external review draft), April 1998. EPA/600/P-98/002Aa.

13. *Waste Incineration and Public Health. 2000.* Committee on Health Effects of Waste Incineration, Board of Environmental Studies and Technology, Commission of Life Sciences, National Research Council, National Academy Press, Washington, D.C., p. 180.

14. Zmirou, D., B. Parent, and J.-L. Potelon. "Etude épidémiologique des effets sur la santé des rejets atmosphériques d'une usine d'incinération de déchets industriels et ménagers." *Revue d'épidémiologie et de Santé Publique,* vol. 32, pp. 391–397, 1984.

15. Shy, C. M., D. Degnan, D. L. Fox, S. Mukerjee, M. J. Hazucha, B. A. Boehlecke, et al. "Do waste incinerators induce adverse respiratory effects? An air quality and epidemiological study of six communities. *Environmental Health Perspectives,* vol. 103(7–8), pp. 714–724, 1995.

16. Elliott, P. G., G. Shaddick, I. Kleinschmidt, D. Jolley, P. Walls, J. Beresford, et al. "Cancer incidence near municipal solid waste incinerators in Great Britain," *British Journal of Cancer,* vol. 73(5), pp. 702–710, 1996.

17. *Waste Incineration and Public Health. 2000.* Committee on Health Effects of Waste Incineration, Board of Environmental Studies and Technology, Commission of Life Sciences, National Research Council, National Academy Press, Washington, D.C., p. 181.

18. Lee, G. F., and Sheehan, W. "Landfills offer false sense of security," *Biocycle,* vol. 37(9), p. 8, 1996.

19. *Code of Federal Regulations,* 40 CFR 257 and 258, and "Solid waste disposal facility criteria: Final rule," *Federal Register,* 9 Oct 1991.

20. Scarlett, L., *Solid Waste Recycling Costs: Issues and Answers,* Reason Public Policy Institute Policy Study No. 193 (Los Angeles: Reason Public Policy Institute, August 1995), p. 2. From http://www.rppi.org/privatization/ps267.html

21. Environmental Liberty and Social Justice for All: How Advocacy Planning Can Help Combat Environmental Racism, by Simmons Buntin, November 1995.

22. Tchobanoglous, G., Theisen, and S. Vigil, *Integrated Solid Waste Management,* McGraw-Hill, New York, p. 374 (1993).

23. Water Resources Information Service, *Ground Water Atlas,* U.S. Geologic Service, Washington, D.C. (2000).

24. *Botany, An Introduction to Plant Science,* by W. Robbins, T. Weir, and C. Stocking, John Wiley, New York (1959).

25. WATER USE CLASSIFICATION OF LANDSCAPE SPECIES: Species Factor Finder http://www.wateright.org/site/reference/wucols.htm

26. Nobel, P. S. *Biophysical Plant Physiology and Ecology.* W. H. Freeman and Co., San Francisco (1983).

27. Salisbury, F. B., and C. W. Ross. *Plant Physiology,* 4th ed. Wadsworth Publishing, Belmont, California (1992).

28. Kaufmann, M. R., *Annual Transpiration in Subalpine Forests: Large Differences Among Four Tree Species.* USDA Forest Service, Rocky Mountain Forest and Range Experiment Station, Fort Collins, Co, 80526-2098, 1985.

29. Schroeder, P. R., J. M. Morgan, T. M. Walski, A. C. Gibson, *The Hydrologic Evaluation of Landfill Performance (HELP) Model Documentation, User's Guide,* EPA/530/SW-84-009, U.S. Environmental Protection Agency, Government Printing Office, Washington, D.C., 1984.

30. Salvato, J. A., *Environmental Engineering and Sanitation,* Wiley, New York, p. 427 (1972).

# 13

# Hazardous Waste Management

## 13–1   THE HAZARD

A **hazardous waste,** is any waste or combination of wastes that poses a substantial danger, now or in the future, to human, plant, or animal life and that therefore must be handled or disposed of with special precautions. The following examples illustrate the potential problems that may arise when special precautions are not taken in the disposal of hazardous waste.

1. Judy Piatt hired Russell Bliss to spray oil around her stables at Moscow Mills, Missouri, to control the dust. A few days later, hundreds of birds fell to the ground and died. Within the next years, 20 of her cats went bald and died. Sixty-two of her horses died. Bliss's oil was waste from a defunct hexachlorophene plant that had paid him to dispose of it. That same waste oil was used to settle the dust in the streets of Times Beach, Missouri. It contained dioxin as a contaminant. It was 1971 and virtually no one knew that this waste oil was hazardous.
2. The lagoon was once a licensed disposal site for toxic wastes. The owner was Berlin & Farro Liquid Incineration, Inc. At the bottom of the mysterious blue liquid in the lagoon were some barrels. They were thought to contain hydrochloric acid. The blue liquid in the lagoon was a cyanide waste. The combination of the two chemicals would result in a lethal cloud of cyanide gas. The citizens of nearby Swartz Creek, Michigan, were evacuated while the State Department of Natural Resources oversaw the cleanup.

These case histories epitomize our concern with hazardous wastes. That which is common practice today may be the seed of disaster for tomorrow. What is considered good disposal practice may become a nightmare if the operators are not responsible or are not good enough business people to make money within the rules and are therefore tempted to stray beyond them.

### Dioxins and PCBs

We would like to elaborate on two particular hazardous wastes that have achieved national prominence: dioxins and PCBs. Because of their newsworthiness, we provide you with a brief summary of the chemistry of these compounds, where they come from, and their environmental effects.

Dioxins are found as over 20 different isomers of a basic chlorodioxin structure (some examples are shown in Figure 13–1). The most common form, 2,3,7,8-tetrachlorodibenzo-*p*-dioxin (TCDD), has become recognized as probably the most poisonous of all synthetic chemicals. Dioxins are a contaminant by-product that may be thermally generated during the manufacture or burning of chlorophenols; pesticides such as 2,4,5-T; Agent Orange, a defoliant made of a 50/50 mix of 2,4-D and 2,4,5-T; algae-controlling herbicides; insecticides; and preservatives. Dioxins are not manufactured for any commercial purpose. They occur only as a contaminant by-product. To date, no dioxin has been found to be formed naturally in the environment. Widespread TCDD contamination has been reported in particulate matter from commercial and domestic combustion processes. Additional background dioxin contamination (0.1–10 ppm) may persist and bioaccumulate following the field application of herbicides.

**FIGURE 13–1**

Some examples of dioxins.

Unsubstituted dioxin     2,7-DCDD     1,3,6,8-TCDD

2,3,7,8-TCDD     1,2,4,6,7,9-HEXA-CDD     OCDD

TCDD is a crystalline solid at room temperature. It is only slightly soluble in water (0.2–0.6 ppb). TCDD is considered to be a highly stable compound. It is thermally degraded at temperatures over 700°C. It is photochemically degraded under ultraviolet light in the presence of a hydrogen-donating solvent such as a solution of olive oil in cyclohexanone.

TCDD contamination was found at levels of parts per million in 2,4,5-T and 2,4-D used for weed control in the United States and as a defoliant in Vietnam; in wastes at the Love Canal disposal sites; in orthochlorophenol crude oil spill residues in the Sturgeon, Missouri, train derailment; and in fallout from an explosion at a chlorophenol manufacturing plant spill in Seveso, Italy. At this last site engineers and scientists were challenged to develop environmentally safe control strategies.

The environmental health effects of dioxin in people are not well documented. However, alleged birth defects in newborns in South Vietnam caused researchers to begin animal toxicological investigations. TCDD is known to cause severe skin disorders, such as chloracne. In test animals it is a carcinogen, teratogen, mutagen, and embryo toxin, and is known to affect immune responses in mammals. It is considered persistent, and it bioaccumulates in aquatic organisms. At this date (2002) no deaths have been directly correlated with low-level TCDD exposure. Nor have epidemiological findings shown any increased incidence of carcinogenesis, teratogenesis, mutagenesis or newborn defects, miscarriages, or similar adverse health effects in people. In May, 2000, the U.S. EPA released a draft report that presented evidence that dioxin, even in trace amounts, may cause adverse human health effects [1]. The draft report states that TCDD is a known human carcinogen and that other dioxins are likely human carcinogens. EPA believes that dioxins may cause a wide range of other effects, including disruption of regulatory hormones, reproductive and immune system disorders, and abnormal fetal development. Levels of dioxins in the environment were negligible until about 1930, peaked about 1970, and have been declining since then. Concentrations of dioxins in human lipid tissue have declined since 1980.

The term **PCB (polychlorinated biphenyl)** refers to a class of organic chemicals produced by the chlorination of a biphenyl molecule. It is composed of ten possible forms and, theoretically, more than 200 isomers. These forms arise from a specified number of chlorine substitutions on the biphenyl molecule and correspond to the chemical nomenclatures monochlorobiphenyl, dichlorobiphenyl, trichlorobiphenyl, and so on. Several isomers for each PCB molecule are possible, the number depending on available substitution sites on each biphenyl portion (2-6, 2′-6′) of the molecule. However, not all possible isomers are likely to be formed during the manufacturing processes. In general, the most common ones are those that have either an equal number of chlorine atoms on both rings or a difference of only one chlorine atom between rings. Some examples are shown in Figure 13–2.

Commercial PCB mixtures were manufactured under a variety of trade names. The chlorine content of any product varied from 18 to 79%, depending on the extent of chlorination during the manufacturing process or on the amount of isomeric mixing engaged in by individual producers.

Molecular structure and names of a few selected polychlorinated biphenyls.

3-Chlorobiphenyl          2,4′-Dichlorobiphenyl          2,4,4′,6-Tetrachlorobiphenyl          2,2′,4,4′,6,6′-Hexachlorobiphenyl

Each company had a specific system for identifying the chlorine content of its product. For example, Aroclor 1248, 1254, and 1260 indicate 48, 54, and 60% chlorine, respectively; Clophen A60, Phenochlor DP6, and Kaneclor 600 designate that these products contain mixtures of hexachlorobiphenyls.

The only important U.S. producer of PCBs was Monsanto Industrial Chemicals Co., which had plants at Anniston, Alabama, where production of PCBs ended in 1970; and Sauget, Illinois, where production ceased in 1977. Sold under Monsanto's registered trademark of Aroclors, mixtures of PCBs had been used originally as a coolant–dielectric for transformers and capacitors, as heat transfer fluids, and as protective coatings for woods when low flammability was essential or desirable. Producers and users alike, apparently unaware of any potential hazards from exposure to PCBs, initially operated in accordance with earlier results of toxicity tests that indicated no effects [2]. The expansion of open-ended applications between 1930 and 1960, incorporating PCBs into such commodities as paints, inks, dedusting agents, and pesticides, led to the widespread dissemination of which we are now aware. By 1937, toxic effects were noted in occupationally exposed workers, and threshold limit values were imposed at manufacturing sites.

The general pattern of release of PCBs to the environment changed significantly during the early 1970s. Until then, essentially no restrictions were imposed either on the use or disposal of PCBs. After evidence became available in 1969 and 1970 that chronic exposure could result in hazards to human health and the environment, Monsanto voluntarily banned sales of PCBs, and the release rate from industrial use was reduced through stringent control measures. However, significant reservoirs of mobile PCBs (those available for transport among environmental media and biota) still exist along with even larger, currently immobile reservoirs. The latter include those materials containing PCBs that are still in service and those deposited in landfills and dumps. The major factor affecting future release of PCBs from these sources will be government regulations controlling storage and disposal of the chemical.

## 13–2  EPA'S HAZARDOUS WASTE DESIGNATION SYSTEM

EPA designates a waste material to be hazardous in two ways [3]: (1) by its presence on EPA-developed lists, or (2) by evidence that the waste exhibits ignitable, corrosive, reactive, or toxic characteristics.

The list of hazardous wastes includes spent halogenated and nonhalogenated solvents; electroplating baths; wastewater treatment sludges from many individual production processes; and heavy ends, light ends, bottom tars, and side-cuts from various distillation processes.

Some commercial chemical products are also listed as being hazardous wastes when discarded. These include "acutely hazardous" wastes such as arsenic acid, cyanides, and many pesticides, as well as "toxic" wastes such as benzene, toluene, and phenols.

EPA has designated five hazardous waste categories. Each hazardous waste is given an EPA hazardous waste number, often referred to as the **hazardous waste code.** Each of the five categories may be identified by the prefix letter assigned by EPA. The five categories may be described as follows:

1. Specific types of wastes from nonspecific sources; examples include halogenated solvents, nonhalogenated solvents, electroplating sludges, and cyanide solutions from plating batches. There are 28 listings in this category. These wastes have a waste code prefix letter F.

2. Specific types of wastes from specific sources; examples include oven residue from the production of chrome oxide green pigments and brine purification muds from the mercury cell process in chlorine production where separated, prepurified brine is not used. There are 111 listings in this category. These wastes have a waste code prefix letter K.

3. Any commercial chemical product or intermediate, off-specification product, or residue that has been identified as an acute hazardous waste. Examples include potassium silver cyanide, toxaphene, and arsenic oxide. There are approximately 203 listings in this category. These wastes have a waste code prefix letter P.

4. Any commercial chemical product or intermediate, off-specification product, or residue that has been identified as hazardous waste. Examples include xylene, DDT, and carbon tetrachloride. There are approximately 450 listings in this category. These wastes have a waste code prefix letter U.

5. Characteristic wastes, which are wastes not specifically identified elsewhere, that exhibit properties of ignitability, corrosivity, reactivity, or toxicity. These wastes have a waste code prefix letter D.

The wastes that appear on one of the lists specified in items one through four are called **listed wastes.** Those wastes that are declared hazardous because of their general properties are called **characteristic wastes.** The characteristics of ignitability, corrosivity, and reactivity may be referred to as ICR. The toxicity characteristic may be referred to as TC.

Figure 13–3 shows a generalized flow scheme for determining if a waste is hazardous according to EPA definitions. Of particular importance in the scheme are those things that are not included in the RCRA regulations. For example, domestic sewage; certain nuclear materials; household wastes, including toxic and hazardous materials; and small quantities (less than $100 \text{ kg} \cdot \text{month}^{-1}$) are excluded from the RCRA regulations. This does not mean that these wastes are not regulated at all. In fact they are regulated under other statutes and, thus, do not need to be regulated under RCRA.

Some waste streams do not come under the purview of RCRA but are, nonetheless, considered hazardous. These special wastes include, for example, PCBs and asbestos. PCBs and asbestos are regulated under the Toxic Substances Control Act (abbreviated TSCA and pronounced "tas-kah").

## 13–3   RCRA AND HSWA

### Congressional Actions on Hazardous Waste

In 1976 Congress passed the Resource Conservation and Recovery Act (abbreviated RCRA and pronounced "rick-rah") directing the EPA to establish hazardous waste regulations. RCRA was amended in 1984 by the Hazardous and Solid Waste Amendments (abbreviated HSWA and pronounced "hiss-wah"). RCRA and HSWA were enacted to regulate the generation and disposal of hazardous wastes. These acts did not address abandoned or closed waste disposal sites or spills. The Comprehensive Environmental Response, Compensation, and Liability Act (abbreviated by CERCLA and pronounced "sir-klah"), commonly referred to as "Superfund," was enacted in 1980 to address these problems. SARA, the Superfund Amendments and Reauthorization Act of 1986, extended the provisions of CERCLA. In the following sections, we shall attempt to tell you about the who, what, where, and how of RCRA, HSWA, CERCLA, and SARA.

### Cradle-to-Grave Concept

The EPA's cradle-to-grave hazardous waste management system is an attempt to track hazardous waste from its generation point (the "cradle") to its ultimate disposal point (the "grave"). The system requires generators to attach a manifest (itemized list describing the contents) form to their hazardous waste shipments. This procedure is designed to ensure that wastes are directed to, and actually reach, a permitted disposal site.

**FIGURE 13-3**

Flow scheme for determining if waste is hazardous. (*Source:* Davis, M. L., and D. A. Cornwell, *Introduction to Environmental Engineering,* WCB/New York: McGraw-Hill, 1998. Reprinted by permission.)

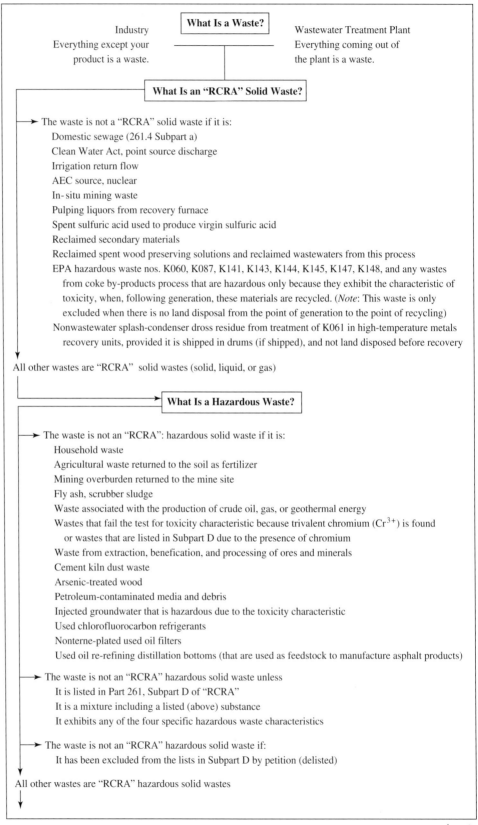

**What Is a Waste?**

Industry
Everything except your product is a waste.

Wastewater Treatment Plant
Everything coming out of the plant is a waste.

**What Is an "RCRA" Solid Waste?**

The waste is not a "RCRA" solid waste if it is:
   Domestic sewage (261.4 Subpart a)
   Clean Water Act, point source discharge
   Irrigation return flow
   AEC source, nuclear
   In-situ mining waste
   Pulping liquors from recovery furnace
   Spent sulfuric acid used to produce virgin sulfuric acid
   Reclaimed secondary materials
   Reclaimed spent wood preserving solutions and reclaimed wastewaters from this process
   EPA hazardous waste nos. K060, K087, K141, K143, K144, K145, K147, K148, and any wastes
      from coke by-products process that are hazardous only because they exhibit the characteristic of
      toxicity, when, following generation, these materials are recycled. (*Note:* This waste is only
      excluded when there is no land disposal from the point of generation to the point of recycling)
   Nonwastewater splash-condenser dross residue from treatment of K061 in high-temperature metals
      recovery units, provided it is shipped in drums (if shipped), and not land disposed before recovery

All other wastes are "RCRA" solid wastes (solid, liquid, or gas)

**What Is a Hazardous Waste?**

The waste is not an "RCRA": hazardous solid waste if it is:
   Household waste
   Agricultural waste returned to the soil as fertilizer
   Mining overburden returned to the mine site
   Fly ash, scrubber sludge
   Waste associated with the production of crude oil, gas, or geothermal energy
   Wastes that fail the test for toxicity characteristic because trivalent chromium ($Cr^{3+}$) is found
      or wastes that are listed in Subpart D due to the presence of chromium
   Waste from extraction, benefication, and processing of ores and minerals
   Cement kiln dust waste
   Arsenic-treated wood
   Petroleum-contaminated media and debris
   Injected groundwater that is hazardous due to the toxicity characteristic
   Used chlorofluorocarbon refrigerants
   Nonterne-plated used oil filters
   Used oil re-refining distillation bottoms (that are used as feedstock to manufacture asphalt products)

The waste is not an "RCRA" hazardous solid waste unless
   It is listed in Part 261, Subpart D of "RCRA"
   It is a mixture including a listed (above) substance
   It exhibits any of the four specific hazardous waste characteristics

The waste is not an "RCRA" hazardous solid waste if:
   It has been excluded from the lists in Subpart D by petition (delisted)

All other wastes are "RCRA" hazardous solid wastes

(continued)

**FIGURE 13–3**

(continued)

---

| What Wastes Are Subject to Regulation? |

The "RCRA" hazardous solid waste is currently not subject to Subtitle C regulations if:

The total combined "RCRA" hazardous waste generated at the site is less than 100 kg/month

It is intended to be legitimately reclaimed or reused, (261.6). However it is subject to RCRA reporting requirements regarding storage and transportion if it is a sludge or contains a Part 261 listed substance.

The "RCRA" hazardous solid waste is temporarily exempt from certain regulations if:

It is a hazardous waste that is generated in a product or raw material storage tank, a product or raw material transport vehicle or vessel, a product or raw material pipeline, or in a manufacturing process unit or an associated nonwaste-treatment-manufacturing unit.

All other "RCRA" hazardous solid wastes are subject to Subtitle C of RCRA regulation with respect to disposal, transport, and storage.

Requirements for Recyclable Materials

Hazardous wastes that are not subject to requirements for generator, transporters, and storage facilities:
Regulated under Subparts C through H (261.6):

Recyclable materials used in a manner constituting disposal

Hazardous wastes burned for energy recovery in boilers and industrial furnaces

Recyclable materials from which precious metals are reclaimed

Spent lead-acid batteries that are being reclaimed

Not subject to regulation or to the notification requirements of RCRA:

Industrial ethyl alcohol that is reclaimed

Used batteries returned to a battery manufacturer for regeneration

Scrap metal

Fuels produced from the refining of oil bearing hazardous wastes

Oil reclaimed from hazardous waste resulting from normal petroleum refining, production, and transportation practices

Hazardous waste fuel produced from oil-bearing hazardous wastes

Petroleum coke produced from petroleum refinery hazardous wastes

Used oil that is recycled and is also a hazardous waste solely because it exhibits a hazardous characteristic is not subject to the requirements of Parts 260–268 of this chapter, but is regulated under Part 279 of this chapter.

## Generator Requirements

Generators of hazardous waste are the first link in the cradle-to-grave chain of hazardous waste management established under RCRA. Generators of more than 100 kg of hazardous waste or 1 kg of acutely hazardous waste per month must (with a few exceptions) comply with all of the generator regulations.

The regulatory requirements for hazardous waste generators include [4]:

1. Obtaining an EPA identification (ID) number
2. Handling of hazardous waste before transport
3. Manifesting of hazardous waste
4. Record keeping and reporting

EPA assigns each generator a unique identification number. Without this number the generator is barred from treating, storing, disposing or transporting, or offering for transportation any hazardous waste. Furthermore, the generator is forbidden from offering the hazardous waste to any transporter, or treatment, storage, or disposal (TSD) facility that does not also have an EPA ID number.

Pretransport regulations are designed to ensure safe transportation of a hazardous waste from origin to ultimate disposal. In developing these regulations, EPA adopted those used by the

Department of Transportation (DOT) for transporting hazardous wastes off-site (49 CFR Parts 172, 173, 178, and 179).

In addition to adopting these DOT regulations, EPA also developed pretransport regulations that cover the accumulation of waste prior to transport. A generator may accumulate hazardous waste on site for 90 days or less as long as they are properly stored, there is an emergency plan, and personnel are trained in the proper handling of hazardous waste.

The 90-day period allows a generator to collect enough waste to make transportation more cost-effective, that is, instead of paying to haul several small shipments of waste, the generator can accumulate waste until there is enough for one big shipment. If the generator accumulates hazardous waste on site for more than 90 days, it is considered an operator of a storage facility and must comply with requirements for such facilities.

The uniform hazardous waste manifest (the **manifest**) is the key to cradle-to-grave waste management (Figure 13–4). Through the use of a manifest, generators can track the movement of hazardous waste from the point of generation to the point of ultimate treatment, storage, or disposal.

HSWA requires that each manifest certify that the generator has in place a program to reduce the volume and toxicity of the waste to the degree that is economically practicable, as determined by the generator, and that the TSD method chosen by the generator is the best practicable method currently available that minimizes the risk to human health and the environment.

The manifest is part of a controlled tracking system. Each time the waste is transferred, that is, from a transporter to the designated facility or from a transporter to another transporter, the manifest must be signed to acknowledge receipt of the waste. A copy of the manifest is retained by each link in the transportation chain. Once the waste is delivered to the designated facility, the owner or operator of the facility must send a copy of the manifest back to the generator. This system ensures that the generator has documentation that the hazardous waste has reached its ultimate destination.

If 35 days pass from the date on which the waste was accepted by the initial transporter and the generator has not received a copy of the manifest from the designated facility, the generator must contact the transporter or the designated facility to determine the whereabouts of the waste. If 45 days pass and the manifest still has not been received, the generator must submit an exception report.

The record keeping and reporting requirements for generators provide EPA and states with a method for tracking the quantities of waste generated and the movement of hazardous wastes.

### Transporter Regulations

Transporters of hazardous waste are the critical link between the generator and the ultimate off-site treatment, storage, or disposal of hazardous waste. The transporter regulations were developed jointly by EPA and the DOT to avoid contradictory requirements coming from the two agencies [4]. Although the regulations are integrated, they are not contained under the same act. A transporter must comply with the regulations under 49 CFR 171–179 (The Hazardous Materials Transportation Act) as well as those under 40 CFR Part 263 (Subtitle C of RCRA).

Even if generators and transporters of hazardous waste comply with all appropriate regulations, transporting hazardous waste can still be dangerous. There is always the possibility that an accident will occur. To deal with this possibility, the regulations require transporters to take immediate action to protect health and the environment if a release occurs by notifying local authorities or diking off the discharge area.

The regulations also give officials special authority to deal with transportation accidents. Specifically, if a federal, state, or local official, with appropriate authority, determines that the immediate removal of the waste is necessary to protect human health or the environment, the official can authorize waste removal by a transporter who lacks an EPA ID and without the use of a manifest.

**FIGURE 13–4**

Uniform hazardous waste manifest.

Please print or type.    *(Form designed for use on elite (12-pitch) typewriter.)*    Form Approved. OMB No. 2000-0404. Expires 7-31-86

| UNIFORM HAZARDOUS WASTE MANIFEST | 1. Generator's US EPA ID No. | Manifest Document No. | 2. Page 1 of | Information in the shaded areas is not required by Federal law. |

3. Generator's Name and Mailing Address

A. State Manifest Document Number

B. State Generator's ID

4. Generator's Phone (   )

5. Transporter 1 Company Name    6.    US EPA ID Number    C. State Transporter's ID

D. Transporter's Phone

7. Transporter 2 Company Name    8.    US EPA ID Number    E. State Transporter's ID

F. Transporter's Phone

9. Designated Facility Name and Site Address    10.    US EPA ID Number    G. State Facility's ID

H. Facility's Phone

| 11. US DOT Description  *(Including Proper Shipping Name, Hazard Class, and ID Number)* | 12. Containers | | 13. Total Quantity | 14. Unit Wt/Vol | I. Waste No. |
|---|---|---|---|---|---|
| | No. | Type | | | |
| a. | | | | | |
| b. | | | | | |
| c. | | | | | |
| d. | | | | | |

GENERATOR

J. Additional Descriptions for Materials Listed Above

K. Handling Codes for Wastes Listed Above

15. Special Handling Instructions and Additional Information

16. GENERATOR'S CERTIFICATION:    I hereby declare that the contents of this consignment are fully and accurately described above by proper shipping name and are classed, packed, marked, and labeled, and are in all respects in proper condition for transport by highway according to applicable international and national government regulations.

Unless I am a small quantity generator who has been exempted by statute or regulation from the duty to make a waste minimization certification under Section 3002(b) of RCRA, I also certify that I have a program in place to reduce the volume and toxicity of waste generated to the degree I have determined to be economically practicable and I have selected the method of treatment, storage, or disposal currently available to me which minimizes the present and future threat to human health and the environment.

Printed/Typed Name    Signature    Month  Day  Year

TRANSPORTER

17. Transporter 1 Acknowledgement of Receipt of Materials

Printed/Typed Name    Signature    Month  Day  Year

18. Transporter 2 Acknowledgement of Receipt of Materials

Printed/Typed Name    Signature    Month  Day  Year

FACILITY

19. Discrepancy Indication Space

20. Facility Owner or Operator: Certification of receipt of hazardous materials covered by this manifest except as noted in Item 19.

Printed/Typed Name    Signature    Month  Day  Year

EPA Form 8700-22 (Rev. 4-85) Previous edition is obsolete.

## Treatment, Storage, and Disposal Requirements

**Treatment, storage, and disposal** facilities (TSDs) are the last link in the cradle-to-grave hazardous waste management system. All TSDs handling hazardous waste must obtain an operating permit and abide by the TSD regulations. The TSD regulations establish performance standards that owners and operators must apply to minimize the release of hazardous waste into the environment.

A TSD facility may perform one or more of the following functions [4]:

1. *Treatment:* Any method, technique, or process, including neutralization, designed to change the physical, chemical, or biological character or composition of any hazardous waste so as to neutralize it or render it nonhazardous or less hazardous; to recover it;

make it safer to transport, store, or dispose of; or make it amenable for recovery, storage, or volume reduction.

2. *Storage:* The holding of hazardous waste for a temporary period, at the end of which the hazardous waste is treated, disposed, or stored elsewhere.

3. *Disposal:* The discharge, deposit, injection, dumping, spilling, leaking, or placing of any solid waste or hazardous waste into or on any land or water so that any constituent thereof may enter the environment or be emitted into the air or discharged into any waters, including groundwaters.

The act establishes standards that consist of administrative–nontechnical requirements and technical requirements.

The purpose of the administrative–nontechnical requirements is to ensure that owners and operators of TSDs establish the necessary procedures and plans to operate a facility properly and to handle any emergencies or accidents. They cover the subject areas shown in the following table:

| Subpart | Subject |
| --- | --- |
| A | Who is subject to the regulations |
| B | General facility standards |
|   |     Waste analysis, security, inspections, training |
|   |     Ignitable, reactive, or incompatible wastes |
|   |     Location standards (permitted facilities) |
| C | Preparedness and prevention |
| D | Contingency plans and emergency procedures |
| E | Manifest system, record keeping, and reporting |

The objective of the technical requirements is to minimize the potential for threats resulting from hazardous waste treatment, storage, and disposal at existing facilities waiting to receive an operating permit. There are two groups of requirements: general standards that apply to several types of facilities and specific standards that apply to a waste management method.

The general standards cover three areas:

1. Groundwater monitoring requirements
2. Closure, postclosure requirements
3. Financial requirements

Groundwater monitoring is only required of owners or operators of a surface impoundment, landfill, land treatment facility, or some waste piles used to manage hazardous waste. The purpose of these requirements is to assess the effect of a facility on the groundwater beneath it. Monitoring must be conducted for the life of the facility except at land disposal facilities, which must continue monitoring for up to 30 years after the facility has closed.

The groundwater monitoring program outlined in the regulations requires a monitoring system of four wells to be installed: one upgradient from the waste management unit and three downgradient. The downgradient wells must be placed so as to intercept any waste migrating from the unit, should such a release occur. The upgradient wells must provide data on groundwater that is not influenced by waste coming from the waste management unit (called background data). If the wells are properly located, comparison of data from upgradient and downgradient wells should indicate if contamination is occurring.

Once the wells have been installed, the owner or operator monitors them for 1 year to establish background concentrations for selected chemicals. These data form the basis for all future data comparisons. Three sets of parameters established for background concentrations: for drinking water, groundwater quality, and groundwater contamination.

Closure is the period when wastes are no longer accepted, during which owners or operators of TSD facilities complete TSD operations; apply final covers to or cap landfills and dispose of or decontaminate equipment, structures, and soil. Postclosure, which applies only to disposal facilities, is the 30-year period after closure during which owners or operators of disposal facilities conduct monitoring and maintenance activities to preserve and look after the integrity of the disposal system.

Financial requirements were established to ensure that funds are available to pay for closing a facility, for rendering postclosure care at disposal facilities, and to compensate third parties for bodily injury and property damage caused by sudden and nonsudden accidents related to the facility's operation (states and federal governments are exempted from abiding by these requirements). There are two kinds of financial requirements: financial assurance for closure–postclosure and liability coverage for injury and property damage.

**Land Ban.**   HSWA significantly expanded the scope of RCRA. HSWA was created, in large part, in response to strongly voiced citizen concerns that existing methods of hazardous waste disposal, particularly land disposal, were not safe. Section 3004 of HSWA sets restrictions on land disposal of specific wastes, commonly called the "land ban," or **land disposal restrictions** (LDR). As specifically required by section 3004(m), the agency established levels or methods of treatment, if any, which substantially reduce the likelihood of migration of hazardous constituents from waste so that short-term and long-term threats to human health and the environment are minimized. On September 18, 1994 the universal treatment standards (UTS) were published by EPA to streamline the process [5].

### Underground Storage Tanks

An **underground storage tank** (UST) system includes an underground storage tank, connected piping, underground ancillary equipment, and containment system, if any. On September 23, 1988, the EPA promulgated the final rules for underground storage tanks [6].

The new regulations include a number of exclusions:

Hazardous waste UST systems
Regulated wastewater treatment facilities
Any equipment or machinery that contains regulated substances for operational purposes
   such as hydraulic lift tanks and electrical equipment tanks
Any UST system of less than 41.5 L
Any UST system containing a de minimis (negligible) concentration of regulated substances
Any emergency spill or overflow containment system that is expeditiously emptied after use

All UST systems installed after December 22, 1988, must have corrosion protection, which can be accomplished in three ways: (1) construction of fiberglass-reinforced plastic, (2) steel- and fiberglass-reinforced plastic composite, or (3) a coated steel tank with cathodic protection. Cathodic protection systems must be regularly tested and inspected. All owners and operators must also provide spill and overfill prevention equipment and a certificate of installation to ensure that the methods of installation were in compliance with the regulations.

Release (leak) detection must be instituted for all UST. Several different methods are allowed for petroleum UST systems. However, some systems have specific requirements, for instance, a pressurized delivery system must be equipped with an automatic line leak detector and have an annual line tightness test. All new or upgraded UST systems storing hazardous substances must have secondary containment with interstitial monitoring.

When release is confirmed, owners and operators must begin corrective action. Immediate corrective action measures include mitigation of safety and fire hazards, removal of saturated soils and floating free product, and an assessment of further corrective action needed. As with any remediation situation, a corrective action plan may be required for long-term cleanups of contaminated soil and groundwater.

## 13-4 **CERCLA AND SARA**

### *The Superfund Law*

The Comprehensive Environmental Response Compensation, and Liability Act (CERCLA) of 1980, better known as "Superfund," became law "to provide for liability, compensation, cleanup and emergency response for hazardous substances released into the environment and the cleanup of inactive hazardous waste disposal sites." CERCLA was generally intended to give EPA authority and funds to clean up abandoned waste sites and to respond to emergencies related to hazardous waste. The law provides for both response and enforcement mechanisms. The four major provisions of the law establish

1. A fund (the "Superfund") to pay for investigations and remedies at sites where the responsible people cannot be found or will not voluntarily pay;
2. A priority list of abandoned or inactive hazardous waste sites for cleanup (the national priority list);
3. The mechanism for action at abandoned or inactive sites (the national contingency plan);
4. Liability for those responsible for cleaning up.

Initially the trust fund was supported by taxes on producers and importers of petroleum and 42 basic chemicals. In its first 5-year period, Superfund collected about $1.6 billion, with 86% of that money coming from industry and the remainder from federal government appropriations. In 1986 the Superfund Amendments and Reauthorization Act (SARA) greatly expanded the money available to remediate Superfund sites. The fund was raised to $8.6 billion for a 5-year period by taxing petroleum products ($2.75 billion), business income ($2.5 billion), and chemical feedstocks ($1.4 billion). The remainder is from general revenues.

### *The National Priority List*

The **national priority list** (NPL) serves as a tool for the EPA to use in identifying sites that appear to present a significant risk to public health or the environment and that may merit use of Superfund money. First published in 1982, it is updated three times a year. In October, 2002, the list contained 1234 sites.

The first NPL was formulated from notification procedures and existing information sources. Subsequently, a numeric ranking system known as the hazard ranking system was developed. Sites with high HRS scores may be added to the list. Sites on the NPL are eligible for Superfund money. Those with lower scores are not likely to be eligible.

### *The Hazard Ranking System*

The **hazard ranking system** (HRS) is a procedure for ranking uncontrolled hazardous waste sites in terms of the potential threat based upon containment of the hazardous substances, route of release, characteristics and amount of the substances, and likely targets. The methodology of the HRS provides a quantitative estimate that represents the relative hazards posed by a site and takes into account the potential for human and environmental exposure to hazardous substances. The HRS score is based on the probability of contamination from four pathways—groundwater, surface water, soil, and air—on the site in question. The groundwater and air migration pathways are evaluated for ingestion and inhalation, respectively. The surface water migration and soil exposure pathways are evaluated for multiple intake routes. Surface water is evaluated for exposure of (1) drinking water, (2) human food chain, and (3) the environment (contact) to hazardous wastes. These exposures are evaluated for two separate migration components—overland/flood migration and groundwater to surface water migration. Soil is evaluated for potential hazardous waste exposure to the (1) resident population and (2) nearby population [7,8].

Use of the HRS requires considerable information about the site and its surroundings, the hazardous substances present, and the geology of the aquifers and the intervening strata. The factors that most affect an HRS site score are the proximity to a densely populated area or source of drinking water, the quantity of hazardous substances present, and the toxicity of those hazardous substances. The HRS methodology has been criticized for the following reasons:

1. There is a strong bias toward human health effects, with only a slight chance of a site in question receiving a high score if it represents a threat or hazard only to the environment.
2. Because of the human health bias, there is an even stronger bias in favor of highly populated affected areas.
3. The air emission migration route must be documented by an actual release, while groundwater and surface water routes have no such documentation requirement.
4. The scoring for toxicity and persistence of chemicals may be based on site containment, which is not necessarily related to a known or potential release of the toxic chemicals.
5. A high score for one migration route can be more than offset by low scores for the other migration routes.
6. Averaging of the route scores creates a bias against a site that has only one hazard, even though that one hazard may pose extreme threat to human health and the environment.

The HRS scores range from 0 to 100, with a score of 100 representing the most hazardous site. Occasional exceptions have been made in the HRS priority ranking to meet the CERCLA requirement that a site designated by a state as its top priority be included on the NPL.

### The National Contingency Plan

The **national contingency plan** (NCP) provides detailed direction on the action to be taken at a hazardous waste site, including initial assessment to determine if an emergency or imminent threat exists, creation of emergency response actions, and a method to rank sites (the HRS) and establish priority for future action. When sufficient indication points to a site posing a potential risk to the environment, a detailed study is required [9,10].

The NCP describes the steps to be taken for the detailed evaluation of the risks associated with a site. Such an evaluation is termed a **remedial investigation** (RI). The process of selecting an appropriate remedy is termed the **feasibility study** (FS). The remedial investigation and the feasibility study are often combined into a single measure, known popularly as a remedial investigation/feasibility study (RI/FS). The requirements of the RI/FS are usually outlined in a written work plan, which must be approved by the relevant federal and state agencies before it may be implemented.

A remedial investigation includes the development of detailed plans that address the following items:

1. *Site characterization:* A description of the hydrogeological and geophysical sampling and analytical procedures to be applied to discover the nature and extent of the waste materials, the physical characteristics of the site, and any receptors that could be affected by the wastes at the site.
2. *Quality control:* The guidelines to be enforced to ensure that all the data collected from the characterization program are valid and satisfactorily accurate.
3. *Health and safety:* The procedures to be employed to protect the safety of the individuals who will work at the site and perform the site characterization.

The RI activities and subsequent evaluation of the data gathered are termed a **risk assessment** or an endangerment assessment. The remedial investigation report documents the evaluation.

The remedial investigation report serves as a basis for the feasibility study, which evaluates various remedial alternatives. The review criteria include overall protection of human health and the environment; compliance with applicable or relevant and appropriate regulations; long-term effectiveness; reduction in toxicity, mobility, or volume; short-term effectiveness; technical and administrative implementability; cost; state acceptance; and community acceptance. All the remedies selected must be capable of reducing the risk at the hazardous waste site to an acceptable level. And, in general, the lowest cost alternative that achieves this objective is chosen as the course of action. The results of the feasibility study are presented in a written report, called the **record of decision** (ROD). This document serves as a preliminary basis for the design of the selected alternative.

One of the keys to the NCP is that it specifies that the degree of cleanup be selected in accordance with several criteria, including the degree of hazard to the "public health, welfare and the environment." Therefore, no predetermined level of remediation can be required or must be achieved at any site. Rather, the degree of correction is established on a site-by-site basis. What is acceptable in one location may not necessarily be acceptable in another.

On completion and approval of the RI/FS, the next step is the preparation of plans and specifications for the selected remedy—the **remedial design** (RD). To complete the process, the construction and other activities are undertaken in accordance with the plans and specifications.

### Liability

Perhaps the most far-reaching provision of CERCLA that has stood the test of the courts was the establishment of *strict joint, and several liability* for cleanup of an NPL site. Those identified by EPA as **potentially responsible parties** (PRPs) may include generators, present owners, or former owners of facilities or real property where hazardous wastes have been stored, treated, or disposed of, as well as those who accepted hazardous waste for transport and selected the facility. PRPs have strict liability; that is, liability without fault. Neither care nor negligence, neither good nor bad faith, neither knowledge nor ignorance, can be claimed as a defense. Congress correctly predicted that there would be instances where the PRPs would contest their contribution to the problem and would, then, be unwilling to share the costs or the responsibility. The strict liability provision orders that the PRP is liable even if the method of disposal was in accordance with prevailing standards, laws, and practice at the time of disposal. In other words, CERCLA is a "pay now, argue later" statute [9].

Although the language specific to "joint and several" liability was removed from CERCLA, the courts have interpreted the law as though the language were included. This means that if a PRP contributed any wastes to a site, that PRP can be held accountable for all costs associated with the cleanup. This concept was strongly reaffirmed in SARA. If the PRP refuses to pay, the federal government can sue to recover costs. These actions have been successful. In certain instances where those liable fail, without sufficient cause, to properly provide for cleanup, they may be liable for triple damages!

### Superfund Amendments and Reauthorization Act

SARA reaffirmed and strengthened many of the provisions and concepts of the CERCLA program. In SARA, Congress clearly expressed a preference but not a requirement, for remedies such as incineration or chemical treatment that render a waste nonhazardous rather than transport to another disposal site or simple containment on site.

Another aspect of SARA is that the level of cleanup should achieve compliance with **applicable or relevant and appropriate requirements** (ARARs). ARARs are environmental standards from programs other than CERCLA and SARA. For example, if a state has a regulation regarding atmospheric emissions from incinerators, then a Superfund cleanup using incineration must meet those applicable standards. Furthermore, if a similar standard appears to be relevant and appropriate then EPA may elect to apply it. For example, if drums of waste found on an uncontrolled hazardous waste site have contents that appear to have the same constituents as F001-F005 spent solvent, then the UTS standards for RCRA waste may be considered relevant and appropriate even though there is no specific evidence to identify the origin of the waste.

SARA significantly strengthens the requirement to consider damages to natural resources, especially those off site. CERCLA also required such observance, but few sites included this factor in practice. SARA provides a mechanism to include the issue in future investigations and remedies.

**Title III.**   SARA includes a major addition to the provisions of CERCLA, namely title III—emergency planning and community right to know. Under the emergency planning provisions facilities must notify the state emergency response commission if they have quantities of extremely hazardous substances that exceed EPA specified **threshold planning quantities** (TPQ). In addition, communities must establish local emergency planning committees (LEPCs) to develop a chemical emergency response plan. This plan must include identification of regulated facilities, emergency response and notification procedures, training programs, and evacuation plans in case of a chemical release.

If a facility accidentally releases chemicals that are on one of two lists (i.e., EPA's extremely hazardous substance list or the CERCLA section 103(a) list), in regulated quantities (RQ), and the release has the potential for exposure off-site, they must notify the LEPC immediately. The law also requires a report on response actions taken, known or anticipated health risks, and advice on medical attention for exposed individuals.

Perhaps the most revolutionary provision of title III is the establishment of the **community's right to know** amounts of chemicals and their location in facilities in their community. Thus, information about potential hazards from chemicals is available to the public. In addition, each year those facilities that release chemicals above specified threshold amounts must submit a **toxic release inventory** (TRI) on an EPA-specified form (form R). This inventory includes both accidental and routine releases, as well as off-site shipments of waste. The publication of these data has resulted in strenuous efforts by industry to control their previously unregulated and, hence, uncontrolled emissions because of the public outcry at the large quantities of materials being dumped into the environment.

## 13–5  HAZARDOUS WASTE MANAGEMENT

A logical priority in managing hazardous waste would be to

1. Reduce the amount of hazardous wastes generated in the first place.
2. Stimulate "waste exchange." (One factory's hazardous wastes can become another's feedstock; for instance, acid and solvent wastes from some industries can be used by others without processing.)
3. Recycle metals, the energy content, and other useful resources contained in hazardous wastes.
4. Detoxify and neutralize liquid hazardous waste streams by chemical and biological treatment.
5. Reduce the volume of waste sludges generated in item four by dewatering.
6. Destroy combustible hazardous wastes in special high-temperature incinerators equipped with proper pollution control and monitoring systems.
7. Stabilize or solidify sludges and ash from items five and six to reduce leachability of metals.
8. Dispose of remaining treated residues in specially designed landfills.

### Waste Minimization

The key elements necessary for the success of a waste minimization program include [11]

Top-level organizational commitment
Financial resources
Technical resources
Appropriate organization, goals, and strategy

The commitment of senior management is the first element that must be in place. Efforts to establish the other elements can follow. The organizational structure adopted should promote communication and feedback from participants. Often, the best ideas come from line operators who work with the processes every day.

Some firms set quantitative waste minimization goals. Other firms are more qualitative in their goal setting.

**Waste Audit.**   An important first step in establishing a strategy for waste minimization is to conduct a waste audit. The audit should proceed stepwise:

1. Identify waste streams
2. Identify sources
3. Establish priority of waste streams for waste minimization activity
4. Screen alternatives
5. Implement
6. Track
7. Evaluate progress

The key question at the outset of a waste audit is "Why is this waste being generated?" You must first establish the primary cause(s) of waste generation before attempting to find solutions. The audit should be waste stream-oriented to produce a list of specific minimization options for additional evaluation or implementation. Once the causes are understood, solution options can be formulated. An efficient materials and waste-tracking system that allows computation of mass balances is useful in establishing priorities. Knowing how much material is going in and how much of it is ending up as waste allows you to decide which process and which waste to address first.

**EXAMPLE 13–1**   A manufacturing company has, as part of its first audit, gathered the following data. Estimate the potential annual air emissions in kilograms of VOCs from the company. Note that 1 U.S. barrel of liquid $= 0.12 \text{ m}^3$

Purchasing Department Records

| Material | Purchase Quantity (barrels) |
|---|---|
| Methylene chloride ($CH_2Cl_2$) | 228 |
| Trichloroethylene ($C_2HCl_3$) | 505 |

Wastewater Treatment Plant Influent

| Material | Average Concentration (mg · L$^{-1}$) |
|---|---|
| $CH_2Cl_2$ | 4.04 |
| $C_2HCl_3$ | 3.25 |

Average flow into treatment plant is $0.076 \text{ m}^3 \cdot \text{s}^{-1}$.

Hazardous Waste Manifests

| Material | Barrels | Concentration (%) |
|---|---|---|
| $CH_2Cl_2$ | 228 | 25 |
| $C_2HCl_3$ | 505 | 80 |

Unused Barrels at End of Year

| | |
|---|---|
| $CH_2Cl_2$ | 8 |
| $C_2HCl_3$ | 13 |

Solution   The materials balance diagram will be the same for each waste.

The mass balance equation is

$$M_{purchase} = M_{air} + M_{ww} + M_{hw} + M_{accum}$$

Solving this equation for $M_{air}$ gives us the estimated VOC emission.

First, we calculate the mass purchased. The density of each compound is found in Appendix A.

Mass Purchased

$$M_{(CH_2Cl_2)} = (228 \text{ barrels} \cdot \text{year}^{-1})(0.12 \text{ m}^3 \cdot \text{barrel}^{-1})(1327 \text{ kg} \cdot \text{m}^{-3})$$
$$= 36,306.72 \text{ kg} \cdot \text{year}^{-1}$$

$$M_{(C_2HCl_3)} = (505 \text{ barrels} \cdot \text{year}^{-1})(0.12 \text{ m}^3 \cdot \text{barrel}^{-1})(1476 \text{ kg} \cdot \text{m}^{-3})$$
$$= 89,445.60 \text{ kg} \cdot \text{year}^{-1}$$

Now we calculate the mass received at the wastewater treatment plant. (Note that $mg \cdot L^{-1} = g \cdot m^{-3}$.)

$$M_{(CH_2Cl_2)} = (4.04 \text{ g} \cdot \text{m}^{-3})(0.076 \text{ m}^3 \cdot \text{s}^{-1})(86,400 \text{ s} \cdot \text{day}^{-1})(365 \text{ days} \cdot \text{year}^{-1})(10^{-3} \text{ kg} \cdot \text{g}^{-1})$$
$$= 9682.81 \text{ kg} \cdot \text{year}^{-1}$$

$$M_{(C_2HCl_3)} = (3.25 \text{ g} \cdot \text{m}^{-3})(0.076 \text{ m}^3 \cdot \text{s}^{-1})(86,400 \text{ s} \cdot \text{day}^{-1})(365 \text{ days} \cdot \text{year}^{-1})(10^{-3} \text{ kg} \cdot \text{g}^{-1})$$
$$= 7789.39 \text{ kg} \cdot \text{year}^{-1}$$

The mass shipped to the hazardous waste disposal facility is calculated next.

$$M_{(CH_2Cl_2)} = (228)(0.12)(1327)(0.25) = 9076.68 \text{ kg} \cdot \text{year}^{-1}$$

$$M_{(C_2HCl_3)} = (505)(0.12)(1476)(0.80) = 71,556.48 \text{ kg} \cdot \text{year}^{-1}$$

Accumulated

$$M_{(CH_2Cl_2)} = (8)(0.12)(1327) = 1273.92 \text{ kg} \cdot \text{year}^{-1}$$

$$M_{(C_2HCl_3)} = (13)(0.12)(1476) = 2302.56 \text{ kg} \cdot \text{year}^{-1}$$

The estimated air emission for each compound is then

$$M_{(CH_2Cl_2)} = 36,306.72 - 9682.81 - 9076.68 - 1273.92$$
$$= 16,273.31, \text{ or } 16,000 \text{ kg} \cdot \text{year}^{-1}$$

$$M_{(CH_2Cl_2)} = 89,445.60 - 7789.39 - 71,556.48 - 2302.56$$
$$= 7797.17, \text{ or } 7800 \text{ kg} \cdot \text{year}^{-1}$$

Note that we round to two significant figures because the volume of the barrels is known to only two significant figures. From this analysis, to reduce the mass of air pollutants emitted, the company should attack the methylene chloride source first. We should also point out that simply counting "barrels in" from the purchasing record and "barrels out" from the hazardous waste manifest would give a highly erroneous picture of the environmental effect of this company's emissions. From a waste minimization point of view, it is also apparent that $C_2HCl_3$, at 80% concentration in barrels going to hazardous waste disposal, is a candidate for recycling.

The first four steps of the waste audit allow you to generate a comprehensive set of waste management options following the hierarchy of source reduction first, waste exchange second, recycling third, and treatment last.

The screening of options begins with source control. The source control investigation should focus on changes in (1) input materials, (2) process technology, and (3) the human aspect of production. Input material changes can be classified into three separate elements: purification, substitution, and dilution.

Purification of input materials is performed to avoid the introduction of inert materials or impurities into the production process. Such an introduction results in waste because the process inventory must be purged to prevent the undesirable accumulation of impurities. Examples of purification of feed materials to lower waste generation include the use of deionized rinse water in electroplating or the use of oxygen instead of air in oxychlorination reactors for production of ethylene dichloride.

Substitution is the replacement of a toxic material with one characterized by lower toxicity or higher environmental desirability. Examples include using phosphates in place of dichromates as cooling water corrosion inhibitors or the use of alkaline cleaners in place of chlorinated solvents for degreasing.

Dilution is a minor component at input material changes and is exemplified by use of more dilute plating solutions to minimize **dragout** (material carried out of one tank and into another).

Technology changes are those made to the physical plant. Examples include process changes; equipment, piping, or layout changes; changes to process operational settings; additional automation; energy conservation; and water conservation.

Procedural or institutional changes consist of improvements in the ways people affect the production process. Also referred to as "good operating practices" or "good housekeeping," these include operating procedures, loss prevention, waste segregation, and material handling improvements.

### Waste Exchange

Waste minimization by consignment of excess unused materials to an independent party for resale to a third party, saves both in waste production and in the cost (environmental and financial) of production from new raw materials. In essence "one person's trash becomes another person's treasure." The difference between a manufacturing by-product, which is costly to treat or dispose, and a usable or salable by-product involves opportunity, knowledge of processes outside the generator's immediate production line, and comparative pricing of virgin material. Waste exchanges serve as information clearinghouses through which the availability and need for various types of materials can be established.

### Recycling

Under RCRA and HSWA, EPA has carefully defined recycling to prohibit bogus recyclers that are really TSDs from taking advantage of more lenient rules for recycling. The definition says that a material is recycled if it is used, reused, or reclaimed (40 CFR 261.1 (c)(7)). A material is "used or reused" if it is either (1) employed as an ingredient (including its use as an intermediate) to make a product (however, a material will not satisfy this condition if distinct components of the material are recovered as separate end products, as when metals are recovered from metal-containing secondary materials); or (2) employed in a particular function as an effective substitute for a commercial product (40 CFR 261.1 (c)(5)). A material is reclaimed if it is processed to recover a useful product or if it is regenerated. Examples include the recovery of lead from spent batteries and the regeneration of spent solvents (40 CFR 261.1 (c)(4)) [12].

Distillation processes can be used to recover spent solvent. The principal characteristics that determine the potential for recovery are the boiling points of the various useful constituents and the water content. The more dilute the waste solvent, the less economical it is to recover. Recovered solvents can be reused by the generator or sold for at least a substantial fraction of the cost of virgin material, and the credit for recovered solvent can more than offset the cost of recovery.

There are several technologies for recovery of metals from metal-plating rinse water. Most are applicable only to waste streams containing a single metal constituent. Examples include ion exchange, electrodialysis, evaporation, and reverse osmosis.

In October 1988 a federal appeals court struck down an EPA policy not to list used oil collected for recycling as a hazardous waste. Prior to that ruling, PCB-contaminated oils, petroleum industry sludges, and leaded tank bottoms were the only oils regulated. The majority of oil and oily wastes generated were not classified as hazardous under EPA regulations. These wastes are amenable either to recovery for use as fuel or to refinement for use as lubricants. Although all waste oil is now deemed hazardous, those oils that were formerly recovered may still be recovered, but the requirements for tracking them are more stringent.

## 13–6   TREATMENT TECHNOLOGIES

The wastes that remain after the implementation of waste minimization must be detoxified and neutralized. A large number of treatment technologies are available to accomplish this, many of which are applications of processes we have discussed in earlier chapters. Examples include biological oxidation (Chapter 10), chemical precipitation, ion exchange, and oxidation–reduction (Chapter 2), and carbon adsorption (Chapter 11). Here we will discuss these as they apply to hazardous waste treatment, and we will introduce some new technologies.

### Biological Treatment

In contrast to naturally occurring compounds, anthropogenic compounds (those created by human beings) are relatively resistant to biodegradation [13]. One reason is that the organisms that are naturally present often cannot produce the enzymes necessary to bring about transformation of the original compound to a point at which the resultant intermediates can enter into common metabolic pathways and be completely mineralized.

Many environmentally important anthropogenic compounds are halogenated, and halogenation is often implicated as a reason for their persistence. The list of halogenated organic compounds includes pesticides, plasticizers, plastics, solvents, and trihalomethanes. Chlorinated compounds are the best known and most studied because of the highly publicized problems associated with DDT and other pesticides and numerous industrial solvents. Hence, chlorinated compounds serve as the basis for most of the information available on halogenated compounds.

Some of the characteristics that appear to confer persistence to halogenated compounds are the location of the halogen atom, the halide involved, and the extent of halogenation. The first step in biodegradation, then, is sometimes dehalogenation, for which there are several biological mechanisms.

Simple generalizations do not appear to be applicable. For example, until recently, oxidative pathways were mostly believed to be the typical means by which halogenated compounds were dehalogenated. Anaerobic, reductive dehalogenation, either biological or nonbiological, is now recognized as the critical factor in the transformation or biodegradation of certain classes of compounds. Compounds that require reductive dechlorination are common among the pesticides, as well as halogenated one- and two-carbon aliphatic compounds.

Reductive dehalogenation involves the removal of a halogen atom by oxidation–reduction. In essence, the mechanism involves the transfer of electrons from reduced organic substances via microorganisms or a nonliving (abiotic) mediator, such as inorganic ions (e.g., $Fe^{3+}$) and biological products [e.g., NAD(P), flavin, flavoproteins, hemoproteins, porphyrins, chlorophyll, cytochromes, and glutathione]. The mediators are responsible for accepting electrons from reduced organic substances and transferring them to the halogenated compounds. The major requirements for the process are believed to be available free electrons and direct contact between the donor, mediator, and acceptor of electrons. Significant reductive dechlorination usually occurs only when the oxidation–reduction potential of the environment is 0.35 V and lower; the exact requirements appear to depend on the compound involved.

Although simple studies using pure cultures of microorganisms and single substrates are valuable, if not essential, for determining biochemical pathways, they cannot always be used to predict biodegradability or transformation in more natural situations. The interactions among environmental factors, such as dissolved oxygen, oxidation–reduction potential, temperature, pH, availability of other compounds, salinity, particulate matter, competing organisms, and concentrations of compounds and organisms, often control the feasibility of biodegradation. The compound's physical or chemical characteristics, such as solubility, volatility, hydrophobicity, and octanol–water partition coefficient, contribute to the compound's availability in solution. Often compounds not soluble in the water are not readily available to organisms for biodegradation. There are some exceptions. For example, DDT, which is only slightly soluble in water, may be degraded by the white rot fungus found on decaying trees. This is because the enzymes involved in the white rot reaction are secreted from the cell.

Simple culture studies are similarly inadequate for predicting the fate of substances in the environment if many interactions occur between different organisms. First, substances that cannot be changed significantly in pure culture studies often will be degraded or transformed under mixed culture conditions. A good example of this type of interaction is **cometabolism,** in which a compound, the nongrowth substrate, is not metabolized as a source of carbon or energy, but is incidentally transformed by organisms using other compounds as growth substrates. The growth substrates provide the energy needed to cometabolize the nongrowth substrates. Second, products of the initial transformation by one organism may subsequently be broken down by a series of different organisms until compounds that can be metabolized by normal metabolic pathways are formed. An example is the degradation of DDT, which is reportedly mineralized directly by only one organism, a fungus; other organisms studied appear to degrade DDT only through cometabolism, resulting in numerous transformation products that subsequently can be used by other organisms. For example, *Hydrogenomonas* can metabolize DDT only as far as *p*-chlorophenylacetic acid (PCPA), whereas *Arthrobacter* species can then remove the PCPA.

Table 13–1 demonstrates that members of almost every class of anthropogenic compound can be degraded by some microorganism. The table also illustrates the wide variety of microorganisms that participate in environmentally significant biodegradation.

The use of novel microorganisms for biological treatment of anthropogenic compounds is a new concept. A number of advancements are required before large-scale application is possible, among the most important of which is an improved knowledge of metabolic pathways for the

**TABLE 13–1**  Examples of Anthropogenic Compounds and Microorganisms That Can Degrade Them

| Compound | Organism | Compound | Organism |
|---|---|---|---|
| Aliphatic (nonhalogenated)<br>  Acrylonitrile | Mixed culture of yeast, mold, protozoan bacteria | Polycyclic aromatics (nonhalogenated)<br>Benzo(a)pyrene, naphthalene, Benzo(a)anthracene | Cunninghamella elegans Pseudomonas |
| Aliphatic (halogenated)<br>  Trichloroethane, trichloroethylene, methyl chloride, methylene chloride | Marine bacteria, soil bacteria, sewage sludge | Polycyclic aromatics (halogenated)<br>  PCBs<br>  4-Chlorobiphenyl | Pseudomonas, Flavobacterium Fungi |
| Aromatic compounds (nonhalogenated)<br>Benzene, 2,6-dinitrotoluene, creosol, phenol | Pseudomonas sp., sewage sludge | Pesticides<br>  Toxaphene<br>  Dieldrin<br>  DDT<br>  Kepone | Corynebacterium pyrogenes<br>Anacystic nidulans<br>Sewage sludge, soil bacteria<br>Treatment lagoon sludge |
| Aromatic compounds (halogenated)<br>1,2-; 2,3-; 1,4-dichlorobenzene, hexachlorobenzene, trichlorobenzene, pentachlorophenol | Sewage sludge Soil microbes | Nitrosamines<br>  Dimethylnitrosamines<br>Phthalate esters | Rhodopseudomonas<br>Micrococcus 12B |

*Source:* Extracted from Table I of Kobayashi, H., and B. P. Rittman, "Microbial removal of hazardous organic compounds," *Environmental Science and Technology,* vol.16, p. 173A, 1982.

biodegradation of specific compounds by different organisms. The metabolic capabilities of many microorganisms, in particular algae and oligotrophic bacteria, are poorly understood. Such knowledge is necessary if limiting reactions are to be determined and the proper types of organisms selected for specific applications. More information about appropriate types of microorganisms to be selected and maintained in real-world treatment systems is needed, especially for the more novel microbial cultures. To develop special-purpose organisms by genetic manipulation, major advances in the understanding of the genetic structure of the many different types of organisms in nature are needed.

Conventional biological treatment processes such as activated sludge and trickling filters have been used to treat hazardous wastes. The major modification to the activated sludge processes has been to extend the mean cell residence time from the conventional values of 4 to 15 days to much longer periods of 3 to 6 months. In a similar fashion, trickling filter loading rates are much lower than those employed in municipal treatment systems. One innovation that has been adopted by TSD facilities is the sequencing batch reactor (SBR). The SBR is a periodically operated, fill-and-draw reactor [14]. Each reactor in an SBR system has five discrete periods in each cycle: fill, react, settle, draw, and idle. Biological reactions are initiated as the raw wastewater fills the tank. During the fill and react phase, the waste is aerated in the same fashion as an activated sludge unit. After the react phase, the mixed liquor suspended solids (MLSS) are allowed to settle. The treated supernatant is discharged during the draw phase. The idle stage, the time between the draw and fill, may be zero or may be a few days depending on wastewater flow demand. The SBR has a major advantage in that wastes may be tested for completeness of treatment before discharge.

### Chemical Treatment

Chemical detoxification is a treatment technology, either employed as the sole treatment procedure or used to reduce the hazard of a particular waste prior to transport, incineration, and burial.

It is important to remember that a chemical procedure cannot magically make a toxic chemical disappear from the **matrix** (wastewater, sludge, etc.) in which it is found but can only convert it to another form. Thus, it is vital to ensure that the products of a chemical detoxification step are less of a problem than the starting material. It is equally important to remember that the reagents for such a reaction can be hazardous.

The spectrum of chemical methods includes complexation, neutralization, oxidation, precipitation, and reduction. An optimum method would be fast, quantitative, inexpensive, and leave no residual reagent, which itself would be a pollution problem. The following paragraphs describe a few of these techniques.

**Neutralization.** Solutions are neutralized by a simple application of the law of mass balance to bring about an acceptable pH. Sulfuric or hydrochloric acid is added to basic solutions, and caustic (NaOH) or slaked lime [$Ca(OH)_2$] is added to acidic solutions. Though a waste is hazardous at pH values less than 2 or greater than 12.5, and it would seem that simply bringing the pH into the range 2–12.5 would be adequate, good treatment practice requires that final pH values be in the range 6–8 to protect natural biota.

**Oxidation.** The cyanide molecule is destroyed by oxidation. Chlorine is the oxidizing agent most frequently used. Oxidation must be conducted under alkaline conditions to avoid the generation of hydrogen cyanide gas. Hence, this process is often referred to as **alkaline chlorination.** In chlorine oxidation, the reaction is carried out in two steps:

$$NaCN + 2NaOH + Cl_2 \rightleftharpoons NaCNO + 2NaCl + H_2O \tag{13-1}$$

$$2NaCNO + 5NaOH + 3Cl_2 \rightleftharpoons 6NaCl + CO_2 + N_2 + NaHCO_3 + 2H_2O \tag{13-2}$$

In the first step, the pH is maintained above 10 and the reaction proceeds in a matter of minutes. In this step, great care must be taken to maintain relatively high pH values because at lower pHs there is a potential for the evolution of highly toxic hydrogen cyanide gas. The second reaction step proceeds most rapidly around a pH of 8, but it is not as rapid as the first step. Higher pH values may be selected for the second step to reduce chemical consumption in the following precipitation steps. This increases the reaction time. Often the second reaction is not carried out because the CNO is considered nontoxic by current regulations.

Ozone also may be used as the oxidizing agent. Ozone has a higher redox potential than chlorine, thus there is a higher driving force toward the oxidized state. When ozone is used, the pH considerations are similar to those discussed for chlorine. Ozone cannot be purchased. It must be made on site as part of the process.

This technology can be applied to a wide range of cyanide wastes: copper, zinc, and brass plating solutions; cyanide from cyanide salt heating baths; and passivating solutions. The process has been practiced on an industrial scale since the early 1940s. For extremely high cyanide concentrations ($>1\%$), oxidation may not be desirable. Cyanide complexes of metals, particularly iron and, to some extent, nickel, cannot be decomposed easily by cyanide oxidation techniques.

Electrolytic oxidation of cyanide is carried out by anodic electrolysis at high temperatures. The theoretical basis of the process is that cyanide reacts with oxygen in solution in the presence of an electric potential. To produce carbon dioxide and nitrogen gas. Normally, the destruction is carried out in a closed cell. Two electrodes are suspended in the solution and a DC current is applied to drive the reaction. The bath temperature must be maintained in the range of 50 to 95°C.

This technology is used for the destruction of cyanide in concentrated spent stripping solutions; in plating solutions for copper, zinc, and brass; in alkaline descalers; and in passivating solutions. It has been more successful for wastes containing high concentrations of cyanide ($50{,}000$–$100{,}000$ mg $\cdot$ L$^{-1}$), but it has also been successfully used for concentrations as low as $500$ mg $\cdot$ L$^{-1}$.

Chemical oxidation methods for treating organic compounds in wastewater have received extensive study. In general, they apply only to dilute solutions and often are considered expensive compared with biological methods. Some examples include wet air oxidation, hydrogen peroxide, permanganate, chlorine dioxide, chlorine, and ozone oxidation. Of these, wet air oxidation and ozonation have shown promise as a pretreatment step for biological processes.

**Wet air oxidation,** also known as the Zimmerman process, operates on the principle that most organic compounds can be oxidized by oxygen given sufficient temperature and pressure. Wet air oxidation may be described as the aqueous phase oxidation of dissolved or suspended organic particles at temperatures of 175 to 325°C and sufficiently high pressure to prevent excessive evaporation. Air is bubbled through the liquid. The process is fuel-efficient; once the oxidation reaction has started, it is usually self-sustaining. Because this method is not limited by reagent cost, it is potentially the most widely applicable of all chemical oxidation methods. The method has been shown to be of use in destroying a wide range of organic compounds, including some pesticides. Although wet oxidation can provide acceptable levels of destruction for many hazardous compounds, it is generally not as complete as incineration. In many instances, the addition of metal salt catalysts can increase the destruction efficiency or allow the process to be run at lower temperature or pressure.

**Precipitation.**   Metals are often removed from plating rinse waters by precipitation. This is a direct application of the solubility product principle (see Chapter 2). By raising the pH with lime or caustic, the solubility of the metal is reduced (Figure 13–5) and the metal hydroxide precipitates. Optimum removal is achieved by selecting the optimum pH as shown in Figure 13–5. Though there is an optimum for each metal, in many cases, the metals are mixed and the lowest value for an individual metal may not be achievable for the mixture.

**FIGURE 13–5**

Solubilities of metal
hydroxides as a function
of pH. (*Source:
Development Document
for Effluent Limitations:
Guideline and Standards
for the Metal Finishing
Point Category* (U.S.
Environmental Protection
Agency Publication
No. EPA/440/1-83-
091), Washington, DC:
U.S. Government Printing
Office, 1981.)

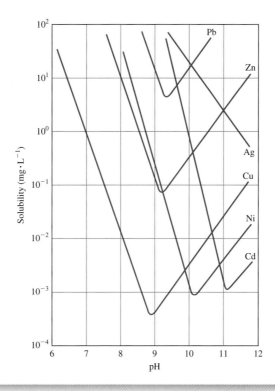

**EXAMPLE 13–2**

A metal plating firm is installing a precipitation system to remove zinc. They plan to use a pH meter to control the feed of hydroxide solution to the mixing tank. What pH should the controller be set at to achieve a zinc effluent concentration of 0.80 mg · L$^{-1}$? The $K_{sp}$ of Zn(OH)$_2$ is $7.68 \times 10^{-17}$.

Solution

From Table A–9 in Appendix A we find that the zinc hydroxide reaction is

$$Zn^{2+} + 2OH^- \rightleftharpoons Zn(OH)_2$$

As shown in Chapter 2, we can write the solubility product equation as

$$K_{sp} = [Zn^{2+}][OH^-]^2$$

Because we want the zinc concentration to be no greater than 0.80 mg · L$^{-1}$, we calculate the moles per liter of zinc.

$$[Zn^{2+}] = \frac{0.80 \text{ mg} \cdot \text{L}^{-1}}{(65.38 \text{ g} \cdot \text{mol}^{-1})(1000 \text{ mg} \cdot \text{g}^{-1})} = 1.224 \times 10^{-5} \text{ mol} \cdot \text{L}^{-1}$$

Now we solve for the hydroxide concentration.

$$[OH^-]^2 = \frac{7.68 \times 10^{-17}}{1.224 \times 10^{-5}} = 6.275 \times 10^{-12}$$

Therefore,

$$[OH^-] = (6.275 \times 10^{-12})^{0.5} = 2.505 \times 10^{-6}$$

The pOH is

$$pOH = -\log(2.505 \times 10^{-6}) = 5.601$$

And the pH set point for the controller is

$$pH = 14 - pOH = 14 - 5.601 = 8.399, \text{ or } 8.4$$

**Reduction.**   Although most heavy metals readily precipitate as hydroxides, hexavalent chromium used in plating solutions must be reduced to trivalent chromium before it will precipitate. Reduction is usually done with sulfur dioxide ($SO_2$) or sodium sulfite ($NaHSO_3$). With $SO_2$ the reaction is

$$3SO_2 + 2H_2CrO_4 + 3H_2O \rightleftharpoons Cr_2(SO_4)_3 + 5H_2O \tag{13-3}$$

Because the reaction proceeds rapidly at low pH, an acid is added to control the pH between 2 and 3.

### Physical/Chemical Treatment

Several treatment processes are used to separate hazardous waste from aqueous solution. The waste is not detoxified but only concentrated for further treatment or recovery.

**Carbon Adsorption.**   Adsorption is a mass-transfer process in which gas vapors or chemicals in solution are held to a solid by intermolecular forces (e.g., hydrogen bonding and van der Waals' interactions). It is a surface phenomenon. Pressure vessels having a fixed bed are used to hold the adsorbent (see Chapter 11). Activated carbon, molecular sieves, silica gel, and activated alumina are the most common adsorbents. The active sites become saturated at some point in time. When the organic material has commercial value, the bed is then regenerated by passing steam through it. The vapor-laden steam is condensed and the organic fraction is separated from the water. If the organic compounds have no commercial value, the carbon may be either incinerated or shipped to the manufacturer for regeneration. Carbon systems for recovery of vapor from degreasers and for polishing wastewater effluents have been in commercial application for more than 30 years.

**Distillation.**   The separation of more volatile materials from less volatile ones by a process of vaporization and condensation is called distillation. When a liquid mixture of two or more components is brought to the boiling point of the mixture, a vapor phase is created above the liquid phase. If the vapor pressures of the pure components are different (which is usually the case), then the constituent(s) having the higher vapor pressure will be more concentrated in the vapor phase than the constituent(s) having the lower vapor pressure. If the vapor phase is cooled to yield a liquid, a partial separation of the constituents will result. The degree of separation depends on the relative differences in the vapor pressures. The larger the differences, the more efficient the separation. If the difference is large enough, a single separation cycle of vaporization and condensation is sufficient to separate the components. If the difference is not large enough, multiple cycles (stages) are required. Four types of distillation may be used: batch distillation, fractionation, steam stripping, and thin film evaporation.*

Both batch distillation and fractionation are well proven technologies for recovery of solvents. Batch distillation is particularly applicable for wastes with high solids concentrations. Fractionation is applicable when multiple constituents must be separated and when the waste contains minimal suspended solids.

When the volatility of the organic compound is relatively high and the concentration relatively low, some form of stripping may be appropriate. Air stripping has been used to purge large quantities of contaminated groundwater of small concentrations of volatile organic matter. The behavior of the process is the inverse of absorption discussed in Chapter 11. Air and contaminated liquid are passed countercurrently through a packed tower. The volatile compounds evaporate into the air, leaving a clean liquid stream. The contaminated air stream must then be treated to avoid an air pollution problem. Frequently this is accomplished by passing the air through an

---

*Air stripping, though not strictly a distillation process because the condensation step is omitted, employs the same general principles of volatilization and, hence, is included in the discussion.

activated carbon column. The carbon is then incinerated. Air stripping has been used to remove tetrachloroethylene, trichloroethylene, and toluene from water [15].

The air stripper design equation may be written as follows:

$$Z_T = \frac{L}{A} \times \frac{\ln\{(C_1/C_2) - (LRT_g/GH_c)[(C_1/C_2) - 1]\}}{K_L a[1 - (LRT_g/GH_c)]} \tag{13-4}$$

where $Z_T$ = packed tower depth (in m)
$L$ = water flow (in $m^3 \cdot min^{-1}$)
$A$ = cross-sectional area of tower (in $m^2$)
$G$ = air flow (in $m^3 \cdot min^{-1}$)
$H_c$ = Henry's constant (in $atm \cdot m^3 \cdot mol^{-1}$)
$R$ = universal gas constant = $8.206 \times 10^{-5}$ $atm \cdot m^3 \cdot mol^{-1} \cdot K^{-1}$
$T_g$ = temperature of air (in K)
$C_1, C_2$ = influent and effluent organic concentration in the water (in $mol \cdot m^{-3}$)
$K_L$ = liquid mass transfer coefficient (in $mol \cdot min^{-1} \cdot m^{-2} \cdot mol^{-1} \cdot m^3$)
$a$ = effective interfacial area of packing per unit volume for mass transfer (in $m^2 \cdot m^{-3}$)

**EXAMPLE 13-3**   Well 12A at the City of Tacoma, WA, is contaminated with $350\,\mu g \cdot L^{-1}$ of 1,1,2,2-tetrachloroethane. The water must be cleaned to the detection limit of $1.0\,\mu g \cdot L^{-1}$. Design a packed tower stripping column to meet this requirement using the following design parameters.

| | |
|---|---|
| Henry's law constant = $5.0 \times 10^{-4}$ $atm \cdot m^3 \cdot mol^{-1}$ | Temperature = 25°C |
| $K_L a = 10 \times 10^{-3}\,s^{-1}$ | Column diameter may not |
| Air flow rate = 13.7 $m^3 \cdot s^{-1}$ | exceed 4.0 m |
| Liquid flow rate = 0.044 $m^3 \cdot s^{-1}$ | Column height may not exceed 6.0 m |

Solution   The Henry's law constants given in Appendix A are in $kPa \cdot m^3 \cdot mol^{-1}$. To convert these to $atm \cdot m^3 \cdot mol^{-1}$, divide by the atmospheric pressure at standard conditions, that is, 101.325 kPa · $atm^{-1}$.

The stripper equation is then solved for $Z_T A$, the column volume.

$$Z_T A = (0.044)\frac{\ln\{(350/1) - [(0.044)(8.206 \times 10^{-5})(298)/(13.7)(5.0 \times 10^{-4})][(350/1) - 1]\}}{10 \times 10^{-3}\{1 - [(0.044)(8.206 \times 10^{-5})(298)/(13.7)(5.0 \times 10^{-4})]\}}$$

$$= (0.044)(674.74) = 29.69\,m^3$$

Any number of solutions are now possible within the boundary conditions of 4-m diameter and 6-m height. For example:

| Diameter (m) | Tower height (m) |
|---|---|
| 4.00 | 2.36 |
| 3.34 | 3.39 |
| 2.58 | 5.68 |

For gases of lower volatility or higher concentration (>100 ppm) **steam stripping** may be employed. The physical arrangement of the process is much like that of an air stripper, except that steam is introduced instead of air. The addition of steam enhances the stripping process by decreasing the solubility of the organic in the aqueous phase and by increasing the vapor pressure. Steam stripping has been used to treat aqueous waste contaminated with chlorinated hydrocarbons, xylenes, acetone, methyl ethyl ketone, methanol, and pentachlorophenol. Concentrations treated range from 100 ppm to 10% organic [16].

Recovery of plating metals by evaporation is accomplished by boiling off sufficient water from the collected rinse stream to allow the concentrate to be returned to the plating bath. The condensed steam is recycled for use as rinse water. The boil-off rate, or evaporator duty, is set to maintain the water balance of the plating bath. Evaporation is usually performed under vacuum to prevent thermal degradation of additives and to reduce the amount of energy required for evaporation of the water.

There are four types of evaporators: rising film, flash evaporators using waste heat, submerged tube, and atmospheric pressure. Rising film evaporators are built so that the evaporative heating surface is covered by a waste water film and does not lie in a pool of boiling wastewater. Flash evaporators are of similar configuration, but the plating solution is continuously recirculated through the evaporator along with the wastewater. This allows the use of waste heat in the plating bath to augment the evaporation process. In the submerged tube design, the heating coils are submerged in the wastewater. Atmospheric evaporators do not recover the distillate for reuse and they do not operate under vacuum.

**Ion Exchange.**   Metals and ionized organic chemicals can be recovered by ion exchange. Ion-exchange chemistry was discussed in Chapter 9. In ion exchange, the waste stream containing the ion to be removed is passed through a bed of resin. The resin is selected to remove either cations or anions. In the exchange process, ions of like charge are removed from the resin surface in exchange for ions in solution. Typically, either hydrogen or sodium is exchanged for cations (metal) in solution. When the bed becomes saturated with the exchanged ion, it is shut down and the resin is regenerated by passing a concentrated solution containing the original ion (hydrogen or sodium) back through the bed. The exchanged pollutant is forced off the bed in a concentrated form that may be recycled. A typical ion-exchange column is shown in Figure 13–6. A prefilter is required to remove suspended material that would hydraulically foul the column. It also removes organics and oils that would foul the resin.

As a rule, ion-exchange systems are suitable for chemical recovery applications in which the rinse water feed has a relatively dilute concentration ($<$1000 mg $\cdot$ L$^{-1}$) and a relatively low concentration is required for recycle. Ion exchange has been demonstrated commercially for recovery of plating chemicals from acid–copper, acid–zinc, nickel, tin, cobalt, and chromium plating baths.

**FIGURE 13–6**

Typical ion-exchange resin column.

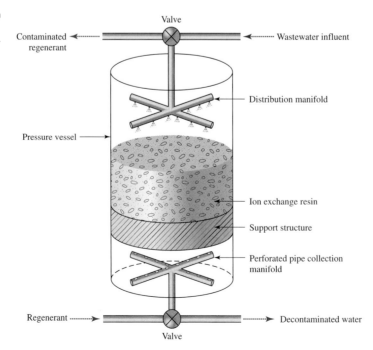

In full-scale operation, the resin bed is not allowed to reach saturation because the concentration of the solute will exceed most discharge standards before this occurs. Normal operation then requires either an operating cycle that will allow regeneration of the spent resin during nonworking hours or, in the case of 24-h, 7-day per week schedules, multiple beds so that one may be taken off-line.

During ion exchange, the normal flow pattern is downward through the bed. The hydraulic loading may range from 25 to 600 $m^3 \cdot day^{-1} \cdot m^{-2}$. Lower hydraulic loadings result in longer contact periods and better exchange efficiency. Because the surface of the bed acts like a filter, regeneration is often countercurrent, that is, the regenerating solution is pumped into the bottom of the column. This results in a cleansing of the column much like the backwashing of a rapid sand filter. Regeneration hydraulic loadings range from 60 to 120 $m^3 \cdot day^{-1} \cdot m^{-2}$.

**Electrodialysis.**  The electrodialysis unit uses a membrane to selectively retain or transmit specific molecules. The membranes are thin sheets of ion-exchange resin reinforced by a synthetic fiber backing. The construction of the unit is such that anion membranes are alternated with cation membranes in stacks of cells in series (Figure 13–7). An electric potential is applied across the membrane to provide the motive force for ion migration. Cation membranes permit passage of only positively charged ions, and anion membranes permit passage of only negatively charged ions. The flow is directed through the membrane in two hydraulic circuits (Figure 13–8). One circuit is ion-depleted and the other is ion-concentrated. The degree of purification achieved in the dilute circuit is set by the electric potential. The ability to pass the charge is proportional to the concentration of the ionic species in the dilute stream. Because ion migration is proportional to

**FIGURE 13–7**

Electrodialysis. (Cations in the feed water show the same behavior as sodium ($Na^+$) and anions show the same behavior as chloride ($Cl^-$). Under the action of an electric field, cation-exchange membranes permit passage only of positive ions, and anion-exchange membranes permit passage only of negatively charged ions.)

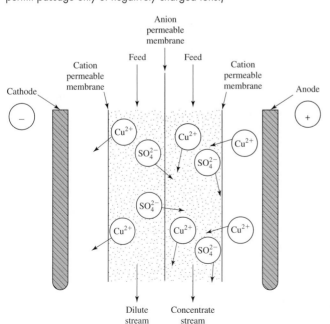

**FIGURE 13–8**

Electrodialysis unit flow schematic.

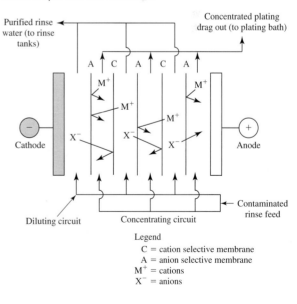

**FIGURE 13–9**

Direct and reverse osmosis.

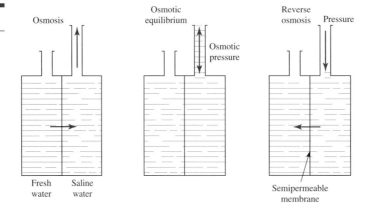

electric potential, the optimum system is a trade-off between energy requirements and degree of contaminant removal.

Electrodialysis has been in commercial operation for more than three decades in the production of potable water from brackish water. It has also been used in deashing of sugars, desalting of food products such as whey, and to recover waste developer in the photo-processing industry and nickel from a metal plating rinse water. Typically, electrodialysis can separate a waste stream containing $1000–5000 \text{ mg} \cdot \text{L}^{-1}$ inorganic salts into a dilute stream that contains $100–500 \text{ mg} \cdot \text{L}^{-1}$ salt and a concentrated stream that contains up to $10,000 \text{ mg} \cdot \text{L}^{-1}$ salt.

**Reverse Osmosis.**   **Osmosis** is the spontaneous transport of a solvent from a dilute solution to a concentrated solution across an ideal semipermeable membrane that impedes passage of the solute but allows the solvent to flow. Solvent flow can be reduced by exerting pressure on the solution side of the membrane, as shown in Figure 13–9. If the pressure is increased above the osmotic pressure on the solution side, the flow reverses. Pure solvent will then pass from the solution into the solvent. As applied to metal finishing wastewater, the solute is the metal and the solvent is pure water.

Many configurations of the membrane are possible. The driving pressure is on the order of 2800 to 5500 kPa. No commercially available membrane polymer has demonstrated tolerance to all extreme chemical factors such as pH, strong oxidizing agents, and aromatic hydrocarbons. However, selected membranes have been demonstrated on nickel, copper, zinc, and chrome baths.

**Solvent Extraction.**   Solvent extraction is also called **liquid extraction** and **liquid–liquid extraction.** Contaminants can be removed from a waste stream using liquid–liquid extraction if the wastewater is contacted with a solvent having a greater solubility for the target contaminants than the wastewater. The contaminants will tend to migrate from the wastewater into the solvent. Although predominately a method for separating organic materials, it may also be applied to remove metals if the solvent contains a material that will react with the metal. **Liquid ion exchange** is one kind of these reactions.

In the solvent extraction process, the solvent and the waste stream are mixed to allow mass transfer of the constituent(s) from the waste to the solvent. The solvent, immiscible in water, is then allowed to separate from the water by gravity. The solvent solution containing the extracted contaminant is called the **extract.** The extracted waste stream with the contaminants removed is called the **raffinate.** As in distillation, the separation may need to be done in one or more stages. In general, more stages result in a cleaner raffinate. The degree of complexity of the apparatus varies from simple mixer–settlers to more exotic contacting devices. If the extract is sufficiently enriched, it may be possible to recover useful material. Distillation is often employed to recover the solvent and reusable organic chemicals. For metal recovery, the ion-exchange material is regenerated by the addition of an acid or alkali. The process has found wide application in the ore processing industry, in food processing, in pharmaceuticals, and in the petroleum industry.

### Incineration

In an incinerator, chemicals are decomposed by oxidation at high temperatures (800°C or greater). The waste, or at least its hazardous components, must be combustible to be destroyed. The primary products from combustion of organic wastes are carbon dioxide, water vapor, and inert ash; however, a multitude of other products can be formed.

**Products of Combustion.**   The percentages of carbon, hydrogen, oxygen, nitrogen, sulfur, halogens, and phosphorus in the waste, as well as the moisture content, need to be known to determine stoichiometric combustion air requirements and to predict combustion gas flow and composition. Actual incineration conditions generally require excess oxygen to maximize the formation of **products of complete combustion** (POCs) and minimize the formation of **products of incomplete combustion** (PICs).

The incineration of halogenated organic compounds results in the formation of halogenated acids, which require further treatment to ensure environmentally acceptable air emissions from the incineration process. Chlorinated organic compounds are the most common halogenated hydrocarbons found in hazardous waste. The incineration of chlorinated hydrocarbons with excess air results in the formation of carbon dioxide, water, and hydrogen chloride. An example is the following reaction for the incineration of dichlorethane [7]:

$$2C_2H_2Cl_2 + 5O_2 \rightleftharpoons 4CO_2 + 2H_2O + 4HCl \tag{13-5}$$

The hydrogen chloride must be removed before the carbon dioxide and steam can be safely exhausted into the atmosphere.

Hazardous waste may contain either organic or inorganic sulfur compounds. When these wastes are incinerated, sulfur dioxide is produced. For example, the destruction of ethyl mercaptan results in the following reaction:

$$2C_2H_5SH + 9O_2 \rightleftharpoons 4CO_2 + 6H_2O + 2SO_2 \tag{13-6}$$

The sulfur dioxide produced by the incineration of sulfur-containing wastes must not exceed air quality standards.

Excess air must be provided to ensure complete combustion. However, the amount of the excess can only be determined empirically. For example, a highly volatile, clean, hydrocarbon waste would probably require much less excess air than would a heavy hydrocarbon sludge within a high solids content. Incineration of sludges and solids may require as much as two to three times excess air above stoichiometric equivalents. Too much excess air should be avoided because it increases the fuel required to heat the waste to destruction temperatures, reduces residence time for the hazardous wastes to be oxidized, and increases the volume of air emissions to be handled by the air pollution control equipment.

By-products from the incineration of hazardous wastes may also result from incomplete combustion as well as from the products of combustion. PICs include carbon monoxide, hydrocarbons, aldehydes, ketones, amines, organic acids, and polycyclic aromatic hydrocarbons (PAHs). In a well-designed incinerator, these products are insignificant in amount. However, in poorly designed or overloaded incinerators, PICs may pose environmental concerns. PCBs, for instance, decompose under such conditions into highly toxic chlorinated dibenzo furans (CDBF). The hazardous material, hexachlorocyclopentadiene (HCCPD), found in many hazardous wastes, is known to decompose into the even more hazardous compound hexachlorobenzene (HCB) [17].

Suspended particulate emissions are also produced during incineration. These include particles of mineral oxides and salts from the mineral constituents in the waste material, as well as fragments of incompletely burned combustibles.

Last, but not least, ash is a product of combustion. The ash is considered a hazardous waste. Metals not volatilized end up in the ash. Unburned organic compounds may also be found in the ash. When organic compounds remain, the ash may simply be incinerated again. The metals must be treated prior to land disposal.

**Design Considerations.**   The most important factors for proper incinerator design and operation are combustion temperature, combustion gas residence time, and the efficiency of mixing the waste with combustion air and auxiliary fuel [17].

Chemical and thermal dynamic properties of the waste that are important in determining its time and temperature requirements for destruction are its elemental composition, net heating value, and any special properties (e.g., explosive properties) that may interfere with incineration or require special design considerations.

In general, higher heating values are required for solids versus liquids or gases, for higher operating temperatures, and for higher excess air rates if combustion is to be sustained without auxiliary fuel consumption. Although sustained combustion (**autogenous combustion**) is possible with heating values as low as 9.3 MJ · kg$^{-1}$, in the hazardous waste incineration industry it is common practice to blend wastes (and fuel oil, if necessary) to obtain an overall heating value of 18.6 MJ · kg$^{-1}$ or greater.

Blending is also used to limit the net chlorine content of chlorinated hazardous waste to a maximum of roughly 30% by weight to reduce chlorine concentrations in the combustion gas. The chlorine and, especially, hydrogen chloride that forms from the chlorine, are very corrosive. They oxidize the fire brick in the incinerator which causes it to fail.

Hazardous waste incinerators must be designed to achieve a 99.99% destruction and removal efficiency (DRE) of the principal organic hazardous components (POHCs) in the waste. This is commonly referred to as "four 9s DRE"; higher DREs may be referred to as five 9s, six 9s, that is, 99.999 and 99.9999% DRE, respectively. Because of the complexity of the wastes being burned, little success has been achieved in predicting the time and temperature requirements for achieving the 99.99% DRE. Empirical tests (**trial burns**) are required to demonstrate compliance. Experience has demonstrated that highly halogenated materials are more difficult to destroy than those with low halogen content.

**Incinerator Types.**   Two technologies dominate the incineration field: liquid injection and rotary kiln incinerators [17]. Over 90% of all incineration facilities use one of these technologies. Of these, more than 90% are liquid injection units. Less commonly used incinerators include fluidized beds and starved air/pyrolysis systems.

Horizontal, vertical, and tangential liquid injection units are used. The majority of the incinerators for hazardous wastes inject liquid hazardous waste at 350–700 kPa through an atomizing nozzle into the combustion chamber. These liquid incinerators vary in size from 300,000 to 9 MJ of heat released per second. An auxiliary fuel such as natural gas or fuel oil is often used when the waste is not autogenous. The liquid wastes are atomized into fine droplets as they are injected. A droplet size in the range 40–100 μm is obtained with atomizers or nozzles. The droplet volatilizes in the hot gas stream and the gas is oxidized. Efficient destruction of liquid hazardous wastes requires minimizing unevaporated droplets and unreacted vapors.

Residence time, temperature, and turbulence (often referred to as the "three Ts") are optimized to increase destruction efficiencies. Typical residence times are 0.5–2 s. Incinerator temperatures usually range between 800 and 1600°C. A high degree of turbulence is desirable for achieving effective destruction of the organic chemicals in the waste. Depending on whether the liquid incinerator flow is axial, radial, or tangential, additional fuel burners and separate waste injection nozzles can be arranged to achieve the desired temperature, turbulence, and residence time. Vertical units are less likely to experience ash buildup. Tangential units have a much higher heat release and generally superior mixing.

The rotary kiln is often used in hazardous waste disposal systems because of its versatility in processing solid, liquid, and containerized wastes. Waste is incinerated in a refractory-lined rotary kiln, as shown in Figure 13–10. The shell is mounted at a slight incline from the horizontal plane to facilitate mixing the waste materials with circulating air. Solid wastes and drummed wastes are usually fed by a conveyor system or a ram. Liquids and pumpable sludges are injected through a nozzle. Noncombustible metal and other residues are discharged as ash at the end of the kiln.

**FIGURE 13–10**

Rotary kiln incinerator.

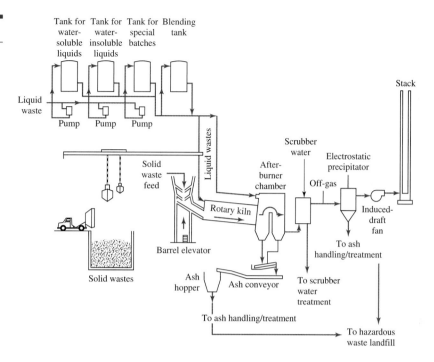

Rotary kilns are typically 1.5–4 m in diameter and range in length from 3 to 10 m. Rotary kiln incinerators usually have a length-to-diameter ratio (L/D) of between 2 and 8. Rotational speeds range from 0.5 to 2.5 cm · s$^{-1}$, depending on kiln periphery. High L/D ratios, along with slower rotational speeds, are used for wastes requiring longer residence times. The feed end of the kiln has airtight seals to adequately control the initial incineration reactions.

Residence times for solid wastes are based on the rotational speed of the kiln and its angle. The residence time to volatilize waste is controlled by the gas velocity. The retention time of solids in the incinerator can be estimated from the following, where the coefficient 0.19 is based on limited experimental data:

$$\theta = \frac{0.19L}{NDS} \tag{13–7}$$

where $\theta$ = retention time (in min)

$L$ = kiln length (in m)

$N$ = kiln rotational speed (in rev · min$^{-1}$)

$D$ = kiln diameter (in m)

$S$ = kiln slope (in m · m$^{-1}$)

Rotary kiln systems typically include secondary combustion chambers or afterburners to ensure complete destruction of the hazardous waste. Kiln operating temperatures range from 800 to 1600°C. Afterburner temperatures range from 1000 to 1600°C. Liquid wastes are often injected into the secondary combustion chamber. The volatilized and combusted wastes leave the kiln and enter the secondary chamber, where additional oxygen is available and high heating value liquid wastes or fuel may be introduced. Both the secondary combustion chamber and the kiln are usually equipped with an auxiliary fuel firing system for startup.

Cement kilns are very efficient at destroying hazardous waste. Their long residence times and high operating temperatures exceed the requirements for destruction of most wastes. Hydrochloric acid generated from chlorinated hydrocarbon wastes is neutralized by the lime in the kiln while slightly lowering the alkalinity of the cement products. Although cement plants can save energy by incinerating liquid wastes, the expense of obtaining permits and public resistance have inhibited use of this process.

**Air Pollution Control (APC).**   Typical APC equipment on an incinerator will include an afterburner, liquid scrubber, demister, and fine particulate control device. Afterburners are used to control emission of unburned organic by-products by providing additional combustion volume at an elevated temperature. Scrubbers are used to physically remove particulate matter, acid gases, and residual organic compounds from the combustion gas stream. Metals, of course, are not destroyed in the incineration process. Some are volatilized and then collected in the air pollution control device. The large liquid droplets that escape from the scrubber are captured in a mist collector. The final stage in gas cleaning is to remove the fine particles that remain. Electrostatic precipitators have been used for this step. Scrubber water and residues from other APC devices are still considered hazardous and must be treated before ultimate land disposal.

**Permitting for Hazardous Waste Incinerators.**   The permitting for hazardous waste incinerators is a complex, multifaceted program conducted simultaneously on federal, state, and local levels [18]. Because of the variety of state and local regulations for the handling, transportation, treatment, and disposal of hazardous wastes, as well as those concerning the operation of incinerators, each startup facility has a unique set of permit requirements.

Generally speaking, hazardous waste incinerators require permits under the following laws: federal RCRA, state RCRA, for PCBs the Toxic Substances and Control Act (TSCA), state and federal wastewater discharge, and state and federal air pollution control. A variety of local permits may also be necessary. Each of these require data substantiating an incinerator's operation at or above performance levels determined by environmental legislation. Each requires a public hearing and discussion of environmental effects as well.

Hazardous waste incinerators must meet three performance standards:

1. *Principal organic hazardous constituents* (POHC). The DRE for a given POHC is defined as the mass percentage of the POHC removed from the waste. The POHC performance standard requires that the DRE for each POHC *designated* in the permit be 99.99% or higher. The DRE performance standard implicitly requires sampling and analysis to measure the amounts of the designated POHC(s) in both the waste stream and the stack effluent gas during a trial burn. (The term *designated POHC* is described in more detail later in this section.) The DRE is determined for each designated POHC from a mass balance of the waste introduced into the incinerator and in the stack gas*:

$$\text{DRE} = \frac{(W_{\text{in}} - W_{\text{out}})}{W_{\text{in}}} \times 100\% \qquad (13\text{--}8)$$

   where $W_{\text{in}}$ = mass feed rate of one POHC in the waste stream
   $W_{\text{out}}$ = mass emission rate of the same POHC present in exhaust emissions prior to release to the atmosphere

2. *Hydrochloric acid.* An incinerator burning hazardous waste and producing stack emissions of more than $1.8 \text{ kg} \cdot \text{h}^{-1}$ of hydrogen chloride (HCl) must control HCl emissions such that the rate of emission is no greater than the larger of either $1.8 \text{ kg} \cdot \text{h}^{-1}$ or 1% of the HCl in the stack gas prior to entering any pollution control equipment.

3. *Particulates.* Stack emissions of particulate matter are limited to $180 \text{ mg} \cdot \text{dscm}^{-1}$ (milligrams per dry standard cubic meter) for the stack gas corrected to 7% oxygen.

---

*Note that this is not a mass balance around the incinerator. Hazardous waste that ends up in the scrubber water, APC residue, and ash are not counted. Hence, the oxidation can be very poor and the incinerator can still meet the 99.99% rule if the scrubber is efficient or the waste ends up in the ash. This is one reason that residues are considered hazardous and must be treated before land disposal.

This adjustment is made by calculating a corrected concentration:

$$P_c = P_m \frac{14}{(21 - Y)} \tag{13–9}$$

where $P_c$ = corrected concentration of particulate (in mg · dscm$^{-1}$)
$P_m$ = measured concentration of particulate (in mg · dscm$^{-1}$)
$Y$ = percent oxygen in the dry flue gas

In this way, a decrease in the particulate concentration due solely to increasing air flow in the stack is not rewarded, and an increase in the particulate concentration due solely to reduction in the air flow in the stack is not penalized.

Compliance with these performance standards is documented by a **trial burn** of the facility's waste streams. As part of the RCRA permit application, a trial burn plan detailing waste analysis, an engineering description of the incinerator, sampling and monitoring procedures, test schedule and protocol, as well as control information, must be developed. If EPA determines that the design is adequate, a temporary or draft permit is issued, allowing the owner or operator to build the incinerator and initiate the trial burn procedure.

The temporary permit covers four phases of operation. During the first phase, immediately following construction, the unit is operated for **shake-down** purposes to identify possible mechanical deficiencies and to ensure its readiness for the trial burn procedures. This phase of the permit is limited to 720 h of operation using hazardous waste feed. The trial burn is conducted during the second phase.

To verify compliance with the POHC performance standard during the trial burn, it is not required that the incinerator DRE be measured for every POHC identified in the waste. The POHCs with the greatest potential for a low DRE, based on the expected difficulty of thermal degradation (incinerability) and the concentration of the POHC in the waste, become the *designated POHCs* for the trial burn. The EPA permit review personnel work with the owners or operators of the incinerator facility in determining which POHCs in a given waste should be designated for sampling and analysis during the trial burn.

If a wide variety of wastes are to be treated, a difficult-to-incinerate POHC at high concentration may be proposed for the trial burn. The substitute POHC is referred to as a **surrogate POHC.** The surrogate POHC does not have to be actually present in the normal waste. It does, however, have to be considered more difficult to incinerate than any POHC found in the waste.

The third phase consists of completing the trial burn and submitting the results. This phase can last several weeks to several months, during which the incinerator is allowed to operate under specified conditions.

Provided that performance standards are met in the trial burn, the facility can begin its fourth and final phase, which continues through the duration of the permit. In the event that the trial burn results do not demonstrate compliance with standards, the temporary permit must be modified to allow for a second trial burn.

**EXAMPLE 13–4**   A test burn waste mixture consisting of three designated POHCs (chlorobenzene, toluene, and xylene) is incinerated at 1000°C. The waste feed rate and the stack discharge are shown in the following table. The stack gas flow rate is 375.24 dscm · min$^{-1}$ (dry standard cubic meters per minute). Is the unit in compliance?

| Compound | Inlet (kg · h$^{-1}$) | Outlet (kg · h$^{-1}$) | Compound | Inlet (kg · h$^{-1}$) | Outlet (kg · h$^{-1}$) |
|---|---|---|---|---|---|
| Chlorobenzene (C$_6$H$_5$Cl) | 153 | 0.010 | HCl | | 1.2 |
| Toluene (C$_6$H$_8$) | 432 | 0.037 | Particulates at 7% O$_2$ | | 3.615 |
| Xylene (C$_8$H$_{10}$) | 435 | 0.070 | | | |

Outlet concentrations were measured in the stack after APC equipment.

Solution    We begin by calculating the DRE for each of the POHCs.

$$DRE = \frac{W_{in} - W_{out}}{W_{in}} \times 100$$

$$DRE_{chlorobenzene} = \frac{153 - 0.010}{153} \times 100 = 99.993\%$$

$$DRE_{toluene} = \frac{432 - 0.037}{432} \times 100 = 99.991\%$$

$$DRE_{xylene} = \frac{435 - 0.070}{435} \times 100 = 99.984\%$$

The DRE for each designated POHC must be at least 99.99%. In this case, the designated POHC xylene fails to meet the standard. The other POHCs exhibit a DRE of greater than 99.99%.

Now we check compliance for the HCl emission. The HCl emission may not exceed $1.8 \text{ kg} \cdot \text{h}^{-1}$ or 1% of the HCl prior to the control equipment, whichever is greater. It is obvious that the $1.2 \text{ kg} \cdot \text{h}^{-1}$ emission meets the $1.8 \text{ kg} \cdot \text{h}^{-1}$ limit. This would be sufficient to demonstrate compliance, but we will calculate the mass emission rate prior to control for the purpose of comparison. To do this we assume all the chlorine in the feed is converted to HCl. The molar feed rate of chlorobenzene ($M_{CB}$) is

$$M_{CB} = \frac{W_{CB}}{(MW)_{CB}} = \frac{(153 \text{ kg} \cdot \text{h}^{-1})(1000 \text{ g} \cdot \text{kg}^{-1})}{112.5 \text{ g} \cdot \text{mol}^{-1}} = 1360 \text{ mol} \cdot \text{h}^{-1}$$

where $M_{CB}$ = molar flow rate of chlorobenzene
$(MW)_{CB}$ = molecular weight of chlorobenzene

Each molecule of chlorobenzene contains one atom of chlorine. Therefore,

$M_{HCl} = M_{CB}$

$\quad = 1360 \text{ mol} \cdot \text{h}^{-1}$

$W_{HCl} = (\text{GMW of HCl})(\text{in mol} \cdot \text{h}^{-1})$

$\quad = (36.5 \text{ g} \cdot \text{mol}^{-1})(1360 \text{ mol} \cdot \text{h}^{-1})$

$\quad = 49,640 \text{ g} \cdot \text{h}^{-1}, \text{ or } 49.64 \text{ kg} \cdot \text{h}^{-1}$

This is the HCl emission prior to control. The emission of $1.2 \text{ kg} \cdot \text{h}^{-1}$ is greater than 1% of the uncontrolled emission, that is,

$1\% \text{ of uncontrolled} = (0.01)(49.64)$

$$= 0.4964 \text{ kg} \cdot \text{h}^{-1}$$

However, the incinerator passes the HCl limits because the HCl emission is less than $1.8 \text{ kg} \cdot \text{h}^{-1}$.

The particulate concentration was measured at 7% $O_2$ and, therefore, does not need to be corrected. The outlet loading ($W_{out}$) of the particulates is

$$W_{out} = \frac{(3.615 \text{ kg} \cdot \text{h}^{-1})(10^6 \text{ mg} \cdot \text{kg}^{-1})}{(375.24 \text{ dscm} \cdot \text{min}^{-1})(60 \text{ min} \cdot \text{h}^{-1})} = 160 \text{ mg} \cdot \text{dscm}^{-1}$$

This is less than the standard of $180 \text{ mg} \cdot \text{dscm}^{-1}$ and is, therefore, in compliance with regard to particulates. However, because the incinerator fails the DRE for xylene, the unit is out of compliance.

**Regulations for PCBs.** Incineration of PCBs is regulated under TSCA rather than RCRA [7]. Thus, some of the permit conditions for incineration of PCBs are different from those for other RCRA hazardous wastes.

The conditions for incineration of liquid PCBs may be summarized as follows:

1. *Time and temperature.* Either of two conditions must be met. The residence time of the PCBs in the furnace must be 2 s at 1200°C ± 100°C with 3% excess oxygen in the stack gas or, alternatively, the furnace residence time must be 1.5 s at 1600°C ± 100°C with 2% excess oxygen in the stack gas.

   The EPA has interpreted these conditions to require a liquid PCB DRE $\geq$ 99.9999%.

2. *Combustion efficiency.* The combustion efficiency shall be at least 99.99%, computed as follows:

$$\text{Combustion efficiency} = \frac{C_{CO_2}}{C_{CO_2} + C_{CO}} \times 100\% \tag{13–10}$$

   where $C_{CO_2}$ = concentration of carbon dioxide in stack gas
   $C_{CO}$ = concentration of carbon monoxide in stack gas

3. *Monitoring and controls.* In addition to these permitted limits, owners or operators of incinerators are required to monitor and control the variables that affect performance. The rate and quantity of PCBs fed to the combustion system must be measured and recorded at regular intervals of no longer than 15 min. The temperatures of the incineration process must be continuously measured and recorded. The flow of PCBs to the incinerator must stop automatically whenever one of the following occurs: the combustion temperature drops below the temperatures specified, that is, 1200 or 1600°C; when there is a failure of monitoring operations; when the PCB rate and quantity measuring and recording equipment fails; or when excess oxygen falls below the percentage specified. Scrubbers must be used for HCl removal during PCB incineration.

   In addition, a trial burn must be conducted and the following exhaust emissions must be monitored:

   | | |
   |---|---|
   | Oxygen ($O_2$) | Total chlorinated organic content |
   | Carbon monoxide (CO) | PCBs |
   | Oxides of nitrogen ($NO_x$) | Total particulate matter |
   | Hydrogen chloride (HCl) | |

An incinerator used for incinerating nonliquid PCBs, PCB articles, PCB equipment, or PCB containers must comply with the same rules as those for liquid PCBs, and the mass air emissions from the incinerator must be no greater than 0.001 g PCB per kilogram of the PCB introduced into the incinerator, that is, a DRE of 99.9999%.

### Stabilization–Solidification

Because of their elemental composition, some wastes, such as nickel, cannot be destroyed or detoxified by physical or chemical means. Thus, once they have been separated from aqueous solution and concentrated in ash or sludge, the hazardous constituents must be bound up in stable compounds that meet the LDR restrictions for leachability.

The terminology for this treatment technology has evolved in the last decade. In the early to mid 1980s "chemical fixation, encapsulation," and "binding" were often used interchangeably with solidification and stabilization. With the promulgation of the LDR restrictions, the EPA established a more precise definition for solidification–stabilization and discouraged the use of the other terms to describe the technology [19]. EPA linked solidification and stabilization because the resultant material from the treatment must be both stable and solid. **Stability** is determined by the degree of resistance of the mixture of the hazardous waste and additive chemical to leaching in the **Toxicity Characteristic Leaching Procedure** (TCLP) [20]. In the EPA definition, then, solidification–stabilization refers to chemical treatment processes that chemically reduce the mobility of the hazardous constituent.

Reduced leachability is accomplished by the formation of a lattice structure or chemical bonds that bind the hazardous constituent and thereby limit the amount of constituent that can be leached when water or a mild acid solution comes into contact with the waste matrix. There are two principal solidification–stabilization processes: cement-based and lime-based. The cement or lime additive is mixed with the ash or sludge and water. It is then allowed to cure to form a solid. The correct mix proportions are determined by trial-and-error experiments on waste samples. In both techniques the stabilizing agent may be modified by other additives such as silicates. In general, this technology is applicable to wastes containing metals with little or no organic contamination, oil, or grease.

## 13-7   LAND DISPOSAL

### Deep Well Injection

**Deep well injection** consists of pumping wastes into geologically secure formations. The general technical requirements of a suitable hazardous waste injection well include [21]

1. A saline-water-bearing formation that is large enough and permeable enough to accept the waste.
2. Overlying and underlying strata (confining layers) that are sufficiently impermeable to confine the waste to the injection strata.
3. The absence of solution-collapse features, faults, joints, and abandoned wells that might permit the escape of the waste.

Obviously, these requirements imply a rigorous understanding of the geologic and hydrologic characteristics of the subsurface. In addition, it is often necessary to pretreat the waste before injection. The purpose of the pretreatment is to modify the waste characteristics so that it is compatible with the injection equipment and the geologic strata. Some waste characteristics of importance are the presence of microorganisms, suspended solids, oils, and entrained or dissolved gases.

Pumping of wastes into these formations has been practiced primarily in Louisiana and Texas. In promulgating the final third of the LDR restrictions, the EPA allowed disposal of waste in class I injection wells for wastes disposed under Clean Water Act regulations [22].

### Land Treatment

Land treatment is sometimes called **land farming** of the waste. In this practice, waste was incorporated with soil material in the manner that fertilizer or manure might be. Microorganisms in the soil degraded the organic fraction of the waste. Under the LDR restrictions, this practice is prohibited.

### The Secure Landfill

Although far from ideal, the use of land for the disposal of hazardous wastes is a major option for the foreseeable future. Furthermore, we recognize that incinerator ash, scrubber bottoms, and the results of biological, chemical, and physical treatment leave residues of up to 20% of the original mass. These residues must be secured in an economical fashion. At this juncture, the secure landfill is the only option.

The basic physical problem with land disposal of hazardous waste stems from the movement of water, originating as precipitation into and through the disposal site. The dissolution of waste material results in contaminants being transported from the waste site to larger regions of the soil zone and, too often, to an underlying aquifer. Problems of groundwater pollution frequently lead to the condemnation of wells and to the contamination of surface water bodies fed by the associated aquifer. In many instances, well contamination is not detected until years after land disposal of waste has begun, owing primarily to the slow movement of the conveying groundwater.

For some chemical species, adsorption to soil particles may also act to retard the movement of the contaminant plume.

Water pollution, caused by a hazardous waste facility, may evolve in a variety of ways. Leachate from landfills may drain out of the side of the landfill and appear as surface runoff. Alternatively, it may seep down slowly through the unsaturated zone, if one exists, and enter an underlying aquifer. Breaks in liners of holding ponds or cracks in the bottom of storage tanks also lead to a downward migration of contaminants toward the water table. Sometimes this migration is impeded by a relatively impermeable geologic barrier, such as a clay layer.

Without the institution of remedial measures, buried waste usually acts as a continuing source of pollution. The waste constituents continue to be transported in the subsurface by infiltrating precipitation. Thus, it is generally recommended that sites that handle hazardous wastes be located above a natural barrier, as well as an applied liner. Moreover, the site should be instrumented to continuously monitor the condition of any associated aquifers. If leachate generation is anticipated, there should be a system for the collection and treatment of the leachate.

The technology of the secure landfill may be divided into two phases: siting and construction. The following discussion is drawn primarily from E. F. Wood and colleagues [23].

**Landfill Siting.** In siting a hazardous waste landfill, the four main considerations are air quality, groundwater quality, surface water quality, and subsurface migration of gases and leachates. Aside from the sociopolitical aspects, the last three components are the major factors to be considered in siting the landfill.

Air quality must be considered to prevent adverse effects to the air caused by volatilization, gas generation, gas migration, and wind dispersal of landfilled hazardous wastes. Generally, these can be controlled by proper construction techniques and do not inhibit the siting.

The hydrogeologic siting problem can be divided into four main areas: hydrology, climate, geology, and soil.

Hydrologic considerations in locating a hazardous waste landfill include distance to the groundwater table, the hydraulic gradient, the proximity of wells, and the proximity to surface waters. The proximity of a site to water supplies and the type of natural materials that occur between a site and a water supply influence contaminant migrations. When distance from the surface to the groundwater table is short, contaminant travel time is also short, allowing for little attenuation before pollutants disperse laterally in the saturated zone. It is desirable to have the average distance to the groundwater table large enough so that contaminants may be significantly attenuated. This also facilitates monitoring of the saturated zone and will permit detection of leaks and implementation remedial action to be undertaken in a timely fashion.

A hydraulic gradient that slopes away from local groundwater supplies is desired. The steeper the hydraulic gradient, the lower the attenuation time and the faster the water movement. Therefore, a moderate hydraulic gradient may be most acceptable.

The distance from the disposal site to water supply wells and surface waters must be as large as possible to protect them from potential contamination in case the landfill leaks. Furthermore, the proximity to surface waters must take into account the potential for flooding. Site flooding will weaken the structure of a land emplacement facility, causing it to fail and leak wastes. Therefore, it is essential that the facility not be built on a floodplain or area subject to local flooding.

Climate is considered a driving force in contaminant migration, but we may exclude it when considering potential sites within the same region, where climate is unlikely to vary significantly.

Structural integrity of host rock is important in terms of seismic risk zones, dipping, and cleavage. Seismic risk zones are areas where earthquakes have occurred or have a high probability of occurring. They indicate the presence of geologic faults and fractures. The presence of faults and fractures is extremely important because they provide a natural pathway for the flow of contaminants, even in low-permeability and low-porosity rock. Future seismic activity could damage the landfill cells and storage tanks of a land disposal facility during or after the construction, filling, and closing of the site, unless it is structurally designed to withstand ground motion.

**Transport capacity** refers to a soil's ability to allow migration of contaminants. Thus, the greater the soil transport capacity, the greater the migration of contaminants, which is undesirable. A soil with a low permeability can lengthen the flow period and act as a natural defense by retarding the movement of contaminants. Glacial outwash plains and deltaic sands are both well-sorted sand and gravel beds with high permeability. Thus, they allow wastes to move faster and further. Clays and silts have lower permeabilities and, thus, inhibit the movement of wastes.

**Sorption capacity** depends on the organic content, predominant minerals, pH, and soil. Sorption includes both absorption and adsorption of contaminants. Sorption is important in limiting the movement of metals, phosphorus, and organic chemicals. **Cation-exchange capacity** (CEC) is a measure of the ability of the soil to trade cations in the soil for those in waste. The higher the CEC, the more cations will be retained. The capacity of soil to retard contaminant migration also depends on the presence of numerous hydrous oxides, particularly iron oxides, and other compounds such as phosphates and carbonates. These compounds precipitate heavy metals from solution.

The hydrogen ion concentration (pH) of soil influences the dominant removal mechanism for metal cations. The dominant removal mechanism for metal cations when pH < 5 is exchange or adsorption; when pH > 6, it is precipitation.

**Landfill Construction.** A secure landfill means, in essence, that no leachate or other contaminant can escape from the fill and adversely affect the surface water or groundwater [24]. Leakage from the site is not acceptable during or after operations. Neither is any external or internal displacement, which could be brought about by slumping, sliding, and flooding. Wastes must not be allowed to migrate from the site.

It is nearly impossible to create an impervious burial vault for hazardous wastes and guarantee its integrity forever. Landfill design and operation is regulated to minimize migration of wastes from the site. The current EPA rules (40 CFR 264.300) for hazardous waste landfills require a minimum of (1) two or more liners, (2) a leachate collection system above and between the liners, (3) surface run-on and run-off control to collect and control at least the water volume resulting from a 24-h, 25-year storm, (4) monitoring wells, and (5) a "cap" (Figure 13–11).

**FIGURE 13–11**

Minimum technology landfill liner, design and recommended final cover design. (*Source: U.S. EPA Seminar Publications,* "Requirements for hazardous waste landfill design, construction and closure," EPA 625/4-89/022, 1989, and "Design and Construction of RCRA/CERCLA Final Covers," EPA 625/4-91/025,1991.)

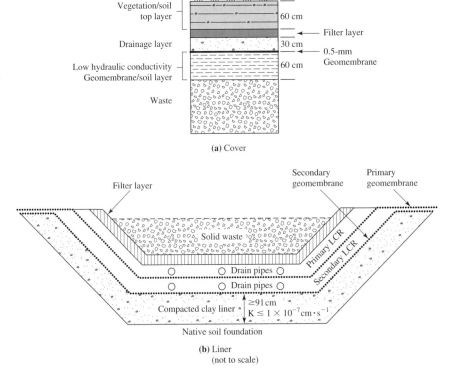

(a) Cover

(b) Liner
(not to scale)

**FIGURE 13–12**

Definition of hydraulic
gradient for landfill liner.

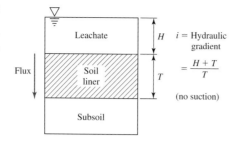

The liner system must include [25]

1. A top liner designed and constructed of materials (e.g., a geomembrane) to prevent migration of hazardous constituents into the liner during the active life and postclosure care period.
2. A composite bottom liner consisting of at least two components. The upper component must be designed and constructed of materials (e.g., a geomembrane) to prevent migration of hazardous constituents into the liner during the active life and postclosure care period. The lower component must be designed and constructed of materials to minimize migration of hazardous constituents if a breach in the upper component were to occur. The lower component must be constructed of at least 91 cm of compacted soil material with a hydraulic conductivity of no more than $1 \times 10^{-7}$ cm $\cdot$ s$^{-1}$.

The leachate collection and removal system (LCR) immediately above the top liner must be designed, constructed, operated, and maintained to collect and remove leachate so that the leachate depth over the liner does not exceed 30 cm. The LCR between the liners and immediately above the bottom liner is also a leak detection system. The LCR must, at a minimum, be

1. Constructed with a bottom slope of 1% or more.
2. Constructed of a granular drainage material with a hydraulic conductivity of $1 \times 10^{-2}$ cm $\cdot$ s$^{-1}$ or more and a thickness of 30 cm or more; or be constructed of synthetic or geonet drainage materials with a transmissibility of $3 \times 10^{-5}$ m$^2$ $\cdot$ s$^{-1}$ or more.
3. Constructed of sufficient strength to prevent collapse and be designed to prevent clogging.

The leachate collection system must include pumps of sufficient size to remove the liquids to prevent leachate from backing up into the drainage layer. The leachate must be treated to meet discharge limits. The treated leachate may be discharged into the municipal wastewater treatment system or into a waterway.

The amount of leachate may be estimated using Darcy's law (see Chapter 6). The hydraulic gradient for a liner is defined as shown in Figure 13–12. The flow rate cannot exceed the amount of water available, that is, the product of the precipitation rate and the area of the landfill. The travel time of a contaminant through a soil layer may be estimated as the linear length of the flow path ($T$) divided by the seepage velocity (Equation 6–10).

**EXAMPLE 13–5**   How long will it take for leachate to migrate through a 0.9-m clay liner with a hydraulic conductivity of $1 \times 10^{-7}$ cm $\cdot$ s$^{-1}$ if the depth of leachate above the clay layer is 30 cm and the porosity of the clay is 55%?

Solution   The Darcy velocity is found using Equation 6–8.

$$v = K\left(\frac{dh}{dr}\right)$$

where the hydraulic gradient ($dh/dr$) is defined as in Figure 13–12.

$$\frac{dh}{dr} = \frac{0.30 \text{ m} + 0.9 \text{ m}}{0.9 \text{ m}} = 1.33$$

The Darcy velocity is then

$$v = (1 \times 10^{-7} \text{ cm} \cdot \text{s}^{-1})(1.33) = 1.33 \times 10^{-7} \text{ cm} \cdot \text{s}^{-1}$$

From Equation 6–10, the seepage velocity is

$$v' = \frac{K(dh/dr)}{\eta} = \frac{1.33 \times 10^{-7} \text{ cm} \cdot \text{s}^{-1}}{0.55} = 2.42 \times 10^{-7} \text{ cm} \cdot \text{s}^{-1}$$

The travel time is then

$$t = \frac{T}{v'} = \frac{(0.9 \text{ m})(100 \text{ cm} \cdot \text{m}^{-1})}{2.42 \times 10^{-7} \text{ cm} \cdot \text{s}^{-1}} = 3.71 \times 10^8 \text{ s, or about 12 years}$$

The site operator must keep careful records of the location and dimensions of each cell and must depict each cell on a map keyed to permanently surveyed vertical and horizontal markers. Records must show the contents of each cell and the approximate location of each hazardous waste type within the cell.

The purpose of groundwater monitoring is to ensure that programs for managing runon, runoff, and leachates are functioning properly so that groundwater remains uncontaminated. If contamination is occurring, early warning can be given and countermeasures taken. The site owner or operator has to place a sufficient number of monitoring wells around the limits of the facility to be able to describe the background (upgradient) and downgradient water quality. The regulations set forth, in detail, how the monitoring wells must be sunk, screened, sealed, sampled, and located, with special emphasis on location of the downgradient wells.

General groundwater quality, especially the suitability of the uppermost aquifer for use as a drinking-water source, must meet EPA's primary drinking-water standards. The flow rate for each sump must be calculated weekly during the active life and closure period, and monthly during the postclosure care period. If the landfill is leaking to the groundwater, the site operator must file an assessment plan with the EPA that shows how the problem is to be remedied.

## 13–8  GROUNDWATER CONTAMINATION AND REMEDIATION

### The Process of Contamination

Hazardous waste landfills are, of course, not the only source of groundwater contamination [7]. Other sources include municipal landfills, septic tanks, mining and agricultural activities, "midnight dumping," and leaking underground storage tanks. It has been estimated that as many as 5000 gasoline storage tanks at local service stations are leaking.

The threat of contamination to groundwater depends on the specific geologic and hydrologic conditions of the site. The process of contamination and the process of transport of contaminants was discussed in Chapter 8.

### EPA's Groundwater Remediation Procedure

The federal program for cleanup of contaminated sites follows a procedural sequence as shown in Figure 13–13. Each of these steps is discussed in the following paragraphs.

**Preliminary Assessment.**  EPA involvement usually begins with the identification of a potential hazardous waste site. The initial information can come from a variety of sources, including local citizens and officials, state environmental agencies, the site owners themselves, or simply from awareness of potential problems associated with particular industries.

EPA has developed an inventory system called the comprehensive environmental response, compensation, and liability information system (CERCLIS) to document all of the sites in the

**FIGURE 13–13**

Steps involved in the Superfund cleanup process.

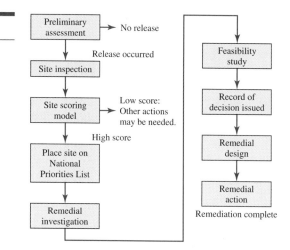

United States that may be candidates for remedial action. This is a continuing program that identifies sites as information about them becomes available. The growth in the number of CERCLIS sites has been dramatic and is expected to continue for the foreseeable future as additional abandoned and contaminated sites are discovered. As of September, 2001, 1238 sites were on the NPL and 43,806 sites were in the CERCLIS inventory [26].

A **preliminary assessment** (PA) is the first step in identifying the potential for contamination from a particular site. The primary objectives of the PA are to determine if a contaminant has been released to the environment, if there is immediate danger to persons living or working near the site, and whether a site inspection is necessary. Samples for environmental analysis are generally not taken during the PA. Following the preliminary assessment, EPA or the designated state agency might determine that an immediate threat to residents or employees at the site requires an immediate removal action. Otherwise, on the basis of the preliminary assessment, the site is classified by EPA into one of the three following categories:

1. No further action is needed, because there is no threat to human health or the environment.
2. Additional information is required to complete the preliminary assessment.
3. Inspection of the site is necessary.

**Site Inspection.**   Site inspection requires sampling to determine the types of hazardous substances present and to identify the extent of contamination and its migration. The actual site inspection includes preparation of a work plan and an on-site safety plan. The site assessment has three objectives:

1. To determine which releases pose no threat to public health and the environment.
2. To determine if there is any immediate threat to persons living or working near the release.
3. To collect data to determine whether or not a site should be included on the NPL.

**HRS, NPL, RI/FS, and ROD.**   The next series of steps in the EPA's procedure include calculations to complete the HRS; inclusion on the NPL if the score is sufficiently high; conduct of a RI/FS; and issuance of an ROD. These steps were discussed in detail in Section 13–4.

**Remedial Design and Remedial Action.**   EPA-funded remedial actions may be taken only at those sites that are on the NPL. This ranking helps ensure that the Superfund dollars are used in the most cost-effective manner and where they will yield the greatest benefit.

Before a remedial action can be taken at a site, a number of questions must be answered. These can be classified as problem definition, design alternatives, and policy.

1. *Problem definition questions.* What are the contaminants and how much contamination is present? How large is the surface area of the contaminated site? What is the size of the contaminated groundwater plume? Where is the exact location of the plume and in what direction is it moving?
2. *Design questions.* Based on the alternatives available, what is the best way to clean up the site? How should these alternatives be implemented? What products will be produced during treatment? How long will it take to complete the remediation and what will it cost?
3. *Policy questions.* What level of protection is adequate? In other words, how clean is clean?

The answers to the first two sets of questions require scientific and engineering background that is supported by extensive sampling of the contaminated site area. The last question cannot be answered objectively; rather it is a subjective and often political question.

The NCP defines three types of responses for incidents involving hazardous substances. In these responses removal is differentiated from remediation. **Removal** is, as its name suggests, the physical relocation of the waste—usually to a secure hazardous waste landfill. **Remediation** means that the waste is to be treated to make it less toxic or less mobile or the site is to be contained to minimize further release. Remediation can take place on site or at a TSD facility. The three types of responses are

1. *Immediate removal* is a prompt response to prevent immediate and significant harm to human health or the environment. Immediate removals must be completed within 6 months.
2. *Planned removal* is an expedited removal when some response, not necessarily an emergency response, is required. The same 6-month limitation also applies to planned removal.
3. *Remedial response* is intended to achieve a site solution that is a permanent remedy for the particular problem involved.

Immediate removals are done to prevent an emergency involving hazardous substances. These emergencies might include fires; explosions; direct human contact with a hazardous substance; human, animal, or food-chain exposure; or contamination of drinking-water sources. An immediate removal involves cleaning up the hazardous site to protect human health and life, containing the hazardous release, and minimizing the potential for damage to the environment. For example, a truck, train, or barge spill could involve an immediate removal determination by EPA to get the spill cleaned up.

Immediate removal responses may include activities such as sample collection and analysis, containment or control of the release, removal of the hazardous substances from the site, provision of alternative water supplies, installation of security fences, evacuation of threatened citizens, or general deterrent of the spread of the hazardous contaminants.

A planned removal involves a hazardous site that does not present an immediate emergency. Under Superfund, EPA may initiate a planned removal if the action will minimize the damage or risk and is consistent with a more effective long-term solution to the problem. Planned removals are carried out by EPA if the responsible party is either unknown or cannot or will not take timely and appropriate action. The state in which the cleanup is located must be willing to match at least 10% of the costs of the removal action, as well as agree to nominate the site in question for the NPL.

### Mitigation and Treatment

Because the spread of contaminants is usually confined to a plume, only localized areas of an aquifer need to be reclaimed and restored [27]. Cleanup of a contaminated aquifer, however, is often troublesome, time-consuming, and costly. The original source of contamination can be eliminated, but the complete restoration of the groundwater is fraught with additional problems, such as defining the site's subsurface environment, locating potential contamination sources, defining potential contaminant transport pathways, determining contaminant extent and concentration, and choosing and implementing an effective remedial process.

Although not a simple task, cleanup is possible. Various methods are being used and have proven successful in certain cases. These efforts have ranged from containment to destruction of the contaminants, either in their original position in the aquifer or by withdrawing the groundwater. Examples of these remedial methods include installing pumping wells to remove contaminated water, building trenches to arrest only the contaminated flow, and stimulating biodegradation of groundwater contaminants.

In many circumstances, the most reasonable and economic remedial approach is to treat the water to attain the necessary quality for a specific use. This treated water may then be used or returned to the aquifer. Certainly, combinations of barriers and treatment methods should be considered. Source control (removal or remediation of the source), physical control, and treatment methods all will have their part in mitigating groundwater contamination problems. Legal implications may also dictate possible strategies.

**Well Systems.**   A well system serves as an example of a common remedial process for treating contaminated groundwater. Well systems manipulate the subsurface hydraulic gradient through injection or withdrawal of water. They are designed to control the movement of the groundwater directly and of the subsurface pollutants indirectly. All require installation of wells at selected sites. It is necessary to first conduct a hydrogeologic study to determine the characteristics of the contaminant plume (width, length, depth, and general shape), the hydraulic gradient across the plume, and the hydrogeologic characteristics of the aquifer. There are three major types of well system: well point, deep well, and pressure ridge systems.

Both well point and deep well systems withdraw water. The former uses closely spaced, shallow wells, each connected to a main pipe (header) that is connected to a centrally located pump. The well point system is used only for shallow water table aquifers. Deep well systems are used for greater depths and are most often pumped individually. Both well point and deep well systems should be designed so that the radius of influence of the system completely intercepts the contaminant plume.

The principle of pressure ridge systems is the inverse of that of a well system. Clean, uncontaminated water is injected to form an upconing of the water table that acts as a barrier to groundwater flow. The injection well is also called a recharge well. The upconing effect of a recharge well is shown in Figure 13–14.

**FIGURE 13-14**

Effect of a recharge well on groundwater flow patterns.

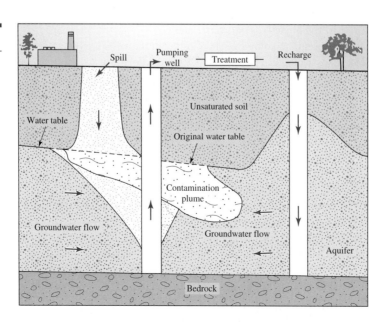

**Nonaqueous phase liquids** (NAPLs) such as gasoline are referred to as "product" because their recovery may have some commercial value. When the NAPL floats on the groundwater table, special recovery techniques may be employed to recover it. Product recovery systems to recover NAPL use wells that terminate in the NAPL plume rather than in the aquifer. Because all hydrocarbons are slightly soluble in water, the product recovery system is usually accompanied by a groundwater pumping system to remove and treat the contaminated groundwater.

**Treatment Technologies.**   The treatment methods used to clean the contaminated groundwater are fundamentally the same as those discussed in Section 13–6. Each must be tailored to the local situation.

## CHAPTER REVIEW

When you have finished studying this chapter you should be able to do the following without the aid of your textbook or notes:

1. Sketch the chemical structure of 2,3,7,8-TCDD.
2. Explain how 2,3,7,8-TCDD occurs or when it is found in nature.
3. Sketch the chemical structure of the PCB 2,4′-dichlorobiphenyl.
4. Explain the origin of PCBs.
5. Define hazardous waste.
6. List the five ways a waste can be found to be hazardous and briefly explain each.
7. Explain why dioxin and PCB are hazardous wastes.
8. State how long generators may store their waste.
9. Define the abbreviations CFR, FR, RCRA, HSWA, CERCLA, and SARA.
10. Explain the major difference (objective) between RCRA/HSWA and CERCLA/SARA.
11. Define the terms *cradle to grave* and *manifest system*.
12. Explain what *land ban,* or *LDR*, means.
13. Define the abbreviations TSD and UST.
14. List the four major provisions of CERCLA.
15. Define the following abbreviations: NPL, NCP, HRS, RI/FS, ROD, and PRP.
16. Explain why it is important for a site to be placed on the NPL.
17. Explain the concept of "joint and several liability" and the implications to those with wastes found in an abandoned hazardous waste site.
18. List and explain four hazardous waste management techniques.
19. List the objectives of a waste audit.
20. Differentiate among waste minimization, waste exchange, and recycling.
21. List six disposal technologies for hazardous wastes.
22. Explain why seismic risk is important in landfill siting.
23. Explain how hydraulic conductivity and sorption capacity of soil limit the migration of hazardous wastes.
24. Explain what hydrologic features are important in siting a landfill.
25. List the minimum EPA requirements for a hazardous waste landfill and sketch a landfill that meets these.
26. Explain the difference between deep well injection and land treatment.
27. Define the following acronyms: PIC, POHC, and DRE, as they apply to incineration.
28. List the most important factors for proper incinerator design and operation.
29. List the two types of incinerators most commonly used for destroying hazardous waste.
30. Explain the terms *designated POHC* and *surrogate* as they apply to a trial burn.
31. Outline the steps in EPA's remediation procedures.
32. Differentiate between "remediation" and "removal" as they pertain to a CERCLA/SARA cleanup.

With the aid of this text, you should be able to do the following:

1. Determine whether or not a waste is an EPA hazardous waste based on its composition, source, or characteristics.
2. Perform a mass balance to identify waste sources or waste minimization opportunities.
3. Write the reactions for oxidation or reduction of chemical contaminants to mineralized form.
4. Perform solubility product calculations to estimate treatment doses for precipitation or the concentration of contaminants that remain in solution.
5. Determine the dimensions of an air stripping column and air or liquid flow rate, given the values for remaining variables.
6. Evaluate a chemical feed to an incinerator to determine whether or not the chlorine content is acceptable and design a mix of waste feeds to achieve a desired chlorine feed rate.
7. Evaluate the operating variables for an incinerator to determine regulatory compliance for DRE, HCl emissions, and particulate emissions.
8. Estimate the hydraulic conductivity of a liner material based on laboratory measurements.
9. Estimate the quantity of leachate given the precipitation rate, area, hydraulic gradient, and hydraulic conductivity.
10. Estimate the seepage velocity and travel time of a contaminant through a soil, given the hydraulic gradient, hydraulic conductivity, porosity, and length of the flow path.

## PROBLEMS

**13–1** Determine whether the following is a RCRA hazardous waste: Municipal wastewater containing $2.0 \text{ mg} \cdot \text{L}^{-1}$ of selenium.

>   **Answer:** Not a hazardous waste

**13–2** Determine whether the following is a RCRA hazardous waste: An empty pesticide container that a homeowner wishes to discard.

**13–3** A dry cleaner accumulates $10 \text{ kg} \cdot \text{month}^{-1}$ of a hazardous waste solvent. To save shipping cost he would like to accumulate 6 months' worth before he ships it to a TSD facility. Can he do this? Explain. (*Note:* This is a "trick" question that requires searching the applicable regulations in the CFR.)

>   **Answer:** Yes

**13–4** Using the data in the following table and Figure P-13–4, use the mass-balance technique to determine the mass flow rate (in kilograms per day) of organic compounds to the condensate collection tank (sample location 4 in Figure P-13–4).

| Sample Location | Flow Rate $(\text{L} \cdot \text{min}^{-1})$ | Total Volatile Organic | Temperature $(°\text{C})$ |
|---|---|---|---|
| 1 | 40.5 | $5858. \text{ mg} \cdot \text{L}^{-1}$ | 25 |
| 2 | 44.8 | $0.037 \text{ mg} \cdot \text{L}^{-1}$ | 80 |
| 3 | 57. (vapor) | 44.13% | 20 |

Notes:
a. % is volume percent
b. Vapor flow rate is corrected to 1 atm and 20°C.
c. Liquid organic density may be assumed to be $0.95 \text{ kg} \cdot \text{L}^{-1}$.
d. Assume the molecular weight of the organic vapor is equal to that of methylene chloride.
e. Steam mass flow rate is $252 \text{ kg} \cdot \text{h}^{-1}$ at 106°C.

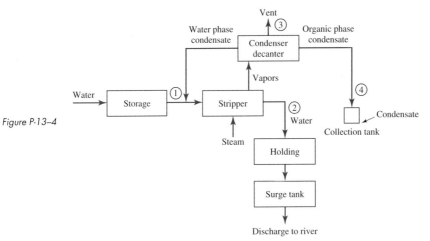

*Figure P-13–4*

**13-5** What is the efficiency of the condenser-decanter in Problem 13–4?

**Answer:** $\eta = 62.5\%$

**13-6** Given the waste constituent and concentration shown in the following table, determine the quantity (in kilograms per day) of hydrated lime ($Ca(OH)_2$) required to neutralize the waste. Estimate the total dissolved solids (TDS) after neutralization. Report your answer in milligrams per liter.

| Constituent | Concentration $(mg \cdot L^{-1})$ | Flow $(L \cdot min^{-1})$ |
|---|---|---|
| HCl | 100 | 5 |

**13-7** Given the constituents and concentrations shown in the following table, determine the quantity (in kilograms per day) of sulfuric acid required to neutralize the waste. Estimate the total dissolved solids (TDS) after neutralization. Report your answer in milligrams per liter.

| Constituent | Concentration $(mg \cdot L^{-1})$ | Flow $(L \cdot min^{-1})$ |
|---|---|---|
| NaOH | 250 | 20 |

**Answers:** $8.82 \, kg \cdot day^{-1}$ of $H_2SO_4$; TDS $= 444 \, mg \cdot L^{-1}$

**13-8** Write the reaction equation to oxidize sodium cyanide using sodium hypochlorite (NaOCl).

**13-9** Write the reaction equation to reduce hexavalent chromium in chromic acid ($H_2Cr_2O_7$) to trivalent chromium using $NaHSO_3$.

**13-10** A metal plating solution contains $20.00 \, mg \cdot L^{-1}$ of copper. Determine the concentration, in moles per liter, to which the hydroxide concentration must be raised to precipitate all but $0.500 \, mg \cdot L^{-1}$ of the copper using lime. The $K_{sp}$ of copper hydroxide is $2.00 \times 10^{-19}$. Estimate the final pH.

**13-11** A metal plating sludge as removed from a clarifier has a solids concentration of 4%. If the volume of sludge is $1.0 \, m^3 \cdot day^{-1}$, what volume will result if the sludge is processed in a filter press to a solids concentration of 30%? If the pressed sludge is dried to 80% solids, what volume will result?

**Answer:** Press $\Psi_2 = 0.133 \, m^3 \cdot day^{-1}$; dryer $\Psi_2 = 0.05 \, m^3 \cdot day^{-1}$

**13-12** In Problem 13–11, ferrocyanide is found in the clarifier sludge at a concentration of 400 mg · kg$^{-1}$ (4% solids). Assuming that the ferrocyanide is part of the precipitate and that none escapes from the filter press, what concentration would be expected in filter cake?

**13-13** A drinking-water supply at Oscoda, Michigan, has been contaminated by trichloroethylene. The average concentration in the water is estimated to be 6000 μg · L$^{-1}$. Using the following design parameters, design a packed-tower stripping column to reduce the water concentration to the State of Michigan discharge limit of 1.5 μg · L$^{-1}$. Note that more than one column in series may be required for reasonable tower heights.

Henry's law constant $= 6.74 \times 10^{-3}$ m$^3$ · atm · mol$^{-1}$    Temperature $= 25°C$
$K_L a = 0.720$ min$^{-1}$    Column diameter may not exceed 4.0 m
Air flow rate $= 60$ m$^3$ · min$^{-1}$    Column height may not exceed 6.0 m
$G/L = 18$

**Answer:** $Z_T = 6$ m; $d = 3.15$ m

**13-14** Well 13 at Watapitae is contaminated with 440 μg · L$^{-1}$ of tetrachloroethylene (perchloroethylene). The water must be remediated to achieve a concentration of 0.2 μg · L$^{-1}$ (the detection limit). Design a packed-tower stripping column to meet this requirement using the following design parameters. Note that more than one column in series may be required for reasonable tower heights.

Henry's law constant $= 100 \times 10^{-4}$ m$^3$ · atm · mol$^{-1}$    Temperature $= 20°C$
$K_L a = 13.5 \times 10^{-3}$ s$^{-1}$    Column diameter may not exceed 4.0 m
Air flow rate $= 15$ m$^3$ · s$^{-1}$    Column height may not exceed 6.0 m
Liquid flow rate $= 0.22$ m$^3$ · s$^{-1}$

**13-15** An incinerator operator receives the following shipments of waste for incineration. Can the operator mix these wastes to achieve 30% by mass of chlorine in the feed?

Trichloroethylene $= 18.9$ m$^3$    Toluene $= 21.3$ m$^3$
1,1,1-Trichloroethane $= 5.3$ m$^3$    $o$-Xylene $= 4.8$ m$^3$

**Answer:** No

**13-16** An incinerator operator receives the following shipments of waste for incineration. What volume of methanol ($CH_3OH$) must the operator mix to achieve 30% by mass of chlorine in the feed? Assume the density of methanol is 0.7913 g · mL$^{-1}$.

Carbon tetrachloride $= 1.2$ m$^3$    Hexachlorobenzene $= 15.3$ m$^3$    Pentachlorophenol $= 25.0$ m$^3$

**13-17** A hazardous waste incinerator is being fed methylene chloride at a concentration of 5858 mg · L$^{-1}$ in a aqueous stream at a rate of 40.5 L · min$^{-1}$. Calculate the mass flow rate of the feed in units of grams per minute.

**Answer:** 237.25 g · min$^{-1}$

**13-18** Methylene chloride was measured in the flue gas of a hazardous waste incinerator at a concentration of 211.86 μg · m$^{-3}$. If the flow rate of gas from the incinerator was 597.55 m$^3$ · min$^{-1}$, what was the mass flow rate of methylene chloride in grams per minute?

**13-19** Assuming that the same incinerator is being evaluated in Problems 13–17 and 13–18, what is the DRE for the incinerator?

**Answer:** DRE $= 99.947\%$

**13-20** Xylene is fed into an incinerator at a rate of 481 kg · h$^{-1}$. If the mass flow rate at the stack is 72.2 g · h$^{-1}$, is the unit in compliance with the EPA rules?

**13-21** 1,2-Dichlorobenzene is being burned in an incinerator under the following conditions:

Operating temperature $= 1150°C$    Stack gas flow rate $= 6.70$ m$^3$ · s$^{-1}$ at standard conditions
Feed flow rate $= 173.0$ L · min$^{-1}$    Stack gas concentrations after APC equipment
Feed concentration $= 13.0$ g · L$^{-1}$     Dichlorobenzene $= 338.8$ μg · dscm$^{-1}$
Residence time $= 2.4$ s     HCl $= 77.2$ mg · dscm$^{-1}$
Oxygen in stack gas $= 7.0\%$     Particulates $= 181.6$ mg · dscm$^{-1}$

Assume all of the chlorine in the feed is converted to HCl. Does the incinerator comply with the EPA rules?

**Answer:** Incinerator fails to comply with HCl limits and with particulate limits.

**13-22** During a trial burn, an incinerator was fed a mixed feed containing trichloroethylene, 1,1,1-trichloroethane, and toluene in an aqueous solution. Each component accounted for 5.0% of the feed solution on a volume basis. The feed rate was $40 \text{ L} \cdot \text{min}^{-1}$. The incinerator was operated at a temperature of 1200°C. The stack gas flow rate was 9.0 dscm $\cdot$ s$^{-1}$ with 7% oxygen. Assuming that all the chlorine in the feed is converted to HCl, is the unit in compliance with the following emissions measured after the APC equipment?

Trichloroethylene = $170 \ \mu\text{g} \cdot \text{dscm}^{-1}$       HCl = $83.2 \text{ mg} \cdot \text{dscm}^{-1}$

1,1,1-Trichloroethane = $353 \ \mu\text{g} \cdot \text{dscm}^{-1}$      Particulates = $123.4 \text{ mg} \cdot \text{dscm}^{-1}$

Toluene = $28 \ \mu\text{g} \cdot \text{dscm}^{-1}$

**13-23** During a trial burn, an incinerator was fed a mixed feed containing hexachlorobenzene (HCB), pentachlorophenol (PCP), and acetone (ACET) in an aqueous solution. Each component accounted for 9.3% of the feed solution on a volume basis, that is, HCB = 9.3%, PCP = 9.3%, and ACET = 9.3%. The feed rate was $140 \text{ L} \cdot \text{min}^{-1}$. The incinerator was operated at a temperature of 1200°C. The stack gas flow rate was 28.32 dscm $\cdot$ s$^{-1}$ with 14% oxygen. Assuming that all the chlorine in the feed is converted to HCl, is the unit in compliance if the following emissions are measured downstream of the APC equipment?

Hexachlorobenzene = $170 \ \mu\text{g} \cdot \text{dscm}^{-1}$      HCl = $83.2 \ \mu\text{g} \cdot \text{dscm}^{-1}$

Pentachlorophenol = $353 \ \mu\text{g} \cdot \text{dscm}^{-1}$      Particulates = $123.4 \text{ mg} \cdot \text{dscm}^{-1}$

Acetone = $28 \ \mu\text{g} \cdot \text{dscm}^{-1}$

**Answer:** Incinerator complies with all emission limits except particulates.

**13-24** A standard permeameter is being considered for testing a clay for a hazardous waste landfill base. If the clay must have a hydraulic conductivity of $10^{-7} \text{ cm} \cdot \text{s}^{-1}$ and the dimensions of the permeameter are as shown here, how long will the test take if a minimum of 100.0 mL of liquid must be collected for an accurate measurement? See Figure P-13-24 for notation and permeameter equation.

$L = 10 \text{ cm}$

$h = 1 \text{ m}$

Diameter of sample = 5.0 cm

*Figure P-13-24*

Standard constant head permeater equation:

$$K = \frac{QL}{hAt}$$

where $K$ = hydraulic conductivity
    $Q$ = quantity of discharge
    $L$ = length of sample
    $h$ = hydraulic head
    $A$ = cross-sectioned area of sample
    $t$ = time

**13-25** A soil sample has been tested to determine hydraulic conductivity using a falling-head permeameter (Figure P-13-25). The following data were recorded:

Diameter of a = 1 mm      Initial head = 1.0 m

Diameter of $A$ = 10 cm      Final head = 25 cm

Length, $L$ = 25 cm      Duration of test = 14 days

*Figure P-13–25*

Falling head permeater equation:

$$K = 2.3 \frac{aL}{At} \log\left(\frac{h_0}{h_1}\right)$$

where $K$ = hydraulic conductivity
$a$ = cross-sectional area of stand pipe
$A$ = cross-sectional area of sample
$L$ = length of sample
$t$ = time
$h_0, h_1$ = head at beginning of test
and at time, $t$, respectively

From these data, calculate the hydraulic conductivity of the sample. Assuming the sample is representative of the landfill site, is this a good soil for a hazardous waste landfill base?

**Answer:** $2.86 \times 10^{-9}$ cm $\cdot$ s$^{-1}$

**13–26** An old hazardous waste landfill was built on a 10-m deep clay liner. An aquifer lies immediately below the clay layer. The clay layer through which the leachate must pass has a hydraulic conductivity of $1 \times 10^{-7}$ cm $\cdot$ s$^{-1}$. If the liquid level (leachate) is 1.0 m deep above the clay layer how much leachate (in cubic meters per day) will reach the aquifer when the clay layer becomes saturated? Assume Darcy's law applies.

**13–27** The three soil layers described here lie between the bottom of a hazardous waste landfill and the underlying aquifer. The depth of leachate above the top soil layer is 0.3 m. How long will it take (in years) for the leachate to migrate to an aquifer located at the bottom of soil C?

**Soil A**
    Depth = 3.0 m
    Hydraulic conductivity = $1.8 \times 10^{-7}$ cm $\cdot$ s$^{-1}$
    Porosity = 55%

**Soil B**
    Depth = 10 m
    Hydraulic conductivity = $2.2 \times 10^{-5}$ m $\cdot$ s$^{-1}$
    Porosity = 25%

**Soil C**
    Depth = 12.0 m
    Hydraulic conductivity = $5.3 \times 10^{-5}$ mm $\cdot$ s$^{-1}$
    Porosity = 35%

**Answer:** 28 years

**13–28** The practical quantitation limit (PQL) for the solvent trichloroethylene is 5 $\mu$g $\cdot$ L$^{-1}$. If a barrel (approximately 0.12 m$^3$) of spent solvent leaked into an aquifer, approximately how many cubic meters of water would be contaminated at the PQL?

## DISCUSSION QUESTIONS

**13–1** What was the outcome of the hazardous waste episode at Times Beach? (*Hint:* You will need to do an Internet search.)

**13–2** Does the "land ban" actually ban the disposal of hazardous waste on the land? Explain.

**13–3** A multimillion dollar company has just learned that one drum out of several hundred found at an abandoned waste disposal site has been identified as theirs. Their attorney explains that they may be potentially responsible for cleanup of all the drums at the site if no other former owners of the drums can be identified. Is this correct? Why or why not?

**13–4** Your boss has proposed that your company institute a recycling program to minimize the generation of waste. Is recycling the best first step to investigate in a waste minimization program? If not, what others would you suggest and in what order?

**13–5** A metal plater is proposing to treat his waste sludge to recover the nickel from it. Would this be

(a) Recycling    (b) Reusing    (c) Reclaiming

State the correct answer(s) and explain why you made your choice(s).

**13–6** It is not necessary to measure every POHC in an incinerator trial burn. True or false? Explain your answer.

## ADDITIONAL READING

### Books

Anderson, W. C., ed., *Innovative Site Remediation Technology,* Volumes 1–8, American Academy of Environmental Engineers, Annapolis, MD (1995).

Bellandi, R., ed., *Hazardous Waste Site Remediation, The Engineers Perspective,* Van Nostrand Reinhold, New York (1988).

Davis, M., and D. Cornwell. *Introduction to Environmental Engineering,* 3rd ed. McGraw-Hill, New York (1998).

Fortuna, R. C., and D. J. Lennett, *Hazardous Waste Regulations, The New Era,* McGraw-Hill, New York (1988).

Freeman, H. M., ed., *Hazardous Waste Minimization,* McGraw-Hill, New York (1990).

Freeman, H. M., ed., *Standard Handbook of Hazardous Waste Treatment and Disposal, 2nd ed.,* McGraw-Hill, New York (1998).

Griffin, R. D., *Principles of Hazardous Materials Management,* Lewis Publishers, Ann Arbor, MI (1988).

Haas, C. N., and R. J. Vamos, *Hazardous and Industrial Waste Treatment,* Prentice Hall, Upper Saddle River, NJ (1995).

Hasan, S., *Geology and Hazardous Waste Management,* Prentice Hall, Upper Saddle River, NJ (1996).

Higgins, T., *Hazardous Waste Minimization Handbook,* Lewis Publishers, Chelsea, MI (1989).

Kamrin, M. A., *Toxicology,* Lewis Publishers, Chelsea, MI (1988).

LaGrega, M. D., P. L. Buckingham, and J. C. Evas, *Hazardous Waste Management,* McGraw-Hill, New York (1994).

Paustenbach, D. J., ed., The *Risk Assessment of Environmental Hazards,* John Wiley, New York (1989).

Quarles, J., *Federal Regulation of Hazardous Wastes,* The Environmental Law Institute, Washington, DC (1982).

Wentz, C. A., *Hazardous Waste Management,* McGraw-Hill, New York (1989).

Wood, E. F., R. A. Ferrara, W. G. Gray, and G. F. Hinder, *Groundwater Contamination from Hazardous Wastes,* Prentice Hall, Upper Saddle River, NJ (1984).

### Journals

*Environmental Progress*

*Environmental Science and Technology*

*Hazardous Waste and Hazardous Materials*

*Journal of Air and Waste Management Association* (formerly *Journal of the Air Pollution Control Association*)

## REFERENCES

1. Hileman, B., "Leaked dioxin report stokes controversy," *C&E News,* p. 13, May 29, 2000.
2. Penning, C. H., "Physical characteristics and commercial possibility of chlorinated diphenyl," *Industrial & Engineering Chemistry,* vol. 22, pp. 1180–1183, 1930.
3. *Code of Federal Regulations,* 40 CFR 260, July 1, 1989. *Note:* CFR means Code of Federal Regulations. The prefix number refers to the volume. Each agency (EPA, DOT, FAA, NRC) has a volume prefix. The suffix number is the paragraph number that spells out the regulation.

4. U.S. Environmental Protection Agency, *RCRA Orientation Manual* (U.S. Environmental Protection Agency Office of Solid Waste, Publication No. EPA/530-SW-86-001), Washington, DC: U.S. Government Printing Office, January 1986.

5. 59 FR 47980,18 SEP 1994. Corrections to the UTS were published on January 3, 1995, 60 FR 242.

6. Portions of this discussion were excerpted from J. B. Bair, "Underground storage tanks (UST)," *Michigan Environmental Law Journal,* vol. 8, no. 2, p. 2, 1989.

7. Wentz, C. A., *Hazardous Waste Management,* McGraw-Hill, New York: pp. 206–207, 277–279, 392–403, 1989.

8. 40 CFR 300, Appendix A, 1 JUL 1994 and 55 FR 51583, 14 DEC 1990.

9. Parts of this discussion were excerpted from O'Brien & Gere Engineers Inc., *Hazardous Waste Site Remediation,* Van Nostrand Reinhold, New York: pp. 11–13, 1988.

10. 40 CFR 300.400, Subpart E, 1 JUL 1994 and 55 FR 8839, 8 MAR 1990.

11. Portions of this discussion were excerpted from C. H. Fromm, A. Bachrach, and M. S. Callahan, "Overview of waste minimization issues, approaches and techniques." In *Transactions of an APCA International Specialty Conference on Performance and Costs of Alternatives to Land Disposal of Hazardous Waste,* E. T. Oppelt, B. L. Blaney, and W. F. Kemner, eds., Pittsburgh, PA. Air Pollution Control Association, pp. 6–20, 1986.

12. *Waste Minimization Opportunity Assessment Manual* (U.S. Environmental Protection Agency Publication No. EPA/625/7-88/003), Cincinnati: Hazardous Waste Engineering Research Lab., p. 2, July 1988.

13. This discussion follows that of H. Kobayashi and B. P. Rittman, "Microbial removal of hazardous organic compounds," *Environmental Science and Technology,* vol. 16, pp. 170A–172A, 1982.

14. Herzbnin, P. A., R. L. Irvine, and K. C. Malinowski, "Biological treatment of hazardous waste in sequencing batch reactors," *Journal of the Water Pollution Control Federation,* vol. 57, pp. 1163–1167, 1985.

15. Gross, R. L., and S. G. TerMaath, "Packed tower aeration strips trichloroethylene from Groundwater," *Environmental Progress,* vol. 4, pp. 119–124, May 1985; U.S. Environmental Protection Agency, *A Compendium of Technologies Used in the Treatment of Hazardous Waste* (U.S. Environmental Protection Agency Publication No. EPA/625/8-87/014), Cincinnati: Center for Environmental Research Information, September 1987.

16. U.S. Environmental Protection Agency, *A Compendium of Technologies Used in the Treatment of Hazardous Waste,* September 1987.

17. Oppelt, E. T., "Thermal destruction options for controlling hazardous wastes," *Civil Engineering ASCE,* pp. 72–75, September 1981.

18. Portions of this discussion were excerpted from L. Theodore and J. Reynolds, *Introduction to Hazardous Waste Incineration,* Wiley, New York: pp. 76–85, 1987.

19. U.S. Environmental Protection Agency, *Best Demonstrated Available Technology (BDAT) Background Document for FOO6* (U.S. Environmental Protection Agency Publication No. EPA/530-SW-88-0009-I), Washington, DC: U.S. Government Printing Office, May 1988.

20. *Federal Register,* 55 FR 26986, June 29, 1990.

21. Warner, D. L., "Subsurface injection of liquid hazardous wastes," In *Standard Handbook of Hazardous Waste Treatment and Disposal, 2nd ed.,* edited by H. M. Freeman, McGraw-Hill, New York: pp. 10.46–10.58, 1998.

22. *Federal Register,* 55 FR 22530, June 1, 1990.

23. Wood, E. F., R. A. Ferrara, W. G. Gray, and G. F. Pinder, *Groundwater Contamination from Hazardous Waste,* Prentice Hall, Englewood Cliffs, NJ: pp. 2–4, 145–158, 1984.

24. This discussion follows that reported by J. Josephson, "Hazardous waste landfill," *Environmental Science and Technology,* vol. 15(3), p. 250, March 1981.

25. *Federal Register,* 57 FR 3462, 29 JAN 1992.

26. U.S. EPA
http://www.epa.gov/superfund/sites/

27. Portions of this discussion were excerpted from R. D. Griffin, *Principles of Hazardous Materials Management,* Lewis Publishers, Ann Arbor, MI: 1988.

# 14

# Agriculture and the Environment*

---

*This chapter was written by Dr. Simon Davies, Department of Agricultural Engineering, Michigan State University.

## 14–1 INTRODUCTION

Agriculture is essential to modern society because it meets our needs for food and fiber. Once most of the workforce was engaged in agriculture; for example, in 1840 nearly 70% of the workforce in the United States were farmers or farm laborers. Agriculture has changed dramatically in the 20th century, especially since the end of World War II; now less than 3% of the population produces the majority of the food and fiber consumed in the United States. However, agriculture is still an important industry. In 1999 farms in the United States produced goods with a value of almost $100 billion. The great increase in agricultural productivity has had many positive effects. However, the need to meet the food and fiber needs of a growing population puts further pressure on limited natural resources, in the United States and elsewhere.

About half of the land area of the United States has been converted to cropland, pastureland, and rangeland. Aside from the obvious effects of the conversion of natural habitats to agricultural use, agriculture has had other effects on the environment, including depleting surface and groundwater resources, increasing erosion, and producing deleterious effects on air and water quality. The widespread use of irrigation has helped agriculture to prosper in arid and semiarid areas. Agriculture in the western United States relies heavily on irrigation, and in many cases the availability of water is a major limiting factor in the growth of agricultural production in these areas. In the past, overgrazing and poor cropping practices lead to major losses of soil from pasture and croplands in some areas of the country. Though much reduced, soil erosion continues to be a serious threat to the environment and the productivity of agricultural land. Agriculture has had an adverse effect on water quality in many areas. The major water quality problems are salinization and contamination of ground and surface waters by nutrients and pesticides. The effects of agricultural activities on air quality are widespread and include smoke from agricultural burning; dust from open feedlots, tillage, and harvesting; pesticide drift from spraying; and emissions of odorous compounds and methane and other greenhouse gases from agricultural operations.

## 14–2 DEPLETION OF SURFACE AND GROUNDWATER RESOURCES

### Water Use

Water use for irrigation is by far the largest consumptive use of water diverted from streams or withdrawn from aquifers in the United States. In 1990, the average daily withdrawals of water for irrigation purposes was about $517 \times 10^6 \, \mathrm{m}^3$, of this amount $288 \times 10^6 \, \mathrm{m}^3 \cdot \mathrm{day}^{-1}$ was consumed. During that year, the water consumption rate for governments, businesses, and households combined was $25.6 \times 10^6 \, \mathrm{m}^3 \cdot \mathrm{day}^{-1}$.

About 86% of the irrigated land in the United States is in the West. Irrigation is critical to crop agriculture in the semiarid West. In addition, eastern farmers may use supplemental irrigation to increase the number of plantings per year and yield per acre, or to supplement any lack of precipitation during droughts.

In the West conflicting demands for water supplies are common. California, in particular, has become very concerned about being able to balance the water needs of agriculture, its growing urban population, and the environment. An example of the controversy that can arise over water rights is the recent actions proposed to protect fisheries and wildlife in the Sacramento Delta in California. The watershed of the Delta provides drinking water to two thirds of the state's population and it supplies some of the state's most productive agricultural areas. The Bay Delta Estuary itself is one of the largest ecosystems for fish and wildlife habitat and production in the United States. Historical and current human activities (e.g., water development, land use, wastewater discharges, introduced species, and harvesting) have degraded the beneficial uses of the

Bay Delta Estuary, as evidenced by the declines in the populations of many biological resources of the estuary. In an effort to reverse this decline, the State of California has proposed that some of the water now diverted from the delta be allowed to flow into the delta. This action created considerable controversy because it affects the water rights of other users.

### Land Subsidence

**Land subsidence,** the loss of surface elevation due to removal of subsurface support, occurs in nearly every state. Common causes of land subsidence from human activity are pumping water, oil, and gas from underground reservoirs; the collapse of underground mines, and the drainage of organic soils. Some of the worst problems are seen in the San Joaquin Valley in California where massive groundwater withdrawals have lead to widespread subsidence. As is shown in Figure 14–1 the loss of surface elevation can be dramatic. The sign on the top of the pole shows where the land surface was back in 1925. In this picture, taken in 1977, the land surface has dropped nearly 9 m during that time.

Many problems result from land subsidence, including

- Damage to bridges, roads, drains, well casings, buildings and other structures.
- Flooding and changes in streamflow patterns.

**FIGURE 14–1**

Land subsidence in the San Joaquin Valley, 10 miles southwest of Mendota, CA. (*Source:* US Geological Survey Professional Paper 1401-A, *Ground Water in the Central Valley, California—A Summary Report* Photo by Dick Ireland, USGS, 1977.)

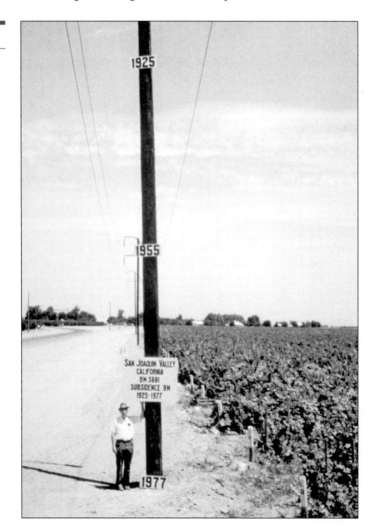

- Loss of groundwater storage. In California more groundwater storage has been lost as a result of subsidence than the volume of all aboveground water storage reservoirs built in the state combined.

The economic damage caused by land subsidence can be significant, for example, the annual cost of subsidence mitigation in the San Joaquin Valley alone is over $180 million.

## 14-3  SOIL EROSION

The problem of soil erosion has been recognized for a long time. The Soil Conservation Service (SCS), now called the Natural Resources Conservation Service (NRCS) was formed in response to the Dust Bowl catastrophe of the mid-1930s. The SCS established a nationwide partnership of federal agencies, local conservation districts, and communities to provide assistance to the rural and urban sectors for the conservation of soil and other natural resources. Through the efforts of these partnerships soil erosion on agricultural land has declined considerably.

Soil erosion due to overgrazing on pasturelands and rangelands and loss of soil from croplands is still a major problem in the United States. In 1997, an estimated 1.7 Pg of soil was lost from cropland and Conservation Reserve Program (CRP)* land in the United States. This translates into an on-farm economic loss of more than $27 billion each year, of which $20 billion is for replacement of nutrients and $7 billion for lost water and soil.

In addition to the economic effect on farmers, erosion can have serious impacts on the environment, including

- Pollution of lakes and streams by nutrients, particularly phosphorus, and agricultural chemicals that are washed away with the soil.
- Flooding due to silt build-up in drains and waterways.
- Build-up of sediments in wetlands, which can lead to serious environmental problems or even loss of these habitats.
- Siltation in reservoirs, which reduces their capacity.
- Siltation in harbors and waterways. The cost for dredging of harbors and waterways in the United States is estimated to be $1 billion per year.

Both water and wind can erode cropland soils. Water erosion results from the removal of soil material by flowing water. When a raindrop strikes the soil surface it can break up soil aggregates. On a slope, water begins to flow downhill carrying the detached soil grains with it. Wind erosion occurs in regions of low rainfall; it can be widespread, especially during periods of drought. Unlike water erosion, wind erosion is generally not related to slope gradient.

As shown in Figure 14–2, water erosion occurs mainly in areas east of the Corn Belt and Southern Plains. Wind erosion takes place mostly in the West, Northern Plains, and Southern Plains. Both water and wind erosion result in major losses of soil from agricultural land. In 1997, erosion due to water on crop and CRP lands was nearly $1.0\,\text{Pg} \cdot \text{year}^{-1}$ and about $0.75\,\text{Pg} \cdot \text{year}^{-1}$ of soil was lost due to wind erosion.

As shown in Figure 14–3, the conservation practices adopted over the past two decades have considerably reduced soil erosion on agricultural lands. The widespread adoption of conservation tillage practices is one of the major contributors to this improvement. Conventional tillage breaks up and buries the crop residue from the previous planting, creating a bare soil surface, which is vulnerable to erosion. Conservation tillage is the practice of leaving some or all of the crop residues on the soil surface to protect it like a mulch. In addition to protecting the soil from erosion

---

*The CRP is a federal program to set aside cropland with the goals of reducing soil erosion, reducing production of surplus commodities, providing income support for farmers, improving environmental quality, and enhancing wildlife habitat.

## FIGURE 14–2

This dot map shows tons of erosion due to wind and water on cropland and CRP land. Each gray dot represents 181 Gg (200,000 tons) of average annual erosion due to water. Each green dot represents 181 Gg (200,000 tons) of average annual erosion due to wind. (*Source:* US Department of Agriculture, National Resource Conservation Service. http://www.nrcs.usda .gov/technical/land/ meta/m5112.html.)

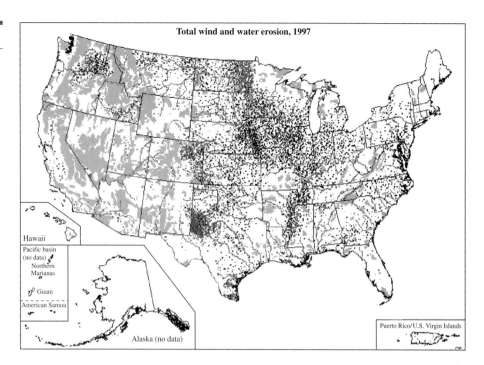

Total wind and water erosion, 1997

## FIGURE 14–3

Wind and water erosion on crop and CRP land from 1982 to 1997. (*Source of data:* US Department of Agriculture, National Resource Conservation Service. http://www.nrcs.usda .gov/technical/land/ meta/m5852.html)

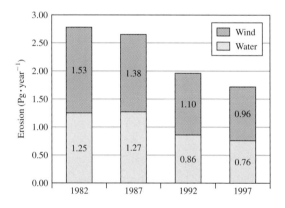

the mulch creates an environment that conserves water in the soil. Conservation tillage has some drawbacks, one of which is an increased dependence on herbicides for weed control. Other practices such as terracing, contour tillage, and crop rotation have helped to reduce water erosion. Diversion of water away from fields or other erosion-sensitive areas can also reduce soil loss.

Measures used to control wind erosion on croplands include conservation tillage, planting windbreaks, and tilling at right angles to the prevailing winds, so that furrows act as small windbreaks to capture blowing soil. Erosion on pastureland and rangeland can be reduced by a number of measures, the single most important of which is control of animal numbers. Animal numbers must be controlled, so that as forage is consumed regrowth has a chance to replace it. For maximum sustained production, plants must be given a period of rest to rebuild these reserves. During droughts the numbers of grazing animals must be tightly controlled, as plants can be injured by a grazing intensity that would not injure them during a less vulnerable season. Proper distribution of animals is also an important grazing management tool. Fences can be used to divide up pastures. On open range land one of the most effective techniques is to provide adequate water facilities that are properly distributed. Ranchers also improve livestock distribution by placing salt and mineral supplies in widespread locations to draw the animals to those areas.

Effective management of soil erosion requires the ability to quantitatively predict the amount of soil loss that would occur under alternative management strategies and practices. Various models have been devised to predict soil loss. The model with the greatest acceptance and use is the universal soil loss equation (USLE) (see Section 7–9). The USLE was developed by U.S. Department of Agriculture's Agricultural Research Service by statistical analyses of rainfall, runoff, and sediment loss data from many small plots located around the United States and has since been modified to improve its predictions [1].

**EXAMPLE 14–1**   A farmer grows corn in Benzie County, MI. The fields on the farm are normally tilled in the spring. One of the fields on the farm is on a hillside, it is 800 ft long with a 6% slope. The soil in this field consists of fine sandy loam soil with an average organic matter content. The field is plowed in the spring and planted with grain corn. The farmer wishes to determine if conservation tillage is needed in this field.

Solution   $A = (R)(K)(LS)(C)(P)$

*Rainfall and runoff factor* $(R)$   From the USDA database the $R$ for this area is 100 (see Figure 7–19)

*Soil erodibility factor* $(K)$   The $K$ factor for this soil is 0.18.

*Slope length-gradient factor* (LS)   The LS factor can be obtained directly or may be calculated using the equation

$$LS = [0.065 + 0.0456\,s + 0.0065\,s^2]\left(\frac{l}{72.5}\right)^{NN}$$

where $s$ = slope steepness (%)
   $l$ = length of slope (ft)
   NN = empirical constant that depends on slope (in this example NN = 0.5)

The LS factor is 1.90

*Crop/vegetation and management factor* $(C)$   The crop type factor is 0.4. The tillage method factor for spring plow is 0.9.

$C$ factor $= 0.4 \times 0.9 = 0.36$

*Support practice factor* $(P)$   Cross slope farming is used on this field. The $P$ factor is 0.75

$A = (R)(K)(LS)(C)(P)$
   $= 100 \times 0.18 \times 1.90 \times 0.36 \times 0.75$
   $= 9.24$ tons $\cdot$ acre$^{-1}$ $\cdot$ year

This soil loss rate of 9.24 tons $\cdot$ acre$^{-1}$ $\cdot$ year is in the moderate range and considerably higher than the "tolerable loss level" of 3 tons $\cdot$ acre$^{-1}$ $\cdot$ year. To reduce the soil losses from this field changes in tillage practice need to be made. By changing the tillage method factor from "spring plow" (tillage method factor 0.9) to "no-till" (tillage method factor 0.25) the $C$ factor is reduced to 0.10. The adjusted annual soil loss value is

$A = (R)(K)(LS)(C)(P)$
   $= 100 \times 0.18 \times 1.90 \times 0.10 \times 0.75$
   $= 2.57$ tons $\cdot$ acre$^{-1}$ $\cdot$ year

which is below the "tolerable soil loss" of 3 tons $\cdot$ acre$^{-1}$ $\cdot$ year.

The wind erosion equation (WEQ) can be used to predict long-term average annual soil losses from a field having specific characteristics. The form of the equation is

$$E = f(IKCLV)$$

where $E =$ estimated average annual soil loss
$\quad I =$ soil erodibility
$\quad K =$ ridge roughness factor
$\quad C =$ climatic factor
$\quad L =$ equivalent unsheltered distance across the field along the prevailing wind erosion direction
$\quad V =$ equivalent vegetative cover

WEQ is an empirical relationship developed primarily from laboratory and field wind tunnel studies in the 1960s [2]. It is still widely used to predict wind erosion. The equation has a number of limitations, including

- It estimates an average annual soil loss. As factors such as vegetative cover vary with season, soil loss also varies seasonally. The model does not take account of this variation.
- Many modern farming systems are not recognized by WEQ.

Consequently, estimates of wind erosion made using WEQ are questionable. The release of the revised wind erosion equation RWEQ, allows advanced farming practices to be evaluated. However, many researchers prefer more sophisticated, process-based erosion models, such as the wind erosion prediction system (WEPS) [3].

## 14–4 WATER QUALITY

The major sources of water quality impairment from agriculture are salts, nutrients (nitrogen and phosphorus), and pesticides.

### Salinization

Much of the water available in the western United States is saline. In many cases the water is "naturally" saline because salts dissolve in the water as it percolates through the soil or rock formations. However, the widespread use of water for irrigation in arid or semiarid areas has increased salinity problems. Evaporation of water from open reservoirs and canals and during application to plants increases salinity. Also, as plants transpire the salts remain in the soil. Salinity problems can also occur when there is shallow saline water table. Irrigation raises the water table, which causes upward movement of saline groundwater into the root zone. Salt accumulation in agricultural soils can lead to a reduction in crop yield, particularly in crops that are sensitive to salinity such as corn, soybeans, rice, lettuce, squash, onion, and bell peppers. Some saline soils can be reclaimed by applying sufficient water to the soil to leach the solutes from the root zone. However, the leaching process may degrade groundwater quality.

Increasing salinity can also cause serious problems in surface waters. As irrigation water percolates through the soil and returns to the river (called return flow or interflow), the salinity increases. The salt concentration increases from the river head waters to the mouth as it is used and reused for irrigation as it flows downstream.

To illustrate this problem we will consider the example of the Salton Sea. The Salton Sea is the largest inland body of water west of the Rockies (surface area of 98,600 ha). It was formed in 1905 when massive flooding caused the Colorado River to break through an irrigation canal headwork and flow freely into the Salton Basin for 18 months. Since then, the sea's existence has been maintained primarily by agricultural return flows from the Imperial, Coachella, and Mexicali valleys. The sea has become a key stop on the Pacific flyway for many species of migratory birds. The Salton Sea National Wildlife Refuge supports over 380 species of birds, among the highest totals of all national refuges. The Salton Sea provides important habitat for several endangered species, including the desert pupfish, Yuma clapper rail, and brown pelican, and it is an important sport fishery.

The Salton Sea is beset by several serious water quality problems. Because it has no outlet, the salt, nutrients, and other pollutants that flow into it are retained within its waters and sediments. Increasing salinity is one of the most serious of these environmental problems. The sea's salinity has been gradually increasing and it has now reached 44 parts per thousand, about 25% higher than ocean water. Many of the native freshwater fish species have disappeared. Beginning in the 1950s, the California Department of Fish and Game introduced marine fish, including orange-mouthed corvina, sargo, gulf croaker, and tilapia, into the Salton Sea. The sea may be becoming too saline for even the marine fish, and the elevated salinity is thought to partially explain the decline in orange-mouthed corvina, the most popular sportfish.

The alternative management options to reducing the effects of irrigation on water quality fall into five categories: (1) source control measures, (2) drainage water reuse, (3) drainage water treatment, (4) drainage water disposal, and (5) institutional changes.

**Source Control.** Irrigation project control measures include using demand schedules, which control the frequency, rate, and duration of water delivery to meet crop water needs. This can be achieved by monitoring soil or crop parameters or by computing the soil–water balance. The first method involves measuring the soil water content or matrix potential (described in Chapter 7) or the leaf water potential. The second method involves a water balance based on an estimate of the storage capacity of water in the soil, crop rooting depth, allowable soil water depletion, and crop evapotranspiration.

There are five basic methods for applying irrigation water: flooding, furrow irrigation, sprinkling, subirrigation, and trickle irrigation. Flooding is relatively inexpensive and it requires a minimum of preparation. Water is brought to the field in permanent ditches and distributed across the fields either by smaller ditches, by overland flow, or by flooding relatively level plots that have been diked. A narrow ditch between rows of plants is used to convey water in furrow irrigation. An important advantage of furrow irrigation is that only 20–50% of the surface area is wetted compared with flooding. This results in reduced evaporation losses. Sprinkler systems are more expensive but can yield advantages in reducing runoff and erosion. In a few areas soil conditions are favorable for subirrigation. A permeable soil in the root zone that is underlain by an impermeable soil layer or a high water table is required. Water is delivered to the field in widely spaced ditches (15–30 m) at a rate that maintains the water table close to the capillary fringe that the plants draw their water from. In trickle or drip irrigation, a perforated pipe is laid along the base of a row of plants. The perforations are designed to allow a flow of $5 \text{ L} \cdot \text{h}^{-1}$ or less and are spaced to produce a wet strip along the crop row. Evaporation from trickle irrigation is minimal, and deep percolation is almost entirely avoided.

Each of these water application methods has advantages and disadvantages. Application efficiency is measured in terms of uniformity of application, deep percolation ratios, and tail-water ratios. The surface methods fall in the range of 50 to 70% compared with the sprinkler and drip systems that are in the range of 75 to 90% [4].

**Drainage Water Reuse.** A second management option is to reuse the drainage water until it is no longer usable. High-quality water is used to irrigate the more salt-sensitive crops. The subsurface drainage from the salt-sensitive crops is used to irrigate more salt-tolerant plants. This process is repeated until the salt concentration is too high for the halophytes that are most salt-tolerant.

**Drainage Water Treatment.** The third management alternative is to treat the water. Reverse osmosis has shown the greatest potential for desalinization of agricultural drainage water. However, the cost is high ($\$880 \cdot 1000 \text{ m}^{-3}$) compared with the cost of raw water ($\$10–20 \cdot 1000 \text{ m}^{-3}$). With reverse osmosis, the brine produced during treatment must still be disposed of.

**Drainage Water Disposal.**   The fourth management option is disposal of the drainage water. Other than return flow, which increases the salinity of the receiving body, the options are disposal in agricultural evaporation ponds and deep well injection. The evaporation ponds occupy a large land area and deep well injection is expensive.

**Institutional Changes.**   Institutional changes to reduce the effect of agriculture on water quality include land retirement or idling, tiered water pricing, water marketing and transfer, and regional planning. The first option essentially means giving up the land for agricultural purposes. Tiered water pricing forces economic choices of minimizing evaporation and percolation losses versus higher water costs for excessive use. Water marketing simply means finding available water outside of the watershed and importing it.

### Nutrients

The release of nutrients from agricultural operations can occur due to the loss of nutrients in runoff or seepage from croplands, rupture of manure storage lagoons, failure of the liner in a manure storage lagoon or the accidental spillage of fertilizers. The loss of nutrients in runoff or seepage from croplands is the major source of nutrient release from agricultural operations.

An adequate supply of the nutrients, such as nitrogen, phosphorus, and potassium, and maintenance of proper soil pH are essential to crop growth. Fertilizers have long been used to increase crop yields. The value of silt deposits from flooding rivers in maintaining soil productivity was recognized more than 5000 years ago by the early Egyptians living along the Nile River. Organic manures have been used in Chinese agriculture for over 3000 years. Today farmers employ both chemical fertilizers and manure to increase crop yield. Intensive crop production like that employed in the United States today requires the addition of fertilizers to sustain crop yields. The most widely used fertilizers are lime (to maintain a proper soil pH), nitrogen (N), phosphorus (P), and potassium (K). The used of lime or K fertilizers causes few environmental problems; however, widespread problems are associated with the use of N and P fertilizers. The primary issues of concern are the eutrophication of surface waters and the contamination of groundwaters with nitrate.

**N and P Cycles on Crop and Grazing Land.**   Figure 7–14 illustrates the complexity of the nitrogen cycle in the soil ecosystem. Nitrogen exists in the soil in both organic and inorganic forms. The principal inorganic forms of N are $NH_3$ or $NH_4^+$ (ammoniacal nitrogen) and nitrate. Usually, over 90% of soil nitrogen is associated with soil organic matter. Plants cannot use organic nitrogen; however, bacteria present in the soil can transform organic N into inorganic N, which is then available to plants. This conversion is called mineralization. The rate of conversion depends on soil moisture conditions, soil acidity, temperature, and microbial activity. The rate of mineralization of organic N in soils is slow, typically, only 15–30% of the organic nitrogen present in the soil is converted to inorganic nitrogen during a growing season. To ensure optimal plant growth nitrogen is usually added to the soil in the form of manure or commercial (chemical) fertilizer. Nitrogen in manure exists primarily in organic and ammoniacal forms. In fresh manure 60–80% of the N exists in the organic form; however, during storage a significant fraction of the organic nitrogen in the manure is converted to ammonia. The most common forms of commercial fertilizer are ammonium nitrate and anhydrous ammonia ($NH_3$).

Continuous cropping of land with a single crop can result in the depletion of the nutrients in the soil. Crop rotation, which is a planned sequence of growing different crops in the same field, is often used, as an alternative to fertilizers, to improve soil fertility. Because legumes (e.g., soybeans) have the ability to fix nitrogen from the atmosphere, they are used in a crop rotation to restore nitrogen to the soil. The growing of legumes also improves the structure of the soil.

Losses of nitrogen from the soil environment may occur as the result of surface runoff; leaching of nitrate; or the release of nitrogen gas ($N_2$), nitrous oxide ($N_2O$), and ammonia to the atmosphere.

**Leaching.**  Although the mobility of ammoniacal and organic nitrogen in the soil environment is limited, nitrate is very mobile. Consequently, leaching losses occur when nitrate is present in the soil water and there is downward movement of water in the soil. Leaching is more likely to occur when rainfall is high. Nitrate can occur in soils if it is added as a fertilizer or if oxygen is present in the soil. If oxygen is present, then the microorganisms present in the soil can convert ammonia to nitrate (nitrification).

**Denitrification.**  A mechanism of nitrogen loss, particularly in waterlogged soils, is denitrification. If oxygen is not present in the soil, then denitrifying bacteria can convert nitrate to nitrogen and nitrous oxide, which can be lost to the atmosphere.

Volatilization of ammonia gas to the atmosphere can also result in nitrogen losses. These losses can be minimized through proper management of fertilizer applications. Anhydrous ammonia must be knifed into the soil to a depth of 8–15 cm, and the soil must be closed behind the applicator shank. Manure should be injected into the soil or if it is applied by spreading. It should be incorporated into the soil using a plough.

The cycling of phosphorus in the soil environment is illustrated in Figure 7–15. Phosphorus can exist in soils in both organic and inorganic forms, the fraction in each form varying greatly, depending on the type of soil. The predominant forms of inorganic phosphorus in the soil environment are dihydrogen phosphate, $H_2PO_4^-$ and monohydrogen phosphate, $HPO_4^{2-}$. Some of the phosphorus may be "available" to plants (i.e., not tightly bound to soil particles); however, most of the phosphorus in the soil is present in a "fixed" form (i.e., tightly bound to the soil particles). The amount of soluble phosphorus present is very small. The mobility of P in the soil is limited; most of the P taken up by a crop during a growing season will probably have moved only a few centimeters or less through the soil to the roots. The soluble P pool is important because it is the pool from which plants take up P and is the only pool that has any measurable mobility in the soil environment.

The phosphate in fertilizers and manure is initially quite soluble and available to plants. Most phosphate fertilizers have been manufactured by treating rock phosphate (the phosphate-bearing mineral that is mined) with acid to make it more soluble. Manure contains soluble phosphate, organic phosphate, and inorganic phosphate compounds that are quite available. When the fertilizer or manure phosphate comes in contact with the soil, various reactions begin occurring that make the phosphate less soluble and less available. The rates and products of these reactions depend on such soil conditions as pH, moisture content, temperature, and the minerals already present in the soil.

**Effect of Fertilizer Use on Surface Water Quality.**  Generally, phosphorus is the limiting nutrient in freshwater aquatic systems, such as lakes. In contrast to freshwater systems, nitrogen is generally the primary limiting nutrient in the seaward portions of estuarine systems. Estuarine waters may be phosphorus-limited when nitrogen concentrations are high and the ratio N:P ratio > 16:1. In such cases, excess phosphorus may trigger eutrophic conditions.

The effect of agriculture on surface water systems can be illustrated by the example of Chesapeake Bay. The Chesapeake Bay is North America's largest estuary. Its watershed covers 166,000 $km^2$ and encompasses parts of six states: Delaware, Maryland, New York, Pennsylvania, Virginia, and West Virginia, as well as the District of Columbia. Excess nutrient inputs into the bay have caused eutrophication and periods of hypoxia (dissolved-oxygen concentrations lower than $1.0 \, mg \cdot L^{-1}$), which in turn have killed or stressed living resources in many areas of the bay. The algal blooms from high nutrient inputs and sediment loads also decrease water clarity, which is largely responsible for the decline of submerged aquatic vegetation. Submerged aquatic vegetation, one of the most important components of the ecosystem, provides critical habitat for shellfish and finfish and food for waterfowl. High nutrient levels in the bay's waters are thought to be responsible for the proliferation of the single-celled organism, *Pfiesteria piscicida,* which causes fish lesions and fish kills.

**FIGURE 14–4**

Nitrogen and phosphorus sources in Chesapeake Bay. (*Source:* US Geological Survey)

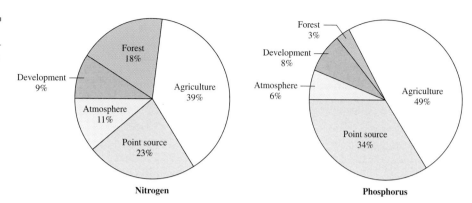

**Nitrogen**

**Phosphorus**

The major source of nutrient pollution in the bay's watershed is runoff from agriculture, which contributes about 40% of the nitrogen and about 50% of the phosphorus entering the Chesapeake Bay (Figure 14–4). The major source of nitrogen is the Susquehanna River, which drains some of the most productive agricultural land in the United States. The sources of nutrient pollution from agricultural land are fertilizer and animal waste. Approximately 1.5 Gg of phosphorus entered the bay from its nine major tributaries from 1990 through 1992. A particular problem within the Chesapeake Bay catchment is that in many areas livestock production is very intensive but crop production is limited. The excessive application of manure to the limited areas of croplands has lead to the accumulation of high levels of phosphorus in the fields. For example, a survey conducted in Sussex County, Delaware, which has a high density of livestock operations, found that in 87% of the fields tested the P levels were excessive. By contrast, in New Castle County, Delaware, which has a low density of livestock operations, less than 10% of the field soils tested had excessive P levels. Phosphorus, which is bound to soil particles can be lost from fields with high P levels in runoff.

Various pollution-reduction strategies were put into place to reduce nutrient pollution in the Chesapeake, including bans on detergents with phosphorus; control of runoff from urban areas, farmland, and pastures; improvements in sewage treatment; and preservation of forest and wetlands, which act as buffers to nutrient-pollution inputs. Controls directed at reducing agricultural and urban erosion also contribute to the lower phosphorus levels. Pollution-reduction strategies are having a positive effect on phosphorus levels in the major tributaries to the bay (the Susquehanna and Potomac Rivers). By contrast, nitrogen levels in the Susquehanna and the Potomac Rivers are increasing. The increase in nitrogen is probably caused by the continued use of nitrogen fertilizer on lawns and cropland, increasing agricultural animal production, and atmospheric deposition of nitrogen from industrial and automotive air pollution.

**Nitrate in Groundwater.**   To protect human health the EPA has established a maximum contaminant level (MCL) of 10 mg · L$^{-1}$ (as nitrogen) for nitrate in drinking water.

The pollution of groundwaters with nitrate is widespread in agricultural areas. A survey by the United States Geological Survey [5] found that in about 12% of domestic supply wells in agricultural areas in the United States the concentration of nitrate exceeded 10 mg · L$^{-1}$. Nitrate concentrations in groundwater were highest in the Northeast, Great Plains, and along the West Coast, where the combination of permeable soils, high rates of fertilizer application, and irrigation provides a large source of nitrate and a high potential for nitrate movement down to the water table.

### Pesticides

**Pesticides** are chemicals used by farmers, households, or industry to regulate and control various types of pests or weeds. The major types of pesticides are herbicides, insecticides, and fungicides. Herbicides are used to kill unwanted plants (i.e., weeds). Insecticides are used to kill

**TABLE 14-1**       Pesticide Use in the United States in 1993

| Most Commonly Used | | Total Mass of Most Commonly Used Pesticides (million lb) | Percentage of Total Mass of That Type of Pesticide (%) |
|---|---|---|---|
| Herbicides | Atrazine, metolachlor and alachlor | 175–190 | 27–29 |
| Insecticides | Chloropyrifos, diazinon, malathion | 23–33 | 9–13 |
| Fungicides | Sulfur, chlorothalonil, mancozeb | ≈59–72 | 49–60 |

*Source:* Aspelin, A. L. *Pesticides Industry Sales and Usage: 1992 and 1993 Market Estimates.* Biological and Economic Analysis Division, Office of Pesticide Programs, Office of Prevention, Pesticides, and Toxic Substances, United States Environmental Protection Agency, Washington, D.C., 1994.

**FIGURE 14-5**

The occurrence of pesticides in agricultural, urban and mixed land use areas within NAWQA study units. (*Source:* U.S. Geological Survey, "The quality of our nation's waters— Nutrients and pesticides," *U.S. Geological Survey Circular 1225,* p. 82, 1999.)

insects that would otherwise destroy crops, gardens, or structures. Fungicides are employed to control the growth of fungi, many of which cause plant diseases. Table 14–1 shows the most commonly used pesticides along with the mass of chemicals used.

**Pesticides in the Environment.** The presence of pesticides in surface- and groundwater is ubiquitous in the United States. In a study conducted by the U.S. Geological Survey (USGS) of 20 national water quality assessment program (NAWQA) study units across the country it was found that more than 90% of water and fish samples from all streams contained one or, more often, several pesticides (Figure 14–5). The most commonly occurring pesticides found in water were primarily those currently in use, whereas those found in fish and sediment are the organochlorine insecticides, such as DDT, that were heavily used decades ago. About 50% of the wells sampled contained one or more pesticides, with the highest detection frequencies in shallow groundwater beneath agricultural and urban areas and the lowest frequencies were in deeper aquifers [5].

In a study of the western Lake Michigan drainage basins (in Wisconsin and Michigan) by the USGS, 33 pesticides were found in surface waters and 15 in groundwater [6]. The most commonly detected pesticides were herbicides used on corn, soybeans, small grains, and hay. Atrazine, the herbicide most commonly used on corn in the study area, was detected in all the surface water samples and more than half of the groundwater samples. The herbicides simazine, metolachlor, prometon, and alachlor were found in more than 50% of the stream samples. The good news is that U.S. EPA drinking-water standards were exceeded in only 11% of the surface water samples. However, the EPA has established maximum contaminant levels (MCLs) for only about 20% of the 88 pesticides analyzed in this study. The western Lake Michigan basin study found that the concentrations of pesticides were approximately 100 times higher in intensively farmed areas

**FIGURE 14–6**

The occurrence of atrazine in aquifers in eastern Wisconsin. (*Source:* Peters, C. A., D. M. Robertson, D. A. Saad, et al. *U.S. Geological Survey Circular 1156* online at http://water.usgs.gov/circ/circ1156)

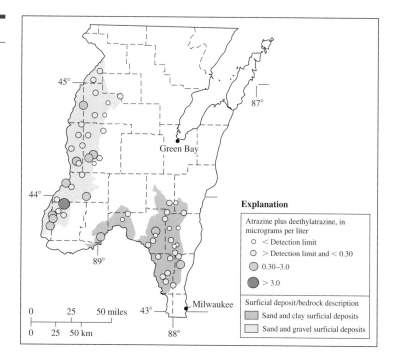

than in nonagricultural or less intensively farmed areas.* Typically, the highest concentrations occurred during the first rainfall events (resulting in runoff) after the application of pesticides. Atmospheric deposition of atrazine was believed to be the cause of the occurrence of this pesticide in two forested streams.

As is illustrated in Figure 14–6, the study also found that the shallow aquifers most vulnerable to contamination were those in intensively cultivated agricultural areas underlain by relatively permeable surficial deposits. Seldom is this shallow groundwater used as a drinking water, lessening the effect of the contamination on human health. Pesticides were also detected in seven drinking-water aquifers. Most of the contaminated water was found in wells drilled in the aquifers not covered by the relatively impermeable confining layer. In conclusion, both USGS studies show the ubiquitous presence of pesticides in the environment. Unfortunately, the presence of pesticides is likely to be underestimated because some of the more difficult to analyze, but widely used, pesticides (e.g., glyphosate, cryolite, and all inorganic pesticides including sulfur and copper) were not included in these studies. Additionally, neither study looked for the presence of the thousands of potential pesticide degradation products that are very rarely included as laboratory analytes.

**Pesticide Degradation.**   **Pesticide degradation,** or the breakdown of pesticides, can occur by three broad groupings of reactions: microbial, chemical (abiotic), and photodegradation. The persistence of pesticides is often described using half-lives. As discussed in Chapter 2, the half-life is the time required for the concentration of a substance to be reduced to one-half of the original amount.

**Microbial degradation** is the breakdown of pesticides by fungi, bacteria, and other microorganisms. The pesticide may be used as a food source or it may be cometabolized by bacteria that use other chemicals as food but serendipitously degrade the pesticide in the process of normal metabolism. Most microbial degradation of pesticides occurs in the soil, much of it in the

---

*Intensive farming was defined as the growing of row crops such as corn, soy beans, and small grains. Nonintensive farming is grazing, hay production, or the growing of less herbicide-intensive crops.

root zone. Soil conditions, such as pH, moisture, temperature, oxygen content, and the amount of organic matter, affect the rate of microbial degradation because of their direct influence on microbial growth and activity. The extent to which the pesticide is sorbed onto soil particles will also control degradation because the stronger the sorption, the less bioavailable the pesticide (and the slower the degradation).

The rate of microbial degradation is also influenced by the frequency of pesticide application. Rapid microbial degradation is more likely when the same pesticide is used repeatedly in the same location because this tends to stimulate the growth of organisms that are capable of degrading the applied pesticide. As the population of these organisms increases, the rate of degradation accelerates.

**Chemical (Abiotic) Degradation.** **Abiotic degradation** is the breakdown of pesticides by processes that do not involve living organisms. In soils, the most common chemical mechanism is hydrolysis. Hydrolysis reactions involve the release of a leaving group (often bromide, iodide, or chloride) and the addition of a hydroxide from water. Because many hydrolysis reactions are acid- or base-catalyzed, the hydrolysis rates will be enhanced at either acidic or alkaline conditions. Temperature, moisture, and the extent to which the pesticide is adsorbed to the soil will also affect the rates of hydrolysis. The chemical nature of the pesticide will also determine which type of hydrolysis reactions will occur and the rate. For example, $t$-butyl chloride ($t_{1/2} = 23$ s) is more rapidly hydrolyzed than is methyl chloride ($t_{1/2} = 340$ days) or isopentyl chloride ($t_{1/2} = 38$ days) [7]. Many organophosphate and carbamate insecticides are particularly susceptible to hydrolysis under alkaline conditions. Some react within a matter of hours when mixed with water having a pH > 8.

**EXAMPLE 14–2**

The half-lives for the hydrolysis of atrazine, a pesticide commonly applied to corn, are 65 days at pH 5 and 200 days at pH 7. Assuming that the rate of hydrolysis of atrazine can be described as first-order, determine the time required for the hydrolysis of 90% of atrazine at pH 5 and pH 7.

**Solution**

The kinetic expression describing the half-life of a chemical can be written as

$$t_{1/2} = -\frac{\ln(0.5)}{k}$$

where $k$ is the first-order rate constant in units of time$^{-1}$. In this case we are given $t_{1/2}$ and we need to find $k$ to determine the time required for 90% of the chemical to degrade. Therefore, we can write

$$k = -\frac{\ln(0.5)}{t_{1/2}}$$

At a pH of 5, $k = -\ln(0.5)/(65 \text{ days}) = 1.07 \times 10^{-2} \text{ day}^{-1}$
At a pH of 7, $k = -\ln(0.5)/(200 \text{ days}) = 3.47 \times 10^{-3} \text{ day}^{-1}$.

If we are looking for the time required for 90% of the pesticide to degrade, we must write the kinetic expression as $t_{90\%} = -\ln(0.1)/t_{1/2}$. The expression is written in this form because under these conditions, 10% of the chemical remains and the expression is written as $C_{remaining}/C_0$.
Thus,

At a pH of 5, $t_{90\%} = -\ln(0.1)/(1.07 \times 10^{-2} \text{ day}^{-1}) = 215 \text{ days}$
At a pH of 7, $t_{90\%} = -\ln(0.1)/(3.47 \times 10^{-3} \text{ day}^{-1}) = 664 \text{ days}$.

For chemicals that are not readily hydrolyzed, reductive dehalogenation (essentially β-elimination reactions) may be important. Among the chemicals that may be reductively dehalogenated under environmental conditions are the polyhalogenated aliphatic hydrocarbons such as 1,1,2,2-tetrachloroethane, 1,2-dibromomethane and 1,1,1-trichloroethane. Although these reactions do occur in nature, the half-lives for these chemicals at pH 7 and 25°C are long (in most cases, decades to centuries).

**Photodegradation.**  **Photodegradation** is the breakdown of pesticides by light, particularly sunlight. Photodegradation can destroy pesticides on foliage, on the soil surface, and even in the air. Factors that influence pesticide photodegradation include the intensity of the sunlight, properties of the application site, the application method, and properties of the pesticide. In most cases, only chemicals that are able to absorb light at wavelengths emitted can be photodegraded.

## 14–5  AIR QUALITY

The effects of agricultural activities on air quality are widespread. The major issues regarding air quality and agriculture have to do with particulate and ammonia emissions in addition to malodorous compounds, greenhouse gases, pesticides, and the effects on the ozone layer.

### Particulate Emissions

Particulate emissions from agriculture mainly result from wind erosion, dust emissions from open feedlots and grain elevators, and smoke from agricultural burning. As discussed in Chapter 11, excessive levels of particulate matter in the air affect visibility and may adversely affect human health and welfare. Particulates (PM-10 and PM-2.5) are "criteria air pollutants" and as such are regulated under the national ambient air quality standards (NAAQS). Some major agricultural areas, such as the San Joaquin Valley of California are nonattainment areas because particulate concentrations in the air do not meet the NAAQS. Under the Clean Air Act, each state must develop a plan to identify the sources of air pollution and to determine what reductions are required to meet federal air quality standards. In California, the state has implemented a smoke management program to reduce the harmful effects of burning in the San Joaquin Valley and elsewhere. Elements of the program include

- Registering and permitting of agricultural and prescribed burns
- Meteorological and smoke management forecasting
- Daily burn authorization
- Enforcement

### Ammonia Emissions

Agriculture is a major source of ammonia emissions to the atmosphere. There are large uncertainties about the accuracy of the estimates of ammonia emissions to the atmosphere, however, existing ammonia inventories indicate that livestock wastes are responsible for 50–70% of ammonia emissions in the United States.

For agriculturally emitted ammonia the central issue is that ammonia is a major source of secondary particulates. These particulates are formed as a result of the reaction of ammonia with acidic compounds, such as sulfuric acid. Ammonia emissions from livestock operations may also contribute to odor problems.

### Malodorous Compounds

Many malodorous compounds, including ammonia; amines; volatile fatty acids and hydrogen sulfide and other sulfur compounds, such as mercaptans, are released from animal feeding operations.

These odors are produced by the decomposition of organic matter (e.g., manure) under anaerobic conditions. The principal sources of odorous emissions include

- Open lot and animal confinement buildings (barns)
- Manure storage facilities (e.g., pits, lagoons, stockpiles, composting operations)
- Land application systems for manure, treated effluent, or open lot runoff
- Animal carcasses

Some of the odorous compounds, such hydrogen sulfide are very toxic. However, the concentrations of these compounds in and around livestock operations are generally below the level where adverse effects on humans have been found.

The release of offensive odors from agricultural operations is not usually regulated by federal or state agencies; however, odors from these operations are a major nuisance. In recent years there has been a dramatic increase in the number of odor-related complaints against farmers. In many states environmental and citizen groups have pressed for legislation to control the problem. The increased size of many livestock operations and the movement of more people into some agricultural areas, as the result of "urban sprawl" is one of the major reasons for the increase in the number of complaints. To address this problem several states have implemented or are considering regulations or other measures to try to reduce odorous emissions from livestock production operations.

### Greenhouse Gases

As is discussed in Chapter 11, the effect of the steady rise of greenhouse gases (carbon dioxide, methane, nitrous oxide) on global surface temperature is an issue of major concern. Agriculture is a significant contributor to greenhouse gas emissions, accounting for an estimated 20% of the global warming potential (GWP).* Agriculture accounts for about 50% of the human-induced methane emissions, about 75% of the human-induced nitrous oxide emissions, and about 5% of the human-induced carbon dioxide emissions. Deforestation and biomass burning, along with other land use changes, account for an additional 14% of the carbon dioxide emissions. The major contribution to carbon dioxide emissions is within the equatorial regions, due to biomass burning and decomposition and mineralization of soil organic carbon.

Agricultural sources of trace gases that contribute to global warming include emissions of methane and nitrogen oxides from animal production facilities and methane emissions from rice production. During animal digestion, methane is produced through the process of enteric fermentation, in which microbes residing in animal digestive systems break down the feed consumed by the animal. Ruminants, which include cattle, buffalo, sheep, and goats, have the highest methane emissions among all animal types because they have a rumen, or large fore-stomach, in which methane-producing fermentation occurs. Methane emissions from animal production account for about 40% of the methane emissions in the United States.

Most of the world's rice, and all of the rice in the United States, is grown on flooded fields. When fields are flooded, anaerobic conditions develop and the organic matter in the soil decomposes, releasing methane to the atmosphere. In 1999, rice cultivation was the source of 2% of U.S. methane emissions. In other countries where rice production is more extensive, the contribution from rice production is more significant.

Although agriculture contributes to GWP, it also reduces atmospheric carbon dioxide emissions through biomass production, tree-planting, and similar activities that sequester significant amounts of carbon and replace fossil fuels. Expansion of these activities could reduce carbon dioxide emissions to the atmosphere.

---

*The concept of global warming potential (GWP) has been developed to compare the ability of each greenhouse gas to trap heat in the atmosphere relative to another gas. Carbon dioxide ($CO_2$) was chosen as the reference gas. The relationship between grams of a gas and g $CO_2$ Eq. thus can be expressed as follows:

g $CO_2$ Eq = (g of gas) $\times$ (GWP)

### Effects on the Ozone Layer

Methyl bromide is a widely used fumigant for controlling insects, nematodes, weeds, and pathogens. Its primary uses are for soil fumigation, postharvest protection, and quarantine treatments. In the 1990s about 3 Gg of methyl bromide was used each year in the United States. However, scientific evidence indicates that methyl bromide contributes significantly to the destruction of earth's stratospheric ozone layer. Under The Montreal Protocol of 1991, methyl bromide was defined as a chemical that contributes to depletion of the earth's ozone layer. Accordingly, the manufacture and importation of methyl bromide will be phased out in developed countries as follows: 25% reduction in 1999, 25% reduction in 2001, 20% reduction in 2003, and complete phase out in 2005. In developing countries, consumption is to be frozen in 2002 at 1995–1998 average levels, followed by 20% reduction in 2005 and complete phase out by 2015. One of the problems facing agriculture is that there is no known single alternative for methyl bromide in efficacy, low cost, ease of use, wide availability, and worker safety. Research on alternatives is underway and it is likely that several substitutes will be developed that may in some cases be pest-specific, and that when used as part of an overall integrated pest management program will reduce pest levels to an acceptable level.

Another potential effect of agriculture on air quality is the release of volatile organic compounds (VOCs) by animal feeding operations that are a precursor to ozone formation. Currently, no recognized emission factors for VOCs exist for these operations from which states can develop reliable emission inventories or cost-effective mitigation measures where required. Research is ongoing to establish the significance of these releases to ozone formation in the lower atmosphere.

### Pesticides

It is important to consider the atmosphere when assessing the effect of pesticides on the environment.* Until the 1960s, atmospheric pollution from pesticide spray drift was generally thought of as a local problem. The detection of DDT, PCBs, and other organochlorine compounds in arctic and antarctic fish and mammals have changed this notion. Long-range transport of pesticides can occur over hundreds to thousands of kilometers. Toxaphene, for example, which was used on cotton in the southern United States and banned in 1982, is still being transported into the Great Lakes region by southerly winds from the Gulf of Mexico. Once deposited on the earth's surface, the pesticide can revolatilize, reenter the atmosphere, and be transported and deposited downwind repeatedly until it is finally degraded. This same process can also occur for the degradation products resulting from chemical or biochemical transformations of pesticides.

## 14-6  ANIMAL WASTE MANAGEMENT

Animal production facilities produce various wastes including manure, dairy washings, silage effluent, and animal carcasses, of which manure is the most significant. Manure can be used as a fertilizer, however, if it is not properly handled and disposed of correctly, manure can create significant environmental problems.

### Manure Handling and Storage

The procedures used for the handling and disposing of animal manures vary greatly. Manure, varies in consistency depending on the animal that produces it, coming in the form of a liquid, slurry, semisolid (paste), or solid. Wastes of different consistencies require different handling techniques. Chickens produce solid manure, which after drying is normally applied to fields in the dry form. By contrast, swine manure is a slurry (which contains a mixture of feces and urine). Swine manure is normally stored in pits, tanks, or lagoons until it is applied to the field. The slurry may be sprayed or spread onto the field. To reduce odor problems and the loss of ammonia, the slurry may also be injected into the soil.

---

*Pesticides in the Atmosphere. U.S. Geological Survey, Fact Sheet FS-152-95.

Although some smaller farm operations collect and apply manure frequently (daily or once every few days), most producers generally only do so occasionally. There are various reasons for this practice, including

- Frequent application is a labor-intensive process.
- Manure is best applied during the early stages of plant growth when plant uptake of nutrients is greatest.
- Manure cannot easily be applied to row crops such as corn when the plants are larger.
- In areas with colder climates manure should not be applied when the ground is frozen.

Operations that produce manure slurries need large storage facilities if they do not apply their manure frequently. Most swine and dairy producers use a lagoon (clay-lined storage basin) to store their manure because this is the cheapest means of storage. Serious problems can result if the lagoon overflows and the waste is released to the environment. In severe cases the lagoon may even collapse as the overflow can erode the lagoon's banks. Lagoons therefore need to be designed to ensure that they have sufficient capacity to hold the manure produced plus any rainfall that may expected.

### Concentrated Animal Feeding Operations

Until the latter part of the 20th century most farms that raised animals integrated crop and animal production. The manure produced by the animals was used to fertilize crops on the farm. As a result of the economics of operation, the average size of animal feeding operations has increased dramatically in the past few decades. Large operations produce a large amount of manure and they often do not have sufficient land to dispose of it properly. Manure only contains a few percent of N or P on a weight basis, so its fertilizer value on a weight basis is small. For swine manure, which contains 90% water, it is not economical to transport the manure more than few kilometers. Even if an operation owns land locally or can negotiate with local crop farmers for them to take the manure, the cost of transporting the manure may exceed its fertilizer value. In this situation some farmers will overapply the manure.

The EPA is concerned about the adverse effects that large animal feeding operations may have on the environment. In February, 2003 it issued a final ruling to regulate discharges from large animal feeding operations [8]. Large operations, referred to as **concentrated animal feeding operations** (CAFOs) are defined as those animal feeding operations with 500 or more animal units (AU).* Under this new rule all CAFOs will be required to apply for a National Pollution Discharge Elimination System (NPDES) permit, submit an annual report, and develop and follow a manure management plan.

### Best Management Practices

Only about 15,500 of the estimated 1.3 million farms with livestock in the United States will be regulated under the new CAFO rules. Some states have themselves regulated animal feeding operations, but on the vast majority of farms the management of manure is unregulated. Although most farms with livestock are not regulated, extensive guidelines govern manure management on farms. These guidelines, often referred to as **best management practices** (BMPs), provide livestock farmers with guidance on how to manage their operations. The guidelines cover when and how much manure should be applied to cropland based on existing soil nutrient levels; manure nutrient content; crop nutrient needs; and site limitations, such as proximity to a water body, slope, and leaching potential. Applying levels that exceed crop nutrient requirements may lead to nutrients entering surface waters or leaching into groundwater. Procedures

---

*An AU is equal to 1000 lb of animal weight. For example, 20 nursery pigs (average weight 50 lb) constitute an animal unit.

that reduce runoff or leaching of pollutants into the environment are also given, examples of which include

- To avoid runoff manure should not be applied to frozen or saturated soils.
- Manure may be applied to the soil by spraying, spreading, or injection into the soil. Where spraying or spreading is used, the manure should be plowed into soil. Incorporation of the manure into the soil reduces odors, nitrogen losses, and the runoff of nutrients and other potential pollutants from the field.
- In steeply sloped fields or areas close to streams or other water bodies the potential for nutrient loss is high. Runoff can be reduced by limiting or not applying manure at all to areas close to streams or other water bodies.
- Manure application should be applied during periods when plant uptake is highest. For most crops this is during the early stages of growth.

### *Manure Application*

Historically, manure application has been based on the crops' N need because (1) it was not necessary to add inorganic N fertilizer to the crop and (2) less land was required to dispose of the manure, which can be important consideration if the operation only has a limited amount of land. Animal manure typically contains a higher ratio of nitrogen-to-phosphorus (N:P) than is required by the crop. As a result, if sufficient manure is added to meet N requirements, the P levels in the manure exceed the P requirements. Long-term application of manure to meet the crops' N needs can lead to the excessive buildup of P in the soil. Concerns regarding P runoff have led several states to adopt BMPs based on providing sufficient P to meet crop needs. In this case, inorganic N fertilizers need to be added to the soil to ensure good crop yields.

**EXAMPLE 14–3**   Measurement of the nutrient levels in the soil in a field indicate that the available N and P in a soil are 100 and 50 $kg \cdot ha^{-1}$, respectively. If the N and P needs for the corn are 170 $kg \cdot ha^{-1}$ and 40 $kg \cdot ha^{-1}$, respectively, calculate the required application rates based on both the crop's P and N needs.

Solution
1. The crop's N need is 170 $kg \cdot N\,ha^{-1}$. The additional N needed is $170 - 100 = 70\,kg \cdot N\,ha^{-1}$.
2. The crop's P need is 40 $kg \cdot ha^{-1}$. Available soil P is 50 $kg \cdot ha^{-1}$. No manure application is needed to meet the crop's P need. Chemical fertilizer is needed to meet the crop's N need of 70 $kg \cdot ha^{-1}$.

## CHAPTER REVIEW

When you have completed studying this chapter you should be able to do the following without the aid of your textbook or notes:

1. Explain the effect that water use for irrigation may have on other water users in arid or semiarid areas.
2. List and explain three problems that can result from land subsidence.
3. Explain the difference between conventional and conservation tillage.
4. List four practices used to reduce soil erosion by water on croplands.
5. List three practices used to reduce wind erosion on croplands.
6. Identify the most important management tool for control of erosion on pastureland and rangeland.
7. Spell out the acronyms USLE and WEQ.
8. List the five factors in the USLE.

9. Given the appropriate information, be able to use the USLE to make management decisions about the effect of alternative management or practices on soil erosion.

10. Explain how the use of water for irrigation can cause salinization and give an example of how salinization can affect the environment.

11. List and explain five measures to control salinization.

12. List the two nutrients used in fertilizers that have the greatest environmental effect.

13. List the chemical forms of nitrogen and phosphorus that are present in the soil environment. Identify which forms are mobile in the soil environment.

14. Sketch and explain the nitrogen and phosphorus cycles on crop- and grazing land.

15. Define the terms *nitrification* and *denitrification*.

16. Identify two environmental problems caused by the excessive use of fertilizers.

17. List the three major types of pesticides used in agriculture.

18. Identify two situations when pesticide use may result in groundwater or surface water contamination (e.g., areas underlain by shallow aquifers).

19. List the three groupings used to describe pesticide degradation.

20. Calculate the rate of degradation of a pesticide given its half-life.

21. List and explain the six effects agriculture has on air quality that are discussed in this chapter.

22. Explain the term *BMP*.

23. Given the appropriate information, be able to calculate appropriate application rates for manure on cropland.

## PROBLEMS

**14-1**  Terraces may be constructed on a sloping field to reduce soil loss. On the farm discussed in Example 14–1 what would be the soil loss from the field if terraces were constructed to reduce the slope length to 200 ft?

**14-2**  Grassy Lake has a 1500-ha catchment. The soils in the catchment contain on average 75 mg $P \cdot kg^{-1}$. Calculate the annual input of phosphorus to the lake from runoff, if the average rate of soil loss is $4 \, t \cdot ha^{-1} \cdot year^{-1}$. (Assume the amount of soluble P in the runoff is negligible.)

**Answer:** 450 kg P

**14-3**  Due to the continued application of manure and poor erosion control, the average soil P concentration in the Grassy Lake catchment (see Problem 14–2) increases to 150 mg $P \cdot kg^{-1}$ and the soil loss rate to $9 \, t \cdot ha^{-1}$. Calculate the percentage increase in the phosphorus input to the lake.

**14-4**  A small lake is surrounded by agricultural land. The lake is 150 m long and 120 m wide, with an average depth of 30 m. The lake is fed by a small pollution-free stream having an average flowrate of $1.5 \, m^3 \cdot s^{-1}$. A herbicide, Greatcrop is detected at a concentration of $45.2 \, \mu g \cdot L^{-1}$ in the lake. Greatcrop degrades biologically with a rate constant of $0.22 \, day^{-1}$. Assuming that the lake is at steady-state conditions and completely mixed at the time of sampling, what would have been the mass input of herbicide? Assume that the stream is the only source of water to the lake and evaporation, precipitation, and seepage can be neglected.

**Answer:** $11.2 \, kg \cdot day^{-1}$

**14-5**  Blue Lake is 3500 m long and 2800 m wide, with an average depth of 20 m. The lake is fed by a stream having an average flowrate of $6.9 \, m^3 \cdot s^{-1}$. The stream flows through agricultural land, and the average concentration of the herbicide, Kill-all in the stream is $33.1 \, \mu g \cdot L^{-1}$. Kill-all degrades biologically with a rate constant of $0.18 \, day^{-1}$. Assuming that the lake is at steady-state conditions and completely mixed, what will the Kill-all concentration in the lake be?

**14-6**  A railroad line runs near the XYZ River, which has an average flow rate of $53 \, m^3 \cdot s^{-1}$. The railroad maintenance company sprays the track easement land with a herbicide, resulting in a herbicide concentration in the river of $65 \, \mu g \cdot L^{-1}$. The city of Clearfield is 18.5 km downstream. The flow velocity in the river is $1.24 \, m \cdot s^{-1}$. If the herbicide degrades with a rate constant of $0.64 \, day^{-1}$, what is the concentration of the herbicide in the river near Clearfield?

**Answer:** 58.2 μg/L.

**14-7** A monitoring well drilled into the Grosser aquifer reveals contamination with the pesticide Ant-away at a concentration of 545 $\mu g \cdot L^{-1}$. A drinking-water well field is 1 km downstream. The hydraulic permeability of the aquifer is $1.2 \times 10^{-4}$ $m \cdot s^{-1}$. The hydraulic gradient is 0.040 $m \cdot m^{-1}$. The retardation factor of Ant-away is 1.6. How long will it take for the pesticide Ant-away to reach the drinking-water well?

**14-8** The XYZ Pesticide Manufacturing Company makes the insecticide Roach-be-gone. The wastewater stream from their manufacturing process contains Roach-be-gone at a concentration of 124 $mg \cdot L^{-1}$. The wastewater flow rate is 2,450,000 $L \cdot day^{-1}$. The wastewater is to be disposed of in the Red Maple River, which has a 10-year low flow of 0.78 $m^3 \cdot s^{-1}$ (just upstream of the outfall). The low-flow velocity in the stream is 0.035 $m \cdot s^{-1}$. Roach-be-gone degrades biologically with a rate constant of 0.45 $day^{-1}$. The Department of Environmental Quality has stipulated that the wastewater stream be treated so that both the following criteria be met:

(a) The concentration of Roach-be-gone in the river just after mixing (at the outfall) be less than 0.50 $mg \cdot L^{-1}$.

(b) The concentration of Roach-be-gone in the river 15 km downstream, at the intake of the Maplecrest City water treatment plant, be less than 0.005 $mg \cdot L^{-1}$.

The 10-year low flow rate must be used in the treatment plant design calculations. What percentage of Roach-be-gone must be removed in a wastewater treatment facility at the XYZ Pesticide Manufacturing Company? Assume that the concentration of Roach-be-gone in the river upstream from the outfall is nondetectable.

**14-9** A farmer has calculated that she needs to add 60 kg N $\cdot ha^{-1}$ to meet crop needs. Calculate the application rate if (1) ammonium nitrate is used to fertilize the fields (2) manure is used to fertilize the fields (the total nitrogen content of the manure is 0.5 wt%, and 43% of that nitrogen is available to the plant during the growing season). The manure contains 0.109 wt% of phosphorus. Calculate the amount of phosphorus applied per hectare if manure is used to fertilize the field to meet crop N needs.

**14-10** Methane, carbon dioxide, and other trace gases are emitted from a manure storage lagoon. The gas emitted is called biogas. Biogas can be collected by placing a cover over the lagoon. The biogas can be burnt to produce heat or electricity, which helps to offset energy costs on the farm. Another benefit of burning the biogas is that it reduces the GWP of the emissions from the lagoon, as the methane (GWP = 21) is converted to carbon dioxide (GWP = 1). If a lagoon produces 50 t of gas and the gas contains 40% $CO_2$ and 60% $CH_4$ on a molar basis, by how many metric tons of $CO_2$ equivalent global warming potential are the emissions reduced by burning the biogas?

**Answer:** 380 tons.

**14-11** Each cow on a 1000-cow dairy produces on average 90 L of manure per day. If the lagoon on the farm is 0.5 ha in area, calculate the average increase in the depth of the manure in the storage after 150 days, if the excess of precipitation over evaporation during this period is 250 mm.

## DISCUSSION QUESTIONS

**14-1** You have been asked to determine the alternatives to manage the available water resources in a semiarid area. What data would you have to gather to make your recommendations?

**14-2** Severe erosion is resulting in siltation in a river. Discuss the possible consequences of siltation and the steps you would take to control or avert any possible problems.

**14-3** A local environmental group claims that nutrients in runoff from several large farms in the area are polluting the local lake. The farmers claim that the pollution comes mainly from the local wastewater treatment plant and from septic systems. What data would you have to gather to determine who is responsible for the pollution of the lake?

## ADDITIONAL READING

### Books and Conference Proceedings

*Environmentally Sound Agriculture.* Proceedings of the Second Conference, Orlando, FL, April 20–22, 1994. American Society for Agricultural Engineering, St. Joseph, MI (1994).

Loehr, R. C. *Pollution Control for Agriculture.* Academic Press, Orlando, FL (1984).

*Animal, Agricultural and Food Processing Wastes.* Proceeding of the 8th International Symposium, Des Moines, IA, October 9–11, 2000. J. A. Moore, ed. American Society for Agricultural Engineering, St. Joseph, MI (2000).

Kiely, G. *Environmental Engineering.* McGraw-Hill, Maidenhead, UK (1996).

### Reports

*America's Private Land, A Geography of Hope.* National Resource Conservation Service, Washington, D.C. (1996).

*Manure Nutrients Relative to the Capacity of Cropland and Pastureland to Assimilate Nutrients: Spatial and Temporal Trends for the United States.* National Resource Conservation Service, Washington, D.C. (2000).

*Water Quality and Agriculture.* National Resource Conservation Service, Washington, D.C. (1997).

### Journals

*Journal of Environmental Quality*

*Journal of Soil and Water Conservation*

*Transactions of the American Society for Agricultural Engineering*

*Water Resources Research*

## REFERENCES

1. Fryrear, D. L., A. Saleh, J. O. Bilbro, et al. 1998. "Revised wind erosion equation (RWEQ) wind erosion and water conservation unit," *USDA-ARS, Southern Plains Area Cropping System Research Laboratory, Technical Bulletin* No. 1.

2. Woodruff, N. P., and F. H. Siddoway. "A wind erosion equation." *Proceedings of the Soil Science Society of America* 1965; 29(5):602–608.

3. Durar, A. A., and E. L. Skidmore. *WEPS Technical documentation: Hydrology submodel.* SWCS. WEPP/WEPS Symposium. Ankeny, IA (1995).

4. National Research Council, *Soil and Water Quality: An Agenda for Agriculture,* National Academy Press, Washington, D.C., p. 390, 1993.

5. U.S. Geological Survey. "The quality of our nation's waters—Nutrients and pesticides," *U.S. Geological Survey Circular 1225,* p. 82, 1999.

6. Peters, C. A., D. M. Robertson, D. A. Saad, et al. 1998. *U.S. Geological Survey Circular 1156,* on line at http://water.usgs.gov/circ/circ1156

7. Schwarzenbach, R. P., P. M. Gschwend, D. M. Imboden, *Environmental Organic Chemistry,* John Wiley and Sons, Inc., New York, p. 366, 1993.

8. *Federal Register,* 68, 7175–7269. February 12, 2003.

# 15

# Noise Pollution

## 15–1   INTRODUCTION

**Noise,** commonly defined as unwanted sound, is an environmental phenomenon to which we are exposed before birth and throughout life. Noise can also be considered an environmental pollutant, a waste product generated in conjunction with various anthropogenic activities. Under the latter definition, noise is any sound—independent of loudness—that can produce an undesired physiological or psychological effect in an individual and that may interfere with the social ends of an individual or group. These social ends include all of our activities—communication, work, rest, recreation, and sleep.

As waste products of our way of life, we produce two general types of pollutants. The general public has become well aware of the first type—the mass residuals associated with air and water pollution—that remain in the environment for extended periods. However, only recently has attention been focused on the second general type of pollution, the energy residuals such as the waste heat from manufacturing processes that creates thermal pollution of our streams. Energy in the form of sound waves constitutes yet another kind of energy residual, but, fortunately, one that does not remain in the environment for a long time. The total amount of energy dissipated as sound throughout the earth is not large compared with other forms of energy; it is only the extraordinary sensitivity of the ear that permits such a relatively small amount of energy to adversely affect us.

It has long been known that noise of sufficient intensity and duration can induce temporary or permanent hearing loss, ranging from slight impairment to nearly total deafness. In general, a pattern of exposure to any source of sound that produces high enough levels can result in temporary hearing loss. Exposure persisting over time can lead to permanent hearing impairment. It has been estimated that 1.7 million workers in the United States between 50 and 59 years of age have enough hearing loss to be awarded compensation. The potential cost to industry could be in excess of $1 billion. Short-term, but frequently serious, effects include interference with speech communication and the perception of other auditory signals, disturbance of sleep and relaxation, annoyance, interference with an individual's ability to perform complicated tasks, and general diminution of the quality of life.

Beginning with the technological expansion of the Industrial Revolution and continuing through a post-World War II acceleration, environmental noise in the United States and other industrialized nations has been gradually and steadily increasing, with more geographic areas becoming exposed to significant levels of noise. Where once noise levels sufficient to induce some degree of hearing loss were confined to factories and occupational situations, noise levels approaching such intensity and duration are today being recorded on city streets and, in some cases, in and around the home.

There are valid reasons why widespread recognition of noise as a significant environmental pollutant and potential hazard or, as a minimum, a detractor from the quality of life, has been slow in coming. In the first place, noise, if defined as unwanted sound, is a subjective experience. What is considered noise by one listener may be considered desirable by another.

Secondly, noise has a short decay time and thus does not remain in the environment for long, as do air and water pollution. By the time the average individual is spurred to action to abate, control, or, at least, complain about sporadic environmental noise, the noise may no longer exist.

Thirdly, the physiological and psychological effects of noise on us are often subtle and insidious, appearing so gradually that it becomes difficult to associate cause with effect. Indeed, to those persons whose hearing may already have been affected by noise, it may not be considered a problem at all.

Furthermore, the typical citizen is proud of this nation's technological progress and is generally happy with the things that technology delivers, such as rapid transportation, labor-saving appliances, and new recreational devices. Unfortunately, many technological advances have been associated with increased environmental noise, and large segments of the population have tended to accept the additional noise as part of the price of progress.

The engineering and scientific community has already accumulated considerable knowledge concerning noise, its effects, and its abatement and control. In that regard, noise differs from most other environmental pollutants. Generally, the technology exists to control most indoor and outdoor noise. As a matter of fact, this is one instance in which knowledge of control techniques exceeds the knowledge of biological and physical effects of the pollutant.

### Properties of Sound Waves

Sound waves result from the vibration of solid objects or the separation of fluids as they pass over, around, or through holes in solid objects. The vibration or separation causes the surrounding air to undergo alternating compression and rarefaction, much in the same manner as a piston vibrating in a tube (Figure 15–1). The compression of the air molecules causes a local increase in air density and pressure. Conversely, the rarefaction causes a local decrease in density and pressure. These alternating pressure changes are the sound detected by the human ear.

Let us assume that you could stand at point A in Figure 15–1. Also let us assume that you have an instrument that will measure the air pressure every 0.000010 s and plot the value on a graph. If the piston vibrates at a constant rate, the condensations and rarefactions will move down the tube at a constant speed. That speed is the speed of sound ($c$). The rise and fall of pressure at point A will follow a cyclic or wave pattern over a period (Figure 15–2). The wave pattern is called sinusoidal.

---

**FIGURE 15–1**

Alternating compression and rarefaction of air molecules resulting from a vibrating piston.

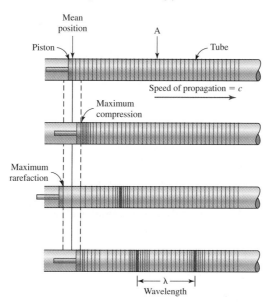

**FIGURE 15–2**

Sinusoidal wave that results from alternating compression and rarefaction of air molecules. The amplitude is shown as $A$ and the period is $P$.

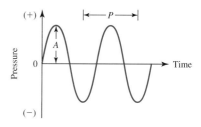

The time between successive peaks or between successive troughs of the oscillation is called the **period** ($P$). The inverse of this, that is, the number of times a peak arrives in one second of oscillations, is called the **frequency** ($f$). Period and frequency are then related as follows:

$$P = \frac{1}{f} \tag{15-1}$$

Because the pressure wave moves down the tube at a constant speed, you would find that the distance between equal pressure readings would remain constant. The distance between adjacent crests or troughs of pressure is called the **wavelength** ($\lambda$). Wavelength and frequency are then related as follows:

$$\lambda = \frac{c}{f} \tag{15-2}$$

The **amplitude** ($A$) of the wave is the height of the peak or depth of the trough measured from the zero pressure line (see Figure 15–2). From Figure 15–2 we can also note that the average pressure could be zero if an averaging time was selected that corresponded to the period of the wave. This would result regardless of the amplitude! This, of course, is not an acceptable state of affairs. The **root mean square** (rms) **sound pressure** ($p_{rms}$) is used to overcome this difficulty.* The rms sound pressure is obtained by squaring the value of the amplitude at each instant in time, summing the squared values, dividing the total by the averaging time, and taking the square root of the total. The equation for rms is

$$\bar{p}_{rms} = (p^2)\frac{1}{2}\left[\frac{1}{t_m}\int p^2(t)\,dt\right]^{1/2} \tag{15-3}$$

where the overbar refers to the time-weighted average and $t_m$ is the time period of the measurement.

### Sound Power and Intensity

**Work** is defined as the product of the magnitude of the displacement of a body and the component of force in the direction of the displacement. Thus, traveling waves of sound pressure transmit energy in the direction of propagation of the wave. The rate at which this work is done is defined as the **sound power** ($W$).

**Sound intensity** ($I$) is the time-weighted average sound power per unit area normal to the direction of propagation of the sound wave. Intensity and power are related as follows:

$$I = \frac{W}{A} \tag{15-4}$$

where $A$ is a unit area perpendicular to the direction of wave motion. Intensity, and hence, sound power, is related to sound pressure in the following manner:

$$I = \frac{(p_{rms})^2}{\rho c} \tag{15-5}$$

where $I$ = intensity (in $W \cdot m^{-2}$)
  $p_{rms}$ = root mean square sound pressure (in Pa)
  $\rho$ = density of medium (in $kg \cdot m^{-3}$)
  $c$ = speed of sound in medium (in $m \cdot s^{-1}$)

Both the density of air and speed of sound are a function of temperature. Given the temperature and pressure, the density of air may be determined from Table A–3 in Appendix A. The speed of sound in air at 101.325 kPa may be determined from the following equation:

$$c = 20.05\sqrt{T} \tag{15-6}$$

where $T$ is the absolute temperature in kelvins (K) and $c$ is in meters per second.

*Sound pressure = (total atmospheric pressure) − (barometric pressure).

### Levels and the Decibel

The sound pressure of the faintest sound that a normal healthy individual can hear is about 0.00002 Pa. The sound pressure produced by a Saturn rocket at liftoff is greater than 200 Pa. Even in scientific notation this is an "astronomical" range of numbers.

To cope with this problem, a scale based on the logarithm of the ratios of the measured quantities is used. Measurements on this scale are called levels. The unit for these types of measurement scales is the **bel,** which was named after Alexander Graham Bell:

$$L' = \log \frac{Q}{Q_0} \tag{15–7}$$

where $L' =$ level, bels
$\quad Q =$ measured quantity
$\quad Q_0 =$ reference quantity
$\quad \log =$ logarithm in base 10

A bel turns out to be a rather large unit, so for convenience it is divided into 10 subunits called **decibels** (dB). Levels in decibels are computed as follows:

$$L = 10 \log \frac{Q}{Q_0} \tag{15–8}$$

The decibel does not represent any physical unit. It merely indicates that a logarithmic transformation has been performed.

**Sound Power Level.** If the reference quantity ($Q_0$) is specified, then the decibel takes on physical significance. For noise measurements, the reference power level has been established as $10^{-12}$ W. Thus, sound power level may be expressed as

$$L_{\mathrm{w}} = 10 \log \frac{W}{10^{-12}} \tag{15–9}$$

Sound power levels computed with Equation 15–9 are reported as decibels re: $10^{-12}$ W.

**Sound Intensity Level.** For noise measurements, the reference sound intensity (Equation 15–4) is $10^{-12}$ W $\cdot$ m$^{-2}$. Thus the sound intensity level is given as

$$L_{\mathrm{I}} = 10 \log \frac{I}{10^{-12}} \tag{15–10}$$

**Sound Pressure Level.** Because sound-measuring instruments measure the $p_{\mathrm{rms}}$, the sound pressure level is computed as follows:

$$L_{\mathrm{p}} = 10 \log \frac{(p_{\mathrm{rms}})^2}{(p_{\mathrm{rms}})_0^2} \tag{15–11}$$

which, after extracting the squaring term, is given as

$$L_{\mathrm{p}} = 20 \log \frac{(p_{\mathrm{rms}})}{(p_{\mathrm{rms}})_0} \tag{15–12}$$

The reference pressure has been established as 20 μPa (micropascals). A scale showing some common sound pressure levels is shown in Figure 15–3.

**Combining Sound Pressure Levels.** Because of their logarithmic heritage, decibels don't add and subtract the way apples and oranges do. Remember: adding the logarithms of

## FIGURE 15-3

Relative scale of sound pressure levels.

## FIGURE 15-4

Graph for solving decibel addition problems.

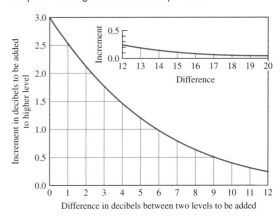

numbers is the same as multiplying them. If you take a 60-dB noise (re: 20 μPa) and add another 60-dB noise (re: 20 μPa) to it, you get a 63-dB noise (re: 20 μPa). If you're strictly an apple-and-orange mathematician, you may take this on faith. For skeptics, this can be demonstrated by converting the decibels to sound power level, adding them, and converting back to decibels. Figure 15–4 provides a graphical solution for this type of problem. For noise pollution work, results should be reported to the nearest whole number. When several levels are to be combined, combine them two at a time, starting with lower valued levels and continuing two at a time with each successive pair until one number remains. Henceforth, in this chapter we will assume levels are all "re: 20 μPa" unless stated otherwise.

**EXAMPLE 15-1**  What sound power level results from combining the following three levels: 68 dB, 79 dB, and 75 dB?

Solution  This problem can be worked by converting the readings to sound power level, adding them, and converting back to decibels.

$$L_p = 10 \log \sum 10^{(68/10)} + 10^{(75/10)} + 10^{(79/10)}$$

$$= 10 \log (117,365,173)$$

$$= 80.7 \text{ dB}$$

Rounding off to the nearest whole number yields an answer of 81 dB re: 20 μPa.

An alternative solution technique using Figure 15–4 begins by selecting the two lowest levels: 68 dB and 75 dB. The difference between the values is 75 − 68 = 7.00. Using Figure 15–4, draw a vertical line from 7.00 on the abscissa to intersect the curve. A horizontal line from the intersection to the ordinate yields about 0.8 dB. Thus, the combination of 68 dB and 75 dB results in a level of 75.8 dB. This, and the remainder of the computation, is shown in the following diagram.

### Characterization of Noise

**Weighting Networks.**  Because our reasons for measuring noise usually involve people, we are ultimately more interested in the human reaction to sound than in sound as a physical phenomenon. Sound pressure level, for instance, can't be taken at face value as an indication of loudness because the frequency (or pitch) of a sound has quite a bit to do with how loud it sounds. For this and other reasons, it often helps to know something about the frequency of the noise you're measuring. This is where weighting networks come in [1]. **Weighting networks** are electronic filtering circuits built into the meter to attenuate certain frequencies. They permit the sound level meter (Figure 15–5) to respond more to some frequencies than to others with a prejudice something like that of the human ear. Writers of the acoustical standards have established three weighting characteristics: A, B, and C. The chief difference among them is that very low frequencies are filtered quite severely by the A network, moderately by the B network, and hardly at all by the C network. Therefore, if the measured sound level of a noise is much higher on C weighting than on A weighting, much of the noise is probably of low frequency. If you really want to know the frequency distribution of a noise (and most serious noise measurers do), it is necessary to use a sound analyzer. But if you are unable to justify the expense of an analyzer, you can still find out something about the frequency of a noise by shrewd use of the weighting networks of a sound level meter.

**FIGURE 15–5**

Precision sound level meter. (Courtesy of Larson-Davis, Inc.)

Figure 15–6 shows the response characteristics of the three basic networks as prescribed by the American National Standards Institute (ANSI) specification number S1.4-1971. When a weighting network is used, the sound level meter electronically subtracts or adds the number of decibels shown at each frequency shown in Table 15–1 from or to the actual sound pressure level at that frequency. It then sums all the resultant numbers by logarithmic addition to give a single reading. Readings taken when a network is in use are said to be "sound levels" rather than "sound pressure levels." The readings taken are designated in decibels in one of the following forms: dB(A); dBa; dBA; dB(B); dBb; dBB; and so on. Tabular notations may refer to $L_A$, $L_B$, $L_C$.

**FIGURE 15–6**

Response characteristics of the three basic weighting networks.

**TABLE 15–1**               Sound Level Meter Network Weighting Values

| Frequency (Hz) | Curve A (dB) | Curve B (dB) | Curve C (dB) | Frequency (Hz) | Curve A (dB) | Curve B (dB) | Curve C (dB) |
|---|---|---|---|---|---|---|---|
| 10 | −70.4 | −38.2 | −14.3 | 500 | −3.2 | −0.3 | 0 |
| 12.5 | −63.4 | −33.2 | −11.2 | 630 | −1.9 | −0.1 | 0 |
| 16 | −56.7 | −28.5 | −8.5 | 800 | −0.8 | 0 | 0 |
| 20 | −50.5 | −24.2 | −6.2 | 1,000 | 0 | 0 | 0 |
| 25 | −44.7 | −20.4 | −4.4 | 1,250 | 0.6 | 0 | 0 |
| 31.5 | −39.4 | −17.1 | −3.0 | 1,600 | 1.0 | 0 | −0.1 |
| 40 | −34.6 | −14.2 | −2.0 | 2,000 | 1.2 | −0.1 | −0.2 |
| 50 | −30.2 | −11.6 | −1.3 | 2,500 | 1.3 | −0.2 | −0.3 |
| 63 | −26.2 | −9.3 | −0.8 | 3,150 | 1.2 | −0.4 | −0.5 |
| 80 | −22.5 | −7.4 | −0.5 | 4,000 | 1.0 | −0.7 | −0.8 |
| 100 | −19.1 | −5.6 | −0.3 | 5,000 | 0.5 | −1.2 | −1.3 |
| 125 | −16.1 | −4.2 | −0.2 | 6,300 | −0.1 | −1.9 | −2.0 |
| 160 | −13.4 | −3.0 | −0.1 | 8,000 | −1.1 | −2.9 | −3.0 |
| 200 | −10.9 | −2.0 | 0 | 10,000 | −2.5 | −4.3 | −4.4 |
| 250 | −8.6 | −1.3 | 0 | 12,500 | −4.3 | −6.1 | −6.2 |
| 315 | −6.6 | −0.8 | 0 | 16,000 | −6.6 | −8.4 | −8.5 |
| 400 | −4.8 | −0.5 | 0 | 20,000 | −9.3 | −11.1 | −11.2 |

**EXAMPLE 15–2** A new type 2 sound level meter is to be tested with two pure tone sources that emit 90 dB. The pure tones are at 1000 Hz and 100 Hz. Estimate the expected readings on the A, B, and C weighting networks.

Solution From Table 15–1 at 1000 Hz, we note that the relative response (correction factor) for each of the weighting networks is zero. Thus for the pure tone at 1000 Hz we would expect the readings on the A, B, and C networks to be 90 dB.

From Table 15–1 at 100 Hz, the relative response for each weighting network differs. For the A network, the meter will subtract 19.1 dB from the actual reading, for the B network, the meter will subtract 5.6 dB from the actual reading, and for the C network, the meter will subtract 0.3 dB. Thus, the anticipated readings would be

A network: $90 - 19.1 = 70.9$, or 71 dB(A)
B network: $90 - 5.6 = 84.4$, or 84 dB(B)
C network: $90 - 0.3 = 89.7$, or 90 dB(C)

**EXAMPLE 15–3** The following sound levels were measured on the A, B, and C weighting networks:

Source 1: 94 dB(A), 95 dB(B), and 96 dB(C)
Source 2: 74 dB(A), 83 dB(B), and 90 dB(C)

Characterize the sources as "low frequency or mid/high frequency."

Solution From Figure 15–6, we can see that readings on the A, B, and C networks will be close together if the source emits noise in the frequency range above about 500 Hz. This range may be classified mid/high frequency because we cannot distinguish between "mid" and "high" frequency using a type 2 sound level meter. Likewise, we can see that below 200 Hz (low frequency), readings on the A, B, and C scale will be substantially different. The readings from the A network will be lower than the readings from the B network, and readings from both the A and B networks will be lower than those from the C network.

*Source 1:* Note that the sound levels on each of the weighting networks differ by 1 dB. From Figure 15–6, it appears that the sound level will be in the mid/high-frequency range.
*Source 2:* Note that the sound levels on each of the weighting networks differ by several decibels and that the reading from the A network is lower than that from the B network and both are below that from the C network. From Figure 15–6, it appears that the sound level will be in the low-frequency range.

**Octave Bands.**    To completely characterize a noise, it is necessary to break it down into its frequency components, or spectra. Normal practice is to consider 8 to 11 octave bands.* The standard octave bands and their geometric mean frequencies (center band frequencies) are given in Table 15–2. Octave analysis is performed with a combination precision sound level meter and an octave filter set.

---

*An octave is the frequency interval between a given frequency and twice that frequency. For example, given the frequency 22 Hz, the octave band is from 22 to 44 Hz. A second octave band would then be from 44 to 88 Hz.

| **TABLE 15–2** | Octave Bands | | |
|---|---|---|---|
| **Octave Frequency Range (Hz)** | **Geometric Mean Frequency (Hz)** | **Octave Frequency Range (Hz)** | **Geometric Mean Frequency (Hz)** |
| 22–44 | 31.5 | 1,400–2,800 | 2,000 |
| 44–88 | 63 | 2,800–5,600 | 4,000 |
| 88–175 | 125 | 5,600–11,200 | 8,000 |
| 175–350 | 250 | 11,200–22,400 | 16,000 |
| 350–700 | 500 | 22,400–44,800 | 31,500 |
| 700–1,400 | 1,000 | | |

Although octave band analysis is frequently sufficient for community noise control (i.e., identifying violators), more refined analysis is required for corrective action and design. One-third octave band analysis provides a slightly more refined picture of the noise source than the full octave band analysis. This improved resolution is usually sufficient for determining corrective action for community noise problems. Narrow band analysis is highly refined and may imply band widths down to 2 Hz. This degree of refinement is only justified in product design and testing or in troubleshooting industrial machine noise and vibration.

**Averaging Sound Pressure Levels.**    Because of the logarithmic nature of the decibel, the average value of a collection of sound pressure level measurements cannot be computed in the normal fashion. Instead, the following equation must be used:

$$\bar{L}_p = 20 \log \frac{1}{N} \sum_{j=1}^{N} 10^{(L_j/20)} \tag{15–13}$$

where $\bar{L}_p$ = average sound pressure level (in dB re: 20 $\mu$Pa)
   $N$ = number of measurements
   $L_j$ = the $j$th sound pressure levels (in dB re: 20 $\mu$Pa)
   $j = 1, 2, 3, \ldots N$

This equation is equally applicable to sound levels in decibels(A). It may also be used to compute average sound power levels if the factors of 20 are replaced with 10s.

**EXAMPLE 15–4**    Compute the mean sound level from the following four readings (all in decibels): 38, 51, 68, and 78.

Solution    First we compute the sum.

$$\sum_{j=1}^{4} = 10^{(38/20)} + 10^{(51/20)} + 10^{(68/20)} + 10^{(78/20)}$$

$$= 1.09 \times 10^4$$

Now we complete the computation.

$$\bar{L}_p = 20 \log \frac{1.09 \times 10^4}{4}$$

$$= 68.7, \text{ or } 69 \text{ dBA}$$

Straight arithmetic averaging would yield 58.7, or 59 dB.

**FIGURE 15–7**

Type A impulse noise.

**FIGURE 15–8**

Type B impulse noise.

**Types of Sounds.**    Patterns of noise may be qualitatively described by one of the following terms: **steady-state,** or **continuous; intermittent;** and **impulse,** or **impact. Continuous noise** is an uninterrupted sound level that varies less than 5 dB during the period of observation. An example is the noise from a household fan. **Intermittent noise** is a continuous noise that persists for more than 1 s that is interrupted for more than 1 s. A dentist's drilling would be an example of an intermittent noise. **Impulse noise** is characterized by a change of sound pressure of 40 dB or more within 0.5 s with a duration of less than 1 s.* The noise from firing a weapon would be an example of an impulsive noise.

Two types of impulse noise generally are recognized. The type A impulse is characterized by a rapid rise to a peak sound pressure level followed by a small negative pressure wave or by decay to the background level (Figure 15–7). The type B impulse is characterized by a damped (oscillatory) decay (Figure 15–8). When the duration of the type A impulse is simply the duration of the initial peak, the duration of the type B impulse is the time required for the envelope to decay to 20 dB below the peak. Because of the short duration of the impulse, a special sound-level meter must be employed to measure impulse noise. You should note that the peak sound pressure level is different from the impulse sound level because of the time-averaging used in the latter.

## 15–2    EFFECTS OF NOISE ON PEOPLE

For the purpose of our discussion, we have classified the effects of noise on people into the following two categories: auditory effects and psychological–sociological effects. **Auditory effects** include both hearing loss and speech interference. **Psychological–sociological effects** include annoyance, sleep interference, effects on performance, and acoustical privacy.

### The Hearing Mechanism

Before we can discuss hearing loss, it is important to outline the general structure of the ear and how it works.

Anatomically, the ear is separated into three sections: the outer ear, the middle ear, and the inner ear (Figure 15–9). The outer and middle ear serve to convert sound pressure to vibrations. In addition, they perform the protective role of keeping debris and objects from reaching the inner ear. The Eustachian tube extends from the middle ear space to the upper part of the throat behind the soft palate. The tube is normally closed. Contraction of the palate muscles during yawning, chewing, or swallowing opens the tubes. This allows the middle ear to ventilate and

---

*The Occupational Safety and Health Administration (OSHA) classifies repetitive events, including impulses, as steady noise if the interval between events is less than 0.5 s.

**FIGURE 15–9**

Anatomical divisions of the ear. (*Source: Seeley, R., T. Stephens, and P. Tate, Anatomy and Physiology, 6th ed., McGraw-Hill, New York, 2003. Reprinted by permission.*)

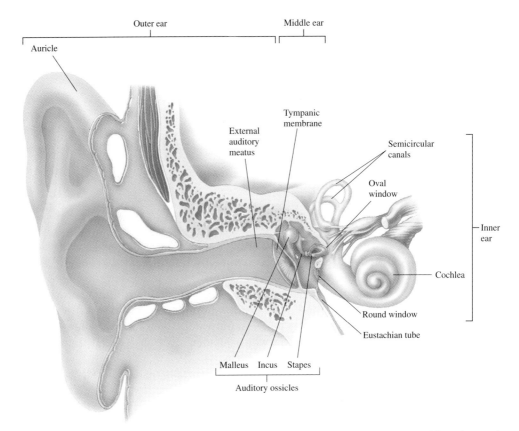

equalize pressure. If external air pressure changes rapidly, for example, by a sudden change in elevation, the tube is opened by involuntary swallowing or yawning to equalize the pressure.

The sound transducer mechanism is housed in the middle ear.* It consists of the **tympanic membrane** (eardrum) and three **ossicles** (bones) (Figure 15–10). The ossicles are supported by ligaments and may be moved by two muscles or by deflection of the tympanic membrane. The muscle movement is involuntary. Loud sounds cause these muscles to contract, which stiffens and diminishes the movement of the ossicular chain. This presumably offers some protection for the delicate inner ear structure from physical injury. According to J. D. Clemis, "More convincing research is still needed to test the validity of this theory of the function of these muscles." The discussion on the middle ear that follows is excerpted from Clemis [2].

> The primary function of the middle ear in the hearing process is to transfer sound energy from the outer to the inner ear. As the eardrum vibrates, it transfers its motion to the malleus. Since the bones of the ossicular chain are connected to one another, the movements of the malleus are passed on to the incus, and finally to the stapes, which is imbedded in the oval window.
>
> As the stapes moves back and forth in a rocking motion, it passes the vibrations into the inner ear through the oval window. Thus, the mechanical motion of the eardrum is effectively transmitted through the middle ear and into the fluid of the inner ear.
>
> The sound-conducting transducer amplifies sound by two main mechanisms. First, the large surface area of the drum as compared to the small surface area of the base of the stapes (footplate) results in a hydraulic effect. The eardrum has about 25 times as much surface area as the oval window. All of the sound pressure collected on the eardrum is transmitted through the ossicular chain and is concentrated on the much smaller area of the oval window. This produces a significant increase in pressure.

---

*A **transducer** is a device that transmits power from one system to another. In this case, sound power is converted to mechanical displacement, which is later measured and interpreted by the brain.

## FIGURE 15–10

The sound transducer mechanism housed in the middle ear. (*Source:* Seeley, R., T. Stephens, and P. Tate, *Anatomy and Physiology,* 6th ed., McGraw-Hill, New York, 2003. Reprinted by permission.)

1. Sound waves strike the tympanic membrane and cause it to vibrate.

2. Vibration of the tympanic membrane causes the three bones of the middle ear to vibrate.

3. The foot plate of the stapes vibrates in the oval window.

4. Vibration of the foot plate causes the perilymph in the scala vestibuli to vibrate.

5. Vibration of the perilymph causes displacement of the basilar membrane. Short waves (high pitch) cause displacement of the basilar membrane near the oval window, and longer waves (low pitch) cause displacement of the basilar membrane some distance from the oval window. Movement of the basilar membrane is detected in the hair cells of the spiral organ, which are attached to the basilar membrane.

6. Vibrations of the perilymph in the scala vestibuli and of the endolymph in the cochlear duct are transferred to the perilymph of the scala tympani.

7. Vibrations in the perilymph of the scala tympani are transferred to the round window, where they are dampened.

The bones of the ossicular chain are arranged in such a way that they act as a series of levers. The long arms are nearest the eardrum, and the shorter arms are toward the oval window. The fulcrums are located where the individual bones meet. A small pressure on the long arm of the lever produces a much stronger pressure on the shorter arm. Since the longer arm is attached to the eardrum and the shorter arm is attached to the oval window, the ossicular chain acts as an amplifier of sound pressure. The magnification effect of the entire sound-conducting mechanism is about 22-to-1.

The inner ear houses both the balance receptors and the auditory receptors. The auditory receptors are in the **cochlea,** a bone shaped like a snail coiled two and one-half times around its own axis (see Figure 15–9). A cross section through the cochlea (Figure 15–11) reveals three compartments: the **scala vestibuli;** the **scala media;** and the **scala tympani.** The scala vestibuli and the scala tympani are connected at the apex of the cochlea. They are filled with a fluid called **perilymph** in which the scala media floats. The hearing organ, the **organ of Corti,** is housed in the scala media. The scala media contains a different fluid, endolymph, which bathes the organ of Corti.

The scala media is triangular in shape and is about 34 mm in length. As shown in Figure 15–11, there are cells growing up from the **basilar membrane.** They have a tuft of hair at one end and are attached to the hearing nerve at the other. A gelatinous membrane (**tectorial membrane**) extends over the hair cells and is attached to the **limbus spiralis.** The hair cells are embedded in the tectorial membrane.

Vibration of the oval window by the stapes causes the fluids of the three scalae to develop a wave-like motion. The movement of the basilar membrane and the tectorial membrane in opposite directions causes a shearing motion on the hair cells. The dragging of the hair cells sets up electrical impulses in the auditory nerves, which are transmitted to the brain.

The nerve endings near the oval and round windows are sensitive to high frequencies. Those near the apex of the cochlea are sensitive to low frequencies.

**FIGURE 15–11**

Cross section through the cochlea.

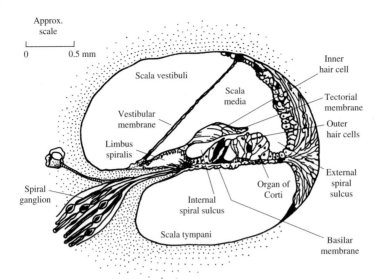

**FIGURE 15–12**

Fletcher–Munson equal loudness contours. (*Source:* Edward B. Magrab, *Environmental Noise Control*, Wiley, New York, 1975. Reprinted by permission.)

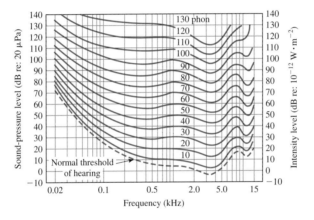

### Normal Hearing

**Frequency Range and Sensitivity.** The ear of the young, audiometrically healthy, adult male responds to sound waves in the frequency range of 20 to 16,000 Hz. Young children and women often have the capacity to respond to frequencies up to 20,000 Hz. The speech zone lies in the frequency range of 500 to 2000 Hz. The ear is most sensitive in the frequency range from 2000 to 5000 Hz. The smallest perceptible sound pressure in this frequency range is 20 μPa.

A sound pressure of 20 μPa at 1.000 Hz in air corresponds to a 1.0-nm displacement of the air molecules. The thermal motion of the air molecules corresponds to a sound pressure of about 1 μPa. If the ear were much more sensitive, you would hear the air molecules crashing against your ear like waves on the beach!

**Loudness.** In general, two pure tones having different frequencies but the same sound pressure level will be heard as different loudness levels. Loudness level is a psychoacoustic quantity.

In 1933, Fletcher and Munson conducted a series of experiments to determine the relationship between frequency and loudness [3]. A reference tone and a test tone were presented alternately to the test subjects, who were asked to adjust the sound level of the test tone until it sounded as loud as the reference. The results were plotted as sound pressure level in decibels versus the test tone frequency (Figure 15–12). The curves are called the **Fletcher–Munson,** or **equal loudness, contours.** The reference frequency is 1000 Hz. The curves are labeled in **phons,** which are the sound pressure levels of the 1000-Hz pure tone in decibels. The lowest contour (dashed line) represents the "threshold of hearing." The actual threshold may vary by as much as ±10 dB between individuals with normal hearing.

**Audiometry.**   Hearing tests are conducted with a device known as an **audiometer.** Basically, it consists of a source of pure tones with variable sound pressure level output into a pair of earphones. If the instrument also automatically prepares a graph of the test results (an **audiogram**), then it will include a weighting network called the **hearing threshold level** (HTL) scale.

The HTL scale is one in which the loudness of each pure tone is adjusted by frequency such that "0" dB is the level just audible for the average normal young ear. Two reference standards are in use: ASA-1951 and ANSI-1969. The ANSI reference values are shown in Figure 15–13. Note the similarity to the Fletcher–Munson contours. The initial audiogram prepared for an individual may be referred to as the baseline HTL or simply as the HTL.

The audiogram shown in Figure 15–14 reflects excellent hearing response. The average normal response may vary ±10 dB from the "0" dB value. As noted on the audiogram, this test was conducted with the ANSI-1969 weighting network.

You may have noted that we keep stressing young in our references to normal hearing. This is because hearing loss occurs due to the aging process, a type of loss called **presbycusis.**

**FIGURE 15–13**

The ANSI reference values for hearing threshold level.

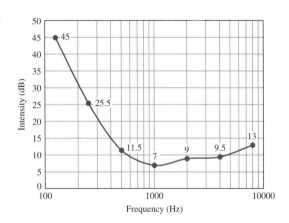

**FIGURE 15–14**

An audiogram illustrating excellent hearing response.

Various degrees of injury
to the hair cells.

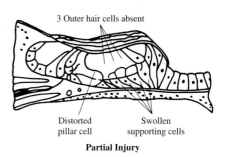

**Normal Organ of Corti**

**Partial Injury**

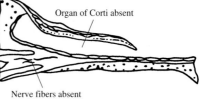

**Severe Injury**

**Total Degeneration**

### Hearing Impairment

**Mechanism.**    With the exception of eardrum rupture from intense explosive noise, the outer
and middle ear rarely are damaged by noise. More commonly, hearing loss is a result of neural
damage involving injury to the hair cells (Figure 15–15). Two theories are offered to explain
noise-induced injury. The first is that excessive shearing forces mechanically damage the hair
cells. The second is that intense noise stimulation forces the hair cells into high metabolic activity, which overdrives them to the point of metabolic failure and consequent cell death. Once
destroyed, hair cells are not capable of regeneration.

**Measurement.**    Because direct observation of the organ of Corti in persons having potential
hearing loss is impossible, injury is inferred from losses in their HTL. The increased sound pressure level required to achieve a new HTL is called **threshold shift.** Obviously, any measurement
of threshold shift depends on having a baseline audiogram taken before the noise exposure.

Hearing losses may be either temporary or permanent. Noise-induced losses must be separated from other causes of hearing loss such as age (presbycusis), drugs, disease, and blows on
the head. **Temporary threshold shift** (TTS) is distinguished from **permanent threshold shift**
(PTS) by the fact that in TTS removal of the noise over stimulation will result in a gradual return
to baseline hearing thresholds.

**Factors Affecting Threshold Shift.**    Important variables in the development of temporary and permanent hearing threshold changes include the following [4].

1. *Sound level.* Sound levels must exceed 60–80 dBA before the typical person will
   experience TTS.
2. *Frequency distribution of sound.* Sounds having most of their energy in the speech
   frequencies are more potent in causing a threshold shift than sounds having most of
   their energy below the speech frequencies.

3. *Duration of sound.* The longer the sound lasts, the greater the amount of threshold shift.

4. *Temporal distribution of sound exposure.* The number and length of quiet periods between periods of sound influences the potentiality of threshold shift.

5. *Individual differences in tolerance.* These differences may vary greatly among individuals.

6. *Type of sound.* (steady-state, intermittent, impulse, or impact) The tolerance to peak sound pressure is greatly reduced by increasing the duration of the sound.

**Temporary Threshold Shift (TTS).**   TTS is often accompanied by a ringing in the ear, muffling of sound, or discomfort of the ears. Most of the TTS occurs during the first 2 h of exposure. Recovery to the baseline HTL after TTS begins within the first hour or two after exposure. Most of the recovery that is going to be attained occurs within 16 to 24 h after exposure.

**Permanent Threshold Shift (PTS).**   There appears to be a direct relationship between TTS and PTS. Noise levels that do not produce TTS after 2–8 h of exposure will not produce PTS if continued beyond this time. The shape of the TTS audiogram will resemble the shape of the PTS audiogram.

Noise-induced hearing loss generally is first characterized by a sharply localized dip in the HTL curve at the frequencies between 3000 and 6000 Hz. This dip commonly occurs at 4000 Hz (Figure 15–16). This is the **high-frequency notch.** The progress from TTS to PTS with continued noise exposure follows a fairly regular pattern. First, the high-frequency notch broadens and spreads in both directions. Although substantial losses may occur above 3000 Hz, the individual will not notice any change in hearing. In fact, the individual will not notice any hearing loss until the speech frequencies between 500 and 2000 Hz average more than a 25-dB increase in HTL on the ANSI-1969 scale. The onset and progress of noise-induced permanent hearing loss is slow and insidious. The exposed individual is unlikely to notice it. Total hearing loss from noise exposure has not been observed.

**Acoustic Trauma.**   The outer and middle ear rarely are damaged by intense noise. However, explosive sounds can rupture the tympanic membrane or dislocate the ossicular chain. The permanent hearing loss that results from very brief exposure to a very loud noise is termed **acoustic trauma** [5]. Damage to the outer and middle ear may or may not accompany acoustic trauma.

**FIGURE 15–16**

An audiogram illustrating hearing loss at the high-frequency notch.

**Protective Mechanisms.** Although the extent and mechanisms are unclear, it appears that the structures of the middle ear offer some protection to the delicate sensory organs of the inner ear [6]. One mechanism of protection is a change in the mode of vibration of the stapes. As noted earlier, there is some evidence that the muscles of the middle ear contract reflexively in response to loud noise. This contraction results in a reduction in the amplification that this series of levers normally produces. Changes in transmission may be on the order of 5 to 10 dB. However, the reaction time of the muscle–bone structure is on the order of 10 ms. Thus, this protection is not effective against steep acoustic wave fronts that are characteristic of impact or impulsive noise.

### Damage-Risk Criteria

A **damage-risk criterion** specifies the maximum allowable exposure to which a person may be exposed if risk of hearing impairment is to be avoided. The American Academy of Ophthalmology and Otolaryngology has defined **hearing impairment** as an average HTL in excess of 25 dB (ANSI-1969) at 500, 1000, and 2000 Hz. This is called the **low fence. Total impairment** is said to occur when the average HTL exceeds 92 dB. Presbycusis is included in setting the 25-dB ANSI low fence. Two criteria have been set to provide conditions under which nearly all workers may be repeatedly exposed without adversely affecting their ability to hear and understand normal speech.

**Continuous or Intermittent Exposure.** The National Institute for Occupational Safety and Health (NIOSH) has recommended that occupational noise exposure be controlled so that no worker is exposed in excess of the limits defined by line B in Figure 15–17. In addition, NIOSH recommends that new installations be designed to hold noise exposure below the limits defined by line A in Figure 15–17. The Walsh–Healey Act, which was enacted by Congress in 1969 to protect workers, used a damage-risk criterion equivalent to the line A criterion.

### Speech Interference

As we all know, noise can interfere with our ability to communicate. Many noises that are not intense enough to cause hearing impairment can interfere with speech communication. The interference, or **masking,** effect is a complicated function of the distance between the speaker and listener and the frequency components of the spoken words. The speech interference level (SIL) was

**FIGURE 15–17**

NIOSH occupational noise exposure limits for continuous or intermittent noise exposure.

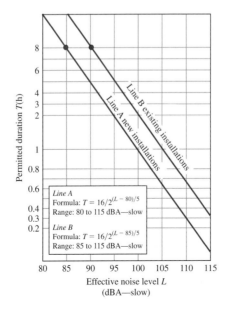

Line A
Formula: $T = 16/2^{(L - 80)/5}$
Range: 80 to 115 dBA—slow

Line B
Formula: $T = 16/2^{(L - 85)/5}$
Range: 85 to 115 dBA—slow

**FIGURE 15–18**

Quality of speech communication as a function of sound level and distance. [*Source:* James D. Miller, *Effects of Noise on People* (U.S. Environmental Protection Agency Publication No. NTID 300.7), Washington, DC: U.S. Government Printing Office, 1971.]

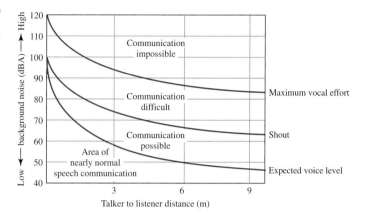

developed as a measure of the difficulty in communication that could be expected with different background noise levels [7]. It is now more convenient to talk in terms of A-weighted background noise levels and the quality of speech communication (Figure 15–18).

**EXAMPLE 15–5**　Consider the problem of a speaker in a quiet zone who wishes to speak to a listener operating a 4.5-Mg truck 6.0 m away. The sound level in the truck cab is about 73 dBA.

Solution　Using Figure 15–18, we can see that she is going to have to shout very loudly to be heard. However, if she moved to within about 1.0 m, she would be able to use her "expected" voice level, that is, the unconscious slight rise in voice level that one would normally use in a noisy situation.

It can be seen that at distances not uncommon in living rooms or classrooms (4.5–6.0 m), the A-weighted background level must be below about 50 dB for normal conversation.

### Annoyance

Annoyance by noise is a response to auditory experience. Annoyance has its base in the unpleasant nature of some sounds, in the activities that are disturbed or disrupted by noise, in the physiological reactions to noise, and in the responses to the meaning of "messages" carried by the noise [8]. For example, a sound heard at night may be more annoying than one heard by day, just as one that fluctuates may be more annoying than one that does not. A sound that resembles another sound that we already dislike and that perhaps threatens us may be especially annoying. A sound that we know is mindlessly inflicted and will not be removed soon may be more annoying than one that is temporarily and regretfully inflicted. A sound, the source of which is visible, may be more annoying than one with an invisible source. A sound that is new may be less annoying. A sound that is locally a political issue may have a particularly high or low annoyance [9].

The degree of annoyance and whether that annoyance leads to complaints, product rejection, or action against an existing or anticipated noise source depend on many factors. Some of these factors have been identified, and their relative importance has been assessed. Responses to aircraft noise have received the greatest attention. There is less information available concerning responses to other noises, however, such as those of surface transportation and industry, and those from recreational activities [8]. Many of the noise-rating or forecasting systems now in existence were developed in an effort to predict annoyance reactions.

**Sonic Booms.**　One noise of special interest with respect to annoyance is called **sonic boom** or, more correctly as we shall see, sonic booms.

**FIGURE 15–19**

Sonic booms resulting from bow wave and tail wave set in motion by supersonic flight.

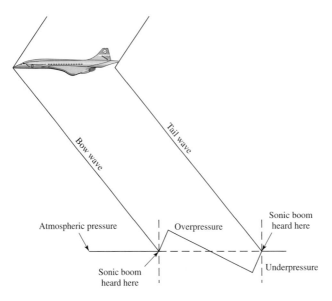

The flow of air around an aircraft or other object whose speed exceeds the speed of sound (supersonic) is characterized by the existence of discontinuities in the air known as **shock wave.** These discontinuities result from the sudden encounter of an impenetrable body with air. At subsonic speeds, the air seems to be forewarned; thus, it begins its outward flow before the arrival of the leading edge. At supersonic speeds, however, the air in front of the aircraft is undisturbed, and the sudden impulse at the leading edge creates a region of overpressure (Figure 15–19) where the pressure is higher than atmospheric pressure. This overpressure region travels outward with the speed of sound, creating a conically shaped shock wave called the **bow wave** that changes the direction of airflow. A second shock wave, the **tail wave,** is produced by the tail of the aircraft and is associated with a region where the pressure is lower than normal. This underpressure discontinuity causes the air behind the aircraft to move sideways.

Major pressure changes are experienced at the ear as the bow and tail shock waves reach an observer. Each of these pressure deviations produces the sensation of an explosive sound [10]. Note that the pressure wave and, hence, the sonic boom exist whenever the aircraft is at supersonic speed and not "just when it breaks the sound barrier."

Both the loudness of the noise and the startling effect of the impulse (it makes us "jump") are found to be very annoying. Apparently we can never get used to this kind of noise. Supersonic flight by commercial aircraft is forbidden in the airspace above the United States. Supersonic flight by military aircraft is restricted to sparsely inhabited areas.

### Sleep Interference

Sleep interference is a special category of annoyance that has received a great deal of attention and study [11]. Almost all of us have been wakened or kept from falling asleep by loud, strange, frightening, or annoying sounds. It is commonplace to be wakened by an alarm clock or clock radio. But it also appears that one can get used to sounds and sleep through them. Possibly, environmental sounds only disturb sleep when they are unfamiliar. If so, disturbance of sleep would depend only on the frequency of unusual or novel sounds. Everyday experience also suggests that sound can help to induce sleep and, perhaps, to maintain it. The soothing lullaby, the steady hum of a fan, or the rhythmic sound of the surf, can serve to induce relaxation. Certain steady sounds can serve as an acoustical shade and mask disturbing transient sounds.

Common anecdotes about sleep disturbance suggest an even greater complexity. A rural person may have difficulty sleeping in a noisy urban area. An urban person may be disturbed by

**FIGURE 15–20**

Effects of brief noise on sleep. [*Source:* J. D. Miller (U.S. Environmental Protection Agency Publication No. NTID 300.7), Washington, DC: U.S. Government Printing Office, 1971.]

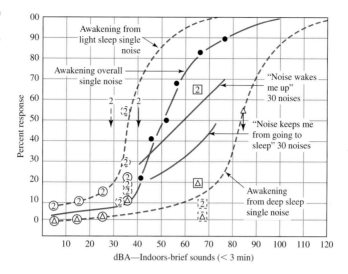

the quiet when sleeping in a rural area. And how is it that a parent may wake to a slight stirring of his or her child, yet sleep through a thunderstorm? These observations all suggest that the relations between exposure to sound and the quality of a night's sleep are complicated.

The effects of relatively brief noises (about 3 min or less) on a person sleeping in a quiet environment have been studied the most thoroughly. Typically, presentations of the sounds are widely spaced throughout a sleep period of 5 to 7 h. A summary of some of these observations is presented in Figure 15–20. The dashed lines are hypothetical curves that represent the percent of awakenings under conditions in which the subject is a normally rested young adult male who has been adapted for several nights to the procedures of a quiet sleep laboratory. He has been instructed to press an easily reached button to indicate that he has awakened, and had been moderately motivated to awake and respond to the noise.

While in light sleep, subjects can awake to sounds that are about 30–40 dB above the level at which they can be detected when subjects are conscious, alert, and attentive. While in deep sleep, the stimulus may have to be 50–80 dB above the level at which they can be detected by conscious, alert, attentive subjects before they will awaken the sleeping subject.

The solid lines in Figure 15–20 are data from questionnaire studies of persons who live near airports. The percentage of respondents who claim that flyovers wake them or keep them from falling asleep is plotted against the A-weighted sound level of a single flyover. These curves are for the case of approximately 30 flyovers spaced over the normal sleep period of 6 to 8 h. The filled circles represent the percentage of sleepers that awake to a 3-min sound at each A-weighted sound level (dBA) or lower. This curve is based on data from 350 persons, each tested in his or her own bedroom. These measures were made between 2:00 and 7:00 A.M. It is reasonable to assume that most of the subjects were roused from a light sleep.

### Effects on Performance

When a task requires the use of auditory signals, speech or nonspeech, then noise at any intensity level sufficient to mask or interfere with the perception of these signals will interfere with the performance of the task.

Where mental or motor tasks do not involve auditory signals, the effects of noise on their performance have been difficult to assess. Human behavior is complicated, and it has been difficult to discover exactly how different kinds of noises might influence different kinds of people doing different kinds of tasks. Nonetheless, the following general conclusions have emerged. Steady noises without special meaning do not seem to interfere with human performance unless the A-weighted noise level exceeds about 90 dB. Irregular bursts of noise (intrusive noise) are more disruptive than steady noises. Even when the A-weighted sound levels of irregular bursts are below 90 dB, they may sometimes interfere with performance of a task. High-frequency components of noise, above about 1000–2000 Hz, may produce more interference with performance than low-frequency components of noise. Noise does not seem to influence the overall rate of work, but high levels of noise may increase the variability of the rate of work. "Noise pauses" may occur followed by compensating increases in work rate. Noise is more likely to reduce the accuracy of work than to reduce the total quantity of work. Complex tasks are more likely to be adversely influenced by noise than are simple tasks.

### Acoustic Privacy

Without opportunity for privacy, either everyone must conform strictly to an elaborate social code or everyone must adopt highly permissive attitudes. Opportunity for privacy avoids the necessity for either extreme. In particular, without opportunity for acoustical privacy, one may experience all of the effects of noise previously described, and, in addition, one is constrained because one's own activities may disturb others. Without acoustical privacy, sound, like a faulty telephone exchange, reaches the "wrong number." The result disturbs both the sender and the receiver.

## 15–3   RATING SYSTEMS

### Goals of a Noise-Rating System

An ideal noise-rating system is one that allows measurements by sound level meters or analyzers to be summarized succinctly and yet represent noise exposure in a meaningful way. In our previous discussions on loudness and annoyance, we noted that our response to sound is strongly dependent on the frequency of the sound. Furthermore, we noted that the type of noise (continuous, intermittent, or impulsive) and the time of day that it occurred (night being worse than day) were significant factors in annoyance.

Thus, the ideal system must take frequency into account. It should differentiate between daytime and nighttime noise. And, finally, it must be capable of describing the cumulative noise exposure. A statistical system can satisfy these requirements.

The practical difficulty with a statistical rating system is that it would yield a large set of parameters for each measuring location. A much larger array of numbers would be required to characterize a neighborhood. It is literally impossible for such an array of numbers to be used effectively in enforcement. Thus, considerable effort has been made to define a single number measure of noise exposure. The following paragraphs describe one of the systems now being used.

### The $L_N$ Concept

The parameter $L_N$ is a statistical measure that indicates how frequently a particular sound level is exceeded [12]. If, for example, we write $L_{30} = 67$ dBA, then we know that 72 dB(A) was exceeded for 30% of the measuring time. A plot of $L_N$ against $N$ where $N = 1\%, 2\%, 3\%$, and so forth, would look like the cumulative distribution curve shown in Figure 15–21.

Allied to the cumulative distribution curve is the probability distribution curve. A plot of this will show how often the noise levels fall into certain class intervals. In Figure 15–22 we can see that 35% of the time the measured noise levels ranged between 65 and 67 dBA; for 15% of the time they ranged between 67 and 69 dBA; and so on. The relationship between this picture and the one for $L_N$ is really quite simple. By adding the percentages given in successive class intervals from right to left, we can arrive at a corresponding $L_N$, where $N$ is the sum of the percentages and $L$ is the lower limit of the left-most class interval added, thus, $L_{30}$

$$L(1 + 2 + 12 + 15) = 67 \text{ dBA}$$

**FIGURE 15-21**

Cumulative distribution curve.

**FIGURE 15-22**

Probability distribution plot.

### The $L_{eq}$ Concept

The equivalent continuous equal energy level ($L_{eq}$) can be applied to any fluctuating noise level [12]. It is that constant noise level that, over a given time, expends the same amount of energy as the fluctuating level over the same period. It is expressed as follows.

$$L_{eq} = 10 \log \frac{1}{t} \int_0^t 10^{L(t)/10} \, dt \qquad (15\text{-}14)$$

where $t$ = the time over which $L_{eq}$ is determined
$\quad L(t)$ = the time varying noise level in dBA

Generally speaking, there is no well-defined relationship between $L(t)$ and time, so a series of discrete samples of $L(t)$ have to be taken. This modifies the expression to

$$L_{eq} = 10 \log \sum_{i=1}^{i=n} 10^{L_i/10} \, t_i \qquad (15\text{-}15)$$

where $n$ = the total number of samples taken
$\quad L_i$ = the noise level in dBA of the $i$th sample
$\quad t_i$ = fraction of total sample time

**EXAMPLE 15-6**   Consider the case where a noise level of 90 dBA exists for 10 min and is followed by a reduced noise level of 70 dBA for 30 min. What is the equivalent continuous equal energy level for the 40-min period? Assume a 5-min sampling interval.

Solution   If the sampling interval is 5 min, then the total number of samples ($n$) is 8, and the fraction of total sample time ($t_i$) for each sample is $1/8 = 0.125$. With these preliminary calculations, we may now compute the sum.

$$\sum_{t=1}^2 = (10^{90/10})(0.250) + (10^{70/10})(0.750)$$

$$= (2.50 \times 10^8) + (7.50 \times 10^6) = 2.58 \times 10^8$$

And finally, we take the log to find

$$L_{eq} = 10 \log(2.58 \times 10^8) = 84.11, \text{ or } 84 \text{ dBA}$$

**FIGURE 15–23**

Graphical illustration of $L_{eq}$ computation given in Example 15–6.

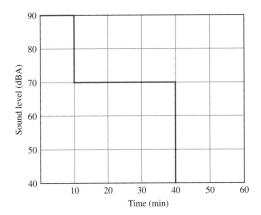

The example calculation is depicted graphically in Figure 15–23. From this you may note that great emphasis is put on occasional high noise levels.

The equivalent noise level was introduced in 1965 in Germany as a rating specifically to evaluate the effect of aircraft noise on the neighbors of airports [13]. It was almost immediately recognized in Austria as appropriate for evaluating the effect of street traffic noise in dwellings and schoolrooms. It has been embodied in the national test standards of Germany for rating the subjective effects of fluctuating noises of all kinds, such as from street and road traffic, rail traffic, canal and river ship traffic, aircraft, industrial operations (including the noise from individual machines), sports stadiums, playgrounds, and the like.

## 15–4   COMMUNITY NOISE SOURCES AND CRITERIA

It is not our intent to provide a detailed discussion of the noise characteristics of all community noise sources. Likewise, we have not attempted to provide a comprehensive list of noise criteria. Rather, we have selected a few examples to provide you with a feeling for the magnitude and range of the numbers.

### *Transportation Noise*

**Aircraft Noise.**   The noise spectra of a wide body fan jet (e.g., the Boeing 747) reveal that sound pressure levels are higher on takeoff than during the approach to land. This is typical of all aircraft. With the notable exception of the turbo jets, smaller aircraft have lower sound pressure levels.

The annoyance criteria for aircraft operations are based on extensive field measurements and opinion surveys. The results of annoyance surveys at nine airports in the United States and Great Britain are summarized in Figure 15–24. $L_{dn}$ is the $L_{eq}$ for a 24-h period with a 10-dB penalty added to the sound levels that occur during the night which is defined as 10 P.M. to 7 A.M.

**Highway Vehicle Noise.**   For most automobiles, exhaust noise constitutes the predominant source for normal operation below about 55 km · h$^{-1}$ (Figure 15–25). Although tire noise is much less of a problem in automobiles than in trucks, it is the dominant noise source at speeds above 80 km · h$^{-1}$. Although not as noisy as trucks, the total contribution of automobiles to the noise environment is significant because of the very large number in operation.

Diesel trucks are 8–10 dB noisier than gasoline-powered ones. At speeds above 80 km · h$^{-1}$, tire noise often becomes the dominant noise source on the truck. The "crossbar" tread is the noisiest.

Motorcycle noise is highly dependent on the speed of the vehicle. The primary source of noise is the exhaust. The noise spectra of two-cycle and four-cycle engines are of somewhat different character. The two-cycle engines exhibit more high-frequency spectra energy content.

**FIGURE 15–24**

Relationship between exposure to aircraft noise and annoyance. (*Source:* K. D. Kryter, G. Jansen, D. Parker, et al., *Non-Auditory Effects of Noise.* Report of WG-63, National Academy of Science–National Research Council Committee on Hearing, Bioacoustics, and Biomechanics, Washington, DC: U.S. GPO, 1971.)

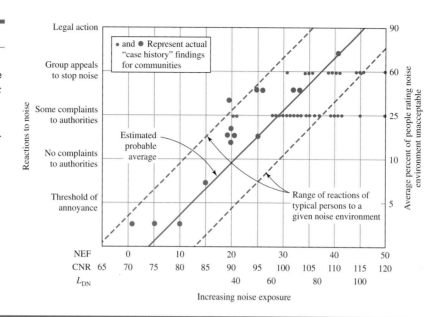

**FIGURE 15–25**

Typical noise spectra of automobiles. (*Source:* U.S. Environmental Protection Agency, *Transportation Noise*, Washington, DC: U.S. Government Printing Office, 1971.)

The U.S. Federal Highway Administration has developed the traffic noise standards shown in Table 15–3. The levels are above those that would be expected to yield no problems but are below those of many existing highways.

### Other Internal Combustion Engines

Because of their ubiquitous nature and the general interest they stimulate, the combustion engines listed in Table 15–4 are included at this point. "In general, these devices are not significant

**TABLE 15-3**                FHA Noise Standards for New Construction

| Land Use Category | Exterior Design Noise Level[a] (dBA) | | Description of Land Use Category |
| | $L_{eq}$ | $L_{10}$ | |
| --- | --- | --- | --- |
| A | 57 | 60 | Tracts of lands in which serenity and quiet are of extraordinary significance and serve an important public need, and where the preservation of those qualities is essential if the area is to continue to serve its intended purpose. For example, such areas could include amphitheaters, particular parks or portions of parks, or open spaces, which are dedicated or recognized by appropriate local officials for activities requiring special qualities of serenity and quiet. |
| B | 67 | 70 | Residences, motels, hotels, public meeting rooms, schools, churches, libraries, hospitals, picnic areas, recreation areas, playgrounds active sports areas, and parks. |
| C | 72 | 75 | Developed lands, properties or activities not included in categories A and B. |
| D | Unlimited | Unlimited | Undeveloped lands. |
| E | 52 (interior) | 55 (interior) | Public meeting rooms, schools, churches, libraries, hospitals, and other such public buildings. |

[a]Either $L_{eq}$ or $L_{10}$ may be used, but not both. The levels are to be based on a 1-h sample.

**TABLE 15-4**                Summary of Noise Characteristics of Internal Combustion Engines

| Source | A-Weighted Noise Energy[a] (kW · h · day$^{-1}$) | Typical A-Weighted Noise Level at 15.2 m (dBA) | 8-h Exposure Level[b] (dBA) | | Typical Exposure Time (h) |
| | | | Average | Maximum | |
| --- | --- | --- | --- | --- | --- |
| Lawn mowers | 63 | 74 | 74 | 82 | 1.5 |
| Garden tractors | 63 | 78 | N/A | N/A | N/A |
| Chain saws | 40 | 82 | 85 | 95 | 1 |
| Snow blowers | 40 | 84 | 61 | 75 | 1 |
| Lawn edgers | 16 | 78 | 67 | 75 | 0.5 |
| Model aircraft | 12 | 78 | 70[c] | 79[c] | 0.25 |
| Leaf blowers | 3.2 | 76 | 67 | 75 | 0.25 |
| Generators | 0.8 | 71 | — | — | — |
| Tillers | 0.4 | 70 | 72 | 80 | 1 |

[a]Based on estimates of the total number of units in operation per day.

[b]Equivalent level for evaluation of relative hearing damage risk.

[c]During engine trimming operation.

*Source:* U.S. Environmental Protection Agency, *Transportation Noise and Noise from Equipment Powered by Internal Combustion Engines,* EPA Pub. No. NTID 300.13, Government Printing Office, Washington, D.C., 1971.

contributors to average residential noise levels in urban areas. However, the relative annoyance of most of the equipment tends to be high [14]." The 8-h exposure level is in reference to the equipment operator.

### Construction Noise

The range of sound levels found for 19 common types of construction equipment is shown in Figure 15–26. Although the sample was limited, the data appear to be reasonably accurate. The noise produced by the interaction of the machine and the material on which it acts often contributes greatly to the sound level.

**FIGURE 15–26**

Range of sound levels from various types of construction equipment (based on limited available data samples). (*Source: Report to the President and Congress on Noise,* 1972.)

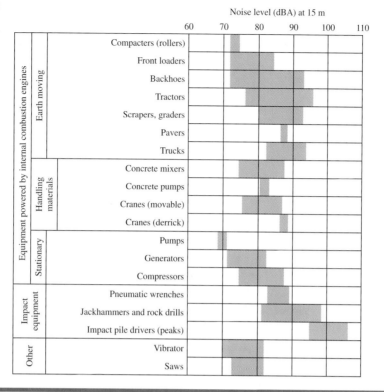

**TABLE 15–5**    HUD Noise Assessment Criteria for New Residential Construction

| General External Exposures | Assessment |
|---|---|
| Exceeds 89 dBA 60 min per 24 hours<br>Exceeds 75 dBA 8 hours per 24 hours<br>CNR zone 3, NEF zone C (airport environs)<br>$L_{NP} > 88$ dB (NP) (exterior) | Unacceptable |
| Exceeds 65 dBA 8 hours per 24 hours<br>Loud repetitive sounds on site<br>CNR zone 2, NEF zone B (airport environs)<br>$L_{NP}$ 74–88 dB (NP) (exterior) | Discretionary: normally unacceptable |
| Does not exceed 65 dBA more than 8 hours per 24 hours<br>$L_{NP}$ 62–74 dB (NP) (exterior) | Discretionary: normally acceptable |
| Does not exceed 45 dBA more than 30 min per 24 hours<br>CNR zone I, NEF zone A (airport environs)<br>$L_{NP} < 62$ dB (NP) (exterior) | Acceptable |

It is difficult, at best, to quantify the annoyance that results from construction noise. The following generalizations appear to hold.

1. Single-house construction in suburban communities will generate sporadic complaints if the boundary line 8-h $L_{eq}$ exceeds 70 dBA.
2. Major excavation and construction in a normal suburban community will generate threats of legal action if the boundary line 8-h $L_{eq}$ exceeds 85 dBA.

### Zoning and Siting Considerations

The U.S. Department of Housing and Urban Development (HUD) set out guideline criteria for noise exposure at residential sites for new construction (Table 15–5). The Federal Aviation

Administration (FAA) has also specified noise levels for land use compatibility. These guidelines, and those given earlier for traffic noise (see Table 15–3), if followed in zoning and siting, will minimize annoyance and complaints.

### Levels to Protect Health and Welfare

In accordance with the directive from Congress, the EPA published noise criteria levels that it deemed necessary to protect the health and welfare of U.S. citizens (Table 15–6) [15]. The EPA maintained that a quiet residential environment is necessary in both urban and rural areas to prevent activity interference and annoyance and to permit the hearing mechanism an opportunity to recuperate if it is exposed to high levels during the day. The $L_{dn}$ of 45 provides a fair margin of safety.

## 15–5 TRANSMISSION OF SOUND OUTDOORS

### Inverse Square Law

If a sphere of radius $\delta$ vibrates with a uniform radial expansion and contraction, sound waves radiate uniformly from its surface. If the sphere is placed such that no sound waves are reflected back in the direction of the source, and if the product $\kappa\delta$, where $\kappa$ is the wave number,* is much less than 1, then the sound intensity at any radial distance $r$ from the sphere is inversely proportional to the square of distance, that is,

$$I = \frac{W}{4\pi r^2} \tag{15–16}$$

where $I$ = sound intensity (in $W \cdot m^{-2}$)
$\quad\quad W$ = sound power of source (in W)

This is the **inverse square law.** It explains that portion of the reduction of sound intensity with distance that is due to wave divergence (Figure 15–27). For a line source such as a roadway or a railroad, the reduction of sound intensity is inversely proportional to $r$ rather than $r^2$. From a practical standpoint it is difficult if not impossible to measure the sound power of the source. In such instances we measure the sound pressure level at some known distance from the source and then use the inverse square law or radial dependence relationships to estimate the sound pressure level at some other distance. For example, using the inverse square law, the sound pressure level, $L_{p2}$, at a distance $r_2$ from the source may be determined if the sound pressure level, $L_{p1}$, at some closer point, $r_1$, is known:

$$L_{p2} = L_{p1} - 10\log\left(\frac{r_2}{r_1}\right)^2 \tag{15–17}$$

For a line source, the sound pressure level, $L_{p2}$, at a distance $r_2$ from the source may be determined at some closer point, $r_1$ by a similar equation.

$$L_{p2} = L_{p1} - 10\log\left(\frac{r_2}{r_1}\right) \tag{15–18}$$

---

*$\kappa = 2\pi/\lambda$, where $\lambda$ wavelength, $\kappa$ has units of reciprocal length, $m^{-1}$.

**FIGURE 15–27**

Illustration of inverse square law.

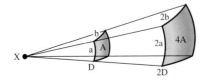

**TABLE 15-6** Yearly Energy Average $L_{eq}$ Identified as Requisite to Protect the Public Health and Welfare with an Adequate Margin of Safety

| | | Indoor | | | Outdoor | | |
|---|---|---|---|---|---|---|---|
| | Measure | Activity Interference | Hearing Loss Consideration | To Protect Against Both Effects[b] | Activity Interference | Hearing Loss Consideration | To Protect Against Both Effects[b] |
| Residential with outside space and farm residences | $L_{dn}$ | 45 | | 45 | 55 | | 55 |
| | $L_{eq(24)}$ | | 70 | | | 70 | |
| Residential with no outside space | $L_{dn}$ | 45 | | 45 | | | |
| | $L_{eq(24)}$ | | 70 | | | | |
| Commercial | $L_{eq(24)}$ | a | 70 | 70[c] | a | 70 | 70[c] |
| Inside transportation | $L_{eq(24)}$ | a | 70 | a | | | |
| Industrial | $L_{eq(24)}$[d] | a | 70 | 70[c] | a | 70 | 70[c] |
| Hospitals | $L_{dn}$ | 45 | | 45 | 55 | | 55 |
| | $L_{eq(24)}$ | | 70 | | | 70 | |
| Educational | $L_{eq(24)}$ | 45 | | 45 | 55 | | 55 |
| | $L_{eq(24)}$[d] | | 70 | | | 70 | |
| Recreational areas | $L_{eq(24)}$ | a | 70 | 70[c] | a | 70 | 70[c] |
| Farm land and general unpopulated land | $L_{eq(24)}$ | | | | a | 70 | 70[c] |

[a] Because different types of activities appear to be associated with different levels, identification of a maximum level for activity interference may be difficult except when speech communication is a critical activity.

[b] Based on lowest level.

[c] Based only on hearing loss.

[d] An $L_{eq(8)}$ of 75 dB may be identified in these situations so long as the exposure over the remaining 16 h per day is low enough to result in negligible contribution to the 24-h average, that is, no greater than an $L_{eq}$ of 60 dB.

Note: Explanation of identified level for hearing loss: The exposure period that results in hearing loss at the identified level is a period of 40 years.

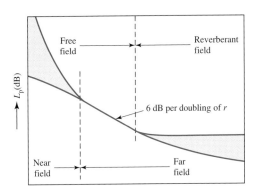

**FIGURE 15–28**

Variation of sound-pressure level in an enclosure along radius $r$ from a noise source. (*Source:* L. L. Beranek, *Noise and Vibration Control*, McGraw-Hill, New York, 1971. Reprinted by permission.)

### Radiation Fields of a Sound Source

The character of the wave radiation from a noise source will vary with distance from the source (Figure 15–28). At locations close to the source, the **near field,** the particle velocity is not in phase with the sound pressure. In this area, $L_p$ fluctuates with distance and does not follow the inverse square law. When the particle velocity and sound pressure are in phase, the location of the sound measurement is said to be in the **far field.** If the sound source is in free space, that is, there are no reflecting surfaces, then measurements in the far field are also **free field measurements.** If the sound source is in a highly reflective space, for example, a room with steel walls, ceiling, and floor, then measurements in the far field are also **reverberant field measurements.** The shaded area in the far field of Figure 15–28 shows that $L_p$ does not follow the inverse square law in the reverberant field.

### Directivity

Most real sources do not radiate sound uniformly in all directions. If you were to measure the sound pressure level in a given frequency band at a fixed distance from a real source, you would find different levels for different directions. If you plotted these data in polar coordinates, you would obtain the directivity pattern of the source.

The **directivity factor** is the numerical measure of the directivity of a sound source. In logarithmic form the directivity factor is called the **directivity index.** For a spherical source it is defined as follows:

$$DI_\theta = L_{p\theta} - L_{ps} \tag{15–19}$$

where $L_{p\theta}$ = sound pressure level measured at distance $r'$ and angle $\theta$ from a directive source radiating power $W$ into an echo-free (**anechoic**) space (in dB)

$L_{ps}$ = sound pressure level measured at distance $r'$ from a nondirective source radiating power $W$ into anechoic space (in dB). This is the same source as the directive source, but acting in the ideal fashion that we assumed in developing the inverse square law.

For a source located on or near a hard, flat surface, the directivity index takes the following form:

$$DI_\theta = L_{p\theta} - L_{ps} + 3 \tag{15–20}$$

The 3-dB addition is made because the measurement is made over a hemisphere instead of a sphere. That is, the intensity at a radius, $r$, is twice as large if a source radiates into a hemisphere rather than the ideal sphere we have used up to this point. Each directivity index is applicable only to the angle at which $L_p$ was measured and only for the frequency at which it was measured.

We assume that the directivity pattern does not change its shape regardless of the distance from the source. This allows us to apply the inverse square law to directive sources simply by measuring the sound pressure level at a distance $r_1$, along the directive angle of interest.

## *Airborne Transmission*

### Effects of Atmospheric Conditions.
Sound energy is absorbed in quiet isotropic air by molecular excitation and relaxation of oxygen molecules and, at very low temperatures, by heat conduction and viscosity in the air. Molecular excitation is a complex function of the frequency of noise, humidity, and temperature. In general, we may say that as the humidity decreases, sound absorption increases. As the temperature increases to about 10–20°C (depending on the noise frequency), absorption increases. Above 25°C, absorption decreases. Sound absorption is higher at higher frequencies.

The vertical temperature profile greatly alters the propagation paths of sound. If a superadiabatic lapse rate exists, sound rays bend upward and noise shadow zones are formed. If an inversion exists, sound rays are bent back toward the ground. This results in an increase in the sound level. These effects are negligible for short distances but may exceed 10 dB at distances over 800 m.

In a similar fashion, wind speed gradients alter the way noise propagates. Sound traveling with the wind is bent down, while sound traveling against the wind is bent upward. When sound waves are bent down, there is little or no increase in sound levels. But when sound waves are bent upward, sound levels can be noticeably reduced.

### Basic Point Source Model.
A point source is one for which $\kappa\delta \ll 1$ and for which Equation 15–16 holds. According to Magrab,

> In practice most noise sources cannot be classified as simple point sources. However, the sound field of a complicated sound source will look as if it were a point source if the following two conditions are met: (1) $r/\delta \gg 1$ that is, the distance from the source is large compared to its characteristic dimension, and (2) $\delta/\lambda \ll r/\delta$, that is, the ratio of the size of the source to the wavelength of sound in the medium is small compared to the ratio of the distance from the source to its characteristic dimension. Recall that $r/\delta \gg 1$ from the first condition. A value of $r/\delta > 3$ is a sufficient approximation; therefore, $\delta\lambda \ll 3$ [16].

The basic point source equation is

$$L_{p2} = L_{p1} - 10\log\left(\frac{r_2}{r_1}\right)^2 - A_e \tag{15–21}$$

where $L_{p2}$ = the desired SPL at angle $\theta$ and distance $r_2$ from source (in dB)
$L_{p1}$ = the measured SPL at angle $\theta$ and distance $r_1$ from source (in dB)
$r_1, r_2$ = distance from source to measurement $L_{p1}$ and $L_{p2}$, respectively
$A_e$ = attenuation for the distance $r_2 - r_1$ (in dB)

With the exception of the last term ($A_e$), it is the inverse square law. The $A_e$ term is the excess attenuation beyond wave divergence. It is caused by environmental conditions and has units of decibels.

The $A_e$ term may be further divided into six terms as follows [17]:

$A_{e1}$ = effect of the difference in value of $\rho c$ from 400 rayls when the ambient temperature and barometric pressure differ appreciably from values that make $\rho c = 400$, for example, 38.9°C and 101.325 kPa. Units are decibels. (1 rayl = 1 N $\cdot$ s $\cdot$ m$^{-3}$)
$A_{e2}$ = attenuation by absorption in the air (in dB)
$A_{e3}$ = attenuation by rain, sleet, snow, or fog (in dB)
$A_{e4}$ = attenuation by barriers (in dB)
$A_{e5}$ = attenuation by grass, shrubbery, and trees (in dB)
$A_{e6}$ = attenuation and fluctuation owing to wind and temperature gradients, to atmospheric turbulence, and to the characteristics of the ground (in dB)

The effect of the difference in $\rho c$ from 400 rayls can be calculated by first computing the change in density ($\rho$) due to temperature and pressure changes (see "Gas Laws" in Chapter 2).

The effect of temperature changes on the speed of sound ($c$) can be calculated using Equation 15–6. The total attenuation, $A_{e1}$, is then computed as follows:

$$A_{e1} = 10 \log \frac{\rho c}{400} \tag{15-22}$$

The sign of $A_{e1}$ is +. Thus, positive values of the right side of Equation 15–22 serve to reduce $L_{p2}$ and negative values increase it.

Results of laboratory tests of the effects of temperature and humidity on attenuation of sound, $A_{e2}$, in the frequency range of 1.25 to 12,500 Hz, for temperatures between $-10$ and $30°C$, and for relative humidities between 10 and 90% have been published by the Society of Automotive Engineers [18]. For a temperature of 20°C, the following formula may be used [19]:

$$A_{e2} = 7.4 \times 10^{-8} \frac{f^2 r}{\phi} \tag{15-23}$$

where $f$ = geometric mean frequency of band (in Hz)
  $r$ = distance between source and receiver (in m)
  $\phi$ = relative humidity (%)

For other temperatures (20 ± 10°C), an approximate solution may be used.

$$A'_{e2} = \frac{A_{e2}}{1 + (\beta)(\Delta T)(f)} \tag{15-24}$$

where $A'_{e2}$ = attenuation at 20°C and $\phi$ = 50% from Equation 15–23 (in dB)
  $\beta = 4 \times 10^{-6}$ for $T$ (in °C)
  $\Delta T = T - 20°C$
  $T$ = temperature (in °C)

The excess attenuation due to rain, mist, fog, hail, sleet, and snow have not been studied extensively. $A_{e3}$ is on the order of $0.5 \times 10^{-3}$ dB · m$^{-1}$ in fog and generally is taken to be zero for conservative estimates.

The attenuation due to barriers ($A_{e4}$) is a complex function of the path length and the wavelength of the sound. This topic is beyond the scope of this text.

The absorption data for grass, shrubbery, and trees ($A_{e5}$) are not easy to generalize. Attenuations range from 0 to 0.30 dB · m$^{-1}$. This analysis, too, is beyond the scope of this text.

The effects of wind and stability ($A_{e6}$) are treated separately for upwind and downwind receptors. For the downwind case, Figure 15–29 is used to calculate $A_{e6}$. For the upwind case,

**FIGURE 15–29**

Downwind excess attenuation, $A_{e6}$. (*Source: L. L. Beranek, Noise and Vibration Control.* Reprinted by permission.)

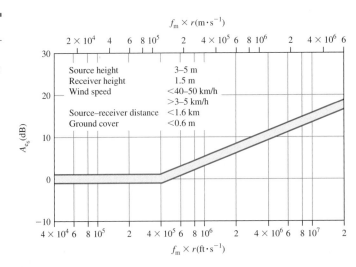

**TABLE 15–7**     Estimates of $X_0$ Upwind, 300–5000 Hz ($\phi = 0$)

| Time | | Sky | | Temperature Profile | | | Wind speed ($m \cdot s^{-1}$) | $X_0$ (m) |
|---|---|---|---|---|---|---|---|---|
| Day | Night | Clear | Overcast | Lapse | Neutral | Inversion | | |
| x | | x | | x | | | 4–8 | 75 |
| x | | | x | | x | | 4–7 | 120 |
| | x | x | | | | x | 1–2 | 600 |

**FIGURE 15–30**

Definition of the "shadow zone" for upwind excess attenuation.
Code:
$x_0$   Distance from source to shadow zone
$\phi$   Angle between wind and sound
$\phi_c$   Critical angle
(*Source:* L. L. Beranek, *Noise and Vibration Control.* Reprinted by permission.)

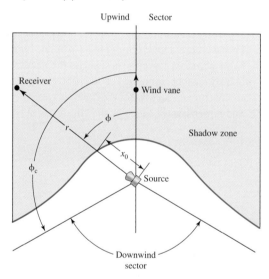

**FIGURE 15–31**

Upwind excess attenuation. (*Source:* L. L. Beranek, *Noise and Vibration Control.* Reprinted by permission.)

one nighttime and two daytime conditions are considered (Table 15–7). The quantity $X_0$ is the estimated distance from the noise source to the edge of the shadow zone (Figure 15–30). This is where the wind and temperature deflection of the sound waves begins to come into play. Once the value of $X_0$ is determined, Figure 15–31 can be used to select the attenuation value.

**EXAMPLE 15–7**     The sound pressure level (SPL) measured 50 m from a compressor is 90 dB at 1000 Hz. Determine the SPL 200 m upwind and downwind on a clear summer afternoon if the wind speed is $5 \ m \cdot s^{-1}$, the temperature is 20°C, the relative humidity is 50%, and the barometric pressure is 100.325 kPa.

Solution     We begin by computing the $A_e$ terms. We assume that the $L_{p1}$ measurement was taken at the same temperature and pressure at which the $L_{p2}$ estimate is to be made. Thus, the value of $A_{e1}$ at $r_2$ is the same as the value at $r_1$, and the attenuation for the distance $r_2 - r_1$ is zero, that is, $A_{e1} = 0.0$.

The attenuation by air absorption is calculated directly from Equation 15–23 with the $r_2 - r_1$ distance being $200 - 50 = 150$ m.

$$A_{e2} = 7.4 \times 10^{-8} \frac{(1000)^2(150)}{50}$$

$$= 0.22 \text{ dB}$$

We assume that $A_{e3}$, $A_{e4}$, and $A_{e5}$ all equal zero for the reasons noted in the text. The attenuation, $A_{e6}$, for downwind may be determined from Figure 15–29 after we have computed the abscissa quantity. Note that we assume that the 50-m measurement was taken under the same conditions as for the prediction at 200 m.

For $r_1$,

$$f_m \times r = (1000 \text{ Hz})(50 \text{ m}) = 5.0 \times 10^4 \text{ m} \cdot \text{s}^{-1}$$

and from Figure 15–29 we find $A_{e6}$ is 0 dB.

For $r_2$,

$$f_m \times r = (1000 \text{ Hz})(200 \text{ m}) = 2.00 \times 10^5 \text{ m} \cdot \text{s}^{-1}$$

and $A_{e6} = 2$ dB from Figure 15–29. The resultant value for $r_2 - r_1$ is then

$$A_{e6} = 2 - 0 = 2 \text{ dB}$$

For the upwind case we must start with Table 15–7. From the problem statement, we find it is a clear summer afternoon. From this we can assume a lapse temperature profile, and because $5 \text{ m} \cdot \text{s}^{-1}$ is within the limits of the table, $X_0 = 75$ m. At lower wind speeds the shadow zone is removed to quite a large distance and probably can be ignored for all practical purposes. At higher wind speeds the howl of the wind quickly moves $X_0$ toward the source.

With $X_0 = 75$, we calculate $r/X_0$ for $r_1$ and $r_2$, separately, and take the difference in $A_{e6}$ values. For $r_1$,

$$\frac{r}{X_0} = \frac{50}{75} = 0.67$$

and from Figure 15–31, $A_{e6} = 0$. For $r_2$,

$$\frac{r}{X_0} = \frac{200}{75} = 2.67$$

and $A_{e6} = 25$ dB from Figure 15–31. The resultant value is

$$A_{e6} = 25 - 0 = 25 \text{ dB}$$

The total downwind attenuation is then

$$\sum = 0 + 0.22 + 0 + 0 + 0 + 2$$

$$= 2.22 \text{ dB}$$

The total upwind attenuation is then

$$\sum = 0 + 0.22 + 0 + 0 + 0 + 25$$

$$= 25.22 \text{ dB}$$

Using Equation 15–21, the downwind SPL is

$$L_{p2} = 90 - 10 \log\left(\frac{200}{50}\right)^2 - 2.22$$

$$= 75.74, \text{ or } 76 \text{ dB at } 1000 \text{ Hz}$$

The upwind SPL is

$$L_{p2} = 90 - 10 \log \left( \frac{200}{50} \right)^2 - 25.22$$

$$= 52.74, \text{ or } 53 \text{ dB at } 1000 \text{ Hz}$$

Obviously, it is much better to be upwind. Note that if you wished to estimate $L_{eq}$, $L_{dn}$, $L_A$, and so on, the value of $L_{p2}$ would have to be calculated at each octave band geometric mean frequency and then summed by decibel addition.

## 15–6  TRAFFIC NOISE PREDICTION

### $L_{eq}$ Prediction

The Ontario Ministry of Transportation and Communications developed a traffic noise prediction equation based on the $L_{eq}$ concept [20]. The empirical equation they developed is as follows:

$$L_{eq} = 42.3 + 10.2 \log(V_c + 6V_t) - 13.9 \log D + 0.13S \qquad (15\text{–}25)$$

where $L_{eq}$ = energy equivalent sound level during 1 h (in dBA)
$V_c$ = volume of automobiles (four tires only) (in vehicles $\cdot$ h$^{-1}$)
$V_t$ = volume of trucks (six or more tires) (in vehicles $\cdot$ h$^{-1}$)
$D$ = distance from edge of pavement to receiver (in m)
$S$ = average speed of traffic flow during 1 h (in km $\cdot$ h$^{-1}$)

This equation does not account for barriers. A nomograph is available to take barriers into account.

### $L_{dn}$ Prediction

The Ontario method is a direct extension of the $L_{eq}$ methodology that enables the calculation of $L_{dn}$. The modified model has the following form:

$$L_{dn} = 31.0 + 10.2 \log[\text{ADDT} + \%T\,\text{ADDT}/20] - 13.9 \log D + 0.13S \qquad (15\text{–}26)$$

where $L_{dn}$ = equivalent A-weighted sound level during 24-h period with 10-dBA weighting
applied to $2200 - 0700$ h (in dBA)
ADDT = annual average daily traffic (in vehicles $\cdot$ day$^{-1}$)
$\%T$ = average percentage of trucks during a typical day (%)

This equation, like Equation 15–25, does not take into account barriers.

## 15–7  NOISE CONTROL

### Source-Path-Receiver Concept

If you have a noise problem and want to solve it, you have to find out something about what the noise is doing, where it comes from, how it travels, and what can be done about it. A straightforward approach is to examine the problem in terms of its three basic elements: that is, sound arises from a source, travels over a path, and affects a receiver or listener [21].

The source may be one or any number of mechanical devices that radiate noise or vibratory energy. Such a situation occurs when several appliances or machines are in operation at a given time in a home or office.

The most obvious transmission path by which noise travels is simply a direct line-of-sight air path between the source and the listener. For example, aircraft flyover noise reaches an observer on the ground by the direct line-of-sight air path. Noise also travels along structural paths. Noise can travel from one point to another via any one path or a combination of several paths. Noise from a washing machine operating in one apartment may be transmitted to another apartment along air passages such as open windows, doorways, corridors, or duct work. Direct physical contact of the washing machine with the floor or walls sets these building components into vibration. This vibration is transmitted structurally throughout the building, causing walls in other areas to vibrate and to radiate noise.

The receiver may be, for example, a single person, a classroom of students, or a suburban community.

Solution of a given noise problem might require alteration or modification of any or all of these three basic elements:

1. Modifying the source to reduce its noise output
2. Altering or controlling the transmission path and the environment to reduce the noise level reaching the listener
3. Providing the receiver with personal protective equipment

### Control of Noise Source by Design

**Reduce Impact Forces.**   Many machines and items of equipment are designed with parts that strike forcefully against other parts, producing noise. Often, this striking action or impact is essential to the machine's function. Several steps can be taken to reduce noise from impact forces. The particular remedy to be applied will be determined by the nature of the machine in question.

A few of the more obvious design modifications are

1. Reduce the weight, size, or height of fall of the impacting mass.
2. Cushion the impact by inserting a layer of shock-absorbing material between the impacting surfaces. In some situations, you could insert a layer of shock-absorbing material behind each of the impacting heads or objects to reduce the transmission of impact energy to other parts of the machine.
3. Whenever practical, one of the impact heads or surfaces should be made of nonmetallic material to reduce resonance (ringing) of the heads.
4. Substitute the application of a small impact force over a long period for a large force over a short period to achieve the same result.

**Reduce Speeds and Pressures.**   Reducing the speed of rotating and moving parts in machines and mechanical systems results in smoother operation and lower noise output. Likewise, reducing pressure and flow velocities in air, gas, and liquid circulation systems lessens turbulence, resulting in decreased noise radiation. Some specific suggestions that may be incorporated in design are discussed the following sections.

**Reduce Frictional Resistance.**   Reducing friction between rotating, sliding, or moving parts in mechanical systems frequently results in smoother operation and lower noise output. Similarly, reducing flow resistance in fluid distribution systems results in less noise radiation. Four of the more important factors that should be checked to reduce frictional resistance in moving parts are alignment, polish, balance, and eccentricity (out-of-roundness).

**Reduce Radiating Area.**   Generally speaking, the larger the vibrating part or surface, the greater the noise output. The rule of thumb for quiet machine design is to minimize the effective radiating surface areas of the parts without impairing their operation or structural strength. This can be done by making parts smaller, removing excess material, or by cutting openings, slots, or perforations in the parts. For example, replacing a large, vibrating sheet-metal safety guard on a machine with a guard made of wire mesh or metal webbing might result in a substantial reduction in noise because of the drastic reduction in surface area of the part.

**Reduce Noise Leakage.**   In many cases, machine cabinets can be made into rather effective soundproof enclosures through simple design changes and the application of some sound-absorbing treatment. Substantial reductions in noise output may be achieved by adopting some of the following recommendations:

1. All unnecessary holes or cracks, particularly at joints, should be caulked.
2. All electrical or plumbing penetrations of the housing or cabinet should be sealed with rubber gaskets or a suitable nonsetting caulk.
3. If practical, all other functional or required openings or ports that radiate noise should be covered with lids or shields edged with soft rubber gaskets to achieve an airtight seal.
4. Other openings required for exhaust, cooling, or ventilation purposes should be equipped with mufflers or acoustically lined ducts.
5. Openings should be directed away from the operator and other people.

**Isolate and Dampen Vibrating Elements.** In all but the simplest machines, the vibrational energy from a specific moving part is transmitted through the machine structure, forcing other component parts and surfaces to vibrate and radiate sound—often with greater intensity than that generated by the originating source itself.

Generally, vibration problems can be considered in two parts. First, we must prevent energy transmission between the source and surfaces that radiate the energy. Second, we must dissipate or attenuate the energy somewhere in the structure. The first part of the problem is solved by isolation. The second part is solved by damping.

The most effective method of vibration isolation involves the resilient mounting of the vibrating component on the most massive and structurally rigid part of the machine. Damping material or structures are those that have some viscous properties. They tend to bend or distort slightly, thus consuming part of the noise energy in molecular motion. The use of spring mounts on motors and laminated galvanized steel and plastic in air-conditioning ducts are two examples.

**Provide Mufflers or Other Silencers.** There is no real distinction between mufflers and silencers. They are often used interchangeably. They are, in effect, acoustical filters and are used when fluid flow noise is to be reduced. The devices can be classified into two fundamental groups: absorptive and reactive mufflers. An **absorptive muffler** is one whose noise reduction is determined mainly by the presence of fibrous or porous materials, which absorb the sound. A **reactive muffler** is one whose noise reduction is determined mainly by geometry. It is shaped to reflect or expand the sound waves with resultant self-destruction.

Although several terms are used to describe the performance of mufflers, the most frequently used appears to be insertion loss (IL). **Insertion loss** is the difference between two sound pressure levels that are measured at the same point in space before and after a muffler has been inserted. Because each muffler IL is highly dependent on the manufacturer's selection of materials and configuration, we will not present general IL prediction equations.

### Noise Control in the Transmission Path

After you have tried all possible ways of controlling the noise at the source, your next line of defense is to set up devices in the transmission path to block or reduce the flow of sound energy before it reaches your ears. This can be done in several ways: (1) absorb the sound along the path, (2) deflect the sound in some other direction by placing a reflecting barrier in its path, or (3) contain the sound by placing the source inside a sound-insulating box or enclosure.

Selection of the most effective technique will depend on various factors, such as the size and type of source, intensity and frequency range of the noise, and the nature and type of environment.

**Separation.** We can make use of the absorptive capacity of the atmosphere, as well as divergence, as a simple, economical method of reducing the noise level. Air absorbs high-frequency sounds more effectively than low-frequency sounds. However, if enough distance is available, even low-frequency sounds will be absorbed appreciably.

If you can double your distance from a point source, you will have succeeded in lowering the sound pressure level by 6 dB. It takes about a 10-dB drop to halve the loudness. If you have to contend with a line source such as a railroad train, the noise level drops by only 3 dB for each doubling of distance from the source. The main reason for this lower rate of attenuation is that line sources radiate sound waves that are cylindrical in shape. The surface area of such waves only increases twofold for each doubling of distance from the source. However, when the distance from the train becomes comparable to its length, the noise level will begin to drop at a rate of 6 dB for each subsequent doubling of distance.

Indoors, the noise level generally drops only from 3 to 5 dB for each doubling of distance in the near vicinity of the source. However, farther from the source, reductions of only 1 or 2 dB occur for each doubling of distance due to the reflections of sound off hard walls and ceiling surfaces.

**Absorbing Materials.**   Noise, like light, will bounce from one hard surface to another. In noise control work, this is called **reverberation.** If a soft, spongy material is placed on the walls, floors, and ceiling, the reflected sound will be diffused and soaked up (absorbed).

Sound-absorbing materials such as acoustical tile, carpets, and drapes placed on ceiling, floor, or wall surfaces can reduce the noise level in most rooms by about 5–10 dB for high-frequency sounds, but only 2–3 dB for low-frequency sounds. Unfortunately, such treatment provides no protection to an operator of a noisy machine who is in the midst of the direct noise field. For greatest effectiveness, sound-absorbing materials should be installed as close to the noise source as possible.

Because of their light weight and porous nature, acoustical materials are ineffectual in preventing the transmission of either airborne or structure-borne sound from one room to another. In other words, if you can hear people walking or talking in the room or apartment above, installing acoustical tile on your ceiling will not reduce the noise transmission.

**Acoustical Lining.**   Noise transmitted through ducts, pipe chases, or electrical channels can be reduced effectively by lining the inside surfaces of such passageways with sound-absorbing materials. In typical duct installations, noise reductions on the order of $10 \, \text{dB} \cdot \text{m}^{-1}$ for an acoustical lining 2.5 cm thick are well within reason for high-frequency noise. A comparable degree of noise reduction for the lower frequency sounds is considerably more difficult to achieve because it usually requires at least a doubling of the thickness or the length of acoustical treatment.

**Barriers and Panels.**   Placing barriers, screens, or deflectors in the noise path can be an effective way of reducing noise transmission, provided that the barriers are large enough in size, and depending on whether the noise is high or low frequency. High-frequency noise is reduced more effectively than low frequency.

The effectiveness of a barrier depends on its location, its height, and its length. Referring to Figure 15–32, we can see that the noise can follow four different paths.

First, the noise follows a direct path to receivers who can see the source well over the top of the barrier. The barrier does not block their line of sight and therefore provides no attenuation. No matter how absorptive the barrier is, it cannot pull the sound downward and absorb it.

**FIGURE 15–32**

Noise paths from a source to a receiver. (*Source: National Cooperative Highway Research Program 174, 1976.*)

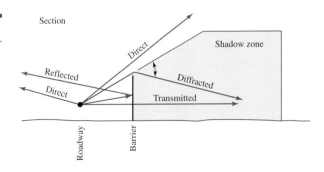

Second, the noise follows a diffracted path to receivers in the shadow zone of the barrier. The noise that passes just over the top edge of the barrier is diffracted (bent) down into the apparent shadow zone in the figure. The larger the angle of diffraction, the more the barrier attenuates the noise in this shadow zone. In other words, less energy is diffracted through large angles than through smaller ones.

Third, in the shadow zone, the noise transmitted directly through the barrier may be significant in some cases. For example, with extremely large angles of diffraction, the diffracted noise may be less than the transmitted noise. In this case, the transmitted noise compromises the performance of the barrier. It can be reduced by constructing a heavier barrier. The allowable amount of transmitted noise depends on the total barrier attenuation desired. More is said about this transmitted noise later.

The fourth path shown in Figure 15–32 is the reflected path. After reflection, the noise is of concern only to a receiver on the opposite side of the source. For this reason, acoustical absorption on the face of the barrier may sometimes be considered to reduce this reflected noise; however, this treatment will not benefit any receivers in the shadow zone. It should be noted that in most practical cases the reflected noise does not play an important role in barrier design. If the source of noise is represented by a line of noise, another short-circuit path is possible. Part of the source may be unshielded by the barrier. For example, the receiver might see the source beyond the ends of the barrier if the barrier is not long enough. This noise from around the ends may compromise, or short-circuit, barrier attenuation. The required barrier length depends on the total net attenuation desired. When 10–15-dB attenuation is desired, barriers must, in general, be very long. Therefore, to be effective, barriers must not only break the line of sight to the nearest section of the source but also to the source far up and down the line.

Of these four paths, the noise diffracted over the barrier into the shadow zone represents the most important parameter from the barrier design point of view. Generally, the determination of barrier attenuation or barrier noise reduction involves only calculation of the amount of energy diffracted into the shadow zone.

**Enclosures.**   Sometimes it is much more practical and economical to enclose a noisy machine in a separate room or box than to quiet it by altering its design, operation, or component parts. The walls of the enclosure should be massive and airtight to contain the sound. Absorbent lining on the interior surfaces of the enclosure will reduce the reverberant buildup of noise within it. Structural contact between the noise source and the enclosure must be avoided, so that the source vibration is not transmitted to the enclosure walls, thus short-circuiting the isolation.

### Control of Noise Source by Redress

The best way to solve noise problems is to design them out of the source. However, we are frequently faced with an existing source that, either because of age, abuse, or poor design, is a noise problem. The result is that we must redress, or correct, the problem as it currently exists. The following identify some measures that might apply if you are allowed to tinker with the source: balance rotating parts; reduce frictional resistance; apply damping materials; seal noise leaks; and perform routine maintenance to repair mufflers, rough road surfaces, and so forth.

### Protect the Receiver

**When All Else Fails.**   When exposure to intense noise fields is required and none of the measures discussed so far is practical, as, for example, for the operator of a chain saw or pavement breaker, then measures must be taken to protect the receiver. The following two techniques are commonly employed.

**Alter Work Schedule.**   Limit the amount of continuous exposure to high noise levels. In terms of hearing protection, it is preferable to schedule an intensely noisy operation for a short interval of time each day over a period of several days rather than a continuous 8-h run for a day or two.

**FIGURE 15–33**

Attenuation of ear protectors at various frequencies. (*Source: National Bureau of Standards Handbook,* p. 119, 1976.)

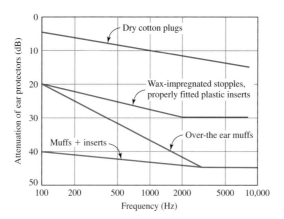

In industrial or construction operations, an intermittent work schedule would benefit not only the operator of the noisy equipment, but also other workers in the vicinity. If an intermittent schedule is not possible, then workers should be given relief time during the day. They should take their relief time at a low-noise-level location and should be discouraged from trading relief time for dollars, paid vacation, or an "early out" at the end of the day!

Inherently noisy operations, such as street repair, municipal trash collection, factory operation, and aircraft traffic, should be curtailed at night and early morning to avoid disturbing the sleep of the community. Remember: operations between 10 P.M. and 7 A.M. are effectively 10 dBA higher than the measured value.

**Ear Protection.**    Molded and pliable earplugs, cup-type protectors, and helmets are commercially available as hearing protectors. Such devices may provide noise reductions ranging from 15 to 35 dB (Figure 15–33). Earplugs are effective only if they are properly fitted by medical personnel. As shown in Figure 15–33, maximum protection can be obtained when both plugs and muffs are employed. Only muffs that have a certification stipulating the attenuation should be used.

These devices should be used only as a last resort, after all other methods have failed to lower the noise level to acceptable limits. Ear protection devices should be used while operating lawn mowers, mulchers, and chippers, and while firing weapons at target ranges. It should be noted that protective ear devices do interfere with speech communication and can be a hazard in some situations where warning calls may be a routine part of the operation (e.g., TIMBERRRR!). A modern ear-destructive device is a portable miniradio–recorder that uses earphones. In this "reverse" muff, high noise levels are directed at the ear without attenuation. If you can hear someone else's radio–recorder, that person is subjecting himself to noise levels in excess of 90–95 dBA!

## CHAPTER REVIEW

When you have completed studying this chapter; you should be able to do the following without the aid of your textbook or notes:

1.  Define frequency, based on a sketch of a harmonic wave you have drawn, and state its units of measure (namely, hertz, Hz).
2.  State the basic unit of measure used in measuring sound energy (namely, the decibel, dB) and explain why it is used.
3.  Define sound pressure level in mathematical terms, that is,

$$\text{SPL} = 20 \log \frac{P_{\text{rms}}}{(P_{\text{rms}})_0}$$

4.  Explain why a weighting network is used in a sound level meter.

5. List the three common weighting networks and sketch their relative frequency response curves. (Label frequencies, that is, 20, 1000, and 10,000 Hz; and relative response, that is, 0, −5, −20, and −45 dB, as in Figure 15–6.)

6. Differentiate between a mid/high-frequency noise source and a low-frequency source on the basis of A, B, and C scale readings.

7. Explain the purpose of octave band analysis.

8. Differentiate among continuous, intermittent, and impulsive noise.

9. Sketch the curves and label the axes of the two typical types of impulsive noise.

10. Sketch a Fletcher–Munson curve, label the axes, and explain what the curve depicts.

11. Define *phon*.

12. Explain the mechanism by which hearing damage occurs.

13. Explain what hearing threshold level (HTL) is.

14. Define *presbycusis* and explain why it occurs.

15. Distinguish between temporary threshold shift (TTS), permanent threshold shift (PTS), and acoustic trauma with respect to cause of hearing loss, duration of exposure, and potential for recovery.

16. Explain why impulsive noise is more dangerous than steady-state noise.

17. Explain the relationship between the allowable duration of noise exposure and the allowable level for hearing protection, that is, damage-risk criteria.

18. List five effects of noise other than hearing damage.

19. List the three basic elements that might require alteration or modification to solve a noise problem.

With the aid of this text, you should be able to do the following:

1. Calculate the resultant sound pressure level from a combination of two or more sound pressure levels.

2. Determine the A-, B-, and C-weighted sound levels from octave band readings.

3. Compute the mean sound level from a series of sound level readings.

4. Compute the following noise statistics if you are provided the appropriate data: $L_p$ or $L_{eq}$.

5. Determine whether or not a noise level will be acceptable given a series of measurements and the criteria listed in Tables 15–3, 15–5, and 15–6.

6. Calculate the sound level at a receptor site after transmission through the atmosphere.

7. Estimate the noise level ($L_{eq}$ or $L_{dn}$) that might be expected for a given roadway configuration and traffic pattern.

## PROBLEMS

**15–1**  A building located near a road is 6.92 m high. How high is the building in terms of wavelengths of a 50.0-Hz sound? Assume that the speed of sound is 346.12 m · s$^{-1}$.

   **Answer:** One wavelength

**15–2**  Repeat Problem 15–1 for a 500-Hz sound if the temperature is 25.0°C.

**15–3**  Determine the sum of the following sound levels (all in decibels): 68, 82, 76, 68, 74, and 81.

   **Answer:** 85.5, or 86 dB

**15–4**  A motorcyclist is warming up his racing cycle at a racetrack approximately 200 m from a sound level meter. The meter reading is 56 dBA. What meter reading would you expect if 15 of the motorcyclist's friends join him with motorcycles having exactly the same sound emission characteristics? You may assume that the sources may be treated as ideal point sources located at the same point.

**15–5**  A law enforcement officer has taken the following readings with her sound level meter. Is the noise source a predominantly low- or middle-frequency emitter? Readings: 80 dBA, 84 dBB, and 90 dBC.

   **Answer:** Predominantly low frequency

**15–6**   The following readings have been made outside the open stage door of the opera house: 109 dBA, 110 dBB, and 111 dBC. Is the singer a bass or a soprano? Explain how you arrived at your answer.

**15–7**   Convert the following octave band measurements to an equivalent A-weighted level.

| Band Center Frequency (Hz) | Band Level (dB) | Band Center Frequency (Hz) | Band Level (dB) |
|---|---|---|---|
| 31.5 | 78 | 1000 | 80 |
| 63 | 76 | 2000 | 80 |
| 125 | 78 | 4000 | 73 |
| 250 | 82 | 8000 | 65 |
| 500 | 81 | | |

**Answer:** 85.5, or 86 dBA

**15–8**   Using the typical noise spectrum for automobiles traveling at 50–60 km · h$^{-1}$ (see Figure 15–25), determine the equivalent A-weighted level using the following octave band geometric mean center frequencies (all in hertz): 63, 125, 250, 500, 1000, 2000, 4000, and 8000.

**15–9**   Compute the average sound pressure level of the following readings by simple arithmetic averaging and by logarithmic averaging (see Equation 15–13) (all readings in decibels): 42, 50, 65, 71, and 47. Does arithmetic averaging underestimate or overestimate the sound pressure level?

**Answers:** $\bar{x} = 55.00$, or 55 dB      $\bar{L}_p = 61.57$, or 62 dB

**15–10**   Repeat Problem 15–9 for the following data (all in decibels): 76, 59, 35, 69, and 72.

**15–11**   The following noise record was obtained in the front yard of a home. Is this a relatively quiet or a relatively noisy neighborhood? Determine the equivalent continuous equal energy level.

| Time (h) | Sound Level (dBa) | Time (h) | Sound Level (dBa) |
|---|---|---|---|
| 0000–0600 | 42 | 1500–1700 | 50 |
| 0600–0800 | 45 | 1700–1800 | 47 |
| 0800–0900 | 50 | 1800–0000 | 45 |
| 0900–1500 | 47 | | |

**Answers:** It is a quiet neighborhood. $L_{eq} = 46.2$, or 46 dBA

**15–12**   A developer has proposed putting a small shopping mall next to a very quiet residential area in Nontroppo, Michigan. Based on the measurements shown in the following table, which were taken at a similar size mall in a similar setting, should the developer expect complaints or legal action? Calculate $L_{eq}$.

| Time (h) | Sound Level (dBA) | Time (h) | Sound Level (dBA) |
|---|---|---|---|
| 0000–0600 | 42 | 1000–2000 | 70 |
| 0600–0800 | 55 | 2000–2200 | 68 |
| 0800–1000 | 65 | 2200–0000 | 57 |

**15–13**   Two oil-fired boilers for a 600-MW (megawatt) power plant produce an 83-dB noise level at 31.5 Hz, 180.0 m from the induced draft fans. Determine the sound pressure level 488.0 m upwind on an overcast day when the wind speed is 4.50 m · s$^{-1}$, the temperature is 20.0°C, the relative humidity is 30.0%, and the barometric pressure is 106.0 kPa.

**Answer:** SPL at 488.0 m = 56 dB at 31.5 Hz

**15-14** The sound pressure level from a jet engine test cell is 90 dB at 125 Hz, and at 1000 Hz at a distance of 400 m. What are the sound pressure levels at 125 and 1000 Hz, 1200 m downwind on a clear evening when the wind speed is 1.50 m · s$^{-1}$, the temperature is 20.0°C, the relative humidity is 50.0%, and the barometric pressure is 103.2 kPa?

**15-15** Consider an ideal single lane of road that carries 1200 vehicles per hour uniformly spaced along the road and determine the following:

(a) The average center-to-center spacing of the vehicles for an average traffic speed of 40.0 km · h$^{-1}$.

(b) The number of vehicles in a 1-km length of the lane when the average speed is 40.0 km · h$^{-1}$.

(c) The sound level (dBA) 60.0 m from a 1-km length of this roadway with automobiles emitting 71 dBA at the edge of an 8.0-m wide roadway. Assume that the autos travel at a speed of 40.0 km · h$^{-1}$, that the sound radiates ideally from a hemisphere, and that contributions of less than 0.3 dBA may be ignored.

> **Answers:** (a) Average center-to-center spacing = 33.3 m
> (b) Number of vehicles in a kilometer length = 30 vehicles · km$^{-1}$
> (c) = 47.47, or 48 dBA

**15-16** Repeat Problem 15–15 if the vehicle speed is increased to 80.0 km · h$^{-1}$ and the spacing is decreased or increased appropriately to maintain 1200 vehicles · h$^{-1}$.

**15-17** In preparation for a public hearing on a proposed interstate bypass at Nontroppo, Michigan, the county road commission has requested that you prepare an estimate of the potential for violation of residential FHA noise standards 75 m from the centerline of the interstate. The edge of the pavement is 28.65 m from the centerline.

Data for I-481 at Pianissimo Avenue
*Estimated traffic*
Automobiles: 7800 per hour at 88.5 km · h$^{-1}$
Heavy trucks: 650 per hour at 88.5 km · h$^{-1}$

Compute the unattenuated $L_{eq}$, at the receiver for autos only.

> **Answer:** $L_{eq} = 70$ dBA

**15-18** Determine the potential for violation of FHA noise standards at the north side of Fermata School 123.17 m from the edge of the interstate highway.

Data for I-481 at Fermata School
*Estimated traffic:* Same as at Pianissimo Avenue (Problem 15–17)

Compute the unattenuated $L_{eq}$ at the school for the combined traffic flow.

## DISCUSSION QUESTIONS

**15-1** Classify each of the following noise sources by type, that is, continuous, intermittent, or impulse. (Not all sources fit these three classifications.)

(a) Electric saw   (b) Air conditioner   (c) Alarm clock (bell type)   (d) Punch press

**15-2** Is the following statement true or false? If it is false, correct it in a nontrivial manner.

"A sonic boom occurs when an aircraft breaks the sound barrier."

**15-3** Is the following statement true or false? If it is false, correct it in a nontrivial manner.

"Excessive continuous noise causes hearing damage by breaking the stapes."

**15-4** As the safety officer of your company, you have been asked to determine the feasibility of reducing exposure time as a method of reducing hearing damage for the following situation:

> The worker is operating a high-speed grinder on steel girders for a high-rise building. The effective noise level at the operator's ear is 100 dBA. She cannot wear protective ear devices because she must communicate with others.

What amount of exposure time would you set as the limit?

## ADDITIONAL READING

Bell, L. H., *Fundamentals of Industrial Noise Control,* Harmony Publications, Trumbull, CT (1973).

Beranek, L. L., ed., *Noise and Vibration Control,* McGraw-Hill, New York (1971).

Davis, M., and D. Cornwell. *Introduction to Environmental Engineering,* 3rd ed. McGraw-Hill, New York (1998).

Lipscomb, D. M., and A. C. Taylor, *Noise Control Handbook of Principles and Practices,* Van Nostrand Reinhold, New York (1978).

Magrab, E. B., *Environmental Noise Control,* Wiley, New York (1975).

Olishifski, J. B., and B. R. Harford, *Industrial Noise and Hearing Conservation,* National Safety Council, Chicago (1975).

## REFERENCES

1. *A Primer of Noise Measurement*, General Radio Company, Concord, MA, 1972.
2. Clemis, J. D., "Anatomy, physiology, and pathology of the ear," *Industrial Noise and Hearing Conservation,* J. B. Olishifski and E. R. Harford, eds., National Safety Council, Chicago, p. 213, 1975.
3. Fletcher, H., and W. A. Munson, "Loudness, its definition, measurement and calculation," *Journal of the Acoustical Society of America,* vol. 5, pp. 82–108, 1935.
4. U.S. Department of Health, Education and Welfare, National Institute for Occupational Safety and Health, *Criteria for a Recommended Standard: Occupational Exposure to Noise,* U.S. Government Printing Office, Washington, D.C., 1972.
5. Davis, H., "Effects of high intensity noise on navy personnel," *U.S. Armed Forces Medical Journal,* vol. 9, pp. 1027–1047, 1958.
6. Davis, H., "The hearing mechanism." In *Handbook of Noise Control,* C. M. Harris, ed., McGraw-Hill, New York, p. 44, 1957.
7. Beranek, L. L., *Acoustics,* McGraw-Hill, New York, 1954.
8. Miller, J. D., *Effects of Noise on People* (U.S. Environmental Protection Agency Publication No. NTID 300.7), U.S. Government Printing Office, Washington, D.C., p. 93, 1971.
9. May, D. N., *Handbook of Noise Assessment,* Van Nostrand Reinhold, New York, p. 5, 1975.
10. Minnix, R. B., "The nature of sound," *Noise Control Handbook of Principles and Practices,* D. M. Lipscomb and A. C. Taylor, eds., Van Nostrand Reinhold, New York, pp. 29–30, 1978.
11. The sections on sleep interference, effects on performance, and acoustic privacy follow J. D. Miller, *Effects of Noise on People* (U.S. Environmental Protection Agency Publication No. NTID 300.7), U.S. Government Printing Office, Washington, D.C., pp. 59, 67–69, 1971.
12. Courtesy of B & K Instruments, Inc., Cleveland.
13. Burck, W., et al., Fluglarm, Gutachten erstatet im Auftrag des Bundesministers für Gesundheitswesen, Göttingen, 1965.
14. U.S. Environmental Protection Agency, *Transportation Noise and Noise from Equipment Powered by Internal Combustion Engines* (Environmental Protection Agency Publication No. NTID 300.13), U.S. Government Printing Office, Washington, D.C., p. 230, 1971.
15. U.S. Environmental Protection Agency, *Information on Levels of Environmental Noise Requisite to Protect Public Health and Welfare with an Adequate Margin of Safety* (Environmental Protection Agency Publication No. 55019-74-004), U.S. Government Printing Office, Washington, D.C., 1974.
16. Magrab, E. B., *Environmental Noise Control,* Wiley, New York, pp. 4, 6, 1975.
17. Beranek, L. L., *Noise and Vibration Control,* McGraw-Hill, New York, p. 169, 1971.
18. Society of Automotive Engineers, *Standard Values of Atmospheric Absorption as a Function of Temperature and Humidity for Use in Evaluating Aircraft Flyover Noise* (ARPSS6), The Society of Automotive Engineers, New York, 1964.
19. Cremer, L., *Raumakustik,* Vol. II (Germany), S. Herzel Verlag, Stuttgart, p. 27, 1961.
20. Hajek, J. J., "$L_{eq}$ traffic noise prediction method," *Environmental Conservation Concerns in Transportation: Energy, Noise and Air Quality,* Transportation Research Record No. 648, Transportation Research Board, National Academy of Sciences, pp. 48–53, 1977.
21. This discussion in large part was taken from R. D. Berendt, E. L. R. Corliss, and M. S. Ojalvo, *Quieting: A Practical Guide to Noise Control* (National Bureau of Standards Handbook 119), U.S. Department of Commerce, Washington, D.C., pp. 16–41, 1976.

# 16

## Ionizing Radiation*

*Ms. Kristin Erickson, Radiation Safety Officer, Office of Radiation. Chemical, and Biological Safety, Michigan State University, contributed to this chapter.

## 16–1 FUNDAMENTALS*

### Atomic Structure

We assume that you are familiar with the Bohr model of atomic structure. In this model the atom is described as consisting of a central nucleus surrounded by a number of electrons in closed orbits about the nucleus. The orbital electrons are grouped in shells.

The nucleus itself can be considered as composed of two distinct kinds of particles: protons, which carry a positive unit charge, $e^+$, and neutrons, which are uncharged. In a particular atom there are $Z$ electrons, each carrying a charge $e^-$, orbiting around the nucleus, and a nucleus composed of $N$ neutrons and $P$ protons. The condition of electrical neutrality for the atom as a whole yields $Pe - Ze = 0$, that is, the number of protons in the nucleus is equal to the number of orbital electrons.

The number $Z$ is the atomic charge or atomic number of the atom, and $Z + N$ is the atomic mass number, usually denoted by $A$. The parameters $A$ and $Z$ completely define a particular atomic species, this being known as a **nuclide.**

The masses of nuclides are measured in terms of the **unified atomic mass unit,** with the symbol u. This is defined as the unit of mass equal to one-twelfth the mass of an atom of carbon of atomic mass number 12. This gives 1 u as $1.6606 \times 10^{-27}$ kg. On this scale, the mass of the neutron is 1.0088665 u, the mass of the proton 1.0088925 u, and the mass of the electron 0.0005486 u.

From the definition of the mass scale, giving proton and neutron masses of the order unity, it is clear that the **atomic mass number** will be a whole number approximation to the nuclidic mass in u. For example, a nuclide of magnesium which contains 12 protons and 12 neutrons has $A = 24$ and a nuclidic mass of 23.985045 u. The difference between the nuclidic mass and the atomic mass number is called the **mass excess.**

The chemical properties of the atom, and hence its designation as a particular element, depend on the number of orbital electrons, that is, on the atomic number $Z$. Given $Z$, the element is uniquely defined. As an example, if a given atom has two orbital electrons, it must be helium (assuming that the atom is not ionized or in some similar nonequilibrium state). Similarly an atom with eight electrons must be oxygen.

A particular nuclide is denoted by $^A_Z X$, where X takes the place of the element symbol. But as $Z$ determines the element, $Z$ and $X$ denote the same thing. Thus, the shorthand can be amended to $^A X$. For example, carbon has six neutrons and six protons. Therefore, this nuclide can be written $^{12}C$, or carbon-12.

For each element (determined only by $Z$) several nuclides (determined by $Z$ and $A$) have the same $Z$ value but different values of $A$. These different nuclides of the same element are called **isotopes.** Hydrogen with $Z = 1$ has three isotopes with atomic mass numbers of 1, 2, and 3. As $Z$ must remain constant at 1, this means that they have zero, one, and two neutrons, respectively. This is illustrated in Figure 16–1. These isotopes all act chemically as hydrogen, but their nuclidic

---

*This discussion follows reference [1].

**FIGURE 16-1**

Three isotopes of hydrogen. (*Source:* R. A. Coombe, *An Introduction to Radioactivity for Engineers,* Macmillan/ St. Martin's Press, New York, 1968.)

○ Electron
◍ Proton
◉ Neutron

Hydrogen — Nucleus $^1_1$H, proton

Deuterium — Nucleus $^2_1$H, deuteron

Tritium — Nucleus $^3_1$H, triton

masses are different. The nuclidic mass of $^1$H is 1.007825 u, that of $^2$H (known as deuterium) is 2.014102 u, and that of $^3$H (known as tritium) is 3.016049 u.

The atomic weight of an element is defined as the combined nuclidic masses of all the isotopes, weighted according to their natural relative abundances. It is denoted by $A$. In the case of hydrogen it follows that the atomic weight is

$$1.007825(0.9844) + 2.014102(0.0156) + 3.016049(0) = 1.00797$$

The masses of the hydrogen isotopes are not obtained by simple addition of neutron masses. For example, the nuclidic mass of $^1$H plus a neutron is 2.016490 u, whereas the mass of deuterium is 2.014102 u. This difference of 0.002388 u is called the **mass defect.** This is because when a proton and a neutron are brought together to form a deuteron (the nucleus of deuterium), energy is released to bind them together. Conversely, energy must be supplied to split them apart. This required energy, the **binding energy,** is obtained from Einstein's equation for the conversion of mass into energy,

$$E = \Delta mc^2 \tag{16-1}$$

where $\Delta m$ is the mass defect and $c$ is the speed of light.

All energies of emitted radiation and particles, as well as the various atomic and nuclear energy levels, are quoted in terms of the **electron volt,** eV. This is the energy that would be acquired by an electron in falling through a potential difference of one volt. From this definition the following equivalent units of energy can be established:

$$1 \text{ eV} = 1.602 \times 10^{-12} \text{ erg} = 1.602 \times 10^{-19} \text{ J}$$

For nuclear energy levels and radiation energies, the electron volt is usually an inconveniently small unit. The units MeV and KeV are then used for $10^6$ eV and $10^3$ eV, respectively. Using Equation 16–1, with the information that $c = 2.99793 \times 10^8$ m $\cdot$ s$^{-1}$, and 1 u = 1.6606 $\times$ $10^{-27}$ kg, then the energy equivalent of 1 u is 931.634 MeV. In other words, this means that if an electron of mass 0.0005486 u were completely annihilated, the energy released would be approximately 0.511 MeV.

### Radioactivity and Radiation

By definition, isotopes have different ratios of neutrons to protons in the nucleus. Some ratios give rise to unstable conditions. This is usually because the neutron-to-proton ratio is too large. Because of this instability, the nucleus changes its state to attain equilibrium, and in so doing emits either a particle or electromagnetic radiation to carry off the excess energy. This phenomenon of nuclear disintegration is known as **radioactivity,** and an isotope that displays such activity is known as a **radioisotope.**

There are three types of isotopes. Some are stable, others are naturally radioactive, and the third group can be artificially produced and are also radioactive. These artificially produced radioisotopes are the isotopes most used in industrial application.

Three major types of decay product carry off the surplus energy when a radioisotope decays: alpha particles, beta particles, and gamma radiation.

**Alpha-Particle Emission.** Conceptually, the source of the instability of the heavy elements is their size; their nuclei are too large. How can they become smaller? One method would be to eject protons or neutrons. Rather than doing this singly, the heavy-element atoms expel them in "packages" containing two protons and two neutrons. This "package" is called an **alpha particle ($\alpha$).** An alpha particle is equivalent to the nucleus of the helium-4 atom, that is, it is simply a body consisting of two protons and two neutrons bound together. Consequently, if an alpha particle is emitted, the nucleus must change to one that has a charge $2e$ less and a mass approximately 4 u less. The general expression is

$$^A_Z X \rightleftharpoons {}^{A-4}_{Z-2}X + {}^4_2He \tag{16-2}$$

Atoms that eject the helium "package" are said to decay through emission of alpha radiation. Alpha-particle emission occurs mainly in radioisotopes whose atomic number is greater than 82. With increasing atomic number, the occurrence of alpha-particle decay increases rapidly, and it is a characteristic of the very heavy elements. It is particularly in evidence in the main decay chains of the natural radioactive isotopes.

You should note that an atom undergoing alpha-particle decay changes into a new element. It is a new element because the product nucleus (often called a **daughter**) contains two fewer protons than the parent atom. Through emission of an alpha particle, uranium becomes thorium. Similarly, radium becomes radon.

**Beta-Particle Emission.**  The instability that is the cause of beta-particle emission arises from the fact that the neutron-to-proton ratio in the nucleus is too high (there are too many neutrons in the nucleus). To achieve stability, a neutron in the nucleus can decay into a proton and an electron. The proton remains in the nucleus so that the neutron-to-proton ratio is decreased, and the electron is ejected. This ejected electron is known as a **beta particle ($\beta$).** The general expression for the decay is

$$\ce{^A_Z X} \rightleftharpoons \ce{^A_{Z+1} X} + \beta^- \tag{16-3}$$

Note that we use the $\beta^-$ to represent an electron of nuclear origin to differentiate it from electrons from other sources. The negative sign is used with the $\beta$ if there is any chance of ambiguity, because a similar particle, called a positron, also exists that carries a positive charge.

Again, as in alpha radiation, emission of a beta particle changes the parent atom into a new element because the number of protons in the nucleus increases by one. If the daughter product also is radioactive, it will, in turn, emit a beta particle, becoming another new element, and so on, until finally a stable neutron-to-proton ratio is reached. Through such a series of changes, for example, the fission-product element krypton becomes rubidium which, in turn, becomes strontium, which finally converts to stable yttrium.

**Gamma-Ray Emission.**  Either alpha or beta particles may be accompanied by gamma radiation. Whereas alpha or beta radiation brings about a change in the size of the nucleus or the number of a particular type of particle therein, the emission of gamma radiation represents only a release of energy. This is the energy that remains in the newly formed nucleus after emission of the alpha or beta particle. Electromagnetic radiation in the form of gamma rays is emitted when a nucleus in an excited state transfers to a more stable state. The nucleus thus retains its original composition, the excess energy being radiated away. If the frequency of the radiation is $v$, and the nucleus changes from a state of energy $E_1$ to a state of energy $E_2$, then the two energies are related by the equation

$$E_1 - E_2 = hv \tag{16-4}$$

where $h$ is Planck's constant, having a value of $6.624 \times 10^{-27}$ ergs. The energy of the emitted gamma ray is thus $hv$. In equations, the gamma ray is represented by the Greek letter gamma ($\gamma$).

**X-Rays.**  Gamma rays are similar to x-rays. Their difference lies only in their source. Gamma rays originate from a nucleus transferring from one nuclear excited state to another, whereas x-rays originate from electrons transferring from a higher to a lower atomic energy state. As atomic energy levels are in general spaced much closer in terms of energy than nuclear levels, it follows from Equation 16–4 that the frequencies of x-rays are much less than those of gamma rays. As far as industrial applications are concerned, the only difference between them is the penetrating power. Because penetrating power increases with frequency, gamma rays have more penetrating power than x-rays.

**Multiple Emissions.**  In the preceding discussions, only single emission has been considered. In practice, two or more different types of emission are possible, and in a great many cases several particles of the same type but of different energies are emitted. This latter effect is due to the multiplicity of nuclear energy levels both in the original isotope nucleus and in the nucleus formed by particle emission.

### Radioactive Decay

Each unstable (radioactive) atom will eventually achieve stability by ejecting an alpha or beta particle. This shift to a more stable form is called **decay.** Each radioactive decay process is characterized by the fact that only a fraction of the unstable nuclei in a given sample will decay in a given time. The probability that a particular nucleus in the sample will decay during a time interval $dt$ is $\lambda\, dt$, where $\lambda$ is the radioactive decay constant. It is defined as the probability that any particular nucleus will disintegrate in unit time.

For a large number of like nuclei together, we make the assumption that $\lambda$ is independent of the age of a nucleus and is the same for all nuclei. This means that $\lambda$ is a constant. If $N$ is the number of nuclei present at a time $t$, then the number of decays occurring in a time $dt$ can be written $\lambda N dt$. As the number of nuclei decreases by $dN$ in this time, we can write

$$dN = -\lambda N dt \tag{16-5}$$

The negative sign denotes that $N$ is decreasing with time. Equation 16–5 shows that the rate of decay is proportional to the number of nuclei present, that is, it is a first-order reaction.

Equation 16–5 can be rearranged and integrated.

$$\int_{N_0}^{N} \frac{dN}{N} = \int_0^t \lambda\, dt$$

$$\ln \frac{N}{N_0} = -\lambda t$$

or

$$N = N_0 \exp(-\lambda t) \tag{16-6}$$

where $N_0$ is the number of radioactive nuclei present at time $t = 0$. Equation 16–6 shows that radioactive decay follows an exponential form. In particular, the time taken for a given number of nuclei to decay to half that number, $T_{1/2}$, is obtained from Equation 16–6 as

$$\ln \frac{N/2}{N_0} = -\lambda T_{1/2}$$

Solving for $T_{1/2}$ yields

$$T_{1/2} = \frac{\ln 2}{\lambda} = \frac{0.693}{\lambda} \tag{16-7}$$

This equation relates two important parameters of a radioactive species: $\lambda$ and the half-life, $T_{1/2}$. These quantities are characteristic properties of a particular species. Half-lives of radioisotopes cover an enormous range of values, from microseconds to millions of years. To illustrate this, some values are given in Table 16–1.

**Specific Activity and the Becquerel.** The quantity $N$ is called the **activity** of a sample. In SI units the becquerel (Bq) is the unit used for activity. One **becquerel** of radioactive material is that quantity of unstable atoms whose frequency of decay is one disintegration per second. This definition covers all modes of disintegration for both single isotopes and mixtures.

For many years the unit used for activity was the curie. One **curie** of radioactive material is that quantity of unstable atoms whose frequency of decay is $3.700 \times 10^{10}$ disintegrations per second. One becquerel is equal to $2.7 \times 10^{-11}$ Ci. The curie is quite a large unit for a lot of

**TABLE 16–1**    Some Radioisotope Half-Lives

| Radioisotope | Half-Life | Radioisotope | Half-Life |
|---|---|---|---|
| Polonium-212 | $3.04 \times 10^{-7}$ s | Calcium-45 | 165 days |
| Carbon-10 | 19.3 s | Cobalt-60 | 5.27 years |
| Oxygen-15 | 2.05 min | Tritium | 12.5 years |
| Carbon-11 | 20.4 min | Strontium-90 | 28 years |
| Radon-222 | 3.825 days | Cesium-137 | 30 years |
| Iodine-131 | 8.06 days | Radium-226 | 1622 years |
| Phosphorus-32 | 14.3 days | Carbon-14 | 5570 years |
| Polonium-210 | 138.4 days | Potassium-40 | $1.4 \times 10^9$ years |

purposes. Millicuries (1 mCi = $10^{-3}$ Ci) or microcuries (1 μCi = $10^{-6}$ Ci) and even picocuries (1 pCi = $10^{-12}$ Ci) were chosen as more manageable units to work with.

The specific activity of a radioisotope is the activity per gram of the pure radioisotope. The number of atoms of a pure radioisotope in one gram is given by

$$N = \frac{N_A}{A} \tag{16–8}$$

where $N_A$ is Avogadro's number ($6.0248 \times 10^{23}$) and $A$ is the nuclidic mass. The specific activity $S$ of a particular radioisotope is an intrinsic property of that radioisotope.

$$S = \frac{\lambda N_A}{A} \text{ disintegrations} \cdot \text{s}^{-1} \tag{16–9}$$

**Growth of Subsidiary Products.**    In the process of decay, a new nuclide is formed, the daughter product. If the daughter product is stable, its concentration will gradually increase as the parent decays. On the other hand, if the daughter product is itself radioactive, the variation in concentrations of parent, daughter, and granddaughter products will very much depend on the relative rates of decay.

In several cases a radioactive isotope decays into another nuclide that is itself radioactive. This can continue for a large number of nuclides, resulting in a decay chain. The characteristics of any particular chain depend largely on the relative decay constants of its various members.

The simplest case is the growth of a radioactive daughter product from the parent atoms. Let us assume we begin with $N_1$ parent atoms of decay constant $\lambda_1$, and $N_2$ daughter atoms of decay constant $\lambda_2$. The rate at which the daughter product is increasing is then the difference between the rate at which it is produced by its parent and the rate at which it decays. This can be written as

$$\frac{dN_2}{dt} = \lambda_1 N_1 - \lambda_2 N_2 \tag{16–10}$$

The rate of production of the daughter is simply the decay rate of the parent.

Using Equation 16–6 with the notation that $N_1$ is the number of nuclei of the parent and $N_{10}$ is the initial number.

$$N_1 = N_{10} \exp(-\lambda_1 t)$$

Substituting in Equation 16–10, we obtain

$$\frac{dN_2}{dt} = \lambda_1 N_{10} \exp(-\lambda_1 t) - \lambda_2 N_2 \tag{16–11}$$

Rearranging, we get

$$\frac{dN_2}{dt} + \lambda_2 N_2 = \lambda_1 N_{10} \exp(-\lambda_1 t) \tag{16-12}$$

This equation can readily be solved by multiplying throughout by the factor $e^{\lambda_2 t}$. Thus,

$$\exp(\lambda_2 t)\frac{dN_2}{dt} + \exp(\lambda_2 t)\lambda_2 (N_2) = \lambda_1 N_{10} \exp(-\lambda_1 t)\exp(\lambda_2 t) \tag{16-13}$$

and

$$\frac{dN_2 e^{\lambda_2 t}}{dt} = \lambda_1 N_{10} \exp[(\lambda_2 - \lambda_1)t] \tag{16-14}$$

On integration this yields

$$N_2 e^{\lambda_2 t} = \frac{\lambda_1 N_{10}}{\lambda_2 - \lambda_1} \exp[(\lambda_2 - \lambda_1)t] + C \tag{16-15}$$

The integration constant $C$ is determined from the boundary conditions. For this case, at $t = 0$, there was no daughter product present, that is, $N_2 = 0$ at $t = 0$. Using these boundary conditions, Equation 16–15 reduces to

$$N_2 e^{\lambda_2 t} = \frac{\lambda_1 N_{10}}{\lambda_2 - \lambda_1}(e^{-\lambda_1 t} - e^{-\lambda_2 t}) \tag{16-16}$$

**Characteristics of Daughter Products.** In the derivation of Equation 16–16, it was assumed that $N_2$ was zero at zero time. Because the daughter nuclide itself decays, then at an infinite time, $N_2$ will again be zero. Between these two times when $N_2 = 0$, there will be a time, say $t'$, when $N_2$ will reach a maximum. At this time, the rate of increase will be passing through a turning point, that is, $dN_2/dt = 0$. Using this fact, together with Equation 16–16, it can be shown that

$$t' = \frac{\ln \lambda_2 - \ln \lambda_1}{\lambda_2 - \lambda_1} \tag{16-17}$$

**Secular Equilibrium.** A limiting case of radioactive equilibrium in which $\lambda_1 \ll \lambda_2$ and in which the parent activity does not decrease measurably during many daughter half-lives is known as **secular equilibrium.** An example of this is $^{238}$U decaying to $^{234}$Th. In this case, a useful approximation of the value of $N_2$ after a large number of half-lives is

$$N_2 = N_{10}\frac{\lambda_1}{\lambda_2} \tag{16-18}$$

**Continuous Production of Parent.** The previous calculations assumed that at zero time a certain number of parent atoms were present and then decayed. In many cases of interest the parent is continuously replenished. Such cases occur for instance in nuclear reactors, where the parent nuclides are continuously being created by neutron bombardment. Another case is the continuous production of carbon-14 by cosmic rays incident on the nuclei present in the upper atmosphere.

**End Products.** Any radioactive decay chain must finally arrive at a nuclide that is stable. The relevant equations can readily be obtained, for any stable nuclide has $\lambda = 0$. For example, consider the case of a radioisotope whose daughter is stable. For this, Equation 16–16 can be used with $\lambda_2 = 0$. Thus,

$$N_2 = N_{10}(1 - e^{-\lambda_1 t}) \tag{16-19}$$

Similar modifications can be made to other equations concerned with longer decay chains.

### Radioisotopes

**Naturally Occurring Radioisotopes.**　Most of the 50 naturally occurring radioisotopes are associated with three distinct series: the thorium series, the uranium series, and the actinium series. Each one of these series starts with an element of high atomic mass (uranium-238, thorium-232, and uranium-235, respectively) and then decays by a long series of alpha- and beta-particle emissions to reach a stable nuclide (lead-206, lead-208, and lead-207, respectively). The three chains are associated with the heavy elements, and very few naturally occurring radioisotopes are found with atomic masses less than 82.

The half-lives of the naturally occurring radioisotopes are very long. Presumably they were constituents of the earth at its formation and their activity has not yet died away beyond detection.

Two other important isotopes that occur in the natural environment but that are not strictly naturally occurring are hydrogen-3 (tritium) and carbon-14. These radioisotopes are artificially produced by cosmic rays bombarding the upper atmosphere of the earth. At present the quantities of these isotopes are in equilibrium, their production rate by cosmic radiation being balanced by their natural decay rate. Because of this phenomenon these isotopes are of particular use in archaeological dating.

**Artificially Produced Radioisotopes.**　The artificial production of radioisotopes is mainly carried out either by nuclear reactors or by particle accelerators. The cyclotron is the accelerator in most general use because the required bombarding particle energies are easily obtained and the output is reasonably high. The transmutation of a stable isotope to a radioactive one is effected by bombarding a target nucleus with a suitable projectile, either electromagnetic or a particle, to produce the required isotope from the resultant nuclear reaction.

When an accelerator is used, the bombarding particles are usually protons, deuterons, or alpha particles. In the nuclear reaction brought about by the bombardment of zinc-64 with energetic deuterons from a cyclotron, the deuteron and zinc-64 nucleus combine to form a new element. The new element has a charge of $30e + e$ and an atomic mass number of $64 + 2$. This compound nucleus is then $^{66}$Ga, gallium-66. This intermediate nucleus disintegrates almost immediately by one of several possible modes of decay. If a proton is emitted, for example, the final nucleus must be left with a nuclear charge of $32e$ and an atomic mass number of 65, so it is $^{65}$Zn. This isotope does not occur in nature.

For the production of radioisotopes for industrial application, the most common nuclear reactions used are those from thermal neutrons. A target sample, in a suitable container, is inserted into the core of a reactor and left there for varying amounts of time. In the core of a reactor there is a copious supply of thermal neutrons. These interact with the target nucleus to produce the required radioisotope, a process known as **neutron activation.**

### Fission

A **nuclear reactor** is an assembly of fissionable material (such as uranium-235, plutonium-239, or uranium-233) arranged in such a way that a self-sustaining **chain reaction** is maintained. When these nuclei are bombarded with neutrons of the appropriate energy, they split up, or **fission,** into fission fragments and neutrons. For the nuclear reaction to continue, at least one of the neutrons produced must be available to produce another fission instead of escaping from the assembly or being used up in some other nuclear reaction. Thus, there is a minimum **(critical)** mass below which the reaction cannot be self-sustaining. Actual reactors are built with an excess mass to make large amounts of neutrons available. The excess neutron production is controlled by the use of **moderators.** The moderators are made of materials with large neutron-capture cross sections, such as boron, cadmium, or hafnium. These are formed into **control rods** that are moved in and out of the reactor to moderate the excess neutrons.

The fission chain reaction is characterized by an enormous release of heat. This heat must be carried away by an efficient cooling system to prevent mechanical failure of the reactor assembly (**meltdown**) and, ultimately, an uncontrolled fission. The ultimate uncontrolled reaction is, of course, an atomic explosion.

The fission fragments are simply lower mass elements. There are, most commonly, two fission fragments from each nucleus with an energy of the order of 200 MeV shared between them. The uranium nucleus does not split into the same two fragments each time. The breakup is far from symmetrical and can occur in more than 30 different ways. The most commonly produced isotopes are grouped around the mass numbers 95 and 139.

The fragments produced from the fission process have very large neutron-to-proton ratios so that they are highly unstable. Many transitions have to occur before a stable nucleus is finally achieved. These successive decays give rise to a decay chain.

Fission fragments, because of their high mass and very high initial charge, have extremely short ranges in matter. Hence, they are contained within the fuel element when a uranium nucleus fissions. The spent nuclear reactor fuel elements thus provide a very intense radioactive source that presents many problems in the subsequent handling and processing. Fission fragments themselves can sometimes be used as a radioactive source for industrial application.

### The Production of X-Rays*

X-rays were discovered in 1895 by Wilhelm Conrad Roentgen. During the course of some studies, he covered a cathode ray tube with a black cardboard box and observed fluorescence on a screen coated with barium platinocyanide near the tube. After further investigation of this phenomenon, he concluded that the effect was caused by the generation of new invisible rays capable of penetrating opaque materials and producing visible fluorescence in certain chemicals. He called these new invisible rays **x-rays.** Because of their discoverer, x-rays are also sometimes referred to as Roentgen rays.

As pointed out previously, x-rays are electromagnetic waves and occupy the same portion of the electromagnetic spectrum as gamma rays. Like gamma rays, x-rays can pass through solid material. The mode of interaction of x-rays with matter is the same, as are the biological and photographic effects.

Whereas gamma rays come from within the nucleus of the atom, x-rays are generated outside the nucleus by the interaction of high-speed electrons with the atom. For this reason, there is a difference in the energy distribution of x- and gamma rays. Gamma rays from any single radionuclide consist only of rays of one or several discrete energies. X-rays consist of a broad, continuous spectrum of energies. The continuous spectrum will be discussed in detail later.

**The X-Ray Tube.**   X-rays are produced whenever a stream of high-speed electrons strikes a substance. This is caused by their sudden stoppage or deflection by atoms within the target material. The x-ray tube (Figure 16–2) is designed to provide the high-speed electrons and the interacting material. Essential components of a x-ray tube are (1) a highly evacuated glass envelope containing the cathode and anode; (2) a source of electrons proceeding from a cathode; and (3) a target (or anode) placed in the path of the electron stream.

The development of the hot filament tube by William D. Coolidge in 1913 was a major advance. Most x-ray tubes in use today are of this type. Here, the free electrons are "boiled out" of an incandescent filament within an evacuated tube and given their velocity by accelerating them through an electric field. In the hot filament tube, the quality and intensity of radiation can be controlled independently by simple electrical means. The intensity of radiation is directly proportional to the current and is proportional to the square of the voltage. This allows a much wider range of wavelengths and intensities, while the characteristics of the tube remain reasonably constant throughout its useful life.

The high voltages required for x-ray tube operation are best obtained by step-up transformers, whose output is always AC. Because the electrons must flow only from cathode to anode

*This discussion follows reference [2].

**FIGURE 16–2**

Typical x-ray tube in self-rectified circuit.

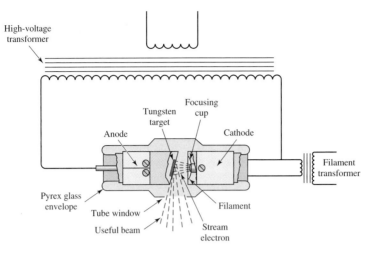

within the tube some means of rectification is necessary. A self-rectified tube acts as its own rectifier. When an alternating voltage is applied to such a tube, electrons flow only from the cathode to anode as long as the anode remains cool. If the anode becomes hot, the flow of electrons reverses during the second half-cycle and the cathode is damaged. Thus the self-rectified tube is limited to low currents and short periods of operation. The use of "valves" (rectifiers) in the power supply circuit eliminates the inverse voltage on the x-ray tube. Thus, more power can be handled by the x-ray tube, the radiation output is increased, and the time of exposure is shortened.

**X-Ray Production Efficiency.** On average, the fraction of the electron energy emitted as electromagnetic radiation increases with the atomic number of the atoms of the target and the velocity of the electrons. This fraction is very small and can be represented by the following empirical equation:

$$F = 1.1 \times 10^{-9} \, ZV \tag{16-20}$$

where $F$ = fraction of the energy of the electrons converted into x-rays
$\quad\quad Z$ = atomic number of the target
$\quad\quad V$ = energy of the electrons (in volts)*

Typically, less than 1% of the electrical power supplied is converted into x-ray energy. The remaining energy (over 99%) appears as heat produced at the target (largely through ionization and excitation). As a result, electron bombardment of the target raises it to a high temperature and, if the heat produced is not dissipated fast enough, the target will melt. This heat production is a serious factor in limiting the capacity of a x-ray tube.

A suitable target must have the following characteristics:

1. A high atomic number because efficiency is directly proportional to $Z$
2. A high melting point because of the high temperatures involved
3. A high thermal conductivity to dissipate the heat
4. Low vapor pressure at high temperatures to prevent target evaporation

**The Continuous Spectrum.** When high-speed electrons are stopped by a target, the radiation produced has a continuous distribution of energies (wavelengths). As the fast-moving electrons enter the surface layers of the target, they are abruptly slowed down by collision with the strong Coulomb field of the nucleus and are diverted from their original direction of motion. Each time the electron suffers an abrupt change of speed, a change in direction, or both, energy in the form of x-rays is radiated. The energy of the x-ray photon emitted depends on the degree

---

*The electron energy is generally expressed in terms of the voltage applied across the tube.

of deceleration. If the electron is brought to rest in a single collision, the energy of the resulting photon corresponds to the kinetic energy of the electron stopped and will be a maximum. If the electron suffers a less drastic collision, a lower energy photon is produced. Because a variety of types of collisions will be occurring, photons of all energies up to the maximum will be produced. This accounts for the continuous distribution of a x-ray spectrum. The maximum intensity (peak of the curve) occurs at a wavelength about 1.5 times the minimum wavelength. The total intensity of radiation from a given x-ray tube is represented by the area under the spectral curve. The intensity has been found, as might be expected, to be directly proportional to the electron current (number of electrons striking the target).

### Radiation Dose*

Fundamentally, the harmful consequences of ionizing radiations to a living organism are due to the energy absorbed by the cells and tissues of the organism. This absorbed energy (or dose) produces chemical decomposition of the molecules present in the living cells. The mechanism of the decomposition appears to be related to ionization and excitation interactions between the radiation and atoms within the tissue. The amount of ionization or number of ion pairs produced by ionizing radiations in the cells or tissues provides some measure of the amount of decomposition or physiological damage that might be expected from a given quantity or dose. The ideal basis for radiation dose measurement could be, therefore, the number of ion pairs (or ionizations) taking place within the medium of interest. For certain practical reasons, the medium chosen for defining exposure dose is air.

**Exposure Dose—the Roentgen.** The exposure dose of x- or gamma radiation within a specific volume is a measure of the radiation based on its ability to produce ionization in air. The unit used for expressing the exposure to x- or gamma radiation is the roentgen (R). Its merit lies in the fact that the magnitude of the exposure dose in roentgens can usually be related to the absorbed dose, which is of importance in predicting or quantifying the expected biological effect (or injury) resulting from the radiation.

The **roentgen** is an exposure dose of x- or gamma radiation such that the associated corpuscular emission per 0.001293 g of air[†] produces, in air, ions carrying one electrostatic unit of quantity of electricity of either sign. Because the ionizing property of radiation provides the basis for several types of detection instruments and methods, such devices may be used to quantify the exposure dose. Note that this is a unit of exposure dose based on ionization of air; it is not a unit of ionization, nor is it an absorbed dose in air.

**Absorbed Dose—the Gray.** The absorbed dose of any ionizing radiation is the energy imparted to matter by ionizing radiations per unit mass of irradiated material at the place of interest. The SI unit of absorbed dose is the gray (Gy). One **gray** is equivalent to the absorption of $1 \ J \cdot kg^{-1}$ (Joule per kilogram). The former unit of absorbed dose was the rad. One **rad** is equivalent to the absorption of $100 \ ergs \cdot g^{-1}$. One Gy = 100 rads. It should be emphasized that although the roentgen unit is strictly applicable only to x- or gamma radiation, the gray unit may be used regardless of the type of ionizing radiation or the type of absorbing medium.

To make a conversion from roentgens to grays two things must be known: the energy of the incident radiation and the mass absorption coefficient of the absorbing material. For example, let us assume that a dose of 1.0 R of gamma radiation was measured in air. What is the equivalent absorbed dose in air?

To form 1 esu per 0.001293 g of air, the radiation must produce $1.61 \times 10^{12}$ ion pairs when absorbed in 1 g of air. From empirical studies it is known that, on the average, 34 eV of energy is

---

*This discussion follows reference [2].

[†]One cubic centimeter of air at STP has a mass of 0.001293 g.

transferred (or absorbed) in the process of forming each ion pair in air. Thus, the total energy absorbed is

$$(34 \text{ eV} \cdot \text{ion pair}^{-1})(1.61 \times 10^{12} \text{ ion pairs} \cdot \text{g}^{-1}) = 5.48 \times 10^{13} \text{ eV} \cdot \text{g}^{-1}$$

Or, in ergs rather than electron volts,

$$(5.48 \times 10^{13} \text{ eV} \cdot \text{g}^{-1})(1.602 \times 10^{-12} \text{ erg} \cdot \text{eV}^{-1}) = 87 \text{ ergs} \cdot \text{g}^{-1}$$

Because $1 \text{ erg} = 1 \times 10^{-7}$ J, then 1 R of exposure dose to a specific volume of air at standard conditions results in the absorbed dose of $8.7 \times 10^{-3}$ Gy.

**Relative Biological Effectiveness (Quality Factor).**  Although all ionizing radiations are capable of producing similar biological effects, the absorbed dose, measured in grays, that will produce a certain effect may vary appreciably from one type of radiation to another. The difference in behavior, in this connection, is expressed by means of a quantity called the **relative biological effectiveness** (RBE) of the particular radiation. The RBE of a given radiation may be defined as the ratio of the absorbed dose (grays) of gamma radiation (of a specified energy) to the absorbed dose of the given radiation required to produce the same biological effect. Thus, if an absorbed dose of 0.2 Gy of slow neutron radiation produces the same biological effect as 1 Gy of gamma radiation, the RBE for slow neutrons would be

$$\text{RBE} = \frac{1 \text{ Gy}}{0.2 \text{ Gy}} = 5$$

The value of the RBE for a particular type of nuclear radiation depends on several factors, such as the energy of the radiation, the kind and degree of the biological damage, and the nature of the organisms or tissue under consideration.

**Tissue Weighting Factor ($W_T$).**  The **tissue weighting factor** ($W_T$) is a modifying factor used in dose calculations to correct for the fact that different tissues and organs have varying degrees of radiosensitivity depending on the radioisotope and the chemical form of the radioisotope. Some tissues and organs are very sensitive; others are not radiosensitive at all. For example, because iodine is easily incorporated in thyroid tissue, the thyroid gland is very sensitive to the radioiodines. The $W_T$ is, therefore, high for the radioiodines. When the tissue or organ is not radiosensitive, the value of $W_T$ may be very small or zero for that tissue.

**The Sievert.**  With the concept of the RBE in mind, it is now useful to introduce another SI unit, known as the sievert (Sv). One **sievert** equals the radiation dose having the same biological effect as a gray of gamma radiation. This was formerly know as the **rem,** an abbreviation of "roentgen equivalent man" (1 Sv = 100 rem). The gray is a convenient unit for expressing energy absorption, but it does not take into account the biological effect of the particular nuclear radiation absorbed. The sievert, however, which is defined by

$$\text{Dose in Sv} = \text{RBE} \times \text{dose in grays} \times W_T$$

provides an indication of the extent of biological injury (of a given type) that would result from the absorption of nuclear radiation. Thus, the sievert is a unit of biological dose.

## 16–2  BIOLOGICAL EFFECTS OF IONIZING RADIATION*

The fact that ionizing radiation produces biological damage has been known for many years. The first case of human injury was reported in the literature just a few months following Roentgen's original paper in 1895 announcing the discovery of x-rays. As early as 1902, the first case of x-ray induced cancer was reported in the literature.

*This discussion follows reference [2].

Early human evidence for harmful effects as a result of exposure to radiation in large amounts existed in the 1920s and 1930s based on the experience of early radiologists, persons working in the radium industry, and other special occupational groups. The long-term biological significance of smaller, chronic doses of radiation, however, was not widely appreciated until the 1950s, and most of our current knowledge of the biological effects of radiation has been accumulated since World War II.

### Sequential Pattern of Biological Effects

The sequence of events following radiation exposure may be classified into three periods: a latent period, a period of demonstrable effect, and a recovery period.

**Latent Period.**  Following the initial radiation event, and often before the first detectable effect occurs, there is a time lag referred to as the **latent period.** There is a vast time range possible in the latent period. In fact, the biological effects of radiation are arbitrarily divided into short-term, or acute, and long-term, or delayed, effects on this basis. Those effects that appear within a matter of minutes, days, or weeks are called **acute effects** and those which appear years, decades, and sometimes generations later are called **delayed effects.**

**Demonstrable Effects Period.**  During or immediately following the latent period, certain discrete effects can be observed. One of the phenomena seen most frequently in growing tissues exposed to radiation is the cessation of mitosis or cell division. This may be temporary or permanent, depending on the radiation dosage. Other effects observed are chromosome breaks, clumping of chromatin, formation of giant cells or other abnormal mitoses, increased granularity of cytoplasm, changes in staining characteristics, changes in motility or ciliary activity, cytolysis, vacuolization, altered viscosity of protoplasm, arid altered permeability of the cell wall. Many of these effects can be duplicated individually with other types of stimuli. The entire gamut of effects however, cannot be reproduced by any single chemical agent.

**Recovery Period.**  Following exposure to radiation, recovery can and does take place to a certain extent. This is particularly manifest in the case of the acute effects, that is, those appearing within a matter of days or weeks after exposure. There is, however, a residual damage from which no recovery occurs, and it is this irreparable injury which can give rise to later delayed effects.

### Determinants of Biological Effects

**The Dose-Response Curve.**  For any biologically harmful agent, it is useful to correlate the dosage administered with the response or damage produced. "Amount of damage" in the case of radiation might be the frequency of a given abnormality in the cells of an irradiated animal, or the incidence of some chronic disease in an irradiated human population. In plotting these two variables, a dose-response curve is produced. With radiation, an important question has been the nature and shape of this curve. Two possibilities are illustrated in Figures 16–3 and 16–4.

Figure 16–3 is a typical "threshold" curve. The point at which the curve intersects the abscissa is the threshold dose, that is, the dose below which there is no response. If an acute and easily observable radiation effect, such as reddening of the skin, is taken as "response," then this type of curve is applicable. The first evidence of the effect does not occur until a certain minimum dose is reached.

Figure 16–4 represents a linear, or nonthreshold, relationship, in which the curve intersects the abscissa at the origin. Here any dose, no matter how small, involves some degree of response. There is some evidence that the genetic effects of radiation constitute a nonthreshold phenomenon, and one of the underlying (and prudent) assumptions in the establishment of radiation protection guidelines and in radiation control activities in public health programs has been the assumption of a nonthreshold effect. Thus, some degree of risk is assumed when large populations of people are

**FIGURE 16–3**

Dose-response curve depicting "threshold" dose.

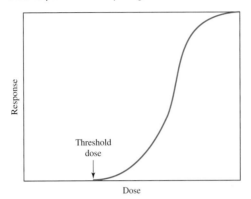

**FIGURE 16–4**

Dose-response curve depicting "no threshold" dose.

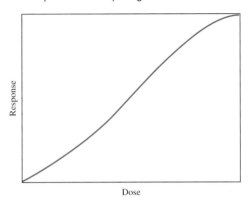

exposed to even very small amounts of radiation. This assumption often makes the establishment of guidelines for acceptable radiation exposure an enormously complex task, because the concept of "acceptable risk" comes into play, in which the benefit to be accrued from a given radiation exposure must be weighed against its hazard.

**Rate of Absorption.**　The rate at which the radiation is administered or absorbed is most important in the determination of what effects will occur. Because a considerable degree of recovery occurs from the radiation damage, a given dose will produce less of an effect if divided (thus allowing time for recovery between dose increments) than if it were given in a single exposure.

**Area Exposed.**　Generally when an external radiation exposure is referred to without qualification as to the area of the body involved, whole-body irradiation is assumed. The portion of the body irradiated is an important exposure parameter because the larger the area exposed, other factors being equal, the greater the overall damage to the organism. Even partial shielding of the highly radiosensitive blood-forming organs such as the spleen and bone marrow can mitigate the total effect considerably. An example of this phenomenon is in radiation therapy, in which doses that would be lethal if delivered to the whole body are commonly delivered to very limited areas, such as to tumor sites.

**Variation in Species and Individual Sensitivity.**　There is a wide variation in the radiosensitivity of various species. Lethal doses for plants and microorganisms, for example, are usually hundreds of times larger than those for mammals. Even among different species of rodents, it is not unusual for one to demonstrate three or four times the sensitivity of another.

　Within the same species, biological variability accounts for a difference in sensitivity among individuals. For this reason the lethal dose for each species is expressed in statistical terms. The $LD_{50}$ for that species, or the dose required to kill 50% of the individuals in a large population, is the standard statistical measure. For people, the $LD_{50}$ is estimated to be approximately 450 R.

**Variation in Cell Sensitivity.**　Within the same individual, a wide variation in susceptibility to radiation damage exists among different types of cells and tissues. In general, cells that are rapidly dividing or have a potential for rapid division are more sensitive than those that do not divide. Furthermore, nondifferentiated cells (i.e., primitive, or nonspecialized) are more sensitive than highly specialized cells. Within the same cell families then, the immature forms, which are generally primitive and rapidly dividing, are more radiosensitive than the older, mature cells, which have specialized in structure and function and have ceased to divide.

### Acute Effects

An acute dose of radiation is one delivered to a large portion of the body during a very short time. If the amount of radiation involved is large enough, acute doses may result in effects that can manifest themselves within a period of hours or days. Here the latent period, or time elapsed between the radiation insult and the onset of effects, is relatively short and grows progressively shorter as the dose level is raised. These short-term radiation effects are composed of signs and symptoms collectively known as acute **radiation syndrome.**

The stages in acute radiation syndrome may be described as follows:

1. *Prodrome.* This is the initial phase of the syndrome and is usually characterized by nausea, vomiting, and malaise. It may be considered analogous to the prodrome state in acute viral infections in which the individual is subject to nonspecific systemic reactions.
2. *Latent stage.* During this phase, which may be likened to the incubation period of a viral infection, the subjective symptoms of illness may subside, and the individual may feel well. Changes, however, may be taking place within the blood-forming organs and elsewhere that will subsequently give rise to the next aspect of the syndrome.
3. *Manifest illness stage.* This phase reflects the clinical picture specifically associated with the radiation injury. Among the possible signs and symptoms are fever, infection, hemorrhage, severe diarrhea, prostration, disorientation, and cardiovascular collapse. Which, if any, of the foregoing phenomena are observed in a given individual largely depend on the radiation dose received.
4. *Recovery or death.*

### Relation of Dose to Type of Acute Radiation Syndrome

As mentioned earlier, each kind of cell has a different sensitivity to radiation. At relatively low doses, for example, the most likely cells to be injured are those with greatest sensitivity, such as the immature white blood cells of lymph nodes and bone marrow. At low doses the observable effects during the manifest illness stage would be in these cells. Thus, you would expect to observe fever, infection, and hemorrhage. This is known as the **hematopoietic form** of the acute radiation syndrome.

At higher doses, usually over 6 Gy cells of somewhat lower sensitivity will be injured. Of particular importance are the epithelial cells lining the gastrointestinal tract, for when these are destroyed a vital biological barrier is broken down. As a result, fluid loss may occur, as well as overwhelming infection, and severe diarrhea in the **gastrointestinal form** of the acute radiation syndrome.

In the **cerebral form,** which may result from doses of 100 Gy or more, the relatively resistant cells of the central nervous system are damaged, and the affected individual undergoes a rapid illness, characterized by disorientation and shock.

Considering the large degree of individual variation that exists in the manifestation of radiation injury, it is difficult to assign a precise dose range to each of these forms of the syndrome. The following generalizations, however, may serve to provide a rough indication of the kinds of doses involved. At 0.5 Gy or less, ordinary laboratory or clinical methods will show no indications of injury. At 1 Gy, most individuals show no symptoms, although a small percentage may show mild blood changes. At 2 Gy, most persons show definite signs of injury; this dose level may prove fatal to those individuals most sensitive to the effects of radiation. At 4.5 Gy, the mean lethal dose has been reached, and 50% of exposed individuals will succumb. Approximately 6 Gy usually marks the threshold of the gastrointestinal form of the acute radiation syndrome, with a very poor prognosis for all individuals involved. A fatal outcome may well be certain at 8–10 Gy.

### Delayed Effects

Long-term effects of radiation are those that may manifest themselves years after the original exposure. The latent period, then, is much longer than that associated with acute radiation syndrome. Delayed radiation effects may result from previous acute, high-dose exposures or from chronic, low-level exposures over a period of years.

No unique disease is associated with the long-term effects of radiation. These effects manifest themselves in human populations simply as a statistical increase in the incidence of certain already existing conditions. Because of the low incidence of these conditions, it is usually necessary to observe large populations of irradiated persons to measure these effects. Biostatistical and epidemiological methods are then used to indicate relationships between exposure and effect. In addition to the large numbers of people needed for human studies of delayed radiation effects, the situation is further complicated by the latent period. In some cases, a radiation-induced increase in a disease may go unrecorded unless the study is continued for many years.

Also note that although it is possible to perform true experiments with animal populations, in which all factors with the exception of radiation exposure are kept identical in study populations, human data are limited to "secondhand" information accrued from populations irradiated for reasons other than radiobiological information. Often a special characteristic of irradiated human populations is the presence of some preexisting disease that makes it extremely difficult to draw meaningful conclusions when these groups are compared with nonirradiated ones.

Despite these difficulties, many epidemiologic investigations of irradiated human beings have provided convincing evidence that ionizing radiation may indeed result in an increased risk of certain diseases long after the initial exposure. This information supplements and corroborates that gained from animal experimentation that demonstrates these same effects.

Among the delayed effects thus far observed have been somatic damage, which may result in an increased incidence of cancer, embryological defects, cataracts, lifespan shortening, and genetic mutations. With proper selection of animal species and strains, and of dose, ionizing radiation may be shown to exert an almost universal carcinogenic action, resulting in tumors in a great variety of organs and tissues. There is human evidence as well that radiation may contribute to the induction of various kinds of neoplastic diseases (cancers).

**Human Evidence.**   Both empirical observations and epidemiologic studies of irradiated individuals have more or less consistently demonstrated the carcinogenic properties of radiation. Some of these findings are summarized here.

Early in this century, when delayed radiation effects were little recognized, luminous numerals on watches and clocks were painted by hand with fine sable brushes, dipped first in radium-containing paint and then often "tipped" on the lips or tongue. Young women commonly were employed in this occupation. Years later, studies of these individuals who had ingested radium paint have disclosed an increased incidence of bone sarcomas and other malignancies resulting from the burdens of radium that had accumulated in their bones.

Some early medical and dental users of x-rays, largely unaware of the hazards involved, accumulated considerable doses of radiation. As early as the year 1910, there were reports of cancer deaths among physicians, presumably attributable to x-ray exposure. Skin cancer was a notable finding among these early practitioners. Dentists, for example, developed lesions on the fingers with which they repeatedly held dental films in their patients' mouths.

Early in this century, certain large mines in Europe were worked for pitchblende, a uranium ore. Lung cancer was highly prevalent among the miners as a result of the inhalation of large quantities of airborne radioactive materials. It was estimated that the risk of lung cancer in the pitchblende miners was at least 50% higher than that of the general population.

One of the strongest supports for the concept that radiation is a leukemogenic agent in people comes from the epidemiologic studies of the survivors of the atomic bombing in Hiroshima, Japan. Survivors exposed to radiation above an estimated dose of approximately 1 Sv showed a significant increase in the incidence of leukemia. In addition, leukemia incidence correlated well with the estimated dose (expressed as distance from the detonation point), thus strengthening the hypothesis that the excess leukemia cases were indeed attributable to the radiation exposure. There is also some indication of an increase in thyroid cancer among the heavily irradiated survivors.

A pioneering study of children of mothers irradiated during pregnancy purported to show an increased risk of leukemia among young children if they had been irradiated in utero as a result of pelvic x-ray examination of the mother. Mothers of leukemic children were questioned as to their radiation histories during pregnancy with the child in question, and these responses were compared with those of a control group, consisting of mothers of healthy playmates of the leukemic children. Originally this work received much criticism, based partly on the questionnaire technique used to elicit the information concerning radiation history. It was believed that differences in recall between the two groups of mothers might have biased the results. A larger subsequent study designed to correct for the objections to the first one corroborated its essential findings and established the leukemogenic effect on the fetus of prenatal x-rays.

Considering the fact that immature, undifferentiated, and rapidly dividing cells are highly sensitive to radiation, it is not surprising that embryonic and fetal tissues are readily damaged by relatively low doses of radiation. It has been shown in animal experiments that deleterious effects may be produced with doses of only 0.10 Gy delivered to the embryo. There is no reason to doubt that the human embryo is equally susceptible.

The majority of the anomalies produced by prenatal irradiation involve the central nervous system, although the specific type of damage is related to the dose and to the stage of pregnancy during which irradiation takes place. In terms of embryonic death, the very earliest stages of pregnancy, perhaps the first few weeks in human beings, are most radiosensitive. From the standpoint of practical radiation protection, this very early sensitivity is of great significance, because it involves a stage in human embryonic development in which pregnancy may well be unsuspected. For this reason, the International Committee on Radiological Protection has recommended that routine nonemergency diagnostic irradiation involving the pelvic area of women in the childbearing years be limited to the 10-day interval following the onset of menstruation. Such precautions would virtually eliminate the possibility of inadvertently exposing a fertilized egg.

The period from approximately the second through the sixth week of human gestation, when pregnancy could still be unsuspected, is the most sensitive for the production of congenital anomalies in the newborn. During this period, embryonic death is less likely than in the extremely early stage, but the production of morphological defects in the newborn is a major consideration.

During later stages of pregnancy, embryonic tissue is more resistant to gross and easily observable damage. However, functional changes, particularly those involving the central nervous system, may result from such late exposures. These would be difficult to measure or evaluate at birth. They usually involve subtle alterations in such phenomena as learning patterns and development and may have a considerable latent period before they manifest themselves. There is some evidence that the decreasing sensitivity of the fetus to gross radiation damage as pregnancy progresses may not apply for the leukemogenic effects of prenatal irradiation. Another important factor to be considered in evaluating the radiation hazard during late pregnancy is that irradiation may produce true genetic mutations in the immature germ cells of the fetus for which no threshold dose has been established.

**Lifespan Shortening.**   In a number of animal experiments, radiation has been demonstrated to have a lifespan-shortening effect. The aging process is complex and largely obscure, and the exact mechanisms involved in aging are as yet uncertain. Irradiated animals in these investigations appear to die of the same diseases as the nonirradiated controls, but they do so at an earlier age. How much of the total effect is due to premature aging and how much to an increased incidence of radiation-induced diseases is still unresolved.

### Genetic Effects
**Background.**   The fertilized egg is a single cell resulting from the union of sperm and egg; millions of cell divisions develop it into a complete new organism. The information that produces the characteristics of the new individual is carried in the nucleus of the fertilized egg on rod-shaped structures called chromosomes, arranged in 23 pairs. In each pair, one member is contributed

by the mother and the other by the father. With each cell division that the rapidly developing embryonic tissue undergoes, all of this information is faithfully duplicated, so that the nucleus in each new cell of the developing organism contains essentially all of the information. This, of course, includes the germ cells in the new organism, which are destined to become sperm or eggs, and thus the information is transmitted from one generation to the next. This hereditary information is often likened to a template or to a code, which is reproduced millions of times over with remarkable accuracy. It is possible to damage the hereditary material in the cell nucleus by means of external influences, and when this is done the garbled or distorted genetic information will be reproduced just as faithfully when the cell divides as was the original message. When this kind of alteration occurs in those cells of the testes or ovaries that will become mature sperm or eggs, it is referred to as **genetic mutation;** if the damaged sperm or egg cell is then used in conception, the defect is reproduced in all of the cells of the new organism that results from this conception, including those that will become sperm or eggs, and thus whatever defect resulted from the original mutation can be passed on for many generations.

Most geneticists agree that the great preponderance of genetic mutations are harmful. By virtue of their damaging effects, they can be gradually eliminated from a population by natural means because individuals afflicted with this damage are themselves less likely to reproduce successfully than are normal individuals. The more severe the defect produced by a given mutation, the more rapidly it will be eliminated and vice versa; mildly damaging mutations may require a great many generations before they gradually disappear.

As a balance to this natural elimination of harmful mutations, fresh ones are constantly occurring. A large number of agents have mutagenic properties, and it is probable that our current knowledge includes just a fraction of these. In addition, mutations can arise within the germ cells of an organism without external insult. Among the various external influences found to be mutagenic are a wide variety of chemicals, certain drugs, and physical factors such as elevated temperatures and ionizing radiation. Natural background radiation probably accounts for a small proportion of naturally occurring mutations. For people, it has been estimated that background radiation probably produces less than 10% of these. Anthropogenic radiation, of course, if delivered to the gonads, can also produce mutations over and above those that occur spontaneously. Radiation, it should be noted, is not unique in this respect and is probably one of a number of environmental influences capable of increasing the mutation rate.

**Animal Evidence.**   The mutagenic properties of ionizing radiation were first discovered in 1927, using the fruit fly as the experimental animal. Since that time, experiments have been extended to include other species, and many investigations have been carried out on mice. Animal experimentation remains our chief source of information concerning the genetic effects of radiation, and as a result of the intensive experimentation, certain generalizations may be made. Among those of health significance are (1) there is no indication of a threshold dose for the genetic effects of radiation, that is, a dose below which genetic damage does not occur; and (2) the degree of mutational damage that results from radiation exposure seems to be dose-rate dependent, so that a given dose is less effective in producing damage if it is protracted or fractionated over a long period.

**Human Evidence.**   A major human study on genetic effects was made with the Japanese who survived the atomic bomb in 1945. As the index of a possible increase of the mutation rate, the sex ratio in the offspring of certain irradiated groups (families, for example, in which the mother had been irradiated but the father had not) was observed. Assuming that some of the mutational damage in the mothers would be recessive, lethal, and sex-linked, a shift in the sex ratio among these families might be expected in the direction of fewer male births than in completely nonirradiated groups, and this seemed to be the case in early reports. Later evaluation of more complete data, however, did not bear out the original suggestion of an effect on the sex ratio.

The preconception radiation histories of the parents of leukemic children compared with those of normal children was a part of the subject of another investigation. From the results, it would appear that there is a statistically significant increase in leukemia risk among children whose mothers had received diagnostic x-rays during this period. The effect here is apparently a genetic rather than an embryonic one because the irradiation occurred prior to the conception of the child.

A somewhat similar study ascertained the radiation exposure histories of the parents of children with Down syndrome. Most of this exposure was prior to the conception of the child. A significantly greater number of the mothers of children with Down syndrome reported receiving fluoroscopy and x-ray therapy than did mothers of the normal children in the control group.

The findings of these two studies may provide evidence that ionizing radiation is a mutational agent in people. However, the findings should be viewed with some reservations because there could be significant differences to begin with between populations of people requiring x-rays and those who do not. These differences alone might account for a slightly higher incidence of leukemia or Down syndrome in the offspring of the former group, irrespective of the radiation received. To date, there has been no incontrovertible evidence found of genetic effects in humans from radiation exposure.

## 16–3   RADIATION STANDARDS

Two population groups are given distinctly different treatment in the establishment of exposure–dose guidelines and rules. Standards are set for those occupationally engaged in work requiring ionizing radiation and for the general public. Although there are many standard-setting bodies, in general, the limits are consistent between groups. The Nuclear Regulatory Commission (NRC) has published guidelines in the *Code of Federal Regulations* (10 CFR 20) that serve as the standard in the United States. The dose guidelines are in addition to the natural background dose.

The allowable dose for occupational exposure is predicated on the following assumptions: the exposure group is under surveillance and control; it is adult; it is knowledgeable of its work and the associated risks; its exposure is at work, that is, $40 \text{ h} \cdot \text{week}^{-1}$; and it is in good health. On this basis, no individual is to receive more than 0.05 Sv per year of radiation exposure.

For the population at large, the allowable whole body dose in one calendar year is 0.001 Sv. This dose does not include medical and dental doses that, for diagnostic and therapeutic reasons, may far exceed this amount.

In addition to these dose rules, the NRC has set standards for the discharge of radionuclides into the environment. Table 16–2 is an extract from that list. These concentrations are measured above the existing background concentration and are annual averages. Discharges must be limited such that the amounts shown are not exceeded in ambient air or natural waters. If a mixture of isotopes is released into an unrestricted area, the concentrations shall be limited so that the following relationship exists:

$$\frac{C_A}{\text{MPC}_A} + \frac{C_B}{\text{MPC}_B} + \frac{C_C}{\text{MPC}_C} \leq 1 \qquad (16\text{–}21)$$

where     $C_A, C_B, C_C$ = concentrations of radionuclides A, B, and C, respectively
(in $\mu\text{Ci} \cdot \text{mL}^{-1}$)
$\text{MPC}_A, \text{MPC}_B, \text{MPC}_C$ = maximum permissible concentrations of radionuclides A, B, and C
from Table II of Appendix B, Part 20 of the *CFR* (10 CFR 20)

**Radon.**   Unlike the standards for exposure and releases to the environment, those for radon in indoor air are established by the EPA. This is because radon is not the result of anthropogenic activity but rather occurs naturally. The EPA guidelines suggest that the annual average radon exposure be limited to $4 \text{ pCi} \cdot \text{L}^{-1}$ of air.

**TABLE 16–2** Selected Maximum Permissible Concentrations of Radionuclides in Air and Water Above Background

| Radionuclide | Class | Occupational Values | | | Effluent Concentrations | | Releases to Sewers |
|---|---|---|---|---|---|---|---|
| | | Oral Ingestion ALI (μCi)[b] | Inhalation ALI (μCi) | Inhalation DAC (μCi)[c] | Air (μCi · mL⁻¹) | Water (μCi · mL⁻¹) | Monthly Average Conc. (μCi · mL⁻¹) |
| Barium-131 | D[a], all compounds | $3 \times 10^3$ | $8 \times 10^3$ | $3 \times 10^{-6}$ | $1 \times 10^{-8}$ | $4 \times 10^{-5}$ | $4 \times 10^{-4}$ |
| Beryllium-7 | W, all compounds except those given for Y | $4 \times 10^4$ | $2 \times 10^4$ | $9 \times 10^{-6}$ | $3 \times 10^{-8}$ | $6 \times 10^{-4}$ | $6 \times 10^{-3}$ |
| | Y, oxides, halides and nitrates | — | $2 \times 10^4$ | $8 \times 10^{-6}$ | $3 \times 10^{-8}$ | — | — |
| Calcium-45 | W, all compounds | $2 \times 10^3$ | $8 \times 10^2$ | $4 \times 10^{-7}$ | $1 \times 10^{-9}$ | $2 \times 10^{-5}$ | $2 \times 10^{-4}$ |
| Carbon-14 | Monoxide | — | $2 \times 10^6$ | $7 \times 10^{-4}$ | $2 \times 10^{-6}$ | — | — |
| | Dioxide | — | $2 \times 10^5$ | $9 \times 10^{-5}$ | $3 \times 10^{-7}$ | — | — |
| | Compounds | $2 \times 10^3$ | $2 \times 10^3$ | $1 \times 10^{-6}$ | $3 \times 10^{-9}$ | $3 \times 10^{-5}$ | $3 \times 10^{-4}$ |
| Cesium-137 | D, all compounds | $1 \times 10^2$ | $2 \times 10^2$ | $6 \times 10^{-8}$ | $2 \times 10^{-10}$ | $1 \times 10^{-6}$ | $1 \times 10^{-5}$ |
| Iodine-131 | D, all compounds | $3 \times 10^1$ Thyroid ($9 \times 10^1$) | $5 \times 10^1$ Thyroid ($2 \times 10^3$) | $2 \times 10^{-8}$ | $2 \times 10^{-10}$ | $1 \times 10^{-6}$ | $1 \times 10^{-5}$ |
| Iron-55 | D, all compounds except those given for W | $9 \times 10^3$ | $2 \times 10^3$ | $8 \times 10^{-7}$ | $3 \times 10^{-9}$ | $1 \times 10^{-4}$ | $1 \times 10^{-3}$ |
| | W, oxides, hydroxides and halides | — | $4 \times 10^3$ | $2 \times 10^{-6}$ | $6 \times 10^{-9}$ | — | — |
| Phosphorus-32 | D, all compounds except those given for W | $6 \times 10^2$ | $9 \times 10^2$ | $4 \times 10^{-7}$ | $1 \times 10^{-9}$ | $9 \times 10^{-6}$ | $9 \times 10^{-5}$ |
| | W, phosphates of $Zn^{2+}$, $S^{3+}$, $Mg^{2+}$, $Fe^{3+}$, $Bi^{3+}$ and lanthanides | — | $4 \times 10^2$ | $2 \times 10^{-7}$ | $5 \times 10^{-10}$ | — | — |
| Radon-222 | With daughters removed | — | $1 \times 10^4$ | $4 \times 10^{-6}$ | $1 \times 10^{-8}$ | — | — |
| | With daughters present | — | $1 \times 10^2$ (or 4 working level months) | $3 \times 10^{-8}$ (or 0.33 working level) | $1 \times 10^{-10}$ | — | — |
| Strontium-90 | D, all soluble compounds except $SrTiO_3$ | $3 \times 10^1$ Bone surface / $4 \times 10^1$ | $2 \times 10^1$ Bone surface / $2 \times 10^1$ | $8 \times 10^{-9}$ | $3 \times 10^{-11}$ | $5 \times 10^{-7}$ | $5 \times 10^{-6}$ |
| | Y, all insoluble compounds and $SrTiO_3$ | — | $4$ | $2 \times 10^{-9}$ | $6 \times 10^{-12}$ | — | — |
| Zinc-65 | Y, all compounds | $4 \times 10^2$ | $3 \times 10^2$ | $1 \times 10^{-7}$ | $4 \times 10^{-10}$ | $5 \times 10^{-6}$ | $5 \times 10^{-5}$ |

[a] D, W, and Y are classes denoting the time of retention in the body, days, weeks and years, respectively.

[b] ALI is the Annual Limit of Intake.

[c] DAC is the derived air concentration.

Source: Excerpted from title 10, CFR, part 20, Appendix B.

## 16–4  RADIATION EXPOSURE

### External and Internal Radiation Hazards

External radiation hazards result from exposure to sources of ionizing radiation of sufficient energy to penetrate the body and cause harm. Generally speaking, it requires an alpha particle of at least 7.5 MeV to penetrate the 0.07 mm protective layer of the skin. A beta particle requires 70 keV to penetrate the same layer [3]. Unless the sources of alpha or beta radiation are quite close to the skin, they pose only a small external radiation hazard. X-rays and gamma rays constitute the most common type of external hazard. When of sufficient energy, both are capable of deep penetration into the body. As a result no radiosensitive organ is beyond the range of their damaging power.

Radioactive materials may gain access to the body by ingestion, by inhalation of air containing radioactive materials, by absorption of a solution of radioactive materials through the skin, and by absorption of radioactive material into the tissue through a cut or break in the skin. The danger of ingesting radioactive materials is not necessarily from swallowing a large amount at one time, but rather from the accumulation of small amounts on the hands, on cigarettes, on foodstuffs, and other objects that bring the material into the mouth.

Any radioactive material that gains entry into the body is an internal hazard. The extent of the hazard depends on the type of radiation emitted, its energy, the physical and biological half-life of the material, and the radiosensitivity of the organ where the isotope localizes. Alpha and beta emitters are the most dangerous radionuclides from the standpoint internal hazard because their specific ionization is very high. Radionuclides with half-lives of intermediate length are the most dangerous because they combine fairly high activity with a half-life sufficiently long to cause considerable damage. Polonium is an example of a potentially very serious internal hazard. It emits a highly ionizing alpha particle of energy 5.3 MeV and has a half-life of 138 days.

### Natural Background

People are exposed to natural radiation from cosmic, terrestrial, and internal sources. Typical gonadal exposures from natural background are summarized in Figure 16–5. Cosmic radiation is that originating outside of our atmosphere. This radiation consists predominately, if not entirely, of

**FIGURE 16–5**

Average dose per year to person living in the United States. (*Source: U.S. Department of Energy.*)

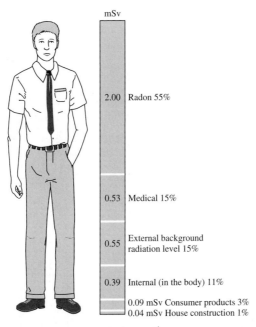

mSv

2.00  Radon 55%

0.53  Medical 15%

0.55  External background radiation level 15%

0.39  Internal (in the body) 11%

0.09 mSv Consumer products 3%
0.04 mSv House construction 1%

Total = 3.60 mSv·year$^{-1}$

protons whose energy spectrum peaks in the range of 1 to 2 GeV. Heavy nuclei are also present. The impact of primary and very high energy secondary cosmic rays produces violent nuclear reactions in which many neutrons, protons, alpha particles, and other fragments are emitted. Most of the neutrons produced by cosmic rays are slowed to thermal energies and, by $n, p$ (neutron–proton) reaction with $^{14}N$, produce $^{14}C$. The lifetime of carbon-14 is long enough that it becomes thoroughly mixed with the exchangeable carbon at the earth's surface (carbon dioxide, dissolved bicarbonate it the oceans, living organisms, etc.). Some of the cosmic radiation penetrates to the earth's surface and contributes directly to our whole body dose. Terrestrial radiation exposure comes from the 50 naturally occurring radionuclides found in the earth's crust. Of these, radon has come to have the most significance as a common environmental hazard to the general public.

Radon is the product of the radioactive decay of its parent, radium. Radium is produced from each of the three major series: $^{235}U$, $^{238}U$, and $^{232}U$. The radon isotopes produced are $^{222}Rn$, $^{220}Rn$, and $^{219}Rn$. These have half-lives of 3.8 days, 55.6 s, and 3.92 s, respectively. $^{222}Rn$, because of its longer half-life and the abundance of its parent uranium in geologic materials, is generally more abundant and, hence, is considered the greater environmental hazard. Because the half-life of radium and its parents is so long, the source is essentially undiminished over human time scales.

The hazard of radon does not come from radon itself but from its radioactive decay products ($^{218}Po$, $^{214}Po$, $^{214}Bi$). The decay products are charged atoms of heavy metals that readily attach themselves to airborne particulates. The main health problem stems from the inhalation of unattached decay products and these particulates. The decay products and particulates become lodged in the lung. As they continue to decay, they release small bursts of energy in the form of alpha, beta, and gamma radiation that damage the lung tissue and could ultimately lead to lung cancer [4].

Radon is a gas. It is colorless, odorless, and generally chemically inert like other noble gases such as helium, neon, krypton, and argon. It does not sorb, hydrolyze, oxidize, or precipitate. Thus, its movement through the ground is not inhibited by chemical interaction with the soil.

Migration of radon occurs by two mechanisms: diffusion as a gas through the pore spaces in the soil and by dissolution and transport in the groundwater. The rate of diffusion or transport is a function of the emanation rate, porosity, structural channels, moisture content, and hydrologic conditions. These migration routes lead to two mechanisms of effect on people. Buildings constructed in areas of high radon emanation may have radon gas penetrate the structure through natural construction openings such as floor drains or joints (Table 16–3) or through structural failures such as cracks that develop from foundation settlement. In areas where the public water supply is drawn from an aquifer that has radon emanation, shower water may release radon. One rule of thumb is that a radon concentration of 10,000 $pCi \cdot L^{-1}$ of water, when heated and agitated, will produce about 1 $pCi \cdot L^{-1}$ of air [5].

**TABLE 16–3**   Radon Gas Measurements in the Floor Drains and in the Basement Air of Seven Houses

| House No. | Radon Concentration in Floor Drain ($pCi \cdot L^{-1}$) | Radon Concentration in Basement Air ($pCi \cdot L^{-1}$) | Ratio Drain/Basement |
|---|---|---|---|
| 1 | 169.3 | 2.51 | 67.5 |
| 2 | 98.4 | 2.24 | 43.9 |
| 3 | 91.4 | 1.43 | 63.9 |
| 4 | 413.3 | 1.87 | 221 |
| 5 | 255.4 | 3.95 | 64.7 |
| 6 | 173.4 | 21.02 | 57.4 |
| 7 | 52.1 | 9.63 | 5.4 |
| Average | 179.0 | 3.52 | |

### X-Rays

X-ray machine use is widespread in industry, medicine, and research. All such uses are potential sources of exposure.

**Medical and Dental Use.**   In addition to the 300,000–400,000 medical-technical personnel that are occupationally exposed to radiation in the use of these machines, a considerable portion of the general population is also exposed. A large portion of the 2,500,000 persons seen daily by physicians have some x-ray diagnostic procedure performed on them.

**Industrial Uses.**   Industrial x-ray devices include radiographic and fluoroscopic units used for the determination of defects in castings, fabricated structures, and welds, and fluoroscopic units used for the detection of foreign material in, for example, airline luggage. Use of these units may result in whole body exposure to the operators and people who are nearby.

**Research Use.**   High-voltage x-ray machines are becoming familiar features of research laboratories in universities and similar institutions. Other x-ray equipment used in research includes x-ray diffraction units used for crystal analysis, electron microscopes, and particle accelerators.

### Radionuclides

**Naturally Occurring.**   Thousands of becquerels of radium is in use in the medical field. In this use, many individuals besides the patient, including other patients, nurses, technicians, radiologists, and physicians, are potentially exposed to radiation.

Static eliminators, employing polonium or radium as the radioactive source, have been widely used in industry. Typical industries where they may be found are the textile and paper trades, printing, photographic processing, and telephone and telegraph companies.

**Artificially Produced.**   Over 6000 universities, hospitals, and research laboratories in the United States are using radionuclides for medical, biological, industrial, agricultural, and scientific research and for medical diagnosis and therapy. Over a million people in the United States receive radiotherapy treatment each year. Possible exposure from such radionuclides is involved with their preparation, handling, application, and transportation. Exposures, internal and external, might also arise through contamination of the environment by wastes originating from the use of these materials.

### Nuclear Reactor Operations

Sources of radiation exposure associated with nuclear reactor operations include the reactor itself; its ventilation and cooling wastes; procedures associated with the removal and reprocessing of its "spent" fuel and the resulting fission product wastes; and procedures associated with the mining, milling, and fabrication of new fuels.

### Radioactive Wastes

There are three principal sources of radioactive wastes: reactors and chemical processing plants, research facilities, and medical facilities. Regulations for the handling and disposal of radioactive wastes are designed to minimize exposure to the general public, but the regulations obviously provide less protection to those handling the waste.

## 16–5   RADIATION PROTECTION*

The principles discussed here are generally applicable to all types or energies of radiation. Their application will vary however, depending on the type, intensity, and energy of the source. For example, beta particles from radioactive materials require different shielding from that for

---

*This discussion follows reference [2].

high-speed electrons from an accelerator. Ideally, we would like to provide protection that results in a radiation exposure of zero. In actuality, technical and economic limitations force us to compromise so that the risks are small compared with the benefits obtained. The radiation standards set the limit above which the risk is deemed to be too great.

### Reduction of External Radiation Hazards

Three fundamental methods are employed to reduce external radiation hazards: distance, shielding, and reduction of exposure time.

**Distance.**   Distance is not only very effective, but also in many instances the most easily applied principle of radiation protection. Beta particles of a single energy have a finite range in air. Sometimes the distance afforded by the use of remote control handling devices will supply complete protection.

The inverse square law for reduction of radiation intensity applies for point sources of x-, gamma, and neutron radiation. The inverse square law states that radiation intensity from a point varies inversely as the square of the distance from the source.

$$\frac{I_1}{I_2} = \frac{(R_2)^2}{(R_1)^2}$$
(16–22)

where $I_1$ is the radiation intensity at distance $R_1$ from the source, and $I_2$ is the radiation intensity at distance $R_2$ from the source. Inspection of this formula will show that increasing the distance by a factor of 3, for example, reduces the radiation intensity to one-ninth of its value. The inverse square law does not apply to extended sources or to radiation fields from multiple sources.

X-ray tubes act sufficiently like point sources so that reduction calculations by this law are valid. Gamma ray sources whose dimensions are small in comparison with the distances involved may also be considered point sources, as can capsule neutron sources.

**Shielding.**   Shielding is one of the most important methods for radiation protection. It is accomplished by placing some absorbing material between the source and the person to be protected. Radiation is attenuated in the absorbing medium. When so used, "absorption," does not imply an occurrence such as a sponge soaking up water, but rather absorption here refers to the process of transferring the energy of the radiation to the atoms of the material through which the radiation passes. X- and gamma radiation energy is lost by three methods: photoelectric effect, Compton effect, and pair production.

The **photoelectric effect** is an all-or-none energy loss. The x-ray, or photon, imparts all of its energy to an orbital electron of some atom. This photon, because it consisted only of energy in the first place, simply vanishes. The energy is imparted to the orbital electron in the form of kinetic energy of motion, and this greatly increased energy overcomes the attractive force of the nucleus for the electron and causes the electron to fly from its orbit with considerable velocity. Thus, an ion pair results. The high-velocity electron (which is called a **photoelectron**) has sufficient energy to knock other electrons from the orbits of other atoms, and it goes on its way producing secondary ion pairs until all of its energy is expended.

The **Compton effect** provides a means of partial energy loss for the incoming x- or gamma ray. Again the ray appears to interact with an orbital electron of some atom, but in the case of Compton interactions, only a part of the energy is transferred to the electron, and the x- or gamma ray "staggers on" in a weakened condition. The high-velocity electron, now referred to as a Compton electron, produces secondary ionization in the same manner as does the photoelectron, and the weakened x-ray continues on until it loses more energy in another Compton interaction or disappears completely via the photoelectric effect. The unfortunate aspect of Compton interaction is that the direction of flight of the weakened x- or gamma ray is different from that of the original. In fact, the weakened x- or gamma ray is frequently referred to as a "scattered" photon, and the entire process is known as Compton scattering. By this mechanism of interaction, the direction of photons in a beam may be randomized, so that scattered radiation may appear around corners and behind shields although at a lesser intensity.

Pair production, the third type of interaction, is much rarer than either the photoelectric or Compton effect. In fact, pair production is impossible unless the x- or gamma ray possesses at least 1 MeV of energy. (Practically speaking, it does not become important until 2 MeV of energy.) **Pair production** may be thought of as the lifting of an electron from a negative to a positive energy state. The pair is a positron–electron pair that results from the photon ejecting an electron and leaving a "hole" the positron. If there is any excess energy in the photon above the 1 MeV required to create two electron masses, it is simply shared between the two electrons as kinetic energy of motion, and they fly out of the atom with great velocity. The negative electron behaves in exactly the ordinary way, producing secondary ion pairs until it loses all of its energy of motion. The positron also produces secondary ionization so long as it is in motion, but when it has lost its energy and slowed almost to a stop, it encounters a free negative electron somewhere in the material. The two are attracted by their opposite charges, and, upon contact, annihilate each other, converting both their masses into pure energy. Thus, two gamma rays of 0.51 MeV arise at the site of the annihilation. The ultimate fate of the annihilation gammas is either photoelectric absorption or Compton scattering followed by photoelectric absorption.

Because the energy of the photon must be greater than 1 MeV for pair production to occur, this process is not a factor in the absorption of x-rays used in dental and medical radiography. The energies of x-rays used in this type of radiography are rarely more than 0.1 MeV.

The predominating mechanism of interaction with the shielding material depends on the energy of the radiation and the absorbing material. The photoelectric effect is most important at low energies, the Compton effect at intermediate energies, and pair production at high energies. As x- and gamma ray photons travel through an absorber, their decrease in number caused by the above-mentioned absorption processes is governed by the energy of radiation, the specific absorber medium, and the thickness of the absorber traversed. The general attenuation may be expressed as follows:

$$\frac{dI}{dx} = -uI_0 \tag{16–23}$$

where $dI$ = reduction of radiation
   $I_0$ = incident radiation
   $u$ = proportionality constant
   $dx$ = thickness of absorber traversed

Integrating yields

$$I = I_0 \exp(-ux) \tag{16–24}$$

Using this formula it is easy to calculate the radiation intensity behind a shield of thickness $x$, or to calculate the thickness of absorber necessary to reduce radiation intensity to a desired level, if the factor $u$ is known. This factor is called the **linear absorption coefficient** when $x$ is a linear dimension. The value of $u$ depends on the energy of the radiation and the absorbing medium. The ratio $I/I_0$ is sometimes called the **transmission.** Tables and graphs are available that give values of $u$ determined experimentally or that give transmission values for varying thickness or different shielding materials (Figures 16–6 through 16–9).

If the radiation being attenuated does not meet narrow-beam conditions, or thick absorbers are involved, the absorption equation becomes

$$I = BI_0 \exp(-ux) \tag{16–25}$$

where $B$ is the buildup factor that takes into account an increasing radiation intensity due to scattered radiation within the absorber.

**FIGURE 16–6**

Transmission through lead of gamma rays from radium; cobalt-60; cesium-137; gold-198; iridium-192; tantalum-182; and sodium-24.

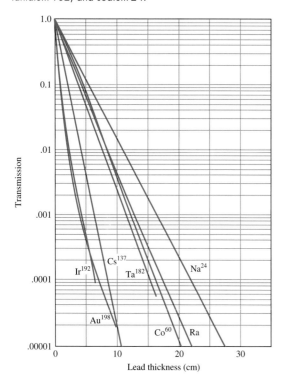

**FIGURE 16–7**

Transmission through concrete (density 147 lb · ft⁻³) of gamma rays from radium; cobalt-60, cesium-137, gold-198; iridium-192.

For alpha and beta emissions from radionuclides (not accelerators), substantial attenuation can be achieved with modest shielding. The amount of shielding required is, of course, a function of the particle energy. For example, a 10-MeV alpha particle has a range of 1.14 m in air, whereas a 1-MeV particle has a range of 2.28 cm. Virtually any solid material of any substance can be used to shield alpha particles. Beta particles can also be shielded relatively easily. For example a $^{32}$P beta at 1.71 MeV can be attenuated 99.8% by 0.25 cm of aluminum. However, materials with high atomic numbers, such as metals, should not be used for high-energy beta shielding due to the production of **Bremsstrahlung radiation** (radiation produced by stopping another kind of radiation). In materials with high atomic numbers, the beta particle is absorbed, but the excess "trapped" energy is released in the form of an x-ray. For this reason, Plexiglas or Lucite, typically 6–12 mm thick, is often used.

Fast neutrons are poorly absorbed by most materials. Therefore, it is necessary to slow them down for efficient absorption. Because the greatest transfer of energy takes place in collisions between particles of equal mass, hydrogenous materials are most effective for slowing down fast neutrons. Water, paraffin, and concrete are all rich in hydrogen, and thus, important in neutron shielding. Once the neutrons have been reduced in energy, they may be absorbed by either boron or cadmium. When a boron atom captures a neutron, it emits an alpha particle, but because of the extremely short range of alpha particles, no additional hazard results. Neutron capture by cadmium results in the emission of gamma radiation. Lead or a similar gamma absorber must be used as a shield against these gammas. A complete shield for a capsule-type neutron source may consist of, first, a thick layer of paraffin to slow down the neutrons, then a surrounding layer of cadmium to absorb the slow neutrons, and finally, an outer layer of lead to absorb both the gammas produced in the cadmium and those emanating from the capsule.

**FIGURE 16–8**

Transmission through iron of gamma rays from radium; cobalt-60, cesium-137; iridium-192.

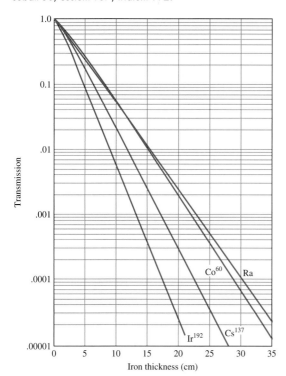

**FIGURE 16–9**

Transmission through lead of x-rays.

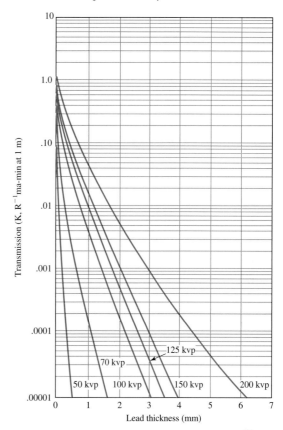

Some care must be exercised in using shielding to reduce exposure. People outside the "shadow" cast by the shield are not necessarily protected. A wall or partition is not necessarily a safe shield for persons on the other side. Their allowable dose may be less than conceived in the design of the barrier. Radiation can "bounce around corners" because it can be scattered.

Scattered radiation is present to some extent whenever an absorbing medium is in the path of radiation. The absorber then acts as a new source of radiation. Frequently, room walls, the floor, and other solid objects are near enough to a source of radiation to make scatter appreciable. When a point source is used under these conditions, the inverse square law is no longer completely valid for computing radiation intensity at a distance. Measurement of the radiation is then necessary to determine the potential exposure at any point.

**Reduction of Exposure Time.**  By limiting the duration of exposure to all radiation sources and by providing ample recuperative time between exposures, the untoward effects of radiation can be minimized. Recognition of the zero threshold theory of damage warrants that exposures, no matter how small, be minimized. The standards established by the NRC are upper bounds to be avoided and not goals to be achieved.

In emergency situations it may occasionally be necessary to work in areas of very high dose rates. This can be done with safety by limiting the total exposure time so that the average permissible value for a day based on the radiation protection guide dose of $1 \times 10^{-3}$ Gy (0.1 rad) per week is not exceeded. This does not imply that a worker should be allowed to extend this practice beyond receiving $1 \times 10^{-3}$ Gy in a short period of time, that is, a dose of $1 \times 10^{-3}$ Gy one day and no dose for 6 days would comply with the rule but would be considered excessive.

Repetitions of this cycle would be unacceptable. Emergency situations may require that work be done in relays of several people in the same job so that the value of the radiation protection guide is not exceeded by any one person.

### *Reduction of Internal Radiation Hazards*

**Occupational.** The prevention and control of contamination is the most effective way to reduce internal hazards in the workplace. The use of protective devices and good handling techniques affords a large measure of protection. Dust should be kept to a minimum by elimination of dry sweeping. Laboratory operations should be carried out in a hood. The exhaust air from the hood must be filtered with a high-efficiency filter. The filter must be replaced regularly in an approved manner. Protective clothing should be worn so that normal street clothes do not become contaminated. Respirators should be worn during emergency operations or when dust is generated. Eating must not be permitted in areas where radioactive materials are handled. Proper training in the care and handling of radioactive materials is, perhaps, the most important method for reducing the potential for internal radiation exposure in the workplace.

**Radon.** Aside from cigarette smoke, the most likely nonoccupational internal radiation hazard is from radon in private dwellings. Because the radon primarily originates in the soil beneath the house, control efforts are aimed at the basement or crawl space.

The EPA suggests two major approaches for new construction: reduction of the pathways for radon entry and reduction of the draft of the house on surrounding and underlying soil. The methods to reduce the pathways for entry are summarized in Figure 16–10. Of particular concern are penetrations into the foundation such as floor drains (see Table 16–3) and cracks in the floor. The use of a polyethylene sheet below the slab is particularly effective for controlling leaks that result from slab cracks that develop as the house settles. Because heat in the upper floors tends to rise, creating a draft much like a chimney, the house has a tendency to create a negative pressure on the basement and, hence, "suck in" radon from the soil pore spaces. Figure 16–11 shows some techniques to minimize the draft effect [5].

For existing structures, the remedies are more difficult to install, will be expensive, and may not yield satisfactory results. If drain tiles are present around the outside or inside of the perimeter footings, these are ideally located to permit vacuum to be drawn near some of the major soil gas entry routes (the joint between the slab and the foundation wall and the footing region where the radon can enter the voids in the block walls). Other efforts have included drilling holes in the slab itself and creating a vacuum system beneath the whole slab. Several suction points (three to seven) are required for this technique to work [6]. One demonstration project showed that jacking the house off the foundation and sealing the block walls was effective. In addition, a proprietary epoxy coating was applied to the floor and walls (Figure 16–12) [7].

### FIGURE 16–10

Methods to reduce pathways for radon entry.

**FIGURE 16–11**

Methods to reduce the vacuum.

- Seal around attic access stairs
- Seal around flue chases and chimneys
- External air supply for fireplace
- External air supply for furnace and other combustible appliances
- Seal around duct and flue chase openings between floors
- Avoid recessed ceiling lights in upper floor
- Storm windows and weather stripping to reduce Venturi effect
- Seal openings around plumbing penetrations
- Grade
- Seal around duct penetration between basement and crawl space
- Solid
- Vents to meet code requirements
- Seal around access door to crawl space
- Vapor barrier between subfloor and finish flooring
- Solid
- Grade
- Furnace
- Crawl space
- Seal
- Footing
- Footing
- Footing

**FIGURE 16–12**

Interior membrane linings and sealants to prevent radon gas infiltration. (*Source: Gallagher & Associates, Inc. April 1987.*)

- Joist
- Sill plate
- Anchor bolt
- 2nd Epoxy coating
- Epoxy to tie systems together
- Fiberglass tail
- Veneer
- 1st Epoxy coating
- Concrete block/ foundation wall
- Membrane sheet

- Concrete block/ foundation wall
- Membrane sheet
- Sealant bead
- Two coats of epoxy
- Bond breaker
- Cant strip (constructed with low mod epoxy gel)
- Concrete slab
- Stone base
- Concrete footing
- Soil

(a)                                    (b)

## 16–6  **RADIOACTIVE WASTE**

### Types of Waste

No single scheme is satisfactory for classifying radioactive waste in a quantitative way. Usage has led us to categorize wastes into "levels." **High-level wastes** are those with activities measured in curies per liter; **intermediate-level wastes** have activities measured in millicuries per liter; **low-level wastes** have activities measured in microcuries per liter. Other classifications skip the intermediate-level wastes and use the terms high-level, **transuranic,** and low-level. The high-level wastes (HLW) are those resulting from reprocessing of spent fuel or the spent fuel itself from nuclear reactors. Transuranic wastes are those containing isotopes above uranium in the periodic table. They are the by-products of fuel assembly, weapons fabrication, and reprocessing. In general their radioactivity is low but they contain long-lived isotopes (those with half-lives greater than 20 years). The bulk of low-level wastes (LLW) has relatively little radioactivity. Most require little or no shielding and may be handled by direct contact.

### Management of High-Level Radioactive Waste

In 1993, there were about 109 operating reactors in the United States [8]. Roughly 10 m$^3$ of spent fuel is generated annually from each of these reactors. The construction of the fuel assembly results in considerably less fission product waste. Approximately 0.1 m$^3$ of the 10 m$^3$ is fission product waste. Of course, it is evenly distributed throughout the assembly and cannot be easily separated. The management choices are (1) store it indefinitely in the form in which it was removed from the reactor, (2) reprocess it to extract the fission products and recycle the other materials, or (3) dispose of it by burial or other isolation technique.

Under the Nuclear Waste Policy Act of 1987, Congress has prescribed that a storage facility be constructed that will not become permanent. Designated the monitored retrievable storage facility, the current and only candidate site is at Yucca Flats, Nevada. The NRC has detailed the rules for the site in the *Code of Federal Regulations* (10 CFR 60). Some of the important provisions are summarized here [9]:

1. The design and operation of the facility should not pose an unreasonable risk to the health and safety of the public. The radiation dose limit is a small fraction of that due to natural background.
2. A multiple barrier is to be used.
3. A thorough site study must be made. Geologic and hydrologic characteristics of the site must be favorable.
4. The repository must be located where there are no attractive resources, be far from population centers, and be under federal control.
5. High-level wastes are to be retrievable for up to 50 years from the start of operations.
6. The waste package must be designed to take into account all of the possible effects from earthquakes to accidental mishandling.
7. The package is to have a design life of 300 years.
8. Groundwater travel time from the repository to the source of public water is to be at least 1000 years.
9. The annual release of radionuclides must be less than 1/1000 of a percent of the amount of the radioactivity that is present 1000 years after the repository is closed.

### Waste Isolation Pilot Plant

The waste isolation pilot plant (WIPP) project was authorized by Congress in 1979. After much political negotiation, the WIPP was authorized as a military transuranic waste facility exempt from licensing by the NRC. Under construction since 1983, the facility consists of 16 km of shafts and tunnels 650 m below ground in southeast New Mexico. The geologic material is a Permian salt basin. It was supposed to begin accepting waste in 1989 but has not done so. Certain risk analyses and compliance with RCRA requirements have delayed its use. The facility was conceived to demonstrate design concepts and to conduct some experiments with military high-level wastes that will later be retrieved. Many design questions about gas generation in the decaying waste and potential contamination scenarios are still being worked out.

### Management of Low-Level Radioactive Waste

**Historical Perspective.**   Between 1962 and 1971, six commercial waste disposal sites were licensed. Three were subsequently closed because they failed. The three sites (Maxey Flats, Kentucky; Sheffield, Illinois; and West Valley, New York) all experienced similar problems. They used shallow land burial to dispose of the waste. This was accomplished by excavating a trench about 3–6 m deep and placing the drums and other containers (often cardboard boxes) of radionuclides in the trench and covering them with excavated soil. The completed trench was covered with a mound of earth and seeded.

Water seeped through the cover material and animals burrowed through it. The heavy clay sites chosen precisely to limit passage to the groundwater system served as holding ponds for the rainwater and ultimately accelerated the corrosion of the drums. At West Valley, when increased radioactivity called attention to this phenomenon, the trenches were opened and pumped to the nearest stream! Concurrently, it was discovered that the drums were often 30–50% empty. This, combined with the fact that the backfill material was heavy clay that did not completely fill the void spaces between the drums, allowed significant settlement of the cover material. This enhanced the collection of precipitation that contributed to the corrosion and failure of the drums.

These episodes led to a major rethinking at how we should manage our radioactive wastes. One result was that in 1980, Congress enacted the Low-Level Waste Policy Act. It says that each state is responsible for providing for the availability of capacity either within or outside of the state for disposal of low-level radioactive waste generated within its borders. The law provided for the formation of **compacts** between states to allow a regional approach to management. As of December 1995, the compact organization was as shown in Figure 16–13. The compacts decide what facilities are required and which states will serve as hosts. Although the compacts were supposed to begin accepting waste in 1986, the negotiation process has taken longer than expected and the deadline has been extended to beyond the year 2000. Many compacts have yet to select sites, let alone begin construction. The three currently available sites will soon run out of capacity, so there is some urgency to solve the problem.

**Waste Minimization.**\*   As with all waste problems we have dealt with in this text, the first step in managing low-level radioactive waste is to minimize its production. Since 1980, considerable strides have been made in reducing the volume of LLRW (Figure 16–14). A number of procedures can be effectively employed.

Immediate sorting of solid radioactive waste from nonradioactive waste is an essential initial step in any scheme for the reduction of the volume of that waste and for the recovery of radionuclides from uranium and transuranium waste. It is optimistic to expect much reduction of that volume of waste by sorting out uncontaminated waste unless it is done at the point of origin. Training plant personnel to do this work at the point of origin has been reasonably successful. To ask radioactive waste management personnel to do the sorting of an unknown mixture of wastes at a subsequent time and place creates an unacceptable hazard of exposure to radiation by inhalation, injury, or ambient external exposure.

Often material only suspected of being radioactively contaminated is labeled and disposed of as such without necessarily actually being radioactive. Much of the so-called "radioactive" waste fits into such a category merely because of the place where it was generated. The cost of assaying such suspected low-level solid wastes to determine their true radioactive content is such

---

\*This discussion follows reference [10].

## FIGURE 16-13

Low-level radioactive waste compacts (December 1995).

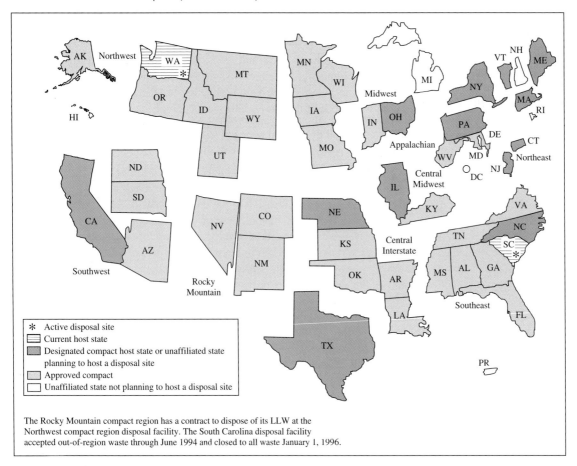

The Rocky Mountain compact region has a contract to dispose of its LLW at the
Northwest compact region disposal facility. The South Carolina disposal facility
accepted out-of-region waste through June 1994 and closed to all waste January 1, 1996.

## FIGURE 16-14

Reduction in low-level
radioactive waste
volume. (*Source: U.S.
Department of Energy
Figures, 1988.*)

that it is often cheaper to combine suspected waste with known radioactive waste than to separate it. This suspicious but not always radioactive waste takes up burial space unnecessarily.
Time, effort, and money are needlessly expended in putting these nonradioactive wastes in the
special radioactive waste landfills.

It has been a general practice to assume that all waste is radioactive if it has been generated
in a laboratory using radioactive materials or by a radiochemical or similar processing activity.

It is termed "radiation zone" or "contaminated area" wastes. Thus, waste that is suitable for disposal in a municipal landfill is mixed with contaminated waste. The burden of proof that the waste is not radioactive is on the person certifying or releasing the waste. Testing of the waste is time-consuming and is often omitted.

Probably the method most likely to succeed in reducing the amount of nonradioactive waste is a careful delineation and reduction of the so-called radiation zone and contamination areas. It is now common to define such areas rather broadly and to include certain zones and areas from which it should be obvious that the waste would not be radioactive. An example would be the office and administrative areas within a radiation zone. Such areas produce much nonradioactive waste that is often included for convenience in the low-level solid radioactive waste from the technical areas. In laboratory situations where nonradioactive wastes are generated alongside the radioactive waste, point source segregation can result in minimal radioactive waste generation.

Separation of combustible or compactible waste at the point of origin both improves waste handling and reduces volume. By sorting, wastes that are not compatible for incineration do not have to be handled at the incinerator. Because the volume reduction in an incinerator is greater than that in a compactor, the more wastes that are capable of incineration that reach the incinerator rather than the compactor, the greater the volume reduction.

### Volume Reduction by Compression.

Compression of solid low-level radioactive waste is suitable for about half the waste generated. There are three kinds of compression devices: compactors, balers, and baggers.

**Compactors** force material into the final storage, shipping, or disposal container. A favorite container is the 0.210-$m^3$ drum. Some space saving is possible. A variant of the compactor is called the **packer.** In this device, the material is compressed into a reusable container. At the burial grounds, the compacted material is dumped directly without any effort to retain its compacted form. Space saving is minimal with packer systems.

**Balers** compress the waste into bales that are wrapped, tied, or banded and then stored, shipped, or disposed of in burial grounds. Considerable space saving is possible with balers.

**Baggers** compress waste into a predetermined shape that is injected into round or rectangular bags, boxes, or drums before storage, shipment, or disposal. Some space saving is possible with this method of compaction.

These three techniques may be suited to general and sometimes even to unique situations. Unfortunately, such treatment does not reduce the possibility of burning while in storage, and only certain materials are suitable for compaction. These include paper, cloth, rubber, plastics, wood, glass, and small light metal objects. Large, rigid metal objects must be excluded because they are usually relatively incompressible and can damage the container and compressing machinery. Moisture (free or absorbed in large quantities by blotting paper or rags) has to be avoided because of its potential forcible release under high pressure, creating a great hazard to operators. Obviously, corrosive, pyrophoric, and explosive waste must be excluded from such processing, whether it is organic or inorganic.

The compression machinery must be economical, reliable, and easy to operate. Many commercial devices are available, but all must be modified by providing air containment, off-gas ventilation, often filtration, and, if necessary, shielding.

### Volume Reduction by Incineration.

Reduction of volumes of solid radioactive waste by incineration has interested managers of low-level radioactive waste, particularly in those parts of the world where land area is at a premium and costs are high. Under these conditions, the advantages of volume reduction are so great that the drawbacks seem only obstacles to be surmounted. In Europe, where land is scarce and more revered, the incineration of solid combustible radioactive waste is a common and apparently satisfactory method of pretreatment before final disposal.

There are certain advantages, such as volume reductions of 80–90%, reported for selected burnable waste. This may be a high estimate if such factors as residues from off-gas treatment and refractory changes are considered. This would represent a considerable saving in land used for burial, in transportation, and in long-term monitoring. In addition, it would free us from the nagging worry about the possible problem of long-burning subterranean fires. Special attention should be given to the problems of burning organic matter (solvents, ion-exchange resins, etc.) and putrescible biological material (animal cadavers, excreta, etc.). Incineration of radioactive waste must be carried out under controlled conditions to prevent the formation of radioactive aerosols and must comply with both RCRA and NRC rules if the wastes are RCRA wastes as well as being radioactive.

### Long-Term Management and Containment

**Site Selection.**   One concern in the burial of radioactive waste is that groundwater or infiltrating surface water will leach the waste and mobilize the radioactive materials. The radionuclides would be carried by this water back to the surface as a part of natural groundwater discharge or through a water well. Because of this concern, hydrogeologic and hydrochemical considerations in site selection become paramount.

The types of hydrogeologic and hydrochemical data that may be needed to determine whether or not a site is adequate include [11]

1. Depth to water table, including perched water tables, if present
2. Distance to nearest points of groundwater, spring water, or surface water usage (including well and spring inventory, and, particularly, wells available to the public)
3. Ratio of pan evaporation to precipitation minus runoff (by month for a period of at least 2 years)
4. Water table contour map
5. Magnitude of annual water table fluctuation
6. Stratigraphy and structure to base of shallowest confined aquifer
7. Baseflow data on perennial streams traversing or adjacent to storage site
8. Chemistry of water in aquifers and aquitards and of leachate from the waste trenches
9. Laboratory measurements of hydraulic conductivity, effective porosity, and mineralogy of core and grab samples (from trenches) of each lithology in unsaturated and saturated (to base of shallowest confined aquifer) zone-hydraulic conductivity to be measured at different water contents and tensions
10. Neutron moisture meter measurements of moisture content of unsaturated zone measurements to be made in specially constructed holes (at least 2 years' record needed)
11. In situ measurements of soil moisture tension in upper 4.5–9 m of unsaturated zone (at least 2 years' record needed)
12. Three-dimensional distribution of head in all saturated hydrostratigraphic units to base of shallowest confined aquifer
13. Pumping, bailing, or slug tests to determine transmissivity and storage coefficients
14. Definition of recharge and discharge areas for unconfined and shallowest confined aquifers
15. Field measurements of dispersivity coefficients
16. Laboratory and field determination of the distribution coefficient for movement of critical nuclides through all hydrostratigraphic units
17. Rates of denudation or slope retreat

These data are necessary for a complete definition of flow and nuclide transport through both the unsaturated and saturated zones.

It is not possible to immobilize a radioactive contaminant in a burial site for long periods of geologic time (i.e., for millions of years) with complete certainty. However, there appear to be hydrogeologic environments in which these contaminants can be kept below the surface and away from people until they have decayed to acceptable levels.

The problem is not merely a matter of ensuring optimum confinement, but also one of ensuring confinement for a minimum but specified time or describing and predicting the performance of these radioactive contaminants in the subsurface until this period has elapsed. For this reason, burial sites having complex hydrogeology in which such predictions are difficult or impossible are probably not suitable for storing radioactive waste.

From a geological standpoint, there appear to be two basic approaches to the long-term control of buried radioactive waste. The simplest approach is to prevent water from reaching the waste and thereby to eliminate the possibility of contaminants in the waste being mobilized. In arid climates, where there is little or no infiltration, this appears to be feasible.

In humid climates, where there is infiltration, some sort of engineered container or facilities that would isolate the waste from the water for hundreds of years is necessary. Whether or not such a facility can be designed, constructed, and demonstrated remains to be seen.

The second approach to long-term control involves burying the waste in a hydrogeologic environment that can be demonstrated to be safe despite the fact that radioactive contaminants can and will be mobilized. Demonstrating that such sites are, in fact, safe requires a quantitative evaluation of the factors influencing contaminant movement. Such an evaluation may be quite difficult but appears to be our only option if we wish to bury radioactive waste in humid climates or in climates where infiltration is capable of mobilizing or leaching the buried waste.

It is also important to give attention to the possible biological and microbiological environment of a burial site. Soil microorganisms, earthworms, larger burrowing animals, and the deep taproots of plants seeking water and nourishment (particularly in desert areas) can all be factors in moving components of waste out of a burial place into the biosphere. Some organisms can release organic compounds into the soil that can serve as complexing agents to mobilize otherwise insoluble contaminants. Some organisms can concentrate radionuclides by surprisingly high factors from their environment and so can change both the biochemical availability and the distribution of a radionuclide.

**Site Selection Criteria.** Michigan's site selection criteria serve to illustrate the factors that need to be considered in selecting disposal sites.

The first objective is to avoid population centers and conflicts with human activities. Michigan established an isolation distance of 1 km and required that projected population growth must not infringe to the extent that it would interfere with health and safety performance objectives of environmental monitoring.

Areas within 1.6 km of a fault where tectonic movement has occurred within the last 10,000 years are excluded as candidate sites. Likewise excluded are areas where significant earthquake intensity has been measured and flood plains exist. Mass wasting, erosion, and similar geologic processes are to be evaluated for possible damage to the facility.

Areas where groundwater flows from sites more than 30 m in 100 years or where groundwater could reach an aquifer in less than 500 years are excluded. The criteria also exclude areas over sole source aquifers and areas where groundwater discharges to the surface within 1 km. The facility may not be built within 16 km of the Great Lakes.

The criteria specify that the safest transportation net will be used. Highways with low accident rates located away from population centers are favored.

The site must have no complex meteorological characteristics and must avoid resource development conflicts. Likewise, environmentally sensitive areas such as wetlands and shorelands must be avoided. Areas that have formally proposed or approved development plans as of January 1, 1988, are excluded.

These criteria are extremely rigorous. Because of these constraints and the more serious problem of public opposition, no new sites have been finalized in the United States. Some compacts have had severe problems and conflicts that have resulted in the expulsion of one of the states. For example, after being selected as the host state, Michigan failed to identify an acceptable site and was expelled from the Midwest Compact.

A few compacts are proceeding quite well. These compacts are involving the public, community officials, regulators, and generators in joint efforts to identify sites, complete licensing applications, secure contractors, and construct the site. The most successful approach appears to be one of identification of actual candidate sites followed by a volunteer applicant.

The two currently operating sites in the United States are at Hanford, Washington, and Barnwell, South Carolina. These sites are accepting low-level radioactive waste from across the United States. There is a tremendous financial advantage to them in doing so. In November 1995, the total cost of disposing of a 0.210-m³ drum was about $3000. Many generators have been storing this waste for several years (e.g., in Michigan, 55 generators have been storing waste for 5 years) and they are willing to pay these prices because of the lack of space.

## CHAPTER REVIEW

When you have completed studying this chapter you should be able to do the following without the aid of your textbook or notes:

1. Explain what an isotope is.
2. Explain why some isotopes are radioactive and others are not.
3. Explain how alpha, beta, x-ray, and gamma ray emissions occur and how they differ.
4. Define the unit becquerel.
5. Explain the process of fission in a nuclear reactor.
6. Explain how x-rays are produced in an x-ray machine.
7. Define the concept of radiation dose and the units of roentgen, rad, Gy, Sv, and rem.
8. Explain the concepts of RBE and WT.
9. List the pattern of biological effects of radiation.
10. Discuss the determinants of biological effects.
11. Discuss the difference between acute and delayed biological effects of radiation.
12. List three possible delayed effects of radiation exposure.
13. State the acceptable occupational and nonoccupational dose of radiation as established by the NRC.
14. Explain the difference between internal and external radiation hazard.
15. Select a material and its thickness to protect against alpha or beta radiation.
16. Describe the sources of background radiation.
17. Explain why radon is a hazard and the mechanism by which the hazard is realized.
18. List three fundamental methods of reducing external radiation hazard.
19. Explain how to reduce occupational exposure to internal radiation hazards.
20. Describe how radon enters a house and give some techniques that may be used to inhibit radon entry.
21. List and describe the three types of radioactive waste (HLW, transuranic, and LLW).
22. Describe how each type of radioactive waste is to be disposed of.
23. Discuss waste minimization practice in reducing the volume of LLW.

With the aid of this text, you should be able to do the following:

1. Determine what particles are emitted in a given decay chain.
2. Determine the activity of a radioisotope given the original activity and the time interval.
3. Determine the activity resulting from the growth of a daughter product from a parent radionuclide.
4. Determine the time to achieve maximum activity of a daughter product.
5. Apply the inverse square law to determine radiation intensity.
6. Determine whether a combination of radionuclides exceeds the permissible concentrations.
7. Calculate the radiation intensity behind a shielding material or the desired thickness of a shielding material to achieve a reduction of radiation intensity.

## PROBLEMS

**16-1** What are the elements $^{40}_{18}X$ and $^{14}_{7}X$?

**Answer:** Argon and nitrogen

**16-2** What are the elements $^{8}_{4}X$ and $^{238}_{92}X$?

**16-3** What particles are emitted in each step in the decay chain represented by

$$^{226}_{88}Ra \longrightarrow \, ^{222}_{80}Rn \longrightarrow \, ^{218}_{84}Po \longrightarrow \, ^{214}_{82}Pb?$$

**Answer:** alpha particle in each case

**16-4** What particles are emitted in each step in the decay chain represented by

$$^{214}_{82}Pb \longrightarrow \, ^{214}_{83}Bi \longrightarrow \, ^{214}_{84}Po \longrightarrow \, ^{210}_{82}Pb \longrightarrow \, ^{210}_{83}Bi \longrightarrow \, ^{210}_{82}Po \longrightarrow \, ^{206}_{82}Pb?$$

**16-5** Show that if a positron and electron are annihilated, then an energy of 1.02 MeV is released.

**16-6** A laboratory solution containing 0.5 $\mu Ci \cdot L^{-1}$ of $^{32}P$ is to be disposed of. How long must the radioisotope be held to meet the allowable discharge activity?

**16-7** If in August 1911, Marie Curie prepared an international standard containing 20.00 mg of $RaCl_2$, what was the radium content of this standard in August 2000?

**Answer:** 14.66 mg

**16-8** An accident has contaminated a laboratory with $^{45}Ca$. The radiation level is ten times the tolerance level. How long must the room be isolated before the tolerance level is reached?

**16-9** What is the mass of a 50 $\mu Ci$ sample of pure $^{131}I$?

**Answer:** $4.04 \times 10^{-10}$ g

**16-10** By emitting an alpha particle, $^{210}Po$ decays to $^{206}Pb$. If the half-life of $^{210}Po$ is 138.4 days, what volume of $^{4}He$ will be produced in 1 year from 50 Ci of $^{210}Po$? Assume the gas is at standard temperature and pressure.

**16-11** Calculate and plot the growth curve of $^{222}Rn$ from an initially pure sample of $^{226}Ra$. Assume no $^{222}Rn$ is present initially.

**16-12** When an x-ray unit is operated at 70 kV and 5 mA, it produces an intensity of D R $\cdot$ min$^{-1}$ at 1.0 m from the source. What intensity will it produce 2.0 m from the source?

**16-13** If the source of x-rays in Problem 16–12 is operated at 15 mA, what intensity will be produced 2.0 m from the source?

**Answer:** 0.75 D

**16-14** What thickness (in centimeters) of lead is required to shield a $^{60}Co$ source so that the transmission is reduced 99.6%?

**16-15** What is the equivalent thickness (in centimeters) of concrete to accomplish the same attenuation as the lead in Problem 16–14?

**Answer:** ~43 cm

**16-16** Determine the proportionality constant ($u$) for lead when it is used to shield $^{137}Cs$.

**16-17** Determine the proportionality constant ($u$) for iron when it is used to shield $^{137}Cs$.

**Answer:** $u = 0.391$

## DISCUSSION QUESTIONS

**16-1** Explain why an archaeological artifact such as wood or bone may be dated by measuring its concentration of carbon-14.

**16-2** Would you expect the tissue weighting factor ($W_T$) for x-rays to the big toe to be greater than, less than, or the same as that for radioiodine to the thyroid? Explain your choice.

**16-3** What kind of radionuclide emitter (alpha, beta, gamma, or x-ray) is most dangerous from an internal hazard point of view? Explain why.

**16-4** A laboratory worker has requested your advice on a shield for work she is doing with high-energy beta particles. What would you recommend?

**16-5** You have an opportunity to purchase an older home with a basement that is serviced by a floor drain. What measures might you request to limit the migration of radon into the basement?

**16-6** What is the status of the proposed Yucca mountain disposal site? How much money has been spent to determine if this site is acceptable.

## ADDITIONAL READING

Davis, M., and D. Cornwell. *Introduction to Environmental Engineering,* 3rd ed. McGraw-Hill, New York (1998).

## REFERENCES

1. Coombe, R. A., *An Introduction to Radioactivity for Engineers,* Macmillan/St. Martin's Press, New York, pp. 1–37, 1968.
2. U.S. Public Health Service, *Introduction to Medical X-Ray Protection, Training and Manpower Development Program,* Rockville, MD, 1968.
3. U.S. Public Health Service, *Radiological Health Handbook* (PHS Publication No. 2016), Rockville, MD, p. 204, 1970.
4. Kuennen, W., and R. C. Roth, *Reduction of Radon Working Level by a Room Air Cleaner,* presented at the 82nd Annual Meeting of the Air & Waste Management Association, Anaheim, CA, June 1989.
5. Murane, D. M., and J. Spears, *Radon Reduction in New Construction,* Indoor Radon II, Proceedings of the Second APCA International Specialty Conference, Cherry Hill, NJ, pp. 183–194, 1987.
6. Henschel, D. B., and A. G. Scott, *Testing of Indoor Radon Reduction Techniques in Eastern Pennsylvania: An Update,* Indoor Radon II, Proceedings of the Second APCA International Specialty Conference, Cherry Hill, NJ, pp. 146–159, 1987.
7. Ibach, M. T., and J. H. Gallagher, *Retrofit and Preoccupancy Radon Mitigation Program for Homes,* Indoor Radon II, Proceedings of the Second APCA International Specialty Conference, Cherry Hill, NJ, pp. 172–182, 1987.
8. Josephson, J., "Nuclear power's dim future," *Environmental Science and Technology,* vol. 27, no. 6, pp. 1007–3009, 1993.
9. Murray, R. L., *Understanding Radioactive Waste,* Battelle Press, Richland, WA, pp. 137–138, 1989.
10. National Research Council, *The Shallow Land Burial of Low-Level Radioactively Contaminated Solid Waste,* Washington, DC: National Academy of Science, 1976.
11. Papadopulos, S. S., and I. J. Winograd, *Storage of Low-Level Radioactive Wastes in the Ground: Hydrogeological and Hydrochemical Factors* (U.S. Environmental Protection Agency Report 520/3-74-009), U.S. Government Printing Office, Washington, DC, 1974.

# Properties of Air, Water, and Selected Chemicals

**TABLE A-1**     Physical Properties of Water at 1 atm

| Temperature (°C) | Density, $\rho$ (kg·m⁻³) | Specific Weight, $\gamma$ (kN·m⁻³) | Dynamic Viscosity, $\mu$ (mPa·s) | Kinematic Viscosity, $\nu$ ($\mu$m²·s⁻¹) |
|---|---|---|---|---|
| 0 | 999.842 | 9.805 | 1.787 | 1.787 |
| 3.98 | 1000.000 | 9.807 | 1.567 | 1.567 |
| 5 | 999.967 | 9.807 | 1.519 | 1.519 |
| 10 | 999.703 | 9.804 | 1.307 | 1.307 |
| 12 | 999.500 | 9.802 | 1.235 | 1.236 |
| 15 | 999.103 | 9.798 | 1.139 | 1.140 |
| 17 | 998.778 | 9.795 | 1.081 | 1.082 |
| 18 | 998.599 | 9.793 | 1.053 | 1.054 |
| 19 | 998.408 | 9.791 | 1.027 | 1.029 |
| 20 | 998.207 | 9.789 | 1.002 | 1.004 |
| 21 | 997.996 | 9.787 | 0.998 | 1.000 |
| 22 | 997.774 | 9.785 | 0.955 | 0.957 |
| 23 | 997.542 | 9.783 | 0.932 | 0.934 |
| 24 | 997.300 | 9.781 | 0.911 | 0.913 |
| 25 | 997.048 | 9.778 | 0.890 | 0.893 |
| 26 | 996.787 | 9.775 | 0.870 | 0.873 |
| 27 | 996.516 | 9.773 | 0.851 | 0.854 |
| 28 | 996.236 | 9.770 | 0.833 | 0.836 |
| 29 | 995.948 | 9.767 | 0.815 | 0.818 |
| 30 | 995.650 | 9.764 | 0.798 | 0.801 |
| 35 | 994.035 | 9.749 | 0.719 | 0.723 |
| 40 | 992.219 | 9.731 | 0.653 | 0.658 |
| 45 | 990.216 | 9.711 | 0.596 | 0.602 |
| 50 | 988.039 | 9.690 | 0.547 | 0.554 |
| 60 | 983.202 | 9.642 | 0.466 | 0.474 |
| 70 | 977.773 | 9.589 | 0.404 | 0.413 |
| 80 | 971.801 | 9.530 | 0.355 | 0.365 |
| 90 | 965.323 | 9.467 | 0.315 | 0.326 |
| 100 | 958.366 | 9.399 | 0.282 | 0.294 |

Pa·s = (mPa·s) × 10⁻³
m²·s⁻¹ = ($\mu$m²·s⁻¹) × 10⁻⁶

**TABLE A–2**   Saturation Values of Dissolved Oxygen in Fresh Water Exposed to a Saturated Atmosphere Containing 20.9% Oxygen Under a Pressure of 101.325 kPa[a]

| Temperature (°C) | Dissolved Oxygen (mg · L$^{-1}$) | Saturated Vapor Pressure (kPa) |
|---|---|---|
| 0 | 14.62 | 0.6108 |
| 1 | 14.23 | 0.6566 |
| 2 | 13.84 | 0.7055 |
| 3 | 13.48 | 0.7575 |
| 4 | 13.13 | 0.8129 |
| 5 | 12.80 | 0.8719 |
| 6 | 12.48 | 0.9347 |
| 7 | 12.17 | 1.0013 |
| 8 | 11.87 | 1.0722 |
| 9 | 11.59 | 1.1474 |
| 10 | 11.33 | 1.2272 |
| 11 | 11.08 | 1.3119 |
| 12 | 10.83 | 1.4017 |
| 13 | 10.60 | 1.4969 |
| 14 | 10.37 | 1.5977 |
| 15 | 10.15 | 1.7044 |
| 16 | 9.95 | 1.8173 |
| 17 | 9.74 | 1.9367 |
| 18 | 9.54 | 2.0630 |
| 19 | 9.35 | 2.1964 |
| 20 | 9.17 | 2.3373 |
| 21 | 8.99 | 2.4861 |
| 22 | 8.83 | 2.6430 |
| 23 | 8.68 | 2.8086 |
| 24 | 8.53 | 2.9831 |
| 25 | 8.38 | 3.1671 |
| 26 | 8.22 | 3.3608 |
| 27 | 8.07 | 3.5649 |
| 28 | 7.92 | 3.7796 |
| 29 | 7.77 | 4.0055 |
| 30 | 7.63 | 4.2430 |
| 31 | 7.51 | 4.4927 |
| 32 | 7.42 | 4.7551 |
| 33 | 7.28 | 5.0307 |
| 34 | 7.17 | 5.3200 |
| 35 | 7.07 | 5.6236 |
| 36 | 6.96 | 5.9422 |
| 37 | 6.86 | 6.2762 |
| 38 | 6.75 | 6.6264 |

[a]For other barometric pressures, the solubilities vary approximately in proportion to the ratios of these pressures to the standard pressures.

*Source:* Calculated by G. C. Whipple and M. C. Whipple from measurements of C. J. J. Fox, *Journal of the American Chemical Society,* vol. 33, p. 362, 1911.

**TABLE A–3** Density of Dry Air in Kilograms per Cubic Meter for Temperature in Degrees Celsius and Absolute Pressure in Kilopascals

| °C | 110.0 | 100.0 | 90.0 | 80.0 | 70.0 | 60.0 | 50.0 | 40.0 | 30.0 | 20.0 | 10.0 |
|---|---|---|---|---|---|---|---|---|---|---|---|
| 0 | 1.4029 | 1.2754 | 1.1478 | 1.0203 | 0.8928 | 0.7652 | 0.6377 | 0.5102 | 0.3826 | 0.2551 | 0.1275 |
| 1 | 1.3978 | 1.2707 | 1.1437 | 1.0166 | 0.8895 | 0.7624 | 0.6354 | 0.5083 | 0.3812 | 0.2541 | 0.1271 |
| 2 | 1.3927 | 1.2661 | 1.1395 | 1.0129 | 0.8863 | 0.7597 | 0.6331 | 0.5064 | 0.3798 | 0.2532 | 0.1266 |
| 3 | 1.3877 | 1.2615 | 1.1354 | 1.0092 | 0.8831 | 0.7569 | 0.6308 | 0.5046 | 0.3785 | 0.2523 | 0.1262 |
| 4 | 1.3827 | 1.2570 | 1.1313 | 1.0056 | 0.8799 | 0.7542 | 0.6285 | 0.5028 | 0.3771 | 0.2514 | 0.1257 |
| 5 | 1.3777 | 1.2525 | 1.1272 | 1.0020 | 0.8767 | 0.7515 | 0.6262 | 0.5010 | 0.3757 | 0.2505 | 0.1252 |
| 6 | 1.3728 | 1.2480 | 1.1232 | 0.9984 | 0.8736 | 0.7488 | 0.6240 | 0.4992 | 0.3744 | 0.2496 | 0.1248 |
| 7 | 1.3679 | 1.2435 | 1.1192 | 0.9948 | 0.8705 | 0.7461 | 0.6218 | 0.4974 | 0.3731 | 0.2487 | 0.1244 |
| 8 | 1.3630 | 1.2391 | 1.1152 | 0.9913 | 0.8674 | 0.7435 | 0.6195 | 0.4956 | 0.3717 | 0.2478 | 0.1239 |
| 9 | 1.3582 | 1.2347 | 1.1112 | 0.9878 | 0.8643 | 0.7408 | 0.6174 | 0.4939 | 0.3704 | 0.2469 | 0.1235 |
| 10 | 1.3534 | 1.2303 | 1.1073 | 0.9843 | 0.8612 | 0.7382 | 0.6152 | 0.4921 | 0.3691 | 0.2461 | 0.1230 |
| 11 | 1.3486 | 1.2260 | 1.1034 | 0.9808 | 0.8582 | 0.7356 | 0.6130 | 0.4904 | 0.3678 | 0.2452 | 0.1226 |
| 12 | 1.3439 | 1.2217 | 1.0995 | 0.9774 | 0.8552 | 0.7330 | 0.6109 | 0.4887 | 0.3665 | 0.2443 | 0.1222 |
| 13 | 1.3392 | 1.2174 | 1.0957 | 0.9740 | 0.8522 | 0.7305 | 0.6087 | 0.4870 | 0.3652 | 0.2435 | 0.1217 |
| 14 | 1.3345 | 1.2132 | 1.0919 | 0.9706 | 0.8492 | 0.7279 | 0.6066 | 0.4853 | 0.3640 | 0.2426 | 0.1213 |
| 15 | 1.3299 | 1.2090 | 1.0881 | 0.9672 | 0.8463 | 0.7254 | 0.6045 | 0.4836 | 0.3627 | 0.2418 | 0.1209 |
| 16 | 1.3253 | 1.2048 | 1.0843 | 0.9638 | 0.8434 | 0.7229 | 0.6024 | 0.4819 | 0.3614 | 0.2410 | 0.1205 |
| 17 | 1.3207 | 1.2007 | 1.0806 | 0.9605 | 0.8405 | 0.7204 | 0.6003 | 0.4803 | 0.3602 | 0.2401 | 0.1201 |
| 18 | 1.3162 | 1.1965 | 1.0769 | 0.9572 | 0.8376 | 0.7179 | 0.5983 | 0.4786 | 0.3590 | 0.2393 | 0.1197 |
| 19 | 1.3117 | 1.1924 | 1.0732 | 0.9540 | 0.8347 | 0.7155 | 0.5962 | 0.4770 | 0.3577 | 0.2385 | 0.1192 |
| 20 | 1.3072 | 1.1884 | 1.0695 | 0.9507 | 0.8319 | 0.7130 | 0.5942 | 0.4753 | 0.3565 | 0.2377 | 0.1188 |
| 21 | 1.3028 | 1.1843 | 1.0659 | 0.9475 | 0.8290 | 0.7106 | 0.5922 | 0.4737 | 0.3553 | 0.2369 | 0.1184 |
| 22 | 1.2984 | 1.1803 | 1.0623 | 0.9443 | 0.8262 | 0.7082 | 0.5902 | 0.4721 | 0.3541 | 0.2361 | 0.1180 |
| 23 | 1.2940 | 1.1763 | 1.0587 | 0.9411 | 0.8234 | 0.7058 | 0.5882 | 0.4705 | 0.3529 | 0.2353 | 0.1176 |
| 24 | 1.2896 | 1.1724 | 1.0551 | 0.9379 | 0.8207 | 0.7034 | 0.5862 | 0.4690 | 0.3517 | 0.2345 | 0.1172 |
| 25 | 1.2853 | 1.1684 | 1.0516 | 0.9348 | 0.8179 | 0.7011 | 0.5842 | 0.4674 | 0.3505 | 0.2337 | 0.1168 |
| 26 | 1.2810 | 1.1645 | 1.0481 | 0.9316 | 0.8152 | 0.6987 | 0.5823 | 0.4658 | 0.3494 | 0.2329 | 0.1165 |
| 27 | 1.2767 | 1.1607 | 1.0446 | 0.9285 | 0.8125 | 0.6964 | 0.5803 | 0.4643 | 0.3482 | 0.2321 | 0.1161 |
| 28 | 1.2725 | 1.1568 | 1.0411 | 0.9254 | 0.8098 | 0.6941 | 0.5784 | 0.4627 | 0.3470 | 0.2314 | 0.1157 |
| 29 | 1.2683 | 1.1530 | 1.0377 | 0.9224 | 0.8071 | 0.6918 | 0.5765 | 0.4612 | 0.3459 | 0.2306 | 0.1153 |
| 30 | 1.2641 | 1.1492 | 1.0343 | 0.9193 | 0.8044 | 0.6895 | 0.5746 | 0.4597 | 0.3448 | 0.2298 | 0.1149 |
| 31 | 1.2599 | 1.1454 | 1.0309 | 0.9163 | 0.8018 | 0.6872 | 0.5727 | 0.4582 | 0.3436 | 0.2291 | 0.1145 |
| 32 | 1.2558 | 1.1416 | 1.0275 | 0.9133 | 0.7991 | 0.6850 | 0.5708 | 0.4567 | 0.3425 | 0.2283 | 0.1142 |
| 33 | 1.2517 | 1.1379 | 1.0241 | 0.9103 | 0.7965 | 0.6827 | 0.5690 | 0.4552 | 0.3414 | 0.2276 | 0.1138 |
| 34 | 1.2476 | 1.1342 | 1.0208 | 0.9074 | 0.7939 | 0.6805 | 0.5671 | 0.4537 | 0.3403 | 0.2268 | 0.1134 |

Pressure (kPa)

(continued)

**TABLE A–3** (Continued)

| | Pressure (kPa) | | | | | | | | | | |
|---|---|---|---|---|---|---|---|---|---|---|---|
| °C | 110.0 | 100.0 | 90.0 | 80.0 | 70.0 | 60.0 | 50.0 | 40.0 | 30.0 | 20.0 | 10.0 |
| 35 | 1.2436 | 1.1305 | 1.0175 | 0.9044 | 0.7914 | 0.6783 | 0.5653 | 0.4522 | 0.3392 | 0.2261 | 0.1131 |
| 36 | 1.2396 | 1.1269 | 1.0142 | 0.9015 | 0.7888 | 0.6761 | 0.5634 | 0.4507 | 0.3381 | 0.2254 | 0.1127 |
| 37 | 1.2356 | 1.1232 | 1.0109 | 0.8986 | 0.7863 | 0.6739 | 0.5616 | 0.4493 | 0.3370 | 0.2246 | 0.1123 |
| 38 | 1.2316 | 1.1196 | 1.0077 | 0.8957 | 0.7837 | 0.6718 | 0.5598 | 0.4479 | 0.3359 | 0.2239 | 0.1120 |
| 39 | 1.2276 | 1.1160 | 1.0044 | 0.8928 | 0.7812 | 0.6696 | 0.5580 | 0.4464 | 0.3348 | 0.2232 | 0.1116 |
| 40 | 1.2237 | 1.1125 | 1.0012 | 0.8900 | 0.7787 | 0.6675 | 0.5562 | 0.4450 | 0.3337 | 0.2225 | 0.1112 |
| 41 | 1.2198 | 1.1089 | 0.9980 | 0.8872 | 0.7763 | 0.6654 | 0.5545 | 0.4436 | 0.3327 | 0.2218 | 0.1109 |
| 42 | 1.2160 | 1.1054 | 0.9949 | 0.8843 | 0.7738 | 0.6633 | 0.5527 | 0.4422 | 0.3316 | 0.2211 | 0.1105 |
| 43 | 1.2121 | 1.1019 | 0.9917 | 0.8815 | 0.7713 | 0.6612 | 0.5510 | 0.4408 | 0.3306 | 0.2204 | 0.1102 |
| 44 | 1.2083 | 1.0984 | 0.9886 | 0.8788 | 0.7689 | 0.6591 | 0.5492 | 0.4394 | 0.3295 | 0.2197 | 0.1098 |
| 45 | 1.2045 | 1.0950 | 0.9855 | 0.8760 | 0.7665 | 0.6570 | 0.5475 | 0.4380 | 0.3285 | 0.2190 | 0.1095 |
| 46 | 1.2007 | 1.0916 | 0.9824 | 0.8732 | 0.7641 | 0.6549 | 0.5458 | 0.4366 | 0.3275 | 0.2183 | 0.1092 |
| 47 | 1.1970 | 1.0882 | 0.9793 | 0.8705 | 0.7617 | 0.6529 | 0.5441 | 0.4353 | 0.3264 | 0.2176 | 0.1088 |
| 48 | 1.1932 | 1.0848 | 0.9763 | 0.8678 | 0.7593 | 0.6509 | 0.5424 | 0.4339 | 0.3254 | 0.2170 | 0.1085 |
| 49 | 1.1895 | 1.0814 | 0.9733 | 0.8651 | 0.7570 | 0.6488 | 0.5407 | 0.4326 | 0.3244 | 0.2163 | 0.1081 |
| 50 | 1.1859 | 1.0780 | 0.9702 | 0.8624 | 0.7546 | 0.6468 | 0.5390 | 0.4312 | 0.3234 | 0.2156 | 0.1078 |
| 51 | 1.1822 | 1.0747 | 0.9673 | 0.8598 | 0.7523 | 0.6448 | 0.5374 | 0.4299 | 0.3224 | 0.2149 | 0.1075 |
| 52 | 1.1786 | 1.0714 | 0.9643 | 0.8571 | 0.7500 | 0.6429 | 0.5357 | 0.4286 | 0.3214 | 0.2143 | 0.1071 |
| 53 | 1.1750 | 1.0681 | 0.9613 | 0.8545 | 0.7477 | 0.6409 | 0.5341 | 0.4273 | 0.3204 | 0.2136 | 0.1068 |
| 54 | 1.1714 | 1.0649 | 0.9584 | 0.8519 | 0.7454 | 0.6389 | 0.5324 | 0.4259 | 0.3195 | 0.2130 | 0.1065 |
| 55 | 1.1678 | 1.0616 | 0.9555 | 0.8493 | 0.7431 | 0.6370 | 0.5308 | 0.4247 | 0.3185 | 0.2123 | 0.1062 |
| 56 | 1.1642 | 1.0584 | 0.9526 | 0.8467 | 0.7409 | 0.6350 | 0.5292 | 0.4234 | 0.3175 | 0.2117 | 0.1058 |
| 57 | 1.1607 | 1.0552 | 0.9497 | 0.8442 | 0.7386 | 0.6331 | 0.5276 | 0.4221 | 0.3166 | 0.2110 | 0.1055 |
| 58 | 1.1572 | 1.0520 | 0.9468 | 0.8416 | 0.7364 | 0.6312 | 0.5260 | 0.4208 | 0.3156 | 0.2104 | 0.1052 |
| 59 | 1.1537 | 1.0488 | 0.9440 | 0.8391 | 0.7342 | 0.6293 | 0.5244 | 0.4195 | 0.3147 | 0.2098 | 0.1049 |
| 60 | 1.1503 | 1.0457 | 0.9411 | 0.8366 | 0.7320 | 0.6274 | 0.5228 | 0.4183 | 0.3137 | 0.2091 | 0.1046 |
| 61 | 1.1468 | 1.0426 | 0.9383 | 0.8340 | 0.7298 | 0.6255 | 0.5213 | 0.4170 | 0.3128 | 0.2085 | 0.1043 |
| 62 | 1.1434 | 1.0394 | 0.9355 | 0.8316 | 0.7276 | 0.6237 | 0.5197 | 0.4158 | 0.3118 | 0.2079 | 0.1039 |
| 63 | 1.1400 | 1.0364 | 0.9327 | 0.8291 | 0.7255 | 0.6218 | 0.5182 | 0.4145 | 0.3109 | 0.2073 | 0.1036 |
| 64 | 1.1366 | 1.0333 | 0.9300 | 0.8266 | 0.7233 | 0.6200 | 0.5166 | 0.4133 | 0.3100 | 0.2067 | 0.1033 |
| 65 | 1.1333 | 1.0302 | 0.9272 | 0.8242 | 0.7212 | 0.6181 | 0.5151 | 0.4121 | 0.3091 | 0.2060 | 0.1030 |
| 66 | 1.1299 | 1.0272 | 0.9245 | 0.8218 | 0.7190 | 0.6163 | 0.5136 | 0.4109 | 0.3082 | 0.2054 | 0.1027 |
| 67 | 1.1266 | 1.0242 | 0.9218 | 0.8193 | 0.7169 | 0.6145 | 0.5121 | 0.4097 | 0.3073 | 0.2048 | 0.1024 |
| 68 | 1.1233 | 1.0212 | 0.9191 | 0.8169 | 0.7148 | 0.6127 | 0.5106 | 0.4085 | 0.3064 | 0.2042 | 0.1021 |
| 69 | 1.1200 | 1.0182 | 0.9164 | 0.8146 | 0.7127 | 0.6109 | 0.5091 | 0.4073 | 0.3055 | 0.2036 | 0.1018 |

| | | | | | | | | | | | |
|---|---|---|---|---|---|---|---|---|---|---|---|
| 70 | 1.1167 | 1.0152 | 0.9137 | 0.8122 | 0.7107 | 0.6091 | 0.5076 | 0.4061 | 0.3046 | 0.2030 | 0.1015 |
| 71 | 1.1135 | 1.0123 | 0.9110 | 0.8098 | 0.7086 | 0.6074 | 0.5061 | 0.4049 | 0.3037 | 0.2025 | 0.1012 |
| 72 | 1.1103 | 1.0093 | 0.9084 | 0.8075 | 0.7065 | 0.6056 | 0.5047 | 0.4037 | 0.3028 | 0.2019 | 0.1009 |
| 73 | 1.1071 | 1.0064 | 0.9058 | 0.8051 | 0.7045 | 0.6039 | 0.5032 | 0.4026 | 0.3019 | 0.2013 | 0.1006 |
| 74 | 1.1039 | 1.0035 | 0.9032 | 0.8028 | 0.7025 | 0.6021 | 0.5018 | 0.4014 | 0.3011 | 0.2007 | 0.1004 |
| 75 | 1.1007 | 1.0006 | 0.9006 | 0.8005 | 0.7004 | 0.6004 | 0.5003 | 0.4003 | 0.3002 | 0.2001 | 0.1001 |
| 76 | 1.0976 | 0.9978 | 0.8980 | 0.7982 | 0.6984 | 0.5987 | 0.4989 | 0.3991 | 0.2993 | 0.1996 | 0.0998 |
| 77 | 1.0944 | 0.9949 | 0.8954 | 0.7959 | 0.6965 | 0.5970 | 0.4975 | 0.3980 | 0.2985 | 0.1990 | 0.0995 |
| 78 | 1.0913 | 0.9921 | 0.8929 | 0.7937 | 0.6945 | 0.5953 | 0.4960 | 0.3968 | 0.2976 | 0.1984 | 0.0992 |
| 79 | 1.0882 | 0.9893 | 0.8904 | 0.7914 | 0.6925 | 0.5936 | 0.4946 | 0.3957 | 0.2968 | 0.1979 | 0.0989 |
| 80 | 1.0851 | 0.9865 | 0.8878 | 0.7892 | 0.6905 | 0.5919 | 0.4932 | 0.3946 | 0.2959 | 0.1973 | 0.0986 |
| 81 | 1.0821 | 0.9837 | 0.8853 | 0.7870 | 0.6886 | 0.5902 | 0.4918 | 0.3935 | 0.2951 | 0.1967 | 0.0984 |
| 82 | 1.0790 | 0.9809 | 0.8828 | 0.7847 | 0.6866 | 0.5886 | 0.4905 | 0.3924 | 0.2943 | 0.1962 | 0.0981 |
| 83 | 1.0760 | 0.9782 | 0.8804 | 0.7825 | 0.6847 | 0.5869 | 0.4891 | 0.3913 | 0.2935 | 0.1956 | 0.0978 |
| 84 | 1.0730 | 0.9754 | 0.8779 | 0.7803 | 0.6828 | 0.5853 | 0.4877 | 0.3902 | 0.2926 | 0.1951 | 0.0975 |
| 85 | 1.0700 | 0.9727 | 0.8754 | 0.7782 | 0.6809 | 0.5836 | 0.4864 | 0.3891 | 0.2918 | 0.1945 | 0.0973 |
| 86 | 1.0670 | 0.9700 | 0.8730 | 0.7760 | 0.6790 | 0.5820 | 0.4850 | 0.3880 | 0.2910 | 0.1940 | 0.0970 |
| 87 | 1.0640 | 0.9673 | 0.8706 | 0.7738 | 0.6771 | 0.5804 | 0.4836 | 0.3869 | 0.2902 | 0.1935 | 0.0967 |
| 88 | 1.0611 | 0.9646 | 0.8682 | 0.7717 | 0.6752 | 0.5788 | 0.4823 | 0.3858 | 0.2894 | 0.1929 | 0.0965 |
| 89 | 1.0582 | 0.9620 | 0.8658 | 0.7696 | 0.6734 | 0.5772 | 0.4810 | 0.3848 | 0.2886 | 0.1924 | 0.0962 |
| 90 | 1.0552 | 0.9593 | 0.8634 | 0.7674 | 0.6715 | 0.5756 | 0.4797 | 0.3837 | 0.2878 | 0.1919 | 0.0959 |
| 91 | 1.0523 | 0.9567 | 0.8610 | 0.7653 | 0.6697 | 0.5740 | 0.4783 | 0.3827 | 0.2870 | 0.1913 | 0.0957 |
| 92 | 1.0495 | 0.9541 | 0.8587 | 0.7632 | 0.6678 | 0.5724 | 0.4770 | 0.3816 | 0.2862 | 0.1908 | 0.0954 |
| 93 | 1.0466 | 0.9514 | 0.8563 | 0.7612 | 0.6660 | 0.5709 | 0.4757 | 0.3806 | 0.2854 | 0.1903 | 0.0951 |
| 94 | 1.0437 | 0.9489 | 0.8540 | 0.7591 | 0.6642 | 0.5693 | 0.4744 | 0.3795 | 0.2847 | 0.1898 | 0.0949 |
| 95 | 1.0409 | 0.9463 | 0.8517 | 0.7570 | 0.6624 | 0.5678 | 0.4731 | 0.3785 | 0.2839 | 0.1893 | 0.0946 |
| 96 | 1.0381 | 0.9437 | 0.8493 | 0.7550 | 0.6606 | 0.5662 | 0.4719 | 0.3775 | 0.2831 | 0.1887 | 0.0944 |
| 97 | 1.0353 | 0.9412 | 0.8471 | 0.7529 | 0.6588 | 0.5647 | 0.4706 | 0.3765 | 0.2824 | 0.1882 | 0.0941 |
| 98 | 1.0325 | 0.9386 | 0.8448 | 0.7509 | 0.6570 | 0.5632 | 0.4693 | 0.3755 | 0.2816 | 0.1877 | 0.0939 |
| 99 | 1.0297 | 0.9361 | 0.8425 | 0.7489 | 0.6553 | 0.5617 | 0.4681 | 0.3744 | 0.2808 | 0.1872 | 0.0936 |
| 100 | 1.0270 | 0.9336 | 0.8402 | 0.7469 | 0.6535 | 0.5602 | 0.4668 | 0.3734 | 0.2801 | 0.1867 | 0.0934 |

*Source: Robert J. List, Smithsonian Meteorological Tables, 6th Revised Edition (Publication 4014 of the Smithsonian Institution), 1951.*

**TABLE A–4**   Viscosity of Dry Air at Approximately 100 kPa[a]

| Temperature (°C) | Dynamic Viscosity (μPa · s) | Temperature (°C) | Dynamic Viscosity (μPa · s) |
|---|---|---|---|
| 0 | 17.1 | 55 | 20.1 |
| 5 | 17.4 | 60 | 20.3 |
| 10 | 17.7 | 65 | 20.6 |
| 15 | 17.9 | 70 | 20.9 |
| 20 | 18.2 | 75 | 21.1 |
| 25 | 18.5 | 80 | 21.4 |
| 30 | 18.7 | 85 | 21.7 |
| 35 | 19.0 | 90 | 21.9 |
| 40 | 19.3 | 95 | 22.2 |
| 45 | 19.5 | 100 | 22.5 |
| 50 | 19.8 | 150 | 25.2 |

$\mu = 17.11 + 0.0536\,T + (P/8280)$ where $T$ is in degrees Celsius and $P$ is in kilopascals.

**TABLE A–5**   Properties of Air at Standard Conditions[a]

| | | |
|---|---|---|
| Molecular weight | $M$ | 28.97 |
| Gas constant | $R$ | $287\ \text{J} \cdot \text{kg}^{-1} \cdot \text{K}^{-1}$ |
| Specific heat at constant pressure | $c_p$ | $1005\ \text{J} \cdot \text{kg}^{-1} \cdot \text{K}^{-1}$ |
| Specific heat at constant volume | $c_v$ | $718\ \text{J} \cdot \text{kg}^{-1} \cdot \text{K}^{-1}$ |
| Density | $\rho$ | $1.185\ \text{kg} \cdot \text{m}^{-3}$ |
| Dynamic viscosity | $\mu$ | $1.8515 \times 10^{-5}\ \text{Pa} \cdot \text{s}$ |
| Kinematic viscosity | $\nu$ | $1.5624 \times 10^{-5}\ \text{m}^2 \cdot \text{s}^{-1}$ |
| Thermal conductivity | $k$ | $0.0257\ \text{W} \cdot \text{m}^{-1} \cdot \text{K}^{-1}$ |
| Ratio of specific heats, $c_p/c_v$ | $k$ | 1.3997 |
| Prandtl number | $Pr$ | 0.720 |

[a]Measured at 101.325 kPa pressure and 298 K temperature.

**TABLE A–6**   Properties of Saturated Water at 298 K

| | | |
|---|---|---|
| Molecular weight | $M$ | 18.02 |
| Gas constant | $R$ | $461.4\ \text{J} \cdot \text{kg}^{-1} \cdot \text{K}^{-1}$ |
| Specific heat | $c$ | $4181\ \text{J} \cdot \text{kg}^{-1} \cdot \text{K}^{-1}$ |
| Prandtl number | $Pr$ | 6.395 |
| Thermal conductivity | $k$ | $0.604\ \text{W} \cdot \text{m}^{-1} \cdot \text{K}^{-1}$ |

**TABLE A–7**   Frequently Used Constants

| | | |
|---|---|---|
| Standard atmospheric pressure | $P_{atm}$ | 101.325 kPa |
| Standard gravitational acceleration | $g$ | $9.8067\ \text{m} \cdot \text{s}^{-2}$ |
| Universal gas constant | $R_u$ | $8314.3\ \text{J} \cdot \text{kg}^{-1} \cdot \text{mol}^{-1} \cdot \text{K}^{-1}$ |
| Electrical permittivity constant | $\epsilon_0$ | $8.85 \times 10^{-12}\ \text{C} \cdot \text{V}^{-1} \cdot \text{m}^{-1}$ |
| Electron charge | $q_e$ | $1.60 \times 10^{-19}\ \text{C}$ |
| Boltzmann's constant | $k$ | $1.38 \times 10^{-23}\ \text{J} \cdot \text{K}^{-1}$ |

**TABLE A–8**   Properties of Selected Organic Compounds

| Name | Formula | M.W. | Density $(g \cdot mL^{-1})$ | Vapor Pressure (mm Hg) | Henry's Law Constant $(kPa \cdot m^3 \cdot mol^{-1})$ |
|------|---------|------|---------|----------------|-------------------|
| Acetone | $CH_3COCH_3$ | 58.08 | 0.79 | 184 | 0.01 |
| Benzene | $C_6H_6$ | 78.11 | 0.879 | 95 | 0.6 |
| Bromodichloromethane | $CHBrCl_2$ | 163.8 | 1.971 | | 0.2 |
| Bromoform | $CHBr_3$ | 252.75 | 2.8899 | 5 | 0.06 |
| Bromomethane | $CH_3Br$ | 94.94 | 1.6755 | 1300 | 0.5 |
| Carbon tetrachloride | $CCl_4$ | 153.82 | 1.594 | 90 | 3 |
| Chlorobenzene | $C_6H_5Cl$ | 112.56 | 1.107 | 12 | 0.4 |
| Chlorodibromomethane | $CHBr_2Cl$ | 208.29 | 2.451 | 50 | 0.09 |
| Chloroethane | $C_2H_5Cl$ | 64.52 | 0.8978 | 700 | 0.2 |
| Chloroethylene | $C_2H_3Cl$ | 62.5 | 0.912 | 2550 | 4 |
| Chloroform | $CHCl_3$ | 119.39 | 1.4892 | 190 | 0.4 |
| Chloromethane | $CH_3Cl$ | 50.49 | 0.9159 | 3750 | 1.0 |
| 1,2-Dibromoethane | $C_2H_2Br_2$ | 187.87 | 2.18 | 10 | 0.06 |
| 1,2-Dichlorobenzene | $1,2\text{-}Cl_2\text{—}C_6H_4$ | 147.01 | 1.3048 | 1.5 | 0.2 |
| 1,3-Dichlorobenzene | $1,3\text{-}Cl_2\text{—}C_6H_4$ | 147.01 | 1.2884 | 2 | 0.4 |
| 1,4-Dichlorobenzene | $1,4\text{-}Cl_2\text{—}C_6H_4$ | 147.01 | 1.2475 | 0.7 | 0.2 |
| 1,1-Dichloroethylene | $CH_2\text{=}CCl_2$ | 96.94 | 1.218 | 500 | 15 |
| 1,2-Dichloroethane | $ClCH_2CH_2Cl$ | 98.96 | 1.2351 | 700 | 0.1 |
| 1,1-Dichloroethane | $CH_3CHCl_2$ | 98.96 | 1.1757 | 200 | 0.6 |
| Trans-1,2-Dichloroethylene | $CHCl\text{=}CHCl$ | 96.94 | 1.2565 | 300 | 0.6 |
| Dichloromethane | $CH_2Cl_2$ | 84.93 | 1.327 | 350 | 0.3 |
| 1,2-Dichloropropane | $CH_3CHClCH_2Cl$ | 112.99 | 1.1560 | 50 | 0.4 |
| Cis-1,3-Dichloropropylene | $ClCH_2CH\text{=}CHCl$ | 110.97 | 1.217 | 40 | 0.2 |
| Ethyl benzene | $C_6H_5CH_2CH_3$ | 106.17 | 0.8670 | 9 | 0.8 |
| Formaldehyde | $HCHO$ | 30.05 | 0.815 | | |
| Hexachlorobenzene | $C_6Cl_6$ | 284.79 | 1.5691 | | |
| Pentachlorophenol | $Cl_5C_6OH$ | 266.34 | 1.978 | | |
| Phenol | $C_6H_5OH$ | 94.11 | 1.0576 | | |
| 1,1,2,2-Tetrachloroethane | $CHCl_2CHCl_2$ | 167.85 | 1.5953 | 5 | 0.05 |
| Tetrachloroethylene | $Cl_2C\text{=}CCl_2$ | 165.83 | 1.6227 | 15 | 3 |
| Toluene | $C_6H_5CH_3$ | 92.14 | 0.8669 | 28 | 0.7 |
| 1,1,1-Trichloroethane | $CH_3CCl_3$ | 133.41 | 1.3390 | 100 | 3.0 |
| 1,1,2-Trichloroethane | $CH_2ClCHCl_2$ | 133.41 | 1.4397 | 25 | 0.1 |
| Trichloroethylene | $ClHC\text{=}CCl_2$ | 131.29 | 1.476 | 50 | 0.9 |
| Vinyl chloride | $H_2C\text{=}CHCl$ | 62.50 | 0.9106 | 2200 | 50 |
| o-Xylene | $1,2\text{-}(CH_3)_2C_6H_4$ | 106.17 | 0.8802 | 6 | 0.5 |
| m-Xylene | $1,3\text{-}(CH_3)_2C_6H_4$ | 106.17 | 0.8642 | 8 | 0.7 |
| p-Xylene | $1,4\text{-}(CH_3)_2C_6H_4$ | 106.17 | 0.8611 | 8 | 0.7 |

Note: Ethene = ethylene; ethyl chloride = chloroethane; ethylene chloride = 1,2-dichloroethane; ethylidene chloride = 1,1-dichloroethane; methyl benzene = toluene; methyl chloride = chloromethane; methyl chloroform = 1,1,1-trichloroethane; methylene chloride = dichloromethane; tetrachloromethane = carbon tetrachloride; tribromomethane = bromoform.

**TABLE A–9**      Typical Solubility Product Constants

| Equilibrium Equation | $K_{sp}$ at 25°C | Equilibrium Equation | $K_{sp}$ at 25°C |
|---|---|---|---|
| $AgCl \rightleftharpoons Ag^+ + Cl^-$ | $1.76 \times 10^{-10}$ | $Fe(OH)_2 \rightleftharpoons Fe^{2+} + 2OH^-$ | $4.79 \times 10^{-17}$ |
| $Al(OH)_3 \rightleftharpoons Al^{3+} + 3OH^-$ | $1.26 \times 10^{-33}$ | $FeS \rightleftharpoons Fe^{2+} + S^{2-}$ | $1.57 \times 10^{-19}$ |
| $BaSO_4 \rightleftharpoons Ba^{2+} + SO_4^{2-}$ | $1.05 \times 10^{-10}$ | $PbCO_3 \rightleftharpoons Pb^{2+} + CO_3^{2-}$ | $1.48 \times 10^{-13}$ |
| $Cd(OH)_2 \rightleftharpoons Cd^{2+} + 2OH^-$ | $5.33 \times 10^{-15}$ | $Pb(OH)_2 \rightleftharpoons Pb^{2+} + 2OH^-$ | $1.40 \times 10^{-20}$ |
| $CdS \rightleftharpoons Cd^{2+} + S^{2-}$ | $1.40 \times 10^{-29}$ | $PbS \rightleftharpoons Pb^{2+} + S^{2-}$ | $8.81 \times 10^{-29}$ |
| $CdCO_3 \rightleftharpoons Cd^{2+} + CO_3^{2-}$ | $6.20 \times 10^{-12}$ | $Mg(OH)_2 \rightleftharpoons Mg^{2+} + 2OH^-$ | $1.82 \times 10^{-11}$ |
| $CaCO_3 \rightleftharpoons Ca^{2+} + CO_3^{2-}$ | $4.95 \times 10^{-9}$ | $MgCO_3 \rightleftharpoons Mg^{2+} + CO_3^{2-}$ | $1.15 \times 10^{-5}$ |
| $CaF_2 \rightleftharpoons Ca^{2+} + 2F^-$ | $1.61 \times 10^{-10}$ | $MnCO_3 \rightleftharpoons Mn^{2+} + CO_3^{2-}$ | $2.23 \times 10^{-11}$ |
| $Ca(OH)_2 \rightleftharpoons Ca^{2+} + 2OH^-$ | $7.88 \times 10^{-6}$ | $Mn(OH)_2 \rightleftharpoons Mn^{2+} + 2OH^-$ | $2.04 \times 10^{-13}$ |
| $Ca_3(PO_4)_2 \rightleftharpoons 3Ca^{2+} + 2PO_4^{3-}$ | $2.02 \times 10^{-33}$ | $NiCO_3 \rightleftharpoons Ni^{2+} + CO_3^{2-}$ | $1.45 \times 10^{-7}$ |
| $CaSO_4 \rightleftharpoons Ca^{2+} + SO_4^{2-}$ | $3.73 \times 10^{-5}$ | $Ni(OH)_2 \rightleftharpoons Ni^{2+} + 2OH^-$ | $5.54 \times 10^{-16}$ |
| $Cr(OH)_3 \rightleftharpoons Cr^{3+} + 3OH^-$ | $6.0 \times 10^{-31}$ | $NiS \rightleftharpoons Ni^{2+} + S^{2-}$ | $1.08 \times 10^{-21}$ |
| $Cu(OH)_2 \rightleftharpoons Cu^{2+} + 2OH^-$ | $2.0 \times 10^{-19}$ | $SrCO_3 \rightleftharpoons Sr^{2+} + CO_3^{2-}$ | $5.60 \times 10^{-10}$ |
| $CuS \rightleftharpoons Cu^{2+} + S^{2-}$ | $1.28 \times 10^{-36}$ | $Zn(OH)_2 \rightleftharpoons Zn^{2+} + 2OH^-$ | $7.68 \times 10^{-17}$ |
| $Fe(OH)_3 \rightleftharpoons Fe^{3+} + 3OH^-$ | $2.67 \times 10^{-39}$ | $ZnS \rightleftharpoons Zn^{2+} + S^{2-}$ | $2.91 \times 10^{-25}$ |
| $FeCO_3 \rightleftharpoons Fe^{2+} + CO_3^{2-}$ | $3.13 \times 10^{-11}$ | | |

**TABLE A–10**      Typical Valences of Elements and Compounds in Water

| Element or Compound | Valence | Element or Compound | Valence |
|---|---|---|---|
| Aluminum | $3^+$ | Manganese | $2^+$ |
| Ammonium ($NH_4$) | $1^+$ | Nickel | $2^+$ |
| Barium | $2^+$ | Oxygen | $2^-$ |
| Boron | $3^+$ | Nitrogen | $3^+, 5^+, 3^-$ |
| Cadmium | $2^+$ | Nitrate ($NO_3$) | $1^-$ |
| Calcium | $2^+$ | Nitrite ($NO_2$) | $1^-$ |
| Carbonate ($CO_3$) | $2^-$ | Phosphorus | $5^+, 3^-$ |
| Carbon dioxide ($CO_2$) | a | Phosphate ($PO_4$) | $3^-$ |
| Chloride (*not* chlorine) | $1^-$ | Potassium | $1^+$ |
| Chromium | $3^+, 6^+$ | Silver | $1^+$ |
| Copper | $2^+$ | Silica | b |
| Fluoride (*not* fluorine) | $1^-$ | Silicate ($SiO_4$) | $4^-$ |
| Hydrogen | $1^+$ | Sodium | $1^+$ |
| Hydroxide (OH) | $1^-$ | Sulfate ($SO_4$) | $2^-$ |
| Iron | $2^+, 3^+$ | Sulfide (S) | $2^-$ |
| Lead | $2^+$ | Zinc | $2^+$ |
| Magnesium | $2^+$ | | |

[a] Carbon dioxide in water is essentially carbonic acid:

$$CO_2 + H_2O \rightleftharpoons H_2CO_3$$

As such, the equivalent weight = GMW/2.

[b] Silica in water is reported as $SiO_2$. The equivalent weight is equal to the gram molecular weight.

**TABLE A–11**    Values of $K_{ow}$, Water Solubilities, and Henry's Law Constants for Selected Organic Compounds

| Compound | log $K_{ow}$ | Water Solubility (mg/L) | $K_H$ (atm/M) | Compound | log $K_{ow}$ | Water Solubility (mg/L) | $K_H$ (atm/M) |
|---|---|---|---|---|---|---|---|
| **Data from Yaws for 25°C** | | | | **Aromatic compounds, continued** | | | |
| **Halogenated aliphatic compounds** | | | | Napthalene | 3.3 | 32 | 0.46 (20°C) |
| Methanes | | | | Phenanthrene | 4.46 | 1.18 | |
| Chloromethane | 0.91 | 5900 | 8.2 | Anthracene | 4.45 | 0.053 | |
| Dichloromethane | 1.25 | 19,400 | 2.5 | Fluorene | 4.18 | 1.89 | |
| Chloroform | 1.97 | 7500 | 4.1 | Other aromatic compounds | | | |
| Bromoform | 2.4 | 3100 | 0.59 | Chlorobenzene | 2.84 | 390 | 4.5 |
| Carbon tetrachloride | 2.83 | 790 | 29 | 1,2-Dichlorobenzene | 3.43 | 92 | 2.8 |
| Dichlorodifluoromethane | 2.16 | 18,800 | 390 | 1,3-Dichlorobenzene | 3.53 | 123 | 3.4 |
| Ethanes | | | | 1,4-Dichlorobenzene | 3.44 | 80 | |
| Chloroethane | 1.43 | 9000 | 6.9 | 1,2,4-Trichlorobenzene | | | 3.0 |
| 1,1-Dichloroethane | 1.79 | 5000 | 5.8 | Hexachlorobenzene | 5.73 | 0.0047 | |
| 1,2-Dichloroethane | 1.48 | 8700 | 1.18 | Nitrobenzene | 1.85 | 1940 | 0.021 |
| 1,1,1-Trichloroethane | 2.49 | 1000 | 22 | 3-Nitrotoluene | 2.45 | 500 | 0.075 |
| 1,1,2-Trichloroethane | 1.89 | 4400 | 0.92 | Phenol | 1.46 | 80,000 | 0.00076 |
| Hexachloroethane | 3.91 | 8 | 25 | Diethyl phthalate | 2.47 | 1000 | 0.00014 |
| Ethenes | | | | 2-Chlorophenol | 2.15 | 25,000 | 0.037 |
| Vinyl chloride | 1.62 | 2700 | 22 | 3-Chlorophenol | 2.5 | 25,000 | 0.00204 |
| 1,1-Dichloroethene | 2.13 | 3400 | 23 | Dibenzofuran | 4.12 | | |
| 1,2-*cis*-Dichloroethene | 1.86 | 3500 | 7.4 | Other aliphatic compounds | | | |
| 1,2-*trans*-Dichloroethene | 2.09 | 6300 | 6.7 | Methyl *t*-butyl ether | 0.94 | 51,000 | 0.54 |
| Trichloroethene | 2.42 | 1100 | 11.6 | Methyl ethyl ketone | 0.29 | 250,000 | 0.030 |
| Tetrachloroethene | 3.4 | 150 | 26.9 | **Data from Schnoor et al. for 20°C** | | | |
| **Aromatic compounds** | | | | 2-Nitrophenol | 1.75 | 2100 | |
| Hydrocarbons | | | | Benzo(a)pyrene | 6.06 | 0.0038 | 0.00049 |
| Benzene | 2.13 | 1760 | 5.6 | Acrolein | 0.01 | 210,000 | 0.0038 |
| Toluene | 2.73 | 540 | 6.4 | Alachlor | 2.92 | 240 | |
| Ethylbenzene | 3.15 | 165 | 8.1 | Atrazine | 2.69 | 33 | |
| Styrene | 2.95 | 322 | 2.6 | Pentachlorophenol | 5.04 | 14 | |
| o-Xylene | 3.12 | 221 | 4.2 | DDT | 6.91 | 0.0055 | 0.038 |
| m-Xylene | 3.2 | 174 | 6.8 | Lindane | 3.72 | 7.52 | 0.0048 |
| p-Xylene | 3.15 | 200 | 6.2 | Dieldrin | 3.54 | 0.2 | 0.0002 |
| 1,2,3-Trimethylbenzene | 3.66 | 36 | 7.4 | 2,4-D | 1.78 | 900 | 0.00000172 |
| 1,2,4-Trimethylbenzene | 4.02 | 35 | | | | | |

*Sources:* C. L. Yaws, "Chemical Properties Handbook." McGraw-Hill, New York, 1999. Schnoor et al., "Processes, Coefficients, and Models for Simulating Toxic Organics and Heavy Metals in Surface Waters," U.S. Environmental Protection Agency, EPA/600/3-87/015, June 1987.

**TABLE A–12**    Henry's Law Constants for Common Gases Soluble in $H_2O$

| Temperature (°C) | $K_H \times 10^{-4}$ (atm) | | | | | | | |
|---|---|---|---|---|---|---|---|---|
| | Air | $N_2$ | $O_2$ | $CO_2$ | CO | $H_2$ | $H_2S$ | $CH_4$ |
| 0 | 4.32 | 5.29 | 2.55 | 0.073 | 3.52 | 5.79 | 0.027 | 2.24 |
| 10 | 5.49 | 6.68 | 3.27 | 0.104 | 4.42 | 6.36 | 0.037 | 2.97 |
| 20 | 6.64 | 8.04 | 4.01 | 0.142 | 5.36 | 6.83 | 0.048 | 3.76 |
| 30 | 7.71 | 9.24 | 4.75 | 0.186 | 6.20 | 7.29 | 0.061 | 4.49 |
| 40 | 8.70 | 10.4 | 5.35 | 0.233 | 6.96 | 7.51 | 0.075 | 5.20 |

*Source:* G. Kiely, *Environmental Engineering.* Copyright © 1996 The McGraw-Hill Companies, New York. Reproduced with permission.

# Index

## Useful Conversion Factors

| Multiply | By | To Obtain |
|---|---|---|
| atmosphere (atm) | 101.325 | kilopascal (kPa) |
| Calorie (international) | 4.1868 | Joules (J) |
| centipoise | $10^{-3}$ | Pa · s |
| centistoke | $10^{-6}$ | $m^2/s$ |
| cubic meter ($m^3$) | 35.31 | cubic feet ($ft^3$) |
| cubic meter | 1.308 | cubic yard ($yd^3$) |
| cubic meter | 1,000.00 | liter (L) |
| cubic meter/s | 15,850.0 | gallons/min (gpm) |
| cubic meter/s | 22.8245 | million gal/d (MGD) |
| cubic meter/$m^2$ | 24.545 | gallons/sq ft (gal/$ft^2$) |
| cubic meter/d · m | 80.52 | gal/d · ft (gpd/ft) |
| cubic meter/d · $m^2$ | 24.545 | gal/d · $ft^2$ (gpd/$ft^2$) |
| cubic meter/d · $m^2$ | 1.0 | meters/d (m/d) |
| days (d) | 24.00 | hours (h) |
| days (d) | 1,440.00 | minutes (min) |
| days (d) | 86,400.00 | seconds (s) |
| dyne | $10^{-5}$ | Newtons (N) |
| erg | $10^{-7}$ | Joules (J) |
| grains (gr) | $6.480 \times 10^{-2}$ | grams (g) |
| grains/U.S. gallon | 17.118 | mg/L |
| grams (g) | $2.205 \times 10^{-3}$ | pounds mass ($lb_m$) |
| hectare (ha) | $10^4$ | $m^2$ |
| hectare (ha) | 2.471 | acres |
| Hertz (Hz) | 1 | cycle/s |
| Joule (J) | 1 | N · m |
| $J/m^3$ | $2.684 \times 10^{-5}$ | Btu/$ft^3$ |
| kilogram/$m^3$ (kg/$m^3$) | $8.346 \times 10^{-3}$ | $lb_m$/gal |
| kilogram/$m^3$ | 1.6855 | $lb_m$/$yd^3$ |
| kilogram/ha (kg/ha) | $8.922 \times 10^{-1}$ | $lb_m$/acre |
| kilogram/$m^2$ (kg/$m^2$) | $2.0482 \times 10^{-1}$ | $lb_m$/$ft^2$ |
| kilometers (km) | $6.2150 \times 10^{-1}$ | miles (mi) |
| kilowatt (kW) | 1.3410 | horsepower (hp) |
| kilowatt-hour | 3.600 | megajoules (MJ) |
| liters (L) | $10^{-3}$ | cubic meters ($m^3$) |
| liters | 1,000.00 | milliliters (mL) |
| liters | $2.642 \times 10^{-1}$ | U.S. gallons |
| megagrams (Mg) | 1.1023 | U.S. short tons |
| meters (m) | 3.281 | feet (ft) |
| meters/d (m/d) | $2.2785 \times 10^{-3}$ | ft/min |
| meters/d | $3.7975 \times 10^{-5}$ | meters/s (m/s) |
| meters/s (m/s) | 196.85 | ft/min |
| meters/s | 3.600 | km/h |
| meters/s | 2.237 | miles/h (mph) |
| micron ($\mu$) | $10^{-6}$ | meters |
| milligrams (mg) | $10^{-3}$ | grams (g) |
| milligrams/L | 1 | g/$m^3$ |
| milligrams/L | $10^{-3}$ | kg/$m^3$ |
| Newton (N) | 1 | kg · m/$s^2$ |
| Pascal (Pa) | 1 | N/$m^2$ |
| Poise (P) | $10^{-1}$ | Pa · s |
| square meter ($m^2$) | $2.471 \times 10^{-4}$ | acres |
| square meter ($m^2$) | 10.7639 | sq ft ($ft^2$) |
| square meter/s | $6.9589 \times 10^6$ | gpd/ft |
| Stoke (St) | $10^{-4}$ | $m^2/s$ |
| Watt (W) | 1 | J/s |
| Watt/cu meter (W/$m^3$) | $3.7978 \times 10^{-2}$ | hp/1,000 $ft^3$ |
| Watt/sq meter · °C (W/$m^2$ · °C) | $1.761 \times 10^{-1}$ | Btu/h · $ft^2$ · °F |